NEW OXFORD
SPELLING DICTIONARY

NEW
OXFORD
SPELLING
DICTIONARY

Edited by
Maurice Waite

OXFORD
UNIVERSITY PRESS

OXFORD
UNIVERSITY PRESS

Great Clarendon Street, Oxford OX2 6DP

Oxford University Press is a department of the University of Oxford.
It furthers the University's objective of excellence in research, scholarship,
and education by publishing worldwide in

Oxford   New York

Auckland   Cape Town   Dar es Salaam   Hong Kong   Karachi
Kuala Lumpur   Madrid   Melbourne   Mexico City   Nairobi
New Delhi   Shanghai   Taipei   Toronto

With offices in

Argentina   Austria   Brazil   Chile   Czech Republic   France   Greece
Guatemala   Hungary   Italy   Japan   South Korea   Poland   Portugal
Singapore   Switzerland   Thailand   Turkey   Ukraine   Vietnam

Oxford is a registered trade mark of Oxford University Press
in the UK and in certain other countries

Published in the United States
by Oxford University Press Inc., New York

© Oxford University Press 2005

Database right Oxford University Press (makers)

First published (as the *Oxford Spelling Dictionary*) 1986
Second edition 1996
This edition 2005

British Library Cataloguing in Publication Data

Data available

Library of Congress Cataloging in Publication Data

Data available

ISBN   0-19-860881-0
ISBN   978-0-19-860881-3

Typeset in Miller by
Interactive Sciences Ltd
Printed in Italy by
Legoprint S.p.A

Contents

Preface

The *New Oxford Spelling Dictionary* replaces the second edition of the *Oxford Spelling Dictionary* (which was also issued as the *Oxford Colour Spelling Dictionary*), the standard work recommended by publishers and editors for guidance in spelling and end-of-line word division. It has been prepared in consultation with the Society for Editors and Proofreaders (SfEP).

The *New Oxford Spelling Dictionary* has been completely re-edited and redesigned to make it easier to use, more comprehensive, and yet at the same time more compact. Its coverage is based on the most-respected single-volume British dictionary, the *Oxford Dictionary of English*, and includes many other words and names as well. The spelling recommendations are based on research into the biggest ever body of English used for the purpose; this is the Oxford English Corpus, Oxford's scientifically selected and indexed collection of machine-readable texts containing many hundreds of millions of words. Finally, the word-division recommendations follow the tried-and-tested Oxford system.

Whether you are an author, copy editor, proofreader, or typesetter, this book provides you with the ideal way to ensure the best spelling practice for any text you are working on, be it a newspaper, magazine, report, thesis, or website. It combines with the *New Oxford Dictionary for Writers and Editors* and *New Hart's Rules* to form the complete reference set that you need, all in a new format that is easier to consult while you are working with proofs or on-screen.

Guide to the dictionary

This dictionary gives specific help to writers, editors, and anyone else working with the written word. It lets you quickly check spellings and shows you where to divide a word at the end of a line of print. Because it has these two main purposes, it omits words which do not normally cause spelling difficulty, including simple words such as *cat*, regular inflections such as *demanded*, and rarer derivatives that are constructed without alteration of their base word, e.g. *hairlessness*. For word division of these types of word, see 2.1 below. For the coverage of compound words, see 1.3.

1 SPELLING

1.1 Indicators
Various indicators are given when necessary to help readers quickly identify the word they wish to spell or divide:

(a) sense indicators

    heroin drug   **heroine** person

(b) similar words which could be confusable

    hare animal; cf. **hair**   **hair** on head; cf. **hare**

(c) word-class (or part-of-speech) labels

    envelop *v.*   **envelope** *n.*

(d) subject-field labels

    bailor *Law*; cf. **bailer, baler**

1.2 Spelling recommendations
A word described as a variant, e.g. *judgment* in

    judgment var. of **judgement**

is the less common spelling, and you are recommended to write *judgement*.

Variants which differ only in the matter of capital letters or whether they are written hyphenated, as two words, or as one, e.g. *communism*, *AIDS*, and *back-up* (as opposed to the recommended *Communism*, *Aids*, and *backup*) are not normally shown. However, pairs of words with capital and lower-case initials are given when each refers to a very different person or thing, e.g.

Balaclava battle   **balaclava** helmet

If an accented foreign word is usually written without its accents in English, the accented form is given as an alternative, e.g.

fete
> *French* **fête**

A spelling labelled *mod.* is the form of a noun used as a modifier, i.e. before another noun, e.g.

top-up *n. & mod.*

This indicates that you should write *a mobile phone top-up* and *a top-up card*, but (as a verb) *top up your mobile here.*

A spelling labelled *attrib.* is the form of an adjective used attributively, i.e. before a noun it qualifies, e.g.

up to date *adj.*   **up-to-date** *attrib.*

This indicates that you should write *the list is up to date* but *an up-to-date list.*

1.3 Hyphenation of compound words and phrases

'Hyphenation' in this section means the use of a 'hard' hyphen in a word such as *south-east* or *de-emphasize* wherever it appears in a line of print. For the use of a hyphen to mark a word division, see section 2 below.

Although standard spelling in English is fixed, hyphenation is not. It would be impossible to include all compounds, so in general only those that are always or most commonly written either as one word ('solid') or hyphenated are shown.

'Syntactic' hyphenated compounds, such as *heat-treat*, *mud-spattered*, or *assembly-line* in *assembly-line workers*, being almost unlimited in number, are given if they contrast with another form, e.g. *vacuum-clean* but *vacuum cleaner.*

1.4 British and US spellings

The labels *Br.* and *US* indicate which spellings to use in British and US English respectively, e.g.

>pretence *Br.*
>>*US* pretense

A *Br.* or *US* label does not necessarily mean that the spelling is used exclusively in that region.

1.5 *-ise* and *-ize*

The verbal ending *-ize* has been in general use since the 16th century. Today it is favoured in US use, and it is the preferred style of Oxford University Press in books published in Britain. However, in British English *-ise* is also acceptable, provided that its use is consistent, and words which can be spelled *-ise* are shown thus:

>**nationalise** *Br.* var. of **nationalize**

1.6 Inflections

All irregular inflections of recommended spellings are shown: inflections not shown follow the normal rules of English. Some regular inflections are shown if they are unexpected or present some particular difficulty, e.g.

>**dragoman** +s

The inflections of borrowed foreign words are shown if they are as in their original language, e.g.

>**bacterium**
>>**bacteria**

When an inflection has different spellings that are not otherwise distinguished, the first one given is recommended, as in

>**cue**
>>**cueing** or **cuing**

2 WORD DIVISION

'Word division' means the splitting of a word at the end of a line of text, with a hyphen added, because there is not enough space for the whole of it. Word division generally improves the overall appearance of text that is justified (i.e. with the lines

expanded to make the right-hand ends align vertically). In unjustified text (i.e. where the right-hand margin is irregular, also known as 'ragged right'), word division is less necessary but is often preferred with narrow columns.

The word divisions given are based on both the pronunciation of words and their internal structure, so that they reflect modern practice and are as unobtrusive as possible, allowing uninterrupted reading.

2.1 Where to divide

A bar (|) indicates a preferred or 'primary' division point, at which a word can be divided under almost any circumstances. A broken bar (¦) indicates a 'secondary' division point, at which a word is best divided only if absolutely necessary, mainly in narrow columns of type, as in newspapers.

Every word division should, ideally, be vetted by eye as a check that it is both the best division possible and better than not dividing at all: for instance, even a primary division may be possible but quite unnecessary at the end of a wide line if the word spaces are not too large. Furthermore, the recommendations in this or any other book should not be regarded as inviolable rules; the typesetter or proofreader should feel free occasionally to allow a division not shown here or vice versa, entirely as appropriate in the context.

Words in categories that may not be shown should be divided as follows:

(a) Simple words
Words of one syllable, such as *branch*, should not be divided.

(b) Regular inflections
Regular inflections that are not shown may be divided if necessary before the following endings:

-ed: only in narrow columns and then only if the word is of at least six letters *and* the ending is pronounced as a separate syllable, as in *part-ed*, but not in *ended* (five letters) or *calmed* (one syllable).

-ing: always, if the word is of more than six letters, e.g. *calm-ing*, but otherwise only in narrow columns, as in *buy-ing*.

-er: only in narrow columns and then only if the word is of at least six letters, as in *calm-er*, but not in *odder*.

-est: always, if the word is of more than six letters, as in *calm-est*, but otherwise, as in *odd-est*, only in narrow columns.

(c) Derivatives

Rarer derivatives that are omitted, such as *hairlessness*, are divisible in the same place(s) as the root word (*hair-lessness*) or before the suffix (i.e. *hairless-ness*).

2.2 Division of hyphenated compounds

A hyphenated compound, such as *after-effect*, can be divided at the hyphen under almost any circumstances. Take care that it is not then assumed to be a solid word: for instance, *re-cover* (meaning 'cover again'), could be mistaken for the more common *recover* (meaning 'reclaim' etc.).

Hyphenated compounds may be divided at the secondary points shown generally at least six letters after the hyphen, e.g. *self-govern¦ment*. Inflections not shown may be divided at the places described in (b) above, but again at least six letters after the hyphen: e.g., *co-presenting* may be divided before *-ing*, but *self-seeded* should not be divided before *-ed*.

As a last resort, in order to avoid very bad spacing, one could divide either (a) the second element at a point fewer than six letters after the hyphen or (b) the first element, in each case following, whenever possible, the recommendations for the elements as words on their own. Care should be taken not to produce an unacceptably obtrusive or misleading result, such as *eco-war-rier* or *cot-ton-picking*.

2.3 Division of personal names

Some writers and typesetters prefer not to divide personal names at all. Those included in this dictionary are shown with both primary and secondary division points, but they are identified as names, e.g.

> **Mac¦ken¦zie, Alex¦an¦der** explorer

so that it is possible to avoid dividing them if one wishes.

Abbreviations used in the dictionary

adj.	adjective	N.	North
adv.	adverb	n.	noun
attrib.	attributive (see 1.2)	NZ	New Zealand
Austral.	Australian	pl.	plural
aux.	auxiliary	prep.	preposition
Br.	British	S.	South
cf.	compare	Scot.	Scottish
conj.	conjunction	sing.	singular
exclam.	exclamation	US	United States
Ind.	Indian	v.	verb
mod.	modifier (see 1.2)	var.	variant

Note on trademarks and proprietary terms

This dictionary includes some words which have, or are asserted to have, proprietary status as trademarks or otherwise. Their inclusion does not imply that they have acquired for legal purposes a non-proprietary or general significance, nor any other judgement concerning their legal status. In cases where the editorial staff have some evidence that a word has proprietary status this is indicated in the entry for that word by the label *trademark*, but no judgement concerning the legal status of such words is made or implied thereby.

A

aa lava
Aa|chen
Aal|borg
aapa
aard|vark
aard|wolf
  aard|wolves
Aar|gau
Aar|hus
Aaron
Ab Jewish month
ab muscle
abaca
aback
aba|cus
Aba|dan in Iran, cf.
  Ibadan
Abad|don the Devil
abaft
aba|lone
aban|don
aban|don|ment
à bas
abase
  abas|ing
abase|ment
abash
abash|ment
abate
  abat|ing
abate|ment
aba|tis
  pl. aba|tis or
  aba|tises
abat|tis var. of
  abatis
ab|at|toir
ab|ax|ial
abaya
Abba God
abba father
ab|bacy
  ab|ba|cies
Abbas, Mah|moud
  'Abu Mazen',
  Palestinian prime
  minister

Ab|basid
ab|ba|tial
abbé
ab|bess nun; cf.
  abyss
Abbe|vil|lian
abbey
abbot
ab|bre|vi|ate
  ab|bre|vi|at|ing
ab|bre|vi|ation
ab|dabs
ab|di|cate
  ab|di|cat|ing
ab|di|ca|tion
ab|di|ca|tor
ab|do|men
ab|dom|in|al
ab|dom|in|al|ly
ab|du|cens
ab|duct
ab|duct|ee
ab|duc|tion
ab|duct|or
Ab|dul|lah
abeam
abe|ce|dar|ian
abed
Abel|lard, Peter
  scholar
abele
abelia
abel|lian
Ab|en|aki var. of
  Abnaki
Abeo|kuta
Aber|deen
Aber|deen|shire
Aber|do|nian
Aber|fan
Aber|nethy
  Aber|neth|ies
ab|er|rance
ab|er|rancy
ab|er|rant
ab|er|rant|ly

ab|er|ra|tion
ab|er|ra|tion|al
Aber|yst|wyth
abet
  abet|ted
  abet|ting
abet|ment
abet|ter
abet|tor var. of
  abbetter
ab extra
abey|ance
abey|ant
abhor
  ab|horred
  ab|hor|ring
ab|hor|rence
ab|hor|rent
ab|hor|rer
abid|ance
abide
  abid|ing
  abid|ing|ly
Abi|djan
abi|gail
abil|ity
  abil|ities
ab ini|tio
abio|gen|esis
abio|gen|ic
abi|ot|ic
Abi|tur
ab|ject
ab|jec|tion
ab|ject|ly
ab|jur|ation
ab|jure
  ab|jur|ing
Ab|khaz
Ab|kha|zia
Ab|kha|zian
ab|late
  ab|lat|ing
ab|la|tion
ab|la|tive
ab|la|tive|ly
ab|laut

ablaze
able
  abler
  ablest
able-bodied
able|ism
able|ist
ablism var. of
  ableism
ablist var. of ableist
abloom
ablush
ab|lu|tion
ab|lu|tion|ary
ably
Ab|naki
ab|ne|gate
  ab|ne|gat|ing
ab|ne|ga|tion
ab|ne|ga|tor
Abney level
ab|nor|mal
ab|nor|mal|ity
  ab|nor|mal|ities
ab|nor|mal|ly
Abo +s *offensive*
aboard
abode
abol|ish
abol|ish|able
abol|ish|er
abol|ish|ment
abo|li|tion
abo|li|tion|ism
abo|li|tion|ist
abo|ma|sum
abo|masa
abom|in|able
abom|in|ably
abom|in|ate
  abom|in|at|ing
abom|in|ation
abom|in|ator
ab|oral
Abo|ri|gi|nal Aus-
  tralian; language

abo|ri|gi|nal else-
where
Abo|ri|gi|nal|ity
Abo|ri|gine Austra-
lian
abo|ri|gine else-
where
aborn|ing
abort
abor|ti|fa|cient
abor|tion
abor|tion|ist
abort|ive
abort|ive|ly
abor|tus fever
Abou|kir Bay
abou|lia var. of
abulia
abou|lic var. of
abulic
abound
about
about face
command
about-face n. & v.
about-facing
about turn
command
about-turn n. & v.
above
ab ovo
abra|ca|dabra
abrade
abrad|ing
abrader
Abra|ham
abra|sion
abra|sive
abra|sive|ly
abra|sive|ness
abrazo +s
ab|react
ab|reac|tion
ab|react|ive
abreast
abridg|able
abridge
abridg|ing
abridge|ment
abridger
abridg|ment var. of
abridgement
abroad
ab|ro|gate
ab|ro|gat|ing

ab|ro|ga|tion
ab|ro|ga|tor
abrupt
abrup|tion
abrupt|ly
abrupt|ness
Abruzzi
Abruz|zi|an
ab|scess
ab|scessed
ab|scise
ab|scis|ing
ab|scissa
ab|scis|sas or
ab|scis|sae
ab|scis|sion
ab|scond
ab|scond|er
ab|seil
ab|seil|er
ab|sence
ab|sent
ab|sen|tee
ab|sen|tee|ism
ab|sent|ly
absent-minded
absent-minded|ly
absent-
minded|ness
ab|sinth plant
ab|sinthe drink
absit omen
ab|so|lute
ab|so|lute|ly
ab|so|lu|tion
ab|so|lut|isa|tion
Br. var. of
absolutization
ab|so|lut|ise *Br.* var.
of absolutize
ab|so|lut|ism
ab|so|lut|ist
ab|so|lut|iza|tion
ab|so|lut|ize
ab|so|lut|iz|ing
ab|solve
ab|solv|ing
ab|son|ant
ab|sorb
ab|sorb|abil|ity
ab|sorb|able
ab|sorb|ance
ab|sorb|ency
ab|sorb|en|cies

ab|sorb|ent
ab|sorb|er
ab|sorb|ing|ly
ab|sorp|ti|om|eter
ab|sorp|tio|met|ric
ab|sorp|tion
ab|sorp|tive
ab|sorp|tiv|ity
ab|squatu|late
ab|squatu|lat|ing
ab|squatu|la|tion
ab|stain
ab|stain|er
ab|ste|mi|ous
ab|ste|mi|ous|ly
ab|ste|mi|ous|ness
ab|sten|tion
ab|sten|tion|ism
ab|stin|ence
ab|stin|ent
ab|stin|ent|ly
ab|stract
ab|strac|tion
ab|strac|tion|ism
ab|strac|tion|ist
ab|stract|ly
ab|stract|or
ab|struse
ab|struse|ly
ab|struse|ness
ab|surd
ab|surd|ism
ab|surd|ist
ab|surd|ity
ab|surd|ities
ab|surd|ly
ABTA Association of
British Travel
Agents
abub|ble
Abu Dhabi
Abuja
Abu|kir Bay var. of
Aboukir Bay
abu|lia
abu|lic
Abu Musa
Abu Mazen
Palestinian prime
minister
Abuna
abun|dance
abun|dant

abun|dant|ly
abura
abus|ing
abuser
Abu Sim|bel
abu|sive
abu|sive|ly
abu|sive|ness
abus|tle
abut
abut|ted
abut|ting
abu|ti|lon
abut|ment
abut|ter
abuzz
abysm
abys|mal
abys|mal|ly
abyss chasm; cf.
abbess
abys|sal
Abys|sinia
Abys|sin|ian
aca|cia
Aca|deme in 'groves
of Academe'
aca|deme the world
of learning
aca|demia
aca|dem|ic
aca|dem|ic|al
aca|dem|ic|al|ly
acad|em|ician
aca|demi|cism
Acad|émie
fran|çaise
acad|em|ism
acad|emy
acad|emies
Aca|dia
Aca|dian of Nova
Scotia; cf.
Akkadian,
Arcadian
aca|jou
acal|cu|lia
acanth|amoeba
acanth|amoe|bae
Acan|tho|ceph|ala
acan|tho|
ceph|al|an
acan|tho|ceph|alid

acan|tho|di|an
acan|thus
a cap|pella
Aca|pulco
acara
Acari
acari|cide
aca|rid
Aca|rina
aca|rine
acar|oid
acar|olo|gist
acar|ology
ACAS Advisory,
Conciliation, and
Arbitration Service
acata|lec|tic
acaus|al
Ac|ca|dian var. of
Akkadian; cf.
Acadian, Arcadian
ac|cede
ac|ced|ing
take up office;
agree; cf. exceed
ac|cel|er|ando
ac|cel|er|andos or
ac|cel|er|andi
ac|cel|er|ant
ac|cel|er|ate
ac|cel|er|at|ing
ac|cel|er|ation
ac|cel|era|tive
ac|cel|er|ator
ac|cel|er|om|eter
ac|cent
ac|cent|or
ac|cen|tual
ac|cen|tu|ate
ac|cen|tu|at|ing
ac|cen|tu|ation
ac|cept receive; cf.
except
ac|cept|abil|ity
ac|cept|able
ac|cept|ably
ac|cept|ance
ac|cep|ta|tion
ac|cept|er generally
ac|cept|or
*Commerce and
Science*
ac|cess
ac|ces|sary var. of
accessory

ac|ces|si|bil|ity
ac|ces|si|bil|ities
ac|cess|ible
ac|cess|ibly
ac|ces|sion
ac|ces|sor|ise Br.
var. of accessorize
ac|ces|sor|ize
ac|ces|sor|iz|ing
ac|ces|sory
ac|ces|sor|ies
ac|ciac|ca|tura
ac|ciac|ca|turas or
ac|ciac|ca|ture
ac|ci|dence
ac|ci|dent
ac|ci|den|tal
ac|ci|den|tal|ly
ac|ci|die
ac|cipi|ter
ac|cipi|trine
ac|claim
ac|clam|ation
ac|cli|mate
ac|cli|mat|ing
ac|cli|ma|tion
ac|cli|ma|tisa|tion
Br. var. of
acclimatization
ac|cli|ma|tise Br.
var. of acclimatize
ac|cli|ma|tiza|tion
ac|cli|ma|tize
ac|cli|ma|tiz|ing
ac|clivi|tous
ac|cliv|ity
ac|cliv|ities
ac|col|lade
ac|com|mo|date
ac|com|mo|dat|ing
ac|com|mo|da|tion
ac|com|mo|da|tion|
ist
ac|com|mo|da|tive
ac|com|pani|ment
ac|com|pan|ist
ac|com|pany
ac|com|pan|ies
ac|com|pan|ied
ac|com|pany|ing
ac|com|plice
ac|com|plish
ac|com|plish|ment
ac|cord
ac|cord|ance

ac|cord|ant
ac|cord|ing|ly
ac|cor|dion
ac|cor|dion|ist
ac|cost
ac|couche|ment
ac|couch|eur *male*
ac|couch|euse
female
ac|count
ac|count|abil|ity
ac|count|abil|ities
ac|count|able
ac|count|ably
ac|count|ancy
ac|count|ant
ac|cou|ter US
ac|cou|ter|ment US
ac|coutre Br.
ac|cout|ring
ac|coutre|ment Br.
Accra city
accra food
ac|credit
ac|credit|ation
ac|crete
ac|cret|ing
ac|cre|tion
ac|cre|tive
ac|crual
ac|crue
ac|cru|ing
ac|cul|tur|ate
ac|cul|tur|at|ing
ac|cul|tur|ation
ac|cul|tur|ative
ac|cu|mu|late
ac|cu|mu|lat|ing
ac|cu|mu|la|tion
ac|cu|mu|la|tive
ac|cu|mu|la|tor
ac|cur|acy
ac|cur|acies
ac|cur|ate
ac|cur|ate|ly
ac|cur|sed
ac|curst *archaic* =
accursed
ac|cusal
ac|cus|ation
ac|cusa|tive
ac|cusa|tor|ial
ac|cusa|tory

ac|cuse
ac|cus|ing
ac|cuser
ac|cus|ing|ly
ac|cus|tom
AC/DC
ace
acing
acedia
acel|lu|lar
acen|tric
aceph|al|ous
acer
acerb
acerb|ic
acerb|ic|al|ly
acerb|ity
acerb|ities
ace|sul|fame
acet|abu|lum
acet|abula
acetal
acet|al|de|hyde
aceta|mide
acet|amino|phen
acet|anil|ide
acet|ate
acet|ic acid; cf.
ascetic
aceto|bac|ter
aceto|gen|ic
aceto|naemia
acet|one
aceto|nitrile
acet|ous
acetyl
acetyl|ate
acetyl|at|ing
acetyl|ation
acetyl|cho|line
acetyl|cholin|ester|
ase
acetyl|ene
acetyl|ide
acetyl|sali|cyl|ic
achaar var. of achar
Achaara
Achaean
Achae|men|ian
Achae|menid
acha|la|sia
achar pickle; cf.
achha
acharne|ment

achar¦ya
Acha¦tes
  pl. Acha¦tes
ache
  ach¦ing
achene
Ach¦eron
Ache¦son, Dean
  politician
Acheu¦lean var. of
  Acheulian
Acheu¦lian
achey var. of achy
achha *Ind. exclam.*;
  cf. achar
achiev¦able
achieve
  achiev¦ing
achieve¦ment
achiev¦er
achil¦lea
Achil¦les
Achil¦les heel
Achil¦les ten¦don
achim¦enes
Achi¦nese
achi¦ote
achir¦al
ach¦kan
achlor¦hydria
Acholi
achon¦drite
achon¦drit¦ic
achon¦dro¦pla¦sia
achon¦dro¦pla¦sic
achon¦dro¦plas¦tic
achro¦mat
achro¦mat¦ic
achy
  achier
  achi¦est
aci¦cu¦lar
acid¦ic
acid¦ifi¦ca¦tion
acid¦ify
  acid¦ifies
  acid¦ified
  acid¦ify¦ing
acid¦im¦etry
acid¦ity
acid¦ly
acido¦phil
acido¦phil¦ic
acido¦oph¦ilus

acid¦osis
acid¦otic
acidu¦late
  acidu¦lat¦ing
  acidu¦la¦tion
acidu¦lous
acidy
aci¦nus
  acini
ack-ack
ackee
ack emma
ack¦ers
ac¦know¦ledge
  ac¦know¦ledg¦ing
ac¦know¦ledge¦able
ac¦know¦ledge¦
    ment
ac¦know¦ledg¦ment
  var. of
  acknowledgement
acme
Acme¦ism
Acme¦ist
acne
Acol
aco¦lyte
Ac¦on¦cagua
acon¦ite
acon¦it¦ine
acorn
acoty¦le¦don
acoty¦le¦don¦ous
acou¦chi
acous¦tic
acous¦tic¦al
acous¦tic¦al¦ly
acous¦ti¦cian
acous¦tics
ac¦quaint
ac¦quaint¦ance
ac¦quaint¦ance¦
    ship
ac¦qui¦esce
  ac¦qui¦es¦cing
ac¦qui¦es¦cence
ac¦qui¦es¦cent
ac¦quir¦able
ac¦quire
  ac¦quir¦ing
ac¦quir¦ee
ac¦quire¦ment
ac¦quir¦er
ac¦qui¦si¦tion

ac¦quisi¦tive
ac¦quisi¦tive¦ness
ac¦quit
  ac¦quit¦ted
  ac¦quit¦ting
ac¦quit¦tal
ac¦quit¦tance
acra¦sia var. of
  akrasia
acrat¦ic var. of
  akratic
Acre town
acre
acre¦age
acre-foot
  acre-feet
acrid
ac¦rid¦ine
ac¦rid¦ity
ac¦rid¦ly
acri¦fla¦vine
Acri¦lan *trademark*
acri¦mo¦ni¦ous
acri¦mo¦ni¦ous¦ly
acri¦mony
acro¦bat
acro¦bat¦ic
acro¦bat¦ic¦al¦ly
acro¦bat¦ics
acro¦cyan¦osis
acro¦lect
acro¦lect¦al
acro¦meg¦al¦ic
ac¦ro¦meg¦aly
acro¦nym
acrop¦etal
acrop¦etal¦ly
acro¦pho¦bia
acro¦pho¦bic
acrop¦olis
across
acros¦tic
acryl¦amide
acryl¦ate
acryl¦ic
acrylo¦nitrile
act¦abil¦ity
act¦able
Ac¦taeon
act¦ant
actin
ac¦tin¦ian
ac¦tin¦ic

ac¦tin¦ide
ac¦tin¦ism
ac¦tin¦ium
ac¦tino¦lite
ac¦tin¦om¦eter
ac¦tino¦morph¦ic
ac¦tino¦morphy
Ac¦tino¦my¦cet¦ales
ac¦tino¦my¦cete
ac¦tion
ac¦tion¦able
ac¦tion¦er
Ac¦tium
ac¦ti¦vate
  ac¦ti¦vat¦ing
ac¦ti¦va¦tion
ac¦ti¦va¦tor
ac¦tive
ac¦tive¦ly
ac¦tiv¦ism
ac¦tiv¦ist
ac¦tiv¦ity
  ac¦tiv¦ities
acto¦myosin
actor
actor¦ish
Actors' Stu¦dio
ac¦tress
ac¦tressy
ac¦tual
ac¦tual¦isa¦tion *Br.*
  var. of
  actualization
ac¦tual¦ise *Br.* var.
  of actualize
ac¦tu¦al¦ité
ac¦tual¦ity
  ac¦tual¦ities
ac¦tual¦iza¦tion
ac¦tual¦ize
  ac¦tual¦iz¦ing
ac¦tu¦al¦ly
ac¦tu¦ar¦ial
ac¦tu¦ari¦al¦ly
ac¦tu¦ary
  ac¦tu¦ar¦ies
ac¦tu¦ate
  ac¦tu¦at¦ing
ac¦tu¦ation
ac¦tu¦ator
actus reus
acu¦ity
acu¦leate
acu¦men

acu|min|ate
acu|point
acu|pres|sure
acu|punc|ture
acu|punc|tur|ist
acushla
acu|tance
acute
  acuter
  acut|est
acute|ly
acute|ness
acyc|lic
acyclo|vir
acyl
acyl|ate
  acyl|at|ing
acyl|ation
adage
ada|gio +s
ad|am|ance
ad|am|ancy
ad|am|ant
ad|am|ant|ine
ad|am|ant|ly
Ad|am|ite
Adams, John US
  president
Adams, John
  Quincy US
  president
Adam's ale
Adam's apple
Adam's Bridge
Adam's nee|dle
Adam's Peak
Adana
adapt
adapt|abil|ity
adapt|able
adapt|ably
adap|ta|tion
adap|ta|tion|ism
adap|ta|tion|ist
adapt|er var. of
  adaptor
adap|tion
adap|tive
adap|tive|ly
adap|tiv|ity
adapto|gen
adapto|gen|ic
adap|tor

Adar Jewish month
ad|ax|ial
Ad|dams, Jane
  reformer
addax
ad|den|dum
  ad|denda
adder
adder's tongue
  plant
ad|dict
ad|dic|tion
ad|dict|ive
ad|dict|ive|ly
add-in *n.*
Ad|ding|ton, Henry
  prime minister of
  Britain
Addis Ababa
Ad|di|son, Jo|seph
  writer
Ad|di|son|ian
addi|tion cf. edition
add|ition|al
add|ition|al|ly
addi|tive
addle
  ad|dling
add-on *n. & mod.*
ad|dorsed
addra
ad|dress
ad|dress|able
ad|dress|ee
ad|dress|er
ad|dres|sor var. of
  addresser
ad|duce
  ad|du|cing
ad|du|cible
ad|duct
ad|duc|tion
ad|duct|or
Adel|aide
Ad|élie Coast; Land
Adel|ine
Aden
Aden|auer,
  Kon|rad chancellor
  of West Germany
ad|en|ine
adeno|car|cin|oma
adeno|car|cin|omas

or adeno|car|cin|
                omata
ad|en|oid|al
ad|en|oids
ad|en|oma
  ad|en|omas or
  ad|en|omata
ad|en|oma|tous
ad|eno|sine
adeno|viral
adeno|virus
ad|enyl|ate
ad|enyl|ic
adept
adept|ly
adept|ness
ad|equacy
  ad|equa|cies
ad|equate
ad|equate|ly
à deux
ad|here
  ad|her|ing
ad|her|ence
ad|her|ent
ad|he|sion
ad|he|sive
ad|hibit
ad|hib|ition
ad hoc
ad|hoc|racy
ad hom|inem
adia|bat|ic
adia|bat|ic|al|ly
adieu
  adieus or adieux
Adi Granth
ad in|fin|itum
ad in|terim
adios
adi|pate
adip|ic
adi|po|cere
adi|po|cyte
adi|pose
adi|pos|ity
Adi|ron|dack
Adis Abeba var. of
  Addis Ababa
adit
Adi|vasi
ad|ja|cency
ad|ja|cent

ad|jec|tival
ad|jec|tival|ly
ad|jec|tive
adjigo +s
adjiko var. of adjigo
ad|join
ad|joint
ad|journ
ad|journ|ment
ad|judge
  ad|judg|ing
ad|judge|ment
ad|judg|ment var.
  of adjudgement
ad|ju|di|cate
  ad|ju|di|cat|ing
ad|ju|di|ca|tion
ad|ju|di|ca|tive
ad|ju|di|ca|tor
ad|junct
ad|junc|tion
ad|junct|ive
ad|jur|ation
ad|jura|tory
ad|jure
  ad|jur|ing
ad|just
ad|just|abil|ity
ad|just|able
ad|just|er
ad|just|ment
ad|ju|tancy
  ad|ju|tan|cies
ad|ju|tant
Ad|ju|tant
  Gen|eral
  Ad|ju|tants
  Gen|eral
ad|ju|vant
ad|land
Adler, Al|fred
  psychologist
Ad|ler|ian
ad lib *adv.*
ad-lib *v.*
ad-libbed
ad-libbing
ad lib|itum
ad litem
adman
admen
ad|meas|ure|ment
admin

ad¦min¦icle
ad¦min¦icu¦lar
ad¦min¦is¦ter
ad¦min¦is¦trable
ad¦min¦is¦trate
  ad¦min¦is¦trat¦ing
ad¦min¦is¦tra¦tion
ad¦min¦is¦tra¦tive
ad¦min¦is¦
          tra¦tive¦ly
ad¦min¦is¦tra¦tor
ad¦min¦is¦tra¦trix
  ad¦min¦is¦tra¦trixes
  or ad¦min¦is¦
          tra¦tri¦ces
ad¦mir¦able
ad¦mir¦ably
ad¦miral
Ad¦mir¦alty depart-
ment
ad¦mir¦alty jurisdic-
tion
ad¦mir¦ation
ad¦mire
  ad¦mir¦ing
ad¦mirer
ad¦mir¦ing¦ly
ad¦mis¦si¦bil¦ity
ad¦mis¦sible
ad¦mis¦sion
admit
  ad¦mit¦ted
  ad¦mit¦ting
ad¦mit¦tance
ad¦mit¦ted¦ly
admix
ad¦mix¦ture
ad¦mon¦ish
ad¦mon¦ish¦ment
ad¦mon¦ition
ad¦moni¦tor
ad¦moni¦tory
ad¦nate
ad nau¦seam
ad¦nexa
ad¦nexal
ad¦nom¦inal
Ad¦nya¦matha¦nha
ado
adobe
adobo +s
ado¦les¦cence
ado¦les¦cent

Ado¦nai
Ado¦nis
adopt
adopt¦able
adopt¦ee
adopt¦er
adop¦tion
adop¦tive
ador¦abil¦ity
ador¦able
ador¦ably
ad¦oral
ad¦or¦ation
adore
  ador¦ing
adorer
ador¦ing¦ly
adorn
adorn¦er
adorn¦ment
ad per¦sonam
ad¦pressed
ad rem
ad¦renal
adren¦alin
adren¦aline var. of
  adrenalin
adren¦al¦ised *Br.*
  var. of adrenalized
adren¦al¦ized
ad¦ren¦er¦gic
adreno|cor¦tico|
          troph¦in
adreno|cor¦tico|
          tropin
  var. of adrenocor-
  ticotrophin
adret
Adrian man's name
Adri¦anne woman's
  name
Adri¦at¦ic
Adri¦enne
adrift
adroit
  adroit¦er
  adroit¦est
adroit¦ly
adroit¦ness
ad¦sci¦ti¦tious
ad¦sorb
ad¦sorb¦able
ad¦sorb¦ate

ad¦sorb¦ent
ad¦sorp¦tion
ad¦sorp¦tive
ad¦strate
ad¦stra¦tum
  ad¦strata
aduki var. of adzuki
adu¦late
  adu¦lat¦ing
adu¦la¦tion
adu¦la¦tor
adu¦la¦tory
Adul¦lam¦ite
adult
adul¦ter¦ant
adul¦ter¦ate
  adul¦ter¦at¦ing
adul¦ter¦ation
adul¦ter¦ator
adul¦ter¦er
adul¦ter¦ess
adul¦ter¦ine
adul¦ter¦ous
adul¦ter¦ous¦ly
adul¦tery
  adul¦ter¦ies
adult¦escent
adult¦hood
adult¦ly
ad¦um¦brate
  ad¦um¦brat¦ing
ad¦um¦bra¦tion
ad¦um¦bra¦tive
ad val¦orem
ad¦vance
ad¦van¦cing
ad¦vance¦ment
ad¦van¦cer
ad¦van¦tage
ad¦van¦ta¦ging
ad¦van¦ta¦geous
ad¦van¦ta¦geous¦ly
ad¦vect
ad¦vec¦tion
ad¦vec¦tive
ad¦vent
Ad¦vent¦ism
Ad¦vent¦ist
ad¦ven¦ti¦tia
ad¦ven¦ti¦tial
ad¦ven¦ti¦tious
ad¦ven¦ture
  ad¦ven¦tur¦ing

ad¦ven¦tur¦er
ad¦ven¦ture¦some
ad¦ven¦tur¦ess
ad¦ven¦tur¦ism
ad¦ven¦tur¦ist
ad¦ven¦tur¦ous
ad¦ven¦tur¦ous¦ly
ad¦ven¦tur¦ous¦
                    ness
ad¦verb
ad¦ver¦bial
ad¦ver¦bi¦al¦ly
ad¦ver¦sar¦ial
ad¦ver¦sary
  ad¦ver¦sar¦ies
ad¦ver¦sa¦tive
ad¦verse
ad¦verse¦ly
ad¦ver¦sity
  ad¦ver¦si¦ties
ad¦vert
ad¦ver¦tise
  ad¦ver¦tis¦ing
ad¦ver¦tise¦ment
ad¦ver¦tiser
ad¦ver¦tor¦ial
ad¦vice *n.*
ad¦vis¦abil¦ity
ad¦vis¦able
ad¦vise *v.*
  ad¦vis¦ing
ad¦vised¦ly
ad¦vise¦ment
ad¦viser
ad¦visor var. of
  adviser
ad¦vis¦ory
ad¦vo¦caat
ad¦vo¦cacy
ad¦vo¦cate
  ad¦vo¦cat¦ing
advocate-depute
  advocates-depute
advocate-general
  advocates-general
ad¦vo¦cate¦ship
ad¦vo¦ca¦tion
ad¦vow¦son
ady¦tum
  adyta
adz *US*
adze *Br.*
  adz¦ing

ad¦zuki
ae¦dile
ae¦dile¦ship
Ae¦gean
aegis
aegro¦tat
Ael¦fric
Ae¦neas
Ae¦neid
ae¦olian *Br.*
  US eolian
aeon *Br.*
  US eon
aepy¦or¦nis
aer¦ate
  aer¦at¦ing
aer¦ation
aer¦ator
aer¦en¦chyma
aer¦en¦chyma¦tous
aer¦ial radio etc.; in
  the air; cf. **areal,**
  ariel
acr¦ial¦ist
aeri¦al¦ity
aeri¦al¦ly
aerie *US*
  Br. eyrie
aero
aero¦batic
aero¦bat¦ics
aer¦obe
aer¦ob¦ic
aer¦ob¦ic¦al¦ly
aer¦obi¦cist
aer¦obics
aero¦biol¦ogy
aero¦brake
  aero¦brak¦ing
aero¦drome
aero¦dynam¦ic
aero¦dynam¦ic¦al¦ly
aero¦dynami¦cist
aero¦dynam¦ics
aero¦elas¦tic
aero¦elas¦ti¦city
aero¦foil
aero¦gel
aero¦gram *US* var.
  of aerogramme
aero¦gramme
aero¦lite
aero¦logic¦al

aer¦ology
aero¦mag¦net¦ic
aero¦medic¦al
aero¦model¦er *US*
aero¦model¦ing *US*
aero¦model¦ler *Br.*
aero¦model¦ling *Br.*
aero¦naut
aero¦naut¦ic
aero¦naut¦ic¦al
aero¦naut¦ics
aer¦onomy
aer¦oph¦agy
aero¦phone
aero¦plane
aero¦shell
aero¦sol
aero¦sol¦ised *Br.*
  var. of aerosolized
aero¦sol¦ized
aero¦space
aero¦stat
Aer¦tex *trademark*
Aes¦chy¦lean
Aes¦chy¦lus drama-
  tist
Aes¦cu¦la¦pian
Æsir Norse gods
  and goddesses
Aesop
aes¦thete
aes¦thet¦ic
aes¦thet¦ic¦al¦ly
aes¦thet¦ician
aes¦theti¦cise *Br.*
  var. of aestheticize
aes¦theti¦cism
aes¦theti¦cize
  aes¦theti¦ciz¦ing
aes¦thet¦ics
aes¦tival *Br.*
  US estival
aes¦tiv¦ate *Br.*
  aes¦tiv¦at¦ing
  US estivate
aes¦tiv¦ation *Br.*
  US estivation
ae¦ther var. of ether
aetio¦logic *Br.*
  US etiologic
aetio¦logic¦al *Br.*
  US etiological

aetio¦logic¦al¦ly *Br.*
  US etiologically
aeti¦ology *Br.*
  aeti¦olo¦gies
  US etiology
Afar people;
  language
afar
afara
afeared
afebrile
af¦fa¦bil¦ity
af¦fable
af¦fably
af¦fair
af | faire love affair
af | fairé busy
af | faire de cœur
  af¦faires de cœur
affaire du cœur
  var. of *affaire de*
  cœur
af¦fcct have an
  effect on; feign; cf.
  effect
af¦fect¦ation
af¦fect¦ing¦ly
af¦fec¦tion
af¦fec¦tion¦al
af¦fec¦tion¦ate
af¦fec¦tion¦ate¦ly
af¦fect¦ive
  concerning
  emotion; cf.
  effective
af¦fect¦iv¦ity emo-
  tional
  susceptibility; cf.
  effectivity
affect¦less
Af¦fen¦pin¦scher
af¦fer¦ent
af¦fi¦ance
  af¦fi¦an¦cing
af¦fi¦ant
af¦fi¦da¦vit
af¦fili¦ate
  af¦fili¦at¦ing
af¦fili¦ation
af¦filia¦tive
af¦final
af¦fine
af¦fined

af¦fin¦ity
  af¦fin¦ities
af¦firm
af¦firm¦ation
af¦firma¦tive
af¦firma¦tive¦ly
af¦firma¦tory
af¦firm¦er
affix
af¦fix¦ation
af¦fla¦tus
af¦flict
af¦flic¦tion
af¦flict¦ive
af¦flu¦ence
af¦flu¦ent
af¦flu¦en¦tial
af¦flu¦enza
af¦flux
af¦ford
af¦ford¦abil¦ity
af¦ford¦able
af¦ford¦ably
af¦for¦est
af¦for¦est¦ation
af¦fran¦chise
  af¦fran¦chis¦ing
af¦fray
af¦fri¦cate
af¦fright
af¦front
af¦fronté
af¦fronty var. of
  affronté
Af¦ghan coat;
  hound
af¦ghan blanket;
  shawl
af¦ghani currency
Af¦ghani¦stan
afi¦cion¦ado +s
afield
afire
aflame
af¦la¦toxin
afloat
aflood
aflut¦ter
à fond thoroughly;
  cf. *au fond*
afoot
afore
afore¦men¦tioned

afore|said
afore|thought
a for|ti|ori
afoul
afraid
A-frame
afreet
afresh
Af|rica
Af|ri|can
Af|ri|cana things; cf. Afrikaner
Af|ri|can|der var. of Afrikander
Af|ri|can|isa|tion Br. var. of Africanization
Af|ri|can|ise Br. var. of Africanize
Af|ri|can|ism
Af|ri|can|ist
Af|ri|can|iza|tion
Af|ri|can|ize
Af|ri|can|iz|ing
Af|ri|kaans
Af|rika Korps
Af|ri|kan|der
Af|ri|kaner person; gladiolus; cf. Africana
Af|ri|kaner|bond
Af|ri|kaner|dom
afrit var. of afreet
Afro +s
Afro|cen|tric
Afro|cen|trism
Afro|cen|trist
af|ror|mo|sia
Afro|trop|ic|al
aft
after
after|birth
after|burn|er
after|care
after|damp
after|deck
after-effect
after|glow
after-image
after|life
after|lives
after|mar|ket
after|math

after|most
after|noon
after|pains
after-party
after-parties
af|ters
after|shave
after|shock
after|sun
after|taste
after|thought
after|touch
after|ward
after|wards
after|word
after|world
Aga stove trademark
aga Muslim chief (Aga in title)
Aga|dir
again
against
Aga Khan
agal
agama
Aga|mem|non
agam|ic asexual
aga|mid lizard
agamma|globu|lin|aemia Br.
agamma|globu|lin|emia US
agamo|sperm|ous
agamo|spermy
aga|pan|thus
agape gaping; fellowship; feast
agar
agar-agar
agar|batti
agar|ic
agar|ose
Agassi, André tennis player
Agas|siz, Jean zoologist
agate
Aga|tha
agave
age
age|ing or aging
age|ism

age|ist discriminatory; cf. agist
age|less
agency
agen|cies
agenda
agent
agent-general
agents-general
agen|tial
agent|ive
agent pro|voca|teur
agents pro|voca|teurs
Ag|ga|dah var. of Haggadah
Ag|gad|ic var. of Haggadic
Ag|gad|ist var. of Haggadist
ag|glom|er|ate
ag|glom|er|at|ing
ag|glom|er|ation
ag|glom|era|tive
ag|glu|tin|ate
ag|glu|tin|at|ing
ag|glu|tin|ation
ag|glu|tin|ative
ag|glu|tin|in
ag|glu|tin|ogen
ag|grad|ation
ag|grand|ise Br. var. of aggrandize
ag|grand|ise|ment Br. var. of aggrandizement
ag|grand|iser Br. var. of aggrandizer
ag|grand|ize
ag|grand|iz|ing
ag|grand|ize|ment
ag|grand|izer
ag|gra|vate
ag|gra|vat|ing
ag|gra|va|tion
ag|gre|gate
ag|gre|gat|ing
ag|gre|ga|tion
ag|gre|ga|tive
ag|gre|ga|tor
ag|gres|sion
ag|gres|sive
ag|gres|sive|ly

ag|gres|sor
ag|grieve
ag|griev|ing
aggro
aghast
Aghios Niko|laos
agile
agile|ly
agil|ity
agin
Agin|court
aging var. of ageing
agio +s
agism var. of ageism
agist feed livestock
agist var. of ageist
agist|er
agist|ment
agi|tate
agi|tat|ing
agi|tated|ly
agi|ta|tion
agi|tato
agi|ta|tor
agit|prop
agleam
aglet
agley
aglow
agma
ag|nail
ag|nate
Ag|natha
ag|nathan
ag|nat|ic
ag|na|tion
agno|lotti
ag|no|sia
ag|nos|tic
ag|nos|ti|cism
Agnus Dei
ago
agog
agogic
agogics
a gogo galore French à gogo; cf. go-go
agogo +s bell
ag|on|ise Br. var. of agonize

ag|on|is|ing|ly *Br.*
  var. of agonizingly
agon|ism
agon|ist
ag|on|is|tic
ag|on|ize
  ag|on|iz|ing
  ag|on|iz|ing|ly
agony
  ag|onies
agora
  agorae or agoras
  market
agora
  ago|rot or ago|roth
  Israeli currency
agora|phobe
agora|pho|bia
agora|pho|bic
agouti
Agra
agram|ma|tism
agran|ulo|cyto|sis
agraphia
agrar|ian
agree
  agrees
  agreed
  agree|ing
agree|able
agree|ably
agree|ment
agres|tal
agres|tic
agri|busi|ness
Agric|ola, Gnaeus
  Ju|lius Roman
  general
agri|cul|tur|al
agri|cul|tur|al|ist
agri|cul|tur|al|ly
agri|cul|ture
agri|cul|tur|ist
agri|mony
  agri|monies
ag|rion
Agrippa, Mar|cus
  Vip|sa|nius Roman
  general
agri|prod|uct
agri|science
agri|scien|tist
agri|tour|ism
agro|bio|logic|al

agro|biolo|gist
agro|biol|ogy
agro|chem|ical
agro-econom|ic
agro|eco|sys|tem
agro|for|est|ry
agro-industrial
agro-industry
  agro-industries
agrolo|gist
agro|nom|ic
agrono|mist
agron|omy
agro|stol|ogy
aground
aguar|di|ente
Aguas|cali|en|tes
ague
agued
aguish
Agul|has
Ahag|gar
ahead
ahem
ahimsa
ahis|tor|ic|al
Ah|mada|bad
Ah|meda|bad var.
  of Ahmadabad
ahole|hole
ahoy
Ah|ri|man
à huis clos
Ahura Mazda
Ahvaz
Ahwaz var. of Ahvaz
ai
aid help
aida fabric
Aidan
aide assistant
aide-de-camp
  aides-de-camp
aide-memoire
  aides-memoires or
  aides-memoire
  French aide-
  mémoire
Aids = acquired
  immune deficiency
  syndrome
aig|rette
ai|guille

ai|guill|ette
ai|kido
ail be ill; cf. ale
ai|lan|thus
Ai|leen
ail|eron
ail|ment
Ailsa
ai|luro|phobe
ai|luro|pho|bia
aim|less
aim|less|ly
aim|less|ness
ain|hum
Ains|ley
ain't
Ain|tree
Ainu
aioli
air gas; tune; breeze
  etc.; cf. e'er, ere,
  eyre, heir
air|bag
air|band
air|base
air|boat
air|borne
air|brick
air|brush
air|burst
air con
air-conditioned
air con|di|tion|er
air con|di|tion|ing
air|craft
air|craft|man
  air|craft|men
air|craft|woman
  air|craft|women
air|crew
air|date
air|drome
air|drop
air|dropped
air|drop|ping
air-dry
  air-dries
  air-dried
  air-drying
Aire|dale
airer
air|fare
air|field

air|flow
air|foil
air|frame
air|freight
air-freshen|er
air|glow
air|gun
air|head
air|ily
airi|ness
air|ing
air|less
air|less|ness
air|lift
air|line air transport
  company
air line pipe supply-
  ing air
air|liner
air|lock
air|mail
air|man
  air|men
air|man|ship
air|miss
air|mobile
air|plane
air|play
air|port
air|screw
air-sea res|cue
air|ship
air|sick
air|sick|ness
air|side
air|space
air|speed
air|stream
air strike
air|strip
air|tight
air|time
air|waves
air|way
air|woman
  air|women
air|worthi|ness
air|worthy
airy
  air|ier
  airi|est
airy-fairy

aisle passage; cf.
  isle
aisled
ait island; cf. ate
aitch
aitch|bone
Ait|ken, Max Lord
  Beaverbrook
Aix-en-Provence
Aix-la-Chapelle
Aiz|awl
Ajac|cio
ajar
Ajax
ajo|wan
ajuga
akara var. of accra
ake|bia
akee var. of ackee
Akela
Akhe|na|ten
  pharaoh
Akhe|na|ton var. of
  Akhenaten
Akhe|ta|ten ancient
  capital of Egypt
Aki|hito emperor of
  Japan
akimbo
akin
akin|esia
akin|et|ic
Akita
Ak|ka|dian of
  Akkad; cf. Acadian,
  Arcadian
akra|sia
akrat|ic
Aksum
Aksum|ite
akva|vit var. of
  aquavit
à la
Ala|bama
Ala|baman
ala|bas|ter
à la carte
alack
alack-a-day
alac|rity
Alad|din
Alain-Fournier
  novelist

ala|meda
Ala|mein, El
Alamo
à la mode
Alana
Åland
ala|nine
Alanna name
alanna Irish my
  child
Alan|nah name
alan|nah var. of
  alanna
Al-Anon organiza-
  tion
Alar trademark
alar of wings
Alar|cón, Pedro
  An|tonio de writer
Al|aric king of
  Visigoths
alarm
alarm|ing|ly
alarm|ism
alarm|ist
al|arum
alas
Alas|dair
Al|aska
Al|askan
Alas|tair
alate
alba
Al|ba|cete
al|ba|core
Al|ba|nia
Al|ba|nian
Al|bany
al|ba|tross
al|bedo +s
Albee, Ed|ward
  dramatist
al|beit
Al|bers, Josef artist
Al|bert
al|bert watch chain
Al|berta
Al|berti, Leon
  Bat|tista Italian
  architect etc.
al|bes|cent
Albi
Al|bi|gen|ses

ala|meda
Al|bi|gen|sian
al|bin|ism
al|bino +s
Al|bi|noni, Tom|aso
  composer
al|bin|ot|ic
Al|bion
alb|ite
al|biz|zia
Ål|borg var. of
  Aalborg
Al|bu|feira
album
al|bu|men white of
  egg
al|bu|min protein
al|bu|min|oid
al|bu|min|ous
al|bu|min|uria
Al|bu|quer|que
al|bur|num
Al|caeus poet
al|ca|hest var. of
  alkahest
al|caic
al|caics
al|calde
Al|ca|traz
al|ca|zar
Al|ces|tis
al|chem|ical
al|che|milla
al|chem|ise Br. var.
  of alchemize
al|chem|ist
al|chem|ize
  al|chem|iz|ing
al|chemy
al|chera
al|cher|inga
Al|cian blue
  trademark
Al|ci|bi|ades
  Athenian general
alcid
Al|cock, John
  aviator
al|co|hol
al|co|hol|ic
al|co|hol|ism
al|co|hol|om|etry
alco|pop

Al|cott, Lou|isa
  May novelist
al|cove
Al|cuin theologian
Al|dabra
Al|deb|aran
Alde|burgh
al|de|hyde
al|de|hydic
al dente
alder
alder|fly
  alder|flies
al|der|man
al|der|men
al|der|man|ic
al|der|man|ship
Al|der|mas|ton
Al|der|ney
al|der|per|son
Al|der|shot
al|der|woman
al|der|women
aldi|carb
Al|dine
Aldis lamp
  trademark
Al|diss, Brian
  writer
aldol
Aldo Ma|nu|zio
  var. of Aldus
  Manutius
al|dos|ter|one
al|dos|ter|on|ism
Al|dous
Al|drin, Buzz
  astronaut
al|drin
Aldus Ma|nu|tius
  Italian scholar
ale beer; cf. ail
alea|tor|ic
alea|tory
alec Br. in 'smart
  alec'
aleck US in 'smart
  aleck'
ale|cost
Alecto
alee
ale|house

Ale|khine,
  Alex|an|der chess
  player
Alem|bert, Jean le
  Rond d'
  philosopher and
  mathematician
alem|bic
Alen|tejo
aleph
Aleppo
alerce
alert
alert|ly
alert|ness
aleth|ic
aleur|one
Aleut
Aleu|tian
A level
al|evin
ale|wife
  ale|wives
Alex|an|der
  Nev|ski var. of
  Alexander Nevsky
Alex|an|der
  Nev|sky Russian
  hero
alex|an|ders plant
Alex|an|dra
Alex|an|dria
Alex|an|drian
alex|an|drine
alex|an|drite
alexia
Al|exis
al|fal|fa
Al Fatah
alfi|sol
al|foil *trademark*
Al|fonso
Al|fred
Al|fredo
al fresco
alga
  algae
algal
Al|garve
al|ge|bra
al|ge|bra|ic
al|ge|bra|ic|al|ly
al|ge|bra|ist

Al|ge|ciras
Alger
Al|geria
Al|ger|ian
Al|ger|non
al|gi|cide
Al|giers
al|gin|ate
Algol
al|go|lag|nia
algo|logic|al
alg|olo|gist
alg|ology
Al|gon|kian var. of
  Algonquian
Al|gon|kin var. of
  Algonquin
Al|gon|quian wide-
  spread N. American
  Indian group
Al|gon|quin Ameri-
  can Indian people
  in Quebec and
  Ontario
al|go|rithm
al|go|rith|mic
al|go|rith|mic|al|ly
al|gua|cil
al|gua|ciles
Al|ham|bra
Al|ham|bresque
Ali, Mu|ham|mad
  boxer
alias
Ali Baba
alibi +s +ed +ing
Ali|cante
Ali|cia
ali|cyc|lic
al|id|ade
alien
alien|abil|ity
alien|able
alien|age
alien|ate
  alien|at|ing
alien|ation
alien|ee
alien|ist
alien|or
ali|form
Ali|garh

Ali|ghieri, Dante
  poet
alight
align
align|ment
alike
ali|ment
ali|men|tary
ali|men|ta|tion
ali|mony
A-line
ali|phat|ic
ali|quot
Alis|dair
Ali|son
ali|sphen|oid
Al|issa
A-list
Alis|tair
alit|er|acy unwill-
  ingness to read; cf.
  illiteracy
alit|er|ate unwilling
  to read; cf.
  illiterate
alive
ali|yah
  ali|yoth
ali|zar|in
al|ka|hest
al|kali
al|kal|ic
al|ka|line
al|ka|lin|ity
al|kal|ise *Br.* var. of
  alkalize
al|kal|ize
  al|kal|iz|ing
al|kal|oid
al|kal|osis
  al|kal|oses
al|kane
al|ka|net
al|kene
alkie var. of alky
alky
  al|kies
alkyd
alkyl
al|kyl|ate
  al|kyl|at|ing
al|kyl|ation
al|kyne

alla breve
alla cap|pella
Allah
Al|lah|abad
alla|manda
al|lan|ite
al|lan|toic
al|lan|toid
al|lan|toin
al|lan|tois
al|lan|to|ides
al|lar|gando
  al|lar|gandi or
  al|lar|gandos
allay
all-clear *n.*
Al|lecto var. of
  Alecto
allée
al|le|ga|tion
al|lege
  al|leging
al|leged|ly
Al|le|gheny
  Al|le|ghen|ies
al|le|giance
al|le|gor|ic|al
al|le|gor|ic|al|ly
al|le|gor|isa|tion
  Br. var. of
  allegorization
al|le|gor|ise *Br.* var.
  of allegorize
al|le|gor|ist
al|le|gor|iza|tion
al|le|gor|ize
  al|le|gor|iz|ing
al|le|gory
  al|le|gor|ies
al|le|gretto +s
Al|le|gri, Gre|gorio
  composer
al|legro +s
al|lele
al|lel|ic
al|lelo|chem|ical
al|lelo|morph
al|lelo|morph|ic
al|lelo|path|ic
al|lelop|athy
al|le|luia
alle|mande

Allen key etc.
trademark
Allen, Woody actor
etc.
Al|lenby, Ed|mund
general
Al|lende, Sal|va|dor
president of Chile
al|ler|gen
al|ler|gen|ic
al|ler|gen|icity
al|ler|gic
al|ler|gist
al|lergy
al|ler|gies
al|le|vi|ate
al|le|vi|at|ing
al|le|vi|ation
al|le|via|tive
al|le|vi|ator
alley lane
alley marble; var. of
ally
alley-oop
al|ley|way
All Fools' Day
all|heal
al|li|aceous
al|li|ance
al|li|cin
al|lied
Al|lier river
al|li|ga|tor
all in tired; in total
all-in complete
Al|li|son
allis shad
al|lit|er|ate
al|lit|er|at|ing
al|lit|er|ation
al|lit|era|tive
al|lit|era|tive|ly
al|lium
all-nighter
Alloa
al|loc|able
al|lo|cate
al|lo|cat|ing
al|lo|ca|tion
al|lo|ca|tive
al|lo|ca|tor
al|loch|thon|ous
al|lo|cu|tion

allod
al|lo|dial
al|lo|dium
al|lo|dia
al|log|am|ous
al|log|amy
allo|gen|eic
allo|gen|ic
allo|graft
allo|graph
allo|met|ric
al|lom|etry
allo|morph
allo|morph|ic
allo|path
allo|path|ic
al|lop|ath|ist
al|lop|athy
allo|pat|ric
al|lop|atry
al|lop|atries
allo|phone
allo|phon|ic
allo|pur|in|ol
allo|saurus
allo|steric
allot
al|lot|ted
al|lot|ting
al|lot|ment
allo|trope
al|lot|rop|ic
al|lot|ropy
al|lot|tee
allow
al|low|able
al|low|ance
al|low|ancing
al|loxan
alloy
all ready entire
number of people
or things in a state
of readiness; cf.
already
all right
all-rounder
All Saints' Day
all-seater
all|seed
All Souls' Day
all|spice

all to|gether all at
once; all in one; cf.
altogether
al|lude
al|lud|ing
refer indirectly; cf.
elude, illude
al|lure
al|lur|ing
al|lure|ment
al|lur|ing|ly
allus
al|lu|sion indirect
reference; cf.
illusion
al|lu|sive containing
an allusion; cf.
elusive, illusive
al|lu|sive|ly in an
allusive way; cf.
elusively
al|lu|sive|ness allu-
sive nature; cf.
elusiveness
al|lu|vial
al|lu|vion
al|lu|vium
ally
al|lies
al|lied
ally|ing
cooperate; partner;
marble
allyl
al|lyl|ic
Alma
Alma-Ata
al|ma|can|tar var.
of almucantar
al|ma|gest
alma mater
al|manac
*Al|man|ach de
Gotha*
Al|man|ack for
Oxford, Whitaker's,
Wisden
al|man|dine
**Alma-Tadema,
Law|rence** painter
Al|maty
Al|me|ría
al|mighty
al|mirah
Al|mir|ante Brown

al|mond
al|mon|er
al|mon|ry
al|mon|ries
Al|mora|vid
Al|mora|vide var. of
Almoravid
al|most
alms charity; cf.
arms
alms|house
al|mu|can|tar
aloe
aloe vera
aloft
alogic|al
aloha
alone
along
along|shore
along|side
aloof
aloof|ly
aloof|ness
alo|pe|cia
Alor Setar
aloud
alow below, in a
ship
Aloy|sius
al|paca
al|par|gata
alpen|glow
alpen|horn
alpen|stock
alpha
al|pha|bet
al|pha|bet|ic
al|pha|bet|ic|al
al|pha|bet|ic|al|ly
al|pha|bet|isa|tion
Br. var. of
alphabetization
al|pha|bet|ise *Br.*
var. of alphabetize
al|pha|bet|iza|tion
al|pha|bet|ize
al|pha|bet|iz|ing
Alpha Cen|tauri
alpha|feto|protein
alpha-hydroxy
alpha|numer|ic
alp|horn

Al|pine of Alps or downhill skiing
al|pine of high mountains
Al|pin|ist
al|prazo|lam
Al Qaeda militant Islamic fundamentalist group
Al Qaida var. of Al Qaeda
al|ready beforehand; as early or as soon as this; cf. all ready
al|right var. of all right
Al|sace
Alsace-Lorraine
Al|sa|tian
al|sike
also
also-ran
al|stroe|me|ria
Altai territory, Russia; mountains
Al|taic
Al|tair star
altar table in church; cf. alter
al|tar|piece
Altay var. of Altai
alt|azi|muth
alt.country
Alt|dor|fer, Al|brecht painter
alter change; cf. altar
al|ter|able
al|ter|ation
al|tera|tive
al|ter|cate
al|ter|cat|ing
al|ter|ca|tion
alter ego
al|ter|ity
al|ter|nant
al|ter|nate
al|ter|nat|ing
al|ter|nate|ly
al|ter|na|tion
al|ter|na|tive
al|ter|na|tive|ly
al|ter|na|tor

Al|thea
Al|thing
alt|horn
al|though
Al|thus|ser, Louis philosopher
al|tim|eter
alti|met|ric
al|tim|etry
alti|plano +s
al|tis|simo
alti|tude
alti|tud|inal
Alt key
Alt|man, Rob|ert film director
alto +s
alto|cumu|lus alto|cumuli
al|together totally; in total; cf. all together
alto-relievo +s
alto|stra|tus
al|tri|cial
al|tru|ism
al|tru|ist
al|tru|is|tic
al|tru|is|tic|al|ly
alu|del
alula
alu|lae
alum
alu|mina
alu|min|ise Br. var. of aluminize
alu|min|ium Br. US aluminum
alu|min|ize
alu|min|iz|ing
alu|mino|sili|cate
alu|min|ous
alu|mi|num US Br. aluminium
alumna female
alum|nae
alum|nus male
alumni
Al|varez, Luis physicist
al|veo|lar
al|veo|late
al|ve|ol|itis

al|veo|lus
al|veoli
alway
al|ways
alys|sum
Alz|heim|er's
ama|crine
ama|da|vat var. of avadavat
ama|dou
amah nursemaid
ama|khosi
Amal Muslim organization
Amalfi
amal|gam
amal|gam|ate
amal|gam|at|ing
amal|gam|ation
Amal|thea
amanu|en|sis
amanu|en|ses
Amapá
am|ar|anth
am|ar|anth|ine
ama|retti biscuits
ama|retto liqueur; cf. amoretto
amar|yl|lis
amass
amass|er
Ama|ter|asu
ama|teur
ama|teur|ish
ama|teur|ish|ly
ama|teur|ish|ness
ama|teur|ism
Amati
ama|tol
ama|tory
am|aur|osis
am|aur|ot|ic
amaze
amaz|ing
amaze|ment
amaz|ing|ly
Ama|zon river; legendary female warrior
ama|zon strong, athletic woman; parrot
ama|zon ant

Ama|zo|nas
Ama|zon dol|phin
Ama|zo|nia
Ama|zon|ian
am|bas|sa|dor
ambassador-at-large
ambassadors-at-large
am|bas|sa|dor|ial
am|bas|sa|dor|ship
am|bas|sa|dress
am|batch
Am|bato
amber
am|ber|gris
am|ber|jack
am|bi|ance Painting
ambi|dex|ter|ity
ambi|dex|trous
ambi|dex|trous|ly
am|bi|ence
am|bi|ent
am|bi|gu|ity
am|bi|gu|ities
am|bigu|ous
am|bigu|ous|ly
ambi|sex|ual
ambi|son|ic
ambi|son|ics
ambit
am|bi|tion
am|bi|tious
am|bi|tious|ly
am|biva|lence
am|biva|lent
am|biva|lent|ly
ambi|ver|sion
ambi|vert
amble
am|bling
am|bler
am|bly|opia
am|bly|opic
ambo
ambos or am|bo|nes
Am|boina var. of Ambon
Am|boin|ese var. of Ambonese
Ambon

Am|bo|nese
am|boyna
Am|brose
am|bro|sia
am|bro|sial
Am|bro|sian of St Ambrose
am|bro|sian of ambrosia
ambry var. of aumbry
am|bu|la|cral
am|bu|la|crum
am|bu|la|cra
am|bu|lance
am|bu|lan|cing
am|bu|lant
am|bu|late
am|bu|lat|ing
am|bu|la|tion
am|bu|la|tory
am|bu|la|tor|ies
Am|bulo|cetus
Am|bulo|ceti
am|bus|cade
am|bus|cad|ing
am|bush
am-dram
ameba US
amebas or amebae Br. amoeba
ameb|ia|sis US Br. amoebiasis
ameb|ic US Br. amoebic
ameb|oid US Br. amoeboid
ame|lan|chier
ameli|or|ate
ameli|or|at|ing
ameli|or|ation
ameli|ora|tive
ameli|or|ator
amen
amen|abil|ity
amen|able
amen|ably
amend improve; cf. emend
amend|able
amende
hon|or|able
amendes
hon|or|ables

amend|er
amend|ment
amends
amen|ity
amen|ities
amen|or|rhea US
amen|or|rhoea Br.
ament
amen|tia
Amer|asian
amerce
amer|cing
amerce|ment
Amer|ica
Ameri|can
Ameri|cana
Ameri|can|isa|tion Br. var. of Americanization
Ameri|can|ise Br. var. of Americanize
Ameri|can|ism
Ameri|can|iza|tion
Ameri|can|ize
Ameri|can|iz|ing
Ameri|can|ness
Amer|ica's Cup
ameri|cium
Amer|ind
Amer|in|dian
Amer|in|dic
Ames|lan = American sign language
Ames test
ameth|yst
ameth|yst|ine
Amex = American Stock Exchange; *trademark* American Express
Am|hara
Am|har|ic
ami|abil|ity
ami|able
ami|ably
ami|an|thus
am|ic|abil|ity
am|ic|able
am|ic|ably
amice
amicus
amici

ami|cus cur|iae
amici cur|iae
amid
Ami|dah
amide
amid|ship
amid|ships
amidst
Am|iens
amigo +s
Am|in|divi
amine
amino +s
amir var. of emir
Amir|ante
Amis, Kings|ley novelist
Amis, Mar|tin novelist
Amish
amiss
ami|tosis
ami|tot|ic
ami|trip|tyl|ine
amity
Amman capital of Jordan
am|meter
ammo
Ammon Greek and Roman name for Amun
am|mo|nia
am|mo|ni|ac|al
am|mo|ni|ated
am|mon|ite
am|mo|nium
am|mon|oid
am|mu|ni|tion
am|nesia
am|nesiac
am|nesic
am|nesty
am|nes|ties
am|nes|tied
am|nesty|ing
amnio +s = amniocentesis
am|nio|cen|tesis
am|nio|cen|teses
am|nion
amnia or
am|ni|ons

am|ni|ote
am|ni|ot|ic
amn't
amoeba Br.
amoe|bas or amoe|bae US ameba
amoeb|ia|sis Br. US amebiasis
amoeb|ic Br. US amebic
amoeb|oid Br. US ameboid
amok
Amon var. of Amun
among
amongst
amon|til|lado +s
amoral
amor|al|ism
amor|al|ist
amor|al|ity
amo|retto
amo|retti
Cupid; cf. *amaretti,* amaretto
am|or|ist
Am|or|ite
amor|oso +s
am|or|ous
am|or|ous|ly
am|or|ous|ness
amorph|ous
amorph|ous|ness
amort|isa|tion Br. var. of amortization
amort|ise Br. var. of amortize
amort|iza|tion
amort|ize
amort|iz|ing
amos|ite
amount
amour
amour cour|tois
amour fou
amour propre
amoxi|cil|lin
amoxy|cil|lin var. of amoxicillin
Am|pa|kine *trademark in the US*

am|pel|op|sis
am|per|age
Am|père, André-
  Marie physicist
am|pere unit
  French ampère
am|per|sand
am|phet|amine
Am|phibia
am|phib|ian
am|phibi|ous
amphi|bole
am|phibo|lite
amphi|bology
  amphi|bolo|gies
am|phib|oly
  am|phib|olies
amphi|brach
amphi|mic|tic
amphi|mixis
amphi|oxus
  amphi|oxi
amphi|path|ic
amphi|phil|ic
amphi|pod
Amphi|poda
am|phip|ro|style
am|phis|baena
Am|phis|bae|nia
am|phis|bae|nian
amphi|theater *US*
amphi|theatre *Br.*
Amphi|trite
am|phit|ryon
amphi|uma
am|phora
  am|phorae or
  am|phoras
ampho|ter|ic
ampi|cil|lin
ample
  amp|ler
  amp|lest
am|plexus
amp|li|fi|ca|tion
amp|li|fier
amp|lify
  amp|li|fies
  amp|li|fied
  amp|li|fy|ing
amp|li|tude
amply
am|poule

ampul *US*
var. of ampoule
am|pule *US*
var. of ampoule
am|pulla
  am|pul|lae
am|pu|tate
  am|pu|tat|ing
am|pu|ta|tion
am|pu|ta|tor
am|pu|tee
amrit
Am|rit|sar
Am|ster|dam
am|trac amphibious
  vehicle
Am|track var. of
  Amtrak
Am|trak US railway
  trademark
am|trak var. of
  amtrac
amuck var. of amok
Amu Darya river
amu|let
Amun Egyptian god
Amund|sen, Roald
  explorer
Amur river
amuse
  amus|ing
amuse-gueule
amuse|ment
amus|ing|ly
amyg|dala
  amyg|da|lae
amyg|dale
amyg|dal|in
amyg|dal|oid
amyg|dal|oid|al
amyl
amyl|ase
amyl|oid
amyl|oid|osis
amylo|pec|tin
amyl|ose
amyo|troph|ic
amy|ot|rophy
Amy|tal *trademark*
ana collection of
  person's sayings
Ana|bap|tism
Ana|bap|tist

anab|asis
anab|ases
ana|bat|ic
ana|bi|osis
ana|bi|ot|ic
ana|bol|ic
an|ab|ol|ism
ana|branch
ana|chron|ic
an|achron|ism
ana|chron|is|tic
ana|chron|is|tic|
    al|ly
ana|clit|ic
ana|co|lu|thic
ana|co|lu|thon
  ana|co|lu|tha
ana|conda
Anac|reon poet
anac|reon|tic
an|acro|nym
ana|cru|sis
  ana|cru|ses
an|adro|mous
an|aemia *Br.*
  US anemia
an|aemic *Br.*
  US anemic
an|aer|obe
an|aer|obic
an|aer|obic|al|ly
an|aes|the|sia *Br.*
  US anesthesia
an|aes|thesi|
    olo|gist *Br.*
  US
  anesthesiologist
an|aes|the|si|ology
  Br.
  US anesthesiology
an|aes|thet|ic *Br.*
  US anesthetic
an|aes|the|tisa|tion
  Br. var. of
  anaesthetization
  US anesthetization
an|aes|the|tise *Br.*
  var. of anaesthetize
  US anesthetize
an|aes|the|tist *Br.*
  US anesthetist
an|aes|the|tiza|tion
  Br.
  US anesthetization

an|aes|the|tize *Br.*
an|aes|the|tiz|ing
  US anesthetize
ana|gen
ana|gen|esis
ana|gen|et|ic
ana|glyph
ana|glyph|ic
Ana|glypta
  trademark
ana|gram
  ana|grammed
  ana|gram|ming
ana|gram|mat|ic
ana|gram|
    ma|tisa|tion
  Br. var. of ana-
  grammatization
ana|gram|ma|tise
  Br. var. of
  anagrammatize
ana|gram|
    ma|tiza|tion
ana|gram|ma|tize
ana|gram|
    ma|tiz|ing
Ana|heim
anal
ana|lecta var. of
  analects
ana|lects
ana|lep|tic
an|al|gesia
an|al|gesic
anal|ly
ana|log *US*
  Br. analogue
ana|logic|al
ana|logic|al|ly
analo|gise *Br.* var.
  of analogize
analo|gize
analo|giz|ing
analo|gous
analo|gous|ly
ana|logue
ana|logy
  ana|lo|gies
an|alpha|bet|ic
anal-retentive
anal-sadistic
ana|lys|able *Br.*
  US analyzable
an|alys|and

ana¦lyse *Br.*
ana¦lys¦ing
US analyze
ana¦lys¦er *Br.*
US analyzer
ana¦lysis
ana¦lyses
ana¦lyst person who
analyses; cf.
annalist
ana¦lyt¦ic
ana¦lyt¦ic¦al
ana¦lyt¦ic¦al¦ly
ana¦lyz¦able *US*
Br. analysable
ana¦lyze *US*
ana¦lyz¦ing
Br. analyse
ana¦lyz¦er *US*
Br. analyser
an¦am¦nesis
an¦am¦neses
an¦am¦nes¦tic
ana¦morph¦ic
ana¦mor¦phosis
ana¦mor¦phoses
an¦anda
An¦angu
Ana¦nias
ana¦paest *Br.*
US anapest
ana¦paest¦ic *Br.*
US anapestic
ana¦pest *US*
Br. anapaest
ana¦pest¦ic *US*
Br. anapaestic
ana¦phase
ana¦phor
an¦aph¦ora
ana¦phor¦ic
ana¦phor¦ic¦al¦ly
an¦aphro¦dis¦iac
ana¦phyl¦actic
ana¦phyl¦axis
anap¦tyc¦tic
anap¦tyxis
an¦arch +s
an¦arch¦ic
an¦arch¦ic¦al¦ly
an¦arch¦ism
an¦arch¦ist
an¦arch¦is¦tic
an¦archy

Ana¦sazi
Ana¦sta¦sia
ana¦stig¦mat
ana¦stig¦mat¦ic
anas¦to¦mose
anas¦to¦mos¦ing
anas¦to¦mosis
anas¦to¦moses
anas¦to¦mot¦ic
anas¦tro¦phe
anath¦ema
anath¦ema¦tise *Br.*
var. of
anathematize
anath¦ema¦tize
anath¦ema¦tiz¦ing
Ana¦to¦lia
Ana¦to¦lian
ana¦tom¦ic
ana¦tom¦ic¦al
ana¦tom¦ic¦al¦ly
anat¦om¦ise *Br.* var.
of anatomize
anat¦om¦ist
anat¦om¦ize
anat¦om¦iz¦ing
anat¦omy
anat¦omies
an¦atto var. of
annatto
an¦ces¦tor
an¦ces¦tral
an¦ces¦tral¦ly
an¦ces¦tress
an¦ces¦try
an¦ces¦tries
ancho +s
an¦chor
an¦chor¦age
an¦chor¦ess
an¦choret
an¦chor¦et¦ic
an¦chor¦ite
an¦chor¦it¦ic
an¦chor¦man
an¦chor¦men
an¦chor¦woman
an¦chor¦women
an¦cho¦veta
an¦chovy
an¦cho¦vies
an¦chusa
an¦cien ré¦gime
an¦ciens ré¦gimes

an¦cient
an¦cient¦ly
an¦cil¦lary
an¦cil¦lar¦ies
ancon
an¦co¦nes
An¦cona
an¦cylo¦stom¦ia¦sis
An¦da¦lu¦cia Span-
ish name for
Andalusia
An¦da¦lu¦sia
An¦da¦lu¦sian
An¦da¦lus¦ite
An¦da¦man islands
an¦dante
an¦dan¦tino +s
An¦dean
An¦der¦sen, Hans
Chris¦tian writer
An¦der¦son,
Eliza¦beth Gar¦rett
physician and
feminist
An¦der¦son,
Mar¦ian singer
An¦der¦son,
Lind¦say film
director
An¦der¦son
shel¦ter
Andes
an¦des¦ite
an¦des¦it¦ic
An¦dhra Pra¦desh
and¦iron
an¦di¦sol var. of
andosol
An¦dorra
An¦dor¦ran
an¦do¦sol
an¦douille
an¦dra¦dite
Andre, Carl sculp-
tor
An¦drea
An¦dreas
An¦drew
An¦drew in 'merry
andrew'
an¦dro¦cen¦tric
An¦dro¦cles
an¦droc¦racy
an¦droc¦ra¦cies

an¦dro¦crat¦ic
an¦droe¦cial
an¦droe¦cium
an¦droe¦cia
an¦dro¦gen
an¦dro¦gen¦ic
an¦dro¦gen¦isa¦tion
Br. var. of
androgenization
an¦dro¦gen¦ise *Br.*
var. of androgenize
an¦dro¦gen¦iza¦tion
an¦dro¦gen¦ize
an¦dro¦gen¦iz¦ing
an¦dro¦gyne
an¦dro¦gyn¦ous
an¦dro¦gyny
an¦droid
An¦drom¦ache
An¦drom¦eda con-
stellation
an¦drom¦eda plant
andro¦pause
An¦dro¦pov, Yuri
Soviet president
andro¦stene¦dione
andro¦ster¦one
an¦ec¦dot¦age
an¦ec¦dotal
an¦ec¦dotal¦ist
an¦ec¦dotal¦ly
an¦ec¦dote
an¦echo¦ic
An¦eirin
anele
anel¦ing
anoint; cf. anneal
an¦emia *US*
Br. anaemia
an¦emic *US*
Br. anaemic
anemo¦graph
anemo¦graph¦ic
an¦emom¦eter
anemo¦met¦ric
an¦emom¦etry
anem¦one
an¦em¦oph¦il¦ous
an¦em¦oph¦ily
an¦en¦ceph¦al¦ic
an¦en¦ceph¦aly
anent
aner¦gia

an¦ergy
an¦er¦oid
an¦es¦the¦sia *US*
  Br. anaesthesia
an¦es¦the¦si¦ologist
  US
  Br.
  anaesthesiologist
an¦es¦the¦si¦ology
  US
  Br.
  anaesthesiology
an¦es¦thet¦ic *US*
  Br. anaesthetic
an¦es¦the¦tist *US*
  Br. anaesthetist
an¦es¦the¦tiza¦tion
  US
  Br.
  anaesthetization
an¦es¦the¦tize *US*
an¦es¦the¦tiz¦ing
  Br. anaesthetize
an¦eu¦ploid
an¦eu¦ploidy
An¦eurin name
an¦eurin vitamin
aneur¦ine var. of
  aneurin
an¦eur¦ism var. of
  aneurysm
an¦eur¦ism¦al var.
  of aneurysmal
an¦eur¦ysm
an¦eur¦ys¦mal
anew
an¦gary
angel
An¦gela
An¦ge¦leno +s per-
  son from Los
  Angeles
angel¦fish
an¦gel¦ic
an¦gel¦ica
an¦gel¦ic¦al¦ly
An¦gel¦ico, Fra
  painter
An¦ge¦lina
An¦ge¦lino var. of
  Angeleno
Angel¦man's
  syn¦drome
angel¦ology

An¦ge¦lou, Maya
  writer
angels-on-
      horseback
an¦ge¦lus
anger
An¦gers city, France
An¦ge¦vin
Ang¦harad
an¦gina
an¦gin¦al
an¦gina pec¦toris
angio¦gen¦esis
angio¦gram
angio¦graph¦ic
angi¦og¦raphy
angi¦oma
  angi¦omas or
  angi¦omata
angio¦neur¦ot¦ic
angio¦plasty
  angio¦plas¦ties
angio¦sperm
angio¦sperm¦ous
angio¦ten¦sin
Ang¦kor
Angle people
angle
  an¦gling
  Geometry; fish
angle¦poise
  trademark
an¦gler
angler¦fish
Angle¦sey
An¦glian
An¦gli¦can
An¦gli¦can¦ism
an¦glice in English
an¦gli¦cisa¦tion *Br.*
  var. of
  anglicization
an¦gli¦cise *Br.* var.
  of anglicize
An¦gli¦cism
an¦gli¦ciza¦tion
an¦gli¦cize
  an¦gli¦ciz¦ing
An¦glis¦tics
Anglo +s
Anglo¦cen¦tric
Anglo¦mania
Anglo¦maniac

Anglo¦phile
Anglo¦philia
Anglo¦phobe
Anglo¦pho¦bia
anglo¦phone
An¦gola
An¦golan
an¦gora
an¦gos¦tura plant
An¦gos¦tura
  bit¦ters *trademark*
an¦grily
angry
  an¦grier
  an¦gri¦est
angst
ang¦strom
angsty
An¦guilla
An¦guil¦lan
an¦guish
an¦gu¦lar
an¦gu¦lar¦ity
an¦gu¦late
  an¦gu¦la¦ting
  an¦gu¦la¦tion
Angus
an¦gwan¦tibo +s
an¦har¦mon¦ic
an¦har¦mon¦icity
an¦he¦do¦nia
an¦he¦don¦ic
an¦he¦dral
an¦hinga
an¦hyd¦ride
an¦hyd¦rite
an¦hyd¦rous
ani bird
an¦il¦ine
ani¦lin¦gus
anima
an¦im¦ad¦ver¦sion
an¦im¦ad¦vert
ani¦mal
ani¦mal¦cu¦lar
ani¦mal¦cule
ani¦mal¦isa¦tion *Br.*
  var. of
  animalization
ani¦mal¦ise *Br.* var.
  of animalize
ani¦mal¦ism
ani¦mal¦ist

ani¦mal¦is¦tic
ani¦mal¦ity
ani¦mal¦iza¦tion
ani¦mal¦ize
  ani¦mal¦iz¦ing
ani¦mate
  ani¦mat¦ing
ani¦mated¦ly
ani¦ma¦teur
ani¦mat¦ic
ani¦ma¦tion
ani¦mato
  ani¦matos or
  ani¦mati
ani¦ma¦tor
anima¦tron¦ic
anima¦tron¦ics
anime Japanese
  animation
ani¦mism
ani¦mist
ani¦mis¦tic
ani¦mos¦ity
  ani¦mos¦ities
ani¦mus
anion
an¦ion¦ic
anise
ani¦seed
an¦is¦ette
an¦is¦ogam¦ous
an¦is¦og¦amy
An¦is¦op¦tera
an¦is¦op¦ter¦an
an¦iso¦trop¦ic
an¦isot¦ropy
Anjou
An¦kara
ankh
ankle
ank¦ling
ank¦let
ankus
an¦kylo¦saur
an¦ky¦lose
an¦ky¦los¦ing
an¦ky¦losis
an¦ky¦loses
an¦ky¦lo¦stom¦ia¦sis
  var. of
  ancylostomiasis
an¦kyl¦ot¦ic

an|lage
  an|lagen
anna money
annal
an|nal|ist writer of
  annals; cf. **analyst**
an|nal|is|tic
Annan, Kofi UN
  Secretary General
An|nap|olis
An|na|purna
an|nates
an|natto +s
Anne queen of Eng-
  land and Scotland;
  Princess Royal
Anne of Cleves
Anne, St
an|neal heat-treat;
  cf. **anele**
an|neal|er
an|ne|lid
An|nel|ida
an|nel|id|an
An|nette
annex *v.*
an|nex|ation
an|nex|ation|ist
an|nexe *n.*
An|ni|goni, Pie|tro
  painter
an|ni|hi|late
  an|ni|hi|lat|ing
an|ni|hi|la|tion
an|ni|hi|la|tor
an|ni|ver|sary
  an|ni|ver|sar|ies
Anno Dom|ini
an|no|tat|able
an|no|tate
  an|no|tat|ing
an|no|ta|tion
an|no|ta|tive
an|no|ta|tor
an|nounce
  an|noun|cing
an|nounce|ment
an|noun|cer
annoy
an|noy|ance
an|noy|er
an|noy|ing|ly
an|nual

an|nu|al|ise *Br.* var.
  of **annualize**
an|nu|al|ize
  an|nu|al|iz|ing
an|nu|al|ly
an|nu|it|ant
an|nuit|ise *Br.* var.
  of **annuitize**
an|nuit|ize
  an|nuit|iz|ing
an|nu|ity
  an|nu|ities
annul
an|nulled
an|nul|ling
an|nu|lar
an|nu|late
an|nu|lated
an|nu|la|tion
an|nu|let
an|nul|ment
an|nu|lus
  an|nuli
an|nun|ci|ate
  an|nun|ci|at|ing
an|nun|ci|ation
an|nun|ci|ator
annus hor|ri|bilis
anni hor|ri|bili
annus mira|bilis
anni mira|bili
anoa
an|odal
anode
an|odic
ano|dise *Br.* var. of
  anodize
ano|diser *Br.* var. of
  anodizer
ano|dize
  ano|diz|ing
ano|dizer
ano|dyne
ano|geni|tal
anoint
anoint|er
anole
anom|al|is|tic
anom|al|ous
anom|al|ous|ly
anom|aly
  anom|al|ies
ano|mia medical
  condition

ano|mic of anomia
anom|ic of anomie
ano|mie lack of
  usual standards
anomy var. of
  anomie
anon soon
anon. = anonymous
ano|nym
an|onym|ise *Br.* var.
  of **anonymize**
ano|nym|ity
an|onym|ize
  an|onym|iz|ing
an|onym|ous
an|onym|ous|ly
anoph|eles
  pl. anoph|eles
anoph|el|ine
an|oph|thal|mia
Ano|plura
ano|plur|an
ano|rak
ano|raky
ano|rec|tal
an|or|ec|tic var. of
  anorexic
an|or|exia ner|vosa
an|or|ex|ic
an|or|gas|mia
an|or|gas|mic
anorth|ite
an|ortho|site
an|os|mia
an|os|mic
an|other
A. N. Other
  unnamed person
an|otherie var. of
  anothery
an|othery
Anouilh, Jean
  writer
ANOVA = analysis
  of variance
an|ovu|lant
an|ovula|tory
an|oxia
an|oxic
an|satz
an|schluss
An|selm
an|ser|ine

an|swer
an|swer|able
an|swer|er
an|swer|phone
Ant|abuse
  trademark
ant|acid
an|tag|on|ise *Br.*
  var. of **antagonize**
an|tag|on|ism
an|tag|on|ist
an|tag|on|is|tic
an|tag|on|is|tic|
  al|ly
an|tag|on|ize
  an|tag|on|iz|ing
An|takya
An|talya
An|tana|na|rivo
Ant|arc|tic
Ant|arc|tica
An|tares
ant|bear
ant|bird
ante
antes
anted
ante|ing
  stake; cf. **anti**
ant|eater
ante|bellum
ante|ce|dence
ante|cedent
ante|cham|ber
ante|chapel
ante|chinus
ante|date
  ante|dat|ing
ante|dilu|vian
ante|lope
ante-mortem
ante|natal
ante|natal|ly
an|tenna *Zoology*
  an|ten|nae
an|tenna aerial
  an|ten|nas or
  an|ten|nae
an|ten|nal
an|ten|nary
an|ten|nule
ante|nup|tial
ante|par|tum

ante|pen|ult
ante|pen|ul|ti|mate
ante-post
an|ter|ior
an|ter|ior|ity
an|teri|or|ly
an|tero|grade
an|tero|lat|eral
ante|room
an|tero|pos|ter|ior
ante|vert|ed
An|thea
ant|he|lion
  ant|he|lia
an|thel|min|tic
an|them
an|them|ic
an|the|mion
  an|the|mia
An|the|mius Greek
  mathematician
an|ther
an|ther|al
an|ther|id|ial
an|ther|id|ium
  an|ther|idia
an|thero|zoid
an|the|sis
ant|hill
antho|cya|nin
an|tholo|gisa|tion
  Br. var. of
  anthologization
an|tholo|gise Br.
  var. of anthologize
an|tholo|gist
an|tholo|giza|tion
an|tholo|gize
  an|tholo|giz|ing
an|thol|ogy
  an|tholo|gies
An|thony, St
An|thony of
  Padua, St
anth|oph|il|ous
Antho|zoa
antho|zoan
an|thra|cene
an|thra|cite
an|thrac|nose
anthra|nilate
anthra|nil|ic
anthra|quin|one

an|thrax
an|throp|ic
an|thropo|cen|tric
an|thropo|
      cen|trism
an|thropo|gen|ic
an|thropo|gen|ic|
          al|ly
an|thro|poid
an|thropo|logic|al
an|thro|polo|gist
an|thro|pol|ogy
an|thropo|met|ric
an|thropo|met|rics
an|thro|pom|etry
an|thropo|
      morph|ic
an|thropo|
  morph|ic|al|ly
an|thropo|morph|
              ise
  Br. var. of
  anthropomorphize
an|thropo|morph|
              ism
an|thropo|morph|
              ize
an|thropo|morph|
          iz|ing
an|thropo|
      morph|ous
an|thro|pop|athy
an|thro|poph|agi
  cannibals
an|thro|
      popha|gous
an|thro|poph|agy
  cannibalism
an|thropo|
      soph|ic|al
an|thro|poso|phy
an|thur|ium
anti against;
  opposer; cf. ante
anti-abortion
anti-abortion|ist
anti-aircraft
anti-apartheid
anti|bac|ter|ial
An|tibes
anti|biosis
anti|biot|ic
anti|body
  anti|bodies

antic
anti|cath|ode
anti-choice
anti|cholin|er|gic
Anti|christ
anti-Christian
an|tici|pate
  an|tici|pat|ing
an|tici|pa|tion
an|tici|pa|tive
an|tici|pa|tor
an|tici|pa|tory
anti|cler|ic|al
anti|cler|ic|al|ism
anti|cli|mac|tic
anti|cli|mac|tic|
            al|ly
anti|cli|max
anti|clinal
anti|cline
anti|clock|wise
anti|coagu|lant
anti|codon
anti-commun|ist
anti-
    constitu|tion|al
anti|con|vul|sant
an|tics
anti|cyc|lone
anti|cyc|lon|ic
anti|depres|sant
anti|diar|rhe|al US
anti|diar|rhoe|al
  Br.
anti|dis|estab|lish|
        ment|arian
anti|dis|estab|lish|
      ment|arian|ism
anti|dotal
anti|dote
anti|drom|ic
anti-emetic
anti-
    establish|ment
anti|feed|ant
anti|ferro|
        mag|net|ic
anti|foul|ing
anti|freeze
anti-g
anti|gen
anti|gen|ic
An|tig|one

an|tig|or|ite
anti|grav|ity
An|tigua
An|ti|guan
anti-hero
  anti-heroes
anti-heroine
anti|his|ta|mine
anti-infect|ive
anti-
    inflam|ma|tory
anti-
    inflam|ma|tories
anti-knock
Anti-Lebanon
An|til|lean
An|til|les
anti-lock
anti|log
anti|log|ar|ithm
an|tilogy
an|tilo|gies
anti|macas|sar
anti-magnet|ic
anti|mal|ar|ial
anti|mat|ter
anti|metab|ol|ite
anti|micro|bial
anti-monarch|ist
an|tim|onial
an|tim|on|ic
an|tim|oni|ous
an|tim|ony chem-
  ical element; cf.
  antinomy
anti-nation|al
anti|node
anti-noise
anti|nomian
anti|nomian|ism
anti|nomy
  anti|nomies
  contradiction
  between laws; cf.
  antimony
anti|novel
anti-nuclear
An|tioch
An|tio|chus Seleu-
  cid kings
anti|oxi|dant
anti|par|al|lel
anti|par|ticle

anti|pasto
anti|pasti
antl|path|et|ic
an|tip|athy
 an|tip|athies
anti-person|nel
anti|per|spir|ant
anti|phon
an|tiph|on|al
an|tiph|on|al|ly
an|tiph|on|ary
 an|tiph|on|ar|ies
an|tiph|ony
 an|tiph|on|ies
anti|podal
anti|pode
An|tipo|dean Australasian
an|tipo|dean generally
An|tipo|des Australasia
an|tipo|des generally
anti|pope
anti|pro|ton
anti|prur|it|ic
anti|psychot|ic
anti|pyr|et|ic
anti|quar|ian
anti|quar|ian|ism
anti|quark
anti|quary
 anti|quar|ies
anti|quated
an|tique
 an|tiquing
an|tiquity
 an|tiqui|ties
anti-racism
anti-racist
anti|retro|viral
anti-roll bar
an|tir|rhi|num
anti|scor|bu|tic
anti-Semite
anti-Semitic
anti-Semitism
anti|sense
anti|sep|sis
anti|sep|tic
anti|sep|tic|al|ly

anti|serum
 anti|sera
anti|social
anti|social|ly
anti|spas|mod|ic
anti-static
An|tis|the|nes
 Greek philosopher
an|tis|tro|phe
anti|sym|met|ric
anti-tank
anti-tetanus
an|tith|esis
 an|tith|eses
anti|thet|ic|al
anti|thet|ic|al|ly
anti|toxic
anti|toxin
anti|trust
anti|type
anti|typ|ical
anti|venin
anti|venom
anti|viral
anti|virus
anti|vivi|sec|tion
anti|vivi|sec|tion|
 ism
anti|vivi|sec|tion|
 ist
ant|ler
ant|lered
Ant|lia
ant lion
An|to|fa|gasta
An|toine
An|toin|ette
An|tonia
An|ton|ine
An|to|ni|nus Pius
 Roman emperor
An|to|ni|oni,
 Mi|chel|an|gelo
 film director
an|tono|ma|sia
An|tony, Mark
 Roman general
ant|onym
ant|onym|ous
an|tral
an|trec|tomy
 an|trec|to|mies
An|trim

An|tron trademark
an|trum
 antra
antsy
 ants|ier
 antsi|est
ant-thrush
Ant|werp
ant-wren
Anu|bis
Anura
Anura|dha|pura
anur|an
an|uria
an|uric
anus
anvil
anx|iety
 anx|ie|ties
anxio|lyt|ic
anx|ious
anx|ious|ly
any
any|body
any|how
any|more US
any more Br.
any|one anybody
any|place anywhere
any road anyway
any|thing
any|time var. of any
 time
any time
any|way
any|ways US
any|where
any|wheres US
any|wise
Anzac
Anzus = Australia,
 New Zealand, and
 United States
A-OK
A-okay var. of
 A-OK
Aor|angi
aor|ist
aor|is|tic
aorta
aor|tic
Aosta
Ao|tea|roa

aou|dad
à ou|trance
Aozou Strip, Chad
apace
Apa|che American
 Indian
apa|che ruffian;
 dance
ap|an|age var. of
 appanage
apart
apart|heid
apart|hotel
apart|ment
apart|otel var. of
 aparthotel
apath|et|ic
apath|et|ic|al|ly
ap|athy
apa|tite mineral
apato|saurus
ape
 aping
Apel|doorn
ape-like
ape|man
ape|men
Ap|en|nines
ap|erçu
aperi|ent
aperi|odic
aperi|od|icity
aperi|tif
aper|ture
apery
 aper|ies
apet|al|ous
Apex airline ticket
 system
apex point
 apexes or api|ces
Apgar
apha|sia
apha|sic
ap|he|lion
ap|he|lia
apher|esis
aph|esis
aphet|ic
aphi|cide
aphid
aphis
 aphi|des

apho|nia
aph|ony var. of
  aphonia
aph|or|ise Br. var.
  of aphorize
aph|or|ism
aph|or|ist
aph|or|is|tic
aph|or|ize
  aph|or|iz|ing
aphro|dis|iac
aphro|dis|iac|al
Aph|ro|dis|ias
Aph|ro|dite
aph|tha
  aph|thae
aph|thous
apian
api|ar|ian
api|ar|ist
api|ary
  api|ar|ies
ap|ical
api|ces
Api|com|plexa
api|cul|tural
api|cul|ture
api|cul|tur|ist
apiece
apish
ap|ish|ness
ap|lanat
ap|lan|at|ic
apla|sia
aplas|tic
aplenty
aplomb
apnea US
ap|noea Br.
apoca|lypse
apoca|lyp|tic
apoca|lyp|tic|al|ly
apo|carp|ous
apo|chro|mat
apo|chro|mat|ic
apoc|ope
apo|crine
apoc|rypha
apoc|ryph|al
apoc|ryph|al|ly
apo|deic|tic var. of
  apodictic
apo|dic|tic

apo|dosis
  apo|doses
apo|dous
apo|gee
apolar
apol|it|ical
Apol|lin|aire,
  Guil|laume writer
Apol|lin|ar|ian
Apol|lin|aris bishop
Apollo Greek god;
  spacecraft
apollo +s butterfly
Apol|lo|nian
Apol|lo|nius math-
  ematician; poet
Apol|lyon
apolo|get|ic
apolo|get|ic|al|ly
apolo|get|ics
apo|lo|gia
apolo|gise Br. var.
  of apologize
apolo|gist
apolo|gize
  apolo|giz|ing
apo|logue
apol|ogy
  apolo|gies
apo|lune
apo|mict
apo|mic|tic
apo|mixis
apo|morph|ine
apo|neur|osis
  apo|neur|oses
apo|neur|ot|ic
apo|phat|ic
apoph|thegm Br.
  US apothegm
  maxim; cf.
  apothem
apoph|theg|mat|ic
  Br.
  US apothegmatic
apophyl|lite
apo|phys|eal
apophy|sis
  apophy|ses
apo|plec|tic
apo|plec|tic|al|ly
apo|plexy
  apo|plex|ies
apo|pro|tein

apop|tosis
apop|tot|ic
apor|et|ic
aporia
apo|sem|at|ic
apo|semat|ism
apo|sio|pesis
  apo|sio|peses
apo|sio|pet|ic
apos|tasy
  apos|tas|ies
apos|tate
apos|tat|ic|al
apos|ta|tise Br. var.
  of apostatize
apos|ta|tize
  apos|ta|tiz|ing
a pos|teri|ori
apos|tle
apostle|bird
apostle|ship
apos|tol|ate
apos|tol|ic
apos|tro|phe
apos|tro|phise Br.
  var. of
  apostrophize
apos|tro|phize
  apos|tro|phiz|ing
apoth|ecary
  apoth|ecar|ies
apo|thegm US
  Br. apophthegm.
  maxim. cf.
  apothem
apo|theg|mat|ic US
  Br.
  apophthegmatic
apo|them Geometry;
  cf. apophthegm,
  apothegm
apothe|osis
apothe|oses
apotheo|sise Br.
  var. of apotheosize
apotheo|size
  apotheo|siz|ing
apo|tro|paic
apo|tro|paic|al|ly
appal Br.
ap|palled
ap|pal|ling
  US appall
Ap|pa|lach|ian

ap|pall US
  Br. appal
ap|pal|ling|ly
Ap|pa|loosa
ap|pan|age
ap|parat
ap|par|at|chik
  ap|par|at|chiks or
  ap|par|at|chiki
ap|par|atus
ap|par|atus
  crit|icus
  ap|par|atus crit|ici
ap|parel
  ap|par|elled Br.
  ap|par|eled US
  ap|parel|ling Br.
  ap|parel|ing US
ap|par|ent
ap|par|ent|ly
ap|par|ition
ap|par|ition|al
ap|peal
ap|peal|able
ap|peal|er
ap|peal|ing|ly
ap|pear
ap|pear|ance
ap|pease
ap|peas|ing
ap|pease|ment
ap|peaser
Appel, Karel
  painter
ap|pel|lant
ap|pel|late
ap|pel|la|tion
ap|pel|la|tive
ap|pel|lee
ap|pend
ap|pend|age
ap|pend|ant
ap|pend|ec|tomy
  ap|pend|ec|to|mies
ap|pen|di|cec|tomy
ap|pen|di|
    cec|to|mies
ap|pen|di|citis
ap|pen|dicu|lar
ap|pen|dix
  ap|pen|di|ces or
  ap|pen|dixes
ap|per|cep|tion
ap|per|cep|tive

ap¦per¦tain
appe|stat
ap¦pe¦tiser *Br.* var.
  of appetizer
ap¦pe¦tis¦ing *Br.* var.
  of appetizing
ap¦pe¦tis¦ing¦ly *Br.*
  var. of appetizingly
ap¦pe¦tite cf.
  apatite
ap¦pe¦ti¦tive
ap¦pe¦tizer
ap¦pe¦tiz¦ing
ap¦pe¦tiz¦ing¦ly
Ap¦pian Way
ap|plaud
ap|plause
apple
apple|jack
apple|sauce *US*
apple sauce *Br.*
app|let
Apple|ton, Ed¦ward
  physicist
apple|wood
appley
ap¦pli¦ance
ap¦pli¦anced
ap¦plic¦abil¦ity
ap¦plic|able
ap¦pli|cant
ap¦pli¦ca¦tion
ap¦pli¦ca¦tion¦al
ap¦pli¦ca¦tive
ap¦pli¦ca¦tor
ap|plier
ap¦pli¦qué
  ap¦pli¦qués
  ap¦pli¦quéd
  ap¦pli¦qué¦ing
apply
ap|plies
ap|plied
ap|ply¦ing
ap¦pog¦gia¦tura
ap¦pog¦gia¦turas or
ap¦pog¦gia¦ture
ap|point
ap|point¦ee
ap|point¦er
ap|point¦ive
ap|point¦ment
ap|port

ap¦por|tion
ap¦por¦tion|able
ap¦por¦tion|ment
ap¦pose
ap|pos¦ing
ap|po|site
ap|po|site¦ly
ap|po|site|ness
ap|pos¦ition
ap|pos¦ition|al
ap|posi|tive
ap|prais|able
ap|prais|al
ap|praise
  ap|prais|ing
ap|praisee
ap|praise|ment
ap|prais¦er
ap|prais|ive
ap|pre¦ciable
ap|pre¦ciably
ap|pre¦ci¦ate
ap|pre¦ci¦at¦ing
ap|pre¦ci¦ation
ap|pre¦cia¦tive
ap|pre¦cia¦tive¦ly
ap|pre¦ci¦ator
ap|pre¦ci¦atory
ap|pre|hend
ap|pre|hen¦si|
         bil¦ity
ap|pre|hen|sible
ap|pre|hen|sion
ap|pre|hen|sive
ap|pre|hen|sive¦ly
ap|pren|tice
  ap|pren|ticing
ap|pren|tice|ship
ap|press
ap|prise *inform*
ap|prize
  ap|priz¦ing
  esteem highly;
  praise
appro
ap|proach
ap|proach|abil¦ity
ap|proach|able
ap|pro|ba¦tion
ap|pro|ba¦tive
ap|pro|ba¦tory
ap|pro|pri¦ate
  ap|pro|pri¦at¦ing

ap|pro|pri¦ate¦ly
ap|pro|pri¦ate|ness
ap|pro|pri¦ation
ap|pro|pri¦ation|ist
ap|pro|pri¦ator
ap|prov|al
ap|prove
  ap|prov¦ing
ap|prov¦ing¦ly
ap|proxi|mant
ap|proxi|mate
  ap|proxi|mat¦ing
ap|proxi|mate¦ly
ap|proxi|ma¦tion
ap|proxi|ma¦tive
ap|pur|ten|ance
ap|pur|ten|ant
apraxia
aprax¦ic
après-ski
après-skiing
apri|cot
April
April Fool's Day
a pri¦ori
apri|or|ism
apron
apron|ful
apro|pos
ap|sara +s
ap|saras
  ap|sar¦ases
  var. of apsara
apse
ap|sidal
apsis
  ap|si|des
ap|ter|ous
Ap|tery|gota
ap|tery|gote
ap|ti|tude
Apu|leius *Roman*
  writer
Apu|lia
Apu|lian
Apus
Aqaba
aqua
aqua aura
aqua|cade
aqua|cul¦ture
aqua for¦tis
aqua|lung

aqua|ma¦nile
aqua|mar¦ine
aqua|naut
aqua|plane
  aqua|plan¦ing
aqua regia
aqua|relle
Aquar|ian
aqua|rist
aquar|ium
  aquaria or
  aquar|iums
Aquar|ius
aqua|robics *US*
  trademark for a
  system of exercises
aquat¦ic
aqua|tint
aqua|vit
aqua vitae
aque|duct
aque|ous
aqui|fer
Aquila
aqui|le¦gia
aquil|ine
Aqui|nas, St
  Thomas
Aqui|taine
aquiver
Ara
Arab
Ara|bella
ar¦ab|esque
ar¦ab|esquing
Ara¦bia
Ara|bian
Arab¦ic
arab¦ic in 'gum
  arabic'
arab|ica
Arabi|cisa|tion *Br.*
  var. of
  Arabicization
Arabi|cise *Br.* var.
  of Arabicize
Arabi|cism
Arabi|ciza|tion
Arabi|cize
  Arabi|ciz¦ing
ara|bin|ose
ara¦bis

Arab|isa|tion *Br.*
  var. of **Arabization**
Arab|ise *Br.* var. of
  Arabize
Arab|ism
Arab|ist
Arab|iza|tion
Arab|ize
  Arab|iz|ing
ar|able
Araby Arabia
ara|cari
  Portuguese **araçari**
ara|chi|don|ic
ara|chis
Ar|achne *Greek*
  Mythology
arach|nid
Arach|nida
arach|nid|an
arach|noid
arachno|phobe
arachno|pho|bia
arachno|pho|bic
Ara|fat, Yas|ser Pal-
  estinian leader
Ara|fura
Ara|gon
ara|gon|ite
arak var. of **arrack**
ara|lia
Aral Sea
Ara|maean var. of
  Aramean
Ara|maic
arame seaweed
Ara|mean
ara|mid
Aran Islands;
  knitwear; cf. **Arran**
Ar|anda var. of
  Arrernte
ara|neid
Ara|nyaka Hindu
  text
Ara|paho +s
ara|paima
Ara|rat
aration|al
Arau|ca|nian
arau|caria
Ara|wak
Ara|wak|an

arb
ar|ba|lest
ar|bi|ter
  ar|bi|ter
  ele|gan|tiae
  ar|bi|ter
  ele|gan|ti|arum
ar|bi|trage
ar|bi|tra|ging
ar|bi|trager var. of
  arbitrageur
ar|bi|tra|geur
ar|bi|tral
ar|bi|tra|ment
ar|bi|trar|ily
ar|bi|trari|ness
ar|bi|trary
ar|bi|trate
  ar|bi|trat|ing
ar|bi|tra|tion
ar|bi|tra|tor
ar|bi|tra|tor|ship
ar|bi|tress
ar|blast var. of
  arbalest
arbor spindle; cf.
  arbour
arbor *US* bower
  Br. **arbour**
ar|bor|eal
ar|bor|eal|ity
ar|bored *US*
  Br. **arboured**
ar|bor|es|cence
ar|bor|es|cent
ar|bor|etum
  ar|bor|etums or
  ar|bor|eta
ar|bori|cul|tural
ar|bori|cul|ture
ar|bori|cul|tur|ist
Ar|borio
ar|bor|isa|tion *Br.*
  var. of **arborization**
ar|bor|ist
ar|bor|iza|tion
arbor vitae
ar|bour *Br.*
  US **arbor**
  bower; cf. **arbor**
ar|boured *Br.*
  US **arbored**
arbo|virus
ar|bu|tus

arc curve; cf. **ark**
ar|cade
Ar|ca|dia district,
  Greece; pastoral
  paradise
Ar|ca|dian of
  Arcadia; cf.
  Acadian, Akkadian
ar|cad|ing
Ar|cady pastoral
  paradise
ar|cane
ar|cane|ly
ar|canum
  ar|cana
Arc de Tri|omphe
arc eye
arc fur|nace
arch
ar|chaea *Biology*
Ar|chaean *Br.*
  Geology
  US **Archean**
ar|chaean *Biology*
archae|bac|ter|ial
archae|bac|ter|ium
  archae|bac|teria
archaeo|
      astron|omy
arch|aeo|logic|al
arch|aeo|logic|al|ly
archae|olo|gise *Br.*
  var. of
  archaeologize
archae|olo|gist
archae|olo|gize
  archae|olo|giz|ing
archae|ology
arch|aeo|magnetic
arch|aeo|mag|net|
      ism
arch|aeo|met|ric
archae|om|etry
archae|op|teryx
ar|chaic
ar|cha|ic|al|ly
archa|ise *Br.* var. of
  archaize
archa|ism
archa|ist
ar|cha|ize
  ar|cha|iz|ing
Arch|angel port,
  Russia

arch|angel
arch|angel|ic
arch|bishop
arch|bishop|ric
arch|board
arch|deacon
arch|deacon|ry
  arch|deacon|ries
arch|deacon|ship
arch|dio|cesan
arch|dio|cese
arch|ducal
arch|duch|ess
arch|duchy
  arch|duch|ies
arch|duke
Ar|chean *US*
  Geology
  Br. **Archaean**
arche|go|nium
arche|go|nia
arch-enemy
  arch-enemies
arch|en|teron
archeo|astron|omy
  US var. of
  archaeoastronomy
archeo|logic|al *US*
  var. of
  archaeological
archeo|logic|al|ly
  US var. of
  archaeologically
arche|olo|gist *US*
  var. of
  archaeologist
arche|olo|gize *US*
  var. of
  archaeologize
arche|ology *US* var.
  of **archaeology**
archeo|mag|net|ic
  US var. of
  archaeomagnetic
archeo|mag|net|
      ism
  US var. of
  archaeomagnetism
archeo|met|ric *US*
  var. of
  archaeometric
arche|om|etry *US*
  var. of
  archaeometry
ar|cher

arch|ery
arche|typal
arche|typ|al|ly
arche|type
arche|typ|ical
arche|typ|ic|al|ly
Archi|bald
archi|diac|onal
archi|diac|on|ate
Ar|chie
archi|epis|co|pacy
archi|
  epis|co|pa|cies
archi|epis|co|pal
archi|epis|cop|ate
ar|chil
Ar|chilo|chus poet
archi|man|drite
Archi|me|dean
Archi|me|des
  mathematician and
  inventor
archi|pel|ago +s
archi|tect
archi|tec|ton|ic
archi|tec|ton|
   ic|al|ly
archi|tec|ton|ics
archi|tec|tural
archi|tec|tur|al|ly
archi|tec|ture
archi|trave
arch|ival
arch|ive
archi|iv|ist
archi|volt
arch|lute
arch|ly
arch|ness
ar|chon
ar|chon|ship
archo|saur
arch|priest
arch-rival
arch|way
arc lamp
arc light
arc min|ute
arco Music
ar|cology
  ar|colo|gies
Arc|tic north polar
  region

arc|tic very cold;
  overshoe; butterfly
Arcto|gaea Br.
Arcto|gaean Br.
Arcto|gea US
Arcto|gean US
arcto|phile
arcto|philia
arct|oph|il|ist
arct|oph|ily
Arc|turus star
ar|cu|ate
arcus sen|ilis
  arci sen|iles
arc weld|ing
ar|dency
ar|den|cies
Ar|dennes
ar|dent
ar|dent|ly
Ar|diz|zone,
  Ed|ward artist
Ard|na|mur|chan
ardor US
ar|dour Br.
ar|du|ous
ar|du|ous|ly
are in 'we are' etc.;
  unit
area
areal pertaining to
  area; cf. aerial,
  ariel
area|way
areca
areg pl. of erg
  sand dunes
areli|gious
arena
ar|en|aceous
arena|virus
aren't
areola n.
  areo|lae
areo|lar adj.
areo|late
areole
areo|logic|al
are|olo|gist
are|ology
Are|opa|gus
Are|quipa
Ares Greek god

arête
'arf = half
'ar|gali
argan
Ar|gand
ar|gent
ar|gent|ifer|ous
Ar|gen|tina
Ar|gen|tine Argen-
  tina; Argentinian
ar|gen|tine
  containing silver
Ar|gen|tin|ian
ar|gil|la|ceous
ar|gil|lite
ar|gin|ine
Ar|give
argle-bargle
Argo constellation
Argo Jason's ship
argol
argon
Ar|go|naut compan-
  ion of Jason
ar|go|naut octopus
Argo Navis
Argos city, ancient
  Greece; cf. Argus,
  argus
ar|gosy
ar|gos|ies
argot
ar|gu|able
ar|gu|ably
argue
ar|gu|ing
ar|guer
ar|gufy
ar|gu|fies
ar|gu|fied
ar|gu|fy|ing
ar|gu|ment
ar|gu|men|ta|tion
ar|gu|men|ta|tive
Argus Greek
  Mythology; cf.
  Argos
argus fish; butterfly;
  pheasant
Argus-eyed
argy-bargy
  argy-bargies
  argy-bargied
  argy-bargying

ar|gyle pattern
Ar|gyll
Ar|gyll|shire
ar|gyro|phil
ar|gyro|philia
ar|gyro|phil|ic
arhat
Århus var. of
  Aarhus
arhyth|mia var. of
  arrhythmia
arhyth|mic var. of
  arrhythmic
arhyth|mic|al|ly
  var. of
  arrhythmically
aria
Ari|adne
Arian relating to
  Aries or Arianism;
  cf. Aryan
Arian|ism early
  Christian heresy
arid
aridi|sol
arid|ity
arid|ly
arid|ness
Ariel spirit in The
  Tempest; moon of
  Uranus
ariel gazelle; cf.
  areal, aerial
Ari|elle name
Arien var. of Arian
Aries constellation;
  sign of zodiac; cf.
  Ares
aright
aril seed covering;
  cf. aryl
aril|late
Ari|ma|thea
ari|oso +s
Ari|osto, Ludo|vico
  poet
arise
arose
aris|ing
arisen
Ar|is|tar|chus
  Greek scholar;
  Greek astronomer

Ar|is|ti|des states-
man and general

Ar|is|tip|pus two
Greek philosophers

aristo +s

ar|is|toc|racy
ar|is|toc|ra|cies

ar|is|to|crat

ar|is|to|crat|ic

ar|is|to|crat|ic|al|ly

Ar|is|toph|anes
Greek dramatist

Ar|is|to|tel|ian

Ar|is|totle Greek
philosopher

Arita porcelain

arith|met|ic

arith|met|ic|al

arith|met|ic|al|ly

arith|met|ician

arith|met|ise Br.
var. of arithmetize

arith|met|ize
arith|met|iz|ing

Ari|zona

Ari|zo|nan

Ar|juna Hinduism

ark Judaism; also in
'Noah's ark'; cf. arc

Ar|kan|san

Ar|kan|sas

ar|kose

ar|kosic

ark shell

Ark|wright,
Rich|ard inventor

Ar|lene

Arles

Ar|lette

Ar|ling|ton

Arlon

ar|mada

ar|ma|dillo +s

Ar|ma|ged|don

Ar|magh

Ar|mag|nac

Arma|lite
trademark

arma|ment

arma|ment|ar|ium
arma|ment|aria

Ar|mani, Gior|gio
couturier

arma|ture

arm|band

arm|chair

Armco trademark

Ar|me|nia

Ar|me|nian of
Armenia; cf.
Arminian

arm|ful

arm|hole

armi|ger

armi|ger|ous

ar|mil|laria

Ar|min|ian of
Arminius; cf.
Armenian

Ar|min|ian|ism

Ar|min|ius theolo-
gian; chieftain

ar|mis|tice

arm|less

arm|let

arm|load

arm|lock

ar|moire

armor US
Br. armour

ar|mor|er US
Br. armourer

ar|mor|ial

Ar|mor|ica

Ar|mor|ican

armor plate US
Br. armour plate

armor-plated US
Br. armour-plated

armor-plating US
Br. armour-plating

ar|mory heraldry;
cf. armoury

ar|mory US
ar|mor|ies
arsenal; weapons.
Br. armoury

ar|mour Br.
US armor

ar|mour|er Br.
US armorer

ar|mour plate Br.
US armor plate

armour-plated Br.
US armor-plated

armour-plating Br.
US armor-plating

ar|moury Br.
ar|mour|ies
US armory
arsenal; weapons;
cf. armory

arm|pit

arm|rest

arms weapons; cf.
alms

arm's-length

Arm|strong, Louis
jazz musician

Arm|strong, Neil
astronaut

arm-wrestle

arm-wrestling

army
ar|mies

Arne, Thomas
composer

Arnel trademark

Arn|hem

Arn|hem Land

ar|nica

Arno

Ar|nold, Mat|thew
writer

Ar|nold, Mal|colm
composer

aroid

arolla

aroma

aroma|thera|
peut|ic

aroma|ther|ap|ist

aroma|ther|apy

aro|mat|ic

aro|mat|ic|al|ly

aroma|ti|city

aroma|tisa|tion Br.
var. of
aromatization

aroma|tise Br. var.
of aromatize

aroma|tiza|tion

aroma|tize
aroma|tiz|ing

arose

around

arous|able

arousal

arouse
arous|ing

Arp, Jean or Hans
painter etc.

ar|peg|gi|ate
ar|peg|gi|at|ing

ar|peg|gi|ation

ar|peg|gi|ator

ar|peg|gio +s

ar|peg|gi|one

arque|bus

ar|rack

ar|raign

ar|raign|ment

Arran island,
Scotland; cf. Aran

ar|range
ar|ran|ging

ar|range|able

ar|range|ment

ar|ran|ger

ar|rant

ar|rant|ly

Arras town, France

arras tapestry; cf.
arris

array

ar|rear

ar|rear|age

Ar|rernte

ar|rest

ar|rest|able

ar|rest|ee

ar|rest|er

ar|rest|ing|ly

ar|rest|ment

ar|res|tor var. of
arrester

Ar|ret|ine pottery

ar|rhyth|mia

ar|rhyth|mia

ar|rhyth|mic

ar|rhyth|mic|al|ly

arrière-pensée

arris Architecture;
rail; cf. arras

ar|rival

ar|rive
ar|riv|ing

ar|riv|isme

ar|riv|iste

ar|ro|gance

ar|ro|gant

ar|ro|gant|ly

ar¦ro¦gate
ar¦ro¦gat¦ing
ar¦ro¦ga¦tion
ar¦ron¦disse¦ment
arrow
arrow¦grass
arrow¦head
arrow¦root
ar¦rowy
ar¦royo +s
arse *Br.*
ars¦ing
vulgar slang;
US ass
arse¦hole *Br.*
vulgar slang;
US asshole
ar¦senal
ar¦sen¦ate
ar¦senic
ar¦sen¦ic¦al
ar¦sen¦ide
ar¦seni¦ous
ar¦seno¦pyr¦ite
arses pl. of arse and
arsis
arsey
ars¦ier
arsi¦est
ars¦ine
arsis
arses
arson
ar¦son¦ist
ars¦phen¦amine
arsy-versy
Arta¦xer¦xes Per-
sian kings
art deco
arte¦fact *Br.*
US artifact
arte¦fac¦tual *Br.*
US artifactual
artel
ar¦tels or ar¦teli
Ar¦te¦mis
ar¦te¦misia
ar¦te¦mi¦si¦nin
Arte Po¦vera
ar¦ter¦ial
ar¦teri¦al¦isa¦tion
Br. var. of
arterialization

ar¦teri¦al¦ise *Br.* var.
of arterialize
ar¦teri¦al¦iza¦tion
ar¦teri¦al¦ize
ar¦teri¦al¦iz¦ing
ar¦teri¦og¦raphy
ar¦teri¦olar
ar¦teri¦ole
ar¦terio¦scler¦osis
ar¦terio¦scler¦ot¦ic
ar¦terio¦ven¦ous
ar¦ter¦itis
ar¦tery
ar¦ter¦ies
ar¦te¦sian
Artex *trademark*
art¦ful
art¦ful¦ly
art¦ful¦ness
arth¦ral¦gia
arth¦rit¦ic
arth¦ritis
arth¦rod¦esis
arthro¦pod
Arthro¦poda
arthro¦scope
arthro¦scop¦ic
arth¦ros¦copy
arth¦ros¦co¦pies
Ar¦thur
Ar¦thur¦ian
artic
arti¦choke
art¦icle
art¦ic¦ling
ar¦tic¦ul¦able
ar¦ticu¦lacy
ar¦ticu¦lar
ar¦ticu¦late
ar¦ticu¦lat¦ing
ar¦ticu¦late¦ly
ar¦ticu¦late¦ness
ar¦ticu¦la¦tion
ar¦ticu¦la¦tor
ar¦ticu¦la¦tory
arti¦fact
Br. artefact
arti¦fac¦tual
Br. artefactual
arti¦fice
ar¦tifi¦cer
arti¦fi¦cial

ar¦ti¦fi¦ci¦al¦ity
ar¦ti¦fi¦ci¦al¦ities
ar¦ti¦fi¦cial¦ly
ar¦til¦ler¦ist
ar¦til¦lery
ar¦til¦ler¦ies
ar¦til¦lery¦man
ar¦til¦lery¦men
art¦ily
arti¦ness
artio¦dac¦tyl
Artio¦dac¦tyla
ar¦ti¦san
ar¦ti¦san¦al
art¦ist painter etc.
ar¦tiste performer
art¦is¦tic
art¦is¦tic¦al¦ly
art¦is¦try
art¦less
art¦less¦ly
art nou¦veau
Ar¦tois
artsy
arts¦ier
artsi¦est
artsy-craftsy var. of
arty-crafty
artsy-fartsy var. of
arty-farty
art¦work
arty
art¦ier
arti¦est
arty-crafty
arty-farty
Aruba
aru¦gula
arum
Ar¦un¦achal
Pra¦desh
Ar¦unta var. of
Arrernte
arvo +s
Arya¦bhata Indian
astronomer and
mathematician
Aryan peoples;
language; cf. Arian
aryl *Chemistry;* cf.
aril
aryt¦en¦oid
as
asses

Roman coin
asa¦fe¦tida US
asa¦foe¦tida *Br.*
asana
Asan¦sol
As¦ante var. of
Ashanti
asap = as soon as
possible
asara¦bacca
as¦bes¦tos
as¦bes¦tosis
as¦car¦ia¦sis
as¦carid
as¦caris
as¦cari¦des
var. of ascarid
as¦cend
as¦cend¦ancy
as¦cend¦an¦cies
as¦cend¦ant
as¦cend¦ency var. of
ascendancy
as¦cend¦ent var. of
ascendant
as¦cend¦er
as¦cen¦sion
as¦cen¦sion¦al
As¦cen¦sion¦tide
as¦cent climb; cf.
assent
as¦cer¦tain
as¦cer¦tain¦able
as¦cer¦tain¦ment
as¦cesis
as¦cet¦ic simple and
disciplined; cf.
acetic
as¦ceti¦cism
As¦cham, Roger
scholar
asch¦el¦minth
asch¦el¦minths or
asch¦el¦min¦thes
as¦cid¦ian
ASCII = American
Standard Code for
Information
Interchange
as¦ci¦tes
as¦cit¦ic
As¦cle¦piad
As¦cle¦pius
asco¦mycete

as|con|oid
as|cor|bate
as|cor|bic
Ascot racecourse
ascot tie
ascrib|able
ascribe
  ascrib|ing
ascrip|tion
ascus
  asci
Asdic
ASEAN = Association of South East Asian Nations
aseis|mic
asep|sis
asep|tic
asep|tic|al|ly
asex|ual
asexu|al|ity
asexu|al|ly
As|gard *Norse Mythology*
ashamed
ashamed|ly
Ash|anti
  pl. Ash|anti
ash|can
Ash|croft, Peggy actress
Ash|dod
Ash|down, Paddy politician
Ashe, Ar|thur tennis player
ashen
ashet
Ash|ga|bat capital of Turkmenistan
ashine
Ash|ke|lon var. of Ashqelon
Ash|ken|azi
Ash|ken|azim
Ash|ken|az|ic
Ash|ken|azy, Vlad|imir pianist
Ash|kha|bad var. of Ashgabat
ash|lar
ash|lar|ing
Ash|mole, Elias antiquary

Ash|molean
Ash|more Reef
Ash|oka var. of Asoka
ashore
ash pan
ash|plant
Ash|qe|lon
ash|ram
ash|rama
ash|tanga
Ash|ton, Fred|erick choreographer
ash|tray
Ashur var. of Assur
ashy
Asia
asi|ago
Asian
Asi|at|ic
A-side
aside
Asi|mov, Isaac writer
as|in|ine
as|in|in|ity
Asir Moun|tains
asity
  asit|ies bird
askance
askant var. of askance
as|kari
askew
Askey, Ar|thur comedian
aslant
asleep
Aslef = Associated Society of Locomotive Engineers and Firemen
AS level
aslope
As|mara
As|mera var. of Asmara
asocial
Asoka Indian emperor
as|para|gine
as|para|gus

as|par|tame
as|par|tate
as|pect
as|pect|ual
Aspen city, US
aspen tree
As|per|ger's syn|drome
as|per|ges
as|per|gil|losis
as|per|gil|lum
as|per|gilla or as|per|gil|lums
as|per|ity
as|per|ities
asper|mia
as|perse
as|pers|ing
as|per|sion
as|phalt
as|phal|tic
aspher|ic
aspher|ic|al
aspher|ic|al|ly
as|pho|del
as|phyxia
as|phyx|ial
as|phyxi|ant
as|phyxi|ate
  as|phyxi|at|ing
as|phyxi|ation
as|phyxi|ator
aspic
as|pi|dis|tra
as|pir|ant
as|pir|ate
  as|pir|at|ing
as|pir|ation
as|pir|ation|al
as|pir|ator
as|pire
  as|pir|ing
as|pirin
asprawl
asquint
As|quith, Her|bert prime minister of Britain
ass donkey
ass *US vulgar slang* buttocks; *Br.* arse

as|sa|gai var. of assegai
assai *Music*
as|sail
as|sail|able
as|sail|ant
Assam
As|sam|ese
as|sart
as|sas|sin
as|sas|sin|ate
  as|sas|sin|at|ing
as|sas|sin|ation
as|sas|sin|ator
as|sault
as|sault|er
as|sault|ive
assay
as|say|er
ass-backwards
as|se|gai +s +ed +ing
as|sem|blage
as|sem|ble
  as|sem|bling
as|sem|blé
as|sem|bler
as|sem|bly
  as|sem|blies
as|sent agree; cf. ascent
as|sent|er
as|sent|or var. of assenter
as|sert
as|sert|er
as|ser|tion
as|sert|ive
as|sert|ive|ly
as|sert|ive|ness
as|sert|or var. of asserter
asses pl. of ass and ass
asses' bridge
as|sess
as|sess|able
as|sess|ment
as|ses|sor
asset
as|sev|er|ate
  as|sev|er|at|ing
as|sev|er|ation

ass|hole *US vulgar*
slang
Br. arsehole
as|sibi|late
as|sibi|lat|ing
as|sibi|la|tion
as|si|du|ity
as|si|du|ities
as|sidu|ous
as|sidu|ous|ly
as|sidu|ous|ness
as|sign
as|sign|able
as|sig|na|tion
as|sign|ee
as|sign|er
as|sign|ment
as|sign|or var. of
assigner
as|sim|il|able
as|simi|late
as|simi|lat|ing
as|simi|la|tion
as|simi|la|tion|ist
as|simi|la|tive
as|simi|la|tor
as|simi|la|tory
As|sisi
as|sist
as|sist|ance
as|sist|ant
as|sist|ant|ship
as|sist|er
as|sist|ive
as|size
as|so|ci|abil|ity
as|so|ci|able
as|so|ci|ate
as|so|ci|at|ing
as|so|ci|ate|ship
as|so|ci|ation
as|so|ci|ation|al
as|so|ci|ation|ism
as|so|ci|ation|ist
as|so|cia|tive
as|so|cia|tory
as|son|ance
as|son|ant
as|son|ate
as|son|at|ing
as|sort
as|sorta|tive
as|sort|ment

as|suage
as|sua|ging
as|suage|ment
As Su|lay|man|iyah
full name of
Sulaymaniyah
as|sum|able
as|sume
as|sum|ing
as|sump|tion
as|sump|tive
Assur
as|sur|ance
as|sure
as|sur|ing
as|sured|ly
as|surer
As|syria
As|syr|ian
As|syrio|logic|al
As|syri|olo|gist
As|syri|ology
astable
As|taire, Fred dan-
cer
As|tana
astanga var. of
ashtanga
As|tarte Phoenician
goddess
astat|ic
as|ta|tine
aster
as|ter|isk
as|ter|ism
astern
as|ter|oid rock in
space; cf. **astroid**
as|ter|oid|al
As|ter|oidea
as|the|nia
as|then|ic
as|theno|sphere
as|theno|spher|ic
asthma
asth|mat|ic
asth|mat|ic|al|ly
Asti
astig|matic
astig|ma|tism
as|tilbe
astir
as|ton|ish

as|ton|ish|ing|ly
as|ton|ish|ment
Astor, Nancy polit-
ician
as|tound
as|tound|ing|ly
astrad|dle
As|traea
as|tra|gal
as|trag|alus
as|trag|ali
As|tra|khan city,
Russia
as|tra|khan fleece
as|tral
astran|tia
astray
As|trid
astride
astrin|gency
astrin|gen|cies
astrin|gent
astrin|gent|ly
astro-archae|ology
astro-archeology
US var. of astro-
archaeology
astro|bio|logic|al
astro|biolo|gist
astro|biol|ogy
astro|bleme
astro|chem|ical
astro|chem|ist
astro|chem|is|try
astro|com|pass
astro|cyte
astro|cyt|ic
astro|dome
astro|ga|tion
astro|ga|tor
as|troid curve; cf.
asteroid
astro|labe
as|trol|oger
astro|logic|al
astro|logic|al|ly
as|trolo|gist
as|trol|ogy
astro|metric
as|trom|etry
astro|naut
astro|naut|ic|al
astro|naut|ics

as|tron|omer
astro|nom|ic
astro|nom|ic|al
astro|nom|ic|al|ly
as|tron|omy
astro|
    pho|tog|raph|er
astro|photo|
            graph|ic
astro|pho|
        tog|raphy
astro|phys|ic|al
astro|physi|cist
astro|phys|ics
Astro'Turf
    trademark
astro|turfed
As|tur|ian
As|tur|ias
as|tute
as|tuter
astut|est
as|tute|ly
as|tute|ness
asty|lar
Asun|ción
asun|der
Asur var. of Assur
asura
Aswan
aswarm
aswim
aswirl
asy|lum
asym|met|ric
asym|met|ric|al
asym|met|ric|al|ly
asym|metry
asym|met|ries
asymp|tom|at|ic
asymp|tote
asymp|tot|ic
asymp|tot|ic|al|ly
asyn|chron|ous
asyn|chron|ous|ly
asyn|chrony
asyn|det|ic
asyn|deton
    asyn|deta
asys|tole
asys|tol|ic
At|ab|rine *US*
    trademark

Br. **Atebrin**
Ata|cama
atac|tic
Ata|lanta *Greek Mythology*
ata|man +s
atap var. of **attap**
at|ar|ac|tic var. of **ataraxic**
at|ar|axia var. of **ataraxy**
at|ar|axic
at|ar|axy
Ata|türk, Kemal president of Turkey
at|av|ism
at|av|is|tic
at|av|is|tic|al|ly
ataxia
ataxic
ataxy var. of **ataxia**
ate past tense of **eat**; cf. **ait**
A-team
At|eb|rin *Br. trademark US* **Atabrine**
atel|ec|tasis
atel|ier
a tempo
atem|poral
atem|por|al|ity
Aten *Egyptian Mythology*
aten|olol
Atha|basca River, Lake
Atha|bas|can var. of **Athabaskan**
Atha|bas|kan
athame
Atha|na|sian
Atha|na|sius, St
atha|nor
Atha|pas|kan var. of **Athabascan**
Atharva Veda *Hinduism*
athe|ism
athe|ist
athe|is|tic
athel|ing

Athel|stan king of England
athe|mat|ic
Athena var. of **Athene**
Athen|aeum
Athe|ne *Greek goddess*
Athen|eum *US Br.* **Athenaeum**
Athen|ian
Ath|ens
athero|gen|esis
  athero|gen|eses
athero|gen|ic
ath|er|oma
ather|oma|tous
ath|ero|scler|osis
  ath|ero|scler|oses
ath|ero|scler|ot|ic
Ather|ton Table|land
athe|toid
athe|tosis
athe|tot|ic
athirst
ath|lete
ath|lete's foot
ath|let|ic
ath|let|ic|al|ly
ath|leti|cism
ath|let|ics
at-home *n.*
Athon|ite
Athos, Mt
athwart
atilt
Ati|van *trademark*
At|kins diet *trademark in the US*
At|kin|son
At|lanta city, US; cf. **Atalanta**
At|lan|tan of Atlanta
At|lan|tean of Atlantis
at|lan|tes pl. of **atlas**, 'columns'
At|lan|tic
At|lan|ti|cism
At|lan|ti|cist

At|lan|tis
Atlas *Greek Mythology*; Mountains
atlas
  at|lases books; vertebrae
  at|lan|tes columns in shape of man
atman +s
at|mos|phere
at|mos|pher|ic
at|mos|pher|ics
atoll
atom
atom|ic
atom|ic|al|ly
atom|icity
  atom|ici|ties
atom|isa|tion *Br.* var. of **atomization**
atom|ise *Br.* var. of **atomize**
atom|iser *Br.* var. of **atomizer**
atom|ism
atom|ist
atom|is|tic
atom|iza|tion
atom|ize
  atom|iz|ing
atom|izer
atomy
  atom|ies
Aton var. of **Aten**
atonal
atonal|ism
atonal|ist
aton|al|ity
aton|al|ly
atone
  aton|ing
atone|ment
atonic
atony
atop
atopic
atopy
atra|bili|ous
atrau|mat|ic
atra|zine
atrem|ble
atre|sia

At|reus *Greek Mythology*
atrial
atrio|ven|tricu|lar
atrium
  atria or **atriums**
atro|cious
atro|cious|ly
atro|city
  atro|ci|ties
atro|phic
at|ro|phy
  at|ro|phies
  at|ro|phied
  at|ro|phy|ing
at|ro|pine
At|ro|pos *Greek Mythology*
atta|boy
at|tacca
at|tach
at|tach|able
at|taché
at|tach|ment
at|tack
at|tack|er
atta|girl
at|tain
at|tain|abil|ity
at|tain|able
at|tain|der
at|tain|ment
at|taint
At|ta|lid
attap
attar
at|tempt
At|ten|bor|ough, David naturalist
At|ten|bor|ough, Rich|ard film director
at|tend
at|tend|ance
at|tend|ant
at|tend|ee
at|tend|er
at|ten|tion
at|ten|tion|al
at|ten|tive
at|ten|tive|ly
at|ten|tive|ness

at¦tenu¦ate
  at¦tenu¦at¦ing
at¦tenu¦ation
at¦tenu¦ator
at¦test
at¦test¦able
at¦test¦ation
at¦test¦or
Attic of Attica;
  language
attic loft
At¦tica
At¦ti¦cism
At¦tila the Hun
at¦tire
  at¦tir¦ing
Attis *Anatolian*
  Mythology
at¦ti¦tude
at¦ti¦tu¦dinal
at¦ti¦tu¦din¦ise *Br.*
  var. of **attitudinize**
at¦ti¦tu¦din¦iser *Br.*
  var. of **attitudinizer**
at¦ti¦tu¦din¦ize
  at¦ti¦tu¦din¦iz¦ing
at¦ti¦tu¦din¦izer
Att¦lee, Clem¦ent
  prime minister of
  Britain
at¦torn
at¦tor¦ney
At¦tor¦ney
  Gen¦eral
At¦tor¦neys
  Gen¦eral
at¦tract
at¦tract¦able
at¦tract¦ant
at¦trac¦tion
at¦tract¦ive
at¦tract¦ive¦ly
at¦tract¦ive¦ness
at¦tract¦or
at¦trib¦ut¦able
at¦tri¦bute *n.*
at¦trib¦ute
  at¦trib¦ut¦ing *v.*
at¦tri¦bu¦tion
at¦tribu¦tive
at¦tribu¦tive¦ly
at¦trit
  at¦trit¦ed or
  at¦trit¦ted

at¦trit¦ing or
  at¦trit¦ting
at¦tri¦tion
at¦tri¦tion¦al
at¦tune
  at¦tun¦ing
at¦tune¦ment
At¦wood,
  Mar¦ga¦ret writer
atyp¦ical
atyp¦ic¦al¦ly
au¦bade
au¦berge
au¦ber¦gine
Au¦beron
au¦bre¦tia
Au¦brey, John
  writer
au¦brie¦tia var. of
  aubretia
au¦burn
Au¦bus¦son
Auck¦land
au con¦traire
au cour¦ant
auc¦tion
auc¦tion¦eer
auc¦tion¦eer¦ing
au¦cuba
au¦da¦cious
au¦da¦cious¦ly
au¦da¦city
Auden, W. H. poet
Audh var. of **Oudh**
aud¦ial
audi¦bil¦ity
aud¦ible
aud¦ibly
audi¦ence
aud¦ile
audio
Audio-
    Animatron¦ic
  trademark
Audio-
    Animatron¦ics
  trademark
audio¦book
audio¦gram
audio¦logic¦al
audi¦olo¦gist
audi¦ology
audi¦om¦eter

audio¦met¦ric
audi¦om¦etry
audio¦phile
audio¦tape *v.*
  audio¦tap¦ing
audio tape *n.*
audio typ¦ist
audio-visual
audit
audit¦abil¦ity
audit¦able
au¦di¦tion
audi¦tive
audi¦tor
audi¦tor¦ial
audi¦tor¦ium
  audi¦tor¦iums or
  audi¦toria
audi¦tory
Aud¦rey
Au¦du¦bon, John
  naturalist and artist
Auer¦bach, Frank
  painter
Auer von
  Wels¦bach, Carl
  chemist
au fait
au fond in essence;
  cf. *à fond*
Auf |klä¦rung
Au¦gean
Au¦geas *Greek*
  Mythology
auger tool; shell; cf.
  augur
Auger ef¦fect
aught anything
aught nought; var.
  of **ought**
aug¦ite
aug¦ment
aug¦men¦ta¦tion
aug¦men¦ta¦tive
Au¦gra¦bies
au gra¦tin
Augs¦burg
augur portend;
  interpreter of
  omens; cf. **auger**
au¦gural
au¦gury
  au¦gur¦ies
Au¦gust month

au¦gust venerable
Au¦gusta
Au¦gust¦an
Au¦gust¦ine, St
Au¦gust¦ine friar
Au¦gust¦in¦ian
au¦gust¦ly
au¦gust¦ness
Au¦gus¦tus
auk bird; cf. **orc**
auk¦let
auld
auld lang syne
aum¦bry
  aum¦bries
au nat¦urel
Aung San Burmese
  political leader
Aung San Suu Kyi
  Burmese political
  leader
aunt
auntie
Aunt Sally
  Aunt Sal¦lies
  game
aunty var. of **auntie**
au pair
aura
  aurae or auras
aural of the ear; cf.
  oral
aur¦al¦ly
Aur¦ang¦zeb Mogul
  emperor
aure¦ate
Aur¦elia
Aur¦elian Roman
  emperor
Aur¦elius, Mar¦cus
  Roman emperor
aure¦ola var. of
  aureole
aure¦ole
aur¦eus
  aurei
au re¦voir
Auric, Georges
  composer
auric
aur¦icle
aur¦ic¦ula
aur¦icu¦lar
aur¦icu¦late

aur|iculo|ther|apy
aur|if|er|ous
Aur|iga
Aur|ig|na|cian
auri|scope
aur|ochs
  pl. aur|ochs
Aur|ora *Roman Mythology*
aur|ora
  aur|oras or
  aur|orae
  atmospheric lights
aur|ora aus|tra|lis
aur|ora bor|ea|lis
aur|oral
auro|scope var. of
  auriscope
Ausch|witz
aus|cul|tate
  aus|cul|tat|ing
aus|cul|ta|tion
aus|cul|ta|tory
Aus|lese
aus|pice
aus|pi|cious
aus|pi|cious|ly
Aus|sie
Aus|ten, Jane
  novelist
aus|ten|ite
aus|ten|it|ic
aus|tere
  aus|terer
  aus|terest
aus|tere|ly
aus|ter|ity
  aus|ter|ities
Aus|ter|litz
Aus|tin friar; city, US
Aus|tin, Her|bert
  car maker
Aus|tin, J. L.
  philosopher
Aus|tin, John jurist
Aus|tral of Australia or Australasia
aus|tral southern
Aus|tra|lasia
Aus|tra|la|sian
Aus|tra|lia
Aus|tra|lian
Aus|tra|li|ana

Aus|tra|lian|ise *Br.* var. of
  Australianize
Aus|tra|lian|ism
Aus|tra|lian|ize
  Aus|tra|lian|iz|ing
Aus|tral|ite
Aus|tral|
Aus|tral|oid
aus|tralo|
       pith|ecine
Aus|tralo|pith|ecus
  Aus|tralo|pith|eci
Aus|tral|orp
Aus|tria
Aus|trian
Austro-Asiatic
Austro-
     Hungar|ian
Austro|nes|ian
au|tarch +s
aut|arch|ic var. of
  autarkic
aut|arch|ist var. of
  autarkist
aut|archy absolute sovereignty
aut|archy
  aut|archies
  self-sufficiency; var. of autarky
aut|ark|ic
aut|ark|ist
aut|arky
  aut|ar|kies
  self-sufficiency; cf. autarchy
aut|eco|logic|al
aut|ecol|ogy
auter|ism var. of
  auteurism
au|teur
au|teur|ism
au|teur|ist
au|then|tic
au|then|tic|al|ly
au|then|ti|cate
  au|then|ti|cat|ing
au|then|ti|ca|tion
au|then|ti|ca|tor
au|then|ti|city
authi|gen|ic
au|thor
author|ess
au|thor|ial

au|thor|isa|tion *Br.* var. of
  authorization
au|thor|ise *Br.* var. of authorize
au|thori|tar|ian
au|thori|tar|ian|
          ism
au|thori|ta|tive
au|thori|ta|tive|ly
au|thor|ity
  au|thor|ities
au|thor|iza|tion
au|thor|ize
  au|thor|iz|ing
author|ship
aut|ism
aut|is|tic
auto +s
auto|anti|body
  auto|anti|bodies
Auto|bahn
auto|biog|raph|er
auto|bio|graph|
       ic|al
auto|bio|graph|
       ic|al|ly
auto|biog|raphy
  auto|biog|raph|ies
auto|car
auto|cataly|sis
auto|cata|lyst
auto|cata|lyt|ic
auto|ceph|al|ous
auto|change
auto|changer
auto|chrome
au|toch|thon
  au|toch|thons or
  au|toch|thones
au|toch|thon|al
au|toch|thon|ic
au|toch|thon|ous
auto|clave
  auto|clav|ing
auto|code
auto|cor|rel|ation
au|toc|racy
  au|toc|ra|cies
auto|crat
auto|crat|ic
auto|crat|ic|al|ly
auto|crine
auto|cross

auto|cue *trademark*
auto-da-fé
auto|dial
  auto|dialled *Br.*
  auto|dialed *US*
  auto|dial|ling *Br.*
  auto|dial|ing *US*
auto|didact
auto|didac|tic
auto|ecol|ogy var. of autecology
auto-erotic
auto-eroticism
auto-exposure
auto|focus
  auto|focuses or
  auto|focus|ses
  auto|focused or
  auto|focussed
  auto|focus|ing or
  auto|focus|sing
au|tog|am|ous
au|tog|amy
auto|gen|ic
au|togen|ous
auto|giro +s
auto|graft
auto|graph
auto|graph|ic
aut|og|raphy
  aut|og|raph|ies
auto|gyro var. of autogiro
auto|harp
auto|hyp|no|sis
auto|hyp|not|ic
auto|immune
auto|immun|ity
auto|intoxi|ca|tion
auto|tolo|gous
auto|toly|sis
auto|lyt|ic
auto|maker
auto|mat
auto|mate
  auto|mat|ing
auto|mat|ic
auto|mat|ic|al|ly
auto|ma|ti|city
auto|ma|tion
au|toma|tisa|tion *Br.* var. of
  automatization

au¦toma¦tise *Br.*
var. of **automatize**
au¦toma¦tism
au¦toma¦tiza¦tion
auto¦ma¦tize
auto¦ma¦tiz¦ing
au¦toma¦ton
au¦tom¦ata or
au¦toma¦tons
auto¦mise *Br.* var. of
automize
auto¦mize
auto¦miz¦ing
auto¦mo¦bile
auto¦mo¦tive
auto¦nomic
au¦tono¦mist
au¦tono¦mous
au¦tono¦mous¦ly
au¦ton¦omy
au¦ton¦omies
auto¦pilot
auto¦pista
aut¦opsy
aut¦op¦sies
aut¦op¦sied
aut¦opsy¦ing
auto¦radio¦gram
auto¦radio¦graph
auto¦radio¦graph¦ic
auto¦radi¦og¦raphy
auto¦rick¦shaw
auto¦rotate
auto¦rotat¦ing
auto¦rota¦tion
auto¦route
auto¦save
auto¦sav¦ing
auto¦shap¦ing
auto¦somal
auto¦some
auto¦strada
auto¦stradas or
auto¦strade
auto¦sug¦ges¦tion
auto¦tel¦ic
au¦tot¦omy
auto¦toxic
auto¦toxin
auto¦trans¦form¦er
auto¦trans¦plant
auto¦trans¦plant¦
ation
auto¦troph

auto¦troph¦ic
au¦tot¦rophy
au¦tot¦ro¦phies
auto¦type
auto¦wind
auto¦wind¦er
aut¦oxi¦da¦tion
aut¦oxi¦dise *Br.* var.
of **autoxidize**
aut¦oxi¦dize
aut¦oxi¦diz¦ing
au¦tumn
au¦tum¦nal
autun¦ite
Au¦vergne
aux¦il¦iary
aux¦il¦iar¦ies
auxin
auxo¦troph
auxo¦troph¦ic
Av var. of **Ab**
ava¦da¦vat
avail
avail¦abil¦ity
avail¦abil¦ities
avail¦able
avail¦ably
ava¦lanche
ava¦lanch¦ing
Ava¦lon
avant-garde
avant-gardism
avant-gardist
Avar people
avar¦ice
avar¦icious
avar¦icious¦ly
avas¦cu¦lar
avast
ava¦tar
avaunt
ave greeting;
farewell
Ave¦bury
Ave Maria
avenge
aven¦ging
aven¦ger
avens
aven¦tur¦ine
av¦enue
aver
averred

aver¦ring
aver¦age
aver¦aging
aver¦age¦ly
aver¦mec¦tin
aver¦ment
Aver¦nus
Aver¦roës
philosopher
averse
aver¦sion
aver¦sive
avert
avert¦able
Aves birds
Avesta
Aves¦tan
Aves¦tic
avgas
avian
avi¦ary
avi¦ar¦ies
avi¦ate
avi¦at¦ing
avi¦ation
avi¦ator
avia¦trix
avi¦at¦ri¦ces
avi¦cul¦lar¦ium
avi¦cu¦llaria
avi¦cul¦tur¦al
avi¦cul¦tur¦al¦ist
avi¦cul¦ture
avi¦cul¦tur¦ist
avid
avidin
avid¦ity
avid¦ly
Avie¦more
avi¦fauna
avi¦faunal
Avi¦gnon
Ávila, St Ter¦esa of
avi¦on¦ics
aviru¦lent
avit¦amin¦osis
avit¦amin¦oses
aviz¦an¦dum
avo +s currency of
Macao
avo¦cado +s
avo¦ca¦tion
avo¦ca¦tion¦al

avo¦cet
Avo¦gadro,
Ame¦deo physicist
avoid
avoid¦able
avoid¦ably
avoid¦ance
avoid¦er
avoir¦du¦pois
Avon
avouch
avouch¦ment
avow
avow¦al
avow¦ed¦ly
avulse
avuls¦ing
avul¦sion
avun¦cu¦lar
avun¦cu¦late
AWACS
pl. **AWACS**
= airborne warning
and control system
Awadh var. of **Oudh**
await
awake
awoke
awak¦ing
awoken
awaken
award
award¦ee
award¦er
aware
aware¦ness
awash
away direction; cf.
aweigh
Awdry, Rev¦er¦end
W. author
awe
awing
aweary
aweigh of anchor;
cf. **away**
awe¦some
awe¦some¦ly
awe¦some¦ness
awe¦stricken
awe¦struck
awful
aw¦ful¦ly

aw¦ful¦ness
awhile
awhirl
awk¦ward
awk¦ward¦ly
awk¦ward¦ness
awl tool; cf. **orle**
awn
awned
awn¦ing
awoke
awoken
AWOL = absent
  without leave
awry
aw-shucks *adj.*
ax *US*
axe *Br.*
  axing
axel skating
  movement; cf. **axil**,
  axle
axe¦man *Br.*
  axe¦men
  US axman
axen¦ic
axen¦ic¦al¦ly
axes pl. of **ax**, **axe**,
  and **axis**
axial
ax¦ial¦ly
axil angle between
  leaf and stem; cf.
  axel, **axle**
ax¦illa
  ax¦il¦lae
ax¦il¦lary
  ax¦il¦lar¦ies
axiom
axio¦mat¦ic
axi¦oma¦tise *Br.* var.
  of **axiomatize**
axi¦oma¦tize
  axi¦oma¦tiz¦ing
axion
axis
  axes
axi¦sym¦met¦ric
axle rod; cf. **axel**,
  axil
axman *US*
  axmen
  Br. axeman
Ax¦min¦ster

axo¦lemma
axo¦lotl
axon
axon¦al
axo¦nemal
axo¦neme
axono¦met¦ric
axo¦plasm
axo¦plas¦mic
Axum var. of
  Aksum
Axum¦ite var. of
  Aksumite
ay yes; vote; var. of
  aye
Aya¦cu¦cho
ayah nurse; cf. **ire**
aya¦huasca
aya¦tol¦lah
Ayck¦bourn, Alan
  playwright
aye yes; vote; always
aye aye *Nautical* yes
aye-aye lemur
Ayer, A. J.
  philosopher
Ayers Rock
Ay¦esha wife of
  Muhammad
Ayles¦bury +s town;
  duck
Ay¦mara
Ayr
Ayr¦shire
Ayub Khan,
  Mu¦ham¦mad
  president of
  Pakistan
Ayur¦veda
Ayur¦vedic
Azad Kash¦mir
aza¦lea
Azande
  pl. Azande
  var. of **Zande**
Aza¦nia
Aza¦nian
aza¦role
azeo¦trope
azeo¦trop¦ic
Azer¦bai¦jan
Azer¦bai¦jani
Azeri

azide
azido¦thy¦mid¦ine
  trademark
Azil¦ian
azi¦muth
azi¦muth¦al
azine
azo
azo¦ben¦zene
azoic
azonal
azoo¦sper¦mia
azoo¦sper¦mic
Azores
azo¦turia
Azov
Az¦rael
Aztec
azu¦lejo +s
azure
azur¦ite
azy¦gos vein
azy¦gous single
Az Zarqa var. of
  Zarqa

————————

B

ba soul
baa
  baas
  baaed or baa'd
  baa¦ing
  bleat
Baal ancient god
Baal¦bek
Baal¦ism
Baath Arab political
  party
Baath¦ism
Baath¦ist
baba in 'rum baba'
baba¦çú var. of
  babassu
baba ga¦noush
baba gha¦nouj var.
  of baba ganoush
ba¦bassu

Bab¦bage, Charles
  mathematician
Bab¦bitt, Mil¦ton
  composer
Bab¦bitt metal;
  complacent
  businessman
bab¦bitt bearing
  lining
Bab¦bitt¦ry
bab¦ble
bab¦bling
babble¦ment
bab¦bler
babby
bab¦bies
Babel, Tower of
babel scene of
  confusion
babe¦li¦cious
ba¦bes¦ia¦sis var. of
  babesiosis
ba¦besi¦osis
Babi adherent of
  Babism; cf. **Barbie**
ba¦biche
babi¦rusa
Bab¦ism
Bab¦ist
ba¦boon
ba¦bouche
Ba¦bru¦isk
Ba¦bru¦ysk var. of
  Babruisk
babu
babul
Babur Mogul
  emperor
ba¦bushka
Babu¦yan
baby
  ba¦bies
  ba¦bied
baby¦ing
baby boom¦er
Baby Doc president
  of Haiti
baby-doll *adj.*
baby¦father
Baby¦gro +s
  trademark
baby¦hood
baby¦ish
Baby¦lon

Baby|lonia
Baby|lon|ian
baby|mother
baby's breath plant
baby|sit
  baby|sat
  baby|sit|ting
baby|sit|ter
baca|lao
Ba|call, Lauren
  actress
bac|ca|laur|eate
bac|carat
Bac|chae *Greek
  Mythology*
bac|cha|nal
Bac|cha|na|lia
  Roman festival
bac|cha|na|lia
  drunken
  celebrations
bac|cha|na|lian
bac|chant
  bac|chants or
  bac|chan|tes *male*
bac|chante *female*
Bac|chic
Bac|chus Greek god
baccy
  bac|cies
Bach, Jo|hann
  Se|bas|tian
  composer
Bach flower
  remedies
bach live alone; cf.
  batch
bach Welsh term of
  endearment
Bach|ar|ach, Burt
  American writer of
  popular songs
ba|chata
bach|elor
bach|elor|ette
bach|elor|hood
ba|cil|lary
ba|cil|li|form
ba|cil|lus
  ba|cilli
back|ache
back-arc
back|bar
back|beat

back|bench *adj.*
back|bench|er
back benches
back|biter
back|bit|ing
back|blocks
back|board
back|bone
back|cast
back|channel
back|chat
back|cloth
back|comb
back|coun|try
back|court
back|crawl
back|cross
back|date
  back|dat|ing
back|down *n.*
back|draft *US*
back|draught *Br.*
back|drop
  back|dropped
  back|drop|ping
back|er
back|field
back|fill
back|fire
  back|fir|ing
back|fist
back|flip
back-formation
back|gam|mon
back|ground
back|ground|er
back|hand
back|hand|ed
back|hand|er
back-heel
back|hoe
back issue
back|land
back|lash
back|less
back|light
  back|lit or
  back|lighted
back|line
back|list
back|load
back|log
back|lot

back|mark|er
back|most
back num|ber
back|pack
back|pack|er
back-pedal
  back-pedals
  back-pedalled *Br.*
  back-pedaled *US*
  back-pedalling *Br.*
  back-pedaling *US*
back|plane
back|plate
back-project
back-projec|tion
back|rest
back-rower
back|scat|ter
back|scratch|er
back-scratch|ing
back|sheesh var. of
  baksheesh
back|shift
back|side
back|sight
back|slap|per
back|slap|ping
back|slash
back|slide
  back|slid|ing
back|slider
back|space
  back|spa|cing
back|spin
back|splash
back|stage
back stairs *n.*
back|stairs *adj.*
back|stamp
back|stay
back|stitch
back|stop
  back|stopped
  back|stop|ping
back|story
  back|stor|ies
back|street
back|stretch on
  racetrack
back|stroke
back|stroker
back|swim|mer
  water boatman

back|swing
back|sword
back talk
back to back *adv.*
back-to-back *adj.
  & n.*
back to front *adv.*
back-to-front *adj.*
back|track
back|up
back|veld
back|veld|er
back|ward
back|ward|ation
back|ward|ly
back|ward|ness
back|wards
back|wash
back|water
back|wind
back|woods
back|woods|man
  back|woods|men
back|yard
bac|lava var. of
  baklava
Bacon, Fran|cis
  philosopher
Bacon, Fran|cis
  painter
Bacon, Roger
  philosopher
bacon
bacon-and-eggs
  plant
bacon|er
Ba|con|ian
bac|ter|aemia *Br.
  US* bacteremia
bac|ter|aem|ic *Br.
  US* bacteremic
bac|ter|emia *US
  Br.* bacteraemia
bac|ter|em|ic *US
  Br.* bacteraemic
bac|teria
bac|ter|ial
bac|ter|ial|ly
bac|teri|cidal
bac|teri|cide
bac|teri|ocin
bac|terio|logic|al
bac|terio|logic|al|ly

bac|teri|olo|gist
bac|teri|ology
bac|teri|oly|sis
bac|terio|lyt|ic
bac|terio|phage
bac|terio|sta|sis
  bac|terio|sta|ses
bac|terio|stat
bac|terio|stat|ic
bac|ter|ium
  bac|teria
bac|teri|uria
Bac|tria
Bac|trian
baculo|virus
bacu|lum
  bac|ula
bad
  bad|der
  bad|dest
  cf. bade
bada bing
bada bing bada
  boom
bad|ass
bad|deley|ite
bad|der|locks
bad|die var. of
  baddy
bad|dish
baddy
  bad|dies
bade archaic past
  tense of bid
Baden town, Austria
Baden-Baden
  town, Germany
Baden-Powell,
  Rob|ert founder of
  Boy Scouts
Baden-
  Württem|berg
Bader, Doug|las
  pilot
badge
  badg|ing
badger
bad|in|age
bad|lands
badly
  worse
  worst
Bad|min|ton horse
  trials

bad|min|ton
bad-mouth v. +s
  +ed +ing
bad|ness
Badon Hill
Bae|deker
Baez, Joan folk
  singer
Baf|fin Bay
Baf|fin Is|land
baf|fle
  baf|fling
baffle|gab
baffle|ment
baf|fler
baf|fling|ly
baft var. of bafta
BAFTA = British
  Association of Film
  and Television Arts
Bafta award
bafta fabric
bag
  bagged
  bag|ging
Ba|ganda
ba|gasse
baga|telle
bagel
bag|ful
bag|gage
bag|ger
Bag|gie trademark
  food bag
baggi|ness
baggy
  bag|gies
  bag|gier
  bag|giest
baggy|wrin|kle
Bagh|dad
bag|man
bag|men
bagnio +s
Bagot goat
bag-o'-wrinkle var.
  of baggywrinkle
bag|piper
bag|pipes
ba gua Chinese
  motif
ba|guette
bag|wash
bag|worm

bah exclam.
ba|ha|dur
Baha'i
Ba|ha'ism
Ba|ha|mas
Ba|ha|mian
Ba|hasa
  In|do|nesia
Ba|ha|sa
  Ma|lay|sia
Bahia
Bah|rain
Bah|raini
baht
  pl. baht
bahu Ind. daughter-
  in-law
Ba|hutu pl. of Hutu
Bai|kal
Bai|ko|nur
bail security for
  prisoner; on cricket
  stumps; bar in
  stable; scoop water;
  cf. bale
bail|able
bail|ee Law
bail|er scoop for
  water; cf. bailor,
  baler
Bai|ley shipping
  area; bridge
Bai|ley, David pho-
  tographer
bai|ley part of castle
bai|lie Scottish
  magistrate
bai|liff
baili|wick
bail|ment
bail|or Law; cf.
  bailer, baler
bail|out n.
Baily's beads
Bain|bridge, Beryl
  novelist
bain-marie
  bains-marie or
  bain-maries
Bai|ram
Baird, John Logie
  pioneer of
  television
bairn

Bair|rada
Bai|sa|khi
bait in hunting or
  fishing; harass;
  torment; cf. bate
bait|cast|er
bait|cast|ing
baiza
baize
Baja Cali|for|nia
Baja Cali|for|nia
  Sur
ba|jada
Bajan
Baka people;
  language
bake
bak|ing
bake|apple
bake|house
Bake|lite trademark
bake-off n. & adj.
Baker, Janet singer
Baker, Jo|seph|ine
  dancer
baker
baker's dozen
bakery
  baker|ies
bake|shop
bake|ware
Bake|well
bak|lava
bak|sheesh
Bakst, Léon painter
  and designer
Baku
Ba|ku|nin, Mikh|ail
  revolutionary
Bala, Lake
Bala|clava battle
bala|clava helmet
bala|fon
bala|laika
bal|ance
bal|an|cing
bal|an|cer
Bal|an|chine,
  George
  choreographer
ba|landa var. of
  balander
ba|lan|der

bal¦an¦itis
balas ruby
bal¦ata
Bala¦ton
Bal¦boa port, Panama
Bal¦boa, Vasco de explorer
bal¦boa Panamanian currency
bal¦brig¦gan
Bal¦con, Mi¦chael film producer
bal¦con¦ied
bal¦cony
　bal¦con¦ies
bal¦da¦chin
bal¦da¦quin var. of baldachin
Bal¦der Norse god
bal¦der¦dash
bald¦head
baldie var. of baldy
bald¦ish
bald¦ly
bald¦money
bald¦ness
bald¦pate
bal¦dric
Bald¦win, James novelist
Bald¦win, Stan¦ley prime minister of Britain
baldy
bale
　bal¦ing
bundle; evil, destruction, etc.; in 'bale out' (of aircraft); cf. bail
Ba¦le¦ar¦ic
ba¦leen
bale¦fire
bale¦ful
bale¦ful¦ly
bale¦ful¦ness
Ba¦len¦ciaga, Cris¦tó¦bal couturier
baler machine; cf. bailer, bailor

Bal¦four, Ar¦thur prime minister of Britain
Bali
bali¦bun¦tal
Bali¦nese
balk US
Br. baulk; cf. bork
Bal¦kan
Bal¦kan¦isa¦tion Br. var. of Balkanization
Bal¦kan¦ise Br. var. of Balkanize
Bal¦kan¦iza¦tion
Bal¦kan¦ize
　Bal¦kan¦iz¦ing
Bal¦kans
Bal¦khash var. of Balqash
balky US
　balk¦ier
　balki¦est
Br. baulky
bal¦lad
bal¦lade
bal¦lad¦eer
bal¦lad¦ry
bal¦lad¦ries
Bal¦lan¦tyne, R. M. author
bal¦lan wrasse
Bal¦la¦rat
Bal¦lard, J. G. novelist
bal¦last
ball bear¦ing
ball¦boy
ball¦cock
bal¦ler¦ina
Bal¦le¦steros, Sev¦eri¦ano ('Sevvy') golfer
bal¦let
bal¦let¦ic
bal¦let¦ic¦al¦ly
bal¦leto¦mane
bal¦leto¦mania
Bal¦lets Russes
ball¦girl
ball¦hawk
bal¦lista
bal¦lis¦tae or bal¦lis¦tas

bal¦lis¦tic
bal¦lis¦tic¦al¦ly
bal¦lis¦tics
bal¦lock vulgar slang; var. of bollock
bal¦lock¦ing vulgar slang; var. of bollocking
bal¦locks vulgar slang; var. of bollocks
bal¦lon Dancing
bal¦loon
bal¦loon¦er
bal¦loon¦fish
bal¦loon¦ist
bal¦lot
bal¦lo¦tin
bal¦lo¦tine
ball¦park
ball¦play¦er
ball¦point
ball¦room
balls vulgar slang
balls-ache vulgar slang
balls-aching vulgar slang
ballsi¦ness
balls-up n. vulgar slang
ballsy
　balls¦ier
　ballsi¦est
bally
bally¦hoo +s +ed +ing
Bally¦mena
bally¦rag
　bally¦ragged
　bally¦rag¦ging
balm ointment; plant; cf. barm
bal¦ma¦caan
bal masqué
bals masqués
Bal¦mer
balm¦ily
balm of Gil¦ead resin; tree
Bal¦moral
bal¦moral cap; boot

bal mus¦ette
bals mus¦ettes
balmy
　balm¦ier
　balmi¦est
soothing; cf. barmy
balm¦yard
balneo¦logic¦al
balne¦olo¦gist
balne¦ology
balneo¦ther¦apy
ba¦lo¦ney
Bal¦qash
balsa
bal¦sam
bal¦sam¦ic
Balt
Bal¦tha¦sar one of the Magi
bal¦tha¦zar wine bottle
Balti person; language
balti food
Bal¦tic
Bal¦ti¦more
Bal¦ti¦mor¦ean
Balti¦stan
Ba¦lu¦chi
Ba¦luchi¦stan
balun electrical transformer
bal¦us¦ter
bal¦us¦trade
bal¦us¦traded
Bal¦zac, Hon¦oré de novelist
Bal¦zac¦ian
Bam¦ako
Bam¦bara
bam¦bino
　bam¦bini or
　bam¦bi¦nos
bam¦boo +s
bam¦boo¦zle
bam¦booz¦ling
bam¦booz¦ler
Bam¦ian
ban
　banned
　ban¦ning
prohibit; prohibition; curse; cf.
banns

Ba¦naba
banal
ban¦al¦ity
  ban¦al¦ities
ban¦al¦ly
ba¦nana
banana¦quit
ban¦ausic
Ban¦bury
banc¦assur¦ance
banc¦assur¦er
Banda, Hast¦ings
  president of Malawi
ban¦dage
  ban¦da¦ging
Band-Aid
  trademark
ban¦dana var. of
  bandanna
ban¦danna
Ban¦da¦ra¦naike,
  Siri¦mavo prime
  minister of Sri
  Lanka
Ban¦dar Lam¦pung
Ban¦dar Seri
  Be¦ga¦wan
Banda Sea
band¦box
ban¦deau
  ban¦deaux
band¦er
ban¦der¦illa
ban¦der¦il¦lero +s
ban¦derol var. of
  banderole
ban¦der¦ole
ban¦der¦snatch
band¦fish
bandi¦coot
ban¦dido var. of
  bandito
ban¦dit
  ban¦dits or
  ban¦ditti
ban¦dito +s
ban¦dit¦ry
Band¦jar¦ma¦sin
  var. of
  Banjarmasin
band¦lead¦er
band¦master
bando¦bast var. of
  bundobust

ban¦dog
ban¦do¦leer var. of
  bandolier
ban¦do¦lier
ban¦do¦neon
ban¦dora
ban¦dore var. of
  bandora
band¦pass
band¦saw
band¦shell
bands¦man
  bands¦men
band¦stand
ban¦dulu
Ban¦dung
ban¦dura
band¦wagon
band¦width
bandy
  ban¦dies
  ban¦died
  bandy¦ing
ban¦dier
bandi¦est
bandy-bandy
  bandy-bandys
bane¦berry
  bane¦berries
bane¦ful
Banff
Banff¦shire
bang noise etc.; cf.
  bhang
Banga¦lore
banga¦rang
bang¦er
Bang¦kok
Ban¦gla
Ban¦gla¦desh
Ban¦gla¦deshi
ban¦gle
Ban¦gor
bang¦tail
Ban¦gui
bang-up *adj.*
ban¦ian var. of
  banyan
ban¦ish
ban¦ish¦ment
ban¦is¦ter
Banja Luka
Ban¦jar¦masin

ban¦jax
banjo
  ban¦jos or ban¦joes
ban¦jo¦ist
Ban¦jul
bank¦abil¦ity
bank¦able
bank¦assur¦ance
  var. of
  bancassurance
bank¦assur¦er var.
  of bancassurer
bank¦er
bank¦note
bank¦roll
bank¦rupt
bank¦rupt¦cy
  bank¦rupt¦cies
bank¦sia
ban¦nable
ban¦ner
ban¦nered
ban¦neret
Ban¦nis¦ter, Roger
  athlete
ban¦nis¦ter var. of
  banister
ban¦nock
Ban¦nock¦burn
banns of marriage
ban¦of¦fee pie; var.
  of banoffi
ban¦offi
ban¦quet
ban¦quet¦er
ban¦quette
ban¦shee
ban¦suri
ban¦tam
ban¦tam¦weight
ban¦teng
ban¦ter
ban¦ter¦er
ban¦ter¦ing¦ly
Ban¦ting,
  Fred¦erick surgeon
Bantu
Ban¦tu¦stan
ban¦yan
ban¦zai
bao¦bab
bap¦tise *Br.* var. of
  baptize

bap¦tism
bap¦tis¦mal
Bap¦tist denomin-
  ation
bap¦tist
bap¦tist¦ery
  bap¦tist¦er¦ies
bap¦tist¦ry var. of
  baptistery
bap¦tize
  bap¦tiz¦ing
bar
  barred
  bar¦ring
  cf. barre
Bar¦ab¦bas
bara brith
bara¦sin¦gha
bara¦thea
ba¦raza
Barb = Broadcasters'
  Audience Research
  Council
barb
Bar¦ba¦dian
Bar¦ba¦dos
Bar¦bara
bar¦bar¦ian
bar¦bar¦ic
bar¦bar¦ic¦al¦ly
bar¦bar¦isa¦tion *Br.*
  var. of
  barbarization
bar¦bar¦ise *Br.* var.
  of barbarize
bar¦bar¦ism
bar¦bar¦ity
  bar¦bar¦ities
bar¦bar¦iza¦tion
bar¦bar¦ize
  bar¦bar¦iz¦ing
Bar¦ba¦rossa,
  Fred¦erick king of
  Germany
bar¦bar¦ous
bar¦bar¦ous¦ly
Bar¦bary
bar¦ba¦stelle
bar¦be¦cue
  bar¦be¦cu¦ing
bar¦bel fish; part of
  fish
bar¦bell weights

Bar¦ber, Sam¦uel
  composer
bar¦ber
bar¦berry
  bar¦berries
barber|shop
bar¦bet bird
bar¦bette gun
  platform
bar¦bi¦can
bar¦bie = barbecue
Bar¦bie doll
  trademark; cf. Babi
Bar¦bi¦rolli, John
  conductor
bar¦bi¦tal
bar¦bi¦tone
bar¦bit¦ur¦ate
Bar¦bi¦zon School
barb|less
bar¦bola
bar¦bo¦tine
Bar|bour *trademark*
  jacket
Bar|bour, John
  poet
Bar¦buda
Bar¦budan
barb|ule
barb|wire *US*
  Br. barbed wire
Barca|Lounger
  trademark
bar¦ca¦role
bar¦ca¦rolle var. of
  barcarole
Bar¦ce¦lona
bar¦chan
Bar¦clay
Bar-Cochba rebel
Bar¦coo
bard
bar¦dee var. of
  bardie
bard¦ic
bar¦die
bard|ol¦ater
bard|ol¦ator var. of
  bardolater
bard|ol¦atry
Bar¦do¦lino +s
Bar¦dot, Bri¦gitte
  actress

bardy
  bar¦dies
bare
  bar¦ing
barer
  bar¦est
  naked, uncover,
  etc.; cf. bear
bare|back
bare|boat
Bare|bones Parlia-
  ment
bare|faced
bare|foot
bar¦ège
bare|hand¦ed
bare|head¦ed
Ba|reilly
bare¦ly
Bar¦en|boim,
  Dan¦iel pianist and
  conductor
bare|ness
Bar|ents Sea
barf
barfi *var. of* burfi
bar¦fly
  bar¦flies
bar|gain
bar|gain¦er
barge
  bar¦ging
barge|board
bar¦gee
Bar|gello
barge|pole
Bari
ba|rilla
Bari|sal
bar|ista
bar¦ite var. of
  baryte
bari|tonal
bari|tone singer; cf.
  baryton
bar¦ium
bark cry of dog; on
  tree trunk; cf.
  barque
bark|cloth
bar|keep
bar¦keep¦er
bar¦ken|tine *US*
  Br. barquentine

bark¦er
Barkly Table|land
  cf. Berkeley
bar¦ley
barley|corn
barley|mow
barm froth; yeast;
  cake; cf. balm
bar¦maid
bar¦man
  bar¦men
barm|brack
barmi|ness
bar mitz|vah +s
  +ed +ing
barmy
  bar¦mier
  bar¦miest
  crazy; cf. balmy
Bar¦na|bas
Bar¦naby
bar¦nacle
Bar¦nard,
  Chris|tiaan
  surgeon
Bar¦nardo, Thomas
  philanthropist
Bar¦nard's star
Bar¦naul
barn|brack var. of
  barmbrack
bar¦net
bar¦ney
Barns|ley
barn|storm
barn|storm¦er
Bar¦num, Phin|eas
  T. showman
barn|yard
Bar¦oda
baro|graph
Ba¦rolo +s
bar¦om¦eter
baro|met¦ric
bar¦om¦etry
baron nobleman;
  beef; cf. barren
bar¦on|age
bar¦on|ess
bar¦on|et
bar¦on|et¦age
bar¦on|et¦cy
  bar¦on|et¦cies
bar¦on|ial

bar¦ony
bar¦on|ies .
bar¦oque
baro|recep¦tor
baro|titis
baro|trauma
bar¦ouche
barque ship; cf.
  bark
bar¦quen|tine *Br.*
  US barkentine
Bar¦qui¦si¦meto
Barra island
bar¦rack
barra|coon
barra|couta long,
  thin food fish
barra|cuda large
  predatory fish
barra|cu¦dina thin
  predatory fish
bar¦rage
bar¦rag|ing
barra|mundi
  pl. barra|mundi or
  barra|mun¦dis
bar¦ranca
bar¦ranco var. of
  barranca
Bar¦ran|quilla
bar¦ra|tor
bar¦ra|trous
bar¦ra|try
barre *Ballet*
barré *Music*
bar¦rel
  bar¦relled *Br.*
  bar¦reled *US*
barrel|ling *Br.*
barrel|ing *US*
barrel|fish
barrel|head
barrel|house
Bar¦ren, Cape
bar¦ren infertile; cf.
  baron
bar¦ren|ly
bar¦ren|ness
barren|wort
Bar¦rett, Eliza|beth
  poet, wife of Robert
  Browning
bar¦rette

barri|cade
barri|cad|ing
Bar|rie, J. M. writer
bar|rier
bar|rio +s
bar|rique
bar|ris|ter
barrister-at-law
  barristers-at-law
bar|room
bar|row
Barrow-in-Furness
Barry, Charles
  architect
barry *Heraldry*
Barry|more
  theatrical family
Bar|sac
bar|tend
bar|tend|er
bar|ter
bar|ter|er
Barth, John writer
Barth, Karl
  theologian
Barthes, Ro|land
  semiotician
Barth|ian
bar|tho|lin|itis
Bar|tho|lin's gland
Bar|tholo|mew
bar|ti|zan
Bart|lett pear
Bar|tók, Béla
  composer
Bart's Hos|pital
bart|sia
bar|wing
bary|centre
bary|cen|tric
ba|ryon
baryon|ic
Ba|rysh|ni|kov,
  Mikh|ail ballet
  dancer
ba|ryta
bar|yte
ba|ry|tes var. of
  baryte
ba|ryt|ic
bary|ton instru-
  ment; cf. baritone
basal

bas|alt
bas|alt|ic
bas|an|ite
bas|ci|net var. of
  basinet helmet; cf.
  bassinet
bas|cule
base
bas|ing
baser
bas|est
  foundation; estab-
  lish; cowardly;
  impure; cf. bass
base|ball
base|board
base|born
base|head
base jump *n. & v.*
base jump|er
base|less
base|less|ly
base|line
base|load
base|ly
base|man
  base|men
base|ment
base|ness
ba|senji
base|plate
bases pl. of base
  and basis
bash
basha shelter; cf.
  basher, bhasha
bash|er person who
  bashes; cf. basha,
  bhasha
ba|shert
bash|ful
bash|ful|ly
bash|ful|ness
Bash|kir
Bash|kiria
bash|ment
basho
  pl. basho or
  bashos
BASIC computer
  language
basic
ba|sic|ally

bas|icity
bas|ici|ties
ba|sidio|mycete
ba|sid|ium
  ba|sidia
Basie, Count jazz
  musician
basil
basi|lar
Bas|il|don
basi|lect
basi|lect|al
Ba|sil|ian
ba|sil|ica
ba|sil|ican
Ba|sili|cata ·
basi|lisk
Bas|ilo|saurus
  Bas|ilo|sauri
basin
basi|net headpiece;
  cf. bassinet
basin|ful
ba|sip|etal
basis
  bases
bask relax; cf.
  basque
bas|ket
bas|ket|ball
bas|ket|ful
Bas|ket Maker
  American Indian
basket-maker
bas|ket|ry
bas|ket|work
Basle
bas|mati
baso|phil
baso|phil|ic
Ba|so|tho
Basque people;
  language
basque bodice; cf.
  bask
Basra
bas-relief
bass *Music;* cf. base
bass fish
Bas|sein
Basse-Norman|die
bas|set horn; hound

Basse|terre capital
  of St Kitts and
  Nevis
Basse-Terre main
  island of
  Guadeloupe
Bas|sey, Shir|ley
  singer
bassi pl. of basso
bas|sinet cradle; cf.
  basinet
bass|ist
bass|let
basso
bas|sos or bassi
basso con|tinuo
basso con|tinuos
bas|soon
bas|soon|ist
basso pro|fundo
basso pro|fun|dos
basso-relievo +s
Bass Strait
bass|wood
bassy
  bass|ier
  bassi|est
bast fibre; cf. baste
bas|tard
bas|tard|isa|tion
  Br. var. of
  bastardization
bas|tard|ise *Br.* var.
  of bastardize
bas|tard|iza|tion
  Br.
bas|tard|ize
  bas|tard|iz|ing
bastard-trench
bas|tardy
baste
bast|ing
  pour fat over; sew;
  thrash; cf. bast
baster
Bas|tet Egyptian
  goddess
Bas|tia
bas|tide
Bas|tille
bas|tin|ado
  pl. bas|ti|nados
  v. bas|tin|adoes
bas|tin|adoed
bas|tin|ado|ing

bas¦tion

bast¦naes¦ite

bast¦näs¦ite var. of
bastnaesite

ba¦suco

Ba¦su¦to¦land

bat

bat¦ted

bat¦ting

Bata port, Equatorial Guinea

Batak people;
language

Batan Islands

ba¦tata

Ba¦ta¦via

Ba¦ta¦vian

batch group etc.; cf.
bach

batch¦mate

Bat¦dam¦bang var.
of Battambang

bate rage; cf. bait

bate

bated

bat¦ing

Falconry; cf. bait

bat¦eau mouche

bat¦eaux mouches

bated in 'with bated
breath'

bat¦el¦eur

Bate¦man, H. M.
cartoonist

Bates, Alan actor

Bates, H. E. writer

Bates¦ian

bat¦fish

Bath city; bun;
chap; Oliver (*trademark*); stone; cf.
Baath

bath

bath¦ing

bathe

bath¦ing

bather

bath¦et¦ic

bath¦house

batho¦chro¦mic

batho¦lith

Bath¦on¦ian

ba¦thos

bath¦robe

bath¦room

Bath¦sheba

bath¦tub

Bath¦urst

bath¦water

bathy¦al

ba¦thym¦eter

bathy¦met¦ric

ba¦thym¦etry

bathy¦pela¦gic

bathy¦scaphe

bathy¦sphere

batik

Ba¦tista, Ful¦gen¦cio
Cuban dictator

bat¦iste

Bat¦man fictional
character

bat¦man

bat¦men
officer's servant

bat mitz¦vah +s
+ed +ing

baton stick used as
implement; cf.
batten

Baton Rouge

baton round

Ba¦tra¦chia

ba¦tra¦chian

bats¦man

bats¦men

bats¦man¦ship

Ba¦tswana pl. of
Tswana

batt thick mat

bat¦tal¦ion

Bat¦tam¦bang

bat¦tels college
account at Oxford
University

batte¦ment

bat¦ten strip of
wood used for
fastening; cf. baton

Bat¦ten¦berg

bat¦ter

bat¦ter¦er

bat¦terie Ballet

*bat¦terie de
cui¦sine*

*bat¦ter¦ies de
cui¦sine*

bat¦tery

bat¦ter¦ies

Bat¦ti¦ca¦loa

bat¦tily

batti¦ness

bat¦tle

bat¦tling
cf. battels

battle¦ax US

battle¦axe Br.

Battle¦born State

battle¦bus

battle¦cruiser

battle¦dore

battle¦dress

battle¦field

battle¦ground

battle¦group

battle¦ment

bat¦tler

battle¦ship

bat¦tue

batty

bat¦ties

bat¦tier

bat¦ti¦est

Batwa pl. of Twa

bat¦wing *adj.*

bat¦woman

bat¦women

bau¦ble

baud

pl. baud or bauds
Computing unit of
speed; cf. bawd,
board, bored

Baude¦laire,
Charles poet

Baude¦lair¦ean

bau¦era

Bau¦haus

baulk Br.
US balk; cf. bork

baulky Br.

baulk¦ier

baulki¦est
US balky

baux¦ite

baux¦it¦ic

bav¦ard¦age

Bav¦aria

Bav¦ar¦ian

bav¦ar¦ois
pl. bav¦ar¦ois

bav¦ar¦oise var. of
bavarois

baw¦bee

bawd prostitute; cf.
baud, board,
bored

bawd¦ily

bawdi¦ness

bawd¦ry

bawdy

bawd¦ier

bawdi¦est

bawl yell

bawl¦er

baw¦ley

bawn fortified
enclosure; meadow;
flat rocks; cf. born,
borne, bourn

Bax, Ar¦nold
composer

bay inlet; cf. bey

baya bird; cf. buyer,
byre

baya¦dère

bay¦berry

bay¦berries

Bayes¦ian

Bayes' the¦orem

Bay¦eux

Bay¦kal var. of
Baikal

Bay¦ko¦nur var. of
Baikonur

Bay¦lis, Lil¦ian
theatre manager

bay¦onet +ed +ing

bayou

Bay¦reuth town,
Germany; cf.
Beirut

baza hawk

ba¦zaar market

ba¦zil¦lion

bazoo +s

ba¦zooka

ba¦zoom

b-ball = basketball

b-boy hip-hop fan

B-cell *Physiology*

bdel¦lium

beach shore; cf.
beech

beach¦comb¦er

beach|front
beach|head
Beach-la-mar
beach|side
beach|wear
Beachy Head
bea¦con
beacon|fish
bead cf. Bede
bead|ily
bea¦dle
bead|let anemone
beads|man
  beads|men
bead|work
beady
  bead|ier
  beadi|est
bea¦gle
  beag|ling
beag|ler
beak
Bea¦ker folk; ware
bea¦ker
beak-like
beaky
beal|ach
beam
Bea¦mer var. of
  Beemer
beam|er *Cricket*; cf.
  bema, bimah
beamy
  beam|ier
  beami|est
bean|bag
bean|ery
  bean|er|ies
bean|feast
beanie
beano +s
bean|pole
bean sprout
bean|stalk
bear animal; cf.
  bare
bear
  bore
  borne
  carry; exert; toler-
  ate; etc.; cf. **bare**
bear
  bore
  born

give birth to; cf.
  bare
bear|abil¦ity
bear|able
bear|ably
bear|berry
  bear|berries
bear|cat
beard
beard|fish
beardie
beard|less
Beard|more
Beards|ley, Aub¦rey
  painter
bear¦er
bear|grass
bear|ish
Béarn|aise
bear|skin
Beas river, India
beast
beastie
beast|li|ness
beast|ly
  beast|lier
  beast|li|est
beat
beaten
  cf. beet
beat|able
beat|box
beat¦er
bea|tif¦ic
bea¦tif¦ic|al¦ly
be|ati¦fi|ca¦tion
be|atify
  be|ati|fies
  be|ati|fied
  be|ati¦fy|ing
be|ati|tude
Beatles pop group
beat|nik
Bea¦ton, Cecil pho-
  tographer
Bea|trice
Bea|trix
Beatty, David
  admiral
Beatty, War¦ren
  actor
beat-up *adj. & n.*
Beau man's name

beau
  beaux or beaus
Beau|fort Sea; scale
beau geste
  beaux gestes
beau idéal
  beaux idéals
Beau|jo¦lais
  pl. Beau|jo¦lais
Beau|jo¦lais
  Nou|veau
Beau|mar¦chais,
  Pierre de drama-
  tist
beau monde
  beaux mondes
Beau|mont,
  Fran¦cis dramatist
Beaune town,
  France; wine
beau sab|reur
  beaux sab|reurs
beaut
beaut|eous
beaut|ician
beau¦ti|fi|ca¦tion
beau¦ti|fier
beau¦ti|ful
beau¦ti|ful¦ly
beaut|ify
  beau¦ti|fies
  beau¦ti|fied
  beau¦ti|fy|ing
beauty
  beaut|ies
Beau|voir, Sim¦one
  de writer
beaux pl. of beau
beaux arts
beaux es|prits
beaux yeux
bea¦ver
bea¦ver|board
Bea¦ver|brook,
  Lord newspaper
  proprietor
bebop
be¦bop|per
be|calm
be|came
bec¦ard
be|cause
béch|amel

Bêche-de-mer var.
  of Bislama
bêche-de-mer
  pl. bêche-de-mer
  or bêches-de-mer
Bech|stein
Bech¦uana|land
Becker, Boris
  tennis player
Becket, St Thomas
  à archbishop
becket
Beck|ett, Sam¦uel
  writer
Beck|ham, David
  footballer
Beck|mann, Ernst
  chemist
beckon
be|cloud
be¦come
  be|came
  be|com¦ing
  be|com¦ing¦ly
bec|querel
bed
  bed¦ded
  bed|ding
be|dab¦ble
be|dab¦bling
bedad
be¦daub
be|daz¦zle
be|daz¦zling
be|dazzle|ment
bed|bug
bed|cham¦ber
bed|clothes
bed|cover
bed|dable
bed¦der
Bede monk and
  writer
be¦deck
bed|eguar
bedel
be¦dell var. of bedel
be|devil
  be|dev¦illed *Br.*
  be|dev¦iled *US*
  be|dev¦il|ling *Br.*
  be|dev¦il|ing *US*
be|devil|ment
bedew

bed|fellow
Bed|ford
Bed|ford|shire
bed|head
be|dight
bedim
 be|dimmed
 be|dim|ming
be|dizen
bed|jacket
bed|lam
bed|linen
Bed|ling|ton
bed|load
bed|maker
Bed|ouin
bed|pan
bed|plate
bed|post
be|drag|gled
bed|rid|den
bed|rock
bed|roll
bed|room
bed|side
bed|sit
bed|sit|ter
bed-sitting room
bed|skirt
bed|sock
bed|sore
bed|spread
bed|stead
bed|straw
bed|time
Bedu var. of
 Bedouin
Bed|uin var. of
 Bedouin
Beeb BBC
beech tree; cf.
 beach
Bee|cham, Thomas
 conductor
beech mar|ten
beech|mast
beech poly|pore
beech|wood
beedi var. of bidi
beef
 beeves
 cattle
 beefs

beefed
beef|ing
 complain;
 complaint
beef|alo
 pl. beef|alo or
 beef|aloes
beef|bur|ger
beef|cake
beef|eat|er
beef|ily
beefi|ness
beef|steak
beef|wood
beefy
 beef|ier
 beefi|est
bee|hive
bee-keeper
bee-keeping
bee|line
Be|el|ze|bub
Bee|mer car; cf.
 beamer, bema,
 bimah
beep|er
beer drink; cf. bier
Beer|bohm, Max
 writer
Beeren|aus|lese
beer|house
beer|ily
Beer|sheba
beery
 beer|ier
 beeri|est
beest|ings
bee-stung
bees|wax
bees|wing crust on
 port wine
beet vegetable; cf.
 beat
Beet|hoven,
 Lud|wig van
 composer
Beet|hoven|ian
bee|tle
beet|ling
 cf. betel
Bee|ton, Mrs cook-
 ery writer
beet|root
beeves

beezer
be|fall
be|fell
be|fallen
befit
be|fit|ted
be|fit|ting
be|fit|ting|ly
befog
be|fogged
be|fog|ging
be|fool
be|fore
be|fore|hand
be|foul
be|friend
be|fud|dle
be|fud|dling
be|fuddle|ment
be|furred
beg
 begged
 beg|ging
begad
began
be|gemmed
beget
 begot or begat
 archaic
 be|get|ting
 be|got|ten
be|get|ter
beg|gar
beg|gar|li|ness
beg|gar|ly
beggar-my-
 neighbor US
beggar-my-
 neighbour Br.
beg|gary
Begin, Men|achem
 prime minister of
 Israel
begin
 began
 be|gin|ning
 begun
be|gin|ner
be|gin|ner's luck
be|gin|ning
begob
be|gone exclam.
be|go|nia
be|gorra

begot
be|got|ten
beg-pardon n.
be|grime
 be|grim|ing
be|grudge
 be|grudg|ing
be|grudger
be|grudg|ing|ly
be|guile
 be|guil|ing
be|guile|ment
be|guiler
be|guil|ing|ly
be|guine
begum
begun
be|half
Behan, Bren|dan
 dramatist
be|have
 be|hav|ing
be|hav|ior US
be|hav|ior|al US
be|hav|ior|al|ism
 US
be|hav|ior|al|ist US
be|hav|ior|al|ly US
be|hav|ior|ism US
be|hav|ior|ist US
be|hav|ior|is|tic US
be|hav|iour Br.
be|hav|iour|al Br.
be|hav|iour|al|ism
 Br
be|hav|iour|al|ist
 Br.
be|hav|iour|al|ly Br.
be|hav|iour|ism Br.
be|hav|iour|ist Br.
be|hav|iour|is|tic
 Br.
be|head
be|held
be|he|moth
be|hest
be|hind
be|hind|hand
be|hold
be|held
be|holden
be|hold|er
be|hoof

be|hoove *US*
  be|hoov|ing
be|hove *Br.*
  be|hov|ing
Bei|der|becke, Bix
  musician
beige
bei|gnet
Bei|jing
Beira region, Portu-
  gal; port,
  Mozambique
beira antelope
Bei|rut capital of
  Lebanon; cf.
  Bayreuth
beisa
Beit Din var. of
  Beth Din
Beja people
be|jab|bers var. of
  bejabers
be|ja|bers
Bé|jart, Maur|ice
  choreographer
be|jee|zus
be|jesus var. of
  bejeezus
be|jew|eled *US*
be|jew|elled *Br.*
Bekaa
Bel var. of Baal
bel 10 decibels; cf.
  bell, belle
be|labor *US*
be|labour *Br.*
Bela|fonte, Harry
  singer
Bela|rus
Bela|rus|ian
be|lated
be|lated|ly
be|lated|ness
Belau var. of Palau
belay
be|lay|er
bel canto
bel|dam
bel|dame var. of
  beldam
be|lea|guer
Belém
bel|em|nite

bel es|prit
  beaux es|prits
Bel|fast
bel|fry
  bel|fries
Bel|gae
Bel|gaum
Bel|gian
Bel|gic
Bel|gium
Bel|gorod
Bel|grade
Bel|gra|via
Bel|gra|vian
Be|lial
belie
  be|ly|ing
be|lief
be|liev|abil|ity
be|liev|able
be|liev|ably
believe
  he|liev|ing
be|liev|er
Be|linda
Beli|sar|ius
Be|li|sha
be|lit|tle
  be|lit|tling
be|little|ment
be|lit|tler
be|lit|tling|ly
Be|li|tung
Be|lize
Be|liz|ean
Be|liz|ian var. of
  Belizean
bell cf. bel, belle
bella|donna
bell|bird
bell-bottomed
bell-bottoms
bell|boy page
bell buoy in sea
belle woman; cf.
  bel, bell
belle époque
  belles époques
Bel|ler|ophon
belles-lettres
bel|let|rism
bel|let|rist
bel|let|ris|tic

bell|flower
bell|hop
bell|li|cose
bell|li|cos|ity
bell|li|ger|ence
bell|li|ger|ency var.
  of belligerence
bell|li|ger|ent
bell|li|ger|ent|ly
Bel|lings|hau|sen
Bel|lini, Gen|tile,
  Gio|vanni, and
  Ja|copo painters
Bel|lini, Vin|cenzo
  composer
Bel|lini cocktail
bell|man
  bell|men
Bel|loc, Hil|aire
  humorist
Bel|low, Saul
  novelist
bell|ow
bell|ows
Bell's palsy
bell|wether
belly
  bell|lies
  bell|lied
  belly|ing
belly|ache
  belly|ach|ing
belly|acher
belly|band
belly|flop
  belly|flopped
  belly|flop|ping
belly|ful
Bel|mondo, Jean-
  Paul actor
Bel|mo|pan
Belo Hori|zonte
be|long
be|long|ings
Belo|rus|sia var. of
  Belarus
Belo|rus|sian var.
  of Belarusian
be|loved
below
below|decks *n.*
below decks *adv.*
Bel Paese
  trademark

Bel|sen
Bel|shaz|zar
Bel|tane
belt|er
belt|man
  belt|men
belt|way
be|luga
bel|ve|dere
be|ly|ing present
  participle of belie
bema
  bemas or bemata
  in church or
  ancient Greece; cf.
  beamer, Beemer
bema in synagogue;
  var. of bimah
Bemba
  pl. Bemba
be|mire
  be|mir|ing
be|moan
be|muse
  be|mus|ing
be|mused|ly
be|muse|ment
Ben|ares var. of
  Varanasi
Ben|bec|ula
bench|er
bench|mark
bench|warm|er
bench|work
bend
  bent
bend|able
bend|ed in 'on
  bended knee'
bend|er
Ben|digo
bendi|ness
bend|let
bendy
bend|ier
bend|iest
be|neath
Bene|di|cite
  canticle
bene|di|cite
  blessing; grace
Bene|dict
Bene|dic|tine
bene|dic|tion

bene|dic|tory

Bene|dict's
re|agent/solu|tion

Bene|dic|tus

bene|fac|tion

bene|fac|tive

bene|fac|tor

bene|fac|tress

ben|efic

bene|fice

ben|efi|cence

ben|efi|cent

ben|efi|cent|ly

bene|fi|cial

bene|fi|cial|ly

bene|fi|ciary
bene|fi|ciar|ies

bene|fi|ci|ate
bene|fi|ci|at|ing

bene|fi|ci|ation

bene|fit
bene|fit|ed or
bene|fit|ted
bene|fit|ing or
bene|fit|ting

Bene|lux

Beneš, Ed|vard
president of
Czechoslovakia

ben|evo|lence

ben|evo|lent

ben|evo|lent|ly

benga

Ben|gal

Ben|gali

ben|gal|ine

Ben|ghazi

Ben|guela

Ben-Gurion, David
prime minister of
Israel

Beni|dorm

be|night|ed

be|night|ed|ness

be|nign

be|nig|nancy

be|nig|nant

be|nig|nity
be|nig|ni|ties

be|nign|ly

Benin

Be|nin|ese

Beni|off

beni|son

Ben|ja|min

ben|ja|min gum

Benn, Tony polit-
ician

benne sesame

ben|net herb

Ben|nett, Alan
writer

Ben|nett, Ar|nold
writer

Ben|nett, Rich|ard
Rod|ney composer

Ben Nevis

Benny, Jack com-
edian

benny
ben|nies
Benzedrine tablet;
benefit

ben|omyl

Be|noni

Ben|tham, Jer|emy
philosopher

Ben|tham|ism

Ben|tham|ite

ben|thic

ben|thos

bento +s

ben|ton|ite

ben tro|vato

bent|wood

Benue-Congo

be|numb

ben|zal|de|hyde

Ben|ze|drine
trademark

ben|zene coal tar
product; ring

ben|zen|oid

ben|zin var. of
benzine

ben|zine petroleum
product

benzo|ate

benzo|caine

benzo|di|azep|ine

ben|zoic

ben|zoin

ben|zol

ben|zole var. of
benzol

benzo|pyr|ene

benzo|quin|one

ben|zoyl

ben|zyl

Beo|wulf

be|queath +s +ed
+ing

be|queath|al

be|queath|er

be|quest

be|rate
be|rat|ing

Ber|ber

Ber|bera

ber|ber|ine

ber|beris

ber|ceuse

Berch|tes|ga|den

be|reave
be|reav|ing

be|reave|ment

be|reft

Bere|nice

beret hat

Berg, Alban
composer

berg ice; adder;
wind; cf. burg

Ber|gamo

ber|ga|mot

Ber|gen city,
Norway

ber|gen rucksack

ber|ge|nia plant

Ber|ger, Hans
psychiatrist

Ber|gerac

Ber|gerac, Cyr|ano
de soldier and
writer

ber|gère

Berg|man, Ing|mar
film and theatre
director

Berg|man, Ing|rid
actress

berg|schrund

Beria, Lav|renti
head of Soviet
secret police

be|rib|boned

beri|beri

Ber|in|gia

Ber|ing|ian

Ber|ing Sea, Strait

Berio, Lu|ciano
composer

berk

Berke|ley Square;
city and university,
US; cf. **Barkly**

Berke|ley, Busby
choreographer

Berke|ley, Len|nox
composer

ber|ke|lium

Ber|koff, Ste|ven
dramatist

Berks. Berkshire

Berk|shire

Ber|lin capital of
Germany

Ber|lin, Ir|ving
songwriter

Ber|lin, Isaiah
philosopher

Ber|lin|er

Ber|lioz, Hec|tor
composer

Ber|lus|coni, Sil|vio
prime minister of
Italy

berm

Ber|muda

Ber|mu|dan

Ber|mu|dian

Bern German name
for **Berne**

Ber|na|dette

Ber|na|dotte, Folke
Swedish statesman

Ber|na|dotte, Jean
French soldier

Ber|nard

Berne

Bern|ese

Bern|hardt, Sarah
actress

Ber|nice

Ber|nini, Gian
Lo|renzo sculptor

Ber|noulli family of
mathematicians
and scientists

Bern|stein,
Leon|ard composer

Berry former prov-
ince, France

berry
ber|ries

ber|ried
berry|ing
fruit; cf. **beret,**
bury
ber|sa|gliere
ber|sa|glieri
ber|serk
ber|serk|er
berth bed; place for
ship; cf. **birth**
Ber|tha
ber|tha collar; cape
Ber|to|lucci,
Ber|nardo film
director
Ber|tram
Ber|trand
Ber|wick|shire
Berwick-upon-
Tweed
beryl
beryl|li|osis
beryl|lium
Bes Egyptian god
Be|san|çon
Bes|ant, Annie
writer and
politician
be|seech
be|sought or
be|seeched
be|seech|ing|ly
beset
be|set|ting
be|side
be|sides
be|siege
be|sieging
be|sieger
be|smear
be|smirch
besom
be|sot|ted
be|sought
be|span|gle
be|span|gling
be|spat|ter
be|speak
be|spoke
be|spoken
be|spec|tacled
be|sprin|kle
be|sprink|ling
Bess|arabia

Bess|arab|ian
Bes|semer, Henry
engineer
Bes|sie
Bessy
Best, Charles
Her|bert
physiologist
Best, George
footballer
bes|tial
bes|tial|ise *Br.* var.
of bestialize
bes|ti|al|ity
bes|ti|al|ities
bes|tial|ize
bes|tial|iz|ing
bes|ti|al|ly
bes|tiary
bes|tiar|ies
be|stir
be|stirred
be|stir|ring
be|stow
be|stow|al
be|strew
be|strewed or
be|strewn
be|stride
be|strode
be|strid|ing
be|strid|den
best-seller
best-selling
be|suit|ed
bet
bet or bet|ted
bet|ting
beta Greek letter
Beta|cam
trademark
beta-carotene
beta|ine
be|take
be|took
be|tak|ing
be|taken
Beta|max
trademark
beta|tron
betel leaf; cf. **beetle**
Betel|geuse
Betel|geux var. of
Betelgeuse

bête noire
bêtes noires
Beth|any
Beth Din
be|think
be|thought
Beth|le|hem
be|tide
be|tid|ing
be|times
bêt|ise
Betje|man, John
poet
be|token
bet|ony
bet|onies
be|took
be|tray
be|tray|al
be|tray|er
be|troth +s +ed
+ing
be|troth|al
bet|ter comparative
of good
bet|ter person who
bets; var. of **bettor**
bet|ter|ment
Betti, Ugo writer
Bet|tina
bet|tong
bet|tor
be|tween
be|twixt
Beu|lah
beurré
beurre blanc
beurre manié
Bevan, An|eurin
(Nye) creator of
British National
Health Service
beva|tron
bevel
bev|elled *Br.*
bev|eled *US*
bev|el|ling *Br.*
bev|el|ing *US*
bev|er|age
Bev|er|idge,
Wil|liam economist
Bev|er|ley town,
England

Bev|erly Hills city,
US
Bevin, Er|nest pol-
itician and trade
unionist
Bevin boy
bev|vied
bevvy
bev|vies
drink
bevy
bev|ies
flock
be|wail
be|wail|er
be|ware
be|war|ing
bewdy
bew|dies
be|whis|kered
Bew|ick, Thomas
artist
Bew|ick's swan
be|wigged
be|wil|der
be|wil|dered|ly
be|wil|der|ing|ly
be|wil|der|ment
be|witch
be|witch|er
be|witch|ing|ly
be|witch|ment
bey Ottoman
governor; cf. **bay**
be|yond
bez|ant
bezel
be|zique
be|zoar
bhad|ra|log var. of
bhadralok
bhad|ra|lok
Bhag|avad|gita
Bhag|wan
bha|jan
bhaji
bha|jia var. of bhaji
bhakti
bhang cannabis; cf.
bang
bhan|gra
bharal
Bha|ra|ta|na|tyam

bha¦sha *Ind.* language; cf. **basher**, **basha**

bha¦van

Bhav|nagar

Bheel var. of **Bhil**

Bheeli var. of **Bhili**

bhel|puri

Bhil people

Bhili

bhindi okra; cf. **bindi**

Bhoj|puri

bhoona var. of **bhuna**

Bho¦pal

Bhu¦ba|nes¦war

bhuna

Bhu¦tan

Bhu¦tan|ese

Bhutto, Ben|azir and **Zul|fikar** prime ministers of Pakistan

bi bisexual

Bi¦afra

Bi¦af¦ran

bialy +s

Bia¦lys|tok

bi-amping

Bi|anca

bi|an¦nual half-yearly; cf. **biennial**

bi|an¦nu¦al|ly half-yearly; cf. **biennially**

Biar|ritz

bias
  biased or biassed
  bias|ing or bias|sing

bi|ath|lete

bi|ath|lon

bi|axial

bi|axial¦ly

bib
  bibbed
  bib|bing garment; fish; drink

bibb lettuce

bib¦ber

bib|elot

bibi *Ind.* wife

Bible Christian or Jewish scriptures

bible individual Bible; other book

bib|lical

bib|lic|al¦ly

bib|li¦cist

bibli|og|raph|er

bib|lio|graph|ic

bib|lio|graph|ic|al

bib|lio|graph|ic| al¦ly

bibli|og|ra|phise *Br.* var. of **bibliographize**

bibli|og|ra|phize

bibli|og|ra|phiz|ing

bibli|og|raphy

bibli|og|raph|ies

bib|lio|mancy

bib|lio|mania

bib|lio|maniac

biblio|met¦ric

biblio|met¦rics

bib|lio|phile

bib|lio|phil¦ic

bibli|oph|ily

bib|lio|pole

bib|lio|ther¦apy

bibu|lous

bibu|lous¦ly

bibu|lous|ness

bi|cam¦eral

bi|cam¦eral|ism

bi|carb

bi|car¦bon|ate

bice

bi|cen¦ten|ary

bi|cen¦ten|ar¦ies

bi|cen¦ten|nial

bi|ceph¦al|ous

bi|ceps

bi|ceps bra|chii

bi|ceps fe|moris

bi¦chir

bi¦chon frise
  bi¦chons frise or bi¦chon frises

bicker

bick|er¦er

bicky
  bick|ies

bi|coast¦al

Bicol var. of **Bikol**

bi|color *US*

bi|col¦ored *US*

bi|col¦our *Br.*

bi|col¦oured *Br.*

bi|con¦cave

bi|con¦vex

bi|cul¦tural

bi|cul¦tur¦al|ism

bi|cus¦pid

bi|cycle

bi|cyc¦ling

bi|cyc¦lic

bi|cyc¦list

bid
  bid or bade *archaic*
  bid|ding
  bid or bid¦den *archaic*

bi|darka

bid|dabil¦ity

bid|dable

bid¦der

biddy
  bid|dies woman

bide
  bid|ing

bidet basin

bidi cigarette

bi|dir¦ec¦tion|al

bid|on|ville

bidri

Bie¦der|meier

Biele|feld

bi|en|nale

bi|en¦nia

bi|en¦nial two-yearly; cf. **biannual**

bi|en¦ni|al¦ly two-yearly; cf. **biannually**

bi|en¦nium
  bi|en¦nia or bi|en¦ni|ums

bien pen|sant adj.

bien-pensant n.

bier coffin stand; cf. **beer**

Bierce, Am|brose writer

bi|face

bi|facial

bif¦fin

bifid

bi|filar

bi|focal

bi|fold

bi|fur¦cate

bi|fur¦cat|ing

bi|fur¦ca¦tion

big
  bigged
  big|ging
  big|ger
  big|gest

bigam|ist

bigam|ous

big¦amy

Big Bang

big-endian

bi|gen¦er¦ic

big|eye tuna

Big|foot

Big|feet creature

big|gie

big|gish

big-head

big|horn

bight inlet; loop; cf. **bite, byte**

big mouth person

big-mouthed

big|ness

big-note

  big-noting

bigot

big|ot|ed

big|ot|ed|ly

big|ot¦ry

big|ot|ries

big time

big-timer

bi|guan¦ide

big|wig

Bihar

Bi¦hari

bi|jec¦tion

bi|jec¦tive

bijou small and elegant

bijou
  bi|joux jewel

bi¦jou|terie

bike
  bik¦ing

biker
bike|way
bikie
Bi|kini atoll
bi|kini garment
bikky var. of bicky
Biko, Steve black
  activist
Bikol
bi|la|bial
bilal
bi|lat|eral
bi|lat|eral|ly
bi|layer
Bil|bao
bil|berry
  bil|berries
bilbo
  bil|bos or bil|boes
  sword
bil|boes ankle
  shackles
bilby
  bil|bies
Bil|dungs|roman
Bil|dungs|romans
  or
Bil|dungs|romane
bi-level
bilge
  bil|ging
bil|har|zia
bil|har|zia|sis
bil|iary
bi|lin|gual
bi|lin|gual|ism
bi|lin|gual|ly
bili|ous
bili|ous|ly
bili|ous|ness
bili|ru|bin
bili|ver|din
bilk
bilk|er
bill|able
billa|bong
bill|board
bil|let
billet-doux
  billets-doux
bil|let|er
bill|fish
bill|fold

bill|head
bill|hook
bil|liard
bil|liards
Bil|lings|gate
Bil|lings method
bill|lion
bil|lion|aire
bil|lionth
Bil|li|ton var. of
  Belitung
bil|lon alloy
bil|low
bil|lowy
bill|post|er
bill|post|ing
bill|stick|er
billy
  bil|lies
billy|can
billy|cart
billy|cock
billy-o
bi|lob|ate
bi|lobed
bi|loca|tion
bil|tong
Bim Barbadian
bim bimbo
bimah in
  synagogue; cf.
  beamer, Beemer,
  bema
bi|manual
bi|manu|al|ly
bimb|lette
bimbo +s
bi-media
bi|met|al|lic
bi|met|al|lism
bi|met|al|list
bi|mil|len|ary
  bi|mil|len|ar|ies
bi|modal
bi|mol|ecu|lar
bi|month|ly
  bi|month|lies
bin
  binned
  bin|ning
bin|ary
  bin|ar|ies
bi|nation|al

bin|aural
bind
  bound
bin|daas
bind|er
bind|ery
  bind|er|ies
bindi Indian fore-
  head mark; cf.
  bhindi
bindi-eye plant
bind|ing
bindle|stiff
bind|weed
bine
bin-end
binge
  binge|ing
  US also bin|ging
bin|ger
bin|gle
bingo
bin|man
  bin|men
bin|nacle
bin|ocs
bin|ocu|lar
bin|ocu|lar|ly
bin|ocu|lars
bi|no|mial
bi|nom|inal
bin|tur|ong
bi|nucle|ate
bio +s
bio|accumu|late
  bio|accumu|lat|ing
  bio|accumu|la|tion
bio|acous|tics
bio|active
bio|activ|ity
bio|assay
bio|avail|abil|ity
bio|avail|able
bio|cen|osis US
  bio|cen|oses
  Br. biocoenosis
bio|cen|tric
bio|cen|trism
bio|cen|trist
bio|chem|ical
bio|chem|ical|ly
bio|chem|ist
bio|chem|is|try

bio|chip
bio|cidal
bio|cide
bio|cir|cuit
bio|clast
bio|clas|tic
bio|cli|mat|ic
bio|coen|osis Br.
  bio|coen|oses
  US biocenosis
bio|com|pati|bil|ity
bio|com|pat|ible
bio|com|puter
bio|com|put|ing
bio|con|trol
bio|data
bio|degrad|abil|ity
bio|degrad|able
bio|deg|rad|ation
bio|degrade
  bio|degrad|ing
bio|diesel
bio|diver|sity
bio|dynam|ic
bio|dynam|ics
bio|elec|tric
bio|elec|tric|al
bio|ener|get|ic
bio|ener|get|ics
bio|engin|eer
bio|engin|eer|ing
bio|ethic|al
bio|ethi|cist
bio|eth|ics
bio|feed|back
bio|film
bio|flavon|oid
bio|foul|ing
bio|fuel
bio|gas
bio|gen|esis
bio|gen|et|ic
bio|gen|ic
bio|geo|chem|ical
bio|geo|chem|ist
bio|geo|chem|istry
bio|geog|raph|er
bio|geo|graph|ic
bio|geo|graph|ic|al
bio|geog|raphy
biog|raphee subject
  of biography

bio|graph|er
bio|graph|ic
bio|graph|ic|al
bio|graph|ic|al|ly
biog|raphy
  biog|raph|ies
bio|haz|ard
bio|indi|ca|tor
bio|infor|mat|ic
bio|infor|mat|ics
Bioko
bio|lis|tic
bio|lis|tics
bio|logic
bio|logic|al
bio|logic|al|ly
biolo|gism
biolo|gist
biolo|gis|tic
biol|ogy
  biol|ogies
bio|lumin|es|cence
bio|lumin|es|cent
bio|mag|net|ism
bio|mark|er
bio|mass
bio|mathe|mat|ics
biome
bio|mech|an|ic|al
bio|mech|an|ic|al|ly
bio|mech|an|ics
bio|mech|an|ist
bio|med|ical
bio|medi|cine
bio|meteor|ology
bio|met|ric
bio|met|ri|cian
bio|met|rics
bi|om|etry
bio|mim|et|ic
bio|mol|ecule
bio|morph
bio|morph|ic
bi|onic
bi|on|ic|al|ly
bi|on|ics
bio|nom|ic
bio|nom|ics
bio|pharma|
        ceut|ical
bio|philia
bio|phys|ic|al

bio|physi|cist
bio|phys|ics
bio|pic
bio|piracy
bio|poly|mer
bio|pros|pect|ing
bio|pros|pect|or
bi|opsy
  bi|op|sies
  bi|op|sied
  bi|opsy|ing
bio|psycho|logic|al
bio|psych|ology
bio|reac|tor
bio|region
bio|region|al
bio|region|al|ism
bio|region|al|ist
bio|remedi|ation
bio|rhythm
bio|rhyth|mic
bio|science
bio|scien|tist
bio|scope
bio|sen|sor
bio|social
bio|solids
bio|sphere
bio|spher|ic
bio|stat|is|tic|al
bio|stat|is|ti|cian
bio|stat|is|tics
bio|stra|tig|raph|er
bio|strati|graph|ic
bio|stra|tig|raphy
bio|sur|gery
bio|syn|thesis
  bio|syn|theses
bio|syn|thet|ic
bio|sys|tem|at|ics
bio|sys|tem|atist
biota
bio|tech
bio|tech|no|logic|al
bio|tech|nolo|gist
bio|tech|nol|ogy
  bio|tech|nolo|gies
bio|tec|ture
bio|ter|ror|ism
bio|ter|ror|ist
bi|ot|ic
bio|tin

bio|tite
bio|tope
bio|trans|form|
              ation
bio|turb|ated
bio|turb|ation
bio|type
bio|war|fare
bio|weapon
bi|par|ti|san
bi|par|ti|san|ship
bi|part|ite
biped
bi|pedal
bi|pedal|ism
bi|pedal|ity
bi|phasic
bi|phenyl
bi|pin|nate
bi|plane
bipod
bi|po|lar
bi|po|lar|ity
bi|racial
bi|ramous
birch
birch|bark
birch|en
Birch|er member of
  John Birch Society
bird
bird|brain
bird|brained
bird|cage
bird|er
bir|die
  birdy|ing
bird-like
bird|lime
bird|seed
bird's-eye plants;
  chilli; maple; pep-
  per; view
bird's-foot +s plant
bird|shot
bird's-nest plant;
  fungus; orchid
bird's-nesting
bird's nest soup
bird|song
bird-strike
bird|watch|er
bird|watch|ing

bird|wing butterfly
bi|refrin|gence
bi|refrin|gent
bi|reme
bi|retta
biri var. of **bidi**
biri|ani var. of
  biryani
biri|yani var. of
  biryani
Bir'|ken|head
Bir'|ken|stock
  trademark
birl spin or whirl;
  cf. **burl**
bir|linn
Bir'|man cat; cf.
  Burman
Bir'|ming|ham
biro +s *trademark*
birr Ethiopian
  currency; cf. **burr**
birth being born; cf.
  berth
birth|date
birth|day
birth|mark
birth|place
birth|right
birth|stone
birth|weight
birth|wort
**Birt|wistle,
  Har'|ri|son** com-
  poser
biry|ani
bis *Music* again
Bis|cay
bis|cotti
bis|cuit
bis|cuity
bis|dithio|
        carba|mate
bi|sect
bi|sec|tion
bi|sect|or
bi|serial
bi|sex|ual
bi|sexu|al|ity
Bish|kek
bishop
bish|op|ric
Bis|lama

Bis|marck
Bis|marck|ian
bis|mil|lah
bis|muth
bison
  pl. bison
bis|phe|nol A
bisque
Bis|sa|gos Islands
Bis|sau
bi|stable
bis|ter *US*
  Br. bistre
bis|tort
bis|toury
  bis|tour|ies
bistre *Br.*
  US bister
bis|tro +s
bi|sul|fate *US*
bi|sul|phate *Br.*
bit
  bit|ted
  bit|ting
  cf. bitt
bitchen var. of
  bitching
bitch|ery
bitch|ily
bitchi|ness
bitch-slap *v.*
  bitch-slapped
  bitch-slapping
bitchy
  bitch|ier
  bitchi|est
bite
  bit
  bit|ing
  bit|ten
  cf. bight, byte
biter
bi|tern|ate
Bi|thynia
bit|ing|ly
bit|map
  bit|mapped
  bit|map|ping
bi|tonal
bi|tonal|ity
Bit|rex *trademark*
bit|ser var. of **bitzer**
bit|stream
bitt post on ship

bit|ter
bitter|cress
bitter-ender
bit|ter|ling
bit|ter|ly
bit|tern
bit|ter|ness
bitter-sweet *adj.*
bitter|sweet plant;
  shell
bit|tily
bit|ti|ness
bitty
  bit|tier
  bit|ti|est
Bitu|mas|tic
  trademark
bitu|men
bi|tu|min|isa|tion
  Br. var. of
  bituminization
bi|tu|min|ise *Br.*
  var. of bituminize
bi|tu|min|iza|tion
bi|tu|min|ize
  bi|tu|min|iz|ing
bi|tu|min|ous
bit|wise
bit|zer
bi|va|lence
  Chemistry
biv|alence *Biology*
bi|valent *Chemistry*
biva|lent *Biology*
bi|valve
bi|vari|ate
biv|ouac
  biv|ou|acked
  biv|ou|ack|ing
bivvy
  biv|vies
  biv|vied
  bivvy|ing
bi|week|ly
  bi|week|lies
bi-wiring
bi|year|ly
biz
bi|zarre
bi|zarre|ly
bi|zarre|ness
bi|zar|rerie
bi|zarro
Bi|zerta

Bi|zerte var. of
  Bizerta
Bizet, Georges
  composer
bizzy
  biz|zies
  police officer; var.
  of busy
blab
  blabbed
  blab|bing
blab|ber
blab|ber|mouth
Black person; var. of
  black
black
black|amoor
black|ball
black|berry
  black|berries
  black|berried
  black|berry|ing
black|bird
black|board
black|boy tree
black|buck
Black|burn
black|butt
black|cap bird
black|cock
black|cur|rant
black|en
black-eyed bean;
  pea; Susan
black|face sheep;
  make-up
black-faced
black|fel|low
black|fish
black|fly
  pl. black|fly or
  black|flies
  aphid
Black|foot
  pl. Black|foot or
  Black|feet
  North American
  Indian
black|guard
black|guard|ly
black|head
black|ish
black|jack
black|lead

black|leg
black|legged
black|leg|ging
black|list
black|ly
black|mail
black|mail|er
black mar|ket|eer
black-
  market|eer|ing
Black|more, R. D.
  writer
black|ness
black|out
black|poll warbler
Black|pool
black|shirt Fascist
black|smith
black|thorn
black|wall tyre
black|water fever
black|wood tree
black|work
  embroidery
blad|der
blad|dered
blad|der|wort
blad|der|wrack
blade
blad|ing
blader
blae|berry
  blae|berries
blag
  blagged
  blag|ging
blag|ger
blah
blah-blah
Blair, Tony prime
  minister of Britain
Blair|ism
Blair|ite
Blake, Peter painter
Blake, Wil|liam
  artist and poet
Blake|ian
Blakey metal plate
  on sole of shoe
Blakey, Art drum-
  mer
blam|able *US*
  Br. blameable

blame
blam¦ing
blame|able *Br.*
  US blamable
blame|ful
blame|less
blame|less¦ly
blame|less|ness
blame|storm|ing
blame|worthi|ness
blame|worthy
blanch
blanc|mange
blanco
  blan|coes
  blan|coed
  blanco|ing
bland|ish
bland|ish|ment
bland¦ly
bland|ness
blan|ket bedding;
  cf. blanquette
blank|ety
blankety-blank
blank¦ly
blank|ness
blan|quette meat
  dish; cf. blanket
Blan|tyre
blare
  blar¦ing
blar|ney
blasé
blas|pheme
  blas|phem¦ing
blas|phemer
blas|phem|ous
blas|phem|ous¦ly
blas|phemy
  blas|phem¦ies
blast¦er
blasto|cyst
blasto|derm
blast-off *n.*
blasto|mere
blasto|myco¦sis
blas|tula
  blas|tu¦lae or
  blas|tu¦las
blat
  blat¦ted
  blat|ting
bla|tancy

bla|tant
bla|tant¦ly
blather
blather|skite
blat|ter
Blaue Reit¦er, Der
  group of painters
blax|ploit|ation
blaze
  blaz¦ing
bla¦zer
blaz|ing¦ly
bla|zon
bla|zon¦ry
bleach
bleach¦er
bleacher|ite
bleak
bleak¦ly
bleak|ness
blear
blear|ily
bleari|ness
bleary
  blear|ier
  bleari|est
bleat
bleat¦er
bleb
bleed
  bled
bleed¦er
bleep
bleep¦er
blem|ish
blend mix; mixture
blende metal
  sulphide
blend¦er
Blen|heim
blenny
  blen|nies
bleo|mycin
bleph|ar|itis
bleph¦aro|plasty
bleph¦aro|spasm
Blér¦iot, Louis
  aviator
bles|bok
bless¦ed
bless¦ed¦ly
bless¦ed|ness
bless|ing

blest var. of blessed
blether var. of
  blather
blether|skate var.
  of blatherskite
blew past tense of
  blow
blewit mushroom;
  cf. bluet
Bligh, Wil|liam
  captain of *The
  Bounty*
blight
blight¦er
Blighty
  Bligh|ties
bli¦mey
blimp|ish
blin
  blini or bliny or
  blinis
blind¦er
blind|fold
blind|ing¦ly
blind¦ly
blind|man's bluff
  US
blind man's buff
  Br.
blind|ness
blind|side *v.*
  blind|sid¦ing
blind|sight
blind|worm
bling-bling
blin|ker
blintze
blip
  blipped
  blip|ping
blip|vert
Bliss, Ar¦thur
  composer
bliss¦ful
bliss|ful¦ly
bliss|ful|ness
blis|ter
blis|ter|ing¦ly
blithe
  blither
  blith¦est
blithe¦ly
blithe|ness

blither var. of
  blather
blith¦er|ing
blithe|some
blitz
blitz|krieg
Blixen, Karen
  writer
bliz|zard
BL Lac ob¦ject
  Astronomy
bloat
bloa¦ter
bloat|ware
blob
  blobbed
  blob|bing
blobby
  blobb¦ier
  blobbi|est
bloc group of
  governments etc.
Bloch, Er¦nest
  composer
block lump;
  prevent; etc.
block|ade
  block|ad¦ing
block|ader
block|age
block|board
block|bust¦er
block|bust¦ing
block¦er
block|head
block|head¦ed
block|hole
block|house
block|ish
block|ship
block|work
blocky
  block¦ier
  blocki|est
Blod|wen
Bloem|fon¦tein
blog
  blogged
  blog|ging
blog|ger
blogo|sphere
Blok, Alex|an¦der
  poet
bloke

bloke|ish
bloke¦ish|ness
blokey
blok¦ish var. of
  blokeish
blond *US*
blonde *Br.*
  blond¦er
  blond¦est
Blon|del minstrel
blonde|ness var. of
  blondness
Blon|din, Charles
  acrobat
blond|ish
blond|ness
Blood North Ameri-
  can Indian
blood
blood|bath
blood-borne
blood|fin
blood|hound
blood|ily
bloodi|ness
blood|less
blood|less|ly
blood|less|ness
blood|let¦ting
blood|line
blood|lust
blood|root
blood|shed
blood|shot
blood sport
blood|stain
blood|stained
blood|stock
blood|stone
blood|stream
blood|suck¦er
blood|suck¦ing
blood|thirst|ily
blood|thirsti|ness
blood|thirsty
  blood|thirst|ier
  blood|thirsti|est
blood|wood
blood|worm
bloody
  blood|ies
  blood|ied
  bloody|ing

blood|ier
bloodi|est
Bloody Mary +s
bloody-minded
bloody-minded¦ly
bloody-
  minded¦ness
blooey awry; cf.
  bluey
blooie var. of blooey
bloom¦er
bloom¦ers
bloom¦ery
  bloom|er¦ies
Bloom¦field,
  Leon¦ard linguist
Bloom¦field|ian
Blooms|bury
bloop¦er
bloopy
bloo|ter
blos|som
blos|somy
blot
  blot|ted
  blot|ting
blotch
blotchi|ness
blotchy
  blotch|ier
  blotchi|est
blot|ter
blotto
blouse
  blous|ing
blou|son
blo|vi¦ate
blo|vi¦ation
Blow, John
  composer
blow
  blew
  blown
  of wind etc.
  blowed
  in 'I'll be blowed'
blow|back
blow|down
blow-drier var. of
  blow-dryer
blow-dry
  blow-dries
  blow-dried
  blow-drying

blow-dryer
blow¦er
blow|fish
blow|fly
  blow|flies
blow|gun
blow|hard
blow|hole
blowie
blow-in
blow|lamp
blown
blow|out *n.*
blow|pipe
blowsy
  blows¦ier
  blowsi|est
blow|torch
blow-up *n.*
blowy
  blow|ier
  blowi|est
blowzy var. of
  blowsy
blub
  blubbed
  blub|bing
blub|ber
blub|bery
blu|cher boot
bludge
  bludg¦ing
bludg¦eon
bludg¦er
blue
  blu¦ing or blue|ing
  bluer
  blu¦est
blue|back
Blue|beard
blue|beat
blue|bell
blue|berry
  blue|berries
blue|bill
blue|bird
blue-black
blue|bot¦tle
blue|coat *US* soldier
Blue|fields
blue|fin
blue|fish
blue|gill

blue|grass
blue|gum
blue|head
blue heel¦er
blue|ish var. of
  bluish
blue|jacket
blue|ness
blue|nose
blue|nosed
Blue Peter
blue|print
blues
Blues and Royals
blue|schist
blues|man
  blues|men
blue|stock¦ing
blue|stone
bluesy
  blues¦ier
  bluesi|est
bluet flowering
  plant; cf. blewit
blue|throat
blue tit
blue|tongue
Blue|tooth
  trademark
Blue Vin¦ney var. of
  Blue Vinny
Blue Vinny
bluey bluish; cf.
  blooey
bluff¦er
bluff¦ly
bluff|ness
blu¦ish
blun|der
blun¦der|buss
blun|der¦er
blunge
  blun|ging
blun|ger
blunt|ly
blunt|ness
blur
  blurred
  blur|ring
blurb
blurry
  blur¦rier
  blur¦ri|est

blurt
blush|er
blush|ing|ly
blus|ter
blus|ter|er
blus|tery
Blu-tack *trademark*
B-lympho|cyte
Bly|ton, Enid writer
B-movie
B'nai B'rith
Bo woman's name
bo +s tree; form of
  address; var. of
  boo; cf. beau, bow
boa snake; feather
  stole
boab var. of baobab
Boa|di|cea var. of
  Boudicca
boak var. of boke
boar pig; cf. boer,
  bore
board wood; coun-
  cil; etc.; cf. baud,
  bawd, bored
board|er lodger; cf.
  border
board|room
board|sail|er
board|sail|ing
board|sail|or var. of
  boardsailer
board|walk
boar|fish
boart diamond; var.
  of bort
Boas, Franz anthro-
  pologist
boast|er
boast|ful
boast|ful|ly
boast|ful|ness
boat|bill
boat|build|er
boat|build|ing
boatel
boat|er
boat|ful
boat|hook
boat|house
boatie
boat|load

boat|man
boat|men
boat|swain
boat|yard
Boa Vista
bob
  bobbed
  bob|bing
bob|ber
Bob|bie
bob|bin
bob|binet
bob|ble
  bob|bling
bob|bly
bobby
bobby-dazzler
bobby socks
bobby sox var. of
  bobby socks
bobby-soxer
bob|cat
bobol
  bob|olled
  bob|ol|ling
bobo|link
bobo|tie
Bo|bru|isk var. of
  Babruisk
Bo|bru|ysk var. of
  Babruisk
bob|skate
bob|sled
  bob|sled|ding
bob|sleigh
bob|stay
bobsy-die
bob|tail
bob|weight
bob|white
boc|age
Boc|cac|cio,
  Gio|vanni writer
bocce game
Boc|cher|ini, Luigi
  composer
boc|cia var. of bocce
boc|con|cini
Boche German
  soldier
Bo|chum
bock|ety
bo|dach

bo|da|cious
bode
  bod|ing
bo|dega
Bode's law
bodge
  bodg|ing
bodger
bodgie
bodh tree; var. of bo
Bodh|gaya
bodhi|sat|tva
bodh|rán
bod|ice
bodi|less
bod|ily
bod|kin
Bod|lcian
Bod|ley, Thomas
  scholar
Bo|doni,
  Giam|bat|tista
  painter
Bod|rum
body
  bod|ies
  bod|ied
  body|ing
body|board
body|board|er
body|board|ing
body|build|er
body|build|ing
body-check
body|guard
body|line
body|shell
body|side
body|suit
body|surf
body|surf|er
body|work
body|work|er
Boe|otia
Boe|otian
Boer early South
  African settler; War
boer Afrikaner
  farmer; goat; cf.
  boar, bore
boer|bul var. of
  boerbull
boer|bull

boere|musiek
boere|wors
boerie var. of
  boerewors
boerewors
Bo|eth|ius Roman
  statesman and
  philosopher
boeuf
  bour|gui|gnon
bof|fin
bof|finy
boffo +s
bof|fola
Bo|fors
bog
  bogged
  bog|ging
bogan
Bo|garde, Dirk
  actor
Bo|gart,
  Hum|phrey actor
bo|gart
bog|bean
bogey in golf; evil;
  enemy aircraft;
  nasal mucus; cf.
  bogie
bo|gey|man
bo|gey|men
bog|gart
bog|gi|ness
bog|gle
  bog|gling
boggy
  bog|gier
  bog|gi|est
bogie wheeled
  undercarriage; rail-
  way carriage; cf.
  bogey
bog|land
bogle
bog|man
bog|men
BOGOF = buy one,
  get one free
Bo|go|mil
Bo|go|mil|ism
bo|gong
Bo|gotá
bog-standard
bog|trot|ter *offen-
  sive*

bogus
bogus|ness
bogy var. of bogey
bogy|man var. of
　bogeyman
Bo Hai
bohea
Bo|he|mia
Bo|he|mian
bo|he|mian uncon-
　ventional
bo|he|mian|ism
boho +s
Bohol
Bohr, Niels physi-
　cist
bohr|ium
bo|hunk
boil
boil|er
boiler|maker
boiler|plate
boi|lie
boil|over
boing
boink US var. of
　bonk
Boise city, US
bois|ter|ous
bois|ter|ous|ly
bois|ter|ous|ness
boîte
Bo|kassa, Jean
　Central African
　dictator
bok choy US var. of
　pak choi
boke
　boking
bokeh Photography
Bo|khara var. of
　Bukhoro
bok|ken
bok|ma|kierie
Bok|mål
bolas
　pl. bolas
　missile; cf. bolus
bold
bold|face
bold|faced
bold|ly
bold|ness

boldo +s
bole trunk of tree;
　clay; cf. boll, bowl
bo|lec|tion
bol|ero +s
bo|lete var. of
　boletus
bo|letus
Bo|leyn, Anne
Bol|ger, James
　prime minister of
　New Zealand
bo|lide
Bol|ing|broke sur-
　name of Henry IV
　of England
Bolí|var, Simón
　Venezuelan patriot
bolí|var Venezuelan
　currency
Bo|livia
Bo|liv|ian
bo|liv|iano +s
Böll, Hein|rich
　writer
boll seed capsule; cf.
　bole, bowl
bol|lard
bol|lito misto
　bol|liti misti
bol|lix vulgar slang
bol|lock vulgar
　slang
bol|locks vulgar
　slang
bol|locky vulgar
　slang
boll|worm
Bolly|wood
bolo +s knife; tie
Bol|ogna
bol|ogna sausage
Bol|ognese
bol|om|eter
bolo|met|ric
bol|om|etry
bo|lo|ney var. of
　baloney
Bol|shevik
Bol|shev|ism
Bol|shev|ist
Bol|shie Bolshevik
bol|shie
　bol|shier

bol|shi|est
　uncooperative
bol|shi|ness
Bol|shoi
bol|shy var. of
　bolshie
bol|ster
bol|ster|er
Bolt, Rob|ert
　dramatist
bolt lock etc.; cf.
　boult
bolt|er
bolt-hole
Bol|ton
bolt-on adj. & n.
Boltz|mann,
　Lud|wig physicist
bolus ball of food
　etc.; cf. bolas
Bol|zano
boma animal
　enclosure
bomb explosive; cf.
　bombe
bom|bard attack
bom|barde musical
　instrument
bom|bard|ier
bom|bard|ment
bom|bar|don
bom|ba|sine var. of
　bombazine
bom|bast
bom|bas|tic
bom|bas|tic|al|ly
Bom|bay
bom|ba|zine
bombe dessert; cf.
　bomb
bombé
bomb|er cf. boma
bom|bin|ate
　bom|bin|at|ing
bomb|let
bom|bora
bomb|proof
bomb|shell
bomb|sight device
　in aircraft
bomb site area
　destroyed by bomb
Bon Japanese Bud-
　dhist festival

Bon, Cape
bona fide
bona fides
Bon|aire
bon|anza
Bona|parte,
　Na|po|leon French
　emperors
Bona|part|ism
Bona|part|ist
bon appétit
bona va|can|tia
Bona|ven|tura, St
bon|bon
bon|bon|nière
bonce
Bond, Ed|ward
　dramatist
Bond, James fic-
　tional secret agent
bond|age
bond|ager
bond|hold|er
Bondi resort,
　Australia
bondi weapon
bon|dieus|erie
bonds|man
　bonds|men
bond|stone
bone|fish
bone|head
bone|head|ed
bone|less
bone|meal
boner
bone|set
bone|shaker
bone|yard
bon|fire
bongo drum
　bon|gos or
　bon|goes
bongo antelope
　pl. bongo or
　bon|gos
bon|ham
Bon|hoef|fer,
　Diet|rich
　theologian
bon|homie
bon|hom|ous
boni|ato +s

Boni|face, St
boni|ness
Bon|ing|ton, Chris
mountaineer
Bon|ita
bo|nito +s
bonk|bust|er
bonk|buster|ing
bonk|bust|ing
bonk|ers
bon mot
bons mots
Bonn city, Germany
Bon|nard, Pierre
artist
bonne maid
bonne bouche
bonne bouches or
bonnes bouches
bonne femme
bon|net
bonnet|head
bonnet|mouth
Bon|ney, Wil|liam
outlaw
Bon|nie first name
Bon|nie Prince
Char|lie
bon|nily
bon|ni|ness
bonny
bon|nier
bon|ni|est
attractive etc.
bo|nobo +s
bon|sai
bon|sela var. of
bonsella
bon|sella
bon|spiel
bonte|bok
bonus
bon viv|ant
bon viv|ants or
bons viv|ants
bon viv|eur
bon viv|eurs or
bons viv|eurs
bon voy|age
bon|xie
bony
boni|er
boni|est

bonza var. of
bonzer
bonze Japanese reli-
gious leader
bon|zer *Austral.*
excellent
boo +s +ed +ing
booai var. of booay
booay *NZ* remote
districts
boob|oisie
boo-boo +s
boo|book
booby
boo|bies
boo|die
boo|dle
boof|head
boo|ga|loo +s +ed
+ing
boo|ger
boo|gie
boo|gie|ing
boogie-woogie
boo|hoo +s +ed
+ing
boo|jum
book|able
book|bind|er
book|bind|ing
book|case
book|cross|ing
book|end
book|er
Book|er Prize
bookie
book|ish
book|ish|ly
book|ish|ness
book|keep|er
book|keep|ing
book|land
book|let
book|louse
book|lice
book|maker
book|mak|ing
book|man
book|men
book|mark
book|mobile
book|plate
book|rest

book|sell|er
book|shelf
book|shelves
book|shop
book|stall
book|store
booksy
book|work
book|worm
Boole, George
mathematician
Bool|ean
boom|er
boom|er|ang
boomi|ness
boom|let
boom|slang
boomy
boom|ier
boomi|est
boon|docks
boon|dog|gle
boon|dog|gling
Boone, Dan|iel
American pioneer
boong *offensive*
boon|ies
boor rude person;
cf. boer
boor|ish
boor|ish|ly
boor|ish|ness
boost|er
booster|ish
booster|ism
boot|able
boot|black
boot|boy
boot-cut
bootee shoe; cf.
booty
Bo|ötes constella-
tion
Booth, Wil|liam
and Cath|er|ine
founders of the Sal-
vation Army
booth
Boo|thia
Pen|in|su|la, Gulf
of
bootie var. of
bootee
boot|jack

boot|lace
Boo|tle
boot|leg
boot|legged
boot|leg|ging
boot|leg|ger
boot|less
boot|lick|er
boot|lick|ing
boot|maker
boot-scooting
boot|strap
boot|strapped
boot|strap|ping
boot-up
booty
boo|ties
stolen goods; per-
son's bottom; cf.
bootee
booty|licious
booze
booz|ing
boozer
booze-up
booz|ily
boozi|ness
boozy
booz|ier
boozi|est
bop
bopped
bop|ping
bo-peep
Bophu|tha|tswana
bop|per
bora
Bora-Bora
bor|acic
bor|age
bor|agin|aceous
bor|ane
Borås
bor|ate
Bor|azon *trademark*
bor|bo|ryg|mic
bor|bo|ryg|mus
bor|bo|rygmi
Bor|deaux
pl. Bor|deaux
bor|de|laise
bor|dello +s
Bor|der collie;
Leicester; terrier

Bor¦der, Allan
cricketer
bor¦der edge; cf.
  boarder
bor¦der¦er
bor¦der¦land
bor¦der¦line
bord¦ure
bore
  bor¦ing
  make hole in; cali-
  bre; boring person;
  wave; past tense of
  bear cf. boar, boer
bor¦eal
bor¦ea¦lis
bored cf. baud,
  bawd, board
bore¦dom
bor¦een
bore¦hole
borer
bore¦scope
Borg, Björn tennis
  player
bor¦gata
  bor¦ga¦tas or
  bor¦gate
Bor¦ges, Jorge Luis
  writer
Bor¦ges¦ian
Bor¦gia, Ce¦sare
  Italian statesman
Bor¦gia, Lu¦cre¦zia
  Italian noblewoman
boric
bor¦ide
bor¦ing
bor¦ing¦ly
bork defame; cf.
  balk, baulk
bor¦lotti bean
Bor¦mann, Mar¦tin
  Nazi politician
Born, Max physicist
born cf. bawn,
  borne, bourn
Borna disease; virus
born-again adj. &
  n.
borne past parti-
  ciple of bear; cf.
  bawn, born, bourn
Bor¦nean

Bor¦neo
Born¦holm
born¦ite
Boro¦bu¦dur
Boro¦din,
  Alek¦sandr
  composer
Boro¦dino
boron
bo¦ro¦nia
boro¦sili¦cate
bor¦ough British
  town; US munici-
  pal corporation;
  division of New
  York City; Alaskan
  county; cf. burgh
Bor¦ro¦mini,
  Fran¦cesco archi-
  tect
Bor¦row, George
  writer
bor¦row
bor¦row¦er
Bor¦sa¦lino +s
  trademark
borsch var. of
  borscht
borscht
bor¦stal
bort diamond; cf.
  bought
bor¦zoi
bosc¦age
Bosch,
  Hier¦ony¦mus
  painter
bosey var. of bosie
bosh nonsense; cf.
  Boche
bosie
bosk¦age var. of
  boscage
bosky
bosk¦ier
boski¦est
Bos¦man Football
  ruling; signing
bo's'n var. of
  boatswain
Bos¦nia
Bosnia–
  Herzegov¦ina
Bos¦nian
bosom

bos¦omed
bos¦omy
boson
Bos¦phorus var. of
  Bosporus
Bos¦porus
BOSS Bureau of
  State Security
bossa nova
boss-cocky
  boss-cockies
boss-eyed
boss¦ily
bossi¦ness
boss¦ism
bossy
  bos¦sies
  boss¦ier
  bossi¦est
bossy¦boots
  pl. bossy¦boots
bost¦hoon
Bos¦ton
Bos¦ton¦ian
bos¦toon var. of
  bosthoon
bosun var. of
  boatswain
Bos¦well, James
  biographer of Dr
  Johnson
Bos¦well¦ian
Bos¦worth
bot larva; robot;
  cadger
bo¦tan¦ic
bo¦tan¦ic¦al
bo¦tan¦ic¦al¦ly
bot¦an¦ise Br. var. of
  botanize
bot¦an¦ist
bot¦an¦ize
  bot¦an¦iz¦ing
Bot¦any wool
bot¦any
  bot¦an¦ies
botch
botch¦er
botch-up
botel var. of boatel
bot¦fly
  bot¦flies
both

Botha, Louis sol-
  dier and prime
  minister of Union
  of South Africa
Botha, P. W. prime
  minister of South
  Africa
Bo¦tham, Ian
  cricketer
bother
bother¦ation
bother¦some
bothie var. of bothy
Both¦nia, Gulf of
Both¦well, James
  Earl, husband of
  Mary, Queen of
  Scots
bothy
  both¦ies
boto +s dolphin
Botox trademark
butry¦oid¦al
bo¦try¦tis
Bot¦swana
Bot¦swa¦nan
botte attack in
  fencing; cf. bot
Bot¦ti¦celli, San¦dro
  painter
bot¦tle
  bot¦tling
bottle¦brush
bottle-feed
bottle-fed
bottle¦ful
bottle¦neck
bottle¦nose
bottle-nosed
bot¦tler
bottle¦screw
bot¦tom
bottom¦land
bottom¦less
bot¦tom¦most
bot¦tom¦ry
  bot¦tom¦ries
  bot¦tom¦ried
  bot¦tom¦ry¦ing
bottom-up adj.
botty
  bot¦ties
botu¦lin
botu¦linum toxin

botu|linus var. of
botulinum
botu|lism
bou|bou
bouchée
Bou|cher, Fran|çois
artist
bou|clé
Bou|dicca queen of
the Iceni
bou|din
bou|doir
bouf|fant
bou|gain|vil|laea
var. of
bougainvillea
Bou|gain|ville
bou|gain|vil|lea
Bou|gain|vil|lian
bough cf. bow
bought cf. bort
bought|en
bou|gie
bouil|la|baisse
bouilli
bouill|lon
boul|der
boul|der|ing
boul|dery
boule French bowls;
cf. boulle
boule Greek council
boules French bowls
var. of boule
boule|vard
boule|vard|ier
Bou|lez, Pierre
composer and
conductor
boulle inlay; cf.
boule
Bou|logne-sur-Mer
Boult, Ad|rian con-
ductor
boult sieve; var. of
bolt
Boult|ing, John
and Roy film
producers and
directors
Boul|ton, Mat|thew
engineer
bounce
boun|cing

bounce-back n. &
mod.
boun|cer
boun|cily
boun|ci|ness
boun|cing Bet
plant
bouncy
boun|cier
boun|ci|est
bound
bound|ary
bound|ar|ies
bound|en
bound|er
bound|less
bound|less|ly
bound|less|ness
boun|teous
boun|teous|ly
boun|teous|ness
boun|ti|ful
boun|ti|ful|ly
bounty
boun|ties
bou|quet
bou|quet garni
bou|quets gar|nis
Bour|baki
Bour|bon French
dynasty; reaction-
ary; biscuit; rose
bour|bon whisky
Bour|bon|nais
bour|don organ
stop
bour|geois
pl. bour|geois
bour|geoise female
bour|geoisie
Bour|guiba, Habib
ben Ali president
of Tunisia
Bourke-White,
Mar|ga|ret photo-
journalist
bourn stream; goal;
limit; cf. bawn,
born, borne
bourne goal; limit;
var. of bourn
Bourne|mouth

bour|rée
bour|rées
bour|réed
bour|rée|ing
bourse
Bour|sin trademark
bous|tro|phedon
bout
bou|tade
bou|tique
bou|ton
bou|ton|nière
Boutros-Ghali,
Bout|ros UN Secre-
tary General
boutu var. of boto
Bou|vet Island
bou|vier
bou|zouki
bovid
bo|vine
Bov|ril trademark
bov|ver
bow incline head or
body; front of ship;
cf. bough
bow knot; ribbon; in
archery; for violin
etc.; cf. beau, bo
bow com|pass
bowd|ler|isa|tion
Br. var. of
bowdlerization
bowd|ler|ise Br. var.
of bowdlerize
bowd|ler|ism
bowd|ler|iza|tion
bowd|ler|ize
bowd|ler|iz|ing
bowel
Bowen, Eliza|beth
writer
bower
bower|bird
Bow|ery
bow|fin
bow|head
bow|hunt|er
bow|hunt|ing
Bowie, David singer
bowie knife
bow|knot
bowl container; cf.
bole, boll

bow-legged
bowl|er
bowl|ful
bow|line rope on
sail; knot
bow line mooring
rope
bowls
bow|man
bow|men
bow|saw
bow|ser trademark
bow|shot
bow|sie
bow|sprit
Bow Street
Run|ner
bow|string
bow|strung
bow-wow
bow|yang
bow|yer
Box and Cox
Boxes and Coxes
Boxed and Coxed
Box|ing and
Cox|ing
box|board
box|car
Boxer member of
Chinese secret
society
boxer in boxing;
dog
box|ercise
trademark
box|fish
box|ful
Box|grove
box-like
box|out
box room
box|thorn
boxty bread
boxy
box|ier
box|iest
boy cf. buoy
boyar
Boyce, Wil|liam
composer
Boy|cott, Geof|frey
cricketer
boy|cott

Boyer, Charles
 actor
boy|friend
boy|hood
boy|ish
boy|ish|ly
boy|ish|ness
Boyle, Rob|ert
 scientist
Boyle's law
boy|lya
Boyne
boyo +s
Boys' Bri|gade
Boy Scout
boy|sen|berry
boy|sen|berries
Boz pseudonym of
 Charles Dickens
bozo +s
B-picture
bra
braai
 braais
 braaied
 braai|ing or
 braa|ing
braai|vleis
Bra|bant
Brab|ham, Jack
 racing driver
brace
bra|cing
brace|let
bracer
bra|cero +s
bra|chial
bra|chi|ate
 bra|chi|at|ing
bra|chi|ation
bra|chi|ator
bra|chio|pod
Bra|chio|poda
bra|chio|saurus
bra|chis|to|chrone
bra|chy|ceph|al|ic
bra|chy|ceph|aly
brachy|ther|apy
bra|cing|ly
brack cake; cf. brak
bracken
bracket
brack|ish

brack|ish|ness
brac|on|id
bract
brac|te|ate
brad|awl
Brad|bury,
 Mal|colm novelist
Brad|bury, Ray science
 ence fiction writer
Bra|den
Brad|en|ham ham
 trademark
Brad|ford
Brad|ley
Brad|man, Don|ald
 cricketer
bra|doon var. of
 bridoon
Brad|shaw
brady|car|dia
brady|ki|nin
brae hill; cf. bray
Brae|burn
Brae|mar
brag
 bragged
 brag|ging
Bra|ganza
Bragg, Wil|liam
 and Law|rence
 physicists
brag|ga|do|cio
brag|gart
brag|ger
Brahe, Tycho
 astronomer
Brahma Hinduism
brahma chicken
Brah|man Hindu
 supreme being;
 member of highest
 Hindu class; cf.
 Brahmin
Brah|mana
Brah|man|ic
Brah|man|ic|al
Brah|man|ism
Brah|ma|putra
brah|ma|pu|tra
 chicken
Brah|min superior
 person; cf.
 Brahman
Brah|min|ic|al

Brah|min|ism var.
 of Brahmanism
Brah|miny
Brahms, Jo|han|nes
 composer
Brahms|ian
Bra|hui
 pl. Bra|hui
braid
brail rope; haul up
Brăila city, Romania
Braille writing for
 the blind
Brain, Den|nis horn
 player
brain organ in
 head; cf. brane
brain|box
brain|case
brain|child
 brain|chil|dren
Braine, John writer
brain fever inflammation
 mation
brain|fever bird
brain|iac
brain|ily
braini|ness
brain|less
brain|less|ly
brain|less|ness
brain|pan
brain|power
brain|stem
brain|storm
brain-teaser
brain-teasing
brain-twister
brain-twisting
brain|wash
brain|wave
brain|work
brainy
 brain|ier
 braini|est
braise
 brais|ing
 cook; cf. braze
brak S. African
 brackish or
 alkaline; cf. brack
brake
 brak|ing
 slow down; device

for slowing; estate
 car; carriage;
 crushing instrument;
 ment; thicket; fern;
 archaic past tense
 of break; cf. break
brake fern
brake har|row
brake horse|power
brake|man
 brake|men
brakes|man
 brakes|men
brake|van
bra|less
Bra|mah, Jo|seph
 inventor
Bra|mante,
 Do|nato architect
bram|ble
bram|bling
bram|bling
bram|bly
Bram|ley
Bram|ley's
 seed|ling
Bran|agh, Ken|neth
 actor and director
bran|chia
 bran|chiae
bran|chial
bran|chi|ate
bran|chio|pod
Bran|chio|poda
branch|let
branch-like
branchy
Bran|cusi,
 Con|stan|tin
 sculptor
bran|dade
Bran|den|burg
brand|er
bran|dish
bran|dish|er
brand|ling
Brando, Mar|lon
 actor
Bran|don
Brands Hatch
Brandt, Bill
 photographer
Brandt, Willy
 chancellor of West

Germany
brandy
bran|dies
brandy-bottle plant
brane *Physics;* cf.
brain
brani|gan var. of
brannigan
branks
branle
bran|ni¦gan
Bran|son, Rich|ard
entrepreneur
Braque, Georges
painter
Brase|nose
brash¦ly
brash|ness
Bra|silia
Bra¦şov
brass
bras|sard
bras|serie
bras|sica
bras|sie golf club
bras|siere
brass|ily
brassi|ness
brass|ware
brassy
  brass|ier
  brassi|est
  like brass
brassy golf club;
var. of **brassie**
Brati|slava
brat|tice
brat|ticed
brat|tish
brat|tish|ness
brat¦tle
  brat|tling
bratty
  brat¦tier
  brat¦ti|est
brat|wurst
Braun, Eva Hitler's
mistress
Braun, Wern|her
von rocket designer
Braun|schweig
bra|vado
brave
  brav¦ing

braver
brav¦est
brav¦ly
brav¦ery
bravo +s shout of
approval
bravo
  bra|vos or **bra¦voes**
  desperado
bra|vura
braw *Scot.* fine
brawl
brawl¦er
braw¦ly
brawn
brawny
  brawn|ier
  brawni|est
Brax|ton Hicks
braxy
Bray, Vicar of
bray cry of donkey;
crush; cf. **brae**
braze
  braz¦ing
  solder; cf. **braise**
bra¦zen
bra|zen¦ly
bra|zen|ness
bra|zier
bra|ziery
  bra|zier|ies
Bra¦zil
Bra|zil|ian
Braz¦za|ville
breach break; fail-
ure; etc.; cf. **breech**
bread food; cf. **bred**
bread|bas¦ket
bread|board
bread|crumb
bread|crumbed
bread¦ed
bread|fruit
bread|head
bread|line
bread|stick
breadth
breadth|ways
breadth|wise var. of
breadthways
bread|win¦ner
bread|win¦ning

break
  broke
  broken
  shatter; make or
  become inoperative;
  etc.; cf. **brake**
break|able
break|age
break|away
break|beat
break|bone fever
break-bulk
break-dance
  break-dancing
  break dan¦cer
break|down n.
break¦er
break-even
break|fall
break|fast
break|fast¦er
break|front
break-in n.
break|neck
break|out n.
break|point
  Computing
break point *Tennis;*
interruption
Break|spear,
Nich|olas English
pope, Adrian IV
break|through n.
break-up n. &
attrib.
break|water
break|wind
Bream, Ju¦lian gui-
tarist
bream fish
  pl. **bream**
bream scrape clean
breast
breast|bonc
breast|feed
  breast|fed
breast|hook
breast|pin
breast|plate
breast|stroke
breast|stroker
breast|sum¦mer
breast|work
breath n.

breath|abil¦ity
breath|able
breath|alyse *Br.*
  breath|alys¦ing
breath|alyser *Br.*
breath|alyze *US*
  breath|alyz¦ing
Breath|alyzer *US*
  trademark
breath|ar¦ian
breathe v.
  breath¦ing
breather
breath|ily
breathi|ness
breath|less
breath|less¦ly
breath|less|ness
breath|tak¦ing
breath|tak¦ing¦ly
breathy
  breath|ier
  breathi|est
brec|cia +s +ed
  +ing
brec¦ci|ate
brec¦ci|at¦ing
brec¦ci|ation
Brecht, Ber|tolt
dramatist
Brecht|ian
Breck¦nock|shire
var. of **Breconshire**
Brecon
Brecon|shire
bred past tense and
past participle of
breed; cf. **bread**
Breda
breech part of gun;
buttocks; put into
breeches; cf.
breach
breech|block
breech|clout
breeches trousers
Breeches Bible
breeches buoy
breech-loader
breech-loading
breed
  bred
  breed¦er
breeks

breeze
  breez|ing
breeze|way
breez|ily
breezi|ness
breezy
  breez|ier
  breezi|est
Bre|genz
brek|kie
brekky var. of
  brekkie
Brel, Jacques singer
Bre|men
brems|strahl|ung
Bren|dan
Bren|del, Al|fred
  pianist
Bren gun
Bren|nan
Bren|ner Pass
Brent
brent goose
bre|saola
Bre|scia
Bres|lau
  German name for
  Wrocław
Bres|son, Rob|ert
  film director
Brest
Brest-Litovsk
breth|ren
Bre|ton person from
  Brittany
Bre|ton, André
  writer
Breu|ghel var. of
  Bruegel
breve
brevet
  brev|et|ed or
  brev|et|ted
  brev|et|ing or
  brev|et|ting
bre|vi|ary
  bre|vi|ar|ies
brev|ity
  brev|ities
brew cf. broo
brew|er
brewer's yeast
brew|ery
  brew|er|ies

brew|house
brew|master
brew|pub
brew|ski
  brew|skis or
  brew|skies
brew-up n.
brey|ani var. of
  biryani
Brezh|nev, Leo|nid
  Soviet leader
Bri|ansk var. of
  Bryansk
briar
briary
brib|able
bribe
  brib|ing
briber
brib|ery
  brib|er|ies
bric-a-brac
brick|bat
brick|field
brickie
brick|lay|er
brick|lay|ing
brick|work
brick|works
brick|yard
brico|lage
brico|leur
bri|dal of a bride;
  cf. bridle
Bride, St
bride|groom
brides|maid
bride|well
Bridge, Frank
  composer
bridge
  bridg|ing
bridge|able
bridge|head
Bridge of Sighs
Bridges, Rob|ert
  poet
Bridge|town
bridge|work
bri|die
bridle
  brid|ling
  for horse; bring

under control; cf.
  bridal
bridle path
bridle|way
bri|doon
Brie
brief
brief|case
brief|less
brief|ly
brier var. of briar
bri|ery var. of
  briary
brig
bri|gade
brig|ad|ier
brig|alow
brig|and
brig|and|age
brig|and|ine
brig|and|ry
brig|an|tine
Briggs, Ray|mond
  writer and
  illustrator
Brig|ham
Bright, John polit-
  ical reformer
bright
bright|en
bright|ish
bright|ly
bright|ness
Brigh|ton
Bright's dis|ease
bright|work
Bri|gitte
brill
  pl. brill
bril|liance
bril|liancy
bril|liant
bril|liant|ine
bril|liant|ined
bril|liant|ly
Brillo pad
  trademark
brim
  brimmed
  brim|ming
brim|ful
brim|less
brim|stone

brin|dle
brin|dled
brine
brin|ing
bring
  brought
bring-and-buy
bring|er
brin|jal
Brink, André writer
brink
brink|man|ship
brinks|man|ship
  US
brinny
  brin|nies
briny
  brini|er
  brini|est
brio
bri|oche
bri|ony
bri|quet var. of
  briquette
bri|quette
bris Jewish
  ceremony
Bris|bane
brisé ballet jump;
  (of a fan) pierced
brisk
bris|ket
brisk|ly
brisk|ness
bris|ling fish
bris|tle
  brist|ling
  stiff hair etc.
bristle|bird
bristle|cone
bristle|tail
bristle|worm
bris|tly
Bris|tol
bris|tols
Brit
Brit|ain
Bri|tan|nia
Bri|tan|nic
Briti|cism
britches var. of
  breeches
Brit|ish

Brit|ish
Col|um|bia prov-
  ince, Canada
Brit|ish|er
Brit|ish|ism var. of
  Briticism
Brit|ish|ness
Briton
Brit|pop
Brit|tany
Brit|ten,
  Ben|ja|min
  composer
brit|tle
brittle|ly
brittle|ness
brittle|star
brit|tly var. of
  brittlely
Brit|ton|ic var. of
  Brythonic
britzka
britzska var. of
  britzka
Brno
bro +s brother
broach pierce; raise
  subject; spire; a
  spit; cf. brooch
broad
broad|acre
broad|band
broad|bill
broad-brush
broad|cast
  past broad|cast
  past participle
  broad|cast or
  broad|cast|ed
broad|cast|er
Broad Church
broad|cloth
broad|en
broad|leaf
  broad|leaves
broad|leaved
broad|loom
broad|loomed
broad|ly
broad-minded
broad-minded|ly
broad-
    minded|ness
Broad|moor

broad|ness
Broads, Nor|folk
broad|scale
broad|sheet
broad|side
  broad|sid|ing
broad|sword
broad|tail
broad|way
broast
Brob|ding|nag
Brob|ding|nag|ian
bro|cade
  bro|cad|ing
Broca's apha|sia
broc|coli
broch tower; cf.
  brock
bro|chette
bro|chure
bro|chure|ware
brock badger; cf.
  broch
Brocken mountain;
  spectre
brocket
bro|derie an|glaise
bro|gan
brogue
broil
broil|er
broke
broken
broken-hearted
broken|ly
broken|ness
bro|ker
broker|age
broker-dealer
brok|ing
brolga
brolly
  brol|lies
bro|mate
brome
bro|meliad
bro|mic
brom|ide
brom|id|ic
brom|ine
brom|ism
bromo|crip|tine
Bromp|ton

bronc
bron|chi
bron|chial
bron|chi|ec|tasis
bron|chi|olar
bron|chi|ole
bron|chio|litis
bron|chit|ic
bron|chitis
bron|cho|cele
bron|cho|dila|tion
bron|cho|dila|tor
bron|cho|gen|ic
bron|cho|
    pneu|mo|nia
bron|cho|scope
bron|chos|copy
  bron|chos|co|pies
broncho|spasm
bron|chus
bron|chi
bronco +s
bronco|bust|er
Bro|now|ski, Jacob
  scientist
Brontë, Anne,
  Char|lotte, and
  Emily writers
bronto|saur var. of
  brontosaurus
bronto|saurus
  bronto|saur|uses
  or bronto|sauri
bronto|there
Bron|wen
Bronx
bronze
  bronz|ing
bronzer
bronze|wing
bronze-winged
bronzy
broo unemployment
  benefit; cf. brew
brooch ornamental
  fastening; cf.
  broach
brood
brood|er
brood|ily
broodi|ness
brood|ing|ly
broody
brood|ier

broodi|est
Brook, Peter stage
  and film director
brook
Brooke, Ru|pert
  poet
Brook|lands
brook|let
brook|lime
Brook|lyn
Brook|lyn|ese
Brook|ner, Anita
  novelist
Brooks, Mel film
  director and actor
brook|weed
broom brush;
  shrub; cf. brume
broom|ball
broomie
broom|rape
broom|stick
brose
broth
brothel
brother
  broth|ers or in
  religious use
  breth|ren
brother-german
  brothers-german
brother|hood
brother-in-law
  brothers-in-law
brother|less
brother|li|ness
brother|ly
brougham
brought
brou|haha
Brou|wer, Adri|aen
  painter
brow|beat
brow|beat|en
brow|beat|er
browed
Brown, Ar|thur
  Whit|ten aviator
Brown, Cap|abil|ity
  landscape gardener
Brown, Ford
  Madox painter
Brown, George
  Mac|kay writer

Brown, James singer

Brown, John abolitionist

brown-bagger

Brown Betty +s

brown|field *adj.*

Brown|ian

Brownie junior Guide

brownie goblin; cake

Brown|ing, Eliza|beth Bar|rett and **Rob|ert** poets

Brown|ing gun

brown|ish

brown|ness

brown-nose brown-nosing

brown-noser

brown-out

Brown|shirt

brown|stone

brown|top bent (grass)

browny

brows|able

browse brows|ing

brows|er

Bru|beck, Dave jazz pianist

bru|bru shrike

Bruce, Lenny comedian

Bruce, Rob|ert king of Scotland

bru|cel|losis

bru|cite

Bruck|ner, Anton composer

Brue|gel, Pie|ter and **Jan**

Brue|ghel var. of **Bruegel**

Bruges

bruin

bruise bruis|ing

bruis|er

bruis|ing|ly

bruit spread rumour; cf. **brut**, **brute**

Brum Birmingham

Bru|maire

brumby brum|bies

brume mist; cf. **broom**

Brum|ma|gem

Brum|mell, Beau

Brum|mie

Brummy var. of **Brummie**

brummy *Austral./ NZ* tawdry

bru|mous

Brundt|land, Gro Har|lem prime minister of Norway

Bru|nei

Bru|nei|an

Bru|nel, Marc Isam|bard and **Isam|bard King|dom** engineers

Bru|nel|les|chi, Fi|lippo architect

bru|net *US* var. of **brunette**

bru|nette

Brun|hild *Germanic Legend*

Bruno, Gior|dano philosopher

Bruns|wick English name for **Braunschweig**

brus|chetta

brush|less

brush-like

brush-off *n.*

brush|stroke

brush|tail

brush-tailed bettong; possum

brush-turkey

brush-up *n.*

brush|wood

brush|work

brushy

brusque brus|quer

brus|quest

brusque|ly

brusque|ness

brus|querie

Brus|sels

Brus|sel sprout var. of **Brussels sprout**

Brus|sels sprout

brut very dry (wine); cf. **bruit**, **brute**

bru|tal

bru|tal|isa|tion *Br.* var. of **brutalization**

bru|tal|ise *Br.* var. of **brutalize**

bru|tal|ism

bru|tal|ist

bru|tal|ity bru|tal|ities

bru|tal|iza|tion

bru|tal|ize bru|tal|iz|ing

bru|tal|ly

brute brutal person; cf. **bruit**, **brut**

bru|tish

bru|tish|ly

bru|tish|ness

Bru|tus

brux|ism

Bry|ansk

Bryl|creem *trademark*

Bryn|ner, Yul actor

bryo|logic|al

bry|olo|gist

bry|ology

bry|ony bry|onies

Bryo|phyta

bryo|phyte

bryo|phyt|ic

Bryo|zoa

bryo|zoan

Bry|thon|ic

B side second team

B-side of record etc.

Bual

bubal

bubba brother

bub|bie grandmother

bub|ble

bub|bling

bubble|gum

bubble|head

bubble|jet

bub|bler

bub|bly bub|blier bub|bli|est

bu|binga

bubo bu|boes swelling

bu|bon|ic

bu|ca|tini

buc|cal of the cheek or mouth; cf. **buckle**

buc|can|eer

buc|cin|ator

Bu|ceph|alus

Buchan, John writer

Bu|chanan, James US president

Bu|cha|rest

Buchen|wald

buchu

Buck, Pearl S. writer

buck|aroo +s

buck|bean

buck|board

buck|brush

buck|een

bucket

bucket|ful

bucket|load

bucket|wheel

buck|eye

buck|horn

buck|hound

Buck|ing|ham

Buck|ing|ham|shire

buck|jump

buck|jump|er

buckle buck|ling cf. **buccal**

buck|ler

Buck|ley's chance

buck|ling

buck|min|ster|
ful|ler|ene

bucko
buck|oes or buckos

buckra

buck|ram

Bucks. Bucking-
hamshire

Buck's Fizz

buck|shee

buck|shot

buck|skin

buck|skinned

buck|thorn

buck|wheat

bucky|ball

bucky|tube

bu|col|ic

bu|col|ic|al|ly

bud
bud|ded
bud|ding

Buda|pest

Bud|dha

Buddh Gaya var. of
Bodhgaya

Bud|dhism

Bud|dhist

Bud|dhis|tic

bud|dhu

bud|dle

bud|dleia

buddy
bud|dies
bud|died
buddy|ing

buddy-buddy

budge
budg|ing

budg|eri|gar

budget

budget|ary

budgie

budo

bud|stick

Bud|weis
German name for
České Budějovice

bud|wood

bud|worm

Buena|ven|tura

Bue|nos Aires

Buer|ger's dis|ease

buf|falo
pl. buf|falo or
buf|fa|loes

buf|fer

buf|fet

buffle|head

buffo +s

buf|foon

buf|foon|ery
buf|foon|er|ies

buf|foon|ish

buff-tip

bug
bugged
bug|ging

bug|aboo +s

Bu|ganda

bug|bane

bug|bear

bug|ger *vulgar
slang*

bug|gery

Bug|gins' turn

buggy
bug|gies
bug|gier
bug|gi|est

bug|house

bugle
bu|gling

bugle-horn

bu|gler

bugle|weed

bu|gloss

buhl var. of boulle

build
built

build|er

build|ers'
mer|chant

build|ing

build-out *n.*

build-up *n.*

Bu|jum|bura

Bu|khara var. of
Bukhoro

Bu|kha|rin,
Niko|lai Soviet
leader

Bu|khoro

Buko|vina

Bula|wayo

bul|bil small bulb

bulb|ous

bul|bul bird

Bul|ga|nin, Niko|lai
Soviet leader

Bul|gar person

bul|gar wheat

Bul|garia

Bul|gar|ian

bulge
bul|ging

bul|gur var. of
bulgar

bulgy
bul|gier
bul|gi|est

bu|lima|rexia

bu|lima|rex|ic

bu|limia ner|vosa

bu|lim|ic

bulk-buy *v.*
bulk-bought
bulk-buying

bulk buy|ing *n.*

bulk|er

bulk|head

bulk|ily

bulki|ness

bulky
bulk|ier
bulki|est

bulla

bul|lae
blister

bul|lace

bul|late

bull|dike var. of
bulldyke

bull|dog
bull|dogged
bull|dog|ging

bull|dog|ger

bull|doze
bull|doz|ing

bull|dozer

bull|dust

bull|dyke

bull|dyker

bul|let

bul|letin

bul|let|proof

bull|fight

bull|fight|er

bull|fight|ing

bull|finch

bull|frog

bull|head

bull|head|ed

bull|headed|ly

bull|headed|ness

bull|horn

bul|lion

bull|ish

bull|ish|ly

bull|ish|ness

bull|lock

bull|locky
bul|lock|ies

bul|lous

bull|pen

bull|ring

bull|rush var. of
bulrush

bulls|eye

bull|shit
bull|shit|ted
bull|shit|ting
vulgar slang

bull|shit|ter *vulgar
slang*

bull|whip
bull|whipped
bull|whip|ping

bully
bul|lies
bul|lied
bully|ing

bully off
bully offs

bully|rag
bully|ragged
bully|rag|ging

bul|rush

bul|wark

Bulwer-Lytton,
Ed|ward writer and
statesman

bum
bummed
bum|ming

bum|bag

bum-bailiff

bum|ber|shoot

bum|ble
bum|bling

bumble|bee

bum|bler

bum|boat

bum|boy

bumf
bum¦fluff
bumi¦pu¦tra
bum¦malo
bum¦ma¦ree
bum¦mer
bump¦er
bumph var. of bumf
bump¦ily
bumpi¦ness
bump¦kin
bump¦kin¦ish
bump-start
bump¦tious
bump¦tious¦ly
bump¦tious¦ness
bumpy
  bump¦ier
  bumpi¦est
bum-rush v.
bum's rush
bum¦sters
Bun¦bury
bunce
bunch
bunch¦berry
  bunch¦berries
bunch¦flower
bunchy
  bunch¦ier
  bunchi¦est
bunco
  bun¦coes
  bun¦coed
  bunco¦ing
bun¦combe var. of
  bunkum
Bun¦des¦bank
Bun¦des¦rat
Bun¦des¦tag
bun¦dle
  bund¦ling
bund¦ler
bundo¦bust
bundu
bun¦fight
bun¦ga¦low
bun¦garo¦toxin
bun¦gee
  bun¦gees
  bun¦geed
  bun¦gee¦ing
bung¦hole

bun¦gle
bun¦gling
bun¦gler
bun¦ion
bun¦ker
bunk¦house
bun¦kum
bunk-up n.
bunny
  bun¦nies
bunny-hop
  bunny-hopped
  bunny-hopping
Bun¦sen
bun¦tal
Bun¦ter, Billy fic-
  tional schoolboy
bunt¦ing
bunt¦line
Bunty
Bu¦ñuel, Luis film
  director
bunya
bunya bunya
Bun¦yan, John
  writer
bun¦yip
Buo¦nar¦roti,
  Mi¦chel¦an¦gelo
  artist
buoy float; cf. boy
buoy¦age
buoy¦ancy
  buoy¦an¦cies
buoy¦ant
buoy¦ant¦ly
bup¦kis
bup¦pie
bu¦pro¦pion
bur var. of burr
Bur¦bage, Rich¦ard
  actor
Bur¦bank
Bur¦berry
  Bur¦berries
  trademark
bur¦ble
  burb¦ling
bur¦bler
bur¦bot
bur¦den
bur¦den¦some
bur¦dock

bur¦eau
  bur¦eaux or
  bur¦eaus
bur¦eau¦cracy
bur¦eau¦cra¦cies
bur¦eau¦crat
bur¦eau¦crat¦ic
bur¦eau¦crat¦ic¦al¦ly
bur¦eau¦crat¦
  isa¦tion
  Br. var. of
  bureaucratization
bur¦eau¦crat¦ise Br.
  var. of
  bureaucratize
bur¦eau¦crat¦
  iza¦tion
bur¦eau¦crat¦ize
bur¦eau¦crat¦iz¦ing
bur¦eau de change
  bur¦eaux de
  change
buret US
bur¦ette Br.
burfi
burg town; cf. berg
burg¦age
Bur¦gas port,
  Bulgaria; cf.
  Burgos
bur¦gee
Bur¦gen¦land
bur¦geon
bur¦ger cf. burgher
Bur¦gess, An¦thony
  novelist
Bur¦gess, Guy spy
bur¦gess
Bur¦gess Shale
  rock
burgh former Scot-
  tish borough
bur¦ghal of a burgh;
  cf. burghul, burgle
bur¦gher citizen; cf.
  burger
Burgh¦ley English
  statesman
bur¦ghul wheat; var.
  of bulgar; cf.
  burghal, burgle
burg¦lar
burg¦lari¦ous
burg¦lar¦ise Br. var.
  of burglarize

burg¦lar¦ize
burg¦lar¦iz¦ing
burg¦lary
burg¦lar¦ies
bur¦gle
  burg¦ling
  steal from; cf.
  burghal, burghul
burgo¦master
bur¦go¦net
bur¦goo +s
Bur¦gos town,
  Spain; cf. Burgas
Bur¦goyne, John
  general and writer
bur¦grave
Bur¦gun¦dian
Bur¦gundy
bur¦gundy
  bur¦gun¦dies
  wine; colour
bur¦ial
burin
burk var. of berk
burka
Burke, Ed¦mund
  writer and
  politician
Burke, Rob¦ert
  O'Hara explorer
Burke, Wil¦liam
  body-snatcher
Burke's Peer¦age
bur¦kha var. of
  burka
Bur¦kina Faso
Bur¦kinan
Bur¦kin¦ese
Bur¦kitt's
  lymph¦oma
burl lump in cloth
  or on tree; cf. birl
bur¦lap
bur¦lesque
  bur¦les¦quing
bur¦les¦quer
bur¦ley tobacco
bur¦li¦ness
Bur¦ling¦ton city,
  Canada
burly
  bur¦lier
  bur¦li¦est
  strong

Burma

Bur¦man of Burma;
cf. **Birman**

bur-marigold

Burm|ese

burn
  burnt *Br.*
  burned *US*

Burne-Jones,
  Ed¦ward painter
  and designer

burn¦er

bur¦net

Bur|nett, Fran|ces
  Hodg¦son novelist

Bur|ney, Fanny
  novelist

Burn|ham scale

burn|ing¦ly

bur|nish

bur|nish¦er

Burn|ley

bur|noose *US*

bur|nous *Br.*

burn|out

Burns, George
  comedian

Burns, Rob¦ert or
  Rob¦bie or Rab¦bie
  poet

burn|side

burnt

buroo var. of **broo**

burp

bur¦pee

burqa var. of **burka**

Burr, Aaron *US*
  statesman

burr cf. **birr**

Burra, Ed¦ward
  painter and
  designer

Burra Din

burra|wang

burra|wong var. of
  burrawang

bur-reed

burr|fish

bur|rito +s

Bur|roughs, Edgar
  Rice writer

Bur|roughs,
  Wil|liam writer

bur¦row

bur|row¦er

Bursa city, Turkey

bursa

  bur¦sae or bur¦sas
  sac in body

bur¦sal

bur¦sar financial
  manager

bur¦sar¦ial

bur¦sary
  bur¦sar¦ies

burse

bur|sitis

burst

burst¦er

bursty

Burt, Cyril
  psychologist

Bur¦ton, Rich|ard
  actor; explorer

bur¦ton

burton-tackle

Burton-upon-
                    Trent

Bu|rundi

Bu¦run¦dian

Bury town

bury
  bur¦ies
  bur¦ied
  bury|ing
  put under ground;
  cf. **beret, berry**

Bur¦yat

Bur¦ya¦tia

Bury St Ed|munds

bus vehicle;
  Computing.
  buses
  US also bus¦ses cf.
  buss

bus convey by bus
  bus¦ses or buses
  bussed or bused
  buss|ing or bus|ing
  cf. **buss**

bus¦bar

bus¦boy

Busby, Matt foot-
  baller

busby
  bus|bies

Bush, George two
  US presidents

bush

bush|baby
  bush|babies

bush|buck

bush|chat

bush|craft

bushel

bushel|ful

bush-hen

bu|shido

bushie var. of **bushy**

bush|ily

bushi|ness

bush|ing

Bush|man
  Bush|men
  in South Africa

bush|man
  bush|men
  in Australia

bush|master

bush|meat

bush|ran¦ger

bush|tit

Bush|veld

bushwa

bush|wah var. of
  bushwa

bush|walk¦er

bush|walk|ing

bush|whack

bush|whack¦er

bushy
  bush|ies
  bush|ier
  bushi|est

busily

busi|ness commerce
  etc.; cf. **busyness**

busi|ness|like

busi|ness|man
  busi|ness|men

busi|ness per¦son

busi|ness people

busi|ness|woman
  busi|ness|women

busk|er

bus|kin

bus|kined

bus|load

bus|man
  bus|men

bus¦man's holi|day

Bu|soni, Fer|ruc|cio
  composer

Buss, Fran|ces edu-
  cationist

buss kiss

bust
  busts
  bust¦ed or bust
  bust|ing

bus|tard

bus|tee

bus¦ter

bus|tier bodice

bust|ier comparative
  of **busty**

busti|ness

bus|tle

bust|ling

bust|line

bust-up *n.*

busty
  bust|ier
  busti|est

bus¦way

busy
  busies
  busied
  busy|ing
  busier
  busi|est

busy|body
  busy|bod|ies

busy Liz|zie

busy|ness being
  busy; cf. **business**

busy|work

but *conj.*; cf. **butt,
  butte**

bu|ta|di|ene

but and ben

bu|tane

bu|ta|noate

bu|ta|noic

bu|ta|nol

butch

butcher

butcher-bird

butcher's look

butch|ery
  butch|er|ies

Bute island,
  Scotland

bute phenylbutazone
  cf. **beaut**

buteo +s

Bu|teyko

Bu|the|lezi,
  Man|go|su|thu
  politician
butle var. of buttle
But|ler, Sam|uel
  poet; novelist
but|ler
butt hit; end; target;
  cask; etc.; cf. but
butte hill; cf. beaut,
  bute
but|ter
butter-and-eggs
  plant
butter|ball
butter|bur
butter|cream
butter|cup
butter|fat
butter|fingered
butter|fingers
butter|fish
butter|fly
  butter|flies
  butter|flied
  but|ter|fly|ing
butter|head
but|teri|ness
butter|milk
butter|nut
butter|scotch
butter|wort
but|tery
  but|ter|ies
but|tie var. of butty
butt|in|sky
  butt|in|skies
but|tle
  but|tling
but|tock
but|ton
button-back mod.
button|ball
button|bush
button-down adj.
button|hole
  button|hol|ing
button|holer
button|hook
but|ton|less
button-quail
But|tons pageboy
button-through
  adj. & n.

button|wood
but|tress
butts shooting range
butty
  but|ties
butut
  pl. butut or bu|tuts
butyl
bu|tyr|ate
buxom
buxom|ness
Bux|te|hude,
  Diet|rich composer
buy
  bought
buy-back n. & mod.
buyer cf. baya, byre
buyer's mar|ket
buy-in n.
buy|out n.
buzz
buz|zard
buzz|er
buzz|word
buzzy
  buzz|ier
  buzz|iest
bwana
by prep. & adv.; in
  'by the by'; cf. bye
Byatt, A. S. writer
Byb|los
by-blow
by-catch
bye Sport; goodbye;
  cf. by
bye-bye
bye-byes
bye-law var. of
  by-law
by-election
bye|line var. of
  byline
Byelo|rus|sia var. of
  Belarus
Byelo|rus|sian var.
  of Belarusian
by-form
by|gone
by-law
by|line
by|name
by|pass

by|path
by|play
by-product
Byrd, Rich|ard
  explorer
Byrd, Wil|liam
  composer
byre barn; cf. baya,
  buyer
by|road
Byron, George poet
Byron|ic
bys|sal
bys|sin|osis
bys|sus
  bys|suses or byssi
by|stand|er
byte Computing; cf.
  bight, bite
Bytom
by|town|ite
byway
by|word
by-your-leave n.
By|zan|tine
By|zan|tin|ism
By|zan|tin|ist
By|zan|tium

———————————

C

Caaba var. of Kaaba
caa|tinga
cab
  cabbed
  cab|bing
cabal
Ca|ba|lah var. of
  Kabbalah
ca|ba|letta
  ca|ba|let|tas or
  ca|ba|lette
Cab|al|ism var. of
  Kabbalism
Cab|al|ist var. of
  Kabbalist
Cab|al|is|tic var. of
  Kabbalistic
Ca|ba|llé,
  Mont|ser|rat singer

ca|bal|lero +s
ca|bana
caba|ret
cab|bage
cabbage|worm
cab|bagy
Cab|bala var. of
  Kabbalah
Cab|bal|ism var. of
  Kabbalism
Cab|bal|ist var. of
  Kabbalist
Cab|bal|is|tic var. of
  Kabbalistic
cab|bie var. of
  cabby
cabby
  cab|bies
caber
Cab|er|net
Cab|er|net Franc
Cab|er|net
  Sau|vi|gnon
cab|ezon
ca|bildo +s
cabin
cabin class
Cab|inda enclave,
  Angola
cab|inet cf.
  Kabinett
cabinet|maker
cabinet|making
cab|in|et|ry
cable
  cab|ling
cable car
cable|gram
cable-knit
cable-laid
cable|way
cab|man
  cab|men
ca|boched var. of
  caboshed
cabo|chon but en
  cabochon
ca|bo|clo +s
ca|boo|dle
ca|boose
ca|boshed
ca|bossed var. of
  caboshed

Cabot, John and
Se¦bas¦tian
explorers
cab¦ot¦age
cab¦over
cab¦rio +s
cab¦ri¦ole
cab¦ri¦olet
ca'¦canny
cacao +s
cac¦cia¦tora var. of
cacciatore
cac¦cia¦tore
ca¦chaca
cach¦alot
cache
cache¦ing or
cach¦ing
store; cf. **cash**
cache¦able
cach¦ec¦tic
cache¦pot
cache-sexe
ca¦chet
cach¦exia
ca¦chou lozenge; cf.
cashew
ca¦chu¦cha
ca¦cique
cack
cack-handed
cack-handed¦ly
cack-handed¦ness
cackle
cack¦ling
caco¦dyl
caco¦dy¦late
cac¦og¦raph¦er
cac¦og¦raphy
caco¦logy
caco¦mis¦tle
cac¦oph¦on¦ous
cac¦oph¦ony
cac¦oph¦onies
cac¦ta¦ceous
cac¦tus
cacti or cac¦tuses
ca¦cu¦min¦al
ca¦das¦tral
ca¦daver
ca¦dav¦er¦ic
ca¦dav¦er¦ous
ca¦dav¦er¦ously

ca¦dav¦er¦ous¦ness
Cad¦bury, George
and Rich¦ard choc-
olate manufacturers
cad¦die
caddy¦ing
in golf; cf. **caddy**
cad¦dis fly; worm
cad¦dish dishonour-
able; cf. **Kaddish**
Cad¦doan
caddy
cad¦dies
for tea; or var. of
caddie
ca¦delle
ca¦dence
ca¦denced
ca¦dency
ca¦den¦tial
ca¦denza
cadet
cadet¦ship
cadge
cadg¦ing
cadger
cadi Muslim judge
Cadiz
Cad¦mean
cad¦mium
Cad¦mus *Greek
Mythology*
cadre
ca¦du¦ceus
ca¦du¦cei
ca¦du¦city
ca¦du¦cous
cae¦cal *Br.
US* cecal
cae¦cil¦ian
cae¦citis *Br.
US* cecitis
cae¦cum *Br.*
caeca
US cecum
Caed¦mon poet
Cae¦lum constella-
tion
Caen city, France
Cae¦no¦zoic var. of
Cenozoic
Caer¦nar¦fon
Caer¦nar¦fon¦shire

Caer¦nar¦von var.
of Caernarfon
Caer¦nar¦von¦shire
var. of
Caernarfonshire
Caer¦philly
Cae¦sar
Cae¦sa¦rea ancient
port
Cae¦sar¦ean *Br.
US* Cesarean
Cae¦sa¦rea
Phil¦ippi ancient
inland city
Cae¦sar¦ian *Br.* var.
of Caesarean
Cae¦sar¦ien¦sis
grammarian
cae¦sium *Br.
US* cesium
caes¦ura
caes¦ural
ca¦fard
cafe
French café
café au lait
cafés au lait
cafe bar
French café bar
café noir
cafe¦teria
cafe¦tière
caff
caf¦fein¦ated
caf¦feine
caffè latte +s
caffè mac¦chi¦ato
+s
Cafod = Catholic
Fund for Overseas
Development
caf¦tan var. of
kaftan
Ca¦gayan
Cage, John
composer
cage
ca¦ging
cagey
cagi¦er
cagi¦est
cagey¦ness var. of
caginess
cagi¦ly
cagi¦ness

Cagli¦ari
Cag¦ney, James
actor
ca¦goule
cagy var. of cagey
ca¦hier
ca¦hoots
Ca¦hora Bassa
ca¦houn var. of
cohune
cahow bird
cai¦man
Cain *Bible*; in 'raise
Cain'
Caine, Mi¦chael
actor
Caino¦zoic var. of
Cenozoic
cai¦pir¦inha
ca¦ique
Cair¦ene person
from Cairo
cairn
Cairn¦gorm region;
mountains
cairn¦gorm mineral
Cairo
cais¦son
Caith¦ness
cai¦tiff
Cait¦lín
caje¦put var. of
cajuput
ca¦jole
ca¦jol¦ing
ca¦jole¦ment
ca¦jol¦ery
ca¦jol¦er¦ies
Cajun
caju¦put
cake
cak¦ing
cake¦hole
cake¦walk
cakey
Cala¦bar
cala¦bash
cala¦baza
cala¦boose
cala¦brese
Ca¦lab¦ria
Ca¦lab¦rian
ca¦la¦dium

Cal¦ais
cala¦manco
  cala¦man¦coes
cala¦man¦der
cala¦mares var. of
  calamari
cala¦mari
cala¦mar¦ies var. of
  calamari
cala¦mine
cala¦mint
cala¦mites
ca¦lam¦itous
ca¦lam¦ity
  ca¦lam¦ities
cala¦mon¦din
cala¦mus
  calami
ca¦lando *Music*
ca¦lan¦dra
ca¦lash
cala¦thea
calc¦alka¦line
cal¦ca¦neum
  cal¦ca¦nea
cal¦ca¦neus
  cal¦ca¦nei
cal¦car¦eous
cal¦car¦ious var. of
  calcareous
cal¦ceo¦laria
cal¦ces pl. of calx
cal¦cic
cal¦ci¦cole
cal¦ci¦col¦ous
cal¦cif¦erol
cal¦cif¦er¦ous
cal¦cif¦ic
cal¦ci¦fi¦ca¦tion
cal¦ci¦fuge
cal¦cify
  cal¦ci¦fies
  cal¦ci¦fied
  cal¦ci¦fy¦ing
cal¦ci¦mine var. of
  kalsomine
cal¦cin¦ation
cal¦cine
  cal¦cin¦ing
cal¦cite
cal¦cit¦ic
cal¦ci¦tonin
cal¦cium

cal¦crete
cal¦cul¦abil¦ity
cal¦cul¦able
cal¦cu¦late
cal¦cu¦lat¦ing
cal¦cu¦lated¦ly
cal¦cu¦la¦tion
cal¦cu¦la¦tive
cal¦cu¦la¦tor
cal¦cu¦lus
  cal¦cu¦luses
  Mathematics
  cal¦culi *Medicine*
Cal¦cutta
Cal¦cut¦tan
cal¦dar¦ium
  cal¦daria
Cal¦de¦cott, Ralph
  artist
Cal¦der, Alex¦an¦der
  artist
cal¦dera
Cal¦derón de la
  Barca, Pedro
  writer
cal¦dron *US* var. of
  cauldron
Cald¦well, Ers¦kine
  writer
ca¦leche
Cale¦do¦nian
cale¦fa¦cient
cal¦en¦dar almanac
cal¦en¦der roll
ca¦len¦dric¦al
cal¦ends
cal¦en¦dula
cal¦en¦ture
calf
  calves
calf-like
calf¦skin
Cal¦gary
Cali city, Colombia
cali¦ber *US*
  Br. calibre
cali¦bered *US*
  Br. calibred
cali¦brate
  cali¦brat¦ing
cali¦bra¦tion
cali¦bra¦tor
cali¦bre *Br.*
  US caliber

cali¦bred *Br.*
  US calibered
ca¦li¦ces pl. of calix
ca¦li¦che
cal¦ico
cali¦coes or cali¦cos
Cali¦cut
Cali¦for¦nia
Cali¦for¦nian
cali¦for¦nium
Ca¦lig¦ula Roman
  emperor
cali¦per
ca¦liph
ca¦liph¦ate
cal¦is¦then¦ic *US*
  Br. callisthenic
cal¦is¦then¦ics *US*
  Br. callisthenics
calix var. of calyx
calk *US* var. of
  caulk
calk¦er *US* var. of
  caulker
call cf. caul
calla plant
Cal¦laghan, James
  prime minister of
  Britain
cal¦la¦loo +s
cal¦la¦lou var. of
  callaloo
Cal¦la¦net¦ics
Cal¦las, Maria
  singer
call¦back
call¦er
call girl
Cal¦lic¦ra¦tes archi¦
  tect
calli¦graph
cal¦lig¦raph¦er
cal¦li¦graph¦ic
cal¦lig¦raph¦ist
cal¦lig¦raphy
Cal¦lima¦chus poet
call¦ing
Cal¦liope Greek and
  Roman Muse
cal¦liope musical
  instrument
cal¦li¦per var. of
  caliper
cal¦li¦ste¦mon

cal¦lis¦then¦ic *Br.*
  US calisthenic
cal¦lis¦then¦ics *Br.*
  US calisthenics
Cal¦listo
cal¦li¦tri¦chid
cal¦lop
cal¦los¦ity
  cal¦los¦ities
cal¦lous unfeeling;
  cf. callus
cal¦loused
cal¦lous¦ly
cal¦lous¦ness
call-out *n.*
call-over *n.*
cal¦low
cal¦low¦ly
cal¦low¦ness
cal¦luna
call-up *n.*
cal¦lus hard skin; cf.
  callous
cal¦lused var. of
  calloused
calm
calma¦tive
calm¦er
calm¦ly
calm¦ness
cal¦modu¦lin
calo¦mel
Calor gas *trademark*
cal¦or¦ic
cal¦or¦ic¦al¦ly
cal¦orie
cal¦or¦if¦ic
cal¦or¦if¦ic¦al¦ly
cal¦or¦im¦eter
cal¦ori¦met¦ric
cal¦or¦im¦etry
calo¦type
calque
  cal¦quing
  loan translation; cf.
  calx
cal¦trap var. of
  caltrop
cal¦trop
calu¦met
ca¦lum¦ni¦ate
  ca¦lum¦ni¦at¦ing
ca¦lum¦ni¦ation

ca¦lum¦ni¦ator
ca¦lum¦ni¦ous
cal¦umny
  cal¦um¦nies
  cal¦um¦nied
  cal¦um¦ny¦ing
calu¦tron
Cal¦va¦dos
Cal¦vary hill
cal¦vary
  cal¦var¦ies
  sculpture etc.
calve
  calv¦ing
  give birth to a calf;
  cf. **carve**
calves pl. of calf
Cal¦vin, John
  theologian
Cal¦vin¦ise Br. var.
  of Calvinize
Cal¦vin¦ism
Cal¦vin¦ist
Cal¦vin¦is¦tic
Cal¦vin¦ize
  Cal¦vin¦iz¦ing
calx
  cal¦ces
  metal oxide; cf.
  calque
Ca¦lypso nymph
ca¦lypso +s music
ca¦lyp¦so¦nian
calyx
  ca¦ly¦ces or ca¦lyxes
cal¦zone
  cal¦zoni or
  cal¦zones
cama¦rad¦erie
Cam¦argue
cama¦rilla
camas plant
ca¦mass var. of
  camas
Cam¦bay
camba¦zola var. of
  cambozola
cam¦ber
cam¦bered
Cam¦ber¦well
cam¦bial
cam¦bium
  cam¦bia or
  cam¦biums

Cam¦bo¦dia
Cam¦bo¦dian
cambo¦zola
  trademark
Cam¦brelle
  trademark
Cam¦brian
cam¦bric
Cam¦bridge
Cam¦bridge¦shire
Cam¦by¦ses Persian
  king
cam¦cord¦er
camel
camel¦back
camel¦eer
cam¦el¦id
cam¦el¦lia
cam¦elo¦pard
Cam¦elo¦par¦da¦lis
  constellation
Cam¦elot *Arthurian*
  Legend
Cam¦em¦bert
cameo +s
cam¦era
cam¦era lu¦cida
  cam¦era lu¦cidas
cam¦era¦man
  cam¦era¦men
cam¦era ob¦scura
  cam¦era ob¦scuras
camera-ready
camera¦work
Cam¦eron, Julia
  Mar¦ga¦ret photog-
  rapher
Cam¦eron, James
  film director
Cam¦er¦oon
Cam¦er¦oon¦ian
Cam¦er¦oun French
  name for
  Cameroon
cami¦knick¦ers
Cam¦illa
Cami¦sard
cami¦sole
camo +s camouflage
Cam¦ões, Luis de
  poet
ca¦mo¦gie
camo¦mile var. of
  chamomile

Ca¦morra
cam¦ou¦flage
  cam¦ou¦fla¦ging
cam¦paign
cam¦paign¦er
Cam¦pa¦nia
Cam¦pa¦nian
cam¦pa¦nile
cam¦pano¦logic¦al
cam¦pan¦olo¦gist
cam¦pan¦ology
cam¦pan¦ula
cam¦panu¦late
Cam¦pari
  trademark
Camp¦bell, Don¦ald
  and Mal¦colm
  speed record
  holders
Camp¦bell, Mrs
  Pat¦rick actress
Campbell-
  Banner¦man,
  Henry prime min-
  ister of Britain
camp¦craft
Cam¦peche state,
  Mexico
camp¦er
camp¦ery
campe¦sino +s
camp¦fire
camp¦ground
cam¦phor
cam¦phor¦ate
  cam¦phor¦at¦ing
cam¦phor¦ic
camp¦ily
camp¦im¦etry
Cam¦pi¦nas
campi¦ness
Cam¦pion, St
  Ed¦mund
Cam¦pion, Jane
  film director
cam¦pion
campo +s
Campo¦basso
Campo Grande
cam¦po¦ree
camp¦site
cam¦pus
campy
  camp¦ier

campi¦est
cam¦pylo¦bac¦ter
CAMRA = Cam-
  paign for Real Ale
cam¦shaft
Camu¦lo¦dunum
Camus, Al¦bert
  writer
cam¦wood
can
  could
can
  canned
  can¦ning
Cana town, Galilee
Ca¦naan
Ca¦naan¦ite
Can¦ada cf.
  Kannada
Can¦ad¦ian
Can¦ad¦ian¦ism
Can¦ad¦ien French
  Canadian
ca¦naille
canal
Cana¦letto painter
can¦al¦isa¦tion Br.
  var. of canalization
can¦al¦ise Br. var. of
  canalize
can¦al¦iza¦tion
can¦al¦ize
  can¦al¦iz¦ing
can¦apé
can¦ard
Can¦ar¦ese var. of
  Kanarese
Can¦ary
  Can¦ar¦ies
  Islands
can¦ary
  can¦ar¦ies
can¦asta
Can¦av¦eral, Cape
Can¦berra
can¦can
can¦cel
  can¦celled Br.
  can¦celed US
  can¦cel¦ling Br.
  can¦cel¦ing US
  can¦cel¦ation US
  var. of cancellation
can¦cel¦bot

can|cel|er *US*
  Br. **canceller**
can|cel|la|tion
can|cel|ler *Br.*
  US **canceller**
can|cel|lous
Can|cer constella-
tion
can|cer
Can|cer|ian
can|cer|ous
Can|cún
Can|dace
can|dela
can|de|la|brum
  can|de|la|bra
Can|dice
can|did
Can|dida name
can|dida fungus
can|di|dacy
  can|di|da|cies
can|di|date
can|di|da|ture
can|did|ia|sis
can|did|ly
can|did|ness
can|diru
can|dle
  cand|ling
candle|berry
  candle|berries
candle|fish
candle|hold|er
candle|light
candle|lit
Candle|mas
candle|nut
candle|power
cand|ler
candle|stick
candle|wick
can-do *adj.*
candomblé
can|dor *US*
cand|our *Br.*
CANDU nuclear
  reactor
candy
  candies
  can|died
  candy|ing
candy-ass

candy|floss
candy|man
  candy|men
candy-stripe
candy-striper
candy|tuft
cane
  can|ing
cane|brake
caner
Canes Ve|nat|ici
Can|field
canid
ca|nine
Canis Major/
  Minor
  constellations
can|is|ter
can|ker
can|ker|ous
canker|worm
Can|more Malcolm
  III of Scotland
canna plant
can|na|bin|oid
can|na|binol
can|na|bis
can|nel|lini bean
can|nel|loni
can|nel|ure
can|ner
can|nery
  can|ner|ies
Cannes resort,
  France
can|ni|bal
can|ni|bal|isa|tion
  Br. var. of
  cannibalization
can|ni|bal|ise *Br.*
  var. of cannibalize
can|ni|bal|ism
can|ni|bal|is|tic
can|ni|bal|is|tic|
          al|ly
can|ni|bal|iza|tion
can|ni|bal|ize
  can|ni|bal|iz|ing
can|ni|kin
can|nily
can|ni|ness
Can|ning, George
  prime minister of
  Britain

can|noli
can|non gun;
  Snooker;
  Engineering; cf.
  canon
can|non|ade
  can|non|ad|ing
cannon|ball
can|non bone
can|non|eer
can|non fod|der
can|not
can|nula
  can|nu|lae or
  can|nu|las
can|nu|late
  can|nu|lat|ing
can|nu|la|tion
canny
  can|nier
  can|ni|est
canoe
  ca|noes
  ca|noed
  ca|noe|ing
canoe|er
ca|noe|ist
can|ola
canon rule; member
  of the clergy; col-
  lection; *Music*; cf.
  cannon
canon can|cri|zans
  canons
  can|cri|zans
canon|ess
ca|non|ic
ca|non|ic|al
ca|non|ic|al|ly
can|on|icity
can|on|isa|tion *Br.*
  var. of
  canonization
can|on|ise *Br.* var.
  of canonize
can|on|ist
can|on|ist|ic
can|on|iza|tion
can|on|ize
  can|on|iz|ing
canon law
canon regu|lar
  canons regu|lar
can|on|ry
  can|on|ries

ca|noo|dle
  ca|nood|ling
Ca|no|pic
Ca|no|pus
can|opy
  can|opies
  can|opied
  can|opy|ing
Ca|nova, An|tonio
  sculptor
canst
cant
can't cannot
Can|tab of Cam-
  bridge University
can|ta|bile
Can|ta|bria region,
  Spain
Can|tab|rian
Can|ta|bri|gian of
  Cambridge or Cam-
  bridge University
can|tal
can|ta|loupe
can|tan|ker|ous
can|tan|ker|ous|ly
can|tan|ker|ous|
          ness
can|tata
cant dog
can|teen
can|ter
Can|ter|bury
can|ter|bury
  can|ter|buries
  furniture
can|thari|des
can|tharus
  can|thari
can|thic
cant hook
can|thus
can|thi
can|ticle
can|ti|lena
can|ti|lever
can|tina
can|tle
canto +s
Can|ton var. of
  Guangzhou city,
  China
can|ton region;
  Heraldry

can|ton|al
Can|ton|ese
can|ton|ment
Canto|pop
can|tor
can|tor|ial
can|toris
cant|rail
can|trip
can|tus
canti
can|tus fir|mus
  can|tus firmi or
  canti firmi
Can|uck
Can|ute Danish
  king of England
can'|vas cloth; cf.
  canvass
canvas|back
can|vass solicit; cf.
  canvas
can|vass|er
can|yon
can|zona Italian
  instrumental song
  arrangement
can|zone
  can|zoni
  Italian or Provençal
  song
can|zon|etta
  can|zon|et|tas or
  can|zon|ette
caou|tchouc
cap
  capped
  cap|ping
cap|abil|ity
  cap|abil|ities
cap|able
cap|ably
cap|acious
cap|acious|ly
cap|acious|ness
cap|aci|tance
cap|aci|tate
  cap|aci|tat|ing
cap|aci|ta|tion
cap|aci|ta|tive var.
  of capacitive
cap|aci|tive
cap|aci|tor

cap|acity
  cap|aci|ties
ca|pari|son
cape
  cap|ing
Cape Bre|ton
  Is|land
Cape col|ored US
Cape col|oured Br.
ca|peesh
Cape John|son
  Depth
Čapek, Karel writer
cap|elin
Ca|pella star; cf. a
  cappella
ca|pel|lini
caper
cap|er|cail|lie
cap|er|cail|zie var.
  of capercaillie
caper|er
cape|skin
Capet, Hugh
  French king
Cap|etian
Cape Town
Cape Verde
Cape Ver|dean
cap|ful
cap|pias
ca|pill|lar|ity
ca|pill|lary
  ca|pill|lar|ies
cap|ital
cap|it|al|isa|tion Br.
  var. of
  capitalization
cap|it|al|ise Br. var.
  of capitalize
cap|it|al|ism
cap|it|al|ist
cap|it|al|is|tic
cap|it|al|is|tic|al|ly
cap|it|al|iza|tion
cap|it|al|ize
  cap|it|al|iz|ing
cap|it|al|ly
capi|tano +s
capi|tate
capi|ta|tion
Cap|itol in ancient
  Rome or Washing-
  ton DC

Cap|itol Hill in
  Washington DC
Ca|pit|ol|ine hill,
  ancient Rome
ca|pitu|lar
ca|pitu|lary
  cap|itu|lar|ies
ca|pitu|late
  ca|pitu|lat|ing
ca|pitu|la|tion
ca|pitu|la|tor
ca|pit|ulum
  ca|pit|ula
cap|let trademark
cap|lin var. of
  capelin
cap'n captain
capo +s
Capo di Monte
capo|eira
capon
capo|nata
Ca|pone, Al gang-
  ster
ca|pon|ier
ca|pon|ise Br. var.
  of caponize
ca|pon|ize
  ca|pon|iz|ing
capot
  ca|pot|ted
  ca|pot|ting
capo tasto +s
Ca|pote, Tru|man
  writer
ca|pote
Cap|pa|do|cia
Cap|pa|do|cian
cap|pel|letti
cap|per
cap|ping
cap|puc|cino +s
Capra, Frank film
  director
Capri
capri pants
ca|pric|cio +s
ca|pric|ci|oso
ca|price
ca|pri|cious
ca|pri|cious|ly
ca|pri|cious|ness
Cap|ri|corn zodiac
  sign

Cap|ri|corn|ian
Cap|ri|cor|nus con-
  stellation
cap|rine
cap|ri|ole
  cap|ri|ol|ing
Ca|privi Strip
cap|ro|ate
capro|lac|tam
cap|ryl|ate
cap|ryl|ic
cap|sa|icin
Cap|sian
cap|si|cum
cap|sid
cap|size
  cap|siz|ing
cap|stan
cap|stone
cap|su|lar
cap|su|late
cap|sule
cap|su|lise Br. var.
  of capsulize
cap|su|lize
  cap|su|liz|ing
cap|tain
Cap|tain Cook|er
  wild boar
cap|tain|cy
  cap|tain|cies
cap|tain gen|eral
  cap|tain gen|erals
cap|tan
cap|tion
cap|tious
cap|tious|ly
cap|tious|ness
cap|tiv|ate
  cap|tiv|at|ing
cap|tiv|at|ing|ly
cap|tiv|ation
cap|tive
cap|tiv|ity
  cap|tiv|ities
cap|tor
cap|ture
  cap|tur|ing
cap|turer
Capu|chin friar;
  hooded cloak
capu|chin monkey;
  pigeon

capy|bara
car cf. carr, ka
cara|bao
  pl. cara|bao
  or cara|baos
cara|bid
cara|bin|eer cavalry
  soldier
cara|biner var. of
  karabiner
cara|bi|nero +s
  Spanish or South
  American guard
cara|bin|ier var. of
  carabineer
cara|bin|iere
  cara|bin|ieri
  Italian paramilitary
  police
cara|cal lynx; cf.
  karakul
Cara|calla Roman
  emperor
cara|cara bird
Ca|ra|cas
cara|cole
  cara|col|ing
  turn made by horse
Ca|rac|ta|cus var. of
  Caratacus
cara|cul var. of
  karakul
ca|rafe
cara|gana
ca|ram|bola
cara|mel
cara|mel|isa|tion
  Br. var. of
  caramelization
cara|mel|ise *Br.* var.
  of caramelize
cara|mel|iza|tion
cara|mel|ize
  cara|mel|iz|ing
ca|ran|gid
cara|pace
carat unit of weight
  for jewels; cf. caret
carat *Br.*
  measure of purity
  of gold
  US karat; cf. caret
Ca|rat|acus British
  chieftain
Cara|vag|gesque

Cara|vag|gio,
  Mi|chel|an|gelo
  painter
cara|van
  cara|vanned
  cara|van|ning
cara|van|ette
cara|van|ner
cara|van|sary *US*
  cara|van|sar|ies
cara|van|serai *Br.*
cara|vel
cara|way
car|ba|mate
carba|maze|pine
car|bam|ic
carb|anion
car|baryl
car|ba|zole
car|bene
car|bide
car|bine
carbo|cat|ion
carbo|hy|drate
car|bol|ic
carbo|load
car|bon
car|bon|aceous
car|bon|ade var. of
  carbonnade
car|bon|ado +s
car|bon|ara
car|bon|ate
  car|bon|at|ing
car|bon|ation
car|bona|tite
car|bon black
car|bon dat|ing
carbon-14
car|bon|ic
Car|bon|ifer|ous
car|bon|isa|tion *Br.*
  var. of
  carbonization
car|bon|ise *Br.* var.
  of carbonize
car|bo|nium
car|bon|iza|tion
car|bon|ize
  car|bon|iz|ing
car|bon|less
car|bon|nade
carbon-12

car|bonyl
car boot sale
car|bor|un|dum
carb|oxy|haemo|
       glo|bin *Br.*
carb|oxy|hemo|
      glo|bin *US*
carb|oxyl
carb|oxyl|ase
carb|oxyl|ate
  carb|oxyl|at|ing
carb|oxyl|ation
car|boy
car|bun|cle
car|bun|cu|lar
car|bur|ation
car|bur|etor *US*
car|bur|et|ter *Br.*
  var. of carburettor
car|bur|et|tor *Br.*
car|bur|isa|tion *Br.*
  var. of
  carburization
car|bur|ise *Br.* var.
  of carburize
car|bur|iza|tion
car|bur|ize
  car|bur|iz|ing
car|ca|jou
car|case var. of
  carcass
car|cass
Car|cas|sonne
car|ceral
Car|che|mish
car|cino|gen
car|cino|gen|esis
car|cino|gen|ic
car|cino|gen|icity
car|cin|oid
car|cin|oma
  car|cin|omas or
  car|cin|omata
car|cin|oma|tosis
car|cin|omat|ous
car|da|mom
Car|da|mom
  Moun|tains
car|da|mum var. of
  cardamom
car|dan joint; shaft
card|board
card-carrying

card|er
card|hold|er
car|dia
car|diac
car|die var. of cardy
Car|diff
Car|di|gan
car|di|gan
Car|di|gan|shire
Car|din, Pierre
  couturier
car|dinal
car|din|al|ate
car|din|al|ity
  car|din|al|ities
car|din|al|ly
car|din|al|ship
car|dio|gram
car|dio|graph
car|dio|graph|er
car|dio|graphy
car|di|oid
car|dio|logic|al
car|di|olo|gist
car|di|ology
car|dio|meg|aly
car|dio|my|op|athy
  car|dio|
      my|op|athies
car|dio|
      pul|mon|ary
car|dio|
      respira|tory
car|dio|thor|acic
car|dio|vas|cu|lar
card|itis
car|doon
card|phone
card sharp
card sharp|er
cardy
  car|dies
  cardigan; cf. cadi
care
  car|ing
car|een
car|eer
car|eer|ism
car|eer|ist
care|free
care|ful
  care|ful|lest

care|ful|ly
care|ful|ness
care|giver
care|giv|ing
care|less
care|less|ly
care|less|ness
care|line
carer
ca|ress
ca|ress|ing|ly
caret omission
  mark; cf. **carat**
care|taker
care|worn
carex
  car|ices
Carey, George
  archbishop of
  Canterbury
Carey, Peter
  novelist
car|fare
car|ful
cargo
  car|goes or car|gos
car|hop
car|iad
cari|ama var. of
  seriema
Carib
Car|ib|an
Carib|bean
cari|bou
cari|ca|tural
cari|ca|ture
cari|ca|tur|ing
cari|ca|tur|ist
CARICOM = Carib-
  bean Community
  and Common
  Market
car|ies
car|il|lon
car|il|lon|neur
Car|ina constella-
  tion
car|ina
  car|inae or
  car|inas *Biology*
car|in|al
car|in|ate
car|in|ated
car|in|ation

car|ing|ly
Car|in|thia in
  Austria
Car|in|thian cf.
  Corinthian
cari|oca
cario|gen|ic
cari|ole var. of
  carriole
cari|ous
cari|tas
car|jack
car|jack|er
cark
cark|ing
carl man; peasant
Car|ley float
car|lin var. of
  carline
car|line thistle;
  ship's timber
Car|ling, Will rugby
  union player
car|ling var. of
  carline
Car|lisle
Carl|ism
Carl|ist
car|load
Car|lo|vin|gian var.
  of Carolingian
Car|low
Carls|bad
Carl|ton
Car|lyle, Thomas
  writer
car|man
  car|men
  driver
Car|mar|then
Car|mar|then|shire
Car|mel name;
  Mount C.
Car|mel|ite
Car|men
Car|michael,
  Hoagy jazz
  musician
car|mina|tive
car|mine
Car|naby Street
Car|nac in France;
  cf. Karnak
car|nage

car|nal
car|nal|ity
car|nal|lite
car|nal|ly
car|nas|sial
Car|nat|ic
car|na|tion
car|nauba
Car|negie, An|drew
  philanthropist
car|ne|lian
car|net
car|ni|val
car|ni|val|esque
Car|niv|ora
car|ni|vore
car|niv|or|ous
carno|saur
car|no|tite
carny carnival
  car|nies
carob
Carol name
carol
  car|olled *Br.*
  car|oled *US*
  car|ol|ling *Br.*
  car|ol|ing *US*
  song; cf. **carrel**
Car|ole name
Caro|lean
car|ol|er *US*
  Br. caroller
Caro|lina, North
  or South
Caro|line name
Caro|lin|gian of
  Charlemagne
Caro|lin|ian of
  North or South
  Carolina
car|ol|ler *Br.*
  US caroler
Caro|lus Mag|nus
  Charlemagne
Caro|lyn
carom
caro|tene
ca|rot|en|oid
ca|rotid
ca|rousal drinking
  party
ca|rouse
  ca|rous|ing

ca|rou|sel merry-go-
  round; conveyor
ca|rous|er
Car|pac|cio,
  Vit|tore painter
car|pac|cio food
car|pal wrist bone;
  cf. carpel
Car|pa|thian
carpe diem
car|pel flower part;
  cf. carpal
car|pel|lary
Car|pen|taria
car|pen|ter
car|pen|try
carp|er
car|pet
carpet bag *n.*
carpet-bag *v.*
  carpet-bagged
  carpet-bagging
carpet|bagger
carpet-bomb
car|pol|ogy
car|pool *US*
car pool *Br.*
car|pool|er *US*
carpo|phore
car|port
car|pus
  carpi
carr marsh; cf. **car,
  ka**
Car|racci family of
  painters
car|rack
car|ra|geen
car|ra|geenan
car|ra|gheen var. of
  carrageen
Car|rara
car|rel cubicle; cf.
  carol
Car|reras, José
  singer
car|riage
car|riage|way
car|rick bend
Carrick-on-
  Shannon
Car|rie
car|rier

car|ri|ole
car|rion
Car|roll, Lewis writer
car|ron|ade
car|rot cf. carat, caret, karat
car|roty
carry
  car|ries
  car|ried
  cf. karri
carry|all
carry|cot
carrying-on n.
  carryings-on
carry-on n. & adj.
carry-out adj. & n.
carry-over n.
carse
car|sick
car|sick|ness
Car|son, Ra|chel zoologist
Car|son City
cart cf. kart, khat, quart
cart|age
Car|ta|gena
carte Fencing; var. of quart
carte blanche
  cartes blanches
carte de visite
  cartes de visite
car|tel
car|tel|ise Br. var. of cartelize
car|tel|ize
  car|tel|iz|ing
Car|ter, An|gela writer
Car|ter, El|li|ott composer
Car|ter, How|ard archaeologist
Car|ter, Jimmy US president
cart|er cf. kata
Car|te|sian
Car|tes|ian|ism
cart|ful
Car|thage
Car|tha|gin|ian

cart|horse
Car|thu|sian
Car|tier Islands
Cartier-Bresson, Henri photographer
car|til|age
car|til|agin|ous
Cart|land, Bar|bara writer
cart|load
carto|gram
car|tog|raph|er
carto|graph|ic|al|ly
car|tog|raphy
carto|man|cer
carto|mancy
car|ton
car|ton|nage
car|toon
car|toon|ish
car|toon|ist
car|toony
cart|oph|il|ist
cart|oph|ily
car|touche
cart|ridge
cart|wheel
cart|wright
car|uncle
car|un|cu|lar
Ca|ruso, En|rico singer
carve
  carv|ing
  cut; cf. calve
car|vel var. of caravel
carvel-built
Car|ver US rush-seated chair
car|ver person who carves; knife; Br. dining chair with arms; cf. cava, kava
car|very
  car|ver|ies
carve-up n.
car wash
cary|atid
  cary|ati|des or cary|atids

Caryl name
caryo|phyl|la|ceous
cary|op|sis
  cary|op|ses
ca|saba
Casa|blanca
Ca|sals, Pablo cellist
Casa|nova philanderer
casa|reep var. of cassareep
cas|bah var. of kasbah
cas|ca|bel
cas|cade
  cas|cad|ing
Cas|cais
cas|cara
cas|cara sa|grada
case
  cas|ing
ca|se|ation
case|book
case-bound
case-harden
ca|sein
case|load
case|mate
Case|ment, Roger Irish nationalist
case|ment
ca|se|ous
case-shot
cas|evac +s +ed +ing
case|work
case|work|er
Cash, Johnny singer
cash money; cf. cache
cash|able
cash|back
cash book
cash box
cash crop|ping
cash dis|pen|ser
cashew nut; cf. cachou
cash|ier
cash|less
cash|mere wool; cf. Kashmir

cash|point trademark
cas|ing
ca|sino +s
cas|ita
cask box; cf. casque
cas|ket
Cas|par one of the Magi
Cas|per
Cas|pian Sea
casque helmet; cf. cask
Cas|san|dra
cas|sa|reep
cas|sata
cas|sa|tion
cas|sava
Casse|grain
cas|ser|ole
  cas|ser|ol|ing
cas|sette
cas|sia
Cas|sie
cas|sin|gle
Cas|sini moon of Saturn
Cas|sini, Gio|vanni astronomer
Cas|sio|peia
cas|sis
cas|sit|er|ite
Cas|sius, Gaius Roman general
cas|sock
cas|socked
cas|sone
cas|sones or cas|soni
cas|sou|let
cas|so|wary
  cas|so|war|ies
cast cf. caste, karst
Cas|ta|lia
Cas|ta|lian
cas|ta|net
cast|away
caste social class; cf. cast, karst
caste|ism
Cas|tel Gan|dolfo papal residence
cas|tel|lan

cas¦tel¦lated
cas¦tel¦la¦tion
cast¦er person or
 machine that casts;
 c. sugar; cf. **castor**
cas¦ti¦gate
cas¦ti¦gat¦ing
cas¦ti¦ga¦tion
cas¦ti¦ga¦tor
cas¦ti¦ga¦tory
Cas¦tile
Cas¦til¦ian
Castilla-La
 Mancha
Castilla-León
Cas¦tle, Bar¦bara
 politician
cas¦tle
 cast¦ling
Castle¦bar
Castle¦reagh,
 Rob¦ert British
 statesman
cast-off *adj. & n.*
Cas¦tor twin of Pol-
 lux; star
cas¦tor sugar
 shaker; wheel; oily
 substance; c.
 action; c. oil; cf.
 caster
cas¦tor sugar var.
 of **caster sugar**
cas¦trate
 cas¦trat¦ing
cas¦tra¦tion
cas¦trato
 cas¦trati
cas¦tra¦tor
Cas¦tries
Cas¦tro, Fidel
 Cuban president
Cas¦tro¦ism
cas¦ual
cas¦ual¦isa¦tion Br.
 var. of
 casualization
cas¦ual¦ise Br. var.
 of casualize
cas¦ual¦iza¦tion
cas¦ual¦ize
 cas¦ual¦iz¦ing
cas¦ual¦ly
cas¦ual¦ness

cas¦ualty
 cas¦ual¦ties
casu¦ar¦ina
casu¦ist
casu¦is¦tic
casu¦is¦tic¦al
casu¦is¦try
casus belli
cat
 cat¦ted
 cat¦ting
cata¦bol¦ic
ca¦tab¦ol¦ism
ca¦tab¦ol¦ite
cata¦chre¦sis
 cata¦chre¦ses
cata¦chres¦tic
cata¦clasis
cata¦clas¦tic
cata¦clysm
cata¦clys¦mal
cata¦clys¦mic
cata¦clys¦mic¦al¦ly
cata¦comb
cata¦di¦op¦tric
ca¦tad¦rom¦ous
cata¦falque
Cata¦lan
cata¦lase
cata¦lec¦tic
cata¦lepsy
 cata¦lep¦sies
cata¦lep¦tic
cata¦log US
cata¦log¦er US
 cata¦loguing
cata¦loguer Br.
 cata¦logue
 rai¦sonné
 cata¦logues
 rai¦son¦nés
Cata¦lo¦nia
Cata¦lo¦nian
ca¦talpa
cata¦lufa
cata¦lyse Br.
 cata¦lys¦ing
 US catalyze
cata¦lyser Br.
 US catalyzer
ca¦taly¦sis
cata¦lyst

cata¦lyt¦ic
cata¦lyt¦ic¦al¦ly
cata¦lyze US
 cata¦lyz¦ing
 Br. catalyse
cata¦lyzer US
 Br. catalyser
cata¦ma¦ran
cata¦mite
cata¦mount
cata¦moun¦tain
cata¦nan¦che
Cat¦ania
cata¦phati¦c
cata¦phor
cat¦aph¦ora
cata¦phor¦ic
cata¦phor¦ic¦al¦ly
cata¦phract
cata¦plasm
cata¦plec¦tic
cata¦plexy
 cata¦plex¦ies
cata¦pult
cata¦ract
ca¦tarrh
ca¦tar¦rhal
cat¦ar¦rhine
ca¦tas¦tro¦phe
cata¦stroph¦ic
cata¦stroph¦ic¦al¦ly
ca¦tas¦troph¦ism
ca¦tas¦troph¦ist
cata¦to¦nia
cata¦ton¦ic
ca¦tawba
cat-bear
cat¦bird
cat¦boat
cat burg¦lar
cat¦call
catch
 caught
 past of **catch**; cf.
 court
catch¦able
catch-all
catch-as-catch-can
catch crop
catch¦er
catch¦fly
 catch¦flies
catch¦ily

catchi¦ness
catch¦light
catch¦line
catch¦ment
catch¦penny
catch¦phrase
catch points
catch-22 +s
catch¦up var. of
 ketchup
catch-up in 'play
 catch-up' etc.
catch¦weight
catch¦word
catchy
 catch¦ier
 catchi¦est
cate *archaic* delicacy
cat¦ech¦esis
cat¦ech¦et¦ic¦al
cat¦ech¦et¦ics
cat¦echin
cat¦ech¦ise Br. var.
 of catechize
cat¦ech¦iser Br. var.
 of catechizer
cat¦ech¦ism
cat¦ech¦is¦mal
cat¦ech¦ist
cat¦ech¦ize
 cat¦ech¦iz¦ing
cat¦ech¦izer
cat¦echol
cat¦echol¦amine
cat¦echu
cat¦echu¦men
cat¦egor¦ial
cat¦egoric
cat¦egor¦ic¦al
cat¦egor¦ic¦al¦ly
cat¦egor¦isa¦tion
 Br. var. of
 categorization
cat¦egor¦ise Br. var.
 of categorize
cat¦egor¦iza¦tion
cat¦egor¦ize
 cat¦egor¦iz¦ing
cat¦egory
 cat¦egor¦ies
ca¦tena
ca¦tenae or
 ca¦tenas
cat¦en¦accio

cat¦en¦ane
ca¦ten¦ary
  ca¦ten¦ar¦ies
cat¦en¦ated
cat¦en¦ation
cat¦en¦ative
cat¦en¦oid
cater
cat¦eran
cater-corner var. of
  cater-cornered
cater-cornered
ca¦ter¦er
cat¦er¦pil¦lar
ca¦ters *Bell-ringing*
cat¦er¦waul
cat¦fight
cat¦fish
cat¦flap
cat¦gut
Cathar
Cath¦ar¦ine
Cath¦ar¦ism
Cath¦ar¦ist
cath¦ar¦sis
  cath¦ar¦ses
cath¦ar¦tic
cath¦ar¦tic¦al¦ly
Ca¦thay
cat¦head part of
  ship
cath¦ec¦tic
cath¦edra in 'ex
  cathedra'
cath¦edral
Cath¦er¦ine de'
  Med¦ici
Cath¦er¦ine of
  Alex¦an¦dria
Cath¦er¦ine of
  Ara¦gon
Cath¦er¦ine the
  Great
Cath¦er¦ine wheel
cath¦eter
cath¦eter¦isa¦tion
  Br. var. of
  catheterization
cath¦eter¦ise *Br. var.
  of* catheterize
cath¦eter¦iza¦tion
cath¦eter¦ize
  cath¦eter¦iz¦ing

cath¦etom¦eter
cath¦exis
cath¦exes
Cath¦leen
cath¦odal
cath¦ode
cath¦ode ray tube
cath¦od¦ic
cath¦odo¦lu¦min¦
  es¦cence
Cath¦olic
  Christianity
cath¦olic generally
cath¦olic¦al¦ly var.
  of catholicly
Cath¦oli¦cise *Br.
  var. of* Catholicize
Cath¦oli¦cism
cath¦ol¦icity
Cath¦oli¦cize
  Cath¦oli¦ciz¦ing
cath¦olic¦ly
Cath¦oli¦cos
  Cath¦oli¦coses or
  Cath¦oli¦coi
cat¦house
Cath¦ryn
Cati¦line Roman
  nobleman
cat¦ion
cat¦ion¦ic
cat¦kin
cat¦lick
cat¦like
cat¦lin¦ite
cat¦mint
cat¦nap
  cat¦napped
  cat¦nap¦ping
cat¦nip
Cato, Mar¦cus
  Por¦cius Roman
  statesman
cat-o'-nine-tails
  pl. cat-o'-nine-tails
cat¦op¦tric
cat¦op¦trics
Cat¦rin
Ca¦tri¦ona
cat's cra¦dle
cat's ear plant
cats¦eye on road
  trademark

cat's eye precious
  stone
cat's foot +s
Cats¦kill
cat's paw person
cat's tail plant
cat¦suit
cat¦sup *US var. of*
  ketchup
cat's whis¦ker wire
  in radio
cat¦tail var. of cat's
  tail
cat¦tery
  cat¦ter¦ies
cat¦tily
cat¦ti¦ness
cat¦tish
cat¦tish¦ly
cat¦tish¦ness
cat¦tle
cattle¦man
  cattle¦men
catt¦leya
catty
  cat¦ties
  cat¦tier
  cat¦ti¦est
catty-cornered var.
  of cater-cornered
Ca¦tul¦lus, Gaius
  Val¦er¦ius poet
cat¦walk
cau¦been
Cau¦ca¦sia
Cau¦ca¦sian
Cau¦cas¦oid
Cau¦ca¦sus
cau¦cus
cau¦dal of or like a
  tail; cf. chordal
caud¦al¦ly
Caud¦ata
caud¦ate having a
  tail; cf. chordate,
  cordate
cau¦dex
cau¦di¦ces
cau¦dillo +s
caught
caul amnion
caul¦dron
cauli¦flower

caulk fill; filler; cf.
  cork
caulk¦er person
  who caulks; cf.
  corker
caus¦able
causal
caus¦algia
caus¦al¦ity
caus¦al¦ly
caus¦ation
causa¦tive
causa¦tive¦ly
cause
  caus¦ing
'cause = because
cause cé¦lèbre
  causes cé¦lèbres
cause¦less
causer
caus¦erie
cause¦way
cau¦sey
caus¦tic
caus¦tic¦al¦ly
caus¦ti¦city
cau¦ter¦isa¦tion *Br.*
  var. of
  cauterization
cau¦ter¦ise *Br.* var.
  of cauterize
cau¦ter¦iza¦tion
cau¦ter¦ize
  cau¦ter¦iz¦ing
cau¦tery
  cau¦ter¦ies
cau¦tion
cau¦tion¦ary
cau¦tious
cau¦tious¦ly
cau¦tious¦ness
Cau¦very river,
  India
cava wine; cf.
  carver, kava
cav¦al¦cade
Cava¦lier in English
  Civil War
cava¦lier
cava¦lier¦ly
cav¦alry
cav¦al¦ries
cav¦al¦ry¦man
  cav¦al¦ry¦men

Cavan
cava|qui|nho +s
cava|tina
  cava|tinas or
  cava|tine
cave
  cav|ing
cave beware
cav|eat
cav|eat emp|tor
cave-dweller
cave|fish
cave-in *n.*
cave-like
Cav|ell, Edith nurse
cave|man
  cave|men
Cav|en|dish, Henry
  scientist
cav|en|dish tobacco
caver
cav|ern
cav|ern|ous
cav|es|son
cave|woman
  cave|women
cav|iar
cavi|are var. of
  caviar
cavil
  cav|illed *Br.*
  cav|iled *US*
  cav|il|ling *Br.*
  cav|il|ing *US*
cav|il|er *US*
cav|il|ler *Br.*
cavi|tary
cavi|ta|tion
cav|ity
  cav|ities
ca|volo nero
ca|vort
Ca|vour, Cam|illo
  Italian statesman
cavy
  cavies
  animal; cf. *cave*
caw bird's cry
Cawn|pore var. of
  Kanpur
Cax|ton, Wil|liam
  printer
cay reef; cf. key,
  quay

Cay|enne capital of
  French Guiana
cay|enne pepper
Cay|ley numbers
Cay|man Islands
cay|man alligator
  var. of caiman
Cay|uga
Cay|use people
cay|use pony
CD-ROM
cea|no|thus
Ceará state, Brazil
cease
  ceas|ing
cease|fire
cease|less
cease|less|ly
Ceau|şescu,
  Nico|lae president
  of Romania
cebid
Cebu
cecal *US*
  Br. caecal
Ce|ci|lia
Ce|cily
ce|citis *US*
  Br. caecitis
ce|cro|pia
cecum *US*
  ceca
  Br. caecum
cedar tree
ce|darn
cedar|wood
cede
  ced|ing
  give up
cedi
  pl. cedi or cedis
  Ghanaian currency
ce|dilla
Ced|ric
Cee|fax *trademark*
ceiba
ceil line the roof of;
  cf. seal
cei|lidh
ceil|ing cf. sealing
cel transparent film;
  cf. cell, sell
cela|don
cel|an|dine

celeb
Cel|ebes Sea;
  former name for
  Sulawesi
Ce|le|bra *trademark*
cele|brant
cele|brate
  cele|brat|ing
cele|bra|tion
cele|bra|tor
cele|bra|tory
ce|leb|rity
  ce|leb|ri|ties
ce|ler|iac
ce|ler|ity
cel|ery
  cel|er|ies
ce|lesta keyboard
  instrument
Cé|leste name
ce|leste organ stop
ce|leste var. of
  celesta
ce|les|tial
ce|les|ti|al|ly
Celia
ce|liac *US*
  Br. coeliac
celi|bacy
celi|bate
cell compartment
  etc.; cf. cel, sell
cella
  cel|lae
  area of ancient
  temple; cf. cellar,
  seller
cel|lar basement; cf.
  cella, seller
cel|lar|age
cel|lar|er
cel|laret
cel|lar|man
  cel|lar|men
celled
Cel|lini,
  Ben|ve|nuto gold-
  smith and sculptor
cell|ist
cell-like
cello +s
cel|lo|phane
  trademark

cell|phone
cel|lu|lar
cel|lu|lar|ity
cel|lu|lase
cel|lu|lite
cel|lu|litis
cel|lu|loid
cel|lu|lose
  cel|lu|los|ing
cel|lu|los|ic
cel|osia
Cel|sius
Celt people; cf. kelt
celt implement
Celt|iber|ian
Cel|tic
Cel|ti|cism
cem|bal|ist
cem|balo +s
ce|ment
ce|men|ta|tion
ce|ment|er
ce|ment|ite
ce|men|ti|tious
ce|men|tum
ceme|tery
  ceme|ter|ies
cen|acle
ceno|bite
ceno|bit|ic
ceno|taph
ce|note
Ceno|zoic
cense
  cens|ing
  to perfume; cf.
  sense
cen|ser vessel for
  incense; cf. censor,
  sensor
cen|sor cut film
  etc.; Roman
  magistrate; cf.
  censer, censure,
  sensor
cen|sor|ial
cen|sori|ous
cen|sori|ous|ly
cen|sori|ous|ness
cen|sor|ship
cen|sur|able

cen|sure
  cen|sur|ing
  criticize; criticism;
  cf. censor
cen|sus
cent monetary unit
  (except of Estonia);
  in 'per cent'; cf.
  scent, sent
cen|tal
cen|tas
  pl. cen|tas
cen|taur
cen|taurea
Cen|taurus
cen|taury
  cen|taur|ies
cen|tavo +s
Cent|com
cen|ten|ar|ian
cen|ten|ary
  cen|ten|ar|ies
cen|ten|nial
cen|ter US
  Br. centre
cen|ter bit US
  Br. centre bit
center|board US
  Br. centreboard
cen|tered|ness US
  Br. centredness
center|field US
  Br. centrefield
center|fielder US
  Br. centrefielder
center|fold US
  Br. centrefold
center|most US
  Br. centremost
center|piece US
  Br. centrepiece
cen|ter stage US
  Br. centre stage
cen|tes|im|al
cen|tésimo +s
  former monetary
  unit of Italy
cen|tesimo +s mon-
  etary unit of Uru-
  guay and Panama
centi|grade
centi|gram
centi|gramme Br.
  var. of centigram
cen|tile

centi|liter US
centi|litre Br.
cen|time
centi|meter US
centimeter-gram-
        second US
centi|metre Br.
centimetre-gram-
        second Br.
cen|timo +s
centi|Morgan var.
  of centimorgan
centi|morgan
centi|pede
cen|tral
cen|tral|isa|tion Br.
  var. of
  centralization
cen|tral|ise Br. var.
  of centralize
cen|tral|ism
cen|tral|ist
cen|tral|ity
cen|tral|iza|tion
cen|tral|ize
  cen|tral|iz|ing
cen|tral|ly
Centre region,
  France
centre Br.
  cen|tring
  US center
centre bit Br.
  US center bit
centre|board Br.
  US centerboard
centred|ness Br.
  US centeredness
centre|field Br.
  US centerfield
centre|field|er Br.
  US centerfielder
centre|fold Br.
  US centerfold
centre|most Br.
  US centermost
centre|piece Br.
  US centerpiece
centre stage Br.
  US center stage
cen|trex
cen|tric
cen|tric|al
cen|tri|city

cen|tri|fu|gal
cen|tri|fu|gal|ly
cen|tri|fu|ga|tion
cen|tri|fuge
  cen|tri|fu|ging
cen|tri|ole
centri|pet|al
centri|pet|al|ly
cen|trism
cen|trist
cen|troid
centro|mere
centro|mer|ic
centro|some
cen|trum
  cen|trums or
  cen|tra
cen|tu|ple
  cen|tu|pling
cen|tur|ial
cen|tur|ion
cen|tury
  cen|tur|ies
cep mushroom
ceph|al|ic
ceph|alin
ceph|al|isa|tion Br.
  var. of
  cephalization
ceph|al|iza|tion
Ceph|alo|chord|ata
ceph|alo|chord|ate
ceph|alo|met|ric
ceph|al|om|etry
ceph|alon
Cepha|lonia
ceph|alo|pod
Ceph|alo|poda
ceph|alo|sporin
ceph|alo|thorax
ce|pheid
Ce|pheus
'cept = except
cer|am|ic
cer|ami|cist
cer|am|ics
Ceram Sea
cer|as|tes
  pl. cer|as|tes
cer|as|tium
cera|tite
cerato|bran|chial
cera|top|sian

Cer|berus
cer|caria
  cer|cariae
cerc|lage
cerco|pith|ecine
cerco|pith|ecoid
cer|cus Zoology
  cerci
cere on bird's beak;
  cf. sear, seer, sere
cer|eal grain used
  for food; cf. serial
cere|bel|lar
cere|bel|lum
  cere|bel|lums or
  cere|bella
cere|bral
cere|bral|ly
cere|brate
  cere|brat|ing
cere|bra|tion
cere|bro|side
cere|bro|spinal
cere|bro|vas|cu|lar
cere|brum
  cere|bra
cere|cloth
Cere|dig|ion
cere|ment
cere|monial
cere|moni|al|ism
cere|moni|al|ist
cere|moni|al|ly
cere|moni|ous
cere|moni|ous|ly
cere|moni|ous|ness
cere|mony
  cere|monies
Ce|ren|kov, Pavel
  physicist; var. of
  Cherenkov
Ce|ren|kov radi-
  ation
cere|olo|gist
cere|ology
cere|op|sis goose
Ceres Roman god-
  dess; asteroid
cer|esin
cer|ise
cer|ium
cer|met

CERN = European Council (or Organization) for Nuclear Research
cero
ceroc
cero|plas|tic
cert
cer|tain
cer|tain|ly
cer|tainty
cer|tain|ties
Cert. Ed. = Certificate in Education
cer|tes
cer|ti|fi|able
cer|ti|fi|ably
cer|tifi|cate
cer|tifi|cat|ing
cer|ti|fi|ca|tion
cer|tify
cer|ti|fies
cer|ti|fied
cer|ti|fy|ing
cer|ti|or|ari
cer|ti|tude
ceru|lean
ceru|men
cer|use
Cer|van|tes, Mi|guel de writer
cer|velat
cer|vical
cervi|citis
cer|vid
cer|vix
cer|vi|ces
Ce|sar|ean US
Br. Caesarean
Ce|sare|witch horse race
ces|ium US
Br. caesium
České Budě|jo|vice
cess
ces|sa|tion
cess|er
ces|sion ceding; territory ceded
cess|pit
cess|pool
c'est la vie
Ces|toda
ces|tode

Ces|toidea var. of Cestoda
cestui que trust
Cet|acea
cet|acean
cet|aceous
ce|tane
cet|eris pari|bus
Cete|wayo var. of Cetshwayo
cetri|mide
Cetsh|wayo Zulu king
Cetti's warb|ler
Cetus
Ceuta
Cé|vennes
ce|vi|che
Cey|lon former name for Sri Lanka
Cey|lon|ese
Cé|zanne, Paul painter
cha var. of char
chaap
chaat Indian dish
chaba|zite
Chab|lis
pl. Chab|lis
Chab|rier, Em|man|uel composer
Chab|rol, Claude film director
cha|cha *Ind.* uncle
cha-cha
cha-chas
cha-cha'd or cha-chaed
cha-chaing dance
cha-cha-cha var. of cha-cha
cha|cha|laca
cha|cham var. of haham
chack
chacma baboon
Chaco plain; War
cha|conne
cha|cun à son goût
Chad country; Lake C.

chad waste from punched card
chad|dar var. of chador
Chad|ian
Chad|ic
cha|dor
Chad|wick, James physicist
chae|bol
pl. chae|bol or chae|bols
chaeta
chae|tae
chae|tog|nath
Chae|tog|natha
chafe
chaf|ing
chafer
chaff
chaf|fer
chaf|fer|er
chaf|finch
chaff|weed
chaffy
Cha|gall, Marc painter
Cha|gas' disease
Cha|gos Archipelago
chag|rin
chai
Chain, Ernst biochemist
chain
chaîné
chain|plate
chain|ring
chain|saw
chain-smoke
chain-smoking
chain-smoker
chair
chair|lady
chair|ladies
chair|lift
chair|man
chair|men
chair|man|ship
chair|per|son
chair|woman
chair|women
chaise
chaise longue
chaises longues

chaise lounge *US* var. of chaise longue
Chaka var. of Shaka
chakka *Ind.* wheel; *cf.* chukka
chakra
chal male Gypsy
chal hostel; var. of chawl
cha|laza
cha|lazae
cha|lazal
Chal|ce|don
Chal|ce|don|ian
chal|ce|don|ic
chal|ced|ony
chal|ced|onies
chal|cid
Chal|cis
Chal|co|lith|ic
chal|co|pyr|ite
Chal|dea
Chal|dean
Chal|dee
chalet
Cha|lia|pin, Fyo|dor singer
chal|ice goblet; *cf.* challis
chal|ico|there
chalk
chalk|board
chalk|face
chalk|hill blue
chalki|ness
chalk-stone
chalky
chalk|ier
chalki|est
chal|lah
chal|lahs or chal|lot or cha|loth
chal|lenge
chal|len|ging
chal|lenge|able
chal|len|ger
chal|len|ging|ly
chal|lis cloth; *cf.* chalice
cha|lone
chalu|meau
chalu|meaux
cha|lupa

cha¦lyb¦eate
Cham people
Cha¦mae¦leon constellation
cha¦mae¦leon animal; var. of **chameleon**
cha¦mae¦leon¦ic var. of **chameleonic**
chamae¦phyte
cham¦ber
Cham¦ber¦lain, Jo¦seph British statesman
Cham¦ber¦lain, Nev¦ille prime minister of Britain
Cham¦ber¦lain, Owen physicist
cham¦ber¦lain
cham¦ber¦lain¦ship
cham¦ber¦maid
Cham¦ber¦tin
Cham¦béry
cham¦bray cloth
cham¦bré brought to room temperature
cham¦cha
cha¦me¦leon
cha¦me¦leon¦ic
cha¦meli
cha¦metz
cham¦fer
cha¦mise
cha¦miso +s var. of **chamise**
cham¦ois
pl. cham¦ois
chamo¦mile var. of **camomile**
Cha¦mo¦nix
Cha¦morro
pl. Cha¦morro or Cha¦mor¦ros
Cham¦pagne region, France
cham¦pagne wine
Champagne-Ardenne
cham¦paign open country
cham¦pak
cham¦pers

cham¦per¦tous
cham¦perty
cham¦per¦ties
cham¦pignon
cham¦pion
cham¦pion¦ship
Cham¦plain, Lake
champ¦levé
Champs Ély¦sées
chana chickpeas
chance
chan¦cing
chan¦cel
chan¦cel¦lery
chan¦cel¦ler¦ies
chan¦cel¦lor
chan¦cel¦lor¦ship
chan¦cer
Chan¦cery UK court
chan¦cery
chan¦cer¦ies
Chan Chan
Chan-chiang var. of **Zhanjiang**
chan¦cily
chan¦ci¦ness
chan¦cre
chan¦croid
chancy
chan¦cier
chan¦ci¦est
chan¦de¦lier
chan¦delle
Chan¦di¦garh
Chand¦ler, Ray¦mond writer
chand¦ler
chand¦lery
chand¦ler¦ies
Chan¦dra¦gupta Maurya Indian emperor
Chan¦dra¦sekhar, Su¦brah¦man¦yan astronomer
Cha¦nel, Coco couturière and perfumer
Chan¦gan former name for **Xian**
Chang-chiakow var. of

Zhangjiakou
Chang¦chun
change
chan¦ging
change¦abil¦ity
change¦able
change¦able¦ness
change¦ably
change¦ful
change¦less
change¦less¦ness
change¦ling
change¦ment
change¦ment de pieds
change¦ments de pieds
change¦over
chan¦ger
change-ringer
change-ringing
change-up *n.*
chan¦ging room
Chang Jiang another name for **Yangtze**
Chang¦sha
Cha¦nia
channa var. of **chana**
chan¦nel
chan¦nelled *Br.*
chan¦neled *US*
chan¦nel¦ling *Br.*
chan¦nel¦ing *US*
chan¦nel¦er *US Br.* **channeller**
channel-graze
channel-grazing
channel-grazer
channel-hop
channel-hopped
channel-hopping
channel-hopper
chan¦nel¦ise *Br.* var. of **channelize**
chan¦nel¦ize
chan¦nel¦iz¦ing
chan¦nel¦ler *Br. US* **channeler**
channel-surf
chan¦son
chan¦son de geste
chant¦er

chan¦ter¦elle
chant¦euse
chan¦tey *US Br.* **shanty**
chan¦ti¦cleer
Chan¦tilly
chan¦try
chan¦tries
chanty var. of **shanty**
Cha¦nuk¦kah var. of **Hanukkah**
cha¦olo¦gist
cha¦ol¦ogy
Chao Phraya
Chaos *Greek Mythology*
chaos
cha¦ot¦ic
cha¦ot¦ic¦al¦ly
chap
chapped
chap¦ping
chapa¦rajos
chapa¦rejos var. of **chaparajos**
chap¦ar¦ral
cha¦patti
chap¦book
chape
chap¦eau
chap¦eaux
chapeau-bras
chapeaux-bras
chapel cf. **chappal**
chap¦el¦ry
chap¦el¦ries
chap¦eron var. of **chaperone**
chap¦eron¦age
chap¦er¦one
chap¦eron¦ing
chap¦er¦onin
chap-fallen
chap¦lain
chap¦lain¦cy
chap¦lain¦cies
chap¦let
chap¦let¦ed
Chap¦lin, Char¦lie actor
Chap¦lin¦esque
Chap¦man, George writer

chap|man
chap|men
chap|pal shoe
Chap|pa|quid|dick
Chap|pell, Greg
  cricketer
chap|pie
cha|prasi
chap|stick
  trademark
chap|tal|isa|tion *Br.*
  var. of
  chaptalization
chap|tal|ise *Br.* var.
  of chaptalize
chap|tal|iza|tion
chap|tal|ize
  chap|tal|iz|ing
chap|ter
char
  charred
  char|ring
  burn; charwoman;
  tea
char fish; var. of
  charr
chara|banc
chara|cin
char|ac|ter
char|ac|ter|ful
char|ac|ter|isa|tion
  Br. var. of
  characterization
char|ac|ter|ise *Br.*
  var. of characterize
char|ac|ter|is|tic
char|ac|ter|is|tic|
    al|ly
char|ac|ter|iza|tion
char|ac|ter|ize
  char|ac|ter|iz|ing
char|ac|ter|less
cha|rade
cha|rango +s
charas
char|broil
char|coal
char|cu|terie
chard vegetable
Char|don|nay
cha|ren|tais
Cha|rente
charge
  char|ging

chargé
charge|able
charge|back
charge-cap
  charge-capped
  charge-capping
chargé d'af|faires
  chargés d'af|faires
charge|hand
char|ger
char|grill
chari|ly
cha|riot
cha|riot|eer
char|ism
cha|risma
  cha|ris|mata
cha|ris|mat|ic
cha|ris|mat|ic|al|ly
char|it|able
char|it|ably
char|ity
  char|ities
cha|ri|vari
charka var. of
  charkha
char|kha
char|lady
  char|ladies
char|la|tan
char|la|tan|ism
char|la|tan|ry
char|la|tan|ries
Charle|magne Holy
  Roman Emperor
Char|lene
Charle|roi
Charles
Charles' Law
Charles Mar|tel
  Frankish ruler
Charles's Law var.
  of Charles' Law
Charles's Wain
Charles|ton cities,
  US
charles|ton dance
char|ley horse
Char|lie
char|lie fool
char|lock
Char|lotte city, US;
  name

char|lotte dessert
Char|lotte Ama|lie
*Char|lotte
  Dun|das*
char|lotte russe
  char|lottes russes
Char|lotte|town
Charl|ton, Bobby
  and **Jack**
  footballers
Char|maine
charm|er
charm|euse
Char|mian
charm|ing
charm|ing|ly
charm|less
charm|less|ly
charm|less|ness
char|mo|nium
  char|mo|nia
char|nel
char|nel house
Cha|ro|lais
  pl. Cha|ro|lais
Cha|rol|lais var. of
  Charolais
Cha|ron
Charo|phyta
char|ophyte
char|poy
charr fish
charro +s
chart|bust|er
char|ter
char|ter|er
Chart|ism
Chart|ist
Char|tres
char|treuse
chart topper
chart-topping
char|woman
  char|women
chary
  chari|er
  chari|est
Cha|ryb|dis
chase
  chas|ing
chaser
Cha|sid var. of
  Hasid

Cha|sid|ic var. of
  Hasidic
Cha|sid|ism var. of
  Hasidism
chasm
chasse liqueur
chassé
  chas|sés
  chas|séd
  chas|sé|ing
  step
Chas|se|las
chas|seur
Chas|sid var. of
  Hasid
Chas|sid|ic var. of
  Hasidic
Chas|sid|ism var. of
  Hasidism
chas|sis
  pl. chas|sis
chaste cf. chased
chaste|ly
chas|ten
chas|ten|er
chaste|ness
chaste tree
chas|tise
  chas|tis|ing
chas|tise|ment
chas|tiser
chas|tity
chas|uble
chat
  chat|ted
  chat|ting
chat|eau
  chat|eaux or
  chat|eaus
  French château,
  châteaux
chat|eau|bri|and
chat|elain
chat|elaine
Chat|ham
chat|line
cha|toy|ance
cha|toy|ancy
cha|toy|ant
chat|tel
chat|ter
chat|ter|bot
chat|ter|box
chat|ter|er

Chat|ter|ton,
  Thomas poet
chat|tery
chat|tl|ly
chat|ti|ness
chatty
  chat|tier
  chat|ti|est
chat-up n. & mod.
Chat|win, Bruce
  writer
Chau|cer, Geof|frey
  writer
Chau|cer|ian
chaud|huri
chauf|feur
chauf|feuse
chaul|moo|gra
Chaumes
chausses
chau|tau|qua
chau|vin|ism
chau|vin|ist
chau|vin|is|tic
chau|vin|is|tic|al|ly
chav
Cha|vín
chaw chew
cha|wal
chawl
chay|ote
cheap cf. cheep
cheap|en
cheapie
cheap|ish
cheap|jack
cheap|ly
cheap|ness
cheapo +s
Cheap|side
cheap|skate
cheat|er cf. cheetah
Che|chen
Che|che|nia var. of
  Chechnya
Chech|nya
check cf. cheque
check US Banking
  Br. cheque
check|able
check|book US
  Br. chequebook
check|box

check|er person or
  thing that checks;
  cashier; cf. chequer
checker US
  pattern
  Br. chequer
checker|berry
checker|berries
checker|board US
  Br. chequerboard
check|ers US
  game
checker|spot
check-in n. & mod.
check|ing ac|count
  US
  Canadian
  chequing account
check|list
check|mate
  check|mat|ing
check|out
check|point
check|room
check-up n.
Ched|dar village,
  England; cheese
cheder
  ched|ar|im or
  ched|ers
  Jewish school
chee|chako +s
chee-chee var. of
  chhi-chhi
cheek|bone
cheek|ily
cheeki|ness
cheek|piece
cheeky
  cheek|ier
  cheeki|est
cheep bird's cry; cf.
  cheap
cheer cf. chir
cheer|ful
cheer|ful|ly
cheer|ful|ness
cheer|ily
cheeri|ness
cheerio +s
cheer|lead|er
cheer|leading
cheer|less
cheer|less|ly

cheer|less|ness
cheers
cheery
  cheer|ier
  cheeri|est
cheese
  chees|ing
cheese|board
cheese|bur|ger
cheese|cake
cheese|cloth
cheese-cutter
cheesed
cheese|mon|ger
cheese-paring
cheese-skipper
cheese|steak
cheese|wood
chees|ily
cheesi|ness
cheesy
  chees|ier
  cheesi|est
chee|tah cf. cheater
chef
chef d'école
  chefs d'école
chef-d'œuvre
  chefs-d'œuvre
Che|foo former
  name for Yantai
Cheka Soviet
  organization
Chek|hov, Anton
  writer
Chek|hov|ian
Che|kiang var. of
  Zhejiang
chela
  che|lae
  claw
chela guru's pupil
che|late
  che|lat|ing
che|la|tion
che|la|tor
che|li|cera
  che|li|cerae
che|li|ceral
Che|li|cer|ata
che|li|cer|ate
Chel|lean
Chelms|ford
Che|lo|nia

che|lo|nian
Chel|sea
Chel|ten|ham
chem|ical
chem|ical|ly
chemi|lu|min|
    es|cence
chemi|lu|min|
    es|cent
che|min de fer
che|mise
che|mis|ette
chemi|sorbed
chemi|sorp|tion
chem|ist
chem|is|try
  chem|is|tries
Chem|nitz
chemo chemother-
  apy
chemo|attract|ant
chemo|auto|troph
chemo|auto|
    troph|ic
chemo|autot|rophy
chemo|
    autot|ro|phies
chemo|prophy|
    lac|tic
chemo|prophy|
    laxis
chemo|recep|tion
chemo|recep|tor
chemo|stat
chemo|syn|thesis
chemo|syn|thet|ic
chemo|tac|tic
chemo|taxis
chemo|ther|ap|ist
chemo|ther|apy
chem|paka var. of
  champak
chem|ur|gic
chem|urgy
Che|nab
che|nar var. of
  chinar
Chen-chiang var. of
  Zhenjiang
Cheng|chow var. of
  Zhenzhou
Chengdu
che|nille

Che|nin blanc
Chen|nai
cheong|sam
Che|ops
cheque *Br. Banking*
  US check
cheque|book *Br.*
  US checkbook
chequer *Br.*
  US checker
chequer|board *Br.*
  US checkerboard
Che|quers home of
  British prime
  minister
che|quers *Br.*
  in 'Chinese
  chequers'
  US checkers
chequing ac|count
  Canadian
  US checking
  account
Cher river, France
Cher singer and
  actress
Cher|bourg
Che|re|mis
Che|ren|kov, Pavel
  physicist
Che|ren|kov radi-
  ation; var. of
  Cerenkov
Che|re|po|vets
Che|rida
cheri|moya
cher|ish
Cher|kasy
Cher|kess
  another name for
  Circassian
Cher|nenko,
  Kon|stan|tin Soviet
  president
Cher|no|byl
cher|no|zem
Chero|kee
che|root
cherry
  cher|ries
cherry-pick
cherry pick|er
cherry|wood
Cher|son|ese

chert
cherty
cherub
  cher|ubs or
  cher|ubim
cher|ub|ic
cher|ub|ic|al|ly
Che|ru|bini, Luigi
  composer
cher|vil
cher|vo|nets
  cher|vontsy
Cher|well, Lord
  physicist
Chesa|peake Bay
Chesh|ire
Chesh|ire,
  Leon|ard airman
  and philanthropist
Chesil Bank/
  Beach
chess|board
chess|man
  chess|men
Ches|ter
Ches|ter|field town
ches|ter|field sofa
Ches|ter|ton, G. K.
  writer
chest|ily
chesti|ness
chest|nut
chesty
  chest|ier
  chesti|est
Ches|van var. of
  Hesvan
Chet|nik
chet|rum
Chetu|mal
che|val glass
Che|va|lier,
  Maur|ice French
  singer and actor
chev|alier
che|val mir|ror
che|vet
Chev|iot sheep;
  Hills
chev|iot wool
chèvre cheese
chev|ron
chev|ro|tain

Chevvy var. of
  Chevy
Chevy +s Chevrolet
  car
chevy var. of chivvy
chew|able
chew|er
chewi|ness
chew|ing gum
chew stick plant
chewy
  chew|ier
  chewi|est
Chey|enne
Cheyne–Stokes
chez
chhaap var. of
  chaap
Chhat|tis|garh
chhi-chhi *Ind.*
  expression of
  disgust; cf. chichi
chi Greek letter; life
  force
Chian from Chios
Chiang Kai-shek
  Chinese statesman
Chiang|mai
Chia|nina
Chi|anti
Chi|apas
chiaro|scuro +s
chi|asma
  chi|as|mata
chi|as|mus
  chi|asmi
chi|as|tic
chi|as|to|lite
chib
  chibbed
  chib|bing
Chib|cha
Chib|chan
chi|bouk
chic
  chic|er
  chic|est
  stylish
Chi|cago
Chi|cago|an
Chi|cana
chi|cane
  chi|can|ing

chi|can|ery
chi|can|er|ies
Chi|cano +s
chi|cha
chi|char|ron
  chi|char|ron|es
Chi|chén Itzá
Chich|es|ter
Chich|es|ter,
  Fran|cis yachtsman
Chi|chewa
chi|chi pretentious;
  cf. chhi-chhi
chi|chi breast
Chi|chi|mec
chick
chicka|biddy
  chicka|biddies
chicka|dee
chicka|ree
Chicka|saw
chick|en cf. chikan
chicken|pox
chicken|shit
chick|pea
chick|weed
chi|cle chewing-gum
  ingredient
chic|ly stylishly
chic|ness
chic|ory
  chic|or|ies
chide
chid|ing
  chid *archaic*
  chid|den *archaic*
chider
chid|ing|ly
chief
chief|dom
chief|ly
chief|tain
chief|tain|cy
  chief|tain|cies
chief|tain|ship
chiff|chaff
chif|fon
chif|fon|ade
chif|fon|ier
chiffo|robe
chig|ger
chi|gnon
chigoe

Chihli, Gulf of
  another name for
  Bo Hai
Chi|hua|hua state
  and city, Mexico
chi|hua|hua dog
chikan embroidery
chi|kun|gunya
chil|blain
child
  chil|dren
child|bear¦ing
child|bed
child|birth
child|care
Childe in 'Childe
  Harold' etc.
Chil¦der|mas
Chil|ders, Er|skine
  Irish nationalist
child|hood
child|ish
child|ish¦ly
child¦ish|ness
child|less
child|less|ness
child|like
child|mind¦er
child-minding
child|proof
chil|dren
Chile country
chile food; var. of
  chilli; cf. **chilly**
Chil|ean
Chile pine
chile rel|leno
  chiles rel|lenos
chili US
  food
  Br. **chilli**
chili|arch +s
chili|asm
chili|ast
chili|as¦tic
chili con carne US
  Br. **chilli con carne**
chili dog
chill
chill-cast
chill¦er
chilli Br.
  chil|lies

US **chili**. food; cf.
  chilly
chilli con carne Br.
  US **chili con carne**
chil|li|ness
chill|ing¦ly
chill-out adj.
chill|some
chil|lum
chilly
  chill|ier
  chilli|est
  cold; cf. **chilli**
chilo|pod
Chilo|poda
Chil|tern Hills;
  Hundreds
Chi|luba
chi|maera var. of
  chimera
chi|maer¦ic var. of
  chimeric
chime
  chim¦ing
chim|enea
chimer
chi|mera
chi|mer¦ic
chi|mer¦ic¦al
chimi|changa
chim|ney
chimo|nan|thus
chim¦pan|zee
Chimu
Chin people
Chin Chinese
  dynasty; var. of **Jin**
Chin Hills, Burma
Ch'in Chinese
  dynasty; var. of **Qin**
China country
china ceramic ware
china|berry
  china|berries
china blue n.
china-blue mod.
china clay
china|graph
China|man
  China|men
  offensive when used
  of a person
chinar
China rose

china stone
China syn|drome
China|town
china|ware
chinch
chin|cher¦in|chee
chin|chilla
chin-chin
Chin|dit
Chin|dwin
chine
  chin¦ing
Chin|ese
Ching in 'I Ching'
Ch'ing Chinese
  dynasty; var. of
  Qing
Chink offensive
  Chinese
chinka|pin var. of
  chinquapin
chin|kara
Chin|kiang var. of
  Zhenjiang
Chinky
  Chink|ies
  offensive
chin|less
chino +s
chi|nois|erie
Chi|nook people
chi|nook wind;
  salmon
chin|qua¦pin
chin|strap
chintz
chintzi|ness
chintzy
  chintz|ier
  chintzi|est
chin-up n.
chin|wag
  chin|wagged
  chin|wag|ging
chi¦ono|doxa
Chios Greek island
chip
  chipped
  chip|ping
chip|board
Chipe|wyan
chip|maker
chip|munk
chipo|lata

chi|potle
Chip|pen|dale,
  Thomas furniture-
  maker; style of
  furniture
chip|per
Chip|pewa
chip|pie var. of
  chippy
chip|ping
chippy
  chip|pies
chip|set
Chi¦rac, Jacques
  president of France
chir|al
chir¦al|ity
chi-rho +s
Chi¦rico, Gior|gio
  de painter
chiri|moya var. of
  cherimoya
chiro|graph¦ic
chir|og|raphy
chiro|mancy
Chiron
chir|ono|mid
chir|opo¦dist
chir|opody
chiro|prac¦tic
chiro|prac¦tor
Chir|optera
chir|op¦ter¦an
chir|op¦ter|ous
chirp
chirp¦er
chirp|ily
chirpi|ness
chirpy
  chirp|ier
  chirpi|est
chirr
chir|rup
  chir|ruped
  chir|rup|ing
chir|rupy
chiru
chisel
  chis|elled Br.
  chis|eled US
  chis¦el|ling Br.
  chis¦el|ing US
chis¦el|er US
chis¦el|ler Br.

Chişi|nă999u

chi-square

Chis|wick

chit
  chit|ted
  chit|ting
chi|tal
chi|tar|rone
  chi|tar|rones or
  chi|tar|roni
chit-chat
  chit-chatted
  chit-chatting
chi|tin
chi|tin|ous
chi|ton
Chit|ta|gong
chit|ter
chit|ter|ling
chitty
  chit|ties
chiv|al|ric
chiv|al|rous
chiv|al|rous|ly
chiv|alry
  chiv|al|ries
chivvy
  chiv|vies
  chiv|vied
  chivvy|ing
chivy var. of chivvy
Chladni patterns/
  figures
chla|mydia
  chla|mydiae
chla|myd|ial
chlamy|do|mo|nas
chlamy|do|spore
chlamys
chlo|asma
chlor|acne
chlor|al
chlor|am|bu|cil
chlor|amine
chlor|am|pheni|col
chlor|ate
chlor|dane
chlor|
      di|az|epox|ide
chlor|ella
chlor|hexi|dine
chlor|ide
chlor|in|ate
  chlor|in|at|ing

chlor|in|ation
chlor|in|ator
chlor|ine
chlor|ite
chlor|it|ic
chlor|it|iza|tion
chlor|it|oid
chloro|dyne
chloro|fluoro|
          car|bon
chloro|form
chloro|phyll
chloro|phyl|lous
Chloro|phyta
chloro|phyte
chloro|plast
chloro|prene
chloro|quine
chlor|osis
  chlor|oses
chloro|thia|zide
chlor|ot|ic
chlor|pro|maz|ine
chlor|tetra|cyc|line
cho|ano|cyte
choc chocolate; cf.
  chock
choc|ahol|ic var. of
  chocoholic
choccy
  choc|cies
chocho +s
chock wedge; cf.
  choc
chocka
chock-a-block
chocker var. of
  chocka
chock|ers
chock-full
chock|stone
choco|hol|ic
choc|olate
choc|olatey
choc|olat|ier
choc|olaty var. of
  chocolatey
Choc|taw
choice
  choicer
  choicest
choil
choir cf. quire

choir|boy
choir|girl
choir|man
  choir|men
choir|master
choi|sya
choke
  chok|ing
choke|berry
  choke|berries
choke-damp
choke|hold
choker
chokey prison; cf.
  choky
cho|ki|dar var. of
  chowkidar
choko +s fruit
cho|kra
Chokwe
choky
  choki|er
  choki|est
choky
  chokies
  prison; var. of
  chokey
chola
chol|an|gio|gram
chol|an|gi|og|raphy
chol|an|gitis
chole|cal|cif|erol
chole|cyst|ec|tomy
  chole|cyst|
        ec|to|mies
chole|cyst|itis
chole|cyst|og|raphy
chole|cysto|kinin
chole|lith|ia|sis
chol|ent
choler anger; bile
chol|era
chol|er|aic
chol|er|ic
chol|er|ic|al|ly
chol|es|terol
choli bodice; cf.
  coaly, coley, coly,
  E. coli
cho|li|amb
cho|li|am|bic
cho|lic
cho|line
cho|lin|er|gic

cho|lin|ester|ase
cholla
cholo +s
cho|metz var. of
  chametz
Chom|skian var. of
  Chomskyan
Chom|sky, Noam
  linguist
Chom|skyan
Chon|drich|thyes
chon|drite
chon|drit|ic
chon|dro|cyte
chon|dro|itin
chond|rule
Chong|qing
choo-choo +s
choof
chook
chookie
choose
  chose
  choos|ing
  chosen
chooser
choosi|ness
choosy
  choos|ier
  choosi|est
chop
  chopped
  chop|ping
chop-chop
chop-fallen var. of
  chap-fallen
chop|house
Cho|pin, Fréd|éric
  composer
chop|per
chop|pily
chop|pi|ness
choppy
  chop|pier
  chop|pi|est
chop|socky
chop|stick
chop suey
choral of a choir or
  chorus
chor|ale hymn tune;
  choir; cf. corral
chor|al|ly

chord in music or
  maths; cf. cord
chord|al cf. caudal
Chord|ata
chord|ate animal;
  cf. caudate,
  cordate
chord line
chordo|phone
chordo|tonal
chore cf. chaw
cho|rea
choreo|graph
chore|og|raph|er
  cf. chorographer
choreo|graph|ic
  cf. chorographic
choreo|graph|ic|
          al|ly
chore|og|raphy
chore|og|raph|ies
  dance; cf.
  chorography
chore|olo|gist
chore|ol|ogy
chori|am|bic
chori|am|bus
chori|ambi
chor|ic
chor|ine
chorio|allan|toic
chorio|car|cin|oma
chorio|car|cin|
            omas
  or chorio|
        car|cin|omata
chor|ion
chori|on|ic
chor|is|ter
cho|rizo +s
chor|og|raph|er cf.
  choreographer
choro|graph|ic cf.
  choreographic
chor|og|raphy
  description and
  mapping of
  regions; cf.
  choreography
chor|oid
chor|oid|al
choro|pleth
chor|ten

chor|tle
chort|ling
chorus
chose
chosen
chota
Chou var. of Zhou
chou|croute
Chou En-lai var. of
  Zhou Enlai
chough bird; cf.
  chuff
choux pastry; bun
chow food; dog; cf.
  ciao
chow chow
chow|der
chow|der|head
chow|der|head|ed
chow|hound
chowk
chowki
chow|ki|dar
chow mein
chres|tom|athy
chres|tom|athies
Chrétien, Jean
  prime minister of
  Canada
Chré|tien de
  Troyes poet
Chrimbo +s
chrism oil
chrisom robe
chrisom-cloth
Chris|sake
Chris|sakes
Chris|sie Christmas
Chrissy var. of
  Chrissie
Christ
Chris|ta|bel
Christa|delph|ian
Christ|church
chris|ten
Chris|ten|dom
chris|ten|er
Christ|er
Christ|hood
Chris|tian
Chris|tian,
  Fletch|er Bounty
  mutineer

Chris|ti|ana
Chris|ti|ania former
  name of Oslo
Chris|tian|isa|tion
  Br. var. of
  Christianization
Chris|tian|ise Br.
  var. of Christianize
Chris|tian|ity
Chris|tian|iza|tion
Chris|tian|ize
  Chris|tian|iz|ing
Chris|tian|ly
Chris|tie, Aga|tha
  writer
Chris|tie, Lin|ford
  sprinter
chris|tie Skiing
Chris|tina
Chris|tine
Christ|ingle
Christ|like
Christ|ly
Christ|mas
Christ|massy
Christo|cen|tric
Christ|ol|atry
Christo|logic|al
Christo|logic|al|ly
Christ|ology
Christ|oph|any
christo|phene var.
  of christophine
Chris|to|pher
  name; herb
chris|to|phine
chroma
chro|maf|fin
chroma|key
chro|mate
chro|mat|ic
chro|mat|ic|al|ly
chro|mati|cism
chro|ma|ti|city
chro|ma|tid
chro|ma|tin
chro|mato|gram
chro|mato|graph
chro|ma|to|
        graph|ic
chro|ma|tog|raphy
chro|ma|top|sia

chrome
chrom|ing
chrome-moly US
  Br. chromoly
chro|mic
chro|mide
chro|min|ance
chro|mite
chro|mium
chromo +s
chromo|dynam|ics
chromo|gen
chromo|gen|ic
chromo|litho|
            graph
chromo|
  lith|og|raph|er
chromo|litho|
            graph|ic
chromo|
  lith|og|raphy
chro|moly
  US chrome-moly
chromo|phore
chromo|phor|ic
chromo|plast
chromo|som|al
chromo|some
chromo|sphere
chromo|spher|ic
chro|mous
chron|ic
chron|ic|al|ly
chron|icity
chron|icle
chron|ic|ling
chron|ic|ler
chrono|biolo|gist
chrono|biol|ogy
chrono|graph
chrono|graph|ic
chrono|logic|al
chrono|logic|al|ly
chron|olo|gist
chron|ology
  chron|olo|gies
chron|om|eter
chrono|met|ric
chron|om|etry
chrono|strati|
            graph|ic
chrono|
  stra|tig|raphy

chrono|ther|apy
chrys|alid
chrys|alis
chrys|an|the|mum
chrys|ele|phant|ine
chryso|beryl
chryso|colla
chryso|lite
chryso|mel|id
chryso|prase
Chrys|os|tom, St
John
chryso|tile
Chrys|tal
chthon|ian
chthon|ic
chub fish
Chubb lock
trademark
chub|bily
chub|bi|ness
chubby
chub|bier
chub|bi|est
Chubu
chuck-a-luck
chuck|er cf. chakka,
chukka
chucker-out
chucker-outs or
chuckers-out
chuck|hole
chuckle
chuck|ling
chuckle|head
chuckle|head|ed
chuck|ler
chuck|walla
chuck-will's-widow
chud|dar var. of
chador
chud|dies
chuddy
chufa
chuff cf. chough
chug
chugged
chug|ging
chug|alug
chug|alugged
chug|alug|ging
chug|ger
chu|kar partridge

Chuk|chi
chukka in polo; cf.
chakka
chuk|ker var. of
chukka
chu|kor var. of
chukar
chum
chummed
chum|ming
Chu|mash
chum|ble
chum|bling
chum|mily
chum|mi|ness
chummy
chum|mier
chum|mi|est
Chün stoneware
chun|der
Chung|king var. of
Chongqing
Chung-shan var. of
Zhongshan
chunk|ily
chun|ki|ness
chunky
chunk|ier
chunk|iest
Chun|nel
chunni
chun|ter
chupa|cabra
chu|patty var. of
chapatti
chuppa var. of
chuppah
chup|pah
chup|pot
Chu|qui|saca
former name for
Sucre
Church body of
Christians
church building;
service; take to
church
church|goer
church|going
Church|ill, Caryl
writer
Church|ill,
Win|ston prime
minister of Britain
Church|ill|ian

churchi|ness
church|key bottle
and can opener
church|man
church|men
church|war|den
church|woman
church|women
churchy
church|ier
churchi|est
church|yard
churi|dar var. of
churidars
churi|dars
chur|inga
churl
churl|ish
churl|ish|ly
churl|ish|ness
churr var. of chirr
chur|ras|caria
chur|rasco +s
Chur|ri|guer|esque
chute cf. shoot
chut|ist
chut|ney
chutty var. of
chuddy
chutz|pah
Chu|vash
Chu|vashia
chyle
chylo|micron
chyl|ous
chyme *Physiology*
chymo|tryp|sin
chym|ous
chy|pre
chy|ron *trademark*
cia|batta
cia|bat|tas
ciao hallo; goodbye
Cib|ber, Col|ley
actor
ci|bor|ium
ci|boria
ci|cada
cica|trice var. of
cicatrix
cica|tri|cial
cica|trisa|tion *Br.*
var. of **cicatrization**

cica|trise *Br.* var. of
cicatrize
cica|trix
cica|tri|ces
cica|triza|tion
cica|trize
cica|triz|ing
ci|cely
ci|cel|lies
Ci|cero, Mar|cus
Tul|lius Roman
statesman
ci|cer|one
ci|cer|oni
Ci|cero|nian
cich|lid
ci|cis|beo
ci|cis|bei or
ci|cis|beos
Cid, El soldier
cider
ci-devant
cigar
cig|aret *US* var. of
cigarette
cig|ar|ette
cig|ar|illo +s
ciggy
cig|gies
cigarette
ci|gua|tera
cil|an|tro
cilia pl. of cilium
cil|iary
cili|ate
cili|ated
cili|ation
cil|ice
Cil|icia in Asia
Minor
Cil|ician
cil|ium
cilia
cill var. of sill
cim|ba|lom
ci|meti|dine
Cim|mer|ian
cinch
cin|chona
cin|chon|ine
Cin|cin|nati
cinc|ture
cinc|tur|ing
cin|der

Cin|der|ella
cin|dery
cine camera
cine|ast var. of
  cineaste
cine|aste
  French **cinéaste**
cin|ema
cinema-goer
cinema-going
Cinema|Scope
  trademark
cine|ma|theque
cine|mat|ic
cine|mat|ic|al|ly
cine|mato|graph
cine|ma|
    tog|raph|er
cine|mato|graph|ic
cine|mato|
   graph|ic|al|ly
cine|ma|tog|raphy
cinéma-vérité
cine|phile
cine|plex *trademark*
cin|er|aria plant
cin|er|ar|ium place
  for cinerary urns
cin|er|ary
cin|er|eous
Cin|gal|ese
  archaic var. of
  Sinhalese
cin|gu|late
cin|gu|lum
cin|gula
cin|na|bar
cin|na|mon
cinq var. of **cinque**
cinque five on dice
cin|que|cento
cinque|foil
Cinque Ports
Cin|tra var. of
  Sintra
ci|pher
cipo|lin
circa
cir|ca|dian
Cir|cas|sian
Circe enchantress
Cir|ce|an
cir|cin|ate

Cir|ci|nus
cir|cle
circ|ling
circ|let
cir|clip
circs circumstances;
  cf. **cirque**
cir|cuit
circuit-breaker
cir|cu|it|ous
cir|cu|it|ous|ly
cir|cu|it|ous|ness
cir|cuit|ry
cir|cuit|ries
cir|cu|lar
cir|cu|lar|isa|tion
  Br. var. of
  circularization
cir|cu|lar|ise *Br.*
  var. of **circularize**
cir|cu|lar|ity
cir|cu|lar|ities
cir|cu|lar|iza|tion
cir|cu|lar|ize
cir|cu|lar|iz|ing
cir|cu|lar|ly
cir|cu|late
cir|cu|lat|ing
cir|cu|la|tion
cir|cu|la|tive
cir|cu|la|tor
cir|cu|la|tory
cir|cum|am|bi|ence
cir|cum|am|bi|ent
cir|cum|am|bu|late
cir|cum|am|bu|
    lat|ing
cir|cum|am|bu|
    la|tion
cir|cum|am|bu|
    la|tory
cir|cum|circle
cir|cum|cise
cir|cum|cis|ing
cir|cum|ci|sion
cir|cum|fer|ence
cir|cum|fer|en|tial
cir|cum|fer|en|
    tial|ly
cir|cum|flex
cir|cum|fuse
cir|cum|fus|ing
cir|cum|ja|cent
cir|cum|lo|cu|tion

cir|cum|lo|cu|
    tion|al
cir|cum|lo|cu|
    tion|ary
cir|cum|lo|cu|tion|
    ist
cir|cum|lo|cu|tory
cir|cum|lunar
cir|cum|navi|gate
cir|cum|navi|
    gat|ing
cir|cum|navi|
    ga|tion
cir|cum|navi|ga|tor
cir|cum|po|lar
cir|cum|scrib|able
cir|cum|scribe
cir|cum|scrib|ing
cir|cum|scriber
cir|cum|scrip|tion
cir|cum|solar
cir|cum|spect
cir|cum|spec|tion
cir|cum|spect|ly
cir|cum|stance
cir|cum|stanced
cir|cum|stan|tial
cir|cum|stan|ti|al|
    ity
cir|cum|
    stan|ti|al|ly
cir|cum|ter|res|
    trial
cir|cum|val|late
cir|cum|val|lat|ing
cir|cum|vent
cir|cum|ven|tion
cir|cum|vo|lu|tion
cir|cus cf. cercus
ciré
Ciren|ces|ter
cire per|due
cirl bunting
cirque hollow; cf.
  circs
cir|rho|sis
cir|rho|ses
  of liver; cf. **sorosis**
cir|rhot|ic
cirri
cirri|ped
cirri|pede
Cirri|pedia
cirro|cumu|lus

cirro|stra|tus
cir|rous of cirrus; cf.
  scirrhous
cir|rus
  cirri
  cloud; cf. **scirrhus**
cis *Chemistry;* cf. **sis**
cis|alpine
cis|at|lan|tic
cisco
cis|coes
Cis|kei
cis|lu|nar
Cis|neros,
  Fran|cisco de
  Spanish statesman
cis|platin
cis|pon|tine
cis|si|fied *Br.* var. of
  sissified
cis|sing of paint
cis|sus
cissy var. of **sissy**
cissy|ish var. of
  sissyish
cist coffin; burial
  chamber; box for
  sacred utensils; cf.
  cyst
Cis|ter|cian
cis|tern
cis|ti|cola
cis|tron
cis|tus
cit|able
cita|del
cit|ation
cite
  cit|ing
  quote; cf. **sight,**
  site
CITES = Conven-
  tion on Inter-
  national Trade in
  Endangered Species
cit|ies
cit|ify
citi|fies
citi|fied
citi|fy|ing
citi|zen
citi|zen|hood

citi|zen|ry
citi|zen|ries
Citi|zens' Ad|vice
Bur|eau
Citi|zens' Ad|vice
Bur|eaux
citi|zen's ar|rest
citi|zens' ar|rests
Citi|zens' Band
Citi|zens' Char|ter
Citi|zens'
Char|ters
citi|zen|ship
Cit|lal|té|petl
cit|ole
cit|ral
cit|rate
cit|ric
citri|cul|ture
cit|ril
cit|rin substance in
fruit
cit|rine mineral
cit|ron
cit|ron|ella
cit|rous relating to
citrus trees or fruit
cit|rus tree; fruit
cit|rusy
cit|tern
city
cit|ies
city|scape
city|ward
city|wards
city|wide
Ciu|dad Bolí|var
Ciu|dad Tru|jillo
Ciu|dad Vic|toria
civet
civic
civ|ic|al|ly
civ|ics
civil
ci|vil|ian
ci|vil|ian|isa|tion
Br. var. of
civilianization
ci|vil|ian|ise Br. var.
of civilianize
ci|vil|ian|iza|tion
ci|vil|ian|ize
ci|vil|ian|iz|ing

civ|il|is|able Br. var.
of civilizable
civ|il|isa|tion Br.
var. of civilization
civ|il|ise Br. var. of
civilize
civ|il|iser Br. var. of
civilizer
ci|vil|ity
ci|vil|ities
civ|il|iz|able
civ|il|iza|tion
civ|il|ize
civ|il|iz|ing
civ|il|izer
civ|il|ly
civvy
clv|vies
Civvy Street
clab|ber
clachan
clack sound;
chatter; cf. claque
clack|er
clacket
Clack|man|nan|
shire
Clac|ton|ian
clad
clad|ded
clad|ding
Clad|dagh ring
clad|ding
clade
clad|ism
cla|dis|tic
cla|dis|tics
Cla|docera
cla|docer|an
clad|ode
clado|gen|esis
clado|gen|et|ic
clado|gram
cla|fou|tis
claggy
clag|gier
clag|gi|est
claim
claim|able
claim|ant cf.
clamant
claim|er
clair|audi|ence
clair|audi|ent

clair-de-lune
clair|voy|ance
clair|voy|ant
clam
clammed
clam|ming
cla|mant insistent;
cf. claimant
clam|bake
clam|ber
clam|diggers trou-
sers
clam|mily
clam|mi|ness
clammy
clam|mier
clam|mi|est
clamor US
Br. clamour
clam|or|ous
clam|or|ous|ly
clam|or|ous|ness
clam|our Br.
US clamor
clamp|down
clamp|er
clam|shell
clan|des|tine
clan|des|tine|ly
clan|des|tin|ity
clang|er mistake
clangor US
Br. clangour;
clanging; uproar
clang|or|ous
clang|our Br.
US clangor;
clanging; uproar;
cf. clanger
clan|nish
clan|nish|ness
clan|ship
clans|man
clans|men
cf. Klansman
clans|woman
clans|women
cf. Klanswoman
clap
clapped
clap|ping
clap|board
clapped-out
clap|per

clap|per|board
Clap|ton, Eric
guitarist
clap|trap
claque supporters;
cf. clack
cla|queur
clara|bella
Clare county,
Republic of Ireland
Clare, St
Clare, John poet
Clar|ence
clar|ence carriage
Clar|en|ceux
Clar|en|don, Earl
of statesman and
historian
claret
Clar|ice
clari|fi|ca|tion
clari|fi|ca|tory
clari|fier
clar|ify
clari|fies
clari|fied
clari|fy|ing
clari|net
clari|net|ist US
clari|net|tist Br.
clar|ion
Clar|issa
clar|ity
clar|ities
Clark, Helen prime
minister of New
Zealand
Clark, Wil|liam
explorer
Clarke, Ar|thur C.
writer
clar|kia
Clark's
nut|crack|er bird
Clar|rie
clar|sach
clart
clarts var. of clart
clarty
clar|tier
clar|ti|est
clary
clar|ies
clasp|er

class-conscious
class
  con|scious|ness
clas|sic
clas|sic|al
clas|sic|al|ism
clas|sic|al|ity
clas|sic|al|ly
clas|si|cise *Br.* var.
  of **classicize**
clas|si|cism
clas|si|cist
clas|si|cize
  clas|si|ciz|ing
Clas|sico Italian
  wine
clas|si|cus in 'locus
  classicus'
clas|si|fi|able
clas|si|fi|ca|tion
clas|si|fi|ca|tory
clas|si|fied
clas|si|fier
clas|sify
  clas|si|fies
  clas|si|fied
  clas|si|fy|ing
class|ily
classi|ness
class|ism
class|ist
class|less
class|less|ness
class|mate
class|room
classy
  class|ier
  classi|est
clast
clas|tic
clath|rate
clat|ter
Claude Lor|rain
  var. of **Claude**
  Lorraine
Claude Lor|raine
  painter
Claud|ette
Clau|dia
clau|di|ca|tion
Claud|ine
Claud|ios
  Ga|le|nos
  full name of **Galen**

Claud|ius Roman
  emperor
Claud|ius
  Ga|le|nus
  Latin name of
  Galen
claus|al
clause
Clau|se|witz, Karl
  von soldier
claus|tral
claus|tra|tion
claus|tro|phobe
claus|tro|pho|bia
claus|tro|pho|bic
claus|tro|pho|bic|
  al|ly
cla|vate
clave
clavi|chord
clav|icle
cla|vicu|lar
cla|vier
clavi|form
claw|back
claw|less
Clay, Cas|sius ori-
  ginal name of
  Muhammad Ali
  the boxer
clayey
clay|ish
clay-like
clay|ma|tion
  trademark in the
  US
clay|more
clay|pan
clean|able
clean-cut
clean|er
clean|ish
clean-limbed
clean|li|ness
clean-living
clean|ly
  clean|lier
  clean|li|est
clean|ness
clean-out *n.*
cleanse
  cleans|ing
cleans|er
clean-shaven

clean|skin
clean-up *n.*
clear|able
clear|ance
clear|cole
  clear|col|ing
clear-cut
  clear-cutting
clear|er
clear-eyed
clear-fell
clear|ing
clear|ly
clear|ness
clear-out *n.*
clear|skin
clear|story *US* var.
  of **clerestory**
clear-thinking
clear-up *n. & mod.*
clear|way
clear|wing
cleat
cleav|able
cleav|age
cleave split
  clove or cleft or
  cleaved
  cleav|ing
  clo|ven or cleft or
  cleaved
cleave adhere
  cleav|ing
cleav|er chopper
cleav|ers plant
cleek hook; golf
  club; cf. **clique**
Cleese, John actor
clef
cleft split; cf. **klepht**
cleg
Cleis|the|nes
  Athenian statesman
cleis|tog|am|ous
cleis|tog|amy
clem|atis
Clem|ence
Cle|men|ceau,
  Georges prime
  minister of France
clem|ency
Clem|ens, Sam|uel
  real name of **Mark**
  Twain

Clem|ent
clem|ent mild
Clem|en|tine
clem|en|tine fruit
Clem|mie
clen|bu|terol
cle|ome
Cleo|patra Egyptian
  queen
cleo|patra butterfly
clep|sy|dra
clere|story
  clere|stor|ies
clergy
  cler|gies
cler|gy|man
cler|gy|men
clergy|woman
  clergy|women
cler|ic
cler|ic|al
cler|ic|al|ism
cler|ic|al|ist
cler|ic|al|ly
cleri|hew
cler|isy
  cleri|sies
clerk
clerk|dom
clerk|ess
clerk|ish
clerk|ly
clerk|ship
Clermont-Ferrand
Cleve|land county,
  England; city, US
Cleve|land, Grover
  US president
clever
clever-clever
clev|er|ly
clev|er|ness
Cleves, Anne of
  wife of Henry VIII
  of England
clevis
clew corner of sail;
  cf. **clou**, clue
clews cords on
  hammock
cli|an|thus
cli|ché
  cli|chés
  cli|chéd

cli¦che var. of cliché
click sound; cf.
  clique, klick
click|able
click-clack
click¦er
clickety-click
click|stream
click-through rate
clicky
cli¦ent
cli¦en|tele
cli¦en|tel|ism
cli¦en|tel|is|tic
cli¦ent|ism
client|ship
Clif|den
  non|par¦eil
cliff|hang¦er
cliff|hang¦ing
cliff-like
Clif|ford
cliff|top
cliffy
  cliff|ier
  cliffi|est
Clift, Mont|gom¦ery
  actor
cli¦mac|ter¦ic
cli¦mac|tic
cli¦mac|tic|al¦ly
cli¦mate
cli¦mat|ic
cli¦mat|ic|al¦ly
cli¦ma|to|logic|al
cli¦ma|to|logic|al¦ly
cli¦mat|olo|gist
cli¦mat|ology
cli¦max
climb ascend; cf.
  clime
climb|able
climb|down
climb¦er
climb-out n.
clime region;
  climate; cf. climb
cli¦nal
clinch¦er
Cline, Patsy singer
cline continuum; cf.
  Klein

cling
  clung
cling¦er
cling film
cling|fish
clingi|ness
cling|stone
clingy
  clingi|er
  clingi|est
clin¦ic
clin|ic¦al
clin|ic|al¦ly
clin|ician
clin|ker furnace
  residue
clink¦er excellent or
  unsatisfactory per-
  son or thing
clinker-built
clink|stone
clin|om¦eter
clino|pyr¦ox|ene
clint
Clin|ton, Bill US
  president
Clin|ton|ite
Clio Muse
clio|met|ric
clio|met|ri|cian
clio|met|rics
clip
  clipped
  clip|ping
clip|board
clip-clop
  clip-clopped
  clip-clopping
clip-on adj. & n.
clip|per
clip|pie
clique exclusive
  group; cf. cleek,
  click, klick
cliquey
  cliqui¦er
  cliqui¦est
cliqu¦ish
cliqu¦ish|ness
clit
clit¦ic
cliti|cisa|tion Br.
  var. of cliticization

cliti|cise Br. var. of
  cliticize
cliti|cize
cliti|ciza|tion
cliti|cize
  cliti|ciz¦ing
clit|or¦al
clit¦ori|dec|tomy
  clit¦ori|dec|tomies
clit|oris
clit|ter
Clive, Rob¦ert
  general
clivia
clo¦aca
  clo|acae
clo|ac¦al
cloak|room
clob|ber
clo|chard
cloche
clock¦er
clock|maker
clock|mak¦ing
clock-watch
clock-watcher
clock|wise
clock|work
Clo|dagh
clod|dish
clod|hop|per
clod|hop|ping
clod|pole
clog
  clogged
  clog|ging
clog|ger
cloggy
  clog|gier
  clog|gi|est
clois|onné
clois|ter
clois|tral
clomi|phene
clompy
  clomp|ier
  clompi|est
clonal
clonal|ity
clone
  clon|ing
cloner
clon¦ic

clonky
  clonk|ier
  clonki|est
Clon|mel
clo¦nus
clop
  clopped
  clop|ping
clo¦qué
clos|able
close
  clos¦ing
  cf. cloze
close
  closer
  clos¦est
  near; stuffy; road;
  etc.
closed-circuit
  television
close-down n.
close¦ly
close-mouthed
close|ness
close-out n.
closer
close-shaven
close-stool
closet
close-up adj. & n.
clos¦ish
clos|trid|ial
clos|trid|ium
  clos|tridia
clos¦ure
  clos|ur¦ing
clot
  clot|ted
  clot|ting
clot|bur
cloth
clothe
  clad archaic or
  literary
cloth¦ing
clothes
clothes line n.
clothes|line v.
  clothes|lin¦ing
clothes peg
clothes|pin
cloth head
clo|thier
cloth¦ing

Clo¦tho one of the Fates
clo|ture
  clo¦tur|ing
  French **clôture**
clou central point or idea; cf. **clew, clue**
cloud|berry
  cloud|berries
cloud|burst
cloud cuckoo land
cloud|ily
cloudi|ness
cloud|land
cloud|less
cloud|let
cloud|scape
cloudy
  cloud|ier
  cloudi|est
clough
clout
clove
clo¦ven
clo¦ver
clo¦ver|leaf +s shape; intersection
clo¦ver leaf
  clo¦ver leaves leaf
Clo¦vis Frankish king; ancient culture
clown|ery
clown|fish
clown|ish
cloy|ing¦ly
clo¦za|pine
cloze test
club
  clubbed
  club|bing
club|babil¦ity
club|bable
club|ber
clubby
  club|bier
  club¦bi|est
club|house
club|land
club|man
  club|men
club|mate
club|moss

club|root
club|rush
clucky
  cluck|ier
  clucki|est
clue
  clue|ing hint; cf. **clew,** ***clou***
clued-in
clued-up
clue|ful
clue|less
  clue|less|ly
  clue|less|ness
Cluj–Napoca
Clum|ber spaniel
clumpy
  clump|ier
  clumpi|est
clum|si¦ly
clum¦si|ness
clumsy
  clum|sier
  clum¦si|est
clunch
Clu|niac
clunk|er
clunky
  clunk|ier
  clunki|est
Cluny
clu¦pe|oid
clus|ter
clutch
clut|ter
Clwyd
Clyde
Clydes|dale
cly|peal
clyp|eus
  clypei
clys|ter
Cly¦tem|nes¦tra
cne|mial
Cni|daria
cni|dar¦ian
Cnut var. of **Canute**
co|acer|vate
coach|build|er
coach-built
coach|load

coach|man
  coach|men
coach|roof
coach|whip
coach|wood
coach|work
co|ad¦ju|tor
co|agul|able
co|agul|ant
co|agu|lase
co|agu|late
  co|agu|lat¦ing
co|agu|la¦tion
co|agu|la|tive
co|agu|la¦tor
co|agu|lum
  co|ag¦ula
coal cf. **cole, kohl**
coal¦er
co|alesce
  co|ales|cing
co|ales|cence
co|ales|cent
coal|face
coal|field
coal|fish
coal-hole
coal|house
co|ali¦tion
  co|ali¦tion|ist
coal|man
  coal|men
coal|mouse
  coal|mice
Coal|port
Coal|sack nebula
coal tit
coaly cf. **coley, coly, choli**
coam|ing raised edge; cf. **comb**
co|ap¦ta¦tion
co|arc|tate
co|arc|ta¦tion
coarse
  coars¦er
  coars¦est rough; cf. **corse, course**
coarse fish
coarse fish|ing
coarse¦ly
coars¦en

coarse|ness
coars¦ish
co|ar¦ticu|lation
coast¦al
coast¦er
coast|guard
coast|land
coast|line
coast|wise
coat cf. **cote**
coatee
coat hang¦er
coati
co¦ati|mundi
Coats Land
coat-tail
co-author
coax
coax¦er
co|axial
  co|axial¦ly
coax|ing¦ly
cob cf. **kob**
co|bala¦min
co|balt
co|balt|ic
co|balt|ous
cob¦ber
Cob¦bett, Wil|liam political reformer
cob¦ble
  cob|bling
cob|bler
cobble|stone
cobby
  cob|bier
  cob¦bi|est
COBE satellite
co-belliger¦ence
co-belliger¦ent
cobia
coble boat
cob|nut
COBOL computer language
cobra
co-brand
cob¦web
cob|webbed
cob|webby
coca
Coca-Cola *trademark*

co|caine
coc|cal
coc|cidia
coc|cid|ian
coc|cidi|oido|
   myco|sis
coc|cidi|osis
cocci|nel|lid
coc|coid
cocco|lith
cocco|litho|phore
cocco|litho|phor|id
coc|cus
  cocci
coc|cy|geal
coc|cyx
  coc|cy|ges or
  coc|cyxes
co-chair
co-chairman
  co-chairmen
Co|chin port, India;
  chicken
Cochin-China
  former name for
  part of Vietnam
Co|chin China var.
  of Cochin (chicken)
coch|in|eal
coch|lea n.
  coch|leae
coch|lear adj.
co|choa
Coch|ran, Charles
  theatrical producer
Coch|ran,
  Jacque|line aviator
Coch|ran, Eddie
  singer and
  songwriter
cocka|bully
  cocka|bul|lies
cock|ade
cock-a-doodle-doo
  +s
cock-a-hoop
cock-a-leekie
cocka|lorum
cocka|mamie
cocka|mamy var. of
  cockamamie
cock and bull
  story
cocka|poo +s

cocka|tiel
cocka|too +s
cocka|trice
cock|boat
cock|chafer
Cock|croft, John
  physicist
cock|crow
cock|er spaniel
cock|erel
Cock|er|ell,
  Chris|to|pher
  engineer
cock|eye bob
cock|eyed
cock|fight
cock|fight|ing
cock|ily
cocki|ness
cockle
  cock|ling
cockle|bur
cock|ler
cockle|shell
cock|loft
cock|ney
cock|ney|ism
cock-of-the-rock
  cocks-of-the-rock
cock-of-the-walk
  cocks-of-the-walk
cock|pit
cock|roach
cocks|comb crest of
  domestic cock; cf.
  coxcomb
cocks|foot
cock|shy
  cock|shies
cocks|man vulgar
  slang
cocks|man|ship
cock|spur
cock|suck|er vulgar
  slang
cock|suck|ing
  vulgar slang
cock|sure
cock|sure|ness
cock|tail
cock-tease vulgar
  slang
cock-teaser vulgar
  slang

cock-up n.
cocky
  cock|ies
  cock|ier
  cocki|est
coco +s coconut tree
cocoa powder or
  drink
coco|bolo +s
coco de mer
  pl. coco de mer
  palms
co-conspira|tor
coco|nut
co|coon
co|coon|er
Cocos Is|lands in
  Indian Ocean
co|cotte
co-counsel|ling
coco|yam
Coc|teau, Jean
  dramatist
cocus wood
cod fish
  pl. cod
cod fake
  cod|ded
  cod|ding
coda concluding
  part
cod|dle
  cod|dling
cod|dler
code
  cod|ing
codec
co|deine
co|depend|ence
co|depend|ency
co|depend|ent
coder cf. coda
code-share
  code-sharing
co-determin|ation
codex
  co|di|ces or
  co|dexes
cod|fish
cod|ger
co|di|cil
co|di|cil|lary
co|di|co|logic|al
co|di|co|logic|al|ly

co|di|col|ogy
co|difi|ca|tion
co|di|fier
co|dify
  co|di|fies
  co|di|fied
  co|di|fy|ing
cod|ling
cod|ology
co|domain
codon
cod|piece
co-driver
cods|wal|lop
Cody, Wil|liam Buf-
  falo Bill
Coe, Se|bas|tian
  runner
coe|cil|ian var. of
  caecilian
coed
co-education
co-education|al
co|ef|fi|cient
coela|canth
coel|en|ter|ate
coel|iac Br.
  US celiac
coelom
  coel|oms or
  coel|omata
coel|om|ate
coel|om|ic
coelo|stat
coel|uro|saur
coeno|bite var. of
  cenobite
coeno|bit|ic var. of
  cenobitic
coeno|cyte
coeno|cyt|ic
co|en|zyme
co|equal
co|equal|ity
co|erce
  co|er|cing
co|er|cible
co|er|cion
co|er|cive
co|er|cive|ly
co|er|civ|ity
co|eter|nal

Coet|zee, J. M.
　novelist
Coeur de Lion,
　Rich|ard English
　king
co|eval
co|eval|ity
co-evolution
co-evolution|ary
co-evolve
　co-evolving
co|ex|ist
co|ex|ist|ence
co|ex|ist|ent
co|ex|ten|sive
co|fac|tor
cof|fee
cof|fer
coffer|dam
cof|fered
cof|fer|er
cof|fin
cof|fle
cof|fret
co-found
co-founder
cog
　cogged
　cog|ging
co|gency
　co|gen|cies
co|gen|er|ation
co|gent
co|gent|ly
cogged
cogit|able
cogi|tate
　cogi|tat|ing
cogi|ta|tion
cogi|ta|tive
cogi|ta|tor
cog|ito, ergo sum
Co|gnac town,
　France
co|gnac
cog|nate
cog|nis|able *Br.* var.
　of cognizable
cog|ni|sance *Br.* var.
　of cognizance
cog|ni|sant *Br.* var.
　of cognizant

cog|nise *Br.* var. of
　cognize
cog|ni|tion
cog|ni|tion|al
cog|ni|tive
cog|ni|tive|ly
cog|ni|tiv|ism
cog|ni|tiv|ist
cog|niz|able
cog|ni|zance
cog|ni|zant
cog|nize
　cog|niz|ing
cog|no|men
co|gnos|cente
　co|gnos|centi
cog|wheel
co|habit
co|habit|ant
co|habit|ation
co|habit|ee
co|habit|er
Cohen, Leon|ard
　singer and writer
cohen var. of kohen
co|here
　co|her|ing
co|her|ence
co|her|ency
　co|her|en|cies
co|her|ent
co|her|ent|ly
co|herer
co|he|sion
co|he|sive
co|he|sive|ly
co|he|sive|ness
coho +s
cohoe var. of coho
co|hort
co|hosh
co-host
COHSE = Confed-
　eration of Health
　Service Employees
co|hune
coif
　coiffed *Br.*
　coifed *US*
　coif|fing *Br.*
　coif|ing *US*
coif|feur *male*
coif|feuse *female*

coif|fure
　coif|fur|ing
coign corner; in
　'coign of vantage';
　cf. coin, quoin
coil
Co|im|ba|tore
Co|im|bra
coin cf. coign,
　quoin
coin|age
co|in|cide
　co|in|cid|ing
co|in|ci|dence
co|in|ci|dent occur-
　ring together; in
　agreement
co|in|ci|den|tal
　chance
co|in|ci|den|tal|ly
　by chance
co|in|ci|dent|ly
　together
coin|er
coin-op
Coin|treau
　trademark
coir
co|it|al
co|ition
co|itus
co|itus
　inter|rup|tus
co|itus
　re|ser|va|tus
co|jo|nes
Coke drink
　trademark
coke
　cok|ing
　fuel; cocaine
col
cola tree; nut;
　drink; cf. coaler
col|an|der
co-latitude
col|can|non
Col|ches|ter
col|chi|cine
col|chi|cum plant
Col|chis ancient
　region, SW Asia
cold-blooded
cold-blooded|ly

cold-call *v.*
cold-caller
cold-cock
cold-drawing
cold-drawn
cold frame
cold-hearted
cold-hearted|ly
cold-hearted|ness
coldie
cold|ish
Cold|itz
cold|ly
cold-molded *US*
cold-molding *US*
cold-moulded *Br.*
cold-moulding *Br.*
cold|ness
cold-rolled
cold-rolling
cold-short
cold-shoulder *v.*
cold-start *v.*
cold-weld *v.*
cold-work *v.*
Cole name
Cole, Nat King
　singer and pianist
cole cabbage etc.; cf.
　coal, kohl
col|ec|tomy
　col|ec|to|mies
Cole|man lantern;
　lamp *trademark*
Cole|man, Or|nette
　saxophonist
cole|man|ite
cole|mouse var. of
　coalmouse
Cole|op|tera
cole|op|ter|an
cole|op|ter|ist
cole|op|ter|ous
cole|op|tile
coleo|rhiza
Cole|raine
Cole|ridge, Sam|uel
　Tay|lor poet
cole|slaw
cole tit var. of coal
　tit
Col|lette novelist
co|leus

cole|wort

coley fish; cf. coaly, coly, choli

colic

coli|cin

col|icky

coli|form

Colin

co|linear|ity

coli|seum stadium; cf. the Colosseum

coll|itis

Coll Scottish island

col|lab|or|ate
col|lab|or|at|ing

col|lab|or|ation

col|lab|ora|tion|ist

col|lab|ora|tive

col|lab|ora|tive|ly

col|lab|or|ator

col|lage

col|la|gen

col|lagist

col|lap|sar

col|lapse
col|laps|ing

col|laps|ibil|ity

col|laps|ible

col|lar cf. choler

col|lar|bone

col|lard

col|lar|less

col|late
col|lat|ing

col|lat|eral

col|lat|eral|ise Br.
var. of collateralize

col|lat|eral|ity

col|lat|eral|ize
col|lat|eral|iz|ing

col|lat|eral|ly

col|la|tion

col|la|tor

col|league

col|lect

col|lect|abil|ity abil-
ity to be collected

col|lect|able able to
be collected

col|lec|ta|nea

col|lect|ibil|ity
value

col|lect|ible worth
collecting; valued
item

col|lec|tion

col|lect|ive

col|lect|ive|ly

col|lect|iv|isa|tion
Br. var. of
collectivization

col|lect|iv|ise Br.
var. of collectivize

col|lect|iv|ism

col|lect|iv|ist

col|lect|iv|is|tic

col|lect|iv|ities

col|lect|iv|iza|tion

col|lect|iv|ize
col|lect|iv|iz|ing

col|lect|or

Col|leen

col|leen Irish girl

col|lege

col|le|gial

col|le|gi|al|ity

col|le|gian

col|le|gi|ate

col|le|gi|ate|ly

col|le|gium
col|le|gia

col|le|gium
mu|sicum
col|le|gia mu|sica

col legno

Col|lem|bola

col|lem|bol|an

col|len|chyma

Colles' frac|ture

col|let

Col|lette

col|licu|lar

col|licu|lus
col|li|culi

col|lide
col|lid|ing

col|lider

col|lie

col|lier

col|liery
col|lier|ies

col|li|gate
col|li|gat|ing

col|li|ga|tion

col|li|ga|tive

col|li|mate

col|li|mat|ing

col|li|ma|tion

col|li|ma|tor

col|lin|ear

col|lin|ear|ity

Col|lins, Joan
actress

Col|lins, Mi|chael
revolutionary

Col|lins, Tom drink

Col|lins, Wil|kie
novelist

col|li|sion

col|li|sion|al

col|lo|cate

col|lo|cat|ing

col|lo|ca|tion

col|lo|dion

col|logue

col|loguing

col|loid

col|loid|al

col|lop

col|lo|quial

col|lo|qui|al|ism

col|lo|qui|al|ly

col|lo|quium
col|lo|qui|ums or
col|lo|quia

col|lo|quy
col|lo|quies

col|lo|type

col|lude
col|lud|ing

col|luder

col|lu|sion

col|lu|sive

col|lu|sive|ly

col|lu|vial

col|lu|vium

col|lyrium
col|lyria

colly|wob|bles

colo|bine

colo|boma

colo|bus

colo|cynth

Co|logne city,
Germany

co|logne

Co|lom|bia in South
America; cf.
Columbia

Co|lom|bian

Col|ombo

Colón port, Panama

colon punctuation;
intestine

colón
co|lo|nes
Costa Rican and
Salvadorean
currency

col|onel officer; cf.
kernel

col|on|el|cy
col|on|el|cies

colonel-in-chief
colonels-in-chief

co|lo|nial

co|lo|ni|al|ism

co|lo|ni|al|ist

co|lo|ni|al|ly

co|lon|ic

col|on|isa|tion Br.
var. of colonization

col|on|ise Br. var. of
colonize

col|on|iser Br. var.
of colonizer

col|on|ist

col|on|iza|tion

col|on|ize
col|on|iz|ing

col|on|izer

col|on|nade

col|ono|scope

col|on|os|copy
col|on|os|copies

col|ony
col|onies

colo|phon

col|oph|ony
col|oph|onies

color US
Br. colour

col|or|able US
Br. colourable

Col|or|adan

Col|or|ado

col|or|ant US
Br. colourant

col|or|ation

col|ora|tura

color-blind US
Br. colour-blind

color blind|ness
  US
  Br. **colour**
  blindness
color code US n.
  Br. **colour code**
color-code US v.
  color-coding
  Br. **colour-code**
colo|rec|tal
col|ored US
  Br. **coloured**
color fast US
  Br. **colour fast**
col|or|ful US
  Br. **colourful**
col|or|ful|ly US
  Br. **colourfully**
col|or|ful|ness US
  Br. **colourfulness**
col|or|im|eter
col|ori|met|ric
col|or|im|etry
col|or|ist US
  Br. **colourist**
col|or|is|tic US
  Br. **colouristic**
col|or|is|tic|al|ly US
  Br. **colouristically**
col|or|iza|tion US
  (*trademark* in the
  US)
  Br. **colourization**
col|or|ize US
  col|or|iz|ing
  Br. **colourize**
col|or|izer US
  (*trademark* in the
  US)
  Br. **colourizer**
col|or|less US
  Br. **colourless**
col|or|less|ly US
  Br. **colourlessly**
col|or|less|ness US
  Br. **colourlessness**
col|or|point US
  Br. **colourpoint**
color wash US n.
  Br. **colour wash**
color-wash US v.
  Br. **colour-wash**
col|or|way US
  Br. **colourway**
col|os|sal

col|os|sal|ly
Col|os|seum in
  Rome
col|os|seum other
  stadium; var. of
  coliseum
Col|os|sians
col|os|sus
  col|ossi
col|os|tomy
  col|os|tomies
col|os|trum
col|our Br.
  US **color**
col|our|able Br.
  US **colorable**
col|our|ant Br.
  US **colorant**
col|our|ation var. of
  coloration
colour-blind Br.
  US **color-blind**
colour blind|ness
  Br.
  US **color blindness**
col|our code Br.
  n.
  US **color code**
colour-code Br.
  colour-coding
  n.
  US **color-code**
col|oured Br.
  US **colored**
col|our fast Br.
  US **color fast**
col|our|ful Br.
  US **colorful**
col|our|ful|ly Br.
  US **colorfully**
col|our|ful|ness Br.
  US **colorfulness**
col|our|isa|tion Br.
  var. of **colorization**
col|our|ise Br. var.
  of **colorize**
col|our|ist Br.
  US **colorist**
col|our|is|tic Br.
  US **coloristic**
col|our|is|tic|al|ly
  Br.
  US **coloristically**
col|our|iza|tion Br.
  var. of **colorization**

col|our|ize Br. var.
  of **colorize**
col|our|izer Br. var.
  of **colorizer**
col|our|less Br.
  US **colorless**
col|our|less|ly Br.
  US **colorlessly**
col|our|less|ness
  Br.
  US **colorlessness**
col|our|point Br.
  US **colorpoint**
col|our wash Br. n.
  US **color wash**
colour-wash Br. v.
  US **color-wash**
col|our|way Br.
  US **colorway**
col|por|tage
col|por|teur
col|po|scope
col|pos|copy
  col|pos|co|pies
col|tan
col|ter US
  Br. **coulter**
colt|ish
Col|trane, John
  saxophonist
colts|foot
colu|brid
colu|brine
co|lugo +s
Col|umba, St
col|um|bar|ium
  col|um|baria or
  col|um|bar|iums
Col|um|bia river,
  city, District, and
  university, US; cf.
  Colombia
Col|um|bine panto-
  mime character
col|um|bine plant
col|um|bite
col|um|bium
Col|um|bus city, US
Col|um|bus,
  Chris|to|pher Ital-
  ian explorer
colu|mella n.
  colu|mel|lae
  colu|mel|lar adj.
col|umn

col|um|nar
col|um|nated
col|um|nist
col|ure
coly
  colies
  bird; cf. **coaly,**
  coley, choli, E. coli
colza
coma
  comas
  unconsciousness
  comae
  cloud in comet
Coma Bere|ni|ces
Com|an|che
co|ma|tose
comb cf. **coaming**
com|bat
  com|bat|ed or
  com|bat|ted
  com|bat|ing or
  com|bat|ting
com|bat|ant
com|bat|ive
com|bat|ive|ly
com|bat|ive|ness
comb-back
combe valley; cf.
  cwm, khoum
comb|er
comb|fish
combi
com|bin|able
com|bin|ation
com|bin|ation|al
com|bina|tive
com|bina|tor|ial
com|bina|tor|ial|ly
com|bina|tor|ics
com|bin|atory
com|bine
  com|bin|ing
com|biner
comb-like
combo +s
comb-over
combs undergar-
  ment; cf. **comms**
com|bust
com|bust|ibil|ity
com|bust|ible
com|bus|tion
com|bus|tive

com|bus|tor
come
  came
  com|ing
  cf. **cum**
come-along
come|back n.
Com|econ
com|edian
com|edic
Com|édie
  Fran|çaise
com|edi|enne
com|edo
  com|edo|nes
com|edo|genic
come|down n.
com|edy
  com|ed|ies
come-hither adj.
come|li|ness
come|ly
  come|lier
  come|li|est
come-on n.
come-outer
comer
com|ess
com|est|ible
comet
com|et|ary
come|up|pance
com|fily
com|fi|ness
com|fit sweet
com|fort ease;
  console
com|fort|able
com|fort|ably
com|fort|er
com|fort|ing|ly
com|fort|less
com|frey
comfy
  com|fier
  com|fi|est
comic
com|ic|al
com|ic|al|ity
com|ic|al|ly
Com|ice pear
Com|in|form Soviet
  organization

Com|ino island,
  Malta
COMINT =
  communications
  intelligence
Com|in|tern com-
  munist organization
com|it|al relating to
  a count or earl; cf.
  committal
com|ity
  com|ities
comm communica-
  tion
comma punctu-
  ation; bacillus;
  butterfly
com|mand
com|mand|ant
com|man|deer
com|mand|er
commander-in-
       chief
  commanders-in-
      chief
com|mander|ship
com|mand|ing|ly
com|mand|ment
com|mando +s
comme ci, comme
  ça
com|media
  dell'arte
comme il faut
com|mem|or|ate
  com|mem|or|at|ing
com|mem|or|ation
com|mem|ora|tive
com|mem|or|ator
com|mence
  com|men|cing
com|mence|ment
com|mend
com|mend|able
com|mend|ably
com|men|da|tion
Com|men|da|tore
  Com|men|da|tori
com|men|da|tory
com|mens|al
com|mens|al|ism
com|mens|al|ity
com|men|sur|
      abil|ity

com|men|sur|able
com|men|sur|ate
com|men|sur|ate|ly
com|ment
com|men|tar|iat
com|men|tary
  com|men|tar|ies
com|men|tate
  com|men|tat|ing
com|men|ta|tor
com|ment|er
com|merce
com|mer|cial
com|mer|cial|
      isa|tion
  Br. var. of
  commercialization
com|mer|cial|ise
  Br. var. of
  commercialize
com|mer|cial|ism
com|mer|ci|al|ity
com|mer|cial|
      iza|tion
com|mer|cial|ize
com|mer|cial|iz|ing
com|mer|cial|ly
com|mère
Com|mie Commun-
  ist; cf. commis
com|min|ation
com|min|gle
  com|min|gling
com|min|ute
  com|min|ut|ing
com|min|ution
com|mis
  pl. com|mis
  chef; cf. Commie
com|mis|er|ate
  com|mis|er|at|ing
com|mis|er|ation
com|mis|era|tive
com|mish
com|mis|saire
com|mis|sar
com|mis|sar|iat
com|mis|sary
  com|mis|sar|ies
com|mis|sion
com|mis|sion|aire
com|mis|sion|er
com|mis|sural
com|mis|sure

com|mit
com|mit|ted
com|mit|ting
com|mit|ment
com|mit|table
com|mit|tal cf.
  comital
com|mit|tee
com|mit|ter
com|mix
com|mix|ture
commo communica-
  tion
com|mode
com|modi|fi|
      ca|tion
com|mod|ify
  com|modi|fies
  com|modi|fied
  com|modi|fy|ing
com|modi|ous
com|modi|ous|ly
com|modi|ous|ness
com|mod|it|
      isa|tion
  Br. var. of
  commoditization
com|mod|it|ise Br.
  var. of
  commoditize
com|mod|it|
      iza|tion
com|mod|it|ize
com|mod|it|iz|ing
com|mod|ity
com|mod|ities
com|mo|dore
Commodore-in-
      Chief
  Commodores-in-
      Chief
com|mon
com|mon|able
com|mon|age
com|mon|al|ity
  com|mon|al|ities
com|mon|alty
  com|mon|al|ties
com|mon|er
com|mon|hold
com|mon|hold|er
com|mon|ly
com|mon|ness
com|mon|place

Com|mons in
Parliament
com|mons daily
fare
com|mon sense
com|mon|sen|sic|al
Com|mon
Ser|jeant
com|mon|wealth
com|mo|tion
comms
communications;
cf. **combs**
com|mu|nal
com|mu|nal|ism
com|mu|nal|ist
com|mu|nal|ity
com|mu|nal|ities
com|mu|nal|ly
com|mu|nard
com|mune
com|mun|ing
com|mu|nic|abil|ity
com|mu|nic|able
com|mu|ni|cant
com|mu|ni|cate
com|mu|ni|cat|ing
com|mu|ni|ca|tion
com|mu|ni|
ca|tion|al
com|mu|ni|ca|tive
com|mu|ni|
ca|tive|ly
com|mu|ni|ca|tor
com|mu|ni|ca|tory
Com|mu|nion
Eucharist
com|mu|nion shar-
ing
com|mu|ni|qué
com|mun|ism
com|mun|ist
com|mun|is|tic
com|mu|ni|tar|ian
com|mu|ni|tar|ian|
ism
com|mu|nity
com|mu|ni|ties
com|mut|abil|ity
com|mut|able
com|mu|tate
com|mu|tat|ing
com|mu|ta|tion
com|mu|ta|tive

com|mu|ta|tor
com|mute
com|mut|ing
com|muter
Como, Lake
Como|doro
Riva|da|via
Com|or|an person
from the Comoros
co-morbid
co-morbid|ity
co-morbid|ities
Com|orin Cape
Com|oros
com|pact
com|pac|tion
com|pact|ly
com|pact|ness
com|pact|or
com|padre
com|pand
com|pand|er
com|pand|or var. of
compander
com|pan|ion
com|pan|ion|able
com|pan|ion|ably
com|pan|ion|ate
companion-in-
arms
companions-in-
arms
com|pan|ion|ship
com|pan|ion|way
com|pany
com|pan|ies
com|pan|ied
com|pany|ing
com|par|abil|ity
com|par|able
com|par|ably
com|para|tist
com|para|tive
com|para|tive|ly
com|para|tor
com|pare
com|par|ing
make comparison;
cf. **compère**
com|pari|son
com|part|ment
com|part|men|tal
com|part|men|tal|
isa|tion

Br. var. of com-
partmentalization
com|part|men|tal|
ise
Br. var. of
compartmentalize
com|part|men|tal|
ism
com|part|men|tal|
iza|tion
com|part|men|tal|
ize
com|part|men|tal|
iz|ing
com|part|
men|tal|ly
com|part|
men|ta|tion
com|pass
com|pas|sion
com|pas|sion|ate
com|pas|sion|ate|ly
com|pati|bil|ity
com|pati|bil|ities
com|pat|ible
com|pat|ibly
com|pat|riot
com|pat|ri|ot|ic
com|peer
com|pel
com|pelled
com|pel|ling
com|pel|lable
com|pel|ling|ly
com|pen|di|ous
com|pen|di|ous|ly
com|pen|dium
com|pen|diums or
com|pen|dia
com|pen|sable
com|pen|sate
com|pen|sat|ing
com|pen|sa|tion
com|pen|sa|tion|al
com|pen|sa|tive
com|pen|sa|tor
com|pen|sa|tory
comp|er
com|père
com|pèr|ing
MC; cf. **compare**
com|pete
com|pet|ing
com|pe|tence

com|pe|tency
com|pe|ten|cies
com|pe|tent
com|pe|tent|ly
com|pe|ti|tion
com|peti|tive
com|peti|tive|ly
com|peti|tive|ness
com|peti|tor
com|pil|ation
com|pile
com|pil|ing
com|piler
com|pla|cence self-
satisfaction; cf.
complaisance
com|pla|cency
com|pla|cent self-
satisfied; cf.
complaisant
com|pla|cent|ly
com|plain
com|plain|ant
com|plain|er
com|plaint
com|plai|sance
acquiescence; cf.
complacence
com|plai|sant
acquiescent; cf.
complacent
com|pleat
archaic var. of
complete
com|plec|ted
com|ple|ment
something that
completes etc.; go
well with; cf.
compliment
com|ple|men|tal
com|ple|
men|tar|ity
com|ple|
men|tar|ities
com|ple|men|tary
forming a whole;
cf. **complimentary**
com|ple|
men|ta|tion
com|ple|ment|iser
Br. var. of
complementizer
com|ple|ment|izer

com|plete
  com|plet|ing
  com|plet|er
  com|plet|est
com|plete|ly
com|plete|ness
com|ple|tion
com|plet|ist
com|plet|ive
com|plex
com|plex|ation
com|plex|ion
com|plex|ity
  com|plex|ities
com|plex|ly
com|pli|ance
com|pli|ant
com|pli|ant|ly
com|pli|cate
  com|pli|cat|ing
com|pli|cated|ly
com|pli|ca|tion
com|pli|cit
com|pli|city
com|pli|ment
  praise; greetings;
  cf. complement
com|pli|men|tary
com|pli|men|tar|ies
  praising; free; cf.
  complementary
com|pline
com|ply
  com|plies
  com|plied
  com|ply|ing
compo +s
com|po|nent
com|po|nen|tial
com|po|nent|ise Br.
  var. of
  componentize
com|po|nent|ize
  com|po|nent|iz|ing
com|pony
com|port
com|port|ment
com|pose
  com|pos|ing
com|posed|ly
com|poser
com|pos|ite
  com|pos|it|ing
com|pos|ition

com|pos|ition|al
com|pos|ition|al|ly
com|posi|tor
com|pos men|tis
com|post
com|post|er
com|pos|ure
com|pote
com|pound
com|pound|able
com|pound|er
com|pra|dor
com|pra|dore var.
  of comprador
com|pre|hend
com|pre|hen|
    si|bil|ity
com|pre|hen|sible
com|pre|hen|sibly
com|pre|hen|sion
com|pre|hen|sive
com|pre|hen|
    sive|ly
com|pre|hen|sive|
    ness
com|pres|ence
com|pres|ent
com|press
com|press|ibil|ity
com|press|ible
com|pres|sion
com|pres|sion|al
com|pres|sive
com|pres|sor
com|prise
  com|pris|ing
com|prom|ise
com|prom|is|ing
com|prom|iser
compte rendu
  comptes rendus
Comp|ton effect
Comp|ton, Denis
  cricketer and
  footballer
Compton-Burnett,
  Ivy novelist
comp|trol|ler
com|pul|sion
com|pul|sive
com|pul|sive|ly
com|pul|sor|ily
com|pul|sory

com|punc|tion
com|punc|tious
com|pur|ga|tion
com|pur|ga|tor
com|pur|ga|tory
com|put|abil|ity
com|put|able
com|pu|ta|tion
com|pu|ta|tion|al
com|pu|ta|tion|al|ly
com|pute
  com|put|ing
com|puter
com|puter|ate
com|pu|ter|isa|tion
  Br. var. of
  computerization
com|pu|ter|ise Br.
  var. of computerize
com|pu|ter|iza|tion
com|pu|ter|ize
  com|pu|ter|iz|ing
com|rade
comrade-in-arms
  comrades-in-arms
com|rade|ly
com|rade|ship
Com|sat *trademark*
Comte, Au|guste
  philosopher
Comt|ism
Comt|ist
con
  conned
  con|ning
  trick; disadvantage;
  a convict; to study;
  convention
con *Br.*
  conned
  con|ning
  steer ship
  US conn
con|acre
Con|akry
con amore
Conan Doyle,
  Ar|thur novelist
con|ation
cona|tive
con brio
con|cat|en|ate
  con|cat|en|at|ing
con|cat|en|ation

con|cave
con|cave|ly
con|cav|ity
  con|cav|ities
concavo-concave
concavo-convex
con|ceal
con|ceal|er
con|ceal|ment
con|cede
  con|ced|ing
con|ceder
con|ceit
con|ceit|ed
con|ceiv|abil|ity
con|ceiv|able
con|ceiv|ably
con|ceive
  con|ceiv|ing
con|cele|brant
con|cele|brate
  con|cele|brat|ing
con|cele|bra|tion
con|cen|ter *US*
  Br. concentre
con|cen|trate
  con|cen|trat|ing
con|cen|trated|ly
con|cen|tra|tion
con|cen|tra|tive
con|cen|tra|tor
con|centre *Br.*
  con|cen|tring
  US concenter
con|cen|tric
con|cen|tric|al|ly
con|cen|tri|city
Con|cep|ción
con|cept
con|cep|tion
con|cep|tion|al
con|cep|tual
con|cep|tu|al|
    isa|tion
  Br. var. of
  conceptualization
con|cep|tu|al|ise *Br.*
  var. of
  conceptualize
con|cep|tu|al|ize
con|cep|tu|al|ism
con|cep|tu|al|ist
con|cep|tu|al|
    iza|tion

con|cep|tu|al|ize
  con|cep|tu|al|iz|ing
con|cep|tu|al¦ly
con|cep¦tus
con|cern
con|cern|ment
con|cert
con|cer¦tante
con|cer¦tina
  con|cer¦tinas
  con|cer¦tinaed or
  con|cer¦tina'd
  con|cer¦tina|ing
con|cer¦tino +s
con|cert¦ise *Br.* var.
  of concertize
con|cert¦ize
  con¦cert|iz¦ing
con¦cert|master
con|certo
  con|cer¦tos or
  con|certi
con|certo grosso
  con|certi grossi
con|ces¦sion
con|ces¦sion|aire
con|ces¦sion|al
con|ces¦sion|ary
con|ces¦sion|naire
  var. of
  concessionaire
con|ces¦sive
conch
  conchs or conches
  shell; domed roof;
  cf. **conk**
con¦cha
  con|chae
  hollow of ear; bone
  in nose; cf. **conker**,
  conquer
con|chie
con|chio¦lin
con|choid
con|choid¦al
con|cho|logic¦al
conch|olo¦gist
conch|ology
con¦chy var. of
  conchie
con|ci¦erge
con|cil|iar
con|cili|ate
  con|cili|at¦ing

con|cili|ation
con|cilia|tive
con|cili|ator
con|cili|atory
con|cise
  con|ciser
  con|cisest
con|cise¦ly
con|cise|ness
con|ci¦sion
con|clave
con|clude
  con|clud¦ing
con|clu¦sion
con|clu¦sive
con|clu¦sive¦ly
con|clu¦sive|ness
con|coct
con|coct|er
con|coc¦tion
con|coct¦or var. of
  concocter
con|comi|tance
con|comi|tancy var.
  of concomitance
con|comi|tant
con|comi|tant¦ly
Con|cord towns,
  US; grape; cf.
  Concorde
con|cord agreement
con|cord|ance
  con|cord|an¦cing
con|cord|ant
con|cordat
Con|corde aircraft;
  cf. **Concord**
*con|cours
  d'élé¦gance*
  pl. con|cours
  d'élé¦gance
con|course
con|cres¦cence
con|cres¦cent
con|crete
  con|cret¦ing
con|crete¦ly
con|crete|ness
con|cre¦tion
con|cre¦tion|ary
con¦cret|isa¦tion
  Br. var. of
  concretization

con¦cret|ise *Br.* var.
  of concretize
con¦cret|iza¦tion
concret|ize
  con¦cret|iz¦ing
con|cu¦bin|age
con|cu¦bin|ary
con|cu¦bine
con|cu¦pis|cence
con|cu¦pis|cent
con¦cur
  con|curred
  con|cur¦ring
con|cur¦rence
con|cur¦rent
con|cur¦rent¦ly
con|cuss
con|cus¦sion
con|cus¦sive
con|demn
con|dem|nable
con|dem|na¦tion
con|dem|na¦tory
con|dens|able
con|den|sate
con|den|sa¦tion
con|dense
  con¦dens|ing
con|den¦ser
con|des¦cend
con|des¦cend|ing¦ly
con|des¦cen|sion
con|dign
con|di¦ment
con|di¦tion
con|di¦tion|al
con|di¦tion|al¦ity
con|di¦tion|al¦ly
con|di¦tion|er
condo +s
con|dole
  con|dol¦ing
con|dol¦ence
con¦dom
con|do¦min|ium
con|don|ation
con|done
  con|don¦ing
con|doner
con¦dor
con|dot¦tiere
con|dot¦tieri

con|duce
  con|du¦cing
con|du¦cive
con|duct
con|duct|ance
con|ducti|bil¦ity
con|duct|ible
con|duc¦tion
con|duct|ive
con|duct|ive¦ly
con|duct|iv¦ity
  con|duct|iv¦ities
con|duct¦or
con|duct¦or|ship
con|duc|tress
con|duc¦tus
  con|ducti
con|duit
con¦dylar
con¦dyl|arth
con¦dyle
con¦dyl|oid
con¦dyl|oma
  con|dyl|omata or
  con|dyl|omas
con|dyl|oma|tous
cone
  con¦ing
cone|flower
cone|head
Con|est¦oga wagon
coney
Coney Is¦land
con¦fab
  con|fabbed
  con|fab|bing
con|fabu|late
  con|fabu|lat¦ing
con|fabu|la¦tion
con|fabu|la¦tory
con|fect
con|fec¦tion
con|fec¦tion|er
con|fec¦tion|ery
  con|fec¦tion|er¦ies
con|fed¦er|acy
  con|fed¦er|acies
con|fed¦er|al
con|fed¦er|ate
  con|fed¦er|at¦ing
con|fed¦er|ation
con¦fer
  con|ferred
  con|fer¦ring

con|fer|ee
con|fer|ence
con|fer|en|cing
con|fer|ment
con|fer|rable
con|fer|ral
con|fess
con|fes|sant
con|fess|ed|ly
con|fes|sion
con|fes|sion|al
con|fes|sion|al|ly
con|fes|sion|ary
con|fes|sor
con|fetti
con|fi|dant *male* trusted person; cf. confident
con|fi|dante *female* trusted person; cf. confident
con|fide
con|fid|ing
con|fi|dence
con|fi|dent self-assured; cf. confidant, confidante
con|fi|den|tial
con|fi|den|ti|al|ity
con|fi|den|ti|al|ities
con|fi|den|tial|ly
con|fi|dent|ly
con|fid|ing|ly
con|fig|ur|able
con|fig|ur|ation
con|fig|ur|ation|al
con|fig|ure
con|fig|ur|ing
con|fine
con|fin|ing
con|fine|ment
con|firm
con|firm|and
con|firm|ation
con|firma|tive
con|firma|tory
con|fis|cate
con|fis|cat|ing
con|fis|ca|tion
con|fis|ca|tor
con|fis|ca|tory
con|fit

Con|fit|eor
con|flab
con|flabbed
con|flab|bing
con|flag|ra|tion
con|flate
con|flat|ing
con|fla|tion
con|flict
con|flict|ual
con|flu|ence
con|flu|ent
con|flux
con|focal
con|form
con|form|abil|ity
con|form|able
con|form|ably
con|form|al
con|form|al|ly
con|form|ance
con|form|ation
con|form|ation|al
con|form|er
con|form|ism
con|form|ist
con|form|ity
con|found
con|found|ed|ly
con|fra|tern|ity
con|fra|tern|ities
con|frère
con|front
con|fron|ta|tion
con|fron|ta|tion|al
Con|fu|cian
Con|fu|cian|ism
Con|fu|cian|ist
Con|fu|cius philosopher
con|fus|abil|ity
con|fus|able
con|fuse
con|fus|ing
con|fused|ly
con|fus|ing|ly
con|fu|sion
con|fut|ation
con|fute
con|fut|ing
conga
con|gas

con|gaed or conga'd
conga|ing dance; cf. conger
congé
con|geal
con|geal|able
con|geal|ment
con|gee
con|gel|ation
con|gener
con|gen|eric
con|gen|er|ous
con|gen|ial
con|geni|al|ity
con|geni|al|ly
con|geni|tal
con|geni|tal|ly
con|ger eel; cf. conga
con|ger|ies *pl.* con|ger|ies
con|gest
con|ges|tion
con|gest|ive
con|glom|er|ate
con|glom|er|at|ing
con|glom|er|ation
Congo river and country, Africa; cf. Kongo
Con|go|lese
con|grats
con|gratu|late
con|gratu|lat|ing
con|gratu|la|tion
con|gratu|la|tor
con|gratu|la|tory
con|gre|gant
con|gre|gate
con|gre|gat|ing
con|gre|ga|tion
Con|gre|ga|tion|al relating to Congregationalism
con|gre|ga|tion|al relating to a congregation
Con|gre|ga|tion|al|ism
Con|gre|ga|tion|al|ist
Con|gress legislative body

con|gress meeting
con|gres|sion|al
con|gres|sion|al|ly
con|gress|man
con|gress|men
con|gress|woman
con|gress|women
Con|greve, William dramatist
con|gru|ence
con|gru|ency
con|gru|en|cies
con|gru|ent
con|gru|ent|ly
con|gru|ity
con|gru|ities
con|gru|ous
con|gru|ous|ly
conic
con|ic|al
con|ic|al|ly
con|ics
co|nidio|phore
co|nid|ium
co|nidia
coni|fer
con|ifer|ous
coni|ine
con|jec|tur|able
con|jec|tural
con|jec|tur|al|ly
con|jec|ture
con|jec|tur|ing
con|join
con|joint
con|joint|ly
con|ju|gacy
con|ju|gacies
con|ju|gal
con|ju|gal|ity
con|ju|gal|ly
con|ju|gate
con|ju|gat|ing
con|ju|ga|tion
con|ju|ga|tion|al
con|junct
con|junc|tion
con|junc|tion|al
con|junc|tiva
con|junc|tivae or con|junc|tivas
con|junc|tival
con|junc|tive

con|junc|tiv|itis
con|junc|ture
con|junto +s
con|jur|ation
con|jure
  con|jur|ing
con|jurer var. of
  conjuror
con|juror
conk nose; head;
  punch; in 'conk
  out'; cf. conch
con|ker horse
  chestnut; cf.
  concha
con man
con moto
conn US
  Br. con; steer ship;
  cf. con
Con|nacht province,
  Republic of Ireland
con|nate
con|nat|ural
con|nat|ur|al|ly
Con|naught var. of
  Connacht
con|nect
con|nect|able
con|nect|ed|ly
con|nect|ed|ness
Con|necti|cut
con|nec|tion
con|nec|tion|al
con|nec|tion|ism
con|nect|ive
con|nect|iv|ity
con|nect|or
Con|ne|mara
  region, Republic of
  Ireland; pony
Con|nery, Sean
  actor
con|nex|ion Br. var.
  of connection
con|nex|ion|al Br.
  var. of
  connectional
Con|nie
con|nip|tion
con|niv|ance
con|nive
  con|niv|ing
con|niver

con|nois|seur
con|nois|seur|ship
Con|nolly, Billy
  comedian
Con|nolly, Cyril
  writer and
  journalist
Con|nolly,
  Maur|een tennis
  player
Con|nors, Jimmy
  tennis player
con|no|ta|tion
con|no|ta|tive
con|note
  con|not|ing
con|nu|bial
con|nu|bi|al|ity
cono|dont
con|oid
con|oid|al
con|quer cf.
  concha, conker
con|quer|able
con|queror
con|quest
con|quis|ta|dor
  con|quis|ta|dores
  or con|quis|ta|dors
Con|rad, Jo|seph
  novelist
Con|ran, Ter|ence
  designer
con rod
con|san|guine
con|san|guin|eous
con|san|guin|ity
con|science
con|science|less
conscience-
             stricken
conscience-struck
con|scien|tious
con|scien|tious|ly
con|scien|tious|
             ness
con|scious
con|scious|ly
con|scious|ness
con|script
con|scrip|tion
con|se|crate
  con|se|crat|ing
con|se|cra|tion

con|se|cra|tor
con|se|cra|tory
con|secu|tive
con|secu|tive|ly
con|secu|tive|ness
con|sen|sual
con|sen|su|al|ly
con|sen|sus
con|sent
con|sen|tient
con|se|quence
con|se|quent
con|se|quen|tial
con|se|quen|tial|
             ism
con|se|quen|tial|ist
con|se|quen|ti|al|
             ity
con|se|quen|tial|ly
con|se|quent|ly
con|ser|vancy
  con|ser|van|cies
con|ser|va|tion
con|ser|va|tion|al
con|ser|va|tion|ist
Con|ser|va|tism
  Politics
con|ser|va|tism
con|ser|va|tive
con|ser|va|tive|ly
con|ser|va|tive|ness
con|ser|va|toire
con|ser|va|tor
con|ser|va|tor|ium
  con|ser|va|tor|iums
  or con|ser|va|toria
con|ser|va|tory
  con|ser|va|tor|ies
con|serve
  con|serv|ing
con|sider
con|sid|er|able
con|sid|er|ably
con|sid|er|ate
con|sid|er|ate|ly
con|sid|er|ate|ness
con|sid|er|ation
con|si|gliere
  con|si|glieri
con|sign
con|sign|ee
con|sign|ment
con|signor

con|sili|ence
con|sili|ent
con|sist
con|sist|ence var. of
  consistency
con|sist|ency
  con|sist|en|cies
con|sist|ent
con|sist|ent|ly
con|sis|tor|ial
con|sis|tory
  con|sis|tor|ies
con|so|ci|ation
con|so|ci|ation|al
con|so|ci|ation|al|
             ism
con|sol|able
con|sola|tion
con|sola|tory
con|sole
  con|sol|ing
con|soler
con|soli|date
  con|soli|dat|ing
con|soli|da|tion
con|soli|da|tor
con|soli|da|tory
con|sol|ing|ly
Con|sols
con|sommé
con|son|ance
con|son|ant
con|son|ant|al
con|son|ant|ly
con sor|dino
con|sort
con|sor|tium
  con|sor|tia or
  con|sor|tiums
con|spe|cif|ic
con|spe|ci|fi|city
con|spec|tus
con|spi|cuity
con|spicu|ous
con|spicu|ous|ly
con|spicu|ous|ness
con|spir|acist
con|spir|acy
  con|spir|acies
con|spir|ator
con|spira|tor|ial
con|spira|tori|al|ly

con|spire
  con|spir|ing
Con|stable, John
  painter
con|stable
con|stabu|lary
  con|stabu|lar|ies
Con|stance name;
  Lake C.
con|stancy
  con|stan|cies
con|stant
Con|stanța
con|stan|tan
Con|stan|tine
Con|stan|tin|ople
  former name of
  Istanbul
con|stant|ly
Con|stanza var. of
  Constanța
con|sta|tive
con|stel|late
  con|stel|lat|ing
con|stel|la|tion
con|ster|nate
  con|ster|nat|ing
con|ster|na|tion
con|sti|pate
  con|sti|pat|ing
con|sti|pa|tion
con|stitu|ency
  con|stitu|en|cies
con|stitu|ent
con|sti|tute
  con|sti|tut|ing
con|sti|tu|tion
con|sti|tu|tion|al
con|sti|tu|tion|al|
        ise
  Br. var. of
  constitutionalize
con|sti|tu|tion|al|
        ism
con|sti|tu|tion|al|
        ist
con|sti|tu|tion|
       al|ity
con|sti|tu|tion|al|
        ize
con|sti|tu|tion|al|
       iz|ing
con|sti|tu|tion|al|ly
con|sti|tu|tive
con|sti|tu|tive|ly

con|strain
con|straint
con|strict
con|stric|tion
con|strict|ive
con|strict|or
con|stru|able
con|stru|al
con|struct
con|struc|tion
con|struc|tion|al
con|struc|tion|al|ly
con|struc|tion|ism
con|struc|tion|ist
con|struct|ive
con|struct|ive|ly
con|struct|ive|ness
con|struct|iv|ism
con|struct|iv|ist
con|struct|or
con|strue
  con|stru|ing
con|sub|stan|tial
con|sub|stan|ti|al|
        ity
con|sub|stan|ti|
       ation
con|sue|tude
con|sue|tud|in|ary
con|sul
con|su|lar
con|sul|ate
con|sul|ship
con|sult
con|sult|ancy
  con|sult|an|cies
con|sult|ant
con|sult|ation
con|sulta|tive
con|sult|ee
con|sum|able
con|sume
  con|sum|ing
con|sumer
con|sumer|ism
con|sumer|ist
con|sumer|is|tic
con|sum|ing|ly
con|sum|mate
con|sum|mat|ing
con|sum|mate|ly
con|sum|ma|tion
con|sum|ma|tor

con|sump|tion
con|sump|tive
con|tact
con|tact|able
contact-breaker
con|tact|ee
con|ta|dina
  con|ta|dine or
  con|ta|di|nas
con|ta|dino
  con|ta|dini or
  con|ta|di|nos
con|ta|gion
con|ta|gious
con|ta|gious|ly
con|ta|gious|ness
con|tain
con|tain|able
con|tain|er
con|tain|er|isa|tion
  Br. var. of
  containerization
con|tain|er|ise Br.
  var. of containerize
con|tain|er|iza|tion
con|tain|er|ize
  con|tain|er|iz|ing
con|tain|ment
con|tam|in|ant
con|tam|in|ate
  con|tam|in|at|ing
con|tam|in|ation
con|tam|in|ator
con|tango +s
Conté pencil etc.
conte story
con|temn
con|temn|er
con|tem|plate
  con|tem|plat|ing
con|tem|pla|tion
con|tem|pla|tive
con|tem|pla|tive|ly
con|tem|pla|tor
con|tem|por|
      an|eity
con|tem|por|
      an|eous
con|tem|por|
      an|eous|ly
con|tem|por|ar|ily
con|tem|por|ari|
       ness

con|tem|por|ary
  con|tem|por|ar|ies
con|tempt
con|tempt|ibil|ity
con|tempt|ible
con|tempt|ibly
con|temp|tu|ous
con|temp|tu|ous|ly
con|tend
con|tend|er
con|tent
con|tent|ed|ly
con|tent|ed|ness
con|ten|tion
con|ten|tious
con|ten|tious|ly
con|ten|tious|ness
con|tent|less
con|tent|ment
con|ter|min|ous
con|tessa
con|test
con|test|abil|ity
con|test|able
con|test|ant
con|test|ation
con|test|er
con|text
con|text|ual
con|text|ual|
      isa|tion
  Br. var. of
  contextualization
con|text|ual|ise Br.
  var. of
  contextualize
con|text|ual|ism
con|text|ual|ist
con|text|ual|
      iza|tion
con|text|ual|ize
  con|text|ual|iz|ing
con|text|ual|ly
con|tigu|ity
con|tigu|ous
con|tigu|ous|ly
con|tin|ence
Con|tin|ent European
  mainland
con|tin|ent
Con|tin|en|tal
  European
con|tin|en|tal

con|tin|en|tal|ly
con|tin|ent|ly
con|tin|gency
  con|tin|gen|cies
con|tin|gent
con|tin|gent|ly
con|tinu|able
con|tin|ual
con|tinu|al|ly
con|tinu|ance
con|tinu|ant
con|tinu|ation
con|tinu|ative
con|tinu|ator
con|tinue
  con|tinu|ing
con|tinu|er
con|tinu|ity
  con|tinu|ities
con|tinu|o +s
con|tinu|ous
con|tinu|ous|ly
con|tinu|ous|ness
con|tinuum
  con|tinua
con|tort
con|tor|tion
con|tor|tion|ist
con|tour
con|tra revolution-
  ary
con|tra prep.
contra|band
contra|band|ist
contra|bass
contra|bas|soon
contra|cep|tion
contra|cep|tive
con|tract
con|tract|able of a
  disease, able to be
  contracted
con|tract|ee
con|tract|ible able
  to be shrunk etc.
con|tract|ile
con|tract|il|ity
con|trac|tion
con|tract|ive
con|trac|tor
con|trac|tor|
  isa|tion
  Br. var. of

contractorization
con|trac|tor|ise *Br.*
  var. of
contractorize
con|trac|tor|
    ization
con|trac|tor|ize
  con|trac|tor|izing
con|trac|tual
con|trac|tu|al|ly
con|trac|tur|al
con|trac|ture
contra|dance
contra|dict
contra|dic|tion
contra|dict|or
contra|dic|tor|ily
contra|dict|ori|
    ness
contra|dict|ory
  contra|dict|or|ies
contra|dis|tinc|tion
contra|dis|tin|
    guish
contra|
  dis|tin|guish|ing
contra|fac|tive
contra|fact|ual
contra|flow
con|trail
contra|indi|cate
  contra|indi|cat|ing
contra|indi|ca|tion
contra|lat|eral
con|tralto +s
con|tra mun|dum
contra|pos|ition
contra|posi|tive
cont|rap|posto
  con|trap|posti
con|tra
  prof|er|entem
con|trap|tion
contra|pun|tal
contra|pun|tal|ly
contra|pun|tist
con|trar|ian
con|trar|ian|ism
con|trar|iety
  con|trar|ieties
con|trar|ily
con|trari|ness
con|trari|wise

contra-rotating
con|trary
  con|trar|ies
con|trast
con|trast|ing|ly
con|trast|ive
con|trasty
contra suggest|ible
contra|vene
  contra|ven|ing
contra|vener
contra|ven|tion
contre|danse
contre-jour
contre|temps
  pl. contre|temps
con|trib|ute
  con|trib|ut|ing
con|tri|bu|tion
con|tribu|tive
con|tribu|tor
con|tribu|tory
  con|tribu|tor|ies
con|trite
con|trite|ly
con|trite|ness
con|tri|tion
con|triv|able
con|triv|ance
con|trive
  con|triv|ing
con|triver
con|trol
  con|trolled
con|trol|ling
con|trol|labil|ity
con|trol|lable
con|trol|lably
con|trol|ler
con|trol|ler|ship
con|tro|ver|sial
con|tro|ver|sial|ist
con|tro|ver|sial|ly
con|tro|versy
  con|tro|ver|sies
con|tro|vert
con|tro|vert|ible
con|tu|ma|cious
con|tu|macy
con|tu|me|li|ous
con|tumely
  con|tume|lies

con|tuse
  con|tus|ing
con|tu|sion
con|un|drum
con|ur|ba|tion
con|ure
conus
coni
conus ar|teri|osus
coni ar|teri|osi
conus me|dul|laris
coni me|dul|lari
con|va|lesce
  con|va|les|cing
con|va|les|cence
con|va|les|cent
con|vect
con|vec|tion
con|vec|tion|al
con|vect|ive
con|vect|or
con|ven|ance
con|vene
  con|ven|ing
con|vener
con|veni|ence
con|veni|ency
  con|veni|en|cies
con|veni|ent
con|veni|ent|ly
con|venor var. of
  convener
con|vent
con|ven|ticle
con|ven|tion
con|ven|tion|al
con|ven|tion|al|ise
  Br. var. of
  conventionalize
con|ven|tion|al|ism
con|ven|tion|al|ist
con|ven|tion|al|ity
  con|ven|tion|
    al|ities
con|ven|tion|al|ize
  con|ven|tion|al|
    iz|ing
con|ven|tion|al|ly
con|ven|tion|eer
con|ven|tual
con|verge
  con|ver|ging
con|ver|gence

con|ver|gency
  con|ver|gen|cies
con|ver|gent
con|ver|sance
con|ver|sancy
con|ver|sa|tion
con|ver|sa|tion|al
con|ver|sa|tion|al|
        ist
con|ver|sa|tion|
       al|ly
conversation-
    stopper
con|ver|saz|ione
  con|ver|saz|ioni or
  con|ver|saz|iones
con|verse
  con|vers|ing
con|verse|ly
con|ver|sion
con|vert
con|vert|er
con|vert|ibil|ity
con|vert|ible
con|ver|tor var. of
  converter
con|vex
con|vex|ity
  con|vex|ities
con|vex|ly
convexo-concave
convexo-convex
con|vey
con|vey|ance
con|vey|an|cer
con|vey|an|cing
con|vey|er var. of
  conveyor
con|vey|or
con|vict
con|vic|tion
con|vince
  con|vin|cing
con|vin|cer
con|vin|cing|ly
con|viv|ial
con|vivi|al|ity
con|vivi|al|ly
con|vo|ca|tion
con|vo|ca|tion|al
con|voke
  con|vok|ing

con|vo|luted
con|vo|lu|tion
con|vo|lu|tion|al
con|vol|vu|lus
  con|vol|vu|luses or
  con|vol|vuli
con|voy
con|vul|sant
con|vulse
  con|vuls|ing
con|vul|sion
con|vul|sive
con|vul|sive|ly
Con|way var. of
  Conwy
Conwy Welsh
  county
cony var. of coney
coo +s +ed +ing soft
  sound; *exclam.*; cf.
  coup
co-occur
  co-occurred
  co-occurring
  co-occurrence
cooee
  coo|ees
  coo|eed
  cooee|ing
Cook, James
  explorer
Cook, Mt
Cook, Peter
  comedian
Cook, Thomas
  tourist pioneer
cook|book
cook-chill
Cooke, Wil|liam
  inventor
cook|er
cook|ery
  cook|er|ies
cook|house
cookie
Cook Islands
cook|out
cook|shop
Cook|son,
  Cath|er|ine novelist
Cook Strait
cook|top
cook|ware
cool cf. koel

coola|bah var. of
  coolibah
cool|ant
cool|er
Coo|ley's an|aemia
Cool|gar|die
cooli|bah
Cool|idge, Cal|vin
  US president
coo|lie labourer; cf.
  coolly, coulee,
  coulis
cool|ish
cool|ly cf. coolie,
  coulee, coulis
Cool|Max
  trademark
cool|ness
coolth
coomb var. of
  combe
coombe var. of
  combe
coon
coon|can
coon|hound
coon|skin
coop cage; cf.
  coupe, couped
co-op cooperative
  enterprise
Coo|per, Gary actor
Coo|per, Henry
  boxer
Coo|per, James
  Feni|more novelist
coop|er
coop|er|age
co|oper|ant
co|oper|ate
  co|oper|at|ing
co|oper|ation
co|opera|tive
co|opera|tive|ly
co|opera|tive|ness
co|oper|ator
Coo|per pair
coop|ery
  coop|er|ies
co|ope|tition
co-opt
co-optation
co-option
co-optive

co|ord|in|ate
co|ord|in|at|ing
co|ord|in|ation
co|ord|ina|tive
co|ord|in|ator
coo|ter
cootie
co-own
co-owner
co-ownership
cop
  copped
  cop|ping
  cf. Kop, kop
Copa|ca|bana
copa|cet|ic
co|paiba
copal
Copán ancient
  Mayan city
co|par|cen|ary
  co|par|cen|ar|ies
co|par|cener
co-parent
co-partner
co-partner|ship
cope
  cop|ing
co|peck var. of
  kopek
Co|pen|hagen
co|pe|pod
Co|pe|poda
coper
Co|per|ni|can
Co|per|ni|cus,
  Nico|laus
  astronomer
cope|stone
copi|able
copier
co-pilot
cop|ing
copi|ous
copi|ous|ly
co|pita
co|pla|nar
co|pla|nar|ity
Cop|land, Aaron
  composer
Cop|ley, John
  painter
co|poly|mer

co|poly|mer|isa|tion
Br. var. of
copolymerization
co|poly|mer|ise *Br.*
var. of
copolymerize
co|poly|mer|iza|tion
co|poly|mer|ize
co|poly|mer|iz|ing
cop-out *n.*
cop|per
cop|peras
Copper|belt region,
Zambia
copper-fasten
copper|head
copper|nob
copper|plate
copper|smith
cop|pery
cop|pice
cop|picing
Cop|pola, Fran|cis
Ford *film director*
copra
co-precipi|tate
co-precipi|tat|ing
co-precipi|ta|tion
co-present
co-present|er
co|proces|sor
co-produce
co-producing
co-producer
co-produc|tion
copro|lalia
copro|lite
copro|pha|gia var.
of coprophagy
copro|pha|gic
cop|ropha|gous
cop|roph|agy
copro|philia
Co-Prosperity
Sphere
copse
Copt
cop|ter
Cop|tic
cop|ula *n.*
copu|lar *adj.*

copu|late
copu|lat|ing
copu|la|tion
copu|la|tive
copu|la|tory
copy
cop|ies
cop|ied
copy|ing
cf. kopi, koppie
copy|book
copy|cat
copy|desk
copy-edit
copy ed|itor
copy|hold
copy|hold|er
copy|ist
copy|left
copy|left|ed
copy|read
copy|read|er
copy|right
copy type
copy typ|ist
copy|writer
copy|writ|ing
coq au vin
coq au vins
co|quet|ry
co|quet|ries
co|quette
co|quet|ting
co|quet|tish
co|quet|tish|ly
co|quet|tish|ness
co|quina *clam*
co|quito +s
cor *exclam.*; cf. caw,
core, corps
Cora *people*; cf.
kora
cor|acle
cor|ac|oid
coral
coral|berry
coral|berries
Cora|lie
cora|lita var. of
corallita
Cor|al|lian
cor|al|line
cor|al|lita

cor|al|lite
cor|al|loid
coral|root *plant*
coram pop|ulo
cor an|glais
cors an|glais
cor|beil *carving of
basket of flowers*
cor|beille *basket of
flowers or fruit*
cor|bel
cor|belled *Br.*
cor|beled *US*
cor|bel|ling *Br.*
cor|bel|ing *US*
cor|bicula
cor|bicu|lae
cor|bie
Cor|bus|ian
Corby
Cor|co|vado
cord *twine etc.*;
vocal membrane;
cf. chord
cord|age
cord|ate *heart-
shaped*; cf.
caudate, chordate
Cor|delia *name*
Cor|del|ier *monk*
cord|grass
cor|dial *polite*;
drink
cor|diale *in 'entente
cordiale'*
cor|di|al|ity
cor|dial|ly
cor|dier|ite
cor|dil|lera
cord|ite
cord|less
Cor|doba *cities,
Argentina and
Spain*
cor|doba *Nicar-
aguan currency*
cor|don
cor|don bleu
cor|dons bleus
dish
cordon-bleu *finch*
cor|don sani|taire
cor|dons
sani|taires

Cor|dova var. of
Cordoba
cor|do|van
Cord|tex *trademark*
Cor|dura *trademark*
cor|du|roy
cord|wain|er
cord|wood
CORE = Congress
of Racial Equality
core
cor|ing
centre etc.; cf. caw,
cor, corps
co|refer|ence
co|refer|en|tial
co-religion|ist
co|rella
Co|relli, Arc|an|gelo
composer
core|op|sis
core|op|ses
corer *utensil*; cf.
Cora, kora
co-respond|ent *in
divorce; shoes*; cf.
correspondent
corf
corves
Corfu
corgi
cori|aceous
cori|an|der
Cor|inna
Cor|inne
Cor|inth
Cor|inth|ian cf.
Carinthian
Corio|lanus *Roman
general*
Cori|olis
cor|ium
Cork *in Republic of
Ireland*
cork cf. calk, caulk
cork|age
cork|er *excellent
person or thing*; cf.
caulker
cork|screw
cork|wood
corky
cork|ier
corki|est

corm
Cor|mac
cor|mel
corm|let
cor|mor|ant
corn|ball
corn beef var. of
  corned beef
corn|brash
corn|bread
corn|cob
corn|cockle
corn|crake
cor|nea
cor|neal
corned beef
Cor|neille, Pierre
  dramatist
cor|nel
Cor|ne|lia
cor|ne|lian var. of
  carnelian
Cor|ne|lius
corn|eous
cor|ner
corner|back
corner|man
  corner|men
corner|stone
corner|wise
cor|net brass instru-
  ment; wafer;
  cavalry officer; cf.
  cornett
cor|net|cy
  cor|net|cies
cornet|fish
cor|net|ist
cor|nett woodwind
  instrument. var. of
  cornetto
cor|net|tist var. of
  cornetist
cor|netto
  cor|netti
corn|field
corn|flake
corn|flour maize
  flour
corn|flower plant
Corn|husk|er State
cor|nice
  cor|nicing
cor|niche

corn|ily
corni|ness
Corn|ish
Cor|nish|man
  Cor|nish|men
Cor|nish|woman
  Cor|nish|women
corn|meal
corn|rows
corn|starch
corn|stone
cornu
  cor|nua
cor|nual
cor|nu|co|pia
cor|nu|co|pian
cor|nus
Corn|wall
corny
  corn|ier
  corni|est
cor|olla
cor|ol|lary
  cor|ol|lar|ies
coro|man|del
cor|ona ring-shaped
  object or
  phenomenon
cor|ona +s cigar
Cor|ona Aus|tra|lis
  constellation
Cor|ona Bor|ealis
coro|nach
cor|ona|graph
cor|onal
cor|on|ary
  cor|on|ar|ies
cor|on|ation
cor|ona|virus
cor|on|er
cor|onet
cor|on|lal
cor|on|oid
Corot, Ca|mille
  painter
Corp Corporal
cor|pora
cor|poral
cor|por|ate
cor|por|ate|ly
cor|por|ation
cor|por|at|isa|tion
  Br. var. of

corporatization
cor|por|at|ise Br.
  var. of corporatize
cor|por|at|ism
cor|por|at|ist
cor|pora|tive
cor|pora|tiv|ism
cor|pora|tiv|ist
cor|por|at|ization
cor|por|at|ize
cor|por|at|iz|ing
cor|por|ator
cor|por|eal
cor|por|eal|ity
cor|por|eal|ly
cor|po|sant
corps
  pl. corps
  body of troops etc.;
  cf. caw, cor, core,
  corpse
corps de bal|let
  pl. corps de bal|let
corps d'elite
  pl. corps d'elite
  French corps
  d'élite
corps
  dip|lo|ma|tique
corps
  dip|lo|ma|tiques
corpse
  corps|ing
  dead body; cf.
  corps
corpse can|dle
cor|pu|lence
cor|pu|lency
cor|pu|lent
cor pul|mo|nale
cor|pus
  cor|pora or
  cor|puses
cor|pus cal|lo|sum
  cor|pora cal|losa
cor|pus
  cav|ern|osum
  cor|pora
  cav|ern|osa
Cor|pus Christi +s
cor|puscle
cor|pus|cu|lar
cor|pus de|licti +s
cor|pus lu|teum
  cor|pora lutea

cor|pus
  spon|gi|osum
  cor|pora
  spon|gi|osa
cor|pus stri|atum
  cor|pora stri|ata
cor|ral
  cor|ralled
  cor|ral|ling
  animal pen; cf.
  chorale
cor|ra|sion
cor|rect
cor|rect|able
cor|rec|tion
cor|rec|tion|al
cor|rec|ti|tude
cor|rect|ive
cor|rect|ly
cor|rect|ness
cor|rect|or
Cor|reg|gio,
  An|tonio Al|legri
  da painter
cor|rel|ate
  cor|rel|at|ing
cor|rel|ation
cor|rel|ation|al
cor|rela|tive
cor|rela|tive|ly
cor|rela|tiv|ity
cor|res|pond
cor|res|pond|ence
cor|res|pond|ent
  letter-writer;
  reporter; cf.
  co-respondent
cor|res|pond|ing|ly
cor|rida
cor|ri|dor
cor|rie
Corrie|dale
cor|ri|gen|dum
  cor|ri|genda
cor|ri|gi|bil|ity
cor|ri|gible
cor|rob|or|ate
  cor|rob|or|at|ing
cor|rob|or|ation
cor|rob|ora|tive
cor|rob|or|ator
cor|rob|ora|tory
cor|robo|ree

cor|rode
cor|rod|ing
cor|rod|ible
cor|rody
cor|rodies
cor|ro|sion
cor|ro|sive
cor|ro|sive|ly
cor|ro|sive|ness
cor|ru|gate
cor|ru|gat|ing
cor|ru|ga|tion
cor|rupt
cor|rupt|er
cor|rupt|ibil|ity
cor|rupt|ible
cor|rup|tion
cor|rup|tive
cor|rupt|ly
cor|rupt|ness
cor|sage
cor|sair
corse *archaic* corpse
corse|let armour
corse|lette woman's
  undergarment
cor|set
cor|set|ière
cor|set|ry
  cor|set|ries
Cor|sica
Cor|sican
cor|tège
Cor|tes Spanish
  legislative assembly
Cor|tés, Her|nando
  conquistador
cor|tex
  cor|ti|ces
Cor|tez var. of
  Cortés
Corti, organ of
cor|tical
cor|ti|cate
cor|ti|cated var. of
  corticate
cor|ti|ca|tion
cor|tici|fugal var. of
  corticofugal
cor|tico|fugal
cor|tico|ster|oid
cor|tico|sterone
cor|tico|troph|in

cor|tico|tropin var.
  of corticotrophin
cor|tile
  cor|tili or cor|ti|les
cor|tina
cor|tin|ate
cor|ti|sol
cor|ti|sone
cor|un|dum
Cor|unna
cor|us|cant
cor|us|cate
  cor|us|cat|ing
cor|us|ca|tion
cor|vée
corves
cor|vette
cor|vid
cor|vina
cor|vine
Cor|vus
cory|ban|tic
cor|yd|alis
cor|ymb
cor|ymb|ose
cor|yne|
          bac|ter|ium
cor|yne|bac|teria
cory|phée
cor|yza
Cos var. of Kos
cos lettuce
cos = cosine;
  because
Cosa Nos|tra
cos|cor|oba
cosec cosecant
co|se|cant
coset *Mathematics*;
  cf. cosset
co-signatory
  co-signator|ies
cosi|ly *Br.*
  US cozily
Cos|ima
Cos|imo de'
  Med|ici Florentine
  statesman and
  banker
co|sine
cosi|ness *Br.*
  US coziness
co-sleep
co-slept

cosme|ceut|ical
cos|met|ic
cos|met|ic|al|ly
cos|met|ician
cos|meto|logic|al
cos|met|olo|gist
cos|met|ology
cos|mic
cos|mic|al|ly
Cosmo
cosmo|drome
cosmo|gen|esis
cosmo|gen|et|ic
cosmo|gen|ic
cos|mogeny
  cos|mogen|ies
cosmo|gon|ic
cosmo|gon|ic|al
cos|mog|on|ist
cos|mog|ony
  cos|mog|onies
cos|mog|raph|er
cosmo|graph|ic|al
cos|mog|raphy
  cos|mog|raph|ies
cosmo|logic|al
cos|molo|gist
cos|mol|ogy
  cos|mol|ogies
cosmo|naut
cos|mop|olis
cosmo|pol|itan
cosmo|pol|it|an|ise
  Br. var. of
  cosmopolitanize
cosmo|pol|it|an|
                 ism
cosmo|pol|it|an|ize
cosmo|pol|it|an|
                iz|ing
cos|mop|ol|ite
cos|mos
COSPAR = Com-
  mittee on Space
  Research
Cos|sack
cos|set
cos|sie
Cos|syra
costa rib; cf. coster
costa +s coast; cf.
  coster
Costa Blanca

Costa Brava
Costa del Sol
Costa-Gavras,
  Con|stan|tin Greek
  film director
cos|tal
co-star
  co-starred
  co-starring
Cos|tard
Costa Rica
Costa Rican
cos|tate
cost–benefit *adj.*
cost-conscious
cost-cutter
cost-cutting
cost-effective
cost-effect|ive|ly
cost-effect|ive|ness
cost-efficiency
cost-efficient
cos|ter costermon-
  ger; cf. costa
cos|ter|mon|ger
cos|tive
cos|tive|ness
cost|ly
  cost|lier
  cost|li|est
cost|mary
  cost|mar|ies
Cost|ner, Kevin
  actor
cost-of-carry
cost-plus
cos|tume
  cos|tum|ing
cos|tumer *US*
cos|tu|mier *Br.*
cosy *Br.*
  cosies
  cosied
cosy|ing
cosi|er
cosi|est
  US cozy
co|tan|gent
cot-case
cot death
cote shelter
Côte d'Azur
cote-hardie
co|terie

co¦ter¦min¦ous
coth hyperbolic
  cotangent
co¦til¦lion
co¦tinga
cot¦ise var. of
  cottise
Cot¦man, John Sell
  painter
co¦to¦neas¦ter
Coto¦nou
Coto¦paxi
co-trimoxa¦zole
Cots¦wold
cotta surplice; cf.
  cottar, cotter
cot¦tage
  cot¦ta¦ging
cot¦tager
cot¦tagey
cot¦tar farm
  labourer; cf. cotta,
  cotter
Cott¦bus
cot¦ter bolt; pin; cf.
  cotta, cottar
cot¦tier
cot¦tise
cot¦ton
cotton-leaf worm
cotton¦mouth
cotton-picking
cotton¦tail
cotton¦weed
cotton¦wood
cot¦ton wool
cot¦tony
cottony-cushion
  scale
coty¦le¦don
coty¦le¦don¦ary
coty¦le¦don¦ous
cou¦cal
couch seat; grass
couch¦ant
couch¦ette
coudé
cou¦gar
cough
cough¦er cf. coffer
could
couldn't

cou¦lee lava; ravine
  French coulée; cf.
  coolie, coolly,
  coulis
couli¦biac
cou¦lis
  pl. cou¦lis
  sauce; cf. coolie,
  coolly, coulee
cou¦lisse
cou¦loir
cou¦lomb unit
Cou¦lomb's law
coul¦ter *Br.*
  US colter
cou¦ma¦rin
cou¦ma¦rone
coun¦cil assembly;
  cf. counsel
coun¦cil¦lor *Br.*
  member of council;
  cf. counsellor
coun¦cil¦lor¦ship
  Br.
coun¦cil¦man
  coun¦cil¦men
coun¦cil¦or *US*
  member of council;
  cf. counselor
coun¦cil¦or¦ship *US*
coun¦cil¦woman
  coun¦cil¦women
coun¦sel
  coun¦selled *Br.*
  coun¦seled *US*
  coun¦sel¦ling *Br.*
  coun¦sel¦ing *US*
  advice; barrister;
  advise; cf. council
coun¦sel¦lor *Br.*
  adviser; in 'Privy
  Counsellor'; cf.
  councillor
coun¦sel¦or *US*
  adviser; cf.
  councilor
counselor-at-law
  counselors-at-law
count¦able
count¦ably
count¦back
count¦down *n.*
coun¦ten¦ance
  coun¦ten¦an¦cing
coun¦ter

coun¦ter¦act
coun¦ter¦action
coun¦ter¦active
counter-attack
counter-attacker
counter-attrac¦tion
coun¦ter¦bal¦ance
  coun¦ter¦
    bal¦an¦cing
coun¦ter¦blast
coun¦ter¦bore
coun¦ter¦bor¦ing
coun¦ter¦change
  coun¦ter¦chan¦ging
coun¦ter¦charge
  coun¦ter¦char¦ging
coun¦ter¦check
coun¦ter¦claim
coun¦ter¦clock¦wise
counter-
  condition¦ing
coun¦ter¦cul¦tural
coun¦ter¦cul¦ture
coun¦ter¦cur¦rent
counter-espion¦age
coun¦ter¦fac¦tual
coun¦ter¦feit
coun¦ter¦feit¦er
coun¦ter¦foil
counter-
  insurgency
counter-
  intelli¦gence
counter-intuitive
counter-
  intuitive¦ly
coun¦ter¦irri¦tant
coun¦ter¦
  irri¦ta¦tion
counter-jumper
coun¦ter¦mand
coun¦ter¦march
coun¦ter¦mark
coun¦ter¦meas¦ure
coun¦ter¦mel¦ody
  coun¦ter¦mel¦odies
coun¦ter¦mine
  coun¦ter¦min¦ing
coun¦ter¦move
  coun¦ter¦mov¦ing
coun¦ter¦move¦
    ment
coun¦ter¦offen¦sive
counter-offer

coun¦ter¦pane
coun¦ter¦part
coun¦ter¦party
coun¦ter¦parties
coun¦ter¦plot
  coun¦ter¦plot¦ted
  coun¦ter¦plot¦ting
coun¦ter¦point
coun¦ter¦poise
  coun¦ter¦pois¦ing
coun¦ter¦pose
  coun¦ter¦pos¦ing
coun¦ter¦pos¦ition
coun¦ter¦
  pro¦duct¦ive
coun¦ter¦pro¦posal
coun¦ter¦punch
coun¦ter¦punch¦er
Counter-
  Reform¦ation
counter-
  revolu¦tion
counter-
  revolu¦tion¦ary
counter-
  revolu¦tion¦ar¦ies
coun¦ter¦rotate
coun¦ter¦rotat¦ing
coun¦ter¦rota¦tion
coun¦ter¦scarp
coun¦ter¦shaded
coun¦ter¦shad¦ing
coun¦ter¦shaft
coun¦ter¦sign
coun¦ter¦
  sig¦na¦ture
coun¦ter¦sink
  coun¦ter¦sunk
coun¦ter¦spy
  coun¦ter¦spies
coun¦ter¦stain
coun¦ter¦stroke
coun¦ter¦sub¦ject
coun¦ter¦tenor
coun¦ter¦terror¦
    ism
coun¦ter¦terror¦ist
coun¦ter¦top
coun¦ter¦trade
counter-
  transfer¦ence
coun¦ter¦vail
coun¦ter¦value

coun|ter|weight
count|ess
coun|tian
count|less
Count Pala|tine
  Counts Pala|tine
coun|tri|fied
coun|try
  coun|tries
coun|try|fied var. of
  countrified
coun|try|made
coun|try|man
  coun|try|men
coun|try|side
coun|try|wide
coun|try|woman
  coun|try|women
count|ship
county
  coun|ties
County Pala|tine
  Coun|ties Pala|tine
coup seizure of
  power
coup de foudre
  coups de foudre
coup de grâce
  coups de grâce
coup de main
  coups de main
coup de maître
  coups de maître
coup d'état
  coups d'état
coup de théâtre
  coups de théâtre
coup d'œil
  coups d'œil
coupe dish; *US* car;
  cf. **coop**
coupé *Br.*
  car
couped *Heraldry*
Cou|pe|rin,
  Fran|çois
  composer
couple
  coup|ling
couple|dom
coup|ler
coup|let
coup|ley var. of
  couply

couply
cou|pon
coupon-clipper
cour|age
cour|age|ous
cour|age|ous|ly
cour|ant
cour|ante
Cour|bet, Gus|tave
  painter
cour|bette
cour|eur de bois
  cour|eurs de bois
cour|gette
cour|ier
cou|rol
Cour|règes, André
  couturier
course
  cours|ing
  route etc.; cf.
  coarse, corse
course|book
cour|ser
course|ware
course|work
court lawcourt etc.;
  cf. **caught**
court bouil|lon +s
cour|te|ous
cour|te|ous|ly
cour|tesan
cour|tesy
  cour|tesies
court|house
court|ier
court|li|ness
court|ly
court|lier
court|li|est
court mar|tial *n.*
  courts mar|tial or
  court mar|tials
court-martial *v.*
  court-martials
  court-martialled
  Br.
  court-martialed
  US
  court-martial|ling
  Br.
  court-martial|ing
  US
Court|ney

Cour|trai
court|room
court|ship
court|yard
cous|cous food; cf.
  cuscus, khus-khus
cousin cf. cozen
cousin-german
  cousins-german
cousin|hood
cousin|ly
cousin|ship
Cous|teau,
  Jacques-Yves
  oceanographer
couth
couthie var. of
  couthy
couthy
cou|ture
cou|tur|ier *male*
cou|turi|ère *female*
cou|vade
cou|vert
cou|ver|ture
co|va|lence
co|va|lency
  co|valen|cies
co|va|lent
co|va|lent|ly
co|vari|ance
co|vari|ant
co|vari|ation
co|vel|line
co|vel|lite
coven group of
  witches; cf. covin
cov|en|ant
cov|en|ant|al
Cov|en|ant|er
  Scottish History
cov|en|ant|or
Cov|ent Gar|den
Cov|en|try
cover
cover|able
cover|age
cover|all
Cov|er|dale, Miles
  biblical scholar
cover|let
cover|slip
cov|ert

cov|ert|ly
cov|er|ture
cover-up *n.*
covet
covet|able
covet|ous
covet|ous|ly
covet|ous|ness
covey
covin fraud; cf.
  coven
cov|ine var. of covin
cowa|bunga
Cow|ard, Noel
  dramatist and actor
cow|ard
cow|ard|ice
cow|ard|li|ness
cow|ard|ly
cow|ardy
cow|bane
cow|bell
cow|berry
  cow|berries
cow|bird
cow|boy
cow|catch|er
Cow|drey, Colin
  cricketer
cower
Cowes town,
  England
cow|fish
cow|girl
cow|herd
cow|hide
cow-house
Cowi|chan sweater
cowl
cowled
cow|lick
cowl|ing
cow|man
  cow|men
co-worker
cow|pat
cow|pea
Cow|per, Wil|liam
  poet
Cow|per's gland
cow|poke
cow|pox
cow|punch|er

cow¦rie shell; cf.
  kauri
co-write
  co-writes
  co-wrote
  co-writing
  co-written
co-writer
cowry var. of cowrie
cow|shed
cow|slip
Cox apple
cox coxswain
coxa
  coxae
coxal
cox|comb dandy; cf.
  cockscomb
cox|comb¦ry
  cox¦comb¦ries
cox|less
cox|opod|ite
Cox|sackie virus
Cox's Bazar
Cox's or¦ange
  pip¦pin
cox|swain
coy shy; cf. koi
coy¦dog
coyly
coy|ness
coy¦ote
coypu
coz cousin
cozen cheat
coz|en|ages
coz|en¦er
cozi¦ly
  Br. cosily
cozi|ness
  Br. cosiness
Cozu|mel
cozy US
  cozies
  cozied
  cozy|ing
  cozi¦er
  cozi|est
  Br. cosy
coz¦zie var. of cossie
crab
  crabbed
  crab|bing

Crabbe, George
  poet
crab|bed¦ly
crab|ber
crab|bily
crab|bi¦ness
crabby
  crab|bier
  crab|bi¦est
crab|eater seal
crab|grass
crab|like
crab|meat
crab|wise
crack|brained
crack|down n.
crack¦er
cracker|jack
crack|ers
crack|head
crack-jaw
crackle
  crack|ling
crack¦ly
  crack|lier
  crack|li¦est
crack|nel
crack|pot
cracks|man
  cracks|men
crack-up n.
cracky
Cra¦cow
cra¦dle
  crad¦ling
cradle|board
cradle-snatch¦er
craft skilled activity;
  cf. kraft
craft¦er
craft|ily
crafti|ness
crafts|man
  crafts|men
crafts¦man|ship
crafts|person
  crafts|people
crafts|woman
  crafts|women
craft|work
craft|work¦er
crafty
  craft¦ier
  crafti¦est

crag¦gily
crag¦gi|ness
craggy
  crag|gier
  crag¦gi|est
crags|man
  crags|men
craic a good time;
  var. of crack
crake
cram
  crammed
  cram|ming
crambo
cram-full
cram|mer
cramp-iron
cram|pon
cran
Cra|nach, Lucas
  two painters
cran¦age
cran|berry
  cran|berries
crane
  cran¦ing
cranes|bill
cra|nial
cra|ni|ate
cra|nio|logic¦al
cra|ni|olo¦gist
cra|ni|ology
cra|nio|met¦ric
cra|ni|om¦etry
cra|nio|sacral
cra|nium
  cra|niums or
  cra|nia
crank|case
crank|ily
cranki|ness
crank|pin
crank|shaft
cranky
  crank¦ier
  cranki¦est
Cran|mer, Thomas
  archbishop
cran|nied
cran|nog
cranny
  cran¦nies

crap
  crapped
crap|ping vulgar
  slang
crape fabric; fern;
  hair; myrtle; cf.
  crêpe
crap|per vulgar
  slang
crap|pie fish
crappy
  crap|pier
crap|pi¦est vulgar
  slang
craps gambling
  game
crap|shoot
crap|shoot¦er
crapu|lence
crapu|lent
crapu|lous
crapy like crape; cf.
  crêpey
craque|lure
crash dive n.
crash-dive v.
  crash-diving
crash|ing¦ly
crash-land
crash test n.
crash-test v.
crash|worthi|ness
crash|worthy
cra¦sis
  cra¦ses
crass
cras|si|tude
crass¦ly
crass|ness
Cras|sus, Mar¦cus
  Li¦cin|ius Roman
  politician
cratch
crate
  crat¦ing
crate|ful
crater
C ra¦tions
craton
cra|ton¦ic
cra¦vat
cra¦vat|ted
crave
  crav¦ing

cra|ven
cra|ven|ly
cra|ven|ness
craver
craw crop of bird or
  insect; cf. crore
craw|dad
craw|fish
Craw|ford, Joan
  actress
crawl|board
crawl|er
crawly
cray
cray|fish
crayon +ed +ing
craze
  craz|ing
crazi|ly
crazi|ness
crazy
  cra|zies
  cra|zier
  crazi|est
creak noise; cf.
  creek
creak|ily
creaki|ness
creak|ing|ly
creaky
  creak|ier
  creaki|est
cream cf. creme
cream|er
cream|ery
  cream|er|ies
cream|ily
creami|ness
cream|ware
creamy
  creami|er
  creami|est
cre|ance
crease
  creas|ing
  cf. kris
cre|at|able
cre|ate
  cre|at|ing
cre|at|ine
cre|atin|ine
cre|ation
cre|ation|ism
cre|ation|ist

cre|ative
cre|ative|ly
cre|ative|ness
cre|ativ|ity
cre|ator
crea|ture
crea|ture|ly
crèche
Crécy
cred
cre|dal
cre|dence
cre|den|tial
  cre|den|tialled Br.
  cre|den|tialed US
  cre|den|tial|ling Br.
  cre|den|tial|ing US
cre|denza
cred|ibil|ity
cred|ible
cred|ibly
credit
cred|it|abil|ity
cred|it|able
cred|it|ably
cred|it|or
credit|worthi|ness
credit|worthy
Credo +s
  Christianity
credo +s
cre|du|lity
credu|lous
credu|lous|ly
credu|lous|ness
Cree
creed
creed|al var. of
  credal
Creek people
creek river; cf.
  creak
creel
creep
  crept
creep|er
creepie
creep|ily
creepi|ness
creep|ing Jenny
  creep|ing Jen|nies
creepy
  creep|ier

creepi|est
creepy-crawly
  creepy-crawlies
creese dagger; var.
  of kris
cre|mas|ter
cre|mate
  cre|mat|ing
cre|ma|tion
cre|ma|tor
crema|tor|ium
  crema|toria or
  crema|tor|iums
crema|tory
  crema|tor|ies
creme product with
  a creamy
  consistency; cf.
  cream
crème an|glaise
crème brû|lée
  crèmes brû|lées or
  crème brû|lées
crème cara|mel
  crèmes cara|mel or
  crème cara|mels
crème de cacao
crème de cas|sis
crème de la crème
crème de menthe
crème fraiche
  French crème
  fraîche
Cre|mona
cren|ate
cren|ated
cren|ation
crenel
cren|el|ate var. of
  crenellate
cren|el|ation var. of
  crenellation
cren|el|late
  cren|el|lat|ing
  provide with
  battlements
cren|el|lation
  battlements
cren|elle var. of
  crenel
crenu|late having a
  notched edge
crenu|lated

crenu|la|tion
  notched edge of
  leaf etc.
creo|dont
Cre|ole
cre|ol|isa|tion Br.
  var. of creolization
cre|ol|ise Br. var. of
  creolize
cre|ol|iza|tion
cre|ol|ize
  cre|ol|iz|ing
creo|sol
creo|sote
creo|sot|ing
crêpe pancake; rub-
  ber; paper; cf.
  crape
crêpe de Chine
crepe myr|tle var.
  of crape myrtle
crêperie
crêpe Su|zette
  crêpes Su|zette
crêpey like crêpe,
  cf. crapy
crépinette
crepi|tant
crepi|tate
  crepi|tat|ing
crepi|ta|tion
crepi|tus
crépon
cre|pus|cu|lar
crêpy var. of crêpey
cres|cendo
  pl. cres|cen|dos or
  cres|cendi
  v. cres|cen|does
  cres|cen|doed
  cres|cen|do|ing
cres|cent
cres|cent|ic
cre|sol
cres|set
Cres|sida
Crest share-trading
  system
Cresta Run
crest|fall|en
crest|fish
crest|less
cre|syl
Cret|aceous

Cre|tan
Crete
cre|tic
cretin
cret|in|ise *Br.* var. of
  cretinize
cret|in|ism
cret|in|ize
  cret|in|iz|ing
cret|in|ous
cret|in|ous|ly
cre|tonne
Creutzfeldt–Jakob
cre|vasse
cre|vette
crev|ice
crew cf. *cru*
Crewe town,
  England
crewel yarn
crew|man
  crew|men
crib
  cribbed
  crib|bing
crib|bage
crib|ber
cri|bel|late
cri|bel|lum
  cri|bella
cribo +s
crib|ri|form
crib|work
Crich|ton, James
  'the Admirable',
  adventurer
Crick, Fran|cis bio-
  physicist
crick
cricket
crick|et|er
cri|coid
crico|thyr|oid
cri de cœur
  cris de cœur
cried
crier
cri|key
crim
Crimbo var. of
  Chrimbo
crime
  crim|ing

Cri|mea
Cri|mean
crime-fighter
crime-fighting
cri|men in|juria
crime pas|sion|nel
  crimes
  pas|sion|nels
crim|inal
crim|in|al|isa|tion
  Br. var. of
  criminalization
crim|in|al|ise *Br.*
  var. of criminalize
crim|in|al|is|tics
crim|in|al|ity
crim|in|al|iza|tion
crim|in|al|ize
  crim|in|al|iz|ing
crim|in|al|ly
crim|ino|genic
crim|ino|logic|al
crim|in|olo|gist
crim|in|ology
crimp|er
crimp|lene
  trademark
crimpy
crim|son
cringe
  crin|ging
cringe-making
crin|ger
cringe|worthy
crin|gle
crin|kle
crink|ling
crinkle-cut
crin|kly
  crink|lier
  crink|li|est
crinkum-crankum
crin|oid
crin|oid|al
Crin|oidea
crino|line
cri|ollo +s
cripes
Crip|pen, Dr mur-
  derer
crip|ple
  crip|pling
cripple|dom

crip|pler
crise de nerfs
  crises de nerfs
cri|sis
  cri|ses
crisp|ate
crisp|bread
crisp|er
Cris|pian
Cris|pin
crispi|ness
crisp|ly
crisp|ness
crispy
  crisp|ier
  crispi|est
cris|sal thrash|er
criss-cross
crista
  cris|tae
cris|tate
cris|to|bal|ite
cri|ter|ial
cri|ter|ion
  cri|teria
crit|ic
crit|ic|al
crit|ic|al|ity
  crit|ic|al|ities
crit|ic|al|ly
criti|cis|able *Br.* var.
  of criticizable
criti|cise *Br.* var. of
  criticize
criti|ciser *Br.* var. of
  criticizer
criti|cism
criti|ciz|able
criti|cize
  criti|ciz|ing
criti|cizer
cri|tique
  cri|tiquing
crit|ter
croak|er
croak|ily
croaky
  croak|ier
  croaki|est
Croat
Cro|atia
Cro|atian
croc crocodile; cf.
  crock

Croce, Bene|detto
  philosopher
cro|chet +ed +ing
  crochet; cf.
  crotchet
cro|chet|er
croci pl. of crocus
cro|cido|lite
crock pot, etc.; cf.
  croc
crock|ery
crocket *Architecture*
Crock|ett, Davy
  frontiersman
Crock|ford's
Crock|pot
  trademark
croco|dile
croco|dil|ian
croco|ite
cro|cos|mia
cro|cus
  cro|cuses or croci
Croe|sus Lydian
  king
croft|er
Crohn's dis|ease
crois|sant
Cro-Magnon
Crom|arty
crom|bec
Cro|mer|ian
crom|lech
cromo|gly|cate
Cromp|ton,
  Rich|mal writer
Cromp|ton,
  Sam|uel inventor
Crom|well, Oli|ver
  general and
  statesman
Crom|well, Thomas
  statesman
cron computer
  command
crone old woman;
  cf. Crohn's disease
cro|ney|ism var. of
  cronyism
Cro|nin, A. J.
  writer
cron|ing
cronk
Cro|nus Greek god

crony
  cro¦nies
cro¦ny¦ism
crook¦back
crook-backed
crook¦ed
crook¦ed¦ly
crook¦ed¦ness
crook¦ery
crook¦neck
croon cf. kroon
croon¦er
crop
  cropped
  crop¦ping
crop-eared
crop¦land
crop-over
crop¦per
cro¦quem¦bouche
croque-monsieur
cro¦quet +ed +ing
  game
cro¦quette food
crore *Ind.* ten
  million; cf. craw
Crosby, Bing singer
  and actor
cro¦sier var. of
  crozier
cross cf. crosse
cross-assembler
cross¦bar
cross-beam
cross-bedding
cross bench
cross-bencher
cross¦bill
cross¦bones
cross¦bow
cross¦bow¦man
  cross¦bow¦men
cross-breed
  cross-bred
cross-check
cross-compiler
cross-connec¦tion
cross-
  contam¦in¦ation
cross-correl¦ate
  cross-correl¦at¦ing
cross-correl¦ation

cross-country
  cross-countries
cross cousin
cross-cultural
cross-current
cross-curricu¦lar
cross-cut
  cross-cutting
cross-dating
cross-dress
cross-dresser
crosse lacrosse stick
cross¦er
cross-examin¦ation
cross-examine
  cross-examin¦ing
cross-examin¦er
cross-eyed
cross-fade
  cross-fading
cross-fertil¦isa¦tion
  Br. var. of cross-
  fertilization
cross-fertil¦ise *Br.*
  var. of cross-
  fertilize
cross-fertil¦iza¦tion
cross-fertil¦ize
  cross-fertil¦iz¦ing
cross¦fire
cross¦flow
cross-grain
cross-grained
cross guard
cross hairs
cross-hatch
cross head
cross-heading
cross index *n.*
cross-index *v.*
cross-infec¦tion
cross-legged
cross link *n.*
cross-link *v.*
cross-linkage
cross¦ly
cross¦match
cross mem¦ber
cross¦ness
cross¦opter¦ygian
cross¦over *n.*
cross-ownership
cross¦patch

cross¦piece
cross-ply
cross-point
cross-pollin¦ate
  cross-pollin¦at¦ing
cross-pollin¦ation
cross-post
cross-pressure
  cross-pressur¦ing
cross prod¦uct
cross-question
cross-rate
cross-refer
  cross-referred
  cross-referring
cross ref¦er¦ence *n.*
cross-reference *v.*
  cross-referen¦cing
cross-rhythm
cross¦road
cross¦roads
cross-ruff
cross sec¦tion *n.*
cross-section *v.*
cross-section¦al
cross-sector¦al
cross-sell
  cross-sold
cross-slide
cross stitch *n.*
cross-stitch *v.*
cross-
  subsid¦isa¦tion
  Br. var. of cross-
  subsidization
cross-subsidise *Br.*
  var. of cross-
  subsidize
cross-
  subsid¦iza¦tion
cross-subsid¦ize
  cross-subsid¦iz¦ing
cross-subsidy
  cross-subsidies
cross¦talk
cross-train
cross¦trees
cross-voting
cross¦walk
cross¦ways
cross¦wind
cross¦wise
cross¦word
cross¦wort

cros¦tini
crotal var. of crottle
cro¦tale cymbal
crotch
crotched
crot¦chet musical
  note; perverse
  belief; cf. crochet
crot¦cheti¦ness
crot¦chety
crotch¦less
cro¦ton
crot¦tle
crouch
croup
croup¦ade
croup¦ier
croupy
crous¦tade
croute
  French croûte
crou¦ton
Crow people
crow
  crowed or crew
crow¦bait
crow¦bar
  crow¦barred
  crow¦bar¦ring
crow¦berry
  crow¦berries
crowd¦ed¦ness
crow¦die
crowd-pleaser
crowd-pleasing
crowd-puller
crowd-pulling
crowd-surf
crowdy var. of
  crowdie
crow¦foot plant; cf.
  crow's foot
crow-pheasant
crow's foot wrinkle;
  cf. crowfoot
crows¦foot
  span¦ner
crow's nest
crow-stepped
croze
Cro¦zet Islands
cro¦zier
cru vineyard; wine

cru|been

cru|ces pl. of crux

cru|cial

cru|ci|al|ity

cru|cial|ly

cru|cian

cru|ci|ate

cru|cible

cru|ci|fer

cru|cif|er|ous

cru|ci|fier

cru|ci|fix

cru|ci|fix|ion

cru|ci|form

cru|cify

  cru|ci|fies

  cru|ci|fied

  cru|ci|fy|ing

cru|ci|ver|bal|ist

cruck

crud

cruddy

  crud|dier

  crud|di|est

crude

  cruder

  cru|dest

crude|ly

crude|ness

cru|di|tés food

cru|dity

  cru|dities

cruel

  cruelled

  cruel|ling

  cruel|ler or

  cruel|er

  cruel|lest or

  cruel|est

  cf. crewel

cruel|ly

cruel|ness

cruelty

  cruel|ties

cruet

Crufts dog show

Cruik|shank,
  George artist

cruise

  cruis|ing
  voyage; cf. cruse

cruiser

cruiser|weight

cruisie var. of
  crusie

cruis|keen

crul|ler

crumb

crumb|ily var. of
  crummily

crumbi|ness var. of
  crumminess

crum|ble

  crum|bling

  crum|bli|ness

  crum|bly

  crum|blies

  crum|blier

  crum|bli|est

crumby

  crumb|ier

  crumbi|est
  like crumbs; cf.
  crummy

crum|horn var. of
  krummhorn

crum|mily

crum|mi|ness

crummy

  crum|mier

  crum|mi|est
  inferior; cf. crumby

crum|pet

crum|ple

  crum|pling

crum|ply

  crum|plier

  crum|pli|est

crunch

  crunch|er

  crunch|ily

  crunchi|ness

crunchy

  crunch|ier

  crunchi|est

crup|per

crural

crus

  crura

cru|sade

  cru|sad|ing

cru|sader

crus cere|bri

  crura cere|bri

cruse jar

crush|able

crush|er

crush|ing|ly

crusie

Crust|acea

crust|acean

crust|ace|ology

crust|aceous

crust|al

crustie n. var. of
  crusty

crust|ily

crusti|ness

crust|ose

crusty

  crust|ies

  crust|ier

  crusti|est

crutch

Crutched Friars

crux

  cruxes or cru|ces

Crux (Aus|tra|lis)

cry

  cries

  cried cf. krai

cry|baby

  cry|babies

cryer var. of crier

cryo|bio|logic|al

cryo|biolo|gist

cryo|biol|ogy

cryo|gen

cryo|gen|ic

cryo|gen|ics

cryo|globu|lin

cryo|lite

cry|on|ic

cry|on|ics

cryo|pre|cipi|tate

cryo|preser|va|tion

cryo|pre|serve

  cryo|pre|serv|ing

cryo|pro|tect|ant

cryo|stat

cryo|sur|gery

cryo|ther|apy

crypt

crypt|analy|sis

crypt|ana|lyst

crypt|ana|lyt|ic

crypt|ana|lyt|ic|al

cryp|tic

cryp|tic|al|ly

cryp|tid

crypto +s

crypto|biont

crypto|biosis

crypto|biot|ic

crypto|coccal

crypto|coc|cosis

crypto|crys|tal|line

crypto|gam

crypto|gam|ic

crypt|og|am|ous

crypto|gen|ic

crypto|gram

crypt|og|raph|er

crypto|graph|ic

crypto|graph|ic|
  al|ly

crypt|og|raphy

crypto|logic|al

crypt|olo|gist

crypt|ology

crypto|meria

crypto|nym

crypt|onym|ous

crypt|orchid

crypt|orchid|ism

crypto|
        spor|idi|osis

crypto|spor|id|ium

  crypto|spor|idia

crypto|zoa

Crypto|zoic Geology

crypto|zoic Ecology

crypto|zoo|logic|al

crypto|zoolo|gist

crypto|zool|ogy

Crys|tal name

crys|tal

crys|tal clear

crystal-clear attrib.

crystal-gazing

crys|tal|lin a
  protein

crys|tal|line like
  crystal

crys|tal|lin|ity

crys|tal|lis|able Br.
  var. of
  crystallizable

crys|tal|lisa|tion Br.
  var. of
  crystallization

crys|tal|lise Br. var.
  of crystallize

crys|tal|lite

crys¦tal¦liz¦able
crys¦tal¦liza¦tion
crys¦tal¦lize
  crys¦tal¦liz¦ing
crys¦tal¦log¦raph¦er
crys¦tal¦lo¦graph¦ic
crys¦tal¦lo¦graph¦ic¦
  al¦ly
crys¦tal¦log¦raphy
crys¦tal¦loid
csar|das
  pl. csar|das
C-section
cten|idium
  cten|idia
cten|oid
Cten|ophora
cteno|phore
Ctesi|phon
cua|drilla
cua¦tro +s
cub
  cubbed
  cub¦bing
Cuba
cu¦bage
Cuba libre +s
Cuban
Cu¦bango var. of
  Okavango
cuba|ture
cubby
  cub¦bies
cubby|hole
cube
  cu¦bing
cubeb
cub|hood
cubic
cu¦bic¦al cube-
  shaped
cu¦bic¦al¦ly
cu¦bicle small room
cu¦bi|form
cu¦bism
cu¦bist
cubit ancient meas-
  ure of length; cf.
  qubit
cu¦bit¦al
cu¦bi¦tus
  cu¦biti
cu¦boid

cu|boid¦al
cucking-stool
cuck|old
cuck|old¦ry
  cuck|old¦ries
cuckoo +s bird that
  lays eggs in others'
  nests; crazy; cf.
  kuku
cuckoo pint
cuckoo-roller
cuckoo-shrike
cu¦cum¦ber
cu¦cur|bit
cu¦cur|bit|aceous
cud
cud¦dle
  cud¦dling
cuddle|some
cud¦dly
  cud¦dlier
  cud¦dli|est
cuddy
  cud¦dies
cudgel
  cudg¦elled *Br.*
  cudg¦eled *US*
  cudgel|ling *Br.*
  cudgel|ing *US*
Cud|lipp, Hugh
  journalist
cud|weed
cue
  cue¦ing or cuing
  signal; hint; in bil-
  liards etc.; cf.
  queue
cueca
cuesta
cuff|link
Cufic var. of Kufic
cui bono?
Cuil|lin Hills
cuir|ass
cuir|ass|ier
cuish var. of cuisse
cuis|ine
cuisse
Cukor, George film
  director
culch var. of cultch
cul|chie
Cul¦dee

cul-de-sac
  culs-de-sac or cul-
  de-sacs
culex
cu¦lices
culi|cine
cul|in|ar¦ily
cu¦lin|ary
Cul¦len skink
cull¦er
cul¦let
Cul¦loden
cully
  cul|lies
Culm strata
culm coal dust
cul¦men
  cul¦mina
culm|if¦er|ous
cul¦min|ant
cul¦min|ate
  cul¦min|at¦ing
cul¦min|ation
cu|lotte *mod.*
cu|lottes
culp|abil¦ity
culp|able
culp|ably
Cul|peper,
  Nich|olas herbalist
cul|prit
cultch
cult¦ic
culti|gen
cult|ish
cult|ish|ness
cult|ism
cult|ist
cul¦tiv|able
cul¦ti|var
cul¦ti|vat|able
cul¦ti|vate
  cul¦ti|vat¦ing
cul¦ti|va¦tion
cul¦ti|va¦tor
cul|tural
cul|tur|al¦ly
cul|tur|ati
cul|ture
  cul|tur|ing
cul|tus
cul|verin
cul|vert

cum combined with
cum¦ber
Cum|ber|land
Cum|ber|nauld
cum¦ber|some
cum¦ber|some¦ly
cum¦ber|some|ness
cum|bia
Cum|bria
Cum|brian
cum|brous
cum|brous¦ly
cum|brous|ness
cumec
cu¦mene
cum grano salis
cumin spice
cum laude
cum|mer|bund
cum¦min var. of
  cumin
cum|mings, e. e.
  writer
cum¦ming|ton|ite
cum|quat var. of
  kumquat
cu¦mu|late
  cu¦mu|lat¦ing
cu¦mu|la¦tion
cu¦mu|la¦tive
cu¦mu|la¦tive¦ly
cu¦mulo|nim|bus
  cu¦mulo|nimbi
cu¦mu|lous *adj.*
cu¦mu|lus *n.*
  cu¦muli
Cuna var. of Kuna
Cu|nard, Sam|uel
  British-Canadian
  shipowner
cu|ne|ate
cu|nei|form
cu-nim cumulonim-
  bus
cun|je|voi
cun|ner
cunni|linc|tus var.
  of cunnilingus
cunni|lin|gus
cun|ning
Cun|ning|ham,
  Merce choreog-
  rapher

cun|ning|ly
Cu|no|be|li|nus var. of **Cymbeline**
cup
  cupped
  cup|ping
cup-bearer
cup|board
cup|cake
cupel
  cu|pelled *Br.*
  cu|peled *US*
  cu|pel|ling *Br.*
  cu|pel|ing *US*
cu|pel|la|tion
cup|ful
Cupid Roman god
cupid winged child
cu|pid|ity
Cupid's bow shape
cupid's dart plant
cu|pola
cu|po|laed
cuppa
cuppy
cu|pram|mo|nium
cu|preous
cu|pric
cu|prif|er|ous
cu|prite
cupro
cupro-nickel
cu|prous
cup tie
cup-tied
cu|pule
cur
cur|abil|ity
cur|able
cur|ably
Cura|çao island
cura|çao +s drink; cf. **curassow**
cura|çoa var. of **curaçao**
cur|acy
  cur|acies
cur|an|dera *female*
cur|an|dero +s *male*
cur|are
cur|as|sow bird; cf. **curaçao**

cur|ate
  cur|at|ing
curate-in-charge
  curates-in-charge
cur|ation
cura|tive
cur|ator
cura|tor|ial
cur|ator|ship
curb restrain; cf. **kerb**
curb *US* pavement edge *Br.* **kerb**
curb bit
curb chain
curb cut *US*
curb roof
curb|side *US* *Br.* **kerbside**
curb|stone *US* *Br.* **kerbstone**
cur|cu|lio +s
cur|cuma
curd cf. **Kurd**
cur|dle
  curd|ling
curd|ler
curdy
cure
  cur|ing
curé priest
cure-all
curer
cur|et|tage
cur|ette
  cur|et|ting
cur|few
Curia
Cur|ial
Curie, Marie and **Pierre** physicists
curie unit
curio +s
curi|osa
curi|os|ity
  curi|os|ities
curi|ous
curi|ous|ly
curi|ous|ness
cur|ium
curl|er
cur|lew

cur|li|cue
curli|ness
curly
  curl|ier
  curli|est
curly-wurly
cur|mudg|eon
cur|mudg|eon|li|ness
cur|mudg|eon|ly
cur|rach coracle
Cur|ragh racecourse
cur|ragh var. of **currach**
curra|jong var. of **kurrajong**
cur|rant dried fruit; c. gall; cf. **current**
cur|ra|wong
cur|rency
  cur|ren|cies
cur|rent cf. **currant**
cur|rent|ly
cur|ricle
cur|ricu|lar *adj.*
cur|ricu|lum
  cur|ric|ula or cur|ricu|lums *n.*
cur|ric|ulum vitae
  cur|ricu|la vitae
cur|rier
cur|rish
curry
  curry|ing
curry comb *n.*
curry-comb *v.*
curse
  curst *archaic*
  curs|ing
curs|ed|ly
curs|ed|ness
curser person who curses; cf. **cursor**
cur|sillo +s
cur|sive
cur|sive|ly
cur|sor indicator; cf. **curser**
cur|sor|ial
cur|sor|ily
cur|sori|ness
curs|ory
curst *archaic* = **cursed**

curt
cur|tail
cur|tail|ment
cur|tain
curtain-raiser
curtain-sider
curtain-up
cur|tal
cur|tana
cur|til|age
Cur|tis, Tony actor
Cur|tiss, Glenn aircraft designer
curt|ly
curt|ness
curt|sey var. of **curtsy**
curtsy
  curt|sies
  curt|sied
  curt|sy|ing
cur|ule
curv|aceous
curv|aceous|ly
curv|aceous|ness
curva|ture
curve
  curv|ing
cur|vet
curvi|lin|ear
curvi|ness
curvy
  cur|vier
  curvi|est
cus|cus animal; cf. **couscous, khus-khus**
cusec
Cush part of ancient Nubia; cf. **Hindu Kush**
cush cushion
cushat
cu|shaw
cush-cush
Cush|ing, Peter actor
Cush|ing's dis|ease/ syn|drome
cush|ion
cush|iony
Cush|it|ic
cushty

cushy
　cush¦ier
　cushi¦est
cusi¦manse
cusk
cusk-eel
cusp
cus¦pate
cusped
cus¦pid
cus¦pid¦al
cus¦pid¦ate
cus¦pi¦dor
cuss
cuss¦ed¦ness
cus¦tard
Cus¦ter, George
　general
cus¦to¦dial
cus¦to¦dian
cus¦to¦dian¦ship
cus¦tody
cus¦tom
cus¦tom¦al var. of
　custumal
cus¦tom¦ar¦ily
cus¦tom¦ary
　cus¦tom¦ar¦ies
custom-built
cus¦tom¦er
cus¦tom¦is¦able Br.
　var. of
　customizable
cus¦tom¦isa¦tion Br.
　var. of
　customization
cus¦tom¦ise Br. var.
　of customize
cus¦tom¦iz¦able
cus¦tom¦iza¦tion
cus¦tom¦ize
　cus¦tom¦iz¦ing
custom-made
cus¦toms
cus¦tos
　ro¦tu¦lorum
cus¦to¦des
　ro¦tu¦lorum
cus¦tu¦mal
cut
　cut¦ting
cut-and-
　　　come-again
n. & mod.

cut-and-cover n.
cut and paste v. &
　n.
cu¦ta¦ne¦ous
cut¦away
cut¦back
cutch
cut-down adj.
cute
　cuter
　cutest
cute¦ly
cute¦ness
cutesy
　cutes¦ier
　cutesi¦est
cut glass n.
cut-glass adj.
Cuth¦bert
cu¦ticle
cu¦ticu¦lar
cutie
cut-in n.
cutin
cutis
cut¦lass
cut¦lass¦fish
cut¦ler
cut¦lery
cut¦let
cut¦line
cut-off adj., n., &
　mod.
cut-out adj., n. &
　mod.
cut¦over
cut-price adj.
cut¦purse
cut-rate
cut¦scene
cut¦ter
cut-throat
cut¦ting
cut¦ting¦ly
cut¦tle
cuttle¦bone
cuttle¦fish
cutty
　cut¦ties
Cutty Sark
cutty-stool
cut up adj. & n.
cut-up attrib.

cut¦water
cut¦work
cut¦worm
cuvée
cu¦vette
Cuzco
cwm hollow; Welsh
　valley; cf. combe,
　khoum
Cwm¦bran
cwtch cupboard;
　cuddle
cyan
cy¦an¦amide
cyan¦ate
cy¦an¦ic
cyan¦ide
cyano¦acryl¦ate
Cyano¦bac¦teria
cyano¦bac¦ter¦ial
cyano¦bac¦ter¦ium
　cyano¦bac¦teria
cyano¦cobala¦min
cyano¦gen
cyano¦gen¦esis
cy¦ano¦gen¦ic
cyano¦hyd¦rin
cyano¦phyte
cyan¦osis
cyan¦ot¦ic
cyano¦type
cy¦ath¦ium
　cy¦athia
Cy¦bele goddess
cyber
cyber¦cafe
cyber¦crime
cyber¦crim¦inal
cyber¦naut
cyber¦net¦ic
cyber¦net¦ician
cyber¦neti¦cist
cy¦ber¦net¦ics
cyber¦phobe
cyber¦pho¦bia
cyber¦pho¦bic
cyber¦punk
cyber¦sex
cyber¦slack¦er
cyber¦slack¦ing
cyber¦space
cyber¦squat¦ter

cyber¦squat¦ting
cyber¦stalk¦er
cyber¦stalk¦ing
cyber¦ter¦ror¦ism
cyber¦ter¦ror¦ist
cyber¦war
cy¦borg
cycad
Cyc¦la¦des
Cyc¦lad¦ic
cyc¦la¦mate
cyc¦la¦men
cycle
　cyc¦ling
cycle¦way
cyc¦lic
cyc¦lic¦al
cyc¦lic¦al¦ly
cyc¦lin
Cycli¦oph¦ora
cyc¦lisa¦tion Br. var.
　of cyclization
cyc¦lise Br. var. of
　cyclize
cyc¦list
cyc¦liza¦tion
cyc¦lize
　cyc¦liz¦ing
cyclo¦add¦ition
cyclo¦alk¦ane
cyclo-cross
cyclo¦hex¦ane
cyclo¦hexyl
cyc¦loid
cyc¦loid¦al
cyc¦lom¦eter
cyc¦lone
cyc¦lon¦ic
cyc¦lon¦ic¦al¦ly
cyclo¦pae¦dia var. of
　cyclopedia
cyclo¦pae¦dic var. of
　cyclopedic
cyclo¦paraf¦fin
cyc¦lo¦pean
cyclo¦pedia
cyclo¦pedic
cyclo¦
　　　phos¦pha¦mide
cyc¦lo¦pian var. of
　cyclopean
cyclo¦pro¦pane

Cyc|lops
  pl. Cyc|lops or
  Cyc|lo|pes
  one-eyed giant
cyc|lops
  cyc|lop|ses
  crustacean
cyclo|rama
cyclo|sporin
cyclo|spor|ine var.
  of cyclosporin
cyc|los|tom|ate
cyclo|stome
cyclo|style
  cyclo|styl|ing
cyclo|thy|mia
cyclo|thy|mic
cyclo|tron
cyder var. of cider
cyg|net young swan;
  cf. signet
Cyg|nus
cy|lin|der
cy|lin|dric|al
cy|lin|dric|al|ly
cym|bal percussion
  instrument; cf.
  symbol
cym|bal|ist cf.
  symbolist
Cym|bel|ine
cym|bid|ium
cyme
cym|ose
Cym|ric
Cymru
Cyne|wulf poet
Cynic philosopher
cynic doubter
cyn|ic|al
cyn|ic|al|ly
cyni|cism
cyno|dont
cyno|sure
Cyn|thia
cy|phel
cy|pher var. of
  cipher
cy|pher|punk
cy-pres
cy|press tree; cf.
  Cyprus
Cyp|rian, St

cyp|rin|id
cyp|rin|oid like carp
Cyp|riot
cyp|ri|pe|dium
Cy|prus cf. cypress
cyp|sela
  cyp|se|lae
Cy|rano de
  Ber|gerac soldier
  and writer
Cyre|na|ic
Cyre|na|ica
Cyre|nai|cism
Cyr|ene region,
  Libya
Cyr|il|lic
Cyrus Persian
  prince; Persian king
cyst sac or cavity in
  body; cf. cist
cyst|ec|tomy
  cyst|ec|to|mies
cyst|eine amino
  acid; cf. cystine,
  Sistine
cys|tic
cysti|cer|coid
cysti|cer|cus
  cysti|cerci
cyst|ine oxidized
  dimer of cysteine;
  cf. cysteine, Sistine
cyst|itis
cysto|scope
cysto|scop|ic
cyst|os|copy
  cyst|os|co|pies
cyst|ot|omy
  cyst|oto|mies
Cythe|rea
Cythe|rean
cyti|dine
cyti|sus
cyto|archi|
        tec|ton|ic
cyto|archi|
        tec|ton|ics
cyto|archi|
        tec|tur|al
cyto|archi|tec|ture
cyto|centri|fuge
cyto|centri|fu|ging
cyto|chrome
cyto|gen|et|ic

cyto|gen|eti|cist
cyto|gen|et|ics
cyto|kine
cyto|kin|esis
cyto|ki|nin
cyto|logic|al
cyto|logic|al|ly
cy|tolo|gist
cy|tology
cy|toly|sis
cyto|lyt|ic
cyto|meg|al|ic
cyto|megalo|virus
cyto|pho|tom|eter
cyto|photo|met|ric
cyto|pho|tom|etry
cyto|plasm
cyto|plas|mic
cyto|sine
cyto|skel|etal
cyto|skel|eton
cyto|sol
cyto|sol|ic
cyto|toxic
cyto|tox|icity
czar var. of tsar
czar|das var. of
  csardas
czar|evich var. of
  tsarevich
czar|ina var. of
  tsarina
czar|ism var. of
  tsarism
czar|ist var. of
  tsarist
Czech
Czecho|slo|vak
Czecho|slo|vakia
Czecho|slo|vak|ian
Czerny, Karl
  composer
Częs|to|chowa

————————————

D

dab
dabbed
dab|bing

dab|ber
dab|ble
  dab|bling
dab|bler
dab|chick
da capo
Dacca var. of Dhaka
dace fish; cf. dais
dacha
Dach|au
dachs|hund
Dacia
Da|cian
da|cite
da|cit|ic
da|coit
da|coity
  da|coi|ties
Dac|ron *trademark*
dac|tyl
dac|tyl|ic
Dada art movement
dada father
dadah illegal drugs
Dada|ism
Dada|ist
Dada|is|tic
Dadd, Rich|ard
  painter
daddy
  dad|dies
daddy-long-legs
  pl. daddy-long-legs
dado +s
Dadra and Nagar
  Ha|veli
Dae|da|lian
Dae|dal|ic
Dae|da|lus
dae|mon divinity;
  inner spirit; com-
  puting process; cf.
  demon
dae|mon|ic cf.
  demonic
daf|fily
daf|fi|ness
daf|fo|dil
daffy
  daf|fier
  daf|fi|est
daft
Daf|ydd

dag
dagged
dag|ging
da Gama, Vasco
explorer
Dag|estan
Dag|es|tan|ian
dagga plant; hemp
dag|ger weapon
dagger|board
daggy
dag|gier
dag|gi|est
Dag|mar
dago
dagos or da|goes
offensive
Dagon
Da|guerre, Louis
photographic
pioneer
da|guerreo|type
da|guerro|type var.
of daguerreotype
Dag|wood
daha|beah var. of
dahabeeyah
daha|bee|yah
dahi yogurt
dahi vada dish
Dahl, Roald writer
dah|lia
Da|ho|mey
Dai man's name
dai midwife
dai|kon
Dáil Éire|ann Irish
parliament
daily
dai|lies
dai|mio var. of
daimyo
Daim|ler, Gott|lieb
engineer
dai|mon divinity;
inner spirit; var. of
daemon
dai|mon|ic var. of
daemonic
dai|myo +s
dain|tily
dain|ti|ness
dainty
dain|ties

dain|tier
dain|ti|est
dai|quiri
dairy
dair|ies
dairy-free
dairy|ing
dairy|maid
dairy|man
dais platform; cf.
dace
daisy
dai|sies
daisy-chainable
daisy-cutter
Dakar capital of
Senegal; cf. Dhaka
Da|kota
Da|ko|tan
daks *Austral./NZ*
trousers
dal var. of dhal
Dalai Lama
da|lasi
pl. da|lasi or
da|la|sis
Dal|croze see
Jaques-Dalcroze
dalek
Dales|man
Dales|men
Dales|woman
Dales|women
Daley name
Dal|hou|sie, James
colonial
administrator
Dali, Sal|va|dor
painter
Dali|esque
Dalit
Dal|la|pic|cola,
Luigi composer
Dal|las
dal|li|ance
Dall sheep
Dall's sheep var. of
Dall sheep
dally
dal|lies
dal|lied
dally|ing
Dal|ma|tia
Dal|ma|tian

dal|mat|ic
Dal|ra|dian
Dal|ri|ada
dal segno
Dal|ton, John
chemist
dal|ton unit
dal|ton|ism
Dal|ton plan
dam
dammed
dam|ming
block; cf. damn
dama gazelle
dam|age
dam|aging
dam|aging|ly
Daman and Diu
damar var. of
dammar
Da|mara
Da|mara|land
Dam|as|cene
Da|mas|cus
dam|ask
Dama|vand
Dam|bust|er
dame
dam|fool
Da|mian
da|mi|ana
Dami|etta
dam|mar
dam|mit
damn condemn; cf.
dam
dam|nable
dam|nably
dam|na|tion
dam|na|tory
damned
damn|ing|ly
dam|num
damna
Damo|clean
Damo|cles
Damon friend of
Pythias
damp-dry
damp-dries
damp-dried
damp-drying

damp|en
damp|en|er
damp|er
Damp|ier, Wil|liam
explorer
damp|ing off
damp|ish
damp|ly
damp|ness
damp-proof
dam|sel
dam|sel|fish
dam|sel|fly
dam|sel|flies
dam|son
dan in judo; buoy
Danae
dan|aid butterfly
Dan|aids *Greek
Mythology*
Dana|kil
Da Nang
dance
dan|cing
dance|able
dance|hall Jamai-
can music style
dan|cer
dan|cer|cise
dan|cer|cize var. of
dancercise
dan|cetté
dan|cetty var. of
dancetté
dance|wear
danda *Ind.* stick; cf.
dander
dan|de|lion
dan|der skin flakes;
stroll; in 'get
someone's dander
up'; cf. danda
dan|diacal
Dan|die Din|mont
dan|dify
dan|di|fies
dan|di|fied
dan|di|fying
dandi|prat
dan|diya raas
dan|dle
dand|ling
Dan|dong
dan|druff

dan|druffy
dandy
  dan|dies
  dan|dier
  dan|di|est
dandy|ish
dandy|ism
Dane
Dane|geld
Dane|law
dane|wort
Dan|forth anchor
dan|ger
dan|ger|ous
dan|ger|ous|ly
dan|gle
  dan|gling
dan|gler
dan|gly
Dan|iel man's name
Dan|iela
Dan|iell cell
Dan|ielle woman's
  name
danio +s
Da|nish
dank|ly
dank|ness
d'An|nun|zio,
  Gab|ri|ele poet
Dano-Norwegian
danse ma|cabre
  danses ma|cabres
dan|seur *male*
dan|seuse *female*
Dante (Ali|ghieri)
  Italian poet
Dan|te|an
Dante-esque var. of
  Dantesque
Dant|esque
dan|tho|nia
Dan|ton, Georges
  revolutionary
Dan|ube
Dan|ub|ian
Dan|zig German
  name for Gdańsk
Dão
dap
  dapped
  dap|ping
daphne shrub

daph|nia
  pl. daph|nia
Daph|nis
Da Ponte, Lor|enzo
  librettist
dap|per
dap|per|ly
dap|per|ness
dap|ple
  dap|pling
Dap|sang
  another name for
  K2
dap|sone
dar|bies handcuffs;
  cf. derby
Darby name; cf.
  Derby
Darby and Joan
Dard
Dar|da|nelles
Dard|ic
dare
  dar|ing
dare|devil
dare|devil|ry
  dare|devil|ries
Dar|ell
Daren
daren't
darer
Dar es Sa|laam
Dar|fur
dar|gah
Dari
Dar|ien province,
  Panama; Gulf
dar|ing
dar|ing|ly
dari|ole
Dar|ius king of
  Persia
Dar|jee|ling
Dar|ji|ling var. of
  Darjeeling
dark|en
dark|en|er
darkie *offensive*
dark|ish
dark|ling
dark|ly
dark|ness
dark|room

dark|some
darky var. of darkie
Dar|lene
Dar|ling, Grace
  heroine
Dar|ling
Dar|ling River
Dar|ling|ton
Darm|stadt
darned|est
dar|nel
darn|er
Darn|ley, Henry
  husband of Mary,
  Queen of Scots
Dar|rell
Dar|ren
Dar|ryl
dar|shan
dart|board
dart|er
Dart|ford
Dart|moor
Dart|mouth
Dar|win city,
  Australia
Dar|win, Charles
  naturalist
Dar|win|ian
Dar|win|ism
Dar|win|ist
Daryl
Das|ehra var. of
  Dussehra
Da|sein existence
dash|board
dash|een
dash|er
dash|iki
dash|ing|ly
dash|pot
das|sie
das|tard
das|tard|li|ness
das|tard|ly
das|toor var. of
  dastur
das|tur
dasy|ure
data
data|base
dat|able
data|comms

data|coms var. of
  datacomms
data|glove
datcha var. of dacha
date
  dat|ing
date|able var. of
  datable
date|book
date|less
Date Line on world
date|line in
  newspaper
da|tive
Datuk
datum
  data
da|tura
daub smear
daube stew
Dau|ben|ton's bat
daub|er
Dau|bigny, Charles
  painter
Dau|det, Al|phonse
  novelist
daugh|ter
daugh|ter|board
daugh|ter|card
daugh|ter|hood
daughter-in-law
  daughters-in-law
daugh|ter|ly
Dau|mier, Hon|oré
  artist
dauno|rubi|cin
daunt
daunt|ing|ly
daunt|less
daunt|less|ly
daunt|less|ness
dau|phin
Dau|phiné
dau|phin|ois
dau|phin|oise var.
  of dauphinois
Davao
daven
daven|port desk
David, Eliza|beth
  cookery writer
David, Jacques-
  Louis painter

Davies, Peter Max|well composer
Davies, Rob|ert|son writer
Davies, W. H. poet
da Vinci, Leo|nardo painter and designer
Davis breathing apparatus
Davis, Bette actress
Davis, Joe, Fred, and **Steve** snooker players
Davis, Miles trumpeter
Davis Cup
Davis Strait
davit
Davos
Davy, Hum|phry chemist
Davy Jones's lock|er
Davy lamp
daw jackdaw; cf. **dor, door**
daw|dle
dawd|ling
dawd|ler
Daw|kins, Rich|ard biologist
dawn
Day, Doris actress
Dayak
Dayan, Moshe politician and general
dayan
  da|yan|im
day|bed
day|boat
day|book
day boy
day|break
day|dream
day|dream|er
day girl
Day-Glo *trademark*
day|glo var. of **Day-Glo**
Day Lewis, Cecil writer
Day-Lewis, Dan|iel actor

day|light
day|mare
day|pack
day|sack
day|sail
day|sail|er *US*
day|sailor *Br.*
day|side
day|spring
day|time
day|timer *trademark*
Day|ton
day|wear
day|work
day|work|er
daze
  daz|ing
dazed|ly
da|zi|bao
  pl. **da|zi|bao**
daz|zle
  daz|zling
dazzle|ment
daz|zler
daz|zling|ly
D-Day
de|ac|ces|sion
dea|con
dea|con|ess
dea|con|ship
de|acti|vate
  de|acti|vat|ing
de|acti|va|tion
de|acti|va|tor
dead
dead|beat
dead|bolt
dead|en
dead|en|er
dead|eye
dead|fall
dead|head
dead|light
dead|line
dead|li|ness
dead|lock
dead|ly
  dead|lier
  dead|li|est
dead|ness
dead-nettle

dead|pan
dead|panned
dead|pan|ning
dead|rise
dead|stick in flying
dead|stock
de|aer|ate
  de|aer|at|ing
de|aer|ation
deaf cf. **def**
deaf-blind *adj.*
deaf|en
deaf|en|ing|ly
de|affer|en|tation
de|affer|ented
deaf mute
deaf|ness
Dea|kin, Al|fred prime minister of Australia
deal
  dealt
  cf. **diel**
de-alcohol|isa|tion *Br.* var. of **de-alcoholization**
de-alcohol|ise *Br.* var. of **de-alcoholize**
de-alcohol|iza|tion
de-alcohol|ize
  de-alcohol|izing
deal|er
deal|er|ship
deal|fish
de|align
de|align|ment
dealt
de|amin|ated
de|amin|ation
Dean, Chris|to|pher ice skater
Dean, James actor
dean cf. **dene**
dean|ery
  dean|er|ies group of parishes; dean's house; cf. **denary**
de-anglicisa|tion *Br.* var. of **de-anglicization**
de-anglicise *Br.* var. of **de-anglicize**

de-angliciza|tion
de-anglicize
de-angliciz|ing
De|anna
dear *adj.*; cf. **deer**
dearie
dear|ly
dear|ness
dearth
deasil clockwise; cf. **diesel**
death
death|bed
death|less
death|less|ness
death|like
death|ly
  death|lier
  death|li|est
death-watch bee|tle
de|at|trib|ute
de|at|trib|ut|ing
de|at|tri|bu|tion
de|bacle
de|bag
de|bagged
de|bag|ging
de|bal|last
de|bar
de|barred
de|bar|ring
de|bark
de|bark|ation
de|bar|ment
de|base
de|bas|ing
de|base|ment
de|baser
de|bat|able
de|bat|ably
de|bate
de|bat|ing
de|bater
de|bauch
de|bauch|ee
de|bauch|er
de|bauch|ery
de|bauch|er|ies
Deb|bie
debby
de|beak
de Beau|voir, Sim|one writer

de|ben|ture
de|bili|tate
  de|bili|tat|ing
  de|bili|tat|ing|ly
de|bili|ta|tion
de|bili|ta|tive
de|bil|ity
  de|bil|ities
debit
deb|it|age
de|blur
  de|blurs
  de|blurred
  de|blur|ring
deb|on|air
deb|on|air|ly
de|bone
  de|boning
Deb|orah
de|bouch
de|bouch|ment
Deb|re|cen
De|brett book on
  British nobility
de|bride|ment
de|brief
  de|brief|er
deb|ris
de Brog|lie, Louis
  French physicist;
  wavelength
de|bruise
  de|bruis|ing
debt
debt|or
de|bug
  de|bugged
  de|bug|ging
debug|ger
de|bunk
de|bunk|er
de|bunk|ery
de|bur var. of
  deburr
de|burr
de|bus
  de|buses
  de|bussed
  de|bus|sing
De|bussy, Claude
  composer
debut +ed +ing
  French début

debu|tant *male*
  French débutant
debu|tante *female*
  French débutante
debye unit
dec|adal
dec|ade
deca|dence
deca|dent
deca|dent|ly
de|caf *trademark in*
  the UK
de|caff var. of decaf
de|caf|fein|ate
  de|caf|fein|at|ing
de|caf|fein|ation
deca|gon
dec|agon|al
deca|he|dral
deca|he|dron
  deca|he|dra or
  deca|he|drons
decal transfer; cf.
  decyl
de|cal|ci|fi|ca|tion
de|cal|ci|fier
de|cal|cify
  de|cal|ci|fy|ing
de|cal|co|ma|nia
deca|liter *US*
deca|litre *Br.*
Deca|logue
De|cam|eron
deca|meter *US*
deca|metre *Br.*
deca|met|ric
de|camp
de|camp|ment
de|can
de|can|al
dec|ane
dc|cani
de|cant
de|cant|er
de|capi|tate
  de|capi|tat|ing
  de|capi|ta|tion
  de|capi|ta|tor
deca|pod
Deca|poda
deca|pod|an
de|cap|su|late
  de|cap|su|lat|ing

de|cap|su|la|tion
de|car|bon|isa|tion
  Br. var. of
  decarbonization
de|car|bon|ise *Br.*
  var. of decarbonize
de|car|bon|iser *Br.*
  var. of
  decarbonizer
de|car|bon|iza|tion
de|car|bon|ize
  de|car|bon|iz|ing
de|car|bon|izer
de|carb|oxyl|ase
de|carb|oxyl|ate
  de|carb|oxyl|at|ing
de|carb|oxyl|ation
de|car|bur|isa|tion
  Br. var. of
  decarburization
de|car|bur|ise *Br.*
  var. of decarburize
de|car|bur|ization
de|car|bur|ize
  de|car|bur|iz|ing
deca|style
deca|syl|lab|ic
dec|ath|lete
dec|ath|lon
decay
Dec|can
de|cease
  de|ceas|ing
de|ce|dent
de|ceit
de|ceit|ful
de|ceit|ful|ly
de|ceit|ful|ness
de|ceiv|able
de|ceive
  de|ceiv|ing
de|ceiver
de|cel|er|ate
  de|cel|er|at|ing
de|cel|er|ation
de|cel|er|ator
De|cem|ber
De|cem|brist
de|cency
  de|cen|cies
de|cen|nial
de|cent

de|cen|ter *US*
  displace from
  centre.
  Br. decentre
de|cent|ly
de|cen|tral|isa|tion
  Br. var. of
  decentralization
de|cen|tral|ise *Br.*
  var. of decentralize
de|cen|tral|ist
de|cen|tral|iza|tion
de|cen|tral|ize
  de|cen|tral|iz|ing
de|centre *Br.*
de|cen|tring
  US decenter
de|cep|tion
de|cep|tive
de|cep|tive|ly
de|cep|tive|ness
de|cere|brate
  de|cere|brat|ing
de|cere|bra|tion
de|cer|ti|fi|ca|tion
de|cer|tify
  de|cer|ti|fies
  de|cer|ti|fied
  de|cer|ti|fy|ing
de-Christian|
  isa|tion
  Br. var. of de-
  Christianization
de-Christian|ise *Br.*
  var. of
  de-Christianize
de-Christian|
  iza|tion
de-Christian|ize
  de-Christian|iz|ing
De|cian
deci|bel
de|cid|able
de|cide
  de|cid|ing
de|cided|ly
de|cider
de|cidua
de|cid|ual
de|cidu|ous
deci|gram
deci|gramme *Br.*
  var. of decigram
de|cile
deci|liter *US*

deci|litre *Br.*
deci|mal
deci|mal|isa|tion
  Br. var. of
  decimalization
deci|mal|ise *Br.* var.
  of **decimalize**
deci|mal|iza|tion
deci|mal|ize
  deci|mal|iz|ing
deci|mal|ly
deci|mate
  deci|mat|ing
deci|ma|tion
deci|ma|tor
deci|meter *US*
deci|metre *Br.*
deci|met|ric
de|cipher
de|cipher|able
de|cipher|ment
de|ci|sion
de|cisive
de|cisive|ly
de|cisive|ness
De|cius, Gaius
  Mes|sius Quin|tus
  Tra|ja|nus Roman
  emperor
deck|chair
deck|hand
deck|head
deck|house
deckle
de|claim
de|claim|er
dec|lam|ation
de|clama|tory
Dec|lan
de|clar|able
de|clar|ant
dec|lar|ation
de|clara|tive
de|clara|tor
de|clara|tory
de|clare
  de|clar|ing
de|clared|ly
de|clarer
de|class
dé|classé *male*
dé|clas|sée *female*
de|clas|si|fi|ca|tion

de|clas|sify
de|clas|si|fies
de|clas|si|fied
de|clas|si|fy|ing
de|claw
de|clen|sion
de|clen|sion|al
de|clin|able
dec|lin|ation
dec|lin|ation|al
de|cline
  de|clin|ing
de|cliner
dec|lin|om|eter
de|cliv|itous
de|cliv|ity
de|cliv|ities
de|clutch
deco art deco;
  decompression; cf.
  dekko
de|coct
de|coc|tion
de|cod|able
de|code
  de|cod|ing
de|coder
de|coke
  de|cok|ing
de|col|late
  de|col|lat|ing
de|col|la|tion
de|col|la|tor
de|colle|ment
dé|col|le|tage
dé|col|leté
dé|col|letée var. of
  décolleté
de|col|on|isa|tion
  Br. var. of
  decolonization
de|col|on|ise *Br.*
  var. of **decolonize**
de|col|on|iza|tion
de|col|on|ize
  de|col|on|iz|ing
de|col|or|isa|tion
  Br. var. of
  decolorization
de|col|or|ise *Br.* var.
  of **decolorize**
de|col|or|iza|tion
de|col|or|ize
  de|col|or|iz|ing

de|com|mis|sion
de|com|mun|isa|
        tion
  Br. var. of
  decommunization
de|com|mun|ise *Br.*
  var. of
  decommunize
de|com|mun|iza|
        tion
de|com|mun|ize
  de|com|mun|iz|ing
de|com|pen|sated
de|com|pen|sa|tion
de|com|pil|ation
de|com|pile
  de|com|pil|ing
de|com|piler
de|com|pos|able
de|com|pose
  de|com|pos|ing
de|com|poser
de|com|pos|ition
de|com|press
de|com|pres|sion
de|com|pres|sor
de|con|di|tion
de|con|gest
de|con|gest|ant
de|con|ges|tion
de|con|se|crate
  de|con|se|crat|ing
de|con|se|cra|tion
de|con|struct
de|con|struc|tion
de|con|struc|tion|
        ism
de|con|struc|tion|
        ist
de|con|struct|ive
de|con|tam|in|ate
de|con|tam|in|
        at|ing
de|con|tam|in|
        ation
de|con|text|ual|
        isa|tion
  Br. var. of decon-
  textualization
de|con|text|ual|ise
  Br. var. of
  decontextualize
de|con|text|ual|
        iza|tion

de|con|text|ual|ize
  de|con|text|ual|
        iz|ing
de|con|trol
de|con|trolled
de|con|trol|ling
de|con|vo|lu|tion
decor
  French décor
dec|or|ate
dec|or|at|ing
dec|or|ation
dec|ora|tive
dec|ora|tive|ly
dec|ora|tive|ness
dec|or|ator
dec|or|ous
dec|or|ous|ly
dec|or|ous|ness
de|cor|ti|cate
  de|cor|ti|cat|ing
de|cor|ti|ca|tion
de|corum
dé|coup|age
de|couple
  de|coup|ling
decoy
de|crease
  de|creas|ing
de|creas|ing|ly
de|cree
  de|crees
  de|creed
  de|cree|ing
de|cree nisi
  de|crees nisi
dec|re|ment
de|crepit
de|crepi|tate
  de|crepi|tat|ing
de|crepi|ta|tion
de|crepi|tude
de|cres|cendo
de|cres|cen|dos or
  de|cres|cendi
de|cres|cent
de|cre|tal
De|cre|tum
de|crier
de|crim|in|al|
        isa|tion
  Br. var. of
  decriminalization

de|crim|in|al|ise Br.
var. of
decriminalize
de|crim|in|al|
iza|tion
de|crim|in|al|ize
de|crim|in|al|iz|ing
decry
de|cries
de|cried
de|cry|ing
de|crypt
de|cryp|tion
de|cubi|tus
de|cum|bent
de|cur|rent
de|cus|sate
de|cus|sat|ing
de|cus|sa|tion
decyl Chemistry;
cf. decal
de|dans
pl. de|dans
de|den|dum
de|denda or
de|den|dums
dedi|cate
dedi|cat|ing
dedi|cated|ly
dedi|catee
dedi|ca|tion
dedi|ca|tor
dedi|ca|tory
de dicto
de|dif|fer|en|ti|ate
de|dif|fer|en|
ti|at|ing
de|dif|fer|en|
ti|ation
de|duce
de|du|cing
de|du|cible
de|duct
de|duct|ibil|ity
de|duct|ible
de|duc|tion
de|duct|ive
de|duct|ive|ly
deed
deedy
dee|jay
deem judge; cf.
deme

de-emphasis
de-emphases
de-emphasise Br.
var. of
de-emphasize
de-emphasize
de-emphasiz|ing
deem|ster
de-energise Br. var.
of de-energize
de-energize
deep|en
deep-freeze v.
deep-freezing
deep-frozen
deep freeze n.
deep freez|er var.
of deep freeze
deep-fry
deep-fries
deep-fried
deep-frying
deep|ly
deep|ness
deep-six
deer
pl. deer
animal; cf. dear
deer|grass
deer|hound
deer|skin
deer|stalk|er
de-escalate
de-escalat|ing
de-escalation
def excellent
de|face
de|facing
de|face|ment
de|facer
de facto
defae|cate Br. var.
of defecate
defae|ca|tion Br.
var. of defecation
defae|cator Br. var.
of defecator
defae|ca|tory Br.
var. of defecatory
de|fal|cate
de|fal|cat|ing
de|fal|ca|tion
de|fal|ca|tor

de Falla, Ma|nuel
composer
def|am|ation
de|fama|tory
de|fame
de|fam|ing
de|famer
de|fa|mil|iar|ise Br.
var. of
defamiliarize
de|fa|mil|iar|ize
de|fa|mil|iar|iz|ing
de|fang
de|fat
de|fat|ted
de|fat|ting
de|fault
de|fault|er
de|feas|ance
de|feas|ibil|ity
de|feas|ible
de|feat
de|feat|ism
de|feat|ist
defe|cate
defe|cat|ing
defe|ca|tion
defe|ca|tor
defe|ca|tory
de|fect
de|fec|tion
de|fect|ive
de|fect|ive|ly
de|fect|ive|ness
de|fect|or
de|femi|nise Br var.
of defeminize
de|femi|nize
de|femi|niz|ing
de|fence Br.
US defense
de|fence|less Br.
US defenseless
de|fence|less|ness
Br.
US
defenselessness
de|fence|man Br.
de|fence|men
US defenseman
de|fend
de|fend|able
de|fend|ant
de|fend|er

de|fen|es|trate
de|fen|es|trat|ing
de|fen|es|tra|tion
de|fense US
Br. defence
de|fense|less US
Br. defenceless
de|fense|less|ness
US
Br. defencelessness
de|fense|man US
de|fense|men
Br. defenceman
de|fens|ibil|ity
de|fens|ible
de|fens|ibly
de|fen|sive
de|fen|sive|ly
de|fen|sive|ness
defer
de|ferred
de|fer|ring
def|er|ence
def|er|ens in 'vas
deferens'
def|er|ent
def|er|en|tial
def|er|en|tial|ly
de|fer|ment
de|fer|rable
de|fer|ral
de|fer|rer
de|fer|vesce
de|fer|ves|cing
de|fer|ves|cence
de|fi|ance
de|fi|ant
de|fi|ant|ly
de|fib|ril|late
de|fi|bril|lat|ing
de|fib|ril|la|tion
de|fib|ril|la|tor
de|fi|ciency
de|fi|cien|cies
de|fi|cient
de|fi|cient|ly
def|icit
de|fier
def|il|ade
def|il|ad|ing
de|file
de|fil|ing
de|file|ment
de|filer

de|fin|able
de|fine
  de|fin|ing
de|finer
de|ˌfini|en|dum
  de|ˌfini|enda
de|ˌfini|ens
  de|ˌfini|en|tia
def|in|ite
def|in|ite|ly
def|in|ite|ness
def|in|ition
def|in|ition|al
def|in|ition|al|ly
de|fini|tive
de|fini|tive|ly
def|la|grate
  def|la|grat|ing
def|la|gra|tion
def|la|gra|tor
de|flate
  de|flat|ing
de|fla|tion
de|fla|tion|ary
de|fla|tion|ist
de|fla|tor
de|flect
de|flec|tion
de|flec|tor
de|flesh
de|flexed
de|flex|ion var. of
  deflection
de|floc|cu|late
  de|floc|cu|lat|ing
de|floc|cu|la|tion
de|flor|ation
de|flower
de|focus
  de|focuses or
  de|focus|ses
  de|focused or
  de|focussed
  de|focus|ing or
  de|focus|sing
Defoe, Dan|iel
  writer
de|fog|ger
de|foli|ant
de|foli|ate
  de|foli|at|ing
de|foli|ation
de|foli|ator

de|force
  de|for|cing
De For|est, Lee
  physicist
de|for|est
de|for|est|ation
de|form
de|form|able
de|form|ation
de|form|ation|al
de|form|ity
  de|form|ities
de|frag|ment
de|frag|men|
    ta|tion
de|frag|ment|er
de|fraud
de|fraud|er
de|fray
de|fray|able
de|fray|al
de|fray|ment
de|frock
de|frost
de|frost|er
def|ter|dar
deft|ly
deft|ness
de|funct
de|fund
de|fuse
  de|fus|ing
defy
  de|fies
  de|fied
  defy|ing
dé|gagé *male*
dé|gagé ballet
  movement
dé|gagée *female*
Degas, Edgar artist
de|gas
  de|gases
  de|gassed
  de|gas|sing
de Gaulle, Charles
  president of France
de|gauss
de|gauss|er
de|gen|er|acy
de|gen|er|ate
  de|gen|er|at|ing
de|gen|er|ation
de|gen|era|tive

de|gen|er|es|cence
de|glaci|ation
de|glam|or|isa|tion
  Br. var. of
  deglamorization
de|glam|or|ise *Br.*
  var. of deglamorize
de|glam|or|ization
de|glam|or|ize
  de|glam|or|izing
de|glaze
  de|glaz|ing
de|glu|ti|tion
de|glu|ti|tive
de|grad|abil|ity
de|grad|able
deg|rad|ation
de|grada|tive
de|grade
  de|grad|ing
de|grader
de|granu|late
  de|granu|lat|ing
de|granu|la|tion
de|greas|ant
de|grease
  de|greas|ing
de|greaser
de|gree
de|gres|sive
degu
de|gus|ta|tion
de haut en bas
de Hav|il|land,
  Geof|frey aircraft
  designer
de|hire
  de|hir|ing
de|hisce
  de|his|cing
de|his|cence
de|his|cent
de Hooch, Pie|ter
  painter
de Hoogh, Pie|ter
  var. of de Hooch
de|horn
de|hors
Dehra Dun
de|hu|man|isa|tion
  Br. var. of
  dehumanization
de|hu|man|ise *Br.*
  var. of dehumanize

de|hu|man|iza|tion
de|hu|man|ize
  de|hu|man|iz|ing
de|hu|midi|fi|
      ca|tion
de|hu|midi|fier
de|hu|midi|fy
  de|hu|midi|fies
  de|hu|midi|fied
  de|hu|midi|fy|ing
de|husk
de|hy|drate
  de|hy|drat|ing
de|hy|dra|tion
de|hy|dra|tor
de|hydro|
    chol|es|terol
de|hydro|gen|ase
de|hydro|gen|ate
  de|hydro|gen|at|ing
de|hydro|gen|ation
Deia|nira
de-ice
  de-icing
de-icer
dei|cidal
dei|cide
deic|tic
deic|tic|al|ly
deid *Scot.* dead
dei|fi|ca|tion
deify
  dei|fies
  dei|fied
  dei|fy|ing
Deigh|ton, Len
  writer
deign
Dei gra|tia
deil *Scot.* devil
Dei|mos
de-index
de|in|dus|trial|
    isa|tion
  Br. var. of deindus-
  trialization
de|in|dus|trial|ise
  Br. var. of
  deindustrialize
de|in|dus|trial|
    iza|tion
de|in|dus|trial|ize
de|in|dus|trial|
    iz|ing

de¦ink
dei¦nony¦chus
deino¦there
deino¦ther¦ium
  deino¦theria or
  deino¦ther¦iums
de¦instal *Br.* var. of
  deinstall
de¦install
de¦install¦la¦tion
de¦instal¦ler
de¦insti¦tu¦tion¦al¦
  isa¦tion
Br. var. of deinsti-
  tutionalization
de¦insti¦tu¦tion¦al¦
  ise
Br. var. of
  deinstitutionalize
de¦insti¦tu¦tion¦al¦
  iza¦tion
de¦insti¦tu¦tion¦al¦
  ize
de¦insti¦tu¦tion¦al¦
  iz¦ing
de¦ion¦isa¦tion *Br.*
  var. of deionization
de¦ion¦ise *Br.* var. of
  deionize
de¦ion¦iser *Br.* var.
  of deionizer
de¦ion¦iza¦tion
de¦ion¦ize
  de¦ion¦iz¦ing
de¦ion¦izer
Deir¦dre
deisal var. of deasil
deism
deist
de¦is¦tic
deity
  de¦ities
de¦ixis
déjà vu
de¦ject
de¦ject¦ed¦ly
de¦jec¦tion
de¦junk
de jure
deka¦liter *US* var.
  of decaliter;
  Br. decalitre
deka¦meter *US* var.
  of decameter;
  Br. decametre

deka¦met¦ric *US*
  var. of decametric
deke
  dek¦ing
Dek¦ker, Thomas
  dramatist
dekko look; cf. deco
de Klerk, F. W.
  president of South
  Africa
del mathematical
  operator
De¦la¦croix,
  Eu¦gène painter
de la Mare,
  Wal¦ter writer
de¦lam¦in¦ate
de¦lam¦in¦at¦ing
de¦lam¦in¦ation
de¦late
  de¦lat¦ing
de¦la¦tion
de¦la¦tor
Dela¦ware
Dela¦war¦ean
delay
de¦lay¦er person
  who delays
de¦layer reduce
  number of layers
dele
  deles
  deled
  dele¦ing
  delete
de¦lect¦abil¦ity
de¦lect¦able
de¦lect¦ably
de¦lect¦ation
del¦eg¦able
dele¦gacy
  dele¦ga¦cies
dele¦gate
  dele¦gat¦ing
dele¦ga¦tion
dele¦ga¦tor
de¦legit¦im¦ate
  de¦legit¦im¦at¦ing
de¦legit¦im¦ation
de¦legit¦ima¦tise *Br.*
  var. of
  delegitimatize
de¦legit¦ima¦tize
  de¦legit¦ima¦tiz¦ing

de¦legit¦im¦isa¦tion
  Br. var. of
  delegitimization
de¦legit¦im¦ise *Br.*
  var. of delegitimize
de¦legit¦im¦iza¦tion
de¦legit¦im¦ize
  de¦legit¦im¦iz¦ing
de¦lete
  de¦let¦ing
dele¦teri¦ous
dele¦teri¦ous¦ly
de¦le¦tion
de¦lex¦ic¦al
Delft city
delft china
Delhi
deli
De¦lian
de¦lib¦er¦ate
  de¦lib¦er¦at¦ing
de¦lib¦er¦ate¦ly
de¦lib¦er¦ate¦ness
de¦lib¦er¦ation
de¦lib¦era¦tive
de¦lib¦er¦ator
De¦libes, Léo
  composer
deli¦cacy
  deli¦ca¦cies
deli¦cate
deli¦cate¦ly
deli¦cate¦ness
deli¦ca¦tes¦sen
de¦licence var. of
  delicense
de¦license
  de¦licen¦sing
de¦li¦cious
de¦li¦cious¦ly
de¦li¦cious¦ness
de¦lict
de¦light
de¦light¦ed¦ly
de¦light¦ful
de¦light¦ful¦ly
de¦light¦ful¦ness
De¦li¦lah
de¦limit
de¦limi¦ta¦tion
de¦lim¦it¦er

de¦lin¦eate
de¦lin¦eat¦ing
de¦lin¦ea¦tion
de¦lin¦ea¦tor
de¦link
de¦lin¦quency
  de¦lin¦quen¦cies
de¦lin¦quent
de¦lin¦quent¦ly
deli¦quesce
  deli¦ques¦cing
deli¦ques¦cence
deli¦ques¦cent
de¦li¦ri¦ant
de¦li¦ri¦ous
de¦li¦ri¦ous¦ly
de¦lir¦ium
  de¦lir¦iums or
  de¦liria
de¦lir¦ium
  tre¦mens
de¦lish delicious
de¦list
De¦lius, Fred¦erick
  composer
de¦liver
de¦liver¦able
de¦liv¦er¦ance
de¦liv¦er¦er
de¦liv¦ery
  de¦liv¦er¦ies
della Fran¦cesca,
  Piero painter
della Quer¦cia,
  Ja¦copo sculptor
della Rob¦bia,
  Luca sculptor
de¦lo¦cal¦isa¦tion
  Br. var. of
  delocalization
de¦lo¦cal¦ise *Br.* var.
  of delocalize
de¦lo¦cal¦iza¦tion
de¦lo¦cal¦ize
  de¦lo¦cal¦iz¦ing
De¦lores name
De¦lors, Jacques
  politician
Delos island
de¦louse
  de¦lous¦ing
delph
Del¦phi
Del¦phian

Del|phic
Del|phine
del|phin|ium
Del|phi|nus
del Sarto, An|drea
  painter
delta
del|ta|ic
delta-v
delta-vee var. of
  delta-v
del|ti|olo|gist
del|ti|ology
del|toid
de|lude
  de|lud|ing
de|luder
del|uge
del|uging
de|lu|sion
de|lu|sion|al
de|lu|sive
de|lu|sory
de|lus|ter US
de|lustre Br.
  de|lus|tring
de luxe
delve
  delv|ing
delver
de|mag|net|isa|tion
  Br. var. of
  demagnetization
de|mag|net|ise Br.
  var. of
  demagnetize
de|mag|net|iser Br.
  var. of
  demagnetizer
de|mag|net|iza|tion
de|mag|net|ize
  de|mag|net|iz|ing
de|mag|net|izer
dema|gog|ic
dema|gogue
dema|goguery
  dema|goguer|ies
dema|gogy
de|mand
de|mand|er
de|mand|ing|ly
de|mant|oid
de|mar|cate
  de|mar|cat|ing

de|mar|ca|tion
de|mar|ca|tor
dé|marche
de|mark
de|mas|si|fi|ca|tion
de|mas|sify
  de|mas|si|fies
  de|mas|si|fied
  de|mas|si|fy|ing
de|materi|al|
  isa|tion
  Br. var. of
  dematerialization
de|materi|al|ise Br.
  var. of
  dematerialize
de|materi|al|
  iza|tion
de|materi|al|ize
  de|materi|al|iz|ing
de Mau|pas|sant,
  Guy writer
Dema|vend var. of
  Damavand
deme Greek political
  division; biological
  subdivision; cf.
  deem
de|mean +ed cf.
  demesne
demean|ing|ly
de|meanor US
de|mean|our Br.
de' Med|ici,
  Cath|er|ine queen
  of France
de' Med|ici,
  Cos|imo statesman
  and banker
de' Med|ici,
  Gio|vanni Pope
  Leo X
de' Med|ici,
  Lor|enzo statesman
  and scholar
de' Med|ici, Maria
  Italian name for
  Marie de Médicis
de Mé|di|cis, Marie
  queen of France
De|melza
de|ment
de|men|ted
de|men|ted|ly
de|men|ted|ness

dé|menti
de|men|tia
de|men|tia
  prae|cox
Dem|er|ara river
dem|er|ara sugar;
  rum
de|merge
  de|mer|ging
de|mer|ger
de|merit
de|meri|tori|ous
Dem|erol
  trademark
de|mer|sal
de|mesne land
Dem|eter
demi-caractère
demi-glace
demi-glaze var. of
  demi-glace
demi|god
demi|god|dess
demi|john
de|mili|tar|isa|tion
  Br. var. of
  demilitarization
de|mili|tar|ise Br.
  var. of demilitarize
de|mili|tar|iza|tion
de|mili|tar|ize
  de|mili|tar|iz|ing
de Mille, Cecil B.
  film producer and
  director
demi|lune
demi-mondaine
demi-monde
de|mine
  de|min|ing
de|miner
de|min|er|al|
  isa|tion
  Br. var. of
  demineralization
de|min|er|al|ise Br.
  var. of
  demineralize
de|min|er|al|
  iza|tion
de|min|er|al|ize
  de|min|er|al|iz|ing
demi-pension
demi|rep

de|mise
  de|mis|ing
demi-sec
demi|semi|quaver
de|mis|sion
de|mist
de|mist|er
demit
de|mit|ted
de|mit|ting
demi|tasse
demi|urge
demi|ur|gic
demo +s +ed +ing
demob
  de|mobbed
  de|mob|bing
de|mo|bil|isa|tion
  Br. var. of
  demobilization
de|mo|bil|ise Br.
  var. of demobilize
de|mo|bil|iza|tion
de|mo|bil|ize
  de|mo|bil|iz|ing
dem|oc|racy
  dem|oc|ra|cies
demo|crat
demo|crat|ic
demo|crat|ic|al|ly
dem|oc|ra|tisa|tion
  Br. var. of
  democratization
dem|oc|ra|tise Br.
  var. of democratize
dem|oc|ra|tiza|tion
dem|oc|ra|tize
  dem|oc|ra|tiz|ing
Dem|oc|ri|tus
  philosopher
démodé
demo|dec|tic
de|modu|late
  de|modu|lat|ing
de|modu|la|tion
de|modu|la|tor
dem|og|raph|er
demo|graph|ic
demo|graph|ic|al|ly
demo|graph|ics
dem|og|raphy
de|mois|elle
de Moivre's
  the|orem

de|mol|ish
de|mol|ish|er
demo|li|tion
demo|li|tion|ist
demon evil spirit;
　cf. daemon
de|mon|et|isa|tion
　Br. var. of
　demonetization
de|mon|et|ise Br.
　var. of demonetize
de|mon|et|iza|tion
de|mon|et|ize
　de|mon|et|iz|ing
de|mon|iac
de|mon|iac|al
de|mon|iac|al|ly
de|mon|ic cf.
　daemonic
de|mon|ic|al|ly
de|mon|isa|tion Br.
　var. of
　demonization
de|mon|ise Br. var.
　of demonize
de|mon|ism
de|mon|iza|tion
de|mon|ize
　de|mon|iz|ing
de|mon|olatry
de|mon|o|logic|al
de|mon|olo|gist
de|mon|ology
　de|mon|olo|gies
de|mon|op|ol|isa|
　　　　tion
　Br. var. of
　demonopolization
de|mon|op|ol|ise
　Br. var. of
　demonopolize
de|mon|op|ol|iza|
　　　　tion
de|mon|op|ol|ize
de|mon|op|ol|iz|ing
dem|on|stra|bil|ity
dem|on|strable
dem|on|strably
dem|on|strate
　dem|on|strat|ing
dem|on|stra|tion
dem|on|stra|tion|al
dem|on|stra|tive
dem|on|stra|tive|ly

dem|on|stra|tor
de Mont|fort,
　Simon founder of
　English parliament
de|mor|al|isa|tion
　Br. var. of
　demoralization
de|mor|al|ise Br.
　var. of demoralize
de|mor|al|iza|tion
de|mor|al|ize
　de|mor|al|iz|ing
de Morgan's laws
demos
　demoi
　common people
De|mos|thenes ora-
　tor
de|mote
　de|mot|ing
dem|ot|ic
de|mo|tion
de|mo|tiv|ate
　de|mo|tiv|at|ing
de|mo|tiv|ation
de|mount
de|mount|able
Demp|sey, Jack
　boxer
de|mul|cent
demur
　de|murred
　de|mur|ring
de|mure
　de|murer
　de|mur|est
de|mure|ly
de|mure|ness
de|mur|rable
de|mur|rage
de|mur|ral
de|mur|rer
de|mutual|isa|tion
　Br. var. of
　demutualization
de|mutual|ise Br.
　var. of demutualize
de|mutual|iza|tion
de|mutual|ize
　de|mutual|iz|ing
demy paper size
de|mye|lin|ate
　de|mye|lin|at|ing
de|mye|lin|ation

de|mys|ti|fi|ca|tion
de|mys|tify
　de|mys|ti|fies
　de|mys|ti|fied
　de|mys|ti|fy|ing
de|myth|olo|gise
　Br. var. of
　demythologize
de|myth|olo|gize
　de|myth|olo|giz|ing
den
　denned
　den|ning
denar Macedonian
　currency; cf. dinar
den|ar|ius
　den|arii
den|ary decimal; cf.
　deanery
de|nation|al|
　　　　isa|tion
　Br. var. of
　denationalization
de|nation|al|ise Br.
　var. of
　denationalize
de|nation|al|
　　　　iza|tion
de|nation|al|ize
de|nation|al|iz|ing
de|natur|al|isa|tion
　Br. var. of
　denaturalization
de|natur|al|ise Br.
　var. of denaturalize
de|natur|al|iza|tion
de|natur|al|ize
　de|natur|al|iz|ing
de|natur|ant
de|natur|ation
de|nature
　de|natur|ing
de|nazi|fi|ca|tion
de|nazify
　de|nazi|fies
　de|nazi|fied
　de|nazi|fy|ing
Den|bigh
Den|bigh|shire
Dench, Judi actress
den|dri|mer
den|drite
den|drit|ic
den|dro|
　　chrono|logic|al

den|dro|chron|
　　　　olo|gist
den|dro|
　　chron|ology
den|dro|gram
den|droid
den|dro|logic|al
den|drolo|gist
den|drol|ogy
den|dron
Dene people
　pl. Dene
dene vale; cf. dean
Deneb
De|neb|ola
de|nerv|ate
　de|nerv|at|ing
de|nerv|ation
De|neuve,
　Cath|érine actress
den|gue fever
Deng Xiao|ping
　Chinese leader
Den Haag Dutch
　name for The
　Hague
deni Macedonian
　currency
deni|abil|ity
deni|able
deni|ably
de|nial
den|ier unit
　pl. den|ier
de|nier person who
　denies
deni|grate
　deni|grat|ing
deni|gra|tion
deni|gra|tor
deni|gra|tory
denim
De Niro, Rob|ert
　actor
Denis, Maur|ice
　painter
Denis patron saint
　of France
De|nise
de|nitri|fi|ca|tion
de|nitrify
　de|nitri|fies
　de|nitri|fied
　de|nitri|fy|ing

deni|zen
deni|zen|ship
Den|mark
Den|nis
de|nom|inal
de|nom|in|ate
  de|nom|in|at|ing
de|nom|in|ation
de|nom|in|ation|al
de|nom|in|ation|al|
  ism
de|nom|ina|tive
de|nom|in|ator
de nos jours
de|nota|tion
de|nota|tion|al
de|nota|tive
de|note
  de|not|ing
de|noue|ment
  French dénouement
de|nounce
  de|noun|cing
de|nounce|ment
de|noun|cer
de novo
Den|pa|sar
dense
  dens|er
  dens|est
dense|ly
dense|ness
densi|fi|ca|tion
dens|ify
  densi|fies
  densi|fied
  densi|fy|ing
dens|im|eter
densi|tom|eter
densi|to|met|ric
densi|to|met|ric|
  al|ly
densi|tom|etry
dens|ity
  dens|ities
den|tal of teeth; cf.
  dentil
den|tal|ise *Br.* var.
  of dentalize
den|ta|lium
  den|ta|lia
den|tal|ize
  den|tal|iz|ing
den|tal|ly

den|tary
den|tar|ies
den|tate
den|telle
den|tex
den|ticle
den|ticu|late
den|ticu|lated
den|ti|frice
den|til *Architecture*;
  cf. dental
denti|lin|gual
dentin *US*
  Br. dentine
den|tinal
den|tine *Br.*
  US dentin
den|tist
den|tis|try
  den|tis|tries
den|ti|tion
den|ture
den|tur|ist
de|nuclear|isa|tion
  Br. var. of
  denuclearization
de|nuclear|ise *Br.*
  var. of
  denuclearize
de|nuclear|iza|tion
de|nuclear|ize
  de|nuclear|iz|ing
de|nuda|tion
de|nude
  de|nud|ing
de|numer|abil|ity
de|numer|able
de|numer|ably
de|nun|ci|ation
de|nun|ci|ator
de|nun|ci|atory
Den|ver
deny
  de|nies
  de|nied
  deny|ing
Denys, St var. of
  Denis
Den|zil
deoch an doris
deo|dar
de|odor|ant
de|odor|isa|tion *Br.*
  var. of

deodorization
de|odor|ise *Br.* var.
  of deodorize
de|odor|iser *Br.* var.
  of deodorizer
de|odor|iza|tion
de|odor|ize
  de|odor|iz|ing
de|odor|izer
Deo gra|tias
de|ontic
de|onto|logic|al
de|ontolo|gist
de|ontol|ogy
Deo vol|ente
de|oxi|da|tion
de|oxi|dise *Br.* var.
  of deoxidize
de|oxi|diser *Br.* var.
  of deoxidizer
de|oxi|dize
  de|oxi|diz|ing
de|oxi|dizer
de|oxy|cor|tico|
  ster|one
de|oxy|gen|ate
de|oxy|gen|at|ing
de|oxy|gen|ation
de|oxy|ribo|
  nucle|ase
de|oxy|ribo|
  nucle|ic
de|oxy|ri|bose
De|par|dieu,
  Gér|ard actor
de|part
dé|parte|ment
  French administra-
  tive district
de|part|ment
de|part|men|tal
de|part|men|tal|
  isa|tion
  Br. var. of depart-
  mentalization
de|part|men|tal|ise
  Br. var. of
  departmentalize
de|part|men|tal|
  ism
de|part|men|tal|
  iza|tion
de|part|men|tal|ize
de|part|men|tal|
  iz|ing

de|part|men|tal|ly
de|part|ure
de|pas|tur|age
de|pas|ture
  de|pas|tur|ing
de|pau|per|ate
dé|paysé male
dé|pay|sée female
de|pend
de|pend|abil|ity
de|pend|able
de|pend|ably
de|pend|ant *Br. n.*
  US dependent
de|pend|ence
de|pend|ency
  de|pend|en|cies
de|pend|ent *adj.*
de|pend|ent *n. US*
  Br. var. of
  dependant
de|pend|ent|ly
de|pend|ing
de|per|son|al|
  isa|tion
  Br. var. of
  depersonalization
de|per|son|al|ise
  Br. var. of
  depersonalize
de|per|son|al|
  iza|tion
de|per|son|al|ize
  de|per|son|al|iz|ing
de|phlo|gis|tic|ated
de|pict
de|pict|er
de|pic|tion
de|pict|ive
de|pig|ment
de|pig|men|tation
dep|il|ate
  dep|il|at|ing
dep|il|ation
dep|il|ator
de|pila|tory
  de|pila|tor|ies
de Pisan,
  Chris|tine writer
de Pizan var. of de
  Pisan
de|plane
  de|plan|ing

de|plete
de|plet|ing
de|pleter
de|ple|tion
de|plor|able
de|plor|ably
de|plore
de|plor|ing
de|ploy
de|ploy|able
de|ploy|ment
de|plume
de|plum|ing
de|polar|isa|tion
Br. var. of
depolarization
de|polar|ise *Br.* var.
of depolarize
de|polar|iza|tion
de|polar|ize
de|polar|iz|ing
de|pol|iti|cisa|tion
Br. var. of
depoliticization
de|pol|iti|cise *Br.*
var. of depoliticize
de|pol|iti|ciza|tion
de|pol|iti|cize
de|pol|iti|ciz|ing
de|poly|mer|
  isa|tion
Br. var. of
depolymerization
de|poly|mer|ise *Br.*
var. of
depolymerize
de|poly|mer|
  iza|tion
de|poly|mer|ize
de|poly|mer|iz|ing
de|pon|ent
de|popu|late
de|popu|lat|ing
de|popu|la|tion
de|port
de|port|able
de|port|ation
de|port|ee
de|port|ment
de|pose
de|pos|ing
de|posit
de|pos|it|ary
de|pos|it|ar|ies
  person; cf.

depository
de|pos|ition
de|pos|it|or
de|posi|tory
de|posi|tor|ies
  storehouse; cf.
depositary
depot
de|power
dep|rav|ation per-
  version, corruption;
  cf. deprivation
de|prave
de|prav|ing
de|prav|ity
de|prav|ities
dep|re|cate
dep|re|cat|ing
  disapprove of
dep|re|cat|ing|ly
dep|re|ca|tion
dep|re|ca|tive
dep|re|ca|tor
dep|re|ca|tory
de|pre|ciable
de|pre|ci|ate
de|pre|ci|at|ing
  lower in value;
  belittle
de|pre|ci|ation
de|pre|cia|tive
de|pre|ci|atory
dep|re|da|tion
dep|re|da|tor
dep|re|da|tory
de|press
de|pres|sant
de|press|ible
de|press|ing|ly
de|pres|sion
de|pres|sive
de|pres|sor muscle
de|pres|sur|isa|tion
Br. var. of
depressurization
de|pres|sur|ise *Br.*
var. of
depressurize
de|pres|sur|iza|
              tion
de|pres|sur|ize
de|pres|sur|iz|ing
De|prez, Jos|quin
var. of des Prez

de|prival
de|priv|ation hard-
  ship, loss; cf.
depravation
de|prive
de|priv|ing
de pro|fun|dis
de|pro|gram *US*
de|pro|grammed
  or de|pro|gramed
de|pro|gram|ming
  or de|pro|gram|ing
de|pro|gramme *Br.*
de|pro|grammed
de|pro|gram|ming
de|pro|tein|isa|tion
Br. var. of
deproteinization
de|pro|tein|ise *Br.*
var. of
deproteinize
de|pro|tein|iza|tion
de|pro|tein|ize
de|pro|tein|iz|ing
depth
depth|less
depu|ta|tion
de|pute
de|put|ing
depu|tise *Br.* var. of
deputize
depu|tize
depu|tiz|ing
dep|uty
dep|uties
dep|uty|ship
de|queue
de|queuing or
de|queue|ing
De Quin|cey,
  Thomas writer
de|racin|ate
de|racin|at|ing
de|racin|ation
déraciné
de|rail
de|rail|leur
de|rail|ment
de|range
de|ran|ging
de|range|ment
de|rate
de|rat|ing
de|ration

Derby
Der|bies
  city; horse race; cf.
  Darby
Derby, Lord prime
  minister of Britain
derby
der|bies
  shoe; hat; cf.
  darbies
Derby|shire
de re
de|real|isa|tion *Br.*
  var. of
derealization
de|real|ised *Br.* var.
  of derealized
de|real|iza|tion
de|real|ized
de|re|cho +s
de|rec|og|nise *Br.*
var. of derecognize
de|rec|og|ni|tion
de|rec|og|nize
de|rec|og|niz|ing
de|refer|ence
de|ref|er|en|cing
de|regis|ter
de|regis|tra|tion
de règle
de|regu|late
de|regu|lat|ing
de|regu|la|tion
de|regu|la|tory
dere|lict
dere|lic|tion
de|re|press
de|re|pres|sion
de|re|qui|si|tion
de|res|trict
de|res|tric|tion
de|ride
de|rid|ing
de|rider
de ri|gueur
de|ris|ible
de|ri|sion
de|ri|sive
de|ri|sive|ly
de|ri|sive|ness
de|ri|sory
de|riv|able
der|iv|ate
der|iv|ation

der|iv|ation|al
de|riva|tive
de|rive
  de|riv|ing
derm
derm|abra|sion
der|mal
Derm|ap|tera
derm|ap|ter|an
derm|ap|ter|ous
derma|titis
der|ma|to|glyph|ic
der|ma|to|glyph|ics
der|ma|to|logic|al
der|ma|to|logic|
    al|ly
derma|tolo|gist
derma|tol|ogy
derma|tome
derm|ato|myco|sis
  derm|ato|myco|ses
derm|ato|myo|sitis
derm|ato|phyte
derm|ato|phyt|ic
derm|ato|phyt|osis
  derm|ato|phyt|oses
derma|tosis
  derma|toses
der|mes|tid
der|mis
Derm|op|tera
derm|op|ter|an
Der|mot
der|nier cri
dero|gate
  dero|gat|ing
dero|ga|tion
de|roga|tive
de|roga|tor|ily
de|roga|tory
Der|rick
der|rick crane
Der|rida, Jacques
  philosopher and
  critic
Der|rid|ean
der|rière
derring-do
der|rin|ger
der|ris
derro +s
Derry =
  Londonderry

derry in 'have a
  derry on'
derv
der|vish
de|sac|ral|isa|tion
  Br. var. of
  desacralization
de|sac|ral|ise *Br.*
  var. of desacralize
de|sac|ral|iza|tion
de|sac|ral|ize
  de|sac|ral|izing
de|sal|in|ate
  de|sal|in|at|ing
de|sal|in|ation
de|sal|in|ator
de|salt
des|apare|cido +s
de|sat|ur|ate
  de|sat|ur|at|ing
de|sat|ur|ation
de|scale
  de|scal|ing
de|scaler
des|cami|sado +s
des|cant
Des|cartes, René
  philosopher and
  mathematician
des|cend
des|cend|ant *n.*
des|cend|ent *adj.*
des|cend|er
des|cen|deur
  climbing
  implement
des|cend|ible
des|cent cf. dissent
de|scram|ble
  de|scram|bling
de|scram|bler
de|scrib|able
de|scribe
  de|scrib|ing
de|scriber
de|scrip|tion
de|scrip|tive
de|scrip|tive|ly
de|scrip|tive|ness
de|scrip|tiv|ism
de|scrip|tiv|ist
de|scrip|tor
des|cry
  des|cries

des|cried
des|cry|ing
Des|de|mona
dese|crate
  dese|crat|ing
dese|cra|tion
dese|cra|tor
de|seed
de|seed|er
de|seg|re|gate
  de|seg|re|gat|ing
de|seg|re|ga|tion
de|select
de|selec|tion
de|sen|si|tisa|tion
  Br. var. of
  desensitization
de|sen|si|tise *Br.*
  var. of desensitize
de|sen|si|tiser *Br.*
  var. of desensitizer
de|sen|si|tiza|tion
de|sen|si|tize
  de|sen|si|tiz|ing
de|sen|si|tizer
des|ert barren
  region; abandon;
  cf. **deserts**, **dessert**
de|sert|er
desert|ifi|ca|tion
de|ser|tion
de|serts as in 'just
  deserts'
de|serve
  de|serv|ing
de|served|ly
de|served|ness
de|sex
de|sexu|al|isa|tion
  Br. var. of
  desexualization
de|sexu|al|ise *Br.*
  var. of desexualize
de|sexu|al|iza|tion
de|sexu|al|ize
  de|sexu|al|iz|ing
dés|ha|billé
deshi var. of desi
desi *Ind.* local
De Sica, Vit|torio
  film director and
  actor
des|ic|cant

des|ic|cate
des|ic|cat|ing
des|ic|ca|tion
des|ic|ca|tive
des|ic|ca|tor
de|sid|er|ate
  de|sid|er|at|ing
de|sid|era|tive
de|sid|er|atum
  de|sid|er|ata
de|sign
des|ig|nate
  des|ig|nat|ing
des|ig|na|tion
des|ig|na|tor
de|sign|ed|ly
de|sign|er
de|sir|abil|ity
de|sir|able
de|sir|able|ness
de|sir|ably
de|sire
  de|sir|ing
Dé|sirée name
De|siree potato
de|sir|ous
de|sist
desk-bound
de|skill
desk|top
des|man +s
des|mid
des|moid
Des Moines
Des|mond
desmo|somal
desmo|some
deso|late
  deso|lat|ing
deso|late|ly
deso|late|ness
deso|la|tion
de|sol|der
de|sorb
de|sorb|ent
de|sorb|er
de|sorp|tion
des|pair
des|pair|ing|ly
des|patch *Br.* var. of
  dispatch
des|patch|er *Br.* var.
  of dispatcher

des|per|ado
  des|per|adoes or
  des|per|ados
des|per|ado|ism
des|per|ate
des|per|ate|ly
des|per|ate|ness
des|per|ation
de|spic|able
de|spic|ably
de Spin|oza,
  Bar|uch
  philosopher
des|pise
  des|pis|ing
des|piser
des|pite
des|pite|ful
de|spoil
de|spoil|er
de|spoil|ment
de|spoli|ation
des|pond
des|pond|ence
des|pond|ency
des|pond|ent
des|pond|ent|ly
des|pot
des|pot|ic
des|pot|ic|al|ly
des|pot|ism
des Prés, Jos|quin
  var. of des Prez
des Prez, Jos|quin
  composer
des|quam|ate
  des|quam|at|ing
des|quam|ation
des|quama|tive
des res
  des reses
Des|sau
des|sert sweet
  course; cf. desert,
  deserts
des|sert|spoon
des|sert|spoon|ful
de|sta|bil|isa|tion
  Br. var. of
  destabilization
de|sta|bil|ise Br.
  var. of destabilize
de|sta|bil|iza|tion

de|sta|bil|ize
de|sta|bil|iz|ing
de Staël, Ma|dame
  novelist
de|stain
De Stijl
des|tin|ation
des|tine
  des|tin|ing
des|tiny
  des|tinies
des|ti|tute
des|ti|tu|tion
de|stock
de-stress
dest|rier
des|troy
des|troy|er
de|struct
de|struct|ibil|ity
de|struct|ible
de|struc|tion
de|struc|tive
de|struc|tive|ly
de|struc|tive|ness
de|struc|tor
de|sue|tude
de|sul|fur|iza|tion
  US
de|sul|fur|ize US
  de|sul|fur|iz|ing
de|sul|fur|izer US
de|sul|phur|
    isa|tion
  Br. var. of
  desulphurization
de|sul|phur|ise Br.
  var. of
  desulphurize
de|sul|phur|iser Br.
  var. of
  desulphurizer
de|sul|phur|
    iza|tion
de|sul|phur|ize
  de|sul|phur|iz|ing
de|sul|phur|izer
des|ul|tor|ily
des|ul|tori|ness
des|ul|tory
de|super|heat|er
de|syn|chron|isa|
    tion
  Br. var. of

desynchronization
de|syn|chron|ise
  Br. var. of
  desynchronize
de|syn|chron|
    ization
de|syn|chron|ize
  de|syn|chron|izing
de|tach
de|tach|abil|ity
de|tach|able
de|tach|ed|ly
de|tach|ment
de|tail
de|tain
de|tain|ee
de|tain|er
de|tain|ment
de|tan|gle
  de|tan|gling
de|tect
de|tect|able
de|tect|ably
de|tec|tion
de|tect|ive
de|tect|or
de|tector|ist
de|tent mechanical
  catch
dé|tente reduction
  in hostility
de|ten|tion
de|tenu
  French détenu
deter
de|terred
de|ter|ring
de|ter|gence
de|ter|gent
de|teri|or|ate
  de|teri|or|at|ing
de|teri|or|ation
de|teri|ora|tive
de|ter|min|able
de|ter|min|acy
de|ter|min|ant
de|ter|min|ate
de|ter|min|ation
de|ter|mina|tive
de|ter|mine
  de|ter|min|ing
de|ter|mined|ly
de|ter|miner

de|ter|min|ism
de|ter|min|ist
de|ter|min|is|tic
de|ter|min|is|tic|
    al|ly
de|ter|rence
de|ter|rent
de|test
de|test|able
de|test|ably
de|test|ation
de|test|er
de|throne
de|thron|ing
de|throne|ment
det|inue
det|on|ate
det|on|at|ing
det|on|ation
det|ona|tive
det|on|ator
de|tor|sion
de|tour
de|tox
de|toxi|cate
de|toxi|cat|ing
de|toxi|ca|tion
de|toxi|fi|ca|tion
de|toxi|fier
de|tox|ify
de|toxi|fies
de|toxi|fied
de|toxi|fy|ing
de|tract
de|trac|tion
de|tract|ive
de|tract|or
de|train
de|train|ment
de|trib|al|isa|tion
  Br. var. of
  detribalization
de|trib|al|ise Br.
  var. of detribalize
de|trib|al|iza|tion
de|trib|al|ize
  de|trib|al|iz|ing
det|ri|ment
det|ri|men|tal
det|ri|men|tal|ly
de|trital
de|triti|vore
det|rit|iv|orous

de|tritus
De|troit
de trop
de Troyes,
  Chré|tien poet
de|trusor
Det|tol *trademark*
de|tu|mesce
  de|tu|mes|cing
de|tu|mes|cence
de|tu|mes|cent
de|tune
Deu|ca|lion son of
  Prometheus
deuce
deuced
deuced|ly
deur|me|kaar
deus ex mach|ina
  deus ex mach|inas
deu|ter|ag|on|ist
deu|ter|an|ope
deu|ter|an|opia
deu|ter|ic
deu|ter|ium
deu|tero|
      canon|ic|al
Deutero-Isaiah
  writer
deu|teron
Deu|tero|nom|ic
Deu|ter|on|om|ist
Deu|ter|on|omy
Deutsche Mark
  var. of
  Deutschmark
Deutsch|mark
deut|zia
Dev, Kapil cricketer
deva divine being
deva|dasi
de Val|era, Eamon
  president of the
  Republic of Ireland
de Val|ois, Nin|ette
  dancer and
  choreographer
de|valu|ation
de|value
  de|valu|ing
Deva|nag|ari
dev|as|tate
  dev|as|tat|ing
  dev|as|tat|ing|ly

dev|as|ta|tion
dev|as|ta|tor
de|vein
de|velop
de|vel|op|able
de|vel|op|er
de|vel|op|ment
de|vel|op|men|tal
de|vel|op|
      men|tal|ly
dé|ve|loppé
De|ven|sian
de|ver|bal
Devi goddess
de|vi|ance
de|vi|ancy
  de|vi|an|cies
de|vi|ant
de|vi|ate
  de|vi|at|ing
de|vi|ation
de|vi|ation|al
de|vi|ation|ism
de|vi|ation|ist
de|vi|ator
de|vice
devil
  dev|illed *Br.*
  dev|iled *US*
  dev|il|ling *Br.*
  dev|il|ing *US*
devil|fish
devil|ish
devil|ish|ly
devil|ish|ness
devil-may-care
devil|ment
dev|il|ry
  dev|il|ries
devils-on-
      horseback
dev|il|try
de|vi|ous
de|vi|ous|ly
de|vi|ous|ness
de|vis|able able to
  be devised; cf.
  divisible
de|vise
  de|vis|ing
de|visee
de|viser inventor;
  cf. devisor, divisor

de|visor person
  leaving property to
  another; cf.
  deviser, divisor
de|vi|tal|isa|tion *Br.*
  var. of
  devitalization
de|vi|tal|ise *Br.* var.
  of devitalize
de|vi|tal|iza|tion
de|vi|tal|ize
de|vi|tal|iz|ing
de|vit|ri|fi|ca|tion
de|vit|rify
  de|vit|ri|fies
  de|vit|ri|fied
  de|vit|ri|fying
de|voice
  de|voi|cing
de|void
de|voir
de|vo|lu|tion
de|vo|lu|tion|ary
de|vo|lu|tion|ist
de|volve
  de|volv|ing
de|volve|ment
Devon
Dev|on|ian
Dev|on|shire
de|voré
  French dévoré
de|vote
  de|vot|ing
de|voted|ly
de|voted|ness
de|votee
de|vo|tion
de|vo|tion|al
de|vo|tion|al|ly
de|vour
de|vour|er
de|vout
de|vout|ly
de|vout|ness
dew moisture; cf.
  due
dewan
Dewar, James
  physicist
dewar flask
de|water
de|wax

dew|berry
  dew|berries
dew|claw
dew|drop
Dewey library
  system
Dewey, John
  philosopher
dew|fall
dew|ily
dewi|ness
dew|lap
de|worm
de|worm|er
Dews|bury
dewy
  dew|ier
  dewi|est
dewy-eyed
dex
dexa|metha|sone
Dexe|drine
  trademark
Dex|ter, Colin
  writer
dex|ter
dex|ter|ity
dex|ter|ous
dex|ter|ous|ly
dex|ter|ous|ness
dex|tral
dex|tral|ity
dex|tral|ly
dex|tran
dex|trin
dex|tro|rota|tion
dex|tro|rota|tory
dex|trose
dex|trous var. of
  dexterous
dex|trous|ly var. of
  dexterously
dex|trous|ness var.
  of dexterousness
dexy
  dex|ies
de|zinci|fi|ca|tion
dhaba
Dhaka capital of
  Bangladesh; cf.
  Dakar
Dhakai
dhal

dhamma var. of
  dharma
dhan|sak
dhar|am|shala var.
  of dharmashala
dharma
dhar|ma|shala
dharna
Dharuk
Dhau|la|giri
dhikr
dhobi washerman;
  cf. dobe
dho|bie itch var. of
  dhobi itch
dhobi itch
dhobi's itch var. of
  dhobi itch
Dho|far
dhol drum; cf.
  dhole, dole
dho|lak
dhole dog; cf. dhol,
  dole
dhoni
dhoti
dhow
dhurra var. of
  durra
dhur|rie rug; cf.
  durry
dhy|ana
dia|base
dia|betes
dia|betes
  in|sipi|dus
dia|betes mel|li|tus
dia|bet|ic
diab||lerie
dia|bol|ic
dia|bol|ical
dia|bol|ic|al|ly
di|ab|ol|ise Br. var.
  of diabolize
di|ab|ol|ism
di|ab|ol|ist
di|ab|ol|ize
  di|ab|ol|iz|ing
di|ab|olo +s
di|acetyl|
  mor|phine
dia|chron|eity
dia|chron|ic

dia|chron|ic|al|ly
di|achron|ism
dia|chron|is|tic
di|achron|ous
di|achron|ous|ly
di|achrony
di|achron|ies
di|ac|onal
di|ac|on|ate
dia|crit|ic
dia|crit|ic|al
dia|crit|ic|al|ly
di|adel|phous
dia|dem +ed
Di|ado|chi Macedo-
  nian generals
di|aer|esis Br.
  di|aer|eses
  US dieresis
dia|gen|esis
dia|gen|et|ic
Di|ag|hi|lev, Ser|gei
  Pav|lo|vich ballet
  impresario
diag|nos|able
diag|nose
diag|nos|ing
diag|no|sis
diag|no|ses
diag|nos|tic
diag|nos|tic|al|ly
diag|nos|ti|cian
diag|nos|tics
di|ag|onal
di|ag|onal|ly
dia|gram
dia|grammed Br.
dia|gramed US
dia|gram|ming Br.
dia|gram|ing US
dia|gram|mat|ic
dia|gram|mat|ic|
  al|ly
dia|grid
dia|kin|esis
  dia|kin|eses
dial
  dialled Br.
  dialed US
  dial|ling Br.
  dial|ing US
  cf. diol
dia|lect
dia|lect|al

dia|lect|al|ly
dia|lect|ic
dia|lect|ic|al
dia|lect|ic|al|ly
dia|lect|ician
dia|lect|ologic|al
dia|lect|olo|gist
dia|lect|ology
dial|er US
dial-in
dial|ler Br.
dia|log US +ed +ing
dia|logic
dia|logic|al
dialo|gism
dialo|gist
dia|logue Br.
  dia|logued
  dia|loguing
dial-up
di|alys|ate Br.
  US dialyzate
dia|lyse Br.
  dia|lys|ing
dia|ly|sis
dia|ly|ses
dia|lyt|ic
di|alyz|ate
  Br. dialysate
dia|lyze US
  dia|lyz|ing
dia|mag|net
dia|mag|net|ic
dia|mag|net|ism
dia|manté
dia|man|tifer|ous
dia|mant|ine
diam|eter
diam|etral
dia|met|ric
dia|met|ric|al
dia|met|ric|al|ly
di|amine
dia|mond
dia|mond|back
diamond-bird
dia|mond|ifer|ous
dia|mor|phine
Diana Roman
  goddess
Diana, Princess of
  Wales
diana butterfly

Diane
Dia|net|ics
Dia|nne
di|an|thus
dia|pa|son
dia|pause
dia|paus|ing
dia|pe|de|sis
dia|per nappy;
  pattern; cf. diapir
di|aph|an|ous
dia|phone
di|aph|or|ase
dia|phor|esis
dia|phor|et|ic
dia|phragm
dia|phrag|mat|ic
di|aph|ysis
di|aph|yses
dia|pir rock
  formation; cf.
  diaper
dia|pir|ic
dia|pir|ism
dia|posi|tive
di|apsid
di|arch|al
di|arch|ic
di|archy
di|arch|ies
diar|ise Br. var. of
  diarize
diar|ist
diar|is|tic
diar|ize
  diar|iz|ing
diar|rhea US
diar|rhe|al US
diar|rhe|ic US
diar|rhoea Br.
diar|rhoe|al Br.
diar|rhoe|ic Br.
diary
  diar|ies
Dias, Bar|tolo|meu
  explorer
dias|pora
dia|spore
dia|stase
dia|stasic
dia|stat|ic
dia|stema
dia|ste|mas or

dia|ste|mata
dia|stereo|iso|mer
dia|stole
dia|stol|ic
dia|thermy
di|ath|esis
  di|ath|eses
dia|tom
dia|tom|aceous
di|atom|ic
di|atom|ite
dia|ton|ic
dia|treme
dia|tribe
Diaz, Bar|tolo|meu
  var. of **Dias**
Díaz, Por|firio
  Mexican president
di|aze|pam
di|azi|non
diazo
diazo|methane
di|azo|nium
di|azo|type
dib
  dibbed
  dib|bing
dib|basic
dib|ber
dib|ble
  dib|bling
dib|bler
di|bor|ane
dice
  pl. **dice**
  v. **dices**
  diced
  di|cing
di|cen|tra
di|cen|tric
dicer
dicey
  dici|er
  dici|est
di|cha|sium
  di|cha|sia
di|chlor|vos
di|chog|am|ous
di|chog|amy
di|chot|ic
di|chot|om|ise *Br.*
  var. of **dichotomize**
di|chot|om|ize
  di|chot|om|iz|ing

di|chot|om|ous
di|chot|om|ous|ly
di|chot|omy
  di|choto|mies
di|chro|ic
di|chro|ism
di|chro|mate
di|chro|mat|ic
di|chro|ma|tism
dick|cis|sel
Dick|ens, Charles
  writer
dick|ens in 'what
  the dickens?' etc.
Dick|ens|ian
dicker
dick|er|er
dickey var. of **dicky**
dick|head *vulgar*
  slang
Dick|in|son, Emily
  poet
dick|wad
dicky
  dick|ies
  dick|ier
  dicki|est
dicot
di|coty|le|don
di|coty|le|don|ous
di|crot|ic
dicta
dic|tam|nus
  dic|tamni
Dic|ta|phone
  trademark
dic|tate
  dic|tat|ing
dic|ta|tion
dic|ta|tor
dic|ta|tor|ial
dic|ta|tori|al|ly
dic|ta|tor|ship
dic|tion
dic|tion|ary
  dic|tion|ar|ies
dic|tum
  dicta or dic|tums
dicty
Dictyop|tera
dictyop|ter|an
di|cyno|dont
di|dac|tic

di|dac|tic|al|ly
di|dac|ti|cism
dida|kai var. of
  didicoi
di|dano|sine
did|di|coy var. of
  didicoi
did|dle
  did|dling
did|dler
diddly-squat
did|dums
diddy
  did|dies
di|de|oxy|cyti|dine
di|de|oxy|ino|sine
Di|derot, Denis
  philosopher
didg|eri|doo +s
didi *Ind.* older sister
didi|coi
did|jeri|du var. of
  didgeridoo
didn't
Dido queen of
  Carthage
dido
  di|does or didos
  antic
didst
Did|yma
di|dym|ium
die
  dying
  cease living; cf. **dye**
die
  dies tools
  dice numbered
  cubes; cf. **dye**
die|back *n.*
die-cast
dief|fen|bachia
die|gesis
  die|geses
die|get|ic
Diego Gar|cia
die|hard
diel relating to 24
  hours; cf. **dial, diol**
diel|drin
di|elec|tric
di|electro|phor|esis
Diels–Alder reac-
  tion

Dien Bien Phu
di|enceph|al|ic
di|enceph|alon
diene organic
  compound
Di|eppe
di|er|esis *US*
  Br. diaeresis
Die|sel, Ru|dolf
  engineer
die|sel fuel; cf.
  deasil
diesel-electric
diesel-hydraulic
diesel|ise *Br.* var. of
  dieselize
diesel|ize
  diesel|iz|ing
die-sinker
die-sinking
Dies Irae
dies non
die-stamping
die|stock
di|es|trus *US*
  Br. dioestrus
diet
diet|ary
  diet|ar|ies
diet|er
diet|et|ic
dict|ct|ic|al|ly
diet|et|ics
di|ethyl
di|ethyl|amide
di|ethyl|ene
di|ethyl|stil|
          bes|trol
di|ethyl|stil|
          boes|trol
diet|ician var. of
  dietitian
diet|itian
Diet of Worms
Diet|rich, Mar|lene
  actress and singer
dif|fer
dif|fer|ence
dif|fer|en|cing
dif|fer|ent
dif|fer|en|tia
dif|fer|en|tiae
dif|fer|en|ti|abil|ity
dif|fer|en|ti|able

dif|fer|en|tial
dif|fer|en|tial|ly
dif|fer|en|ti|ate
  dif|fer|en|ti|at|ing
dif|fer|en|ti|ation
dif|fer|en|ti|ator
dif|fer|ent|ly
dif|fer|ent|ness
dif|fi|cult
dif|fi|culty
  dif|fi|cul|ties
dif|fi|dence
dif|fi|dent
dif|fi|dent|ly
dif|fract
dif|frac|tion
dif|fract|ive
dif|fract|om|eter
dif|fuse
  dif|fus|ing
dif|fuse|ly
dif|fuse|ness
dif|fuser
dif|fus|ible
dif|fu|sion
dif|fu|sion|ism
dif|fu|sion|ist
dif|fu|sive
dif|fu|siv|ity
  dif|fu|siv|ities
dif|fusor var. of
  diffuser
dig
  dug
  dig|ging
Di|gam|bara
di|gamma
di|gas|tric
di|gen|ean
di|ger|ati
di|gest
di|gest|er
di|gest|ibil|ity
di|gest|ible
di|ges|tif
di|ges|tion
di|gest|ive
dig|ger
dight
digi|cam *trademark*
digit
digit|al
digi|talin

digi|talis
digit|al|isa|tion *Br.*
  var. of
  digitalization
digit|al|ise *Br.* var.
  of digitalize
digit|al|iza|tion
digit|al|ize
  digit|al|iz|ing
digit|al|ly
digi|tate
digi|ta|tion
digi|ti|grade
digit|isa|tion *Br.*
  var. of digitization
digit|ise *Br.* var. of
  digitize
digit|iser *Br.* var. of
  digitizer
digit|iza|tion
digit|ize
  digit|iz|ing
digit|izer
digi|toxin
di|glos|sia
di|glos|sic
dig|ni|fied|ly
dig|nify
  dig|ni|fies
  dig|ni|fied
  dig|ni|fy|ing
dig|ni|tary
  dig|ni|tar|ies
dig|nity
  dig|ni|ties
di|goxin
di|graph
di|graph|ic
di|gress
di|gress|er
di|gres|sion
di|gres|sive
di|gres|sive|ly
di|gres|sive|ness
di|he|dral
di|hy|brid
di|hy|dric
di|hydro|
  tes|tos|ter|one
di|hy|droxy|
  acet|one
Dijon
dik-dik
dike var. of dyke

dik|kop
dik|tat
Di|lan|tin
  trademark
di|lapi|date
di|lapi|dat|ing
di|lapi|da|tion
di|lat|able
di|lat|ancy
dila|ta|tion
di|late
  di|lat|ing
dila|tion
di|la|tor
dila|tor|ily
dila|tori|ness
dila|tory
dildo
  dil|dos or dil|does
di|lemma
dil|et|tante
  dil|et|tanti or
  dil|et|tan|tes
dil|et|tant|ish
dil|et|tant|ism
dili|gence
dili|gent
dili|gent|ly
dilly
  dil|lies
  dil|lier
  dil|li|est
dilly|bag
dilly-dally
  dilly-dallies
  dilly-dallied
  dilly-dallying
di|lo|pho|saurus
  di|lo|pho|saur|uses
  or di|lopho|sauri
di|lu|ent
di|lute
  di|lut|ing
di|luter
di|lu|tion
di|lu|tive
di|lu|vial
di|lu|vian
dim
  dimmed
  dim|ming
dim|mer
dim|mest
Di|Maggio, Joe
  baseball player

Dim|bleby,
  Rich|ard, David,
  and Jona|than
  broadcasters
dime
di|men|sion
di|men|sion|al
di|men|sion|al|ly
di|men|sion|less
dimer
di|mer|cap|rol
di|mer|ic
di|mer|isa|tion *Br.*
  var. of
  dimerization
di|mer|ise *Br.* var.
  of dimerize
di|mer|iza|tion
di|mer|ize
  di|mer|iz|ing
di|mer|ous
dim|eter
di|metho|ate
di|methyl
di|met|ric
di|met|ro|don
di|midi|ate
di|midi|at|ing
di|midi|ation
di|min|ish
di|min|ish|able
di|minu|endo
  pl. di|minu|en|dos
  or di|minu|endi
  v. di|minu|en|dos
  di|minu|en|doed
  di|minu|en|do|ing
dim|in|ution
di|minu|tive
di|minu|tive|ly
di|minu|tive|ness
di|mis|sory
dim|ity
dimly
dim|mable
dim|mer
dim|mish
dim|ness
di|morph|ic
di|morph|ism
di|morpho|theca
di|morph|ous

dimple
dim|pling
dim|ply
 dim|plier
 dim|pli|est
dim sim var. of dim
 sum
dim sum
dim|wit
dim-witted
dim-witted|ly
dim-witted|ness
DIN technical
 standard
din
 dinned
 din|ning
dinar currency of
 various countries;
 cf. denar
Di|naric
din-din var. of din-
 dins
din-dins
dine
 din|ing
 eat; cf. dyne
diner
di|nero
diner-out
 diners-out
din|ette
ding-a-ling
Ding an sich
 Dinge an sich
ding|bat
ding-dong
ding|er
din|ges var. of
 dingus
din|ghy
 din|ghies
 boat; cf. dingy
din|gily
din|gi|ness
din|gle
dingle|berry
 dingle|berries
dingo
 din|goes or din|gos
din|gus
dingy
 din|gier
 din|gi|est
 dull; cf. dinghy

di|nitro|gen
dink
Dinka
dinki-di var. of
 dinky-di
din|kum
Dinky *trademark*
 toy
dinky
 din|kies
 dink|ier
 dinki|est
dinky-di
dinna *Scot.* did not
din|nae var. of
 dinna
din|ner
dinner|ware
dino|fla|gel|late
dino|saur
dino|saur|ian
di|nucleo|tide
dio|cesan
dio|cese +s
dioch
Dio|cle|tian Roman
 emperor
diode
di|oe|cious
di|oecy
d|oes|trus *Br.*
 US diestrus
Di|oge|nes
 philosopher
di|ogen|ite
diol chemical
 compound; cf. dial
Dione moon of
 Saturn
Dio|nys|iac
Dio|nys|ian
Dio|nys|ius I and
 II, rulers of
 Syracuse
Dio|nys|ius
 Ex|ig|uus Scythian
 monk and scholar
Dio|nys|ius of
 Hali|car|nas|sus
 Greek historian
Dio|nys|ius the
 Are|opa|gite
 Greek churchman

Dio|nysus Greek
 god
Dio|phan|tine
Dio|phan|tus
 mathematician
di|op|side
di|op|tase
di|opter *US*
di|optre *Br.*
di|op|tric
di|op|trics
Dior, Chris|tian
 couturier
dio|rama
di|or|ite
di|or|it|ic
Dio|scuri Castor
 and Pollux
di|os|genin
di|oxan var. of
 dioxane
di|oxane
di|ox|ide
di|oxin
dip
 dipped
 dip|ping
dip-dye
 dip-dyeing
Dip. Ed. Diploma
 in Education
di|pep|tide
di|phen|
              hydra|mine
di|phenyl|amine
di|phenyl|thio|
          car|ba|zone
di|phos|phate
diph|theria
diph|ther|ial
diph|ther|it|ic
diph|ther|oid
diph|thong
diph|thong|al
diph|thong|isa|tion
 Br. var. of
 diphthongization
diph|thong|ise *Br.*
 var. of
 diphthongize
diph|thong|iza|tion
diph|thong|ize
 diph|thong|iz|ing
di|phy|cer|cal

di|ple|gia
diplo|blast|ic
diplo|coc|cus
 diplo|cocci
dip|lod|ocus
dip|loid
dip|loidy
dip|loma
dip|lo|macy
dip|lo|mat official;
 tactful person
dip|lo|mate holder
 of diploma
dip|lo|mat|ic
dip|lo|mat|ic|al|ly
dip|lo|ma|tist
dip|lont
dip|lo|pia
diplo|pod
Diplo|poda
diplo|tene
Di|plura
di|pluran
di|polar
di|pole
dip pen
dip|per
dippy
 dip|pier
 dip|pi|est
dip|shit *vulgar
 slang*
dipso +s
dipso|mania
dipso|maniac
dipso|mani|ac|al
dip|stick
DIP switch in
 computer
dip switch for car
 headlights
Dip|tera
dip|teral
dip|teran
dip|ter|ist
dip|tero|carp
dip|ter|ous
dip|tych
di|pyr|id|amole
di|quat
diram currency of
 Tajikistan; cf.
 dirham

dire
  direr
  dir|est
  serious; cf. **dyer**
dir|ect
dir|ec|tion
dir|ec|tion|al
dir|ec|tion|al|ity
dir|ec|tion|al|ly
dir|ec|tion|less
Dir|ect|oire
dir|ect|or
dir|ect|or|ate
dir|ect|or gen|eral
  dir|ect|ors gen|eral
dir|ect|or|ial
dir|ect|or|ship
Dir|ec|tory *French History*
dir|ec|tory
  dir|ec|tor|ies
dir|ec|tress
dir|ec|trice
dir|ec|trix
  dir|ec|tri|ces
dire|ful
dire|ly
dire|ness
dire wolf
dirge
dirge|ful
dir|ham currency of Morocco, UAE, Libya, and Qatar; cf. **diram**
diri|gible
diri|gisme
diri|giste
dirk
dirndl
dirt|bag
dirt|ily
dirti|ness
dirty
  dirt|ies
  dirt|ied
  dirty|ing
  dirt|ier
  dirti|est
dis
  disses

dissed
dis|sing
dis|abil|ity
dis|abil|ities
dis|able
dis|ab|ling
dis|able|ment
dis|ablist
dis|abuse
dis|abus|ing
di|sac|char|ide
dis|ad|van|tage
dis|ad|van|ta|ging
dis|ad|van|ta|geous
dis|af|fect|ed
dis|af|fect|ed|ly
dis|af|fec|tion
dis|af|fili|ate
dis|af|fili|at|ing
dis|af|fili|ation
dis|af|firm
dis|af|firm|ation
dis|af|for|est
dis|af|for|est|ation
dis|af|for|est|ment
dis|ag|gre|gate
dis|ag|gre|gat|ing
dis|ag|gre|ga|tion
dis|agree
dis|agrees
dis|agreed
dis|agree|ing
dis|agree|able
dis|agree|ably
dis|agree|ment
dis|allow
dis|allow|ance
dis|am|bigu|ate
dis|am|bigu|at|ing
dis|am|bigu|ation
dis|amen|ity
  dis|amen|ities
dis|appear
dis|appear|ance
dis|appli|ca|tion
dis|apply
  dis|ap|plies
  dis|ap|plied
  dis|apply|ing
dis|ap|point
dis|ap|point|ed|ly
dis|ap|point|ing|ly
dis|ap|point|ment
dis|ap|pro|ba|tion

dis|ap|proval
dis|ap|prove
  dis|ap|prov|ing
dis|ap|prov|er
  dis|ap|prov|ing|ly
dis|arm
dis|arma|ment
dis|arm|er
dis|arm|ing
dis|arm|ing|ly
dis|ar|range
  dis|ar|ran|ging
dis|ar|range|ment
dis|array
dis|ar|ticu|late
  dis|ar|ticu|lat|ing
dis|ar|ticu|la|tion
dis|as|sem|ble
  dis|as|sem|bling
dis|as|sem|bler
dis|as|sem|bly
dis|as|so|ci|ate
  dis|as|so|ci|at|ing
dis|as|so|ci|ation
dis|as|ter
dis|as|trous
dis|as|trous|ly
dis|avow
dis|avowal
dis|band
dis|band|ment
dis|bar
  dis|barred
  dis|bar|ring
dis|bar|ment
dis|be|lief
dis|be|lieve
  dis|be|liev|ing
dis|be|liever
dis|be|liev|ing|ly
dis|bene|fit
dis|bound
dis|bud
  dis|bud|ded
  dis|bud|ding
dis|bur|den
dis|bur|sal
dis|burse
  dis|burs|ing
dis|burse|ment
dis|bur|ser

disc *Br.*
  US & Computing
  disk
dis|calced
dis|card
dis|card|able
dis|car|nate
disc|ec|tomy
dis|cern
dis|cern|er
dis|cern|ible
dis|cern|ibly
dis|cern|ing|ly
dis|cern|ment
dis|cerp|ti|bil|ity
dis|cerp|tible
dis|cerp|tion
dis|charge
  dis|char|ging
dis|charge|able
dis|char|ger
dis|ciple
dis|ciple|ship
dis|cip|lic
dis|cip|lin|able
dis|cip|linal
dis|cip|lin|ar|ian
dis|cip|lin|ary
dis|cip|line
  dis|cip|lin|ing
dis|cipu|lar
dis|claim
dis|claim|er
dis|close
  dis|clos|ing
dis|closer
dis|clos|ure
disco
  pl. dis|cos
  v. dis|coes
  dis|coed
  dis|co|ing
  discotheque; cf. **Disko**
disc|ob|olus
  disc|ob|oli
disc|og|raph|er
disc|og|raphy
  disc|og|raph|ies
dis|coid
dis|coid|al
dis|color *US*
dis|col|or|ation

dis|col¦our *Br.*
dis|col¦our|ation
　var. of
　discoloration
dis|com¦bobu|late
dis|com¦bobu|
　　lat¦ing
dis|com¦fit baffle;
　thwart
dis|com¦fit|ure
dis|com¦fort
　unease; make
　uneasy
dis|com¦mode
dis|com¦mod¦ing
dis|com¦mo¦di¦ous
dis|com¦mod¦ity
dis|com¦pose
dis|com¦pos¦ing
dis|com¦pos¦ure
dis|con¦cert
dis|con¦cert|ing¦ly
dis|con¦firm
dis|con¦firm|able
dls|con¦firm|ation
dis|con¦firm|atory
dis|con¦form|ity
dis|con¦form|ities
dis|con¦nect
dis|con¦nect¦ed¦ly
dis|con¦nect¦ed|
　　　　　　ness
dis|con¦nec¦tion
dis|con¦nex¦ion var.
　of disconnection
dis|con¦so¦late
dis|con¦so¦late¦ly
dis|con¦sol|ation
dis|con¦tent
dis|con¦tent¦ed¦ly
dis|con¦tent¦ed|
　　　　　　ness
dis|con¦tent|ment
dis|con¦tinu|ance
dis|con¦tinu|ation
dis|con¦tinue
dis|con¦tinu¦ing
dis|con¦tinu|ity
dis|con¦tinu|ities
dis|con¦tinu¦ous
dis|con¦tinu¦ous¦ly
dis|cord
dis|cord|ance
dis|cord|ant

dis|cord|ant¦ly
disco|theque
　French discothèque
dis|count
dis|count|able
dis|coun¦ten|ance
dis|coun¦te¦nan|
　　　　　　cing
dis|count¦er
dis|cour¦age
dis|cour¦aging
dis|cour¦age|ment
dis|cour¦aging¦ly
dis|course
dis|cours¦ing
dis|cour¦teous
dis|cour¦teous¦ly
dis|cour¦tesy
dis|cour¦tesies
dis|cover
dis|cov¦er|able
dis|cov¦er¦er
dis|cov¦ery
　dis|cov¦er|ies
dis|credit
dis|cred¦it|able
dis|cred¦it|ably
dis|creet circum-
　spect; tactful; cf.
　discrete
dis|creet¦ly
dis|crep|ancy
dis|crep|an¦cies
dis|crep|ant
dis|crete separate;
　cf. discreet
dis|crete¦ly
dis|crete|ness
dis|cre¦tion
dis|cre¦tion|ary
dis|cret¦isa|tion *Br.*
　var. of
　discretization
dis|cret¦ise *Br.* var.
　of discretize
dis|cret|ization
dis|cret|ize
　dis|cret|iz¦ing
dis|crim¦in|abil¦ity
dis|crim¦in|able
dis|crim¦in|ant
dis|crim¦in|ate
　dis|crim¦in|at¦ing
dis|crim¦in|ate¦ly

dis|crim¦in|ation
dis|crim¦ina|tive
dis|crim¦in|ator
dis|crim¦in|atory
dis|cur¦sive
dis|cur¦sive¦ly
dis|cur¦sive|ness
dis|cus disc
dis|cuss dcbate
dis|cuss|able
dis|cuss|ant
dis|cus¦sion
dis|dain
dis|dain|ful
dis|dain|ful¦ly
dis|ease
dis|eased
dis|econ¦omy
　dis|econ¦omies
dis|em¦bark
dis|em¦bark|ation
dis|em¦bar¦rass
dis|em¦bar¦rass|
　　　　　　ment
dis|em¦bodi|ment
dis|em¦body
dis|em¦bod¦ies
dis|em¦bod¦ied
dis|em¦body|ing
dis|em¦bogue
dis|em¦boguing
dis|em¦bowel
dis|em¦bow¦elled
　Br.
dis|em¦bow¦eled
　US
dis|em¦bowel|ling
　Br.
dis|em¦bowel|ing
　US
dis|em¦bowel|ment
dis|em¦broil
dis|em¦power
dis|em¦power|ment
dis|en¦chant
dis|en¦chant|ing¦ly
dis|en¦chant|ment
dis|en¦cum¦ber
dis|en¦dow
dis|en¦dow|ment
dis|en¦fran¦chise
dis|en¦fran¦chis¦ing

dis|en¦fran¦chise|
　　　　　　ment
dis|en¦gage
dis|en¦gaging
dis|en¦gage|ment
dis|en¦tail
dis|en¦tail|ment
dis|en¦tan¦gle
dis|en¦tan¦gling
dis|en¦tangle|ment
dis|en¦thral *Br.*
dis|en¦thralled
dis|en¦thral|ling
dis|en¦thrall *US*
dis|en¦thrall|ment
　US
dis|en¦thral|ment
　Br.
dis|en¦title
dis|en¦titling
dis|en¦title|ment
dis|en¦tomb
dis|en¦tomb|ment
dis|equi¦lib¦rium
dis|equi¦lib¦ria
dis|es¦tab¦lish
dis|es¦tab¦lish|
　　　　　　ment
dis|es¦teem
dis¦eur male
dis|euse female
dis|favor *US*
dis|favour *Br.*
dis|fel¦low|ship
dis|fel¦low|shipped
dis|fel¦low|ship|
　　　　　　ping
dis|fig¦ur|ation
dis|fig¦ure
dis|fig¦ur¦ing
dis|fig¦ure|ment
dis|for¦est
dis|for¦est|ation
dis|fran¦chise
dis|fran¦chis¦ing
dis|fran¦chise|
　　　　　　ment
dis|frock
dis|gorge
dis|gor¦ging
dis|gorge|ment
dis|gor¦ger
dis|grace
dis|gra¦cing

dis|grace|ful
dis|grace|ful|ly
dis|grun|tled
dis|gruntle|ment
dis|guise
 dis|guis|ing
dis|guise|ment
dis|gust
dis|gust|ed|ly
dis|gust|ful
dis|gust|ing|ly
dis|gust|ing|ness
dis|ha|bille var. of
 déshabillé
dis|har|mo|ni|
  ous|ly
dis|har|mon|ise Br.
 var. of
 disharmonize
dis|har|mon|ize
 dis|har|mon|iz|ing
dis|har|mony
 dis|har|monies
dish|cloth
dish|dash var. of
 dishdasha
dish|dasha
dis|heart|en
dis|heart|en|ing|ly
dis|heart|en|ment
dish|evel
 dish|ev|elled Br.
 dish|ev|eled US
 dish|ev|el|ling Br.
 dish|ev|el|ing US
dish|ev|el|ment
dish|ful
dis|hon|est
dis|hon|est|ly
dis|hon|esty
 dis|hon|est|ies
dis|honor US
dis|hon|or|able US
dis|hon|or|ably US
dis|hon|our Br.
dis|hon|our|able
 Br.
dis|hon|our|ably
 Br.
dish|pan
dish|rag
dish|wash|er
dish|wash|ing
dish|water

dishy
 dish|ier
 dishi|est
dis|il|lu|sion
dis|il|lu|sion|ment
dis|in|car|nate
dis|in|cen|tive
dis|in|clin|ation
dis|in|cline
 dis|in|clin|ing
dis|in|cor|por|ate
 dis|in|cor|por|
  at|ing
dis|in|fect
dis|in|fect|ant
dis|in|fec|tion
dis|in|fest
dis|in|fest|ation
dis|in|fla|tion
dis|in|fla|tion|ary
dis|in|for|ma|tion
dis|in|genu|ity
dis|in|genu|ous
dis|in|genu|ous|ly
dis|in|genu|ous|
   ness
dis|in|herit
dis|in|herit|ance
dis|in|hibit
dis|in|hib|ition
dis|in|te|grate
 dis|in|te|grat|ing
dis|in|te|gra|tion
dis|in|te|gra|tive
dis|in|te|gra|tor
dis|in|ter
 dis|in|terred
 dis|in|ter|ring
dis|in|ter|est
dis|in|ter|est|ed
dis|in|ter|est|ed|ly
dis|in|ter|est|ed|
   ness
dis|inter|medi|ate
 dis|inter|
   medi|at|ing
dis|inter|medi|
   ation
dis|inter|ment
dis|invent
dis|invest
dis|invest|ment
dis|invite
 dis|invit|ing

dis|in|vol|tura
dis|jecta mem|bra
dis|join
dis|joint
dis|joint|ed|ly
dis|joint|ed|ness
dis|junct
dis|junc|tion
dis|junct|ive
dis|junct|ive|ly
dis|junc|ture
disk US &
 Computing; cf. disc
disk|ette
disk|less
Disko island; cf.
 disco
dis|lik|able var. of
 dislikeable
dis|like
 dis|lik|ing
dis|like|able
dis|liker
dis|locate
 dis|locat|ing
dis|loca|tion
dis|lodge
 dis|lodg|ing
dis|lodge|able
dis|lodge|ment
dis|lodg|ment var.
 of dislodgement
dis|loyal
dis|loyal|ist
dis|loy|al|ly
dis|loy|alty
 dis|loy|al|ties
dis|mal
dis|mal|ly
dis|mal|ness
dis|man|tle
 dis|mant|ling
dis|mantle|ment
dis|mant|ler
dis|mast
dis|may
dis|mem|ber
dis|mem|ber|ment
dis|miss
dis|mis|sal
dis|miss|ible
dis|mis|sive
dis|mis|sive|ly

dis|mis|sive|ness
dis|mount
Dis|ney, Walt car-
 toon producer
Dis|ney|esque
dis|obedi|ence
dis|obedi|ent
dis|obedi|ent|ly
dis|obey
dis|obey|er
dis|oblige
dis|obli|ging
di|somic
di|somy
dis|order
dis|order|li|ness
dis|order|ly
dis|or|gan|isa|tion
 Br. var. of
 disorganization
dis|or|gan|ise Br.
 var. of disorganize
dis|or|gan|iza|tion
dis|or|gan|ize
 dis|or|gan|iz|ing
dis|orient
dis|orien|tate
 dis|orien|tat|ing
dis|orien|ta|tion
dis|own
dis|own|er
dis|own|ment
dis|par|age
 dis|para|ging
dis|par|age|ment
dis|para|ging|ly
dis|par|ate
dis|par|ate|ly
dis|par|ity
 dis|par|ities
dis|pas|sion
dis|pas|sion|ate
dis|pas|sion|ate|ly
dis|patch
dis|patch|er
dis|pel
 dis|pelled
 dis|pel|ling
dis|pel|ler
dis|pens|abil|ity
dis|pens|able
dis|pens|ary
 dis|pens|ar|ies

dis|pen|sa|tion
dis|pen|sa|tion|al
dis|pen|sa|tion|al|
  ism
dis|pen|sa|tion|al|
  ist
dis|pense
  dis|pens|ing
dis|pen|ser
dis|per|sal
dis|pers|ant
dis|perse
  dis|per|sing
dis|perser
dis|pers|ible
dis|per|sion
dis|per|sive
dis|pirit
dis|pir|it|ed|ly
dis|pir|it|ing|ly
dis|place
  dis|placing
dis|place|ment
dis|play
dis|play|er
dis|please
  dis|pleas|ing
dis|pleas|ing|ly
dis|pleas|ure
  dis|pleas|ur|ing
dis|port
dis|pos|abil|ity
dis|pos|able
dis|posal
dis|pose
  dis|pos|ing
dis|poser
dis|pos|ition
dis|posi|tive
dis|posi|tor
dis|pos|sess
dis|pos|ses|sion
dis|praise
  dis|prais|ing
dis|proof
dis|pro|por|tion
dis|pro|por|tion|al
dis|pro|por|tion|
  al|ity
dis|pro|por|tion|
  al|ly
dis|pro|por|tion|
  ate

dis|pro|por|tion|
  at|ing
dis|pro|por|tion|
  ate|ly
dis|pro|por|tion|
  ation
dis|prov|able
dis|prove
  dis|prov|ing
Dis|pur
dis|put|able
dis|put|ably
dis|pu|tant
dis|pu|ta|tion
dis|pu|ta|tious
dis|pu|ta|tious|ly
dis|pu|ta|tious|ness
dis|pu|ta|tive
dis|pute
  dis|put|ing
dis|puter
dis|quali|fi|ca|tion
dis|qual|ify
  dis|quali|fies
  dis|quali|fied
  dis|quali|fy|ing
dis|quiet
dis|quiet|ing|ly
dis|quiet|ude
dis|quisi|tion
dis|quisi|tion|al
Dis|raeli,
  Ben|ja|min prime
  minister of Britain
dis|rate
  dis|rat|ing
dis|re|gard
dis|rel|ish
dis|re|mem|ber
dis|re|pair
dis|rep|ut|able
dis|rep|ut|able|ness
dis|rep|ut|ably
dis|re|pute
dis|res|pect
dis|res|pect|ful
dis|res|pect|ful|ly
dis|robe
  dis|rob|ing
dis|rupt
dis|rupt|er
dis|rup|tion
dis|rup|tive

dis|rup|tive|ly
dis|rup|tive|ness
dis|rupt|or var. of
  disrupter
diss var. of dis
dis|sat|is|fac|tion
dis|sat|is|fac|tory
dis|sat|isfy
  dis|sat|is|fies
  dis|sat|is|fied
  dis|sat|is|fy|ing
dis|saver
dis|sav|ing
dis|sect
dis|sec|tion
dis|sect|or
dis|sem|blance
dis|sem|ble
  dis|sem|bling
dis|sem|bler
dis|sem|in|ate
  dis|sem|in|at|ing
dis|sem|in|ation
dis|sem|in|ator
dis|sem|in|ule
dis|sen|sion
dis|sen|sus
dis|sent disagree;
  disagreement; cf.
  descent
Dis|sent|er Non-
  conformist
dis|sent|er
dis|sen|tient
dis|sepi|ment
dis|ser|ta|tion
dis|ser|ta|tion|al
dis|ser|vice
dis|si|dence
dis|si|dent
dis|simi|lar
dis|simi|lar|ity
  dis|simi|lar|ities
  dis|simi|lar|ly
dis|simi|late
  dis|simi|lat|ing
  change; cf.
  dissimulate
dis|simi|la|tion
  change; cf.
  dissimulation
dis|simi|la|tory
dis|sim|ili|tude

dis|simu|late
  dis|simu|lat|ing
  conceal; cf.
  dissimilate
dis|simu|la|tion
  concealment; cf.
  dissimilation
dis|simu|la|tor
dis|si|pate
  dis|si|pat|ing
dis|si|pater var. of
  dissipator
dis|si|pa|tion
dis|si|pa|tive
dis|si|pa|tor
dis|soci|able
dis|soci|ate
  dis|soci|at|ing
dis|soci|ation
dis|socia|tive
dis|solu|bil|ity
dis|sol|uble
dis|sol|ubly
dis|sol|ute
dis|sol|ute|ly
dis|sol|ute|ness
dis|sol|ution
dis|solv|able
dis|solve
  dis|solv|ing
dis|solv|ent
dis|son|ance
dis|son|ant
dis|son|ant|ly
dis|suade
  dis|suad|ing
dis|suader
dis|sua|sion
dis|sua|sive
dis|syl|lab|ic var. of
  disyllabic
dis|syl|lable var. of
  disyllable
dis|sym|met|ric
dis|sym|metry
  dis|sym|metries
dis|taff
dis|tal
dis|tal|ly
dis|tance
  dis|tan|cing
dis|tant
dis|tan|ti|ate
  dis|tan|ti|at|ing

dis|tan|ti|ation
dis|tant|ly
dis|taste
dis|taste|ful
dis|taste|ful|ly
dis|taste|ful|ness
dis|tem|per
dis|tend
dis|ten|si|bil|ity
dis|ten|sible
dis|ten|sion
dis|tich +s
dis|tich|ous
dis|til *Br.*
  dis|tilled
  dis|til|ling
dis|till *US*
dis|til|late
dis|til|la|tion
dis|til|la|tory
dis|til|ler
dis|til|lery
  dis|til|ler|ies
dis|tinct
dis|tinc|tion
dis|tinct|ive
dis|tinct|ive|ly
dis|tinct|ive|ness
dis|tinct|ly
dis|tinct|ness
dis|tin|gué male
dis|tin|guée female
dis|tin|guish
dis|tin|guish|able
dis|tort
dis|tort|ed|ly
dis|tor|tion
dis|tor|tion|al
dis|tor|tion|less
dis|tract
dis|tract|ed|ly
dis|tract|ing|ly
dis|trac|tion
dis|tract|or
dis|train
dis|train|er
dis|train|ment
dis|traint
dis|trait *male*
dis|traite *female*
dis|traught
dis|tress

dis|tress|ful
dis|tress|ing|ly
dis|trib|ut|able
dis|tribu|tary
  dis|tribu|tar|ies
dis|trib|ute
  dis|trib|ut|ing
dis|tri|bu|tion
dis|tri|bu|tion|al
dis|tribu|tive
dis|tribu|tive|ly
dis|tribu|tor
dis|trict
dis|tro +s
dis|trust
dis|trust|er
dis|trust|ful
dis|trust|ful|ly
dis|turb
dis|turb|ance
dis|turb|er
dis|turb|ing|ly
di|sub|sti|tuted
di|sul|fide *US*
disulfiram
di|sul|phide *Br.*
dis|union
dis|unite
  dis|unit|ing
dis|unity
  dis|uni|ties
dis|use
  dis|us|ing
dis|util|ity
di|syl|lab|ic
di|syl|lable
ditch
ditch|er
ditch|water
di|ter|pene
di|ter|pen|oid
di|theism
di|theist
dither
dith|er|er
dith|ery
di|thion|ite
di|thi|zone
dithy|ramb
dithy|ramb|ic
di|transi|tive
ditsi|ness var. of
  ditziness

ditsy var. of ditzy
dit|tany
  dit|tanies
ditto
  pl. dit|tos
  v. dit|toes
  dit|toed
  ditto|ing
dit|to|graph|ic
dit|tog|raphy
  dit|tog|raph|ies
ditty
  dit|ties
ditz
ditzi|ness
ditzy
  ditz|ier
  ditzi|est
Diu island
di|ur|esis
  di|ur|eses
di|ur|et|ic
di|ur|nal
di|ur|nal|ly
diva
di|va|gate
  di|va|gat|ing
di|va|ga|tion
di|va|lent
Di|vali var. of
  Diwali
divan
di|vari|cate
  di|vari|cat|ing
di|vari|ca|tion
dive
  dove *US*
  div|ing
dive-bomb
dive-bomber
diver
di|verge
  di|ver|ging
di|ver|gence
di|ver|gency
  di|ver|gen|cies
di|ver|gent
di|ver|gent|ly
di|vers sundry
di|verse
di|verse|ly
di|ver|si|fi|ca|tion
di|ver|sify
  di|ver|si|fies

di|ver|si|fied
di|ver|si|fy|ing
di|ver|sion
di|ver|sion|ary
di|ver|sity
  di|ver|sities
di|vert
di|ver|ticu|lar
di|ver|ticu|litis
di|ver|ticu|losis
di|ver|ticu|lum
  di|ver|tic|ula
di|ver|ti|mento
  di|ver|ti|menti or
  di|ver|ti|men|tos
di|vert|ing|ly
di|ver|tisse|ment
Dives rich man
di|vest
di|vesti|ture
di|vest|ment
di|vest|ure
divi var. of divvy
div|ide
  div|id|ing
divi|dend
div|ider
divi-divi
div|in|ation
div|in|atory
div|ine
  div|in|ing
div|iner
div|inest
div|ine|ly
div|iner
div|in|ise *Br.* var. of
  divinize
div|in|ity
  div|in|ities
div|in|ize
  div|in|iz|ing
div|isi
div|isi|bil|ity
div|is|ible capable
  of being divided; cf.
  devisable
div|ision
div|ision|al
div|ision|al|isa|tion
  Br. var. of
  divisionalization
div|ision|al|ise *Br.*
  var. of divisionalize

div|ision|al|iza|tion
div|ision|al|ize
div|ision|al|iz|ing
div|ision|ism
div|isive
div|isive|ly
div|isive|ness
div|isor number; cf.
  deviser, devisor
di|vorce
di|vor|cing
di|vorcé US male
di|vor|cee Br.
di|vor|cée US
  female
di|vorce|ment
divot
di|vul|ga|tion
di|vulge
di|vul|ging
di|vulge|ment
di|vul|gence
divvy
  div|vies
  div|vied
  divvy|ing
Di|wali
diwan
Dixie southern
  states of US
dixie cooking pot
Dixie|crat
Dixie|land
diya
Di|yar|ba|kir
di|zyg|ot|ic
di|zy|gous
diz|zily
diz|zi|ness
dizzy
  diz|zies
  diz|zied
  dizzy|ing
  diz|zier
  diz|zi|est
Dja|karta var. of
  Jakarta
djebel var. of jebel
djel|laba
djembe
Djerba
djib|bah var. of
  jibba
Dji|bouti

Dji|bou|tian
djinn var. of jinn
D-layer
D.Litt. = Doctor of
  Literature
D-lock
D-mark
D.Mus. = Doctor of
  Music
DNase
Dnie|per
Dnies|ter
Dni|pro|
    dzer|zhinsk
Dni|pro|pet|rovsk
D-notice
do
  pl. dos or do's
  v. does
  did
  doing
  done
do Music; var. of
  doh; cf. doe,
  dough
do|able
dob
  dobbed
  dob|bing
dob|ber
dob|bin
dobby
  dob|bies
dobe adobe; cf.
  dhobi
Do|ber|man
  (pin|scher) US +s
Do|ber|mann
  (pin|scher)
dobra
dobro +s trademark
dob|son|fly
  dob|son|flies
Dob|son|ian
Dob|son unit
doc doctor; cf. dock
do|cent
Do|cet|ic
Do|cet|ism
Do|cet|ist
doch an dorris var.
  of deoch an doris
do|cile
do|cile|ly

do|cil|ity
dock cf. doc
dock|age
docken
dock|er
docket
dock|land
docko|min|ium
dock|side
dock|yard
Doc Mar|tens var.
  of Dr Martens
doc|tor
doc|tor|al
doc|tor|ate
doc|tor|ial
doc|tor|ly
doc|tor|ship
doc|trin|aire
doc|tri|nal
doc|tri|nal|ly
doc|trine
docu|drama
docu|ment
docu|ment|able
docu|men|tal
docu|men|tal|ist
docu|men|tar|ian
docu|men|tar|ist
docu|men|tary
  docu|men|tar|ies
docu|men|ta|tion
docu|men|ta|tive
docu|soap
docu|tain|ment
dod|der
dod|der|er
dod|deri|ness
dod|dery
dod|dle
do|deca|gon
do|deca|he|dral
do|deca|he|dron
  do|deca|he|dra or
  do|deca|he|drons
Do|decan|ese
do|deca|phon|ic
dodge
dodg|ing
dodge|ball
Dodge City
dodgem

dodger
dodg|ily
dodgi|ness
Dodg|son, Charles
  'Lewis Carroll',
  writer
dodgy
  dodgi|er
  dodgi|est
dodo
  dodos or do|does
Do|doma
doe deer; cf. doh,
  dough
doe-eyed
doek
doer
doe|skin
doesn't
doest
doeth
dog
  dogged
  dog|ging
dog|bane
dog|berry
  dog|berries
dog|dom
doge ruler of Venice
dog-end
dog|face
dog|fight
dog|fight|er
dog|fight|ing
dog|fish
dog|ged
dog|ged|ly
dog|ged|ness
dog|ger boat; geo-
  logical feature
Dog|ger Bank
dog|gerel
dog|gie var. of
  doggy
dog|gi|ness
dog|gish
doggo
dog|gone
doggy
  dog|gies
  dog|gi|er
  dog|gi|est
doggy-paddle
  doggy-paddling

dog|house
dogie calf
dog-leg
dog|like
dogma
dog|man
  dog|men
dog|mat|ic
dog|mat|ic|al|ly
dog|mat|ics
dog|ma|tise Br. var. of dogmatize
dog|ma|tism
dog|ma|tist
dog|ma|tize
  dog|ma|tiz|ing
dog|nap
  dog|napped
  dog|nap|ping
dog|nap|per
do-good n. & adj.
do-gooder
do-goodery
do-goodism
dog-paddle US
  dog-paddling
  Br. doggy-paddle
Dog|rib
dogs|body
dogs|bodies
dogs|body|ing
dog|shore
dog|skin
dog|sled
dogs|tail grass
dogs|tooth pattern; var. of dog-tooth
dog's-tooth vio|let
dog-tired
dog-tooth
  dog-teeth
dog|trot
  dog|trot|ted
  dog|trot|ting
dog|watch
dog|wood
doh musical note; exclam.; cf. doe, dough
Doha
dohyo +s
doily
  doi|lies
doit

doit|ed
do-it-yourself
do-it-yourself|er
dojo +s
Dolby trademark
dolce
dolce far ni|ente
Dolce|latte trademark
dolce vita, la
doll|drums
dole
  dol|ing
  benefit; woe; distribute; cf. dhol, dhole
dole-bludger
dole|ful
dole|ful|ly
dole|ful|ness
doler|ite
doli capax
doli|cho|ceph|al|ic
doli|cho|ceph|aly
doli in|capax
Dolin, Anton dancer and choreographer
do|lina var. of doline
do|line
D'Oliveira, Basil cricketer
Doll, Rich|ard physician
doll
dol|lar
dollar|bird
dol|lar|isa|tion Br. var. of dollarization
dol|lar|iza|tion
Doll|fuss, Engel|bert chancellor of Austria
doll|house US Br. doll's house
dol|lop
doll's house US dollhouse
dolly
  dol|lies
  dol|lied
  dolly|ing

Dolly Var|den
dolma
dol|mas or dol|ma|des
dol|man +s sleeve
dol|men +s tomb
dol|mus
dolo|mite mineral or rock
Dolo|mites mountains
dolo|mit|ic
dolor US Br. dolour
Do|lores
dol|or|im|eter +s
dol|or|im|etry
dol|or|ous
dol|or|ous|ly
dolo|stone
dol|our Br. US dolor
dol|phin
dol|phin|ar|ium dol|phin|ar|iums or dol|phin|aria
dol|phin|fish
dolt|ish
dolt|ish|ly
dolt|ish|ness
Dom Roman Catholic title
dom palm var. of doum
do|main realm
do|maine vineyard
domal
do|man|ial
dome
  dom|ing
dome-like
Domes|day Book; cf. doomsday
do|mes|tic
do|mes|tic|able
do|mes|tic|al|ly
do|mes|ti|cate
  do|mes|ti|cat|ing
do|mes|ti|ca|tion
do|mes|ti|city
  do|mes|ti|ci|ties
domic|al
domi|cil var. of domicile

domi|cile
domi|cil|ing
domi|cil|iary
dom|in|ance
dom|in|ant
dom|in|ant|ly
dom|in|ate
  dom|in|at|ing
dom|in|ation
dom|in|ator
dom|in|atrix
  dom|in|atrixes or dom|in|atri|ces
dom|in|eer
dom|in|eer|ing|ly
Dom|ingo, Pla|cido singer
Dom|inic, St
Do|min|ica island
do|min|ical
Do|min|ic|an
dom|inie
do|min|ion
Dom|in|ique
do|min|ium
Dom|ino, Fats musician
dom|ino
  dom|inoes
Dom|itian Roman emperor
Don rivers; Spanish male title
don
  donned
  don|ning
  university teacher; put on
Don|ald
do|nate
  do|nat|ing
Dona|tello sculptor
don|atio mor|tis causa
don|ationes mor|tis causa
do|na|tion
Donat|ism
Donat|ist
do|na|tor
Do|na|tus, Ae|lius Roman grammarian

Donau geological system

Don|cas|ter

done cf. **dun**

donee

Don|egal

done|ness

doner kebab; cf. **dona, donna, donor**

Don|ets river; Basin

Don|etsk city

donga

don|gle

dong quai

Doni|zetti, Gae|tano composer

don|jon castle keep; cf. **dungeon**

Don Juan legendary libertine

don|key

donkey|man donkey|men

donna Italian, Spanish, or Portuguese lady; cf. **dona, doner, donor**

Don|nan

Donne, John poet

donné var. of **donnée**

don|née

don|nish

don|nish|ly

don|nish|ness

donny|brook

donor giver; cf. **dona, doner, donna**

do-nothing

Dono|van

Don Quix|ote fictional hero

don|ship

don't

don't-know

donut US var. of **doughnut**

doo|bie

doo|brie var. of **doobry**

doo|bry

doo|bries

doo|dad

doo|dah

doo|dle

dood|ling

doodle|bug

dood|ler

dood|ling

doodly

doodly-squat

doo-doo +s excrement; cf. **doudou**

doo|fus

doo|hickey

doo|jig|ger

doo|lally

doom cf. **doum**

doom|ily

doomi|ness

doom|say|er

doom|say|ing

dooms|day last day; cf. **Domesday**

doom|ster

doom|watch

doom|watch|er

doomy doom|ier doomi|est

doona Austral. trademark duvet

door cf. **daw, dor**

door|bell

door|case

door|keeper

door|knob

door|man door|men

door|mat

door|nail

door|post

door|step door|stepped door|step|ping

door|stop

door|stop|per

door|way

door|yard

doo-wop

doo-wopper

doo|zie var. of **doozy**

doozy doo|zies

dopa amino acid; cf. **doper**

dopa|mine

dopa|min|ergic

dop|ant

dope dop|ing

doper cf. **dopa**

dope|ster

dopey

dopi|er dopi|est

dopi|aza

dop|ily

dopi|ness

dop|pel|gän|ger

Dop|per

dop|pie

Dop|pler

dopy var. of **dopey**

dor beetle; cf. **daw, door**

Dor|ado constellation

dor|ado +s fish

do-rag

Dor|cas

dor|cas gazelle

Dor|ches|ter

Dor|dogne

Dor|drecht

Doré, Gus|tave illustrator

doré

Dor|een

Dor|ian

Doric

Dor|inda

dork

dorki|ness

dorky dork|ier dorki|est

dor|mancy dor|man|cies

dor|mant

dor|mer

Dor|mi|tion

dor|mi|tory dor|mi|tor|ies

Dor|mo|bile trademark

dor|mouse dor|mice

dormy

do|ron|icum

Doro|thea

Doro|thy

dor|sal

dor|sal|ly

Dor|set

dorsi|flex

dorsi|flex|ion

dorsi|flex|or

dorsi|ven|tral

dorsi|ven|tral|ly

dorso|lat|eral

dorso|lat|eral|ly

dorso|ven|tral

dorso|ven|tral|ly

dor|sum dorsa

Dort|mund

dory dor|ies

DOS disk operating system

dosa dosas or dosai

dos-à-dos

dos|age

dose dos|ing

do-se-do var. of **do-si-do**

dose|meter var. of **dosimeter**

dosha energy

do-si-do do-si-dos do-si-doed do-si-doing

dos|im|eter

dosi|met|ric

dos|im|etry

doss

dos|sal

doss|er

dos|seret

doss|house

dos|sier

dost in 'thou dost'; cf. **dust**

Dos|to|ev|sky,
　Fyodor novelist
dot
　dot|ted
　dot|ting
dot|age
dot|ard
dot-com
dote
　dot|ing
doter
doth
dot|ing|ly
dot|ish
dot mat|rix
　print|er
dot|ter
dot|terel
dot|tily
dot|ti|ness
dot|tle
dotty
　dot|tier
　dot|ti|est
Dou|ala
Douay Bible
double
　doub|ling
double-banking
double-cross
double-crosser
double-dealer
double-dealing
double-decker
double-ender
double en|ten|dre
　double en|ten|dres
double-header
　train; sports event
double|ness
double quick
doub|ler
double|speak
doub|let
double|talk
double|think
double|ton
double|tree
doub|loon
doub|lure
doubly
doubt uncertainty;
　cf. **dout**

doubt|able
doubt|er
doubt|ful
doubt|ful|ly
doubt|ful|ness
doubt|ing|ly
doubt|less
doubt|less|ly
douce
dou|ceur
dou|ceur de vie
dou|ceur de vivre
douche
　douch|ing
douc lan|gur
douc mon|key
dou|dou *W. Ind.*
　darling; cf. **doo-
　doo**
dough mixture for
　bread etc.; cf. **doe,
　doh**
dough|boy
doughi|ness
dough|nut
dough|nut|ting
dought|ily
doughti|ness
doughty
　dought|ier
　doughti|est
doughy
　dough|ier
　doughi|est
Doug|las capital of
　the Isle of Man; fir;
　pine; spruce
Doug|las, Kirk and
　Mi|chael actors
Douglas-Home,
　Alec prime minis-
　ter of Britain
doula
Doul|ton *trademark*
　pottery
doum palm; cf.
　doom
dour
dour|ly
dour|ness
Douro river
dou|rou|couli
douse
　dous|ing

drench; extinguish;
　cf. **dowse**
dout extinguish; cf.
　doubt
dove bird
dove *US* past tense
　of **dive**
dove|cot var. of
　dovecote
dove|cote
dove|kie
dove|like
Dover
dove's-foot +s
dove's-foot
　cranes|bill
dove|tail
dov|ish
dow|ager
dowd
dow|dily
dow|di|ness
Dow|ding, Hugh
　Marshal of the RAF
dowdy
　dow|dies
　dow|dier
　dow|di|est
dowel
dow|elled *Br.*
dow|eled *US*
dowel|ling *Br.*
dowel|ing *US*
dower
dow|itcher
Dow Jones
Down county, Nor-
　thern Ireland
down and out *adj.*
down-and-out
　attrib. & n.
down|beat
down|burst
down|case
　down|cas|ing
down|cast
down|change
　down|chan|ging
down|comer
down|con|ver|sion
down|con|vert|er
down|coun|try
down|curved

down|cut
down|cut|ting
down|draft *US*
down|draught *Br.*
down|drift
down|er
down|fall
down|field
down|fold
down|force
down|grade
　down|grad|ing
down|haul
down|heart|ed
down|hill
down|hill|er
down|hole
down-home
Down|ing Street
down|land
down|light
down|light|er
down|light|ing
down|link
down|load
down|load|able
down|mar|ket
down|most
down pay|ment
down|pipe
down|play
down|pour
down|rate
down|rat|ing
down|right
down|river
Downs hills; sea
　area
down|scale
down|scal|ing
down|shift
down|side
down|size
　down|siz|ing
down|slope
down|spout
Down's syn|drome
down|stage
down|stairs
down|state
down|stater
down|stream

down|stroke
down|swing
down|tempo
down|throw
  down|threw
  down|thrown
down|time
down to earth *adj.*
down-to-earth
  attrib.
down-to-earthness
down|town
down|town|er
down|trend
down|trod|den
down|turn
down|ward
down|ward|ly
down|wards
down|warp
down|wash
down|well|ing
down|wind
down|wind|er
downy
  down|ier
  downi|est
down|zone
  down|zon|ing
dowry
  dow|ries
dowse
  dows|ing
  search for water; cf.
  douse
dowser
dowt *var.* of dout
dox|as|tic
doxo|logic|al
dox|ology
  dox|ologies
doxo|rubi|cin
doxy
  doxies
doxy|cyc|line
doyen *male*
doy|enne *female*
Doy|enne du
  Co|mice
  Doy|ennes du
  Co|mice
Doyle, Ar|thur
  Conan novelist

D'Oyly Carte,
  Rich|ard
  impresario
doze
  doz|ing
dozen
doz|enth
dozer
dozi|ly
dozi|ness
dozy
  dozi|er
  dozi|est
D.Phil. = Doctor of
  Philosophy
drab
  drab|ber
  drab|best
Drab|ble,
  Mar|ga|ret novelist
drab|ble
  drab|bling
drab|ly
drab|ness
dra|caena
drachm unit; cf.
  DRAM, dram
drachma
  drach|mas or
  drach|mae
  former Greek
  currency
drack
Draco Athenian
  legislator;
  constellation
drac|one
dra|co|nian
dra|con|ic
Drac|ula, Count
  fictional character
draeger|man
  draeger|men
draff
draft preliminary
  writing or drawing;
  money order; *US
  Military;* cf.
  draught
draft *US*
  current of air; act
  of drinking;
  drawing in; depth
  of water; d. horse.
  Br. draught

draft dodger
draft dodg|ing
draft|ee
draft|er
draft|ily *US*
  Br. draughtily
drafti|ness *US*
  Br. draughtiness
draft|proof *US*
  Br. draughtproof
drafts|man *US*
  drafts|men
  Br. draughtsman
drafts|man|ship
  US
  Br.
  draughtsmanship
drafts|person
  drafts|people
  Br. draughtsperson
drafts|woman *US*
  drafts|women
  Br.
  draughtswoman
drafty *US*
  draft|ier
  drafti|est
  Br. draughty
drag
  dragged
  drag|ging
dra|gée
drag|ger
drag|gle
  drag|gling
draggy
  drag|gier
  drag|gi|est
drag|line
drag|net
drago|man
  drago|mans or
  drago|men
dragon
drag|onet
dragon|fish
dragon|fly
  dragon|flies
drag|on|nade
drag|oon
drag|ster
drail
drain
drain|age
drain|board

drain|cock
drain|er
drain|pipe
Draize test
Drake, Fran|cis
  explorer; equation;
  Passage
drake
Drak|ens|berg
Dra|lon *trademark*
DRAM = dynamic
  random access
  memory; cf.
  drachm
dram drink; cf.
  drachm
drama
drama-
    documen|tary
drama-
    documen|tar|ies
Dram|amine
  trademark
dra|mat|ic
dra|mat|ic|al|ly
dra|mat|ics
drama|tisa|tion *Br.*
  var. of
  dramatization
drama|tise *Br.* var.
  of dramatize
drama|tis
  per|sonae
drama|tist
drama|tiza|tion
drama|tize
  drama|tiz|ing
drama|turg var. of
  dramaturge
drama|turge
drama|tur|gic|al
drama|tur|gic|al|ly
drama|turgy
  drama|tur|gies
Dram|buie
  trademark
dra|medy +s
drape
  drap|ing
draper
dra|pery
  dra|per|ies
dras|tic
dras|tic|al|ly

drat|ted

draught *Br.*
current of air; act
of drinking;
drawing in; depth
of water; d. horse;
cf. **draft**;
US **draft**

draught|board

draught|ily *Br.*
US **draftily**

draughti|ness *Br.*
US **draftiness**

draught|proof *Br.*
US **draftproof**

draughts game

draughts|man *Br.*
draughts|men
US **draftsman**

draughts|man|ship
Br.
US **draftsmanship**

draughts|person
draught|speople
US **draftsperson**

draughts|woman
Br.
draughts|women
US **draftswoman**

draughty *Br.*
draught|ier
draughti|est
US **drafty**

Dra|vid|ian

draw
drew
drawn
sketch; attract;
even score; in 'prize
draw'; etc.; cf.
drawer

draw|back

draw|bar

draw|bridge

draw|card

draw|cord

draw|down

draw|ee

drawer sliding
compartment; cf.
draw

draw|er person who
draws cheque, pic-
ture, beer, etc.; cf.
draw

drawer|ful

draw|knife
draw|knives

drawl

drawl|er

drawly

drawn

draw-off

draw|string

dray cart; cf. **drey**

dray|man
dray|men

dread

dread|ful

dread|ful|ly

dread|ful|ness

dread|locked

dread|locks

dread|nought

dream
dreamed or
dreamt

dream|boat

dream|catch|er

dream|er

dream|ful

dream|ily

dreami|ness

dream|land

dream|less

dream|like

dream|scape

Dream|time

dream|work

dream|world

dreamy
dream|ier
dreami|est

drear

drear|ily

dreari|ness

dreary
drear|ier
dreari|est

dreck

dreck|ish

drecky

dredge
dredg|ing

dredg|er

dree
drees
dreed
dree|ing

dreggy

D-region

dregs

dreich

dreidel

dreidl var. of
dreidel

drek var. of dreck

Dres|den

dress|age

dress|er

dressing-down *n.*

dress|maker

dress|mak|ing

dressy
dress|ier
dressi|est

drew past tense of
draw

drey squirrel's nest;
cf. **dray**

Drey|fus, Al|fred
French army officer

drib|ble

drib|bling

drib|bler

drib|bly

drib|let

dribs and drabs

driech var. of
dreich

dried

drier comparative of
dry; cf. **dryer**

drift|er

drift|fish

drift|way

drift|wood

drifty
drift|ier
drifti|est

drill|er

drily

drink
drank
drunk

drink|able

drink-drive *adj.*

drink-driver

drink-driving

drink|er

drip
dripped
drip|ping

drip-dry
drip-dries
drip-dried
drip-drying

drip-feed
drip-fed

drip feed

drip|pily

drip|pi|ness

drippy
drip|pier
drip|pi|est

drip|stone

driv|abil|ity var. of
driveability

driv|able var. of
driveable

drive
drove
driv|ing
driven

drive|abil|ity

drive|able

drive-by *adj. & n.*
+s

drive-in *adj. & n.*

drivel
driv|elled *Br.*
driv|eled *US*
driv|el|ling *Br.*
driv|el|ing *US*
driv|el|er *US*

drive|line

driv|el|ler *Br.*

driven

drive-on *adj.*

drive-on/drive-off
adj.

driver

driver|less

drive|shaft

drive-through *adj.*
& n.

drive-thru +s *adj.*
& n. US var. of
drive-through

drive|train

drive|way

driz|zle

driz|zling

driz|zly
driz|zlier
driz|zli|est

Dr Mar|tens
trademark

Dro|gheda
drogue
droid
droit
droit de sei|gneur
droll
droll|ery
　droll|er|ies
droll|ness
drolly
dro|maeo|saur
dro|maeo|saurid
drome
drom|ed|ary
　drom|ed|ar|ies
drom|ond
dromos
　dromoi
drone
　dron|ing
drongo
　dron|gos or
　dron|goes
droob
droog
drool
droop cf. drupe
droop|ily
droopi|ness
droop-snoot
droop-snooted
droopy
　droop|ier
　droopi|est
drop
　dropped
　drop|ping
drop-dead *adj.*
drop-down *adj.*
drop-forge
　drop-forging
drop|head
drop-in *n. & adj.*
drop kick *n.*
drop-kick *v.*
drop-leaf
　drop-leaves
drop|let
drop-off *n.*
drop|out
drop|pable
drop|per
drop|seed

drop-ship
　drop-shipped
　drop-shipping
drop ship|ment
drop shot
drop|si|cal
drop|side
drop-stitch
dropsy
　drop|sies
drop-top
drop|wort
dros|era
droshky
　drosh|kies
dros|oph|ila
drossy
　dros|sier
　drossi|est
Drott|ning|holm
drought
drouth
drouthy
drove
　drov|ing
drover
drown
drowse
　drows|ing
drows|ily
drow|si|ness
drowsy
　drows|ier
　drowsi|est
drub
　drubbed
　drub|bing
drudge
　drudg|ing
drudg|ery
　drudg|er|ies
drug
　drugged
　drug|ging
drug|get
drug|gie var. of
　druggy
drug|gist
druggy
　drug|gies
drug|store
Druid
Druid|ess
Dru|id|ic

Dru|id|ic|al
Dru|id|ism
drum
　drummed
　drum|ming
drum|beat
drum|fire
drum|fish
drum|head
drum|lin
drum|lin|oid
drum|mer
drum|stick
drunk
drunk|ard
drunk|en
drunk|en|ly
drunk|en|ness
drup|aceous
drupe fruit; cf.
　droop
dru|pel
drupe|let
Drury Lane
Druse var. of Druze
druse cavity
Dru|silla
drusy
druth|ers
Druze sect; cf.
　druse
dry
　adj. drier
　dri|est
　v. dries
　dried
　dry|ing
　pl. dries or drys
dryad
dryas
dry-clean
dry-cleaner
Dry|den, John
　writer
dryer device; cf.
　drier
dry-fry
　dry-fries
　dry-fried
　dry-frying
dry|ish
dry|land land with
　low rainfall
dry land not sea

dryly var. of drily
dry|ness
dry-nurse
dryo|pith|ecine
Dryo|pith|ecus
　Dryo|pith|eci
dry|stone
dry|suit
dry|wall
DTs
dual
　dualled *Br.*
　dualed *US*
　dual|ling *Br.*
　dual|ing *US*
　double; cf. duel
dual|ise *Br.* var. of
　dualize
dual|ism
dual|ist believer in
　dualism; cf. duelist,
　duellist
dual|is|tic
dual|ity
　dual|ities
dual|ize
　dual|iz|ing
dual|ly
dub
　dubbed
　dub|bing
Dubai
Du Barry, Marie
　mistress of Louis
　XV
dub|bin
dubby
Dub|ček,
　Alex|an|der leader
　of Czechoslovakia
du|bi|ety
du|bi|ous
du|bi|ous|ly
du|bi|ous|ness
du|bi|ta|tion
du|bi|ta|tive
Dub|lin
Dub|lin|er
dub|nium
Du|bon|net
　trademark
Du|brov|nik
ducal
ducat

Duc¦cio di
  Buon¦in¦segna
  painter
Duce, Il Mussolini
Du¦champ, Mar¦cel
  artist
Du¦chenne
duch¦ess noble-
  woman
du¦chesse furniture;
  fabrics; potatoes
duchy
  duch¦ies
  dukedom; cf.
  dutchie
duck cf. DUKW
duck¦bill
duck-billed
duck¦board
duck-dive
  duck-diving
duck-egg blue
duckie var. of ducky
duck¦ling
duck¦pin
duck-shove
  duck-shoving
duck¦tail
duck¦walk
duck¦weed
Duckworth–Lewis
ducky
  duck¦ies
ductal
duc¦tile
duc¦til¦ity
duct¦less
duct¦ular
duct¦ule
ductus
  ducti
duct¦work
dude
  dud¦ing
dudg¦eon
dud¦ish
Dud¦ley, Rob¦ert
  Earl of Leicester
due owing; cf. dew
duel
  duelled Br.
  dueled US
  duel¦ling Br.
  duel¦ing US

fight; cf. dual
duel¦er US
duel¦ist US cf.
  dualist
duel¦ler Br.
duel¦list Br; cf.
  dualist
du¦ende
du¦enna
duet
  duet¦ted
  duet¦ting
duet¦tist
Dufay, Guil¦laume
  composer
duf¦fel bag/coat
duf¦fer
duf¦fle var. of duffel
dufus var. of doofus
Dufy, Raoul artist
du¦gite
du¦gong
dug¦out
dui¦ker
Duis¦burg
du jour
Dukas, Paul
  composer
duke
  duk¦ing
duke¦dom
DUKW +s amphibi-
  ous vehicle; cf.
  duck
dul¦ca¦mara
dul¦cet
dul¦cian
dul¦ci¦ana
Dul¦cie
dul¦ci¦mer
dul¦ci¦tone
dulia
dull¦ard
Dul¦les, John
  Fos¦ter politician
dull¦ish
dull¦ness
dulls¦ville
dully
dul¦ness var. of
  dullness
du¦lo¦sis
du¦lot¦ic

dulse
Du¦luth
duly
dum Ind. steamed
Duma Russian
  council
Dumas, Alex¦andre
  père and fils,
  writers
Du Maur¦ier,
  Daphne writer
Du Maur¦ier,
  George illustrator
  and writer
dumb
Dum¦bar¦ton town
Dum¦bar¦ton Oaks
Dum¦bar¦ton¦shire
  var. of
  Dunbartonshire
dumb-bell
dumb¦found
dumb¦head
dumb¦ly
dumb¦ness
dumbo +s
dumb¦show
dumb¦size
  dumb¦siz¦ing
dumb¦struck
dum¦dum bullet
dum-dum stupid
  person
dum¦found var. of
  dumbfound
Dum¦fries
Dum¦fries¦shire
dumka
  dum¦kas or dumky
dummy
  dum¦mies
  dum¦mied
  dummy¦ing
du¦mor¦tier¦ite
dump¦er
dump¦ily
dumpi¦ness
dump¦ling
dump¦ster
dumpy
  dump¦ies
  dump¦ier
  dumpi¦est

dun
  dunned
  dun¦ning
  colour; horse; may-
  fly; pester; fort; cf.
  done
dunam
Dun¦bar, Wil¦liam
  poet
dun-bar moth
Dun¦bar¦ton¦shire
  cf. Dumbarton
Dun¦can, Isa¦dora
  dancer
dunce
Dun¦dalk
Dun¦dee
dun¦der¦head
dun¦der¦head¦ed
Dun¦edin
Dun¦ferm¦line
dun¦garee
Dun¦gar¦van
Dun¦ge¦ness
dun¦geon under-
  ground prison; cf.
  donjon
dung¦heap
dung¦hill
dung¦worm
dun¦ite
Dunk¦ard
Dunk¦er sect
dunk¦er
Dun¦kirk
Dun Lao¦ghaire
dun¦lin
Dun¦lop, John
  Boyd Scottish
  inventor
Dun¦lop town;
  cheese
Dun¦mow flitch
dun¦nage
dun¦nart
Dunne, John
  Wil¦liam
  philosopher
Dun¦net Head
dunno +s = don't
  know
dun¦nock
dunny
  dun¦nies

Duns Sco¦tus,
  John theologian
Dun|stable, John
  composer
Dun|stan, St
duo +s
duo|deci¦mal
duo|deci¦mal¦ly
duo|decimo +s
duo|denal
duo|den|itis
duo|de¦num
  duo|de¦nums or
  duo|dena
duo|logue
duomo +s
du|op¦ol|is¦tic
du|op¦oly
  du|op¦olies
duo|tone
dup¦able
du|patta
dupe
  dup|ing
duper
dup¦ery
  dup¦er¦ies
du|pion
duple
du¦plet
du|plex
du|plic¦able
du¦pli|cate
  du|pli|cat¦ing
du|pli|ca¦tion
du|pli|ca¦tor
du¦pli|ci¦tous
du¦pli|ci¦tous¦ly
du|pli¦city
  du|pli¦ci¦ties
du|pon¦dius
  du|pon¦dii
duppy
  dup|pies
du Pré, Jacque¦line
  cellist
Du|puy|tren's
  con|trac¦ture
dura var. of **durra**
dur|abil¦ity
dur¦able
dur¦ably
dural

Dur|alu|min
  trademark
dura mater
dur|amen
dur|ance
Du|rango
dur|ation
dur|ation¦al
dura|tive
Dur¦ban
dur¦bar
durch|kom¦pon|
              iert
Dürer, Al|brecht
  artist
dur¦ess
Durex *trademark*
  pl. **Durex**
Durga Hindu
  goddess
Dur¦ga|pur
Dur¦ham
dur¦ian
duri|crust
dur¦ing
Durk|heim, Émile
  philosopher
Durk¦heim|ian
durn *US* var. of
  darn
Duroc
durra
Dur|rell, Ger¦ald
  zoologist and writer
Dur|rell, Law|rence
  writer
Dur¦rës
dur¦rie rug; var. of
  dhurrie
durry
  dur|ries
  cigarette; cf.
  dhurrie
durst *archaic* past
  of **dare**
durum wheat
dur¦wan
durzi
Du¦shanbe
dusk|ily
duski|ness
dusky
  dusk|ies
  dusk|ier

duski|est
Dus¦sehra
Düs¦sel|dorf
dust particles; cf.
  dost
dust|ball
dust|bin
Dust|bust¦er
  trademark
dust|cart
dust|coat
dust¦er
dust|heap
dust¦ily
Dus¦tin
dusti|ness
dust|less
dust|man
dust|men
dust|pan
dust-up *n.*
dusty
  dust¦ier
  dusti|est
Dutch of the Neth-
  erlands etc.; in 'go
  Dutch'
dutch wife
dutchie cooking
  pot; cf. **duchy**
Dutch|man
  Dutch|men
Dutch|woman
  Dutch|women
du|teous
du|teous¦ly
du|teous|ness
duti|able
duti|ful
duti|ful¦ly
duti|ful|ness
duty
  du¦ties
duty-bound
duty-free
duty-paid
du|um¦vir
du|um¦vir|ate
Du|val¦ier, Papa
  Doc and **Baby Doc**
  presidents of Haiti
duvet
dux
  duces

top pupil
dux¦elles
Dvořák, An|tonín
  composer
dwaal
dwale
dwam
dwarf
  pl. **dwarfs** or
  dwarves
  v. **dwarfs**
  dwarfed
  dwarf|ing
dwarf|ish
dwarf|ism
dweeb
dweeb|ish
dweeby
  dweeb|ier
  dweeb|iest
dwell
  dwelt or **dwelled**
dwell¦er
dwin¦dle
  dwin|dling
dyad
dyad¦ic
Dyak var. of **Dayak**
dy|arch¦al var. of
  diarchal
dy|arch¦ic var. of
  diarchic
dy|archy var. of
  diarchy
dyb¦buk
  dyb|buks or
  dyb|bukim
dye
  dye¦ing
  colour, stain; cf. **die**
dye|able
dyed-in-the-wool
dye|line
dyer cf. **dire**
dye|stuff
Dyfed
dying present parti-
  ciple of **die**; cf.
  dyeing
dyke
dyk¦ing
dykey
dykier
dyki|est

Dylan, Bob singer
  and songwriter
Dymphna
dyn = dyne(s)
dy|nam|ic
dy|nam|ic|al
dy|nam|ic|al|ly
dy|nami|cist
dy|nam|ics
dyna|misa|tion *Br.*
  var. of
  dynamization
dyna|mise *Br.* var.
  of dynamize
dyna|mism
dyna|mist
dyna|mite
  dyna|mit|ing
dyna|miter
dyna|miza|tion
dyna|mize
  dyna|miz|ing
dy|namo +s
dyna|mom|eter
dyn|ast
dyn|as|tic
dyn|as|tic|al|ly
dyn|asty
  dyn|as|ties
dyne unit; cf. dine
dyno
  dynos
  dyno'd or dynoed
  dyno|ing
dyn|ode
dys|aes|the|sia *Br.*
  dys|aes|the|siae or
  dys|aes|the|sias
  US dysesthesia
dys|arth|ria
dys|cal|cu|lia
dys|cra|sia
dys|cra|sic
dys|en|ter|ic
dys|en|tery
dys|es|the|sia
  dys|es|the|siae or
  dys|es|the|sias
  Br. dysaesthesia
dys|func|tion
dys|func|tion|al
dys|func|tion|al|ly
dys|gen|ic
dys|graphia

dys|graph|ic
dys|kin|esia
dys|lalia
dys|lec|tic
dys|lexia
dys|lex|ic
dys|men|or|rhea
  US
dys|men|or|rhoea
  Br.
dys|morphia
dys|morph|ic
dys|par|eunia
dys|pep|sia
dys|pep|tic
dys|pha|gia
dys|pha|sia
dys|pha|sic
dys|phem|ism
dys|pho|nia
dys|phoria
dys|phor|ic
dys|pla|sia
dys|plas|tic
dys|pnea *US*
dys|pneic *US*
dys|pnoea *Br.*
dys|pnoeic *Br.*
dys|praxia
dys|pro|sium
dys|rhyth|mia
dys|rhyth|mic
dys|thymia
dys|thym|ic
dys|tocia
dys|tonia
dys|ton|ic
dys|topia
dys|topian
dys|trophia
  myo|ton|ica
dys|troph|ic
dys|troph|in
dys|trophy
  dys|tro|phies
dys|uria
dy|tis|cid
Dzaou|dzi
Dzer|zhinsk
Dzer|zhin|sky,
  Fe|liks
  Ed|mund|ovich
  Bolshevik leader

dzho var. of dzo
dzo
  pl. dzo or dzos
Dzong|kha

─────────────

E

eager
eager|ly
eager|ness
eagle
  eag|ling
eag|let
eagre wave
Eal|ing
Eamon
Ea|monn
ear|ache
ear|bash
ear|bash|er
ear|bud
ear de|fend|ers
ear|drum
ear|ful
ear|hole
earl
earl|dom
ear|less
Earl Grey
earli|ness
Earl Mar|shal
ear|lock
Earl Pal|at|ine
  Earls Pal|at|ine
early
  earl|ies
  earl|ier
  earli|est
ear|mark
ear|muff
earn gain; cf. ern,
  erne, urn
earn|er
earn|est
earn|est|ly
earn|est|ness
earn|ings
EAROM = electric-
  ally alterable read-

only memory
Earp, Wyatt Ameri-
  can marshal
ear|phone
ear|piece
ear|plug
ear|ring
ear|shot
earth
earth|bound
earth|en
earth|en|ware
earth|ily
earthi|ness
earth|light
earth|li|ness
earth|ling
earth|ly
  earth|lier
  earth|li|est
earth|nut
earth|quake
earth|shine
earth|star
earth|ward
earth|wards var. of
  earthward
earth|work
earth|worm
earthy
  earth|ier
  earthi|est
ear|wax
ear|wig
  ear|wigged
  ear|wig|ging
ear|wit|ness
ease
  eas|ing
ease|ful
easel
ease|ment
easer
eas|ily
easi|ness
east|bound
East|bourne
East Ender
Easter
east|er|ly
  east|er|lies
east|ern
east|ern|er

east¦ern¦most
East India¦man
  East India¦men
east¦ing
East Kil¦bride
east-north-east
east-south-east
east¦ward
east¦ward¦ly
east¦wards var. of
  eastward
East¦wood, Clint
  actor
easy
  eas¦ier
  easi¦est
easy-peasy
eat
  ate
  eaten
eat¦able
eat¦ery
  eat¦er¦ies
eat-in
eau de co¦logne
  eaux de co¦logne
eau de Nil
eau de toi¦lette
  eaux de toi¦lette
eau de vie
  eaux de vie
eaves
eaves¦drop
  eaves¦dropped
  eaves¦drop¦ping
eaves¦drop¦per
eaves¦trough
ebb
Eben¦ezer
Ebla city, ancient
  Syria
E-boat
Ebola virus, fever
ebon
Ebon¦ics
ebon¦ise Br. var. of
  ebonize
ebon¦ite
ebon¦ize
  ebon¦iz¦ing
ebony
  ebon¦ies
e-book
Ebor¦acum

Ebro
ebul¦li¦ence
ebul¦li¦ency
ebul¦li¦ent
ebul¦li¦ent¦ly
ebul¦li¦tion
ecad
écarté
e-cash
ec¦bol¦ic
Ecce Homo +s
ec¦cen¦tric strange;
  not centred; cf.
  excentric
ec¦cen¦tric¦al¦ly cf.
  excentrically
ec¦cen¦tri¦city
  ec¦cen¦tri¦ci¦ties
ec¦chym¦osis
  ec¦chym¦oses
Ec¦cles
ec¦cle¦sial
ec¦cle¦si¦arch +s
Ec¦cle¦si¦as¦tes
ec¦cle¦si¦as¦tic
ec¦cle¦si¦as¦tic¦al
ec¦cle¦si¦as¦ti¦cism
Ec¦cle¦si¦as¦ti¦cus
ec¦cle¦sio¦logic¦al
ec¦cle¦si¦olo¦gist
ec¦cle¦si¦ology
ec¦crine
ec¦dysi¦al
ec¦dysi¦ast
ec¦dy¦sis
  ec¦dy¦ses
ec¦dys¦one
échappé
ech¦elon
eche¦veria
ech¦idna
ech¦in¦acea
ech¦ino¦derm
Ech¦ino¦der¦mata
ech¦in¦oid
Ech¦in¦oidea
ech¦inus
Echi¦ura
echi¦uran
echi¦ur¦oid
echo
  echoes
  echoed

echo¦ing
echo¦car¦dio¦gram
echo¦car¦dio¦graph
echo¦car¦dio¦
      graph¦ic
echo¦car¦di¦
      og¦raphy
echo¦er
echoey
echo¦gram
echo¦graph
echo¦ic
echo¦la¦lia
echo¦less
echo¦loca¦tion
echo¦praxia
echo¦virus
echt
eclair
  French éclair
éclair¦cisse¦ment
eclamp¦sia
eclamp¦tic
éclat
eclec¦tic
eclec¦tic¦al¦ly
eclec¦ti¦cism
eclipse
  eclips¦ing
eclip¦tic
eclog¦ite
ec¦logue
eclose
  eclos¦ing
eclo¦sion
eco¦cen¦tric
eco¦cen¦trism
eco¦cide
eco¦fem¦in¦ism
eco¦fem¦in¦ist
eco¦freak
eco-friend¦ly
eco-label
eco-labeling US
eco-labelling Br.
E. coli
eco¦lodge
eco¦logic¦al
eco¦logic¦al¦ly
eco¦lo¦gist
ecol¦ogy
  ecol¦ogies
e-commerce

econo¦met¦ric
econo¦met¦ri¦cian
econo¦met¦rics
econo¦met¦rist
eco¦nom¦ic
eco¦nom¦ic¦al
eco¦nom¦ic¦al¦ly
eco¦nom¦ics
econo¦misa¦tion Br.
  var. of
  economization
econo¦mise Br. var.
  of economize
econo¦miser Br. var.
  of economizer
econo¦mism
econo¦mist
econo¦miza¦tion
econo¦mize
  econo¦miz¦ing
econo¦mizer
econ¦omy
  econ¦omies
écorché
eco¦region
eco¦sphere
ecos¦saise
  French écossaise
eco¦sys¦tem
eco¦ter¦ror¦ism
eco¦ter¦ror¦ist
eco¦tonal
eco¦tone
eco¦tour
eco¦tour¦ism
eco¦tour¦ist
eco¦toxico¦logic¦al
eco¦toxi¦colo¦gist
eco¦toxi¦col¦ogy
eco¦type
eco-warrior
ecru
ec¦sta¦sise Br. var.
  of ecstasize
ec¦sta¦size
  ec¦sta¦siz¦ing
ec¦stasy
  ec¦sta¦sies
ec¦stat¦ic
ec¦stat¦ic¦al¦ly
ecto¦derm
ecto¦der¦mal
ecto¦gene
ecto¦gen¦esis

ecto|gen|et|ic
ecto|gen|ic
ec|togen|ous
ecto|morph
ecto|morph|ic
ecto|morphy
  ecto|morphies
ecto|para|site
ecto|para|sit|ic
ec|top|ic
ecto|plasm
ecto|plas|mic
ecto|proct
Ecto|procta
ecto|therm
ecto|ther|mic
ecto|thermy
  ecto|ther|mies
ec|tro|pion
ecu
  pl. ecu *or* ecus
  European currency
  unit
écu +s French coin
Ecua|dor
Ecua|dor|ean
Ecua|dor|ian var. of
  Ecuadorean
ecu|men|ic|al
ecu|men|ic|al|ly
ecu|men|ism
ec|zema inflamma-
  tion; cf. excimer
ec|zema|tous
eda|city
Edam
eda|mame
ed|aph|ic
edapho|saurus
Edda book
eddo
  ed|does
eddy
  ed|dies
  ed|died
  eddy|ing
Eddy|stone
edel|weiss
edema *US*
  ede|mas *or*
  ede|mata
  Br. oedema
edema|tous *US*
  Br. oedematous

Eden
Edent|ata
edent|ate
eden|tu|lous
edge
  edging
Edge|hill
edge|less
edger
edge-tool
edge|ways *Br.*
edge|wise *US*
edgi|ly
edgi|ness
edg|ing
edg|less var. of
  edgeless
edgy
  edgi|er
  edgi|est
edh letter; var. of
  eth
edi|bil|ity
ed|ible
edict
edict|al
edi|fi|ca|tion
edi|fice
edify
  edi|fies
  edi|fied
  edify|ing
edify|ing|ly
Ed|in|burgh
Edi|son, Thomas
  inventor
edit|able
edi|tion version of
  book etc.; cf.
  addition
edi|tio prin|ceps
  edi|ti|ones
  prin|cipes
edi|tor
edi|tor|ial
edi|tori|al|ise *Br.*
  var. of editorialize
edi|tori|al|ist
edi|tori|al|ize
  edi|tori|al|iz|ing
edi|tori|al|ly
edit|or|ship
edit|ress

edi|trix
  edi|trices
Ed|mond
Ed|mon|ton
Ed|mund
Edo
  pl. Edo *or* Edos
Edom|ite
educ|abil|ity
educ|able
edu|cate
  edu|cat|ing
edu|ca|tion
edu|ca|tion|al
edu|ca|tion|al|ist
edu|ca|tion|al|ly
edu|ca|tion|ist
edu|ca|tive
edu|ca|tor
educe
  edu|cing
edu|cible
educ|tion
educ|tive
edu|tain|ment
Ed|ward
Ed|wardes
Ed|ward|ian
Ed|ward|iana
Ed|wards
Ed|wina
eejit
eel|grass
eel-like
eel|pout
eel|worm
eely
Eem
Eem|ian
e'en = even
eensy
eensy-weensy
e'er = ever; cf. air,
  ere, eyre, heir
eerie
  eer|ier
  eeri|est
  weird; cf. Erie,
  eyrie
eer|ily
eeri|ness
Eeyore|ish var. of
  Eeyorish

Eeyor|ish
ef|face
  ef|facing
ef|face|ment
ef|fect result; bring
  about; cf. **affect**
ef|fect|ive having an
  effect; efficient; cf.
  affective
ef|fect|ive|ly in an
  effective way; cf.
  affectively
ef|fect|ive|ness
ef|fect|iv|ity degree
  of being effective;
  cf. **affectivity**
ef|fect|or
ef|fec|tual
ef|fec|tu|al|ity
ef|fec|tu|al|ly
ef|fec|tu|ate
  ef|fec|tu|at|ing
ef|fec|tu|ation
ef|fem|in|acy
  ef|fem|in|acies
ef|fem|in|ate
ef|fem|in|ate|ly
ef|fendi
ef|fer|ent
ef|fer|vesce
  ef|fer|ves|cing
ef|fer|ves|cence
ef|fer|ves|cent
ef|fete
ef|fete|ly
ef|fete|ness
ef|fi|ca|cious
ef|fi|ca|cious|ly
ef|fi|ca|cious|ness
ef|fi|cacy
ef|fi|ciency
  ef|fi|cien|cies
ef|fi|cient
ef|fi|cient|ly
ef|figy
  ef|fi|gies
ef|fleur|age
  ef|fleur|aging
ef|flor|esce
  ef|flor|es|cing
ef|flor|es|cence
ef|flor|es|cent
ef|flu|ence
ef|flu|ent

ef¦flu|vium
  ef¦flu|via
ef¦flux
ef¦flux|ion
ef¦fort
ef¦fort|ful
ef¦fort|less
ef¦fort|less|ly
ef¦fort|less|ness
ef¦front|ery
  ef¦front|eries
ef¦ful|gence
ef¦ful|gent
ef¦ful|gent|ly
ef¦fuse
  ef¦fus|ing
ef¦fu|sion
ef¦fu|sive
ef¦fu|sive|ly
ef¦fu|sive|ness
Efik
e-fit
EFTA European
  Free Trade
  Association
EFTPOS electronic
  funds transfer at
  point of sale
egad
egali|tar|ian
egali|tar|ian|ism
Eg¦bert
Eger
egest
eges¦tion
egg-and-spoon
  race
eggar
egg-beater
egger var. of eggar
egg-flip
egg|head
egg|less
egg¦nog
egg|plant
eggs and bacon
  plant
eggs Bene|dict
egg|shell
egg-tooth
  egg-teeth
eggy
  egg¦ier

eggi|est
eg¦lan|tine
Eg¦mont
ego +s
ego|cen¦tric
ego|cen¦tric|al¦ly
ego|cen¦trl|cïty
ego|cen¦trism
ego-ideal
ego¦ism
ego¦ist
ego|is¦tic
ego|is¦tic|al
ego|is¦tic|al¦ly
ego|less
ego|mania
ego|maniac
ego|mani¦ac|al
ego-psycholo¦gist
ego-psychol¦ogy
ego|surf
ego|tise Br. var. of
  egotize
ego|tism
ego|tist
ego|tis¦tic
ego|tis¦tic|al
ego|tis¦tic|al¦ly
ego|tize
  ego|tiz|ing
egre|gious
egre|gious|ly
egre|gious|ness
egress
egres|sion
egres|sive
egret
Egypt
Egyp¦tian
Egyp¦tian|isa¦tion
  Br. var. of
  Egyptianization
Egyp¦tian|ise Br.
  var. of Egyptianize
Egyp¦tian|iza¦tion
Egyp¦tian|ize
Egyp¦tian|iz¦ing
Egypto|logic¦al
Egypt|olo¦gist
Egypt|ology
Eich|mann, Adolf
  Nazi administrator

ei¦cosa|penta|
      eno¦ic
Eid Muslim festival
eider
ei¦der|down quilt
eider down eider
  duck's feathers
ei|det¦ic
ei¦do|lon
  ei¦do|lons or
  ei¦dola
eidos
Eid ul-Adha
Eid ul-Fitr
Eifel German region
Eif¦fel Tower
eigen|fre¦quency
  eigen|fre|quen|cies
eigen|func¦tion
eigen|state
eigen|value
eigen|vector
Eiger Swiss
  mountain
Eigg Scottish island
eight number; cf.
  ait, ate
eight|een
eight|eenmo +s
eight|eenth
eight|fold
eighth
eighth¦ly
eight|ieth
eight-iron
eights
eight|some
8vo = octavo
eighty
  eight¦ies
eighty-first,
  eighty-second,
  etc.
eighty|fold
eighty-one, eighty-
  two, etc.
Eilat
Ei¦leen
eina
Eind|hoven city
Ein|fühl|ung
ein|korn
Ein|stein, Al¦bert

Ein|stein|ian
ein|stein|ium
Eint|hoven,
  Wil|lem
  physiologist
Eire
Eir¦ene goddess of
  peace
eir|en¦ic var. of
  irenic
eir¦eni|con
Ei|sen|hower,
  Dwight ('Ike') US
  president
Ei|sen|stadt
Ei|sen|stein,
  Ser¦gei
  Mikh|ail|ovich film
  director
ei|stedd|fod
  ei|stedd|fods or
  ei|stedd|fodau
ei|stedd|fod¦ic
Eis|wein
  Eis|weins or
  Eis|weine
ei¦ther
either/or
eius|dem gen|eris
  var. of *ejusdem*
  generis
ejacu|late
  ejacu|lat¦ing
ejacu|la¦tion
ejacu|la¦tor
ejacu|la¦tory
eject
ejecta lava etc.; cf.
  ejector
ejec¦tion
eject|ive
eject|ment
eject¦or device; cf.
  ejecta
ejido +s Mexican
  farm
ejus|dem gen|eris
eke
  eking
El elevated railway
El Aaiún
elab|or|ate
  elab|or|at¦ing
elab|or|ate¦ly

elab¦or¦ate¦ness
elab¦or¦ation
elab¦ora¦tive
elab¦or¦ator
Elaine
El Ala¦mein
Elam
Elam¦ite
elan
  French élan
eland
elapse
  elap¦sing
elasi¦pod
elasmo¦branch +s
elasmo¦saur
elas¦tane
elas¦tase
elas¦tic
elas¦tic¦al¦ly
elas¦ti¦cated
elas¦ti¦cise *Br.* var.
  of elasticize
elas¦ti¦city
  elas¦ti¦ci¦ties
elas¦ti¦cize
  elas¦ti¦ciz¦ing
elas¦tin
elasto¦mer
elasto¦mer¦ic
Elasto¦plast
  trademark
Elat var. of Eilat
elate
  elat¦ing
elated¦ly
elated¦ness
ela¦tion joy; cf.
  illation
E-layer
Elba island
El¦ba¦san city
Elbe river
elbow
El¦brus mountain,
  Russia
El¦burz mountains,
  Iran
Elche
El Cid
elder
elder¦berry
  elder¦berries

Elder Brother
  Elder Breth¦ren
  of Trinity House
elder¦care
elder¦flower
elder¦li¦ness
eld¦er¦ly
elder¦ship
eld¦est
El Djem
El Dor¦ado ficti-
  tious country
el¦dor¦ado +s any
  imaginary rich
  place
el¦dritch
Elea¦nor of
  Aqui¦taine
Elea¦nor of
  Cas¦tile
Ele¦at¦ic
ele¦cam¦pane
elect
elect¦abil¦ity
elect¦able
elec¦tion
elec¦tion¦eer
elect¦ive
elect¦or
elect¦or¦al
elect¦or¦al¦ly
elect¦or¦ate
elect¦or¦ship
Elec¦tra
elect¦ress
elec¦tret
elec¦tric
elec¦tric¦al
elec¦tric¦al¦ly
elec¦tri¦cian
elec¦tri¦city
elec¦tri¦fi¦ca¦tion
elec¦tri¦fier
elec¦trify
  elec¦tri¦fies
  elec¦tri¦fied
  elec¦tri¦fy¦ing
elec¦tro +s
electro-acoustic
elec¦tro¦car¦dio¦
            gram
elec¦tro¦car¦dio¦
            graph

elec¦tro¦car¦dio¦
          graph¦ic
elec¦tro¦car¦di¦
          og¦raphy
elec¦tro¦cautery
elec¦tro¦chem¦ical
elec¦tro¦
        chem¦ical¦ly
elec¦tro¦chem¦ist
elec¦tro¦chem¦is¦try
elec¦tro¦chro¦mic
elec¦tro¦chro¦mism
elec¦tro¦
      coagu¦la¦tion
elec¦tro¦
      con¦vul¦sive
elec¦tro¦cor¦tico¦
            gram
elec¦tro¦cute
  elec¦tro¦cut¦ing
elec¦tro¦cu¦tion
elec¦tro¦cyte
elec¦trode
elec¦tro¦der¦mal
elec¦tro¦di¦aly¦sis
elec¦tro¦dynam¦ic
elec¦tro¦dynam¦ics
elec¦tro¦
      enceph¦alo¦gram
elec¦tro¦
      enceph¦alo¦graph
elec¦tro¦en¦ceph¦al¦
            og¦raphy
elec¦tro¦fish
elec¦tro¦genic
elec¦tro¦jet
elec¦tro¦kinetic
elec¦tro¦less
elec¦tro¦lier
elec¦tro¦lumin¦
          es¦cence
elec¦tro¦lumin¦
          es¦cent
elec¦tro¦lyse *Br.*
  elec¦tro¦lys¦ing
  US electrolyze
elec¦tro¦lyser *Br.*
  US electrolyzer
elec¦troly¦sis
  elec¦troly¦ses
elec¦tro¦lyte
elec¦tro¦lyt¦ic
elec¦tro¦lyt¦ic¦al¦ly

elec¦tro¦lyze *US*
  elec¦tro¦lyz¦ing
  Br. electrolyse
elec¦tro¦lyzer *US*
  Br. electrolyser
elec¦tro¦mag¦net
elec¦tro¦mag¦net¦ic
elec¦tro¦mag¦net¦ic¦
            al¦ly
elec¦tro¦mag¦net¦
            ism
elec¦tro¦
      mech¦an¦ic¦al
elec¦trom¦eter
elec¦tro¦met¦ric
elec¦trom¦etry
elec¦tro¦mo¦tive
elec¦tro¦myo¦gram
elec¦tro¦myo¦graph
elec¦tro¦myo¦
          graph¦ic
elec¦tro¦myog¦
          raphy
elec¦tron
elec¦tro¦nega¦tive
elec¦tro¦nega¦tiv¦ity
elec¦tron¦ic
elec¦tron¦ica
elec¦tron¦ic¦al¦ly
elec¦tron¦ics
elec¦tron¦volt
electro-oculogram
electro-
      oculograph¦ic
electro-
      oculog¦raphy
electro-optic
electro-optical
electro-optics
electro-osmosis
electro-osmotic
elec¦tro¦phile
elec¦tro¦phil¦ic
elec¦tro¦phor¦ese
elec¦tro¦phor¦es¦ing
elec¦tro¦phor¦esis
elec¦tro¦phor¦et¦ic
elec¦tro¦
      phor¦et¦ic¦al¦ly
elec¦troph¦orus
elec¦tro¦
      physio¦logic¦al
elec¦tro¦
      physi¦olo¦gist

elec|tro|
 physi|ology
elec|tro|plaque
elec|tro|plate
 elec|tro|plat|ing
elec|tro|plater
elec|tro|plax
elec|tro|plexy
elec|tro|polish
elec|tro|por|ate
 elec|tro|por|at|ing
elec|tro|por|ation
elec|tro|posi|tive
elec|tro|recep|tion
elec|tro|recep|tor
elec|tro|retino|
 gram
elec|tro|scope
elec|tro|scop|ic
electro-select|ive
elec|tro|shock
elec|tro|stat|ic
elec|tro|stat|ics
elec|tro|sur|gery
elec|tro|sur|gi|cal
elec|tro|tech|nic|al
elec|tro|tech|nics
elec|tro|tech|
 nol|ogy
elec|tro|thera|
 peut|ic
elec|tro|ther|ap|ist
elec|tro|ther|apy
elec|tro|ther|mal
elec|tro|type
 elec|tro|typ|ing
elec|tro|typer
elec|tro|valence
elec|tro|valency
elec|tro|valent
elec|tro|weak
elec|trum
elec|tu|ary
 elec|tu|ar|ies
ele|emo|syn|ary
ele|gance
ele|gant
ele|gant|ly
ele|giac
ele|giac|al|ly
ele|giacs
ele|gise *Br.* var. of
 elegize

ele|gist
ele|gize
 ele|giz|ing
elegy
ele|gies
elem|ent
elem|en|tal
elcm|en|tal|ism
elem|en|tar|ily
elem|en|tary
elem|en|tar|ies
elemi
elen|chus
elen|chi
 Logic
Eleo|nora
Eleo|nora's falcon
ele|phant
ele|phant|ia|sis
ele|phant|ine
ele|phant|oid
ele|vate
ele|vat|ing
ele|va|tion
ele|va|tion|al
ele|va|tor
ele|va|tory
eleven
eleven|fold
eleven-plus
elev|enses
elev|enth
elev|von
elf
 elves
elfin
elf|ish
Elgar, Ed|ward
 composer
Elgin town; Marbles
Elgon mountain
El Greco painter
Elias
elicit draw out; cf.
 illicit
elicit|ation
elicit|or
elide
 elid|ing
eli|gi|bil|ity
eli|gible
Eli|jah
elim|in|able

elim|in|ate
elim|in|at|ing
elim|in|ation
elim|in|ator
elim|in|atory
Elint electronic
 intelligence-
 gathering
Eliot, George
 English novelist
Eliot, T. S. Anglo-
 American poet
Elisa|beth
Elisa|beth|ville
Eli|sha
eli|sion
elite
 French élite
elit|ism
elit|ist
elixir
Eliza
Eliza|beth English
 and British queens
Eliza|bethan
elk|horn
el|lagic
Elles|mere
El|lice Is|lands
 former name of
 Tuvalu; cf. Ellis
 Island
El|ling|ton, Duke
 jazz musician
El|liot
El|liott
el|lipse
el|lip|sis
el|lip|ses
el|lips|oid
el|lips|oid|al
el|lip|tic
el|lip|tic|al
el|lip|tic|al|ly
el|lip|ti|city
Ellis, Have|lock
 psychologist
Ellis Is|land in
 New York; cf.
 Ellice Islands
Ells|worth
Elmo in 'St Elmo's
 fire'

El Niño +s changes
 including warming
 of water; cf. **La
 Niña**
elo|cu|tion
elo|cu|tion|ary
elo|cu|tion|ist
elo|dea plant
Elo|him
Elo|hist
elong|ate
elong|at|ing
elong|ation
elope
 elop|ing
elope|ment
eloper
elo|quence
elo|quent
elo|quent|ly
El Paso
El Sal|va|dor
Elsan *trademark*
else|where
Elsie
El|si|nore
El|speth
El|ster
El|ster|ian
elu|ant var. of
 eluent
elu|ate
elu|ci|date
 elu|ci|dat|ing
elu|ci|da|tion
elu|ci|da|tive
elu|ci|da|tor
elu|ci|da|tory
elude avoid; escape;
 cf. allude, illude
elu|ent
Elul Jewish month
elu|sion act of
 eluding; cf.
 allusion, illusion
elu|sive difficult to
 catch; avoiding the
 point; cf. allusive,
 illusive
elu|sive|ly in an
 elusive way; cf.
 allusively
elu|sive|ness elusive
 nature; cf.

allusiveness
elute
elut¦ing
elu¦tion
elu¦tri¦ate
  elu¦tri¦at¦ing
elu¦tri¦ation
elvan rock
elven elf-like
elver
elves
El¦vira
elv¦ish
Ely city, England
Ély¦sée Pal¦ace
Elys¦ian
Elys¦ium
ely¦tron
  ely¦tra
El¦ze¦vir family of
  Dutch printers
em printing measure
ema¦ci¦ated
ema¦ci¦ation
email
email¦er
ema¦lan¦geni pl. of
  lilangeni
em¦an¦ate
  em¦an¦at¦ing
em¦an¦ation
eman¦ci¦pate
  eman¦ci¦pat¦ing
eman¦ci¦pa¦tion
eman¦ci¦pa¦tor
eman¦ci¦pa¦tory
Eman¦uel name; cf.
  Emmanuel
emas¦cu¦late
  emas¦cu¦lat¦ing
emas¦cu¦la¦tion
emas¦cu¦la¦tor
emas¦cu¦la¦tory
em¦balm
em¦balm¦er
em¦balm¦ment
em¦bank
em¦bank¦ment
em¦bargo
  em¦bar¦goes
  em¦bar¦goed
  em¦bargo¦ing
em¦bark

em¦bar¦ras de
  choix
em¦bar¦ras de
  ri¦chesses
em¦bar¦rass
em¦bar¦rass¦ing¦ly
em¦bar¦rass¦ment
em¦bas¦sage
em¦bassy
  em¦bas¦sies
em¦bat¦tle
em¦bat¦tling
em¦bay
em¦bay¦ment
embed
em¦bed¦ded
em¦bed¦ding
em¦bed¦ded¦ness
em¦bed¦ment
em¦bel¦lish
em¦bel¦lish¦er
em¦bel¦lish¦ment
ember
em¦bez¦zle
  em¦bez¦zling
em¦bezzle¦ment
em¦bez¦zler
Embi¦optera
embi¦opter¦an
em¦bit¦ter
em¦bit¦ter¦ment
em¦bla¦zon
em¦bla¦zon¦ment
em¦blem
em¦blem¦at¦ic
em¦blem¦at¦ise Br.
  var. of
  emblematize
em¦blem¦atist
em¦blem¦at¦ize
  em¦blem¦at¦iz¦ing
em¦bodi¦ment
em¦body
  em¦bodies
  em¦bodied
  em¦body¦ing
em¦bold¦en
em¦bol¦ec¦tomy
  em¦bol¦ec¦to¦mies
em¦bol¦ic
em¦bol¦isa¦tion
  Br. var. of
  embolization

em¦bol¦ism
em¦bol¦iza¦tion
em¦bolus
  em¦boli
em¦bon¦point
em¦bosom
em¦boss
em¦boss¦er
em¦boss¦ment
em¦bouch¦ure
em¦bour¦geoise¦
         ment
em¦bowel
  em¦bow¦elled Br.
  em¦bow¦eled US
  em¦bowel¦ling Br.
  em¦bowel¦ing US
em¦bower
em¦brace
  em¦bra¦cing
em¦brace¦able
em¦brace¦ment
em¦bracer
em¦bras¦ure
em¦bras¦ured
em¦brit¦tle
  em¦brit¦tling
em¦brittle¦ment
em¦bro¦ca¦tion
em¦broi¦der
em¦broi¦der¦er
em¦broi¦dery
  em¦broi¦der¦ies
em¦broil
em¦broil¦ment
em¦bryo +s
em¦bryo¦gen¦esis
em¦bryo¦gen¦ic
em¦bry¦ogeny
em¦bry¦oid
em¦bryo¦logic
em¦bryo¦logic¦al
em¦bryo¦logic¦al¦ly
em¦bry¦olo¦gist
em¦bry¦ology
em¦bry¦on¦al
em¦bry¦on¦ic
em¦bus
  em¦buses
  em¦bused or
  em¦bussed
  em¦bus¦ing or
  em¦bus¦sing

emcee
  em¦cees
  em¦ceed
  em¦cee¦ing
emend remove
  errors; cf. amend
emend¦ation
emen¦da¦tory
em¦er¦ald
emerge
  emer¦ging
emer¦gence
emer¦gency
emer¦gen¦cies
emer¦gent
emeri¦tus
emerse
emersed
  Botany above
  water; cf. immerse,
  immersed
emer¦sion Botany
  emergence; cf.
  immersion
Emer¦son, Ralph
  Waldo philosopher
emery
Emesa
em¦esis
emet¦ic
emet¦ine
emic
emics
emi¦grant
emi¦grate
  emi¦grat¦ing
emi¦gra¦tion
emi¦gra¦tory
émi¦gré
Emilia-Romagna
emi¦nence
émi¦nence grise
  émi¦nences grises
emi¦nent
emi¦nent¦ly
emir
emir¦ate
emis¦sary
  emis¦sar¦ies
emis¦sion
emis¦sive
emis¦siv¦ity
emit
  emit¦ted

emit|ting
give off; cf. omit
emit|ter
Emlyn
Em|man|uel
Christianity; cf.
  Emanuel
Em|me|line
em|mena|gogue
Em|men|tal
Em|men|thal var. of
  Emmental
emmer wheat
emmet ant
Emmy
  Em|mies
emo
emo|core
emol|li|ence
emol|li|ent
emolu|ment
emote
  emot|ing
emoter
emoti|con
emo|tion
emo|tion|al
emo|tion|al|ise *Br.*
  var. of
  emotionalize
emo|tion|al|ism
emo|tion|al|ist
emo|tion|al|ity
emo|tion|al|ize
  emo|tion|al|iz|ing
emo|tion|al|ly
emo|tion|less
emo|tive
emo|tive|ly
emo|tiv|ism
emo|tiv|ist
emo|tiv|ity
em|pa|nada
em|panel var. of
  impanel
em|panel|ment var.
  of impanelment
em|path
em|path|et|ic
em|path|et|ic|al|ly
em|path|ic
em|pa|thise *Br.* var.
  of **empathize**

em|pa|thist
em|pa|thize
em|pa|thiz|ing
em|pathy
  em|pathies
em|pen|nage
em|peror
em|per|or|ship
em|phasis
  em|phases
em|pha|sise *Br.* var.
  of emphasize
em|pha|size
  em|pha|siz|ing
em|phat|ic
em|phat|ic|al|ly
em|phy|se|ma
em|pire
Em|pire line
em|pir|ic
em|pir|ic|al
em|pir|ic|al|ly
em|piri|cism
em|piri|cist
em|place|ment
em|plane
  em|plan|ing
em|ploy
em|ploy|abil|ity
em|ploy|able
em|ploy|ee
em|ploy|er
em|ploy|ment
em|pol|der var. of
  impolder
em|por|ium
  em|poria or
  em|por|iums
em|power
em|power|ment
emp|ress
em|presse|ment
Emp|son, Wil|liam
  poet and critic
emp|ti|ly
emp|ti|ness
empty
  emp|ties
  emp|tied
  empty|ing
  emp|tier
  emp|ti|est
empty-nester

em|pur|ple
  em|purp|ling
em|py|ema
em|pyr|eal
em|pyr|ean
Emrys
emu bird
emu|late
  emu|lat|ing
emu|la|tion
emu|la|tive
emu|la|tor
emu|lous
emu|lous|ly
emul|si|fi|able
emul|si|fi|ca|tion
emul|si|fier
emul|sify
  emul|si|fies
  emul|si|fied
  emul|si|fy|ing
emul|sion
emul|sive
emu-wren
en printing measure
en|able
  en|ab|ling
en|able|ment
en|abler
en|act
en|act|able
en|action
en|act|ive
en|act|ment
en|act|or
en|amel
  en|am|elled *Br.*
  en|am|eled *US*
  en|am|el|ling *Br.*
  en|am|el|ling *US*
  en|am|el|er *US*
  en|am|el|ler *Br.*
en|amel|work
en|amor *US*
en|am|our *Br.*
en|an|thema
en|antio|mer
en|antio|mer|ic
en|antio|merically
en|antio|morph
en|antio|morph|ic

en|antio|morph|
        ism
en|antio|morph|
        ous
en|arg|ite
en|arth|ro|sis
  en|arth|ro|ses
en|ation
en bloc
en brosse
en cabo|chon
En|cae|nia
en|cage
  en|caging
en|camp
en|camp|ment
en|cap|si|date
  en|cap|si|dat|ing
  en|cap|si|da|tion
en|cap|su|late
  en|cap|su|lat|ing
  en|cap|su|la|tion
en|case
  en|cas|ing
en|case|ment
en|cash
en|cash|able
en|cash|ment
en|caus|tic
en|ceinte
en|ceph|al|ic
en|ceph|alin var. of
  enkephalin
en|ceph|al|isa|tion
  Br. var. of
  encephalization
en|ceph|al|it|ic
en|ceph|al|itis
en|ceph|al|itis
  leth|ar|gica
en|ceph|al|iza|tion
en|ceph|alo|gram
en|ceph|alo|graph
en|ceph|alo|
        graph|ic
en|ceph|al|
        og|raphy
en|ceph|alo|
        my|eli|tis
en|ceph|alon
en|ceph|al|op|athy
en|ceph|al|
        op|athies
en|chain

en|*chaîne*|*ment*
  Ballet
en|chain|ment
en|chant
en|chant|er
en|chant|er's
  night|shade
en|chant|ing|ly
en|chant|ment
en|chant|ress
en|chase
  en|chas|ing
en|chil|ada
en|chir|id|ion
  en|chir|id|ions or
  en|chir|idia
en|cipher
en|cipher|ment
en|cir|cle
  en|circ|ling
en|circle|ment
en clair
en|clasp
en|clave
en|clit|ic
en|close
  en|clos|ing
en|clos|ure
en|code
  en|cod|ing
en|coder
en|comi|ast
en|comi|as|tic
en|comi|enda
en|co|mium
  en|co|miums or
  en|co|mia
en|com|pass
en|com|pass|ment
enco|pre|sis
en|core
  en|cor|ing
en|coun|ter
en|cour|age
  en|cour|aging
en|cour|age|ment
en|cour|ager
en|cour|aging|ly
en|croach
en|croach|er
en|croach|ment
en croute
  French en croûte

en|crust
en|crust|ation
en|crypt
en|cryp|tion
en|cul|tur|ation var.
  of inculturation
en|cum|ber
en|cum|brance
en|cyc|lic|al
en|cyclo|pae|dia
  var. of
  encyclopedia
en|cyclo|pae|dic
  var. of
  encyclopedic
en|cyclo|pae|dism
  var. of
  encyclopedism
en|cyclo|pae|dist
  var. of
  encyclopedist
en|cyclo|pe|dia
en|cyclo|pe|dic
en|cyclo|ped|ism
en|cyclo|ped|ist
en|cyst
en|cyst|ation
en|cyst|ment
en|dan|ger
en|dan|ger|ment
end-around
end|arter|ec|tomy
  end|arter|
    ec|to|mies
end|arter|itis
en daube
en|dear
en|dear|ing|ly
en|dear|ment
en|deavor *US*
en|deav|our *Br.*
en|dem|ic
en|dem|ic|al|ly
en|dem|icity
en|dem|ism
End|erby Land
ender|gon|ic
end|game
end|gate
end|ite
en|dive
end|less
end|less|ly

end|less|ness
end|member
end|most
end|note
endo|car|dial
endo|car|dit|ic
endo|car|di|tis
endo|car|di|um
endo|carp
endo|carp|ic
endo|cen|tric
endo|crine
endo|crino|logic|al
endo|crin|olo|gist
endo|crin|ology
endo|cyto|sis
endo|cytot|ic
endo|derm
endo|der|mal
endo|der|mis
en|dog|am|ous
en|dog|amy
endo|gen|esis
endo|gen|ic
en|dogen|ous
en|dogen|ous|ly
en|dogeny
endo|lith|ic
endo|lymph
endo|met|rial
endo|met|ri|osis
endo|met|ri|tis
endo|met|rium
endo|morph
endo|morph|ic
endo|morphy
endo|nucle|ase
endo|para|site
endo|para|sit|ic
endo|pep|tid|ase
en|doph|ora
endo|phor|ic
endo|phyte
endo|phyt|ic
endo|plasm
endo|plas|mic
endo|pod
en|dopo|dite
en|dor|phin
en|dors|able
en|dorse
  en|dors|ing

en|dor|see
en|dorse|ment
en|dor|ser
endo|scope
endo|scop|ic
endo|scop|ic|al|ly
en|dos|co|pist
en|dos|copy
en|dos|co|pies
endo|skel|etal
endo|skel|eton
endo|sperm
endo|spore
endo|sym|bi|ont
endo|sym|bi|osis
endo|sym|bi|otic
endo|the|lial
endo|the|lium
  endo|the|lla
endo|therm
endo|ther|mal
endo|ther|mic
endo|thermy
endo|toxin
endo|tracheal
endow
en|dow|er
en|dow|ment
end|paper
end-play
en|drin
en|due
  en|du|ing
en|dur|abil|ity
en|dur|able
en|dur|ance
en|dure
  en|dur|ing
en|dur|ing|ly
en|duro +s
end|ways
end|wise
En|dym|ion
en échelon
enema
enemy
en|emies
Eneo|lith|ic
en|er|get|ic
en|er|get|ic|al|ly
en|er|get|ics
ener|gise *Br.* var. of
  energize

en¦er¦giser *Br.* var.
  of **energizer**
ener¦gize
  ener¦giz¦ing
en¦er¦gizer *Br.* var.
  of **energiser**
en¦er¦gu¦men
en¦ergy
  en¦er¦gies
ener¦vate
  ener¦vat¦ing
en¦er¦va¦tion
Ene¦we¦tak var. of
  Eniwetok
en face
en fam¦ille
en¦fant gâté
  en¦fants gâtés
en¦fant ter¦rible
  en¦fants ter¦ribles
en¦fee¦ble
  en¦feeb¦ling
en¦feeble¦ment
en¦feoff
en¦feoff¦ment
en fête
en¦fet¦ter
en¦fil¦ade
  en¦fil¦ad¦ing
en¦flesh
en¦flesh¦ment
en¦fleur¦age
en¦flur¦ane
en¦fold envelop; cf.
  infolded, infolding
en¦force
  en¦for¦cing
en¦force¦abil¦ity
en¦force¦able
en¦force¦ment
en¦for¦cer
en¦fran¦chise
  en¦fran¦chis¦ing
en¦fran¦chise¦ment
en¦gage
  en¦gaging
en¦gagé
en¦gage¦ment
en¦ga¦ging¦ly
Engel¦mann
  spruce
En¦gels, Fried¦rich
  political
  philosopher

en¦gen¦der
en¦gine
en¦gin¦ing
en¦gin¦eer
en¦gin¦eer¦ing
en¦gine¦less
en¦gin¦ery
en¦gird
en¦gir¦dle
  en¦gird¦ling
en¦glacial
Eng¦land
Eng¦lish
Eng¦lish¦man
  Eng¦lish¦men
Eng¦lish¦ness
Eng¦lish¦woman
  Eng¦lish¦women
en¦globe
  en¦glob¦ing
en¦gorge
  en¦gor¦ging
en¦gorge¦ment
en¦graft
en¦graft¦ment
en¦grain var. of
  ingrain
en¦grained var. of
  ingrained
en¦gram
en¦gram¦mat¦ic
en¦grave
  en¦grav¦ing
en¦graver
en¦gross
en¦gross¦ing¦ly
en¦gross¦ment
en¦gulf
en¦gulf¦ment
en¦hance
  en¦han¦cing
en¦hance¦ment
en¦han¦cer
en¦har¦mon¦ic
en¦har¦mon¦ic¦al¦ly
en¦igma
en¦ig¦mat¦ic
en¦ig¦mat¦ic¦al¦ly
en¦isle
  en¦isl¦ing
En¦iwe¦tok Pacific
  island
en¦jambed

en¦jambe¦ment
en¦jamb¦ment var.
  of enjambement
en¦join
en¦join¦der
en¦join¦ment
en¦joy
en¦joy¦abil¦ity
en¦joy¦able
en¦joy¦able¦ness
en¦joy¦ably
en¦joy¦er
en¦joy¦ment
en¦keph¦alin
en¦kin¦dle
  en¦kind¦ling
en¦lace
  en¦lacing
en¦large
  en¦lar¦ging
en¦large¦ment
en¦lar¦ger
en¦light¦en
en¦light¦en¦er
en¦light¦en¦ment
en¦list
en¦list¦er
en¦list¦ment
en¦liven
en¦liven¦er
en¦liven¦ment
en masse
en¦mesh
en¦mesh¦ment
en¦mity
  en¦mi¦ties
en¦nea¦gram
Ennis
En¦nis¦kil¦len
en¦noble
  en¦nob¦ling
en¦noble¦ment
ennui
Enoch
enoki
eno¦logic¦al *US*
  Br. oenological
en¦olo¦gist *US*
  Br. oenologist
en¦ol¦ogy *US*
  Br. oenology
eno¦phile *US*
  Br. oenophile

en¦oph¦il¦ist *US*
  Br. oenophilist
enor¦mity
  enor¦mities
enor¦mous
enor¦mous¦ly
enor¦mous¦ness
eno¦sis
enough
en pa¦pil¦lote
en pas¦sant
en pen¦sion
en¦plane var. of
  emplane
en plein air
en poste
en pri¦meur
en¦print
en prise
en¦queue
  en¦queuing or
  en¦queue¦ing
en¦quire var. of
  inquire
en¦quir¦er var. of
  inquirer
en¦quir¦ing¦ly var.
  of inquiringly
en¦quiry var. of
  inquiry
en¦rage
  en¦raging
en rap¦port
en¦rapt
en¦rap¦ture
  en¦rap¦tur¦ing
en¦rich
en¦rich¦ment
en¦robe
  en¦rob¦ing
enrol *Br.*
  en¦rolled
  en¦rol¦ling
en¦roll *US*
en¦rol¦lee
en¦rol¦ler
en¦roll¦ment *US*
en¦rol¦ment *Br.*
en route
ENSA =
  Entertainments
  National Service
  Association
En¦schede

en¦sconce
  en¦scon¦cing
en¦sem¦ble
en¦sheath
  en¦sheathes
  en¦sheathed
  en¦sheath¦ing
en¦sheath¦ment
en¦shrine
  en¦shrin¦ing
en¦shrine¦ment
en¦shroud
en¦si¦form
en¦sign
en¦sil¦age
  en¦sil¦aging
en¦sile
  en¦sil¦ing
en¦slave
  en¦slav¦ing
en¦slave¦ment
en¦slaver
en¦snare
  en¦snar¦ing
en¦snare¦ment
en¦snarl
Ensor, James artist
en¦sor¦cel *US* var. of
  ensorcell
en¦sor¦cell
en¦sor¦cell¦ment
en¦soul
en¦soul¦ment
en¦sta¦tite
en¦sue
  en¦su¦ing
en suite
en¦sure
  en¦sur¦ing
  make sure; cf.
  insure
en¦swathe
  en¦swath¦ing
en¦tab¦la¦ture
en¦table¦ment
en¦tail
en¦tail¦ment
ent¦ameba *US*
  ent¦amebae or
  ent¦amebas
ent¦amoeba *Br.*
  ent¦amoe¦bae or
  ent¦amoe¦bas

en¦tan¦gle
  en¦tan¦gling
en¦tangle¦ment
en¦tasis
  en¦tases
En¦tebbe
en¦tel¦echy
  en¦tel¦echies
en¦tel¦lus
en¦telo¦dont
en¦tendre in 'double
  entendre' etc.
en¦tente
  en¦ticing
En¦tente Cor¦di¦ale
enter
en¦ter¦al
en¦ter¦ic
en¦ter¦itis
en¦tero¦coccus
  en¦tero¦cocci
en¦tero¦coel
en¦tero¦coel¦ic
en¦tero¦coely
  en¦tero¦coelies
en¦tero¦coli¦tis
en¦tero¦cyte
en¦tero¦hepat¦ic
en¦ter¦op¦athy
  en¦ter¦op¦athies
en¦ter¦os¦tomy
  en¦ter¦os¦tomies
en¦tero¦tox¦aemia
  Br.
en¦tero¦tox¦emia
  US
en¦tero¦toxi¦gen¦ic
en¦tero¦toxin
en¦tero¦virus
en¦ter¦prise
en¦ter¦priser
en¦ter¦pris¦ing
en¦ter¦pris¦ing¦ly
en¦ter¦tain
en¦ter¦tain¦er
en¦ter¦tain¦ing¦ly
en¦ter¦tain¦ment
en¦thalpy
  en¦thal¦pies
en¦thral *Br.*
  en¦thrals
  en¦thralled
  en¦thral¦ling
en¦thrall *US*
en¦thrall¦ment *US*

en¦thral¦ment *Br.*
en¦throne
  en¦thron¦ing
en¦throne¦ment
en¦thuse
  en¦thus¦ing
en¦thu¦si¦asm
en¦thu¦si¦ast
en¦thu¦si¦as¦tic
en¦thu¦si¦as¦tic¦al¦ly
en¦thy¦meme
en¦tice
  en¦ticing
en¦tice¦ment
en¦ticer
en¦ticing¦ly
en¦tire
en¦tire¦ly
en¦tir¦ety
  en¦tir¦eties
enti¦sol
en¦ti¦ta¦tive
en¦title
  en¦titling
en¦title¦ment
en¦tity
  en¦tities
en¦tomb
en¦tomb¦ment
en¦to¦mo¦logic¦al
en¦to¦molo¦gist
en¦to¦mol¦ogy
en¦to¦mopha¦gist
en¦to¦mopha¦gous
en¦to¦mophagy
en¦to¦moph¦il¦ous
en¦to¦mophily
ento¦proct
Ento¦procta
ent¦optic
en¦tou¦rage
en¦tr'acte
en¦trails
en¦train board a
  train; carry along
en¦train enthusiasm
en¦train¦ment
en¦tram¦mel
  en¦tram¦melled *Br.*
  en¦tram¦meled *US*
  en¦tram¦mel¦ling
  Br.

en¦tram¦mel¦ing
  US
en¦trance
  en¦tran¦cing
en¦trance¦ment
en¦tran¦cing¦ly
en¦trant
en¦trap
  en¦trapped
  en¦trap¦ping
en¦trap¦ment
en tra¦vesti
en¦treat
en¦treaty
  en¦treaties
entre¦chat
en¦tre¦côte
en¦trée
entre¦mets
en¦trench
en¦trench¦ment
entre nous
entre¦pôt
entre¦pre¦neur
entre¦pre¦neur¦ial
entre¦pre¦neur¦ial¦
  ism
entre¦pre¦neur¦
  ial¦ly
entre¦pre¦neur¦ism
entre¦pre¦neur¦
  ship
entre¦sol
en¦trism var. of
  entryism
en¦trist var. of
  entryist
en¦trop¦ic
en¦tro¦pion
en¦tropy
  en¦tro¦pies
en¦trust
en¦trust¦ment
entry
  en¦tries
entry¦ism
entry¦ist
entry¦phone
  trademark
entry¦way
ents =
  entertainments
en¦twine
  en¦twin¦ing

en|twine|ment
enu|cle|ate
  enu|cle|at|ing
enu|cle|ation
E-number
enu|mer|able
  countable; cf.
  innumerable
enu|mer|ate
  enu|mer|at|ing
  mention; count; cf.
  innumerate
enu|mer|ation
enu|mera|tive
enu|mer|ator
enun|ci|ate
  enun|ci|at|ing
enun|ci|ation
enun|cia|tive
enun|ci|ator
enure
  en|ur|ing
  Law take effect; cf.
  inure
en|ur|esis
en|ur|et|ic
enurn var. of inurn
en|velop v.
en|ve|lope n.
en|velop|ment
en|venom
en|venom|ate
  en|venom|at|ing
en|venom|ation
en ventre sa mère
Enver Pasha
  Turkish leader
en|vi|able
en|vi|ably
en|vi|er
en|vi|ous
en|vi|ous|ly
en|viron
en|vir|on|ment
en|vir|on|men|tal
en|vir|on|men|tal|
          ism
en|vir|on|men|tal|
         ist
en|vir|on|
      men|tal|ly
en|vir|ons
en|vis|age
  en|vis|aging

en|vi|sion
envoi concluding
  stanza or passage
envoy messenger,
  representative; also
  var. of envoi
envy
  en|vies
  en|vied
  envy|ing
en|wrap
  en|wrapped
  en|wrap|ping
en|wreathe
  en|wreath|ing
Enzed
En|zed|der
en|zo|ot|ic
en|zym|at|ic
en|zyme
en|zym|ic
en|zymo|logic|al
en|zym|olo|gist
en|zym|ology
Eo|cene
eo|hip|pus
eo ipso
eo|lian *US*
  Br. aeolian
eo|lith
Eo|lith|ic
eon *US*
  Br. aeon
Eos Greek goddess
eosin
eo|sino|phil
eo|sino|philia
eo|sino|phil|ic
epact
ep|arch
ep|archy
  ep|arch|ies
ep|au|let *US*
ep|au|lette *Br.*
ep|axial
épée
épée|ist
epeiro|gen|esis
epeiro|gen|ic
epeir|ogeny
epen|dyma
epen|dymal

epen|thesis
  epen|theses
epen|thet|ic
ep|ergne
ep|exe|gesis
ep|exe|geses
ep|exc|get|ic
ephah
eph|ebe
eph|ebic
eph|edra
ephe|drine
ephem|era
ephem|eral
ephem|eral|ity
ephem|eral|ly
ephem|eris
  ephem|er|ides
ephem|er|ist
Ephem|er|op|tera
ephem|er|op|ter|an
Ephe|sian
Eph|esus
ephod
ephor
eph|or|ate
Eph|raim
eph|yra
  eph|yrae
epi|ben|thic
epi|ben|thos
epi|blast
epic
epic|al
ep|ic|al|ly
epi|can|thic
epi|car|dial
epi|car|dium
  epi|car|dia
epi|carp
epi|ce|dian
epi|ce|dium
  epi|ce|dia
epi|cene
epi|cen|ter *US*
epi|cen|tral
epi|centre *Br.*
epi|con|dy|lar
epi|con|dyle
epi|con|dyl|itis
epi|con|tin|en|tal
epi|cor|mic
epi|cotyl

epi|crit|ic
epi|cure
Epi|cur|ean of
  Epicurus
epi|cur|ean devoted
  to enjoyment
Epi|cur|ean|ism
epi|cur|ism
Epi|curus
  philosopher
epi|cuticle
epi|cuticu|lar
epi|cycle
epi|cyc|lic
epi|cyc|loid
epi|cyc|loid|al
Epi|daurus
epi|deic|tic
epi|dem|ic
epi|demio|logic|al
epi|demi|olo|gist
epi|demi|ology
epi|der|mal
epi|der|mic
epi|der|mis
epi|derm|oid
epi|derm|oly|sis
  (bul|losa)
epi|dia|scope
epi|didy|mal
epi|didy|mis
  epi|didy|mides
epi|dote
epi|dural
epi|fauna
epi|faun|al
epi|fluor|es|cence
epi|gas|tric
epi|gas|trium
  epi|gas|tria
epi|geal
epi|gene
epi|gen|esis
epi|gen|esist
epi|gen|et|ic
epi|gen|eti|cist
epi|gen|et|ics
epi|glot|tal
epi|glot|tic
epi|glot|tis
epi|gone
  epi|gones or
  epig|oni

epi|gram
epi|gram|mat|ic
epi|gram|mat|ic|
    al|ly
epi|gram|ma|tise
    Br. var. of
    epigrammatize
epi|gram|ma|tist
epi|gram|ma|tize
    epi|gram|
        ma|tiz|ing
epi|graph
epig|raph|er
epi|graph|ic
epig|raph|ist
epig|raphy
epi|gy|nous
epi|gyny
    epi|gynies
epil|ate
    epil|at|ing
epil|ation
epil|ator
epi|lepsy
epi|lep|tic
epi|lepto|gen|ic
epi|lim|nion
    epi|lim|nia
epi|lith|ic
epi|log *US* var. of
    epilogue
epi|logue
epi|medium
epi|mer
epi|mer|ic
epim|er|ise *Br.* var.
    of epimerize
epi|mer|ism
epim|er|ize
    epim|er|iz|ing
epi|meron
    epi|mera or
    epi|mer|ons
epi|my|sium
epi|neph|rine
epi|ni|clan
Epi|palaeo|lith|ic
    Br.
Epi|paleo|lith|ic
    US
epi|phan|ic
epiph|any
    epiph|anies
epi|phe|nom|en|al

epi|phe|nom|enon
    epi|phe|nom|ena
epiph|ora
epi|phyl|lum
epi|phys|eal
epiphy|sis
    epiphy|ses
epi|phyt|al
epi|phyte
epi|phyt|ic
Epi|rus
epis|co|pacy
    epis|co|pa|cies
epis|co|pal
epis|co|pa|lian
epis|co|pa|lian|ism
epis|co|pal|ism
epis|co|pate
epi|scope
epi|sem|at|ic
episi|ot|omy
    episi|oto|mies
epi|sode
epi|sod|ic
epi|sod|ic|al|ly
epi|some
epis|ta|sis
    epis|ta|ses
epi|stat|ic
epi|staxis
    epi|staxes
epi|stem|ic
epis|temo|logic|al
epis|temo|log|ic|
        al|ly
epis|tem|olo|gist
epis|tem|ol|ogy
    epis|tem|olo|gies
epi|ster|num
    epi|sterna or
    epi|ster|nums
epis|tle
epis|tol|ary
epis|trophe
epi|style
epi|taph
epi|tax|ial
epi|taxy
epi|tha|lam|ic
epi|tha|la|mium
    epi|tha|la|miums
    or epi|tha|la|mia

epi|thal|amus
    epi|thal|ami
epi|the|lial
epi|the|lium
    epi|the|lia
epi|thet
epi|thet|ic
epit|ome
epit|om|isa|tion *Br.*
    var. of
    epitomization
epit|om|ise *Br.* var.
    of epitomize
epit|om|ist
epit|om|iza|tion
epit|om|ize
    epit|om|iz|ing
epi|tope
epi|zoic
epi|zo|ite
epi|zoon
    epi|zoa
epi|zo|ot|ic
epoch
epoch|al
epode
ep|onym
eponym|ous
eponym|ously
EPOS = electronic
    point of sale
ep|ox|ide
epoxy
    epox|ies
epox|ied
epoxy|ing
EPROM = erasable
    programmable
    read-only memory
ep|si|lon
Ep|stein, Jacob
    sculptor
Epstein–Barr
epyl|lion
    epyl|lia
equa|bil|ity
equ|able
equ|ably
equal
    equalled *Br.*
    equaled *US*
    equal|ling *Br.*
    equal|ing *US*

equal|isa|tion *Br.*
    var. of equalization
equal|ise *Br.* var. of
    equalize
equal|iser *Br.* var. of
    equalizer
equali|tar|ian
equali|tar|ian|ism
equal|ity
    equal|ities
equal|iza|tion
equal|ize
    equal|iz|ing
equal|izer
equal|ly
equa|nim|ity
equani|mous
equant
equat|able
equate
    equat|ing
equa|tion
equa|tion|al
equa|tive
equa|tor
equa|tor|ial
equa|tori|al|ly
equerry
    equer|ries
eques
    equi|tes
eques|trian
eques|tri|an|ism
eques|tri|enne
    female
equi|angu|lar
equid
equi|dis|tance
equi|dis|tant
equi|dis|tant|ly
equi|final
equi|final|ity
equi|lat|eral
equili|brate
    equili|brat|ing
equili|bra|tion
equili|bra|tor
equi|lib|rial
equili|brist
equi|lib|rium
    equi|lib|ria or
    equi|lib|riums
equine

equi|noc|tial
equi|nox
equip
  equipped
  equip|ping
equip|age
equi|par|ti|tion
equi|par|tl|tioned
equip|ment
equi|poise
  equi|pois|ing
equi|pol|ence
equi|pol|lence
equi|pol|lency
equi|pol|lent
equipo|tent
equi|poten|tial
equip|per
equi|prob|abil|ity
equi|prob|able
equi|setum
  equi|seta or
  equi|setums
equit|abil|ity
equit|able
equit|ably
equit|ant
equi|ta|tion
equity
  equi|ties
equiva|lence
equiva|lency
  equiva|len|cies
equiva|lent
equiva|lent|ly
equivo|cal
equivo|cal|ity
equivo|cal|ly
equivo|cate
  equivo|cat|ing
equivo|ca|tion
equivo|ca|tor
equivo|ca|tory
Equu|leus
er hesitation; cf. err
era
erad|ic|able
eradi|cant
eradi|cate
  eradi|cat|ing
eradi|ca|tion
eradi|ca|tor
eras|able

erase
eras|ing
eraser
Eras|mus,
  Desi|der|ius Dutch
  scholar
Eras|tian
Eras|tian|ism
Eras|tus
  Swiss theologian
  and physician
eras|ure
Erato
Era|tos|thenes
  Greek scholar
er|bium
Ere|bus
Erech|theum
erect
erect|able
erect|ile
erec|tion
erect|ly
erect|ness
erect|or
er|em|ite
er|em|it|ic
er|em|it|ic|al
ereth|ism
Ere|van var. of
  Yerevan
ere|while
erf plot of land
  erfs or erven
Er|furt
erg unit of energy
erg sand dunes
  ergs or areg
erga|tive
erga|tiv|ity
ergo
ergo|cal|cif|erol
erg|odic
ergo|di|city
erg|om|eter
ergo|met|rine
ergo|nom|ic
ergo|nom|ic|al|ly
ergo|nom|ics
er|gono|mist
ergo|sphere

er|gos|terol
ergot
er|gota|mine
er|got|ism
erhu
erica
eri|ca|ceous
Erics|son, John
  Swedish engineer
Erics|son, Leif
  Norse explorer
Eri|danus
Erie, Lake
erig|eron
Eriks|son, Leif var.
  of Ericsson, Leif
Erin
Erinys
  Erinyes
  Greek Fury
eris|tic
Eri|trea
Eri|trean
erk naval rating; air-
  craftman; disliked
  person; cf. irk
Er|len|meyer
erl-king
er|mine
er|min|ois
Er|min|trude
ern US
  eagle; cf. earn, urn
erne Br.
  eagle; cf. earn, urn
Er|nest
Er|nest|ine
Ernst, Max artist
erode
  erod|ing
erod|ible
er|ogen|ous
Eros
ero|sion
ero|sion|al
ero|sive
erot|ic
erot|ica
erot|ic|al|ly
eroti|cisa|tion
  Br. var. of
  eroticization

eroti|cise Br.
  var. of eroticize
eroti|cism
eroti|ciza|tion
eroti|cize
  eroti|ciz|ing
crot|ism
eroto|gen|ic
erot|ogen|ous
erot|ology
eroto|mania
eroto|maniac
err be mistaken; cf.
  er
er|rancy
er|rand
er|rant
er|rant|ry
  er|rant|ries
er|rat|ic
er|rat|ic|al|ly
er|rati|cism
er|ratum
  er|rata
Er Rif
Errol
er|ro|ne|ous
er|ro|ne|ous|ly
error
error|less
er|satz
Erse
erst
erst|while
Erté designer
eru|cic
eruc|ta|tion
eru|dite
eru|dite|ly
eru|di|tion
erupt break out
  suddenly; eject
  lava; cf. irrupt
erup|tion breakout;
  ejection of lava; cf.
  irruption
erup|tive
eruv
eru|vim
eryn|gium
eryngo
eryn|gos or
eryn|goes

ery|sip|elas
ery|sip|eloid
ery|thema
ery|themal
ery|them|at|ic
ery|thema|tous
eryth|rism
eryth|ri|tol
erythro|blast
erythro|blast|ic
erythro|blast|osis
erythro|cyte
erythro|cyt|ic
erythro|gen|ic
eryth|roid
erythro|
  leu|kae|mia Br.
erythro|leu|ke|mia
  US
erythro|mycin
eryth|ro|nium
  eryth|ro|niums or
  eryth|ro|nia
erythro|poi|esis
erythro|poi|etic
erythro|poi|etin
Erz|ge|birge
Erzu|rum
Es|bjerg
esca|beche
es|ca|drille
es|cal|ade
es|cal|ate
  es|cal|at|ing
es|cal|ation
es|cal|ator
es|cal|lo|nia
es|cal|lop Heraldry
es|cal|ope meat
es|cap|able
es|cap|ade
es|cape
  es|cap|ing
es|capee
es|cape|ment
es|caper
es|cap|ism
es|cap|ist
es|cap|olo|gist
es|cap|ology
es|car|got
es|ca|role
es|carp|ment

es|char
eschato|logic|al
eschat|olo|gist
eschat|ology
es|ch|aton
es|cheat
Escher, M. C. artist
es|chew
es|chew|al
esch|scholt|zia var.
  of eschscholzia
esch|schol|zia
Es|cof|fier,
  Georges-Auguste
  chef
es|co|llar
Es|cor|ial
es|cort
es|cri|toire
es|crow
es|cudo +s
es|cu|lent
es|cut|cheon
Es|dras
eser|ine
Es|fa|han var. of
  Isfahan
Es|kimo +s may
  cause offence
Eskimo-Aleut
esky
  es|kies trademark
Es|mer|alda
Es|mond
ESOL = English for
  speakers of other
  languages
esopha|geal US
  Br. oesophageal
esopha|gitis US
  Br. oesophagitis
esoph|ago|scope
  US
  Br.
  oesophagoscope
esopha|gus US
  esoph|agi
  Br. oesophagus
eso|ter|ic
eso|ter|ica
eso|ter|ic|al|ly
eso|teri|cism
eso|teri|cist
es|pada

es|pa|drille
es|pal|ier
es|parto +s
es|pe|cial
es|pe|cial|ly
Es|per|ant|ist
Es|per|anto
es|pial
es|pi|on|age
Es|pír|ito Santo
es|plan|ade
cs|pousal
es|pouse
  es|pous|ing
es|pouser
es|pres|sivo
es|presso +s
es|prit
es|prit de corps
es|prit de
  l'es|cal|ier
espy
  espies
  espied
  espy|ing
Es|qui|pu|las
es|quire
essay
es|say|ist
essay|ist|ic
esse
Essen
es|sence
Es|sene
es|sen|tial
es|sen|tial|ism
es|sen|tial|ist
es|sen|ti|al|ity
es|sen|tial|ly
Esse|quibo
Essex
es|tab|lish
cs|tab|lish|er
es|tab|lish|ment
es|tab|lish|ment|
    arian
es|tab|lish|ment|
    arian|ism
es|tam|inet
estan|cia
es|tate
es|teem
Es|telle

ester
es|ter|ase
es|ter|ify
  es|teri|fies
  es|teri|fied
  es|teri|fy|ing
Es|ther
es|thete US var. of
  aesthete
es|thet|ic US var. of
  aesthetic
es|thet|ic|al|ly US
  var. of aesthetically
es|thet|ician US
  var. of aesthetician
es|theti|cism US
  var. of aestheticism
es|thet|ics US var.
  of aesthetics
Es|tima
es|tim|able
es|tim|ably
es|ti|mate
  es|ti|mat|ing
es|ti|ma|tion
es|tima|tive
es|ti|ma|tor
es|tival US
  Br. aestival
es|tiv|ate US
  es|tiv|at|ing
  Br. aestivate
es|tiv|ation US
  Br. aestivation
es|toile
Es|tonia
Es|to|nian
estop
es|topped
es|top|ping
es|top|pel
Esto|ril
est|overs
es|tra|diol US
  Br. oestradiol
es|trange
es|tran|ging
es|trange|ment
es|treat
es|treat|ment
Es|tre|ma|dura
  Spanish name for
  Extremadura

es|triol *US*
  Br. oestriol
es|tro|gen *US*
  Br. oestrogen
es|tro|gen|ic *US*
  Br. oestrogenic
es|trone *US*
  Br. oestrone
es|trous *US adj.*
  Br. oestrous
es|trum *US*
  Br. oestrum
es|trus *US n.*
  Br. oestrus
es|tu|ar|ial
es|tu|ar|ine
es|tu|ary
  es|tu|ar|ies
es|tufa
esuri|ent
Esz|ter|gom
ETA Basque separ-
  atist movement
eta Greek letter
eta|gere
  French étagère
e-tailer
eta|lon
et cet|era
et|cet|eras
etch
etch|ant
etch|er
eter|nal
eter|nal|ise *Br.* var.
  of eternalize
eter|nal|ity
eter|nal|ize
  eter|nal|iz|ing
eter|nal|ly
eter|nise *Br.* var. of
  eternize
eter|nity
  eter|nities
eter|nize
  eter|niz|ing
Et|es|ian
eth
etha|cryn|ic
eth|am|butol
Ethan
etha|nal
eth|ana|mide
eth|ane

eth|ane|dioic
eth|ane|diol
eth|ano|ate
eth|an|oic
etha|nol
eth|chlor|vynol
Ethel
Ethel|red
eth|ene
ether
ether|eal
ether|eal|ise *Br.* var.
  of etherealize
ethere|al|ity
ether|eal|ize
  ether|eal|iz|ing
ether|eal|ly
ether|ial var. of
  ethereal
ether|ial|ly var. of
  ethereally
eth|er|ic
eth|er|isa|tion *Br.*
  var. of etherization
eth|er|ise *Br.* var. of
  etherize
eth|er|iza|tion
eth|er|ize
  eth|er|iz|ing
Ether|net
ethic
eth|ic|al
eth|ic|al|ity
eth|ic|al|ly
ethi|cist
eth|ics
eth|idium
Ethi|opia
Ethi|op|ian
Ethi|op|ic
eth|moid
eth|moid|al
Ethna
eth|nic
eth|nic|al|ly
eth|ni|city
ethno|archaeo|
      logic|al
ethno|archae|
      olo|gist
ethno|archae|ology
ethno|archeo|
      logic|al *US*

var. of ethno-
  archaeological
ethno|arche|
      olo|gist *US*
var. of ethno-
  archaeologist
ethno|arche|ology
  US var. of
  ethnoarchaeology
ethno|botan|ic|al
ethno|botan|ist
ethno|botany
ethno|cen|tric
ethno|cen|tric|al|ly
ethno|cen|tri|city
ethno|cen|trism
ethno|cide
ethno|cul|tur|al
ethno|gen|esis
eth|nog|raph|er
ethno|graph|ic
ethno|graph|ic|
      al|ly
eth|nog|raphy
  eth|nog|raph|ies
ethno|his|tor|ian
ethno|his|toric
ethno|his|tor|ic|al
ethno|his|tory
ethno|lin|guist
ethno|lin|guis|tic
ethno|lin|guis|tics
ethno|logic|al
ethno|logic|al|ly
eth|nolo|gist
eth|nol|ogy
ethno|meth|odo|
      logic|al
ethno|meth|od|
      olo|gist
ethno|method|
      ology
ethno|musico|
      logic|al
ethno|music|
      olo|gist
ethno|music|ology
ethno|science
etho|gram
etho|logic|al
etho|logic|al|ly
eth|olo|gist
eth|ol|ogy
ethos

eth|oxy|ethane
ethyl
ethyl|ben|zene
ethyl|ene
ethyl|ene|di|amine
eth|yne
etic
eti|ol|ated
eti|ola|tion
etio|logic *US*
  Br. aetiologic
etio|logic|al *US*
  Br. aetiological
etio|logic|al|ly *US*
  Br. aetiologically
eti|ology *US*
  eti|olo|gies
  Br. aetiology
eti|quette
Etna
Eton
Eton|ian
Eto|sha Pan
étouffée
etrier
  French étrier
Etru|ria
Etru|rian
Etrus|can
Etrusc|ol|ogy
étude
etui
  French étui
etymo|logic|al
etymo|logic|al|ly
ety|molo|gise *Br.*
  var. of etymologize
ety|molo|gist
ety|molo|gize
  ety|molo|giz|ing
ety|mol|ogy
  ety|molo|gies
ety|mon
  ety|mons or etyma
eu|bac|ter|ial
eu|bac|ter|ium
eu|bac|teria
Eu|boea
eu|ca|lypt
eu|ca|lyp|tus
  eu|ca|lyp|tuses or
  eu|ca|lypti
eu|cary|ote var. of
  eukaryote

eu|cary|ot|ic var. of
   eukaryotic
Eu|char|ist
Eu|char|is|tic
eu|chre
   euch|ring
eu|chro|mat|ic
eu|chroma|tin
Eu|clid
   mathematician
Eu|clid|ean
eu|crite
eu|cryphia
eu|daemon|ism
eu|daemon|ist
eu|daemon|is|tic
eu|demon|ism var.
   of eudaemonism
eu|demon|ist var. of
   eudaemonist
eu|demon|is|tic var.
   of eudaemonistic
eudi|om|et|er
eudio|met|ric
eudi|om|etry
Eu|dora
Eu|gene
Eu|ge|nia
eu|gen|ic
eu|gen|ic|al|ly
eu|geni|cist
eu|gen|ics
Eugé|nie French
   empress
eu|gen|ist
eu|gen|ol
eu|glena
eu|glen|oid
eu|he|dral
eu|kary|ote
eu|kary|ot|ic
eu|la|chon
Euler, Leon|hard
   mathematician
eu|lo|gise Br. var. of
   eulogize
eu|lo|gist
eu|lo|gis|tic
eu|lo|gis|tic|al|ly
eu|lo|gium
   eu|lo|giums or
   eu|lo|gia

eu|lo|gize
eu|lo|giz|ing
eu|logy
eu|logies
Eu|men|ides
Eu|nice
eu|nuch
eu|ony|mus
eu|pep|tic
eu|phau|siid
Eu|phe|mia
eu|phem|ise Br. var.
   of euphemize
eu|phem|ism
eu|phem|is|tic
eu|phem|is|tic|al|ly
eu|phem|ize
eu|phem|iz|ing
eu|phon|ic
eu|pho|ni|ous
eu|pho|ni|ous|ly
eu|phon|ise Br. var.
   of euphonize
eu|pho|nium
eu|phon|ize
eu|phon|iz|ing
eu|phony
eu|phonies
eu|phor|bia
eu|phoria
eu|phori|ant
eu|phor|ic
eu|phor|ic|al|ly
eu|phra|sia
Eu|phra|tes
eu|phu|ism
eu|phu|ist
eu|phu|is|tic
eu|ploid
eu|ploidy
eu|ploi|dies
Eur|asia
Eur|asian
Eur|atom
eur|eka
eu|rhyth|mics Br.
   US eurythmics
eu|rhythmy Br.
   US eurythmy
Eu|ripi|des
   dramatist
Euro European

euro
   pl. euros or euro
   currency
euro +s animal
Euro|bond
Euro|cen|tric
Euro|cen|tri|city
Euro|cen|trism
Euro|
      com|mun|ism
Euro|com|mun|ist
Euro|crat
euro|creep
Euro|cur|rency
Euro|dol|lar
Euro-election
Euro|land
Euro|mar|ket
Euro-MP
Eur|opa
Euro|par|lia|ment
Euro|par|lia|men|
      tar|ian
Euro|par|lia|ment|
      ary
Eur|ope
Euro|pean
Euro|pean|isa|tion
   Br. var. of
   Europeanization
Euro|pean|ise Br.
   var. of
   Europeanize
Euro|pean|ism
Euro|pean|iza|tion
Euro|pean|ize
   Euro|pean|iz|ing
Euro|phile
euro|pium
Euro|poort
Euro|pop
Euro-sceptic
Euro-scepticism
Euro|star
   trademark
Euro|style cf.
   urostyle
Euro|trash
Euro|vision
Euro|zone
eury|apsid
Eury|dice
eury|hal|ine

eur|yp|terid
eury|ther|mal
eu|ryth|mics US
   Br. eurhythmics
eu|rythmy US
   Br. eurhythmy
eury|topic
Eu|se|bio, Fer|raira
   da Silva footballer
Eu|se|bius early
   bishop
Eus|kara
eu|social
eu|soci|al|ity
eusol
Eus|tace
Eus|ta|chian
eu|stasy
eu|stat|ic
Eus|ton
eu|tec|tic
eu|tec|toid
Eu|terpe
eu|than|asia
eu|than|ise
   Br. var. of
   euthanize
eu|than|ize
eu|than|iz|ing
Eu|theria
eu|ther|ian
eu|thyr|oid
eu|troph|ic
eu|trophi|cate
eu|trophi|cat|ing
eu|trophi|ca|tion
evacu|ant
evacu|at|ing
evacu|ation
evacu|ative
evac|uee
evad|able
evade
evad|ing
evader
Evadne
eva|gin|ate
eva|gin|at|ing
eva|gin|ation
evalu|ate
evalu|at|ing
evalu|ation

evalu|ative
evalu|ator
evan|esce
　evan|es|cing
evan|es|cence
evan|es|cent
evan|es|cent|ly
evan|gel
evan|gel|ic|al
evan|gel|ic|al|ism
evan|gel|ic|al|ly
Evan|gel|ine
evan|gel|isa|tion
　Br. var. of
　evangelization
evan|gel|ise Br. var.
　of evangelize
evan|gel|iser Br.
　var. of evangelizer
evan|gel|ism
evan|gel|ist
evan|gel|is|tic
evan|gel|iza|tion
evan|gel|ize
　evan|gel|iz|ing
evan|gel|izer
evap|or|able
evap|or|ate
　evap|or|at|ing
evap|or|ation
evap|ora|tive
evap|or|ator
evap|or|ite
evapo|
　trans|pir|ation
eva|sion
eva|sive
eva|sive|ly
eva|sive|ness
evec|tion
Eve|lyn
even|ing
eve|ning|er
Evenki
even|ly
even|ness
even|song
even-steven
even-stevens var. of
　even-steven
event
event|er
event|ful

event|ful|ly
event|ful|ness
even|tide
event|ive
event|less
even|tual
even|tu|al|ity
even|tu|al|ly
even|tu|ate
　even|tu|at|ing
even|tu|ation
ever
Ever|est
Ever|glades
ever|green
ever|last|ing
ever|last|ing|ly
ever|more
evers|ible
ever|sion
Evert, Chris tennis
　player
evert turn inside out
every
every|body every-
　one
every body each
　body
every|day ordinary
every day each day
Every|man
every|one every per-
　son, everybody
every one each one
every|place
every|thing
every way
every|where
Every|woman
eve-teaser
eve-teasing
Ev|ette
evict
evic|tion
evict|or
evi|dence
　evi|den|cing
evi|dent
evi|den|tial
evi|den|ti|al|ity
evi|den|tial|ly
evi|den|tiary

evi|dent|ly
evil
evil-doer
evil-doing
evil|ly
evince
　evin|cing
evis|cer|ate
　evis|cer|at|ing
evis|cer|ation
Evita
evi|ter|nal
evi|tern|ity
evo|ca|tion
evoca|tive
evoca|tive|ly
evoca|tive|ness
evoke
　evok|ing
evoker
evo|lute
evo|lu|tion
evo|lu|tion|al
evo|lu|tion|al|ly
evo|lu|tion|ar|ily
evo|lu|tion|ary
evo|lu|tion|ism
evo|lu|tion|ist
evo|lu|tive
evolv|able
evolve
　evolv|ing
evolve|ment
Ev|onne
ev|zone
Ewart
Ewe people
ewe sheep; cf. yew,
　you
ewer jug
ex|acer|bate
　ex|acer|bat|ing
ex|acer|ba|tion
exact
exacta bet
exact|able
exact|ing|ly
exac|tion
exac|ti|tude
exact|ly
exact|ness
exact|or

ex|ag|ger|ate
　ex|ag|ger|at|ing
ex|ag|ger|ated|ly
ex|ag|ger|ation
ex|ag|gera|tive
ex|ag|ger|ator
exalt
exalt|ation
exalté
exam
exa|men de
　con|science
exa|mens de
　con|science
exam|in|able
exam|in|ation
examination-in-
　　　　chief
exam|ine
　exam|in|ing
exam|inee
exam|in|er
ex|ample
ex ante
ex|an|thema
　ex|an|the|mas or
　ex|an|the|mata
ex|an|the|mat|ic
ex|an|thema|tous
ex|ap|ta|tion
ex|arch +s
ex|arch|ate
ex|as|per|ate
　ex|as|per|at|ing
ex|as|per|at|ing|ly
ex|as|per|ation
Ex|cali|bur
ex cath|edra
ex|ca|vate
　ex|ca|vat|ing
ex|ca|va|tion
ex|ca|va|tor
ex|ceed go beyond;
　cf. accede
ex|ceed|ing|ly
excel
ex|celled
ex|cel|ling
ex|cel|lence
ex|cel|lency
　ex|cel|len|cies
ex|cel|lent
ex|cel|lent|ly
ex|cel|sior

ex|cen|tric *Biology*;
cf. eccentric
ex|cen|tric|al|ly
Biology; cf.
eccentrically
ex|cept leave out;
not including; cf.
accept
ex|cep|tion
ex|cep|tion|able
ex|cep|tion|al
ex|cep|tion|al|ism
ex|cep|tion|al|ity
ex|cep|tion|al|ly
ex|cerpt
ex|cerpt|ible
ex|cerp|tion
ex|cess
ex|ces|sive
ex|ces|sive|ly
ex|change
ex|chan|ging
ex|change|abil|ity
ex|change|able
ex|chan|ger
ex|chequer
ex|cimer chemical
compound; cf.
eczema
ex|cipi|ent
ex|cise
ex|cis|ing
ex|cise|man
ex|cise|men
ex|ci|sion
ex|ci|sion|al
ex|cit|abil|ity
ex|cit|able
ex|cit|ably
ex|cit|ant
ex|ci|ta|tion
ex|ci|ta|tory
ex|cite
ex|cit|ing
ex|cited|ly
ex|cite|ment
ex|citer
ex|cit|ing|ly
ex|citon
ex|claim
ex|clam|ation
ex|clama|tory
ex|clave

ex|clos|ure
ex|clud|able
ex|clude
ex|clud|ing
ex|cluder
ex|clu|sion
ex|clu|sion|ary
ex|clu|sion|ist
ex|clu|sive
ex|clu|sive|ly
ex|clu|sive|ness
ex|clu|siv|ism
ex|clu|siv|ist
ex|clu|siv|ity
ex|cogi|tate
ex|cogi|tat|ing
ex|cogi|ta|tion
ex|com|mu|ni|cant
ex|com|mu|ni|cate
ex|com|mu|ni|
cat|ing
ex|com|mu|ni|
ca|tion
ex|com|mu|ni|
ca|tive
ex|com|mu|ni|
ca|tor
ex|com|mu|ni|
ca|tory
ex-con
ex|cori|ate
ex|cori|at|ing
ex|cori|ation
ex|cre|ment
ex|cre|men|tal
ex|cres|cence
ex|cres|cent
ex|creta body waste;
cf. excreter
ex|crete
ex|cret|ing
ex|creter person or
thing that excretes;
cf. excreta
ex|cre|tion
ex|cre|tive
ex|cre|tory
ex|cru|ci|at|ing
ex|cru|ci|at|ing|ly
ex|cul|pate
ex|cul|pat|ing
ex|cul|pa|tion
ex|cul|pa|tory
ex|cur|rent

ex|cur|sion
ex|cur|sion|ist
ex|cur|sus
ex|cus|able
ex|cus|ably
ex|cusal
ex|cusa|tory
ex|cuse
ex|cus|ing
ex|cuse me apology
excuse-me dance
ex-directory
ex div. = ex
dividend
ex divi|dend
Exe river
exeat
exec
exe|crable
exe|crably
exe|crate
exe|crat|ing
exe|cra|tion
exe|cra|tive
exe|cra|tory
ex|ecu|tant
exe|cute
exe|cut|ing
exe|cu|tion
exe|cu|tion|er
ex|ecu|tive
exe|cu|tor of a will
exe|cu|tor of a plan
etc.
exe|cu|tor|ship
ex|ecu|tory
ex|ecu|trix *female*
ex|ecu|tri|ces
exe|dra
exe|drae
exe|gesis
exe|geses
exe|gete
exe|get|ic|al
exe|ge|tist
ex|em|plar
ex|em|plar|ity
ex|em|plary
ex|em|pli|fi|ca|tion
ex|em|pli|fies
ex|em|pli|fied

ex|em|pli|fy|ing
ex|em|plum
ex|em|pla
ex|empt
ex|emp|tion
ex|en|ter|ation
exe|qua|tur
exe|quy
exe|quies
ex|er|cis|able
ex|er|cise
ex|er|cis|ing
mental or physical
activity; cf.
exorcize
ex|er|ciser
exer|cycle
trademark
ex|er|gon|ic
ex|ergue
exert exercise; cf.
exsert
ex|er|tion
Exe|ter
exe|unt
ex|fil|trate
ex|fil|trat|ing
ex|fil|tra|tion
ex|foli|ant
ex|foli|ate
ex|foli|at|ing
ex|foli|ation
ex|folia|tive
ex|foli|ator
ex gra|tia
ex|hal|able
ex|hal|ation
ex|hale
ex|hal|ing
ex|haust
ex|haust|ed|ly
ex|haust|er
ex|haust|ibil|ity
ex|haust|ible
ex|haust|ing|ly
ex|haus|tion
ex|haust|ive
ex|haust|ive|ly
ex|haust|ive|ness
ex|hibit
ex|hib|ition
ex|hib|ition|er
ex|hib|ition|ism

ex|hib|ition|ist
ex|hib|ition|is|tic
ex|hib|it|or
ex|hil|ar|ant
ex|hil|ar|ate
ex|hil|ar|at|ing
ex|hil|ar|at|ing|ly
ex|hil|ar|ation
ex|hil|ara|tive
ex|hort
ex|hort|ation
ex|hor|ta|tive
ex|hor|ta|tory
ex|hort|er
ex|hum|ation
ex|hume
ex|hum|ing
ex hy|poth|esi
exil|gence
exil|gency
exi|gen|cies
exil|gent
exil|gible
exi|gu|ity
ex|igu|ous
ex|igu|ous|ly
exile
ex|il|ing
exil|ic
exine
exist
ex|ist|ence
ex|ist|ent
ex|ist|en|tial
ex|ist|en|tial|ism
ex|ist|en|tial|ist
ex|ist|en|tial|ly
exit
ex lib|ris
Ex|moor
ex ni|hilo
exo|atmos|pher|ic
exo|bio|logic|al
exo|biolo|gist
exo|biol|ogy
exo|carp
exo|cen|tric
Exo|cet *trademark*
exo|crine
exo|cyt|osis
exo|cyt|ot|ic
exo|der|mis

exo|dus
exo|enzyme
ex of|fi|cio
ex|og|am|ous
ex|og|amy
exo|gen|ic
ex|ogen|ous
ex|ogen|ous|ly
exon *Biochemistry*;
  commander of Yeo-
  men of the Guard
ex|on|er|ate
  ex|on|er|at|ing
ex|on|er|ation
ex|on|era|tive
exo|nucle|ase
exo|pep|tid|ase
ex|oph|ora
exo|phor|ic
ex|oph|thal|mia
  var. of
  exophthalmos
ex|oph|thal|mic
ex|oph|thal|mos
ex|oph|thal|mus
  var. of
  exophthalmos
exo|planet
exo|pod
ex|opo|dite
ex|or|bi|tance
ex|or|bi|tant
ex|or|bi|tant|ly
ex|or|cise *Br.* var. of
  exorcize
ex|or|cism
ex|or|cist
ex|or|cize
  ex|or|ciz|ing
  drive away evil
  spirit; cf. exercise
ex|or|dial
ex|or|dium
  ex|or|diums or
  ex|or|dia
exo|skel|etal
exo|skel|eton
exo|sphere
exo|spher|ic
exo|sto|sis
  exo|sto|ses
exo|ter|ic
exo|ther|mal
exo|ther|mic

exot|ic
exot|ica
exot|ic|al|ly
exoti|cism
exo|toxin
ex|pand
ex|pand|abil|ity
ex|pand|able
ex|pand|er
ex|panse
ex|pan|si|bil|ity
ex|pan|sible
ex|pan|sile
ex|pan|sion
ex|pan|sion|ary
ex|pan|sion|ism
ex|pan|sion|ist
ex|pan|sion|is|tic
ex|pan|sive
ex|pan|sive|ly
ex|pan|sive|ness
ex|pan|siv|ity
ex parte
expat
ex|pati|ate
  ex|pati|at|ing
ex|pati|ation
ex|patri|ate
  ex|patri|at|ing
ex|patri|ation
ex|pect
ex|pect|able
ex|pect|ancy
  ex|pect|an|cies
ex|pect|ant
ex|pect|ant|ly
ex|pect|ation
ex|pect|ed|ly
ex|pec|tor|ant
ex|pec|tor|ate
  ex|pec|tor|at|ing
ex|pec|tor|ation
ex|pec|tor|ator
ex|pe|di|ence
ex|pe|di|ency
  ex|pe|di|en|cies
ex|pe|di|ent
ex|pe|di|ent|ly
ex|ped|ite
  ex|ped|it|ing
ex|ped|iter
ex|ped|ition
ex|ped|ition|ary

ex|ped|itious
ex|ped|itious|ly
ex|ped|itor var. of
  expediter
expel
  ex|pelled
  ex|pel|ling
ex|pel|lable
ex|pel|lee
ex|pel|ler
ex|pend
ex|pend|abil|ity
ex|pend|able
ex|pend|ably
ex|pend|iture
ex|pense
ex|pen|sive
ex|pen|sive|ly
ex|pen|sive|ness
ex|peri|ence
  ex|peri|en|cing
ex|peri|ence|able
ex|peri|en|cer
ex|peri|en|tial
ex|peri|en|tial|ism
ex|peri|en|tial|ly
ex|peri|ment
ex|peri|men|tal
ex|peri|men|tal|
           ism
ex|peri|men|tal|ist
ex|peri|men|tal|ly
ex|peri|men|ta|tion
ex|peri|ment|er
ex|pert
ex|pert|ise skill
ex|pert|ise *Br.* var.
  of expertize give
  expert opinion
ex|pert|ize
  ex|pert|iz|ing
  give expert opinion
ex|pert|ly
ex|pert|ness
ex|pi|able
ex|pi|ate
  ex|pi|at|ing
ex|pi|ation
ex|pi|ator
ex|pi|atory
ex|pir|ation
ex|pira|tory

ex|pire
  ex|pir|ing
ex|piry
  ex|pir|ies
ex|plain
ex|plain|able
ex|plain|er
ex|plan|an|dum
  ex|plan|anda
ex|plan|ans
  ex|plan|an|tia
ex|plan|ation
ex|plana|tor|ily
ex|plana|tory
ex|plant
ex|plant|ation
ex|ple|tive
ex|plic|able
ex|pli|can|dum
  ex|pli|canda
ex|pli|cans
  ex|pli|can|tia
ex|pli|cate
  ex|pli|cat|ing
ex|pli|ca|tion
ex|plica|tive
ex|pli|ca|tor
ex|pli|ca|tory
ex|pli|cit
ex|pli|cit|ly
ex|pli|cit|ness
ex|plode
  ex|plod|ing
ex|plo|der
ex|ploit
ex|ploit|able
ex|ploit|ation
ex|ploit|ative
ex|ploit|er
ex|ploit|ive
ex|plor|ation
ex|plor|ation|al
ex|plora|tive
ex|plora|tory
ex|plore
  ex|plor|ing
ex|plor|er
ex|plo|sion
ex|plo|sive
ex|plo|sive|ly
ex|plo|sive|ness
Expo +s
ex|po|nent

ex|po|nen|tial
ex|po|nen|tial|ly
ex|po|nen|ti|ate
  ex|po|nen|ti|at|ing
ex|po|nen|ti|ation
ex|port
ex|port|abil|ity
ex|port|able
ex|port|ation
ex|port|er
ex|pose
  ex|pos|ing
ex|posé
ex|poser
ex|pos|ition
ex|pos|ition|al
ex|posi|tor
ex|posi|tory
ex post
ex post facto
ex|pos|tu|late
  ex|pos|tu|lat|ing
ex|pos|tu|la|tion
ex|pos|tu|la|tor
ex|pos|tu|la|tory
ex|pos|ure
ex|pound
ex|pound|er
ex|press
ex|press|er
ex|press|ible
ex|pres|sion
ex|pres|sion|al
ex|pres|sion|ism
ex|pres|sion|ist
ex|pres|sion|is|tic
ex|pres|sion|less
ex|pres|sion|less|ly
ex|pres|sion|less|
      ness
ex|pres|sive
ex|pres|sive|ly
ex|pres|sive|ness
ex|pres|siv|ity
ex|press|ly
ex|presso var. of
  espresso
ex|press|way
ex|pro|pri|ate
  ex|pro|pri|at|ing
ex|pro|pri|ation
ex|pro|pri|ator
ex|pul|sion

ex|pul|sive
ex|punc|tion
ex|punge
  ex|pun|ging
ex|punge|ment
ex|pun|ger
ex|pur|gate
  ex|pur|gat|ing
ex|pur|ga|tion
ex|pur|ga|tor
ex|pur|ga|tory
ex|quis|ite
ex|quis|ite|ly
ex|san|guin|ate
  ex|san|guin|at|ing
ex|san|guin|ation
ex|san|guine
ex|sert *Biology* put
  forth; cf. **exert**
ex-service
ex-serviceman
ex-servicemen
ex-servicewoman
ex-servicewomen
ex si|len|tio
ex|solu|tion
ex|solve
  ex|solv|ing
ex|tant
ex|tem|por|an|eous
ex|tem|por|
    an|eous|ly
ex|tem|por|ar|ily
ex|tem|por|ary
ex|tem|pore
ex|tem|por|isa|tion
  Br. var. of
  extemporization
ex|tem|por|ise *Br.*
  var. of extemporize
ex|tem|por|iza|tion
ex|tem|por|ize
  ex|tem|por|iz|ing
ex|tend
ex|tend|abil|ity
ex|tend|able
ex|tend|er
ex|tend|ibil|ity var.
  of extendability
ex|tend|ible var. of
  extendable
ex|ten|si|bil|ity
ex|ten|sible
ex|ten|sile

ex|ten|sion
ex|ten|sion|al
ex|ten|sive
ex|ten|sive|ly
ex|ten|sive|ness
ex|tens|om|eter
ex|ten|sor
ex|tent
ex|tenu|ate
  ex|tenu|at|ing
ex|tenu|ation
ex|tenu|atory
ex|ter|ior
ex|ter|ior|isa|tion
  Br. var. of
  exteriorization
ex|ter|ior|ise *Br.*
  var. of exteriorize
ex|ter|ior|ity
ex|ter|ior|iza|tion
ex|ter|ior|ize
  ex|ter|ior|iz|ing
ex|ter|ior|ly
ex|ter|min|ate
  ex|ter|min|at|ing
ex|ter|min|ation
ex|ter|min|ator
ex|ter|min|atory
ex|tern
ex|ter|nal
ex|ter|nal|isa|tion
  Br. var. of
  externalization
ex|ter|nal|ise *Br.*
  var. of externalize
ex|ter|nal|ism
ex|ter|nal|ist
ex|ter|nal|ity
ex|ter|nal|ities
ex|ter|nal|iza|tion
ex|ter|nal|ize
  ex|ter|nal|iz|ing
ex|ter|nal|ly
ex|tern|ment
ex|tero|cep|tion
ex|tero|cep|tive
ex|tero|cep|tiv|ity
ex|tero|cep|tor
ex|tinct
ex|tinc|tion
ex|tin|guish
ex|tin|guish|able
ex|tin|guish|er

ex|tin|guish|ment
ex|tir|pate
  ex|tir|pat|ing
ex|tir|pa|tion
ex|tir|pa|tor
extol
  ex|tolled
  ex|tol|ling
cx|tol|ler
ex|tol|ment
ex|tort
ex|tort|er
ex|tor|tion
ex|tor|tion|ate
ex|tor|tion|ate|ly
ex|tor|tion|er
ex|tor|tion|ist
ex|tort|ive
extra
extra|cel|lu|lar
extra|
    chro|mo|som|al
extra|cor|por|eal
ex|tract
ex|tract|abil|ity
ex|tract|able
ex|trac|tion
ex|tract|ive
ex|tract|or
extra-curricu|lar
extra|dit|able
extra|dite
  extra|dit|ing
extra|di|tion
ex|tra|dos
extra|dural
extra|famil|ial
extra|flor|al
extra|gal|ac|tic
extra|judi|cial
extra|judi|cial|ly
extra|legal
extra|limit|al
extra|lin|guis|tic
extra|mari|tal
extra|mari|tal|ly
extra|mural
extra|mural|ly
extra|music|al
ex|tra|ne|ous
ex|tra|ne|ous|ly
extra|net

extra|or|din|aire
extra|or|din|ar|ily
extra|or|din|ary
  extra|or|din|ar|ies
ex|trapo|late
  ex|trapo|lat|ing
ex|trapo|la|tion
ex|trapo|la|tive
ex|trapo|la|tor
extra|pos|ition
extra|pyr|am|id|al
extra|sens|ory
extra|solar
extra|sys|tole
extra|ter|res|trial
extra|ter|ri|tor|ial
extra|ter|ri|tori|
     al|ity
extra|trop|ic|al
extra|uter|ine
ex|trava|gance
ex|trava|gant
ex|trava|gant|ly
ex|trava|ganza
ex|trava|sate
  ex|trava|sat|ing
ex|trava|sa|tion
extra|vas|cu|lar
extra|vehicu|lar
extra|ver|sion var.
  of extroversion
extra|vert var. of
  extrovert
extra|vert|ed var. of
  extroverted
ex|trema pl. of
  extremum
Ex|tre|ma|dura
ex|treme
  ex|trem|est
ex|treme|ly
ex|tremis in *'in
  extremis'*
ex|trem|ism
ex|trem|ist
ex|trem|ity
  ex|trem|ities
ex|tremo|phile
ex|tremum
  ex|trem|ums or
  ex|trema
ex|tric|able
ex|tri|cate
  ex|tri|cat|ing

ex|tri|ca|tion
ex|trin|sic
ex|trin|sic|al|ly
ex|tro|pian
ex|tropy
ex|trorse
ex|tro|ver|sion
ex|tro|vert
ex|tro|vert|ed
ex|trud|able
ex|trude
  ex|trud|ing
ex|tru|sile
ex|tru|sion
ex|tru|sive
ex|uber|ance
ex|uber|ant
ex|uber|ant|ly
ex|ud|ate
ex|ud|ation
ex|uda|tive
exude
  ex|ud|ing
exult
ex|ult|ancy
  ex|ult|an|cies
ex|ult|ant
ex|ult|ant|ly
ex|ult|ation
ex|ult|ing|ly
Exuma Cays
exurb
ex|urban
ex|ur|ban|ite
ex|ur|bia
ex|uviae
ex|uvial
ex|uvi|ate
  ex|uvi|at|ing
ex|uvi|ation
ex-voto +s
ex-works
eyas
  ey|asses or ey|ases
eye
  eye|ing or eying
eye|ball
eye|bath
eye|black
eye|bright
eye|brow
eye-catcher
eye-catching

eye-catchingly
eye|cup
eye|ful
eye|glass
eye|hole
eye|lash
eye|less
eye|let
eye|lid
eye|line
eye|liner
eye|patch
eye|piece
eye|shade
eye|shadow
eye|shot
eye|sight
eye|sore
eye splice
eye|spot
eye|stalk
Eye|tie *offensive*
eye|wash
eye|water
eye|wear
eye|wit|ness
eyot var. of **ait**
eyra
eyre court; cf. **air,
  e'er, ere, heir**
eyrie *Br.* nest; *US*
  aerie; cf. **Erie,
  eerie**
Ey|senck, Hans
  psychologist
Eze|kiel
e-zine

fa *Music*; var. of **fah**
fab
  fabbed
  fab|bing
  = fabulous;
  fabricate
faba bean; var. of
  fava
fabbo

fabby

Fab|ergé, Peter
Carl jeweller

Fabia

Fa|bian

Fa|bian|ism

Fa|bian|ist

Fa|bius Cunc|tator
general and
statesman

fable
fab|ling

fa|bler

fab|less

fab|liau
fab|li|aux

Fab|lon *trademark*

Fabre, Jean ento-
mologist

Fab|ri|ano, Gen|tile
da painter

fab|ric

fab|ri|cate
fab|ri|cat|ing

fab|ri|ca|tion

fab|ri|ca|tor

Fab|ri|cius, bursa
of

Fabry–Pérot

fabu|late
fabu|lat|ing

fabu|la|tion

fabu|la|tor

fabu|list

fabu|los|ity

fabu|lous

fabu|lous|ly

fabu|lous|ness

fa|cade
French fa|çade

face
fa|cing

face|ache

face|cloth

face|less

face|less|ness

face|lift

face-off *n.*

face|plate

facer

face-saver

face-saving

facet

fa|cet|ed

fa|cetiae

fa|cetious

fa|cetious|ly

fa|cetious|ness

facety

face|work|er

facia var. of **fascia**

fa|cial of a face; cf.
fascial

fa|cial|ly

fa|cies
pl. fa|cies

fa|cile

fa|cile|ly

fa|cile|ness

fa|cili|tate
fa|cili|tat|ing

fa|cili|ta|tion

fa|cili|ta|tive

fa|cili|ta|tor

fa|cili|ta|tory

fa|cil|ity

fa|cil|ities

fac|sim|ile

fac|sim|ile|ing

fact|find|er

fact-finding

fac|ti|city

fac|tion

fac|tion|al

fac|tion|al|ise *Br.*
var. of **factionalize**

fac|tion|al|ism

fac|tion|al|ize
fac|tion|al|iz|ing

fac|tion|al|ly

fac|tious

fac|tious|ly

fac|tious|ness

fac|ti|tious

fac|ti|tious|ly

fac|ti|tious|ness

fac|ti|tive

fac|tive

fac|toid

fac|tor

fac|tor|able

fac|tor|age

fac|tor eight var. of
factor VIII

fac|tor VIII

fac|tor|ial

fac|tori|al|ly

fac|tor|isa|tion *Br.*
var. of
factorization

fac|tor|ise *Br.* var. of
factorize

fac|tor|iza|tion

fac|tor|ize
fac|tor|iz|ing

fac|tory
fac|tor|ies

fac|to|tum

fac|tual

factu|al|ity

fact|ual|ly

fact|ual|ness

fac|tum
fac|tums or **facta**

fac|ture

fac|ula *n.*
facu|lae

facu|lar *adj.*

fac|ul|ta|tive

fac|ul|ta|tive|ly

fac|ulty
fac|ul|ties

fad|dily

fad|di|ness

fad|dish

fad|dish|ly

fad|dish|ness

fad|dism

fad|dist

faddy
fad|dier
fad|di|est

fade
fad|ing

fade-in *n.*

fade|less

fade-out *n.*

fader

fade-up *n.*

fado +s

fae|cal *Br.*
US **fecal**

fae|ces *Br.*
US **feces**

Fa|enza

fae|rie *archaic* fairy-
land; fairy; cf. **fairy**

Faeroe Islands; var.
of **Faroe**

Faero|ese var. of
Faroese

faery *archaic*; var. of
faerie

fag
fagged
fag|ging

fag|got homosexual;
food

fag|got *Br.*
bundle; embroider.
US **fagot**

fag|goty

faggy

Fagin character in
Dickens

fagot *US*
bundle; embroider.
Br. **faggot**; cf.
faggot

fah *Music*

fahl|erz

Fahr|en|heit

fai|ence
French **faïence**

fail not succeed; cf.
faille, fale

faille fabric; cf. **fail,
fale**

fail|over

fail-safe

fáilte welcome

fail|ure

fain gladly; cf. **fane,
feign**

fai|né|ant

faint lose conscious-
ness; pale, dim; cf.
feint

faint|ly

faint|ness

fair just; light-col-
oured; moderate; of
weather; beautiful;
entertainment;
streamline; cf. **fare,
fayre**

Fair|banks,
Doug|las two
actors

Fair|fax, Thomas
English general

fair|ground

fair|ing streamlin-
  ing; cf. **faring**
fair|ish
Fair Isle island;
  knitwear
fair|lead
fair¦ly
fair|ness
fair|water
fair|way
fairy
  fair¦ies
  imaginary being;
  homosexual; small
  animal; cf. **faerie**
fairy|land
fairy|like
Fai¦sal kings of Iraq
Fai¦sal|abad
fais|an¦dé
fait ac|com|pli
  faits ac|com|plis
faith
faith|ful
faith|ful¦ly
faith|ful|ness
faith|less
faith|less¦ly
faith|less|ness
fa¦jita
fake
  fak¦ing
faker person who
  fakes
fak¦ery
  fak¦er¦ies
fakie
fakir religious
  ascetic
Fala|bella
fala|fel
Fa¦lange Spanish
  Fascist movement;
  cf. **Phalange**
Fa¦lan|gism
Fa¦lan|gist member
  of Falange; cf.
  Phalangist
Fa|la¦sha
fal|cate
fal|cated
fal|chion
fal|ci|form
fal|cip¦arum

fal¦con
fal|con¦er
fal|con¦et
fal|con¦ry
fal|deral var. of
  folderol
Faldo, Nick golfer
fald|stool
fale Samoan house;
  cf. **fail, faille**
Fa¦ler|nian
Fal|kirk
Falk|land
fall
  fell
  fall¦en
Falla, Ma¦nuel de
  composer
fal|la¦cious
fal|la¦cious|ly
fal|la¦cious|ness
fal|lacy
  fal|la¦cies
fall|away
fall|back
fall¦en
fall|en|ness
fall¦er
fall|fish
fal|li|bil|ism
fal|li|bil|ist
fal|li|bil|ity
fall|ible
fall|libly
falling-off
  fallings-off
falling-out
  fallings-out
fall-off *n.*
Fal|lo|pian
Fal|lot, tet¦ral|ogy
  of
fall|out
fal|low
fal|low|ness
false
  fals¦er
  fals¦est
false|hood
false¦ly
false|ness
fal|setto +s
false|work

fal¦sies
fal|si|fi|abil¦ity
fal|si|fi|able
fal|si|fi|ca¦tion
fals|ify
  fal¦si|fies
  fal¦si|fied
  fal¦si|fy|ing
fal|sity
  fal|sities
Fal|staff|ian
Fal|ster
fal¦ter
fal|ter¦er
fal|ter|ing¦ly
Falun Dafa var. of
  Falun Gong
Falun Gong
Fama|gusta
fa|mi¦lia
  fa|mi¦liae
  historical
  household
fa|mil¦ial
fa|mil¦iar well
  known
fa|mil¦iar|isa¦tion
  Br. var. of
  familiarization
fa|mil¦iar|ise *Br.*
  var. of **familiarize**
fa|mil¦iar|ity
  fa|mil¦iar|ities
fa|mil¦iar|iza¦tion
fa|mil¦iar|ize
  fa|mil¦iar|iz¦ing
fa|mil¦iar¦ly
fam¦il|ist
fam¦il|is¦tic
fa¦mille in *'en
  famille'*
fa¦mille jaune
fa¦mille noire
fa¦mille rose
fa¦mille verte
fam¦ily
  fam¦ilies
fam¦ine
fam¦ish
fam¦ous
fam¦ous¦ly
fam¦ous|ness
famu|lus
  fam¦uli

Fan people;
  language; var. of
  Fang
fan
  fanned
  fan|ning
Fana|galo var. of
  Fana|kalo
Fana|kalo
fan|at¦ic
fan|at|ic¦al
fan|at|ic¦al¦ly
fan|ati|cise *Br.* var.
  of **fanaticize**
fan|ati|cism
fan|ati|cize
  fan|ati|ciz¦ing
fan|boy
fan|ci|able
fan|cier
fan|ci|ful
fan|ci|ful¦ly
fan|ci|ful|ness
fan|cily
fan|ci|ness
fancy
  fan|cies
  fan|cied
  fancy|ing
  fan|cier
  fan|ci|est
fancy-free
fancy|work needle-
  work etc.
fan|dan|gle
fan|dango
  fan|dan¦goes or
  fan|dan¦gos
fan|dom
fane temple; cf.
  fain, feign
fan|fare
fan|faro|nade
Fang people;
  language
**Fan|gio, Juan
  Ma¦nuel** racing
  driver
fang|less
fango
fan-jet
fan|kle
  fank|ling
fan|light

fan-like
fan¦ner
fanny
  fan¦nies
  Br. vulgar slang
Fanny Adams
fan¦tabu¦lous
fan¦tail
fan-tailed
fan-tan
fan¦ta¦sia
fan¦ta¦sise *Br. var.*
  of fantasize
fan¦ta¦sist
fan¦ta¦size
  fan¦ta¦siz¦ing
fan¦tast
fan¦tas¦tic
fan¦tas¦tic¦al
fan¦tas¦tic¦al¦ity
fan¦tas¦tic¦al¦ly
fan¦tasy
  fan¦ta¦sies
  fan¦ta¦sied
  fan¦tasy¦ing
Fante
Fanti *var. of Fante*
fan¦tods
fan¦zine
fa¦quir *var. of fakir*
far
  fur¦ther *or* far¦ther
  fur¦thest *or*
  far¦thest
  cf. fah
farad
fara¦daic
Fara¦day, Mi¦chael
  scientist
fara¦day unit
fa¦rad¦ic *var. of*
  faradaic
far¦an¦dole
fa¦rang
far¦away *adj.*
farce
far¦ceur
far¦ci¦cal
far¦ci¦cal¦ity
far¦ci¦cal¦ly
farcy illness; *cf.*
  Farsi
far¦del

fare
far¦ing
  get on; payment for
  travel; food; *cf.*
  fair, fayre
fare-thee-well *n.*
fare¦well
fare-you-well *n.*
far¦falle
Fa¦rida¦bad
far¦ina
far¦in¦aceous
farkle¦berry
  farkle¦berries
farl
farm¦able
far¦man *var. of*
  firman
farm¦er *cf.* pharma
farm¦er's lung
farm¦ers' mar¦ket
farm¦hand
farm¦house
farm¦ing *cf.*
  pharming
farm¦land
farm¦stead
farm¦yard
Farn¦borough
Farne Islands
Far¦nese Italian
  ducal family
Faro port, Portugal
faro game
Faroe Islands
Faro¦ese
fa¦rouche
Far¦ouk king of
  Egypt
Far¦quhar, George
  writer
far¦ra¦gin¦ous
far¦rago
  far¦ra¦gos *Br.*
  far¦ra¦goes *US*
Far¦rell, J. G.
  English novelist
Far¦rell, J. T.
  American novelist
far¦rier
far¦riery
  far¦rier¦ies
far¦row
far¦ruca

farse
fars¦er
fars¦est
Farsi language; *cf.*
  farcy
far¦ther
far¦ther¦most *var.*
  of furthermost
far¦thest *var. of*
  furthest
far¦thing
far¦thin¦gale
fart¦lek
fas¦ces
fa¦scia +s board etc.
fa¦scia
fa¦sciae *Anatomy*
fa¦scial *Anatomy of*
  a fascia; *cf.* facial
fa¦sci¦ated
fa¦scia¦tion
fas¦cicle
fas¦ci¦cu¦lar
fas¦ci¦cu¦late
fas¦ci¦cu¦la¦tion
fas¦ci¦cule instal-
  ment; *var. of*
  fascicle
fas¦cic¦ulus
  fas¦cic¦uli
  Anatomy bundle;
  var. of fascicle
fas¦ci¦itis
fas¦cin¦ate
  fas¦cin¦at¦ing
  fas¦cin¦at¦ing¦ly
fas¦cin¦ation
fas¦cin¦ator
fas¦cine
fas¦ciol¦ia¦sis
fas¦cism
fas¦cist
fas¦cis¦tic
fash¦ion
fash¦ion¦abil¦ity
fash¦ion¦able
fash¦ion¦able¦ness
fash¦ion¦ably
fash¦ion¦er
fash¦ion¦ista
Fass¦bin¦der,
  Rai¦ner Wer¦ner
  film director
fast¦back

fast¦ball
fas¦ten
fas¦ten¦er
Fas¦text
fas¦tidi¦ous
fas¦tidi¦ous¦ly
fas¦tidi¦ous¦ness
fas¦tigi¦ate
fast¦ness
Fast¦net
fat
  fat¦ted
  fat¦ting
  fat¦ter
  fat¦test
Fatah, Al
fatal
fa¦tal¦ism
fa¦tal¦ist
fa¦tal¦is¦tic
fa¦tal¦is¦tic¦al¦ly
fa¦tal¦ity
  fa¦tal¦ities
fa¦tal¦ly
Fata Mor¦gana
fat¦back
fate
  fat¦ing
  destiny; *cf.* fete
fate¦ful
fate¦ful¦ly
fate¦ful¦ness
fat¦head
fat-headed
fat-headed¦ness
father *cf.* farther
father¦hood
father-in-law
  fathers-in-law
father¦land
father¦less
father¦less¦ness
father¦like
father¦li¦ness
father¦ly
Father's Day
fathom
fathom¦able
Fath¦om¦eter
  trademark
fathom¦less
fat¦ig¦abil¦ity *var. of*
  fatiguability

fat¦ig¦able var. of
  fatiguable
fat¦igu¦abil¦ity
fat¦igu¦able
fa¦tigue
  fa¦tiguing
Fat¦iha
Fat¦ihah var. of
  Fatiha
Fat¦ima daughter of
  Muhammad
Fá¦tima village,
  Portugal
Fat¦lmid
Fat¦im¦ite
fat¦ism var. of
  fattism
fat¦ist var. of fattist
fat¦less
fat¦ling
fatly
fat¦ness
fa¦toush
fatso
  fat¦soes
fat¦stock
fat¦ten
fat¦ti¦ness
fat¦tish
fat¦tism
fat¦tist
fatty
  fat¦ties
  fat¦tier
  fat¦ti¦est
fa¦tu¦ity
  fa¦tu¦ities
fatu¦ous
fatu¦ous¦ly
fatu¦ous¦ness
fatwa
fau¦bourg
fau¦ces
fau¦cet
fau¦cial
faugh expression of
  disgust
fauj¦dar
fauji¦dar var. of
  faujdar
Faulk¦ner, Wil¦liam
  novelist
fault
fault¦ily

faulti¦ness
fault¦less
fault¦less¦ly
faulty
  fault¦ier
  faulti¦est
faun Roman deity;
  cf. fawn
fauna
  fau¦nae or fau¦nas
faun¦al
faun¦is¦tic
Faunt¦leroy
Fau¦nus Roman god
Fauré, Gab¦riel
  composer
Faust astronomer
  and necromancer
Faust¦ian
Faustus var. of
  Faust
faute de mieux
fau¦teuil
Fauve
Fauv¦ism
Fauv¦ist
faux false; cf. foe
faux naïf +s
faux pas
  pl. faux pas
fava bean
fave
fa¦vela
favor US
  Br. favour
fa¦vor¦able US
  Br. favourable
fa¦vor¦able¦ness US
  Br. favourableness
fa¦vor¦ably US
  Br. favourably
fa¦vor¦er US
  Br. favourer
fa¦vor¦ite US
  Br. favourite
fa¦vor¦it¦ism US
  Br. favouritism
fa¦vour Br.
  US favor
fa¦vour¦able Br.
  US favorable
fa¦vour¦able¦ness
  Br.
  US favorableness

fa¦vour¦ably Br.
  US favorably
fa¦vour¦er Br.
  US favorer
fa¦vour¦ite Br.
  US favorite
fa¦vour¦it¦ism Br.
  US favoritism
fav¦rile
Fawkes, Guy con-
  spirator
fawn deer; brown;
  behave servilely; cf.
  faun
fawn¦ing¦ly
fax
fay *literary* fairy; cf.
  fey
faya¦lite
fayre *pseudo-archaic*
  fête, sale; food; cf.
  fair, fare
faze
  faz¦ing
  disconcert; cf.
  phase
fa¦zenda
faz¦en¦deiro +s
fealty
  feal¦ties
fear¦ful
fear¦ful¦ly
fear¦ful¦ness
fear¦less
fear¦less¦ly
fear¦less¦ness
fear¦some
fear¦some¦ly
fear¦some¦ness
feart afraid
fea¦sant in 'damage
  feasant'
feasi¦bil¦ity
feas¦ible
feas¦ibly
feast¦er
feat achievement; cf.
  feet
fea¦ther
feather¦back
feather-brain
fea¦ther¦cut *n.*
feather-cut *v.*
feather-cutting

fea¦theri¦ness
fea¦ther¦less
fea¦ther¦tail
fea¦ther¦weight
fea¦thery
fea¦ture
  fea¦tur¦ing
fea¦ture¦less
fea¦tur¦ette
feb¦ri¦fugal
feb¦ri¦fuge
fe¦brile
fe¦brile¦ly
fe¦bril¦ity
Feb¦ru¦ary
  Feb¦ru¦ar¦ies
fecal US
  Br. faecal
feces US
  Br. faeces
feck¦less
feck¦less¦ly
feck¦less¦ness
fecu¦lence
fecu¦lent
fec¦und
fe¦cund¦abil¦ity
fe¦cund¦ate
  fe¦cund¦at¦ing
fe¦cund¦ation
fe¦cund¦ity
Fed Federal Reserve
fed past tense and
  past participle of
  feed; FBI agent
fed¦ay¦een
fed¦eral
fed¦er¦al¦isa¦tion
  Br. var. of
  federalization
fed¦er¦al¦ise Br. var.
  of federalize
fed¦er¦al¦ism
fed¦er¦al¦ist
fed¦er¦al¦iza¦tion
fed¦er¦al¦ize
  fed¦er¦al¦iz¦ing
fed¦er¦al¦ly
fed¦er¦ate
  fed¦er¦at¦ing
fed¦er¦ation
fed¦er¦ation¦ist
fed¦er¦ative

fe¦dora
fee
feeb
fee¦bate
fee¦ble
  fee¦bler
  feeb¦lest
feeble¦ness
feebly
feed
  fed
feed¦back
feed¦er
feed¦forward
feed¦lot
feed¦stock
feed¦stuff
feed¦through
feel
  felt
feel¦er
feel-good *adj.*
feel-goodism
feel¦ing¦less
feel¦ing¦ly
fee sim¦ple
  fees sim¦ple
feet pl. of foot; cf.
  feat
fee tail
  fees tail
Feh¦ling's re¦agent
Feh¦ling's
  so¦lu¦tion
feign pretend; cf.
  fain, fane
fei¦joa
fei¦joada
feint sham attack;
  pretend; of ruled
  lines; cf. faint
feis
  feis¦eanna
feist¦ily
feisti¦ness
feisty
  feist¦ier
  feisti¦est
fela¦fel var. of
  falafel
Fel¦den¦krais
feld¦spar
feld¦spath¦ic
feld¦spath¦oid

feld¦spath¦oidal
feli¦cif¦ic
fe¦lici¦tate
  fe¦lici¦tat¦ing
  fe¦lici¦ta¦tion
fe¦lici¦tous
  fe¦lici¦tous¦ly
fe¦li¦city
  fe¦li¦ci¦ties
felid
fe¦line
fe¦lin¦ity
felix culpa
Felix¦stowe
fella fellow
fel¦lah
  fel¦la¦hin
  Egyptian peasant;
  cf. feller
fel¦late
  fel¦lat¦ing
fel¦la¦tio
fel¦la¦tor
fell¦er person who
  fells; fellow; cf.
  fellah
fel¦lies var. of
  felloes
Fel¦lini, Fe¦de¦rico
  film director
fel¦loes wheel rim
fel¦low person
fel¦low¦ship
fellow-travel¦er *US*
fellow-travel¦ing
  US
fellow-travel¦ler *Br.*
fellow-travel¦ling
  Br.
fell-walker
fell-walking
felo de se
  felos de se
felon
fe¦loni¦ous
  fe¦loni¦ous¦ly
fel¦ony
  fel¦on¦ies
fels¦ic
fel¦spar var. of
  feldspar
felt past tense and
  past participle of
  feel; fabric; cf. veld

felty
fel¦lucca
fel¦wort
fem var. of femme
fe¦male
fe¦male¦ness
feme cov¦ert
  femes cov¦ert or
  femes cov¦erts
feme sole
  femes sole or
  femes soles
fem¦inal
fem¦in¦al¦ity
fem¦in¦eity
fem¦in¦ine
fem¦in¦ine¦ly
fem¦in¦ine¦ness
fem¦in¦in¦ity
  fem¦in¦in¦ities
fem¦in¦isa¦tion *Br.*
  var. of
  feminization
fem¦in¦ise *Br.* var. of
  feminize
fem¦in¦ism
fem¦in¦ist
fem¦in¦ity
fem¦in¦iza¦tion
fem¦in¦ize
  fem¦in¦iz¦ing
femme
femme fa¦tale
  femmes fa¦tales
femme sole var. of
  feme sole
fem¦oral
femur
  fe¦murs or fem¦ora
fen marsh
fen
  pl. fen
  Chinese currency
fen¦berry
  fen¦berries
fence
  fen¦cing
fence¦less
fen¦cer
fence¦row
fen¦cible
Fen¦der, Leo guitar-
  maker
fend¦er

Fen¦ella
fen¦es¦tella
fen¦es¦tra
  fen¦es¦trae
  fen¦es¦tra ova¦lis
  fen¦es¦tra ro¦tunda
fen¦es¦trate
fen¦es¦tra¦tion
fen-fire
feng shui
Fe¦nian
Fe¦nian¦ism
fen¦land
fen¦nec
fen¦nel plant; cf.
  phenyl
Fenno¦scan¦dia
fenny
fen¦tanyl
fenu¦greek
feo¦dary
  feo¦dar¦ies
feof¦fee
feoff¦ment
feof¦for
feral
fer¦ber¦ite
fer de lance
  fers de lance or
  fer de lances
Fer¦di¦nand
Fer¦gal
Fer¦gus
Fer¦guson, Alex
  football manager
feria
fer¦ial
fer¦in¦ghee
fer¦in¦ghi var. of
  feringhee
Fer¦man¦agh
Fer¦mat, Pierre de
  mathematician
fer¦mata
fer¦ment turn sugar
  into alcohol;
  agitation; cf.
  foment
fer¦ment¦able
fer¦men¦ta¦tion
  turning sugar into
  alcohol; cf.
  fomentation
fer¦men¦ta¦tive

fer|ment|er container; organism; cf. **fomenter**

Fermi, En|rico physicist

fermi unit

Fermi-Dirac

fer|mion

fer|mium

fern
 pl. **fern** or **ferns**
 plant; cf. **firn, föhn**

Fer|nando Póo

fern|bird

fern|brake

fern|ery
 fern|er|ies

ferny

fer|ocious

fer|ocious|ly

fer|ocious|ness

fer|ocity
 fer|oci|ties

ferox

Fer|ranti, Se|bas|tian de electrical engineer

Fer|rara city, Italy

Fer|rari, Enzo car maker

fer|rate

fer|rel var. of **ferrule**

Fer|rel's law

fer|ret

ferret-badger

fer|ret|er

fer|rety

fer|ri|age

fer|ric

ferri|cyan|ide

Fer|rier, Kath|leen singer

ferri|mag|net|ic

ferri|mag|net|ism

Fer|ris wheel

fer|rite

fer|rit|ic

fer|ritin

ferro|cene

ferro|con|crete

ferro|cyan|ide

ferro|elec|tric

ferro|elec|tri|city

ferro|fluid

ferro|mag|ne|sian

ferro|mag|net|ic

ferro|mag|net|ism

fer|rous

fer|ru|gin|ous

fer|rule metal cap; cf. **ferule**

ferry

fer|ries

fer|ried

ferry|ing

ferry|man
 ferry|men

fer|tile

fer|til|is|able *Br.* var. of **fertilizable**

fer|til|isa|tion *Br.* var. of **fertilization**

fer|til|ise *Br.* var. of **fertilize**

fer|til|iser *Br.* var. of **fertilizer**

fer|til|ity

fer|til|iz|able

fer|til|iza|tion

fer|til|ize
 fer|til|iz|ing

fer|til|izer

fer|ula

fer|ule
 fer|ul|ing
 cane; cf. **ferrule**

fer|vency
 fer|ven|cies

fer|vent

fer|vent|ly

fer|vid

fer|vid|ly

fer|vor *US*

fer|vour *Br.*

Fès var. of **Fez**

Fes|cen|nine

fes|cue

fess

fesse *Heraldry* var. of **fess**

festa Italian festival; cf. **fester**

fes|tal

fes|tal|ly

fes|ter become septic; cf. **festa**

fes|ti|val

fes|tive

fes|tive|ly

fes|tiv|ity
 fes|tiv|ities

fes|toon

Fest|schrift
 Fest|schrift|en or **Fest|schrifts**

feta cheese; cf. **fetter, fetor**

fetal
 Br. (*non-technical*) also **foetal**

fetch

fetch|er

fetch|ing|ly

fete
 fet|ing
 fair; festival; honour or entertain lavishly
 French **fête**; cf. **fate**

fête cham|pêtre
 fêtes cham|pêtres

fête gal|ante
 fêtes gal|antes

feti|cide
 Br. (*non-technical*) also **foeticide**

fetid

fetid|ly

fetid|ness

fet|ish

fet|ish|isa|tion *Br.* var. of **fetishization**

fet|ish|ise *Br.* var. of **fetishize**

fet|ish|ism

fet|ish|ist

fet|ish|is|tic

fet|ish|iza|tion

fet|ish|ize
 fet|ish|iz|ing

fet|lock

fetor foul smell

fetta cheese; var. of **feta**

fet|ter shackle

fet|ter|lock

fet|tle
 fet|tling

fet|tler

fet|tuc|cine

fet|tu|cini var. of **fettuccine**

fetus
 Br. (*non-technical*) also **foetus**

feu +s +ed +ing

feud

feu|dal

feu|dal|isa|tion *Br.* var. of **feudalization**

feu|dal|ise *Br.* var. of **feudalize**

feu|dal|ism

feu|dal|ist

feu|dal|is|tic

feu|dal|ity

feu|dal|iza|tion

feu|dal|ize
 feu|dal|iz|ing

feu|dal|ly

feud|atory
 feud|ator|ies

feu de joie
 feux de joie

feud|ist

feuille|té

feuille|ton

fever

fever|few

fe|ver|ish

fe|ver|ish|ly

fe|ver|ish|ness

fe|ver|ous

few not many; cf. **phew**

fey strange etc.; cf. **fay**

Fey|deau, Georges playwright

feyly

fey|ness

Feyn|man, Rich|ard physicist

Fez city, Morocco

fez hat
 fezzes
 fezzed

Ffes|tin|iog

f-hole

fi|acre

fi|ancé *male*

fi|an|cée *female*

fian|chetto
  fian|chet|toes
  fian|chet|toed
  fian|chetto|ing
Fianna Fáil
fi|asco +s
fiat
fib
  fibbed
  fib|bing
fib|ber
fiber US
  Br. fibre
fiber|board US
  Br. fibreboard
fiber|fill US
  Br. fibrefill
fiber|glass US
  Br. fibreglass
fiber|less US
  Br. fibreless
fiber-optic US mod.
  Br. fibre-optic
fiber op|tics US
  Br. fibre optics
fiber|scope US
  Br. fibrescope
Fi|bo|nacci num-
  ber; series
fibre Br.
  US fiber
fibre|board Br.
  US fiberboard
fibre|fill Br.
  US fiberfill
fibre|glass Br.
  US fiberglass
fibre|less Br.
  US fiberless
fibre-optic Br. mod.
  US fiber-optic
fibre op|tics Br.
  US fiber optics
fibre|scope Br.
  US fiberscope
fi|bril
fi|bril|lar
fi|bril|lary
fib|ril|late
  fib|ril|lat|ing
fib|ril|la|tion
fi|brin
fi|brino|gen
fi|brin|oid
fi|brin|oly|sis

fi|brino|lyt|ic
fi|brin|ous
fibro +s
fibro|aden|oma
  fibro|aden|omas or
  fibro|aden|omata
fibro|blast
fibro|cyst|ic
fi|broid
fi|broin
fibro|lite
fi|broma
  fi|bro|mas or
  fi|bro|mata
fibro|myal|gia
fibro|plasia
fibro|sar|coma
  fibro|sar|co|mas or
  fibro|sar|co|mata
fibro|
    sar|co|ma|tous
fi|bro|sis
fi|bro|ses
fi|bro|sit|ic
fi|bro|si|tis
fi|brot|ic
fi|brous
fib|ula n.
  fibu|lae or fibu|las
fibu|lar adj.
fiche
Fichte, Jo|hann
  philosopher
fichu
fickle
  fick|ler
  fick|lest
fickle|ness
fickly
fic|tile
fic|tion
fic|tion|al
fic|tion|al|isa|tion
  Br. var. of
  fictionalization
fic|tion|al|ise Br.
  var. of fictionalize
fic|tion|al|ity
fic|tion|al|iza|tion
fic|tion|al|ize
  fic|tion|al|iz|ing
fic|tion|al|ly
fic|tion|ist
fic|ti|tious

fic|ti|tious|ly
fic|ti|tious|ness
fic|tive
fic|tive|ness
ficus
  pl. ficus or fi|cuses
fid|ay|een var. of
  fedayeen
fid|dle
  fid|dling
fiddle|back pattern;
  spider
fiddle-back chair
fiddle-de-dee
fiddle-faddle
  fiddle-faddling
fiddle|head
fid|dler
Fid|dler's Green
fiddle|stick
fid|dly
  fid|dlier
  fid|dli|est
Fidei De|fen|sor
fide|ism
fide|ist
fide|is|tic
fi|del|ity
  fi|del|ities
fidget
fidget|er
fidgeti|ness
fidgety
Fido fog dispersal
  device; dog's name
fi|du|cial
fi|du|ciary
  fi|du|ciar|ies
fidus Acha|tes
fie exclam.; cf. phi
fief
fief|dom
Field, John
  composer
field
field|craft
field|er
field|fare
Field|ing, Henry
  writer
Fields, Gracie
  singer
Fields, W. C.
  comedian

fields|man
fields|men
field|stone
field|work
field|work|er
fiend
fiend|ish
fiend|ish|ly
fiend|ish|ness
fiend|like
fierce
  fier|cer
  fier|cest
fierce|ly
fierce|ness
fieri fa|cias
fier|ily
fieri|ness
fiery
  fier|ier
  fieri|est
fi|esta
FIFA soccer
  governing body
Fife region
fife musical
  instrument
fif|ing
fifer
FIFO = first in, first
  out
fif|teen
fif|teenth
fifth
fifth|ly
Fifth-monarchy-
    man
Fifth-monarchy-
    men
fif|ti|eth
fifty
  fif|ties
fifty-fifty
fifty-first, fifty-
  second, etc.
fifty|fold
fifty-one, fifty-two,
  etc.
fig
  figged
  fig|ging
fig|bird
fight
  fought

fight|back
fight|er
fighter-bomber
fig|ment
fi|gura
  fi|gurae
fig|ural
fig|ur|ant *male*
fig|ur|ante *female*
fig|ur|ation
fig|ura|tive
fig|ura|tive|ly
fig|ure
  fig|ur|ing
fig|ure|head
fig|ure|less
fig|ure of eight *n.*
  fig|ures of eight
figure-of-eight
  mod.
figure-skater
figure-skating
fig|ur|ine
fig|wort
Fiji
Fiji|an
fila|beg var. of
  filibeg
fila|gree var. of
  filigree
fila|ment
fila|men|tary
fila|ment|ous
fill|aria
  fill|ariae
fill|ar|ial
fill|ar|ia|sis
fila|ture
fil|bert
filch|er
file
  fil|ing
  cf. phial
filé herb
file|fish
file|name
filer person or thing
  that files; cf. phyla
filet net; French
  spelling of fillet
filet mi|gnon
  fi|lets mi|gnons
fil|ial

fili|al|ly
fili|ation
fili|beg
fili|bus|ter
fili|cide
Fili|cop|sida
fili|form
fili|gree
  fili|greed
Filio|que
Fili|pina *female*
Fili|pino +s *male*
fille de joie
  filles de joie
fill|er
fill|let meat; strip;
  band; cf. filet
fil|let|er
fil|lip +ed +ing
fil|lis
fill|lis|ter
Fill|more, Mil|lard
  US president
fill-up *n.*
filly
  fill|lies
film|goer
film-going
film|ic
film|ily
filmi|ness
film-maker
film-making
film noir
  films noirs
film|og|raphy
  film|og|raph|ies
film|set *Printing*
  film|set|ting
film set *Film-
  making*
film|set|ter
film|strip
filmy
  film|ier
  filmi|est
filo *Br.*
  US phyllo
Filo|fax *trademark*
filo|podial
filo|podium
  filo|podia
filo|selle

filo|virus
fils currency
  pl. fils
fils son
fil|ter remove
  impurities; cf.
  philtre
fil|ter|able
filter-feeder
filter-feeding
filth
filth|ily
filthi|ness
filthy
  filth|ier
  filthi|est
fil|trable var. of
  filterable
fil|trate
fil|tra|tion
fim|bria
  fim|briae
fim|brial
fim|bri|ate
fim|bri|ated
fin
  finned
  fin|ning
fin|agle
  fin|ag|ling
fin|agler
final
fi|nale
fi|nal|isa|tion *Br.*
  var. of finalization
fi|nal|ise *Br.* var. of
  finalize
fi|nal|ism
fi|nal|ist
fi|nal|is|tic
fi|nal|ity
  fi|nal|ities
fi|nal|iza|tion
fi|nal|ize
  fi|nal|iz|ing
fi|nal|ly
fi|nance
  fi|nan|cing
fi|nan|cial
fi|nan|cial|ly
fi|nan|cier
fin|back
Fin|bar
finca

find
  found
find|able
find|er
fin de siècle
  fins de siècle
Find|horn
find-spot
fine
  fin|ing
  finer
  fin|est
fine|able
fine cham|pagne
fine-draw
  fine-drew
  fine-drawn
Fine Gael
fine|ly
fine|ness
fin|ery
  fin|eries
fines herbes
fi|nesse
  fi|ness|ing
fine-tooth comb
fine-toothed comb
  var. of fine-tooth
  comb
fine-tune
  fine-tuning
fin|foot
Fin|gal's Cave
fin|ger
fin|ger|board
finger-dry
  finger-dries
  finger-dried
  finger-drying
finger|fish
fin|ger|less
fin|ger|ling
fin|ger|mark
fin|ger|nail
finger-paint
fin|ger|pick
finger|pick|er
finger|plate
finger|post
fin|ger|print
finger|stall
finger|tip
fin|gle
  fin|gling

fin|ial
fini|cal
fini|cal|ity
fini|cal|ly
fini|cal|ness
fin|ick|ing
fin|icky
finis
fin|ish end; cf.
  Finnish
fin|ish|er
Fin|is|terre
fi|nite
fi|nite|ly
fi|nite|ness
fi|nit|ism
fi|nit|ist
fi|nito
fini|tude
Fin|land
Fin|land|isa|tion
  Br. var. of
  Finlandization
Fin|land|ise *Br.* var.
  of **Finlandize**
Fin|land|iza|tion
Fin|land|ize
  Fin|land|iz|ing
fin|less
Finn
fin|nan had|dock
fin|nesko
  pl. fin|nesko
Finn|ic
Finn|ish
Finn Mac|Cool
  Irish mythological
  hero
Finn Mac
  Cumhaill var. of
  Finn MacCool
Finno-Ugrian
Finno-Ugric
finny
fino +s
fi|noc|chio
fiord var. of **fjord**
fi|ori|tura
  fi|ori|ture
fip|ple
fiqh *Islamic law*
fir tree; cf. **fur**

fire
  fir|ing
fire|arm
fire|back
fire|ball
fire|ball|er
fire|ball|ing
fire|bomb
fire|box
fire|brand
fire|brat
fire|break
fire|brick
fire|bug
fire|clay
fire|crack|er
fire|crest
fire|damp
fire|dog
fire|drake
fire-eater
fire|fight
fire|fight|er
fire|fight|ing
fire|finch
fire|fish
fire|fly
  fire|flies
fire|guard
fire|hall
fire|house
fire|less
fire|light
fire|light|er
fire|lit
fire|lock
fire|man
  fire|men
fire|master
fire|place
fire|plug
fire|power
fire|proof
firer
fire-raiser
fire-raising
fire|ship
fire|side
fire|storm
fire|thorn
fire-walker
fire-walking

fire|wall
fire-watcher
fire-watching
fire|water
fire|weed
Fire|Wire
  trademark
fire|wood
fire|work
fir|kin
firm
firma|ment
firma|men|tal
fir|man +s
firm|ly
firm|ness
firm|ware
firn snow; cf. **fern**,
  föhn
firry of fir trees; cf.
  furry
first
first aid *n.*
first-aid *mod.*
first-aider
first|born
first-foot *n. & v.*
first-footer
first|ly
first-nighter
Firth, J. R. linguist
firth
fisc in ancient
  Rome; cf. **fisk**
fis|cal
fis|cal|ity
fis|cal|ly
Fisch|er, Bobby
  chess player
Fischer-Dieskau,
  Diet|rich singer
fish|able
fish|bowl
fish|cake
Fish|er shipping
  area
Fish|er, Geof|frey
  20th-cent.
  archbishop
Fish|er, Ron|ald
  Ayl|mer English
  statistician

Fish|er, St John
  bishop, d. 1535
fish|er cf. **fissure**
fish|er|folk
fish|er|man
  fish|er|men
fish|er|man bat;
  knit
fish|er|man's bend
fish|er|man's knot
fish|er|man's rib
fish|er|woman
  fish|er|women
fish|ery
  fish|er|ies
fish|eye lens
fish|ily
fishi|ness
fish|ing cf. **phishing**
fish|like
fish|meal
fish|mon|ger
fish|net
fish|plate
fish|tail
fish|way
fish|wife
  fish|wives
fishy
  fish|ier
  fishi|est
fisk in Scotland, var.
  of **fisc**
fis|sile
fis|sil|ity
fis|sion
fis|sion|able
fis|sip|ar|ous
fis|sure
  fis|sur|ing
  crack; cf. **fisher**
fist|ful
fist|ic
fisti|cuffs
fis|tula *n.*
  fis|tulas or
  fis|tu|lae
fis|tu|lar *adj.*
fis|tu|lous
fit
  fit|ted
  fit|ting
  fit|ter
  fit|test

cf. fytte
fitch
fitché
fit|chew
fitchy var. of fitché
fit|ful
fit|ful|ly
fit|ful|ness
fitly
fit|ment
fitna
fitnah var. of fitna
fit|ness
fit-out *n.*
fit|ter
fit|ting
fit|ting|ly
fit|ting|ness
Fit|ti|paldi,
  Emer|son racing
  driver
fit-up *n.*
Fitz|ger|ald,
  Ed|ward scholar
  and poet
Fitz|ger|ald, Ella
  jazz singer
Fitz|ger|ald, F.
  Scott and Zelda
  writers
FitzGerald–
       Lorentz
Fitz|roy
Fitz|wil|liam
Fiume
five
five-a-side
five-corner shrub
five-corners var. of
  five-corner
five-eighth rugby
  player
five fin|ger plant
five fin|gers var. of
  five finger
five|fold
five-iron
five o'clock
  shadow
fiver
five-spice
five|stones
fix|able

fix|ate
fix|at|ing
fix|ation
fixa|tive
fixed-do var. of
  fixed-doh
fixed-doh
fix|ed|ly
fix|ed|ness
fixer
fixer-upper
fixit
fix|ity
  fix|ities
fix|ture
fiz|gig
fizz effervesce; hiss;
  cf. phiz
fizz|er
fizz|ily
fizzi|ness
fiz|zle
  fiz|zling
fiz|zog
fizzy
  fizz|ier
  fizzi|est
fjord
flab|ber|gast
flab|bi|ly
flab|bi|ness
flabby
  flab|bier
  flab|bi|est
flac|cid
flac|cid|ity
flac|cid|ly
flack publicity
  agent; promote; cf.
  flak
flack|ery
fla|con
flag
  flagged
  flag|ging
fla|gel|lant
fla|gel|lar
fla|gel|late
  fla|gel|lat|ing
  fla|gel|la|tion
  fla|gel|la|tor
  fla|gel|la|tory
fla|gel|li|form

fla|gel|lum
  fla|gella
fla|geo|let
flag|fish
flag|ger
fla|gi|tious
flag|man
  flag|men
flagon
flag|pole
fla|grancy
  fla|gran|cies
fla|grant
fla|grant|ly
flag|ship
flag|staff
flag|stone
flag|stoned
flail
flair instinct; talent;
  cf. flare
flak anti-aircraft
  fire; criticism; cf.
  flack
flake
  flak|ing
flaki|ly
flaki|ness
flaky
  flaki|er
  flaki|est
flambé +s +ed +ing
flam|beau
  flam|beaus or
  flam|beaux
Flam|bor|ough
  Head
flam|boy|ance
flam|boy|ancy
  flam|boy|an|cies
flam|boy|ant
flam|boy|ant|ly
flame
  flam|ing
flame|less
flame|like
fla|men
  fla|mens or
  fla|mi|nes
fla|menco +s
flame|out
flame-projector
flame|proof
flamer

flame-thrower
fla|mingo
  fla|min|gos or
  fla|min|goes
flam|ma|bil|ity
flam|mable
flam|mu|lated
Flam|steed, John
  astronomer
flamy
  flami|er
  flami|est
Flan|ders
Flan|drian
flân|erie
flân|eur
flange
  flan|ging
flange|less
flan|ger
flank|er
flan|nel
  flan|nelled *Br.*
  flan|neled *US*
  flan|nel|ling *Br.*
  flan|nel|ing *US*
flan|nel|board
flan|nel|ette
flan|nel|graph
flannel|mouth
flap
  flapped
  flap|ping
flap|doo|dle
flap|jack
flap|per
flappy
  flap|pier
  flap|pi|est
flap|shell
flap-shelled
flare
  flar|ing
  widen; flame; cf.
  flair
flare|path
flare-up *n.*
flash|back
flash|board
flash|bulb
flash|card
flash|cube
flash|er
flash|gun

flash|ily
flashi|ness
flash lamp
flash|light
flash|over
flash|point
flashy
  flash|ier
  flashi|est
flask
flat
  flat|ted
  flat|ting
  flat|ter
  flat|test
flat|bed
flat|hill
flat|boat
flat|bread
flat|bug
flat|car
flat|fish
flat|foot
  flat|foots or
  flat|feet
  police officer
flat-footed
flat-footed|ly
flat-footed|ness
flat-four
flat|head
flat iron
flat|land
flat|let
flat|line
  flat|lin|ing
flat|liner
flat|ly
flat|mate
flat|ness
flat-pack
flat race
flat ra|cing
flat|ten
flat|ten|er
flat|ter
flat|ter|er
flat|ter|ing|ly
flat|tery
  flat|ter|ies
flat|tie
flat|tish
flat-top

flatty var. of flattie
flatu|lence
flatu|lency
flatu|lent
flatu|lent|ly
fla|tus
flat|ware
flat-weave
flat|worm
flat-woven
Flau|bert, Gus|tave
  novelist
flaunt
flaunt|er
flaunty
flaut|ist Br.
  US flutist
fla|ves|cent
Fla|via
Fla|vian
fla|vin yellow dye
fla|vine antiseptic
fla|vonc
fla|von|oid
flavo|pro|tein
fla|vor US
fla|vor|ful US
fla|vor|less US
fla|vor|ous
fla|vor|some US
fla|vour Br.
fla|vour|ful Br.
fla|vour|less Br.
fla|vour|some Br.
flaw imperfection;
  squall; cf. floor,
  flor
flaw|less
flaw|less|ly
flax
flax|en
flax-lily
  flax-lilies
flax|seed
F-layer
flay|er
flea insect; cf. flee
flea|bag
flea|bane
flea bite
flea-bitten
fleadh

flea|pit
flea|wort
flèche
flech|ette
Fleck|er, James
  Elroy poet
flec|tion var. of
  flexion
fledge
  fledg|ing
fledge|ling var. of
  fledgling
fledg|ling
flee
  fled
  run away; cf. flea
fleece
  flee|cing
fleece|able
flee|cily
fleeci|ness
fleecy
  flee|cier
  flee|ci|est
fleer
fleet
fleet|ing
fleet|ing|ly
fleet|ly
fleet|ness
Fleet Street
fleh|men
Flem|ing people
Flem|ing,
  Alex|an|der
  bacteriologist
Flem|ing, Ian
  novelist
Flem|ish
flense
  flen|sing
flen|ser
flesh|er
fleshi|ness
flesh|ings
flesh|less
flesh|ly
  flesh|lier
  flesh|li|est
flesh|pots
fleshy
  flesh|ier
  fleshi|est
fletch

Fletch|er, John
  dramatist
fletch|er
fleur-de-lis
  pl. fleur-de-lis
fleur-de-lys var. of
  fleur-de-lis
fleuron
fleury
Flevo|land
flew past tense of
  fly; cf. flu, flue
flews lips of
  bloodhound
flex
flexi|bil|ity
flex|ible
flex|ibly
flex|ile
flex|il|ity
flex|ion
flexi|time
flexo
flexo|graph|ic
flex|og|raphy
flex|or
flex|time
flexu|os|ity
flexu|ous
flex|ural
flex|ure
flex|wing
flib|ber|ti|gib|bet
flic computer
  animation; French
  policeman
flick flip
flicker
flicky
flier var. of flyer
flight
flight|ily
flighti|ness
flight|less
flight|less|ness
flight|line
flight|see|ing
flighty
  flight|ier
  flighti|est
flim|flam
  flim|flammed
  flim|flam|ming

flim|flam|mer
flim|flam|mery
flim|sily
flim|si|ness
flimsy
  flim|sies
  flim|sier
  flim|si|est
flinch|er
flinch|ing|ly
flin|ders splinters
Flin|ders bar
Flin|ders Is|land
fling
  flung
fling|er
flint|ily
flinti|ness
flint|lock
Flint|shire
flinty
  flint|ier
  flinti|est
flip
  flipped
  flip|ping
flip-flop
  flip-flopped
  flip-flopping
flip|pancy
  flip|pan|cies
flip|pant
flip|pant|ly
flip|per
flip-top
flir|ta|tion
flir|ta|tious
flir|ta|tious|ly
flir|ta|tious|ness
flirty
  flirt|ier
  flirti|est
flit
  flit|ted
  flit|ting
flitch
flit|ter
flitter|mouse
  flitter|mice
fliv|ver
flix|weed
float|able
float|ation var. of
  flotation

floatel
float|er
floating-point
float|plane
floaty
  float|ier
  floati|est
floc mass of fine
  particles; cf. flock,
  phlox
flocci|nauci|nihili|
    pili|fi|ca|tion
floc|cose
floc|cu|lant
floc|cu|late
  floc|cu|lat|ing
  floc|cu|la|tion
floc|cule
floc|cu|lence
floc|cu|lent
floc|cu|lus
  floc|culi
floc|cus
  flocci
flock group;
  wallpaper; cf. floc,
  phlox
flock|master
flocky
  flock|ier
  flocki|est
Flod|den
floe ice; cf. flow
Flo|ella
flog
  flogged
  flog|ging
flog|ger
flo|kati
flood
flood|gate
flood|light
  flood|lit
floor cf. flaw, flor
floor|board
floor|cloth
floor|pan
floor|walk|er
floo|sie var. of
  floozy
floo|zie var. of
  floozy
floozy
  floo|zies

flop
  flopped
  flop|ping
flop|house
flop|peroo +s
flop|pily
flop|pi|ness
floppy
  flop|pies
  flop|pier
  flop|pi|est
flor film on surface
  of wine; cf. flaw,
  floor
Flora
flora
  floras or florae
  plants
floral
flor|al|ly
Floréal
flor|eat
Flor|ence
Flor|en|tine
flore pleno
Flores islands,
  Indonesia and
  Azores
flor|es|cence
floret
Florey, How|ard
  pathologist
Flor|ian|ópo|lis
flori|bunda
flori|can
flori|cul|tural
flori|cul|ture
flori|cul|tur|ist
florid
Flor|ida
Flor|ida Keys
Flor|id|ian
flor|id|ity
flor|id|ly
flor|id|ness
flor|ifer|ous
flori|le|gium
  flori|le|gia or
  flori|le|giums
florin
Florio, John scholar
flor|ist
flor|is|tic
flor|is|tic|al|ly

flor|is|tics
flor|is|try
  flor|is|tries
flor|uit
flory
flossy
  floss|ier
  flossi|est
flo|ta|tion
flo|tel var. of floatel
flo|tilla
flot|sam
flounce
  floun|cing
flouncy
  floun|cier
  floun|ci|est
floun|der
floun|der|er
flour ground grain;
  cf. flower
flour bee|tle cf.
  flower beetle
flouri|ness cf.
  floweriness
flour|ish
flour|ish|er
flour moth
floury
  flour|ier
  flouri|est
  cf. flowery
flout
flow run; pour; cf.
  floe
flower cf. flour
flower bee|tle cf.
  flour beetle
flower|er
flow|eret
flow|eri|ness cf.
  flouriness
flower|less
flower|like
flower|peck|er
flower|pot
flowery
  flower|ier
  floweri|est
  having flowers;
  ornate; cf. floury
flow|ing|ly
flow|meter
flown

flow-on *n.*
flow|sheet
flow|stone
flu illness; cf. flew,
　flews, flue
flub
　flubbed
　flub|bing
fluc|tu|ant
fluc|tu|ate
　fluc|tu|at|ing
fluc|tu|ation
flue smoke duct; cf.
　flew, flews, flu
flue-cure
　flue-curing
flu|el|len
flu|ence
flu|ency
flu|ent
flu|ent|ly
fluff
fluf|fily
fluf|fi|ness
fluffy
　fluff|ier
　fluffi|est
flu|gel|horn
　German
　Flügelhorn
fluid
fluid drachm
flu|id|ic
flu|id|ics
flu|id|ify
　flu|idi|fies
　flu|idi|fied
　flu|idi|fy|ing
flu|id|isa|tion *Br.*
　var. of fluidization
flu|id|ise *Br.* var. of
　fluidize
flu|id|ity
flu|id|iza|tion
flu|id|ize
　flu|id|iz|ing
flu|id|ly
flu|id|ounce *US* var.
　of fluid ounce
flui|dram *US* var. of
　fluid drachm
fluke
　fluk|ing
flukey var. of fluky

fluki|ly
fluki|ness
fluky
　fluki|er
　fluki|est
flu-like
flume
　flum|ing
flum|mery
　flum|mer|ies
flum|mox
flun|key
flun|key|ism
flunky var. of
　flunkey
flunky|ism var. of
　flunkeyism
fluor|esce
　fluor|es|cing
fluor|es|cein
fluor|es|cence
fluor|es|cent
fluor|id|ate
　fluor|id|at|ing
fluor|id|ation
fluor|ide
fluor|im|eter var. of
　fluorometer
fluor|in|ate
　fluor|in|at|ing
fluor|in|ation
fluor|ine
fluor|ite
fluoro|car|bon
fluoro|chrome
fluoro|graph
fluor|og|raphy
fluoro|om|eter
fluoro|met|ric
fluoro|met|ric|al|ly
fluor|om|etry
fluoro|poly|mer
fluoro|quino|lone
fluoro|scope
fluoro|scop|ic
fluoro|scopy
　fluor|os|co|pies
fluor|osis
fluor|spar
flu|ox|et|ine
flurry
　flur|ries
　flur|ried
　flurry|ing

flush|er
Flush|ing
　English name for
　Vlissingen
flush|ness
flus|ter
flute
　flut|ing
flute-like
flutey var. of fluty
flut|ist *US*
　Br. flautist
flut|ter
flut|ter|er
flut|ter|ing|ly
flutter-tonguing
flut|tery
fluty
　fluti|er
　fluti|est
flu|vial
flu|via|tile
flu|vio|gla|cial
flu|vio|lacus|trine
flu|vi|om|eter
flu|vox|amine
flux
flux|gate
flux|ion
flux|ion|al
fly
　flies
　flew
　fly|ing
　flown
insect; move
through air; etc.
fly
　flys or flies
carriage
fly +er +est clever
fly|able
fly|away
fly|back *Electronics*
fly ball
fly|blow
fly|blown
fly boy
fly|bridge
fly-by *n.*
fly-by-night
fly-by-nighter
fly|catch|er
flyer

fly-fish
fly half
fly-in *n.*
fly|leaf
　fly|leaves
fly|man
fly|men
fly|ness
Flynn, Errol actor
fly|over
fly|paper
fly-past *n.*
fly-pitcher
fly-pitching
fly-post
fly-poster
flysch
fly|sheet
fly|speck
fly|specked
fly-through *n.*
fly-tip
　fly-tipped
　fly-tipping
fly-tipper
fly|trap
fly|way
fly|weight
fly|wheel
f-number
Fo, Dario play-
　wright
foal
foam
foam|less
foamy
　foam|ier
　foami|est
fob
　fobbed
　fob|bing
fo|cac|cia
focal
fo|cal|isa|tion *Br.*
　var. of focalization
fo|cal|ise *Br.* var. of
　focalize
fo|cal|iza|tion
fo|cal|ize
　fo|cal|iz|ing
fo|cal|ly
Foch, Fer|di|nand
　French marshal

fo'c's'le = forecastle
focus
  pl. fo|cuses or foci
  v. fo|cuses or
  fo|cusses
  fo|cused or
  fo|cussed
  fo|cus|ing or
  fo|cus|sing
fo|cus|er
fo|cus|ser var. of
  focuser
fod|der
fody
  fo|dies
foe enemy; cf. faux
foehn var. of föhn
foe|tal Br. non-
  technical var. of
  fetal
foeti|cide Br. non-
  technical var. of
  feticide
foe|tid var. of fetid
foe|tid|ly var. of
  fetidly
foe|tid|ness var. of
  fetidness
foe|tus Br. non-
  technical var. of
  fetus
fog
  fogged
  fog|ging
fog|bound
fog|bow
fogey
fogey|dom
fogey|ish
fogey|ism
Fo|ggia
fog|gily
fog|gi|ness
foggy
  fog|gier
  fog|gi|est
fog|horn
fogou
fogy
  fo|gies
  var. of fogey
fogy|dom var. of
  fogeydom
fogy|ish var. of
  fogeyish

fogy|ism var. of
  fogeyism
föhn wind; cf. fern,
  firn
foi|ble
foie gras
foil
foil|ist
foist
Fo|kine, Mi|chel
  choreographer
Fok|ker, An|thony
  aircraft designer
fola|cin
fol|ate
fold
fold|able
fold|away
fold|er
fol|de|rol
fold-out adj. & n.
foley Film-making
fo|li|aceous
fo|li|age
fo|liar
fo|li|ate
fo|li|ation
folic
folie à deux
  folies à deux
folie de gran|deur
Folies-Bergère
folio +s
fo|li|ose
fo|lium
  folia
foli|vore
fol|iv|or|ous
folk
Folke|stone
folkie folk music
  fan; cf. folky
folki|ness
folk|ish
folk|life
folk|lore
folk|lor|ic
folk|lor|ist
folk|lor|is|tic
folks
folk|si|ness
folksy
  folks|ier

folksi|est
folk|ways
folk|weave
folky
folk|ier
folki|est
  adj.; cf. folkie
fol|licle
fol|licu|lar
fol|licu|late
fol|licu|lated
fol|licul|itis
fol|lis
  fol|les
fol|low
fol|low|er
fol|low|er|ship
follow-my-leader
follow-on n.
follow-the-leader
follow-through n.
follow-up n.
folly
  fol|lies
Fol|som
Fom|al|haut
fo|ment stir up; cf.
  ferment
fo|men|ta|tion stir-
  ring up; cf.
  fermentation
fo|ment|er stirrer-
  up of trouble; cf.
  fermenter
fo|mi|tes
Fon people
Fonda, Henry,
  Jane, Peter, and
  Bridget actors
fon|dant
fon|dle
  fond|ling
fond|ler
fond|ly
fond|ness
fondu Ballet
fon|due Cooking
fons et origo
font
Fon|taine|bleau
fon|tal
fon|ta|nel US
fon|ta|nelle Br.

Fon|teyn, Mar|got
  ballet dancer
fon|tina
Foo|chow var. of
  Fuzhou
food|grain
foodie
food|stuff
foody var. of foodie
foo fight|er cf. fou
foo-foo var. of fufu
fool|ery
  fool|er|ies
fool|har|dily
fool|hardi|ness
fool|hardy
  fool|har|dier
  fool|hardi|est
fool|ish
fool|ish|ly
fool|ish|ness
fool|proof
fools|cap
fool's er|rand
fool's gold
fool's mate
fool's para|dise
fool's pars|ley
foo|ster
foot
  pl. feet
  v. foots
  foot|ed
  foot|ing
foot|age
foot-and-mouth
foot|ball
foot|ball|er
foot|bath
foot|bed
foot|board
foot|brake
foot|bridge
foot-candle
foot-dragger
foot-dragging
foot|er
foot|fall
foot|gear
foot|hill
foot|hold
footie var. of footy

foo¦tle
  foot¦ling
foot¦less
foot¦lights
foot¦locker
foot¦loose
foot¦man
  foot¦men
foot¦mark
foot¦note
  foot¦not¦ing
foot¦pad
foot¦path
foot¦plate
foot-pound
foot-pound-second
foot¦print
foot¦rest
Foot¦sie Stock
  Exchange index
  trademark
foot¦sie amorous
  play with feet
foot¦slog
  foot¦slogged
  foot¦slog¦ging
foot¦slog¦ger
foot¦sore
foot¦stalk
foot¦step
foot¦stool
foot¦sure
foot¦wall
foot¦way
foot¦wear
foot¦well
foot¦work
footy
foo yong cf. fou
foo¦zle
  fooz¦ling
fop¦pery
  fop¦per¦ies
fop¦pish
fop¦pish¦ly
fop¦pish¦ness
for on behalf of etc.;
  cf. fore, 'fore, four
for¦age
  for¦aging
for¦ager
for¦amen
  for¦am¦ina

for¦amen
  mag¦num
for¦amen
  mag¦nums or
  for¦am¦ina magna
for¦am¦in¦ifer
  for¦am¦in¦ifers or
  for¦am¦in¦ifera
for¦am¦in¦if¦eral
for¦am¦in¦if¦er¦an
for¦am¦in¦ifer¦ous
for'ard = forward
for'as¦tero +s
foray
foray¦er
forb
for¦bade
for¦bear
  for¦bore
  for¦borne
  refrain; abstain; cf.
  forebear
for¦bear¦ance
for¦bid
  for¦bade or for¦bad
  for¦bid¦ding
  for¦bid¦den
for¦bid¦ding¦ly
forby var. of forbye
for¦bye
force
  for¦cing
force¦able able to
  be forced; cf.
  forcible
forced land¦ing cf.
  force-land
force-feed
  force-fed
force¦ful
force¦ful¦ly
force¦ful¦ness
force-land v.
force ma¦jeure
force¦meat
force¦out
for¦ceps
for¦cer
for¦cible involving
  force; cf. forceable
for¦cibly
Ford, Ford Madox
  writer

Ford, Ger¦ald US
  president
Ford, Har¦ri¦son
  actor
Ford, Henry car
  maker
Ford, John film
  director
ford¦able
Ford¦ism
Ford¦ist
ford¦less
for¦do
  for¦does
  for¦did
  for¦done
fore front; cf. for,
  four
'fore = before
fore¦arm
fore¦bear ancestor;
  cf. forbear
fore¦bode
  fore¦bod¦ing
fore¦bod¦ing
  fore¦bod¦ing¦ly
fore¦brain
fore¦cabin
fore¦cad¦die
fore¦cast
  past and past
  participle fore¦cast
  or fore¦cast¦ed
fore¦cast¦er
fore¦castle
fore¦check
fore¦check¦er
fore¦close
  fore¦clos¦ing
fore¦clos¦ure
fore¦court
fore¦dawn
fore¦deck
for¦edge var. of
  fore¦edge
fore¦do var. of fordo
fore¦doom
fore¦dune
fore-edge
fore¦father
fore¦fend var. of
  forfend
fore¦fin¦ger

fore¦foot
  fore¦feet
fore¦front
fore¦gather
fore¦go
  fore¦goes
  fore¦went
  fore¦gone
  precede; in 'fore-
  gone conclusion';
  cf. forgo
fore¦go¦er
fore¦ground
fore¦gut
fore¦hand
fore¦head
fore¦hock
for¦eign
for¦eign¦er
for¦eign¦ness
fore¦know
  fore¦knew
  fore¦known
fore¦know¦ledge
fore¦lady
  fore¦ladies
fore¦land
fore¦leg
fore¦limb
fore¦lock
Fore¦man, George
  boxer
fore¦man
  fore¦men
fore¦mast
fore¦most
fore¦mother
fore¦name
fore¦noon
fo¦ren¦sic
fo¦ren¦sic¦al¦ly
fo¦ren¦sics
fore¦or¦dain
fore¦or¦din¦ation
fore¦part
fore¦paw
fore¦peak
fore¦person
fore¦play
fore¦quar¦ter
fore¦rib
fore¦run
  fore¦ran
  fore¦run¦ning

fore|run|ner
fore|sail
fore|see
  fore|saw
  fore|seen
fore|see|abil|ity
fore|see|able
fore|see|ably
fore|seer
fore|shadow
fore|sheet
fore|shock
fore|shore
fore|short|en
fore|show
  fore|shown
fore|sight
fore|sight|ed
fore|sight|ed|ly
fore|skin
for|est
fore|stall
fore|stall|er
fore|stal|ment
for|est|ation
fore|stay
For|est|er, C. S.
  novelist
for|est|er
for|est|ry
fore|taste
  fore|tast|ing
fore|tell
  fore|told
fore|tell|er
fore|thought
fore|to|ken
fore|told
fore|top
fore-top|gallant
fore-top|gallant-
          mast
fore-top|gallant-
          sail
fore|top|mast
fore|top|sail
fore|tri|angle
for|ever
for ever var. of
  forever
for|ever|more *US*
for ever|more *Br.*
fore|warn

fore|warn|er
fore|went
fore|wing
fore|woman
  fore|women
fore|word
forex
fore|yard
For|far
For|far|shire
for|feit
for|feit|able
for|feit|er
for|feit|ure
for|fend
for|gather var. of
  foregather
for|gave
forge
  for|ging
forge|able
for|ger
for|gery
  for|ger|ies
for|get
  for|got
  for|get|ting
  for|got|ten
for|get|ful
for|get|ful|ly
for|get|ful|ness
forget-me-not
for|get|table
for|get|ter
for|giv|able
for|giv|ably
for|give
  for|gave
  for|giv|ing
  for|given
for|give|ness
for|giver
for|giv|ing|ly
for|go
  for|goes
  for|went
  for|gone
  go without; cf.
  forego
for|got
for|got|ten
for|int
fork|ball

Fork|beard, Sweyn
  king of Denmark
  and England
fork|ful
fork|lift
fork|tail
form cf. forme
forma
  for|mas or for|mae
  Botany; cf. former
form|abil|ity
form|able
for|mal
for|mal|de|hyde
for|ma|lin
for|mal|isa|tion *Br.*
  var. of
  formalization
for|mal|ise *Br.* var.
  of formalize
for|mal|ism
for|mal|ist
for|mal|is|tic
for|mal|ity
  for|mal|ities
for|mal|iza|tion
for|mal|ize
  for|mal|iz|ing
for|mal|ly officially;
  cf. formerly
For|man, Milos
  film director
form|ant
for|mat
  for|mat|ted
  for|mat|ting
for|mate
for|ma|tion
for|ma|tion|al
for|ma|tive
for|ma|tive|ly
Formby, George
  comedian
forme *Printing.* cf.
  form
For|men|tera
for|mer previous; cf.
  forma
form|er person or
  thing that forms;
  cf. forma

for|mer|ly previ-
  ously; cf. **formally**
for|mic
For|mica *trademark*
for|mic|ar|ium
  for|mic|aria
for|mi|ca|tion
for|mid|able
for|mid|able|ness
for|mid|ably
form|less
form|less|ly
form|less|ness
for|mol
For|mosa
for|mula
  for|mu|lae or
  for|mu|las
for|mul|able
for|mu|la|ic
for|mu|la|ic|al|ly
for|mu|lar|ise *Br.*
  var. of formularize
for|mu|lar|ize
  for|mu|lar|iz|ing
for|mu|lary
  for|mu|lar|ies
for|mu|late
  for|mu|lat|ing
for|mu|la|tion
for|mu|la|tor
for|mu|lism
form|work
for|myl
For|nax
for|nenst var. of
  for|nent
for|nent
for|ni|cate
  for|ni|cat|ing
for|ni|ca|tion
for|ni|ca|tor
for|nix
for|nices
for|nix cere|bri
  for|nices cere|bri
for|rard
  non-standard
  forward
For|rest, John
  explorer and pre-
  mier of Western
  Australia

for|sake
  for|saken
for|saken|ness
for|saker
for|sooth
For|ster, E. M.
  novelist
for|ster|ite
for|swear
  for|swore
  for|sworn
For|syth, Fred|erick
  writer
for|sythia
fort cf. fought
For|ta|leza
for|ta|lice
Fort-de-France
forte strong point;
  Music loudly
Fort|ean
Fort|eana
forte|piano +s
  musical instrument
forte piano *Music*
  loud then soft
Forth
forth forward; cf.
  fourth
forth|com|ing
forth|right
forth|right|ly
forth|right|ness
forth|with
for|ti|eth
for|ti|fi|able
for|ti|fi|ca|tion
for|ti|fier
for|tify
  for|ti|fies
  for|ti|fied
  for|ti|fy|ing
for|tis
for|tis|simo
  for|tis|simos or
  for|tis|simi
for|ti|tude
Fort Knox
Fort Lamy
fort|let
fort|night
fort|night|ly
  fort|night|lies
For|tran

fort|ress
for|tuit|ous
for|tuit|ous|ly
for|tuit|ous|ness
for|tu|ity
  for|tu|ities
for|tu|nate
for|tu|nate|ly
for|tune
Fort Wil|liam
Fort Worth
forty
  for|ties
forty-first, forty-
  second, etc.
Forty-five 1745
  rebellion
forty-five gramo-
  phone record
forty|fold
forty-niner
forty-one, forty-
  two, etc.
forum
  for|ums or fora
for|ward
for|ward|er
for|ward|ly
for|ward|ness
for|wards
for|went
Fos|bury flop
fossa
  fos|sae *Anatomy*
  fos|sas animal
fosse
Fosse Way
fos|sick
fos|sick|er
fos|sil
fos|sil|ifer|ous
fos|sil|isa|tion *Br.*
  var. of fossilization
fos|sil|ise *Br.* var. of
  fossilize
fos|sil|iza|tion
fos|sil|ize
  fos|sil|iz|ing
fos|sor|ial
Fos|ter, Jodie
  actress
Fos|ter, Nor|man
  architect
fos|ter

fos|ter|age
foster-brother
foster-child
foster-daughter
fos|ter|er
foster-father
fos|ter|ling
foster-mother
foster-parent
foster-sister
foster-son
fou *Scot.* drunk; cf.
  foo fighter, foo
  yong
Fou|caul|dian
Fou|cault, Jean
  Ber|nard Léon
  physicist
Fou|cault, Mi|chel
  philosopher
Fou|cault|ian var.
  of Foucauldian
fou|letté
fought cf. fort
foul disgusting; cf.
  fowl
Foulah var. of Fula
fou|lard
foul|ly
foul|ness
foul-up *n.*
fou|mart
found
foun|da|tion
foun|da|tion|al
found|er person
  who founds
foun|der sink; fail;
  horse disorder
found|ling
found|ress
foun|dry
  foun|dries
fount source;
  fountain;
  Printing Br. var. of
  font
foun|tain
foun|tain|head
four number; cf. for,
  fore, 'fore
four-by-four
four|chette

four-eyes
  pl. four-eyes
four-flush
four-flusher
four|fold
Fou|rier analysis;
  series; transform
Fou|rier|ism
Fou|rier|ist
four-in-hand
four-iron
four|penny
four-ply
four-poster
four|score
four|some
four-square
four-stroke
four|teen
four|teenth
fourth in number;
  cf. forth
fourth|ly
4to = quarto
fovea
  fo|veae
fovea cen|tra|lis
  fo|veae cen|tra|lis
fo|veal
fo|ve|ate
fowl bird; cf. foul
Fowl|er, H. W.
  lexicographer
fowl|er
Fowles, John
  novelist
fowl pest
fowl plague
Fox people
  pl. Fox
Fox, Charles
  politician
Fox, George
  founder of Quakers
Fox, Edward and
  James actors
fox
Foxe, John author
  of *The Book of
  Martyrs*
fox|fire
fox|glove
fox|hole

fox|hound
fox hunt n.
fox-hunt v.
Fox|hunt|er horse
fox-hunter
foxie Austral./NZ
fox terrier; cf. foxy
fox|ily
foxi|ness
fox|like
fox|tail
Fox Tal|bot,
Wil|liam Henry
photography
pioneer
fox|trot
fox|trot|ted
fox|trot|ting
foxy
fox|ier
foxi|est
adj; cf. foxie
foyer
Fra Italian monk;
see Angelico, Fra
etc.
frab|jous
fra|cas
pl. fra|cas
US also fra|cases
frac|tal
frac|tion
frac|tion|al
frac|tion|al|isa|tion
var. of
fractionalization
frac|tion|al|ise Br.
var. of fractionalize
frac|tion|al|iza|tion
frac|tion|al|ize
frac|tion|al|iz|ing
frac|tion|al|ly
frac|tion|ate
frac|tion|at|ing
frac|tion|ation
frac|tious
frac|tious|ly
frac|tious|ness
frac|ture
frac|tur|ing
frae Scot. from; cf.
fray
frae|nu|lum var. of
frenulum

frae|num var. of
frenum
frag
fragged
frag|ging
fra|gile
fra|gile|ly
fra|gil|ity
frag|ment
frag|men|tal
frag|men|tar|ily
frag|men|tary
frag|men|ta|tion
Fra|go|nard, Jean-
Honoré painter
fra|grance
fra|grancy
fra|gran|cies
fra|grant
fra|grant|ly
'fraid non-standard
afraid
frail
frail|ly
frail|ness
frailty
frail|ties
fraise strawberry;
drink
Frak|tur
fram|able var. of
frameable
fram|be|sia US
fram|boe|sia Br.
fram|boise
frame
fram|ing
frame|able
frame|less
framer
frame|set
frame|shift
frame-up n.
frame|work
franc currency; cf.
frank
France
France, Ana|tole
writer
Fran|ces woman's
name; cf. Francis
Fran|cesca
Franche-Comté

fran|chise
fran|chis|ing
fran|chisee
fran|chiser
fran|chisor var. of
franchiser
Fran|cine
Fran|cis man's
name; cf. Frances
Fran|cis, Dick
writer
fran|cisa|tion var.
of francization
Fran|cis|can
fran|cise var. of
francize
Fran|cis of As|sisi,
St
Fran|cis of Sales,
St
Fran|cis Xa|vier,
St
fran|cium
fran|ciza|tion
also francisation
fran|cize
fran|ciz|ing
also francise
Franck, César
composer
Franco, Fran|cisco
Spanish head of
state
Franco- French
and...
Franco|ism
Franco|ist
fran|co|lin
Franco|mania
Fran|conia
Fran|co|nian
Franco|phile
Franco|phobe
Franco|pho|bia
franco|phone
fran|gible
fran|gi|pane
almond paste; cake
fran|gi|pani tree
fran|glais
Frank Germanic
tribe
Frank, Anne diarist

frank stamp;
candid; cf. franc
Fran|ken|food
Fran|ken|stein, Dr
scientist in novel
frank|er
Frank|fort in US
Frank|furt am
Main in western
Germany
Frank|furt an der
Oder in eastern
Germany
frank|furt|er
frank|in|cense
Frank|ish
Frank|lin, Aretha
singer
Frank|lin,
Ben|ja|min states-
man and scientist;
F. stove
Frank|lin,
Rosa|lind scientist
frank|lin
frank|ly
frank|ness
fran|tic
fran|tic|al|ly
fran|tic|ness
Franz Josef
emperor of Austria
Franz Josef Land
frap
frapped
frap|ping
frappé
Fras|cati
Fra|ser River
Fra|ser, Mal|colm
prime minister of
Australia
frass
fra|ter
fra|ter|nal
fra|ter|nal|ism
fra|ter|nal|ly
frat|er|nisa|tion Br.
var. of
fraternization
frat|er|nise Br. var.
of fraternize
fra|ter|nity
fra|ter|nities

frat¦er¦niza¦tion
frat¦er¦nize
  frat¦er¦niz¦ing
frat¦ri¦cidal
frat¦ri¦cide
Frau
  Frauen
  German-speaking
  woman; cf. vrou
fraud
fraud¦ster
fraudu¦lence
fraudu¦lent
fraudu¦lent¦ly
fraught
Fräu¦lein
fraxi¦nella
fray battle; cf. frae
Fray Ben¦tos
Fra¦zer, James
  anthropologist
Frazier, Joe boxer
fra¦zil ice crystals in
  stream
fraz¦zle
  fraz¦zling
  exhaustion; to
  exhaust
freak
freak¦ily
freaki¦ness
freak¦ish
freak¦ish¦ly
freak¦ish¦ness
freak-out n.
freaky
  freak¦ier
  freaki¦est
freckle
  freck¦ling
freckly
  freck¦lier
  freck¦li¦est
Fred¦die
Freddy
Fred¦erick
Fred¦eric¦ton
free
  freed
  freer
  freest
free-associ¦ate
free-associ¦at¦ing

free¦base
free¦bas¦ing
free¦bie
free¦board
free¦boot
free¦boot¦er
free¦born
freed¦man
  freed¦men
free¦dom
Free¦fone
  trademark var. of
  Freephone
free-for-all
free¦hand drawing
free hand freedom
  to act
free-handed
free-handed¦ly
free-handed¦ness
free¦hold
free¦hold¦er
free¦lance
  free¦lan¦cing
  free¦lan¦cer
free-living
free¦load
free¦load¦er
free¦ly
free¦man
  free¦men
free¦mar¦tin
Free¦mason
Free¦mason¦ry of
  Freemasons
free¦mason¦ry fel-
  low feeling
free¦ness
Free¦phone var. of
  Freefone
Free¦post
freer
free-range
free¦ride
  free¦rid¦ing
free¦sia
free-spoken
freest
free-standing
Free Stater
free¦stone
free¦style
  free¦styl¦ing

free¦styler
free-swimming
free¦think¦er
free¦think¦ing
free-to-air
Free¦town
free¦ware
free¦way
free¦wheel ratchet
  assembly; to coast
free wheel wheel
freez¦able
freeze
  froze
  freez¦ing
  fro¦zen
  solidify; cf. frieze
freeze-dry
  freeze-dries
  freeze-dried
  freeze-drying
freeze-frame
  freeze-framing
freeze-out n.
freez¦er
freeze-up n.
Frege, Gott¦lob
  philosopher and
  mathematician
Frei¦burg in
  Germany; cf.
  Fribourg
freight
freight¦age
freight¦er
Freight¦liner
  trademark
Fre¦limo
Fre¦man¦tle
Fré¦mont, John
  explorer
French
Fren¦chie var. of
  Frenchy
French¦ifi¦ca¦tion
French¦ify
  Frenchi¦fies
  Frenchi¦fied
  Frenchi¦fy¦ing
French¦man
  French¦men
French¦ness
French¦woman
  French¦women

Frenchy
  French¦ies
  French¦ier
  Frenchi¦est
fre¦net¦ic
fre¦net¦ic¦al¦ly
fre¦neti¦cism
frenu¦lum
fre¦num
fren¦zied¦ly
frenzy
  fren¦zies
  fren¦zied
freon trademark
fre¦quency
  fre¦quen¦cies
fre¦quent
fre¦quen¦ta¦tion
fre¦quen¦ta¦tive
fre¦quent¦er
fre¦quent¦ly
fresco
  fres¦coes or
  fres¦cos
  fres¦coed
fresco secco
fresh¦en
fresh¦en¦er
fresh¦er
freshet
freshie
fresh¦ly
fresh¦man
  fresh¦men
fresh¦ness
fresh¦water adj.
fresh¦woman
  fresh¦women
freshy var. of
  freshie
fres¦nel lens
Fresno
fret
  fret¦ted
  fret¦ting
fret¦board
fret¦ful
fret¦ful¦ly
fret¦ful¦ness
fret¦less
fret¦saw
fret¦work
Freud, Lu¦cian
  painter

Freud, Sig|mund
  psychotherapist
Freud|ian
Freud|ian|ism
Frey Scandinavian
  god
Freya Scandinavian
  goddess
Freyr var. of Frey
fri|abil|ity
fri|able
fri|able|ness
friar monk; cf. fryer
friar|bird
friar|ly
Friar Minor
  Friars Minor
friar's bal|sam
fri|ary
  fri|ar|ies
frib|ble
Fri|bourg in
  Switzerland; cf.
  Freiburg
fri|can|deau
  fri|can|deaux
fric|as|see
  fric|as|sees
  fric|as|seed
  fric|as|see|ing
frica|tive
fric|tion
fric|tion|al
fric|tion|less
Fri|day
fridge
fridge-freezer
Fried|man, Mil|ton
  economist
Fried|rich, Cas|par
  David painter
friend
friend|less
friend|lily
friend|li|ness
friend|ly
  friend|lies
  friend|lier
  friend|li|est
friend|ship
frier var. of fryer;
  cf. friar
Frie|sian cattle; cf.
  Frisian

Fries|land
frieze wall decor-
  ation; cloth; cf.
  freeze
frig
  frigged
  frig|ging vulgar
  slang
frig|ate
Frigga Scandinavian
  goddess
fright
fright|en
fright|en|er
fright|en|ing|ly
fright|ful
fright|ful|ly
fright|ful|ness
fri|gid
fri|gid|ar|ium
  fri|gid|aria
fri|gid|ity
fri|gid|ly
fri|gid|ness
fri|jo|les
frill|ery
  frill|er|ies
fril|li|ness
frilly
  frill|ies
  frill|ier
  frilli|est
Fri|maire
fringe
  frin|ging
fringe|less
fringy
Frink, Elisa|beth
  sculptor and artist
frip|pery
  frip|per|ies
frip|pet
fris|bee trademark
Frisch, Karl von
  zoologist
Frisch, Max writer
Frisch, Otto physi-
  cist
frisé fabric
fri|sée lettuce
Frisia
Fris|ian of Friesland
  or Frisia; person;
  language; Islands;

  cf. Friesian
frisk|er
fris|ket
frisk|ily
friski|ness
frisky
  frisk|ier
  friski|est
fris|son
frit
  frit|ted
  frit|ting
Frith, Wil|liam
  painter
fri|til|lary
  fri|til|lar|ies
frit|tata
frit|ter
fritto misto
Fritz
fritz in 'on the fritz'
Fri|uli
Friuli|an
Friuli-Venezia
  Giu|lia
frivol
  friv|olled Br.
  friv|oled US
  friv|ol|ling Br.
  friv|ol|ing US
fri|vol|ity
  fri|vol|ities
friv|olous
friv|olous|ly
friv|olous|ness
frizz
friz|zante
friz|zi|ness
friz|zle
  friz|zling
friz|zly
frizzy
  friz|zies
  friz|zi|er
  friz|zi|est
fro in 'to and fro'; cf.
  froe
'fro = Afro
  (hairstyle); cf. froe
Fro|bi|sher,
  Mar|tin explorer
froe tool; cf. fro
Froe|bel, Fried|rich
  educationist

Froe|bel|ian
Froe|bel|ism
frog
  frogged
  frog|ging
frog|bit
frog|fish
Froggy
  Frog|gies
  derogatory French
  person
froggy adj.
frog|hop|per
frog|let
frog|man
  frog|men
frog|march
frog|mouth
frog|spawn
froid|eur
fro|ing in 'toing and
  froing'
frolic
  frol|icked
  frol|ick|ing
  frol|ick|er
  frol|ic|some
from|age blanc
from|age frais
Fromm, Erich
  psychoanalyst
frond plant part
frond|age
Fronde French civil
  wars
frond|ose
frons
  frontes
front
front|age
front|ager
front|al
front|al|ly
front bench
front|bench|er
fron|tier
fron|tier|less
fron|tiers|man
  fron|tiers|men
fron|tiers|woman
  fron|tiers|women
fron|tis|piece
front|less
front|let

front|man
 front|men
front|most
fron|ton
front-runner
front-running
front|side
front|ward
front|wards
frore
frosh
Frost, Rob|ert poet
frost|bite
frost|bitten
frost|ily
frosti|ness
frost|less
frost stat
frosty
 frost|ier
 frosti|est
froth
froth|ily
frothi|ness
frothy
 froth|ier
 frothi|est
frot|tage
frot|teur
frot|teur|ism
frot|tola
 frot|tole
Froude num|ber
frou-frou
frounce
fro|ward
fro|ward|ly
fro|ward|ness
frown
frow|si|ness var. of
 frowziness
frowst
frow|sti|ness
frow|sty
 frow|stier
 frow|sti|est
frowsy var. of
 frowzy
frow|zi|ness
frowzy
 frow|zier
 frow|zi|est
froze

frozen
fro|zen|ly
Fruc|ti|dor
fruc|ti|fi|ca|tion
fruc|tify
 fruc|ti|fies
 fruc|ti|fied
 fruc|ti|fy|ing
fruc|tose
fruc|tu|ous
frug
 frugged
 frug|ging
fru|gal
fru|gal|ity
fru|gal|ly
fru|gal|ness
fru|gi|vore
fru|giv|or|ous
fruit
fruit|age
fruit|ar|ian
fruit|ar|ian|ism
fruit|bat
fruit|cake person
fruit cake cake
fruit|crow
fruit|er
fruit|er|er
fruit|ful
fruit|ful|ly
fruit|ful|ness
fruit|ily
fruiti|ness
fru|ition
fruit|less
fruit|less|ly
fruit|less|ness
fruit|let
fruit|wood
fruity
 fruit|ier
 fruiti|est
fru|menty
frump|ily
frumpi|ness
frump|ish
frump|ish|ly
frumpy
 frump|ier
 frumpi|est
fru|sem|ide

frus|trate
frus|trat|ing
frus|trated|ly
frus|trater
frus|trat|ing|ly
frus|tra|tion
frust|ule
frus|tum
 frusta or frus|tums
fru|ti|cose
Fry, Chris|to|pher
 writer
Fry, Eliza|beth
 reformer
fry
 fries
 fried
 fry|ing
fryer person who
 fries; device for
 frying; cf. friar
fry|pan
fry-up n.
f-stop
Fuad kings of Egypt
fubsy
 fub|sier
 fub|si|est
Fuchs, Klaus physi-
 cist
Fuchs, Viv|ian
 explorer
fuch|sia
fuch|sin
fuchs|ine var. of
 fuchsin
fuck|able vulgar
 slang
fuck|er vulgar slang
fuck|head vulgar
 slang
fuck-me adj. vulgar
 slang
fuck-up n. vulgar
 slang
fuck|wit vulgar
 slang
fu|coid
fuco|xan|thin
fucus
 fuci
fud|dle
 fud|dling
fuddy-duddy
 fuddy-duddies

fudge
 fudg|ing
fueh|rer var. of
 führer
fuel
 fuelled Br.
 fueled US
 fuel|ling Br.
 fuel|ing US
fuel|wood
Fuen|tes, Car|los
 writer
fufu
fug
 fugged
 fug|ging
fu|ga|cious
fu|ga|city
fugal
fu|gal|ly
Fu|gard, Athol
 playwright
fu|gato +s
Fug|gle
fuggy
 fug|gier
 fug|gi|est
fu|gi|tive
fugle|man
fugle|men
fugu Japanese fish
 dish
fugue
fu|guing
 musical form
füh|rer
Fu|jai|rah
Fuji
Fu|jian
Fu|ji|yama
Fu|kien var. of
 Fujian
Fu|ku|oka
Fula
Fu|lani
Fulbe
Ful|bright,
 Wil|liam US sen-
 ator; education
 awards
ful|crum
 ful|cra or
 ful|crums
ful|fil Br.
 ful|filled

ful¦fill¦ing
ful¦fill *US*
ful¦fill¦able
ful¦fill¦er
ful¦fill¦ment *US*
ful¦fil¦ment *Br.*
Ful¦fulde
ful¦gent
ful¦gur¦ant
ful¦gur¦ate
ful¦gur¦at¦ing
ful¦gur¦ation
ful¦gur¦ite
ful¦gur¦ous
fu¦li¦gin¦ous
full¦back
full-blood
full-bottomed
Ful¦ler,
  Buck¦min¦ster
  designer
ful¦ler¦ene
full face *adv.*
full-face *adj.*
full-fashioned
full-fledged
full-frontal
full-grown
full-length *adj.*
full¦ness
fully
ful¦mar
ful¦min¦ant
ful¦min¦ate
ful¦min¦at¦ing
ful¦min¦ation
ful¦ness var. of
  fullness
ful¦some
ful¦some¦ly
ful¦some¦ness
Ful¦ton, Rob¦ert
  engineer
ful¦ves¦cent
ful¦vous
fu¦mar¦ate
fu¦mar¦ic
fu¦ma¦role
fu¦ma¦rol¦ic
fum¦ble
fum¦bling
fum¦bler
fum¦bling¦ly

fumet
fu¦mi¦gant
fu¦mi¦gate
fu¦mi¦gat¦ing
fu¦mi¦ga¦tion
fu¦mi¦ga¦tor
fum¦ing¦ly
fu¦mi¦tory
fu¦mi¦tor¦ies
fumy
fumi¦er
fumi¦est
fun
funned
fun¦ning
Fu¦na¦futi
fu¦nam¦bu¦list
fun¦board
Fun¦chal
func¦tion
func¦tion¦al
func¦tion¦al¦ism
func¦tion¦al¦ist
func¦tion¦al¦ity
  func¦tion¦al¦ities
func¦tion¦al¦ly
func¦tion¦ary
  func¦tion¦ar¦ies
func¦tion¦less
func¦tor
fun¦dal
fun¦da¦ment
fun¦da¦men¦tal
fun¦da¦men¦tal¦ism
fun¦da¦men¦tal¦ist
fun¦da¦men¦tal¦ity
  fun¦da¦men¦tal¦
  ities
fun¦da¦men¦tal¦ly
fund¦er
fund¦hold¦er
fund¦hold¦ing
fundi *expert;*
  enthusiast
fun¦die *fundamen-*
  talist
fun¦dus
  fundi
Fundy, Bay of
fu¦neral
fu¦ner¦ary
fu¦ner¦eal
fu¦ner¦eal¦ly

fun¦fair
fun¦gal
fungi
fun¦gi¦bil¦ity
fun¦gible
fun¦gi¦cidal
fun¦gi¦cide
fun¦gi¦form
fun¦gi¦stat¦ic
fun¦giv¦or¦ous
fungo
  fun¦goes or fungos
fun¦goid
fun¦gous *adj.*
fun¦gus *n.*
  fungi or fun¦guses
fun¦house
fu¦nicle
fu¦nicu¦lar
fu¦nicu¦lus
  fu¦niculi
fun¦kia
funk¦ily
funki¦ness
funk¦ster
funky
  funk¦ier
  funki¦est
fun¦nel
  fun¦nelled *Br.*
  fun¦neled *US*
  fun¦nel¦ling *Br.*
  fun¦nel¦ing *US*
funnel-web spi¦der
fun¦nily
fun¦ni¦ness
fun¦ni¦os¦ity
  fun¦ni¦os¦ities
funny
  fun¦nies
  fun¦nier
  fun¦ni¦est
funny-face
  humorous
funny-ha-ha
funny-peculiar
fun¦ster
Fur people
  pl. Fur
fur
  furred
  fur¦ring
  animal hair;
  coating; cf. fir

furan
fur¦below
fur¦bish
furca
  fur¦cae
fur¦cal
fur¦cate
  fur¦cat¦ing
  fur¦ca¦tion
fur¦cula *n.*
  fur¦cu¦lae
fur¦cu¦lar *adj.*
fur¦fur¦aceous
fur¦fural
fur¦fur¦al¦de¦hyde
furi¦oso
furi¦ous
furi¦ous¦ly
furl
furl¦able
fur¦less
fur¦long
fur¦lough
fur¦mety var. of
  frumenty
fur¦nace
  fur¦na¦cing
Fur¦neaux Is¦lands
fur¦nish
fur¦nish¦er
fur¦ni¦ture
furor *US*
fur¦ore *Br.*
fur¦osem¦ide var. of
  frusemide
fur¦phy
  fur¦phies
fur¦rier
fur¦riery
fur¦ri¦ness
fur¦row
furry
  fur¦rier
  fur¦ri¦est
  cf. firry
fur¦ther
fur¦ther¦ance
fur¦ther¦er
fur¦ther¦more
fur¦ther¦most
fur¦thest
fur¦tive
fur¦tive¦ly

fur|tive|ness
Furt|wän|gler,
  Wil|helm con-
  ductor
fu|runcle
fu|run|cu|lar
fu|run|cu|lo|sis
fu|run|cu|lous
Fury *Greek*
  Mythology
  Fur|ies
fury
  fur|ies
furze
furzy
fu|sain
fu|sar|ium
  fu|saria or
  fu|sar|iums
fus|cous
fuse
  fus|ing
fusee *Br.*
  US **fuzee**
fusel oil; cf. fusil
fu|sel|lage
fuse|way
fusi|bil|ity
fus|ible
fu|si|form
fusil musket; cf.
  fusel
fu|si|leer *US*
  var. of fusilier
fu|si|lier
fu|sil|lade
  fu|sil|lad|ing
fu|silli
fusi|motor
fu|sion
fu|sion|al
fu|sion|ism
fu|sion|ist
fuss|er
fuss|ily
fussi|ness
fuss|pot
fussy
  fuss|ier
  fussi|est
fus|ta|nella
fus|tian
fus|tic

fus|tily
fusti|ness
fusty
  fus|tier
  fus|ti|est
fu|thark
fu|thorc var. of
  futhark
fu|thork var. of
  futhark
fu|tile
fu|tile|ly
fu|tili|tar|ian
fu|til|ity
  fu|til|ities
futon
fut|tock
fu|ture
future-proof
fu|tur|ism
fu|tur|ist
fu|tur|is|tic
fu|tur|is|tic|al|ly
fu|tur|ity
  fu|tur|ities
fu|turo|logic|al
fu|tur|olo|gist
fu|tur|ology
futz
fuze *US* var. of **fuse**
fuzee *US* var. of
  fusee
Fu|zhou
fuzz|box
fuzz|ily
fuzzi|ness
fuzzy
  fuzz|ies
  fuzz|ier
  fuzzi|est
fuzzy-wuzzy
  fuzzy-wuzzies
  offensive
F-word
fyke
fyl|fot
fyn|bos
fyrd
fytte section of
  poem; var. of **fit**

G

gab
  gabbed
  gab|bing
gab|ar|dine *US*
  Br. gaberdine
gab|ble
  gab|bling
gab|bler
gab|bro +s
gab|bro|ic
gab|broid
gabby
  gab|bier
  gab|bi|est
gab|er|dine *Br.*
  US gabardine
Gabès
gab|fest
ga|bion
ga|bion|age
Gable, Clark actor
gable
gab|let
Gabo, Naum sculp-
  tor
Gabon
Gab|on|ese
ga|boon mahogany
Ga|boon viper
Gabor, Den|nis
  electrical engineer
Gab|or|one
Gab|riel man's
  name
Gab|ri|eli,
  Gio|vanni
  composer
Gab|ri|elle woman's
  name
Gad Hebrew
  patriarch
gad
  gad|ded
  gad|ding
gad|about
Gad|ar|ene
Gad|dafi,
  Mu'am|mer

Mu|ham|mad al
  president of Libya
gad|fly
  gad|flies
gadget
gadget|eer
gadget|ry
  gadget|ries
gadgety
Gad|hel|ic
gadid
gad|oid
gado|lin|ite
gado|lin|ium
gad|roon
gad|wall
gad|zooks
Gaea goddess; var.
  of **Gaia**
Gael
Gael|dom
Gael|ic Celtic; cf.
  Gallic
Gael|tacht
Gae|nor
gaff spear; spar; in
  'blow the gaff'
gaffe blunder
gaf|fer
gag
  gagged
  gag|ging
gaga
Ga|garin, Yuri
  cosmonaut
gage
  ga|ging
  pledge; greengage;
  position relative to
  wind;
  US var. of **gauge**
gage|able *US* var. of
  gaugeable
gager *US* var. of
  gauger
gag|gle
  gag|gling
gag|ster
Gaia Greek goddess;
  theory of earth; cf.
  Gaya
Gaian
gai|ety
  gai|eties

gai¦jin
 pl. gai¦jin

gail¦lar¦dia

gaily

gain¦able

gain¦er

gain¦ful

gain¦ful¦ly

gain¦ful¦ness

gain¦say
 gain¦said

gain¦say¦er

Gains¦bor¦ough,
 Thomas painter

'gainst = against

gait manner of
 walking; cf. gate

gaita musical
 instrument

gai¦ter legging

Gait¦skell, Hugh
 politician

gal girl; unit of
 acceleration

gala festivity; cf.
 galah

gal¦ac¦ta¦gogue

gal¦ac¦tic

gal¦ac¦tic¦al¦ly

gal¦ac¦tor¦rhoea

gal¦act¦osa¦mine

gal¦act¦ose

gal¦ago +s

galah bird; cf. gala

Gala¦had Arthurian
 knight

gal¦an¦gal ginger-
 like plant; cf.
 galingale

gal¦ant style of
 music; cf. gallant

gal¦an¦tine

Gal¦apa¦gos

Gal¦atea *Greek
 Mythology*

Gal¦aţi city,
 Romania

Gal¦atia region of
 Asia Minor

Gal¦atian

gal¦axy
 gal¦ax¦ies

Galba, Ser¦vius
 Sul¦pi¦cius Roman
 emperor

gal¦ba¦num

Gal¦braith, John
 Ken¦neth econo-
 mist

gale

galea
 ga¦leae or ga¦leas

gal¦eate

gal¦eated

Galen Greek
 physician

ga¦lena

gal¦en¦ic

galère

gal¦ette

galia melon

Gal¦icia regions,
 Spain and E
 Europe

Gal¦ician

Gali¦lean

Gali¦lee region; Sea
 of

gali¦lee church
 porch

Gali¦leo Gali¦lei
 astronomer

gal¦in¦gale sedge; cf.
 galangal

gal¦iot var. of galliot

gali¦pot resin; cf.
 gallipot

gal¦joen
 pl. gal¦joen

gall

gal¦lant brave;
 chivalrous; cf.
 galant

gal¦lant¦ly

gal¦lant¦ry
 gal¦lant¦ries

gall¦ate

gall¦berry
 gall¦berries

gall¦leon

gall¦le¦ria

gall¦lery
 gall¦ler¦ies
 gall¦ler¦ied

gal¦let

gal¦ley

gal¦li¦am¦bic

Gal¦lia
 Nar¦bon¦en¦sis

Gal¦li¦ano +s

gal¦li¦ard

gal¦li¦ass

Gal¦lic Gaulish;
 French; cf. Gaelic

gal¦lic acid

Gal¦lican

Gal¦lican¦ism

gal¦lice in French

Gal¦li¦cise *Br.* var. of
 Gallicize

Gal¦li¦cism

Gal¦li¦cize
 Gal¦li¦ciz¦ing

gal¦li¦gas¦kins

gal¦li¦maufry
 gal¦li¦mauf¦ries

gal¦li¦mi¦mus

gal¦lin¦aceous

gall¦ing¦ly

gal¦li¦nule

gal¦liot

Gal¦lip¦oli

gal¦li¦pot pot; cf.
 galipot

gal¦lium

gal¦li¦vant

galli¦wasp lizard; cf.
 gall wasp

gallo¦glass

Gallo¦mania

Gallo¦maniac

gal¦lon

gal¦lon¦age

gal¦loon

gal¦lop +ed +ing
 horse's pace; cf.
 galop

gal¦lop¦er

Gallo¦phile

Gallo¦phobe

Gallo¦pho¦bia

gal¦lous var. of
 gallus

Gal¦lo¦way region;
 cattle

gallow¦glass var. of
 galloglass

gal¦lows

gall¦stone

Gal¦lup poll
 trademark

gal¦lus

gall wasp cf.
 galliwasp

gal¦oot

galop dance; cf.
 gallop

gal¦ore

gal¦osh

Gals¦worthy, John
 writer

Gal¦tieri, Leo¦poldo
 president of
 Argentina

Gal¦ton, Fran¦cis
 scientist

gal¦umph

Gal¦vani, Luigi
 anatomist

gal¦van¦ic

gal¦van¦ic¦al¦ly

gal¦van¦isa¦tion *Br.*
 var. of
 galvanization

gal¦van¦ise *Br.* var.
 of galvanize

gal¦van¦is¦er *Br.* var.
 of galvanizer

gal¦van¦ism

gal¦van¦iza¦tion

gal¦van¦ize
 gal¦van¦iz¦ing

gal¦van¦iz¦er

gal¦van¦om¦eter

gal¦vano¦met¦ric

gal¦vano¦scope

gal¦vano¦scop¦ic

Gal¦ves¦ton

galvo +s

Gal¦way

Gama, Vasco da
 explorer

Gamay

gamba

gam¦bade

gam¦bado
 gam¦ba¦dos or
 gam¦ba¦does

Gam¦bia country
 and river, W.
 Africa; cf. Gambier

Gam¦bian

gam¦bier plant

Gam|bier Is|lands
  in French
  Polynesia; cf.
  Gambia
gam|bit
gam|ble
  gam|bling
  bet; cf. gambol
gam|bler
gam|boge
gam|bol
  gam|bolled Br.
  gam|boled US
  gam|bol|ling Br.
  gam|bol|ing US
  frolic; cf. gamble
gam|brel
gam|busia
game
  gam|ing
  gamer
  gamest
game|cock
game|fowl
  pl. game|fowl
game|keep|er
game|keep|ing
gam|elan
game|ly
game|ness
game|pad
game|play
gamer
games|man
  games|men
games|man|ship
game|some
games|play|er
game|ster
gam|et|an|gium
  gam|et|an|gia
gam|ete
gam|et|ic
gam|eto|cyte
gam|eto|gen|esis
gam|eto|gen|ic
gam|et|ogeny
  gam|et|ogenies
gam|eto|phyte
gam|eto|phyt|ic
gamey var. of gamy
gam|gee
gami|ly
gamin male

gam|ine female
gami|ness
gamma Greek
  letter; cf. gammer
gamma-
    aminobu|tyr|ic
gamma-linolen|ic
gam|mer old
  woman; cf. gamma
gam|mon
gammy
  gam|mier
  gam|mi|est
gamut
gamy
  gami|er
  gami|est
ga|nache
Ga|na|pati
Gäncä
Gance, Abel film
  director
Ganda language
Gan|der town and
  airport, Canada
gan|der male goose;
  look
Gan|dhi,
  Ma|hatma, In|dira,
  and Rajiv Indian
  politicians
Gan|dhi|nagar
gandy dan|cer
ganef
Gan|esh Hindu
  deity
Gan|esha var. of
  Ganesh
gang band, group;
  cf. gangue
gang|board
gang|bust|er
gang|er
Gan|ges
Gan|get|ic
gang|land
gan|gle
  gan|gling
gan|gliar adj.
gan|gli|form
gan|glion
  gan|glia or
  gan|glions
gan|gli|on|ated

gan|gli|on|ic
gan|glio|side
gan|gly
gan|glier
gan|gli|est
gang|mast|er
gang|plank
gan|grene
gan|gren|ing
gan|gren|ous
gang|sta music
gang|ster criminal
gang|ster|ism
Gang|tok
gangue earth; cf.
  gang
gang|way
gan|is|ter
ganja
gan|net
gan|net|ry
  gan|net|ries
gan|oid
gan|sey
Gansu
gant|let US var. of
  gauntlet
gant|line
gan|try
  gan|tries
Gantt chart
Gany|mede Greek
  Mythology; moon
  of Jupiter
ganz|feld
gaol Br. var. of jail
gaol|bird Br. var. of
  jailbird
gaol|break Br. var.
  of jailbreak
gaol|er Br. var. of
  jailer
gap
  gapped
  gap|ping
gape
  gap|ing
gaper
gape|worm
gap|ing|ly
gappy
  gap|pier
  gap|pi|est
gar fish

gar|age
  gar|aging
garam ma|sala
garba Indian dance
  and song
gar|bage
gar|banzo +s
gar|ble
  garb|ling
garb|ler
Garbo, Greta
  actress
garbo +s
gar|board
garb|olo|gist
garb|ology
Gar|cía Lorca,
  Fe|de|rico Spanish
  poet and dramatist
Gar|cía Már|quez,
  Gab|riel Colombian
  novelist
gar|con
gar|con|nière
Garda
  Gar|dai
  Irish police; cf.
  guardee
Garda, Lake
gar|den
gar|den|er
gardener-bird
gar|den|er
  bower|bird
gar|denia
garde|robe
Gard|ner, Ava
  actress
Gard|ner, Erle
  Stan|ley novelist
Gar|eth
Gar|field, James
  US president
gar|fish
gar|ganey
gar|gan|tuan
gar|get
gar|gle
garg|ling
gar|goyle
gar|goyl|ism
Ga|ri|baldi,
  Giu|seppe Italian
  military leader

ga¦ri¦baldi biscuit; fish; blouse

ga¦rim¦peiro +s

gar¦ish

gar¦ish¦ly

gar¦ish¦ness

Gar¦land, Judy actress

gar¦land

gar¦lic

gar¦licky

gar¦ment

gar¦ner

gar¦net

gar¦nier¦ite

gar¦nish

gar¦nish¦ee
  gar¦nish¦ees
  gar¦nish¦eed
  gar¦nish¦ee¦ing

gar¦nish¦ment

gar¦ni¦ture

Ga¦ronne

gar¦otte var. of garrotte

Ga¦roua

gar¦pike

gar¦ret

Gar¦rick, David actor

gar¦rison

gar¦ron

gar¦rote US
  gar¦rot¦ing

gar¦rotte Br.
  gar¦rott¦ing

gar¦ru¦lity

gar¦rul¦ous

gar¦rul¦ous¦ly

gar¦rul¦ous¦ness

gar¦rya

garry¦owen

gar¦ter

Ga¦ruda

Gar¦vey, Mar¦cus political activist

gas
  gases
  pl. also gas¦ses *US*
  gassed
  gas¦sing
gas¦bag

Gas¦con native of Gascony

gas¦con braggart

gas¦con¦ade

Gas¦cony

gas¦eous

gas¦eous¦ness

gas¦hold¦er

gas¦ifi¦ca¦tion

gas¦ify
  gasi¦fies
  gasi¦fied
  gasi¦fy¦ing

Gas¦kell, Mrs Eliza¦beth novelist

gas¦ket

gas¦kin

gas¦light

gas¦lit

gas¦man
  gas¦men

gaso¦hol

gas oil

gas¦olene var. of gasoline

gas¦oline

gas¦om¦eter

gasp¦er

gas-proof

gas¦ser

gas¦si¦ness

gassy
  gas¦sier
  gas¦si¦est

Gast¦ar¦bei¦ter
  pl. Gast¦ar¦bei¦ter
  or *Gast¦ar¦bei¦ters*

gas¦tero¦pod var. of gastropod

Gast¦haus
  Gast¦häuser

Gast¦hof
  Gast¦höfe or
  Gast¦hofs

gas¦tor¦nis

gas¦trec¦tomy
  gas¦trec¦tomies

gas¦tric

gas¦trin

gas¦tri¦tis

gastro¦cne¦mius
  gastro¦cne¦mii

gastro¦colic

gastro¦enter¦ic

gastro¦enter¦itis

gastro¦entero¦
       logic¦al

gastro¦enter¦
       olo¦gist

gastro¦enter¦ology

gastro¦intes¦tinal

gastro¦lith

gastro¦nome

gastro¦nom¦ic

gastro¦nom¦ic¦al¦ly

gas¦tron¦omy

gastro¦pod

Gastro¦poda

gas¦trop¦odous

gastro¦pub

gastro¦scope

gastro¦scop¦ic

gas¦tros¦copy
  gas¦tros¦co¦pies

gas¦tros¦tomy
  gas¦tros¦to¦mies

gastro¦trich +s

Gastro¦tricha

gas¦trula
  gas¦tru¦lae

gas¦tru¦la¦tion

gas¦works

gat gun; cf. ghat

gate
  gat¦ing
  barrier; cf. gait

gat¦eau
  gat¦eaus or
  gat¦eaux
  French gâteau,
  gâteaux

gate¦crash

gate¦crash¦er

gate¦fold

gate¦house

gate¦keep¦er

gate¦leg
  gate¦legged

gate¦man
  gate¦men

gate¦post

Gates, Bill computer entrepreneur

Gates¦head

gate¦way

Gatha Zoroastrian poem

gather

gath¦er¦er

Gat¦ling

gator = alligator

Gatso +s

GATT = General Agreement on Tariffs and Trade

Gat¦wick

gauche

gauche¦ly

gauche¦ness

gauch¦erie

Gau¦cher's dis¦ease

gau¦cho +s

Gaudí, An¦tonio architect

Gaudier-Brzeska, Henri sculptor

gaud¦ily

gaudi¦ness

gaudy
  gau¦dies
  gaud¦ier
  gaud¦iest

gauge
  gauging
  measure; cf. gage

gauge¦able

gauger

Gau¦guin, Paul painter

Gau¦hati

Gaul

Gau¦lei¦ter

Gaul¦ish

Gaulle, Charles de president of France

Gaull¦ism

Gaull¦ist

Gault geological series

gault clay

Gaunt, John of son of Edward III of England

gaunt

gaunt¦let

gaunt¦ly

gaunt¦ness

gaur

Gauss, Karl Fried¦rich mathematician

gauss unit

Gauss¦ian

Gau|tama family
  name of **Buddha**
Gau|teng
gauze
gauz|ily
gauzl|ness
gauzy
  gauz|ier
  gauzi|est
gav|age
Gav|as|kar, Sunil
  cricketer
gavel
  gav|elled *Br.*
  gav|eled *US*
  gav|el|ling *Br.*
  gav|el|ing *US*
gavel|kind
ga|vial
ga|votte
Ga|wain Arthurian
  knight
Gawd = God in
  exclamations
gawk
gawk|er
gawk|ily
gawki|ness
gawk|ish
gawky
  gawk|ier
  gawki|est
gawp stare; cf. **gorp**
gawp|er
Gay, John dramatist
Gaya city, India; cf.
  Gaia
gayal Indian ox; cf.
  gayelle
gay|dar
Gaye, Mar|vin
  singer
gay|elle *W. Ind.*
  arena; cf. **gayal**
gay|ety *US* var. of
  gaiety
Gay-Lussac
gay|ness
Gaza
gaz|ania
Ga|zan|kulu
gazar
gaze
  gaz|ing

gaz|ebo +s
gaz|elle
gazer
gaz|ette
  gaz|et|ting
gaz|et|teer
Gazi|an|tep
ga|zil|lion
gaz|pa|cho +s
gaz|ump
gaz|ump|er
gaz|un|der
Gdańsk
g'day *Austral./NZ*
  good day
Gdy|nia
Ge goddess. var. of
  Gaia
gean cherry; cf.
  gene, jean, jeans
ge|anti|cline
gear
gear|box
gear|stick
gear|wheel
Geber chemist
gecko
  geckos or geck|oes
gee|bung
Gee|chee
gee|gaw *US* var. of
  gewgaw
gee-gee
geek|dom
geeky
  geek|ier
  geek|iest
Gee|long
geese
gee-string var. of
  G-string
gee whiz
Geez var. of **Jeez**
Ge'ez language
gee|zer person; cf.
  geyser
ge|filte fish
gegen|schein
Ge|henna
Geh|rig, Lou base-
  ball player; disease
Gehry, Frank archi-
  tect

Gei|ger count|er
Geiger-Müller
  count|er
Gei|kie, Archi|bald
  geologist
gei|sha
  pl. gei|sha or
  gei|shas
Geiss|ler tube
Geist
gei|ton|og|am|ous
gei|ton|og|amy
gel
gelled
gel|ling
gel|ada
gel|atin
gel|atine var. of
  gelatin
gel|at|in|isa|tion *Br.*
  var. of
  gelatinization
gel|at|in|ise *Br.* var.
  of gelatinize
gel|at|in|iza|tion
gel|at|in|ize
gel|at|in|iz|ing
gel|at|in|ous
gel|at|in|ous|ly
gel|ation
gel|ato
gel|ati
gel|coat
Gel|der|land
geld|ing
gelid
gel|ig|nite
Gell-Mann,
  Mur|ray physicist
gelly gelignite; cf.
  jelly
gel|se|mium
Gel|sen|kir|chen
gem
  gemmed
  gem|ming
Gem|ara
ge|ma|tria
Ge|mayel, Pierre
  Lebanese political
  leader
Ge|mein|schaft
gem|in|al
gem|in|al|ly

gemin|ate
  gemin|at|ing
gemin|ation
Gem|ini
Gemi|nian
Gem|in|ids
gem-like
gemma
gem|mae
gem|ma|tion
gem|mip|ar|ous
gem|mo|logic|al
gem|molo|gist
gem|mology
gem|mu|la|tion
gem|mule
gemmy having
  gems; cf. **jemmy**
gemo|logic|al var.
  of gemmological
gem|olo|gist var. of
  gemmologist
gem|ology var. of
  gemmology
gems|bok
gem|stone
ge|müt|lich
Ge|müt|lich|keit
gen
  genned
  gen|ning
gena *Zoology*
genae
genal
gen|darme
gen|darm|erie
gen|der
gen|dered
Gene man's name;
  cf. **Jean**
gene *Biology*; cf.
  gean, jean, jeans
ge|nea|logic|al
ge|nea|logic|al|ly
ge|nea|logise *Br.*
  var. of genealogize
ge|neal|ogist
ge|neal|ogize
ge|neal|ogiz|ing
ge|neal|ogy
ge|neal|ogies
gen|era
gen|er|able
gen|eral

gen|er|al|is|abil|ity
  Br. var. of
  generalizability
gen|er|al|is|able *Br.*
  var. of
  generalizable
gen|er|al|isa|tion
  Br. var. of
  generalization
gen|er|al|ise *Br.* var.
  of generalize
gen|er|al|iser *Br.*
  var. of generalizer
gen|er|al|ism
gen|er|al|is|simo +s
gen|er|al|ist
gen|er|al|ity
  gen|er|al|ities
gen|er|al|iz|abil|ity
gen|er|al|iz|able
gen|er|al|iza|tion
gen|er|al|ize
  gen|er|al|iz|ing
gen|er|al|izer *US*
gen|er|al|ly
gen|er|al|ship
gen|er|ate
  gen|er|at|ing
gen|er|ation
gen|er|ation|al
gen|er|ation|al|ly
gen|era|tive
gen|era|tiv|ity
gen|er|ator
gen|er|atrix
  gen|er|atri|ces
gen|er|ic
gen|er|ic|al|ly
gen|er|os|ity
gen|er|ous
gen|er|ous|ly
gen|esis
Genet, Jean writer
genet catlike
  mammal; cf. jennet
gen|et|ic
gen|et|ical
gen|et|ic|al|ly
gen|eti|cist
gen|et|ics
Gen|ette name
Gen|eva city

gen|eva gin;
  literary var. of
  genever
gen|ever
Gene|vieve
Gen|ghis Khan
gen|ial
geni|al|ity
geni|al|ly
genic
gen|icu|late
genie
  ge|nies
genii pl. of genius
genip
geni|pap var. of
  genipapo
geni|papo +s
gen|ista
geni|tal
geni|talia
geni|tal|ly
geni|tival
geni|tival|ly
geni|tive
geni|tor
genito-urinary
geni|ture
ge|nius
  ge|niuses
  persons
  genii
  spirits; influences
ge|nius loci
  genii loc|orum
Ge|ni|zah
gen|lock
genny
  gen|nies
  sail; cf. jenny
Genoa port, Italy;
  cake
genoa sail
geno|cidal
geno|cide
Geno|ese
gen|ome
gen|om|ic
gen|om|ics
geno|type
  geno|typ|ing
geno|typ|ic
genre

gens
  gen|tes
  group of people
Gent
  Flemish name for
  Ghent
gen|ta|mi|cin
gen|teel
gen|teel|ism
gen|teel|ly
gen|teel|ness
gen|tes pl. of gens
gen|tian
Gen|tile non-
  Jewish; non-Jew
gen|tile indicating
  nationality
Gen|tile da
  Fab|ri|ano painter
gen|til|ity
  gen|til|ities
gen|tle
  gent|ling
  gent|ler
  gent|lest
gentle|folk
gentle|man
  gentle|men
gentleman-at-arms
  gentlemen-at-arms
gentle|man
  farm|er
  gentle|men
  farm|ers
gentle|man|li|ness
gentle|man|ly
gentle|man's
  agree|ment +s
gentle|man's
  gentle|man
  gentle|men's
  gentle|men
Gentle|man's
  Rel|ish *trademark*
gentle|men's
  agree|ment var. of
  gentleman's
  agreement
gentle|ness
gentle|woman
  gentle|women
gen|tly
gen|too +s
gen|tri|fi|ca|tion
gen|tri|fier

gen|tri|fy
  gen|tri|fies
  gen|tri|fied
  gen|tri|fy|ing
gen|try
genu
  genua
  Anatomy knee
genu|flect
genu|flec|tion
genu|flect|or
genu|flex|ion *Br.*
  var. of genuflection
genu|ine
genu|ine|ly
genu|ine|ness
genus
  gen|era
geo|botan|ic|al
geo|bot|an|ist
geo|bot|any
geo|caching
geo|cen|tric
geo|cen|tric|al|ly
geo|cen|trism
geo|chem|ical
geo|chem|ist
geo|chem|is|try
geo|chrono|logic|al
geo|chron|olo|gist
geo|chron|ology
geo|chrono|met|ric
geo|chron|om|etry
geode
geo|des|ic
geo|des|ist
geo|desy
geo|det|ic
geo|dic
geo|duck
Geof|frey of
  Mon|mouth
  chronicler
geog|raph|er
geo|graph|ic
geo|graph|ic|al
geo|graph|ic|al|ly
geog|raphy
  geog|raph|ies
geoid
geo|logic
geo|logic|al
geo|logic|al|ly

geolo|gise *Br.* var. of
  geologize
geolo|gist
geolo|gize
  geolo|giz|ing
geol|ogy
geo|mag|net|ic
geo|mag|net|ic|al|ly
geo|mag|net|ism
geo|mancy
geo|man|tic
geo|mat|ic
geom|eter
geo|met|ric
geo|met|ric|al
geo|met|ric|al|ly
geom|etri|cian
geo|met|rid
geom|etry
  geom|etries
geo|morph|ic
geo|mor|pho|
          logic|al
geo|morph|olo|gist
geo|morph|ology
ge|oph|agy
geo|phys|ic|al
geo|physi|cist
geo|phys|ics
geo|pol|it|ical
geo|pol|it|ic|al|ly
geo|pol|it|ician
geo|pol|it|ics
Geor|die
George automatic
  pilot
George Town cap-
  ital of the Cayman
  Islands; port,
  Malaysia
George|town cap-
  ital of Guyana
Geor|gette name
geor|gette fabric
Geor|gia
Geor|gian
Geor|giana
geor|gic
Geor|gie
Geor|gina
geo|science
geo|sci|en|tist
geo|spa|tial

geo|sphere
geo|sta|tion|ary
geo|stra|tegic
geo|strat|egy
geo|stroph|ic
geo|syn|chron|ous
geo|syn|cline
geo|tac|tic
geo|taxis
geo|tech|nic|al
geo|tech|nics
geo|ther|mal
geo|ther|mal|ly
geo|trop|ic
geo|trop|ism
Gera
Ger|aint
Ger|ald
Ger|ald|ine
Ger|ald|ton
ge|ra|nial
ge|ra|niol
ge|ra|nium
Ger|ard, John
  herbalist
ger|bera
ger|bil
ger|enuk
geri|at|ric
geria|tri|cian
Gé|ri|cault,
  Théo|dore painter
germ
Ger|maine
Ger|man
ger|man having
  same parents; cf.
  germen
ger|man|der
ger|mane
ger|mane|ly
ger|mane|ness
Ger|man|ic
ger|man|ic
  Chemistry of
  germanium
Ger|mani|cism
Ger|man|isa|tion
  Br. var. of
  Germanization
Ger|man|ise *Br.* var.
  of Germanize

Ger|man|iser *Br.*
  var. of Germanizer
Ger|man|ism
Ger|man|ist
ger|ma|nium
Ger|man|iza|tion
Ger|man|ize
  Ger|man|iz|ing
Ger|man|izer
Ger|many
  Ger|manies
ger|men *Botany*; cf.
  german
ger|mi|cidal
ger|mi|cide
Ger|mi|nal month
ger|min|al
ger|min|al|ly
ger|min|ate
  ger|min|at|ing
ger|min|ation
ger|mina|tive
ger|min|ator
Ger|mis|ton
germy
  germ|ier
  germi|est
Ger|on|imo Apache
  chief
ger|on|tic
ger|on|toc|racy
  ger|on|toc|ra|cies
ger|on|to|crat
ger|onto|crat|ic
ger|on|to|logic|al
ger|on|tolo|gist
ger|on|tol|ogy
Ger|rard
ger|ry|man|der
ger|ry|man|der|er
Gersh|win, George
  composer
Ger|son therapy
Ger|trude
ger|und
ger|und|ial
ger|und|ival
ger|und|ive
Ger|vaise
Ger|vase
Ge|sell|schaft
ges|ner|iad

gesso
ges|soes
ge|stalt
ge|stalt|ism
ge|stalt|ist
Ge|stapo
ges|tate
ges|tat|ing
ges|ta|tion
ges|ta|tion|al
ges|ticu|late
ges|ticu|lat|ing
ges|ticu|la|tion
ges|ticu|la|tive
ges|ticu|la|tor
ges|ticu|la|tory
ges|tural
ges|ture
ges|tur|ing
ge|sund|heit
get
got
get|ting
got|ten *US*
get-at-able
get|away
get-go
Geth|sem|ane
get-out *n. & mod.*
get|table
get|ter
get|ter|ing
get-together
Getty, Jean Paul
  industrialist
Gettys|burg
get-up *n.*
get-up-and-go
Getz, Stan sax-
  ophonist
geum
gew|gaw
Ge|würz|tram|iner
gey *Scot.* very
gey|ser hot spring;
  water heater; cf.
  geezer
gey|ser|ite
Ghana
Ghan|aian
gha|rana
gha|rara
ghar|ial

gharry
  ghar|ries
ghast|lily
ghast|li|ness
ghastly
  ghast|lier
  ghast|li|est
ghat flight of river-
  steps etc.; cf. **gat**
gha|tam
Ghats mountains
gha|zal
ghazi
Gha|zia|bad
Ghaz|na|vid
ghee clarified butter;
  cf. **gi, gie**
Gheg
Ghent
ghe|rao +s +ed +ing
gher|kin
ghetto
  pl. **ghet|tos** or
  ghet|toes
  v. **ghet|toes**
  ghet|toed
  ghetto|ing
ghetto|isa|tion var.
  of **ghettoization**
ghetto|ise *Br.* var. of
  ghettoize
ghetto|iza|tion
ghetto|ize
  ghetto|iz|ing
ghi var. of **ghee**
Ghib|el|line
Ghib|el|lin|ism
Ghi|berti, Lo|renzo
  sculptor
ghibli
ghil|lie var. of **gillie**
Ghir|lan|daio
  painter
ghost
ghost|bust|er
ghost|like
ghost|li|ness
ghost|ly
  ghost|lier
  ghost|li|est
ghost|write
  ghost|wrote
  ghost|writing
  ghost|written

ghost|writer
ghoul
ghoul|ish
ghoul|ish|ly
Ghul|ghu|leh
ghusl
ghyll ravine; stream
  var. of **gill**
gi judo jacket; cf.
  ghee, gie
Gia|co|metti,
  Al|berto artist
giant
giant|ism
giant-killer
giant-killing
giant|like
Giant's Cause|way
giaour
giar|dia|sis
Gib Gibraltar; cf. **jib**
gib|ber speak inco-
  herently; stone; cf.
  jibba, jibber
gibber|bird
gib|ber|el|lic
gib|ber|el|lin
gib|ber|ish
gib|bet
Gib|bon, Ed|ward
  historian
gib|bon
Gib|bons, Grin|ling
  sculptor
Gib|bons, Or|lando
  composer
gib|bous of the
  moon; cf. **gibus**
gibbs|ite
gibe
  gib|ing
  var. of **jibe**; cf.
  gybe
gib|lets
Gib|ral|tar
Gib|ral|tar|ian
Gib|ran, Kha|lil
  writer and artist
Gib|son, Mel actor
Gib|son Des|ert
Gib|son girl
gibus hat; cf.
  gibbous

gid disease
gid|dap
  US var. of **giddy-up**
gid|di|ly
gid|di|ness
giddy
  gid|dies
  gid|died
  giddy|ing
  gid|dier
  gid|di|est
giddy-up
Gide, André writer
Gid|eon
gidgee
gie
  gies
  gied
  gie|ing
  gien
  Scot. give; cf. **ghee,**
  gi
Giel|gud, John
  actor
GIF image file
  format
GIFT = gamete
  intrafallopian
  transfer
gift|able
gift|ed|ness
gift|ware
gig
  gigged
  gig|ging
giga|bit
giga|byte
giga|flop
giga|hertz
gi|gan|tic
gi|gan|tic|al|ly
gi|gant|ism
gi|gant|om|achy
  gi|gant|om|achies
Gi|gan|to|pith|ecus
  Gi|gan|to|pith|eci
giga|watt
gig|gle
  gig|gling
gig|gler
gig|gly
  gig|glier
  gig|gli|est
Gigli, Ben|ia|mino
  singer

GIGO = garbage in,
  garbage out
gig|olo +s
gigot meat; sleeve
gigue
Gijón
Gila mon|ster
Gil|bert,
  Hum|phrey
  explorer
Gil|bert, Wil|liam
  scientist
Gil|bert, W. S.
  librettist
Gil|bert|ese
Gil|bert|ian
Gil|bert Is|lands
gild cover with gold;
  cf. **guild**
gild|er person who
  gilds; cf. **guilder**
gilet
gil|gai
Gil|ga|mesh legend-
  ary Sumerian king
Gill, Eric sculptor
  etc.
gill
gil|la|roo
  pl. **gil|la|roo** or
  gil|la|roos
  fish; cf. **jillaroo**
Gil|les|pie, Dizzy
  trumpeter
Gil|lian
gil|lie
gilli|flower var. of
  gillyflower
Gil|ling|ham
gilly|flower
Gil|son|ite
  trademark
gilt covered with
  gold; gold layer;
  government secur-
  ity; pig; cf. **guilt**
gilt|wood
gim|bal
  gim|balled
  gim|bal|ling
gim|crack
gim|crack|ery
gim|let
gimme

gim¦mer
gim¦mick
gim¦mick¦ry
gim¦micky
gimp trimming;
 lame person; limp;
 cf. guimpe
gimpy
gin
 ginned
 gin¦ning
gin¦ger
gin¦ger¦bread
gin¦ger¦li¦ness
gin¦ger¦ly
gin¦gery
ging¦ham
gin¦gival
gin¦gi¦vitis
gingko var. of
 ginkgo
gin¦gly¦mus
gin¦glymi
gink
ginkgo
 gink¦gos or
 gink¦goes
gin¦nel
gin¦ner
gin¦nery
 gin¦ner¦ies
gi¦nor¦mous
Gins¦berg, Allen
 poet
gin¦seng
ginzo +s
Gio¦conda, La
Gior¦gione painter
Giotto di
 Bon¦done painter
gip var. of gyp
gippo offensive var.
 of gyppo
gippy tummy
gipsy var. of Gypsy
gipsy¦ish var. of
 gypsyish
gipsy¦wort var. of
 gypsywort
girl¦affe
gir¦an¦dole
gira¦sol
gira¦sole var. of
 girasol

gird
 gird¦ed or girt
gir¦der
gir¦dle
 gird¦ling
gird¦ler
girl¦friend
girl¦hood
girlie
girl¦ish
girl¦ish¦ly
girl¦ish¦ness
girly var. of girlie
girn var. of gurn
girn¦er var. of
 gurner
giro is credit
 transfer; cf. gyro
Gi¦ronde
Gi¦ron¦din var. of
 Girondist
Gi¦rond¦ist
girt
girth
Gis¦borne
Gis¦card
 d'Es¦taing, Val¦éry
 president of France
Gi¦selle
Gish, Lil¦lian
 actress
gismo var. of gizmo
Gis¦sing, George
 writer
gist
Gita
gîte
git¦tern
give
 gave
 giv¦ing
 given
give¦away
give¦back
giver
Giza, El
gizmo +s
giz¦zard
Gje¦tost
gla¦bella n.
 gla¦bellae
gla¦bel¦lar adj.
glab¦rous

glacé
gla¦cial
gla¦ci¦al¦ly
gla¦ci¦ated
gla¦ci¦ation
gla¦cier
gla¦cio¦logic¦al
gla¦ci¦olo¦gist
gla¦ci¦ology
gla¦cis
 pl. gla¦cis
glad
 glad¦ded
 glad¦ding
 glad¦der
 glad¦dest
glad¦den make glad;
 cf. gladdon
glad¦die
glad¦don flower; cf.
 gladden
gladi¦ator
gladia¦tor¦ial
gladi¦olus
 gladi¦oli
glad¦ly
glad¦ness
glad¦some
Glad¦stone,
 Wil¦liam Ewart
 prime minister of
 Britain; bag
Glad¦ston¦ian
Gladys
Gla¦go¦lit¦ic
glai¦kit
glair egg white
 adhesive; cf. glare
glairy
glaive
glam
 glammed
 glam¦ming
glam¦azon
glamor US var. of
 glamour
Gla¦mor¦gan
glam¦or¦isa¦tion Br.
 var. of
 glamorization
glam¦or¦ise Br. var.
 of glamorize
glam¦or¦iza¦tion

glam¦or¦ize
 glam¦or¦iz¦ing
glam¦or¦ous
glam¦or¦ous¦ly
glam¦our
glam¦our¦isa¦tion
 Br. var. of
 glamorization
glam¦our¦ise Br.
 var. of glamorize
glam¦our¦iza¦tion
 var. of
 glamorization
glam¦our¦ize var. of
 glamorize
glance
glan¦cing
glan¦cing¦ly
glan¦ders
glan¦du¦lar
glans
 glan¦des
glare
 glar¦ing
 stare; shine; cf.
 glair
glare¦shield
glar¦ing¦ly
glary
 glar¦ier
 glari¦est
Glas¦gow
glas¦nost
Glass, Philip
 composer
glass
glass¦fish
glass¦ful
glass¦house
glassie n. var. of
 glassy
glass¦ily
glass¦ine
glassi¦ness
glass¦less
glass-like
glass¦paper
glass¦ware
glass¦work
glass¦works
glass¦wort
glassy
 glass¦ies
 glass¦ier

glassi|est
Glas|ton|bury
Glas|we|gian
glatt ko|sher
Glau|ber's salts
glau|coma
glau|comat|ous
glau|con|ite
glau|con|it|ic
glauco|phane
glau|cous
glaze
  glaz|ing
glazer
glaz|ier
glaz|iery
  glaz|ier|ies
Glaz|unov,
  Alek|sandr
  composer
glazy
  glaz|ier
  glazi|est
gleam
gleam|ing|ly
gleamy
glean
glean|er
glebe
glee
glee|ful
glee|ful|ly
glee|ful|ness
glee|man
  glee|men
glee|some
gleet
gleety
Gleich|schal|tung
Glen|coe
Glenda
Glen|dower, Owen
  Welsh prince
Glen|eagles
glen|garry
  glen|gar|ries
glen|oid
Glen|rothes
Glenys
gley
glia
glial

glib
glib|ber
glib|best
glib|ly
glib|ness
glide
  glid|ing
glider
glim|mer
glimpse
  glimps|ing
Glinka, Mikh|ail
  Ivan|ovich
  composer
glio|blast|oma
  glio|blast|omas or
  glio|blast|omata
gli|oma
  gli|omas or
  gli|omata
glis|sade
  glis|sad|ing
glis|sando
  glis|sandi or
  glis|san|dos
glissé
glis|ten
glis|ter
glitch
glitchy
glit|ter
glit|ter|ati
glit|ter|ing|ly
Glit|ter|tind
glit|tery
glitz
glitz|ily
glitzi|ness
glitzy
  glitz|ier
  glitzi|est
gloam|ing
gloat
gloat|er
gloat|ing|ly
glo|bal
glo|bal|isa|tion *Br.*
  var. of
  globalization
glo|bal|ise *Br.* var.
  of globalize
glo|bal|ism
glo|bal|ist
glo|bal|iza|tion

glo|bal|ize
  glo|bal|iz|ing
glo|bal|ly
globe
  glob|ing
globe|fish
globe|flower
globe-like
globe|trot
  globe|trotted
  globe|trot|ting
globe|trot|ter
glo|bi|ger|ina
  glo|bi|ger|inas or
  glo|bi|ger|inae
glo|bi|ger|inal
glo|boid
glo|bose
globu|lar
globu|lar|ity
glob|ule
globu|lin
globu|lous
glo|bus
  hys|ter|icus
glo|bus pal|li|dus
  globi pal|lidi
glo|chid
glo|chid|ium
  glo|chidia
glock|en|spiel
glögg
glom
  glommed
  glom|ming
glom|eru|lar
glom|er|ulo|
       neph|ritis
glom|eru|lus
  glom|eruli
gloom cf. glume
gloom|ily
gloomi|ness
gloomy
  gloom|ier
  gloomi|est
gloopy
glop
  glopped
  glop|ping
gloppy
  glop|pier
  glop|pi|est
Gloria

Glori|ana
glori|fi|ca|tion
glori|fier
glor|ify
  glori|fies
  glori|fied
  glori|fy|ing
glori|ole
glori|ous
glori|ous|ly
glori|ous|ness
glory
  glor|ies
  glor|ied
  glory|ing
glory-of-the-snow
gloss|ar|ial
gloss|ar|ist
gloss|ary
  gloss|ar|ies
gloss|ator
gloss|er
gloss|ily
glossi|ness
gloss|itis
glos|sog|raph|er
glos|so|lalia
glos|so|lalic
glosso|
       pha|ryn|geal
glossy
  glossies
gloss|ier
  glossi|est
glost
glot|tal
glot|tic
glot|tis
glotto|chrono|
       logic|al
glotto|chron|ol|ogy
Glouces|ter
Glouces|ter|shire
glove
  glov|ing
glove|box
glove|less
glover
glow
glower
glower|ing|ly
glow|ing|ly
glow-worm

glox|inia
gloze
  gloz|ing
glu|ca|gon
glu|can
Gluck, Chris|toph
  Wil|li|bald von
  composer
gluco|cortic|oid
glu|cosa|mine
glu|cose
glu|co|side
glu|co|sid|ic
glu|cur|on|ate
glu|cur|on|ic
glue
  glu|ing or glue|ing
glue-like
gluey
  glu|ier
  glui|est
gluey|ness
glug
  glugged
  glug|ging
glugg var. of glögg
glug|gable
glüh|wein
glum
  glum|mer
  glum|mest
glu|ma|ceous
glume Botany; cf.
  gloom
glum|ly
glum|ness
glu|mose
gluon
glut
  glut|ted
  glut|ting
glu|tam|ate
glu|tam|ic
glu|tam|ine
gluta|thi|one
glute
glu|teal
glu|ten
glu|teus max|imus
  glu|tei max|imi
glu|tin|ous
glu|tin|ous|ly
glu|tin|ous|ness
glut|ton

glut|ton|ise Br. var.
  of gluttonize
glut|ton|ize
  glut|ton|iz|ing
glut|ton|ous
glut|ton|ous|ly
glut|tony
gly|caemia Br.
gly|caem|ic Br.
gly|cemia US
gly|cem|ic US
gly|cer|ide
gly|cerin US
gly|cer|ine Br.
gly|cerol
gly|ceryl
gly|cine
glyco|gen
glyco|gen|esis
glyco|gen|ic
gly|col
gly|col|ic
gly|col|lic var. of
  glycolic
gly|coly|sis
glyco|lyt|ic
glyco|pro|tein
glyco|side
glyco|sid|ic
glyco|suria
glyco|sur|ic
Glynde|bourne
Glyn|dwr, Owain
  Welsh form of
  Owen Glendower
Glynis
Glyn|nis
glyph
glyph|ic
gly|pho|sate
glyp|tic
glyp|to|dont
glyp|tog|raphy
G-man
  G-men
gnamma
gnarl
gnarly
  gnarl|ier
  gnarli|est
gnash
gnash|er
gnat

gnat|catch|er
gnatho|sto|mu|lid
Gnatho|
  sto|mu|lida
gnaw chew; cf. nor
gnaw|ing|ly
gneiss
gneiss|ic
gneiss|oid
gneiss|ose
gnoc|chi
gnome cf. nome
gno|mic
gnom|ic|al|ly
gnom|ish
gnomon
gnom|on|ic
  Geometry; cf.
  mnemonic
gno|sis
Gnos|tic early
  Christian heretic
gnos|tic relating to
  knowledge
Gnos|ti|cism
gnoto|biot|ic
gnu
go
  goes
  went
  gone
Goa state, India
goa gazelle
goad
go-ahead n. & adj.
goal
goal|ball
goal|hang|er
goalie
goal|keep|er
goal|keep|ing
goal|less
goal|mouth
goal|post
goal|scorer
goal|scor|ing
goal|tend|er
goal|tend|ing
goal|wards
Goan
Goan|ese
go|anna
go-around n.

goat-antelope
goatee
goateed
goat|fish
goat|herd
goat|ish
goat's beard plant
goat|skin
goat's rue
goat|suck|er
goaty
  goat|ier
  goati|est
go-away bird
gob
  gobbed
  gob|bing
Göb|bels, Jo|seph
  var. of Goebbels
gob|bet
Gobbi, Tito singer
gob|ble
  gob|bling
gobble|de|gook
gobble|dy|gook var.
  of gobbledegook
gob|bler
gob|daw
Gobe|lin tapestry;
  cf. goblin
Gobe|lins French
  tapestry factory
go-between n.
gobi Ind. cauliflower
  or cabbage; cf.
  goby
Gobi Des|ert
Gobi|neau, Jo|seph
  Ar|thur de anthro-
  pologist
gob|let
gob|lin creature in
  folklore; cf.
  Gobelin
gobo +s
go|bony
gob|shite vulgar
  slang
gob|smacked
gob|smack|ing
gob|stop|per
goby
  go|bies
  fish; cf. gobi

go-by *n.* snub
go-cart handcart; cf.
  go-kart
God¦ard, Jean-Luc
  film director
God-awful
god¦child
  god¦chil¦dren
god¦dam
god¦damn var. of
  goddam
god¦damned var. of
  goddam
God¦dard, Rob¦ert
  Hutch¦ings
  physicist
god-daughter
god¦dess
Gödel's incomplete-
  ness theorem
godet
go¦de¦tia
go-devil
god¦father
God-fearing
god¦for¦saken
God¦frey
God-given
god¦head
god¦hood
God¦iva, Lady
god¦less
god¦less¦ness
god¦like
god¦li¦ness
godly
  god¦lier
  god¦li¦est
god-man
  god-men
god¦mother
go¦down warehouse
god¦par¦ent
god¦send
god¦ship
god¦son
God¦speed
Godu¦nov, Boris
  tsar of Russia
god¦ward
god¦wards
Godwin-Austen
god¦wit

God¦wot¦tery
God¦zilla
Goeb¦bels, Jo¦seph
  Nazi leader
goer cf. goa
Goe¦ring,
  Her¦mann Nazi
  leader
Goes, Hugo van
  der painter
goest
goeth
Goe¦the, Jo¦hann
  Wolf¦gang von
  writer
Goe¦thean
Goe¦thian var. of
  Goethean
goeth¦ite
gofer person who
  runs errands; cf.
  gopher
gof¦fer
Gog and Magog
go-getter
go-getting
gogga
gog¦gle
  gog¦gling
goggle-box
goggle-eye
goggle-eyed
go-go dancer;
  assertive; cf.
  a gogo, agogo
Gogol, Ni¦ko¦lai
  writer
Goi¦del¦ic
going-over
  goings-over
goings-on
goi¦ter US
goi¦tered US
goitre Br.
goitred Br.
goi¦trous
go-kart racing car;
  cf. go-cart
Golan Heights
Gol¦conda
gold¦brick
gold¦brick¦er
gold¦bug
gold¦crest

gold¦en
golden¦eye
gold¦en¦ly
gold¦en¦rod
golden¦seal
gold¦field
gold¦finch
gold¦fish
goldi¦locks
  pl. goldi¦locks
Gold¦ing, Wil¦liam
  novelist
Gold¦schmidt,
  Vic¦tor Mor¦itz
  chemist
Gold¦smith, Oli¦ver
  writer
gold¦smith
gold¦wasser
gold¦work
gold¦work¦ing
Gold¦wyn, Sam¦uel
  film director
golem
golf ball for golf
golf¦ball in
  typewriter
golf¦er
gol¦gappa
Golgi, Ca¦millo Ital-
  ian histologist; G.
  body, apparatus
Gol¦gotha
Gol¦iath
Gol¦lancz, Vic¦tor
  publisher
gol¦li¦wog
gol¦lop +ed +ing
golly
gol¦lies
gom¦been
gomer
Gom¦or¦rah
gonad
go¦nadal
go¦nado¦troph¦ic
go¦nado¦troph¦in
go¦nado¦tropic var.
  of **gonadotrophic**
go¦nado¦tropin var.
  of **gonadotrophin**
Gon¦cha¦rov, Ivan
  novelist

Gon¦court,
  Ed¦mond and
  Jules de writers;
  Prix G.
Gond
Gondi var. of **Gond**
gon¦dola
gon¦do¦lier
Gon¦dwana
Gond¦wana¦land
gone
goner doomed per-
  son etc.; cf. **gonna**
gon¦fa¦lon
gon¦fa¦lon¦ier
gong
gon¦gooz¦ler
go¦nia¦tite
gonif
gon¦iff var. of gonif
goni¦om¦eter
go¦nio¦met¦ric
goni¦om¦etry
Gonk *trademark*
gonna = going to;
  cf. **goner**
gono¦coc¦cal
gono¦coc¦cus
gono¦cocci
gono¦lek
gon¦or¦rhea US
gon¦or¦rhe¦al US
gon¦or¦rhoea Br.
gon¦or¦rhoe¦al Br.
gonzo
goo¦ber
good
  bet¦ter
  best
Good¦all, Jane
  zoologist
good¦by +s US var.
  of goodbye
good¦bye
good¦fella
good-for-nothing
goodie var. of goody
good¦ish
good¦li¦ness
good¦ly
  good¦lier
  good¦li¦est

Good|man, Benny
clarinettist
good|ness
good|night parting
wish
goodo *Austral./NZ*
good
good-oh *dated
exclam.*
good-time *adj.*
good-timer
good|wife
good|wives
good|will
Good|win Sands
Good|wood
goody
good|ies
Good|year, Charles
inventor
goody-goody
goody-goodies
gooey
goo|ier
gooi|est
gooey|ness
goof|ball
goof|ily
goofi|ness
goof-off *n.*
goof-up *n.*
goo|fus
goofy
goof|ier
goofi|est
Goo|gle *trademark*
search engine; cf.
googol
goo|gle *v.*
goog|ling
googly
goog|lies
goo|gol number; cf.
Google
goo|gol|plex
goo-goo
goolie
gooly var. of goolie
goom|bah
goom|bay
goonda
goo|ney
goony var. of
gooney

goopi|ness
goopy
goop|ier
goopi|est
goos|an|der
goose
geese
birds
gooses
tailor's irons
v. goos|ing
goose|berry
goose|berries
goose|fish
goose|flesh
goose|foot +s plant
goose|gog
goose|grass
goose|herd
goose-like
goose|neck
goose|skin
goose-step
goose-stepped
goose-stepping
goosey
goos|ier
goosi|est
**Goos|sens,
Eu|gene, Leon,
Marie,** and
Sid|onie musicians
goosy var. of goosey
gopak
go|pher rodent; tor-
toise; snake; wood;
cf. gofer
gopher|wood tree
gopik
go|pura
go|puram
Gor|ak|pur
goral
**Gor|ba|chev,
Mikh|ail** Soviet
president
Gor|bals
gor|bli|mey
gor|cock
Gor|dian knot
gor|dian worm
Gor|dium
gordo +s

Gor|don setter;
Riots
**Gor|don, Charles
George** British
general
Gor|don Ben|nett
exclam.
gore
gor|ing
Gó|recki, Hen|ryk
composer
Gö|reme
Gore-tex *trademark*
gorge
gor|ging
gor|geous
gor|geous|ly
gor|geous|ness
gor|ger
gor|get
gor|gio +s
gor|gon
gor|gon|eion
gor|gon|eia
gor|gon|ian
Gor|gon|zola
gor|illa ape; cf.
guerrilla
gor|ily
gori|ness
Gö|ring, Her|mann
var. of Goering
Gor|khali var. of
Gurkhali
Gorky, Ar|shile
painter
Gorky, Maxim
writer
Gor|lovka
gor|mand|ise *Br.*
var. of
gourmandize; cf.
gourmandise
gor|mand|iser *Br.*
var. of
gourmandizer
gor|mand|ize
gor|mand|iz|ing
var. of
gourmandize; cf.
gourmandise
gor|mand|izer var.
of gourmandizer
gorm|less
gorm|less|ly

gorm|less|ness
Gorno-Altai
Gorno-Altaisk
go-round *n.*
gorp food; cf. gawp
gorse
Gor|sedd
Gor|sedds or
Gor|sed|dau
gorsy
gor|sier
gor|si|est
gory
gor|ier
gori|est
gos|hawk
gosht
gos|ling
go-slow *n.*
gos|pel
gos|pel|er *US
Br.* gospeller
gos|pel|ize var. of
gospelize
gos|pel|ize
gos|pel|iz|ing
gos|pel|ler *Br.
US* gospeler
gos|samer
gos|sa|mery
gos|san
gos|sip +ed +ing
gos|sip|er
gos|sipy
gos|soon
gossy|pol
gotcha
gotcher var. of
gotcha
Goth people
goth music; fan
Gotha
Gotham
Goth|am|ite
Goth|en|burg
Goth|ic people; lan-
guage; architecture;
lettering; horrifying
goth|ic relating to
goths or their
music
Goth|ic|al|ly
Gothi|cise *Br.* var.
of Gothicize

Gothi|cism
Gothi|cize
Gothi|ciz|ing
gotta = got a; got to
got|ten
Göt|ter|däm|mer|
ung
Göt|tingen
gou|ache
Gouda
gouge
gou|ging
gou|ger
Gough Island
gou|jon
gou|jons
gou|lash
Gould, Glenn
pianist
Gould, Ste|phen
Jay palaeontologist
Gou|nod, Charles
composer
gou|rami
gourd plant; fruit
gourde Haitian
currency
gourd|ful
gour|mand glutton
gour|mand|ise
gluttony;
also Br. var. of
gourmandize
gour|mand|iser Br.
var. of
gourmandizer
gour|mand|ism
gour|mand|ize
gour|mand|iz|ing
eat voraciously; cf.
gourmandise
gour|mand|izer
gour|met connois-
seur
gout
gouti|ness
gout|weed
gouty
gout|ier
gouti|est
gov|ern
gov|ern|abil|ity
gov|ern|able
gov|ern|ance

gov|ern|ess
gov|ern|essy
gov|ern|ment
gov|ern|men|tal
gov|ern|men|tal|ly
gov|ern|or
gov|er|nor|ate
Gov|ern|or
Gen|eral
Gov|ern|ors
Gen|eral
gov|er|nor|ship
gowan
gowk
goy
goyim or goys
Goya, Fran|cisco
painter
goy|isch var. of
goyish
goy|ish
Gozo
Graaf|ian
grab
grabbed
grab|bing
grab|ber
grab|ble
grab|bling
grabby
grab|bier
grab|bi|est
gra|ben
pl. gra|ben or
gra|bens
Grac|chus
Grac|chi
Roman tribunes
Grace, W. G.
cricketer
grace
gra|cing
grace|ful
grace|ful|ly
grace|ful|ness
grace|less
grace|less|ly
grace|less|ness
Graces Greek
Mythology
Gra|cias a Dios,
Cape
Gra|cie
gra|cile

gra|ci|lis
gra|cil|ity
gra|cious
gra|cious|ly
gra|cious|ness
grackle
grad|abil|ity
grad|able
grad|ate
grad|at|ing
grad|ation
grad|ation|al
Grade, Lew tele-
vision producer
grade
grad|ing
grade|ly
grader
Grad|grind
gra|di|ence
gra|di|ent
gra|din var. of
gradine
gra|dine
gradi|om|eter
grad|ual
grad|ual|ism
grad|ual|ist
grad|ual|is|tic
grad|ual|ly
grad|ual|ness
gradu|and
gradu|ate
gradu|at|ing
gradu|ation
gradus
Grae|cise Br. var. of
Graecize
Grae|cism
Grae|cize
Grae|ciz|ing
Graeco-
Greek and ...
Graeco|mania
Graeco|maniac
Graeco|phile
Graf, Steffi tennis
player
graf|fiti +s +ed
+ing
graf|fi|tist
graft
graft|er

Graf|ton, Duke of
prime minister of
Britain
Gra|ham, Mar|tha
dancer
Gra|ham, Thomas
physical chemist;
law
Gra|ham, Billy
evangelical
preacher
gra|ham cracker,
flour, etc.
Gra|hame,
Ken|neth writer
Gra|ham Land
Grail
grain
grain|er
Grain|ger, Percy
composer
graini|ness
grain|less
grainy
grain|ier
graini|est
gral|loch
gram
gram-equiva|lent
grami|ci|din
gram|in|aceous
grami|niv|or|ous
gramma grand-
mother
gram|ma|logue
gram|mar cf.
gramma
gram|mar|ian
gram|mat|ical
gram|mat|ical|
isa|tion
Br. var. of gram-
maticalization
gram|mat|ical|ise
Br. var. of
grammaticalize
gram|mat|ical|ity
gram|mat|ical|
ization
gram|mat|ical|ize
gram|mat|ical|
iz|ing
gram|mat|ical|ly
gramme var. of
gram

gram-molecule
Grammy
  Grammys or
  Gram|mies
Gram-negative
gramo|phone
gramo|phon|ic
gramp
Gram|pian
Gram-positive
gramps var. of
  gramp
gram|pus
Gram|sci, An|tonio
  political theorist
Gram stain
grana *Botany*
Gran|ada cities,
  Spain and
  Nicaragua; cf.
  Grenada
gran|adilla
gran|ary
  gran|ar|ies
Gran Can|aria
Gran Chaco
gran|dad
gran|daddy
  gran|dad|dies
gran|dam
gran|dame var. of
  grandam
grand-aunt
grand|child
  grand|chil|dren
grand cru
  grands crus
grand|dad var. of
  grandad
grand|daddy
  grand|daddies
  var. of grandaddy
grand|daugh|ter
Grande Co|more
grande dame
  grandes dames
gran|dee
*grande
  hori|zon|tale*
  *grandes
  hori|zon|tales*
grand|eur
grand|father
grand|father|ly

Grand Gui|gnol
  Grand Gui|gnols
gran|di|flora
grand|ilo|quence
grand|ilo|quent
grand|ilo|quent|ly
gran|di|ose
gran|di|ose|ly
gran|di|os|ity
grand jeté
  grands jetés
grand|kid
grand|ly
grand|ma
grand mal
  grands mals
grand|mama
grand|mamma var.
  of grandmama
Grand Mar|nier
  Grand Mar|niers
  trademark
Grand Mas|ter of
  knighthood,
  Freemasons, etc.
grand|mas|ter
  Chess
grand|mother
grand|mother|ly
grand-nephew
grand|ness
grand-niece
grand|pa
grand|papa
grand|pappy
  grand|pap|pies
grand|par|ent
grand|paren|tal
grand|parent|hood
Grand Prix
  Grands Prix
grand sei|gneur
  grands sei|gneurs
grand siècle
grand|sire
grand|son
grand|stand
grand-uncle
grange
gran|ger|isa|tion
  Br. var. of
  grangerization
gran|ger|ise *Br.* var.
  of grangerize

gran|ger|iza|tion
gran|ger|ize
  gran|ger|iz|ing
gran|ifer|ous
grani|form
gra|nita
  gra|ni|tas or
  gra|nite
  crushed ice drink
gran|ite rock
gran|ite|ware
gran|it|ic
gran|it|isa|tion *Br.*
  var. of
  granitization
gran|it|ise *Br.* var.
  of granitize
gran|it|iza|tion
gran|it|ize
  gran|it|iz|ing
gran|it|oid
grani|vore
gran|iv|or|ous
gran|ma var. of
  grandma
gran|nie var. of
  granny
granny
grano|di|or|ite
gran|ola
grano|lith|ic
grano|phyre
grano|phyric
gran|pa var. of
  grandpa
Grant, Cary actor
Grant, Ulys|ses S.
  US president
grant|able
grant-aid *v.*
grant|ee
grant|er generally;
  cf. grantor
Granth = Adi
  Granth
Gran|tha Indian
  alphabet
Gran|thi person
  who reads from Adi
  Granth
Granth Sahib
  another term for
  Adi Granth

grant-in-aid
  grants-in-aid
grant|or Law; cf.
  granter
gran tur|ismo +s
granu|lar
granu|lar|ity
granu|late
granu|lat|ing
granu|la|tion
granu|la|tor
gran|ule
granu|lite
granu|lit|ic
gran|ulo|cyte
gran|ulo|cyt|ic
granu|loma
  granu|lomas or
  granu|lomata
granu|loma|tous
gra|nu|lo|met|ric
granum
grape|fruit
  pl. grape|fruit
grape|seed
grape|shot
grape|vine
grapey
grapi|er
grapi|est
graph
graph|em|at|ic
graph|eme
graph|em|ic
graph|em|ics
graph|ic
graphi|cacy
graph|ic|al
graph|ic|al|ly
graph|ic|ness
graph|ics
graph|ite
graph|it|ic
graph|it|isa|tion *Br.*
  var. of
  graphitization
graph|it|ise *Br.* var.
  of graphitize
graph|it|iza|tion
graph|it|ize
  graph|it|iz|ing
grapho|logic|al
graph|olo|gist

graph|ology
grap|nel
grappa
Grap|pelli,
  Ste|phane jazz
  violinist
grap|ple
  grap|pling
grap|pler
grap|to|lite
grapy var. of grapey
Gras|mere
grasp|able
grasp|er
grasp|ing|ly
grasp|ing|ness
Grass, Gün|ther
  writer
grass|bird
grass|cloth
grass|hop|per
grassi|ness
grass|land
grass|less
grass-like
grass|quit
grass|veld
grassy
  grass|ier
  grassi|est
grate
  grat|ing
  scrape; hearth; cf.
  great
grate|ful
grate|ful|ly
grate|ful|ness
grater
grati|cule
grati|fi|ca|tion
grati|fier
grat|ify
  grati|fies
  grati|fied
  grati|fy|ing
grati|fy|ing|ly
gratin
grat|iné
grat|inée var. of
  gratiné
grat|inéed
grat|ing|ly
gra|tis

grati|tude
gra|tuit|ous
gra|tuit|ous|ly
gra|tuit|ous|ness
gra|tu|ity
  gra|tu|ities
graunch
grau|pel
grav|ad|lax
gra|va|men
gra|va|mina
grave
  grav|ing
  graved or graven
  graver
  grav|est
grave|dig|ger
gravel
  grav|elled Br.
  grav|eled US
  grav|el|ling Br.
  grav|el|ing US
gravel-blind
grav|el|ly of or like
  gravel; deep voiced
  etc.
grave|ly seriously
graven
grave|ness
Gra|ven|stein
graver
Graves, Rob|ert
  writer
Graves wine
  pl. Graves
Graves' dis|ease
grave|side
grave|stone
Gra|vet|tian
grave|yard
gravid
grav|im|eter
gravi|met|ric
grav|im|etry
grav|itas
gravi|tate
  gravi|tat|ing
gravi|ta|tion
gravi|ta|tion|al
gravi|ta|tion|al|ly
gravi|ton
grav|ity
  grav|ities
grav|lax

grav|ure
gravy
  gra|vies
Gray, Asa botanist
Gray, Thomas poet
gray US
  colour
  Br. grey
gray unit; cf. grey
gray|beard US
  Br. greybeard
Gray code
gray|hen US
  Br. greyhen
gray|ish US
  Br. greyish
gray|lag US
  Br. greylag
gray|ling
gray|ly US
  Br. greyly
gray|ness US
  Br. greyness
gray|scale US
  Br. greyscale
gray|wacke US
  Br. greywacke
Graz city, Austria
graze
  graz|ing
grazer
gra|zier
grease
  greas|ing
grease|ball
grease|less
grease|paint
grease|proof
greaser
grease|wood
greas|ily
greasi|ness
greasy
  greas|ier
  greasi|est
great big etc.; cf.
  grate
great-aunt
great|coat
great-grand|child
great-
  grand|chil|dren
great-
  grand|daughter

great-grand|father
great-
      grand|mother
great-
      grand|par|ent
great-grand|son
great|ly
great-nephew
great|ness
great-niece
great-uncle
greave armour; cf.
  grieve
grebe
grebo +s
Gre|cian
Gre|cise Br. var. of
  Graecize
Gre|cism var. of
  Graecism
Gre|cize var. of
  Graecize
Greco, El painter
Greco- var. of
  Graeco-
Greece
greed
greed|ily
greedi|ness
greedy
  greed|ier
  greedi|est
greedy guts
  pl. greedy guts
gree|gree
Greek
Greek|ness
Green|away, Kate
  artist
green|back
green|bottle
green|bul
Greene, Gra|ham
  novelist
Green|er shotgun
green|ery
  green|er|ies
greenery-yallery
green|eye fish
green|feed
green|field adj.
green|finch
green|fly
  pl. green|fly or

green|flies
green|gage
green|gro|cer
green|gro|cery
green|gro|cer|ies
green|head fly
green|heart
green|hide
green|horn
green|house
greenie
green|ish
green|keep|er Br.
  US greenskeeper
green|keep|ing Br.
  US greenkeeping
Green|land
Green|land|er
Green|land|ic
green|let
green|ling
green|ly
green|mail
green|mail|er
green|ness
Green|ock
green|ock|ite
Green|peace
green|sand
green|shank
green|sick|ness
greens|keep|er US
  Br. greenkeeper
greens|keep|ing US
  Br. greenkeeping
green|stick
  frac|ture
green|stone
green|stuff
green|sward
green|ware
green|wash
green|wash|ing
green|way
Green|wich
green|wood
greeny
Greer, Ger|maine
  writer
greet|er
greg|ar|ine
gre|gari|ous
gre|gari|ous|ly

gre|gari|ous|ness
Gre|gor|ian
Greg|ory
greige
grei|sen
grem|lin
Gre|nache
Gren|ada island,
  West Indies; cf.
  Granada
gren|ade
Gren|adian
gren|adier
gren|adilla var. of
  granadilla
gren|adine fabric;
  cordial
Gren|adine
  Is|lands
Gren|del
Gren|fell, Joyce
  entertainer
Gre|noble
Gren|ville, George
  prime minister of
  Britain
Gres|ham, Thomas
  financier; G's law
Gres|ley, Nigel
  railway engineer
Gre|tel
Gretna Green
Greuze, Jean-
  Baptiste painter
gre|vil|lea
Grey, George prime
  minister of New
  Zealand
Grey, Lady Jane
  queen of England
Grey, Lord prime
  minister of Britain
Grey, Zane writer
grey Br.
  US gray; cf. gray
grey|beard Br.
  US graybeard
grey|hen Br.
  US grayhen
grey|hound
grey|ish Br.
  US grayish
grey|lag Br.
  US graylag

grey|ly Br.
  US grayly
Grey|mouth
grey|ness Br.
  US grayness
grey|scale Br.
  US grayscale
grey|wacke Br.
  US graywacke
grib|ble
gricer
gricing
grid
grid|ded
grid|ding
grid|der
grid|dle
grid|dling
G-ride
grid|iron
grid|lock
grief
grief-stricken
Grieg, Ed|vard
  composer
griev|ance
grieve
griev|ing
  mourn; cf. greave
griever
griev|ous
griev|ous|ly
griev|ous|ness
grif|fin mythical
  creature; cf. griffon
Grif|fith, Ar|thur
  Irish president
Grif|fith, D. W.
  film director
grif|fon vulture;
  dog; cf. griffin
grift|er
gri-gri var. of gris-
  gris
grike
grill cooking appar-
  atus; food; cf. grille
grill|ade
grill|age
grille grating; cf.
  grill
grill|er
grilse

grim
grim|mer
grim|mest
grim|ace
grim|acing
grim|acer
Gri|maldi,
  Fran|cesco
  physicist
Gri|maldi, Jo|seph
  clown
gri|mal|kin
grime
grim|ing
grimi|ly
grimi|ness
grim|ly
Grimm, Jacob and
  Wil|helm
  philologists and
  folklorists
Grimm's Fairy
  Tales
Grimm's law
grim|ness
grim|oire
Grim|ond, Jo
  politician
Grims|by
grimy
grimi|er
grimi|est
grin
grinned
grin|ning
Grinch
grind
  ground
grind|er
grind|ing|ly
grind|stone
gringo +s
grin|ner
grin|ning|ly
griot
grip
  gripped
grip|ping
gripe
grip|ing
griper
grippe influenza
grip|per
grip|ping|ly

grippy
  grip|pier
  grip|pi|est
Gri|qua
Gris, Juan painter
gri|saille
Gri|selda
griseo|ful|vin
gri|sette
gris-gris
gris|kin
gris|li|ness
grisly
  gris|lier
  gris|li|est
  horrible; cf. **gristly**,
  grizzly
grison animal
Gri|sons canton,
  Switzerland
gris|sini
gris|tle
gris|tly
  grist|lier
  grist|li|est
  containing gristle;
  cf. **grisly**, **grizzly**
grist|mill
grit
  grit|ted
  grit|ting
grit|stone
grit|ter
grit|tily
grit|ti|ness
gritty
  grit|tier
  grit|ti|est
Gri|vas, George
  Greek Cypriot
  patriot
grivet
griz|zle
  griz|zling
griz|zler
griz|zly
  griz|zlies
  griz|zlier
  griz|zli|est
  bear; grey;
  complaining; cf.
  grisly, **gristly**
groan
groan|er
groat coin

groats grain
Gro-bag
  trademark for
  growbag
gro|cer
gro|cery
  gro|cer|ies
groce|teria
grockle
Grodno
grog
  grogged
  grog|ging
grog|gily
grog|gi|ness
groggy
  grog|gier
  grog|gi|est
grog|ram
groin *Anatomy;*
  Architecture
groin *US*
  on seashore
  Br. **groyne**
grok
  grokked
  grok|king
grom|met
grom|well
Gro|myko, An|drei
  Soviet president
Gro|ning|en
groom|er
grooms|man
  grooms|men
groove
  groov|ing
groov|er
groov|ily
groovi|ness
groovy
  groov|ier
  groovi|est
grope
  grop|ing
groper
grop|ing|ly
Gro|pius, Wal|ter
  architect
gros|beak
gro|schen
gros|grain
gros point

gross
  pl. **gross**
Grosse|teste,
  Rob|ert churchman
Gross|glock|ner
gross|ly
gross|ness
gross-out
gros|su|lar
gros|su|lar|ite
Gros Ventre
Grosz, George
  painter
grosz
  groszy or **grosze**
gro|tesque
gro|tesque|ly
gro|tesque|ness
gro|tesque|rie
grotti|ness
grotto
  grot|toes or
  grot|tos
  grottoed
grotty
  grot|tier
  grot|ti|est
grouch|ily
grouchi|ness
grouchy
  grouch|ier
  grouchi|est
ground|bait
ground|break|er
ground|break|ing
ground|er
ground|hog
ground|hop|per
ground|less
ground|less|ly
ground|less|ness
ground|ling
ground|mass
ground|nut
ground|out
ground-roller
ground|sel
ground|sheet
grounds|keep|er
grounds|man
  grounds|men
ground|swell
ground|water

ground|work
group
group|age
group|er
groupie
group|set
group|think
group|us|cule
group|ware
grouse
  grous|ing
grouser
grout
grout|er
Grove, George
  musicologist
grove
grovel
  grov|elled *Br.*
  grov|eled *US*
  grov|el|ling *Br.*
  grov|el|ing *US*
  grov|el|er *US*
  grov|el|ing|ly *US*
  grov|el|ler *Br.*
  grov|el|ling|ly *Br.*
grovy
grow
  grew
  grow|ing
  grown
grow|able
grow|bag
grow|er
growl|er
growly
  growl|ier
  growli|est
grow|more
grown past parti-
  ciple of **grow**; cf.
  groan
grown-up *adj. & n.*
growth
groyne *Br.*
  US **groin**; on
  seashore; cf. **groin**
groz|ing iron
Grozny
grrrl assertive young
  woman
grub
  grubbed
  grub|bing

grub|ber
grub|bily
grubbi|ness
grubby
  grub|bier
  grub|bi|est
grub|stake
  grub|stak|ing
grudge
  grudg|ing
grudger
grudg|ing|ly
grudg|ing|ness
gruel
gruel|ing US
gruel|ing|ly US
gruel|ling Br.
gruel|ling|ly Br.
grue|some
grue|some|ly
grue|some|ness
gruff|ly
gruff|ness
grum|ble
  grum|bling
grum|bler
grum|bling|ly
grum|bly
grump|ily
grumpi|ness
grump|ish
grumpy
  grump|ier
  grumpi|est
Grundy
  Grun|dies
Grundy|ism
Grüne|wald,
  Ma|thias painter
grun|gi|ness
grungy
  grun|gier
  grun|gi|est
grun|ion
grunt|er
grun|tled
Grus constellation
Gruy|ère
gryke var. of grike
gryphon var. of
  griffin
grys|bok
Gryt|vi|ken

G spot
Gstaad
G-string
G-suit
gua|ca|mole
gua|charo +s
Gua|da|la|jara
Gua|dal|ca|nal
Gua|dal|qui|vir
Gua|de|loupe
Gua|de|loup|ian
guaiac
guai|ac|ol
guai|acum
Guam
Guam|an|ian
guan
gua|naco +s
Guan|che
Guang|dong
Guangxi Zhu|ang
Guang|zhou
guan|idine
guan|ine
guano +s
guano|sine
Guan|tá|namo
guar
gua|ra|che var. of
  huarache
gua|rana
Gua|rani S. Ameri-
  can Indian;
  language
gua|rani Paraguayan
  currency
guar|an|tee
  guar|an|tees
  guar|an|teed
  guar|an|tee|ing
  promise
guar|an|tor
guar|anty
  guar|an|ties
  undertaking of
  liability
guard
guard|ant Heraldry
guard|ed|ly
guarded|ness
guard|ee cf. Gardai
guard|house

Guardi, Fran|cesco
  painter
guard|ian
guard|ian|ship
guard|room
guards|man
  guards|men
Guar|neri,
  Giu|seppe violin-
  maker
Guar|ner|ius
Gua|te|mala
Gua|te|mal|an
guava
guaya|bera
guay|ule
gub|bins
gu|ber|na|tor|ial
gud|dle
  gud|dling
gud|dler
gudgeon
Gud|run
guel|der rose
Guelph
Guelph|ic
Guelph|ism
gue|non
guer|don
Gue|ricke, Otto von
  engineer
guer|illa var. of
  guerrilla
Guer|nica
Guern|sey island;
  cattle
guern|sey garment
guer|rilla cf. gorilla
guess
guess|able
guess|er
guess|ti|mate
  guess|ti|mat|ing
guess|work
guest
guest|book
gues|ti|mate var. of
  guesstimate
Gue|vara, Che
  revolutionary
guf|faw
Gug|gen|heim

Gui|ana region, S.
  America; French,
  British, etc.; G.
  Highlands; cf.
  Guyana
guid
  Scot. spelling of
  good
guid|able
guid|ance
guide
  guid|ing
guide|book
guide|line
guide|post
guider
guide|way
gui|don
Gui|enne var. of
  Guyenne
Gui|gnol
Gui|gnol|esque
guild association; cf.
  gild
guil|der Dutch
  currency; cf. gilder
Guild|ford
guild|hall
guilds|man
  guilds|men
guile
guile|ful
guile|ful|ly
guile|less
guile|less|ly
guile|less|ness
Guillain–Barré
guille|met punctu-
  ation mark
guil|le|mot bird
guil|loche
guil|lo|tine
  guil|lo|tin|ing
guilt culpability; cf.
  gilt
guilt|ily
guilti|ness
guilt|less
guilt|less|ly
guilt|less|ness
guilty
  guilt|ier
  guilti|est

guimp var. of gimp, guimpe

guimpe blouse; cf. gimp

Guinea in W. Africa

guinea money

Guinea-Bissau

guinea|fowl
  pl. guinea|fowl

Guin|ean

guinea pig

Guinea worm

guinep var. of genip

Guin|evere

Guin|ness, Alec
  actor

gui|pure

guiro +s

guise

guiser

gui|tar

guitar|fish

gui|tar|ist

Gu|ja|rat state,
  India

Gu|ja|rati

Gu|je|rat var. of
  Gujarat

Gu|je|rati var. of
  Gujarati

Guj|rat city,
  Pakistan

gulab jamun

Gulag system

gulag camp

gular

Gul|ben|kian,
  Ca|louste philan-
  thropist

gulch

gul|den

gules

gulet boat; cf. gullet

gulf|weed

Gul|lah

gull|ery
  gull|er|ies

gul|let oesophagus;
  cf. gulet

gul|ley var. of gully

gul|li|bil|ity

gul|lible

gul|libly

gully

gul|lies

gul|lied

gully|ing

gulp|er

gulpy

gum

gummed

gum|ming

Gumbo patois

gumbo +s okra;
  soup; soil; music

gum|boil

gum|boot

gum|drop

gumma
  gum|mas or
  gum|mata

gum|ma|tous

gum|mily

gum|mi|ness

gum|mosis

gummy
  gum|mies
  gum|mier
  gum|miest

gump|tion

gum|shield

gum|shoe

gun
  gunned
  gun|ning

gun|boat

gundi animal

gundy in 'no good
  to gundy'

gun|fight

gun|fight|er

gun|fire

gunge
  gunge|ing

gung-ho

gungy
  gun|gier
  gun|gi|est

gun|ite

gunk

gunk|hole
  gunk|hol|ing

gun|less

gun|lock

gun|maker

gun|man
  gun|men

gun|metal

Gunn, Thom poet

gun|nel fish; cf.
  gunwale

Gun|nell, Sally ath-
  lete

gun|ner

gun|nera

gun|nery

gunny
  gun|nies

gunny|sack

gun|play

gun|point

gun|pow|der

gun|room

gun|run|ner

gun|run|ning

gun|sel

gun|ship

gun|shot

gun|sight sight on
  gun

gun site emplace-
  ment

gun|sling|er

gun|sling|ing

gun|smith

gun|stock

gun|ter sail; rig

Gun|ter's chain

Gun|ther character
  in *Nibelungenlied*

Gun|tur city, India

gun|wale part of
  ship; cf. gunnel

gun|yah

Günz

Guo|min|dang var.
  of Kuomintang

guppy
  gup|pies

Gupta

Gup|tan

Gur language

gur sugar

Gur|djieff, George
  spiritual leader

gurd|wara

gur|gle
  gurg|ling

gur|jun

Gur|kha

Gur|khali

Gur|mukhi

gurn

gur|nard

gurn|er

Gur|ney, Ivor poet
  and composer

gur|ney

gur|rier

gurry

guru

gush|er

gush|ily

gushi|ness

gush|ing|ly

gushy
  gush|ier
  gushi|est

gus|set

gussy
  gus|sies
  gus|sied
  gussy|ing

gus|ta|tion

gus|ta|tive

gus|ta|tory

Gus|tavus
  Adol|phus king of
  Sweden

gust|ily

gusti|ness

gusto

gusty
  gust|ier
  gusti|est

gut
  gut|ted
  gut|ting

gut|bucket

Guten|berg,
  Jo|han|nes printer

Guth|rie, Woody
  folk singer-
  songwriter

Guth|rie test

gut|kha

gut|less

gut|less|ly

gut|less|ness

gut-rot

gut|ser

guts|ily

gutsi|ness

gutsy
  guts|ier
  guts|est
gutta-percha
gut|tate
gut|ta|tion
gut|ter
gut|ter|snipe
gut|tur|al
gut|tur|al|ly
gutty
  gut|ties
  gut|tier
  gut|ti|est
gut|zer var. of
  gutser
guv'nor
guy man; rope;
  cf. gey
Guy|ana country, S.
  America; cf.
  Guiana
Guy|an|ese
Guy|enne region,
  France
guyot
guz|zle
  guz|zling
guz|zler
Gwa|lior
gweilo +s
Gwen|do|len
Gwen|do|line
Gwent
Gwyn|edd county,
  Wales
Gwyn|eth name
gwyn|iad
Gwynn, Nell actress
gyan
gybe Br. sailing
  gyb|ing
  US jibe; cf. jibe,
  gibe
gym
gym|khana
gym|na|sial
gym|na|sium
  gym|na|siums or
  gym|na|sia
gym|nast
gym|nas|tic
gym|nas|tic|al|ly
gym|nas|tics

gymno|gene
gym|noso|phist
gym|noso|phy
  gym|noso|phies
gymno|sperm
gymno|sperm|ous
gym|nure
gymp var. of gimp
gym|slip
gy|nae|ceum
  gy|nae|cea
  women's
  apartments; cf.
  gynoecium
gy|nae|coc|racy Br.
  gy|nae|coc|ra|cies
  US gynecocracy
gy|nae|co|logic|al
  Br.
  US gynecological
gy|nae|co|logic|
    al|ly Br.
  US gynecologically
gy|nae|colo|gist Br.
  US gynecologist
gy|nae|col|ogy Br.
  US gynecology
gy|nae|co|mas|tia
  Br.
  US gynecomastia
gy|nae|co|phobia
  Br.
  US gynecophobia
gy|nan|dro|morph
gy|nan|dro|
    morph|ic
gy|nan|dro|
    morphy
gy|nan|dro|
    morphies
gy|nan|drous
gy|narchy
  gy|nar|chies
gyne|coc|racy US
  gyne|coc|ra|cies
  Br. gynaecocracy
gyne|co|logic|al US
  Br. gynaecological
gyne|co|logic|al|ly
  US
  Br.
  gynaecologically
gyne|colo|gist US
  Br. gynaecologist
gyne|cology US
  Br. gynaecology

gyne|co|mas|tia US
  Br. gynaecomastia
gyne|co|phobia US
  Br. gynaecophobia
gyno|cen|tric
gy|noe|cium
  gy|noe|cia
  part of flower; cf.
  gynaeceum
gyno|pho|bia
gyno|phobic
gyp
gypped
gyp|ping
gyppo +s *offensive*
gyp|seous
gyp|sif|er|ous
gyp|soph|ila
gyp|sum
Gypsy
  Gyp|sies
gypsy|ish
gypsy moth
gypsy|wort
gyral
gyr|ate
  gyr|at|ing
gyr|ation
gyr|ator
gyr|atory
  gyr|ator|ies
gyre
  gyr|ing
gyr|fal|con
gyri
gyro +s gyroscope;
  gyrocompass; cf.
  giro
gyro|com|pass
gyro|cop|ter
gyro|mag|net|ic
gyron
gyr|onny
gyro|pilot
gyro|plane
gyro|scope
gyro|scop|ic
gyro|scop|ic|al|ly
gyro|sta|bil|ised Br.
  var. of
  gyrostabilized
gyro|sta|bil|iser Br.
  var. of
  gyrostabilizer

gyro|sta|bil|ized
gyro|sta|bil|izer
gyrus
  gyri
gyt|tja
gyve shackle; cf. **jive**

H

haaf area of sea
haar fog
Haar|lem in the
  Netherlands; cf.
  Harlem
HAART = highly
  active antiretroviral
  therapy
Hab|ak|kuk
haba|nera
hab|dabs
Hab|da|lah
hab|eas cor|pus
ha|ben|dum
Haber–Bosch
hab|er|dash|er
hab|er|dash|ery
  hab|er|dash|er|ies
hab|er|geon
Ha|ber|mas,
  Jürgen social
  philosopher
ha|bili|ment
ha|bili|tate
  ha|bili|tat|ing
  ha|bili|ta|tion
habit
hab|it|abil|ity
hab|it|able
hab|it|ant
habi|tat
habi|ta|tion
habi|ta|tive
hab|it|ed
ha|bit|ual
ha|bit|ual|ly
ha|bitu|ate
  ha|bitu|at|ing
ha|bitu|ation
ha|bi|tué

hab|itus

ha|boob

Habs|burg

háček

ha|cen|dado +s

hach|ure
hach|ur|ing

ha|ci|enda

ha|ci|en|dado var.
of hacendado

hacka|more

hack|berry
hack|berries

hack|er

hack|ery
hack|er|ies

hack|ette

hackle
hack|ling

hack|ma|tack

Hack|ney

hack|ney car|riage

hack|neyed

hack|saw

hack|tiv|ism

hack|tiv|ist

ha|dada

hadal

had|dock

hade
had|ing

Ha|dean

ha|deda var. of
hadada

Hades

Hadhra|maut

Had|ith

Had|lee, Rich|ard
cricketer

Had|ley cell

hadn't

Ha|drian Roman
emperor

had|ron

had|ron|ic

had|ro|saur

hadst

haec|ce|ity
haec|ce|ities

Haeckel, Ernst
biologist and
philosopher

haem *Br.*
  US heme

haem|agglu|tin|
  ation *Br.*
  US
  hemagglutination

haem|agglu|tin|in
  Br.
  US hemagglutinin

haem|al *Br.*
  US hemal

haem|angi|oma *Br.*
  haem|angi|omas or
  haem|angi|omata
  US hemangioma

haema|tem|esis *Br.*
  US hema|tem|esis

haem|at|ic *Br.*
  US hematic

haem|atin *Br.*
  US hematin

haem|atite *Br.*
  US hematite

haem|ato|cele *Br.*
  US hematocele

haem|ato|crit *Br.*
  US hematocrit

haema|togen|ous
  Br.
  US hematogenous

haem|ato|logic *Br.*
  US hematologic

haem|ato|logic|al
  Br.
  US hematological

haema|tolo|gist *Br.*
  US hematologist

haema|tol|ogy *Br.*
  US hematology

haema|toma *Br.*
  haema|tomas or
  haema|to|mata
  US hematoma

haema|topha|gous
  Br.
  US
  hematophagous

haem|ato|poi|esis
  Br.
  US hematopoiesis

haem|ato|poi|etic
  Br.
  US hematopoietic

haema|toxy|lin *Br.*
  US hematoxylin

haema|turia *Br.*
  US hematuria

haemo|chroma|
  tosis *Br.*
  US
  hemochromatosis

haemo|coel *Br.*
  US hemocoel

haemo|cya|nin *Br.*
  US hemocyanin

haemo|cyt|om|eter
  Br.
  US
  hemocytometer

haemo|di|aly|sis *Br.*
  US hemodialysis

haemo|dynam|ic
  Br.
  US hemodynamic

haemo|dynam|ic|
  al|ly *Br.*
  US
  hemodynamically

haemo|dynam|ics
  Br.
  US hemodynamics

haemo|glo|bin *Br.*
  US hemoglobin

haemo|globin|
  opathy *Br.*
  US
  hemoglobinopathy

haemo|globin|uria
  Br.
  US
  hemoglobinuria

haemo|lymph *Br.*
  US hemolymph

haem|oly|sis *Br.*
  haem|oly|ses
  US hemolysis

haemo|lyt|ic *Br.*
  US hemolytic

haemo|philia *Br.*
  US hemophilia

haemo|phil|iac *Br.*
  US hemophiliac

haemo|phil|ic *Br.*
  US hemophilic

haemo|poi|esis *Br.*
  US hemopoiesis

haemo|poi|etic *Br.*
  US hemopoietic

haem|op|ty|sis *Br.*
  US hemoptysis

haem|or|rhage *Br.*
  haem|or|rha|ging
  US hemorrhage

haem|or|rhagic *Br.*
  US hemorrhagic

haem|or|rhoid *Br.*
  US hemorrhoid

haem|or|rhoid|al
  Br.
  US hemorrhoidal

haemo|sta|sis *Br.*
  US hemostasis

haemo|stat *Br.*
  US hemostat

haemo|stat|ic *Br.*
  US hemostatic

haere mai

hafiz

Haf|lin|ger

haf|nium

haft

Haf|torah
  Haf|toroth

Hagar *Bible*

Hagen city, Germany; character in
  Nibelungenlied

hag|fish

Hag|ga|dah
  Hag|ga|doth

Hag|gad|ic

Hag|gad|ist

Hag|gai

Hag|gard, Rider
writer

hag|gard

hag|gis

hag|gish

hag|gle

hag|gling

hag|gler

Hagia So|phia
another name for
St Sophia

Hagi|og|rapha part
of Bible

hagi|og|raph|er
writer

hagio|graph|ic

hagio|graph|ic|al

hagi|og|raphy
hagi|og|raph|ies

hagi|ol|ater

hagi|ol|atry

hagio|logic|al
hagi|olo|gist
hagi|ology
hagio|scope
Hague, The
ha ha laughter
ha-ha ditch
haham
Hahn, Otto chemist
hahn|ium
haick var. of haik
Haida
Haifa
Haig, Doug|las field marshal
haik Arab garment; cf. hake, hike
Hai|kou capital of Hainan
haiku poem
pl. haiku or hai|kus
hail frozen rain; greet; cf. hale
hail|er
Haile Sel|as|sie emperor of Ethiopia
hail-fellow-well-met
Hail Mary +s
hail|stone
hail|storm
Hai|nan
Hai|nault in Essex, England
Hai|naut in Belgium
Hai|phong
hair cf. hare
hair|ball
hair|band
hair|brush
hair|care
hair|cloth
hair|cut
hair|do +s
hair|dress|er
hair|dress|ing
hair|drier var. of hairdryer
hair|dryer
hair|grip

hairi|ness
hair|less
hair-like
hair|line
hair|net
hair|piece
hair|pin
hair-raising
hair's breadth
hair|slide
hair|spray
hair|spring
hair|streak
hair|style
hair|styl|ing
hair|styl|ist
hairy
hair|ier
hairi|est
Haiti
Hai|tian
Hai|tink, Ber|nard conductor
haj pilgrimage
haji pilgrim
hajj var. of haj
hajji var. of haji
haka Maori dance; cf. Hakka
hak|ama
hake fish; cf. haik
hakim
Hakka people; cf. haka
Hak|luyt, Rich|ard geographer and historian
Hako|date
Ha|la|cha
Ha|la|ch|ic
Halaf
Ha|laf|ian
Ha|la|kah var. of Halacha
Ha|la|kha var. of Halacha
halal
ha|lala
hal|ation
hal|berd
hal|berd|ier
hal|bert var. of halberd

hal|cyon
haldi
hale
hal|ing
healthy; drag; cf. hail
Hale–Bopp
hale|ness
haler currency
hale|some
Hales|owen
Haley, Bill rock-and-roll singer
half
halves
cf. haaf
half|back
half-ball
half|beak
half-blue
half-boot
half-bottle
half-breed offensive
half-brother
half-caste offensive
half-century
half-centur|ies
half-cock
half-crown
half-cut
half-deck
half-dozen
half-duplex
half-hardy
half-hardies
half-hose
half-hour
half-hourly
half-hunter
half-inch unit; steal
half-integer
half-integral
half-lap
half-length
half-life
half-lives or half-lifes
half-light
half-marathon
half-moon
half-move
half|penny
half|pen|nies or

half|pence
half|penny|worth
half-pie
half-pipe
half-relief
half-sister
half-sovereign
half-standard
half-term
half-tester
half-timber|ing
half-time
half-title
half-tone
half-track
half-truth
half-uncial
half-volley
half|way
half|wit
half-witted
hali|but
Hali|car|nas|sus
hal|ide
hal|ier
hali|eut|ic
Hali|fax
hal|ite
hali|tosis
hali|tot|ic
Hall, Rad|clyffe writer
hall room; cf. haul
Halle city, Germany
Hallé, Charles conductor; H. Orchestra
Hal|lel
hal|le|lu|jah
Hal|ler, Al|brecht von anatomist and physiologist
Hal|ley's Comet
hal|liard var. of halyard
Hal|li|day, Mi|chael linguist
hall|mark
hallo var. of hello
hal|loo +s +ed +ing
hal|loumi
hal|low
Hal|low|een

hall|stand
Hall|statt
hal|lu;ces
hal;lu;cin|ant
hal;lu;cin|ate
hal;lu;cin|at;ing
hal;lu;cin|ation
hal;lu;cin|ator
hal;lu;cin|atory
hal;lu;cino|gen
hal;lu;cino|gen;ic
hal;lux
hal;lu;ces
hall|way
halma
Hal;ma;hera
halo
pl. ha;loes or halos
v. ha;loes
ha;loed
ha;lo;ing
halo|car;bon
halo|form
halo|gen
halo|gen|ate
halo;gen|at;ing
halo;gen|ation
halo|gen;ic
halon
halo|peri;dol
halo|phile
halo|phil;ic
halo|phyte
halo|thane
Hals, Frans painter
halt
hal;ter
halter-break
halter-broke
halter-broken
hal;tere
halter-neck
halt;ing;ly
halva
hal;vah var. of halva
halve v.
halv;ing
halv;ers
halves pl. of half
halwa
halwah var. of
halwa
hal;yard

Ham son of Noah
ham
hammed
ham|ming
hama|dryad
nymph; snake
hama|dryas baboon
hama|me;lis
hama|me;lises
ham-and-egger
ha;mar;tia
Hamas organization
ham;ate
ham|bone
Ham|burg
ham|bur;ger food
Ham|elin
German Hameln
hamer|kop
hames
ham|fat
Ham;il;car Cartha-
ginian general
Ham;il;ton cities
Ham;il;ton, Emma
mistress of Lord
Nelson
Ham;il;ton|ian
Ham;il;ton|ian|ism
Ha;mish
Ham;ite
Ham;it;ic
Hamito-Semitic
Ham;let Danish
prince
ham;let village
Hamm city,
Germany
Ham;mar|skjöld,
Dag UN secretary
general
ham;mer
Ham;mer|fest
ham;mer|head
shark; bird
ham;mer head
head of hammer
ham;mer|kop var.
of hamerkop
ham;mer|less
ham;mer|lock
Ham;mer|stein,
Oscar librettist

Ham|mett,
Dash|iell writer
ham|mily
ham|mi;ness
ham|mock
Ham|mond, Joan
singer
Ham|mond organ
Ham;mu;rabi king
of Babylonia
hammy
ham|mier
ham;mi;est
Ham|nett,
Kath|ar;ine fashion
designer
ham|per
Hamp|shire
Hamp|stead
Hamp|ton city, US;
H. Court, Wick,
Roads
ham|ster
ham|string
ham|strung
Ham|sun, Knut
novelist
ham|ulus
ham|uli
hamza
Han Chinese
dynasty
Han|cock, Tony
comedian
hand|bag
hand|bagged
hand|bag;ging
hand|ball
hand|basin
hand|bell
hand|bill
hand|book
hand|brake
hand|car
hand|cart
hand|clap
hand|clap;ping
hand|craft
hand|cuff
hand|ed;ness
Han;del, George
Frid;eric composer
Han;del|ian
hand|ful

hand|glass
hand|grip
hand|gun
hand-held
hand|hold
hand-holding
handi cooking pot;
cf. handy
handi|cap
handi|capped
handi|cap;ping
han;di|cap;per
han;di|craft
hand|ily
handi|ness
han;di|work
hand|job vulgar
slang
hand|ker;chief
hand|ker;chiefs or
hand|ker;chieves
hand-knit
hand-knitted
hand-knitting
han;dle
hand|ling
handle|abil;ity
handle|able
handle|bar
handle|less
hand|ler
hand|less
Hand|ley Page,
Fred;erick aircraft
designer
hand|list
hand|made
hand|maid
hand|maiden
hand-me-down
hand|off
hand|out
hand|over
hand|phone
hand-pick
hand|print
hand|pump
hand|rail
hand|saw
hand|sel var. of
hansel
hand|set
hands-free

hand|shake
hand|shak|ing
hands-off *adj.*
hand|some
  hand|somer
  hand|som|est
  good-looking; cf.
  hansom
hand|some|ly
hand|some|ness
hands-on
hand|span
hand|spike
hand|spring
hand|stand
hand|stroke
hand|work
hand|woven
hand|writ|ing
hand|writ|ten
Handy, W. C.
  musician
handy
  hand|ier
  handi|est
  convenient; skilful;
  cf. handi
handy|man
handy|men
hane|poot
hang
  hung
  suspended
  hanged
  executed
hangar shed; cf.
  hanger
hangar|age
Hang|chow var. of
  Hangzhou
hang|dog
hang|er coathanger
  etc.; cf. hangar
hanger-on
  hangers-on
hang-glide
  hang-gliding
hang-glider
hangi
hang|man
hang|nail
hang-out *n.*
hang|over
Hang Seng

hang-up *n.*
Hang|zhou
han|ker
han|ker|er
han|kie var. of
  hanky
Hanks, Tom actor
hanky
  han|kies
hanky-panky
Han|ni|bal Cartha-
  ginian general
Hanoi
Han|over
  German Hannover
Han|over|ian
Hansa
Han|sard
Hanse var. of
  Hansa
Han|se|at|ic
Han|sel in *Hansel
  and Gretel*
  German Hänsel
han|sel gift
  han|selled *Br.*
  han|seled *US*
  han|sel|ling *Br.*
  han|sel|ing *US*
Han|sen's dis|ease
han|som cab cf.
  handsome
hanta|virus
Hants = Hampshire
Han|uk|kah Jewish
  festival
Hanu|man Hindu
  divine being
hanu|man monkey
Haora var. of
  Howrah
hap
  happed
  hap|ping
hapax le|gom|enon
  hapax le|gom|ena
ha'|penny var. of
  halfpenny
hap|haz|ard
hap|haz|ard|ly
hap|haz|ard|ness
Haph|torah var. of
  Haftorah
hap|kido

hap|less
hap|less|ly
hap|less|ness
haplo|chrom|ine
haplo|dip|loid
hap|log|raphy
hap|loid
hap|loidy
  hap|loid|ies
hap|lol|ogy
  hap|lol|ogies
haplo|type
ha'p'orth var. of
  halfpennyworth
hap|pen
hap|pen|stance
happi Japanese coat
hap|pily
hap|pi|ness
happy
  hap|pier
  hap|pi|est
  cf. happi
happy-clappy
  happy-clappies
happy-go-lucky
Haps|burg var. of
  Habsburg
hap|ten
hap|tic
hapto|glo|bin
hapu
hara-kiri
haram
har|am|bee
har|angue
  har|anguing
har|anguer
Har|are
har|ass
har|ass|er
har|ass|ment
har|bin|ger
har|bor *US*
  Br. harbour
har|bor|age *US*
  Br. harbourage
harbor|less *US*
  Br. harbourless
harbor|master *US*
  Br. harbour
  master
har|bour *Br.*
  US harbor

har|bour|age *Br.*
  US harborage
har|bour|less *Br.*
  US harborless
har|bour mas|ter
  Br.
  US harbormaster
hard|back
hard|ball
hard|bit|ten
hard|board
hard|bodied
hard|body
  hard|bodies
  athletic person
hard-code
  hard-coding
hard core nucleus;
  rubble
hard|core music;
  pornography
hard|cover
Harde|canute king
  of Denmark
hard|en
hard|en|er
hard|gain|er
hard|head duck;
  catfish
hard-headed
hard-headed|ly
hard-headed|ness
hard|heads plant
Har|die, Keir polit-
  ician
hardi|hood
har|dily
hardi|ness
Hard|ing, War|ren
  US president
hard|ish
hard line *n.*
  unyielding adher-
  ence to policy
hard-line *adj.*
hard|liner
hard lines bad luck
hard|ly
hard|ness
hard-on *vulgar
  slang*
hard|pan
hard|scrab|ble

hard-shell suitcase etc.

hard|shell clam

hard|ship

hard|stand¦ing

hard|stone

hard|top car roof; car; road

Har|dwar

hard|ware

hard-wire
  hard-wiring

hard|wood

Hardy, Oli|ver comedian

Hardy, Thomas writer

hardy
  har|dier
  har|di¦est

Hare, David dramatist

Hare, Wil|liam body-snatcher

hare
  har¦ing
  animal; cf. **hair**

hare|bell

hare-brained

Ha¦redi
  Ha|redim

Hare|foot, Har¦old king of England

Hare Krishna

hare|lip
  hare|lipped
  offensive

harem

hare's-foot +s plant

hare's-tail plant

hare|wood

Har|geisa

Har|geysa var. of
  Hargeisa

Har|greaves, James inventor

hari|cot

Hari|jan

har|issa

hark¦en var. of
  hearken

Har|lech

Har¦lem in New York City; H.

Globetrotters, Renaissance; cf.
  Haarlem

Har|le¦quin pantomime character

har|le¦quin multicoloured; duck; fish

har|le¦quin|ade

Har¦ley Street

har|lot

har|lot¦ry

Har¦low

Har¦low, Jean film actress

har|mat¦tan

harm|ful

harm|ful¦ly

harm|ful|ness

harm|less

harm|less¦ly

harm|less|ness

harmo|lod¦ic

harmo|lod¦ics

har|mon¦ic

har|mon¦ica

har|mon¦ic|al¦ly

har|mo¦ni|ous

har|mo¦ni|ous¦ly

har|mo¦ni|ous|ness

har|mon|isa|tion
  Br. var. of
  harmonization

har|mon¦ise *Br.* var.
  of **harmonize**

har|mon|iser *Br.*
  var. of **harmonizer**

har|mon|ist

har|mo|nium

har|mon|iza|tion

har|mon|ize
  har|mon|iz¦ing

har|mon|izer

har|mony
  har|monies

Harms|worth, Al¦fred
  Lord Northcliffe

har|ness

har|ness¦er

Har|old

Haroun-al-
  Raschid
  var. of **Harun ar-Rashid**

---

har¦per

Har|pers Ferry

harp|ist

Har|poc¦ra|tes
  Greek Mythology

har|poon

har|poon¦er

harp¦si|chord

harp¦si|chord|ist

harpy
  har|pies

har|que|bus var. of
  arquebus

har|ri|dan

har|rier

Har|riet

Har|rin|gton

Har¦ris Scottish
  island; tweed; hawk

Har¦ris, Ar¦thur
  'Bomb¦er' Marshal
  of the RAF

Har¦ris, Frank writer

Har¦ris|burg

Har¦ri|son, Ben|ja¦min US
  president

Har¦ri|son, George guitarist

Har¦ri|son, Rex actor

Har¦ri|son, Wil|liam Henry US president

Har¦ro|vian

Har¦row London
  borough; school

har¦row

har|row¦er

har|row|ing¦ly

har|rumph

harry
  har¦ries
  har|ried
  harry|ing
  ravage; worry

harsh¦en

harsh¦ly

harsh|ness

hart deer; cf.
  HAART, heart

har¦tal

har¦te|beest

Hart|ford in US; cf.
  Hertford

Hart¦le|pool

Hart|ley, L. P. novelist

harts|horn

hart's tongue

harum-scarum

Harun ar-Rashid
  caliph of Baghdad

har¦us|pex

har¦us|pi¦ces

har¦us|pic¦al

har¦us|picy

har¦us|picies

Har|vard University; classification

har|vest

har|vest|able

har|vest¦er

har|vest|man
  har¦vest|men

Har|vey, Wil|liam
  English physician

Har¦vey
  Wall¦bang¦er

Har|wich

Ha¦ry|ana

Harz mountains

harz¦burg|ite

has-been

Has|dru|bal two
  Carthaginian generals

Hašek, Jaro|slav writer

Hash¦em|ite

Hashi|moto's
  dis|ease

hash|ish

Hasid
  Has|id¦im

Ha|sid¦ic

Has|id|ism

has¦let

Has|mon|ean

hasn't = has not

Has|selt

has|sium

has¦sle
  has|sling

has|sock

hast

hast|ate

haste
  hast¦ing
  hurry
has¦ten
hasti¦ly
hasti¦ness
Hast¦ings town and battle
Hast¦ings, War¦ren governor general of India
hasty
  hasti¦er
  hasti¦est
hat
  hat¦ted
hat¦able deserving hate
hat¦band
hat¦box
hatch¦back
hatchel var. of hackle
hatch¦ery
  hatch¦er¦ies
hatchet
hatchet¦fish
hatch¦ling
hatch¦ment
hatch¦way
hate
  hat¦ing
hate¦able var. of hatable
hate¦ful
hate¦ful¦ly
hate¦ful¦ness
hater
hat¦ful
hath
Hath¦away, Anne wife of Shakespeare
hatha yoga
Hathor Egyptian goddess
hat¦less
hat¦pin
hat¦red
Hat¦shep¦sut Egyptian queen
hat¦stand
hat¦ter
Hatti people
Hat¦tic

Hat¦tie
hat-trick
Hat¦tusa
hau¦berk
haugh river plain; cf. haw, hoar, whore
haught¦ily
haughti¦ness
haughty
  haught¦ier
  haught¦iest
Hau-Hauism
haul pull; cf. hall
haul¦age
haul¦er
haul¦ier
haulm
haunch
haunt
haunt¦er
haunt¦ing¦ly
Haupt¦mann, Ger¦hart dramatist
haur¦ient
Hausa
haus¦frau
hau¦stel¦late
hau¦stel¦lum
hau¦stella
hau¦stor¦ial
hau¦stor¦ium
  hau¦storia
haut¦boy
haute bour¦geoisie
haute cou¦ture
haute cuis¦ine
haute école
Haute-Normandie
haut¦eur
haut monde
haut-relief
ha¦vala var. of hawala
havan
Ha¦vana
Hav¦ant
ha¦varti
Hav¦da¦lah var. of Habdalah
have
  has
  had

hav¦ing
  pl. haves
Havel, Vác¦lav Czech writer and president
hav¦eli
haven
have-not
haven't = have not
haver
hav¦er¦sack
hav¦er¦sin var. of haversine
hav¦er¦sine
hav¦il¦dar
havoc
  hav¦ocked
  hav¦ock¦ing
haw hawthorn fruit; eyelid; in 'hum and haw'; cf. haugh, hoar, whore
Ha¦waii
Ha¦wai¦ian
ha¦wala
haw¦finch
hawk
hawk¦bit
Hawke, Bob prime minister of Australia
Hawke Bay bay, New Zealand
hawk¦er
Hawke's Bay region, New Zealand
hawk-eyed
Hawk¦eye State
hawk¦fish
Hawk¦ing, Ste¦phen physicist; radiation
Haw¦kins, Cole¦man saxophonist
Haw¦kins, John naval commander
hawk¦ish
hawk¦ish¦ly
hawk¦ish¦ness
hawk¦like
hawk¦moth
Hawks, How¦ard film director

hawks¦beard
hawks¦bill
hawk¦shaw
Hawks¦moor, Nich¦olas architect
hawk¦weed
Haw¦kyns, John var. of Hawkins
hawse
hawse¦hole
hawse¦pipe
haw¦ser
hawser-laid
haw¦thorn
Haw¦thorne, Na¦than¦iel writer
Haw¦thorne ef¦fect
hay dried grass; dance; cf. heigh, hey
hay¦box
hay¦cock
Hay diet
Haydn, Jo¦seph composer
Hayek, Fried¦rich Au¦gust von economist
Hayes, Ruth¦er¦ford US president
hay¦field
hay¦lage
Hay¦ley
hay¦loft
hay¦maker
hay¦mak¦ing
hay¦mow
hay¦rick
hay¦ride
hay¦seed
hay¦stack
hay¦wire
Hay¦worth, Rita actress
haz¦ard
haz¦ard¦ous
haz¦ard¦ous¦ly
haz¦ard¦ous¦ness
haz¦chem = hazardous chemicals
haze
  haz¦ing
hazel

hazel|nut
haz|ily
hazi|ness
Haz|litt, Wil|liam
  essayist
haz|mat
hazy
  hazi|er
  hazi|est
haz|zan
  haz|zan|im
H-block
H-bomb
head
head|ache
head|achy
head|age
head|band
head|bang|er
head|bang|ing
head|board
head|butt
head|case
head|cheese
head|cloth
head|count
head|dress
head|end in cable
  television
head|er
head|gear
head|hunt
head|hunt|er
head|ily
headi|ness
head|lamp
head|land
head|less
head|light
head|line
  head|lin|ing
  in newspaper
head line Palmistry
head|liner
head|lock
head|long
head|man
  head|men
head|master
head|master|ly
head|mis|tress
head|mis|tressy
head|most

head|note
head-on
head|phone
head|piece
head|quar|ters
head|rail
head|rest
head|room
head|sail
head|scarf
  head|scarves
head|set
head|ship
head|shrink|er
heads|man
  heads|men
head|space
head|spring
head|square
head|stall
head|stand
head|stand|er
head|stay
head|stock
head|stone
head|stream
head|strong
heads-up n. & adj.
head teach|er
head|tie
head-up adj.
head|ward
head|wards
head|water
head|way
head|wind
head|word
head|work
head|wrap
heady
  head|ier
  headi|est
heal cure; cf. heel
heal|able
heal-all
heald part of loom
heal|er
health
health|ful
health|ful|ly
health|ful|ness
health|ily

healthi|ness
healthy
  health|ier
  healthi|est
Hea|ney, Sea|mus
  poet
heap
hear
  heard
hear|able
Heard Is|land
hear|er
hark|en
hear|say
hearse
Hearst, Wil|liam
  Ran|dolph news-
  paper publisher
heart organ in body;
  cf. HAART, hart
heart|ache
heart|beat
heart|break
heart|break|er
heart|break|ing
heart|break|ing|ly
heart|broken
heart|burn
heart|en
heart|en|ing|ly
heart|felt
hearth
hearth|rug
hearth|stone
heart|ily
hearti|ness
heart|land
heart|less
heart|less|ly
heart|less|ness
hearts|ease
heart|sick
heart|sick|ness
heart|sink
heart|sore
heart|strings
heart-throb
heart-to-heart adj.
  & n.
heart|wood
heart|worm
hearty
  heart|ies

heart|ier
hearti|est
heat
heated|ly
heat|er
heat cx|chan|ger
Heath, Ed|ward
  ('Ted') prime min-
  ister of Britain
heath
hea|then
hea|then|dom
hea|then|ish
hea|then|ism
hea|ther
hea|thery
heath|land
Heath Rob|in|son
Heath|row
heathy
heat|proof
heat|stroke
heat-treat
heat treat|ment
hcat|wave
heave
  hove Nautical
  heav|ing
heave-ho
heaven
heav|en|li|ness
heav|en|ly
heav|en|ward
heav|en|wards
heaver
heav|ily
heavi|ness
Heavi|side, Oli|ver
  English physicist;
  layer
Heaviside–
        Kennelly
heavy
  heav|ies
  heav|ier
  heavi|est
heavy|ish
heavy|set
heavy|weight
heb|dom|adal
Hebe Greek Myth-
  ology; asteroid;
  (offensive) Jewish
  person

hebe shrub
Hebei in China
hebe|phre|nia
hebe|phren|ic
hebe|tude
Heb|raic
Heb|ra|ise *Br.* var.
  of Hebraize
Heb|ra|ism
Heb|ra|ist
Heb|ra|is|tic
Heb|ra|ize
  Heb|ra|iz|ing
Heb|rew
Heb|ri|dean
Heb|ri|des
Heb|ron
Heb|ros
Hec|ate Greek
  goddess
heca|tomb
heck|el|phone
heckle
  heck|ling
heck|ler
hec|tar|age
hec|tare
hec|tic
hec|tic|al|ly
hecto|coty|lus
  hecto|cotyli
hecto|gram
hecto|gramme *Br.*
  var. of **hectogram**
hecto|liter *US*
hecto|litre *Br.*
hecto|meter *US*
hecto|metre *Br.*
Hec|tor
hec|tor bully
hec|tor|ing|ly
Hec|uba *Greek*
  Mythology
he'd
hed|dle
hedge
  hedg|ing
hedge|hog
hedger
hedge|row
he|don|ic
he|don|ism
he|don|ist

he|don|is|tic
he|don|is|tic|al|ly
heebie-jeebies
heed *cf.* he'd
heed|ful
heed|ful|ly
heed|ful|ness
heed|less
heed|less|ly
heed|less|ness
hee-haw
heel back of foot; *cf.*
  heal
heel|ball
heel|less
heel|tap
Hefei
heft|ily
hefti|ness
hefty
  heft|ier
  hefti|est
Hegel, Georg
  philosopher
He|gel|ian
He|gel|ian|ism
hege|mon|ic
he|gem|ony
  he|gem|onies
He|gira
  Muhammad's
  departure from
  Mecca to Medina
he|gira any
  migration
heiau
Hei|deg|ger,
  Mar|tin
  philosopher
Hei|del|berg
heifer
heigh *archaic*
  exclam. expressing
  encouragement or
  enquiry; *cf.* hay,
  hey
heigh-ho
height highness; *cf.*
  hight
height|en
height|ism
height|ist
Heil|bronn
Hei|long

Hei|long|jiang
Heim|lich
Heine, Hein|rich
  poet
hei|nie
hein|ous
hein|ous|ly
hein|ous|ness
heir inheritor; *cf.*
  air
heir-at-law
  heirs-at-law
heir|dom
heir|ess
heir|less
heir|loom
heir|ship
Hei|sen|berg,
  Wer|ner physicist;
  uncertainty
  principle
heist
hel-tiki
Hejaz
Hej|ira var. of
  Hegira
Hekla volcano
HeLa cells
Hel|den|tenor
Helen daughter of
  Zeus and Leda
Hel|ena
hel|en|ium
he|li|acal
he|li|an|the|mum
he|li|an|thus
hel|ic|al
hel|ic|al|ly
heli|ces
heli|chry|sum
he|li|city
heli|coid
heli|coid|al
Heli|con, Mt
heli|con tuba
heli|conia
heli|cop|ter
he|lic|tite
Heli|go|land
helio|cen|tric
helio|cen|tric|al|ly
Helio|ga|balus
  Roman emperor

helio|gram
helio|graph
helio|graph|ic
helio|g|raphy
helio|gra|vure
he|li|om|eter
helio|pause
He|li|opo|lis
Hel|ios Greek god
helio|sphere
helio|spher|ic
helio|stat
helio|stat|ic
helio|ther|apy
helio|trope
helio|trop|ic
helio|trop|ism
helio|type
Helio|zoa
helio|zoan
heli|pad
heli|port
heli-ski
heli-skier
he|lium
helix
  heli|ces
he'll = he shall; he
  will
hell|acious
hell|acious|ly
Hell|lad|ic
hell|bend|er
hell-bent
hell|cat
hell|e|bore
hell|e|bor|ine
Hel|len son or
  brother of
  Deucalion
Hel|lene
Hel|len|ic
Hel|len|isa|tion *Br.*
  var. of
  Hellenization
Hel|len|ise *Br.* var.
  of **Hellenize**
Hel|len|iser *Br.* var.
  of **Hellenizer**
Hel|len|ism
Hel|len|ist
Hel|len|is|tic
Hel|len|iza|tion

Hel¦len¦ize
  Hel¦len¦iz¦ing
Hel¦len¦izer
Hel¦ler, Jo¦seph
  novelist
hel¦ler
Hel¦ler|work
Hel¦les|pont
hell|fire
hell|gram|mite
hell|hole
hell|hound
hel|lion
hell|ish
hell|ish¦ly
hell|ish|ness
hell-like
Hell|man, Lil¦lian
  dramatist
hello
  pl. hel¦los
  v. hel¦loes
hel|loed
hel¦lo|ing
hell|raiser
hell|rais¦ing
hell|luva = hell of a
hell|ward
Hel|mand
helm¦er
hel¦met
Helm|holtz,
  Her|mann von
  physiologist and
  physicist
hel|minth
hel¦minth|ia¦sis
hel¦minth¦ic
hel¦minth|oid
hel¦mintho|logic¦al
hel¦minth|olo¦gist
hel¦minth|ology
Hel|mont,
  Jo¦an¦nes Bap|tista
  van chemist and
  physician
helms|man
helms|men
Hélo¦ïse lover of
  Peter Abelard
helot
helot|age
hel¦ot|ism
hel¦ot¦ry

help¦er
help|ful
help|ful¦ly
help|ful|ness
help|less
help|less¦ly
help|less|ness
help|line
Help|mann,
  Rob¦ert choreog-
  rapher
help|mate
help|meet var. of
  helpmate
Hel¦sing|borg
Hel¦sing|fors
Hel¦sing|ør
Hel|sinki
helter-skelter
helve
Hel|ve¦tian
Hel|vet¦ic
hem
  hemmed
  hem|ming
hem|agglu¦tin|
      ation *US*
  Br.
  haemagglutination
hem|agglu¦tin|in
  US
  Br. haemagglutinin
hemal *US*
  Br. haemal
he-man
  he-men
hem|angi¦oma *US*
  hem|angi¦omas or
  hem|angi¦omata
  Br. haemangioma
hema|tem¦esis *US*
  Br. haematemesis
hem|at¦ic *US*
  Br. haematic
hema|tin *US*
  Br. haematin
hema|tite *US*
  Br. haematite
hem¦ato|cele *US*
  Br. haematocele
hem¦ato|crit *US*
  Br. haematocrit
hema|togen¦ous *US*
  Br. haematogenous

hema¦to|logic *US*
  Br. haematologic
hema¦to|logic¦al
  US
  Br. haematological
hema|tolo¦gist *US*
  Br. haematologist
hema|tol¦ogy *US*
  Br. haematology
hema|toma *US*
  Br. haematoma
hema|topha¦gous
  US
  Br.
  haematophagous
hem|ato|poi¦esis
  US
  Br. haematopoiesis
hem¦ato|poi¦etic
  US
  Br. haematopoietic
hema|toxy¦lin *US*
  Br. haematoxylin
hema|turia *US*
  Br. haematuria
heme *US*
  Br. haem
Hemel
  Hemp|stead
hem¦ero|cal¦lis
  pl. hem¦ero|cal¦lis
hemi|an¦opia
hemi|an¦op¦sia var.
  of hemianopia
hemi|cel¦lu¦lose
Hemi|chord¦ata
hemi|chord¦ate
hemi|circle
hemi|cycle
hemi|cylin¦drical
hemi|demi|semi|
      quaver
hemi|hy¦drate
hemi|meta¦bol¦ic
hemi|metabol¦ous
hemi|morph¦ite
Hem|ing|way,
  Er¦nest novelist
hemi|ola
hemi|para¦site
hemi|par¦esis
hemi|penis
  hemi|penes
hemi|ple¦gia
hemi|ple¦gic

hemi|pode
Hem|ip¦tera
hem|ip¦ter¦an
hem|ip¦ter¦ous
hemi|sphere
hemi|spher¦ic
hemi|spher¦ic¦al
hemi|spher¦ic¦al¦ly
hemi|stich +s
Hem|kund
hem|line
hem|lock
hemo|chroma|tosis
  US
  Br.
  haemochromatosis
hemo|coel *US*
  Br. haemocoel
hemo|cya¦nin *US*
  Br. haemocyanin
hemo¦cyt|om¦eter
  US
  Br.
  haemocytometer
hemo|di¦aly¦sis *US*
  Br. haemodialysis
hemo|dynam¦ic *US*
  Br. haemodynamic
hemo|dynam¦ic|
      al¦ly *US*
  Br.
  haemodynamically
hemo|dynam¦ics
  US
  Br.
  haemodynamics
hemo|glo¦bin *US*
  Br. haemoglobin
hemo|globin|
      opathy *US*
  Br. haemoglobin-
  opathy
hemo|globin|uria
  US
  Br.
  haemoglobinuria
hemo|lymph *US*
  Br. haemolymph
hem|oly¦sis *US*
  Br. haemolysis
hemo|lyt¦ic *US*
  Br. haemolytic
hemo|philia *US*
  Br. haemophilia

hemo|phil|iac US
 Br. **haemophiliac**
hemo|phil|ic US
 Br. **haemophilic**
hemo|poi|esis US
 Br. **haemopoiesis**
hemo|poi|etic US
 Br. **haemopoietic**
hem|op|ty|sis US
 Br. **haemoptysis**
hem|or|rhage US
 hem|or|rha|ging
 Br. **haemorrhage**
hem|or|rhagic US
 Br. **haemorrhagic**
hem|or|rhoid US
 Br. **haemorrhoid**
hem|or|rhoid|al US
 Br. **haemorrhoidal**
hemo|sta|sis US
 Br. **haemostasis**
hemo|stat US
 Br. **haemostat**
hemo|stat|ic US
 Br. **haemostatic**
hemp|en
hemp-nettle
hemp|seed
hem|stitch
Henan
hen and chick|ens
 pl. hen and
 chick|ens
 plant
hen|bane
hen|bit
hence
hence|forth
hence|for|ward
hench|man
 hench|men
hen-coop
hen|deca|gon
hen|dec|agon|al
hen|deca|syl|lab|ic
hen|deca|syl|lable
hen|dia|dys
Hen|drix, Jimi rock
 musician
Hen|dry, Ste|phen
 snooker player
hen|equen
henge

Hen|gist Jutish
 leader
hen|house
Henle loop
Henley-on-Thames
henna +s +ed +ing
heno|the|ism
hen|peck
Henri, Rob|ert
 painter
Hen|rician
Henri|etta
hen-run
Henry
henry unit
 hen|ries or hen|rys
Henry's law
Henze, Hans
 Wer|ner composer
hep|arin
hep|ar|in|isa|tion
 Br. var. of
 heparinization
hep|ar|in|ise Br.
 var. of heparinize
hep|ar|in|iza|tion
hep|ar|in|ize
 hep|ar|in|iz|ing
hep|at|ic
hep|at|ica
Hep|at|icae
hepa|titis
hep|ato|cyte
hepa|toma
 hepa|to|mas or
 hepa|to|mata
hep|ato|meg|aly
hep|ato|pan|creas
hep|ato|toxic
hep|ato|tox|icity
hep|ato|toxin
Hep|burn, Aud|rey
 and Kath|ar|ine
 actresses
hep|cat
Heph|aes|tus Greek
 Mythology
Heph|zi|bah
Hepple|white
hepta|chlor
hepta|chord
hep|tad
hepta|gon

hept|agon|al
hepta|he|dral
hepta|he|dron
 hepta|he|dra or
 hepta|he|drons
hept|am|er|ous
hept|am|eter
hept|ane
hept|arch|ic
hept|archy
 hept|arch|ies
Hepta|teuch
hept|ath|lete
hept|ath|lon
hepta|va|lent
hep|tyl
Hep|worth,
 Bar|bara sculptor
Hera Greek goddess
Hera|cles Greek
 form of **Hercules**
Hera|cli|tus
 philosopher
Her|ak|lion
her|ald
her|al|dic
her|al|dic|al|ly
her|ald|ist
her|ald|ry
Herat
herb|aceous
herb|age
herb|al
herb|al|ism
herb|al|ist
herb|al|ly
herb|ar|ium
 herb|aria
herb|ary
 herb|aries
herb ben|net
herb Chris|to|pher
Her|bert, A. P.
 humorist
Her|bert, George
 poet
her|bert undistin-
 guished man or
 youth
herb Ger|ard
herbi|cide
herbi|vore
herb|iv|or|ous

herb Paris
herb Rob|ert
herby
herb|ier
herbi|est
Her|ce|gov|ina var.
 of Herzegovina
Her|ce|gov|in|ian
 var. of
 Herzegovinian
Her|cu|la|neum
Her|cu|lean
Her|cu|les
Her|cyn|ian
herd group of
 animals; cf. **heard**
herd|boy
herd|er
herds|man
 herds|men
Herd|wick
here cf. hear
here|about var. of
 hereabouts
here|abouts
here|after
here|at
here|by
here|edit|able
here|edita|ment
here|edi|tarian
here|edi|tar|ian|ism
here|edi|tar|ily
here|edi|tari|ness
here|edi|tary
here|ed|ity
Here|ford
Here|ford|shire
here|in
here|in|after
here|in|before
here|of
Her|ero
 pl. Her|ero or
 Her|eros
her|esi|arch +s
her|esy
 her|esies
her|et|ic
her|et|ic|al
her|et|ic|al|ly
here|to
here|to|fore

here|under
here|unto
here|upon
Here|ward the
Wake
here|with
her|iot
her|it|abil|ity
her|it|able
her|it|ably
heri|tage
heri|tor
herky-jerky
herl piece of feather;
cf. hurl
Herm Channel
Island
herm pillar
Her|man
herm|aph|ro|dite
herm|aph|ro|dit|ic
herm|aph|ro|dit|
ism
Herm|aph|ro|ditus
Greek Mythology
her|men|eut|ic
her|men|eut|ic|al
her|men|eut|ic|al|ly
her|men|eut|ics
Her|mes *Greek
Mythology*
Her|mes
Tris|me|gis|tus
Mythology
her|met|ic
her|met|ic|al|ly
her|meti|cism
Her|mia
Her|mione
her|mit
her|mit|age
Her|mit|ian
her|mit|ic
her|nia
her|nias or
her|niae
her|nial
her|ni|ate
her|niat|ing
her|nia|tion
Hero Greek mytho-
logical priestess

Hero Greek
mathematician
hero
her|oes
Herod Agrippa
two rulers of
ancient Palestine
Herod Anti|pas
ruler of ancient
Palestine
Herod|ian
Her|od|otus Greek
historian
hero|ic
hero|ic|al|ly
hero|ics
her|oin drug
hero|ine person
hero|ise *Br.* var. of
heroize
hero|ism
hero|ize
hero|iz|ing
heron
her|on|ry
her|on|ries
Her|oph|ilus Greek
anatomist
hero wor|ship *n.*
hero-worship *v.*
hero-worshipped
Br.
hero-worshiped
US
hero-worship|ping
Br.
hero-worship|ing
US
hero-worship|er
US
hero-worship|per
Br.
her|pes sim|plex
her|pes|virus
her|pes zos|ter
her|pet|ic
her|peto|fauna
her|peto|faunal
her|peto|logic|al
her|pe|tolo|gist
her|pe|tol|ogy
herp|tile
Her|rick, Rob|ert
poet
her|ring

her|ring|bone
her|ring|bon|ing
Her|riot, James
writer and veterin-
ary surgeon
Herrn|huter
Her|schel, John
and Wil|liam Brit-
ish astronomers
her|self
her|story
her|stories
Hert|ford in
England; cf.
Hartford
Hert|ford|shire
Herts. =
Hertfordshire
Hertz, Hein|rich
physicist
hertz unit
pl. hertz
Hertz|ian
Hertzsprung–
Russell
Herut Israeli polit-
ical party
Her|ze|gov|ina
Her|ze|gov|in|ian
Herzl, Theo|dor
writer and Zionist
leader
Her|zog, Wer|ner
film director
he's
Hesh|van var. of
Hesvan
He|siod Greek poet
hesi|tance
hesi|tancy
hesi|tan|cies
hesi|tant
hesi|tant|ly
hesi|tate
hesi|tat|ing
hesi|tat|er
hesi|tat|ing|ly
hesi|ta|tion
hesi|ta|tive
Hes|per|ian
Hes|peri|des Greek
nymphs
hes|per|idium
hes|per|idia

Hes|perus
Hess, Myra pianist
Hess, Ru|dolf Nazi
politician
Hess, Vic|tor
Fran|cis physicist
Hesse state,
Germany
Hesse, Her|mann
novelist
Hes|sen German
name for Hesse
Hes|sian of Hesse;
boot; fly
hes|sian cloth
Hes|ter
Hes|van Jewish
month
Hesy|chast
het|aera
het|aeras or
het|aerae
het|aira var. of
hetaera
het|ero +s
het|ero|aromatic
het|ero|cercal
het|ero|chro|mat|ic
het|ero|
chro|ma|tin
het|ero|clite
het|ero|clit|ic
het|ero|cyc|lic
het|ero|dox
het|ero|doxy
het|ero|dox|ies
het|ero|dyne
het|ero|dyn|ing
het|ero|gam|etic
heter|og|am|ous
heter|og|amy
het|ero|gen|eity
het|ero|ge|neous
diverse; cf.
heterogenous
het|ero|ge|neous|ly
het|ero|ge|neous|
ness
heter|ogen|ous
originating outside
the organism; cf.
heterogeneous
het|ero|glos|sia
het|ero|glos|sic

heter|og|ony
het|ero|graft
heter|ol|ogous
heter|ology
　heter|ologies
heter|om|er|ous
het|ero|morph
het|ero|morph|ic
het|ero|morph|ism
het|ero|morph|ous
het|ero|morphy
　het|ero|morphies
heter|on|om|ous
heter|on|omy
het|ero|nym
het|ero|nym|ic
het|er|onym|ous
het|ero|polar
Het|er|op|tera
het|er|op|ter|an
het|er|op|ter|ous
het|ero|sex|ism
het|ero|sex|ist
het|ero|sex|ual
het|ero|sexu|al|ity
het|ero|sexu|al|ly
het|er|osis
het|ero|styled
het|ero|stylous
het|ero|styly
het|er|otic
het|ero|trans|plant
het|ero|troph
het|ero|troph|ic
het|ero|trophy
　het|ero|trophies
het|ero|zy|gos|ity
het|ero|zy|gote
het|ero|zy|gous
het|man
　het|men
heu|chera
heur|is|tic
heur|is|tic|al|ly
hevea
hew
　hewn
　chop; cf. hue
hewer
hexa|chord
hexad
hexa|deci|mal
hexa|deci|mal|ly

hexa|gon
hex|agon|al
hexa|gram
hexa|he|dral
hexa|he|dron
　hexa|he|dra or
　hexa|he|drons
hexa|hydroxy|
　cyclo|hex|ane
hex|am|er|ous
hex|am|eter
hex|ane
hex|apla
hexa|ploid
hexa|ploidy
　hexa|ploi|dies
hexa|pod
Hexa|poda
hexa|style
Hexa|teuch
hexa|va|lent
hex|ose
hexyl
hey *exclam.* used to
　attract attention
　etc.; cf. hay, heigh
hey|day
Heyer, Geor|gette
　writer
Heyer|dahl, Thor
　anthropologist
Heyhoe-Flint,
　Ra|chael cricketer
hey presto
Hez|bol|lah
H-hour
hi *exclam.*; cf. high
hia|tal
hia|tus
Hia|watha legend-
　ary American
　Indian
Hib bacterium
hiba tree
hi|bachi
hiba|kusha
　pl. hiba|kusha
hi|ber|nate
hi|ber|na|ting
hi|ber|na|tion
hi|ber|na|tor
Hi|ber|nian
Hi|ber|nia|nism

Hi|ber|ni|cism
hi|bis|cus
hic sound of hiccup;
　cf. hick
hic|cough var. of
　hiccup
hic|coughy var. of
　hiccupy
hic|cup
hic|cupy
hic jacet
hick person; cf. hic
hickey
Hickok, Wild Bill
　frontiersman and
　marshal
hick|ory
　hick|or|ies
Hi|dalgo state,
　Mexico
hi|dalgo +s Spanish
　gentleman
Hi|datsa
hid|den
hid|den|ite
hid|den|ness
hide
　hid
　hid|ing
　hid|den
hide-and-seek
hide|away
hide|bound
hided in 'thick-
　hided' etc.
hid|eos|ity
　hid|eos|ities
hid|eous
hid|eous|ly
hid|eous|ness
hide|out
hider
hidey-hole
hid|rosis
hid|rot|ic
hidy-hole var. of
　hidey-hole
hie go
　hie|ing or hying
hie|la|man
hier|arch +s
hier|arch|ic|al
hier|arch|ic|al|ly

hier|arch|isa|tion
　Br. var. of
　hierarchization
hier|arch|ise *Br.*
　var. of hierarchize
hier|arch|iza|tion
hier|arch|ize
　hier|arch|iz|ing
hier|archy
　hier|arch|ies
hier|at|ic
hier|at|ic|al|ly
hier|oc|racy
　hier|oc|ra|cies
hiero|crat|ic
hiero|glyph
hiero|glyph|ic
hiero|glyph|ic|al|ly
hiero|gram
hiero|graph
hier|ol|atry
hier|ology
hiero|phant
hiero|phant|ic
hi-fi
hig|gle
　hig|gling
higgledy-piggledy
　higgledy-
　　piggle|dies
hig|gler
Higgs boson
Higgs par|ticle
high cf. hi
high|ball
high|bind|er
high|boy
high|brow
higher-up
high|fa|lu|tin
high|fa|lu|ting var.
　of highfalutin
high-flier var. of
　high-flyer
high-flyer
high-flying
high hat *n.* hat;
　person; fish; cf.
　hi-hat
high-hat *adj. & v.*
　high-hatted
　high-hatting
high jump
high jump|er

High|land *mod.* of e.g. Scotland
high|land high land
High|land¦er of e.g. Scotland
high|land¦er of high land
High|land|man
High|land|men of e.g. Scotland
high|land|man
high|land|men of high land
High|lands of e.g. Scotland
high life extravagant living
high|life music
high|light
high|light¦er
high-low boot
high¦ly
high muck-a-muck
high muckety-muck var. of high muck-a-muck
high|ness
high-res var. of hi-res
high-rise
High|smith, Pa¦tri¦cia writer
high-strung
hight *archaic* named; cf. **height**
high|tail
high tech *n.*
high-tech *adj.*
high-tensile
high-top shoe
high-up *n.*
high|veld
high-water mark
high|way
high¦way|man
high¦way|men
hi-hat cymbals; cf. **high hat**
hijab
hi¦jack
hi¦jack¦er
Hijaz var. of **Hejaz**
Hijra var. of **Hegira**

hijra *Ind.* transvestite or eunuch
hike
hik¦ing
cf. **haik**
hiker
hila pl. of **hilum**; cf. **hyla**
hilar *adj.*
hil¦ari|ous
hil¦ari|ous¦ly
hil¦ari|ous|ness
hil¦ar|ity
Hil¦ary, St
Hil¦ary term
Hil|bert space
Hil¦de|gard of Bin¦gen, St
Hil¦des|heim
Hili|gay¦non
Hill, Gra¦ham and Damon racing drivers
Hill, Row|land founder of penny post
Hil|lary, Ed¦mund mountaineer
hill|billy
hill|bil¦lies
hil¦li|ness
hill|man
hill|men
hil|lock
hil|locky
hill|side
hill|star
hill|top
hill|walk¦er
hill|walk¦ing
hilly
hill|ier
hilli|est
hilum
hila
hilus
hili
Hil¦ver|sum
Hi¦ma|chal Pra|desh
Hima|layan
Hima|layas
hi¦mat|ion

Himm|ler, Hein|rich Nazi leader
Hims var. of **Homs**
him|self
Him¦yar|ite
Hi¦na|yana Buddhism
hind
hind|brain
Hin¦de|mith, Paul composer
Hin¦den|burg, Paul von president of Germany; H. Line
hin¦der
Hindi
hind leg
hind|limb
hind|most
Hin¦doo *archaic* var. of **Hindu**
hind|quar¦ters
hin|drance
hind|sight
Hindu
Hin¦du|ise *Br.* var. of **Hinduize**
Hin¦du|ism
Hin¦du|ize
Hin¦du|iz¦ing
Hindu Kush
Hin¦du|stan
Hin¦du|stani
Hin|dutva
hind|wing
hinge
hinge|ing or **hin|ging**
hinge|less
hinge-like
Hing|lish
hinky
hink|ier
hinki|est
hinnie term of endearment; var. of **hinny**
hinny
hin|nies
hi|noki
hin¦ter|land

hip
hip¦per
hip¦pest
hip hop
hip-hopper
hip|ness
Hip|par¦chus astronomer
hip¦pe|as¦trum
hipped
hip¦pie var. of **hippy**
hippie|dom
hippi|ness
hippo +s
hippo|cam¦pus
hippo|campi
hippo|cras
Hip¦poc|ra¦tes physician
Hippo|crat¦ic
Hippo|crene
hippo|drome
hippo|griff
hippo|gryph var. of **hippogriff**
Hip¦poly¦tus Greek mythological figure
hippo|pot¦amus
hippo|pot¦amuses or **hippo|pot¦ami**
Hippo Re¦gius
hip|pur¦ate
hip|pur¦ic
hip¦pus
hippy
hip|pies
hip|pier
hip|pi¦est
hippy-dippy
hippy-dippier
hippy-dippiest
hippy|ish
hip|shot
hip|ster
hip¦ster|ism
hir¦able *US* var. of **hireable**
hira|gana
hir|cine
hire
hir¦ing
hire|able
hire|ling
hirer

hi-res
Hiri Motu
Hiro|hito Japanese
  emperor
hi|rola
Hiro|shima
hir|ple
  hirp|ling
Hirsch|sprung's
  dis|ease
Hirst, Da|mien
  artist
hir|sute
hir|sute|ness
hir|sut|ism
hi|run|dine
His|pan|ic
His|pani|cise Br.
  var. of Hispanicize
His|pani|cist
His|pani|cize
  His|pani|ciz|ing
His|pani|ola
His|pan|ist
his|pid
hissy fit
his|ta|mine
his|ta|min|ic
his|ti|dine
his|tio|cyte
histo|chem|ical
histo|chem|is|try
histo|com|pati|
          bil|ity
histo|gen|esis
  histo|gen|eses
histo|gen|et|ic
histo|gen|ic
hist|ogeny
histo|gram
histo|logic
hist|olo|gist
hist|ology
hist|oly|sis
histo|lyt|ic
his|tone
histo|patho|logic|al
histo|patho|logic|
          al|ly
histo|path|olo|gist
histo|path|ology
histo|plas|mo|sis

his|tor|ian
his|tori|ated
his|tor|ic
his|tor|ic|al
his|tor|ic|al|ly
his|tori|cisa|tion
  Br. var. of
  historicization
his|tori|cise Br. var.
  of historicize
his|tori|cism
his|tori|cist
his|tor|icity
his|tori|ciza|tion
his|tori|cize
  his|tori|ciz|ing
his|tori|ograph|er
his|torio|graph|ic
his|torio|
          graph|ic|al
his|torio|graph|ic|
          al|ly
his|tori|og|raphy
his|tory
  his|tor|ies
history-sheeter
histo|sol
his|tri|on|ic
his|tri|on|ic|al|ly
his|tri|on|ics
hit
  hit|ting
hitch
Hitch|cock, Al|fred
  film director
Hitch|ens, Ivon
  painter
hitch|er
hitch|hike
  hitch|hik|ing
hitch|hiker
Hite, Shere feminist
hi-tech var. of high-
  tech
hither
hith|er|to
hith|er|ward
Hit|ler, Adolf Nazi
  leader
Hit|ler|ian
Hit|ler|ism
Hit|ler|ite
hit-out n.

hit|ter
Hit|tite
hive
  hiv|ing
hives
hiya greeting
Hiz|bul|lah var. of
  Hezbollah
Hmong
  pl. Hmong
ho
  hos or hoes
  exclam.;
  prostitute; cf. hoe
hoa|gie
hoar grey; frost; cf.
  haugh, haw, whore
hoard store; cf.
  horde
hoard|er
hoar|hound var. of
  horehound
hoar|ily
hoari|ness
hoarse
  hoars|er
  hoars|est
  of voice; cf. horse
hoarse|ly
hoars|en
hoarse|ness
hoar|stone
hoary
  hoar|ier
  hoari|est
hoat|zin
hoax
hoax|er
Ho|bart
Hob|bema,
  Mein|dert painter
Hobbes, Thomas
  philosopher
Hobbes|ian
hob|bit
hob|ble
  hob|bling
hobble|bush
hobble|de|hoy
hob|bler
Hobbs, Jack
  cricketer
hobby
  hob|bies

hobby horse
hob|by|ist
hob|day
hob|gob|lin
hob|nail
hob|nob
  hob|nobbed
  hob|nob|bing
hobo
  ho|boes or hobos
Hob|son's choice
Ho Chi Minh
  president of North
  Vietnam
hock leg joint; wine;
  pawn; cf. hough
hocket
hockey
Hock|ney, David
  painter
Hock|tide
hocus
  ho|cus|ses or
  ho|cuses
  ho|cussed or
  ho|cused
  ho|cus|sing or
  ho|cus|ing
hocus-pocus
hod|den
Ho|deida
Hodge farmworker
hodge|podge US
  Br. hotchpotch
Hodg|kin's
  dis|ease
hod|man
  hod|men
hodo|graph
hod|om|eter var. of
  odometer
hodo|scope
Hoe, Rich|ard
  inventor and
  industrialist
hoe tool; cf. ho
hoe|cake
hoe|down
hoer person who
  hoes
Hofei var. of Hefei
Hoffa, Jimmy trade
  union leader
Hoff|man, Dus|tin
  actor

Hoff|mann,
E. T. A. novelist
Hof|manns|thal,
Hugo von drama-
tist
hog
hogged
hog|ging
hogan
Ho|garth, Wil|liam
artist
Ho|garth|ian
hog|back
hog|fish
Hogg, James poet
hogg sheep; var. of
hog
Hog|gar
Moun|tains
hog|ger
hog|gery
hog|ger|ies
hog|get
hog|gin
hog|gish
hog|gish|ly
hog-like
Hog|ma|nay
hog|nose snake
hog-nosed
hog|nut
hogs|head
hog-tie
hog-tying
hog|wash
hog|weed
hog-wild
Hohen|stau|fen
Hohen|zol|lern
Hoh|hot
ho ho
ho-hum
hoick
hoi pol|loi
hoi|sin
hoist
hoist|er
hoity-toity
hoke
hoking
hokey
hoki|er
hoki|est

sentimental; cf.
hoki
hokey-cokey
hokey|ness
hokey-pokey
hoki
pl. hoki
fish; cf. hokey
hoki|ly
hoki|ness var. of
hokeyness
Hok|kaido
Hok|kien
pl. Hok|kien
hokku
pl. hokku
var. of haiku
hoko|nui
hokum
Hoku|sai,
Kat|su|shika artist
Hol|arc|tic
Hol|bein, Hans
painter
hold
held
hold|able
hold|all
hold|back
hold|er
Höl|der|lin,
Fried|rich poet
hold|fast
hold|out
hold|over
hold-up n.
hole
hol|ing
hollow; cf. whole
holey full of holes;
cf. holy, wholly
Holi Hindu festival;
cf. holy, wholly
Holi|day, Bil|lie
singer
holi|day
holi|day|maker
holier-than-thou
Holi|ness title of
pope
holi|ness
Hol|in|shed,
Raph|ael chronicler
hol|ism

hol|ist
hol|is|tic
hol|is|tic|al|ly
Hol|land
hol|land linen
hol|land|aise
Hol|land|er
Hol|lands gin
hol|ler
Hol|ler|ith
hol|low
hol|low|ly
hol|low|ness
hol|low|ware
Holly, Buddy musi-
cian
holly
hol|lies
holly|hock
Holly|wood
holm islet; oak tree;
cf. hom, home
holme islet. var. of
holm
Holmes, Kelly run-
ner
Holmes, Oli|ver
Wen|dell physician
and writer
Holmes, Sher|lock
fictional detective
Holmes|ian
hol|mium
holo +s
holo|caust
Holo|cene
holo|en|zyme
Holo|fer|nes
holo|gram
holo|graph
holo|graph|ic
holo|graph|ic|al|ly
hol|og|raphy
holo|phrase
holo|phr|asis
holo|phras|tic
holo|phyt|ic
holo|thur|ian
holo|thur|oid
Holo|thur|oidea
holo|type
Holst, Gus|tav
composer

Hol|stein
Hol|stein|ian
hol|ster
holus-bolus
holy
holies
holi|er
holi|est
sacred; cf. holey,
Holi, wholly
Holy|head
holy|stone
holy|ston|ing
hom plant; juice; cf.
holm, home
homa var. of hom
hom|age
hom|bre man; cf.
ombre, ombré
hom|burg
home
hom|ing
residence; cf. hom,
holm
home|body
home|bodies
home|boy
home brew
home-brewed
home|buy|er
home|com|ing
home|girl
home-grown
home|land
home|less
home|less|ness
home|like
home|li|ness
home|ly
home|lier
home|li|est
home-made
home|maker
home|mak|ing
homeo|box
homeo|morph|ic
homeo|morph|ism
homeo|path
homeo|path|ic
homeo|path|ic|al|ly
hom|eop|ath|ist
hom|eop|athy
hom|eop|athies

home|osis
home|oses
homeo|sta|sis
  homeo|sta|ses
homeo|stat|ic
homeo|therm
homeo|ther|mal
homeo|ther|mic
homeo|thermy
home|otic
home|owner
home own|er|ship
Homer *Greek poet*
homer *Baseball*;
  pigeon
Hom|er|ic
home|room
home|sick
home|sick|ness
home|site
home|spun
home|stead
home|stead|er
home|stead|ing
home|style
home|ward
home|wards
home|work
home|work|er
homey
  homi|er
  homi|est
cosy; cf. homie
homey|ness
homi|cidal
homi|cidal|ly
homi|cide
homie *local*
  acquaintance; cf.
  homey
homi|let|ic
ho|mil|iary
ho|mil|iar|ies
hom|il|ist
hom|ily
  hom|ilies
homi|ness var. of
  homeyness
hom|inid
hom|in|oid
hom|iny
Homo *genus*

homo +s homo-
  sexual
homo|cen|tric
homo|cer|cal
homo|cyst|eine
hom|oeo|box *Br.*
  var. of homeobox
hom|oeo|path *Br.*
  var. of homeopath
hom|oeo|path|ic
  Br. var. of
  homeopathic
hom|oeo|path|ic|
    al|ly
  Br. var. of
  homeopathically
hom|oe|op|ath|ist
  Br. var. of
  homeopathist
hom|oe|op|athy *Br.*
  var. of homeopathy
homoe|osis *Br.* var.
  of homeosis
hom|oeo|sta|sis *Br.*
  var. of homeostasis
hom|oeo|stat|ic *Br.*
  var. of homeostatic
homoe|ot|ic *Br.* var.
  of homeotic
homo|erot|ic
homo|eroti|cism
homo|gam|et|ic
hom|og|am|ous
hom|og|amy
  hom|og|amies
hom|ogen|ate
homo|gen|eity
homo|ge|neous
  uniform; cf.
  homogenous
homo|ge|neous|ly
homo|ge|neous|
      ness
hom|ogen|isa|tion
  Br. var. of
  homogenization
hom|ogen|ise *Br.*
  var. of homogenize
hom|ogen|iser *Br.*
  var. of
  homogenizer
hom|ogen|iza|tion
hom|ogen|ize
  hom|ogen|iz|ing
hom|ogen|izer

homo|gen|ous *Biol-
  ogy* with common
  descent; cf.
  homogeneous
hom|ogeny
homo|graft
homo|graph
homo|graph|ic
hom|oio|therm var.
  of homeotherm
hom|oio|ther|mal
  var. of
  homeothermal
hom|oio|ther|mic
  var. of
  homeothermic
hom|oio|thermy
  var. of
  homeothermy
hom|oio|us|ian cf.
  homoousian
homo|log *US* var. of
  homologue
hom|olo|gate
hom|olo|gat|ing
hom|olo|ga|tion
hom|olo|gise *Br.*
  var. of homologize
hom|olo|gize
  hom|olo|giz|ing
hom|olo|gous
homo|logue
hom|ology
  hom|olo|gies
homo|morph|ic
homo|morph|ic|
      al|ly
homo|morph|ism
homo|morphy
  homo|morphies
homo|nym
homo|nym|ic
hom|onym|ous
hom|onymy
homo|ous|ian cf.
  homoiousian
homo|phobe
homo|pho|bia
homo|pho|bic
homo|phone
homo|phon|ic
homo|phon|ic|al|ly
hom|oph|onous
hom|oph|ony

homo|polar
Hom|op|tera
hom|op|ter|an
hom|op|ter|ous
hom|or|gan|ic
Homo sa|pi|ens
homo|sex|ual
homo|sexu|al|ity
homo|sexu|al|ly
homo|social
homo|trans|plant
hom|ous|ian var. of
  homoousian
homo|zy|gos|ity
homo|zy|gote
homo|zy|gous
Homs *city, Syria*
hom|un|cule var. of
  homunculus
hom|un|cu|lus
hom|un|culi
homy var. of homey
hon = honey
hon|cho
  pl. hon|chos
  v. hon|choes
  hon|choed
  hon|choing
Hon|duran
Hon|duras
Hon|ecker, Erich
  *East German head
  of state*
Hon|eg|ger, Ar|thur
  composer
hon|est
hon|est|ly
honest-to-God
honest-to-
      goodness
hon|esty
hone|wort
honey
honey|bird
honey|bun
honey|bunch
honey|comb
honey|creep|er
honey|dew
honey|eater
hon|eyed
honey|guide
honey|moon

honey|moon|er

honey|pot

honey|suck|er

honey|suckle

honey|trap

honey|wort

hongi

Hong Kong

Ho|ni|ara

hon|ied var. of
honeyed

*Honi soit qui mal
y pense*

Honi|ton

honk|er

honky
  hon|kies

honky-tonk

hon|nête homme
  hon|nêtes hommes

Hono|lulu

honor US
  Br. honour

hon|or|able US
  Br. honourable

hon|or|able|ness
  US
  Br.
  honourableness

hon|or|ably US
  Br. honourably

hon|or|and

hon|or|ar|ium
  hon|or|ar|iums or
  hon|or|aria

hon|or|ary

hon|or|ee US

hon|or|if|ic

hon|or|if|ic|al|ly

hon|oris causa

hon|our Br.
  US honor

hon|our|able Br.
  US honorable

hon|our|able|ness
  Br.
  US honorableness

hon|our|ably Br.
  US honorably

Hon|shu

Hooch, Pie|ter de
  painter

hooch

Hood, Thomas poet

hoodia

hoodie var. of
  hoody

hood|less

hood-like

hood|lum

hoo|doo +s +ed
  +ing

hood|wink

hoody
  hood|ies

hooey

hoof
  pl. hoofs or hooves
  v. hoofs
  hoofed
  hoof|ing

hoof|er

Hoogh var. of
  Hooch

Hoo|ghly

hoo-ha

hoo|kah pipe; cf.
  hooker

hook|bait

Hooke, Rob|ert sci-
  entist

Hook|er, Jo|seph
  botanist

hook|er rugby
  player; prostitute;
  cf. hookah

Hooke's law

hookey in 'play
  hookey'; cf. hooky

hook|less

hook|let

hook-like

hook|tip

hook-up n.

hook|worm

hooky easy to
  remember; cf.
  hookey

hoo|ley

hoo|li|gan

hooli|gan|ism

hoo|lock

hoop|er

hoopla

hoo|poe

hoo|ray

Hoo|ray Henry
  Hoo|ray Hen|rys

or Hoo|ray
  Hen|ries

hoo|roo +s

hoose|gow

Hoo|sier

hootch var. of
  hooch

hoote|nanny
  hoote|nan|nies

hoot|er

hoots *exclam.*

Hoo|ver, Her|bert
  US president

Hoo|ver, J. Edgar
  FBI director

Hoo|ver vacuum
  cleaner *trademark*

hoo|ver v.

Hoo|ver|ville

hooves

hop
  hopped
  hop|ping

Hope, Bob com-
  edian

hope
  hop|ing

hope|ful

hope|ful|ly

hope|ful|ness

hope|less

hope|less|ly

hope|less|ness

hoper

hop|head

Hopi

Hop|kins, An|thony
  actor

Hop|kins, Ger|ard
  Man|ley poet

hop|lite

Hop|per, Ed|ward
  painter

hop|per

hop|ple
  hop|pling

hoppy

hop|pier
  hop|pi|est

hop|sack

hop|scotch

hora dance

Hor|ace Roman
  poet

horah var. of hora

horal

hor|ary

Hor|atia

Hor|atian

Hor|atio

hor|chata

horde large group;
  cf. hoard

Hor|dern, Mi|chael
  actor

hore|hound

hori|zon

hori|zon|tal

hori|zon|tal|ity

hori|zon|tal|ly

Hor|licks
  trademark

hor|mo|nal

hor|mo|nal|ly

hor|mone

Hor|muz

Horn, Cape

horn|beam

horn|bill

horn|blende

horn|book

hor|nero +s

Hor|ner's
  syn|drome

hor|net

horn|fels

horn|ily

horni|ness

horn|ist

horn|less

horn-like

horn|pipe

horn|swog|gle
  horn|swog|gling

horn|tail

Hor|nung, Er|nest
  novelist

horn|worm

horn|wort

horny
  horn|ier
  horni|est

horo|loge

hor|ol|oger

horo|logic|al

hor|olo|gist

Horo|lo|gium

hor|ol|ogy
hor|op|ter
horo|scope
horo|scop|ic
hor|os|copy
Horo|witz,
  Vlad|imir pianist
hor|ren|dous
hor|ren|dous|ly
hor|rent
hor|rible
hor|rible|ness
hor|ribly
hor|rid
hor|rid|ly
hor|rid|ness
hor|rif|ic
hor|rif|ic|al|ly
hor|ri|fi|ca|tion
hor|rify
  hor|ri|fies
  hor|ri|fied
  hor|ri|fy|ing
hor|ri|fy|ing|ly
hor|rip|il|ate
  hor|rip|il|at|ing
hor|ri|pil|ation
hor|ror
hor|ror vacui
Horsa Jutish leader
hors con|cours
hors de com|bat
hors d'oeuvre
horse
  hors|ing
  animal; cf. hoarse
horse|back
horse|bean
horse-block
horse|box
horse-coper
horse|flesh
horse|fly
  horse|flies
horse|hair
Horse|head
  Neb|ula
horse|leech
horse|less
horse-like
horse|man
  horse|men
horse|man|ship

horse|mint
horse|play
horse|play|er
horse|power
  pl. horse|power
horse|rad|ish
horse|shit *vulgar
  slang*
horse|shoe
horse-trade
  horse-trading
  horse-trader
horse|whip
  horse|whipped
  horse|whip|ping
horse|woman
  horse|women
horsey
  hors|ier
  horsi|est
  var. of horsy
hors|ily
horst
Horst Wes|sel
  Song
horsy var. of horsey
Horta, Vic|tor
  architect
hor|ta|tion
hor|ta|tive
hor|ta|tory
Hor|tense
hor|ten|sia
horti|cul|tural
horti|cul|tur|al|ist
horti|cul|ture
horti|cul|tur|ist
hor|tus sic|cus
  horti sicci
Horus Egyptian god
hos|anna
Hosay Muslim
  festival
hose
  hos|ing
Hosea
hose-in-hose
hosel
hose|pipe
hoser
ho|sier
ho|siery
hos|pice

hos|pit|able
hos|pit|ably
hos|pital
hos|pi|tal|er *US
  Br.* hospitaller
hos|pi|tal|isa|tion
  Br. var. of
  hospitalization
hos|pi|tal|ise *Br.*
  var. of hospitalize
hos|pi|tal|ism
hos|pi|tal|ity
hos|pi|tal|iza|tion
hos|pi|tal|ize
  hos|pi|tal|iz|ing
hos|pi|tal|ler *Br.
  US* hospitaler
hos|po|dar
hosta
hos|tage
hos|tel
hos|tel|er *US
  Br.* hosteller
hos|tel|ing *US
  Br.* hostelling
hos|tel|ler *Br.
  US* hosteler
hos|tel|ling *Br.
  US* hosteling
hos|tel|ry
  hos|tel|ries
host|ess
hos|tile
hos|tile|ly
hos|til|ity
  hos|til|ities
host|ler var. of
  ostler
hot
  hot|ted
  hot|ting
  hot|ter
  hot|test
hot|bed
hotch|pot *Law*
hotch|potch
  US hodgepodge
hot cross bun
hot-desking
hot dog *n.*
hot|dog *v.*
  hot|dogged
  hot|dog|ging
hot|dog|ger

hotel
ho|tel|ier
hotel|keep|er
ho|tel|ling
hot|foot +s +ed
  +ing *adv. & v.*
hot|head
hot-headed
hot-headed|ly
hot-headed|ness
hot|house
  hot|hous|ing
hot|line
hot|link
hot|list
hotly
hot|ness
hot|plate
hot|pot
hot rod *n.*
hot-rod
  hot-rodded
  hot-rodding *v.*
hot-rodder
hot-short
hot|shot
Hot|spur, Harry Sir
  Henry Percy
hot|spur
hot-swap
  hot-swapped
  hot-swapping
hot-swappable
hotsy-totsy
Hot|ten|tot
hot|ter
hot|tie
hot|tish
hotty var. of hottie
hot-water bag
hot-water bot|tle
hot-wire
  hot-wiring
hou|bara
Hou|dini, Harry
  escapologist
hough joint of meat
  above hock; to
  hamstring; cf. hock
houm|mos var. of
  hummus
hou|mos var. of
  hummus

hound
hound|fish
hound's tongue
  plant
hounds|tooth +s
  pattern
houn|gan
hour
hour|glass
houri
hour'|ly
house
  hous|ing
house|boat
house|bound
house|boy
house|break
  house|broke
  house|broken
house|break'|er
house|build'|er
house|build'|ing
house|buy'|er
house|carl
house|carle var. of
  housecarl
house|coat
house|craft
house|father
house|fly
  house|flies
house|ful
house|group
house|hold
house|hold'|er
house-hunt
house-hunter
house hus|band
house|keep
  house|kept
house|keep'|er
house|keep'|ing
house|leek
house|less
house|maid
house|man
  house|men
house|master
house|mate
house|mis'|tress
house|mother
house|parent
house-proud

house|room
house-sit
  house-sat
  house-sitting
house-sitter
house|top
house-train
house-warming
house|wife
  house|wives
house|wife'|ly
house|wif'|ery
house|work
housey
housey-housey
housie-housie var.
  of housey-housey
Hous|man, A. E.
  poet
Hous|ton
hout|ing
hovel
hover
hov'|er|craft
  pl. hov'|er|craft
hov'|er|er
hov'|er|fly
  hov'|er|flies
hov'|er|port
hov'|er|train
How'|ard,
  Cath'|er'|ine wife of
  Henry VIII of
  England
How'|ard, John
  prison reformer
How'|ard, John
  prime minister of
  Australia
How'|ard, Les'|lie
  actor
How'|ard, Trevor
  actor
how'|be'|it
how'|dah
how-de-do var. of
  how-do-you-do
how-do-you-do +s
  awkward situation
howdy
how|dies
how-d'ye-do var. of
  how-do-you-do

howe mound;
  hollow
how'|e'er = however
How'|erd, Fran|kie
  comedian
how|ever
howff
how|itz'|er
howk
howl'|er
how|let
howl|ing'|ly
How'|rah
how|so'e'er =
  howsoever
how|so'|ever
how-to +s
how|tow'|die
how'|zat Cricket
Hoxha, Enver
  prime minister of
  Albania
Hox|nian
hoya shrub
hoy'|den
hoy'|den|ish
Hoyle in 'according
  to Hoyle'
Hoyle, Fred
  astrophysicist
Hra|dec Krá|lové
Hrodna
hryvna
hryv|nia var. of
  hryvna
Huai|nan
Hual|laga
Huambo
Huang Hai Chinese
  name for the
  Yellow Sea
Huang Ho Chinese
  name for the
  Yellow River
hua|ra|che
Huas|ca|rán
hubba hubba
Hub|bard squash
Hub'|ble, Edwin
  astronomer; classi-
  fication; telescope;
  constant; law; time
hubble-bubble
hub|bub

hubby
  hub|bies
hub'|cap
Hubei
Hu'|bert
Hubli
Hubli-Dharwar
  var. of Hubli
hu'|bris
hu'|bris|tic
hu'|chen
  pl. hu'|chen
hucka|back
huckle-back
huckle|berry
  huckle|berries
huck|ster
huck|ster|ism
Hud'|ders|field
hud'|dle
hud|dling
Hu'|di|bras|tic
Hud'|son, Henry
  explorer; River
Hud'|son Bay
Hud'|son|ian
Hud'|son's Bay
  Company; blanket
Hué city, Vietnam
hue colour; in 'hue
  and cry'; cf. hew
hue|less
huff'|er
huff'|ily
huffi|ness
huff'|ish
huffy
  huff'|ier
  huffi|est
hug
  hugged
  hug|ging
huge
huger
hug'|est
huge'|ly
huge|ness
hug|gable
hug'|ger
hugger-mugger
Hughes, How'|ard
  industrialist and
  film producer
Hughes, Ted poet

Hugo, Vic|tor writer
Hu|gue|not
hui gathering in NZ
or Hawaii
huia extinct bird
hula dance
Hula-Hoop toy;
US trademark for
hula hoop
hula-hula var. of
hula
hulk|ing
hul|la|ba|loo +s
hullo var. of hello
hum
  hummed
  hum|ming
human +s
hu|mane
  hu|maner
  hu|man|est
hu|mane|ly
hu|mane|ness
hu|man|isa|tion *Br.*
var. of
humanization
hu|man|ise *Br.* var.
of **humanize**
hu|man|ism
hu|man|ist
hu|man|is|tic
hu|man|is|tic|al|ly
hu|mani|tar|ian
hu|mani|tar|ian|
            ism
hu|man|ity
  hu|man|ities
hu|man|iza|tion
hu|man|ize
  hu|man|iz|ing
hu|man|kind
hu|man|ly
hu|man|ness
hu|man|oid
Hum|ber
Hum|ber|side
hum|ble
  hum|bling
  hum|bler
  hum|blest
humble-bee
hum|ble|ness
hum|bly

Hum|boldt,
  Fried|rich explorer;
  H. Current
hum|bug
  hum|bugged
  hum|bug|ging
hum|bug|gery
hum|ding|er
hum|drum
Hume, David
  philosopher
Hume|an
hu|mec|tant
hu|meral relating to
  the humerus; Cath-
  olic vestment; cf.
  humoral
hu|merus
  hu|meri
  bone; cf. **humorous**
humic
humid
hu|midi|fi|ca|tion
hu|midi|fier
hu|mid|ify
  hu|midi|fies
  hu|midi|fied
  hu|midi|fy|ing
hu|midi|stat
hu|mid|ity
  hu|mid|ities
hu|mid|ly
hu|mi|dor
hu|mifi|ca|tion
hum|ify
  humi|fies
  humi|fied
  humi|fy|ing
hu|mili|ate
  hu|mili|at|ing
  hu|mili|at|ing|ly
hu|mili|ation
hu|mili|ator
hu|mil|ity
Hum|int
hum|mable
hum|mel
hum|mer
hum|ming|bird
hum|mock
hum|mocky
hum|mus chickpea
  spread; cf. **humous**,
  humus

hu|mon|gous
humor *US*
  Br. **humour**
hu|moral relating to
  body fluids; cf.
  humeral
hu|mor|esque
hu|mor|ist
hu|mor|is|tic
hu|mor|less *US*
  Br. **humourless**
hu|mor|less|ly *US*
  Br. **humourlessly**
hu|mor|less|ness
  US
  Br.
  humourlessness
hu|mor|ous cf.
  humerus
hu|mor|ous|ly
hu|mor|ous|ness
hu|mour *Br.*
  US **humor**
hu|mour|less *Br.*
  US **humorless**
hu|mour|less|ly *Br.*
  US **humorlessly**
hu|mour|less|ness
  Br.
  US **humorlessness**
hum|ous consisting
  of humus; cf.
  hummus
hump|back
hump|backed
Hum|per|dinck,
  Engel|bert
  composer
humph
Hum|phrey
Hum|phry
hump|less
humpty-dumpty
  humpty-dumpties
humpy
  hump|ies
  hump|ier
  humpi|est
hu|mun|gous var. of
  humongous
humus soil
  constituent; cf.
  hummus, humous
hu|mus|ify
  hu|musi|fies

hu|musi|fied
hu|musi|fy|ing
Hum|vee *trademark*
Hun Asiatic people
Hunan
hunch|back
hunch|backed
hun|dred
hun|dred|fold
hun|dredth
hun|dred|weight
**Hun|dred Years
  War**
Hun|gar|ian
Hun|gary
hun|ger
hung|over
hun|grily
hun|gri|ness
hun|gry
  hun|grier
  hun|gri|est
hun|ker
hun|kers
hunky
  hunk|ier
  hunki|est
hunky-dory
Hun|nish
Hunt, Hol|man
  painter
hunt-and-peck
hunt|away
hunt|er
hunter-gather|er
hunter-killer
Hun|ting|don town,
  England
**Hun|ting|don,
  Count|ess of**
  religious leader
Hun|ting|don|shire
Hun|ting|ton city,
  West Virginia
**Hun|ting|ton
  Beach** city,
  California
**Hun|ting|ton's
  cho|rea**
**Hun|ting|ton's
  dis|ease**
hunt|ress
hunts|man
  hunts|men

Hunts|ville
hun¦yak
Huon pine
hur¦dle
  hurd|ling
hurd|ler
hurdy-gurdy
  hurdy-gurdies
hurl throw; cf. herl
hurl¦er
Hur¦ler's
  syn|drome
hur¦ley
hurly-burly
Huron people; Lake
hur¦rah
hur¦ray var. of
  hooray
Hurri
Hur|rian
hur¦ri|cane
hur¦ried¦ly
hur¦ried|ness
hur¦roo var. of
  hooroo
hurry
  hur|ries
  hur|ried
  hurry|ing
hurry-up adj.
hurst
hurt
hurt|ful
hurt|ful¦ly
hurt|ful|ness
hur¦tle
  hurt|ling
hurty
  hurt|ier
  hurti|est
Hus¦ain var. of
  Hussein
Husák, Gus¦táv
  president of
  Czechoslovakia
hus|band
hus¦band|hood
hus¦band|less
hus¦band¦ly
hus¦band|man
  hus¦band|men
hus¦band¦ry
hush|aby

hush|abye var. of
  hushaby
hush-hush
husk|ily
huski|ness
husky
  husk|ies
  husk|ier
  huski|est
Huss, John reli-
  gious reformer
huss fish
  pl. huss
hus¦sar
Hus|sein,
  Ab¦dul|lah ibn king
  of Jordan, 1946–51
Hus|sein, Sad¦dam
  president of Iraq
Hus|sein ibn Talal
  king of Jordan,
  1953–99
Hus|serl, Ed¦mund
  philosopher
Huss|ite
Huss¦it|ism
hussy
  hus|sies
hust|ings
hus¦tle
  hust|ling
hust|ler
Hus¦ton, John film
  director
hut
  hut|ted
  hut|ting
hutch
hutia
hut-like
hut|ment
Hut¦ter|ite
Hut|ton, Len
  cricketer
Hutu
  pl. Hutu or Hutus
  or Ba¦hutu
Hux|ley, Al¦dous
  writer
Hux|ley, An|drew
  physiologist
Hux|ley, Ju¦lian
  biologist
Hux|ley, Thomas
  biologist

Huy|gens,
  Chris|tiaan physi-
  cist; eyepiece; space
  probe
huzza
huzzah var. of
  huzza
Hwange
hwyl fervour
hya|cinth
hya¦cinth|ine
Hya|cin¦thus Greek
  Mythology
Hya¦des star cluster
hy¦aena var. of
  hyena
hy¦aeno|don
hya¦lin n.
hya|line adj.
hya|lite
hya|loid
hya|lur¦on|ate
hya|lur¦on|ic
hy¦brid
hy¦brid|is|able Br.
  var. of hybridizable
hy¦brid|isa¦tion Br.
  var. of
  hybridization
hy¦brid|ise Br. var.
  of hybridize
hy¦brid|iser Br. var.
  of hybridizer
hy¦brid|ism
hy¦brid|ity
hy¦brid|iz|able
hy¦brid|iza¦tion
hy¦brid|ize
  hy¦brid|iz¦ing
hy¦brid|izer
hy|dan¦toin
hyda|thode
hyda|tid
Hyde, Ed¦ward Earl
  of Clarendon
Hyde in 'Jekyll and
  Hyde'
Hyde Park
Hy¦dera|bad
Hydra Greek Myth-
  ology; constellation
hydra invertebrate;
  problem
hy¦dram|nios

hy¦dran|gea
hy|drant
hy|drat¦able
hy|drate
  hy¦drat|ing
hy¦dra|tion
hy¦dra|tor
hy|draul¦ic
hy¦draul|ic|al¦ly
hy¦draul|icity
hy¦draul|ics
hy¦dra|zine
hy|dria
  hy|driae or
  hy|driai
hy¦dric
hy|dride
hy¦dri|od¦ic
hydro +s
hydro|bro¦mic
hydro|car¦bon
hydro|cele
hydro|ceph¦al¦ic
hydro|ceph|alus
hydro|ceph¦aly
hydro|chlor¦ic
hydro|chlor¦ide
hydro|chloro|
  fluoro|car¦bon
hydro|col¦loid
hydro|cor¦ti¦sone
hydro|cul¦ture
hydro|cyan¦ic
hydro|dynam¦ic
hydro|dynami¦cist
hydro|dynam¦ics
hydro|elec¦tric
hydro|elec¦tri|city
hydro|fluor¦ic
hydro|fluoro|
  car¦bon
hydro|foil
hydro|frac¦tur¦ing
hydro|gel
hydro|gen
hy¦dro|gen|ase
hy¦dro|gen|ate
  hy¦dro|gen|at¦ing
hy¦dro|gen|ation
hy¦dro|gen|ous
hydro|geo|logic¦al
hydro|geolo¦gist
hydro|geol¦ogy

hy¦drog¦raph¦er
hydro¦graph¦ic
hydro¦graph¦ic¦
     al¦ly
hy¦drog¦raphy
hy¦droid
hydro¦lase
hydro¦logic
hydro¦logic¦al
hydro¦logic¦al¦ly
hy¦drolo¦gist
hy¦drol¦ogy
hy¦drol¦ys¦ate
hydro¦lyse *Br.*
  hydro¦lys¦ing
  US hydrolyze
hy¦droly¦sis
  hy¦droly¦ses
hydro¦lyt¦ic
hydro¦lyze *US*
  hydro¦lyz¦ing
  Br. hydrolyse
hydro¦mag¦net¦ic
hydro¦mag¦net¦ics
hydro¦mas¦sage
hydro¦
    mech¦an¦ic¦al
hydro¦mech¦an¦ics
hydro¦medusa
  hydro¦medu¦sae
hydro¦mel
hydro¦meteor
hy¦drom¦eter
hydro¦met¦ric
hy¦drom¦et¦ry
hy¦dron¦ic
hy¦dro¦nium
hydro¦path¦ic
hy¦drop¦ath¦ist
hy¦drop¦athy
hydro¦phil¦ic
hydro¦phil¦icity
hy¦droph¦il¦ous
hy¦droph¦ily
hydro¦pho¦bia
hydro¦pho¦bic
hydro¦pho¦bi¦city
hydro¦phone
hydro¦phyte
hydro¦phyt¦ic
hydro¦plane
  hydro¦plan¦ing
hydro¦pon¦ic

hydro¦pon¦ic¦al¦ly
hydro¦pon¦ics
hydro¦power
hydro¦quin¦one
hydro¦speed
hydro¦speed¦ing
hydro¦sphere
hydro¦stat¦ic
hydro¦stat¦ic¦al¦ly
hydro¦stat¦ics
hydro¦sul¦phite
hydro¦ther¦apist
hydro¦ther¦apy
hydro¦ther¦mal
hydro¦ther¦mal¦ly
hydro¦thorax
hydro¦trop¦ism
hy¦drous
hy¦drox¦ide
hy¦drox¦onium
hy¦droxy¦apa¦tite
hy¦droxyl
hy¦drox¦yl¦ate
  hy¦drox¦yl¦at¦ing
hy¦drox¦yl¦ation
Hydro¦zoa
hydro¦zoan
Hy¦drus
hyena
hy¦giene
hy¦gien¦ic
hy¦gien¦ic¦al¦ly
hy¦gien¦ist
hy¦grom¦eter
hygro¦met¦ric
hy¦grom¦etry
hy¦grophil¦ous
hygro¦phyte
hygro¦scope
hygro¦scop¦ic
hygro¦scop¦ic¦al¦ly
hying
Hyk¦sos
hyla tree frog; cf.
  hila
hylo¦morph¦ic
hylo¦morph¦ism
hylo¦zo¦ism
hymen
hy¦men¦al of hymen
hy¦men¦eal of
  marriage

hy¦men¦ial of
  hymenium
hy¦men¦ium
  hy¦menia
  surface of fungus
Hy¦men¦op¦tera
hy¦men¦op¦ter¦an
hy¦men¦op¦ter¦ous
Hymie
hymn song
hym¦nal
hym¦nary
  hym¦nar¦ies
hym¦nic
hym¦nist
hym¦nod¦ist
hym¦nody
hymn¦og¦raph¦er
hymn¦og¦raphy
hymno¦logic¦al
hymn¦olo¦gist
hymn¦ology
hyoid
hyos¦cine
hyos¦cya¦mine
hyp¦aes¦the¦sia *Br.*
  US hypesthesia
  abnormally low
  sensitivity; cf.
  hyperaesthesia
hyp¦aes¦thet¦ic *Br.*
  US hypesthetic
  with abnormally
  low sensitivity; cf.
  hyperaesthetic
hyp¦aeth¦ral
hyp¦al¦lage
hyp¦an¦thial
hyp¦an¦thium
  hyp¦an¦thia
Hyp¦atia
  philosopher and
  mathematician
hype
  hyp¦ing
hyper
hyper¦active
hyper¦active¦ly
hyper¦activ¦ity
hyper¦aemia *Br.*
  US hyperemia
hyper¦aem¦ic *Br.*
  US hyperemic

hyper¦aes¦the¦sia
  Br.
  US hyperesthesia
  abnormally high
  sensitivity; cf.
  hypaesthesia
hyper¦aes¦thet¦ic
  Br.
  US hyperesthetic
  with abnormally
  high sensitivity; cf.
  hypaesthetic
hyper¦alge¦sia
hyper¦alge¦sic
hyper¦ali¦men¦
    ta¦tion
hyper¦bar¦ic
hyper¦ba¦ton
hyper¦bola curve
  hyper¦bolas or
  hyper¦bolae
hyper¦bole exagger-
  ation
hyper¦bol¦ic
hyper¦bol¦ic¦al¦ly
hyper¦bol¦ism
hyper¦bol¦oid
hyper¦bol¦oid¦al
Hyper¦bor¦ean
  Greek Mythology
hyper¦bor¦ean per-
  son; of extreme
  north
hyper¦chol¦es¦
    ter¦ol¦aemia *Br.*
hyper¦chol¦es¦
    ter¦ol¦emia *US*
hyper¦cor¦rect
hyper¦cor¦rec¦tion
hyper¦crit¦ic¦al
  over-critical; cf.
  hypocritical
hyper¦crit¦ic¦al¦ly
  over-critically; cf.
  hypocritically
hyper¦cube
hyper¦drive
hyper¦emia *US*
  Br. hyperaemia
hyper¦em¦ic *US*
  Br. hyperaemic
hyper¦es¦the¦sia *US*
  Br. hyperaesthesia.
  abnormally high
  sensitivity; cf.

hypesthesia
hyper|es|thet|ic US
Br. hyperaesthetic
with abnormally
high sensitivity; cf.
hypesthetic
hyper|extend
hyper|exten|sion
hyper|gamy
hyper|gly|caemia
Br.
excess of glucose;
cf. hypoglycaemia
hyper|gly|caem|ic
Br.
of hyperglycaemia;
cf. hypoglycaemic
hyper|gly|cemia US
excess of glucose;
cf. hypoglycemia
hyper|gly|cem|ic
US
of hyperglycemia;
cf. hypoglycemic
hy|per|gol|ic
hy|peri|cin
hy|peri|cum
hyper|immune
hyper|immun|ized
hyper|in|fla|tion
hyper|instru|ment
Hy|perion
hyper|kera|tosis
hyper|kin|esia
hyper|kin|esis
hyper|kin|et|ic
hyper|link
hyper|lip|aemia Br.
hyper|lip|aem|ic
Br.
hyper|lip|emia US
hyper|lip|em|ic US
hyper|lip|id|aemia
Br.
hyper|lip|id|aem|ic
Br.
hyper|lip|id|emia
US
hyper|lip|id|em|ic
US
hyper|mar|ket
hyper|media
hyper|me|tro|pia
hyper|me|trop|ic

hyper|mnesia
hyper|mut|able
hyper|muta|tion
hyper|nym more
general term; cf.
hyponym
hyp|eron
hyper|opia
hyper|op|ic
hyper|para|site
hyper|para|sit|ic
hyper|para|sit|ism
hyper|
          para|thyr|oid
hyper|
          para|thyr|oid|ism
hyper|pig|men|
          ta|tion
excessive pigmenta-
tion of the skin; cf.
hypopigmentation
hyper|pla|sia
hyper|real
hyper|real|ism
hyper|real|ist
hyper|real|is|tic
hyper|real|ity
hyper|real|ities
hyper|sen|si|tive
hyper|sen|si|tive|
          ness
hyper|sen|si|tiv|ity
hyper|son|ic
hyper|son|ic|al|ly
hyper|space
hyper|spa|tial
hyper|sthene
hyper|ten|sion
abnormally high
blood pressure; cf.
hypotension
hyper|ten|sive with
hypertension; cf.
hypotensive
hyper|text
hyper|ther|mia
abnormally high
temperature; cf.
hypothermia
hyper|ther|mic
with hyperthermia;
cf. hypothermic
hyper|thy|roid
relating to
hyperthyroidism; cf.

hypothyroid
hyper|thy|roid|ic
with
hyperthyroidism; cf.
hypothyroidic
hyper|thy|roid|ism
excessive thyroid
activity; cf.
hypothyroidism
hyper|tonia
hyper|ton|ic
hyper|ton|icity
hyper|troph|ic
hyper|tro|phied
hyper|trophy
hyper|tro|phies
hyper|ven|ti|late
hyper|ven|ti|lat|ing
breathe abnormally
rapidly; cf.
hypoventilate
hyper|ven|ti|la|tion
abnormally rapid
breathing; cf.
hypoventilation
hyp|es|the|sia US
Br. hypaesthesia.
abnormally low
sensitivity; cf.
hyperesthesia
hyp|es|thetic US
Br. hypaesthetic
with abnormally
low sensitivity; cf.
hyperesthesic
hyp|eth|ral var. of
hypaethral
hypha
hy|phae
hy|phal
Hy|pha|sis
hy|phen
hy|phen|ate
hy|phen|at|ing
hy|phen|ation
hypna|gogic
hypno|gogic var. of
hypnagogic
hypno|pae|dia Br.
hypno|pe|dia US
hypno|pom|pic
Hyp|nos Greek god
hyp|no|sis
hyp|no|ses
hypno|ther|ap|ist

hypno|ther|apy
hyp|not|ic
hyp|not|ic|al|ly
hyp|no|tis|able Br.
var. of
hypnotizable
hypno|tise Br. var.
of hypnotize
hypno|tism
hypno|tist
hypno|tiz|able
hypno|tize
hypno|tiz|ing
hypo +s
hypo|aller|gen|ic
hypo|blast
hypo|cal|cae|mia
Br.
hypo|cal|ce|mia US
hypo|caust
hypo|centre
hypo|chlor|ite
hypo|chlor|ous
hypo|chon|dria
hypo|chon|driac
hypo|chon|driac|al
hypo|chon|dria|sis
hypo|cor|ism
hypo|cor|is|tic
hypo|cotyl
hyp|oc|risy
hyp|ocri|sies
hypo|crite
hypo|crit|ical
showing hypocrisy;
cf. hypercritical
hypo|crit|ic|al|ly
with hypocrisy; cf.
hypercritically
hypo|cyc|loid
hypo|cyc|loid|al
hypo|der|mic
hypo|der|mic|al|ly
hypo|gas|tric
hypo|gas|trium
hypo|gas|tria
hypo|geal
hypo|gean
hypo|gene
hypo|gen|ic
hypo|geum
hypo|gea
hypo|glos|sal

hypo|gly|caemia *Br.*
glucose deficiency;
cf. **hyperglycaemia**
hypo|gly|caem|ic
Br.
having
hypoglycaemia; cf.
hyperglycaemic
hypo|gly|cemia *US*
glucose deficiency;
cf. **hyperglycemia**
hypo|gly|cem|ic *US*
having
hypoglycemia; cf.
hyperglycemic
hypo|gonad|al
hypo|gonad|ic
hypo|gonad|ism
hyp|ogyn|ous
hyp|ogyny
hyp|ogynies
hy|poid
hypo|kal|aemia *Br.*
hypo|kal|aem|ic *Br.*
hypo|kal|emia *US*
hypo|kal|em|ic *US*
hypo|lim|nion
hypo|lim|nia
hypo|mag|nes|
aemia *Br.*
hypo|mag|nes|
aem|ic *Br.*
hypo|mag|nes|emia
US
hypo|mag|nes|
em|ic *US*
hypo|mania
hypo|man|ic
hypo|nym more
specific term; cf.
hypernym
hyp|onymy
hyp|onym|ies
hypo|para|thyr|oid
hypo|para|thyr|oid|
ism
hypo|phys|eal
hypo|phys|ial var.
of hypophyseal
hyp|ophy|sis
hyp|ophy|ses
hypo|pig|men|
ta|tion
inadequate pigmen-
tation of the skin;

cf. hyperpigmenta-
tion
hypo|pitu|it|ar|ism
hypo|pitu|it|ary
hypo|spa|dias
hypo|spray
trademark in the
US
hy|pos|tasis
hy|pos|tases
hy|pos|ta|sise *Br.*
var. of hypostasize
hy|pos|ta|size
hy|pos|ta|siz|ing
US hypostatize
hypo|stat|ic
hy|pos|ta|tlse *Br.*
var. of hypostasize
hy|pos|ta|tize *US*
hy|pos|ta|tiz|ing
Br. hypostasize
hypo|style
hypo|sul|phite *Br.*
& *US*
hypo|tac|tic
hypo|taxis
hypo|ten|sion
abnormally low
blood pressure; cf.
hypertension
hypo|ten|sive with
abnormally low
blood pressure; cf.
hypertensive
hypot|en|use
hypo|thal|am|ic
hypo|thal|amus
hypo|thal|ami
hypo|thec
hy|pothe|cary
hy|pothe|cate
hy|pothe|cat|ing
hy|pothe|ca|tion
hypo|ther|mia
abnormally low
temperature; cf.
hyperthermia
hypo|ther|mic with
hypothermia; cf.
hyperthermic
hy|poth|esis
hy|poth|eses
hy|pothe|sise *Br.*
var. of hypothesize

hy|pothe|siser *Br.*
var. of
hypothesizer
hypo|thesizer
hy|pothe|sist
hy|pothe|size
hy|pothe|siz|ing
hy|pothe|sizer
hypo|thet|ic|al
hypo|thet|ic|al|ly
hypothetico-
deduct|ive
hypo|thy|roid relat-
ing to
hypothyroidism; cf.
hyperthyroid
hypo|thy|roid|ic
with
hypothyroidism; cf.
hyperthyroidic
hypo|thy|roid|ism
subnormal thyroid
activity; cf.
hyperthyroidism
hypo|tonia
hypo|ton|ic
hypo|ton|icity
hypo|ven|ti|late
hypo|ven|ti|lat|ing
breathe abnormally
slowly; cf.
hyperventilate
hypo|ven|ti|la|tion
abnormally slow
breathing; cf.
hyperventilation
hypo|vol|aemia *Br.*
hypo|vol|aem|ic *Br.*
hypo|vol|emia *US*
hypo|vol|em|ic *US*
hyp|ox|aemia *Br.*
hypo|xan|thine
hyp|ox|emia *US*
hyp|oxia
hyp|ox|ic
hypsi|lopho|don
hypsi|lopho|dont
hypsi|
lopho|dont|id
hypso|graph|ic
hypso|graph|ic|al
hyp|sog|raphy
hyp|som|eter
hypso|met|ric
hyra|coid

Hyra|coidea
hyr|aco|ther|ium
hyrax
hyr|axes or
hyr|aces
hyson
hys|sop
hys|ter|ec|tom|ise
Br. var. of
hysterectomize
hys|ter|ec|tom|ize
hys|ter|
ec|tom|iz|ing
hys|ter|ec|tomy
hys|ter|ec|to|mies
hys|ter|esis
hys|teria
hys|ter|ic
hys|ter|ic|al
hys|ter|ic|al|ly
hys|teron
pro|teron
hys|trico|morph
Hys|trico|morpha
Hy|trel *trademark*

I

iamb
iam|bic
iam|bus
iam|buses or iambi
Iap|etus
Iaşi
IATA = Inter-
national Air Trans-
port Association
iatro|chem|ical
iatro|chem|ist
iatro|chem|is|try
iatro|gen|esis
iatro|gen|eses
iat|ro|gen|ic
Iba|dan in Nigeria;
cf. **Abadan**
Iban
pl. Iban
Ibár|ruri Gómez,
Dol|ores 'La Pas-
ionaria', politician

I-beam
Iberia
Iber|ian
iberis
  pl. iberis
Ibero- Iberian and...
ibex
Ibi|bio
  pl. Ibi|bio or
  Ibibios
ibid.
ibis
ibis|bill
Ibiza
Ibi|zan
Ibn Ba|tuta
  explorer
Ibo var. of Igbo
iboga|ine
Ibsen, Hen|rik
  dramatist
ibu|pro|fen
Icar|ian
Ica|rus *Greek*
  Mythology
ice
  icing
ice|berg
ice|blink
ice|block lolly
ice|boat
ice|box
ice|break|er
ice cream
ice|fall
ice|fish *n.*
ice-fish *v.*
Ice|land
Ice|land|er
Ice|land|ic
ice|man
  ice|men
Iceni
ice skate *n.*
ice-skate *v.*
  ice-skating
ice skater
ice skat|ing *n.*
I Ching
ich|neu|mon
ich|nog|raphy
  ich|nog|raph|ies
ichor

ich|or|ous
ich|thus
ich|thyic
ich|thy|oid
ich|thyo|lite
ich|thyo|logic|al
ich|thy|olo|gist
ich|thy|ol|ogy
ich|thy|opha|gous
ich|thy|oph|agy
ich|thy|or|nis
ich|thyo|saur
ich|thyo|saurus
  ich|thyo|sauri or
  ich|thyo|saur|uses
ich|thy|osis
ich|thy|ot|ic
I-chun var. of
  Yichun
icicle
icily
ici|ness
icing
ick sticky substance
icki|ness
Ick|nield Way
icky
  ick|ier
  icki|est
icon
icon|ic
icon|ic|al|ly
icon|icity
icon|ify
  iconi|fies
  iconi|fied
  iconi|fy|ing
icon|ise *Br.* var. of
  iconize
icon|ize
  icon|iz|ing
icono|clasm
icono|clast
icono|clas|tic
icono|clas|tic|al|ly
icono|dule
icono|dul|ist
icon|og|raph|er
icono|graph|ic
icono|graph|ic|al
icono|graph|ic|al|ly
icon|og|raphy
  icon|og|raph|ies

icon|ol|atry
icono|logic|al
icon|ology
  icon|olo|gies
icon|osta|sis
  icon|osta|ses
icosa|he|dral
icosa|he|dron
  icosa|he|dra or
  icosa|he|drons
ictal
ic|ter|ic
ic|ter|ine
ic|terus
Ic|ti|nus architect
ictus
  pl. ictus or ic|tuses
icy
  icier
  ici|est
Id var. of Eid
I'd = I had; I
  should, I would.
id *Psychology*
Ida name; asteroid;
  Mount
Idaho
Idaho|an
id|dings|ite
ide
idea
ideal
ideal|isa|tion *Br.*
  var. of idealization
ideal|ise *Br.* var. of
  idealize
ideal|iser *Br.* var. of
  idealizer
ideal|ism
ideal|ist
ideal|is|tic
ideal|is|tic|al|ly
ideal|ity
  ideal|ities
ideal|iza|tion
ideal|ize
  ideal|iz|ing
ideal|izer
ideal|ly
ide|ate
  ideat|ing
idea|tion
idea|tion|al
idea|tion|al|ly

idée fixe
  idées fixes
idée reçue
  idées reçues
idem
idem|po|tent
ident
iden|ti|cal
iden|ti|cal|ly
iden|ti|fi|able
iden|ti|fi|ably
iden|ti|fi|ca|tion
iden|ti|fier
iden|tify
  iden|ti|fies
  iden|ti|fied
  iden|ti|fy|ing
iden|ti|kit
  trademark
iden|tity
  iden|tities
ideo|gram
ideo|graph
ideo|graph|ic
ideog|raphy
ideo|logic|al
ideo|logic|al|ly
ideolo|gist
ideo|logue
ideol|ogy
  ideolo|gies
ides
idigbo +s tree
idi|ocy
  idi|ocies
idio|graph|ic
idio|lect
idiom
idiom|at|ic
idiom|at|ic|al|ly
idio|path|ic
idi|op|athy
  idi|op|athies
idio|phone
idio|syn|crasy
  idio|syn|cra|sies
idio|syn|crat|ic
idio|syn|crat|ic|
             al|ly
idiot
idi|ot|ic
idi|ot|ic|al|ly

idiot sav¦ant
  pl. idiot sav¦ants or
  idiots sav¦ants
idio|type
idle
  id¦ling
  lazy; be inactive; cf.
  idol
idle|ness
idler
idli food
  pl. idli or idlis
idly
Ido language
ido|crase
idol object of
  worship; cf. idle
idol|ater
idol|atrous
idol|atry
  idol|atries
idol|isa¦tion *Br* var
  of idolization
idol|ise *Br.* var. of
  idolize
idol|iser *Br.* var. of
  idolizer
idol|iza¦tion
idol|ize
  idol|iz¦ing
idol|izer
Idome|neus *Greek*
  Mythology
idyl var. of idyll
idyll
idyl¦lic
idyl¦lic|al¦ly
Ife city, Nigeria
iff = if and only if
iffy
  if¦fier
  if¦fi|est
Ifni
Iftar
Igbo
  pl. Igbo or Igbos
Igle|sias, Julio
  singer
igloo +s
Ig¦na|tius Loy¦ola,
  St
ig¦ne|ous
ig¦nim|brite

ignis fat¦uus
  ignes fatui
ig¦nit|abil¦ity
ig¦nit|able
ig¦nite
  ig¦nit|ing
ig¦niter
ig¦ni|tion
ig¦ni|tron
ig¦no|bil¦ity
ig¦noble
  ig¦nobler
  ig¦nob¦lest
ig¦nobly
ig¦no|mini¦ous
ig¦no|mini¦ous¦ly
ig¦no|mini¦ous|
         ness
ig¦no|miny
  ig¦no|minies
ig¦nor|able
ig¦nor|amus
ig¦nor|ance
ig¦nor|ant
ig¦nor|ant¦ly
ig¦nor|atio elen¦chi
  ig¦nor|atio¦nes
  elen¦chi
ig¦nore
  ig¦nor|ing
ig¦norer
ig¦no|tum per
  ig¦no|tius
Iguaçu
iguana
igua|nid
iguano|don
iiwi
Ijaw var. of Ijo
Ijo
IJs¦sel
IJs¦sel|meer
ikat
ike|bana
Ikh¦na|ton var. of
  Akhenaten
ikki|ness var. of
  ickiness
ikky var. of icky
ikon var. of icon
ilang-ilang var. of
  ylang-ylang
ilea pl. of ileum

ileac of the ileum;
  cf. iliac
ileal
Île-de-France
ile|itis
ile|os¦tomy
  ile¦os¦tomies
Il¦esha
ileum
  ilea
  part of small
  intestine; cf. ilium
ileus
ilex
ilia pl. of ilium
iliac relating to the
  ilium; cf. ileac
ili¦acus
  ili¦aci
Iliad
Ilium ancient Greek
  city
ilium
  ilia
  pelvic bone; cf.
  ileum
I'll I shall; I will.
ill
il¦la|tion inference;
  cf. elation
il¦la|tive
Illa|warra
il¦legal
il¦legal|ity
  il¦legal|ities
il¦legal¦ly
il¦legi|bil¦ity
il¦legible
il¦legibly
il¦legit¦im|acy
  il¦legit¦im|acies
il¦legit¦im|ate
il¦legit¦im|ate¦ly
il¦lib|eral
il¦lib¦er¦al|ity
il¦li¦ber¦al¦ly
Il¦lich, Ivan educa-
  tionalist
il¦licit unlawful; cf.
  elicit
il¦licit¦ly
il¦licit|ness
il¦lim¦it|abil¦ity
il¦lim¦it|able

il¦lim¦it|ably
Illi|noi¦an *Geology*
Illi|nois
Illi|nois¦an of
  Illinois
il¦liquid
il¦liquid|ity
il¦lite
il¦lit¦er|acy
  il¦lit¦er|acies
il¦lit¦er|ate
ill|ness
il¦lo|cu¦tion
il¦lo|cut¦ion|ary
il¦logic
il¦logic|al
il¦logic|al|ity
  il¦logic|al|ities
il¦logic|al¦ly
ill-treat
ill-treatment
il¦lude
  il¦lud|ing
  deceive; cf. allude,
  elude
il¦lume
  il¦lum|ing
il¦lu|min|ance
il¦lu|min|ant
il¦lu|min|ate
  il¦lu|min|at¦ing
il¦lu|min|ati
il¦lu|min|at¦ing¦ly
il¦lu|min|ation
il¦lu|mina|tive
il¦lu|min|ator
il¦lu|mine
  il¦lu|min|ing
il¦lu|min|ism
il¦lu|min|ist
ill use *n.*
ill-use *v.*
  ill-using
il¦lu|sion false
  perception; cf.
  allusion
il¦lu|sion|al
il¦lu|sion|ary
il¦lu|sion|ism
il¦lu|sion|ist
il¦lu|sion|is¦tic
il¦lu|sive deceptive;
  cf. allusive, elusive

il·lu·sor·ily
il·lu·sori·ness
il·lu·sory
il·lus·trate
il·lus·trat·ing
il·lus·tra·tion
il·lus·tra·tion·al
il·lus·tra·tive
il·lus·tra·tive·ly
il·lus·tra·tor
il·lus·tri·ous
il·lus·tri·ous·ly
il·lus·tri·ous·ness
il·lu·vial
il·lu·vi·ated
il·lu·vi·ation
Il·lyria
Il·lyr·ian
il·ly·whack·er
il·men·ite
Ilo·cano
Ilo·ilo
Ilorin
ilva·ite
I'm = I am
image
im·aging
image·able
image·less
imager
im·agery
im·ager·ies
image·set·ter
im·agin·able
im·agin·ably
im·agi·nal
im·agin·ar·ily
im·agin·ary
im·agin·ation
im·agina·tive
im·agina·tive·ly
im·agina·tive·ness
im·agine
im·agin·ing
im·agin·eer
im·agin·er
im·agines pl. of
  imago
im·agism
im·agist
im·agis·tic
imago
  im·agos or

im·agi·nes
imam
imam·ate
Imam Bay·ildi
Imari
IMAX *trademark*
im·bal·ance
im·be·cile
im·be·cil·ic
im·be·cil·ity
  im·be·cil·ities
im·bed var. of
  embed
im·bed·ded·ness
  var. of
  embeddedness
im·bibe
  im·bib·ing
im·biber
im·bi·bi·tion
im·bizo +s
Im·bolc
im·bongi
  izim·bongi or
  iim·bongi or
  im·bongis
im·bri·cate
  im·bri·cat·ing
im·bri·ca·tion
im·bro·glio +s
Im·bros
im·brue
  im·bru·ing
imbue
  im·bu·ing
Im·ho·tep architect
  and scholar
imid·azole
imide
imine
im·ipra·mine
im·it·able
imi·tate
  imi·tat·ing
imi·ta·tion
imi·ta·tive
imi·ta·tive·ly
imi·ta·tive·ness
imi·ta·tor
imli
im·macu·lacy
im·macu·late
im·macu·late·ly

im·macu·late·ness
im·ma·nence
  inherency; cf.
  imminence
im·ma·nent inher-
  ent; cf. imminent
im·ma·nent·ism
im·ma·nent·ist
Im·man·uel var. of
  Emmanuel
im·ma·ter·ial
im·ma·teri·al·ism
im·ma·teri·al·ist
im·ma·teri·al·ity
im·ma·teri·al·ly
im·ma·ture
im·ma·ture·ly
im·ma·tur·ity
im·meas·ur·abil·ity
im·meas·ur·able
im·meas·ur·ably
im·me·di·acy
  im·me·di·acies
im·me·di·ate
im·me·di·ate·ly
im·med·ic·able
Im·mel·mann
im·me·mor·ial
im·me·mori·al·ly
im·mense
im·mense·ly
im·mens·ity
  im·mens·ities
im·merse
im·mers·ing
  dip; cf. emerse
im·mer·sion dip-
  ping; cf. emersion
im·mer·sive
im·mi·grant
im·mi·grate
  im·mi·grat·ing
im·mi·gra·tion
im·mi·nence
  impending nature;
  cf. immanence
im·mi·nent
  impending; cf.
  immanent
im·mi·nent·ly
im·mis·ci·bil·ity
im·mis·cible
im·mis·cibly

im·mis·er·ate
im·mis·er·at·ing
im·mis·er·ation
im·mis·er·isa·tion
  Br. var. of
  immiserization
im·mis·er·ise *Br.*
  var. of immiserize
im·mis·er·iza·tion
im·mis·er·ize
im·mis·er·izing
im·mit·ig·able
im·mit·ig·ably
im·mit·tance
im·mix·ture
im·mo·bile
im·mo·bil·isa·tion
  Br. var. of
  immobilization
im·mo·bil·ise *Br.*
  var. of immobilize
im·mo·bil·iser *Br.*
  var. of immobilizer
im·mo·bil·ism
im·mo·bil·ity
  im·mo·bil·ities
im·mo·bil·iza·tion
im·mo·bil·ize
  im·mo·bil·iz·ing
im·mo·bil·izer
im·mod·er·ate
im·mod·er·ate·ly
im·mod·er·ate·ness
im·mod·er·ation
im·mod·est
im·mod·est·ly
im·mod·esty
  im·mod·est·ies
im·mol·ate
  im·mol·at·ing
im·mol·ation
im·mol·ator
im·moral
im·mor·al·ism
im·mor·al·ist
im·mor·al·ity
  im·mor·al·ities
im·mor·al·ly
im·mor·tal
im·mor·tal·isa·tion
  Br. var. of
  immortalization
im·mor·tal·ise *Br.*
  var. of immortalize

im¦mor¦tal¦ity
 im¦mor¦tal¦ities
im¦mor¦tal¦iza¦tion
im¦mor¦tal¦ize
 im¦mor¦tal¦iz¦ing
im¦mor¦tal¦ly
im¦mor¦telle flower
im¦mo¦tile
im¦mov¦abil¦ity
im¦mov¦able
im¦mov¦ably
im¦move¦abil¦ity
 var. of
 immoveability
im¦move¦able var.
 of immovable
im¦move¦ably var.
 of immovably
im¦mune
im¦mun¦isa¦tion Br.
 var. of
 immunization
im¦mun¦ise Br. var.
 of immunize
im¦mun¦iser Br. var.
 of immunizer
im¦mun¦ity
 im¦mun¦ities
im¦mun¦iza¦tion
im¦mun¦ize
 im¦mun¦iz¦ing
im¦mun¦izer
im¦muno¦assay
im¦muno¦blot¦ting
im¦muno¦
 chem¦is¦try
im¦muno¦
 com¦pe¦tence
im¦muno¦
 com¦pe¦tent
im¦muno¦
 com¦prom¦ised
im¦muno¦cyto¦
 chem¦ical
im¦muno¦cyto¦
 chem¦istry
im¦muno¦
 defi¦ciency
im¦muno¦defi¦cien¦
 cies
im¦muno¦
 dif¦fu¦sion
im¦muno¦
 electro¦phor¦esis

im¦muno¦
 fluor¦es¦cence
im¦muno¦
 fluor¦es¦cent
im¦muno¦gen¦ic
im¦muno¦gen¦icity
im¦muno¦globu¦lin
im¦muno¦logic
im¦muno¦logic¦al
im¦muno¦logic¦al¦ly
im¦mun¦olo¦gist
im¦mun¦ology
im¦muno¦sorb¦ent
im¦muno¦sup¦pres¦
 sant
im¦muno¦
 sup¦pressed
im¦muno¦
 sup¦pres¦sion
im¦muno¦
 sup¦pres¦sive
im¦muno¦ther¦apy
im¦muno¦
 ther¦apies
im¦mure
 im¦mur¦ing
im¦mure¦ment
im¦mut¦abil¦ity
 im¦mut¦abil¦ities
im¦mut¦able
im¦mut¦ably
i-Mode
Imo¦gen
im¦pact
im¦pac¦tion
im¦pact¦ive
im¦pact¦or
im¦pair
im¦pair¦ment
im¦pala
im¦pale
im¦pal¦ing
im¦pale¦ment
im¦paler
im¦palp¦abil¦ity
im¦palp¦able
im¦palp¦ably
im¦pan¦ate
im¦pan¦ation
im¦panel
 im¦pan¦elled Br.
 im¦pan¦eled US
 im¦panel¦ling Br.
 im¦panel¦ing US

im¦panel¦ment
im¦park
im¦part
im¦par¦ta¦tion
im¦par¦tial
im¦par¦ti¦al¦ity
im¦par¦tial¦ly
im¦pass¦abil¦ity of
 road etc.; cf.
 impassibility
im¦pass¦able impos-
 sible to travel over;
 cf. impassible
im¦pass¦ably in an
 impassable way; cf.
 impassibly
im¦passe
im¦passi¦bil¦ity
 impassivity; cf.
 impassability
im¦pass¦ible impas-
 sive; cf. impassable
im¦pass¦ibly impas-
 sively; cf.
 impassably
im¦pas¦sion
im¦pas¦sive
im¦pas¦sive¦ly
im¦pas¦sive¦ness
im¦pas¦siv¦ity
im¦pasto +s
im¦pa¦tience lack of
 patience
im¦pa¦tiens plant
im¦pa¦tient
im¦pa¦tient¦ly
im¦peach
im¦peach¦able
im¦peach¦ment
im¦pec¦cabil¦ity
im¦pec¦cable
im¦pec¦cably
im¦pe¦cu¦ni¦os¦ity
im¦pe¦cu¦ni¦ous
im¦pe¦cu¦ni¦ous¦
 ness
im¦ped¦ance
im¦pede
 im¦ped¦ing
im¦pedi¦ment
im¦pedi¦menta
im¦pedi¦men¦tal
impel
 im¦pelled

im¦pel¦ling
im¦pel¦ler
im¦pel¦lor var. of
 impeller
im¦pend
im¦pend¦ent
im¦pene¦tra¦bil¦ity
im¦pene¦trable
im¦pene¦trably
im¦peni¦tence
im¦peni¦tency
im¦peni¦tent
im¦peni¦tent¦ly
im¦pera¦tival
im¦pera¦tive
im¦pera¦tive¦ly
im¦pera¦tive¦ness
im¦per¦ator
im¦pera¦tor¦ial
im¦per¦cepti¦bil¦ity
im¦per¦cept¦ible
im¦per¦cept¦ibly
im¦per¦cep¦tive
im¦per¦cipi¦ence
im¦per¦cipi¦ent
im¦per¦fect
im¦per¦fec¦tion
im¦per¦fect¦ive
im¦per¦fect¦ly
im¦per¦for¦ate
im¦per¦ial
im¦peri¦al¦ise Br.
 var. of imperialize
im¦peri¦al¦ism
im¦peri¦al¦ist
im¦peri¦al¦is¦tic
im¦peri¦al¦is¦tic¦
 al¦ly
im¦peri¦al¦ize
 im¦peri¦al¦iz¦ing
im¦peri¦al¦ly
im¦peril
 im¦perilled Br.
 im¦periled US
 im¦peril¦ling Br.
 im¦peril¦ing US
im¦peri¦ous
im¦peri¦ous¦ly
im¦peri¦ous¦ness
im¦per¦ish¦abil¦ity
im¦per¦ish¦able
im¦per¦ish¦ably
im¦per¦ium

im|per|man|ence
im|per|man|ency
im|per|man|ent
im|per|man|ent|ly
im|per|me|abil|ity
im|per|me|able
im|per|mis|si|
          bil|ity
im|per|mis|sible
im|per|son|al
im|per|son|al|ity
im|per|son|al|ly
im|per|son|ate
 im|per|son|at|ing
im|per|son|ation
im|per|son|ator
im|per|tin|ence
im|per|tin|ent
im|per|tin|ent|ly
im|per|turb|abil|ity
im|per|turb|able
im|per|turb|ably
im|per|vi|ous
im|per|vi|ous|ly
im|per|vi|ous|ness
im|pe|ti|gin|ous
im|pe|tigo
im|pe|trate
 im|pe|trat|ing
im|petu|os|ity
im|petu|ous
im|petu|ous|ly
im|petus
Im|phal
impi
im|pi|ety
 im|pi|eties
im|pinge
 im|pin|ging
im|pinge|ment
im|pin|ger
im|pious
im|pious|ly
imp|ish
imp|ish|ly
imp|ish|ness
im|plac|abil|ity
im|plac|able
im|plac|ably
im|plant
im|plant|ation
im|plaus|ibil|ity

im|plaus|ible
im|plaus|ibly
im|plead
im|ple|ment
im|ple|men|ta|tion
im|ple|ment|er
im|pli|cate
 im|pli|cat|ing
im|pli|ca|tion
im|pli|ca|tion|al
im|pli|ca|tive
im|pli|ca|ture
im|pli|cit
im|pli|cit|ly
im|pli|cit|ness
im|plied|ly
im|plode
 im|plod|ing
im|plore
 im|plor|ing
im|plor|ing|ly
im|plo|sion
im|plo|sive
im|plu|vium
 im|plu|via
imply
 im|plies
 im|plied
 im|ply|ing
im|pol|der
im|pol|ite
im|pol|ite|ly
im|pol|ite|ness
im|pol|it|ic
im|pol|it|ic|ly
im|pon|der|abil|ity
 im|pon|der|
         abil|ities
im|pon|der|able
im|pon|der|ably
im|port
im|port|able
im|port|ance
im|port|ant
im|port|ant|ly
im|port|ation
im|port|er
im|por|tun|ate
im|por|tun|ate|ly
im|por|tune
 im|por|tun|ing
im|por|tun|ity
 im|por|tun|ities

im|pose
 im|pos|ing
 im|pos|ing|ly
im|pos|ing|ness
im|pos|ition
im|pos|si|bil|ism
im|pos|si|bil|ist
im|pos|si|bil|ity
 im|pos|si|bil|ities
im|pos|sible
im|pos|sibly
im|post
im|pos|ter var. of
 impostor
im|pos|tor
im|pos|ture
im|po|tence
im|po|tency
 im|po|tencies
im|po|tent
im|po|tent|ly
im|pound
im|pound|able
im|pound|er
im|pound|ment
im|pov|er|ish
im|pov|er|ish|ment
im|prac|tic|abil|ity
 im|prac|tic|
         abil|ities
im|prac|tic|able
im|prac|tic|ably
im|prac|tic|al
im|prac|ti|cal|ity
 im|prac|ti|cal|ities
im|prac|tic|al|ly
im|pre|cate
 im|pre|cat|ing
im|pre|ca|tion
im|pre|ca|tory
im|pre|cise
im|pre|cise|ly
im|pre|ci|sion
im|preg|na|bil|ity
im|preg|nable
im|preg|nably
im|preg|nate
 im|preg|nat|ing
im|preg|na|tion
im|pres|ario +s
im|pre|script|ible
im|press
im|press|ible

im|pres|sion
im|pres|sion|
         abil|ity
im|pres|sion|able
im|pres|sion|ably
im|pres|sion|al
Im|pres|sion|ism
Im|pres|sion|ist
 painter etc.
im|pres|sion|ist
 entertainer
im|pres|sion|is|tic
im|pres|sion|is|tic|
         al|ly
im|pres|sive
im|pres|sive|ly
im|pres|sive|ness
im|press|ment
im|prest
im|pri|ma|tur
im|print
im|prison
im|pris|on|ment
impro +s
im|prob|abil|ity
 im|prob|abil|ities
im|prob|able
im|prob|ably
im|prob|ity
 im|prob|ities
im|promptu
im|proper
im|prop|er|ly
im|pro|pri|ate
 im|pro|pri|at|ing
im|pro|pri|ation
im|pro|pri|ator
im|pro|pri|ety
 im|pro|pri|eties
im|prov
im|prov|abil|ity
im|prov|able
im|prove
 im|prov|ing
im|prove|ment
im|prover
im|provi|dence
im|provi|dent
im|provi|dent|ly
im|pro|visa|tion
im|pro|visa|tion|al
im|pro|visa|tor|ial
im|pro|visa|tory

im¦pro¦vise
  im¦pro¦vis¦ing
im¦pro¦viser
im¦pru¦dence
im¦pru¦dent
im¦pru¦dent¦ly
im¦pu¦dence
im¦pu¦dent
im¦pu¦dent¦ly
im¦pu¦di¦city
im¦pugn
im¦pugn¦able
im¦pugn¦ment
im¦pu¦is¦sance
im¦pu¦is¦sant
im¦pulse
im¦pul¦sion
im¦pul¦sive
im¦pul¦sive¦ly
im¦pul¦sive¦ness
im¦pul¦siv¦ity
im¦pun¦ity
im¦pure
im¦pure¦ly
im¦pure¦ness
im¦pur¦ity
  im¦pur¦ities
im¦put¦able
im¦put¦ation
im¦pu¦ta¦tive
im¦pute
  im¦put¦ing
imshi
in¦abil¦ity
  in¦abil¦ities
in ab¦sen¦tia
in¦access¦ibil¦ity
in¦access¦ible
in¦access¦ibly
in¦accur¦acy
  in¦ac¦cur¦acies
in¦accur¦ate
in¦accur¦ate¦ly
in¦action
in¦acti¦vate
  in¦acti¦vat¦ing
in¦acti¦va¦tion
in¦acti¦va¦tor
in¦active
in¦active¦ly
in¦activ¦ity
in¦ad¦equacy
  in¦ad¦equa¦cies

in¦ad¦equate
in¦ad¦equate¦ly
in¦ad¦mis¦si¦bil¦ity
in¦ad¦mis¦sible
in¦ad¦mis¦sibly
in¦ad¦ver¦tence
in¦ad¦ver¦tency
  in¦ad¦ver¦ten¦cies
in¦ad¦vert¦ent
in¦ad¦vert¦ent¦ly
in¦ad¦vis¦abil¦ity
in¦ad¦vis¦able
in¦ali¦en¦abil¦ity
in¦ali¦en¦able
in¦ali¦en¦ably
in¦alter¦abil¦ity
in¦alter¦able
in¦alter¦ably
in¦am¦or¦ata *female*
in¦am¦or¦ato +s
  male
inane
in¦ane¦ly
in¦anga
in¦ani¦mate
in¦ani¦mate¦ly
in¦ani¦ma¦tion
in¦an¦ition
in¦an¦ity
  in¦an¦ities
in¦appar¦ent
in¦appe¦tence
in¦appe¦tent
in¦applic¦abil¦ity
in¦applic¦able
in¦applic¦ably
in¦appo¦site
in¦appo¦site¦ly
in¦appo¦site¦ness
in¦appre¦ciable
in¦appre¦ciably
in¦appre¦ci¦ation
in¦appre¦cia¦tive
in¦appro¦pri¦ate
in¦appro¦pri¦ate¦ly
in¦appro¦pri¦ate¦
  ness
in¦apt
in¦apti¦tude
in¦apt¦ly
in¦arch
in¦argu¦able

in¦argu¦ably
in¦articu¦lacy
  in¦articu¦lacies
in¦articu¦late
in¦articu¦late¦ly
in¦articu¦late¦ness
in¦art¦is¦tic
in¦art¦is¦tic¦al¦ly
in¦as¦much
in¦atten¦tion
in¦atten¦tive
in¦atten¦tive¦ly
in¦atten¦tive¦ness
in¦audi¦bil¦ity
in¦aud¦ible
in¦aud¦ibly
in¦aug¦ural
in¦aug¦ur¦ate
  in¦aug¦ur¦at¦ing
in¦aug¦ur¦ation
in¦aug¦ur¦ator
in¦aug¦ur¦atory
in¦aus¦pi¦cious
in¦aus¦pi¦cious¦ly
in¦aus¦pi¦cious¦ness
in¦authen¦tic
in¦authen¦tic¦al¦ly
in¦authen¦ti¦city
in-between *adj. &*
  n.
in-between¦er
in¦board
in¦born
in¦bound
in-box
in¦breathe
  in¦breath¦ing
in¦breed
  in¦bred
in¦built
in-by var. of in-bye
in-bye
Inc. = Incorporated
Inca people
inca bird
Inca¦ic
in¦cal¦cul¦abil¦ity
in¦cal¦cul¦able
in¦cal¦cul¦ably
Incan
in¦can¦desce
  in¦can¦des¦cing
in¦can¦des¦cence

in¦can¦des¦cent
in¦can¦des¦cent¦ly
in¦cant
in¦can¦ta¦tion
in¦can¦ta¦tion¦al
in¦can¦ta¦tory
in¦cap¦abil¦ity
in¦cap¦able
in¦cap¦ably
in¦cap¦aci¦tant
in¦cap¦aci¦tate
  in¦cap¦aci¦tat¦ing
in¦cap¦aci¦ta¦tion
in¦cap¦acity
  in¦cap¦aci¦ties
in¦car¦cer¦ate
  in¦car¦cer¦at¦ing
in¦car¦cer¦ation
in¦car¦cer¦ator
in¦car¦na¦dine
  in¦car¦na¦din¦ing
in¦car¦nate
  in¦car¦nat¦ing
in¦car¦na¦tion
in¦case var. of
  encase
in¦cau¦tion
in¦cau¦tious
in¦cau¦tious¦ly
in¦cau¦tious¦ness
in¦cen¦di¦ar¦ism
in¦cen¦di¦ary
  in¦cen¦di¦ar¦ies
in¦cen¦sa¦tion
in¦cense
  in¦cens¦ing
in¦cens¦ory
  in¦cens¦or¦ies
in¦center *US*
  Br. incentre
in¦cen¦tive
in¦cen¦tiv¦ise *Br.*
  var. of **incentivize**
in¦cen¦tiv¦ize
  in¦cen¦tiv¦iz¦ing
in¦centre
  US incenter
in¦cept
in¦cep¦tion
in¦cep¦ti¦sol
in¦cep¦tive
in¦cept¦or
in¦cer¦ti¦tude

in|ces|sancy
in|ces|sant
in|ces|sant|ly
in|cest
in|ces|tu|ous
in|ces|tu|ous|ly
in|ces|tu|ous|ness
inch|meal
in|cho|ate
in|cho|ate|ly
in|cho|ate|ness
in|cho|ative
In|chon
inch|worm
in|ci|dence
in|ci|dent
in|ci|den|tal
in|ci|den|tal|ly
in|cin|er|ate
  in|cin|er|at|ing
in|cin|er|ation
in|cin|er|ator
in|cipi|ence
in|cipi|ency
  in|cipi|en|cies
in|cipi|ent
in|cipi|ent|ly
in|cipit
in|circle
in|cise
  in|cis|ing
in|ci|sion
in|ci|sion|al
in|ci|sive
in|ci|sive|ly
in|ci|sive|ness
in|ci|sor
in|ci|sura
  in|ci|surae
  var. of incisure
in|cisure
in|cit|ation
in|cite
  in|cit|ing
stir up; cf. **insight**
in|cite|ful offering
incitement; cf.
insightful
in|cite|ment
in|citer
in|civil|ity
  in|civil|ities

in|clem|ency
in|clem|en|cies
in|clem|ent
in|clem|ent|ly
in|clin|able
in|clin|ation
in|cline
  in|clin|ing
in|cliner
in|clin|om|eter
in|close var. of
  enclose
in|clos|ure var. of
  enclosure
in|clude
  in|clud|ing
in|clu|sion
in|clu|sion|ary
in|clu|sive
in|clu|sive|ly
in|clu|sive|ness
in|clu|siv|ism
in|clu|siv|ist
in|cog|ni|sance var.
  of incognizance
in|cog|ni|sant var.
  of incognizant
in|cog|nito +s
in|cog|ni|zance
in|cog|ni|zant
in|co|her|ence
in|co|her|ency
  in|co|her|en|cies
in|co|her|ent
in|co|her|ent|ly
in|co|he|sion
in|com|bust|ibil|ity
in|com|bust|ible
in|come
in|comer
in|com|ing
in|com|men|sur|
          abil|ity
in|com|men|sur|
          able
in|com|men|sur|
          ably
in|com|men|sur|ate
in|com|mode
  in|com|mod|ing
in|com|mo|di|ous
in|com|mu|nic|
          abil|ity

in|com|mu|nic|able
in|com|mu|ni|cado
in|com|mu|ni|
          ca|tive
in|com|par|abil|ity
in|com|par|able
in|com|par|ably
in|com|pati|bil|ity
in|com|pat|ible
in|com|pe|tence
in|com|pe|tency
  in|com|pe|tencies
in|com|pe|tent
in|com|pe|tent|ly
in|com|plete
in|com|plete|ly
in|com|plete|ness
in|com|ple|tion
in|com|pre|hen|
          si|bil|ity
in|com|pre|
          hen|sible
in|com|pre|
          hen|sibly
in|com|pre|
          hen|sion
in|com|press|
          ibil|ity
in|com|press|ible
in|con|ceiv|abil|ity
in|con|ceiv|able
in|con|ceiv|ably
in|con|clu|sive
in|con|clu|sive|ly
in|con|clu|sive|ness
In|co|nel trademark
in|con|gru|ence
in|con|gru|ent
in|con|gru|ent|ly
in|con|gru|ity
  in|con|gru|ities
in|con|gru|ous
in|con|gru|ous|ly
in|con|gru|ous|ness
in|connu
in|con|secu|tive
in|con|se|quence
in|con|se|quent
in|con|se|quen|tial
in|con|se|
    quen|ti|al|ity
in|con|se|
    quen|ti|al|ities

in|con|se|
    quen|tial|ly
in|con|se|quent|ly
in|con|sid|er|able
in|con|sid|er|ate
in|con|sid|er|ate|ly
in|con|sid|er|ate|
          ness
in|con|sid|er|ation
in|con|sist|ency
  in|con|sist|en|cies
in|con|sist|ent
in|con|sist|ent|ly
in|con|sol|abil|ity
in|con|sol|able
in|con|sol|ably
in|con|spicu|ous
in|con|spicu|ous|ly
in|con|spicu|ous|
          ness
in|con|stancy
in|con|stan|cies
in|con|stant
in|con|test|abil|ity
in|con|test|able
in|con|test|ably
in|con|tin|ence
in|con|tin|ent
in|con|tin|ent|ly
in|con|tro|vert|
          ibil|ity
in|con|tro|vert|ible
in|con|tro|vert|ibly
in|con|veni|ence
in|con|veni|en|cing
in|con|veni|ent
in|con|veni|ent|ly
in|con|vert|ible
in|co|ord|in|ation
in|corp|or|ate
  in|corp|or|at|ing
in|corp|or|ation
in|corp|or|ative
in|corp|or|ator
in|cor|por|eal
in|cor|por|eal|ity
in|cor|por|eal|ly
in|cor|por|eity
  in|cor|por|eities
in|cor|rect
in|cor|rect|ly
in|cor|rect|ness
in|cor|ri|gi|bil|ity

in|cor|ri|gible
in|cor|ri|gibly
in|cor|rupt|ibil|ity
in|cor|rupt|ible
in|creas|able
in|crease
  in|creas|ing
in|creas|ing|ly
in|cre|ate
in|credi|bil|ity
in|cred|ible
in|cred|ibly
in|credu|lity
in|credu|lous
in|credu|lous|ly
in|credu|lous|ness
in|cre|ment
in|cre|men|tal
in|cre|men|tal|ism
in|cre|men|tal|ist
in|cre|men|tal|ly
in|crim|in|ate
  in|crim|in|at|ing
in|crim|in|ation
in|crim|in|atory
in-crowd
in|crust var. of
  encrust
in|crust|ation
in|cu|bate
  in|cu|bat|ing
in|cu|ba|tion
in|cu|ba|tive
in|cu|ba|tor
in|cu|ba|tory
in|cub|ous *Botany*
in|cu|bus demon
  in|cu|buses or
  in|cubi
in|cu|des pl. of
  incus
in|cul|cate
  in|cul|cat|ing
in|cul|ca|tion
in|cul|ca|tor
in|cul|pate
  in|cul|pat|ing
in|cul|pa|tion
in|cul|pa|tory
in|cul|tur|ation
in|cum|bency
  in|cum|ben|cies
in|cum|bent

in|cun|able
in|cu|nabu|lum
  in|cu|nab|ula
incur
  in|curred
  in|cur|ring
in|cur|abil|ity
in|cur|able not
  curable; cf.
  incurrable
in|cur|ably
in|curi|os|ity
in|curi|ous
in|cur|rable liable
  to be incurred; cf.
  incurable
in|cur|rence
in|cur|rent
in|cur|sion
in|cur|sive
in|cur|vate
  in|cur|vat|ing
in|curv|ation
in|curve
  in|curv|ing
incus
  in|cu|des
in|cuse
  in|cus|ing
in|daba
In|de|bele pl. of
  Ndebele
in|debt|ed
in|debt|ed|ness
in|decency
  in|decen|cies
in|decent
in|decent|ly
in|de|cipher|able
in|de|cipher|ably
in|deci|sion
in|deci|sive
in|deci|sive|ly
in|deci|sive|ness
in|declin|able
in|decom|pos|able
in|dec|or|ous
in|dec|or|ous|ly
in|decorum
in|deed
in|deedy
in|defat|ig|abil|ity
in|defat|ig|able

in|defat|ig|ably
in|defeasi|bil|ity
in|defeas|ible
in|defeas|ibly
in|defect|ible
in|defens|ibil|ity
in|defens|ible
in|defens|ibly
in|defin|able
in|defin|ably
in|def|in|ite
in|def|in|ite|ly
in|def|in|ite|ness
in|dehis|cence
in|dehis|cent
in|deli|bil|ity
in|del|ible
in|del|ibly
in|deli|cacy
  in|deli|ca|cies
in|deli|cate
in|deli|cate|ly
in|dem|ni|fi|ca|tion
in|dem|ni|fier
in|dem|nify
  in|dem|ni|fies
  in|dem|ni|fied
  in|dem|ni|fy|ing
in|dem|nity
  in|dem|nities
in|dem|on|strable
in|dene
in|dent
in|den|ta|tion
in|dent|er device
in|den|tion
in|dent|or person
in|den|ture
  in|den|tur|ing
in|den|ture|ship
in|de|pend|ence
in|de|pend|ent
in|de|pend|ent|ly
in|des|crib|abil|ity
in|des|crib|able
in|des|crib|ably
in|des|truct|ibil|ity
in|des|truct|ible
in|des|truct|ibly
in|de|ter|min|able
in|de|ter|min|acy
  in|de|ter|min|acies
in|de|ter|min|ate

in|de|ter|min|ation
in|de|ter|min|ism
in|de|ter|min|ist
in|de|ter|min|is|tic
index
  pl. in|dexes or
  in|di|ces
in|dex|able
in|dex|ation
in|dex|er
index|ible var. of
  indexable
in|dex|ic|al
*Index Libr|orum
  Pro|hib|it|orum*
India
India|man
  India|men
In|dian
In|di|ana
In|di|an|an
In|dian|apo|lis
In|dian|isa|tion *Br.*
  var. of
  Indianization
In|dian|ise *Br.* var.
  of Indianize
In|dian|ism
In|dian|iza|tion
In|dian|ize
  In|dian|iz|ing
In|dian|ness
india|rubber var. of
  India rubber
Indic
in|di|can
in|di|cant
in|di|cate
  in|di|cat|ing
in|di|ca|tion
in|di|ca|tive
in|di|ca|tive|ly
in|di|ca|tor
in|di|ca|tory
in|di|ca|trix
  in|di|ca|tri|ces
in|di|ces pl. of
  index
in|di|cia
in|di|co|lite
in|dict accuse; cf.
  indite
in|dict|able
in|dict|ee

in|dict|er
in|dic|tion
in|dict|ment
indie independent
  pop group etc.; cf.
  Indy
In|dies
in|dif|fer|ence
in|dif|fer|ent
in|dif|fer|ent|ism
in|dif|fer|ent|ist
in|dif|fer|ent|ly
in|di|gence
in|di|gene
in|di|gen|isa|tion
  Br. var. of
  indigenization
in|di|gen|ise *Br.* var.
  of indigenize
in|di|gen|iza|tion
in|di|gen|ize
  in|di|gen|iz|ing
in|di|gen|ous
in|di|gen|ous|ly
in|di|gent
in|di|gest|ibil|ity
in|di|gest|ible
in|di|gest|ibly
in|di|ges|tion
in|di|gest|ive
In|di|girka
in|dig|nant
in|dig|nant|ly
in|dig|na|tion
in|dig|nity
  in|dig|nities
in|di|go
  in|di|gos or
  in|di|goes
indigo|bird
in|di|goid
in|di|go|tin
Indio +s
in|dir|ect
in|dir|ec|tion
in|dir|ect|ly
in|dir|ect|ness
in|dis|cern|ibil|ity
in|dis|cern|ible
in|dis|cern|ibly
in|dis|cip|line
in|dis|creet not dis-
  creet; injudicious;

cf. indiscrete
in|dis|creet|ly
in|dis|crete not
  divided into dis-
  tinct parts; cf.
  indiscreet
in|dis|cre|tion
in|dis|crim|in|ate
in|dis|crim|in|
      ate|ly
in|dis|crim|in|ate|
        ness
in|dis|crim|in|
       at|ing
in|dis|crim|in|ation
in|dis|pens|abil|ity
in|dis|pens|able
in|dis|pens|ably
in|dis|pose
  in|dis|pos|ing
in|dis|pos|ition
in|dis|put|abil|ity
in|dis|put|able
in|dis|put|ably
in|dis|soci|able
in|dis|solu|bil|ity
in|dis|sol|uble
in|dis|sol|ubly
in|dis|tinct
in|dis|tinct|ive
in|dis|tinct|ly
in|dis|tinct|ness
in|dis|tin|guish|
        able
in|dis|tin|guish|
        ably
in|dite
  in|dit|ing
  put into words; cf.
  indict
in|dium
in|di|vid|ual
in|di|vidu|al|
      isa|tion
  Br. var. of
  individualization
in|di|vidu|al|ise *Br.*
  var. of
  individualize
in|di|vidu|al|ism
in|di|vidu|al|ist
in|di|vidu|al|is|tic
in|di|vidu|al|ity
  in|di|vidu|al|ities

in|di|vidu|al|
      iza|tion
in|di|vidu|al|ize
  in|di|vidu|al|iz|ing
in|di|vidu|al|ly
in|di|vidu|ate
  in|di|vidu|at|ing
in|di|vidu|ation
in|di|vis|ibil|ity
in|di|vis|ible
in|di|vis|ibly
Indo- Indian and ...
Indo|china
Indo|chin|ese
indo|chin|ite
in|docile
in|docil|ity
in|doc|trin|ate
  in|doc|trin|at|ing
in|doc|trin|ation
in|doc|trin|ator
in|doc|trin|atory
in|dole
in|dole|acet|ic
in|do|lence
in|do|lent
in|do|lent|ly
Indo|logic|al
Ind|olo|gist
Ind|ology
indo|meth|acin
in|dom|it|abil|ity
in|dom|it|able
in|dom|it|ably
Indo|nesia
Indo|nes|ian
in|door
in|doors
In|dore
in|dorse *US & Law*
  var. of endorse
in|dorse|ment *US*
  & Law var. of
  endorsement
in|dor|ser *US &*
  Law var. of
  endorser
in|doxyl
Indra Hindu god
in|draft *US*
in|draught *Br.*
in|drawn
indri

in|dub|it|able
in|dub|it|ably
in|duce
  in|du|cing
in|duce|ment
in|ducer
in|du|cible
in|duct
in|duct|ance
in|duct|ee
in|duc|tion
in|duct|ive
in|duct|ive|ly
in|duct|iv|ism
in|duct|iv|ist
in|duct|or
indue var. of endue
in|dulge
  in|dul|ging
in|dul|gence
in|dul|gent
in|dul|gent|ly
in|dul|ger
in|du|line
in|dult
in|du|men|tum
  in|du|menta
in|duna
In|du|rain, Mi|guel
  cyclist
in|dur|ate
  in|dur|at|ing
in|dur|ation
in|dura|tive
Indus
in|du|sium
  in|du|sia
in|dus|trial
in|dus|tri|al|isa|
        tion
  Br. var. of
  industrialization
in|dus|tri|al|ise *Br.*
  var. of
  industrialize
in|dus|tri|al|ism
in|dus|tri|al|ist
in|dus|tri|al|iza|
        tion
in|dus|tri|al|ize
  in|dus|tri|al|iz|ing
in|dus|tri|al|ly
in|dus|tri|ous

in|dus|tri|ous|ly
in|dus|tri|ous|ness
in|dus|try
  in|dus|tries
in|dwell
  in|dwelt
in|dwell|er
Indy = Indianapolis;
  cf. indie
Indy|car
in|ebri|ate
  in|ebri|at|ing
in|ebri|ation
in|ebri|ety
in|edi|bil|ity
in|ed|ible
in|educ|abil|ity
in|educ|able
in|effa|bil|ity
in|effable
in|effably
in|ef|face|abil|ity
in|ef|face|able
in|ef|fcct|ive
in|ef|fect|ive|ly
in|ef|fect|ive|ness
in|ef|fec|tual
in|ef|fec|tu|al|ity
in|ef|fec|tu|al|ly
in|ef|fec|tu|al|ness
in|ef|fi|ca|cious
in|ef|fi|cacy
  in|ef|fi|ca|cies
in|ef|fi|ciency
  in|ef|fi|cien|cies
in|ef|fi|cient
in|ef|fi|cient|ly
in|egali|tar|ian
in|elas|tic
in|elas|tic|al|ly
in|elas|ti|city
in|ele|gance
in|ele|gant
in|ele|gant|ly
in|eli|gi|bil|ity
in|eli|gible
in|eli|gibly
in|eluct|abil|ity
in|eluct|able
in|eluct|ably
in|ept
in|epti|tude
in|ept|ly

in|ept|ness
in|equable
in|equal|ity
  in|equal|ities
in|equit|able
in|equit|ably
in|equity
  in|equi|ties
in|equi|valve
in|erad|ic|able
in|erad|ic|ably
in|err|ancy
  in|err|ancies
in|err|ant
in|err|ant|ist
inert
in|er|tia
in|er|tial
in|er|tia|less
in|ert|ly
in|ert|ness
in|escap|abil|ity
in|escap|able
in|escap|ably
in|es|cutch|eon
in esse
in|es|sen|tial
in|estim|able
in|estim|ably
in|ev|it|abil|ity
  in|ev|it|abil|ities
in|ev|it|able
in|ev|it|ably
in|exact
in|exacti|tude
in|exact|ly
in|exact|ness
in|ex|cus|able
in|ex|cus|ably
in|ex|haust|ibil|ity
in|ex|haust|ible
in|ex|haust|ibly
in|ex|or|abil|ity
in|ex|or|able
in|ex|or|ably
in|ex|pedi|ency
in|ex|pedi|ent
in|ex|pen|sive
in|ex|pen|sive|ly
in|ex|pen|sive|ness
in|ex|peri|ence
in|ex|peri|enced

in|ex|pert
in|ex|pert|ly
in|ex|pi|able
in|ex|pi|ably
in|ex|plic|abil|ity
in|ex|plic|able
in|ex|plic|ably
in|ex|pli|cit
in|ex|press|ible
in|ex|press|ibly
in|ex|pres|sive
in|ex|pugn|able
in|ex|ten|sible
in ex|tenso
in|ex|tin|guish|able
in ex|tre|mis
in|ex|tric|abil|ity
in|ex|tric|able
in|ex|tric|ably
in|fall
in|fal|li|bil|ity
in|fal|lible
in|fal|libly
in|fam|ous
in|fam|ous|ly
in|famy
  in|famies
in|fancy
  in|fan|cies
in|fant
in|fanta *female*
in|fante *male*
in|fanti|cidal
in|fanti|cide
in|fant|ile
in|fant|il|isa|tion
  Br. var. of
  infantilization
in|fant|il|ise *Br.* var.
  of infantilize
in|fant|il|ism
in|fant|il|ity
in|fant|il|ization
in|fant|il|ize
  in|fant|il|iz|ing
in|fant|ine
in|fan|try
  in|fan|tries
in|fan|try|man
  in|fan|try|men
in|farct
in|farc|tion

in|fatu|ate
  in|fatu|at|ing
in|fatu|ation
in|fauna
in|faun|al
in|feasi|bil|ity
in|feas|ible
in|fect
in|fec|tion
in|fec|tious
in|fec|tious|ly
in|fec|tious|ness
in|fect|ive
in|fect|iv|ity
in|fect|or
in|fec|und
in|fec|und|ity
in|feed
in|fe|li|ci|tous
in|fe|li|ci|tous|ly
in|feli|city
  in|feli|ci|ties
infer
  in|ferred
in|fer|ring
in|fer|able
in|fer|ence
in|fer|en|tial
in|fer|en|tial|ly
in|fer|ior
in|fer|ior|ity
  in|fer|ior|ities
in|fer|ior|ly
in|fer|nal
in|fer|nal|ly
in|ferno +s
in|fer|rable var. of
  inferable
in|fer|tile
in|fer|til|ity
in|fest
in|fest|ation
in|fibu|late
  in|fibu|lat|ing
in|fibu|la|tion
in|fi|del
in|fi|del|ity
  in|fi|del|ities
in|field
in|field|er
in|fight|er
in|fight|ing
in|fill

in|fil|trate
  in|fil|trat|ing
in|fil|tra|tion
in|fil|tra|tor
in|fi|mum
in fine
in|fin|ite
in|fin|ite|ly
in|fin|ite|ness
in|fini|tesi|mal
in|fini|tesi|mal|ly
in|fini|tival
in|fini|tival|ly
in|fini|tive
in|fini|tude
in|fin|ity
  in|fin|ities
in|firm
in|firm|ar|er
in|firm|ary
  in|firm|ar|ies
in|firm|ity
  in|firm|ities
in|firm|ly
in|fix
in|fix|ation
in fla|grante
  de|licto
in|flame
  in|flam|ing
in|flam|ma|bil|ity
in|flam|mable
in|flam|ma|tion
in|flam|ma|tory
in|flat|able
in|flate
  in|flat|ing
in|fla|ter
in|fla|tion
in|fla|tion|ary
in|fla|tion|ism
in|fla|tion|ist
in|fla|tor var. of
  inflater
in|flect
in|flec|tion
in|flec|tion|al
in|flec|tion|less
in|flect|ive
in|flexed
in|flex|ibil|ity
  in|flex|ibil|ities
in|flex|ible

in|flex|ibly
in|flex|ion var. of
  inflection
in|flex|ion|al var. of
  inflectional
in|flex|ion|less var.
  of inflectionless
in|flict
in|flict|able
in|flict|er
in|flic|tion
in|flict|or var. of
  inflicter
in|flor|es|cence
in|flow
in|flu|ence
  in|flu|en|cing
in|flu|ence|able
in|flu|en|cer
in|flu|ent
in|flu|en|tial
in|flu|en|tial|ly
in|flu|enza
in|flu|en|zal
in|flux
info
info|bahn
in|fold fold in; cf.
  enfold
info|medi|ary
info|medi|aries
info|mer|cial
info|naut
in|form
in|for|mal
in|for|mal|ity
  in|for|mal|ities
in|for|mal|ly
in|form|ant
in|form|at|ics
in|for|ma|tion
in|for|ma|tion|al
in|for|ma|tion|al|ly
in|form|ative
in|form|ative|ly
in|form|ative|ness
in|forma|tory
in|form|er
info|tain|ment
info|tech
info|war
infra below
in|fra|class

in|fract
in|frac|tion
in|fract|or
in|fra|dian
infra dig
in|fra|lap|sar|ian
in|fran|gi|bil|ity
in|fran|gible
in|fran|gibly
infra|order
in|fra|red
in|fra|renal
in|fra|son|ic
in|fra|son|ic|al|ly
in|fra|sound
infra|specif|ic
in|fra|struc|tural
in|fra|struc|ture
in|fre|quency
  in|fre|quen|cies
in|fre|quent
in|fre|quent|ly
in|fringe
  in|frin|ging
in|fringe|ment
in|frin|ger
in|fruct|es|cence
in|fula
  in|fu|lae
in|fun|dibu|lar
in|fun|dibu|lum
  in|fun|dibula
in|furi|ate
  in|furi|at|ing
in|furi|at|ing|ly
in|fus|able able to
  be infused; cf.
  infusible
in|fuse
  in|fus|ing
in|fuser
in|fus|ibil|ity
in|fus|ible not fus-
  ible or meltable; cf.
  infusable
in|fu|sion
in|fus|oria
in|gather
in|gem|in|ate
  in|gem|in|at|ing
Ingen|housz, Jan
  scientist
in|geni|ous clever

in|geni|ous|ly
  cleverly
in|geni|ous|ness
  cleverness
in|génue
in|genu|ity
  cleverness
in|genu|ous
  innocent
in|genu|ous|ly
  innocently
in|genu|ous|ness
  innocence
in|gest
in|gesta
in|ges|tion
in|gest|ive
ingle
ingle|nook
in|glori|ous
in|glori|ous|ly
in|glori|ous|ness
in|going
ingot
in|graft var. of
  engraft
in|grain
in|grate
in|grati|ate
  in|grati|at|ing
in|grati|at|ing|ly
in|grati|ation
in|grati|tude
in|grav|es|cence
in|grav|es|cent
in|gre|di|ent
Ingres, Jean painter
in|gress
in|gres|sion
in|gres|sive
In|grid
in-group
in|grow|ing
in|grown
in|growth
in|guin|al
in|gur|gi|tate
  in|gur|gi|tat|ing
in|gur|gi|ta|tion
in|gush
in|habit
in|hab|it|abil|ity
in|hab|it|able

in|hab|it|ance
in|hab|it|ancy
in|hab|it|ant
in|hab|it|ation
in|hal|ant
in|hal|ation
in|hal|ator
in|hale
　in|hal|ing
in|haler
in|har|mon|ic
in|har|mon|icity
in|har|mo|ni|ous
in|haul
in|here
　in|her|ing
in|her|ence
in|her|ent
in|her|ent|ly
in|herit
in|her|it|abil|ity
in|her|it|able
in|her|it|ance
in|heri|tor
in|he|sion
in|hibin
in|hibit
in|hib|ition
in|hibi|tive
in|hibi|tor
in|hibi|tory
in|homo|gen|eity
in|homo|gen|eous
in|hos|pit|able
in|hos|pit|able|ness
in|hos|pit|ably
in|hos|pi|tal|ity
in|human
in|hu|mane
in|hu|mane|ly
in|human|ity
　in|human|ities
in|human|ly
in|hum|ation
in|hume
　in|hum|ing
in|imi|cal
in|imi|cal|ly
in|im|it|abil|ity
in|im|it|able
in|im|it|ably
inion

ini|qui|tous
ini|qui|tous|ly
ini|quity
　ini|qui|ties
ini|tial
　ini|tialled *Br.*
　ini|tialed *US*
　ini|tial|ling *Br.*
　ini|tial|ing *US*
ini|tial|isa|tion *Br.*
　var. of
　initialization
ini|tial|ise *Br.* var.
　of **initialize**
ini|tial|ism
ini|tial|iza|tion
ini|tial|ize
　ini|tial|iz|ing
ini|tial|ly
ini|ti|ate
　ini|ti|at|ing
ini|ti|ation
ini|tia|tive
ini|ti|ator
ini|ti|atory
in|ject
in|ject|able
in|jec|tion
in|ject|ive
in|ject|or
in|jera
in-joke
in|ju|di|cious
in|ju|di|cious|ly
in|ju|di|cious|ness
Injun *offensive*; in
　'honest Injun'
in|junct
in|junc|tion
in|junct|ive
in|jure
　in|jur|ing
in|jurer
in|juri|ous
in|juri|ous|ly
in|juri|ous|ness
in|jury
　in|jur|ies
in|just|ice
In|ka|tha
ink|berry
　ink|berries
inker
ink|horn

inki|ness
ink|jet
inkle
ink|ling
ink-pad
ink|stand
ink|well
inky
ink|ier
inki|est
in|laid
in|land
in|land|er
in-law
in|lay
　in|laid
in|lay|er
in|let
in|lier
in-line
in-liner
in loco par|en|tis
inly
in|ly|ing
In|mar|sat
in|mate
in med|ias res
in me|mor|iam
in|most
inn
in|nards
in|nate
in|nate|ly
in|nate|ness
inner
in|ner|ly
in|ner|most
in|ner|ness
in|nerv|ate
　in|nerv|at|ing
　supply with nerves;
　cf. **innovate**
in|nerv|ation sup-
　ply of nerves; cf.
　innovation
in|ning *Baseball*
in|nings
　pl. in|nings or
　in|ningses
　Cricket; period of
　office etc.
innit = isn't it
inn|keep|er

in|no|cence
in|no|cency
　in|no|cen|cies
in|no|cent
in|no|cent|ly
In|no|cents' Day
in|nocu|ous
in|nocu|ous|ly
in|nocu|ous|ness
in|nom|in|ate
in|nov|ate
　in|nov|at|ing
　bring in something
　new; cf. **innervate**
in|nov|ation new
　thing; cf.
　innervation
in|nov|ation|al
in|nova|tive
in|nova|tive|ly
in|nov|ator
in|nov|atory
Inns|bruck
in|nu|endo
　pl. in|nu|en|does or
　in|nu|en|dos
In|nuit var. of **Inuit**
in|nu|mer|abil|ity
in|nu|mer|able too
　many to count; cf.
　enumerable
in|nu|mer|ably
in|nu|mer|acy
in|nu|mer|ate not
　numerate; cf.
　enumerate
in|nu|tri|tious
in|ob|ser|vance
in|ocul|able
in|ocu|lant
in|ocu|late
　in|ocu|lat|ing
in|ocu|la|tion
in|ocu|la|tive
in|ocu|la|tor
in|ocu|lum
　in|oc|ula
in|odor|ous
in-off
in|offen|sive
in|offen|sive|ly
in|offen|sive|ness
in|op|er|abil|ity
in|op|er|able

in|op|er|ably
in|op|era|tive
in|op|por|tune
in|op|por|tune|ly
in|op|por|tune|ness
in|or|din|ate
in|or|din|ate|ly
in|or|gan|ic
in|or|gan|ic|al|ly
in|oscu|late
  in|oscu|lat|ing
in|oscu|la|tion
in|osine
in|osi|tol
ino|trop|ic
in|patient
in per|so|nam
in po|ten|tia
in|pour|ing
in pro|pria
per|sona
in|put
  in|put or in|put|ted
  in|put|ting
in|put|ter
in|quest
in|qui|et|ude
in|quil|ine
in|quire *US*
  in|quir|ing
  Br. enquire
in|quirer *US*
  Br. enquirer
in|quir|ing|ly *US*
  Br. enquiringly
in|quiry *US*
  in|quir|ies
  Br. enquiry
in|qui|si|tion
in|qui|si|tion|al
in|quisi|tive
in|quisi|tive|ly
in|quisi|tive|ness
in|quisi|tor
In|quisi|tor
  Gen|eral
In|quisi|tors
  Gen|eral
in|quisi|tor|ial
in|quisi|tori|al|ly
in|quor|ate
in re
in rem

inro
  pl. inro or inros
in|road
in|rush
in|salu|bri|ous
in|salu|brity
in|sane
in|sane|ly
in|sani|tary
in|san|ity
  in|san|ities
in|sati|abil|ity
in|sati|able
in|sati|ably
in|sati|ate
in|scape
in|scrib|able
in|scribe
  in|scrib|ing
in|scriber
in|scrip|tion
in|scrip|tion|al
in|scrip|tive
in|scrut|abil|ity
in|scrut|able
in|scrut|ably
in|seam
in|sect
in|sect|an
in|sect|arium
in|sect|ary
  in|sect|ar|ies
in|secti|cidal
in|secti|cide
in|sect|ile
In|sect|iv|ora
in|sect|ivore
in|sect|iv|or|ous
in|se|cure
in|se|cure|ly
in|se|cur|ity
  in|se|cur|ities
in|sel|berg
in|sem|in|ate
  in|sem|in|at|ing
in|sem|in|ation
in|sem|in|ator
in|sens|ate
in|sens|ibil|ity
in|sens|ible
in|sens|ibly
in|sensi|tive
in|sensi|tive|ly

in|sensi|tiv|ity
  in|sensi|tiv|ities
in|sen|tience
in|sen|tient
in|sep|ar|abil|ity
in|sep|ar|able
in|sep|ar|ably
in|sert
in|sert|able
in|sert|er
in|ser|tion
INSET = in-service
  education and
  training
in|set
  in|set or in|set|ted
  in|set|ting
in|set|ter
in|shal|lah
in|shore
in|side
in|sider
in|sidi|ous
in|sidi|ous|ly
in|sidi|ous|ness
in|sight
  understanding; cf.
  incite
in|sight|ful cf.
  inciteful
in|sight|ful|ly
in|sig|nia
in|sig|nifi|cance
in|sig|nifi|cancy
  in|sig|nifi|can|cies
in|sig|nifi|cant
in|sig|nifi|cant|ly
in|sin|cere
in|sin|cere|ly
in|sin|cer|ity
  in|sin|cer|ities
in|sinu|ate
  in|sinu|at|ing
in|sinu|at|ing|ly
in|sinu|ation
in|sinu|ative
in|sinu|ator
in|sinu|endo +s
in|sipid
in|sip|id|ity
  in|sip|id|ities
in|sip|id|ly
in|sip|id|ness

in|sist
in|sist|ence
in|sist|ency
in|sist|ent
in|sist|ent|ly
in situ
in|so|bri|ety
in|so|far
in|so|la|tion exposure to sun; cf.
  insulation
in|sole
in|so|lence
in|so|lent
in|so|lent|ly
in|solu|bil|ise *Br.*
  var. of insolubilize
in|solu|bil|ity
in|solu|bil|ize
  in|solu|bil|iz|ing
in|sol|uble
in|sol|ubly
in|solv|able
in|solv|ency
  in|solv|en|cies
in|solv|ent
in|som|nia
in|som|niac
in|so|much
in|sou|ci|ance
in|sou|ci|ant
in|sou|ci|ant|ly
in|source
  in|sour|cing
in|span
  in|spanned
  in|span|ning
in|spect
in|spec|tion
in|spect|or
in|spect|or|ate
in|spect|or
  gen|eral
in|spect|ors
  gen|eral
in|spect|or|ial
in|spect|or|ship
in|spir|ation
in|spir|ation|al
in|spir|ation|al|ly
in|spir|ation|ism
in|spir|ation|ist
in|spira|tory

in|spire
in|spir|ing
in|spired|ly
in|spirer
in|spir|ing|ly
in|spirit
in|spis|sate
in|spis|sat|ing
in|spis|sa|tion
in|spis|sa|tor
in|stabil|ity
in|stabil|ities
in|stal
in|stalled
in|stall|ing
Br. var. of install
in|stall
in|stall|la|tion
in|stall|er
in|stall|ment US
in|stal|ment Br.
in|stance
in|stan|cing
in|stancy
in|stant
in|stant|an|eity
in|stant|an|eous
in|stant|an|eous|ly
in|stant|an|eous|
ness
in|stan|ter
in|stan|ti|ate
in|stan|ti|at|ing
in|stan|ti|ation
in|stant|ly
In|stants lottery
tickets trademark
in|star
in|state
in|stat|ing
in statu
pu|pil|lari
in|staur|ation
in|staur|ator
in|stead
in|step
in|sti|gate
in|sti|gat|ing
in|sti|ga|tion
in|sti|ga|tor
in|stil Br.
in|stilled
in|still|ling
in|still US

in|stil|la|tion
in|still|ment US
in|stil|ment Br.
in|stinct
in|stinct|ive
in|stinct|ive|ly
in|stinct|ual
in|stinc|tu|al|ly
in|sti|tute
in|sti|tut|ing
in|sti|tu|tion
in|sti|tu|tion|al
in|sti|tu|tion|al|
isa|tion
Br. var. of institu-
tionalization
in|sti|tu|tion|al|ise
Br. var. of
institutionalize
in|sti|tu|tion|al|ism
in|sti|tu|tion|al|
iza|tion
in|sti|tu|tion|al|ize
in|sti|tu|tion|al|
iz|ing
in|sti|tu|tion|al|ly
INSTRAW = Inter-
national Research
and Training Insti-
tute for the
Advancement of
Women
in|struct
in|struc|tion
in|struc|tion|al
in|struct|ive
in|struct|ive|ly
in|struct|or
in|struct|or|ship
in|struc|tress
in|stru|ment
in|stru|men|tal
in|stru|men|tal|ism
in|stru|men|tal|ist
in|stru|men|tal|ity
in|stru|men|tal|
ities
in|stru|men|tal|ly
in|stru|men|ta|tion
in|sub|or|din|ate
in|sub|or|din|ate|ly
in|sub|or|din|ation
in|sub|stan|tial
in|sub|stan|ti|al|ity

in|sub|stan|tial|ly
in|suf|fer|able
in|suf|fer|ably
in|suf|fi|ciency
in|suf|fi|cien|cies
in|suf|fi|cient
in|suf|fi|cient|ly
in|suf|flate
in|suf|flat|ing
in|suf|fla|tion
in|suf|fla|tor
in|sula n.
in|su|lae
in|su|lant
in|su|lar adj.
in|su|lar|ity
in|su|lar|ly
in|su|late
in|su|lat|ing
in|su|la|tion separ-
ation; cf. insolation
in|su|la|tor
in|su|lin
in|su|litis
in|sult
in|sult|er
in|sult|ing|ly
in|su|per|abil|ity
in|su|per|able
in|su|per|ably
in|sup|port|able
in|sup|port|ably
in|sur|abil|ity
in|sur|able
in|sur|ance
in|sure
in|sur|ing
secure payment
against damage,
theft, etc.; cf.
ensure
in|surer
in|sur|gence
in|sur|gency
in|sur|gen|cies
in|sur|gent
in|sur|mount|able
in|sur|mount|ably
in|sur|rec|tion
in|sur|rec|tion|ary
in|sur|rec|tion|ist
in|sus|cep|ti|bil|ity
in|sus|cep|tible

in|swing
in|swing|er
in|tact
in|tact|ness
in|tagli|ated
in|taglio
pl.
in|taglios
v. in|taglioes
in|taglioed
in|taglio|ing
in|take
in|tan|gi|bil|ity
in|tan|gible
in|tan|gibly
in|tar|sia
in|te|ger
in|te|gra|bil|ity
in|te|grable
in|te|gral
in|te|gral|ity
in|te|gral|ly
in|te|grand
in|te|grant
in|te|grate
in|te|grat|ing
in|te|gra|tion
in|te|gra|tion|ist
in|te|gra|tive
in|te|gra|tor
in|teg|rin
in|teg|rity
in|tegu|ment
in|tegu|men|tal
in|tegu|ment|ary
in|tein
intel military
intelligence
in|tel|lect
in|tel|lec|tion
in|tel|lect|ive
in|tel|lec|tual
in|tel|lec|tual|ise
Br. var. of
intellectualize
in|tel|lec|tual|ism
in|tel|lec|tual|ist
in|tel|lec|tu|al|ity
in|tel|lec|tual|ize
in|tel|lec|tual|iz|ing
in|tel|lec|tual|ly
in|tel|li|gence
in|tel|li|gen|cer

in|tel|li|gent
in|tel|li|gen|tial
in|tel|li|gent|ly
in|tel|li|gent|sia
in|tel|li|gi|bil|ity
in|tel|li|gible
in|tel|li|gibly
In|tel|sat
in|tem|per|ance
in|tem|per|ate
in|tem|per|ate|ly
in|tem|per|ate|ness
in|tend
in|tend|ancy
  in|tend|an|cies
in|tend|ant
in|tend|er
in|tend|ment
in|tense
  in|tenser
  in|tens|est
in|tense|ly
in|tense|ness
in|tensi|fi|ca|tion
in|ten|si|fier
in|ten|sify
  in|ten|si|fies
  in|ten|si|fied
  in|ten|si|fy|ing
in|ten|sion *Logic*;
  determination; cf.
  intention
in|ten|sion|al *Logic*;
  cf. intentional
in|ten|sion|al|ity
  Logic; cf.
  intentionality
in|ten|sion|al|ly
  Logic; cf.
  intentionally
in|ten|sity
  in|ten|sities
in|ten|sive
in|ten|sive|ly
in|ten|sive|ness
in|tent
in|ten|tion purpose;
  cf. intension
in|ten|tion|al delib-
  erately; cf.
  intensional
in|ten|tion|al|ism
in|ten|tion|al|ity
  deliberateness; cf.

intensionality
in|ten|tion|al|ly
  deliberately; cf.
  intensionally
in|tent|ly
in|tent|ness
in|ter
  in|terred
  in|ter|ring
  bury
inter|act
inter|act|ant
inter|action
inter|action|al
inter|action|ism
inter|action|ist
inter|active
inter|active|ly
inter|activ|ity
inter-agency
inter alia
inter alios
inter-allied
inter|ar|ticu|lar
inter|atom|ic
inter|bank
inter|breed
  inter|bred
inter|cal|ary
inter|cal|ate
  inter|cal|at|ing
  inter|cal|ation
inter|cede
  inter|ced|ing
inter|ceder
inter|cel|lu|lar
inter|cen|sal
inter|cept
inter|cep|tion
inter|cep|tive
inter|cept|or
inter|ces|sion inter-
  ceding; cf.
  intersession
inter|ces|sion|al
inter|ces|sor
inter|ces|sory
inter|change
  inter|chan|ging
inter|change|
           abil|ity
inter|change|able
inter|change|ably

Inter|City
  trademark
inter|city
inter-class
inter|col|le|gi|ate
inter|co|lo|nial
inter|colum|nar
inter|
    colum|ni|ation
inter|com
inter|com|mu|ni|
           cate
  inter|com|mu|ni|
          cat|ing
  inter|com|mu|ni|
          ca|tion
  inter|com|mu|ni|
          ca|tive
inter|com|mu|nion
inter|com|mu|nity
inter|con|nect
inter|con|nect|ed|
           ness
inter|con|nec|tion
inter|con|tin|en|tal
inter|con|ver|sion
inter|con|vert
inter|con|vert|ible
inter|cool
inter|cool|er
inter|cor|rel|ate
  inter|cor|rel|at|ing
  inter|cor|rel|ation
inter|cos|tal
inter|cos|tal|ly
inter|course
inter|crop
  inter|cropped
  inter|crop|ping
inter|cross
inter|crural
inter|cur|rent
inter|cut
  inter|cut|ting
inter|denom|in|
          ation|al
inter|denom|in|
        ation|al|ly
inter|dental
inter|depart|
         men|tal
inter|depart|
       men|tal|ly
inter|depend

inter|depend|ence
inter|depend|ency
  inter|depend|en|
           cies
inter|depend|ent
inter|dict
inter|dic|tion
inter|dict|or
inter|dict|ory
inter|digit|al
inter|digi|tate
  inter|digi|tat|ing
inter|dis|cip|lin|ary
inter|est
inter|est|ed|ly
inter|est|ed|ness
inter|est|ing|ly
inter|face
inter|facing
inter|facial
inter|facing
inter|faith
inter|fere
inter|fer|ing
inter|fer|ence
inter|fer|en|tial
inter|ferer
inter|fer|ing|ly
inter|fero|gram
inter|fero|gramme
  var. of
  interferogram
inter|fer|om|eter
inter|fero|met|ric
inter|fero|met|ric|
          al|ly
inter|fer|om|etry
inter|feron
inter|file
  inter|fil|ing
inter|flow
inter|fluve
inter|flu|vial
inter|fuse
  inter|fus|ing
inter|fusion
inter|gal|act|ic
inter|gal|act|ic|al|ly
inter|gen|er|ic
inter|gla|cial
inter|gov|ern|
        men|tal

inter|gov|ern|
   men|tal|ly
inter|grad|ation
inter|grade
  inter|grad|ing
inter|grow
  inter|grew
  inter|grown
inter|growth
in|terim
in|ter|ior
in|ter|ior|ise *Br.*
  var. of interiorize
in|ter|ior|ity
in|ter|ior|ize
  in|ter|ior|iz|ing
in|ter|ior|ly
inter|ject
inter|jec|tion
inter|jec|tion|al
inter|ject|ory
inter|knit
  inter|knit|ted or
  inter|knit
  inter|knit|ting
inter|lace
  inter|lacing
inter|lace|ment
In|ter|laken
inter|lan|guage
inter|lap
  inter|lapped
  inter|lap|ping
inter|lard
inter|lay
  inter|laid
inter|layer
inter|leaf
  inter|leaves
inter|leave
  inter|leav|ing
inter|leu|kin
inter|lib|rary
inter|line
  inter|lin|ing
inter|lin|ear
inter|lin|eate
  inter|lin|eat|ing
inter|lin|ea|tion
inter|lin|gua
inter|lin|gual
inter|link
inter|link|age
inter|lobu|lar

inter|lock
inter|lock|er
inter|loc|tion
inter|locu|tor
inter|locu|tory
inter|locu|trix
inter|lope
  inter|lop|ing
inter|loper
inter|lude
inter|mar|riage
inter|marry
  inter|mar|ries
  inter|mar|ried
  inter|marry|ing
inter|medi|acy
  inter|medi|acies
inter|medi|ary
  inter|medi|ar|ies
inter|medi|ate
  inter|medi|at|ing
  inter|medi|ate|ly
  inter|medi|ate|ness
inter|medi|ation
inter|medi|ator
inter|medium
  inter|media
in|ter|ment
inter|mesh
inter|mezzo
  inter|mezzi or
  inter|mezzos
in|ter|min|able
in|ter|min|ably
inter|min|gle
  inter|min|gling
inter|mis|sion
inter|mit
  inter|mit|ted
  inter|mit|ting
inter|mit|tence
inter|mit|tency
  inter|mit|ten|cies
inter|mit|tent
inter|mit|tent|ly
inter|mix
inter|mix|able
inter|mix|ture
inter|modal
inter|mo|lecu|lar
in|tern cf. in-turn
in|tern|al
in|tern|al|isa|tion
  Br. var. of

internalization
in|tern|al|ise *Br.*
  var. of internalize
in|tern|al|ity
in|tern|al|iza|tion
in|tern|al|ize
  in|tern|al|iz|ing
in|tern|al|ly
inter|nation|al
Inter|nation|ale
  song
inter|nation|al|
    isa|tion
  Br. var. of inter-
  nationalization
inter|nation|al|ise
  Br. var. of
  internationalize
inter|nation|al|ism
inter|nation|al|ist
inter|nation|al|ity
inter|nation|al|
    iza|tion
inter|nation|al|ize
  inter|nation|al|
    iz|ing
inter|nation|al|ly
inter|naut
in|terne *n.* var. of
  intern
inter|necine
in|tern|ee
inter|nega|tive
Inter|net
inter|neuron
inter|neur|on|al
inter|neur|one var.
  of interneuron
in|tern|ist
in|tern|ment
inter|node
inter|ship
inter|nuclear
inter|nun|cial
inter|ocean|ic
in|tero|cep|tive
in|tero|cep|tor
inter|oper|abil|ity
inter|oper|able
inter|oper|ate
  inter|oper|at|ing
inter|osse|ous
in|ter|pel|late
  in|ter|pel|lat|ing

question minister;
  Philosophy; cf.
interpolate
interpellate
in|ter|pel|la|tion
  action of
  interpellating; cf.
  interpolation
in|ter|pel|la|tor
  person who
  interpellates; cf.
  interpolator
inter|pene|trate
  inter|pene|trat|ing
inter|pene|tra|tion
inter|pene|tra|tive
inter|per|son|al
inter|per|son|al|ly
inter|phase
inter|plan|et|ary
inter|plant
inter|play
inter|plead|er
Inter|pol
in|ter|pol|ate
  in|ter|pol|at|ing
  insert; interject; cf.
  interpellate
in|ter|pol|ation
  insertion;
  interjection; cf.
  interpellation
in|ter|pola|tive
in|ter|pol|ator
  person who
  interpolates; cf.
  interpellator
inter|pole
inter|pose
  inter|pos|ing
inter|pos|ition
in|ter|pret
in|ter|pret|abil|ity
in|ter|pret|able
in|ter|pret|ation
in|ter|pret|ation|al
in|ter|pret|ative
in|ter|pret|ative|ly
in|ter|pret|er
in|ter|pret|ive
in|ter|pret|ive|ly
inter|pro|vin|cial
inter|quar|tile
inter|racial
inter|racial|ly

inter|reg|num
  inter|reg|nums or
  inter|regna
inter|relate
  inter|relat|ing
inter|related|ness
inter|rela|tion
inter|rela|tion|ship
in|ter|ro|gate
  in|ter|ro|gat|ing
in|ter|ro|ga|tion
in|ter|ro|ga|tion|al
inter|roga|tive
inter|roga|tive|ly
in|ter|ro|ga|tor
inter|roga|tory
  inter|roga|tor|ies
inter|rupt
inter|rupt|er
inter|rupt|ible
inter|rup|tion
inter|rup|tive
inter|rupt|or var. of
  interrupter
inter se
inter|sect
inter|sec|tion
inter|sec|tion|al
inter|seg|men|tal
inter|
    seg|men|tal|ly
inter|sep|tal
inter|ses|sion
  period; cf.
  intercession
inter|sex
inter|sex|ual
inter|sexu|al|ity
inter|space
  inter|spacing
inter|spe|cif|ic
inter|spe|cif|ic|al|ly
inter|sperse
  inter|spers|ing
inter|sper|sion
inter|spinal
inter|spin|ous
inter|sta|dial
inter|state
inter|stel|lar
in|ter|stice
inter|sti|tial
inter|sti|tial|ly

inter|sub|ject|ive
inter|sub|ject|ive|ly
inter|sub|ject|iv|ity
inter|text|ual
inter|text|ual|ity
  inter|text|ual|ities
inter|text|ual|ly
inter|tidal
inter|track
inter|tribal
inter|trigo
inter|twine
  inter|twin|ing
inter|twine|ment
inter|twist
inter|val
inter|val|lic
inter|val|om|eter
inter|vene
  inter|ven|ing
inter|vener var. of
  intervenor
inter|ve|ni|ent
inter|venor
inter|ven|tion
inter|ven|tion|al
inter|ven|tion|ism
inter|ven|tion|ist
inter|ver|te|bral
inter|view
inter|view|ee
inter|view|er
inter vivos
inter|vocal|ic
inter|vocal|ic|al|ly
inter|war
inter|weave
  inter|weav|ing
  inter|woven
inter|wind
inter|wound
inter|work
in|tes|tacy
  in|tes|ta|cies
in|tes|tate
in|tes|tinal
in|tes|tin|al|ly
in|tes|tine
in|thrall var. of
  enthrall
in|ti|chi|uma
in|ti|fada

in|tima
  in|timae
in|tim|acy
  in|tim|acies
in|timal
in|tim|ate
  in|tim|at|ing
in|tim|ate|ly
in|tim|ation
in|timi|date
  in|timi|dat|ing
in|timi|dat|ing|ly
in|timi|da|tion
in|timi|da|tor
in|timi|da|tory
in|tim|ism
in|tim|ist
in|tinc|tion
in|tit|ule
  in|tit|ul|ing
into
in|toler|able
in|toler|ably
in|toler|ance
in|toler|ant
in|toler|ant|ly
in|ton|ate
  in|ton|at|ing
in|ton|ation
in|ton|ation|al
in|tone
  in|ton|ing
in|toner
in toto
in|toxi|cant
in|toxi|cate
  in|toxi|cat|ing
in|toxi|cat|ing|ly
in|toxi|ca|tion
in|toxi|meter
intra|cel|lu|lar
intra|cel|lu|lar|ly
in|tract|abil|ity
in|tract|able
in|tract|ably
intra|day
intra|der|mal
intra|der|mal|ly
in|tra|dos
intra|mo|lecu|lar
intra|mo|lecu|lar|ly

intra|mural
intra|mur|al|ly
intra|mus|cu|lar
intra|mus|cu|lar|ly
intra|nation|al
intra|net
in|transi|gence
in|transi|gency
  in|transi|gen|cies
in|transi|gent
in|transi|gent|ly
in|transi|tive
in|transi|tive|ly
in|transi|tiv|ity
intra|per|son|al
intra|pre|neur
intra|spe|cif|ic
intra|thecal
intra|thecal|ly
intra|uter|ine
intra|vas|cu|lar
intra|vas|cu|lar|ly
intra|ven|ous
intra|ven|ous|ly
in tray
intra|zonal
in|trepid
in|trep|id|ity
in|trep|id|ly
in|tri|cacy
  in|tri|ca|cies
in|tri|cate
in|tri|cate|ly
in|tri|gant *male*
in|trigue
  in|tri|guing
in|tri|guer
in|tri|guing|ly
in|trin|sic
in|trin|sic|al|ly
intro +s
intro|duce
  intro|du|cing
intro|ducer
intro|duc|tion
intro|duc|tory
intro|gres|sion
intro|gres|sive
in|troit
intro|ject
intro|jec|tion
intro|mis|sion

in|tron
in|tron|ic
in|trorse
intro|spect
intro|spec|tion
intro|spect|ive
intro|spect|ive|ly
intro|ver|sion
intro|ver|sive
intro|vert
intro|vert|ive
in|trude
  in|trud|ing
in|truder
in|tru|sion
in|tru|sive
in|tru|sive|ly
in|tru|sive|ness
in|tub|ate
  in|tub|at|ing
in|tub|ation
in|tuit
in|tuit|able
in|tu|ition
in|tu|ition|al
in|tu|ition|al|ism
in|tu|ition|ism
in|tu|ition|ist
in|tui|tive
in|tui|tive|ly
in|tui|tive|ness
in|tui|tiv|ist
in|tu|mes|cent
in-turn *Curling*; cf.
  intern
in|tus|sus|cep|tion
Inuit *pl. n.*
Inuk
  pl. Inuit
Inuk|ti|tuk var. of
  Inuk|ti|tut
Inuk|ti|tut
inu|lin
in|unc|tion
in|un|date
  in|un|dat|ing
in|un|da|tion
In|upi|aq
  pl. Inu|piaq
In|upi|at var. of
  Inupiaq
In|upik var. of
  Inupiaq

inure accustom; cf.
  enure
in|ure|ment
in|urn
in utero
in|utile
in|util|ity
in vacuo
in|vade
  in|vad|ing
in|vader
in|va|gin|ate
  in|va|gin|at|ing
in|va|gin|ation
in|valid
in|vali|date
  in|vali|dat|ing
in|vali|da|tion
in|val|id|ism
in|val|id|ity
  in|val|id|ities
in|val|id|ly
in|valu|able
in|valu|ably
Invar *trademark*
in|vari|abil|ity
in|vari|able
in|vari|ably
in|vari|ance
in|vari|ant
in|va|sion
in|va|sive
in|va|sive|ly
in|vect|ed
in|vec|tive
in|veigh
in|vei|gle
  in|veig|ling
in|veigle|ment
in|vent
in|ven|tion
in|vent|ive
in|vent|ive|ly
in|vent|ive|ness
in|vent|or
in|ven|tory
  in|ven|tor|ies
  in|ven|tor|ied
  in|ven|tory|ing
in|ver|acity
  in|ver|aci|ties
In|ver|car|gill
In|ver|ness

Inverness-shire
in|verse
in|verse|ly
in|ver|sion
in|ver|sive
in|vert
in|vert|ase
in|ver|te|brate
in|vert|er
in|vert|ibil|ity
in|vert|ible
in|vest
in|vest|able
in|vest|ible var. of
  investable
in|ves|tig|able
in|ves|ti|gate
  in|ves|ti|gat|ing
in|ves|ti|ga|tion
in|ves|ti|ga|tion|al
in|ves|ti|ga|tive
in|ves|ti|ga|tor
in|ves|ti|ga|tory
in|ves|ti|ture
in|vest|ment
in|vest|or
in|vet|er|acy
  in|vet|er|acies
in|vet|er|ate
in|vet|er|ate|ly
in|viabil|ity
in|viable
in|vidi|ous
in|vidi|ous|ly
in|vidi|ous|ness
in|vigi|late
  in|vigi|lat|ing
in|vigi|la|tion
in|vigi|la|tor
in|vig|or|ate
  in|vig|or|at|ing
  in|vig|or|at|ing|ly
in|vig|or|ation
in|vig|ora|tive
in|vig|or|ator
in|vin|ci|bil|ity
in|vin|cible
in|vin|cibly
in vino veri|tas
in|viol|abil|ity
in|viol|able
in|viol|ably

in|viol|acy
in|viol|ate
in|viol|ate|ly
in|viol|ate|ness
in|vis|cid
in|visi|bil|ity
in|vis|ible
in|vis|ibly
in|vi|ta|tion
in|vi|ta|tion|al
in|vi|ta|tory
in|vite
  in|vit|ing
in|vitee
in|viter
in|vit|ing|ly
in vitro
in vivo
in|vo|ca|tion
in|vo|ca|tory
in|voice
  in|voi|cing
in|voke
  in|vok|ing
in|voker
in|vola|tile
in|vo|lucre
in|vol|un|tar|ily
in|vol|un|tary
in|vo|lute
in|vo|luted
in|vo|lu|tion
in|vo|lu|tion|al
in|volve
  in|volv|ing
in|volve|ment
in|vul|ner|abil|ity
in|vul|ner|able
in|vul|ner|ably
in|wale
in|ward
in|ward|ly
in|ward|ness
in|wards
in|wrap var. of
  enwrap
in|wreathe var. of
  enwreathe
in|wrought
in|yanga
  in|yangas or
  iz|in|yanga

Io *Greek Mythology*;
  moon of Jupiter
io moth
iod¦ate
iod¦ide
iod¦in¦ate
  iod¦in¦at¦ing
iod¦in¦ation
iod¦ine
iod¦isa¦tion *Br.* var.
  of iodization
iod¦ise *Br.* var. of
  iodize
iod¦ism
iod¦iza¦tion
iod¦ize
  iod¦iz¦ing
iodo¦form
iodo¦met¦ric
iod¦om¦etry
iodo¦phor
ion charged mol-
  ecule etc.; cf. **iron**
Iona
Ion¦esco, Eu¦gène
  dramatist
Ionia
Ion¦ian
Ionic architectural
  order; Greek dialect
ionic of ions
ion¦ic¦al¦ly
ion¦is¦able *Br.* var.
  of ionizable
ion¦isa¦tion *Br.* var.
  of ionization
ion¦ise *Br.* var. of
  ionize
ion¦iser *Br.* var. of
  ionizer
ion¦iz¦able
ion¦iza¦tion
ion¦ize
  ion¦iz¦ing
ion¦izer
iono¦mer
iono¦pause
iono¦phore
iono¦sphere
iono¦spher¦ic
ionto¦phor¦esis
iora
Ios Greek island; cf.
  Eos

iota
Iowa
Iowan
ipe¦cac
ipe¦cacu¦anha
Iphi¦ge¦nia
Ipoh
ipo¦moea
ippon
ipro¦nia¦zid
ipse dixit
ip¦si¦lat¦eral
ip¦sis¦sima verba
ipso facto
Ips¦wich
Ips¦wich¦ian
Iqbal, Mu¦ham¦mad
  politician
Iqui¦tos
Iran
Iran¦gate
Iran¦ian
Iraq
Iraqi
iras¦ci¦bil¦ity
iras¦cible
iras¦cibly
irate
ir¦ate¦ly
ir¦ate¦ness
ire anger; cf. **ayah**
ire¦ful
Ire¦land
Ire¦naeus, St
iren¦ic
iren¦icon var. of
  eirenicon
Irgun
Irian Jaya
iri¦da¦ceous
iri¦dec¦tomy
  iri¦dec¦to¦mies
iri¦des¦cence
iri¦des¦cent
iri¦des¦cent¦ly
irid¦ium
iri¦dolo¦gist
iri¦dol¦ogy
irie
iris
Irish

Ir¦ish¦man
  Ir¦ish¦men
Ir¦ish¦ness
Ir¦ish¦woman
  Ir¦ish¦women
ir¦itis
irk irritate; cf. **erk**
irk¦some
irk¦some¦ly
irk¦some¦ness
Ir¦kutsk
iroko +s
iron cf. **ion**
iron¦bark
iron¦clad
iron¦er
iron¦ic
iron¦ic¦al
iron¦ic¦al¦ly
iron¦ise *Br.* var. of
  ironize
iron¦ist
iron¦ize
  iron¦iz¦ing
iron-like
Iron¦man
  trademark sporting
  contest
iron¦master
iron¦mon¦ger
iron¦mon¦gery
  iron¦mon¦ger¦ies
Iron¦side Edmund
  II of England
Iron¦sides Oliver
  Cromwell; his
  cavalry
iron¦stone
iron¦ware
iron¦wood
iron¦work
iron¦works
irony
  iron¦ies
  like iron;
  expression
Iro¦quoi¦an
Iro¦quois
  pl. **Iro¦quois**
ir¦radi¦ance
ir¦radi¦ant
ir¦radi¦ate
  ir¦radi¦at¦ing
ir¦radi¦ation

ir¦ration¦al
ir¦ration¦al¦ise *Br.*
  var. of **irrationalize**
ir¦ration¦al¦ism
ir¦ration¦al¦ist
ir¦ration¦al¦ity
  ir¦ration¦al¦ities
ir¦ration¦al¦ize
  ir¦ration¦al¦iz¦ing
ir¦ration¦al¦ly
Ir¦ra¦waddy
ir¦re¦but¦table
ir¦re¦claim¦able
ir¦re¦con¦cil¦abil¦ity
ir¦re¦con¦cil¦able
ir¦re¦con¦cil¦ably
ir¦re¦cov¦er¦able
ir¦re¦cov¦er¦ably
ir¦re¦deem¦abil¦ity
ir¦re¦deem¦able
ir¦re¦deem¦ably
ir¦re¦den¦tism
ir¦re¦den¦tist
ir¦re¦du¦ci¦bil¦ity
ir¦re¦du¦cible
ir¦re¦du¦cibly
ir¦re¦flex¦ive
ir¦re¦form¦able
ir¦ref¦rag¦able
ir¦ref¦rag¦ably
ir¦re¦fut¦abil¦ity
ir¦re¦fut¦able
ir¦re¦fut¦ably
ir¦re¦gard¦less
ir¦regu¦lar
ir¦regu¦lar¦ity
  ir¦regu¦lar¦ities
ir¦regu¦lar¦ly
ir¦rele¦vance
ir¦rele¦vancy
  ir¦rele¦van¦cies
ir¦rele¦vant
ir¦rele¦vant¦ly
ir¦re¦li¦gion
ir¦re¦li¦gious
ir¦re¦li¦gious¦ly
ir¦re¦li¦gious¦ness
ir¦re¦me¦di¦able
ir¦re¦me¦di¦ably
ir¦re¦mis¦sible
ir¦re¦mov¦abil¦ity
ir¦re¦mov¦able

ir|re|mov|ably
ir|rep|ar|abil|ity
ir|rep|ar|able
ir|rep|ar|ably
ir|re|place|able
ir|re|place|ably
ir|re|press|ibil|ity
ir|re|press|ible
ir|re|press|ibly
ir|re|proach|
    abil|ity
ir|re|proach|able
ir|re|proach|ably
ir|re|pro|du|cible
ir|re|sist|ibil|ity
ir|re|sist|ible
ir|re|sist|ibly
ir|re|solu|ble
ir|reso|lute
ir|reso|lute|ly
ir|reso|lute|ness
ir|reso|lu|tion
ir|re|solv|able
ir|re|spect|ive
ir|re|spon|si|bil|ity
ir|re|spon|sible
ir|re|spon|sibly
ir|re|spon|sive
ir|re|triev|abil|ity
ir|re|triev|able
ir|re|triev|ably
ir|rev|er|ence
ir|rev|er|ent
ir|rev|er|en|tial
ir|rev|er|ent|ly
ir|re|ver|si|bil|ity
ir|re|vers|ible
ir|re|vers|ibly
ir|rev|oc|abil|ity
ir|rev|oc|able
ir|rev|oc|ably
ir|rig|able
ir|ri|gate
  ir|ri|gat|ing
ir|ri|ga|tion
ir|ri|ga|tive
ir|ri|ga|tor
ir|rit|abil|ity
ir|rit|able
ir|rit|ably
ir|ri|tancy
  ir|ri|tan|cies

ir|ri|tant
ir|ri|tate
  ir|ri|tat|ing
ir|ri|tated|ly
ir|ri|tat|ing|ly
ir|ri|ta|tion
ir|ri|ta|tive
ir|ri|ta|tor
ir|rota|tion|al
ir|rupt enter
  forcibly; cf. erupt
ir|rup|tion forcible
  entry; cf. eruption
ir|rup|tive
Ir|ving, Henry
  actor-manager
Ir|ving,
  Wash|ing|ton
  writer
Ir|ving|ite
Isa, Mount town,
  Australia
Isaac Bible
Isa|bel
Isa|bella queen of
  Castile; wife of
  Edward II of Eng-
  land; colour
Isa|belle
isa|bel|line
is|ab|gul var. of
  ispaghula
Isa|dora
isa|gogic
isa|gogics
Isaiah
is|allo|bar
is|allo|bar|ic
isa|tin
is|chae|mia Br.
is|chae|mic Br.
is|che|mia US
is|che|mic US
Is|chia
is|chial
is|chior|rho|gic
is|chium
  is|chia
is|en|trop|ic
is|ethion|ate
is|ethi|on|ic
Is|eult lover of
  Tristram

Is|fa|han
Ish|er|wood,
  Chris|to|pher
  novelist
Ishi|guro, Kazuo
  novelist
Ishi|hara
Ish|mael
Ish|mael|ite
Ish|tar Babylonian
  and Assyrian
  goddess
Isi|dore mathemat-
  ician and engineer
Isi|dore, St
is|in|glass
Isis Egyptian god-
  dess; river
Is|ken|de|run
Islam
Is|lama|bad
Is|lam|ic
Is|lami|cisa|tion
  var. of
  Islamicization
Is|lami|cise var. of
  Islamicize
Is|lami|ciza|tion
Is|lami|cize
  Is|lami|ciz|ing
Is|lam|isa|tion Br.
  var. of Islamization
Is|lam|ise Br. var. of
  Islamize
Is|lam|ism
Is|lam|ist
Is|lam|ite
Is|lam|it|ic
Is|lam|iza|tion
Is|lam|ize
  Is|lam|iz|ing
Is|lamo|pho|bia
is|land
is|land|er
Islay Scottish island
isle island; cf. aisle
Isle of Man
Isle of Wight
isles|man
  isles|men
islet
is|lets of
  Lang|er|hans

Is|mail Arabic
  spelling of Ishmael
Is|maili
Is|mail Sa|mani
  Peak
Isnik var. of Iznik
isn't = is not
iso|agglu|tin|ation
iso|bar
iso|bar|ic
Iso|bel
iso|butane
iso|butyl
iso|butyl|ene
iso|cheim
iso|chro|mat|ic
iso|chron
isoch|ron|ous
isoch|ron|ous|ly
iso|clinal
iso|cline
iso|clin|ic
iso|crates orator
iso|crat|ic
iso|cyan|ate
iso|cyan|ide
iso|dia|met|ric
iso|dynam|ic
iso|elec|tric
iso|elec|tron|ic
iso|en|zyme
iso|fla|vone
iso|gam|ete
isog|am|ous
isog|amy
iso|gen|ic
iso|geo|therm
iso|geo|ther|mal
iso|gloss
iso|gon|ic
iso|hel
iso|hyet
iso|kin|et|ic
iso|lable
iso|lat|able
iso|late
  iso|lat|ing
iso|la|tion
iso|la|tion|ism
iso|la|tion|ist
iso|la|tor
Is|olde

iso|leu|cine
iso|line
iso'mer
isom|er|ase
iso|mer'ic
isom|er'ise *Br.* var.
of isomerize
isom|er|ism
isom|er|ize
  isom|er|iz|ing
isom|er|ous
iso|met'ric
iso|met'ric|al|ly
iso|met'rics
isom|etry
iso|morph
iso|morph'ic
iso|morph|ism
iso|morph|ous
iso|nia'zid
iso|ni'trile
iso|oc'tane
iso|pach +s
iso|phote
iso|pleth
iso'pod
Iso|poda
iso|pren'aline
iso|prene
iso|pro'pa'nol
iso|pro'pyl
iso|proterenol
Isop|tera
isop|ter'an
iso|pyc'nal
iso|pyc'nic
iso|rhyth'mic
isos|bes'tic
isos|celes
iso|seis'mal
iso|seis'mic
isos|mot'ic
iso|spin
isos|tasy
iso|stat'ic
iso|tactic
iso|there
iso|therm
iso|ther'mal
iso|ther'mal'ly
iso|thio|cyan'ate
iso|ton'ic

iso|ton'ic|al'ly
iso|ton'icity
iso|tope
iso|top'ic
iso|top'ic|al'ly
isot|opy
  isot|opies
iso|trop'ic
iso|trop'ic|al'ly
isot|ropy
  isot|ro'pies
iso|zyme
is'pa|ghul var. of
  ispaghula
is'pa|ghula
Is'pa|han var. of
  Isfahan
Is|rael
Is|raeli
Is|rael|ite
Is|ra|fel angel
Issa
Is'sa|char *Bible*
issei
  pl. issei
Is'si|gonis, Alec
  car designer
is|su'able
is|su'ance
is|su'ant
issue
  is|su'ing
is|sue|less
is|suer
Is|tan|bul
Isth|mian of the
  Isthmus of Corinth
isth|mian of any
  isthmus
isth|mus
  isth|muses strips
  of land
  isthmi *Anatomy*
istle var. of ixtle
Is|tria
Is|trian
Itaipu
ital food
Ital|ian
Ital|ian|ate
Ital'ian|ise *Br.* var.
  of Italianize
Ital'ian|ism

Ital'ian|ist
Ital'ian|ize
  Ital'ian|iz'ing
Ital'ic of Italy
ital'ic sloping type
itali|cisa'tion *Br.*
  var. of italicization
itali|cise *Br.* var. of
  italicize
itali|ciza'tion
itali|cize
  itali|ciz'ing
Ital|iot
Italy
Ita|nagar
ITAR-Tass Russian
  news agency
itch
itchi|ness
itchy
  itch|ier
  itch|iest
it'd
item
item|isa'tion *Br.*
  var. of itemization
item|ise *Br.* var. of
  itemize
item|iser *Br.* var. of
  itemizer
item|iza'tion
item|ize
  item|iz'ing
item|izer
it'er|ate
it'er|at|ing
it'er|ation
it'era|tive
it'era|tive|ly
It girl
Ith|aca
ithy|phal'lic
it|in'er|acy
it|in'er|ancy
it|in'er|ant
it|in'er|ary
  it|in'er|ar'ies
it|in'er|ate
  it|in'er|at|ing
itin'er|ation
it'll
Ito, Hiro|bumi
  Japanese prince
its of it

it's = it is
it'self
itsy-bitsy
itty-bitty
Ivan rulers of Russia
I've
iver|mec'tin
Ives, Charles
  composer
ivied
Ivor|ian
ivor|ine *trademark*
Ivory, James film
  director
ivory
iv'or|ies
iv'or|ied
ivy
  ivies
  ivied
iwi
  pl. iwi
  Maori community
Iwo Jima
ixia
Ixion *Greek*
  Mythology
ixnay
ixtle
Iyen|gar
Iyyar *Jewish month*
izard
Izmir
Izmit
Iznik
Izod test
Iz'ves|tia

J

jab
  jabbed
  jab|bing
Jab'al|pur
jab'ber
jab'ber|wocky
  jab'ber|wockies
jab'iru
jabo|randi
jabot

jacal
ja|ca|les
hut; cf. **jackal**
jaca|mar
jac|ana
  Portuguese ja|çana
jaca|randa
ja|cinth
jackal animal; cf.
  jacal
jacka|napes
  pl. jacka|napes
jack|aroo +s +ed
  +ing
jack|ass
jack|boot
Jack-by-the-hedge
jack|daw
jack|een
jack|eroo var. of
  jackaroo
jack|et
jack|fish
Jack Frost
jack|fruit
  pl. jack|fruit or
  jack|fruits
jack|ham|mer
jack-in-office
  jacks-in-office
jack-in-the-box
Jack-in-the-pulpit
jack|knife
  pl. jack|knives
  v. jack|knifes
jack|knifed
jack|knif|ing
jack|leg
Jack|lin, Tony
  golfer
jack of all trades
  jacks of all trades
jack-o'-lantern
jack|pot
jack|rab|bit
Jack Rus|sell ter-
  rier
jacks toilet
jack|shit *vulgar*
  slang
jack|sie
Jack|son, An|drew
  US president

Jack|son, Glenda
  actress and
  politician
Jack|son, Jesse pol-
  itician and
  clergyman
Jack|son, Mi|chael
  singer
Jack|son, Thomas
  'Stone|wall' Ameri-
  can general
Jack|son|ian
Jack|son|ville
jack|staff
jack|stay
jack|stone
jack|straw
jacksy var. of
  jacksie
Jack Tar
jack-up
Jacky
  Jack|ies
  offensive Australian
  Aboriginal
Jacky Jacky
  Jacky Jack|ies
  offensive Australian
  Aboriginal
Jacky liz|ard
Jacky Win|ter
Jacob *Bible*
Jaco|bean relating
  to James II of
  England; cf.
  Jacobian
Jaco|bethan
Jac|obi, Derek
  actor
Ja|cobi, Karl
  mathematician
Ja|cobi|an relating
  to Karl Jacobi; cf.
  Jacobean
Jaco|bin extreme
  radical; friar
jaco|bin pigeon
Jaco|bin|ic
Jaco|bin|ic|al
Jaco|bin|ism
Jaco|bite
Jaco|bit|ic|al
Jaco|bit|ism
Ja|cobs, W. W.
  writer

Ja|cob|sen, Arne
  architect and
  furniture designer
Ja|cob|son's organ
jaco|net
jac|quard
Jacque|line
Jacque|lyn
jac|querie
Jac|quetta
Jac|qui
jacti|ta|tion
ja|cuzzi *trademark*
jaded|ly
jaded|ness
jade|ite
j'adoube
jae|ger
Jaffa city, Israel;
  (*trademark*) orange
jaf|fle
Jaffna
Jag car
jag
jagged
jag|ging
Jag|an|na|tha
jag|ged|ly
jag|ged|ness
Jag|ger, Mick singer
jag|ger
jag|gery
jag|gie prickly. var.
  of **jaggy**
jaggy
  jag|gier
  jag|gi|est
jag|uar
jag|uar|undi
Jah God
Jah|veh var. of
  Yahweh
jai alai
jail
jail|bait
jail|bird
jail|break
jail|er
jail|house
Jain adherent of
  Jainism
Jain|ism
Jain|ist

Jai|pur
Ja|karta var. of
  Djakarta
jake all right
jakes toilet
Ja|kob|son, Roman
  linguist
Jal|ala|bad
Jalal ad-Din
  ar-Rumi founder
  of whirling
  dervishes
Jal|an|dhar var. of
  Jullundur
jalap
Jal|apa En|ri|quez
jala|peño +s
ja|lebi
jaleo +s
jal|frezi
jali
Jal|isco
jal|opy
  jal|op|ies
jal|ou|sie
jam
  jammed
  jam|ming
  squeeze; stick;
  conserve; cf. **jamb**
jama|dar
Ja|maica
Ja|mai|can
jamb part of door
  frame; cf. **jam**
jam|ba|laya
jam|beau
  jam|beaux or
  jam|beaus
jam|bo|ree
James, C. L. R.
  novelist
James, Henry
  novelist
James, Jesse outlaw
James, M. R. writer
  of ghost stories
James, P. D. writer
  of detective fiction
James Bay
James|ian
Jame|son Raid
James|town
jam jar

jam¦mer
Jammu
jammy
 jam¦mier
 jam¦mi¦est
Jam¦nagar
jam-packed
jam¦rool
Jam¦shed¦pur
Jam¦shid legendary
 Persian king
jamun
Janá¦ček, Leoš
 composer
Jan¦cis
jan¦dal trademark
Jane Doe
JANET = Joint Aca-
 demic Network
Janet
Jan¦ette
jan¦gle
 jan¦gling
jan¦gly
 jan¦glier
 jan¦gli¦est
Jan¦ice
Jan¦ine
Janis
jan¦is¦sary
 jan¦is¦sar¦ies
jani¦tor
jani¦tor¦ial
jani¦zary var. of
 janissary
jank¦ers
Jan Mayen
Jan¦sen, Cor¦ne¦lius
 theologian
Jan¦sen¦ism
Jan¦sen¦ist
Jan¦sens,
 Cor¦ne¦lius painter;
 var. of Johnson
Janu¦ary
 Janu¦ar¦ies
Janus
Japan
japan
 ja¦panned
 ja¦pan¦ning
 varnish
Ja¦pani¦ma¦tion

jape
 jap¦ing
jap¦ery
 jap¦er¦ies
Ja¦pheth Bible
Ja¦phet¦ic
Jap¦lish
ja¦pon¦ica
Jaques-Dalcroze,
 Émile music
 teacher
jar
 jarred
 jar¦ring
jar¦di¦nière
jar¦ful
jar¦gon language;
 stone
Jar¦gon¦elle
jar¦gon¦ic
jar¦gon¦ise Br. var.
 of jargonize
jar¦gon¦is¦tic
jar¦gon¦ize
 jar¦gon¦iz¦ing
jar¦goon stone var.
 of jargon
jar¦head
jarl
Jarls¦berg
 trademark
ja¦rool var. of jarul
jar¦rah
jar¦ring¦ly
Jar¦row
Jarry, Al¦fred
 dramatist
jarul
Jaru¦zel¦ski,
 Woj¦ciech presi-
 dent of Poland
Jas¦min name
Jas¦mine name
jas¦mine
Jason Greek
 Mythology
jaspé
Jas¦per
jas¦per stone
jas¦per¦ware
Jat
Jat¦aka
jatha
jati

jato +s = jet-assisted
 take-off
jaun¦dice
jaunt
jaunt¦ily
jaunti¦ness
jaunty
 jaunt¦ier
 jaunti¦est
Java island; Man;
 programming lan-
 guage (trademark)
Java coffee
Javan
Ja¦van¦ese
jav¦elin
jave¦lina
jaw
jaw¦bone
 jaw¦bon¦ing
jaw¦break¦er
jaw¦fish
 jaw¦fishes
jaw-jaw
jaw¦less
jaw¦line
jay bird
Jay¦cee member of
 Junior Chamber of
 Commerce
jay¦walk
jay¦walk¦er
jazz
jazz¦bo +s
jazz¦er
jazz¦er¦cise
 trademark in the
 US
jazz¦ily
jazzi¦ness
jazz¦man
 jazz¦men
jazzy
 jazz¦ier
 jazzi¦est
J-cloth trademark
jeal¦ous
jeal¦ous¦ly
jeal¦ousy
 jeal¦ousies
Jean woman's name;
 cf. Gene
jean cloth; cf. gean,
 gene

Jean¦ette
Jeanie
Jean¦ne¦ret,
 Charles Édou¦ard
 architect,
 'Le Corbusier'
Jean¦nette
Jean¦nie
Jean Paul novelist
Jeans, James
 physicist
jeans trousers; cf.
 genes
jebel
Jed¦dah
Jedi
jeep trademark
jee¦pers
jee¦pers cree¦pers
jeer
jeer¦ing¦ly
jeet kune do
Jeeves valet in P. G.
 Wodehouse novels
Jeez exclam.
jefe
Jef¦feries, Rich¦ard
 writer
Jef¦fer¦son,
 Thomas US
 president
Jef¦fer¦son¦ian
Jef¦frey
Jef¦freys, George
 judge
jehad var. of jihad
je¦hadi var. of jihadi
jehad¦ist var. of
 jihadist
Je¦hosa¦phat var. of
 Jehoshaphat
Je¦hosha¦phat Bible
Je¦ho¦vah
Je¦hov¦ist
Jehu Bible
je¦junal
je¦june
je¦june¦ly
je¦june¦ness
je¦juno¦ileal
je¦junum
 je¦juna or
 je¦junums

Je¦kyll, Ger¦trude
  gardener
Jek¦yll and Hyde
jell var. of gel
jel¦laba var. of
  djellaba
Jel¦li¦coe, Earl
  admiral
jel¦li¦fi¦ca¦tion
jel¦lify
  jel¦li¦fies
  jel¦li¦fied
  jel¦li¦fy¦ing
Jell-O +s *trademark*
jello +s generally
jelly
  jel¦lies
  jel¦lied
  jelly¦ing
  food etc.; cf. **gelly**
jelly¦fish
jelly-like
jelu¦tong
jema¦dar var. of
  jamadar
Jem¦ima
jemmy
  jem¦mies
  jem¦mied
  jemmy¦ing
  crowbar; cf.
  gemmy.
  US jimmy
Jena
je ne sais quoi
Jeni¦fer
Jen¦kins, Roy polit-
  ician
Jen¦kins's Ear,
  War of
Jen¦ner, Ed¦ward
  physician
jen¦net horse; cf.
  genet
Jen¦ni¦fer
Jenny
jenny
  jen¦nies
  spinning jenny;
  female donkey;
  wren; crane; cf.
  genny
jeon
  pl. jeon

jeop¦ard¦ise *Br.* var.
  of **jeopardize**
jeop¦ard¦ize
  jeop¦ard¦iz¦ing
jeop¦ardy
Jeph¦thah *Bible*
Jerba var. of Djerba
jer¦boa
jere¦miad
Jere¦miah
Jer¦emy
jere¦pigo
Jerez de la
  Fron¦tera
Jeri¦cho
jerk¦er
jerk¦ily
jer¦kin
jerki¦ness
jerk¦water
jerky
  jerk¦ier
  jerk¦iest
jero¦boam
Je¦rome
Je¦rome, Je¦rome
  K. writer
jerri¦can var. of
  jerrycan
Jerry
  Jer¦ries
jerry
  jer¦ries
  pot
jerry-builder
jerry-building
jerry-built
jer¦ry¦can
Jer¦sey Channel
  Island; cattle
jer¦sey garment
Je¦ru¦sa¦lem
Jer¦vis, John
  admiral
Jer¦vis Bay
  Ter¦ri¦tory
Jes¦per¦sen, Otto
  philologist
Jesse man's name;
  tree; window
Jesse tree
Jesse win¦dow
Jes¦sica

Jes¦sie woman's
  name
jes¦sie effeminate
  man
jessy var. of jessie
jest¦er
Jesu
Jes¦uit
Jesu¦it¦ic¦al
Jesu¦it¦ic¦al¦ly
Jes¦uits' bark
Jesus
JET = Joint Euro-
  pean Torus
jet
  jet¦ted
  jet¦ting
jet¦boat
jeté
jet¦foil
jet-lagged
jet¦liner
jet¦sam
jet set *n.*
jet-set *mod.*
jet-setter
jet-setting
jet ski *n. trademark*
jet-ski +s +ed +ing
  v.
jet-skier
jet¦ti¦son
jet¦ton
jetty
  jet¦ties
jet¦way *trademark*
jeu d'es¦prit
jeux d'es¦prit
jeun¦esse dorée
jewel
  jew¦elled *Br.*
  jew¦eled *US*
  jew¦el¦ling *Br.*
  jew¦el¦ing *US*
jew¦el¦er *US*
  Br. jeweller
jew¦el¦er's rouge
  US
  Br. jeweller's rouge
jewel¦fish
jew¦el¦ler *Br.*
  US jeweler
jew¦el¦ler's rouge
  Br.

  US jeweler's rouge
jew¦el¦lery *Br.*
  US jewelry
jew¦el¦ry *US*
  Br. jewellery
Jew¦ess
jew¦fish
Jew¦ish
Jew¦ish¦ly
Jew¦ish¦ness
Jewi¦son, Nor¦man
  film director and
  producer
Jewry
  Jew¦ries
  cf. jury
jez¦ail
Jez¦ebel
Jhansi
Jhar¦kand
jheel var. of jhil
Jhe¦lum
Jheri curl
jhil
jhuggi
Jiang Jie Shi var.
  of Chiang Kai-
  shek
Jiangsu
Jiangxi
jiao
  pl. jiao
jib
  jibbed
  jib¦bing
jibba Muslim's coat;
  cf. **gibber, jibber**
jib¦bah var. of jibba
jib¦ber person who
  jibs; cf. **gibber,
  jibba**
jibe *US*
  jib¦ing
  Sailing.
  Br. gybe; cf. **gibe**
jibe
  jib¦ing
  agree; cf. **gibe,
  gybe**
Ji¦buti var. of
  Djibouti
ji¦cama
Jid¦dah var. of
  Jeddah
jiff

jiffy
jif|fies
Jiffy bag *trademark*
jig
 jigged
 jig|ging
jiga|boo
jig|ger
jiggery-pokery
jig|gle
 jig|gling
jig|gly
jiggy
jig|saw
jihad
ji|hadi
jihad|ist
jil|bab
Jilin
jill female ferret var.
 of gill
jill|aroo female
 farmhand; cf.
 gillaroo
Jil|lian
jil|lion large number
jilt
Jim Crow *offensive
 when used of a
 person*
Jim Crow|ism
jim-dandy
 jim-dandies
Ji|mé|nez de
 Cis|neros,
 Fran|cisco Grand
 Inquisitor
Jim|iny
jim-jams
Jimmu legendary
 Japanese emperor
Jimmy name
jimmy *US*
 jim|mies
 jim|mied
 jimmy|ing
 Br. jemmy
Jimmy Wood|ser
jimp|son var. of
 jimson
jim|son weed
Jin Chinese dynasty
Jina teacher in
 Jainism

Jinan city, China
jing|bang
jin|gle
jin|gling
jin|gler
jin|gly
jin|glier
jin|gli|est
jingo
 jin|goes
jin|go|ism
jin|go|ist
jin|go|is|tic
jink dodge; in 'high
 jinks'; cf. jinx
jin|ker
jinn
 pl. jinn or jinns
 intelligent spirit; cf.
 gin
Jin|nah,
 Mu|ham|mad Ali
 president of
 Pakistan
jin|rick|sha
jin|riki|sha var. of
 jinricksha
jinx spell; cf. jinks
jird
jit
jit|ney
jit|ter
jit|ter|bug
 jit|ter|bugged
 jit|ter|bug|ging
jit|teri|ness
jit|tery
jiu-jitsu var. of
 ju-jitsu
Ji|varo
 pl. Ji|varo or
 Ji|va|ros
Ji|va|roan
jive
 jiv|ing
 dance; cf. gyve
jiver
jivey
jizz
jo
 joes
Joa|chim, St
Joa|chim, Jo|seph
 violinist

Joan, Pope legend-
 ary female pope
Jo|anna
jo|anna piano
Jo|anne
Joan of Arc, St
João Pes|soa
Job *Bible*
job
 jobbed
 job|bing
job|ber
job|bery
job|bie
job|centre
job|less
job|less|ness
Jobs, Steve com-
 puter entrepreneur
Job's com|fort|er
job-share
 job-sharing
job-sharer
Job's tears
jobs|worth
Jo|burg =
 Johannesburg
job|work
Jo|casta *Greek
 Mythology*
Joce|lyn
Jock name;
 Scotsman
jock disc jockey;
 pilot; sports fan
jockey
jockey|ship
jock|ish
jock|strap
joc|ose
joc|ose|ly
joc|ose|ness
joc|os|ity
 joc|os|ities
jocu|lar
jocu|lar|ity
jocu|lar|ly
joc|und
joc|und|ity
 joc|und|ities
joc|und|ly
Jodh|pur
jodh|purs

Jod|rell Bank
Joel *Bible*
joe-pye weed
joey
Joffre, Jo|seph
 French marshal
jog
 jogged
 jog|ging
jog|ger
jog|gle
 jog|gling
Jog|ja|karta var. of
 Yogyakarta
jog-shuttle
jog|trot
Jo|hanna
Jo|han|nes|burg
 city
Jo|han|nine
Jo|han|nis|berg
 grape
John, Aug|us|tus
 painter
John, Barry rugby
 player
John, Elton singer-
 songwriter
John, Gwen painter
john toilet
Johna|than cf.
 Jonathan
john|boat
John
 Chrys|os|tom, St
John Doe
John Dory
 John Dories
Johne's dis|ease
johnny
 john|nies
 fellow
johnny|cake
johnny-come-
 lately
 johnny-come-
 latelies
Johnny-on-the-
 spot
 Johnnies-on-the-
 spot
John o'Groats
Johns, Jas|per
 artist

John|son, Amy
  aviator
John|son, An|drew
  US president
John|son,
  Cor|ne|lius painter
John|son, Dr
  Sam|uel lexicog-
  rapher
John|son, Jack
  boxer
John|son, Lyn|don
  Baines US
  president
John|son, Magic
  basketball player
John|son, Mi|chael
  sprinter
john|son penis
John|son|ian
Johor
Johor Ba|haru
Jo|hore ver. of
  Johor
joie de vivre
join|able
join|der
join|er
join|ery
joint|er
joint|less
joint|ly
joint|ress
join|ture
  join|tur|ing
joist
jo|joba
joke
  jok|ing
joker
jokey
  jok|ier
  joki|est
joki|ly
joki|ness
jok|ing|ly
joky var. of jokey
Jo|lene
jolie laide
  jolies laides
joli|otium
jol|li|fi|ca|tion
jol|lily
jol|li|ness

jol|lity
  jol|lities
jol|lof rice
jolly
  jol|lies
  jol|lied
  jolly|ing
  jol|lier
  jol|li|est
jolly|tail
Jol|son, Al singer
  and actor
jolty
  jolt|ier
  jolti|est
Jo|lyon
Jomon
Jona|gold
Jonah *Bible*
Jona|than *Bible*;
  apple
Jona|thon
Jones, Bobby golfer
Jones, Dan|iel
  phonetician
Jones, Inigo
  architect
Jones, John Paul
  American admiral
Jones, Steve
  geneticist
Jones, Tom pop
  singer
jones addiction; be
  addicted
joneses
jonesed
jones|ing
Joneses
jon|gleur
Jön|kö|ping
jon|quil
Jon|son, Ben
  dramatist
Jon|son|ian
Jop|lin, Janis rock
  singer
Jop|lin, Scott
  musician
Joppa
Jor|daens, Jacob
  painter
Jor|dan country;
  river; name

Jor|dan, Mi|chael
  basketball player
Jor|dan|ian
jorum
Jor|vik
Josce|line
Jo|seph
Jo|seph ben
  Mat|thias
  historian
Jo|seph|ine French
  empress
Jo|seph|son
  junc|tion
Jo|se|phus, Fla|vius
  historian and
  general
josh|er
Joshua
Jos|iah
Jos|quin des Prez
  composer
joss|er
jos|tle
  jost|ling
jot
  jot|ted
  jot|ting
jota dance
jot|ter
Jotun giant
Jotun|heim
jougs
jouis|sance
jouk
Joule, James physi-
  cist; effect; law
joule unit
Joule–Thomson
jounce
  joun|cing
jour|nal
jour|nal|ese style of
  writing
jour|nal|ise *Br.* var.
  of journalize
jour|nal|ism
jour|nal|ist
jour|nal|is|tic
jour|nal|is|tic|al|ly
jour|nal|ize
  jour|nal|iz|ing
  enter in a journal
jour|ney

jour|ney|er
jour|ney|man
  jour|ney|men
journo +s
joust
joust|er
J'Ouvert
Jove Roman god; in
  'by Jove'
jo|vial
jovi|al|ity
jo|vial|ly
Jo|vian
jowl
jowly
  jowl|ier
  jowli|est
Joyce, James writer
Joy|cean
joy|ful
joy|ful|ly
joy|ful|ness
joy|less
joy|less|ly
joy|less|ness
joy|ous
joy|ous|ly
joy|ous|ness
joy|pad
joy|ride
joy|rid|ing
joy|rider
joy|stick
J-pop
Juan Car|los king
  of Spain
Juan Fer|nan|dez
  Is|lands
Juá|rez, Ben|ito
  president of Mexico
Juba city, Sudan
juba dance
Jubba river, E.
  Africa
jube
ju|bi|lance
ju|bi|lant
ju|bi|lant|ly
Ju|bi|late canticle
ju|bi|late
  ju|bi|lat|ing
  rejoice
ju|bi|la|tion

ju¦bi¦lee
Ju¦bi¦lee clip
  trademark
Ju¦daea
Ju|daean
Judaeo- *Br*
  US Judeo-
Judah
Ju¦da¦ic
Juda|isa|tion var. of
  Judaization
Juda|ise var. of
  Judaize
Juda|ism
Juda|ist
Ju¦da|iza|tion
Juda|ize
  Juda|iz¦ing
judas hole
Judas Is¦car¦iot
  Apostle; traitor; J.
  kiss, tree
Judas kiss
Judas
  Mac¦ca|baeus
  Jewish leader
Judas tree
jud¦der
jud|dery
Jude name
Judea var. of
  Judaea
Ju¦dean var. of
  Judaean
Juden|rat
Juden|rate
Judeo- *US*
  Br. Judaeo-
Ju|dezmo +s
judge
  judg¦ing
judge|ment
judge|men¦tal
judge|men¦tal|ly
judge|ship
Judges' Rules
judg|ment var. of
  judgement
judg|men¦tal var. of
  judgemental
judg¦men¦tal¦ly var.
  of judgementally
ju¦di¦ca¦tory
ju¦di¦ca¦ture

ju¦di¦cial
ju¦di¦cial¦ly
ju¦di¦ciary
  ju¦di¦ciar¦ies
ju¦di¦cious
ju¦di¦cious¦ly
ju¦di¦cious|ness
Ju¦dith
judo
judo|ist
ju¦doka
ju¦do¦kas
Judy
  Ju¦dies
  name; woman
jug
  jugged
  jug|ging
jugal
Ju¦gend|stil
jug|ful
Jug¦ger|naut Hindu
  god
jug¦ger|naut
  vehicle; force
jug|gins
jug|gle
  jug|gling
jug|gler
jug|glery
  jug|gler|ies
Jugo|slav var. of
  Yugoslav
Jugo|slavia var. of
  Yugoslavia
Jugo|slav|ian var. of
  Yugoslavian
jugu|lar
jugu|late
  jugu|lat¦ing
jugum
  juga
Ju¦gur¦tha king of
  Numidia
Ju¦gurth|ine
juice
  juic¦ing
  liquid from fruit or
  vegetables; cf. *jus*
juice|less
juicer
juici¦ly
juici|ness

juicy
  juici¦er
  juici¦est
ju-jitsu
juju
ju¦jube
ju-jutsu var. of
  ju-jitsu
juke
  juk¦ing
juke|box
julep
julia butterfly
Ju¦lian of Julius
  Caesar; calendar;
  Alps
Ju¦lian Roman
  emperor
Ju¦lian of
  Nor|wich female
  mystic
Julia set
Julie name; cf. July
ju¦li|enne
  ju¦li|en¦ning
Ju¦liet name; cap
Ju¦lius Cae¦sar
Jul¦lun|dur
July +s month; cf.
  Julie
jumar
jum¦bie spirit; bird
jum¦ble
  jum|bling
jumbo +s
jum|buck
Jumna
jump|able
jump|cut *n.*
jump-cut *v.*
  jump-cuts
  jump-cutting
jump¦er
jump|ily
jumpi|ness
jump-off *n.*
jump-start
jump|station
jump|suit
jump-up *n.*
jumpy
  jump|ier
  jumpi|est

jun
  pl. jun
  N. Korean currency
junco
  jun¦cos or jun|coes
junc|tion
junc|ture
June
Ju|neau port, US
june|berry
  june|berries
junc|teenth
Jung, Carl
  psychologist
Jung|frau
Jung|ian
jun¦gle
jungle|fowl
jun¦gli *Indian*
  uncultured
jung|list
jun¦gly
  jun|glier
  jun|gli¦est
  of jungle music
jun¦ior
jun|ior|ity
ju|ni|per
Jun¦ka|noo
Jun¦ker
jun|ker|dom
jun|ker|ism
jun|ket
junkie
junky var. of junkie
junky
  junk|ies
junk|yard *US*
Juno Roman god-
  dess; asteroid;
  D-Day beach
Juno|esque
junta
junto +s
Ju¦pi¦ter
Jura French/Swiss
  mountain range;
  Scottish island
jural
Jur¦as|sic
jurat
jur¦id¦ic¦al
jur¦id¦ic¦al¦ly
jur¦is|con¦sult

jur¦is|dic¦tion
jur¦is|dic¦tion¦al
jur¦is|pru¦dence
jur¦is|pru¦dent
jur¦is|pru¦den¦tial
jur¦ist
jur¦is¦tic
juror
jury
  jur¦ies
  jur¦ied
  jury|ing
  people giving
  verdict; cf. **Jewry**
jury|man
  jury|men
jury-rigged
jury|woman
  jury|women
jus thin gravy; cf.
  juice
jus co¦gens
jus gen¦ilum
Jus|sieu, An|toine
  French botanist
jus|sive
juste mi|lieu
just|ice
just|ice|ship
jus¦ti|ciable
jus¦ti|ciar
jus¦ti|ciary
  jus¦ti|ciar¦ies
jus¦ti|fi¦abil¦ity
jus¦ti|fi¦able
jus¦ti|fi¦ably
jus¦ti|fi¦ca¦tion
jus¦ti|fi¦ca¦tory
jus¦ti|fier
jus|tify
  jus¦ti|fies
  jus¦ti|fied
  jus¦ti|fy¦ing
Jus|tin, St
Jus|tine
Jus¦tin|ian Roman
  emperor
just|ly
just|ness
jut
  jut¦ted
  jut¦ting
Jute people
jute fibre

Jut¦ish
Jut|land
Juv|enal Roman
  satirist
ju|ven|es¦cence
ju|ven|es¦cent
ju|ven|ile
ju|ven|ilia
ju|ven|il¦ise *Br.* var.
  of juvenilize
ju|ven|il¦ity
ju|ven|il¦ize
  ju|ven|il¦izing
juvie
juxta|glo¦meru¦lar
juxta|pose
  juxta|pos¦ing
juxta|pos¦ition
juxta|pos¦ition¦al
Jy¦väs|kylä

K

ka spirit; cf. car,
  carr
Kaaba
ka|baddi
ka|baka
Kaba|lega
Kabarda-Balkar
Ka|bard|ian
Kabardino-
    Balkaria
Kab|bala var. of
  Kabbalah
Kab|ba¦lah *Juda-
  ism*; cf. Karbala
Kab|bal|ism
Kab|bal|ist
Kab|bal|is¦tic
ka|bel|jou
Kab|inett wine
ka|bloona
  ka|bloo¦nas or
  ka|bloo¦nat
kabob *US* var. of
  kebab
ka|boodle var. of
  caboodle
ka|boom

ka¦buki
Kabul
Kabwe
Ka¦byle
kachha var. of
  kuccha
Ka¦chin
ka|china
ka-ching
kach|ori
kadai var. of karahi
ka¦dai|tcha
Kádár, János prime
  minister of
  Hungary
Kad|dish Jewish
  prayer; cf. caddish
kadi var. of cadi
Ka¦di|köy
kaffee|klatsch
Kaf¦fir lily; *offensive*
  black person; cf.
  Kafir
kaf¦fir *offensive*
  beer; corn
kaf¦fi|yeh var. of
  keffiyeh
Kafir NE Afghan
  people; cf. Kaffir
kafir non-Muslim
Ka¦firi
Kafka, Franz
  novelist
Kaf¦ka|esque
kaf¦tan
Kago|shima
kagu
kaha|wai
  pl. kaha|wai
kahi¦ka|tea
ka¦huna
Kai|feng
kail var. of kale
kain¦ic
kain|ite
kairo|mone
kai¦ros
Kair|ouan
Kai¦ser, Georg
  dramatist
kai¦ser
kai¦ser|ship
Kai¦sers|lau¦tern

kai¦zen
kajal
kaka
kaka-bill
ka¦kapo +s
kake|mono +s
kaki fruit; cf. khaki
Ka|kie¦mon
kala-azar
Kala|hari
kal¦am|kari
kal¦an|choe
Ka¦lash|ni¦kov
kale
kal¦eido|scope
kal¦eido|scop¦ic
kal¦eido|scop¦ic|
    al¦ly
kal|ends var. of
  calends
Kale|vala
Kal|goor¦lie
Kali Hindu goddess
kali plant
Kali|dasa Indian
  poet and dramatist
Kali|man¦tan
ka|limba
Ka¦li|nin, Mikh|ail
  Soviet head of state
Ka¦li|nin|grad
Ka¦lisz
Kal¦mar
kal|mia
Kal|muck var. of
  Kalmyk
Kal¦myk
Kal|mykia
Kalmykia-Khalmg
  Tangch
ka|long
kalpa
kal¦so|mine
  kal¦so|min¦ing
Kama Hindu god
kama|cite
ka¦mahi
Kama Sutra
Kamba
  pl. Kamba or
  Kam¦bas or
  Wa|kamba
Kam|chatka

kame glacial deposit
ka¦meez
  pl. ka¦meez or
  ka¦meezes
kami
  pl. kami
  Shinto divine being
kami¦kaze
Ka¦mila¦roi
  pl. Ka¦mila¦roi
Kam¦pala
kam¦pong
Kam¦pong Cham
  var. of Kompong
  Cham
Kam¦pong Som
  var. of Kompong
  Som
Kam¦pu¦chea
  former name for
  Cambodia
Kam¦pu¦chean
kam¦pung var. of
  kampong
kana Japanese
  writing
ka¦naka
kana¦my¦cin
Kan¦ar¦ese
kanat var. of qanat
Kan¦awa, Kiri Te
  singer
kan¦ban
Kan¦chen¦junga
Kan¦da¦har
Kan¦din¦sky,
  Was¦sily artist
Kandy town, Sri
  Lanka
Kan¦dy¦an
kanga kangaroo;
  prison warder; cf.
  khanga
Kan¦gar city,
  Malaysia
kan¦ga¦roo +s
Kang¦chen¦junga
  var. of
  Kanchenjunga
kan¦gha
Kango *trademark*
Kan¦goes
kan¦gri
Ka¦Ngwane
kanji

Kan¦nada language
Kano city, Nigeria
Kan¦pur
Kan¦san
Kan¦sas
Kansu var. of
  Gansu
Kant, Im¦man¦uel
  philosopher
Kant¦ian
Kant¦ian¦ism
KANU = Kenya
  African National
  Union
ka¦nuka
kanzu
Kao¦hsiung
kao¦liang
kao¦lin
kao¦lin¦ise *Br.* var.
  of kaolinize
kao¦lin¦ite
kao¦lin¦ize
  kao¦lin¦iz¦ing
kaon
Ka¦onde
Kapa¦chira
ka¦pell¦mei¦ster
Kapil Dev cricketer
kapok
Ka¦poor, Raj actor
  and film-maker
Ka¦posi's sar¦coma
kappa
kapur tree
kaput
Kara Sea
kara bangle
kara¦bi¦ner in
  mountaineering; cf.
  carabineer
Kara¦chai-
  Cherkess
Karachai-
  Cherkes¦sia
Kara¦chay var. of
  Karachai
Karachay-Balkar
Ka¦ra¦chi
ka¦rahi
Kara¦ite

Kara¦jan, Her¦bert
  von conductor
ka¦raka
Kara¦kal¦pak
Kara¦koram moun-
  tains west of the
  Himalayas; Pass;
  Highway
Kara¦korum city,
  Mongolia
kara¦kul sheep; cf.
  caracal
Kara Kum
kar¦anga
kara¦oke
karat *US*
  Br. **carat.** measure
  of purity of gold; cf.
  carat, caret, carrot
ka¦rate
ka¦ra¦teka
Kar¦bala city, Iraq;
  cf. Kabbalah
karee var. of karree
Ka¦re¦lia
Ka¦re¦lian
Karen people; lan-
  guage; State; cf.
  karren
ka¦rezza
Ka¦riba
Kari¦tane
Karl-Marx-Stadt
Kar¦loff, Boris
  actor
Kar¦lovy Vary
Karls¦bad
Karls¦ruhe
karma Hindu and
  Buddhist doctrine;
  yoga; cf. Kama
kar¦mic
kar¦mic¦al¦ly
Kar¦nak in Egypt;
  cf. Carnac
Kar¦na¦taka
Kar¦naugh
  Mathematics
karo +s shrub
Karoo
Kar¦pov, Ana¦toli
  chess player
kar¦ree tree

kar¦ren *Geology*; cf.
  Karen
karri tree
kar¦roid
Kar¦roo var. of
  Karoo
Kars city, Turkey
Karsh, You¦suf
  photographer
karst *Geology*; cf.
  cast, caste
karst¦ic
karst¦ifi¦ca¦tion
karst¦ify
karsti¦fies
karsti¦fied
karsti¦fy¦ing
kart motor-racing
  vehicle; cf. cart,
  carte, khat, quart
Kart¦ve¦lian
karyo¦kin¦esis
kary¦oly¦sis
karyo¦type
karyo¦typ¦ing
karyo¦typ¦ic
karzy
  kar¦zies
  var. of khazi
kas¦bah
Kasha *trademark*
  fabric
kasha porridge
Kash¦mir region;
  goat; cf. cashmere
Kash¦miri
kash¦rut
kash¦ruth var. of
  kashrut
Ka¦shu¦bian
Kas¦parov, Garry
  chess player
Kas¦sel
kata martial-arts
  training
ka¦ta¦bat¦ic
ka¦tab¦ol¦ism var. of
  catabolism
kata¦kana
ka¦tana
Ka¦tanga
Kat¦ang¦ese
Kathak
Katha¦kali

kath|ar|ev|ousa
Kath|ar|ine
kath|ar|om|eter
Kath|er|ine
Kathia|war
Kath|leen
Kath|mandu
Kath|ryn
katipo +s
Kat|mandu var. of
  Kathmandu
Kato|wice
ka|tsina
ka|tsi|nam
  var. of kachina
kat|suo|bushi
kat|sura
Kat|te|gat
ka|ty|did
kat|zen|jam|mer
Kauai
Kauff|mann,
  An|gel|ica artist
kau|ma|tua
Kau|nas
Ka|unda, Ken|neth
  president of
  Zambia
kau|papa
kauri tree; cf.
  cowrie
kava shrub; drink;
  cf. carver, cava
Ka|válla
Ka|veri var. of
  Cauvery
Kawa|bata,
  Yasu|nari novelist
kawa-kawa
Kawa|saki
Kaw|thoo|lay
Kaw|thu|lei var. of
  Kawthoolay
kayak
kaya|keet
kayak|er
Kaye, Danny actor
  and comedian
kayo
  pl. kayos
  v. kayoes
kayoed
kayo|ing
Kay|seri

kaza|choc
Kaz|akh or
  Kaz|akhi
Kaz|akh|stan
Kazan capital of
  Tatarstan
Kazan, Elia film
  and theatre director
ka|zil|lion
kazoo +s
kea bird
keaki
Kean, Ed|mund
  actor
Keat|ing, Paul
  prime minister of
  Australia
Kea|ton, Bus|ter
  actor
Keats, John poet
Keats|ian
kebab
Koble, John
  churchman
Keb|ne|kaise
keck
kecks
Kedah state,
  Malaysia
kedge
  kedg|ing
kedg|eree
keech
Kee|gan, Kevin
  footballer
keek
keel|back
keel|boat
Kee|ler, Chris|tine
  model
keel|er
keel|haul
kee|lie
Keel|ing Is|lands
keel|less
keel|son
keema
Kee|mun
Keene, Charles
  caricaturist
keen|er
keen|ly
keen|ness

keep
  kept
keep|able
keep|er
keeper|ship
keep-fit n. & adj.
keep|net
keep|sake
kees|hond
kees|ter var. of
  keister
kef var. of kif
Ke|fal|linía Greek
  name for
  Cephalonia
kef|fi|yeh
Kef|la|vik
kef|te|des
keg|ger
kei|retsu
  pl. kei|retsu
keis|ter
Kejia
Ke|lan|tan
kelim var. of kilim
Kel|ler, Helen
  social reformer
Kellogg–Briand
  Pact
Kells, Book of
Kelly, Gene dancer
  and actor
Kelly, Grace actress
Kelly, Ned
  bushranger
Kelly, Petra polit-
  ician
ke|loid
kelp|fish
kel|pie
kel|son var. of
  keelson
kelt fish; cf. Celt,
  celt
kel|ter var. of kilter
Kel|vin scale
kel|vin unit
Kem|ble, Fanny
  actress
Kem|ble, John and
  Charles actors
Kempe, Mar|gery
  mystic

Kem|pis, Thomas à
  theologian
kempt
kempy
ken
  kenned or kent
  ken|ning
kenaf
Ken|dal
kendo
kendo|ist
Ken|eally, Thomas
  novelist
Ken|elm
Ken|nedy, Ed|ward
  ('Teddy') US
  politician
Ken|nedy, John
  Fitz|ger|ald US
  president
Ken|nedy, Rob|ert
  ('Bobby') US
  politician
ken|nel
  ken|nelled Br.
  ken|neled US
  ken|nel|ling Br.
  ken|nel|ling US
Kennelly–
         Heaviside
kennel|maid
kennel|man
kennel|men
Ken|neth
ken|ning
keno
ken|osis
ken|ot|ic
Ken|sing|ton
ken|speckle
Kent county,
  England
kent past tense and
  past participle of
  ken
kente cloth
ken|tia
Kent|ish
Ken|ton, Stan
  bandleader
Ken|tuck|ian
Ken|tucky
Kenya country;
  Mount

Ken¦yah people
Ken¦yan
Ken¦yatta, Jomo
  president of Kenya
kep
  kepped
  kepping
kepi
  French képi
Kep¦ler, Jo¦han¦nes
  astronomer
Kep¦ler¦ian
Ker¦ala
Ker¦al¦ite
kera¦tec¦tomy
  kera¦tec¦to¦mies
kera¦tin
kera¦tin¦isa¦tion *Br.*
  var. of
  keratinization
kera¦tin¦ise *Br.* var.
  of **keratinize**
kera¦tin¦iza¦tion
kera¦tin¦ize
  kera¦tin¦iz¦ing
kera¦tino¦cyte
ker¦at¦in¦ous
kera¦titis
kerato¦mileu¦sis
kerato¦plasty
  kerato¦plas¦ties
kera¦tosis
  kera¦toses
kera¦tot¦omy
  kera¦toto¦mies
kerb *Br.*
  US **curb**. pavement
  edge; cf. **curb**
kerb-crawler *Br.*
kerb-crawling *Br.*
kerb¦side *Br.*
  US **curbside**
kerb¦stone *Br.*
  US **curbstone**
Kerch city, Ukraine
ker¦chief
ker¦chiefed
ker-ching var. of
  ka-ching
ker¦eru
Keres
  pl. **Keres**
Keres¦an
kerf

ker¦fuf¦fle
Ker¦gue¦len
Kerk¦rade
Ker¦madec
ker¦mes
  pl. **ker¦mes**
  insects; oak
ker¦mis carnival;
  fair
Kern, Je¦rome
  composer
kern Irish soldier;
  Printing
kerne soldier var. of
  kern
ker¦nel nut; cf.
  colonel
kern¦ite
Ker¦now
  Cornish name for
  Cornwall
kero¦gen
kero¦sene
kero¦sine var. of
  kerosene
Ker¦ouac, Jack
  novelist
Kerr ef¦fect
ker¦ria
Kerry
  Ker¦ries
  Irish county; cattle
ker¦sey
ker¦sey¦mere
keru¦ing
kes var. of **kesh**
kesh
kes¦ki¦dee var. of
  kiskadee
kes¦trel
Kes¦wick
keta¦mine
ketch
ketch¦up
ke¦tene
keto acid
keto¦naemia *Br.*
ke¦tone
keto¦nemia *US*
ke¦ton¦ic
ke¦to¦nuria
ke¦to¦sis
ke¦tot¦ic
ket¦tle

kettle¦drum
kettle¦drum¦mer
kettle¦ful
Keu¦per rock; cf.
  Kuiper
keur¦boom
kevel
Kev¦lar *trademark*
Kew Gar¦dens
kew¦pie *trademark
  in the US*
key for lock; cf. **cay**,
  quay
key¦board
key¦board¦er
key¦board¦ist
keyer
key¦hold¦er
key¦hole
Key Largo
key¦less
Key lime
Keynes, John
  May¦nard econo
  mist
Keynes¦ian
Keynes¦ian¦ism
key¦note
key¦noter
key¦pad
key¦pal
key¦punch
key¦punch¦er
key¦stone stone
Key¦stone Kops
key¦stroke
key¦way
Key West
key¦word
Kha¦ba¦rovsk
Kha¦cha¦tur¦ian,
  Aram composer
khad¦dar var. of
  khadi
khadi cloth
Kha¦kas¦sia
khaki colour; cf.
  kaki
Khaki Camp¦bell
kha¦lasi
Khali¦stan
Khal¦kha
Khalsa

Khama, Ser¦etse
  president of
  Botswana
Kham¦bat var. of
  Cambay
kham¦sin
Khan, Imran crick
  eter and politician
Khan, Ja¦han¦gir
  squash player
khan ruler; inn
khana
khan¦ate
khanga fabric; cf.
  kanga
khan¦sama
khapra
Kharg Is¦land
Khar¦kiv
Khar¦kov Russian
  name for **Kharkiv**
Khar¦toum
khat shrub; cf. **cart**,
  carte, **kart**, **quart**
kha¦yal
Khay¦yám, Omar
  poet
Kha¦zar
khazi
  kha¦zies
Khe¦dival
Khe¦dive
Khe¦div¦ial
Kher¦son
Khi¦tai var. of
  Cathay
Khmer
Khmer Rouge
Khoi var. of
  Khoikhoi
Khoi¦khoi
  pl. **Khoi¦khoi**
Khoi-khoin var. of
  Khoikhoi
Khoi¦san
Khoja
Kho¦meini,
  Aya¦tol¦lah Iranian
  leader
Khon¦su Egyptian
  god
Khor¦ram¦shahr
khoum Mauritanian
  currency; cf.

combe, cwm

Khrush¦chev,
Ni¦kita Soviet
leader

Khrush¦chev¦ian

Khufu Egyptian
name for **Cheops**

khula Islamic
divorce

Khulna

Khun¦jerab

khus-khus aromatic
root; cf. **couscous,**
cuscus

khyal var. of **khayal**

Khy¦ber

ki life force; var. of
chi

kiaat

kiang

kia ora NZ greeting

kib¦ble
    kib¦bling

kib¦butz
    kib¦butz¦im or
    kib¦butzes

kib¦butz¦nik

kibe

ki¦bitka

kib¦itz

kib¦itz¦er

kib¦lah var. of **qibla**

ki¦bosh

kick¦able

kick-and-rush

Kicka¦poo
    pl. **Kicka¦poo** or
    Kicka¦poos

kick-ass

kick¦back

kick¦ball

kick-boxer

kick-boxing

kick-down n.

kick¦er

kick-off n.

kick-pleat

kick¦shaw

kick¦sort¦er

kick¦stand

kick-start

kick-turn

kicky
    kick¦ier
    kicki¦est

kid
    kid¦ded
    kid¦ding

Kidd, Cap¦tain
    (Wil¦liam) pirate

kid¦der

Kid¦der¦min¦ster

kid¦die

kiddie¦wink

kid¦ding¦ly

kid¦dle

kid¦dush

kiddy var. of **kiddie**

kideo +s

kid¦nap
    kid¦napped
    US also **kid¦naped**
    kid¦nap¦ping
    US also
    kid¦nap¦ing
    kid¦nap¦per
    US also
    kid¦nap¦er

kid¦ney

kid¦ology

kid¦skin

kid¦stakes

kid¦ult

kid¦vid

kie¦kie

Kiel

kiel¦basa

Kielce

Kiel¦der

kier vat; cf. **Kir**

kierie

Kier¦ke¦gaard,
    Søren philosopher

Kier¦ke¦gaard¦ian

kie¦sel¦guhr

kie¦ser¦ite

Kies¦low¦ski,
    Krzysz¦tof film
    director

Kiev

kif

Ki¦gali

kike offensive

kikoi

Ki¦kongo

Ki¦kuyu

Ki¦lauea

Kil¦dare

kil¦der¦kin

kilim

Kili¦man¦jaro

Kil¦kenny

Kil¦lar¦ney

kill¦deer

kill¦er

kill file n.

kill¦file v.
    kill¦fil¦ing

kil¦lick

killi¦fish

kill¦ing¦ly

kill¦joy

Kil¦mar¦nock

kiln-dry
    kiln-dries
    kiln-dried
    kiln-drying

Kil¦ner jar
    trademark

kilo +s

kilo¦base

kilo¦bit

kilo¦byte

kilo¦cal¦orie

kilo¦cycle

kilo¦gram

kilo¦gramme Br.
    var. of **kilogram**

kilo¦hertz
    pl. **kilo¦hertz**

kilo¦joule

kilo¦liter US

kilo¦litre Br.

kilo¦meter US

kilo¦metre Br.

kilo¦met¦ric

kilo¦ton

kilo¦tonne var. of
    kiloton

kilo¦volt

kilo¦watt

kilowatt-hour

Kil¦roy mythical
    person

kil¦ter

kil¦tie

kilty var. of **kiltie**

Kim¦ber¦ley city,
    South Africa

Kim¦ber¦leys
    region, Australia

kim¦ber¦lite

Kim¦berly name

Kim¦bundu

kim¦chi

Kim Il Sung presi-
    dent of Korea

Kim Jong Il presi-
    dent of Korea

ki¦mono +s +ed

kina
    pl. **kina**
    currency of Papua
    New Guinea

Kina¦balu

kin¦aes¦the¦sia Br.
    US **kinesthesia**

kin¦aes¦thet¦ic Br.
    US **kinesthetic**

kin¦ase

Kin¦car¦dine¦shire

Kin¦chin¦junga var.
    of **Kanchenjunga**

kinda = **kind** of

kin¦der =
    kindergarten

kin¦der¦gar¦ten

kin¦der¦gar¦ten¦er

kin¦der¦gart¦ner
    US var. of
    kindergartener

Kin¦der Scout

kin¦dle
    kind¦ling

kind¦ler

kind¦li¦ness

kind¦ly
    kind¦lier
    kind¦li¦est

kind¦ness

kin¦dred

kindy
    kin¦dies

kine cows

kine¦mat¦ic

kine¦mat¦ic¦al¦ly

kine¦mat¦ics

kine¦mato¦graph

kine¦scope

kin¦es¦ics

kin¦esio¦logic¦al

kin¦esi¦olo¦gist

kin¦esi¦ology

kin|esis
kin|eses
kin|es|the|sia US
Br. kinaesthesia
kin|es|thet|ic US
Br. kinaesthetic
kin|et|ic
kin|et|ic|al|ly
kin|et|ics
kin|etin
kin|eto|chore
kin|eto|plast
kin|eto|scope
kin|folk
King, B. B. blues
musician
King, Bil|lie Jean
tennis player
**King, Mar|tin
Lu|ther** civil rights
leader
King, Ste|phen
writer
**King, Wil|liam
Lyon Mac|ken|zie**
prime minister of
Canada
king|bird
king|bolt
king|craft
king|cup
king|dom
king|fish
king|fish|er
king-hit
king-hitted
king-hitting
king|hood
king|klip
King Kong
king|less
king|let
king|like
king|li|ness
king|ly
king|lier
king|li|est
king|maker
king|pin
king post
king|ship
king|side
Kings|ley, Charles
writer

king|snake
Kings|ton in
Jamaica or Canada
**Kingston-upon-
Hull**
**Kingston-upon
Thames**
Kings|town capital
of St Vincent
kinin
kin|ka|jou
Kinki region, Japan
kink|ily
kinki|ness
kinky
kink|ier
kinki|est
kin|less
Kin|neret
kinni|kin|nic var. of
kinnikinnick
kinni|kin|nick
kinni|kin|nik var. of
kinnikinnick
kino gum
kino|rhynch
Kino|rhyncha
Kin|ross
Kinross-shire
Kin|sey, Al|fred sex
researcher
kins|folk
Kin|shasa
kin|ship
kins|man
kins|men
kins|woman
kins|women
Kin|tyre
kiosk
kip
kipped
kip|ping
sleep; animal hide
kip
pl. kip or kips
Laotian currency
kipa var. of kippa
kipah var. of kippa
Kip|ling, Rud|yard
writer
Kip|ling|esque
kippa skull cap
kip|per fish; tie

Kir trademark
drink; cf. kier
Kirbi|grip
trademark var. of
kirby grip
kirby grip
Kirch|hoff, Gus|tav
physicist
Kirch|ner, Ernst
painter
Kir|ghiz var. of
Kyrgyz
Kiri|bati
Kiri|ti|mati
kirk
Kirk|caldy
Kirk|cud|bright
Kirk|cud|bright|
shire
kirk|man
kirk|men
Kir|kuk
Kirk|wall
kirk|yard
Kir|lian
Kir|man
Kirov
Ki|rova|bad
kir|pan
kirsch
kirsch|was|ser
Kir|sten
Kir|stie
kir|tan
kir|tle
Ki|runa
Ki|rundi
Ki|san|gani
kish
Kishi|nyov
kishke
kis|ka|dee
Kis|lev Jewish
month
Kis|lew var. of
Kislev
kis|met
kiss|able
kiss-ass
kiss-curl
kis|sel
kiss|er

Kis|sin|ger, Henry
diplomat
kiss-off n.
kisso|gram
kissy
kissy-face
kist coffin, burial
chamber; var. of
cist
Ki|swa|hili
kit
kit|ted
kit|ting
kitab
kit|bag
kit-cat portrait
Kit-Cat Club
kit|chen
kit|chen|alia
kitchen-diner
Kit|chener city,
Canada
**Kit|chener,
Her|bert** British
soldier
kit|chen|er cooking
range
kit|chen|ette
kit|chen|ware
kite
kit|ing
kite|board|er
kite|board|ing
Kite|mark
trademark
ki|tenge
kite|surf|er
kite|surf|ing
kith
kitsch
kitschi|ness
kitschy
kitsch|ier
kitschi|est
kit|ten
kit|ten|ish
kit|ten|ish|ly
kitti|wake
kit|tle
kittle-cattle
kitty
kit|ties
kitty-corner var. of
cater-cornered

Kitty Hawk
Kitwe
Kitz|bühel
kiva
Kivu, Lake
Ki|wan|ian
Ki|wa|nis
Kiwi New Zealander
kiwi bird; fruit
Kla|gen|furt
Klai|peda
Klan Ku Klux Klan
Klans|man
Klans|men
Klans|woman
Klans|women
klatch
klatsch var. of
klatch
klaxon *trademark*
kleb|si|ella
Klebs-Löffler
Klee, Paul *painter*
Klee|nex *trademark*
pl. Klee|nex or
Klee|nexes
Klein, Cal|vin
fashion designer
Klein, Mel|anie
psychoanalyst
Klein bot|tle cf.
cline
Klem|perer, Otto
conductor
klepht Greek
fighter; cf. cleft
klept|oc|racy
klept|oc|ra|cies
klep|to|crat
klep|to|crat|ic
klep|to|mania
klep|to|maniac
klep|to|para|site
klep|to|para|sit|ic
klep|to|para|sit|
ism
Klerk, F. W. de
president of South
Africa
Klerks|dorp
klez|mer
klez|mor|im
klick kilometre; cf.
click, clique

klieg
klik var. of klick
Klimt, Gus|tav
painter
Kline|fel|ter's
syn|drome
Kling|on
klip|fish
klip|spring|er
Klon|dike
klong
kloof
Klos|ters
kludge
kludg|ing
klutz
klutzi|ness
klutzy
klutz|ier
klutzi|est
Klux|er
klys|tron
K-meson
knack
knacker
knack|wurst
knag stump of
branch; cf. nag
knai|del
knai|dels or
knaid|lach
knap
knapped
knap|ping
shape stones; crest
of hill; cf. nap,
nappe
knap|per stone
shaper; cf. nappa,
napper
knap|sack
knap|weed
knar projection on
tree
knave rogue; cf.
nave
knav|ery
knav|er|ies
knav|ish
knav|ish|ly
knav|ish|ness
kna|wel plant
knead work dough
knead|able

knead|er
knee
knee|board
knee|board|er
knee|board|ing
knee|cap
knee|capped
knee|cap|ping
knee|hole
knee-jerk
kneel
knelt or kneeled
kneel|er
knee-slapper
knee-slapping
knees-up
knee-trembler
knei|del var. of
knaidel
knell
knelt
Knes|set
knew past tense of
know; cf. new, nu
knicker *mod.*; cf.
nicker
Knick|er|bocker
New Yorker; K.
Glory
knick|er|bock|ered
knick|er|bock|ers
garment
knick|ered
knicker|less
knick|ers
knick-knack
knick-knackery
knick-knacker|ies
knick point
knicks = knickers
knife
pl. knives
v. knifes
knifed
knif|ing
knife-edge
knife|fish
knife-like
knife|man
knife|men
knife|point
knifer
knight person; cf.
night, nite

knight er|rant
knights er|rant
knight-errant|ry
knight|hood
Knight
Hos|pit|al|ler
Knights
Hos|pit|al|ler
knight|like
knight|li|ness
knight|ly
knight|lier
knight|li|est
cf. nightly
knight mar|shal
knights mar|shal
Knights|bridge
Knight Temp|lar
Knights Temp|lar
kni|pho|fia
knish
knit
knit|ted
knit|ting
make with yarn
and needles; cf. nit
knit|bone
knit|ter
knit|wear
knives
knob
knobbed
knob|bing
handle; cf. nob
knob|ble small
knob; cf. nobble
knob|bly
knob|blier
knob|bli|est
knobby
knob|bier
knob|bi|est
knob|ker|rie
knob|kerrie|ing
knob|kierie var. of
knobkerrie
knob-like
knob|stick
knock cf. nock
knock|about
knock-back *n.*
knock-down *adj. &*
n.
knock-down-drag-
out *n.*

knock|er
knocker-up
  knockers-up
knock-kneed
knock knees
knock-off *n.*
knock-on *n. &*
  mod.
knock|out
knock-up *n.*
knock|wurst var. of
  knackwurst
Knole sofa
knoll
knop
knop|per
Knos|sos
knot
  knot|ted
  knot|ting
knot|grass
knot|hole
knot|less
knot|ter
knot|tily
knot|ti|ness
knotty
  knot|tier
  knot|ti|est
knot|weed
knot|work
knout whip; cf.
  nowt
know
  knew
  known
know|able
know-all
know|bot
  trademark
know|er
know-how
know|ing|ly
know|ing|ness
know-it-all
know|ledg|abil|ity
  var. of
  knowledgeability
know|ledg|able var.
  of knowledgeable
know|ledg|ably var.
  of knowledgeably
know|ledge
know|ledge|abil|ity
know|ledge|able

know|ledge|ably
know-nothing
know-nothing|ism
Knox, John Prot-
  estant reformer
Knox, Ron|ald
  theologian
Knox|ville
knuckle
  knuck|ling
knuckle|ball
knuckle|ball|er
knuckle|dust|er
knuckle|head
knuckle|headed
knuckly
knur
knurl
Knut var. of Cnut
KO
  KO's
  KO'd
  KO'ing
koa
koala
koan
kob
  pl. kob
  antelope; fish;
  cf. cob
Kobe port, Japan
kobo
  pl. kobo
ko|bold
Koch, Rob|ert bac-
  teriologist
Kö|chel
kochia
KO'd = knocked out
Ko|dály, Zol|tán
  composer
Ko|diak
koek|sister
koel bird
koe|sister var. of
  koeksister
Koest|ler, Ar|thur
  writer
kofta
koft|gari
ko|hanga reo +s
kohen
  ko|han|im
Ko|hima
Koh-i-noor

Kohl, Hel|mut
  chancellor of
  Germany
kohl powder; cf.
  coal, cole
kohl|rabi
  kohl|rabies
koi
  pl. koi
  carp; cf. coy
koine
koi|no|nia
ko|kako +s
ko|ka|nee
Ko|koschka, Oskar
  artist
koko|wai
kola tree var. of cola
Kola Pen|in|sula
Kol|ha|pur
kol|in|sky
  kol|in|skies
Kol|kata
  kol|khoz
  kol|khozes or
  kol|khozy
Kol Nidre
kolo +s
Kolyma
ko|mati|ite
ko|mati|it|ic
koma|tik
Ko|modo
Kom|on|dor
Kom|pong Cham
Kom|pong Som
Kom|so|mol
Kom|so|molsk
Kon|dra|tiev
kon|eke
Kongo
  pl. Kongo or
  Kon|gos
  people; language;
  cf. Congo
kon|goni
kon|im|eter
Kon|kani
Kon-Tiki
Konya
kook crazy person
kooka|burra
kook|ily
kooki|ness

kooky
kook|ier
kooki|est
Koon|ing, Wil|lem
  de painter
Koori
Kop soccer stand;
  cf. cop
kop hill; cf. cop
ko|peck var. of
  copeck
kopek var. of
  copeck
ko|piyka
kopje var. of koppie
kop|pie small hill
kora musical
  instrument; cf.
  Cora, corer
kor|adji
Koran
Ko|ran|ic
Kor|but, Olga gym-
  nast
Korch|noi, Vik|tor
  chess player
Korda, Alex|an|der
  film producer and
  director
Kor|do|fan
kore
  korai
  Greek statue
Korea
Ko|rean
kor|ero +s
korf|ball
kor|haan
kori bustard
korma
Kor|sa|koff's
  psych|osis
Kor|sa|koff's
  syn|drome
Kort|rijk
koru
kor|una Czech or
  Slovak currency
Korup national
  park, Cameroon
Kor|yak
Kos Greek island; cf.
  cos
Kos|ciusko,
  Thad|deus Polish

patriot; Mount K.
ko¦sher
Ko¦šice
Kos|ovan
Kos|ovar
Kos|ovo
Kos|suth, Lajos
Hungarian patriot
Ko¦sy|gin, Alek¦sei
Soviet leader
Kota city, India
Kota Ba¦haru
Kota Kina|balu
Kotka port, Finland
koto +s
kot¦wal
kot|wali
Kotze|bue, Au¦gust
von dramatist
kou|miss
kou|prey
kour|bash var. of
kurbash
kou¦ros
kou¦roi
Kou¦rou
kow¦hai
Kow|loon
kow¦tow
kow|tow¦er
kraal
Krafft-Ebing,
Rich|ard von
physician and
psychologist
kraft paper cf.
craft
Kra¦gu|jevac
krai Russian admin-
istrative territory
Kra Isth|mus
krait
Kraka|toa
kra¦ken
Kra¦ków
Kras¦no|dar
Kras¦no|yarsk
Kraut offensive
Kraut|rock
Kraut|rock¦er
Krav Maga
kray var. of krai
Krebs cycle

kreef
Kre|feld
Kreis|ler, Fritz vio-
linist
Krem¦en|chuk
Krem|lin Russian
government
krem|lin citadel
Krem¦lin|olo¦gist
Krem|lin|ology
krep|lach
krieg|spiel
Kriem|hild
Germanic
Mythology
krill
pl. krill
krim|mer
Krio
kris
Krishna Hindu
god; River
Krishna|ism
Krish|na|murti,
Jiddu spiritual
leader
Kris|tall|nacht
Kris¦ti|ania var. of
Christiania
Kris¦tian|sand
kro|mesky
kro|mes¦kies
krona
kro¦nor
Swedish currency
krona
kro¦nur
Icelandic currency
krone
kro¦ner
Danish or Norwe-
gian currency
Kro¦nos var. of
Cronus
kroon
kroons or krooni
Estonian currency;
cf. croon
Kro|pot|kin, Prince
Peter anarchist
Kroto, Harry
chemist
Kru
pl. Kru
people; language;
Coast

Kru¦ger, Paul South
African soldier and
statesman
kru|ger|rand
krumm|holz
krumm|horn
Krupp, Al¦fred
arms manufacturer
kryp|ton
kryp|ton|ite
kry|tron
Kshat|riya
K/T bound|ary
K2 mountain
Kuala Lum¦pur
Kuala
Te¦reng|ganu var.
of Kuala
Trengganu
Kuala Treng|ganu
Kuan|tan
Kuan Yin Chinese
Buddhist goddess
Ku-band
Ku¦blai Khan
emperor of China
Ku|brick, Stan|ley
film director
kuccha
ku¦chen
pl. ku¦chen
Ku|ching
kudos
kudu
kudzu
Kufic
kugel
Kui¦per belt region
of solar system; cf.
Keuper
Ku Klux¦er
Ku Klux Klan
Ku Klux
Klans|man
Ku Klux
Klans|men
kukri
kuku NZ pigeon; cf.
cuckoo
kula
kulak
kulan
kulcha
kulfi
kul|tarr

Kul¦tur
Kul¦tur|kampf
Kum var. of Qom
ku¦mara
pl. ku¦mara
Kumbh Mela
Ku¦mina
kumis var. of
koumiss
ku¦miss var. of
koumiss
ku¦mite
kum¦kum
küm¦mel
kum|quat
Kuna
kuna
kune
Croatian currency
kun¦da|lini
Kun¦dera, Milan
novelist
Kung people
pl. Kung
kung fu
Kun¦lun Shan
kun|zite
Kuo|min|tang
Kuo¦pio
Kupf|fer cell
kur|bash
kur¦cha|tov¦ium
Kurd
kur|dai¦tcha var. of
kadaitcha
Kurd|ish
Kur¦di|stan
Kur¦gan city, Rus-
sia; people
kur¦gan burial
mound
kuri dog
Kuril var. of Kurile
Ku¦rile Is|lands
Kuro|sawa, Akira
film director
Kuro|shio
kurra|jong
kur|saal
Kursk
kurta
kur¦tha var. of
kurta
kur|tosis

kuru disease
kurus
  pl. **kurus**
  Turkish currency
  Turkish **kuruş**
Kuşa|dasi
Kushan
kusi|manse var. of
  cusimanse
kusti
Kuta|isi
Ku|tani
Kutch, Gulf of
Kutch, Rann of
Ku|wait
Ku|waiti
Kuz|nets Basin
Kuz|netsk var. of
  Kuznets
kvass
kvell
kvetch
Kwa language
kwa|cha
kwaito
Kwa|kiutl
Kwa|Nde|bele
Kwang|chow var. of
  Guangzhou
Kwangju
Kwangsi Chuang
  var. of **Guangxi**
  Zhuang
Kwang|tung var. of
  Guangdong
kwanza
  pl. **kwanza** or
  kwan|zas
Kwan|zaa
kwashi|or|kor
Kwa|Zulu
KwaZulu-Natal
kwela
KWIC = keyword in
  context
kyan|ise *Br.* var. of
  kyanize
kyan|ite
kyan|it|ic
kyan|ize
  kyan|iz|ing
kyat
  pl. **kyat** or **kyats**
  Burmese currency

ky|bosh var. of
  kibosh
Kyd, Thomas
  dramatist
kyle
kylie
kylin
kylix
  ky|likes or **ky|lixes**
kyloe
kymo|graph
kymo|graph|ic
Kyoto
kype
ky|phosis
  ky|phoses
ky|phot|ic
Ky|re|nia
Kyr|gyz
  pl. **Kyr|gyz**
Kyr|gyz|stan
Kyrie elei|son
kyte
kyu
kyudo
Kyu|shu
Kyzyl
Kyzyl Kum

L

la *Music*; var. of **lah**
laa|ger encamp-
  ment; cf. **lager**
Laa|youne var. of
  La'youn
Laban, Ru|dolf von
  choreographer
lab|arum
lab|da|num var. of
  ladanum
labe|fac|tion
label
  la|belled *Br.*
  la|beled *US*
  la|bel|ling *Br.*
  la|bel|ing *US*
  la|bel|er *US*
  la|bel|ler *Br.*
  la|bel|lum
  la|bella

labia
la|bial
la|bial|ise *Br.* var. of
  labialize
la|bial|ize
  la|bial|iz|ing
la|bi|al|ly
labia ma|jora
labia mi|nora
la|bi|ate
la|bile
la|bil|ity
la|bio|den|tal
la|bio|velar
la|bium
  labia
lab|lab
labor *US*
  Br. **labour**
la|bora|tory
  la|bora|tor|ies
la|bor|er *US*
  Br. **labourer**
la|bori|ous
  la|bori|ous|ly
  la|bori|ous|ness
labor|ism *US*
  Br. **labourism**
labor|ist
  Br. **labourist**
La|bor|ite *US*
  Br. **Labourite**
la|bour *Br.*
  US **labor**
la|bour|er *Br.*
  US **laborer**
la|bour|ism *Br.*
  US **laborism**
la|bour|ist
  US **laborist**
La|bour|ite *Br.*
  US **Laborite**
labra
labra|doodle
Lab|ra|dor
lab|ra|dor|es|cence
lab|ra|dor|es|cent
lab|ra|dor|ite
la|bral
la|bret
lab|rish
la|brum
  labra
La|brusca

La Bru|yère, Jean
  de moralist
La|buan
la|bur|num
laby|rinth
laby|rin|thian
laby|rin|thine
laby|rinth|itis
laby|rinth|odont
lac resin; insect; cf.
  lack, lakh
Lacan, Jacques
  psychoanalyst
La|can|ian
La|can|ian|ism
Lac|ca|dive
lac|case
lac|co|lith
lace
  la|cing
lace|bark
lace|cap
Lace|dae|mon|ian
La Ceiba
lace|maker
lace|mak|ing
la|cer|able
la|cer|ate
  la|cer|at|ing
la|cer|ation
La|certa
la|cer|tid
La|cer|tilia
la|cer|til|ian
lace-up *adj. & n.*
lace|wing
lace|wood
lace|work
lacey var. of **lacy**
la|ches
La|che|sis *Greek*
  Mythology
Lach|lan
lach|ryma Christi
lach|ry|mal
lach|ry|ma|tion
lach|ry|ma|tor
lach|ry|ma|tory
  lach|ry|ma|tor|ies
lach|ry|mose
lach|ry|mose|ly
lach|ry|mos|ity
laci|ly
laci|ness

la¦cini¦ate
la¦cini¦ated
la¦cini¦ation
lack want; cf. lac,
lakh
lacka|dai|si|cal
lacka|dai|si|cal¦ly
lack|aday
lackey
Lack|land, John
son of Henry II of
England
lack|lus¦ter US
lack|lustre Br.
La¦clos, Pierre
Cho|der|los de
novelist
La¦co|nia
La¦co|nian
la|con|ic
la|con|ic|al¦ly
la|con|icism
la|con|icum
la|con|ica
lac|on|ism
La Co|ruña
lac¦quer
lac¦quer¦er
lac¦quer¦ware
lac¦quer¦work
lac¦ri¦mal var. (esp.
in *Anatomy*) of
lachrymal
lac¦ri¦ma¦tion var.
of lachrymation
lac¦ri¦ma¦tor var. of
lachrymator
lac¦ri¦ma¦tory
lac¦ri¦ma¦tor¦ies
var. of
lachrymatory
la|crosse
lac¦ry¦mal var. of
lachrymal
lac¦ry¦ma¦tion var.
of lachrymation
lact|al¦bu|min
lac¦tam
lac¦tase
lac¦tate
lac¦tat¦ing
lac¦ta¦tion
lac¦ta¦tion|al
lac¦teal

lac¦tes¦cence
lac¦tes¦cent
lac¦tic
lac¦tif¦er¦ous
lacto|ba|cil|lus
lacto|ba|cilli
lacto|fer¦rin
lacto|fla¦vin
lacto|gen¦ic
lacto|globu¦lin
lac|tom¦eter
lac|tone
lacto-ovo-
  vegetar¦ian
lacto|pro¦tein
lacto|scope
lac¦tose
lacto|suria
lacto-vegetar¦ian
lac¦tu|lose
la¦cuna
la¦cu|nae or
  la¦cu|nas
la¦cu|nal
la¦cu|nar
la¦cu|nary
la¦cu|nate
la¦cu|nose
la¦cus|trine
lacy
laci¦er
laci¦est
La¦dakh
La|da¦khi
lada|num plant
resin; cf. laudanum
lad¦der
ladder-back
ladder|tron
lad¦die
lad|dish
lad|dish|ness
laddu
lade
lad¦ing
load; cf. laid
lad|ette
la-di-da
la¦dies
la¦dies' chain
Dancing
la¦dies' fin|gers
okra; cf. ladyfinger,

lady's finger
la¦dies' man
la¦dies' night
la¦dies' room
la¦dies' tresses
  plant *US*
  Br. lady's tresses
la¦dify var. of ladyfy
Ladin
La¦dino +s dialect;
person
la¦dino +s plant
La¦dis|laus, St king
of Hungary
La¦dis|laus king of
Poland
ladle
lad¦ling
ladle|ful
ladler
La¦doga
ladoo var. of laddu
lad's love plant
lady
la¦dies
lady|bird
lady|boy
lady|bug
lady|fin¦ger *US*
  cake
  Br. lady's finger; cf.
  ladies' fingers
lady|fish
lady|fy
lady|fies
lady|fied
lady|fy|ing
lady|hood
lady-in-waiting
ladies-in-waiting
lady|kill¦er
lady|like
lady|like|ness
lady-love
lady's bed|straw
lady's com|pan|ion
lady's fin|ger vetch;
cf. ladies' fingers
lady's fin|ger *Br.*
sponge cake.
US ladyfinger
lady|ship
lady's maid

lady's man var. of
ladies' man
lady's man¦tle
Lady|smith
lady's slip|per plant
lady's smock plant
lady's tresses plant
  Br.
  US ladies' tresses
Laen|nec's cirrhosis
Lae|ti¦tia
Lae|trile *trademark*
laevo|rota¦tion *Br.*
  US levorotation
laevo|rota¦tory *Br.*
  US levorotatory
lae¦vu|lose *Br.*
  US levulose
La|fay¦ette,
Mar|quis de
French soldier
Laf¦fer curve
La Fon|taine, Jean
de poet
lag
lagged
lag|ging
lagan
lagar
la|gares
Lag b'Omer
la¦gena
la|ge¦nae
la|ge¦nar
lager beer; cf.
laager
La¦ger|löf, Selma
novelist
lag|gard
lag|gard¦ly
lag|gard|ness
lag|ger
La Gio|conda
la¦gniappe
lago|morph
Lago|morpha
la|goon
la|goon¦al
Lagos
La|grange, Jo¦seph
Louis, Comte de
mathematician
La¦gran|gian
lah *Music;* cf. lar

lahar
lah-di-dah var. of
la-di-da
Lahnda
La¦hore
Lahu
laic
laic¦al¦ly
lai¦cisa¦tion Br. var.
of laicization
lai¦cise Br. var. of
laicize
lai¦cism
lai¦city
lai¦ciza¦tion
lai¦cize
lai¦ciz¦ing
laid past tense and
past participle of
lay; paper; cf. lade
lain past participle
of lie; cf. lane
Laing, R. D.
psychoanalyst
lair animal's den; cf.
layer
lair¦age
laird
laird¦ship
lairy
lair¦ier
lairi¦est
laissez-aller
laissez-faire
laissez-faireism
laissez-passer
lais¦sez vi¦brer
laity
la¦ities
Laius Greek
Mythology
Lake¦land = Lake
District etc.
lake¦less
lake¦let
laker
lake¦side
lakh hundred
thousand; cf. lac,
lack
La¦ko¦nia var. of
Laconia
La¦kota
laksa

Lak¦shad¦weep
Lak¦shmi Hinduism
La¦lage
la-la land
lala¦pa¦looza var. of
lollapalooza
laldy
La¦lique, René jew-
eller
Lal¦lan
Lal¦lans
lal¦la¦tion
lally¦gag var. of
lollygag
Lalo, Édouard
composer
La Lou¦vière
lam
  lammed
lam¦ming
  hit; escape; cf.
  lamb
lama monk; cf.
  llama
Lama¦ism
Lama¦ist
La¦marck, Jean
  Bap¦tiste de natur-
  alist
La¦marck¦ian
La¦marck¦ism
La¦mar¦tine,
  Al¦phonse de poet
la¦ma¦sery
la¦ma¦ser¦ies
La¦maze
Lamb, Charles and
  Mary writers
lamb young sheep;
  cf. lam
lam¦bada
lam¦bast var. of
  lambaste
lam¦baste
  lam¦bast¦ing
lambda
lambd¦oid
lambd¦oid¦al
lam¦bency
  lam¦ben¦cies
lam¦bent
lam¦bent¦ly
lamb¦er

Lam¦bert,
Con¦stant
  composer
lam¦bert
lamb¦kin
lamb¦like
lamb¦bre¦quin
Lam¦brusco +s
lamb's ears plant
lamb's fry
lamb¦skin
lamb's let¦tuce
lamb's quar¦ter
lamb's-tails catkins
lamb's tongue
  plant
lambs¦wool
lame
  lam¦ing
  lamer
  lam¦est
lamé
lame¦brain
la¦mella n.
  la¦mel¦lae
la¦mel¦lar adj.
la¦mel¦late
la¦melli¦branch +s
la¦melli¦
      bran¦chi¦ate
la¦melli¦corn
la¦melli¦form
la¦melli¦podial
la¦melli¦podium
  la¦melli¦podia
la¦mel¦lose
lame¦ly
lame¦ness
la¦ment
lam¦ent¦able
lam¦ent¦ably
lam¦en¦ta¦tion
la¦ment¦er
lamia
  la¦miae or la¦mias
lam¦ina n.
  lam¦inae
lamin¦able
lam¦inal
lam¦inar adj.
lamin¦ate
  lamin¦at¦ing
lamin¦ation

lamin¦ator
lamin¦ec¦tomy
  lamin¦ec¦to¦mies
lam¦ing¦ton
lam¦inin
lamin¦itis
lamin¦ose
lam¦ish
la¦mium
Lam¦mas
lam¦mer¦geier
lam¦mer¦geyer var.
  of lammergeier
lam¦pas
lamp¦black
Lam¦pe¦dusa,
  Giu¦seppe di
  novelist
lamp¦er
lam¦pern
lamp¦hold¦er
lamp¦less
lamp¦light
lamp¦light¦er
lamp¦lit
lam¦poon
lam¦poon¦er
lam¦poon¦ery
  lam¦poon¦er¦ies
lam¦poon¦ist
lam¦prey
lampro¦phyre
lamp¦shade
LAN = local area
  network
lanai porch
Lan¦ark¦shire
Lan¦ca¦shire
Lan¦cas¦ter
Lan¦cas¦ter, Burt
  actor
Lan¦cas¦trian
lance
  lan¦cing
  weapon; pipe;
  pierce; cut open; cf.
  launce
lance¦jack
lance¦let
Lance¦lot Arthurian
  knight
lan¦ceo¦late
lan¦cer

lan|cet
lancet|fish
lance|wood
Lan|chow var. of
Lanzhou
Lan|cing in Eng-
land; College; cf.
Lansing
Lancs. = Lancashire
Land
Län|der
a state of Germany
or Austria
land dry land etc.
Lan|dau, Lev physi-
cist
lan|dau
lan|dau|let
land|er
Landes department,
France
land|fall
land|fill
land|form
land-grab
land-grabber
land-grabbing
land|grave
land|hold|er
land|hold|ing
land|ing
land|lady
land|ladies
Länd|ler
land|less
land|less|ness
land|line
land|locked
land|lord
land|lord|ism
land|lub|ber
land|mark
land|mine
Lan|dor, Wal|ter
Sav|age writer
land|owner
land|owner|ship
land|owning
land|plane
land|race
land|rail
Land|sat

land|scape
land|scap|ing
land|scaper
land|scap|ist
Land|seer, Edwin
painter
Land's End
Lands|hut
land|side
lands|knecht
land|slide
land|slip
Lands|mål
lands|man
lands|men
Land|steiner, Karl
physician
land|tie
land|ward
land|wards
lane track etc.; cf.
lain
Lang, Fritz film
director
lan|gar kitchen;
meal; cf. languor,
langur
Lang|land,
Wil|liam poet
lang|lauf
Lang|ley, Sam|uel
Pier|point astron-
omer and aviation
pioneer
lan|gosta var. of
langouste
lan|gouste
lan|gous|tine
lan|gra
lang syne
Lang|ton, Ste|phen
archbishop of
Canterbury
Lang|try, Lil|lie
actress
lan|guage
langue
langued *Heraldry*
langue de chat
langues de chat
Langue|doc prov-
ince
langue d'oc lan-
guage

Languedoc-
Roussil|lon
langue d'oïl
lan|guid
lan|guid|ly
lan|guid|ness
lan|guish
lan|guish|er
lan|guish|ment
lan|guor idleness;
cf. langar, langur
lan|guor|ous
lan|guor|ous|ly
lan|gur monkey; cf.
langar, languor
lan|iard var. of
lanyard
La Niña cooling of
water; cf. El Niño
lank
lank|ily
lanki|ness
lank|ly
lank|ness
lanky
lank|ier
lank|iest
lan|ner
lan|neret
lan|olin
Lan|sing city, US;
cf. Lancing
lans|que|net
lan|tana
Lan|tau
lan|tern
lantern|fish
lan|than|ide
lan|than|oid
lan|thanum
la|nugo
lan|yard
Lan|zar|ote
Lan|zhou
Lao
pl. Lao or Laos
Laoc|oon *Greek*
Mythology
Lao|di|cean
lao|gai
Laoighis var. of
Laois
Laois Irish county

Laos Asian country
Lao|tian
Lao-tzu traditional
founder of Taoism
Laoze var. of Lao-
tzu
lap
lapped
lap|ping
lapa courtyard
La Palma one of
the Canary Islands;
cf. Las Palmas
lap|aro|scope
lap|aro|scop|ic
lap|aro|scop|ic|al|ly
lapar|os|copy
lapar|os|co|pies
lapar|ot|omy
lapar|oto|mies
La Paz
lap|dog
lapel
la|pelled
US also la|peled
lap|ful
lapi|dary
lapi|dar|ies
la|pilli
lapis laz|uli
La|pita
Lap|ith *Greek*
Mythology
La|place, Pierre,
Mar|quis de
mathematician
and physicist
Lap|land
Lap|land|er
La Plata
Lapp
lap|pet
Lapp|ish
lap|sang sou|chong
lapse
laps|ing
lap|stone
lap|strake
lap|sus ca|lami
pl. lap|sus ca|lami
lap|sus lin|guae
pl. lap|sus lin|guae
Lap|tev Sea
lap|top

lap|wing
lar gibbon; cf. **lah**
Lara, Brian
cricketer
Lara|mie
lar|board
lar|cen|er
lar|cen|ist
lar|cen|ous
lar|ceny
lar|cenies
larch
lard|ass
lar|der
lar|don
lar|doon var. of
lardon
lardy
lard|ier
lardi|est
lares Roman gods
Lar|gac|til
trademark
large
lar|ging
lar|ger
lar|gest
large|ly
large|mouth fish
large|ness
lar|gess var. of
largesse
lar|gesse
lar|ghet|to +s
lar|gish
largo +s
lari
pl. lari or laris
currency of Georgia
or the Maldives
Lar|iam *trademark*
lar|iat
La Rioja
La|ris|sa
Lar|kin, Philip poet
lar|ki|ness
lark|spur
larky
La
Roche|fou|cauld,
Fran|çois de
Mar|sil|lac, Duc de
writer
La Ro|chelle

La|rousse, Pierre
lexicographer
lar|ri|kin
lar|rup
Larry
larva
lar|vae
form of insect; cf.
lava
Larv|acea
larv|acean
lar|val
larvi|cide
Lar|wood, Har|old
cricketer
la|ryn|geal
la|ryn|ges
laryn|git|ic
laryn|gi|tis
laryn|golo|gist
laryn|gol|ogy
la|ryn|go|scope
laryn|gos|copy
laryn|gos|co|pies
laryn|got|omy
laryn|goto|mies
lar|ynx
la|ryn|ges
la|sagne
La Salle, Rob|ert
explorer
La Scala
Las|car
Las|caux
las|civi|ous
las|civi|ous|ly
las|civi|ous|ness
lase
las|ing
laser
laser|disc
Laser|Vision
trademark
lash|er
lash|less
lash-up *n.*
Las Pal|mas capital
of the Canary
Islands; cf. La
Palma
La Spe|zia
lasque
Lassa fever
lassi drink

las|sie girl
las|si|tude
lasso
pl. las|sos or
las|soes
v. las|soes
las|soed
lasso|ing
las|so|er
Las|sus, Or|lande
de composer
last|ing|ly
last|ing|ness
last|ly
Las Vegas
lat
pl. lati or lats
Latvian currency
lat muscle
La|ta|kia
latch
latchet
latch|key
late
later
lat|est
late|comer
la|teen
late|ish var. of
latish
late|ly
la|tency
la|ten|cies
La Tène
late|ness
la|tent
la|tent|ly
lat|eral
lat|eral|isa|tion *Br.*
var. of
lateralization
lat|eral|ise *Br.* var.
of lateralize
lat|eral|ity
lat|eral|iza|tion
lat|eral|ize
lat|eral|iz|ing
lat|eral|ly
Lat|eran
lat|er|ite
lat|er|it|ic
latex
la|texes or la|ti|ces
lath thin strip

lathe
lath|ing
machine
la|ther
la|thery
lathi stick
lath|yr|ism
la|tici|fer
lati|cif|er|ous
lati|fun|dium
lati|fun|dia
Lati|mer, Hugh
martyr
Latin
La|tina
Lat|in|ate
Lat|in|isa|tion *Br.*
var. of Latinization
Lat|in|ise *Br.* var. of
Latinize
Lat|in|iser *Br.* var.
of Latinizer
Lat|in|ism
Lat|in|ist
Lat|in|ity
Lat|in|iza|tion
Lat|in|ize
Lat|in|iz|ing
Lat|in|izer
La|tino +s
lat|ish
la|tis|si|mus dorsi
la|tis|simi dorsi
lati|tude
lati|tu|din|al
lati|tu|din|al|ly
lati|tu|din|ar|ian
lati|tu|din|ar|ian|
ism
La|tium
latke
La|tona *Roman
Mythology*
La Tour, Georges
de painter
la|tria
la|trine
latte coffee
lat|ten
lat|ter
latter-day
lat|ter|ly

lat|tice
  lat|ti|cing
lattice|work
latti|cinio
latti|cino var. of
  latti|cinio
Lat|via
Lat|vian
Laud, Wil|liam
  archbishop of
  Canterbury
laud praise; cf. lord
Lauda, Niki racing
  driver
laud|abil|ity
laud|able
laud|ably
laud|anum drug; cf.
  ladanum
laud|ation
laud|atory
Lau|der, Harry
  comedian
lauds prayers; cf.
  lords
laugh
laugh|able
laugh|ably
laugh|er
laugh|ing|ly
laughing-thrush
laugh|ter
Laugh|ton, Charles
  actor
launce fish; cf.
  lance
Launce|lot Arthur-
  ian knight; var. of
  Lancelot
Laun|ces|ton
launch
launch|er
laun|der
laun|der|er
laun|der|ette
laun|dress
laun|drette var. of
  launderette
laun|dro|mat
  trademark in the
  US
laun|dry
  laun|dries

laun|dry|man
laun|dry|men
Laur|asia
Laur|asian
laure|ate
laure|ate|ship
laurel
  laur|elled Br.
  laur|eled US
  laurel|ling Br.
  laurel|ing US
Laurel and Hardy
  comedians
Lau|ren
Laur|ence,
  Mar|ga|ret novelist
Laur|en|tian
Laur|en|tius
  Latin name of St
  Lawrence
Lau|rie
Laur|ier, Wil|frid
  prime minister of
  Canada
lau|rus|ti|nus
Lau|sanne
LAUTRO = Life
  Assurance and Unit
  Trust Regulatory
  Organization
lava volcanic rock;
  cf. larva, laver
la|vabo +s
lava|tera
lav|ation
lava|tor|ial
lav|atory
  lav|ator|ies
lave
  lav|ing
lav|en|der
Laver, Rod tennis
  player
laver seaweed;
  bread; basin; cf.
  lava, larva
La|vin|ia
lav|ish
lav|ish|ly
lav|ish|ness
La|vois|ier,
  An|toine scientist
Law, Bonar prime
  minister of Britain

law cf. lor. lore
law|break|er
law|break|ing
law|ful
law|ful|ly
law|ful|ness
law|giver
lawks
law|less
law|less|ly
law|less|ness
law|maker
law-making
law|man
  law|men
lawn grass; linen; cf.
  lorn
lawn|mow|er
lawny
Law|rence, St
Law|rence, D. H.
  writer
Law|rence, Er|nest
  physicist
Law|rence, Thomas
  painter
Law|rence, T. E. 'of
  Arabia'
law|ren|cium
Law|son's cy|press
law|suit
law|yer
law|yer|ly
lax
laxa|tive
lax|ity
lax|ities
laxly
lax|ness
lay
  laid
  cf. lei, ley
lay|about
Laya|mon poet and
  priest
lay|away
lay|back
lay-by +s n.
layer person or
  thing that lays;
  thickness; cf. lair
layer-out
lay|ette

lay|man
  lay|men
lay-off n.
La'youn
lay|out
lay|over
lay|per|son
  lay|per|sons or
  lay|people
lay|shaft
lay-up n.
lay|woman
  lay|women
lazar
laza|ret
lazar|ette
lazar|etto +s
Laz|ar|ist
laze
  laz|ing
lazi|ly
lazi|ness
Lazio
laz|ull
laz|ur|ite
lazy
  lazi|er
  lazi|est
lazy|bones
  pl. lazy|bones
lazy Susan
l-dopa
L-driver
lea meadow; cf. lee,
  ley, li
Leach, Ber|nard
  potter
leach percolate; cf.
  leech
leach|ate
Lea|cock, Ste|phen
  humorist and
  economist
lead
  lead|ed
  metal; cf. led
lead
  led
  guide; cf. lead, lied
Lead|beater's
  pos|sum
lead|en
lead|er
  person who leads;

cf. lieder
lead¦er¦ene
lead¦er|less
lead¦er|ship
lead-in n.
lead-off adj. & adv.
lead-up n.
lead|work
lead|wort
leaf on tree; paper;
etc.; cf. lief
  pl. leaves
  v. leafs
leaf|age
leaf|bird
leaf|cut¦ter
leaf-fall
leaf|hop¦per
leafi|ness
leaf|less
leaf|let
leaf-like
leaf|love
leafy
  leaf|ier
  leafi|est
league
lea¦guing
lea¦guer
leak escape of liquid
etc.; cf. leek
leak|age
leak¦er
Lea¦key, Louis,
  Mary, and
  Rich¦ard
  anthropologists
leaki|ness
leak|proof
leaky
  leak|ier
  leaki|est
Leam¦ing|ton
Lean, David film
  director
lean
  leaned
  Br. also leant
slope; thin; cf. lien
lean-burn
Le|an¦der Greek
  Mythology
lean¦ly
Le¦anne

lean|ness
leant
  Br. var. of leaned
lean-to +s
leap
  leaped
  Br. also leapt
leap¦er
leap|frog
  leap|frogged
  leap|frog|ging
Lear, Ed¦ward artist
  and poet
Lear, King Shake-
  spearean character
learn
  learned
  Br. also learnt
learn|abil¦ity
learn|able
learn¦ed knowledge-
  able
learn|ed¦ly
learn|ed|ness
learn¦er
learn|fare
learnt v.
  Br. var. of learned
Leary, Tim¦o|thy
  drug pioneer
leas|able
lease
  leas¦ing
lease|back
lease|hold
lease|hold¦er
Lease-Lend
leas¦er
leash
least
least|ways
least|wise
leat watercourse; cf.
  leet, lied
lea¦ther
lea¦ther|back
lea¦ther|cloth
lea¦ther|ette
lea¦theri|ness
lea¦ther|jacket
  larva of crane fly
lea¦thern
lea¦ther|neck
lea¦ther|oid

lea¦ther|wear
lea¦ther|wood
lea¦thery
leave
  left
  leav¦ing
leaved as in 'yellow-
  leaved'
leaven
leav¦er
leave-taking
Lea¦vis, F. R.
  literary critic
Leavis|ite
Leba|nese
Leba|non
Le¦bens|raum
Le Carré, John
  novelist
leccy
lech
Le Cha|tel¦ier's
  prin|ciple
lech¦er
lech¦er|ous
lech¦er|ous¦ly
lech¦er|ous|ness
lech¦ery
  lech¦er¦ies
lechwe
leci|thin
leci|thin|ase
lecker var. of lekker
Le|clan¦ché,
  Georges chemist;
  L. cell
Le|conte de Lisle,
  Charles poet
Le Cor|bu¦sier
  architect
lec|tern
lec¦tin
lec|tion
lec|tion|ary
  lec|tion|ar¦ies
lec¦tor
lec|trice
lec|ture
  lec|tur|ing
lec|tur¦er
lec|tur¦er|ship
lec|ture|ship
lecy|thus
lecy|thi

led past tense and
  past participle of
  lead = guide; cf.
  lead = metal
Leda Greek
  Mythology
leder|hosen
ledge
ledger
ledger line in
  music; var. of leger
  line
ledgy
  ledgi¦er
  ledgi¦est
Lee, Bruce actor
Lee, Chris|to¦pher
  actor
Lee, Gypsy Rose
  striptease artist
Lee, Har¦per
  American novelist
Lee, Laurie English
  writer
Lee, Rob¦ert E.
  American general
Lee, Spike film
  director
lee shelter; cf. lea,
  ley, li
lee|board
leech worm; doctor;
  on sail; cf. leach
leech|craft
Leeds
Lee-Enfield
leek vegetable; cf.
  leak
leer look slyly; cf.
  lehr
leeri|ness
leer|ing|ly
leer|vis
leery
  leer¦ier
  leeri|est
lees
leet court; cf. leat,
  lied
Leeu|war¦den
Leeu|wen|hoek,
  An¦toni van
  naturalist
lee|ward
lee|ward¦ly

lee¦way
Le Fanu, Jo¦seph
  Sheri¦dan novelist
left-hander
leftie var. of lefty
left¦ish
left¦ism
left¦ist
left¦most
left¦over
left¦ward
left¦wards
left-winger
lefty
  left¦ies
leg
  legged
  leg¦ging
leg¦acy
  leg¦acies
legal
lo¦gal¦ese
le¦gal¦isa¦tion Br.
  var. of legalization
le¦gal¦ise Br. var. of
  legalize
le¦gal¦ism
le¦gal¦ist
le¦gal¦is¦tic
le¦gal¦is¦tic¦al¦ly
le¦gal¦ity
  le¦gal¦ities
le¦gal¦iza¦tion
le¦gal¦ize
  le¦gal¦iz¦ing
le¦gal¦ly
leg¦ate
leg¦ate a lat¦ere
  leg¦ates a lat¦ere
lega¦tee
leg¦ate¦ship
lega¦tine
le¦ga¦tion
  diplomats;
  building; cf.
  ligation
le¦gato +s
lega¦tor
leg-cutter Cricket
le¦gend
le¦gend¦ar¦ily
le¦gend¦ary remark-
  able; of or

connected with
  legends
le¦gend¦ry legends
  collectively
Léger, Fer¦nand
  painter
Leger, St horse race
le¦ger¦de¦main
leger line in music;
  cf. ledger
leg¦ger
leg¦gi¦ness
leg¦ging
leggy
  leg¦gier
  leg¦gi¦est
leg¦hold
Leg¦horn old name
  for Livorno;
  chicken
leg¦horn straw; hat
le¦gi¦bil¦ity
le¦gible
le¦gibly
le¦gion
le¦gion¦aire var. of
  legionnaire
le¦gion¦ary
  le¦gion¦ar¦ies
le¦gion¦ella
  le¦gion¦el¦lae
le¦gion¦naire
le¦gion¦naires'
  dis¦ease
le¦gis¦late
  le¦gis¦lat¦ing
le¦gis¦la¦tion
le¦gis¦la¦tive
  le¦gis¦la¦tive¦ly
le¦gis¦la¦tor
le¦gis¦la¦ture
legit = legitimate
le¦git¦im¦acy
  le¦git¦im¦acies
le¦git¦im¦ate
  le¦git¦im¦at¦ing
le¦git¦im¦ate¦ly
le¦git¦im¦ation
le¦git¦ima¦tisa¦tion
  Br. var. of
  legitimatization
le¦git¦ima¦tise Br.
  var. of legitimatize
le¦git¦ima¦tiza¦tion

le¦git¦ima¦tize
  le¦git¦ima¦tiz¦ing
le¦git¦im¦isa¦tion
  Br. var. of
  legitimization
le¦git¦im¦ise Br. var.
  of legitimize
le¦git¦im¦ism
le¦git¦im¦ist
le¦git¦im¦iza¦tion
le¦git¦im¦ize
  le¦git¦im¦iz¦ing
leg¦less
leg¦man
  leg¦men
Lego trademark
leg-over vulgar
  slang
leg-pull
leg-pulling
leg¦room
leg-show
leg spin
leg-spinner
leg¦uaan var. of
  leguan
leg¦uan
leg¦ume
le¦gu¦min¦ous
leg-up
leg¦work
Leh town, India
Lehár, Franz
  composer
Le Havre
lehnga
lehr furnace; cf. leer
lei garland; cf. lay,
  ley
lei pl. of leu; cf. lay,
  ley
Leib¦niz, Gott¦fried
  philosopher
Leib¦niz¦ian
Lei¦bo¦vitz, Annie
  photographer
Leices¦ter
Leices¦ter¦shire
Leich¦hardt,
  Lud¦wig explorer
Lei¦den city, the
  Netherlands; cf.
  Leyden

Leigh, Viv¦ien
  actress
Leigh¦ton,
  Fred¦eric painter
  and sculptor
Lein¦ster
leio¦thrix
Leip¦zig
leish¦mania
  leish¦manias or
  leish¦maniae
leish¦man¦ia¦sis
Leis¦ler's bat
leis¦ter
leis¦ure
leis¦ured
leis¦ure¦less
leis¦ure¦li¦ness
leis¦ure¦ly
leis¦ure¦wear
leit¦motif
leit¦motiv var. of
  leitmotif
Lei¦trim
Leix var. of Laois
lek
lek¦ker
lek¦king
Lely, Peter painter
LEM = lunar excur-
  sion module
leman lover; cf.
  lemon
Le Mans
lemma
  lem¦mas or
  lem¦mata
lemma¦tisa¦tion Br.
  var. of
  lemmatization
lemma¦tise Br. var.
  of lemmatize
lemma¦tiza¦tion
lemma¦tize
  lemma¦tiz¦ing
lem¦ming
Lem¦mon, Jack
  actor
Lem¦nos
lemon fruit; cf.
  leman
lem¦on¦ade
lemon-squeezer
lemon¦wood

lem¦ony
lem¦pira
lemur
lem¦ur¦ine
lem¦ur¦oid
Len¦clos, Ninon de
courtesan
lend
lent
lend¦able
lend¦er
Lendl, Ivan tennis
player
Lend-Lease
len¦gha var. of
lehnga
length
length¦en
length¦en¦er
length¦ily
lengthi¦ness
length¦man
length¦men
length¦ways
length¦wise
lengthy
length¦ier
length¦iest
le¦ni¦ence
le¦ni¦ency
le¦ni¦en¦cies
le¦ni¦ent
le¦ni¦ent¦ly
Lenin, Vlad¦imir
Ilich Soviet
premier
Len¦in¦akan
Len¦in¦grad
Len¦in¦ism
Lenin¦ist
Lenin¦ite
lenis
lenes
len¦ition
leni¦tive
len¦ity
len¦ities
Len¦non, John rock
musician
Len¦nox
leno +s
Le¦nora
lens

lens¦less
lens¦man
lens¦men
Lent period before
Easter
lent past tense and
past participle of
lend; cf. leant
Lent¦en
len¦tic
len¦ti¦cel
len¦ticu¦lar
lenti¦form
len¦tigo
len¦ti¦gi¦nes
len¦til
len¦tisk
lenti¦virus
lent lily
lento +s
len¦toid
Lenz's law
Leo
León
Leon¦ard, El¦more
writer
Leo¦nardo da
Vinci painter and
scientist
Leon¦berg
Leon¦ca¦vallo,
Rug¦giero
composer
Leone, Ser¦gio film
director
leone Sierra Leone
currency
Leo¦nian
Leo¦nids
Léo¦nie
Leo¦nine of Pope
Leo; verse
leo¦nine of lions
Leo¦nora
leop¦ard
leop¦ard¦ess
Leo¦pold kings of
Belgium
Léo¦pold¦ville
leo¦tard
lepak +ed +ing
Le¦panto
Lep¦cha
leper

lepido¦cro¦cite
lepido¦lite
Lepi¦dop¦tera
lepi¦dop¦ter¦an
lepi¦dop¦ter¦ist
lepi¦dop¦ter¦ous
Lepi¦dus, Mar¦cus
Ae¦mil¦ius Roman
statesman
lep¦or¦ine
lepo¦spon¦dyl
lep¦re¦chaun
lep¦roma¦tous
lepro¦sar¦ium
lepro¦sar¦iums or
lepro¦saria
lep¦rosy
lep¦rous
lepta pl. of lepton
lep¦tin
Lep¦tis Magna
lepto¦ceph¦al¦ic
lepto¦ceph¦al¦ous
lepto¦kur¦tosis
lepto¦kur¦toses
lepto¦men¦in¦geal
lepto¦men¦in¦ges
lep¦ton
lepta
coin
lep¦ton +s particle
lep¦ton¦ic
lepto¦spir¦osis
lepto¦tene
Lepus
Ler¦mon¦tov,
Mikh¦ail novelist
and poet
Ler¦ner, Alan J.
lyricist
Ler¦wick
les = lesbian
Le¦sage, Alain-
René novelist and
playwright
Les¦bian of Lesbos
les¦bian female
homosexual
les¦bian¦ism
lesbi¦gay
lesbo +s = lesbian
Les¦bos island
Lesch–Nyhan

lese-majesty
French **lèse-
majesté**
le¦sion
Les¦ley chiefly
woman's name
Les¦lie chiefly man's
name
Le¦so¦tho
les¦see
les¦see¦ship
less¦en diminish; cf.
lesson
Les¦seps,
Fer¦di¦nand de
canal builder
less¦er not so great;
cf. lessor
Les¦sing, Doris
English novelist
Les¦sing, Gott¦hold
German dramatist
Les Six French
composers
les¦son tuition etc.;
cf. lessen
les¦sor person who
lets property by
lease; cf. lesser
Les¦ter
let
let¦ted
in sense 'hindered'
let¦ting
letch var. of lech
let-down *n. & adj.*
le¦thal
le¦thal¦ity
le¦thal¦ly
leth¦ar¦gic
leth¦ar¦gic¦al¦ly
leth¦argy
leth¦ar¦gies
Lethe *Greek
Mythology*
Le¦the¦an
Le¦ti¦cia port,
Colombia
Le¦ti¦tia name
Leto *Greek
Mythology*
let-off *n.*
let-out *n. & mod.*
let's

Lett *archaic* var. of
  Latvian
let¦ter
let¦ter box for mail
letter¦box video for-
  mat
letter-card
let¦ter car¦rier
letter¦form
letter¦head
let¦ter head¦ing
let¦ter¦ing
let¦ter¦press
letter¦set
Let¦tic
Let¦tice name
Lett¦ish
let¦tuce salad
let-up *n.*
Letze¦buerg¦esch
  var. of
  Lëtzebuergesch
Letze¦burg¦esch
leu
  lei
  Romanian currency
leu¦cine
leu¦cis¦tic
leu¦cite
leuco¦cyte *Br.*
  US **leukocyte**
leuco¦cyt¦ic *Br.*
  US **leukocytic**
leuco¦cyt¦osis *Br.*
  US **leukocytosis**
leuco¦cyt¦ot¦ic *Br.*
  US **leukocytotic**
leuco¦derma
leu¦coma *Br.*
  US **leukoma**
leuco¦penia *Br.*
  US **leukopenia**
leuco¦pen¦ic *Br.*
  US **leukopenic**
leuco¦plast
leu¦cor¦rhea *US* var.
  of **leukorrhea**
  Br. **leucorrhoea**
leu¦cor¦rhoea *Br.*
  US **leukorrhea**
leu¦co¦sis *Br.*
  US **leukosis**
leu¦cot¦ic *Br.*
  US **leukotic**

leu¦cot¦omy *Br.*
leu¦coto¦mies
  US **leukotomy**
leu¦kae¦mia *Br.*
  US **leukemia**
leu¦kaem¦ic *Br.*
  US **leukemic**
leu¦kaemo¦gen *Br.*
  US **leukemogen**
leu¦kaemo¦gen¦esis
  Br.
  US
  leukemogenesis
leu¦kaemo¦gen¦ic
  Br.
  US **leukemogenic**
leu¦ke¦mia *US*
  Br. **leukaemia**
leu¦kem¦ic *US*
  Br. **leukaemic**
leu¦kemo¦gen *US*
  Br. **leukaemogen**
leu¦kemo¦gen¦esis
  US
  Br.
  leukaemogenesis
leu¦kemo¦gen¦ic *US*
  Br. **leukaemogenic**
leuko¦cyte *US*
  Br. **leucocyte**
leuko¦cyt¦ic *US*
  Br. **leucocytic**
leuko¦cyt¦osis *US*
  Br. **leucocytosis**
leuko¦cyt¦ot¦ic *US*
  Br. **leucocytotic**
leuko¦derma var. of
  leucoderma
leu¦koma *US*
  Br. **leucoma**
leuko¦penia *US*
  Br. **leucopenia**
leuko¦pen¦ic *US*
  Br. **leucopenic**
leu¦kor¦rhea *US*
  Br. **leucorrhoea**
leu¦ko¦sis *US*
  Br. **leucosis**
leu¦kot¦ic *US*
  Br. **leucotic**
leu¦kot¦omy *US*
leu¦koto¦mies
  Br. **leucotomy**
Leu¦ven
lev Bulgarian
  currency

le¦vade
Le¦val¦lois
Le¦val¦lois¦ean
lev¦ami¦sole
Le¦vant E.
  Mediterranean
le¦vant abscond
le¦vant¦er
Lev¦an¦tine
le¦vator
levee reception;
  embankment; cf.
  levy; *French* **levée**
level
lev¦elled *Br.*
lev¦eled *US*
lev¦el¦ling *Br.*
lev¦el¦ing *US*
lev¦el¦er *US*
  Br. **leveller**
Lev¦el¦ler dissenter
lev¦el¦ler *Br.*
  US **leveler**
lev¦el¦ly
lev¦el¦ness
lever
le¦ver¦age
le¦ver¦aging
lev¦eret
Le¦ver¦hulme, Lord
  industrialist
Le¦ver¦ku¦sen
Levi *Bible*
Levi, Primo novelist
levi¦able
le¦via¦than
levi¦gate
levi¦gat¦ing
levi¦ga¦tion
lev¦ir¦ate
le¦vir¦at¦ic
**Lévi-Strauss,
  Claude** social
  anthropologist
levi¦tate
levi¦tat¦ing
levi¦ta¦tion
levi¦ta¦tor
Le¦vite
Le¦vit¦ic¦al
Le¦vit¦icus
lev¦ity
lev¦ities
levo¦dopa

levo¦nor¦ges¦trel
levo¦rota¦tion *US*
  Br. **laevorotation**
levo¦rota¦tory *US*
  Br. **laevorotatory**
le¦vu¦lose *US*
  Br. **laevulose**
levy
  lev¦ies
  lev¦ied
  levy¦ing
  tax; impose; cf.
  levee
lewd
lewd¦ly
lewd¦ness
Lewes town,
  England
Lewis L. acid, acid-
  ity, base, gun
Lewis island, Scot-
  land; name
Lewis, Carl athlete
Lewis, C. S.
  religious writer
Lewis, Jerry Lee
  singer and pianist
Lewis, Len¦nox
  boxer
Lewis, Meri¦wether
  explorer
Lewis, Sin¦clair
  novelist
Lewis, Wynd¦ham
  novelist and painter
lewis lifting device
Lewis¦ian
lewis¦ite
Lexan *trademark*
lex¦eme
lex fori
lex¦ic¦al
lex¦ical¦ise *Br.* var.
  of **lexicalize**
lex¦ical¦ize
lex¦ical¦iz¦ing
lex¦ical¦ly
lexi¦cog¦raph¦er
lex¦ico¦graph¦ic
lex¦ico¦graph¦ic¦al
lex¦ico¦graph¦ic¦
  al¦ly
lexi¦cog¦raphy
lex¦ico¦logic¦al

lex¦ico‖logic¦al¦ly
lexi¦colo¦gist
lexi¦col¦ogy
lexi¦con
lexi¦gram
Lex¦ing¦ton
lexis
lex loci
lex tali¦onis
ley temporary pasture; line between
ancient sites; cf.
lay, lea, lee, lei, li
Ley¦den town; var.
of Leiden
Ley¦den, Lucas van
painter
Ley¦den jar
Ley¦land cy¦press
ley¦landii
Leyte island,
Philippines
lez var. of les
lezzy
lez¦zies
Lhasa
Lhasa apso +s
li
pl. li
Chinese unit of
distance; cf. lea,
lee, ley
li¦abil¦ity
li¦abil¦ities
li¦able
li¦aise
li¦ais¦ing
li¦aison
liana
liane var. of liana
Liao
Liao¦dong
Liao¦ning
liar person who tells
a lie; l. dice; cf.
lyre
liard
Lias geological
epoch
lias stone
li¦as¦sic
lia¦tris
pl. lia¦tris
lib = liberation

li¦ba¦tion
lib¦ber
Lib Dem = Liberal
Democrat
li¦bec¦cio +s
libel
li¦belled *Br.*
li¦beled *US*
li¦bel¦ling *Br.*
li¦bel¦ing *US*
li¦bel¦er *US*
li¦bel¦ler *Br.*
li¦bel¦lous *Br.*
li¦bel¦lous¦ly *Br.*
li¦bel¦ous *US*
li¦bel¦ous¦ly *US*
Li¦ber¦ace pianist
and entertainer
lib¦eral
lib¦er¦al¦isa¦tion *Br.*
var. of
liberalization
lib¦er¦al¦ise *Br.* var.
of liberalize
lib¦er¦al¦iser *Br.* var.
of liberalizer
lib¦er¦al¦ism
lib¦er¦al¦ist
lib¦er¦al¦is¦tic
lib¦er¦al¦ity
lib¦er¦al¦ities
lib¦er¦al¦iza¦tion
lib¦er¦al¦ize
lib¦er¦al¦iz¦ing
lib¦er¦al¦izer
lib¦er¦al¦ly
lib¦er¦al¦ness
lib¦er¦ate
lib¦er¦at¦ing
lib¦er¦ation
lib¦er¦ation¦ist
lib¦er¦ator
Li¦beria
Li¦ber¦ian
li¦bero +s
lib¦er¦tar¦ian
lib¦er¦tar¦ian¦ism
lib¦er¦tin¦age
lib¦er¦tine
lib¦er¦tin¦ism
lib¦erty
lib¦er¦ties
Lib¦erty ship
li¦bid¦in¦al

li¦bid¦in¦al¦ly
li¦bid¦in¦ous
li¦bid¦in¦ous¦ness
li¦bido +s
Lib-Lab = Liberal
and Labour
Li Bo var. of Li Po
LIBOR = London
Inter-Bank Offered
Rate
Libra constellation;
sign of zodiac
libra
li¦brae
Roman unit of
weight
Li¦bran
li¦brar¦ian
li¦brar¦ian¦ship
li¦brary
li¦brar¦ies
li¦brate
li¦brat¦ing
li¦bra¦tion
li¦bret¦tist
li¦bretto
li¦bretti or
li¦bret¦tos
Libre¦ville
Lib¦rium *trademark*
Libya
Lib¦yan
lice
li¦cence *Br. n.*
li¦cens¦able
li¦cense *v. & US n.*
li¦cens¦ing
li¦cen¦see
li¦cen¦ser var. of
licensor
li¦cen¦sor
li¦cen¦ti¦ate
li¦cen¦ti¦ate¦ship
li¦cen¦tious
li¦cen¦tious¦ly
li¦cen¦tious¦ness
li¦chee var. of lychee
li¦chen
li¦chen¦ology
li¦chen¦ous
Lich¦field
lich¦gate
licht
Scot. var. of light

Lich¦ten\stein, Roy
painter and
sculptor
licit
licit¦ly
lick¦er
lick¦er¦ish lecherous; cf. liquorish
lick¦er¦ish¦ly
lickety-split
lick¦spit¦tle
lic¦orice *US*
Br. liquorice
lic¦tor
lidar detection
system
lid¦ded
Lid\dell, Eric athlete
Lid\dell Hart,
Basil military
historian
Li¦dingö
lid¦less
lido +s public pool
lido¦caine
Lido di
Mala¦mocco
island and resort
off Venice
Lie, Tryg¦ve
Halv¦dan UN Secretary General
lie
lay
lying
lain
be horizontal; cf.
lye
lie
lying
tell untruths; cf. lye
Lieb¦chen
Lieb¦frau¦milch +s
Lie¦big, Jus¦tus von
German chemist
Liech¦ten\stein
country
Liech¦ten\stein¦er
lied
lie¦der
German song; cf.
lead, leader, leat,
leet
lie-down *n.*

lief gladly; cf. **leaf**
Liège
liege
liege|man
　liege|men
lie-in *n.*
lien right to hold
　another's property;
　cf. **lean**
li|erne
lieu in 'in lieu (of)'
lieu|ten|ancy
　lieu|ten|an|cies
lieu|ten|ant
life
　lives
life|belt
life|blood
life|boat
life|boat|man
　life|boat|men
life|buoy
life-expired
life|guard on beach
　etc.
Life Guards British
　regiment
life|less
life|less|ly
life|less|ness
life|like
life|like|ness
life|line
life|long
lifer
life|saver
life size *n.*
life-size *adj.*
life-sized
life|span
life|style
life|time
life|world
Liffe = London
　International
　Financial Futures
　Exchange
Lif|fey
Lif|ford
LIFO = last in, first
　out
lift|able
lift|er

lift-off *n.*
lig
　ligged
　lig|ging
liga|ment
liga|men|tal
liga|men|tary
liga|ment|ous
lig|and
lig|ase
li|gate
li|gat|ing
li|ga|tion tying off;
　cf. **legation**
liga|ture
　liga|tur|ing
liger lion-tigress
　cross
Lig|eti, György
　composer
lig|ger
light
　lit or light|ed
　visible radiation;
　illuminate; bright;
　not heavy; (*lights*)
　lungs; cf. **lite**
light|en
　light|en|ing
　make or become
　lighter; cf.
　lightning
light|er
light|er|age
light|er|man
　light|er|men
light|fast
light|fast|ness
light|house
lighting-up time
light|ish
light|less
light|ly
light|ness
light|ning electric
　discharge; cf.
　lightening
light|proof
light|ship
light|some
light|some|ly
light|some|ness
light|weight
light|wood

lig|neous
lig|nifi|ca|tion
lig|nify
　lig|ni|fies
　lig|ni|fied
　lig|ni|fy|ing
lig|nin
lig|nite
lig|nit|ic
lig|no|caine
ligno|cel|lu|lose
ligno|tuber
lig|num vitae
lig|roin
lig|ula
　ligu|lae
ligu|lar
ligu|late
lig|ule
Li|guria
Li|gur|ian
li|gus|trum
lik|abil|ity var. of
　likeability
lik|able var. of
　likeable
lik|able|ness var. of
　likeableness
lik|ably var. of
　likeably
like
　lik|ing
like|abil|ity
like|able
like|able|ness
like|ably
like|li|hood
like|ly
　like|lier
　like|li|est
liken
like|ness
Li|kert scale
like|wise
Likud
lilac
li|lan|geni
　ema|lan|geni
lili|aceous
Lil|ian
lil|ied
Li|lien|thal, Otto
　aviator

Lil|ith *Jewish
　Mythology*
Lille city, France
Lil|lee, Den|nis
　cricketer
Lil|lian
Lil|li|bur|lero
lil|li|pu|tian
lilly-pilly
　lilly-pillies
lilo +s
Li-lo +s *trademark*
　var. of lilo
Li|longwe
lily
　lil|ies
lily-trotter
lily-white
Lima capital of Peru
lima bean
Lim|as|sol
limb arm, leg, etc.;
　Astronomy;
　Botany; cf. **limn**
Limba people
limba tree
lim|ber supple; part
　of gun carriage; l.
　pine
lim|ber|neck
lim|ber|ness
limb|less
limbo
　lim|bos
　lim|boed
　limbo|ing
Lim|burg
Lim|burg|er
lim|bus
　limbi
lime
　lim|ing
　fruit; chemical; cf.
　Lyme disease
lime|ade
lime|burn|er
lime|kiln
lime|less
lime|light
limen
　li|mens or li|mina
lime|pit
Lim|er|ick Irish
　county and town

lim|er¦ick poem
lime|scale
lime|stone
lime|wash
Limey Briton; cf.
　limy
lim|inal
lim¦in¦al|ity
limit
limit|able
limit|ary
limi|ta¦tion
limi|ta¦tive
limit|ed|ness
limit¦er
limit|less
limit|less¦ly
limit|less|ness
limn paint; cf. limb
lim¦ner
lim¦no|logic¦al
lim¦nolo|gist
lim¦nol|ogy
limo +s
Li|moges
Limón
lim¦on|ene
lim¦on|ite
lim¦on|it¦ic
Li¦mou|sin
lim|ou¦sine
lim¦pet
lim¦pid
lim¦pid|ity
lim¦pid¦ly
lim¦pid|ness
limp|kin
limp¦ly
limp|ness
Lim|popo
lim|ulus
　lim¦uli
limy
　limi¦er
　limi¦est
　containing lime; cf.
　Limey
linac = linear
　accelerator
Lin|acre, Thomas
　physician and
　scholar

lin|age number of
　lines; cf. lineage
Lin Biao politician
linch|pin
Lin|coln cities
Lin|coln, Abra|ham
　US president
Lin|coln|shire
Lin|coln's Inn
Lin|crusta
　trademark
Lincs. =
　Lincolnshire
linc|tus
Lind, James phys-
　ician
Lind, Jenny singer
lin|dane
Lind|bergh,
　Charles aviator
lin|den
Lin|dis|farne
Lind|say, Lio|nel
　and Nor|man
　Australian artists
line
　lin¦ing
lin|eage ancestry; cf.
　linage
lin¦eal
lin|eal¦ly in a direct
　line of descent; cf.
　linearly
lin¦ea|ment
lin¦ear
lin¦ear|isa¦tion var.
　of linearization
lin¦ear|ise Br. var.
　of linearize
lin¦ear|iser var. of
　linearizer
lin¦ear|ity
lin¦ear|iza¦tion
lin¦ear|ize
　lin¦ear|iz¦ing
lin¦ear|izer
lin¦ear¦ly in a
　straight line; cf.
　lineally
lin¦ea|tion
line|back¦er
line dance n.
line-dance v.
　line-dancing

line dan¦cer
line dan¦cing n.
line-engraved
line en|graver
line en|grav¦ing
line|feed
line|fish
line-in n.
Line Is¦lands
Lin|eker, Gary foot-
　baller
line|man
　line|men
linen
linen|fold
line-out n.
liner
line|side
lines|man
　lines|men
line-up n.
Lin|ford
linga Hindu symbol;
　cf. linger. var. of
　lingam
Lin|gala
lin¦gam
ling|cod
　pl. ling|cod
lin¦ger be slow to
　leave; cf. linga
lin|ger¦er
lin|ge¦rie
lin|ger|ing¦ly
lingo
　lin¦gos or lin¦goes
lingon|berry
　lingon|berries
lin|gua franca
　lin|gua francas
lin|gual
lin|gual¦ly
lin|guine
lin|guist
lin|guis¦tic
lin|guis¦tic|al¦ly
lin|guis¦ti¦cian
lin|guis¦tics
lin|gu|late
lingy
lin¦hay
lini|ment
lin¦ish

lin|ish¦er
link|age
link¦er
link|man
　link|men
Lin|köp¦ing
links golf course; cf.
　lynx
links|land
link|span
link-up n.
link|work
Lin|lith|gow
linn waterfall
Lin|naean of
　Linnaeus; cf.
　Linnean
Lin|naeus, Caro|lus
　naturalist
Lin|nean So¦ciety
　cf. Linnaean
lin¦net
lino +s
lino|cut
lino¦cut|ting
lino|le¦ate
lino|leic
lino|len|ate
lino|len¦ic
lino|leum
Lino|type
　trademark
Lin Piao var. of Lin
　Biao
lin|sang
lin|seed
linsey-wolsey var.
　of linsey-woolsey
linsey-woolsey
lin|stock
lin|tel
　lin|teled US
　lin|telled Br.
lint¦er
lin|tie Scot. linnet
linty like or full of
　lint
Linux trademark in
　the US
liny
　lini¦er
　lini¦est
Linz
lion

Lio¦nel

lion¦ess

lion¦head fish

lion¦heart

lion¦heart¦ed

lion¦isa¦tion *Br.* var. of lionization

lion¦ise *Br.* var. of lionize

lion¦iser *Br.* var. of lionizer

lion¦iza¦tion

lion¦ize
  lion¦iz¦ing

lion¦izer

lion-like

lip
  lipped
  lip¦ping

lipa
  pl. lipa or lipas

lip¦aemia *Br.*
  US lipemia

Li¦pari

lip¦ase

Lip¦chitz, Jacques
  sculptor

lip¦emia *US*
  Br. lipaemia

Li¦petsk

lipid

lip¦id¦osis
  lip¦id¦oses

Lip¦iz¦za¦ner

lip¦less

lip¦like

lip¦line

lip¦liner

Li Po Chinese poet

lipo¦gen¦esis

lipo¦gen¦ic

lipo¦gram

lipo¦gram¦mat¦ic

lip¦oid

lip¦oid¦osis
  lip¦oid¦oses
  var. of lipidosis

lip¦oly¦sis

lipo¦lyt¦ic

lip¦oma
  lip¦omas or
  lip¦omata

lipo¦phil¦ic

lipo¦poly¦sac¦char¦
  ide

lipo¦pro¦tein

lipo¦some

lipo¦suc¦tion

lipo¦troph¦in var. of lipotropin

lipo¦tropin

Lip¦pes loop

Lippi, Fil¦ip¦pino
  and Fra Fi¦lippo
  painters

lip¦pie = lipstick var. of lippy

Lip¦pi¦za¦ner var. of Lipizzaner

Lipp¦mann,
  Gab¦riel physicist

lippy

lip¦pier

lip¦pi¦est

lip-read

lip reader

lip¦salve

lip¦stick

lip-sync

lip-syncer

lip-synch var. of lip-sync

lip-syncher var. of lip-syncer

li¦quate
  li¦quat¦ing

li¦qua¦tion

li¦que¦fa¦cient

li¦que¦fac¦tion

li¦que¦fac¦tive

li¦que¦fi¦able

li¦que¦fier

li¦quefy
  li¦que¦fies
  li¦que¦fied
  li¦que¦fy¦ing

li¦ques¦cent

li¦queur

li¦quid

li¦quid¦am¦bar

li¦quid¦ate
  li¦quid¦at¦ing

li¦quid¦ation

li¦quid¦ator

li¦quid¦ise *Br.* var. of liquidize

li¦quid¦iser *Br.* var. of liquidizer

li¦quid¦ity

li¦quid¦ize
  li¦quid¦iz¦ing

li¦quid¦izer

li¦quid¦ly

li¦quid¦ness

li¦quor

li¦quor¦ice *Br.*
  US licorice

li¦quor¦ish fond of liquor; cf. **lickerish**

lira

lire

lirio¦den¦dron

liri¦pipe

lis
  pl. lis or lisses
  = fleur-de-lis

lis alibi pen¦dens
  lites alibi
  pen¦dentes

Lis¦bon capital of Portugal

Lis¦burn town, Nor¦thern Ireland

Lis¦doon¦varna

li¦sente *pl.* of sente

Li¦sieux, St Ter¦esa of

lisle

Lisp computer language

lisp speech defect

lis pen¦dens
  lites pen¦dentes

lisp¦er

lisp¦ing¦ly

Lissa¦jous fig¦ure

lis¦som *Br.*

lis¦some *US*

lis¦some¦ly *US*

lis¦some¦ness *US*

lis¦som¦ly *Br.*

lis¦som¦ness *Br.*

list¦able

lis¦tel

lis¦ten

lis¦ten¦abil¦ity

lis¦ten¦able

lis¦ten¦er

Lis¦ter, Jo¦seph surgeon

list¦er

lis¦teria

lis¦teri¦osis

list¦less

list¦less¦ly

list¦less¦ness

Lis¦ton, Sonny
  boxer

LIST¦SERV +s
  trademark

Liszt, Franz
  composer

Liszt¦ian

Li T'ai Po var. of Li Po

lit¦any

lit¦anies

litas
  pl. litas
  Lithuanian currency

lit¦chi var. of lychee

lit. crit. = literary criticism

lite low-calorie, simplified; cf. **light**

liter *US*
  Br. litre

lit¦er¦acy

lit¦er¦acies

lit¦erae
  hu¦ma¦ni¦ores

liter¦age *US*
  Br. litreage

lit¦eral to the letter; misprint; cf. **littoral**

lit¦er¦al¦ise *Br.* of literalize

lit¦er¦al¦ism

lit¦er¦al¦ist

lit¦er¦al¦is¦tic

lit¦er¦al¦ity

lit¦er¦al¦ize
  lit¦er¦al¦iz¦ing

lit¦er¦al¦ly

literal-minded

lit¦er¦al¦ness

lit¦er¦ar¦ily

lit¦er¦ari¦ness

lit¦er¦ary

lit¦er¦ate

lit¦er¦ate¦ly

lit¦er¦ati

lit¦er|atim
lit¦era|ture
lith photographic
  film
lith|arge
lithe
  lither
  lith¦est
  supple and graceful
lithe¦ly
lithe|ness
lithe|some
lithia
lith|ia¦sis
lith¦ic
lithi¦fi¦ca¦tion
lith¦ify
  lithi|fies
  lithi¦fied
  lithi¦fy¦ing
lith|ium
litho
  pl. lithos
  v. lithoes
lithoed
litho|ing
litho|graph
lith|og|raph¦er
litho|graph¦ic
litho|graph¦ic|al¦ly
lith|og¦raphy
litho|logic
litho|logic¦al
litho|logic¦al¦ly
lith|ology
litho|phane
litho|phyte
litho|pone
litho|sol
litho|sphere
litho|spher¦ic
lith|ot¦om¦ise *Br.*
  var. of lithotomize
lith|ot¦om¦ist
lith|ot¦om¦ize
  lith|ot¦om¦iz¦ing
lith|ot¦omy
  lith|oto¦mies
litho|tripsy
litho|trip¦ter
litho|trip¦tic
litho|trip¦tor var. of
  lithotripter
litho|trite

lith|ot¦rity
  lith|ot¦rities
Lithu|ania
Lithu|anian
lit¦ig|able
liti|gant
liti|gate
  liti|gat¦ing
liti|ga¦tion
liti|ga¦tor
li¦ti¦gious
li¦ti¦gious¦ly
li¦ti¦gious|ness
lit¦mus
lit|op¦tern
li|to¦tes
litre *Br.*
  US liter
litre|age *Br.*
  US literage
LittD = Doctor of
  Letters
lit¦ter
lit¦tér|ateur
lit¦ter|bug
lit¦tle
lit¦tler
lit¦tlest
little-endian
little|ness
Little Rhody
Little|wood, Joan
  theatre director
lit|toral shore; cf.
  literal
Lit¦tré, Émile
  philosopher and
  lexicographer
li¦tur|gic¦al
li¦tur|gic¦al¦ly
li¦tur|gics
li¦tur|gio|logic¦al
li¦tur|gi¦olo|gist
li¦tur|gi|ology
lit|ur¦gist
lit|urgy
  lit¦ur|gies
Lit¦vak
Liu|zhou
liv|abil¦ity *US*
  Br. liveability
liv|able *US*
  Br. liveable

live *v.*
liv¦est *archaic*
liv¦ing
live *adj.*
  liv¦est
live|abil¦ity
  US livability
live|able
  US livable
live|bear¦er
live-bearing
live-born
live-in *adj. & n.*
live¦li|hood
live|lily
live¦li|ness
live|long
live¦ly
  live|lier
  live¦li|est
liven
liver
liv|er¦ied
liv|er¦ish
liv|er¦ish|ness
Liv|er|pool
Liv|er|pud¦lian
liver spot
liver-spotted
liver|wort
liv¦ery
  liv|er¦ies
liv|ery|man
  liv|ery|men
lives pl. of life
live|stock
live|ware
livid
liv|id¦ity
liv|id¦ly
liv|id|ness
Liv¦ing|stone,
  David missionary
  and explorer
liv¦ing stone plant
Li|vo¦nia
Li|vo¦nian
Li|vorno
Livy Roman
  historian
lix¦ivi|ate
  lix¦ivi|at¦ing
lix¦ivi|ation

Liz¦ard promontory,
  England
liz¦ard
lizard|fish
Liz¦zie
Lizzy
Ljub¦ljana
llama animal; cf.
  lama
Llan|drin|dod
  Wells
Llan|dudno
lla|nero +s
Llan|gollen
llano +s
Lle|we|lyn Welsh
  prince
Llosa, Mario
  Var¦gas writer
Lloyd, Har¦old
  actor
Lloyd, Marie
  music-hall singer
Lloyd George,
  David prime minis-
  ter of Britain
Lloyd's *Insurance*
Lloyd's List
Lloyd's Regis¦ter
Lloyd Web¦ber,
  An¦drew composer
Lly|welyn ap
  Gruf|fydd
  Welsh name of
  Llewelyn
lo *exclam.*; cf. low
loa
  pl. loa or loas
  voodoo god
Loach, Ken film
  director
loach
load burden; to
  carry; cf. lode
load¦er
load|master
loadsa = loads of
load|space
load|stone var. of
  lodestone
loaf
  pl. loaves
  v. loafs
loafed
loaf|ing

loaf¦er idler
loaf¦er shoe
  trademark in US
loam
loami¦ness
loamy
  loam¦ier
  loami¦est
loan lend; something lent; lane; cf.
  lone
loan¦able
loan¦ee
loan¦er lender; cf.
  loner
loan¦ing lane
loan¦word
loath reluctant
loathe despise
loath¦er
loath¦some
loath¦some¦ness
loaves
lob
  lobbed
  lob¦bing
Lo¦ba¦chev¦sky,
  Ni¦ko¦lai
  Ivan¦ovich
  mathematician
lobar
lo¦bate
lob¦ation
lobby
  lob¦bies
  lob¦bied
  lobby¦ing
lobby¦ist
lobe
lob¦ec¦tomy
  lob¦ec¦to¦mies
lobe¦fin
lobe-finned
lobe¦less
lo¦belia
Lo¦bito
lob¦lolly
  lob¦lol¦lies
lobo +s
lo¦bola
lo¦bolo var. of
  lobola
lobo¦pod
lobo¦podial

lobo¦po¦dium
  lobo¦po¦dia
lob¦ot¦om¦isa¦tion
  var. of
  lobotomization
lob¦ot¦om¦ise *Br.*
  var. of lobotomize
lob¦ot¦om¦iza¦tion
lob¦ot¦om¦ize
  lob¦ot¦om¦iz¦ing
lob¦ot¦omy
  lo¦boto¦mies
lob¦scouse
lob¦ster
lobu¦lar
lobu¦late
lob¦ule
lob¦worm
local nearby; pub
lo¦cale place
lo¦cal¦is¦able *Br.* var.
  of localizable
lo¦cal¦isa¦tion *Br.*
  var. of localization
lo¦cal¦ise *Br.* var. of
  localize
lo¦cal¦ism
lo¦cal¦ist
lo¦cal¦ity
  lo¦cal¦ities
lo¦cal¦iz¦able
lo¦cal¦iza¦tion
lo¦cal¦ize
  lo¦cal¦iz¦ing
lo¦cal¦ly
lo¦cal¦ness
Lo¦carno
lo¦cat¦able
lo¦cate
  lo¦cat¦ing
lo¦ca¦tion
lo¦ca¦tion¦al
loca¦tive
lo¦ca¦tor
loc. cit. = loco citato
loch Scottish lake;
  cf. lough
lochan
lo¦chia
lo¦chial
Loch Lo¦mond
Loch Maree
Loch Ness

loch¦side
loci pl. of locus
locie
lock cf. lox
lock¦able
lock¦age
lock¦box
lock¦down
Locke, John
  philosopher
Locke, Jo¦seph
  railway engineer
Lock¦ean
locker
Lock¦er¦bie
locket
lock¦fast
lock-in *n. & mod.*
lock¦jaw
lock-keeper
lock-knit
lock¦less
lock¦nut
lock¦out
lock¦smith
lock¦step
lock-up *adj. & n.*
Lock¦yer, Nor¦man
  astronomer
loco +s
loco¦mo¦tion
loco¦mo¦tive
loco¦motor
loco¦mo¦tory
loco¦weed
Loc¦rian
locu¦lar
loc¦ule
locu¦lus
  loc¦uli
locum
locum ten¦ency
  locum ten¦en¦cies
locum ten¦ens
  locum ten¦en¦tes
locus
  loci
locus clas¦si¦cus
  loci clas¦sici
locus standi
  loci standi
lo¦cust
lo¦cu¦tion

lo¦cu¦tion¦ary
lode vein of metal
  ore; cf. load
loden
lode¦star
lode¦stone
Lodge, David
  novelist
Lodge, Oli¦ver
  physicist
lodge
  lodg¦ing
  small house; cf.
  loge
lodge¦ment
lodge¦pole
lodg¦er
lodi¦cule
Łódź
loerie var. of lourie
loess
loes¦sial
loes¦sic
Loewi, Otto
  physiologist
lo-fi
Lo¦fo¦ten
loft¦er
loft¦ily
lofti¦ness
lofts¦man
  lofts¦men
lofty
  loft¦ier
  lofti¦est
log
  logged
  log¦ging
Logan, Mt
logan stone
lo¦gan¦berry
  lo¦gan¦berries
loga¦rithm
loga¦rith¦mic
loga¦rith¦mic¦al¦ly
log¦book
loge box in theatre;
  cf. lodge
log_e natural
  logarithm
log¦ger
log¦ger¦head
log¦gia open-sided
  gallery; cf. logia

logia pl. of logion;
　cf. loggia
logic
lo|gic|al
logic|al|ity
　logic|al|ities
logic|al|ly
lo|gi|cian
logi|cism
logi|cist
login
log|ion
　logia
lo|gis|tic
lo|gis|tic|al
lo|gis|tic|al|ly
lo|gis|tics
log|jam
log-log
log-normal
log-normal|ity
log-normal|ly
logo +s
logo|cen|tric
logo|cen|trism
log|off
logo|gram
logo|graph
logo|graph|ic
logon
logo|phile
log|or|rhea US
log|or|rhe|ic US
log|or|rhoea Br.
log|or|rhoe|ic Br.
Logos word of God
logo|type
log|out
log|roll|er
Lo|groño
log|run|ner
log|wood
logy
　logier
　logi|est
Lo|hen|grin legend-
　ary figure
lo|iasis
loin|cloth
Loire river, France
Loir-et-Cher
　department, France
Lois

loi|ter
loi|ter|er
lokey var. of locie
Loki Scandinavian
　god
Lok Sabha
Lo|lita
Lol|land
lol|la|pa|looza
Lol|lard
Lol|lard|ism
Lol|lardy
loll|er
lolli|pop
lol|lop
lollo rosso
lolly
　lol|lies
lolly|gag
　lolly|gagged
　lolly|gag|ging
Lolly|wood
Lom|bard
Lom|bard|ic
Lom|bardy
Lom|bok
Lomé
lo|ment
lo|ment|aceous
lo|men|tum
　lo|menta
Lo|mond, Loch
Lomu, Jonah rugby
　player
Lon|don
Lon|don, Jack
　novelist
Lon|don|derry
Lon|don|er
lone solitary; cf.
　loan
lone|li|ness
lone|ly
　lone|lier
　lone|li|est
loner solitary
　person; cf. loaner
lone|some
lone|some|ly
lone|some|ness
lon|gan
long|bill
long|board

long|boat
long|bow
long|dog
longe
　longe|ing
　rein; var. of lunge
lon|geron
lon|gev|ity
Long|fel|low,
　Henry
　Wads|worth poet
Long|ford
long|hair person;
　cat
long|hand
long|horn
long|house
lon|gi|corn
long|ing|ly
Lon|gi|nus writer
long|ish
lon|gi|tude
lon|gi|tu|din|al
lon|gi|tu|din|al|ly
long johns
long jump
long jump|er
long|leaf pine
long|line fish|ing
long|liner
long|list
long|neck beer
　bottle
Long|shan
long|ship
long|shore
long|shore|man
　long|shore|men
long-sleever glass
　of beer
long|spur
long|stop
lon|gueur
long|wall mining
　method
long|ways
long|wise
long|wool sheep
lo|ni|cera
lon|ning lane; var.
　of loaning
Lons|dale

loo +s toilet; card
　game; l. table; cf.
　lieu
looey lieutenant; cf.
　louis
loo|fah
looie var. of looey
look|alike
look-and-say
look|er
looker-on
look-in n.
look|ism
look|ist
look|out
look-see n.
look|up
loon silly person;
　bird; cf. lune
loon|ie Canadian
　coin; cf. loony
looni|ness
loony
　loon|ies
　loon|ier
　looni|est
　mad (person); cf.
　loonie
loop|er
loop|hole
loop|hol|ing
loop|ily
loopi|ness
loop-the-loop n.
loopy
　loop|ier
　loopi|est
loose
　loos|ing
　loos|er
　loos|est
　release; not tight;
　cf. lose, luce
loose|ly
loos|en
loos|en|er
loose|ness
loose|strife
loosey-goosey
loos|ish
loot booty; cf. lute
loot|er
lop
　lopped

lop|ping

lope
 lop|ing
lop-eared
lop-ears
lo|pera|mide
lopho|dont
lo|phoph|orate
lopho|phore
Lop Nor
Lop Nur var. of
 Lop Nor
lopo|lith
lop|per
lop|sided
lop|sided|ly
lop|sided|ness
lo|qua|cious
lo|qua|cious|ly
lo|qua|city
lo|quat
lo|qui|tur
lor *exclam.*; cf. **law**,
 lore
Loran navigation
 system
lor|an|thus
lor|aze|pam
Lorca, Fe|de|rico
 Gar|cía poet and
 dramatist
lord noble; ruler; in
 'lord it'; cf. **laud**,
 lauds
Lord Howe
 Is|land
lord|less
lord-like
lord|li|ness
lord|ling
lord|ly
 lord|lier
 lord|li|est
lor|do|sis
 lor|do|ses
lor|do|tic
Lord's cricket
 ground, London
lords and ladies
 plant
lord|ship
Lordy *exclam.*
lore traditions; side
 of bird's or snake's

head; cf. **law**, **lor**
Lore|lei
Loren, So|phia
 actress
Lor|entz, Hen|drik
 physicist; L. con-
 traction, force,
 transformation
Lor|enz, Kon|rad
 zoologist
Lor|enz L. attractor,
 curve
lo-res
Lor|eto
Lor|etta
lor|gnette
lor|gnon
lor|ica
 lor|icae or loricas
lori|cate
Lori|ent
lori|keet
lori|let
lori|mer var. of
 loriner
lori|ner
loris
lorn abandoned; cf.
 lawn
Lor|rain, Claude
 var. of **Lorraine**
Lor|raine, Claude
 painter
Lor|raine region,
 France; name; L.
 cross
Lorre, Peter actor
lorry
 lor|ries
 vehicle
lorry|load
lory
 lor|ies
 parrot
Los Ala|mos
Los Angel|eno +s
Los An|geles
lose
 lost
 los|ing
 cease to have; cf.
 loose
losel
lose-lose

loser
losing|est
Lo Spa|gno|letto
 painter and etcher
loss
loss-leader
loss|less
lossy
Lot in the Bible;
 river, France
lot
 lot|ted
 lot|ting
lota water pot
lo-tech var. of **low-**
 tech
loth var. of **loath**
Lo|thario +s
Lo|thian
Loti, Pierre novelist
loti
 ma|loti
 Lesotho currency
lote
lo|tion
Lotka–Volterra
lotsa = lots of
lotta = lot of
lot|tery
 lot|ter|ies
Lot|tie
Lotto, Lo|renzo
 painter
lotto game
lotus
lotus|bird
lotus-eater
lotus-eating
Lotus Sutra
 Buddhism
Lou
Lou|ang|phra|bang
 var. of **Luang**
 Prabang
louche
loucher
louch|est
loud|en
loud|hail|er
loud|ish
loud|ly
loud|mouth
loud-mouthed
loud|ness

loud|speak|er
Lou|ella
Lou Geh|rig's
 dis|ease
lough Irish lake; cf.
 loch
Lough|bor|ough
Louis kings of
 France and
 Hungary
Louis, Joe boxer
louis
 pl. louis
 = louis d'or; cf.
 looey
Lou|isa
louis d'or
 pl. louis d'or
Lou|ise
Lou|isi|ana
Lou|isi|an|an
Lou|isi|an|ian var.
 of **Louisianan**
Louis Joseph de
 Montcalm Gozon
 French general
Louis-Napoleon
 Napoleon III of
 France
 French **Louis-**
 Napoléon
Louis Phil|ippe
 king of France
Louis|ville
lounge
 loun|ging
lounge|core
loun|ger
loun|gey
loup
 Scot. & N. English
 var. of **leap**
loupe magnifying
 glass
loup|ing ill
lour frown; look
 threatening; cf.
 lower
lour|dan var. of
 lurdan
Lourdes
Lou|renço
 Mar|ques
lourie
lour|ing|ly

loury

louse
  pl. lice
  v. louses
  loused
  lousing
lous|er
louse|wort
lous|ily
lousi|ness
lousy
  lous|ier
  lousi|est
Louth
lout|ish
lout|ish|ly
lout|ish|ness
Lou|vain
lou|var fish
lou|ver *US*
  slat
  Br. louvre
Louvre museum
lou|vre slat
  US louver
lov|abil|ity
lov|able
lov|able|ness
lov|ably
lov|age
lovat
love
  lov|ing
love|abil|ity var. of
  lovability
love|able var. of
  lovable
love|able|ness var.
  of lovableness
love|ably var. of
  lovably
love|bird
love-hate
love-in
love-in-a-mist
love-in-idleness
Love|lace,
  Count|ess of
  mathematician
Love|lace, Rich|ard
  poet
love|less
love|less|ly
love|less|ness

love-lies-bleeding
  plant
love|lily
love|li|ness
Lov|ell, Ber|nard
  astronomer
Love|lock, James
  scientist
love|lock
love|lorn
love|ly
  love|lies
  love|lier
  love|li|est
love|mak|ing
lover
lover|less
love|sick
love|sick|ness
love|some
love|worthy
lovey darling; cf.
  luvvie
lovey-dovey
lov|ing|ly
lov|ing|ness
Low, David artist
low not high; moo;
  cf. lo
lowan
low|ball *Baseball*
low|boy
low|brow
low-down
Low|ell, Amy poet
Low|ell, James poet
  and critic
Low|ell, Per|ci|val
  astronomer
Low|ell, Rob|ert
  poet
low-end
lower comparative
  of low; let down;
  make lower; cf. loa,
  lour
Lower Hutt
lower|most
Low|es|toft
low-fi var. of lo-fi
low|ish
low|land
low|land|er

low|life +s disreput-
  able person
low life disreputable
  people or activities
low-lifer
low|light dull fea-
  ture; dark tint
low|lily
low|li|ness
low-loader
lowly
  low|lier
  low|li|est
low|ness
low-res var. of
  lo-res
low-rider
low-rise
Lowry, L. S. painter
Lowry, Mal|colm
  novelist
low tech *n.*
low-tech *adj.*
low|veld
low-water mark
lox liquid oxygen;
  smoked salmon
loxo|drome
loxo|drom|ic
loyal
loyal|ism
loyal|ist
loy|al|ly
loy|alty
  loy|al|ties
loz|enge
Lozi
L-plate
Lua|laba
Lu|anda
Luang Pra|bang
luau
  pl. luau or luaus
Luba
lub|ber
lub|ber|like
lub|ber|ly
Lub|bock
lube
  lubing
Lü|beck
Lu|bianka var. of
  Lubyanka

Lub|lin
lubra *offensive*
lu|bri|cant
lu|bri|cate
lu|bri|cat|ing
lu|bri|ca|tion
lu|bri|ca|tive
lu|bri|ca|tor
lu|bri|cious
lu|bri|cious|ly
lu|bri|city
Lu|bum|bashi
Lu|byanka
Lucan of St Luke
Lucan poet
Lucan, Lord
  missing Earl
Lucas, George film
  director
Lucas van Ley|den
  painter
Lucca
luce
  pl. luce
  fish; cf. loose
lu|cency
lu|cen|cies
lu|cent
lu|cern var. of
  lucerne
Lu|cerne in
  Switzerland
lu|cerne plant
Lu|cian writer
lucid
lu|cid|ity
lu|cid|ly
Lu|ci|fer Satan;
  planet Venus
lu|ci|fer match
lu|cifu|gous
Lu|cille
Lu|cinda
lu|cine
lu|cite *trademark*
luck|ily
luck|less
luck|less|ly
luck|less|ness
Luck|now
lucky
  luck|ier
  lucki|est

lu|cra|tive
lu|cra|tive|ly
lu|cra|tive|ness
lucre
Lu|cre|tia in
  Roman legend
Lu|cre|tius poet
lucu|brate
  lucu|brat|ing
lucu|bra|tion
Lu|cul|lan
lud in 'm'lud'
Lud|dism
Lud|dite
Lud|dit|ism
Lu|den|dorff, Erich
  German general
lu|der|ick
  pl. lu|der|ick
Lud|hiana
ludic
ludi|crous
ludi|crous|ly
ludi|crous|ness
Ludo = Ludovic
ludo game
Lu|do|vic
Lud|wig kings of
  Bavaria
Lud|wigs|hafen
lues (ven|erea)
lu|et|ic
luff
Luft|waffe
lug
  lugged
  lug|ging
Lu|ganda
Lu|gano
luge
  lu|ging
Luger trademark in
  the US
lug|gable
lug|gage
lug|ger ship
lug|hole
Lu|gosi, Bela actor
lug|sail
lu|gu|bri|ous
lu|gu|bri|ous|ly
lu|gu|bri|ous|ness
lug|worm

Lu|hansk
Lu|kács, György
  philosopher
luke|warm
luke|warm|ly
luke|warm|ness
lul|laby
  lul|la|bies
Lully, Jean-Baptiste
  composer
lulu
lum
luma
lum|bago
lum|bar relating to
  the lower back
lum|ber useless
  objects; timber;
  move awkwardly;
  encumber
lum|ber|er
lum|ber|jack
lum|ber|jacket
lum|ber|man
lum|ber|men
lum|ber|some
lum|ber|some|ness
lumen
  pl. lumen Physics
lumen
lu|mina Anatomy
Lu|mière, Au|guste
  and Louis pioneers
  of cinema
lu|min|aire
Lu|min|al drug
  trademark
lu|min|al of a
  lumen
lu|mi|nance
lu|mi|nary
  lu|mi|nar|ies
lu|mi|nesce
lu|mi|nes|cing
lu|mi|nes|cence
lu|mi|nes|cent
lu|mi|nif|er|ous
lu|mi|nos|ity
  lu|mi|nos|ities
lu|mi|nous
lu|mi|nous|ly
lu|mi|nous|ness
lumme exclam.
lum|mox

lump|ec|tomy
  lump|ec|to|mies
lump|en
lump|en|pro|le|
      tar|iat
lump|er
lump|fish
lump|ily
lumpi|ness
lump|ish
lump|ish|ly
lump|ish|ness
lump|suck|er
lumpy
  lump|ier
  lumpi|est
Luna Soviet moon
  probes
lu|nacy
  lu|na|cies
luna moth
lunar
lunar caus|tic
Lu|nar|ian
lu|nate
lu|na|tic
lu|na|tion
lunch|eon
lunch|eon|ette
lunch|er
lunch|room
lunch|time
Lund city, Sweden
Lunda
  pl. Lunda or
  Lun|das or
  Ba|lunda
Lundy
lune crescent; cf.
  loon
lu|nette
lung in body
lunge
  lunge|ing or
  lun|ging
  thrust etc.
lunge
  lunge|ing
  exercise horse on
  rein
lung|fish
lung|ful
lungi
lung|less

lung|worm
lung|wort
luni|solar
luni|tidal
lunk
lun|ker
lunk|head
lun|ula n.
  lunu|lae
lunu|lar adj.
lunu|late
lun|ule
Luo
  pl. Luo or Luos
Luo|yang city,
  China
lu|para
Lu|per|cal var. of
  Lupercalia
Lu|per|calia
Lu|per|cal|ian
lupin flower
lu|pine like a wolf
lu|pine var. of lupin
lu|poid
lu|pous relating to
  lupus
lu|pu|lin
Lupus constellation
lupus disease
lupus
  ery|the|ma|to|sus
lupus vul|garis
lur ancient trumpet
lurch
lurch|er
lur|dan
lure
  lur|ing
  entice; enticement
lurex trademark
lurgy
  lur|gies
lurid
lur|id|ly
lur|id|ness
lurk
lurk|er
Lu|saka
Lu|sa|tian
lus|cious
lus|cious|ly
lus|cious|ness

lush|ly
lush|ness
Lu|shun
Lu|si|ta|nia ancient
province, SW
Europe
Lu|si|ta|nia Cunard
liner
Lu|si|ta|nian
luso|phone
lust|er US
Br. lustre
lust|er|less US
Br. lustreless
lust|er|ware US
Br. lustreware
lust|ful
lust|ful|ly
lust|ful|ness
lust|ily
lusti|ness
lus|tra
lus|tral
lustre Br.
US luster
lustre|less Br.
US lusterless
lustre|ware Br.
US lusterware
lus|trine var. of
lustring
lus|tring
lus|trous
lus|trous|ly
lus|trous|ness
lus|trum
lus|tra or
lus|trums
lusty
lust|ier
lusti|est
lusus na|turae
pl. lusus na|turae
lu|tan|ist var. of
lutenist
lutchet
lute
lut|ing
musical instru-
ment; sealant; cf.
loot
lu|teal
lu|te|cium var. of
lutetium

lu|tein pigment; cf.
Lutine
lu|tein|is|ing Br.
var. of luteinizing
lu|tein|iz|ing
lu|ten|ist
luteo|ful|vous
luteo|troph|ic
luteo|trop|ic var. of
luteotrophic
lu|teous
lute|string
lu|te|tium
Lu|ther, Mar|tin
theologian
Lu|ther|an
Lu|ther|an|ise Br.
var. of Lutheranize
Lu|ther|an|ism
Lu|ther|an|ize
Lu|ther|an|iz|ing
lu|thern
lu|thier
Lu|thuli, Al|bert
politician
Lu|tine Bell cf.
lutein
lu|tino +s
lut|ist
Lu|to|mer
Ries|ling
Luton
Lu|to|sław|ski,
Wi|told composer
Lu|tuli var. of
Luthuli
Lut|yens, Edwin
architect
Lut|yens, Elisa|beth
composer
lutz
Lu|vale
pl. Lu|vale
Lu|vian var. of
Luwian
luv|vie effusive actor
or actress; cf. lovey
luvvie|dom
luvvy
luv|vies
var. of lovey, luvvie
Lu|wian
lux
pl. lux

unit of illumin-
ation; cf. de luxe
lux|ate
lux|at|ing
lux|ation
luxe luxury; in 'de
luxe'; cf. lux
Lux|em|bourg
Lux|em|bourg|er
Lux|em|burg, Rosa
revolutionary
Lux|em|burg|ish
Luxor
lux|uri|ance
lux|uri|ant
lux|uri|ant|ly
lux|uri|ate
lux|uri|at|ing
lux|uri|ous
lux|uri|ous|ly
lux|uri|ous|ness
lux|ury
lux|ur|ies
Luzon
Lviv
Lvov Russian name
for Lviv
lwei
pl. lwei
Lwena
another name for
Luvale
L-word
Ly|all|pur
lyase
ly|caen|id
ly|can|thrope
ly|can|throp|i|c
ly|can|thropy
lycée
Ly|ceum Philosophy
ly|ceum lecture hall
etc.
ly|chee
lych|gate
lych|nis
Lycia
Ly|cian
lyco|pene
lyco|pod
lyco|po|dium
ly|cop|sid
Ly|cop|sida

Lycra trademark
Ly|cur|gus reputed
founder of Sparta
lydd|ite explosive;
cf. lydite
Lyd|gate, John poet
Lydia
Lyd|ian
lyd|ite stone; cf.
lyddite
lye alkaline liquid;
cf. lie
Lyell, Charles
geologist
lying
lying-in +s n.
lying-in-state n.
lyings-in-state
ly|ing|ly
lyke wake
Lyly, John writer
Lyman ser|ies
Lyme dis|ease cf.
lime
Lyme Regis
lymph
lymph|aden|itis
lymph|aden|
op|athy
lymph|angio|gram
lymph|angio|
graph|ic
lymph|angi|
og|raphy
lymph|an|gitis
lymph|at|ic
lympho|blast
lympho|blast|ic
lympho|cyte
lympho|cyt|ic
lymph|oid
lympho|kine
lymph|oma
lymph|omas or
lymph|omata
lympho|reticu|lar
Lynch, David film
director
lynch
lynch|er
lyn|chet
lynch|pin var. of
linchpin
Lyn|ette

Lynn, Vera singer
Lyn¦sey
lynx animal; cf.
  links
Lyon
  French name for
  Lyons
Lyon herald
lyon¦naise
Lyons city, France
lyo|phil|ic
ly¦oph¦il¦isa|tion
  Br. var. of
  lyophilization
ly¦oph¦il¦ise Br. var.
  of lyophilize
ly¦oph¦il¦iza|tion
  ly¦oph¦il¦iz¦ing
lyo|pho¦bic
Lyo|tard, Jean-
  François philo-
  sopher and critic
Lyra constellation
lyr¦ate
lyre musical
  instrument; cf. liar
lyre|bird
lyre|tail
lyric
lyr¦ic¦al
lyr¦ic¦al¦ly
lyri¦cism
lyri¦cist
lyr¦ist
Ly¦san|der Spartan
  general
lys¦ate
lyse
  lys¦ing
Ly¦senko|ism
ly¦ser|gic
lys|im¦eter
lysin antibody
ly¦sine amino acid
Ly¦sip|pus Greek
  sculptor
lysis
Lysol trademark
lyso|somal
lyso|some
lyso|zyme
lytic

lyt¦ic¦al¦ly
Lyt¦ton, Lord
  title of Edward
  Bulwer-Lytton

—————————

M

ma = mother; cf.
  mar, maar
ma'am = madam; cf.
  malm
maar crater; cf. ma,
  mar
Maas river
maas soured milk
Maa¦sai var. of
  Masai
maas|bank¦er
Maas|trich
Maat Egyptian
  goddess
ma¦bela cereal
ma¦bele var. of
  mabela
Mabi|no¦gion
  Welsh text
Ma¦buse, Jan
  painter
Mac Scotsman; form
  of address
mac = mackintosh
ma¦cabre
mac¦adam
mac¦adamed
maca|da¦mia
mac¦ad¦am|ise Br.
  var. of macadamize
mac¦ad¦am|ize
  mac¦ad¦am|iz¦ing
maca|juel
McAleese, Mary
  president of
  Republic of Ireland
Mac¦Alpin,
  Ken¦neth king of
  Scotland
Maca|nese
Macao
Ma¦capá
ma¦caque

Maca¦ro|nesia
Maca¦ro|nes¦ian
maca|roni +s pasta;
  penguin
maca|roni
  maca¦ro|nies
  dandy
maca|ron¦ic
maca|roon
Mac¦Arthur,
  Doug|las US
  general
Ma¦cas|sar
Mac¦aulay, Rose
  writer
Mac¦aulay, Thomas
  Bab¦ing|ton
  historian
macaw
Mac¦beth king of
  Scotland
Mac¦ca|baeus,
  Judas Jewish
  leader
Mac¦ca|bean
Mac¦ca|bee
McCarthy, Jo¦seph
  R. US politician
McCarthy, Mary
  writer
McCarthy|ism
McCarthy|ist
McCarthy|ite
McCart|ney, Paul
  singer and
  songwriter
mac¦chi¦ato +s
McCoy in 'the real
  McCoy'
McCul¦lers,
  Car¦son writer
Mac¦Diarmid,
  Hugh poet
Mac¦Donald, Flora
  Scottish heroine
Mac¦Donald,
  Ram¦say prime
  minister of Britain
Mac¦don¦ald, John
  prime minister of
  Canada
Mac¦Donnell
  Ranges
Mace trademark
Mac¦ing

(spray with)
  chemical
mace club; spice
ma¦cé|doine
Ma¦ce|don
Ma¦ce|do¦nia
Ma¦ce|do¦nian
Ma¦ceió
McEnroe, John
  tennis player
macer
ma¦cer|ate
  ma¦cer|at¦ing
ma¦cer|ation
ma¦cer|ator
McEwan, Ian
  novelist
mac|far|lane over-
  coat
Mac|gil|li|cuddy's
  Reeks
McGona¦gall,
  Wil|liam writer
McGui¦nn
Mach, Ernst physi-
  cist
Mach as in 'Mach 1',
  'Mach 2', etc.
mach|air
ma¦chan
mache
macher
ma|chete
Ma¦chia|vel
Ma¦chia|velli,
  Nic|colò political
  philosopher
Ma¦chia|vel|lian
Ma¦chia|vel|lian|
    ism
ma¦chico|late
ma¦chico|lat¦ing
ma¦chico|la¦tion
ma¦chin|abil¦ity
ma¦chin|able
ma¦chin|ate
  ma¦chin|at¦ing
ma¦chin|ation
ma¦chin|ator
ma¦chine
  ma¦chin¦ing
machine-gunner
ma¦chin¦ery
ma¦chin¦er¦ies

ma|chin|ist
mach|ismo
Mach|meter
macho +s
Macht|poli|tik
Machu Pic|chu
Ma|chupo virus
McIntosh variety of
apple
mac|in|tosh var. of
mackintosh
McJob
mack var. of mac
Mac|kay port,
Australia
Mac|ken|zie,
Alex|an|der
explorer
Mac|ken|zie,
Comp|ton writer
Mac|ken|zie,
Wil|liam Canadian
politician
mack|erel
mackinaw
McKinlay, John
explorer
McKinley, Mt
McKinley, Wil|liam
US president
Mack|in|tosh,
Charles Ren|nie
architect and
designer
mack|in|tosh
raincoat
mackle printing
blemish
macle twin crystal;
spot in a mineral
Mac|lean, Ali|stair
writer
Mac|lean, Don|ald
spy
McLuhan,
Mar|shall
communications
scholar
Mac|mil|lan,
Har|old prime
minister of Britain
McNagh|ten rules
McNaugh|ten
rules var. of
McNaghten rules

Mac|Neice, Louis
poet
Mâcon
Mac|qua|rie,
Lach|lan Austra-
lian administrator
mac|ramé
macro +s
macro|bi|ot|ic
macro|carpa
macro|ceph|alic
macro|ceph|al|ous
macro|ceph|aly
macro|cosm
macro|cos|mic
macro|cos|mic|al|ly
macro|cycle
macro|cyc|lic
macro|eco|nom|ic
macro|econ|omy
macro|econ|omies
macro|evo|lu|tion
macro|evo|lu|tion|
ary
macro|gam|ete
macro lens
macro|lepi|
dop|tera
macro|mol|ecu|lar
macro|mol|ecule
mac|ron
macro|nu|tri|ent
macro|phage
macro|
photog|raphy
macro|phyte
macro|pod
macro|scop|ic
macro|scop|ic|al|ly
macro|struc|tural
macro|struc|ture
ma|cruran
ma|crur|ous
McTim|oney
mac|ula *n.*
macu|lae
mac|ula lutea
macu|lae lu|teae
macu|lar *adj.*
macu|late
macu|lat|ing
macu|la|tion
mac|ule

ma|cumba
ma|cushla
mad
mad|ded
mad|ding
mad|der
mad|dest
Mada|gas|can
Mada|gas|car
madam form of
address; conceited
girl; brothel-keeper
Ma|dame
Mes|dames
French-speaking
woman
mad|cap
mad|den
mad|den|ing|ly
mad|der plant; red
dye
Mad|die
Maddy
made past tense and
past participle of
make; cf. maid
Ma|deira
Ma|deir|an
Mad|elaine name
Mad|eleine name
madeleine cake
Mad|eline name
Ma|de|mois|elle
Mes|de|mois|elles
mad|er|isa|tion *Br.*
var. of
maderization
mad|er|ised *Br.* var.
of maderized
mad|er|iza|tion
mad|er|ized
made-up wearing
make-up; invented;
prepared for sale;
surfaced; delighted
mad|house
Madhya Pra|desh
Madi|son city;
dance
Madi|son, James
US president
madison cycle race
madly
mad|man
mad|men

mad|ness
mado +s
Ma|donna the Vir-
gin Mary; singer
ma|donna represen-
tation of the
Madonna; virtuous
woman
ma|donna lily
Ma|dras port, India
ma|dras striped
cotton
ma|drasa
Mad|re|por|aria
mad|re|por|ar|ian
mad|re|pore
mad|re|por|ite
Ma|drid
mad|ri|gal
mad|ri|gal|ian
mad|ri|gal|ist
mad|ri|lene soup
Mad|ri|len|ian
Mad|ri|leño +s
ma|droña var. of
ma|droño
ma|droño +s
mad|tom catfish
Ma|dura island,
Indonesia
Madu|rai city, India
Madur|ese person
from Madura
mad|woman
mad|women
Mae|an|der
Mae|ce|nas, Gaius
writer
maedi
mael|strom
mae|nad
mae|nad|ic
maes|toso +s
maes|tro
maes|tri or
maes|tros
Mae|ter|linck,
Maur|ice writer
Mafe|king
Mafia in Sicily, US,
etc.
mafia any sinister
organized group
mafic *Geology*

Mafi|keng
modern spelling of
Mafeking
mafi|oso
mafi|osi
Mag|adha ancient
kingdom, India
Ma|gadi, Lake in
Kenya
Mag|ahi
maga|logue
maga|zine
mag|da|len
reformed prostitute
Mag|da|lena river,
Colombia; name
Magd|alen College,
Oxford
Mag|da|lene, Mary
Bible
Magd|alene
Col|lege, Cambridge
Mag|da|len|lan
Archaeology
Mag|de|burg
Ma|gel|lan,
Fer|di|nand
explorer
Mag|el|lan|ic
Clouds
Magen David
ma|genta
Mag|gid
Mag|gid|im
Mag|gie
mag|gie bird
Mag|giore, Lake
mag|got
mag|goty
Magh|reb var. of
Maghrib
Magh|rib
Magi the 'wise men'
magi pl. of magus
Ma|gian of the Magi
or magi
magic
ma|gicked
ma|gick|ing
magic|al
magic|al|ly
ma|gi|cian
ma|gilp var. of
megilp

Magi|not Line
magis|ter
magis|ter|ial
magis|teri|al|ly
magis|ter|ium
magis|tracy
magis|tra|cies
magis|tral
magis|trate
magis|trate|ship
magis|tra|ture
Mag|le|mo|sian
mag|lev
magma
magmas or
mag|mata
mag|mat|ic
mag|ma|tism
Magna Carta
Magna Charta var.
of Magna Carta
magna cum laude
Magna Grae|cia
mag|na|nim|ity
mag|nani|mous
mag|nani|mous|ly
mag|nate
mag|ne|sia
mag|nes|ian
mag|ne|site
mag|ne|sium
mag|net
mag|ne|tar
mag|net|ic
mag|net|ic|al|ly
mag|net|is|able Br.
var. of
magnetizable
mag|net|isa|tion
Br. var. of
magnetization
mag|net|ise Br. var.
of magnetize
mag|net|iser Br.
var. of magnetizer
mag|net|ism
mag|net|ite
mag|net|iz|able
mag|net|iza|tion
mag|net|ize
mag|net|iz|ing
mag|net|izer
mag|neto +s

magneto-electric
magneto-
electri|city
mag|neto|graph
mag|neto|hydro|
dynam|ic
mag|net|om|eter
mag|net|om|etry
mag|ne|ton
magneto-optical
mag|neto|pause
mag|neto|
resist|ance
mag|neto|resist|ive
mag|neto|sphere
mag|neto|spher|ic
mag|neto|tail
mag|ne|tron
mag|ni|fi|able
Mag|nifi|cat can-
ticle
mag|nifi|cat song of
praise
mag|ni|fi|ca|tion
mag|nifi|cence
mag|nifi|cent
mag|nifi|cent|ly
mag|nif|ico
mag|nif|icoes
mag|ni|fier
mag|nify
mag|ni|fies
mag|ni|fied
mag|ni|fy|ing
mag|nilo|quence
mag|nilo|quent
mag|nilo|quent|ly
Mag|nito|gorsk
mag|ni|tude
mag|no|lia
Mag|nox fuelled
with magnox
mag|nox alloy
mag|num
mag|num opus
mag|num opuses
or magna opera
Mag|nus
Magog in 'Gog and
Magog'
mag|pie
Ma|gritte, René
painter

mags|man
mags|men
ma|guey
magus
magi
Mag|yar
maha
Maha|bad
Maha|bhar|ata
ma|ha|jan
mahal
Ma|ha|mad Sephar-
dic synagogue
trustees; cf.
Muhammad
ma|hant
maha|raja Indian
prince
maha|ra|jah var. of
maharaja
maha|ra|nee var. of
maharani
maha|rani
maharaja's wife
Maha|rash|tra
Maha|rishi
ma|hatma
Maha|weli
Maha|yana
Buddhism
Mahdi *Islam*
Mahd|ism
Mahd|ist
Mah|fouz, Na|guib
writer
Ma|hi|can American
Indian people for-
merly of New York
State; cf. Mohegan,
Mohican
Ma|hil|lyow
mahi|mahi
mah-jong
mah-jongg var. of
mah-jong
Mah|ler, Gus|tav
composer
Mah|ler|ian
mahl|stick
mahoe
ma|hog|any
ma|hog|anies
Mahon, Port
ma|ho|nia

Ma¦hore
ma¦hout
Mah¦ratta var. of
  Maratha
Mah¦ratti var. of
  Marathi
mah¦seer
mahua
ma¦hurat
mahwa var. of
  mahua
maid servant; girl
mai¦dan open space
maid¦en girl
maid¦en¦hair
Maid¦en¦head
  town, England
maid¦en¦head vir-
  ginity
maid¦en¦hood
maid¦en¦ish
maiden-like
maid¦en¦ly
maid¦ser¦vant
Maid¦stone
mai¦eu¦tic
maigre fast day
Mai¦gret fictional
  detective
Mai¦kop
mail post; flexible
  armour; cf. male
mail¦able
mail¦bag
mail¦boat
mail¦box
Mail¦er, Nor¦man
  writer
mail¦er person
  sending post;
  something sent by
  post
mail¦lot
mail¦man
  mail¦men
mail-out n.
mail¦shot
  mail¦shot¦ted
  mail¦shot¦ting
maim
Mai¦moni¦des
  philosopher

Main river,
  Germany; cf.
  Maine
main principal;
  pipe, cable; ocean;
  cf. mane
main¦board
main¦crop mod.
Maine state, US; cf.
  Main
Mainer
main¦frame
Main¦land islands,
  Orkney and
  Shetland
main¦land country
  excluding islands
main¦land¦er
main¦line
  main¦lin¦ing
  inject drugs
  intravenously
main line railway
  line; principal vein
main¦liner
main¦ly
main¦mast
main¦plane
main¦sail
main¦sheet
main¦spring
main¦stay
main¦stream
main¦tain
  main¦tain¦abil¦ity
main¦tain¦able
main¦tain¦er
main¦ten¦ance
Main¦te¦non,
  Fran¦çoise,
  Mar¦quise de wife
  of Louis XIV of
  France
main¦top
main¦top¦mast
Mainz
mai¦ol¦ica fine Ital-
  ian earthenware; cf.
  majolica
Mai¦sie
mai¦son¦ette
mais¦try
  mais¦tries
mai tai

Mai¦thili
maître d'
  maître d's
maître d'hôtel
  maîtres d'hôtel
Mai¦treya Buddha
maize cereal; cf.
  maze
ma¦jes¦tic
ma¦jes¦tic¦al¦ly
maj¦esty
  maj¦es¦ties
maj¦lis
  pl. maj¦lis
ma¦jol¦ica imitation
  maiolica
Major, John prime
  minister of Britain
major
Ma¦jorca
Ma¦jor¦can
major-domo +s
ma¦jor¦ette
major gen¦eral
  major gen¦erals
Ma¦jor¦ism
ma¦jor¦itar¦ian
ma¦jor¦itar¦ian¦ism
ma¦jor¦ity
  ma¦jor¦ities
major-leaguer
ma¦jor¦ly
maj¦us¦cule
mak¦able
Ma¦ka¦rios arch-
  bishop, president of
  Cyprus
Ma¦kasar var. of
  Makassar
Ma¦kas¦ar¦ese
Ma¦kas¦sar
Ma¦kas¦sar¦ese var.
  of Makasarese
make
  made
  mak¦ing
make¦able var. of
  makable
make-and-break
  electrical switch
make-believe
  make-believ¦ing
make-do makeshift

make-or-break n.
  & mod.
make¦over n.
maker
make¦shift
make-up n.
make¦weight
make-work adj. &
  n.
Mak¦ga¦dik¦gadi
  Pans
Makh¦ach¦kala
ma¦khani
maki zushi
  Japanese dish
mako
  pl. mako or makos
Ma¦konde
  pl. Ma¦konde or
  Ma¦kon¦des
Makua
  pl. Makua or
  Makuas
ma¦kutu sorcery
mala string of
  prayer beads
Mala¦bar Coast
Ma¦labo
mal¦ab¦sorp¦tion
Ma¦lacca Strait;
  former name of
  Melaka
ma¦lacca cane
Mal¦achi Bible
mal¦ach¦ite
malaco¦logic¦al
mala¦colo¦gist
mala¦col¦ogy
Mala¦cos¦traca
mala¦cos¦tra¦can
mal¦adap¦ta¦tion
mal¦adapt¦ed
mal¦adap¦tive
mal¦adjust¦ed
mal¦adjust¦ment
mal¦admin¦is¦ter
mal¦admin¦is¦
  tra¦tion
mal¦adroit
mal¦adroit¦ly
mal¦adroit¦ness
mal¦ady
  mal¦ad¦ies

mala fide in bad
faith

mala fides bad faith

Mal¦aga city, Spain;
wine

Mala¦gasy
pl. Mala¦gasy or
Mala¦gas¦ies
Madagascan;
language

mala¦gueña
Spanish dance

mala¦gueta var. of
malaguetta

mala¦guetta =
grains of Paradise

mal¦aise

Mala¦mud,
Ber¦nard writer

mala¦mute

ma¦langa

mala¦pert

mala¦prop

mala¦prop¦ism

mal¦apro¦pos

malar

Mäla¦ren

mal¦aria

mal¦ar¦ial

mal¦ar¦ian

mal¦ario¦logic¦al

mal¦ari¦olo¦gist

mal¦ari¦ology

mal¦ari¦ous

ma¦lar¦key

mal¦ate

mala¦thion

Ma¦lawi

Ma¦la¦wian

Malay

Ma¦laya

Ma¦lay¦alam lan-
guage

Ma¦lay¦alee var. of
Malayali

Ma¦lay¦ali
Malayalam-speaker

Ma¦lay¦an

Malayo- Malay or
Malayan and ...

Ma¦lay¦sia

Ma¦lay¦sian

Mal¦bec

mal¦coha var. of
malkoha

Mal¦colm

mal¦con¦tent

mal¦con¦tent¦ed

mal de mer

mal¦devel¦op¦ment

mal¦dis¦trib¦uted

mal¦dis¦tri¦bu¦tion

Mal¦dives

Mal¦div¦ian

mal du siècle

Male city

male masculine; cf.
mail

male¦ate

mal¦edic¦tion

mal¦edic¦tive

mal¦edic¦tory

mal¦efac¦tion

mal¦efac¦tor

mal¦efic

mal¦efi¦cence

mal¦efi¦cent

Male¦gaon

ma¦leic

mal¦emute var. of
malamute

male¦ness

Ma¦len¦kov, Ge¦orgi
Soviet leader

Mal¦esia

Mal¦esian

Mal¦evich, Kazi¦mir
painter

mal¦evo¦lence

mal¦evo¦lent

mal¦evo¦lent¦ly

mal¦fatti

mal¦fea¦sance

mal¦fea¦sant

mal¦for¦ma¦tion

mal¦formed

mal¦func¦tion

Mal¦herbe,
Fran¦çois de poet

Mali country

mali gardener

Mali¦an

Mal¦ibu resort, US;
surfboard

malic

mal¦ice

ma¦li¦cious

ma¦li¦cious¦ly

ma¦li¦cious¦ness

ma¦lign malignant;
slander; cf. moline

ma¦lig¦nancy

ma¦lig¦nan¦cies

ma¦lig¦nant

ma¦lig¦nant¦ly

ma¦lign¦er

ma¦lig¦nity

ma¦lign¦ly

malik

ma¦limbe

Malin

ma¦lin¦ger

ma¦lin¦ger¦er

Ma¦linke
pl. Ma¦linke or
Ma¦lin¦kes

Mal¦in¦ow¦ski,
Bron¦isław
Kas¦par anthro-
pologist

mal¦ison

mal¦koha

mall walk; shopping
centre; cf. maul

mal¦lam

mal¦lard

Mal¦lar¦mé,
Sté¦phane poet

Malle, Louis film
director

mal¦le¦abil¦ity

mal¦le¦able

mal¦le¦ably

mal¦lee eucalyptus

mal¦lee¦fowl
pl. mal¦lee¦fowl

mal¦lee hen

mal¦lei *pl.* of
malleus

mal¦le¦olus

mal¦le¦oli

mal¦let

mal¦leus

mal¦lei

mal¦ling

Mal¦loph¦aga

mal¦loph¦agan

Mal¦lor¦can var. of
Majorcan

mal¦low

malm rock; brick;
cf. ma'am

Malmö

malm¦sey

mal¦nour¦ished

mal¦nour¦ish¦ment

mal¦nu¦tri¦tion

mal¦occlu¦sion

mal¦odor *US*

mal¦odor¦ous

mal¦odour *Br.*

malo¦lac¦tic

mal¦on¦ate

mal¦on¦ic

Mal¦ory, Thomas
writer

ma¦loti *pl.* of loti

mal¦per¦form¦ance

Mal¦pi¦ghi,
Mar¦cello micro-
scopist

Mal¦pig¦hian

Mal¦pla¦quet

mal¦pr ac¦tice

mal¦pre¦sen¦ta¦tion

Mal¦raux, André
novelist

Malta

malt¦ase

Mal¦tese

malt¦house

Mal¦thus, Thomas
economist

Mal¦thu¦sian

Mal¦thu¦sian¦ism

malti¦ness

malt¦ing

malto¦dex¦trin

mal¦tose

mal¦treat

mal¦treat¦er

mal¦treat¦ment

malt¦ster

malty

malt¦ier

malti¦est

mal¦va¦ceous

Mal¦vasia

Mal¦vern

mal¦ver¦sa¦tion

mal¦voisie

mal¦ware

mama = mother

mama|guy
mama-san
mamba snake
mambo
  pl. mam|bos
  v. mam|boes
  mam|boed
  mambo|ing
mamee var. of
  mammee
mam|elon
Mam|eluke
Mamet, David
  dramatist
ma|milla *Br.*
  ma|mil|las or
  ma|mil|lae
  US mammilla
mam|il|lary *Br.*
  US mammillary
mam|il|late *Br.*
  US mammillate
mam|il|lated *Br.*
  US mammillated
mamma
  mam|mae
  breast
mamma +s var. of
  mama
mam|mal
Mam|ma|lia
mam|ma|lian
mammal-like
mam|malo|gist
mam|mal|ogy
mam|mary
  mam|mar|ies
mam|mee tree; cf.
  mammy
mam|mee sa|pote
mam|mi|form
mam|milla *US*
  mam|mil|las or
  mam|mil|lae
  Br. mamilla
mam|mil|lary *US*
  Br. mamillary
mam|mil|late *US*
  Br. mamillate
mam|mil|lated *US*
  Br. mamillated
mam|mo|gram
mam|mog|raphy
Mam|mon
Mam|mon|ish
Mam|mon|ism
Mam|mon|ist
Mam|mon|ite
mam|moth
mammy
  mam|mies
  mother; cf.
  mammee
Ma|mou|tzu
mam|para var. of
  mompara
Mam'selle
Man, Isle of
man
  pl. men
  v. mans
  manned
  man|ning
mana supernatural
  power; cf. manna
man|acle
  man|ac|ling
man|age
  man|aging
man|age|abil|ity
man|age|able
man|age|ably
man|age|ment
man|ager
man|ager|ess
man|ager|ial
man|ager|ial|ism
man|ager|ial|ist
man|ageri|al|ly
man|ager|ship
Ma|na|gua
man|akin American
  bird; cf. manikin,
  mannequin,
  mannikin
Ma|nama
ma|ñana
Mana Pools
Ma|nas|seh *Bible*
Ma|nas|ses, Prayer
  of
manat
  pl. manat
  currency of
  Azerbaijan or
  Turkmenistan
man-at-arms
  men-at-arms
mana|tee

Ma|naus
Mana|watu
Man|chego
Man|ches|ter city,
  England
man|ches|ter
  household linen
man|chet
man|chi|neel
Man|chu
Man|chu|ria
Man|chu|rian
man|ciple
Man|cu|nian
Man|dae|an
man|dala circular
  symbol
Man|da|lay port,
  Burma
man|dal|ic
man|da|mus
  man|da|mus|es
Man|dan
  pl. Man|dan or
  Man|dans
man|dap
man|da|pam var. of
  mandap
Man|da|rin Chinese
  language
man|da|rin official;
  orange; m. collar,
  duck
man|da|rin|ate
man|da|rine
  orange; var. of
  mandarin
man|da|tary
  man|da|tar|ies
  receiver of a
  mandate; cf.
  mandatory
man|date
man|dat|ing
man|da|tor|ily
man|da|tory com-
  pulsory; cf.
  mandatary
man-day
Mande
  pl. Mande or
  Mandes
Man|de|an var. of
  Mandaean

Man|dela, Nel|son
  president of South
  Africa
Man|del|brot,
  Be|noit
  mathematician
Man|del|stam,
  Osip poet
Man|de|ville, John
  reputed author of
  travellers' tales
man|dible
man|dibu|lar
man|dibu|late
Man|ding
  pl. Man|ding or
  Man|dings
Man|dingo
  pl. Man|dingo or
  Man|din|gos
Man|dinka
  pl. Man|dinka or
  Man|din|kas
  Mande-speaking
  people; language
man|dir
man|dola large
  mandolin; cf.
  mandorla
man|do|lin musical
  instrument
man|do|line
  vegetable slicer
man|do|lin|ist
man|dora var. of
  mandola
man|dorla almond-
  shape; cf. mandola
man|drag|ora
man|drake
Man|drax
  trademark
man|drel shaft; rod
man|drill baboon
man|du|cate
  man|du|cat|ing
man|du|ca|tion
man|du|ca|tory
mane hair on horse,
  lion, etc.; cf. main
maneb
maned
ma|nège
mane|less

Manes founder of
 Manichaeism
manes deified souls
Manet, Édouard
 painter
Ma|netho Egyptian
 priest
man|eu|ver *US*
 Br. manoeuvre
man|eu|ver|abil|ity
 US
 Br.
 manoeuvrability
man|eu|ver|able
 US
 Br. manoeuvrable
man|eu|ver|er *US*
 Br. manoeuvrer
Man|fred
man|ful
man|ful|ly
man|ful|ness
manga
man|ga|bey
man|ga|nate
man|ga|nese
man|gan|ic
Man|gan|in
 trademark
man|gan|ite
man|gan|ous
mange
man|gel beet; cf.
 mangle
mangel-wurzel
man|ger
mange|tout
 pl. mange|tout or
 mange|touts
man|gey var. of
 mangy
man|gily
man|gi|ness
man|gle
 man|gling
 laundry machine;
 mutilate; cf.
 mangel
man|gler
mango
 man|goes or
 man|gos
man|gold
man|gonel

man|go|steen
man|grove
mangy
 man|gier
 man|gi|est
man|handle
 man|hand|ling
Man|hat|tan island,
 New York City
man|hat|tan cock-
 tail
man|hole
man|hood
man-hour
man|hunt
mania
ma|niac
ma|ni|acal
ma|ni|acal|ly
manic
Ma|nica|land
man|ic|al|ly
manic de|pres|sion
manic-depres|sive
Mani|chae|an
Mani|chaean|ism
Mani|chae|ism
Mani|che|an var. of
 Manichaean
Mani|chean|ism
 var. of
 Manichaeanism
Mani|chee
Mani|che|ism var.
 of Manichaeism
mani|cotti
mani|cure
 mani|cur|ing
 mani|cur|ist
mani|fest
mani|fest|ation
mani|fest|ly
mani|festo +s
mani|fold various;
 branching pipe; cf.
 manyfold
mani|fold|ly
mani|kin little man;
 cf. manakin,
 mannequin,
 mannikin
Ma|nila city, Philip-
 pines; fibre; paper

Ma|nilla fibre;
 paper; var. of
 Manila
ma|nilla bracelet
man|ioc
man|iple
ma|nipu|la|bil|ity
ma|nipu|lable
ma|nipu|lar
ma|nipu|lat|able
ma|nipu|late
 ma|nipu|lat|ing
ma|nipu|la|tion
ma|nipu|la|tive
ma|nipu|la|tive|ly
ma|nipu|la|tive|
 ness
ma|nipu|la|tor
ma|nipu|la|tory
Mani|pur
Mani|puri
Mani|toba
Mani|to|ban
mani|tou
man|kind
manky
 mank|ier
 mank|iest
man|less
Man|ley, Mi|chael
 prime minister of
 Jamaica
man|like
man|li|ness
manly
 man|lier
 man|li|est
man-made
Mann, Thomas
 writer
manna food; cf.
 manner, manor
Man|nar island and
 town, Sri Lanka;
 Gulf
manned
man|ne|quin
 dressmaker's
 model; cf.
 manakin, manikin,
 mannikin
man|ner way;
 behaviour; cf.
 manna, manor

man|nered
man|ner|ism
man|ner|ist
man|ner|is|tic
man|ner|less
man|ner|li|ness
man|ner|ly
Mann|heim
man|nie
man|ni|kin Old
 World bird; cf.
 manakin, manikin,
 mannequin
Man|ning, Olivia
 novelist
man|nish
man|nish|ly
man|nish|ness
man|ni|tol
man|nose
manny var. of
 mannie
Mano river
mano-a-mano +s
man|oeuv|ra|bil|ity
 Br.
 US
 maneuverability
man|oeuv|rable *Br.*
 US maneuverable
man|oeuvre *Br.*
 man|oeuv|ring
 US maneuver
man|oeuv|rer *Br.*
 US maneuverer
man-of-war
 men-of-war
man|oir
man|om|eter
mano|met|ric
ma non troppo
 Music
manor house;
 district; cf. manna,
 manner
man|orial
man-o'-war
 men-o'-war
 var. of man-of-war
man|power
man|qué
man|sard
Man|sart, Fran|çois
 architect

manse

Man|sell, Nigel
racing driver

man|ser|vant
men|ser|vants or
man|ser|vants

**Mans|field,
Kath|er|ine** writer

man|sion

man|slaugh|ter

Man|son, Charles
cult leader

man|sue|tude

manta

man|teau

**Man|tegna,
An|drea** painter

man|tel mantel-
piece; cf. **mantle**

**Man|tell, Gid|eon
Al|ger|non**
geologist

man|tel|letta
man|tel|let|tas or
man|tel|lette

man|tel|piece

man|tel|shelf
pl. man|tel|shelves
v. man|tel|shelfs
man|tel|shelfed
man|tel|shelf|ing

mantel|tree

man|tic

man|ti|core

man|tid

man|tilla

man|tis
pl. man|tis or
man|tises

man|tissa

man|tle
mant|ling
cloak; in gas lamp;
layer of the earth;
cf. **mantel**

mantle|piece var. of
mantelpiece

mantle|shelf var. of
mantelshelf

mant|let

man to man
frankly

man-to-man attrib.
marking one
opponent; frank

Man|toux test

man|tra

man|trap

man|tric

Man|tua city, Italy

man|tua gown

Man|tuan

Manu Hindu
Mythology

manu|al

manu|al|ly

ma|nu|brial

ma|nu|brium
ma|nu|bria or
ma|nu|briums

manu|code

Man|uel|ine

manu|fac|tory

manu|fac|tor|ies

manu|fac|tur|
       abil|ity

manu|fac|tur|able

manu|fac|ture
manu|fac|tur|ing

manu|fac|tur|er

ma|nuka

manul

manu|mis|sion

manu|mit
manu|mit|ted
manu|mit|ting
manu|mit|ter

ma|nure
ma|nur|ing

manus
pl. manus

manu|script

Manu|tius, Aldus
printer

Manx Logh|tan
sheep

**Manx|man
Manx|men**

**Manx|woman
Manx|women**

many

man|yatta

many|fold by many
times; cf. **manifold**

man|za|nilla sherry

man|za|nita shrub

**Man|zoni,
Ales|san|dro** writer

Mao|ism

Mao|ist

mao|mao +s fish;
cf. **Mau Mau, mau-
mau**

Maori
pl. **Maori** or
Maoris
New Zealand
people and
language; cf. **Mari**

Maori|dom

Maori|land

Maori|tanga

mao-tai

Mao Tse-tung var.
of **Mao Zedong**

Mao Ze|dong
Chinese leader

map

mapped

map|ping

ma|pant|sula
pl. of **pantsula**

mape|pire

maple

map|less

Mappa Mundi map
in Hereford
Cathedral

mappe|monde
medieval world
map

map|per

Ma|puche
pl. **Ma|puche** or
Ma|pu|ches

Ma|puto

ma|quette

ma|quila

ma|quila|dora

ma|quill|age

Ma|quis French
resistance
movement

ma|quis
pl. ma|quis
member of the
Maquis; dense
scrub; cf. **marquee**

ma|quis|ard

mar

marred

mar|ring
spoil; cf. **ma, maar**

mara

mara|bou stork;
feather

mara|bout Muslim
hermit; shrine

mara|bunta wasp

ma|raca

Mara|caibo

Mara|dona, Diego
footballer

marae
pl. marae

mar|aging steel

Ma|ramba

Mara|nhão state,
Brazil

Mara|ñón river,
Peru

ma|ranta

ma|rari
pl. ma|rari or
ma|raris

mar|as|chino +s

mar|as|mic

mar|as|mus

Marat, Jean French
revolutionary

Ma|ra|tha member
of a Hindu caste

Ma|ra|thi language

mara|thon

mara|thon|er

ma|raud

ma|raud|er

mara|vedi

Mar|bella

mar|ble
marb|ling

marble|ise Br. var.
of **marbleize**

marble|ize
marble|iz|ing

marb|ler

marbly

Mar|burg

Marc name

marc brandy; cf.
mark, marque

Marc|an of St Mark

mar|cas|ite

mar|cato Music

Mar|ceau, Mar|cel
mime artist

Mar|cel name

mar|cel
  mar|celled
  mar|cel|ling
  (put) wave in hair
Mar|cella
mar|ces|cence
mar|ces|cent
March month
march walk; mili-
  tary music
Mar|che region,
  Italy
march|er
Mar|ches region,
  English-Welsh
  border
mar|chesa
  mar|chese
  female
mar|chese
  mar|chesi
  male
mar|chion|ess
march|pane
march past n.
  march pasts
Mar|cia
Mar|ci|ano, Rocky
  boxer
Mar|coni,
  Gu|glielmo
  electrical engineer
Marco Polo travel-
  ler
Mar|cus
Mar|cus Aur|elius
  Roman emperor
Mar|cuse, Her|bert
  philosopher
Mar del Plata
Mardi Gras
Mar|duk
  Babylonian
  Mythology
mardy
  mar|dier
  mar|di|est
Mare, Wal|ter de la
  writer
mare female horse;
  cf. mayor
mare
  maria or mares
  sea; flat area on the
  moon or Mars

mare clau|sum
  maria clausa
Marek's dis|ease
mare li|berum
  maria li|bera
ma|remma
  ma|remme
  marshy land
Ma|rengo
mare's nest
mare's tail
Ma|reva
  in|junc|tion
Mar|fan's
  syn|drome
Mar|ga|ret
mar|gar|ine
Mar|ga|rita port,
  Venezuela
mar|ga|rita cocktail
Mar|gate town
mar|gate fish
mar|gay
marge margin;
  edge; margarine
Mar|gery
mar|gin
mar|gin|al
mar|gi|na|lia
mar|gin|al|isa|tion
  Br. var. of
  marginalization
mar|gin|al|ise *Br.*
  var. of marginalize
mar|gin|al|ity
mar|gin|al|iza|tion
mar|gin|al|ize
  mar|gin|al|iz|ing
mar|gin|al|ly
mar|gin|ate
  mar|gin|at|ing
mar|gin|ation
Margo
Mar|got
mar|grav|ate
mar|grave
mar|grav|ine
Mar|guer|ite name
mar|guer|ite flower
Mari ancient city,
  Syria
Mari
  pl. Mari or Maris
  people and

language of Russia;
  cf. Maori
Maria name
maria pl. of mare
mari|achi
mari|age blanc
  mari|ages blancs
mari|age de
  con|ve|nance
  mari|ages de
  con|ve|nance
Mar|ian of the Vir-
  gin Mary; name
Mari|ana Is|lands,
  Trench
Mari|anne
Maria Ther|esa
  Habsburg queen
Mari|bor
mari|cul|ture
Marie An|toin|ette
  queen of France
Marie Byrd Land
Marie Ce|leste var.
  of *Mary Celeste*
Marie de Mé|di|cis
  queen of France
Mari El republic,
  Russia
Marie Rose
Mari|gold name
mari|gold flower
ma|ri|huana var. of
  marijuana
ma|ri|juana
Mari|lyn
ma|rimba
Mar|ina name
mar|ina harbour for
  pleasure boats etc.
mar|in|ade
  mar|in|ad|ing
mari|nara
marin|ate
  marin|at|ing
marin|ation
mar|ine
mari|ner
Mari|netti, Fi|lippo
  writer
marin|ise *Br.* var. of
  marinize
marin|ize
  marin|iz|ing

Mari|ol|atry
Mario|logic|al
Mari|ology
Mar|ion
mar|io|nette
mari|posa
Mar|isa
Maris Piper
Mar|ist
mari|tal
mari|tal|ly
mari|time
Ma|ritsa
Ma|riu|pol
Mar|ius, Gaius
  Roman general
mar|joram
Mar|jorie
Mark name; Apostle
mark sign etc.; cf.
  marc, marque
Mark An|tony
mark|down n.
mark|ed|ly
mark|ed|ness
mark|er cf. markka
mar|ket
mar|ket|abil|ity
mar|ket|able
mar|ket|eer
mar|ket|er
market|isa|tion *Br.*
  var. of
  marketization
market|ise *Br.* var.
  of marketize
market|iza|tion
market|ize
  market|iz|ing
market|place
market|space
mark|hor
markka former
  Finnish currency
Mar|kova, Ali|cia
  dancer
Mar|kov model
marks|man
  marks|men
marks|man|ship
marks|woman
  marks|women
mark|up

Marl|bor|ough
town and school,
England; region,
New Zealand;
Duke of
Marl|bur|ian
Mar|lene
Mar|ley, Bob musician
mar|lin fish
mar|line thin rope
mar|lin|spike
Mar|lon
Mar|lov|ian
Mar|lowe,
Chris|to|pher
dramatist
marly
marl|ier
marli|est
Mar|ma|duke
mar|ma|lade
mar|mal|ise Br. var.
of marmalize
mar|mal|ize
mar|mal|iz|ing
Mar|mara, Sea of
Mar|mite yeast
extract trademark
mar|mite cooking
pot
mar|mor|eal
mar|mor|eal|ly
mar|mo|set
mar|mot
Marne river, France
maro|cain
Maro|nite
Ma|roon descendant of runaway
slaves
ma|roon colour;
leave trapped and
alone
marque make of
car; licence; cf.
marc, mark
mar|quee tent; cf.
maquis
mar|quesa Spanish
marchioness
Mar|que|san
Mar|que|sas
Is|lands

mar|quess British
nobleman; cf.
marquis
mar|quess|ate var.
of marquisate
mar|quet|ry
Mar|quette,
Jacques missionary
Már|quez, Gab|riel
Gar|cía novelist
mar|quis
mar|quises
non-British
nobleman; cf.
marquess
mar|quis|ate
mar|quise
non-British
noblewoman
mar|qui|sette fabric
Marra|kech var. of
Marrakesh
Marra|kesh
mar|ram
Mar|rano +s
marri tree; cf.
marry
mar|riage
mar|riage|abil|ity
mar|riage|able
mar|ron
mar|ron glacé
mar|rons glacés
mar|row
marrow|bone
mar|row|fat
marrow|less
mar|rowy
marry
mar|ries
mar|ried
marry|ing
wed; cf. marri
Mar|ryat, Cap|tain
novelist
Mars Roman god;
planet
Mar|sala town,
Sicily; wine; cf.
masala
Mar|sanne
Mar|seil|laise
Mar|seilles
French Marseille
Mar|sha

mar|shal
mar|shalled Br.
mar|shaled US
mar|shal|ling Br.
mar|shal|ing US
officer; arrange; cf.
martial
mar|shal|er US
Mar|shall, George
C. American
general
mar|shal|ler Br.
Mar|shall|ese of the
Marshall Islands
Mar|shall Is|lands
Mar|shal|sea
former prison
mar|shal|sea
former court
mar|shal|ship
marsh|bird
marshi|ness
marsh|land
marsh|mal|low
confection
marsh mal|low
plant
marsh|wort
marshy
marshi|er
marshi|est
Mars|ton Moor
mar|su|pial
mar|su|pium
mar|su|pia
Mar|syas Greek
Mythology
Mar|ta|ban, Gulf of
Mar|tel, Charles
Frankish ruler
Mar|tello +s tower
mar|ten weasel-like
animal; cf. martin
Mar|tens, Dr
trademark
mar|tens|ite
mar|tens|it|ic
Mar|tha
Mar|tial Roman
poet
mar|tial warlike; cf.
marshal
mar|tial|ly
Mar|tian
Mar|tin, St

Mar|tin, Dean
singer and actor
mar|tin bird; cf.
marten
Mar|tina
Mar|tine
Mar|ti|neau,
Har|riet writer
mar|tinet
mar|tin|et|ish var.
of martinettish
mar|tin|et|tish
mar|tin|gale
Mar|tini vermouth
trademark
Mar|tini cocktail
Mar|tin|ican var. of
Martiniquan
Mar|ti|niquan
Mar|ti|nique
Mar|tin|ism
Mar|tin|ist
Mar|tin|mas
Martin|ware
mart|let
mar|tyr
mar|tyr|dom
mar|tyr|isa|tion Br.
var. of
martyrization
mar|tyr|ise Br. var.
of martyrize
mar|tyr|iza|tion
mar|tyr|ize
mar|tyr|iz|ing
mar|tyro|logic|al
mar|tyr|olo|gist
mar|tyr|ology
mar|tyr|ol|ogies
mar|tyry
mar|tyr|ies
Mar|uts Hinduism
mar|vel
mar|velled Br.
mar|veled US
mar|vel|ling Br.
mar|vel|ing US
mar|vel|er US
Mar|vell, An|drew
poet
mar|vel|ler Br.
mar|vel|lous Br.
mar|vel|lous|ly Br.

mar¦vel|lous|ness
Br.
mar¦vel|ous *US*
mar¦vel|ous|ly *US*
mar¦vel|ous|ness
US
Mar¦vin
marvy
Mar|wari language
Marx, Karl political
philosopher
Marx Broth|ers
Marx|ian
Marx|ism
Marx|ist
Mary Ce|leste
Mary Jane shoe;
marijuana
Mary|land
Mary|land|er
Mary Mag|da|len
var. of Mary
Magdalene
Mary Mag|da|lene
Bible
mar¦zi|pan
mar¦zi|panned
mar¦zi|pan|ning
masa dough
Ma|sac¦cio painter
Ma¦sada
Masai
pl. Masai or
Mas¦ais
ma|sala spice; dish;
cf. Marsala
Mas¦aryk, Tomáš
president of
Czechoslovakia
Mas|bate
Mas|cagni, Pie¦tro
composer
mas|cara
mas|caraed
Mas|car¦ene
Is|lands
mas|car|pone
mas|cle
mas|con
mas|cot
mas¦cu|line
mas¦cu|line|ly
mas¦cu|lin|isa|tion
Br. var. of

masculinization
mas¦cu|lin|ise *Br.*
var. of masculinize
mas¦cu|lin|ist
mas¦cu|lin|ity
mas¦cu|lin|ities
mas¦cu|lin|iza|tion
mas¦cu|lin|ize
mas¦cu|lin|iz¦ing
mas¦cu|list
Mase|field, John
poet
maser electronic
device; cf. mazer
Mas¦eru
mash|er
Mash|had
mashie
Ma|shona
pl. Ma|shona or
Ma|sho|nas
Ma|shona|land
ma*s|jid*
mask cover; cf.
masque
mask|er
mas¦kin|onge
maso|chism
maso|chist
maso|chis¦tic
maso|chis¦tic|al¦ly
Mason = Freemason
mason builder in
stone
Ma|son¦ic
Mason|ite fibre-
board *trademark*
Mason jar
Ma|son¦ry =
Freemasonry
ma|son¦ry stone-
work
mason's mark
mason wasp
ma|soor
Ma|sorah
Mas|or|ete
Mas|or|et¦ic
masque dramatic
entertainment; cf.
mask
mas|quer
mas|quer|ade
mas|quer|ad¦ing

mas|quer|ader
Mass Eucharist
mass quantity of
matter etc.
Mas|sa|chu|setts
mas|sacre
mas|sac¦ring
mas|sage
mas|sa¦ging
mas|sager
mas|sa|sauga
Mas|sawa
massé billiards
stroke
mas|seter
mas|seur
mas|seuse
mas|si|cot
mas|sif group of
mountains; cf.
massive
Mas|sine, Léo|nide
dancer
Mas|sin|ger, Philip
dramatist
mas|sive huge; cf.
massif
mas|sive|ly
mas|sive|ness
mass|less
Mas|son, André
painter
Mas|so|rah var. of
Masorah
mass-produce
mass-producing
mass-producer
mass pro|duc¦tion
massy
mas|taba
mast|ec|tomy
mast|ec¦to|mies
mas|ter
master-at-arms
masters-at-arms
master|class
master|dom
master|ful
master|ful¦ly
master|ful|ness
master|hood
master|less
master|li|ness
mas|ter|ly

master|mind
Mas|ter of the
Rolls
master|piece
master|ship
master|stroke
master|work
master|wort
mas|tery
mast|head
mas|tic
mas¦ti|cate
mas¦ti|cat¦ing
mas¦ti|ca¦tion
mas¦ti|ca¦tor
mas¦ti|ca¦tory
mas|tiff
Mas¦ti|goph¦ora
mas¦ti|goph|or¦an
mas|titis
mas|to|don
mas|to|don¦tic
mas|toid
mas|toid|itis
mas¦tur|bate
mas¦tur|ba¦ting
mas¦tur|ba¦tion
mas¦tur|ba¦tor
mas¦tur|ba¦tory
Ma|suria
Ma|sur|ian
mat
mat|ted
mat|ting
floor covering;
entangle; matrix;
cf. matt, matte
mat *US*
dull
Br. matt
Mata|bele
Mata|bele|land
mata|dor
Mata Hari
matai tree
mata|mata turtle
match|able
match|board
match|book
match|box
matchet
match|less
match|less|ly

match|lock
match|maker
match|mak|ing
match|stick
match|up
match|wood
mate
  mat|ing
  friend, partner;
  copulate
maté herbal tea
  Spanish mate
mate|lassé fabric
mate|less
mate|lot sailor
mate|lote fish stew
mater
mater dol|or|osa
mater|fami|lias
  matres|fami|lias
ma|ter|ial matter;
  fabric; physical;
  significant; cf.
  materiel
ma|teri|al|isa|tion
  Br. var. of
  materialization
ma|teri|al|ise *Br.*
  var. of materialize
ma|teri|al|ism
ma|teri|al|ist
ma|teri|al|is|tic
ma|teri|al|is|tic|
  al|ly
ma|teri|al|ity
ma|teri|al|ities
ma|teri|al|iza|tion
ma|teri|al|ize
  ma|teri|al|iz|ing
ma|teri|al|ly
ma|teria med|ica
ma|ter|iel military
  materials; cf.
  material;
  French matériel
ma|ter|nal
ma|ter|nal|ism
ma|ter|nal|ist
ma|ter|nal|is|tic
ma|ter|nal|ly
ma|ter|nity
mate|ship
matey
  mati|er

mati|est
ma|tey|ness
math|em|at|ic|al
math|em|at|ic|al|ly
math|em|at|ician
math|em|at|ics
math|em|at|isa|
        tion
  Br. var. of
  mathematization
math|em|at|ise *Br.*
  var. of
  mathematize
math|em|at|iza|
        tion
math|em|at|ize
math|em|at|izing
Mathew
Ma|thias
Ma|thilda
Ma|tilda name;
  bundle
mati|ly
matin morning
  birdsong
mat|inal
mat|inee
  French mat|inée
mati|ness var. of
  mateyness
mat|ins
Ma|tisse, Henri
  painter
Mat|lock
Mat|mata
Mato Grosso
  plateau and state,
  Brazil
Mato Grosso do
  Sul state, Brazil
matres|fami|lias pl.
  of materfamilias
ma|tri|arch +s
ma|tri|arch|al
ma|tri|arch|ate
ma|tri|archy
  ma|tri|arch|ies
ma|tric =
  matriculation
matri|ces pl. of
  matrix
matri|cidal
matri|cide

ma|tricu|late
ma|tricu|lat|ing
ma|tricu|la|tion
matri|focal
matri|lin|eal
matri|lin|eal|ly
matri|local
matri|local|ity
matri|mo|nial
matri|mo|ni|al|ly
matri|mony
ma|trix
  ma|tri|ces or
  ma|trixes
ma|tron
ma|tron|hood
ma|tron|ly
matro|nym|ic
matry|oshka
  matry|oshki
mat|suri
Mat|su|yama
Matt name
matt *Br.*
  dull; *US* mat; cf.
  mat, matte
matte smelting
  product; mask; cf.
  mat, matt
mat|ter
Mat|ter|horn
mat|ter of fact *n.*
matter-of-fact *adj.*
matter-of-factly
matter-of-factness
Mat|thau, Wal|ter
  actor
Mat|thew name;
  Apostle
Mat|thew Paris
  chronicler
Mat|thews,
  Stan|ley footballer
Mat|thias
mat|tify
  mat|ti|fies
  mat|ti|fied
  mat|ti|fy|ing
mat|tins var. of
  matins
mat|tock
mat|tress
mat|ur|ate
  mat|ur|at|ing

mat|ur|ation
mat|ur|ation|al
ma|tur|ative
ma|ture
  ma|tur|ing
ma|turer
ma|tur|est
ma|ture|ly
ma|tur|ity
  ma|tur|ities
ma|tu|tinal
maty
  mat|ies
  mat|ier
  mat|iest
  var. of matey
mat|zah
mat|zoth
  var. of matzo
matzo
  matzos or
  mat|zoth
  unleavened biscuit
matzoh
  var. of matzo
mauby
maud|lin
Maugham,
  Som|er|set writer
Maui
maul hammer;
  mutilate; cf. mall
mau|lana learned
  Muslim; cf.
  Mawlana
maul|er
maul|stick var. of
  mahlstick
Mau Mau African
  secret society; cf.
  maomao, mau-
  mau
mau-mau +s +ed
  +ing terrorize; cf.
  maomao, Mau
  Mau
Mauna Kea
Mauna Loa
maun|der
Maun|der
  mini|mum
Maundy
Mau|pas|sant, Guy
  de writer
Maur|een

Maure|ta|nia part
of Morocco and
Algeria; cf.
Mauritania
Maure|ta|nian
Maur|iac, Fran|çois
writer
Maur|ice
Maur|ist
Mauri|ta|nia coun-
try, W. Africa; cf.
Mauretania
Mauri|ta|nian
Maur|itian
Maur|itius
Maury, Mat|thew
oceanographer
Mau|rya Indian
dynasty
Mau|ryan
Mau|ser *trademark*
mau|so|leum
mau|so|leums or
mau|so|lea
mauve
mauve|ine
mauv|ish
maven
mav|er|ick
Mavis name
mavis bird
maw stomach;
throat; cf. **mor,
moor, more**
ma|washi
mawk|ish
mawk|ish|ly
mawk|ish|ness
Maw|lana alterna-
tive name for **Jalal
ad-Din ar-Rumi**;
cf. **maulana**
maxi
max|illa
max|il|lae
max|il|lary
max|illi|ped
max|illo|facial
Maxim, Hiram
Ste|vens engineer;
M. gun
maxim principle
max|ima
max|imal

maxi|mal|ism
max|imal|ist
max|imal|ly
maxim|and
Max|imil|ian
maxi|min
maxi|misa|tion *Br.*
var. of
maximization
maxi|mise *Br.* var.
of **maximize**
maxi|miser *Br.* var.
of **maximizer**
maxi|miza|tion
maxi|mize
maxi|miz|ing
maxi|mizer
max|imum
max|ima or
max|imums
Max|ine
max|ixe
Max|well, James
Clerk physicist
Max|well, Rob|ert
publisher
max|well unit
Maya
pl. Maya or Mayas
Central American
people; language;
name
maya *Hinduism;
Buddhism*
Maya|kov|sky,
Vlad|imir poet
Mayan
may|apple
maybe perhaps;
possibility
May bug
May Day 1 May
May|day radio dis-
tress signal
Mayer, Louis B.
film executive
may|est
May Fair fair held
in May
May|fair district,
London
may|flower
may|fly
may|flies

may|hap
may|hem
may|ing
May|nooth
mayn't
Mayo county,
Republic of Ireland
mayo +s =
mayonnaise
may|on|naise
mayor council
official; cf. **mare**
may|or|al
may|or|alty
may|or|al|ties
may|or|ess
may|or|ship
May|otte
may|pole
may|pop
Mayr, Ernst zoolo-
gist
mayst
may|weed
Mazar-e-Sharif
Maza|rin, Jules
French statesman
maza|rine blue
butterfly
Maz|at|lán
Mazda|ism
Mazda|ist
maz|door
maze labyrinth; cf.
maize
mazel tov
mazer bowl; cf.
maser
ma|zuma
ma|zurka
mazy
mazi|er
mazi|est
maz|zard
Maz|zini, Giu|seppe
Italian political
leader
Mba|bane
mbalax
mba|qanga
Mbeki, Thabo
president of South
Africa
mbira

Mbundu
pl. Mdundu
people; language
Mbuti
pl. Mbuti or
Mbutis
people
m-commerce
me
objective case of **I**;
note in tonic sol-fa
mea culpa
Mead, Mar|ga|ret
anthropologist
mead drink,
meadow; cf. **meed**
meadow
meadow|land
meadow|lark
meadow|sweet
mead|owy
mea|ger *US*
lacking; thin
mea|ger|ly *US*
mea|ger|ness *US*
meagre *Br.*
lacking; thin
meagre
fish
meagre|ly *Br.*
meagre|ness *Br.*
mealie maize; cf.
mealy
mealie|pap
meali|ness
meal|time
meal|worm
mealy
meali|er
meali|est
powdery; pale; cf.
mealie
mean
meant
intend; signify; not
generous; unkind;
inferior; average;
cf. **mien, mesne**
Me|ander var. of
Maeander
me|ander wind;
wander
meanie
mean|ing
mean|ing|ful

mean|ing|ful|ly
mean|ing|ful|ness
mean|ing|less
mean|ing|less|ly
mean|ing|less|ness
mean|ing|ly
mean|ly
mean|ness
meant
mean|time meanwhile; intervening period
mean time time on ordinary clock
mean|while
meany var. of meanie
mea|sles
measly
meas|lier
meas|li|est
meas|ur|abil|ity
meas|ur|able
meas|ur|ably
meas|ure
meas|ur|ing
meas|ured|ly
meas|ure|less
meas|ure|less|ly
meas|ure|ment
meas|urer
meat flesh; cf. meet, mete
meat|ball
Meath
meat|head
meat|hook
meat|ily
meati|ness
meat|less
meat|space
me|atus
    pl. me|atus or me|atuses
meaty
meat|ier
meati|est
mebos
Mecca
Mec|can
Mec|cano
    trademark
mech mechanic; gear mechanism

mech|an|ic
mech|an|ic|al
mech|an|ic|al|ly
mech|an|ician
mech|an|isa|tion
    Br. var. of mechanization
mech|an|ise Br. var. of mechanize
mech|an|iser Br. var. of mechanizer
mech|an|ism
mech|an|ist
mech|an|is|tic
mech|an|is|tic|al|ly
mech|an|iza|tion
mech|an|ize
mech|an|iz|ing
mech|an|izer
mech|ano|
    recep|tive
mech|ano|
    recep|tor
mecha|tron|ics
Me|che|len city, Belgium
Mech|lin lace
Mecklenburg-West Pom|er|ania
meco|nium
mecon|opsis
mecon|opses
Mec|op|tera
mec|op|ter|an
mé|dail|lon
me|daka
medal
    med|alled Br.
    med|aled US
medal|ling Br.
medal|ing US
    award; gain a medal; cf. meddle
med|al|ist US
med|al|lic
med|al|lion
med|al|list Br.
Medan
Meda|war, Peter immunologist
med|dle
med|dling
    interfere; cf. medal

med|dler busybody; cf. medlar
meddle|some
meddle|some|ness
Mede
Medea Greek Mythology
Me|de|llín
med|evac
med|evacked
med|evack|ing
med|fly
med|flies
Media country of the Medes
media pl. of medium; newspapers, television, etc.
media Anatomy
med|iae
me|di|acy
medi|aeval var. of medieval
medi|aeval|ise Br. var. of medievalize
medi|aeval|ism var. of medievalism
medi|aeval|ist var. of medievalist
medi|aeval|ly var. of medievally
media|gen|ic
med|ial
medi|al|ly
Me|dian of Media; Mede
me|dian of the middle, mean, or midpoint; median value
me|di|ant third note of a diatonic scale
media|scape
me|di|as|tin|al
medi|as|ti|num
medi|as|tina
me|di|ate
me|di|at|ing
me|di|ate|ly
me|di|ation
me|di|ator
me|di|atory
Medi|bank
medic doctor; cf. medick

med|ic|able
Me|dic|aid
med|ic|al
med|ical|isa|tion
    Br. var. of medicalization
med|ical|ise Br. var. of medicalize
med|ical|iza|tion
med|ical|ize
med|ical|iz|ing
med|ic|al|ly
med|ic|ament
Medi|care
medi|cate
medi|cat|ing
medi|ca|tion
med|ica|tive
Me|di|cean
Med|ici Florentine family
me|di|cin|al
me|di|cin|al|ly
medi|cine
med|ick plant; cf. medic
med|ico +s
medi|eval
medi|eval|ise Br. var. of medievalize
medi|eval|ism
medi|eval|ist
medi|eval|ize
medi|eval|iz|ing
medi|eval|ly
Me|dina city, Saudi Arabia
me|dina district of N. African town
medi|oc|racy
medi|oc|ra|cies
me|di|ocre
me|di|ocre|ly
me|di|oc|rity
me|di|oc|rities
medi|tate
medi|tat|ing
medi|ta|tion
medi|ta|tive
medi|ta|tive|ly
medi|ta|tive|ness
medi|ta|tor
Medi|ter|ra|nean

me¦dium +s
spiritualist
me¦dium
media or
me¦diums
other senses
me¦dium¦ism
me¦dium¦is¦tic
medium-pacer
me¦dium¦ship
medi¦vac var. of
medevac
med¦lar tree; cf.
meddler
med¦ley
med¦leyed or
med¦lied
Médoc region,
France; wine
me¦drese var. of
madrasa
me¦dulla
me¦dul¦lae or
me¦dul¦las
me¦dulla
ob¦lon¦gata
me¦dul¦lae
ob¦lon¦ga¦tae
me¦dul¦lary
Me¦dusa Greek
Mythology
me¦dusa jellyfish
me¦du¦sae or
me¦dusas
me¦dus¦oid
Meech Lake
meed reward; cf.
mead
meek¦ly
meek¦ness
meer¦kat
meer¦schaum
Mee¦rut
meet
met
encounter;
gathering; suitable;
cf. meat, mete
meet¦er person who
meets; cf. meter,
metre
meet¦ly
meet¦ness
mef¦lo¦quine
mega¦bit

mega¦bucks
mega¦byte
Mega¦chir¦op¦tera
mega¦chir¦op¦
ter¦an
mega¦cycle
mega¦death
mega¦dose
Me¦gaera Greek
Mythology
mega¦fauna
mega¦faun¦al
mega¦flop
mega¦gam¦ete
mega¦hertz
pl. mega¦hertz
mega¦lith
mega¦lith¦ic
meg¦alo¦blast
meg¦alo¦blast¦ic
Megal¦oceros
meg¦alo¦mania
meg¦alo¦maniac
meg¦alo¦mani¦ac¦al
meg¦alo¦man¦ic
meg¦alop¦olis
meg¦alop¦olises
meg¦alo¦pol¦itan
meg¦alo¦saurus
mega¦mouth
mega¦phone
mega¦phon¦ing
mega¦phon¦ic
mega¦pixel
mega¦pode
mega¦ron
mega¦spore
mega¦star
mega¦star¦dom
mega¦store
mega¦struc¦ture
mega¦ther¦ium
mega¦ther¦iums or
mega¦theria
mega¦ton
mega¦tonne var. of
megaton
mega¦volt
mega¦watt
Meg¦ger trademark
Meg¦ha¦laya
Me¦giddo
Me¦gil¦lah

meg¦ilp
meg¦ohm
meg¦rim
mehndi henna
tattoo
mci¦bo¦mian
Meiji Tenno
Japanese emperor
meio¦fauna
mei¦osis
mei¦oses
cell division; litotes;
cf. miosis
mei¦ot¦ic of meiosis;
cf. miotic
mei¦otic¦al¦ly
Meir, Golda prime
minister of Israel
Meis¦sen city, Ger-
many; porcelain
Meiss¦ner ef¦fect
Meis¦ter¦singer
pl. Meis¦ter¦singer
or Meis¦ter¦singers
meit¦ner¦ium
Me¦kele
Mek¦nès
Me¦kong
mela Hindu festival
me¦laena Br.
US melena
Me¦laka
mela¦leuca
mela¦mine
mel¦an¦cho¦lia
mel¦an¦chol¦ic
mel¦an¦chol¦ic¦al¦ly
mel¦an¦choly
Mel¦anch¦thon,
Phil¦ipp Protestant
reformer
Mela¦nesia
Mela¦nes¦ian
me¦lange
French mélange
mel¦an¦ic
Mel¦anie
mel¦anin
mel¦an¦ism
mel¦an¦ite
mel¦ano¦cyte
mel¦an¦oid
mel¦an¦oma
mel¦an¦osis

mel¦an¦ot¦ic
mela¦tonin
Melba, Nel¦lie
opera singer
Mel¦bourne city,
Australia; Lord
Mel¦chior Bible
Mel¦chiz¦edek Bible
Me¦le¦ager Greek
poet
melee
French mêlée
me¦lena US
Br. melaena
melic to be sung
mel¦ick grass
Me¦lilla
meli¦lot
Me¦linda
meli¦oid¦osis
meli¦or¦ate
meli¦or¦at¦ing
meli¦or¦ation
meli¦ora¦tive
meli¦or¦ism
meli¦or¦ist
meli¦or¦is¦tic
me¦lisma
me¦lis¦mata or
me¦lis¦mas
mel¦is¦mat¦ic
Me¦lissa
Mel¦kite
mel¦lif¦er¦ous
mel¦lif¦lu¦ence
mel¦lif¦lu¦ent
mel¦lif¦lu¦ous
mel¦lif¦lu¦ous¦ly
mel¦lif¦lu¦ous¦ness
Mel¦lon, An¦drew
financier
mello¦phone
mello¦tron
mel¦low
mel¦low¦ly
mel¦low¦ness
me¦lo¦deon
me¦lod¦ic
me¦lod¦ica
me¦lod¦ic¦al¦ly
me¦lo¦dion var. of
melodeon
me¦lo¦di¦ous

me|lo|di|ous|ly
me|lo|di|ous|ness
melo|dise *Br.* var. of
  melodize
melo|dist
melo|dize
  melo|diz|ing
melo|drama
melo|dra|mat|ic
melo|dra|mat|ic|
    al|ly
melo|drama|tise
  Br. var. of
  melodramatize
melo|drama|tist
melo|drama|tize
melo|drama|tiz|ing
Mel|ody name
mel|ody
  mel|od|ies
  tune
melon
Melos
Mel|pom|ene Muse
  of tragedy
melt|able
melt|down
mel|temi
melt|er
melt|ing|ly
mel|ton cloth
Mel|ton Mow|bray
melt|water
Mel|ville, Her|man
  writer
Mel|vin
mem|ber
mem|bered
mem|ber|less
mem|ber|ship
mem|bran|aceous
mem|brane
mem|bran|eous
mem|brano|phone
mem|bran|ous
mem|brum vi|rile
meme *Biology*
me|mento
  me|men|tos or
  me|men|toes
me|mento mori
me|met|ic

Mem|non *Greek*
  Mythology
memo +s
mem|oir
mem|oir|ist
mem|ora|bilia
mem|or|abil|ity
mem|or|able
mem|or|able|ness
mem|or|ably
memo|ran|dum
  memo|randa or
  memo|ran|dums
me|mor|ial
me|mor|ial|ise *Br.*
  var. of memorialize
me|mor|ial|ist
me|mor|ial|ize
  me|mor|ial|iz|ing
mem|or|is|able *Br.*
  var. of
  memorizable
mem|or|isa|tion *Br.*
  var. of
  memorization
mem|or|ise *Br.* var.
  of memorize
mem|or|iser *Br.* var.
  of memorizer
mem|or|iz|able
mem|or|iza|tion
mem|or|ize
  mem|or|iz|ing
mem|or|izer
mem|ory
  mem|or|ies
Mem|phis
mem|sahib
men|ace
  men|acing
men|acer
men|acing|ly
mena|dione
mé|nage
mé|nage à trois
mé|nages à trois
men|agerie
Menai Strait
Me|nan|der
Me|nap|ian
mena|quin|one
me|nar|che
Men|cius Chinese
  philosopher

Men|cken, H. L.
  writer
mend|able
men|da|cious
men|da|cious|ly
men|da|city
  untruthfulness; cf.
  mendicity
Mende
  pl. Mende
Men|del, Gre|gor
  geneticist
Men|de|leev,
  Dmi|tri chemist
men|del|evium
Men|del|ian
Men|del|ism
Men|dels|sohn
  (-Bartholdy), Felix
  composer
mend|er
Men|deres
men|di|cancy
men|di|cant
men|di|city beg-
  ging; cf. mendacity
Men|dip Hills
Men|doza
Mene|laus *Greek*
  Mythology
Menes pharaoh
men|folk
men|haden
men|hir
me|nial
me|ni|al|ly
Mé|nière's dis|ease
men|in|geal
men|in|ges *pl.* of
  meninx
men|ingi|oma
  pl. men|ingi|omas
  or men|ingi|omata
men|in|git|ic
men|in|gi|tis
men|in|go|cele
men|in|go|coc|cal
men|in|go|coc|cus
  men|in|go|cocci
men|in|go|
  enceph|al|itis
men|inx
men|in|ges

men|isc|ec|tomy
men|isc|ec|to|mies
me|nis|cus
me|nisci
Men|non|ite
meno|logion
meno|logia
Men|om|inee
  pl. Men|om|inee or
  Men|om|inees
Men|om|ini var. of
  Menominee
meno mosso *Music*
meno|pausal
meno|pause
me|norah
Men|orca Spanish
  name for **Minorca**
Men|or|can var. of
  Minorcan
men|or|rha|gia
men|or|rhea *US*
men|or|rhoea *Br.*
mensch
men|ses
mensh var. of
  mensch
Men|she|vik
mens rea
men|strua *pl.* of
  menstruum
men|strual
men|stru|ate
  men|stru|at|ing
men|stru|ation
men|stru|ous
men|struum
  men|strua
men|sur|able
men|sural
men|sur|ation
mens|wear
men|tal
men|tal|ism
men|tal|ist
men|tal|is|tic
men|tal|ity
  men|tal|ities
men|tal|ly
men|ta|tion
men|thol
men|thol|ated
men|tion

men¦tion¦able
mento +s
men¦tor
men¦tum
  Entomology
menu
me¦nudo +s
Men¦uhin, Ye¦hudi
  violinist
Men¦zies, Rob¦ert
  prime minister of
  Australia
Meo
  pl. Meo or Meos
meow var. of miaow
mepa¦crine
me¦peri¦dine
Meph¦is¦to¦
      phe¦lean
  var. of
  Mephistophelian
Moph¦is¦toph¦eles
Meph¦is¦to¦
      phe¦lian
meph¦it¦ic
me¦ranti
mer¦bau
mer¦bro¦min
Merc Mercedes car
merc mercenary
mer¦cado +s
Mer¦calli scale
mer¦can¦tile
mer¦can¦til¦ism
mer¦can¦til¦ist
mer¦cap¦tan
Mer¦ca¦tor,
  Ger¦ar¦dus geog-
  rapher
Mer¦ce¦des
mer¦cen¦ary
  mer¦cen¦ar¦ies
mer¦cer
mer¦cer¦ise *Br.* var.
  of mercerize
mer¦cer¦ize
  mer¦cer¦iz¦ing
mer¦cery
  mer¦cer¦ies
mer¦chan¦dis¦able
mer¦chan¦dise n. &
  v.
  mer¦chan¦dis¦ing
mer¦chan¦diser

mer¦chan¦diz¦able
  var. of
  merchandisable
mer¦chan¦dize v.
  var. of
  merchandise
mer¦chan¦dizer var.
  of merchandiser
Mer¦chant, Is¦mail
  film producer
mer¦chant trader
mer¦chant¦able
mer¦chant¦man
  mer¦chant¦men
Mer¦cia ancient
  kingdom, central
  England; cf.
  Murcia
Mer¦cian
mer¦ci¦ful
mer¦ci¦ful¦ly
mer¦ci¦less
mer¦ci¦less¦ly
mer¦ci¦less¦ness
Merckx, Eddy
  racing cyclist
Merco¦sur
Mer¦couri, Me¦lina
  actress and
  politician
Mer¦cur¦ial of the
  planet Mercury
mer¦cur¦ial volatile;
  containing mercury
mer¦curi¦al¦ity
mer¦curi¦al¦ly
Mer¦cur¦ian
mer¦cur¦ic
Mer¦curo¦chrome
  trademark
mer¦cur¦ous
Mer¦cury Roman
  god; planet
mer¦cury
  mer¦curies
  metal; plant
mercy
  mer¦cies
merde
mere
  mer¦est
Mere¦dith, George
  writer
mere¦ly

mer¦en¦gue dance;
  cf. meringue
mereo¦logic¦al
mere¦ology
mere¦tri¦cious
mere¦tri¦cious¦ly
mere¦tri¦cious¦ness
mer¦gan¦ser
merge
  mer¦ging
mer¦ger
mer¦guez
  pl. mer¦guez
Mé¦rida
me¦rid¦ian
me¦rid¦ion¦al
Me¦riel
mer¦ingue confec-
  tion; cf. merengue
me¦rino +s
Meri¦on¦eth¦shire
meri¦stem
meri¦stem¦at¦ic
merit
mer¦it¦oc¦racy
  mer¦it¦oc¦ra¦cies
merito¦crat
mer¦ito¦crat¦ic
meri¦tori¦ous
meri¦tori¦ous¦ly
meri¦tori¦ous¦ness
mer¦kin
Merle name
merle blackbird
Mer¦lin magician;
  name
mer¦lin falcon
mer¦lon parapet
Mer¦lot
Mer¦lyn name
mer¦maid
mer¦maid's purse
  +s
mer¦man
  mer¦men
Meroe
Mero¦itic
mero¦nym
me¦ron¦ymy
Mero¦vin¦gian
mer¦rily
mer¦ri¦ment

merry
  mer¦rier
  mer¦ri¦est
merry-go-round
merry¦maker
merry¦mak¦ing
merry¦thought
  wishbone
Mersa Ma¦truh
Mer¦senne
  num¦ber
Mer¦sey
Mer¦sey¦side
Mer¦sin
Mer¦thyr Tyd¦fil
Meru
  pl. Meru or Merus
mer¦veille du jour
  mer¦veilles du jour
Mer¦vin
Mer¦vyn
mesa
més¦al¦li¦ance
Mesa Verde
mes¦cal
mes¦ca¦lin var. of
  mescaline
mes¦ca¦line
mes¦clun
Mes¦dames
Mes¦de¦moi¦selles
mes¦em¦bry¦
      an¦the¦mum
mes¦en¦ceph¦al¦ic
mes¦en¦ceph¦alon
mes¦en¦chy¦mal
mes¦en¦chy¦mat¦
        ous
mes¦en¦chyme
mes¦en¦ter¦ic
mes¦en¦ter¦itis
mes¦en¦teron
mes¦en¦tery
  mes¦en¦ter¦ies
Me¦shed
me¦shuga crazy
me¦shu¦gaas crazi-
  ness
me¦shugga var. of
  meshuga
me¦shug¦gen¦er
  crazy person
mesia

me¦sial
me¦si¦al¦ly
mesic
Mes¦mer, Franz
  physician
mes¦mer¦ic
mes¦mer¦ic¦al¦ly
mes¦mer¦isa¦tion
  Br. var. of
  mesmerization
mes¦mer¦ise Br. var.
  of mesmerize
mes¦mer¦iser Br.
  var. of mesmerizer
mes¦mer¦is¦ing¦ly
  Br. var. of
  mesmerizingly
mes¦mer¦ism
mes¦mer¦ist
mes¦mer¦iza¦tion
mes¦mer¦ize
  mes¦mer¦iz¦ing
mes¦mer¦izer
mes¦mer¦iz¦ing¦ly
mesne Law
  intermediate
Meso-America
Meso-American
meso|blast
meso|carp
meso|ceph¦al¦ic
meso|derm
meso|der¦mal
meso|fauna
meso|gas¦tric
meso|gas¦trium
  meso|gas¦tria
meso|kur¦tosis
  meso|kur¦toses
Meso|lith¦ic
meso|mer¦ic
me|som¦er|ism
meso|morph
meso|morph¦ic
meson
mes|on¦ic
meso|pause
meso|pel¦agic
meso|phyll
meso|phyte
meso|phyt¦ic
Meso|po¦ta¦mia
Meso|po¦ta¦mian

meso|saur
meso|scale
meso|sphere
meso|the¦lial
meso|theli¦oma
meso|the¦lium
  meso|the¦lia
meso|thor¦acic
meso|thorax
meso|zoan
Meso|zo¦ic
mes|pi¦lus
  mes|pi¦luses
mes|quite
mes|sage
  mes¦sa¦ging
Mes¦sa¦lina,
  Val¦eria Roman
  empress
Mes¦sei¦gneurs
mes¦sen|ger
Mes¦ser¦schmitt,
  Willy aircraft
  designer
Mes|siaen, Oli|vier
  composer
Mes|siah promised
  Jewish deliverer
mes|siah leader or
  saviour
mes¦siah|ship
mes¦si|an¦ic
mes¦si|an¦ism
Mes¦si|dor month
Mes|sier, Charles
  astronomer
Mes|sieurs
mess¦ily
Mes|sina city, Sicily;
  Strait
messi|ness
mess|mate
Messrs = Messieurs
mes|suage
messy
  mess¦ier
  messi|est
mes¦tiza female
mes|tizo +s male
meta in 'meta key';
  cf. metta
meta|bi¦sul¦fite US
meta|bi¦sul¦phite
  Br.

meta|bol¦ic
meta|bol¦ic¦al¦ly
me¦tab¦ol¦is¦able
  Br. var. of
  metabolizable
me¦tab¦ol¦ise Br.
  var. of metabolize
me¦tab¦ol¦iser Br.
  var. of metabolizer
me¦tab¦ol¦ism
me¦tab¦ol¦ite
me¦tab¦ol¦iz¦able
me¦tab¦ol¦ize
  me¦tab¦ol¦iz¦ing
me¦tab¦ol¦izer
meta|car¦pal
meta|car¦pus
  meta|carpi
meta|cen¦ter US
meta|centre Br.
meta|cen¦tric
meta|chrom¦asia
meta|chrom¦at¦ic
meta|chro¦sis
meta|cog¦ni¦tion
meta|cog¦ni¦tive
meta|data
meta|fic¦tion
meta|fic¦tion|al
meta|file
me|tage
meta|gen¦esis
  meta|gen¦eses
meta|ge¦net¦ic
metal
  met|alled Br.
  met|aled US
  met¦al|ling Br.
  met¦al|ing US
  iron, copper, etc.;
  cf. metol, mettle
meta|lan¦guage
met|al¦de|hyde
metal|flake
meta|lin¦guis¦tic
metal|iza¦tion US
  Br. metallization
metal|ize US
  Br. metallize
me¦tal|lic
me¦tal|lic¦al¦ly
metal|li¦city
metal|li¦ci¦ties
metal|lif¦er¦ous

metal|line
metal|lisa|tion Br.
  var. of
  metallization
metal|lise Br. var. of
  metallize
metal|liza|tion Br.
  US metalization
metal|lize Br.
  metal|liz|ing
  US metalize
met|al|lo|gen¦ic
met|al|lo|graph¦ic
metal|log¦raphy
metal|loid
me|tal|lo|phone
metal|lur¦gic|al
metal|lur¦gic¦al¦ly
metal|lur¦gist
me|tal|lurgy
metal|mark
metal|ware
metal|work
metal|work¦er
metal|work¦ing
meta|mathe|mat|
        ic¦al
meta|
  mathe|mat|ic¦al|ly
meta|mathe|mat|
        ician
meta|mathe|mat|
        ics
meta|mer chemical
  compound
meta|mere body
  segment
meta|mer¦ic
meta|mer¦ic¦al¦ly
me|tam|er|ism
meta|mes|sage
meta|morph¦ic
meta|morph¦ism
meta|morph¦ose
  meta|morph¦os|ing
meta|mor¦phosis
  meta|mor¦phoses
meta|noia
meta|phase
meta|phor
meta|phor¦ic
meta|phor¦ic¦al
meta|phor¦ic¦al¦ly
meta|phos|phate

meta|phos|phor|ic
meta|phrase
 meta|phras|ing
meta|phras|tic
meta|phys|ic
Meta|phys|ic|al
 metaphysical poet
meta|phys|ic|al of
 metaphysics
meta|phys|ic|al|ly
meta|phys|ician
meta|physi|cise Br.
 var. of
 metaphysicize
meta|physi|cize
 meta|physi|ciz|ing
meta|pla|sia
meta|plas|tic
meta|psy|cho|
 logic|al
meta|psych|ology
meta|somat|ic
meta|soma|tise Br.
 var. of
 metasomatize
meta|soma|tism
meta|soma|tize
 meta|soma|tiz|ing
meta|sta|bil|ity
meta|sta|ble
me|tas|ta|sis
 me|tas|ta|ses
me|tas|ta|sise Br.
 var. of metastasize
me|tas|ta|size
 me|tas|ta|siz|ing
meta|stat|ic
meta|tar|sal
meta|tar|sus
 meta|tarsi
me|tate
Meta|theria
meta|ther|ian
me|tath|esis
 me|tath|eses
meta|thet|ic
meta|thet|ic|al
meta|thor|acic
meta|thorax
Meta|zoa
meta|zoan
mete
 met|ing
 apportion;

boundary; cf. **meat**,
 meet
met|em|psy|chosis
met|em|psy|choses
met|em|psy|chos|
 ist
met|em|psy|chot|ic
me|teor
Met|eora
me|teor|ic
me|teor|ic|al|ly
me|teor|ite
me|teor|it|ic
me|teoro|graph
me|teor|oid
me|teor|oid|al
me|teoro|logic|al
me|teoro|logic|al|ly
me|teor|olo|gist
me|teor|ology
meter measuring
 device; measure
 with a meter; cf.
 metre
meter US
 metric unit; poetic
 rhythm.
 Br. metre
meter|age US
 Br. metreage
meth|acryl|ate
meth|acryl|ic
metha|done
meth|aemo|glo|bin
 Br.
 US
 methemoglobin
meth|aemo|
 glo|bin|aemia Br.
 US methemo-
 globinemia
meth|am|pheta|
 mine
metha|nal
me|thane
meth|ano|gen
meth|ano|gen|esis
meth|ano|gen|ic
metha|nol
meth|aqua|lone
 trademark
methe|drine
 trademark
meth|eg|lin

meth|emo|glo|bin
 US
 Br.
methaemoglobin
meth|emo|glo|bin|
 emia US
 Br. methaemo-
 globinaemia
methi|cil|lin
me|thinks
 me|thought
methio|carb
me|thio|nine
metho +s
method
mé|thode
 cham|pen|oise
meth|od|ic
meth|od|ic|al
method|ic|al|ly
Meth|od|ism
Meth|od|ist
Meth|od|is|tic|al
Me|tho|dius
meth|odo|logic|al
meth|odo|logic|
 al|ly
meth|od|olo|gist
meth|od|ology
 meth|od|olo|gies
metho|trex|ate
me|thought
Me|thu|selah patri-
 arch; very old
 person
me|thu|selah wine
 bottle
me|thyl
methy|late
 methy|lat|ing
methy|la|tion
methyl|ben|zene
methy|lene
me|thyl|
 phen|id|ate
metic
meti|cal
me|ticu|lous
me|ticu|lous|ly
me|ticu|lous|ness
mé|tier
Metis
 pl. Metis

metol photographic
 developer; cf.
 metal, mettle
Me|ton|ic
meto|nym
meto|nym|ic
meto|nym|ic|al
meto|nym|ic|al|ly
me|ton|ymy
 me|ton|ymies
met|ope
meto|pro|lol
metre Br.
 metric unit; poetic
 rhythm; US meter;
 cf. **meter**
metre|age Br.
 US meterage
met|ric
met|ric|al
met|ric|al|ly
met|ri|cate
 met|ri|cat|ing
met|ri|ca|tion
me|tri|tis
metro +s
Metro|land
metro|logic|al
me|trol|ogy
metro|nida|zole
metro|nome
metro|nom|ic
metro|nom|ic|ally
metro|nym|ic var.
 of matronymic
metro|plex
metro|pole
me|trop|olis
 me|trop|olises or
 me|trop|oles
metro|pol|itan
metro|pol|it|an|ate
metro|pol|it|an|
 ism
metro|polit|ic|al
me|tror|rha|gia
metro|sexual
metta Buddhist
 meditation; cf.
 meta
Met|ter|nich,
 Kle|mens Austrian
 statesman

met¦tle courage,
spirit; cf. metal,
metol
mettle|some
Metz
Me¦ucci, An¦tonio
Italian engineer
meu|nière
Meur|sault
Meuse river, NW
Europe
mew cat's cry; gull;
cage for hawks; cf.
mu
mewl whimper; cf.
mule
mews stabling; cf.
muse
Mexi|cali
Mexi|can
Mexi|cano +s
Mex¦ico
Meyer|beer,
Gia|como
composer
Meyer|hof, Otto
biochemist
meze
me¦zer|eon
me¦zu¦zah
me¦zu¦zahs or
me¦zu¦zoth
mezza|luna
mezza|nine
mezza voce
mezzo +s
mezzo forte
Mezzo|giorno
mezzo piano
mezzo-relievo +s
mezzo-soprano +s
mezzo|tint
mezzo|tint¦er
mho +s unit; cf. mo,
mow
mi var. of me (in
tonic sol-fa)
Miami
mia-mia
Miao people
pl. Miao
miaow cat's cry
miasm

mi¦asma
mi¦as|mata or
mi|asmas
mi¦as|mal
mi¦as|mat¦ic
mi¦as|mic
mi¦as|mic|al¦ly
mic microphone; cf.
mick
mica mineral
mi¦ca|ceous
Micah Bible
Mi¦caw|ber
Mi¦caw|ber|ish
Mi¦caw|ber|ism
mi|cel¦lar
mi|celle
Mi¦chael
Mi¦chaela
Mi¦chaelis
con|stant
Mich¦ael|mas
Mi¦chel|an¦gelo
Buon|ar|roti artist
Mi¦chèle
Mi¦che|lin, André
and Édu|ard tyre
manufacturers
Mi¦chelle
Mi¦chel|ozzo
architect
Mi¦chel|son,
Al¦bert physicist
Mich|igan state,
US; Lake
Mich|igan|der
Mi¦cho|acán
mick reverse side of
a coin; cf. mic
mick|erie var. of
mickery
mick|ery
mick|er|ies
Mickey name
mickey in 'take the
mickey'
Mickey Finn
Mickey Mouse
mickle
Micky name
micky var. of
mickey

Mic¦mac
pl. Mic¦mac or
Mic|macs
mic|rite
micro +s
micro|aero|phile
micro|aero|phil¦ic
micro|ana¦lyser Br.
micro|analy¦sis
micro|ana¦lyt|ic¦al
micro|ana¦lyz|er
US
micro|array
micro|bal|ance
mi|crobe
mi|cro¦bial
mi|cro¦bic
micro|bio|logic¦al
micro|bio|logic|
al¦ly
micro|biolo¦gist
micro|biol¦ogy
micro|biota
micro|brew
micro|brew¦ery
micro|brew¦er¦ies
micro|brows¦er
micro|burst
micro|cap¦sule
micro|car
micro|cel¦lu¦lar
micro|ceph¦al¦ic
micro|ceph¦alous
micro|ceph¦aly
micro|check
micro|chem¦is¦try
micro|chip
Micro|chir|op¦tera
micro|chir|op|
ter¦an
micro|cir¦cuit
micro|cir¦cuit¦ry
micro|cir¦cuit¦ries
micro|cir¦cu|la¦tion
micro|cir¦cu|
la¦tory
micro|cli¦mate
micro|cli¦mat¦ic
micro|cli¦mat¦ic|
al¦ly
micro|cline
micro|coc¦cal

micro|coc¦cus
micro|cocci
micro|code
micro|com¦puter
micro|con¦tin¦ent
micro|con¦trol|ler
micro|copy
micro|copies
micro|copied
micro|copy|ing
micro|cosm
micro|cos¦mic
micro|cos¦mic|al¦ly
micro|credit
micro|crys¦tal|line
micro|cyte
micro|cyt¦ic
micro|
densi¦tom¦eter
micro|derm|
abra¦sion
micro|dot
micro|eco¦nom¦ic
micro|elec¦tron¦ic
micro|envir¦on|
ment
micro|evo¦lu¦tion
micro|evo¦lu¦tion|
ary
micro|farad
micro|fauna
micro|fiber US
micro|fibre Br.
micro|fib¦ril
micro|fiche
micro|fich¦ing
micro|fila¦ment
micro|fil¦aria
micro|fil¦ar¦iae
micro|film
micro|flora
micro|form
micro|fos¦sil
micro|fungus
micro|fungi
micro|gam¦ete
micro|glia
micro|glial
micro|gram
micro|gramme Br.
var. of microgram
micro|gran¦ite
micro|graph

micro|graph|ic
mi|crog|raphy
micro|grav|ity
micro|groove
micro|habi|tat
micro|inject
micro|injec|tion
micro|in|struc|tion
micro|kernel
micro|
    lepi|dop|tera
micro|light
micro|liter US
micro|lith
micro|lith|ic
micro|litre Br.
micro|manage
  micro|managing
micro|manage|
    ment
micro|manager
micro|mesh
micro|meteor|ite
micro|meteor|oid
micro|meteoro|
    logic|al
micro|meteor|
    ology
mi|crom|eter gauge
micro|meter US
  unit
micro|metre Br.
  unit
mi|crom|etry
micro|mini|atur|
    isa|tion
  Br. var. of micro-
  miniaturization
micro|mini|atur|
    iza|tion
mi|cron
Micro|nesia
Micro|nes|ian
mi|cron|isa|tion Br.
  var. of
  micronization
mi|cron|ise Br. var.
  of micronize
mi|cron|iser Br. var.
  of micronizer
mi|cron|iza|tion
mi|cron|ize
  mi|cron|iz|ing
mi|cron|izer

micro|nu|trient
micro|organ|ism
micro|pay|ment
micro|phage
micro|phagic
mi|cropha|gous
micro|phone
micro|phon|ic
micro|photo|graph
micro|photo|
    graph|ic
micro|pho|tog|
    raphy
micro|phyll
micro|phys|ic|al
micro|phys|ics
micro|pip|ette
micro|pore
micro|por|os|ity
micro|por|ous
micro|print
micro|print|ing
micro|prism
micro|probe
micro|pro|ces|sor
micro|pro|gram
micro|
    propa|ga|tion
mi|crop|sia
mi|crop|ter|ous
micro|pyle
micro|read|er
micro|sat|el|lite
micro|scoot|er
micro|scope
micro|scop|ic
micro|scop|ic|al
micro|scop|ic|al|ly
mi|cro|scop|ist
Micro|sco|pium
mi|cros|copy
micro|sec|ond
micro|seism
micro|seis|mic
micro|somal
micro|some
micro|species
  pl. micro|species
micro|sphere
micro|
  spor|an|gium
micro|spor|an|gia
micro|spore

micro|struc|tur|al
micro|struc|ture
micro|sur|geon
micro|sur|gery
micro|sur|gi|cal
micro|switch
micro|
  techno|logic|al
micro|tech|nol|ogy
micro|tome
micro|tonal
micro|tonal|ity
micro|tonal|ly
micro|tone
micro|tubule
micro|vascu|lar
micro|vil|lar
micro|vil|lus
  micro|villi
micro|wav|able var.
  of microwaveable
micro|wave
  micro|wav|ing
micro|wave|able
mic|rur|gic|al
mic|rurgy
mic|tur|ate
  mic|tur|at|ing
mic|tur|ition
mid-air
Midas Greek
  Mythology
mid-Atlantic
mid|brain
mid|day
middel|manne|tjie
mid|den
mid|dle
  mid|dling
middle|brow
Mid|dle
  Eng|land|er
Middle-European
middle|man
  middle|men
Middles|brough
mid|dles|cence
mid|dles|cent
Middle|sex
Middle|ton,
  Thomas dramatist
middle|veld
middle|ware

middle|weight
mid|dling
mid|dling|ly
middy
  mid|dies
Mid|east
mid-European
mid|field
mid|field|er
Mid|gard
  Scandinavian
  Mythology
midget
Mid Gla|mor|gan
mid|gut
mid|heaven
MIDI = musical
  instrument digital
  interface
Midi region, France
midi dress etc.
midi|bus
midi|nette
Midi Pyrénées
mid|iron
Mid|land of the
  Midlands; central
  US
mid|land middle
  part of a country
mid|land|er
Mid|lands central
  England
mid|life
mid|line
Mid|lothian
mid|most
mid|night
mid-off Cricket
mid-on Cricket
mid|point
Mid|rash
  Mid|rash|im
mid|rib
mid|riff
mid|sec|tion
mid|ship
mid|ship|man
  mid|ship|men
mid|sole
mid|stream
mid|sum|mer
Mid|sum|mer Day

mid|sum|mer
  mad|ness
Mid|sum|mer's
  Day var. of
  Midsummer Day
mid|term
mid|town
mid-Victor|ian
mid|way
mid|week
Mid|west
Mid|west|ern
Mid|west|ern|er
mid|wicket
mid|wife
  pl. mid|wives
  v. mid|wifes
  mid|wifed
  mid|wifing
mid|wif|ery
mid|win|ter
mie|lie var. of
  mealie
mien look; bearing;
  cf. mean, mesne
Mies|ian
Mies van der
  Rohe, Lud|wig
  architect
mife|pris|tone
miffy
MiG
might *v.*; strength;
  cf. mite
might|est
might-have-been
  n.
might|ily
mighti|ness
mightn't
mighty
  might|ier
  mighti|est
mig|ma|tite
mi|gnon|ette
mi|graine
mi|grain|eur
mi|grain|ous
mi|grant
mi|grate
  mi|grat|ing
mi|gra|tion
mi|gra|tion|al
mi|gra|tor

mi|gra|tory
Mi|hail|ović,
  Drag|oljub soldier
mih|rab
mi|kado +s
Mike name
mike
  mik|ing
  microphone; idle
  time away
Mi'k|maq
  pl. Mi'k|maq or
  Mi'k|maqs
  var. of Micmac
mikva
mil thousandth of
  an inch; also var. of
  mille in 'per mille';
  cf. mill
Milad
mi|lady
  mi|la|dies
mil|age var. of
  mileage
Milan
Mil|an|ese
milch
mil|dew
mil|dewy
mild|ish
mild|ly
mild|ness
Mil|dred
mile unit; cf. myall
mile|age
mile|ometer var. of
  milometer
mile|post
miler
miles glori|osus
  mili|tes glori|osi
Mi|le|sian
mile|stone
Mi|le|tus
mil|foil
Mil|haud, Da|rius
  composer
milia pl. of milium
mili|aria
mil|iary
mi|lieu
  mi|lieux or
  mi|lieus
mil|ing

mili|tancy
  mili|tan|cies
mili|tant
mili|tant|ly
mili|taria
mili|tar|ily
mili|tar|isa|tion *Br.*
  var. of
  militarization
mili|tar|ise *Br.* var.
  of militarize
mili|tar|ism
mili|tar|ist
mili|tar|is|tic
mili|tar|is|tic|al|ly
mili|tar|iza|tion
mili|tar|ize
  mili|tar|iz|ing
mili|tary
mili|tate
  mili|tat|ing
mil|itia
mil|itia|man
  mil|itia|men
mil|ium
  milia
milk|er
milk|fish
milk-glass
milk|ily
milki|ness
milk|maid
milk|man
  milk|men
milk|shake
milk|sop
milk|weed
milk|wort
milky
  milk|ier
  milki|est
mill building or
  apparatus for
  grinding; cf. mil
mill|able
Mil|lais, John
  Ever|ett painter
mill|board
Mille, Cecil B. de
  film producer and
  director
mille in 'per mille'
mille|feuille
mille|fiori

mille|fleurs
mil|len|ar|ian
mil|len|ar|ian|ism
mil|len|ar|ian|ist
mil|len|ary
  mil|len|ar|ies
mil|len|nial
mil|len|nial|ism
mil|len|nial|ist
mil|len|nium
  mil|len|niums or
  mil|len|nia
mille|pede var. of
  millipede
mille|pore
Mil|ler, Ar|thur
  playwright
Mil|ler, Glenn
  bandleader
Mil|ler, Henry
  novelist
mill|er
mill|er|ite
mill|er's thumb
  mill|er's thumbs
  fish
mil|lesi|mal
mil|lesi|mal|ly
Mil|let, Jean
  painter
mil|let
Mil|lett, Kate fem-
  inist
mill|hand
milli|am|meter
milli|amp
milli|am|pere
Mil|lian
mil|liard
milli|bar
Mil|li|cent
Mil|lie
mil|lieme
  French millième
Milli|gan, Spike
  comedian
milli|gram
milli|gramme *Br.*
  var. of milligram
Mil|li|kan, Rob|ert
  physicist
milli|liter *US*
milli|litre *Br.*
milli|meter *US*

milli|metre *Br.*
mill|iner
mill|in|ery
  mill|in|eries
mil|lion
mil|lion|aire
mil|lion|air|ess
mil|lion|fold
mil|lionth
milli|pede
milli|sec|ond
milli|volt
milli|watt
mill|pond
mill|stone
mill|stream
mill|work|er
mill|wright
Milne, A. A. *writer*
Milo *name*
millo *sorghum*
mil|om|eter
mi|lord
Milos *Greek spelling of Melos*
Mi|lose|vic,
  Slobo|dan *polit-
  ician*
Milque|toast
mil|reis
milt|er
Mil|ton, John *poet*
Mil|ton|ian
Mil|ton|ic
Mil|ton Keynes
Mil|wau|kee
Mimas
mim|bar var. of
  minbar
mime
  mim|ing
mimeo +s
mimeo|graph
mimer
mi|mesis
mi|met|ic
mi|met|ic|al|ly
mime|tite
mimic
  mim|icked
  mim|ick|ing
mim|ick|er

mim|ic|ry
mim|ic|ries
mi|mosa
mimsy
mimu|lus
mimu|luses
min|able var. of
  mineable
Mina|mata
Mi|nang|ka|bau
min|aret
min|aret|ed
Minas Ge|rais
min|atory
mi|nau|dière
min|bar
mince
  min|cing
minced meat *meat*
mince|meat *mix-
  ture of currants,
  apples, etc.*
min|cer
min|cing|ly
mind *intellect; look
  after; etc.;* cf.
  mined
Min|da|nao
Min|del
mind|er
mind|ful
mind|ful|ly
mind|ful|ness
mind|less
mind|less|ly
mind|less|ness
Min|doro
mind|set
mind|share
mind-your-own-
              business
  plant
mine
  min|ing
mine|able
mine|field
mine|hunt|er
mine|hunt|ing
mine|lay|er
mine|lay|ing
miner *mineworker;*
  cf. minor, mynah
min|eral

min|eral|isa|tion
  Br. var. of
  mineralization
min|eral|ise *Br.* var.
  of mineralize
min|eral|iza|tion
min|eral|ize
  min|eral|iz|ing
min|eralo|
          cor|tic|oid
min|eral|ogic|al
min|eral|ogic|al|ly
min|eral|ogist
min|eral|ogy
Min|erva *Roman
  Mythology*
Mi|ner|vois *wine;
  French district*
min|es|trone
mine|sweep|er
mine|sweep|ing
mine|work|er
ming|er
min|gily
min|gling
min|gle
  min|gling
Min|gus, Char|lie
  musician
mingy
min|gier
min|gi|est
min|hag
  min|hag|im
Minho
Mini *car trademark*
mini *dress etc.;* cf.
  minnie
mini|ature
mini|atur|ing
mini|atur|isa|tion
  Br. var. of
  miniaturization
mini|atur|ise *Br.*
  var. of miniaturize
mini|atur|ist
mini|atur|iza|tion
mini|atur|ize
  mini|atur|iz|ing
mini|bar
mini|beast
mini-break
mini|bus
  mini|buses

mini|cab
mini|cam
mini|camp
Mini|com
  trademark
mini|com|puter
Mini|coy Is|lands
mini|disc
mini|dress
mini|fun|dium
  mini|fun|dia
mini-golf
mini|gun
mini|kin
minim
mini|ma pl. of
  minimum
min|imal
min|im|al|ism
min|im|al|ist
mini-mall
min|im|al|ly
mini|mart
mini|max
mini-me
mini|misa|tion *Br.*
  var. of
  minimization
min|im|ise *Br.* var.
  of minimize
min|im|iser *Br.* var.
  of minimizer
mini|miza|tion
min|im|ize
  min|im|iz|ing
min|im|izer
min|imum
min|ima or
  min|imums
min|ion
mini-pill
mini-roundabout
mini rugby
mini|ser|ies
  pl. mini|ser|ies
mini|skirt
min|is|ter
min|is|ter gen|eral
  min|is|ter
  gen|erals
min|is|ter|ial
min|is|teri|al|ly
min|is|ter|ship

min¦is¦trant
min¦is¦tra¦tion
min¦is¦try
  min¦is¦tries
mini¦tower
Mini Van
  trademark
mini¦van general
min¦iver
mini¦vet
mink stoatlike
  animal
minke whale
minna¦ritchi var. of
  minnerichi
Min¦ne¦ap¦olis
min¦ne¦ola
minne¦richi
Minne¦sing¦er
Min¦ne¦sota
Min¦ne¦so¦tan
Min¦nie name
min¦nie in 'moaning
  minnie'; cf. mini
min¦now
Min¦oan
minor below legal
  age; unimportant;
  cf. miner, mynah
Min¦orca
Min¦or¦can
Mi¦nor¦ite
mi¦nor¦ity
  mi¦nor¦ities
minor-leaguer
Minos legendary
  Cretan king
Mino¦taur
mino¦taur beetle
min¦oxi¦dil
min¦ster
min¦strel
min¦strel¦sy
mint¦age
mint¦er
Min¦ton
minty
  mint¦ier
  minti¦est
minu¦end
min¦uet
minus
min¦us¦cu¦lar

min¦us¦cule
mi¦nute
  mi¦nuter
  minut¦est
  tiny
min¦ute
  min¦ut¦ing
  60 seconds;
  (*minutes*)
  proceedings; to
  record
mi¦nute¦ly
min¦ute¦man
  min¦ute¦men
mi¦nute¦ness
mi¦nu¦tia var. of
  minutiae
mi¦nu¦tiae
minx
minx¦ish
minxy
min¦yan
  min¦yan¦im
Mio¦cene
mi¦osis eye
  disorder; cf.
  meiosis
mi¦ot¦ic of miosis;
  cf. meiotic
Mi¦que¦llet lock
Mi¦que¦llon
Mira¦beau,
  Hon¦oré French
  revolutionary
Mira¦bel name
mira¦belle plum-
  like fruit
mira¦bile dictu
mira¦cid¦ium
  mira¦cidia
mir¦acle
mi¦racu¦lous
mi¦racu¦lous¦ly
mi¦racu¦lous¦ness
mira¦dor
mir¦age
Mi¦randa
MIRAS = mortgage
  interest relief at
  source
mire
  mir¦ing
mire¦poix
  pl. *mire¦poix*
mirex

Mir¦iam
mirid
mirin
mir¦li¦ton
mirn¦yong var. of
  mirrnyong
Miró, Joan painter
miro +s tree
mirrn¦yong
mir¦ror
mirror¦ball
mirth¦ful
mirth¦less
mirth¦less¦ly
mirth¦less¦ness
MIRV = multiple
  independently-
  targeted re-entry
  vehicle
miry
  miri¦er
  miri¦est
mis¦ad¦dress
mis¦ad¦ven¦ture
mis¦align
mis¦align¦ment
mis¦alli¦ance
mis¦allo¦cate
  mis¦allo¦cat¦ing
  mis¦allo¦ca¦tion
mis¦ally
  mis¦allies
  mis¦allied
  mis¦ally¦ing
mis¦an¦drist
mis¦andry
mis¦an¦thrope
mis¦an¦throp¦ic
  mis¦an¦throp¦ic¦
    al¦ly
mis¦an¦thro¦pise
  Br. var. of
  misanthropize
mis¦an¦thro¦pist
mis¦an¦thro¦pize
  mis¦an¦thro¦piz¦ing
mis¦an¦thropy
mis¦ap¦pli¦ca¦tion
mis¦ap¦ply
  mis¦ap¦plies
  mis¦ap¦plied
  mis¦ap¦ply¦ing
mis¦ap¦pre¦hend

mis¦ap¦pre¦hen¦
            sion
mis¦appro¦pri¦ate
  mis¦appro¦
       pri¦at¦ing
  mis¦appro¦
       pri¦ation
mis¦attrib¦ute
  mis¦attrib¦ut¦ing
mis¦attri¦bu¦tion
mis¦be¦got¦ten
mis¦be¦have
  mis¦be¦hav¦ing
mis¦be¦hav¦ior *US*
mis¦be¦hav¦iour *Br.*
mis¦be¦lief
mis¦believ¦er
mis¦cal¦cu¦late
  mis¦cal¦cu¦lat¦ing
  mis¦cal¦cu¦la¦tion
mis¦call
mis¦car¦riage
mis¦carry
  mis¦car¦ries
  mis¦car¦ried
  mis¦carry¦ing
mis¦cast
mis¦ce¦gen¦ation
mis¦cel¦la¦nea
mis¦cel¦lan¦eous
mis¦cel¦lan¦eous¦ly
mis¦cel¦lan¦eous¦
            ness
mis¦cel¦lan¦ist
mis¦cel¦lany
  mis¦cel¦lanies
mis¦chance
mis¦chief
mis¦chiev¦ous
mis¦chiev¦ous¦ly
mis¦chiev¦ous¦ness
misch metal
mis¦ci¦bil¦ity
mis¦cible
mis¦classi¦fi¦ca¦tion
mis¦clas¦sify
  mis¦clas¦si¦fies
  mis¦clas¦si¦fied
  mis¦clas¦si¦fy¦ing
mis¦com¦mu¦ni¦
         ca¦tion
mis¦con¦ceive
  mis¦con¦ceiv¦ing
mis¦con¦ceiver

mis|con|cep|tion
mis|con|duct
mis|con|fig|ur|
　　　　　ation
mis|con|fig|ure
　mis|con|fig|ur|ing
mis|con|struc|tion
mis|con|strue
　mis|con|stru|ing
mis|copy
　mis|cop|ies
　mis|cop|ied
　mis|copy|ing
mis|count
mis|cre|ant
mis|cue
　mis|cue|ing or
　mis|cuing
mis|date
　mis|dat|ing
mis|deal
　mis|dealt
mis|dec|lar|ation
mis|deed
mis|deliv|ery
　mis|deliv|er|ies
mis|de|mean|ant
mis|de|meanor US
mis|de|mean|our
　Br.
mis|de|scribe
　mis|de|scrib|ing
mis|de|scrip|tion
mis|diag|nose
　mis|diag|nos|ing
mis|diag|nosis
　mis|diag|noses
mis|dial
　mis|dialled Br.
　mis|dialed US
　mis|dial|ling Br.
　mis|dial|ing US
mis|dir|ect
mis|dir|ec|tion
mis|doing
mis|doubt
mis|edu|cate
　mis|edu|cat|ing
mis|edu|ca|tion
mis|edu|ca|tive
mise en place
mise en scène
　mises en scène
mis|em|ploy

mis|em|ploy|ment
miser
mis|er|abil|ism
mis|er|abil|ist
mis|er|able
mis|er|ably
mi|sère
mi|sère ou|verte
mis|er|ere
mis|eri|cord
miser|li|ness
miser|ly
mis|ery
　mis|er|ies
mis|esti|mate
　mis|esti|mat|ing
mis|esti|ma|tion
mis|feas|ance
mis|feed
mis|field
mis|file
　mis|fil|ing
mis|fire
　mis|fir|ing
mis|fit
mis|for|tune
mis|give
　mis|gave
　mis|giv|ing
　mis|given
mis|gov|ern
mis|gov|ern|ment
mis|guided
　mis|guided|ly
　mis|guided|ness
mis|handle
　mis|hand|ling
mis|hap
mis|hear
Mish|ima, Yukio
　writer
mis|hit
　mis|hit|ting
mish|mash
Mish|nah
Mish|na|ic
mis|iden|ti|fi|
　　　　ca|tion
mis|iden|tify
　mis|iden|ti|fies
　mis|iden|ti|fied
　mis|iden|ti|fy|ing
mis|in|form
mis|in|for|ma|tion

mis|in|ter|pret
mis|in|ter|pret|
　　　　　ation
mis|in|ter|pret|er
mis|judge
　mis|judg|ing
mis|judge|ment
mis|judg|ment var.
　of misjudgement
mis|key
mis|kick
Mis|kito
　pl. Mis|kito or
　Mis|kitos
Mis|kolc
mis|label
　mis|labelled Br.
　mis|labeled US
　mis|label|ling Br.
　mis|label|ling US
mis|lay
　mis|laid
mis|lead
　mis|lead|er
　mis|lead|ing|ly
mis|like
　mis|lik|ing
mis|man|age
　mis|man|aging
mis|man|age|ment
mis|match
mis|mate
　mis|mat|ing
mis|meas|ure
　mis|meas|ur|ing
mis|meas|ure|ment
mis|name
　mis|nam|ing
mis|nomer
mis|num|ber
miso
mis|ogyn|ist
mis|ogyn|is|tic
mis|ogyn|ous
mis|ogyny
mis|per|ceive
　mis|per|ceiv|ing
mis|per|cep|tion
mis|pickel
mis|place
　mis|placing
mis|place|ment
mis|play
mis|print

mis|pro|nounce
　mis|pro|noun|cing
mis|pro|nun|ci|
　　　　　ation
mis|quo|ta|tion
mis|quote
　mis|quot|ing
mis|read
mis|rec|og|nise Br.
　var. of
　misrecognize
mis|rec|og|ni|tion
mis|rec|og|nize
　mis|rec|og|niz|ing
mis|re|mem|ber
mis|re|port
mis|rep|re|sent
mis|rep|re|sen|
　　　　　ta|tion
mis|rep|re|sen|
　　　　　ta|tive
mis|route
　mis|rout|ing
mis|rule
　mis|rul|ing
miss|able
mis|sal book
mis-sell
　mis-sold
mis|sel thrush var.
　of mistle thrush
mis|shape
　mis|shap|ing
mis|sha|pen
　mis|sha|pen|ly
　mis|sha|pen|ness
mis|sile projectile
mis|sil|ery
missio|logic|al
mis|siol|ogy
mis|sion
mis|sion|ary
　mis|sion|ar|ies
mis|sion|er
mis|sis var. of
　missus
miss|ish
Mis|sis|sauga
Mis|sis|sippi
Mis|sis|sip|pian
mis|sive
Mis|so|lon|ghi
Mis|souri
Mis|souri|an

mis|speak
  mis|spoke
  mis|spoken
mis|spell
  mis|spelled
  Br. also mis|spelt
mis|spend
  mis|spent
mis|state
  mis|stat|ing
mis|state|ment
mis|step
mis|sus
missy
  mis|sies
mis|tak|able
mis|tak|ably
mis|take
  mis|took
  mis|tak|ing
  mis|taken
mis|take|able var.
  of mistakable
mis|take|ably var.
  of mistakably
mis|taken|ly
mis|taken|ness
mis|teach
  mis|taught
mis|ter
mist|ily
mis|time
  mis|tim|ing
misti|ness
mis|title
  mis|titling
mis|tle thrush cf.
  missal
mistle|toe
mistle|toe|bird
mis|took past tense
  of mistake
mis|tral
mis|trans|late
  mis|trans|lat|ing
mis|trans|la|tion
mis|treat
mis|treat|ment
mis|tress
mis|trial
mis|trust
mis|trust|ful
misty
  mist|ier

misti|est
mis|type
  mis|typ|ing
mis|un|der|stand
  mis|un|der|stood
mis|us|age
mis|use
  mis|us|ing
mis|user
Mi|tanni
Mi|tan|nian
Mitch|ell, Joni
  singer-songwriter
Mitch|ell,
  Mar|ga|ret novelist
Mitch|ell, R. J.
  aeronautical
  designer
Mitchum, Rob|ert
  actor
mite arachnid; small
  amount; cf. might
miter *US*
  Br. mitre
Mit|ford, Jes|sica
  writer
Mit|ford, Nancy
  writer
mi|thai Indian
  sweets
mi|ther
Mith|ra|da|tes var.
  of Mithridates
Mith|raeum
  Mith|raea
Mith|ra|ic
Mith|ra|ism
Mith|ra|ist
Mith|ras *Roman*
  Mythology
Mith|ri|da|tes
mith|ri|dat|ic
mith|ri|da|tism
miti|gable
miti|gate
  miti|gat|ing
miti|ga|tion
miti|ga|tor
miti|ga|tory
Mitla
mito|chon|drial
mito|chon|drion
  mito|chon|dria
mito|gen

mito|gen|ic
mi|tosis
  mi|toses
mi|tot|ic
mi|tral
mitre *Br.*
  mitr|ing
  US miter
Mit|siwa var. of
  Massawa
Mittel|land Canal
mit|ten
mit|tened
Mit|ter|rand,
  Fran|çois president
  of France
mit|ti|mus
Mitty, Wal|ter
  Wal|ter Mittys
mi|tumba
mitz|vah
  mitz|voth
  see also
  bar mitzvah,
  bat mitzvah
mix|able
mixer
mixie
Mix|master food
  processor
  trademark
mix|master
  accomplished mixer
  of music
mix|olo|gist
mix|ology
Mixo|lyd|ian mode
Mix|tec
  pl. Mix|tec or
  Mix|tecs
mix|ture
mix-up *n.*
mizen var. of
  mizzen
Mizo
  pl. Mizo or Mizos
Mi|zo|ram
mi|zuna
miz|zen
mizzen|mast
mizzen|sail
miz|zle
  miz|zling

miz|zly
  miz|zlier
  miz|zli|est
m'lud = my lord
Mma|batho
M'Nagh|ten rules
  var. of McNaghten
  rules
mne|mon|ic
  remembering
  device; cf.
  gnomonic
mne|mon|ic|al|ly
mne|mon|ist
Mne|mos|yne *Greek*
  Mythology
mnemo|tech|nic
mo +s = moment; cf.
  mho, mow
moa bird; cf. mower
Moab
Moab|ite
moan plaintive
  sound; make a
  moan; complain; cf.
  mown
moan|er
moan|ful
moat ditch; cf. mote
mob
  mobbed
  mob|bing
mob|ber
mobe mobile phone
mobey mobile
  phone
Mo|bile city, US
mo|bile
mo|bil|is|able *Br.*
  var. of mobilizable
mo|bil|isa|tion *Br.*
  var. of
  mobilization
mo|bil|ise *Br.* var. of
  mobilize
mo|bil|iser *Br.* var.
  of mobilizer
mo|bil|ity
mo|bil|iz|able
mo|bil|iza|tion
mo|bil|ize
  mo|bil|iz|ing
mo|bil|izer
Mö|bius strip

mobo +s mother-
board
mob|oc|racy
  mob|oc|ra|cies
mob|ster
Mo|butu, Sese Seko
  president of Zaire
moc moccasin; cf.
  mock
moc|ca|sin
Mocha stone;
  pottery
mocha coffee;
  leather; cf. **mocker**
mocha|ccino +s
mock laugh at;
  inauthentic;
  examination; cf.
  moc
mock|able
mock|er person who
  mocks; cf. **mocha**
mock|ery
  mock|er|ies
mock-heroic
mock|ing|bird
mock|ing|ly
mock|ney
mocku|men|tary
  mocku|men|taries
mock-up n.
mocky
  mock|ies
mo|cock
Mod Gaelic
  competition
mod modern; 1960s
  stylish young per-
  son; modulo
mod|acryl|ic
modal
modal|ism
modal|ist
mo|dal|ity
  mo|dal|ities
mo|dal|ly
mode manner;
  fashion
model
  mod|elled *Br.*
  mod|eled *US*
  mod|el|ling *Br.*
  mod|el|ing *US*
  mod|el|er *US*
  mod|el|ler *Br.*

modem
Mod|ena
mod|er|ate
  mod|er|at|ing
  mod|er|ate|ly
mod|er|ation mod-
  erate conduct
Mod|er|ations
  examination
mod|er|at|ism
mod|er|ato +s
mod|er|ator
mod|er|ator|ship
mod|ern recent; up
  to date
mo|derne of a form
  of art deco; ultra-
  modern
mod|ern|isa|tion
  Br. var. of
  modernization
mod|ern|ise *Br.* var.
  of **modernize**
mod|ern|iser *Br.*
  var. of **modernizer**
mod|ern|ism
mod|ern|ist
mod|ern|is|tic
mod|ern|ity
  mod|ern|ities
mod|ern|iza|tion
mod|ern|ize
  mod|ern|iz|ing
mod|ern|izer
mod|ern|ly
mod|ern|ness
mod|est
mod|est|ly
mod|esty
  mod|esties
modi|cum
modi|fi|able
modi|fi|ca|tion
modi|fi|ca|tory
modi|fier
mod|ify
  modi|fies
  modi|fied
  modi|fy|ing
**Modi|gliani,
  Ame|deo** painter
mo|dil|lion
modi|olus
  modi|oli

mod|ish
mod|ish|ly
mod|ish|ness
mod|iste
modu|lar
modu|lar|ity
modu|late
  modu|lat|ing
modu|la|tion
modu|la|tor
mod|ule
mod|ulo
modu|lus
  mod|uli
modus op|er|andi
  modi op|er|andi
modus po|nens
modus tol|lens
modus vi|vendi
  modi vi|vendi
Moeri|ther|ium
Moe|sia
mo|fette
mof|fle
Moga|di|shu
Moga|don
  trademark
  pl. **Moga|don** or
  Moga|dons
mog|gie
moggy
  mog|gies
  var. of **moggie**
Mogh|lai var. of
  Mughlai
Mo|ghul var. of
  Mogul
Mog|lai var. of
  Mughlai
Mogul Muslim ruler
  in India
mogul important
  person; hump on
  ski slope
Mo|hács
mo|hair
mo|halla
Mo|ham|med var.
  of **Muhammad**
Mo|ham|med|an
  var. of
  Muhammadan
**Mo|ham|med|an|
  ism**

  var. of
  Muhammadanism
Mo|have Des|ert
  var. of **Mojave
  Desert**
Mo|hawk
  pl. **Mo|hawk** or
  Mo|hawks
Mo|he|gan Ameri-
  can Indian people
  formerly of Massa-
  chusetts and
  Connecticut; cf.
  Mahican, Mohican
mohel
  mo|hels or
  mo|hel|im or
  mo|hal|im
Mohenjo-Daro
Mo|hi|can hairstyle;
  also var. of
  Mohegan or
  Mahican
Moho = Mohorovi-
  čić discontinuity
**Moholy-Nagy,
  László** artist
**Moho|ro|vi|čić
  dis|con|tinu|ity**
Mohs' scale
moi|dore
moi|ety
  moi|eties
moire silk; with
  rippled, lustrous
  finish
moiré var. of **moire**
mois|ten
moist|ly
moist|ness
mois|ture
mois|ture|less
mois|tur|ise *Br.* var.
  of **moisturize**
mois|tur|iser *Br.*
  var. of **moisturizer**
mois|tur|ize
  mois|tur|iz|ing
mois|tur|izer
moisty
mo|jarra
Mo|jave Des|ert
mo|jito +s
mojo +s
moko +s

mok|sha
mol *Chemistry* short
  for **mole**
mola
molal
mol|al|ity
molar
mo|lar|ity
mo|las|ses
Mold town, Wales
mold *US*
  Br. mould
mold|able *US*
  Br. mouldable
Mol|davia
Mol|davian
mold|board *US*
  Br. mouldboard
mold|er *US* person
  who moulds; rot;
  Br. moulder
mol|di|ness *US*
  Br. mouldiness
mold|ing *US*
  Br. moulding
Mol|dova
Mol|do|van
moldy *US*
  Br. mouldy
mo|lecu|lar
mo|lecu|lar|ity
mo|lecu|lar|ly
mol|ecule
mole|hill
mole|skin
mo|lest
mo|lest|ation
mo|lest|er
Mol|ière dramatist
mo|line *Heraldry*;
  cf. **malign**
Mo|lise
Mol|lie
mol|li|fi|ca|tion
mol|li|fier
mol|lify
  mol|li|fies
  mol|li|fied
  mol|li|fy|ing
molli|sol
mol|lusc *Br.*
mol|lus|can *Br.*
mol|lusc|oid *Br.*
mol|lusc|ous *Br.*

mol|lus|cum
  con|ta|gi|osum
mol|lusk *US*
mol|lus|kan *US*
mol|lusk|oid *US*
mol|lusk|ous *US*
Moll|weide
  pro|jec|tion
Molly name
molly
  mol|lies
  fish
molly|cod|dle
molly|cod|dling
molly|doo|ker
molly|mawk
Mo|loch idol
mo|loch lizard
mo|los|sus
  mo|lossi
Molo|tov,
  Vyache|slav Soviet
  foreign minister;
  M. cocktail
molt *US*
  Br. moult
mol|ten
molto
Mo|lucca Is|lands
Mo|luc|can
molvi var. of **moulvi**
moly
  molies
mo|lyb|date
mo|lyb|den|ite
mo|lyb|denum
mom *US*
  Br. mum
Mom|basa
mo|ment
mo|menta
mo|ment|ar|ily
mo|ment|ari|ness
mo|ment|ary
mo|ment|ly
mo|men|tous
mo|men|tous|ly
mo|men|tous|ness
mo|men|tum
  mo|menta
mom|ism
momma
Momm|sen,
  Theo|dor historian

mommy *US*
mom|mies
  Br. mummy
mom|para
Momus
  Mo|muses or
  Momi
Mon people
  pl. Mon or Mons
Mon|acan
Mon|aco
monad
mona|del|phous
mo|nad|ic
mon|ad|ism
mon|ad|nock
Mona|ghan
monal
Mona Lisa
mon|amine var. of
  monoamine
mona mon|key
mo|nan|drous
mo|nan|dry
mon|arch +s
Mo|nar|chian
mo|nar|chic
mo|nar|chic|al
mon|arch|ism
mon|arch|ist
mon|archy
  mon|arch|ies
Mon|ash, John
  Australian general
mon|as|tery
  mon|as|ter|ies
mo|nas|tic
mo|nas|tic|al|ly
mo|nas|ti|cise *Br.*
  var. of **monasticize**
mo|nas|ti|cism
Mon|as|tir
Mo|nas|tral
  trademark
mon|atom|ic
mon|aural
mon|aural|ly
mona|zite
Mon|ba|zil|lac
Mön|chen|
         glad|bach
Monck, George
  general

mon|daine
Mon|day
mon|dial
mondo
Mon|drian, Piet
  painter
Moné|gasque
Monel *trademark*
Monet, Claude
  painter
mon|et|ar|ily
mon|et|ar|ise *Br.*
  var. of **monetarize**
mon|et|ar|ism
mon|et|ar|ist
mon|et|ar|ize
mon|et|ar|iz|ing
mon|et|ary
mon|et|isa|tion *Br.*
  var. of
  monetization
mon|et|ise *Br.* var.
  of **monetize**
mon|et|iza|tion
mon|et|ize
  mon|et|iz|ing
money
  moneys or mon|ies
money bag bag for
  money
money|bags
  pl. money|bags
  person
mon|eyed
mon|ey|er
money-grubber
money-grubbing
money|lend|er
money|lend|ing
money|less
money|maker
money|mak|ing
money|wort
mon|ger
mongo
  pl. mongo or
  mon|gos
Mon|gol member of
  Asian people
mon|gol *offensive*
  person with Down's
  syndrome
Mon|go|lia
Mon|go|lian

mon¦gol¦ism *offen-*
  sive
Mon¦gol¦oid
  characteristic of
  Mongolians;
  Mongoloid type
mon¦gol¦oid *offen-*
  sive affected with
  Down's syndrome
mon¦goose +s
mon¦grel
mon¦grel¦isa¦tion
  Br. var. of
  mongrelization
mon¦grel¦ise *Br.*
  var. of mongrelize
mon¦grel¦ism
mon¦grel¦iza¦tion
mon¦grel¦ize
  mon¦grel¦iz¦ing
mo¦nial
monic
Mon¦ica
mon¦icker var. of
  moniker
mon¦ickered var. of
  monikered
mon¦ied var. of
  moneyed
mon¦ies pl. of
  money
moni¦ker
mon¦ikered
mo¦nilia
  mo¦nil¦iae
mo¦nili¦form
mon¦ism
mon¦ist
mon¦is¦tic
moni¦tor
moni¦tor¦ial
moni¦tor¦ship
Monk, The¦lo¦nious
  musician
monk¦ery
monk¦ey
mon¦key¦ish
monkey¦shines
monk¦fish
monk¦ish
monk¦ish¦ly
monk¦ish¦ness
monks¦hood plant
Mon¦mouth

Mon¦mouth¦shire
mono +s
mono¦acid
mono¦amine
mono¦basic
mono¦bloc
mono¦brow
mono¦browed
mono¦car¦pic
mono¦car¦pous
mono¦caus¦al
Mon¦oceros
mono¦cha¦sium
  mono¦cha¦sia
mono¦chord
mono¦chro¦mat¦ic
mono¦chro¦mat¦ic¦
  al¦ly
mono¦
  chro¦ma¦tism
mono¦chrom¦ator
mono¦chrome
mono¦chro¦mic
mon¦ocle
mon¦ocled
mono¦cli¦nal
mono¦cline
mono¦clin¦ic
mono¦clo¦nal
mono¦coque
mono¦cot
mono¦coty¦le¦don
mono¦coty¦le¦don¦
  ous
mon¦oc¦racy
  mon¦oc¦ra¦cies
mono¦crat
mono¦crat¦ic
mono¦crys¦tal¦line
mon¦ocu¦lar
mono¦cul¦ture
mono¦cycle
mono¦cyc¦lic
mono¦cyte
mono¦dac¦tyl
mono¦dac¦tyly
mon¦od¦ic
mono¦dis¦perse
mon¦od¦ist
mono¦drama
mon¦ody
  mon¦odies
mon¦oe¦cious

mon¦oecy
mono¦fil
mono¦fila¦ment
mon¦og¦amist
mon¦og¦am¦ous
mon¦og¦am¦ous¦ly
mon¦og¦amy
mono¦gen¦ean
mono¦gen¦esis
mono¦gen¦et¦ic
mono¦gen¦ic
mono¦gen¦ic¦al¦ly
mono¦gen¦ism
mono¦gen¦ist
mon¦ogeny
mono¦glot
mono¦gram
  mono¦grammed
  mono¦gram¦ming
mono¦gram¦mat¦ic
mono¦graph
mono¦graph¦ic
mono¦gyne
mon¦ogyny
mono¦hull
mono¦hy¦brid
mono¦hy¦drate
mono¦hy¦dric
mono¦kini
mon¦ol¦ater
mon¦ol¦atrist
mon¦ol¦atrous
mon¦ol¦atry
mono¦layer
mono¦lin¦gual
mono¦lin¦gual¦ism
mono¦lith
mono¦lith¦ic
mono¦logic
mono¦logic¦al
mon¦olo¦gise *Br.*
  var. of monologize
mon¦olo¦gist
mon¦olo¦gize
  mon¦olo¦giz¦ing
mono¦logue
mon¦olo¦guist var.
  of monologist
mono¦mania
mono¦maniac
mono¦mani¦ac¦al
mono¦mer

mono¦mer¦ic
mon¦om¦eter
mono¦met¦ric
mono¦mial
mono¦mo¦lecu¦lar
mono¦mor¦phem¦ic
mono¦morph¦ic
mono¦morph¦ism
mono¦morph¦ous
mono¦nuclear
mono¦nucle¦osis
mono¦opha¦gous
mono¦phon¦ic
mono¦oph¦ony
  mon¦oph¦onies
mono¦ph¦thong
mono¦ph¦thong¦al
mono¦phy¦let¦ic
Mon¦ophy¦site
Mon¦ophy¦sit¦ism
mono¦plane
mono¦ple¦gia
mono¦ple¦gic
mono¦ploid
mono¦pod
mono¦podial
mono¦podium
  mono¦podia
mono¦pole
mon¦op¦ol¦isa¦tion
  Br. var. of
  monopolization
mon¦op¦ol¦ise *Br.*
  var. of monopolize
mon¦op¦ol¦iser *Br.*
  var. of
  monopolizer
mon¦op¦ol¦ist
mon¦op¦ol¦is¦tic
mon¦op¦ol¦is¦tic¦
  al¦ly
mon¦op¦ol¦iza¦tion
mon¦op¦ol¦ize
  mon¦op¦ol¦iz¦ing
mon¦op¦ol¦izer
mon¦op¦oly
  mon¦op¦olies
mono¦pro¦pel¦lant
mon¦op¦sony
  mon¦op¦so¦nies
mon¦op¦ter¦al
mon¦op¦teros
  mon¦op¦ter¦oses

mono|rail
mon|orchid
mon|orchid|ism
mono|sac|char|ide
mono|semic
mono|semous
mono|semy
mono|ski
mono|ski¦er
mono|ski¦ing
mono|so¦dium
  glu¦ta|mate
mono|some
mono|som¦ic
mono|somy
mono|spe¦cif¦ic
mono|stable
mono|stroph¦ic
mono|syl¦lab¦ic
mono|syl¦lab¦ic|
      al¦ly
mono|syl¦lable
mono|sym¦met¦ric
mono|sym¦metry
 mono|sym¦metries
mono|synap¦tic
mono|tech¦nic
mono|the¦ism
mono|the¦ist
mono|the¦is¦tic
mono|the¦is¦tic|
      al¦ly
Mon|oth¦elete var.
 of **Monothelite**
Mon|oth¦elite
mono|ther¦apy
 mono|ther¦apies
mono|tint
mono|tone
mono|ton¦ic
mono|ton¦ic|al¦ly
mono|ton¦icity
mon|ot¦on|ise Br.
 var. of **monotonize**
mon|ot¦on|ize
 mon|ot¦on|iz¦ing
mon|ot¦on|ous
mon|ot¦on|ous¦ly
mon|ot¦ony
mono|treme
mono|trope
mon|ot¦ropy

Mono|type machine
 trademark
mono|type print
 made on glass or
 metal
mono|typ¦ic
mono|un¦satu|
      rated
mono|va¦lent
mon|ox¦ide
mono|zy¦gos¦ity
mono|zy¦got¦ic
mono|zy¦gous
Mon|roe, James
 American presi-
 dent; M. doctrine
Mon|roe, Mari¦lyn
 actress
Mon|ro¦via
Mon|sei¦gneur
 Mes|sei¦gneurs
 title of French
 prince, cardinal,
 etc.
Mon|sieur
 Mes|sieurs
Mon|si¦gnor
 Mon|si¦gnors or
 Mon|si¦gnori
 Roman Catholic
 title
mon|soon
mon|soon¦al
mons pubis
 mon¦tes pubis
mon|ster
mon|stera
mon|strance
mon|stros¦ity
 mon|stros¦ities
mon|strous
mon|strous¦ly
mon|strous¦ness
mons Ven|eris
 mon¦tes Ven|eris
mon|tage
Mon|tagna,
 Bar¦to|lom¦meo
 Cin|cani painter
Mon|tagn¦ais
 pl. Mon|tagn¦ais
Mon|tagn¦ard
Mon|ta|gue
Mon|tagu's
 har¦rier

Mon|taigne,
 Mi¦chel de writer
Mon|tana
Mon|tan¦an
mon|tane
Mon|tan|ism
Mon|tan|ist
Mont Blanc
mont|bre¦tia
Mont|calm,
 Mar|quis de
 French general
monte card game
Monte Albán
Monte Carlo
Monte Cas|sino
Mon|tego Bay
Mon|te|neg¦rin
Mon|te|negro
Monte|pul¦ciano +s
Mon|terey city, US;
 M. cypress; M. Jack
Mon|ter|rey city,
 Mexico
Mon|tes|pan,
 Mar|quise de mis-
 tress of Louis XIV
Mon|tes|quieu,
 Charles political
 philosopher
Mon¦tes|sori,
 Maria educationist
Mon|te|verdi,
 Clau¦dio composer
Mon¦te|video
Mon|tez, Lola dan-
 cer and mistress of
 Ludwig I of Bavaria
Mon¦te|zuma Aztec
 ruler
Mont|fort, Simon
 de founder of Eng-
 lish parliament
Mont|gol¦fier,
 Jo¦seph Mi¦chel
 and **Jacques**
 Étienne French
 balloonists
Mont|gom¦ery city,
 US
Mont|gom¦ery,
 Ber¦nard Law
 general
Mont|gom¦ery,
 Lucy Maud

 novelist
Mont¦gom¦ery|
      shire
month¦ly
 month|lies
Mont|martre
mont|mor¦il|lon|ite
Monto|nero +s
Mont|par¦nasse
Mont Pelée
Mont|pel¦ier city,
 US
Mont|pel¦lier city,
 France
Mont|rachet
Mon|treal
Mon|treux
Mon|trose,
 Mar|quis of
 general
Mont St Mi¦chel
Mont|ser¦rat
Mont|ser¦ra¦tian
mon|tuno +s
Monty name
monty in 'the full
 monty'
monu|ment
monu|men¦tal
monu|men¦tal|ise
 Br. var. of
 monumentalize
monu|men¦tal|ism
monu|men¦tal|ity
monu|men¦tal|ize
 monu|men¦tal|
      iz¦ing
monu|men¦tal¦ly
mon|zon|ite
mon|zon|it¦ic
moo +s +ed +ing
 cattle sound; cf.
 moue
mooch¦er
moo-cow
mood¦ily
moodi|ness
moody
 mood¦ier
 moodi|est
Moog, Rob¦ert
 inventor

moo¦lah

mooli

moomba

moon¦beam

moon¦calf
  moon¦calves

moon-eye

moon¦fish

moon¦flower

moong var. of **mung**

Moonie *offensive*
  member of Unifica-
  tion Church; cf.
  muni

moon¦less

moon¦let

moon¦light +ed

moon¦light¦er

moon¦like

moon¦lit

moon¦quake

moon¦raker

moon¦rat

moon¦rise

moon¦scape

moon¦seed

moon¦set

moon¦shee
  var. of **munshi**

moon¦shine

moon¦shiner

moon¦stomp

moon¦stone

moon¦struck

moon¦walk

moon¦walk¦er

moon¦wort

moony
  moon¦ier
  mooni¦est

Moor N. African
  people

moor open land; tie
  up a boat; cf. **maw,**
  mor, more

moor¦age

moor¦burn

moor¦cock

Moore, Bobby
  footballer

Moore, Dud¦ley
  actor

Moore in 'Old
  Moore's Almanac'

Moore, G. E.
  philosopher

Moore, George
  novelist

Moore, Henry
  sculptor

Moore, John
  general

Moore, Thomas
  poet

Mooré language;
  var. of **More**

moor¦fowl
  pl. moor¦fowl or
  moor¦fowls

moor¦hen

moor¦ings

Moor¦ish of Moors;
  cf. **moreish**

moor¦land

Moor¦park apricot

moory

moose
  pl. moose
  elk; cf. **mousse**

moose¦wood

moo shi

moo shoo var. of
  moo shi

moo shu roo var. of
  moo shi

moot
  moot¦ed
  moot¦ing
  debatable; raise
  (topic); cf. **mute**

mop
  mopped
  mop¦ping

mo¦pane

mo¦pani var. of
  mopane

mop¦board

mope
  mop¦ing

moped motor cycle

moper

mopery

mopey

mopi¦er

mopi¦est

mop¦head

mopi¦ly

mopi¦ness

mop¦ish

mo¦poke

mop¦pet

moppy
  mop¦pi¦er
  mop¦pi¦est

Mopti

mop¦top

mopy var. of **mopey**

mo¦quette

mor humus; cf.
  maw, moor, more

Mora¦da¦bad

mo¦rainal

mo¦raine

mo¦rain¦ic

moral concerned
  with acceptable
  behaviour; lesson

mor¦ale mental
  attitude

mor¦al¦isa¦tion *Br.*
  var. of
  moralization

mor¦al¦ise *Br.* var.
  of moralize

mor¦al¦iser *Br.* var.
  of moralizer

mor¦al¦ism

mor¦al¦ist

mor¦al¦is¦tic

mor¦al¦is¦tic¦al¦ly

mor¦al¦ity
  mor¦al¦ities

mor¦al¦iza¦tion

mor¦al¦ize
  mor¦al¦iz¦ing

mor¦al¦izer

mor¦al¦ly

moran

Morar, Loch

mor¦ass

mora¦tor¦ium
  mora¦tor¦iums or
  mora¦toria

Mor¦avia

Mor¦avian

Moray former
  county, Scotland

moray eel

Moray¦shire

mor¦bid

mor¦bid¦ity

mor¦bid¦ly

mor¦bif¦ic

mor¦billi

mor¦billi¦virus

mor¦ceau
  mor¦ceaux

morcha

mor¦da¦cious

mor¦dancy

mor¦dant corrosive
  substance

mor¦dant¦ly

mor¦dent musical
  ornament

Mor¦dred
  Arthurian Legend

Mordva var. of
  Mordvin

Mord¦vin

Mord¦vinia

Mord¦vin¦ian

More language

More, St Thomas
  English statesman

more greater in
  number etc.; cf.
  maw, mor, moor

Mo¦reau, Jeanne
  actress

More¦cambe

mor¦een

more¦ish pleasant
  to eat; cf. **Moorish**

morel

Mor¦elia

mor¦ello +s

Mor¦elos

more¦over

more¦pork var. of
  mopoke

mores customs

Mor¦esco var. of
  Morisco

Mor¦esque

More¦ton Bay
  chest¦nut

Mor¦gan horse

Mor¦gan, J. P.
  financier

mor¦ga¦nat¦ic

mor¦ga¦nat¦ic¦al¦ly

mor¦gan¦ite

Mor¦gan le Fay
  Arthurian Legend

mor¦gen measure of land

morgue

mori¦bund

mori¦bun¦dity

mor¦ine var. of moreen

mor¦ion

Mor¦isco
Mor¦is¦cos or Mor¦is¦coes

Mori¦sot, Berthe painter

Mor¦land, George painter

Mor¦ley, Thomas composer

Mor¦mon

Mor¦mon¦ism

morn morning; cf. mourn

mor¦nay

morn¦ing time of day; cf. mourning

Mor¦ning¦side

Moro +s

Mo¦roc¦can

Mo¦rocco country

mo¦rocco +s leather

moro¦coy tortoise

moron

Mo¦roni

mor¦on¦ic

mo¦ron¦ic¦al¦ly

mor¦ose

mor¦ose¦ly

mor¦ose¦ness

Mor¦peth

morph¦al¦lac¦tic

morph¦al¦laxis

mor¦pheme

mor¦phem¦ic

mor¦phem¦ic¦al¦ly

mor¦phem¦ics

Mor¦pheus *Roman Mythology*

mor¦phia

mor¦phine

morph¦ing

mor¦phin¦ism

mor¦pho +s

mor¦pho¦gen

mor¦pho¦gen¦esis

mor¦pho¦genet¦ic

mor¦pho¦gen¦ic

mor¦pho¦line

mor¦pho¦logic

mor¦pho¦logic¦al

mor¦pho¦logic¦al¦ly

morph¦olo¦gist

morph¦ology
morph¦olo¦gies

mor¦pho¦met¦ric

mor¦pho¦met¦ric¦al¦ly

mor¦pho¦met¦rics

morph¦om¦etry

mor¦pho¦phon¦eme

mor¦pho¦
    phon¦emic

mor¦pho¦phono¦
    logic¦al

mor¦pho¦phono¦
    logic¦al¦ly

mor¦pho¦
    phon¦ology

mor¦pho¦syn¦tac¦tic

mor¦pho¦
    syn¦tac¦tic¦al¦ly

mor¦pho¦syn¦tax

Mor¦ris, Wil¦liam designer

Mor¦ris, Wil¦liam Rich¦ard Lord Nuffield, motor manufacturer

Mor¦ris chair

mor¦ris dance

mor¦ris dan¦cer

mor¦ris dan¦cing

Mor¦ri¦son, Jim rock singer

Mor¦ri¦son, Toni novelist

Mor¦ri¦son, Van musician

Mor¦ri¦son shel¦ter

mor¦row

Morse
Mors¦ing (use) code

morse clasp

Morse taper

mor¦ta¦della
mor¦ta¦del¦las or mor¦ta¦delle

mor¦tal

mor¦tal¦ity
mor¦tal¦ities

mor¦tal¦ly

mor¦tar

mor¦tar¦ium
mor¦taria

mor¦tar¦less

mort¦gage

mort¦ga¦ging

mort¦gage¦able

mort¦ga¦gee

mort¦ga¦ger var. of mortgagor

mort¦ga¦gor

mor¦tice var. of mortise

mor¦ticer var. of mortiser

mor¦ti¦cian

mor¦ti¦fi¦ca¦tion

mor¦tify

mor¦ti¦fies

mor¦ti¦fied

mor¦ti¦fy¦ing

mor¦ti¦fy¦ing¦ly

Mor¦ti¦mer, Roger de English noble

mor¦tise

mor¦tis¦ing

mor¦tiser

mort¦main

Mor¦ton, Jelly Roll musician

Mor¦ton, John archbishop of Canterbury

mor¦tu¦ary
mor¦tu¦ar¦ies

mor¦ula
mor¦ulae

Mor¦wenna

mor¦wong

Mo¦saic of Moses

mo¦saic
mo¦saicked
mo¦saick¦ing
(decorate with) picture made up of pieces

mo¦sai¦cism

mo¦sai¦cist

Mos¦an¦der, Carl chemist

mosa¦saur

mos¦bolle¦tjie

mos¦cato +s

mos¦cha¦tel plant; cf. muscatel

Mos¦cow

Mosel German name for the Moselle

Mose¦ley, Henry physicist

Mo¦selle

Moses *Bible*

Moses, Ed athlete

Moses, Grand¦ma painter

mosey

mo¦shav

mo¦shav¦im

mos¦kon¦fyt

Mos¦lem var. of Muslim

Mos¦ley, Os¦wald Fascist leader

Mos¦ley¦ite

Mo¦sotho

mosque

Mos¦quito +s var. of Miskito

mos¦quito
mos¦qui¦toes insect

Mos¦sad

moss¦back

moss¦backed

Möss¦bauer ef¦fect

Mos¦sel Bay

Mossi
pl. Mossi or Mos¦sis

mos¦sie bird; cf. mossy, mozzie

mos¦si¦ness

moss-like

mosso *Music*

moss¦troop¦er

mossy
moss¦ier
moss¦iest covered with moss; cf. mossie

Mos¦tar

most¦est

most¦ly

Mosul

mot girlfriend; cf.
  motte
mote speck of dust;
  cf. **moat**
motel
motet
moth|ball
mother
mother|board
Mother Carey's
  chicken
mother|craft
mother|fuck|er
  vulgar slang
mother|fuck|ing
  vulgar slang
mother|hood
Mother Hub|bard
Mother|ing
  Sun|day
mother-in-law
  mothers-in-law
mother|land
mother|less
mother-like
mother|li|ness
mother|ly
mother-of-pearl
Mother's Day
Mother Ship|ton
mother-to-be
  mothers-to-be
mother|wort
moth|proof
mothy
  moth|ier
  mothi|est
motif decoration;
  recurring idea; cf.
  motive
mo|tile
mo|til|ity
Mo|tion, An|drew
  poet
mo|tion
mo|tion|al
mo|tion|less
mo|tion|less|ly
mo|tiv|ate
  mo|tiv|at|ing
mo|tiv|ation
mo|tiv|ation|al
mo|tiv|ation|al|ly
mo|tiv|ator

mo|tive reason;
  causative; cf. **motif**
mo|tive|less
mo|tive|less|ly
mo|tive|less|ness
mo|tiv|ic
mo|tiv|ity
mot juste
  mots justes
mot|ley
  mot|lier
  mot|li|est
mot|mot
moto|cross
moto|cross|er
moto|neuron var.
  of **motor neuron**
moto per|petuo
  moto per|petui
motor
motor|able
motor|bike
motor|boat
motor|cade
motor|cycle
motor|cyc|ling
motor|cyc|list
motor|home
motor|ial
motor|isa|tion *Br.*
  var. of
  motorization
motor|ise *Br.* var. of
  motorize
motor|ist
motor|iza|tion
motor|ize
  motor|iz|ing
motor|man
  motor|men
motor|mouth
motor|mouthed
motor|sail|er
motor|sport
motor|way
mo|tory
Mo|town
mot|ser
motte castle mound;
  cf. **mot**
mot|tle
  mot|tling

motto
  mot|tos or
  mot|toes
Motu
  pl. **Motu**
motu prop|rio *+s*
motza var. of
  motser
moue pout; cf. **moo**
mouf|flon var. of
  mouflon
mouf|lon
mouillé
mou|jik var. of
  muzhik
Mou|lay Id|riss
mould *Br.*
  US **mold**
mould|able *Br.*
  US **moldable**
mould|board *Br.*
  US **moldboard**
mould|er *Br.*
  person who
  moulds; rot;
  US **molder**
mouldi|ness *Br.*
  US **moldiness**
mould|ing *Br.*
  US **molding**
mouldi|warp var. of
  mouldwarp
mould|warp
mouldy *Br.*
  mould|ier
  mould|iest
  US **moldy**
mouldy|warp var.
  of **mouldwarp**
moules (à la)
  ma|ri|nière
Mouli *trademark*
mou|lin
Mou|lin Rouge
Moul|mein
moult *Br.*
  US **molt**
moulvi
mount|able
moun|tain
moun|tain|board
moun|tain|
      board|er
moun|tain|eer
moun|tain|ous

moun|tain|ous|ly
moun|tainy
mount|ant
Mount|bat|ten,
  Louis Earl Mount-
  batten of Burma,
  admiral
moun|te|bank
moun|te|bank|ery
mount|er
Moun|tie
Mount Isa town,
  Australia
mourn feel sorrow;
  cf. **morn**
Mourne
  Moun|tains
mourn|er
mourn|ful
mourn|ful|ly
mourn|ful|ness
mourn|ing
  sorrowing; cf.
  morning
mou|saka var. of
  moussaka
Mou|salla var. of
  Musala
mouse
  pl. **mice**
  v. **mouses**
  moused
  mous|ing
  rodent; computer
  device; cf. **mousse**
mouse|bird
mouse-ear chick-
  weed
mouse-like
mouser
mouse|trap
  mouse|trapped
  mouse|trap|ping
mousey var. of
  mousy
mous|ily
mousi|ness
mous|saka
mousse
  mouss|ing
  dish; foam; cf.
  moose, mouse
mous|se|line
mous|seron
mous|seux

Mous|sorg|sky
var. of Mussorgsky

mous|tache *Br.*
US mustache

mous|tached *Br.*
US mustached

Mous|ter|ian

mousy
mous|ier
mousi|est

Mou|tan peony; cf.
mouton

mouth +s +ed +ing

mouth|brood|er

mouth|er

mouth|ful

mouth|less

mouth|part

mouth|piece

mouth|wash

mouthy
mouth|ier
mouthi|est

mou|ton sheepskin;
cf. Moutan

mov|abil|ity

mov|able

mov|ably

mov|ant

move
mov|ing

move|abil|ity var. of
movability

move|able var. of
movable

move|ably var. of
movably

move|less

move|ment

mover

movie

movie|goer

movie|going

movie|maker

mov|ing|ly

movi|ola *trademark*

mow
past participle
mowed or mown
cut grass etc.; cf.
mho, mo

mower grass-cutter;
cf. moa

mown past parti-
ciple of mow; cf.
moan

moxa

moxi|bus|tion

moxie

Moy|ga|shel
trademark

Mo|zam|bi|can

Mo|zam|bique

Moz|arab

Moz|arab|ic

Moz|art, Wolf|gang
Ama|deus
composer

Moz|art|ian

mo|zetta var. of
mozzetta

mozo +s

mozz in 'put the
mozz on'

moz|za|rella

moz|zetta

moz|zette

moz|zie mosquito;
cf. mossie

moz|zle

mpingo +s

Mpu|ma|langa

mr|danga var. of
mridangam

mri|dan|gam

msasa

mu Greek letter; cf.
mew

Mu|ba|rak, Hosni
president of Egypt

much cf. mutch

Mucha, Al|phonse
artist

mu|chacha female

mu|chacho +s male

Mu|chinga
Moun|tains

much|ly

much|ness

mucho

muci|lage

muci|lagi|nous

mucin

mu|cin|ous

mucka|muck

muck|er

mucki|ness

muckle var. of
mickle

muck|rake

muck|rak|ing

muck|raker

mucky
muck|ier
mucki|est

mucky-muck var. of
muckamuck

mu|coid

muco|poly|
sac|char|ide

mu|cosa
mu|cosae

mu|co|sal

mu|cos|ity

mu|cous *adj.*; cf.
mucus

mucro

mu|cro|nes or
mucros

mu|cron|ate

mu|cuna

mucus *n.*; cf.
mucous

mud|bank

mud|bath

mud|bug

mud|dily

mud|di|ness

mud|dle

mud|dling

mud|dler

mud|dling|ly

mud|dly

muddy
mud|dies
mud|died
muddy|ing
mud|dier
mud|di|est

Mu|de|jar
Mu|de|jares
Spanish Mudéjar

mud|fish

mud|flap

mud|flat

mud|flow

mud|guard

mud|lark

mud|lark|er

mud|minnow

mud-nester bird

mudra

mud|skip|per

mud|slide

mud|stone

Mud|ville

mud|wort

muesli

muez|zin

muf|fin

muf|fle

muf|fling

muf|fler

mufti

mug
mugged
mug|ging

Mu|gabe, Rob|ert
president of
Zimbabwe

Mu|ganda

mug|ful

mug|ger

mug|gi|ness

mug|gins
pl. mug|gins or
mug|ginses

mug|gle

Muggle|ton|ian

muggy
mug|gier
mug|gi|est

Mug|hal var. of
Mogul

Mugh|lai

mug|shot

mug|wort

mug|wump

Mu|ham|mad
founder of Islam;
cf. Mahamad

Mu|ham|mad
Ahmad Sudanese
Mahdi

Mu|ham|mad Ali
boxer; pasha of
Egypt

Mu|ham|mad|an
may cause offence

Mu|ham|mad|an|
ism
may cause offence

Mu|har|ram

Muir, Edwin poet

Muir, Jean fashion designer

muis|hond
pl. muis|hond or muis|honds or muis|honde

mu|ja|hed|din var. of mujahedin

mu|ja|he|din Islamic guerrilla fighters

mu|ja|hi|deen var. of mujahedin

mu|ja|hi|din var. of mujahedin

Mu|ji|bur Rah|man president of Bangladesh

muj|tahid
muj|tahids or *muj|tahi|dūn* Islamic legal authority

Mu|kalla

Muk|den

mukh|tar

muk|luk

mukti

muk|tuk

mu|latto
mu|lat|tos or mu|lat|toes

mul|berry
mul|berries

mulch

mulct

Mul|doon, Rob|ert prime minister of New Zealand

mule animal; slipper; cf. mewl

mules|ing

mu|leta

mule|teer

muley deer; hornless

mulga

mul|gara

Mul|ha|cén

Mül|heim

Mul|house

mulie *n.* var. of muley (deer)

muli|eb|rity

mul|ish

mul|ish|ly

mul|ish|ness

mul|lah Muslim scholar; cf. muller

mul|lein

Mul|ler, Her|mann geneticist

Mül|ler, Max philologist

mul|ler grinding stone; cf. mullah

Mül|ler|ian

Müller-Thurgau

mul|let

mul|li|gan

mul|li|ga|tawny

Mul|lin|gar

mul|lion

mul|lioned

mul|lock

mul|lo|way

Mul|ready +s

Mul|ro|ney, Brian prime minister of Canada

Mul|tan

multi-access

multi-agency

multi|axial

multi|buy

multi|cast

multi|cel|lu|lar

multi|cel|lu|lar|ity

multi|chan|nel

multi|color *US*

multi|col|ored *US*

multi|col|our *Br.*

multi|col|oured *Br.*

multi|culti

multi|cul|tur|al

multi|cul|tur|al|ism

multi|cul|tur|al|ist

multi|cul|tur|al|ly

multi|di|men|sion|al

multi|di|men|sion|al|ity

multi|di|men|sion|al|ly

multi|dir|ec|tion|al

multi|dis|cip|lin|ary

multi-ethnic

multi|fa|cet|ed

multi|fac|tor|ial

multi-faith

multi|fari|ous

multi|fari|ous|ly

multi|fari|ous|ness

multi|fid

multi|fila|ment

multi|flora

multi|focal

multi|foil

multi|fold

multi|form

multi|form|ity

multi|func|tion

multi|func|tion|al

multi|gen|er|ation|al

multi|grade *trademark in the US for photographic paper*

multi|grain

multi|grav|ida
multi|grav|idae

multi|gym

multi|hull

multi|lat|eral

multi|lat|eral|ism

multi|lat|eral|ist

multi|lat|eral|ly

multi|layer

multi|layered

multi|level

multi|lin|gual

multi|lin|gual|ism

multi|lin|gual|ly

multi|media

multi|meter

multi|mil|lion

multi|mil|lion|aire

multi|modal

multi|mode

multi|nation|al

multi|nation|al|ly

multi|nomial

multi-occupancy

multi-occupan|cies

multi-occupa|tion

multi-occupy

multi-occupies

multi-occupied

multi-occupy|ing

multi|pack

mul|tip|ara

mul|tip|arae

mul|tip|ar|ous

multi|par|tite

multi|party

multi|phase

multi|play

multi|play|er

mul|tiple

multi|plet

multi|plex

multi|plex|er

multi|plex|or var. of multiplexer

multi|pli|able

multi|plic|able

multi|pli|cand

multi|pli|ca|tion

multi|plica|tive

multi|pli|city

multi|pli|ci|ties

multi|plier

multi|ply

multi|plies

multi|plied

multi|ply|ing

multi|polar

multi|po|lar|ity

multi|pole

multi|pro|cess|ing

multi|pro|ces|sor

multi|pro|gram|ming

multi-purpose

multi|racial

multi|racial|ism

multi|racial|ist

multi|racial|ly

multi-role

multi|ses|sion

multi|spec|tral

multi-stage

multi-storey

multi|task

multi|task|er

multi|thread|ed

multi|thread|ing

multi|track

multi|tuber|cu|late

multi|tude

multi|tu|di|nous

multi-user
multi-utility
  multi-utilities
multi|va|lence
multi|va|lency
  multi|va|len|cies
multi|va|lent
multi|valve
multi|vari|ate
multi|vend|or
multi|verse
multi|vi|bra|tor
multi|vita|min
multi|way
mul|tum in parvo
mul|ture
mum *Br.* mother;
  US mom
mum silent; act in
  mummers' play
  mummed
  mum|ming
Mum|bai
mum|ble
  mum|bling
mum|bler
mumblety-peg
mum|bling|ly
mumbo-jumbo
mum|chance
mu-meson
mum|mer
Mum|mer|set
mum|mery
  mum|mer|ies
mummi|chog
mum|mify
  mum|mi|fies
  mum|mi|fied
  mum|mi|fy|ing
mummy *Br.* mother
  mum|mies
  US mommy
mummy
  mum|mies
  preserved body
mump|ish
mump|si|mus
mumsy
Munch, Ed|vard
  painter

Munch|ausen,
  Baron fictional
  hero
munch|er
munch|ies
munch|kin
Munda
  pl. Munda or
  Mundas
mun|dane
mun|dane|ly
mun|dan|ity
  mun|dan|ities
mung bean
Mungo name
mungo +s cloth
muni municipal
  bond; *Ind.* holy
  person; cf. Moonie
munia
Mun|ich
mu|ni|ci|pal
mu|ni|ci|pal|
      isa|tion
  Br. var. of
  municipalization
mu|ni|ci|pal|ise *Br.*
  var. of
  municipalize
mu|ni|ci|pal|ity
  mu|ni|ci|pal|ities
mu|ni|ci|pal|
      iza|tion
mu|ni|ci|pal|ize
  mu|ni|ci|pal|iz|ing
mu|ni|ci|pal|ly
mu|nifi|cence
mu|nifi|cent
mu|nifi|cent|ly
mu|ni|ment
mu|ni|tion
Munro +s Scottish
  mountain
Munro, Hec|tor
  Hugh real name of
  Saki
Mun|sell
mun|shi
Munsi
mun|sif
Mun|ster province,
  Republic of Ireland
Mün|ster city,
  Germany

mun|tin
mun|tined
munt|jac
Muntz metal
mun|yeroo +s
mun|yeru var. of
  munyeroo
muon
muon|ic
mup|pet
Muq|disho
mur|age
mural
mural|ist
Mu|rano glass
Murat, Joa|chim
  king of Naples
Mur|chi|son Falls;
  Rapids
Mur|cia city and
  region, Spain; cf.
  Mercia
mur|der
mur|der|er
mur|der|ess
mur|der|ous
mur|der|ous|ly
mur|der|ous|ness
Mur|doch, Iris
  writer
Mur|doch, Ru|pert
  media entrepreneur
mure
  mur|ing
murex
  muri|ces or
  mur|exes
murgh
muri|ate
muri|cate
murid
Mur|iel
Mu|rillo,
  Bar|to|lomé
  Este|ban painter
mur|ine
mu|ri|qui
murk
murk|ily
murki|ness
murky
  murk|ier
  murki|est
Mur|mansk

mur|mur
mur|mur|ation
mur|mur|er
mur|mur|ing|ly
mur|mur|ous
Mur|nau, F. W.
  film director
Mur|phy, Eddie
  actor
mur|phy
  mur|phies
  potato
Mur|phy's Law
mur|rain
mur|ram
Mur|ray name
Mur|ray, Gil|bert
  scholar
Mur|ray, James
  lexicographer
murre bird; cf.
  myrrh
mur|re|let
mur|rey
Mur|rum|bidgee
Muru|roa
Mu|sala, Mt
mu|sambi
Musca
mus|ca|del var. of
  muscatel
Mus|ca|delle wine
  grape
Mus|ca|det wine
mus|ca|dine wine
  grape
mus|cae
  voli|tan|tes
mus|car|ine poison-
  ous compound
mus|car|in|ic
Mus|cat capital of
  Oman
mus|cat grape; wine
mus|ca|tel grape;
  wine; raisin; cf.
  moschatel
Muschel|kalk
Musci
mus|cid
mus|ci|mol
muscle
  musc|ling
  Anatomy; cf.

mussel
muscle|less
muscle|man
muscle|men
muscly
musc|lier
muscli|est
mus|co|vado +s sugar
Mus|co|vite citizen of Moscow
mus|co|vite mineral
Mus|covy former principality, Russia; duck
mus|cu|lar
mus|cu|lar|ity
mus|cu|lar|ly
mus|cu|la|ture
mus|cu|lo|skel|etal
Muse Greek and Roman Mythology
muse
mus|ing ponder; inspiration; cf. mews
museo|graph|ic
museo|graph|ic|al
muse|og|raphy
museo|logic|al
muse|olo|gist
muse|ol|ogy
mu|sette
mu|seum
Mu|sev|eni, Yow|eri president of Uganda
mu|shaira
Mu|shar|raf, Per|vez president of Pakistan
mush|er
mush|ily
mushi|ness
mush|rat
mush|room
mush|roomy
mushy
mush|ier
mushi|est
music
mu|sica ficta
mu|sic|al of music; play with music

musi|cale musical gathering
mu|sic|al|ise Br. var. of musicalize
mu|sic|al|ity
mu|sic|al|ize
mu|sic|al|iz|ing
mu|sic|al|ly
mu|si|cian
mu|si|cian|ly
mu|si|cian|ship
music lover
mu|sico|logic|al
mu|sic|olo|gist
mu|sic|ology
Musil, Rob|ert novelist
mus|ing|ly
mu|sique con|crète
mus|keg
mus|kel|lunge
mus|ket
mus|ket|eer
mus|ket|ry
muski|ness
Mus|ko|gean
Mus|kogee pl. Mus|kogee or Muskogees
musk|rat
musk|wood
musky
musk|ier
muski|est
Mus|lim
Mus|limah
mus|lin
mus|lined
muso +s
mus|quash
mus|sel mollusc; cf. muscle
mussel|crack|er
Mus|so|lini, Ben|ito leader of Italy
Mus|sorg|sky, Mo|dest composer
mussy
must frenzy
mus|tache US Br. moustache
mus|tached US Br. moustached

mus|tachi|oed
mus|tang
mus|tard
mus|tardy
mus|te|lid
mus|ter
mus|ter|er
musth var. of must
must-have adj. & n.
must|ily
musti|ness
Mus|tique
mustn't
musty
must|ier
musti|est
Mut Egyptian goddess; cf. mutt
mut|abil|ity
mut|able
muta|gen
mu|ta|gen|esis
mu|ta|gen|ic
mu|ta|gen|ise Br. var. of mutagenize
mu|ta|gen|ize
mu|ta|gen|iz|ing
mu|tant
Mu|tare
mu|tate
mu|tat|ing
mu|ta|tion
mu|ta|tion|al
mu|ta|tion|al|ly
mu|ta|tis mu|tan|dis
mu|ta|tive
mu|ta|tor
mutch cap
mutch|kin
mute
mut|ing silent; muffle; cf. moot
mute|ly
mute|ness
muti
mu|ti|late
mu|ti|lat|ing
mu|ti|la|tion
mu|ti|la|tor
mu|tin|eer

mu|tin|ous
mu|tin|ous|ly
mu|tiny
mu|tin|ies
mu|tin|ied
mu|tiny|ing
mut|ism
muton
Mut|su|hito original name of Meiji Tenno
mutt dog
mut|ter
mut|terer
mut|ter|ing|ly
mut|ton
mutton|head
mutton|head|ed
mut|tony
mu|tual reciprocal; (company) owned by its members; cf. mutuel
mu|tual|ise Br. var. of mutualize
mu|tual|ism
mu|tual|ist
mu|tual|is|tic
mu|tu|al|ity
mu|tual|ize
mu|tual|iz|ing
mu|tu|al|ly
mu|tuel totalizator; cf. mutual
mu|tule
muu|muu
mux = multiplex
Muzaf|fara|bad
muzak background music trademark
mu|zhik Russian peasant
Muz|tag
muz|zily
muz|zi|ness
muz|zle
muz|zling
muzzle-loader
muzzy
muz|zier
muz|zi|est
my|al|gia
my|al|gic
my|al|ism

myall tree; cf. mile
Myan|mar
Myan|mar|ese
my|as|the|nia
my|as|the|nia
  gravis
my|ce|lial
my|ce|lium
  my|ce|lia
My|ce|nae
My|ce|nae|an
My|ce|ne|an var. of
  Mycenaean
my|ce|toma
myco|bac|ter|ial
myco|bac|ter|ium
  myco|bac|teria
myco|logic|al
myco|logic|al|ly
my|colo|gist
my|col|ogy
myco|plasma
  myco|plas|mas or
  myco|plas|mata
myco|pro|tein
mycor|rhiza
  mycor|rhizae
mycor|rhizal
my|co|sis
  my|co|ses
my|cot|ic
myco|toxin
myco|troph|ic
my|cot|ro|phy
my|dria|sis
mye|lin
mye|lin|ated
mye|lin|ation
mye|li|tis
mye|loid
mye|loma
  mye|lo|mas or
  mye|lo|mata
myel|op|athy
my|enter|ic
My|fanwy
myg|alo|morph
Myko|layiv
Myk|onos
Mylar trademark
my|lo|don
my|lon|ite
My|men|singh

myna var. of mynah
mynah bird; cf.
  miner, minor
myo|car|dial
myo|car|di|tis
myo|clon|ic
myo|clo|nus
myo|fib|ril
myo|gen|ic
myo|glo|bin
myo|logic|al
my|olo|gist
my|ol|ogy
myo|mere
myo|me|trium
myo|morph
Myo|morpha
myo|path|ic
my|op|athy
  my|op|athies
myope
my|opia
my|opic
my|opic|al|ly
my|osin
my|osis var. of
  miosis
myo|sitis
myo|sotis
  myo|sotises
my|otis
  my|otises
myo|tome
myo|tonia
myo|ton|ic
myr|iad
myr|ia|pod
myr|in|got|omy
myr|is|tate
myr|ist|ic
myr|me|co|logic|al
myr|me|colo|gist
myr|me|col|ogy
myr|meco|phile
myr|mec|oph|il|ous
myr|mec|oph|ily
myr|mi|don
myr|oba|lan
myrrh resin,
  incense; cf. murre
myr|rhy
myr|ta|ceous
Myr|tle name

myr|tle shrub
my|self
Mysia
Mys|ian
mysid
My|sore
mys|ta|gogue
mys|ta|gogy
  mys|ta|gogies
mys|teri|ous
mys|teri|ous|ly
mys|teri|ous|ness
mys|tery
  mys|ter|ies
mys|tic
mys|tic|al
mys|tic|al|ly
mys|ti|cete
Mys|ti|ceti
mys|ti|cism
mys|ti|fi|ca|tion
mys|ti|fier
mys|tify
  mys|ti|fies
  mys|ti|fied
  mys|ti|fy|ing
  mys|ti|fy|ing|ly
mys|tique
myth
mythi pl. of mythus
myth|ic
myth|ic|al
myth|ic|al|ly
mythi|cise Br. var.
  of mythicize
mythi|cism
mythi|cist
mythi|cize
  mythi|ciz|ing
mythi|fi|ca|tion
myth|ify
  mythi|fies
  mythi|fied
  mythi|fy|ing
myth|og|raph|er
myth|og|raphy
mythoi pl. of
  mythos
myth|olo|ger
mytho|logic|al
mytho|logic|al|ly
myth|olo|gise Br.
  var. of mythologize

myth|olo|giser Br.
  var. of
  mythologizer
myth|olo|gist
myth|olo|gize
  myth|olo|giz|ing
myth|olo|gizer
myth|ology
  myth|olo|gies
mytho|mania
mytho|maniac
mytho|poeia
mytho|poeic
mytho|poet|ic
my|thos
  my|thoi
  myth; narrative
  theme
my|thus
  mythi
  myth; mythos
Myti|lene
myx|edema US
myx|oe|dema Br.
myx|oma
  myx|omas or
  myx|omata
myx|oma|tosis
myx|oma|tous
myxo|my|cete
myxo|virus
mzungu

N

NAAFI = Navy,
  Army, and Air
  Force Institutes
naam name
naan bread; var. of
  nan
naar|tjie
Naas
nab
  nabbed
  nab|bing
Naba|taean
Naba|tean var. of
  Nabataean

nabe = neighbour-
hood; neighbour
Na¦beul
Nabi
Nab¦lus
nabob
Nab¦okov,
Vlad¦imir writer
Na¦cala
na¦celle
nachas var. of
naches
naches
nacho +s
NACODS =
National Associ-
ation of Colliery
Overmen, Deputies,
and Shotfirers
nacre mother-
of-pearl; cf. naker
nac¦re¦ous
nada
Na-Dene
Nader, Ralph safety
campaigner
Nader¦ism
Na¦dine
nadir
nae¦vus Br.
naevi
US nevus
naff¦ness
Naffy var. of NAAFI
NAFTA = North
American Free
Trade Agreement;
cf. naphtha
nag
nagged
nag¦ging
pester; horse; cf.
knag
Naga people;
language
naga Hinduism
Naga¦land
na¦gana
nagar Ind. town
Naga¦saki
nag¦ger
nag¦ging¦ly
naggy
nag¦gi¦er

nag¦gi¦est
Nagorno-
Karabakh
Na¦goya
Nag¦pur
nag¦ware
Nagy, Imre prime
minister of
Hungary
nah nonstandard
spelling of no
Naha
Na¦huatl
pl. Na¦huatl or
Na¦huatls
Na¦huat¦lan
Nahum Bible
naiad
naiads
also nai¦ades
nai¦ant
naif naive person;
cf. naïve
French naïf
nail¦er
nail¦ery
nail¦er¦ies
nail¦head
nail¦less
nail¦tail wal¦laby
nain¦sook
Nai¦paul, V. S.
writer
naira
Nairn¦shire
Nai¦robi
nais¦sant
naive adj.; cf. naif
naiver
naivest
French naïve
naive¦ly
naive¦ness
naiv¦ety
naiv¦eties
French naïveté
Najaf
naked
naked¦ly
naked¦ness
naker drum; cf.
nacre
Na¦khon Sawan
Na¦kuru

nala var. of nullah
Nal¦chik
nali¦dix¦ic
na¦lox¦one
nal¦trex¦one
Nam short for
Vietnam
Nama
pl. Nama or
Namas
namak
Nam¦an¦gan
Na¦ma¦qua¦land
nam¦as¦kar
nam¦aste
namaz
namby-pamby
namby-pambies
name
nam¦ing
name¦able
name¦check
name child
name-children
name¦less
name¦less¦ly
name¦less¦ness
name¦ly
name¦plate
name¦sake
name¦space
Namib Des¦ert
Na¦mibia
Na¦mib¦ian
nam¦kin
namma var. of
gnamma
Namur
Nan name
nan grandmother;
Indian bread
nana grandmother
Na¦naimo
Nanak, Guru
founder of Sikhism
Nan¦chang
Nancy city, France;
name
nancy
nan¦cies
offensive effeminate
or homosexual man
nancy story W. Ind.
folk tale

Nanda Devi
Nandi Hinduism
nan¦dina
nan¦dro¦lone
Nan¦ette
Nanga Par¦bat
Nan¦jing
nan¦keen
Nan¦king var. of
Nanjing
nanna var. of nana
Nan¦ning
nanno¦fos¦sil
nanno¦plank¦ton
var. of
nanoplankton
nanny
nan¦nies
nan¦nied
nanny¦ing
nanny¦gai
nano +s
nano¦bac¦ter¦ium
nano¦bac¦teria
nano¦bot
nano¦fos¦sil var. of
nannofossil
nano¦gram
nano¦gramme Br.
var. of nanogram
nano¦meter US
nano¦metre Br.
nano¦plank¦ton
nano¦scale
nano¦sec¦ond
nano¦tech¦no¦
logic¦al
nano¦tech¦nolo¦gist
nano¦tech¦nol¦ogy
nano¦tube
Nan¦sen, Fridt¦jof
explorer
Nantes
Nan¦tucket
naos
naoi
nap
napped
nap¦ping
short sleep; pile on
textiles; card game;
tip as winner; cf.
knap, nappe
napa cab¦bage

na¦palm
nap¦ery
Naph¦tali *Bible*
naph¦tha oil; cf.
  NAFTA
naph¦tha¦lene
naph¦thal¦ic
naph¦thene
naph¦then¦ic
naph¦thol
Na¦pier port, New
  Zealand
Na¦pier, John
  mathematician
Na¦pier¦ian
nap¦kin
Na¦ples
nap¦less
Na¦po¦leon three
  rulers of France;
  French Napoléon
na¦po¦leon coin;
  game
na¦po¦leon boot
Na¦po¦leon¦ic
nappa leather; cf.
  knapper, napper
nappe *Geology*; cf.
  knap, nap
nap¦per head; cf.
  knapper, nappa
nappy
  nap¦pies
  nap¦pier
  nap¦pi¦est
  absorbent pad;
  frizzy
na¦proxen
Nara
Na¦ra¦yan, R. K.
  writer
Na¦ra¦ya¦nan, K. R.
  president of India
Na¦ra¦yan¦ganj
Nar¦bonne
narc narcotics
  agent; cf. nark
nar¦cis¦sism
nar¦cis¦sist
nar¦cis¦sis¦tic
nar¦cis¦sis¦tic¦al¦ly
Nar¦cis¦sus youth
nar¦cis¦sus
  pl. nar¦cis¦sus or

nar¦cissi or
nar¦cis¦suses
  flower
nar¦cis¦sus fly
narco +s
nar¦co¦lepsy
nar¦co¦lep¦tic
nar¦co¦sis
narco¦ter¦ror¦ism
narco¦ter¦ror¦ist
nar¦cot¦ic
nar¦cot¦ic¦al¦ly
nar¦co¦tisa¦tion *Br.*
  var. of
  narcotization
nar¦co¦tise *Br.* var.
  of narcotize
nar¦co¦tism
nar¦co¦tiza¦tion
nar¦co¦tize
  nar¦co¦tiz¦ing
nar¦doo +s
nares
  sing. naris
nar¦ghile
nar¦iyal
nark informer;
  annoying person;
  annoy; cf. narc
narky
  nark¦ier
  nark¦iest
Nar¦mada
Nar¦nia
Narra¦gan¦set var.
  of Narragansett
Narra¦gan¦sett
  pl. Narra¦gan¦sett
  or Narra¦gan¦setts
nar¦rat¦able
nar¦rate
  nar¦rat¦ing
nar¦ra¦tion
nar¦ra¦tive
nar¦ra¦tive¦ly
nar¦ra¦tiv¦ise *Br.*
  var. of narrativize
nar¦ra¦tiv¦ity
nar¦ra¦tiv¦ize
  nar¦ra¦tiv¦iz¦ing
nar¦rato¦logic¦al
nar¦ra¦tolo¦gist
nar¦ra¦tol¦ogy
nar¦ra¦tor

nar¦ra¦tor¦ial
nar¦row
nar¦row¦band
nar¦row¦boat
nar¦row¦cast
  past and past
  participle
  nar¦row¦cast or
  nar¦row¦cast¦ed
nar¦row¦cast¦er
nar¦row¦ish
nar¦row¦ly
nar¦row¦ness
nar¦thex
Nar¦vik
nar¦whal
nary
NASA = National
  Aeronautics and
  Space
  Administration
nasal
na¦sal¦isa¦tion *Br.*
  var. of nasalization
na¦sal¦ise *Br.* var. of
  nasalize
na¦sal¦ity
na¦sal¦iza¦tion
na¦sal¦ize
  na¦sal¦iz¦ing
nas¦al¦ly
nas¦cency
nas¦cent
nase¦berry
nase¦berries
Naseby
Nash, Beau dandy
Nash, John
  architect
Nash, Ogden writer
Nash, Paul artist
Nashe, Thomas
  writer
Nash equi¦lib¦rium
nashi
Nash¦ville
Nasik
Na¦smyth, James
  engineer
naso¦gas¦tric
naso¦pha¦ryn¦geal
naso¦phar¦ynx
naso¦pha¦ryn¦ges
Nas¦sau

Nas¦ser, Gamal
  Abdel president of
  Egypt
nas¦tic
nas¦tily
nas¦ti¦ness
na¦stur¦tium
nasty
  nasties
  nas¦tier
  nasti¦est
natak
Natal former prov-
  ince, South Africa;
  port, Brazil
natal of one's birth
Nat¦alie
na¦tal¦ity
na¦tant
Na¦ta¦sha
na¦ta¦tion
nata¦tor¦ial
na¦ta¦tor¦ium
na¦ta¦tory
nates
NATFHE =
  National Associ-
  ation of Teachers in
  Further and Higher
  Education
Nath¦alie
Na¦than
Na¦than¦iel
nathe¦less
nath¦less var. of
  natheless
na¦tion
na¦tion¦al
na¦tion¦al¦isa¦tion
  Br. var. of
  nationalization
na¦tion¦al¦ise *Br.*
  var. of nationalize
na¦tion¦al¦iser *Br.*
  var. of nationalizer
na¦tion¦al¦ism
na¦tion¦al¦ist
na¦tion¦al¦is¦tic
na¦tion¦al¦is¦tic¦
  al¦ly
na¦tion¦al¦ity
na¦tion¦al¦ities
na¦tion¦al¦iza¦tion

na|tion|al|ize
  na|tion|al|iz|ing
na|tion|al|izer
na|tion|al|ly
na|tion|hood
na|tion|wide
na|tive
na|tive|ly
na|tive|ness
na|tiv|ism
na|tiv|ist
na|tiv|is|tic
na|tiv|ity
  na|tiv|ities
NATO = North
  Atlantic Treaty
  Organization
natri|uresis
natri|uret|ic
Nat|ron, Lake
nat|ron salt
nat|ter
nat|ter|er
nat|ter|jack
Nat|tier blue
nat|tily
nat|ti|ness
natty
  nat|tier
  nat|ti|est
Na|tu|fian
nat|ural
nat|ur|al|isa|tion
  Br. var. of
  naturalization
nat|ur|al|ise *Br.* var.
  of naturalize
nat|ur|al|ism
nat|ur|al|ist
nat|ur|al|is|tic
nat|ur|al|is|tic|al|ly
nat|ur|al|iza|tion
nat|ur|al|ize
  nat|ur|al|iz|ing
nat|ur|al|ly
nat|ur|al|ness
na|ture
na|tured
na|tur|ism
na|tur|ist
na|turo|path
na|turo|path|ic
na|tur|op|athy

Nauga|hyde
  trademark in the
  US
naught nothing; cf.
  nought
naught *US* var. of
  nought
naugh|tily
naugh|ti|ness
naughty
  naugh|tier
  naugh|ti|est
nau|plius
  nau|plii
Nauru
Nau|ru|an
nau|sea
nau|se|ate
  nau|se|at|ing
  nau|se|at|ing|ly
nau|se|ous
nau|se|ous|ly
nau|se|ous|ness
nautch
naut|ical
naut|ical|ly
naut|il|oid
Naut|ilus submar-
  ine
naut|ilus mollusc
  naut|iluses or
  naut|ili
Nav|aho var. of
  Navajo
nav|aid
Nav|ajo
  pl. Nav|ajo or
  Nav|ajos
naval of navies; cf.
  navel
na|val|ly
Navan
Nava|nagar
Nava|ratra var. of
  Navaratri
Nava|ratri
nav|arin casserole
Nava|rino battle
Na|varre in Spain
nave part of church
  or wheel; cf. **knave**
navel *Anatomy*; cf.
  naval
na|vel|wort

na|vicu|lar
nav|ig|abil|ity
nav|ig|able
navi|gate
navi|gat|ing
navi|ga|tion
navi|ga|tion|al
navi|ga|tion|al|ly
navi|ga|tor
Nav|ra|ti|lova,
  Mar|tina tennis
  player
navvy
  nav|vies
navy
  na|vies
nawab
Naxa|lite
Nax|çi|van
Naxos
nay no; cf. **né, née,
  neigh**
nay|aka
Naya|rit
nay|say
  nay|said
nay|say|er
Naz|ar|ene person
  from Nazareth
Naz|ar|eth
Naz|ar|ite var. of
  Nazirite
Nazca Lines
Nazi
Nazi|dom
Nazi|fi|ca|tion
Nazify
  Nazi|fies
  Nazi|fied
  Nazi|fy|ing
Nazi|ism var. of
  Nazism
Naz|ir|ite Israelite
  abstainer
Naz|ism
Nde|bele
  pl. Nde|bele or
  Nde|beles
N'Dja|mena
Ndola
né before man's pre-
  vious name; cf. **nay,
  née, neigh**
Neagh, Lough

Ne|an|der|thal
neap tide; cf. **neep**
Nea|pol|itan
near|by
Ne|arc|tic
Near East|ern
near|ish
near|ly
near|ness
near|shore
near|side
near|sighted
near|sighted|ly
near|sighted|ness
neat tidy
neat
  pl. neat or neats
  bovine
neat|en
Neath town, Wales
neath beneath
neat|ly
neat|ness
neat's-foot oil
Neb|bi|olo +s
neb|bish
neb|bishy
Neb|lina, Pico da
Neb|raska
Neb|ras|kan
Nebu|chad|nez|zar
  king of Babylon
nebu|chad|nez|zar
  wine bottle
neb|ula
  nebu|lae or
  nebu|las
  space cloud; cf.
  nebuly
nebu|lar *adj.*
nebu|lise *Br.* var. of
  nebulize
nebu|liser *Br.* var.
  of nebulizer
nebu|lize
  nebu|liz|ing
nebu|lizer
nebu|los|ity
nebu|lous
nebu|lous|ly
nebu|lous|ness
neb|uly *Heraldry*;
  cf. **nebulae**

né¦ces¦saire
ne¦ces¦sar¦ian
ne¦ces¦sar¦ian¦ism
ne¦ces¦sar¦ily
ne¦ces¦sary
  ne¦ces¦sar¦ies
ne¦ces¦si¦tar¦ian
ne¦ces¦si¦tar¦ian¦
  ism
ne¦ces¦si¦tate
ne¦ces¦si¦tat¦ing
ne¦ces¦si¦tous
ne¦ces¦sity
  ne¦ces¦sities
Nech¦tans¦mere
neck part of body,
  clothing, violin,
  etc.; impudence;
  kiss; cf. nek
Neckar river,
  Germany
neck¦band
neck¦cloth
Neck¦er, Jacques
  banker
neck¦er kisser
neck¦er¦chief
Neck¦er cube
neck¦lace
  neck¦lacing
neck¦less
neck¦let
neck¦line
neck¦tie
neck¦wear
necro¦bi¦osis
necro¦bi¦ot¦ic
ne¦crol¦atry
necro¦logic¦al
ne¦crolo¦gist
ne¦crol¦ogy
  ne¦crolo¦gies
necro¦man¦cer
necro¦mancy
necro¦man¦tic
necro¦phile
necro¦philia
necro¦phil¦iac
necro¦phil¦ic
ne¦croph¦il¦ism
ne¦croph¦il¦ist
necro¦pho¦bia
ne¦crop¦olis

nec¦ropsy
  nec¦rop¦sies
ne¦cro¦sis
nec¦rot¦ic
nec¦ro¦tise Br. var.
  of necrotize
nec¦ro¦tize
  nec¦ro¦tiz¦ing
nec¦tar
nec¦tar¦ean
nec¦tar¦eous
nec¦tar¦if¦er¦ous
nec¦tar¦ine
nec¦tar¦ivor¦ous
nec¦tar¦ous
nec¦tary
  nec¦tar¦ies
neddy
  ned¦dies
née before woman's
  maiden name; cf.
  nay, né, neigh
need require; cf.
  knead
need¦ful
need¦ful¦ly
need¦ful¦ness
Need¦ham, Jo¦seph
  scientist
needi¦ness
nee¦dle
  need¦ling
needle¦cord
needle¦craft
needle¦fish
needle¦ful
needle¦lace
needle¦point
need¦less
need¦less¦ly
need¦less¦ness
needle¦tail
needle¦woman
  needle¦women
needle¦work
needle¦work¦er
needn't
needy
  need¦ier
  needi¦est
neep turnip; cf.
  neap
ne'er
ne'er-do-well

ne¦fari¦ous
ne¦fari¦ous¦ly
ne¦fari¦ous¦ness
Nef¦er¦titi Egyptian
  queen
neg¦ate
  neg¦at¦ing
neg¦ation
nega¦tive
  nega¦tiv¦ing
nega¦tive¦ly
nega¦tive¦ness
nega¦tiv¦ism
nega¦tiv¦ist
nega¦tiv¦is¦tic
nega¦tiv¦ity
  nega¦tiv¦ities
neg¦ator
neg¦atory
neg¦entrop¦ic
neg¦entropy
  neg¦entro¦pies
Negev
neg¦lect
neg¦lect¦ful
neg¦lect¦ful¦ly
neg¦lect¦ful¦ness
neg¦li¦gee
  French négligé
neg¦li¦gence
neg¦li¦gent
neg¦li¦gent¦ly
neg¦ligi¦bil¦ity
neg¦li¦gible
neg¦li¦gibly
Ne¦gombo
ne¦go¦ti¦abil¦ity
ne¦go¦ti¦able
ne¦go¦ti¦ant
ne¦go¦ti¦ate
  ne¦go¦ti¦at¦ing
ne¦go¦ti¦ation
ne¦go¦ti¦ator
Ne¦gress offensive
Neg¦rillo +s African
Negri Sem¦bi¦lan
Neg¦rito +s Austro-
  nesian
Neg¦ri¦tude
Negro
  Ne¦groes offensive
Negro, Rio river
Ne¦groid

Negro¦ism
ne¦groni
Negro¦phobe
Negro¦pho¦bia
Negro¦pho¦bic
Neg¦ros island,
  Philippines
Negus title of ruler
  of Ethiopia
negus drink
Ne¦he¦miah Bible
Nehru,
  Ja¦wa¦har¦lal prime
  minister of India
neigh of a horse; cf.
  nay, né, née
neigh¦bor US
neigh¦bor¦hood US
neigh¦bor¦less US
neigh¦bor¦li¦ness
  US
neigh¦bor¦ly US
neigh¦bor¦ship US
  Br. neighbourship
neigh¦bour Br.
neigh¦bour¦hood
  Br.
neigh¦bour¦less Br.
neigh¦bour¦li¦ness
  Br.
neigh¦bour¦ly Br.
neigh¦bour¦ship Br.
Neil name
Neill, A. S. educa-
  tionist
Neill, Sam actor
Nei¦sse rivers
nei¦ther
Nejd
nek mountain col;
  cf. neck
nek¦ton
nek¦ton¦ic
Nel¦lore
nelly
  nel¦lies
Nel¦son port, New
  Zealand
Nel¦son, Ho¦ra¦tio
  admiral
Nel¦son, Wil¦lie
  singer
nel¦son wrestling
  hold

Nel|spruit
Neman
nem|at|ic
nem|ati|cidal var.
of nematocidal
nem|ati|cide var. of
nematocide
nem|ato|cidal
nem|ato|cide
nem|ato|cyst
Nema|toda
nema|tode
nem|at|olo|gist
nem|at|ology
nem|ato|morph
Nem|ato|morpha
Nem|bu|tal
trademark
nem. con.
Nem|er|tea
nem|er|tean
nem|er|tine
nem|esia
Nem|esis Greek
goddess; retributive
justice personified
nem|esis
nem|eses
agent of downfall
nemo dat
nemo dat quod
non habet
nene goose
ne-ne var. of nene
Nenets
pl. Nenets or
Nentsy or Nentsi
Nen|nius writer
neo|clas|sic
neo|clas|sic|al
neo|clas|si|cism
neo|clas|si|cist
neo|co|lo|nial
neo|co|lo|nial|ism
neo|co|lo|nial|ist
neo|con
neo-Confucian
neo-Confucian|ism
neo|con|ser|va|
　　　　　　tism
neo|con|ser|va|tive
neo|cor|tex
　neo|cor|ti|ces

neo|cor|tical
neo-Darwin|ian
neo-Darwin|ism
neo-Darwin|ist
neo|dym|ium
neo-fascism
neo-fascist
Neo|gaea *Br.*
Neo|gaean *Br.*
Neo|gea *US*
Neo|gean *US*
Neo|gene
neo-Georgian
neo-Gothic
Neo|gram|mar|ian
neo-
　　Impres|sion|ism
neo-
　　Impres|sion|ist
neo-Latin
neo|liberal
neo|liberal|ism
Neo|lith|ic
neolo|gise *Br.* var.
of neologize
neolo|gism
neolo|gist
neolo|gize
　neolo|giz|ing
neo-Malthu|sian
neo-
　Malthu|sian|ism
neo-Marxism
neo-Marxist
Neo-Melanesian
neo|my|cin
neon
neo|natal
neo|natal|ly
neo|nate
neo|nat|olo|gist
neo|nat|ology
neo-Nazi
neo-Nazism
ne|onto|logic|al
neont|ology
neo|pagan
neo|pagan|ism
neo|pen|tane
neo|pho|bia
neo|pho|bic
neo|phyte

neo|pla|sia
neo|plasm
neo|plas|tic
neo|plasti|cism
Neo|pla|ton|ic
Neo|pla|ton|ism
Neo|pla|ton|ist
neo|prene
Neop|tole|mus
　Greek Mythology
neo-realism
neo-realist
neo|stig|mine
neo|ten|ic
neot|enous
neot|eny
neo|ter|ic
Neo|trop|ic|al
neo|trop|ics
Neo|zo|ic
Nepal
Nep|al|ese
Nep|ali
　pl. Nep|ali or
　Nep|alis
ne|pen|the the drug;
var. of nepenthes
ne|pen|thes
　pl. ne|pen|thes
drug in the *Ody-
sey*; similar potion;
plant
neper
ne|peta
neph|el|ine
nepheline-syenite
neph|el|in|ite
neph|el|om|eter
nephew
neph|rec|tomy
　neph|rec|to|mies
neph|rid|ial
neph|rid|ium
　neph|ridia
neph|rite
neph|rit|ic
neph|ritis
nephro|logic|al
neph|rolo|gist
neph|rol|ogy
neph|ron
neph|rosis

neph|rot|ic
nephro|toxic
nephro|tox|icity
nephro|toxin
Nepia, George
rugby player
ne plus ultra
nepo|tism
nepo|tist
nepo|tis|tic
Nep|tune Roman
god; planet
Nep|tun|ian
nep|tun|ian dyke
Nep|tun|ism
Nep|tun|ist
nep|tun|ium
nerd
nerd|ish
nerd|ish|ness
nerdy
　nerd|ier
　nerdi|est
Ner|eid sea nymph;
satellite of Neptune
ner|eid bristle worm
Ner|eus Greek
Mythology
ner|ine
Ner|issa
ner|ite
ner|it|ic
Nernst, Wal|ther
chemist
Nero
ner|oli
Nero|nian
Ne|ruda, Pablo
poet
Nerva, Mar|cus
Coc|ceius Roman
emperor
nerv|ation
nerve
nerv|ing
nerve|less
nerve|less|ly
nerve|less|ness
nerve-racking
nerve-wracking
var. of nerve-
racking
Nervi, Pier Luigi
engineer

ner|vily
nerv|ine
nervi|ness
ner|vous
ner|vous|ly
ner|vous|ness
nerv|ure
nervy
  ner|vier
  ner|vi|est
Nes|bit, Edith
  writer
nes|ci|ence
nes|ci|ent
nesh|ness
Nes|sie Loch Ness
  monster
Nes|sus mythical
  character
nest|er
nest|ful
nes|tle
  nest|ling
nest-like
nest|ling
Nes|tor *Greek*
  Mythology
Nes|tor|ian
Nes|tor|ian|ism
net
  net|ted
  net|ting
neta *Ind.* politician;
  leader
Net|an|yahu,
  Ben|ja|min prime
  minister of Israel
net|ball
net|ful
nether
Neth|er|land|er
Neth|er|land|ish
Neth|er|lands
neth|er|most
neth|er|world
neti|quette
neti|zen
net|suke
  pl. net|suke or
  net|sukes
nett *adj. & v.* var. of
  net in financial
  senses
net|ter

net|tle
  net|tling
nettle|rash
nettle|some
netty
  net|ties
net|work
net|work|able
net|work|er
Neu|châ|tel
Neue Sach|lich|keit
neum var. of neume
Neu|mann, John
  computer pioneer
neume
neur|al
neur|al|gia
neur|al|gic
neur|al|ly
neur|amin|ic
neur|amin|id|ase
neur|as|the|nia
neur|as|the|nic
neur|ec|tomy
  neur|ec|to|mies
neuri|lemma
  neuri|lem|mas or
  neuri|lem|mata
neuri|lem|mal
neur|it|ic
neur|itis
neuro|ana|tom|
      ic|al
neuro|anat|om|ist
neuro|anat|omy
neur|obics
neuro|bio|logic|al
neuro|biolo|gist
neuro|biol|ogy
neuro|blast
neuro|blast|oma
neuro|chem|ical
neuro|chem|ist
neuro|chem|istry
neuro|epi|the|lial
neuro|epi|the|lium
neuro|fib|ril
neuro|fib|ril|lary
neuro|fibroma
neuro|fibro|mas or
neuro|fibro|mata
neuro|fibroma|
      tosis

neuro|gen|esis
neuro|gen|ic
neur|oglia
neuro|hor|mone
neuro|hyp|ophy|sis
  neuro|hyp|ophy|ses
neuro|lep|tic
neuro|lin|guis|tic
neuro|logic
neuro|logic|al
neuro|logic|al|ly
neur|olo|gist
neur|ology
neur|oma
  neur|omas or
  neur|omata
neuro|mast
neuro|mus|cu|lar
neuron
neur|on|al
neur|one var. of
  neuron
neur|on|ic
neuro|path
neuro|path|ic
neuro|patho|
      logic|al
neuro|path|olo|gist
neuro|path|ol|ogy
neur|opathy
neuro|pep|tide
neuro|pharma|co|
      logic|al
neuro|pharma|
      colo|gist
neuro|pharma|
      col|ogy
neuro|physio|
      logic|al
neuro|
      physi|olo|gist
neuro|physi|ology
neuro|pil
neuro|pile var. of
  neuropil
neuro|psychi|atric
neuro|psych|iatrist
neuro|psych|iatry
neuro|psycho|
      logic|al
neuro|psych|
      olo|gist
neuro|psych|ology

Neur|op|tera
neur|op|ter|an
neur|op|ter|ous
neuro|sci|ence
neuro|sci|en|tist
neur|osis
  neur|oses
neuro|sur|geon
neuro|sur|gery
neuro|sur|gi|cal
neuro|syph|ilis
neuro|syph|il|it|ic
neur|ot|ic
neur|ot|ic|al|ly
neur|oti|cism
neur|ot|omy
neuro|toxic
neuro|tox|icity
neuro|toxi|col|ogy
neuro|toxin
neuro|trans|
      mis|sion
neuro|trans|mit|
        ter
neuro|troph|ic of
  the growth of ner-
  vous tissue
neuro|trop|ic
  attacking the ner-
  vous system
neuro|trop|ism
Neu|sied|ler See
neu|ston
neu|ston|ic
neu|ter
neu|tral
neu|tral|isa|tion *Br.*
  var. of
  neutralization
neu|tral|ise *Br.* var.
  of neutralize
neu|tral|iser *Br.*
  var. of neutralizer
neu|tra|lism
neu|tra|list
neu|tral|ity
neu|tral|iza|tion
neu|tral|ize
  neu|tral|iz|ing
neu|tral|izer
neu|tral|ly
neu|trino +s
neu|tron

neu|tro|penia
neu|tro|pen|ic
neu|tro|phil
neu|tro|phil|ic
Neva
Nev|ada
Nev|ad|an
névé
never
never|more
Never-Never Australian outback
never-never hire purchase
Never-Never Coun|try var. of Never-Never Land
Never-Never Land region, N. Australia
never-never land utopian place
Ne|vers city, France
never|the|less
Nevil
Nev|ille
Nevis island, West Indies
Nevis, Ben
Ne|vis|ian
Nev|sky, Alex|an|der Russian hero
nevus *US*
nevi
Br. naevus
new recent; unused; cf. knew, nu
New|ark
new|bie
new|born
new-build ship
new-build housing
new|build|ing ship
New|burg
Newby, Eric travel writer
New|cas|tle
Newcastle-under-Lyme
Newcastle-upon-Tyne
New|comen, Thomas engineer
new|comer

newel
new|fan|gled
New|fie
New|found|land
New|found|land|er
New|gate
New Guin|ean
New Hamp|shir|ite
newie
Ne Win president of Burma
new|ish
New Jer|sey|an
New Jer|sey|ite
New|lands, John industrial chemist
newly
newly-wed *n.*
New|man, Bar|nett painter
New|man, John Henry churchman
New|man, Paul actor
New|mar|ket
new|ness
New|port
Newry
news|agent
news|boy
news|cast
news|cast|er
news|feed
news|flash
news|group
newsie *n.* var. of newsy
news|let|ter
news|man
news|men
news|paper
news|paper|man
news|paper|men
new|speak
news|print
news|read|er
news|reel
news|room
news-sheet
news-stand
news|vend|or
news|wire

news|worthi|ness
news|worthy
newsy
news|ies
news|ier
news|iest
New|ton, Isaac mathematician and physicist
new|ton unit
New|ton|ian
New|town|abbey
New York|er
New Zea|land|er
nexus
Ney, Mi|chel soldier
Nez Percé
  pl. Nez Percé or Nez Percés people
ngaio +s
Ngami|land
Ngata, Apl|ana Tar|upa Maori leader
Ng|bandi
ngoma
Ngoni people
  pl. Ngoni or Ngo|nis
ngoni drum
Ngoro|ngoro
ngul|trum
  pl. ngul|trum
Nguni
  pl. Nguni or Ngu|nis
ngwee
  pl. ngwee
Nhu|lun|buy
nia|cin
Nia|mey
nib|bana var. of nirvana
nibbed
nib|ble
nib|bling
nib|bler
Nibel|ung
  Nibel|ungs or Nibel|ungen
Nibel|ung|en|lied
nib|let
nib|lick

NiCad
Nicad *trademark in the US*
Ni|caea
Ni|cae|an
Nicam
Nic|ar|agua
Nic|ar|aguan
Nice city, France
nice
  nicer
  nicest
nice|ish var. of nicish
nice|ly
Ni|cene
nice|ness
ni|cety
ni|ceties
niche
nich|ing or niche|ing
Nich|iren
Nich|ol|as, St; cf. Nicolas
Nich|ol|son, Ben artist
Nich|ol|son, Jack actor
ni|chrome *trademark*
nicish
nickel
nick|elled *Br.*
nick|eled *US*
nickel|ling *Br.*
nickel|ing *US*
nickel-and-dime
  nickel-and-diming
nick|el|ic
nick|el|odeon
nick|el|ous
nick|er whinny; cf. knicker
nicker
  pl. nicker pound in money; cf. knicker
Nick|laus, Jack golfer
nick-nack var. of knick-knack
nick|name
nick|nam|ing
Nico|bar|ese

Nico|bar Is|lands
Ni¦çois male
  pl. Ni¦çois
Ni|çoise female
Nicol man's name;
  N. prism
Nic¦ola
Nico|las, Saint can-
  tata by Benjamin
  Britten; cf.
  Nicholas
Ni¦cole woman's
  name
Ni¦col|ette
Nico|sia
ni¦coti|ana
nico¦tina|mide
nico¦tin|ate
nico¦tine
nico¦tin|ise Br. var.
  of nicotinize
nico¦tin|ism
nico¦tin|ize
  nico¦tin|iz|ing
nic|ti¦tate
  nic|ti¦tat|ing
nic|ti¦ta|tion
nid|ation
nid|icol|ous
nidi¦fi|ca|tion
nidi|fu¦gous
nid¦ify
  nid|ifies
  nid|ified
  nid¦ify|ing
nidus
  nidi or nid¦uses
niece
ni¦ello
ni¦el|loed
niels|bohr|ium
Niel|sen, Carl
  composer
Nie|meyer, Oscar
  architect
Nie|möller, Mar¦tin
  pastor
niente Music
Nier|stein|er
Nie|tzsche,
  Fried¦rich
  philosopher
Nie|tzsche¦an
Nie|tzsche¦an|ism

ni|fedi|pine
niffy
  niff|ier
  nif¦fi|est
Nifl|heim
nif|tily
nif¦ti|ness
nifty
  nif¦tier
  nif¦ti|est
Ni|gella name
ni|gella plant
Niger river and
  country, Africa
Ni|geria
Ni|ger¦ian of
  Nigeria
Ni|ger¦ien of Niger
nig|gard
nig¦gard¦li|ness
nig¦gard¦ly
nig¦ger offensive
nigger|head
nig¦gle
  nig|gling
nig|gling¦ly
nig¦gly
  nig|glier
  nig|gli|est
nigh
night period of
  darkness; cf. knight
night|bird
night|cap
night|clothes
night|club
night|club¦ber
night|club|bing
night|dress
night|fall
night|gown
night|hawk
nightie
Night|in|gale,
  Flor|ence nurse
night|in|gale
night|jar
night|less
night|life
night¦ly in the
  night; every night;
  cf. knightly
night|mare

night|mar¦ish
night|mar¦ish|ly
night|shade
night|shirt
night|side
night|spot
night|stand
night|stick
night|watch|man
  night|watch|men
night|wear
nig¦iri zushi
Ni¦hang
ni¦hil|ism
ni¦hil|ist
ni¦hil|is¦tic
nihil ob¦stat
Nii|gata
Ni¦jin|sky, Vas¦lav
  dancer
Nij|megen
nikah
Nike Greek goddess
Nik¦kei index
nil des¦per|an¦dum
Nile river
nil|gai
Nil|giri
Nilo-Saharan
Nil|ot¦ic
nil|po¦tent
Nils|son, Bir¦git
  singer
nim¦ble
  nim|bler
  nim|blest
nim|ble|ness
nim|bly
nimbo|stratus
nim¦bus
  nimbi or
  nim|buses
Nimby +s
Nimby|ism
Nîmes
niminy-piminy
Nim¦rod Bible
nim¦rod hunter
Nim¦rud Mesopota-
  mian city
nin|com|poop
nine days' won|der
nine|fold

nine|pins
nine|teen
nine|teenth
nine|ti¦eth
nine-to-five adj. &
  n.
nine-to-fiver
ninety
  nine|ties
ninety-first,
  ninety-second,
  etc.
ninety|fold
ninety-one,
  ninety-two, etc.
Nin|eveh
ning-nong
Ning|sia var. of
  Ningxia
Ning|xia
nin|hyd|rin
Nin|ian
ninja
nin|jutsu
ninny
  nin|nies
ninon
ninth
ninth¦ly
Niobe Greek
  Mythology
nio¦bic
nio|bium
nio|bous
nip
  nipped
nip|ping
nipa palm
nip¦per
nip|pily
nippi|ness
nip¦ple
nip¦pled
nipple|wort
Nip|pon|ese
Nippy
  Nip|pies
  waitress
nippy
  nip|pier
  nip¦pi|est
  nimble
niqab Muslim veil

NIREX = Nuclear
  Industry Radio-
  active Waste
  Executive
Niro, Rob¦ert De
  actor
nir¦vana
Nir¦vana prin¦ciple
Niš
Nisan
nisei
Nish var. of **Niš**
nisi
nisin
Nis¦sen hut
nit louse; stupid
  person; cf. **knit**
niter *US*
  Br. **nitre**
nit¦erie
Ni¦te¦rói
nit¦inol
ni¦trate
  ni¦trat¦ing
ni¦tra¦tion
ni¦traze¦pam
nitre *Br.*
  US **niter**
ni¦tric
ni¦tride
  ni¦trid¦ing
  ni¦tri¦fi¦able
  ni¦tri¦fi¦ca¦tion
ni¦trify
  ni¦tri¦fies
  ni¦tri¦fied
  ni¦tri¦fy¦ing
ni¦trile
ni¦trite
nitro +s
nitro¦ben¦zene
nitro¦blue
nitro¦cel¦lu¦lose
nitro¦chalk
nitro¦fur¦an¦toin
ni¦tro¦gen
ni¦tro¦gen¦ous
nitro¦gly¦cerin *US*
nitro¦gly¦cer¦ine *Br.*
nitro¦methane
ni¦troph¦il¦ous
ni¦tro¦sa¦mine
ni¦trous

ni¦trox
nitty
nitty-gritty
nit¦wit
nit¦wit¦ted
nit¦wit¦ted¦ness
nit¦wit¦tery
Niue
nival
niv¦ation
niv¦eous
Ni¦ver¦nais
Ni¦vose
  French **Nivôse**
nix nothing; cancel;
  water sprite;
  warning; cf. **Nyx**
nixer
nixie
Nixon, Rich¦ard
  Mil¦hous *US*
  president
Nizam ruler of
  Hyderabad
nizam the Turkish
  army
Niz¦ari
Nizhni Nov¦go¦rod
Nizhni Tagil
Nkomo, Joshua
  vice-president of
  Zimbabwe
Nkru¦mah, Kwame
  president of Ghana
No Japanese drama;
  var. of **Noh**; cf.
  know, no
no
  noes
  negative; cf. **know,
  Noh**
no-account *adj.* &
  n.
No¦ach¦ian
Noah *Bible*
noah shark
nob upper-class per-
  son; head; cf. **knob**
no-ball *n.* & *v.*
nob¦ble
  nob¦bling
  tamper with; cf.
  knobble
nob¦bler

nobby
nob¦bier
nob¦bi¦est
Nobel, Al¦fred
  chemist
No¦bel¦ist
no¦bel¦ium
Nobel Prize
**Nobel
  prize¦win¦ner**
no¦bil¦iary
no¦bil¦ity
no¦bil¦ities
noble
  no¦bler
  nob¦lest
noble¦man
  noble¦men
noble¦ness
no¦blesse
no¦blesse ob¦lige
noble¦woman
  noble¦women
nobly
no¦body
  no¦bodies
no-brainer
no¦cebo +s
noci¦cep¦tive
noci¦cep¦tor
nock notch; cf.
  knock
nocti¦luca
  nocti¦lucae
nocti¦lucent
noc¦tuid
noc¦tule
noc¦turn part of
  matins; cf.
  nocturne
noc¦tur¦nal
noc¦tur¦nal¦ly
noc¦turne piece of
  music; painting; cf.
  nocturn
nocu¦ous
nod
  nod¦ded
  nod¦ding
nodal
nod¦dle
  nod¦dling
noddy
  nod¦dies

node of Ran¦vier
nodi pl. of **nodus**
nod¦ic¦al
nod¦ose
nod¦os¦ity
nodu¦lar
nodu¦lated
nodu¦la¦tion
nod¦ule
nodu¦lose
nodu¦lous
Noel Christmas;
  man's name
Noelle woman's
  name
Noe¦ther, Emmy
  mathematician
no¦et¦ic
Nof¦re¦tete var. of
  Nefertiti
nogal
nog¦gin
nog¦ging
no-good *adj.* & *n.*
Noh Japanese
  drama; cf. **know,
  no**
no-hoper
nohow in no way;
  cf. **know-how**
noir of film or
  fiction genre
noir¦ish
noise
  nois¦ing
noise¦less
noise¦less¦ly
noise¦less¦ness
noise¦maker
nois¦ette
nois¦ily
noisi¦ness
noi¦some
noi¦some¦ness
noisy
  nois¦ier
  noisi¦est
Nok ancient Niger-
  ian civilization
Nolan, Sid¦ney
  painter
no¦lens vo¦lens
noli me tan¦gere

nolle pros
  nolle prosses
  nolle prossed
  nolle pros|sing
nolle pro|sequi
nolo con|ten|dere
nomad
no|mad|ic
no|mad|ic|al|ly
no|mad|ism
no-man's-land
nom|arch +s
  Egyptian
  governor; Greek
  administrator
nom|archy
  nom|arch|ies
no-mark unsuccess-
  ful person
nom|bril
nom de guerre
  noms de guerre
nom de plume
  noms de plume
Nome city
nome territorial
  division; cf. gnome
nomen
  nomens or
  nom|ina
no|men|cla|tive
no|men|cla|tor
no|men|cla|tural
no|men|cla|ture
no|men|kla|tura
  Soviet elite
nom|ina pl. of
  nomen
nom|in|al
nom|in|al|isa|tion
  Br. var. of
  nominalization
nom|in|al|ise *Br.*
  var. of nominalize
nom|in|al|ism
nom|in|al|ist
nom|in|al|is|tic
nom|in|al|iza|tion
nom|in|al|ize
  nom|in|al|iz|ing
nom|in|al|ly
nom|in|ate
  nom|in|at|ing
nom|in|ation

nom|ina|tive
nom|in|ator
nom|inee
nomo|gram
nomo|graph
nomo|graph|ic
nomo|graph|ic|al|ly
nom|og|raphy
nomo|logic|al
nomo|logic|al|ly
nomo|thet|ic
non-addict|ive
non|age
nona|gen|ar|ian
non-aggres|sion
non|agon
non|agon|al
non-alcohol|ic
non-aligned
non-alignment
non-allergen|ic
non-allergic
no-name unknown
  (person)
non|ane
non-appear|ance
non-associa|tive
non-attend|ance
non-attrib|ut|able
non-attrib|ut|ably
non-availabil|ity
non-being
non-believer
non-belliger|ence
non-belliger|ent
non-
  biodegrad|able
non-biologic|al
non-capital
nonce
non|cha|lance
non|cha|lant
non|cha|lant|ly
non-cleric|al
non-clinic|al
non-coding
non-com
non-combat|ant
non-commer|cial
non-
  commis|sioned
non-commit|tal

non-commit|tal|ly
non-communi|cant
non-competi|tive
non-compli|ance
non com|pos
  men|tis
non-conduct|ing
non-conduct|or
non-
  confiden|tial|ly
Non|con|form|ism
  Religion
non|con|form|ism
  general
Non|con|form|ist
  Religion
non|con|form|ist
  general
Non|con|form|ity
  Religion
non|con|form|ity
  general
non-content
non-conten|tious
non-
  contra|dic|tory
non-contribu|tory
non-contro|ver|sial
non-cooper|ation
non-count
non-custodial
nonda
non-dairy
non-delivery
non-
  denomin|ation|al
non|de|script
non|de|script|ly
non|de|script|ness
non-destruc|tive
non-direction|al
non-disjunc|tion
non-drinker
non-drip
non-driver
none not any; cf.
  nun
none Christian
  service; cf. known
non-emergency
non-empty
non|en|tity
  non|en|tities

nones *pl. n.* day in
  Roman calendar
nones *sing. n.*
  Christian service;
  var. of none
non-essential
non est fac|tum
  non est facta
none|such excellent
  person or thing;
  var. of nonsuch
nonet
none|the|less
non-Euclid|ean
non-event
non-executive
non-existence
non-existent
non-factive
non-fatal
non|feas|ance
non-ferrous
non-fiction
non-fiction|al
non-figura|tive
non-finite
non-flam
non-flammable
non-fulfill|ment
  US
non-fulfil|ment *Br.*
non-function|al
non-
  govern|men|tal
non-Hodgkin's
non-human
non-infectious
non-inflam|mable
non-inherent
non-insulin-
  dependent
non-interfer|ence
non-interlaced
non-interven|tion
non-
  interven|tion|ism
non-
  interven|tion|ist
non-invasive
non-iron
non-ism
non-issue
non|join|der

non-judgemen|tal
non-judgmen|tal
  var. of **non-judgemental**
Non|juror
non-jury
non-league
non licet
non-linear
non-linear|ity
non-linear|ly
non-linguis|tic
non-logical
non-magnet|ic
non-malignant
non-medical
non-member
non-member|ship
non-metal
non-metallic
non-military
non-moral
non-morally
non-Muslim
non-native
non-natural
non-negative
non-negoti|able
non-net
non-nuclear
no-no +*s n.*
non-object|ive
non-observance
non-operation|al
non-organic
non-paramet|ric
non|par|eil
non-partici|pat|ing
non-partisan
non-party
non-payer
non-payment
non-penetra|tive
non-perform|ing
non-person
non-person|al
non-physic|al
non-physical|ly
non placet
non-playing
non|plus
  non|plusses

non|plussed
non|plus|sing
non-political
non poss|umus
non-prescrip|tion
non-price
non-product|ive
non-profes|sion|al
non-profit
non-profit-making
non-prolifer|ation
non-propri|etary
non-qualify|ing
non-reader
non-refund|able
non-religious
non-renewable
non-reproduc|tive
non-residence
non-resident
non-resistance
non-restrict|ive
non-return
non-return|able
non-rhotic
non-rigid
non-scene
non-scientif|ic
non-scientist
non-secretor
non-sectar|ian
non-select|ive
non|sense
non|sens|ical
non|sens|ical|ity
non|sens|ical|ly
non sequi|tur
non-sexist
non-sexual
non-sexual|ly
non-skid
non-slip
non-smoker
non-smoking
non-solid
non-special|ist
non-specif|ic
non-standard
non-starter
non-statutory
non-stick

non-stoichio|met|ric
non-stop
non|such
non|suit *Law*
non-surgical
non-swimmer
non-taxable
non-taxpay|er
non-teaching
non-technical
non-technic|al|ly
non-threaten|ing
non-toxic
non-tradition|al
non-transfer|able
non-treaty
non-trivial
non-tropic|al
non-U
non-uniform
non-uniform|ity
non-uniform|ly
non-union
non-urgent
non-usage
non-use
non-user
non-verbal
non-verbal|ly
non-vintage
non-violence
non-violent
non-volatile
non-voter
non-voting
non-word
Nonya
nonyl
non-zero
noo|dle
  nood|ling
noo|gie
Noo|goora burr
nookie var. of
  nooky
nooky
noon|day
no one
noon|er
noo|noo +**s** var. of
  nunu

noon|tide
noon|time
Noord|hin|der
noose
  noos|ing
noo|sphere
noo|spher|ic
Nootka
  pl. **Nootka** or
   Noot|kas
noo|trop|ic
nopal
nope
NOR Boolean
  operator
nor and not; cf.
  gnaw
nor' = north
NORAD = North
  American Aero-
  space Defence
  Command
nor|adren|aline
Nor|bert
Nor|bert|ine
Nor|dic
Nord|kyn
Nord-Pas-
   de-Calais
Nor|een
nor|epin|eph|rine
Nor|folk
nori
noria
Nori|ega, Ma|nuel
  Panamanian head
  of state
nor|ite
nor|mal
nor|malcy
nor|mal|isa|tion *Br.*
  var. of
  normalization
nor|mal|ise *Br.* var.
  of **normalize**
nor|mal|iser *Br.*
  var. of **normalizer**
nor|mal|ity
nor|mal|iza|tion
nor|mal|ize
nor|mal|iz|ing
nor|mal|izer
nor|mal|ly

Nor|man of Normandy; name
Nor|man, Greg golfer
Nor|man, Jes|sye soprano
Nor|mandy
Nor|man|esque
Nor|man|ise *Br.* var. of **Normanize**
Nor|man|ism
Nor|man|ize
    Nor|man|iz|ing
nor|ma|tive
nor|ma|tive|ly
nor|ma|tive|ness
normo|gly|caemia *Br.*
normo|gly|caem|ic *Br.*
normo|gly|cemia *US*
normo|gly|cem|ic *US*
normo|ten|sive
Norn language; Scandinavian goddess
Nor|plant *trademark*
Nor|ris
Norr|kö|ping
Nor|roy *Heraldry*
Norse
Norse|man
    Norse|men
nor|teño +s
North|al|ler|ton
North|amp|ton
North|amp|ton| shire
North|ants = Northamptonshire
north|bound
North|cliffe, Al|fred newspaper proprietor
north- country|man
north-country|men
north-east
north|east|er
north-easter|ly
    north-easter|lies

north-eastern
north-eastward
north-eastwards
no-show *n.*
nosh-up
nosi|ly
nosi|ness
noso|co|mial
nos|ode
noso|graph|ic
nos|og|raphy
noso|logic|al
nos|olo|gist
nos|ology
nos|tal|gia
nos|tal|gic
nos|tal|gic|al|ly
nos|tal|gie de la boue
nos|tal|gist
nos|toc
Nos|tra|da|mus astrologer
Nos|trat|ic
nos|tril
nos|triled *US*
nos|trilled *Br.*
nos|tro
nos|trum
nosy
    nosies
    nosied
    nosy|ing
    nosi|er
    nosi|est
nosy par|ker
NOT Boolean operator
Not type of paper
not negative word; cf. **knot**
nota pl. of **notum**
nota bene
not|abil|ity
    not|abil|ities
not|able
not|able|ness
not|ably
notal
notam
nota|phil|ic
not|aph|il|ist
not|aph|ily
no|tar|ial

nosh|ery
    nosh|er|ies
nosh-up
nosi|ly
nosi|ness

no|tari|al|ly
no|tar|ise *Br.* var. of **notarize**
no|tar|ize
    no|tar|iz|ing
no|tary
    no|tar|ies
no|tary pub|lic
    no|tar|ies pub|lic
no|tate
    no|tat|ing
no|ta|tion
nota|tion|al
nota|tion|al|ly
no|tator
not-being *n.*
notch|back
notch|er
notchy
    notch|ier
    notchi|est
note
    not|ing
note|book
note|card
note|case
note|let
note|pad
note|paper
notes in|égales
note|worthi|ness
note|worthy
noth|ing
noth|ing|ness
notho|saur
no|tice
    no|ticing
no|tice|able
no|tice|ably
no|tice|board
no|ti|fi|able
no|ti|fi|ca|tion
no|tify
    no|ti|fies
    no|ti|fied
    no|ti|fy|ing
no|tion
no|tion|al
no|tion|al|ist
no|tion|al|ly
no|titia
noto|chord
Noto|gaea

nose
    nos|ing
nose|bag
nose|band
nose|bleed
nose|dive
    nose|div|ing
no-see-um
nose|gay
nose|less
no|sema
nose|piece
nosey var. of **nosy**

norther wind
north|er|ly
    north|er|lies
north|ern
Nor|thern blot
north|ern|er
north|ern|most
north|ing
north|land
North|man
    North|men
north-north-east
north-north-west
North|um|ber|land
North|um|bria
North|um|brian
north|ward
north|ward|ly
north|wards
north-west
north|wester
north-wester|ly
    north-wester|lies
north-western
North|west Ter|ri|tor|ies in Canada
North|west Ter|ri|tory region, US
north-westward
north-westwards
Nor|walk
Nor|way
Nor|we|gian
nor'|wester
Nor|wich

Noto|gaean
Noto|gea *US* var. of
  Notogaea
Noto|gean *US* var.
  of Notogaean
no|tori|ety
no|tori|ous
no|tori|ous|ly
no|tor|nis
noto|ungu|late
not-out *n.*
Notre Dame uni-
  versity, US
Notre-Dame cath-
  edral, Paris
no-trumper
Not|ting|ham
Not|ting|ham|shire
Not|ting Hill
notum
  nota
not|with|stand|ing
Nou|ad|hi|bou
Nou|ak|chott
nou|gat
nou|gat|ine
nought the digit 0;
  cf. naught
noughth before first
nought|ies years
  2000-09
Nou|méa
nou|menal
nou|men|al|ly
nou|menon
  nou|mena
noun
noun|al
nour|ish
nour|ish|er
nour|ish|ing|ly
nour|ish|ment
nous common sense
nouse var. of nous
nou|veau
nou|veau riche
nou|veau roman
  nou|veaux
  ro|mans
nou|velle cuis|ine
nou|velle vague
nova
  novae or novas

nov|acu|lite
Nova Lis|boa
Nova Sco|tia
Nova Sco|tian
nov|ate
nov|at|ing
nov|ation
Nov|aya Zem|lya
novel
nov|el|ese
nov|el|esque
nov|el|ette
nov|el|et|tish
nov|el|isa|tion *Br.*
  var. of novelization
nov|el|ise *Br.* var. of
  novelize
nov|el|ist
nov|el|is|tic
nov|el|iza|tion
nov|el|ize
nov|el|liz|ing
nov|ella
Nov|ello, Ivor
  composer
nov|el|ly
nov|elty
  nov|el|ties
No|vem|ber
nov|ena
No|verre, Jean-
  Georges choreog-
  rapher
Nov|go|rod
nov|ice
novi|ci|ate var. of
  novitiate
Novi Sad
no|viti|ate
Novo|cain
  trademark
novo|caine
No|vo|kuz|netsk
Novo|si|birsk
No|votný, Anto|nín
  president of
  Czechoslovakia
now|adays
noway var. of no
  way
no way not at all
no|ways var. of no
  way
nowed *Heraldry*

Nowel Christmas
  var. of Noel
No|well Christmas
  var. of Noel
no|where
no|wheres|ville
no-win
no|wise
now|ness
now-now
nowt nothing; cf.
  knout
NOx pollutants
nox|ious
nox|ious|ly
nox|ious|ness
noy|ade
noyau
  noy|aux
noz|zle
n-tuple
nu Greek letter; cf.
  knew, new
nu|ance
nu|an|cing
Nuba
  pl. Nuba or Nubas
nub|bin
nub|ble
nub|bled
nub|bly
  nub|blier
  nub|bli|est
nubby
  nub|bier
  nub|bi|est
Nubia
Nu|bian
nu|bile
nu|bil|ity
Nu|buck
nu|cel|lar
nu|cel|lus
nu|celli
nu|chal
nu|cif|er|ous
nu|clear
nu|cle|ase
nu|cle|ate
nu|cle|at|ing
nu|cle|ation
nu|clei
nu|cle|ic

nu|cleo|cap|sid
nu|cle|olar
nu|cle|olus
  nu|cle|oli
nu|cleon
nu|cleon|ic
nu|cleon|ics
nu|cleo|phile
nu|cleo|phil|ic
nu|cleo|plasm
nu|cleo|pro|tein
nu|cleo|side
nu|cleo|som|al
nu|cleo|some
nu|cleo|syn|thesis
nu|cleo|syn|thet|ic
nu|cleo|tide
nu|cleus
nu|clei
nu|clide
nu|clid|ic
nuddy
nudge
nudg|ing
nudger
nudi|branch +s
Nudi|bran|chia
nudi|bran|chi|ate
nudie
nud|ism
nud|ist
nud|ity
nud|nick var. of
  nudnik
nud|nik
nuée ar|dente
  nuées ar|dentes
Nuer
  pl. Nuer or Nuers
Nuevo León
nuevo sol
  nuevo soles
Nuf|field, Wil|liam
  motor
  manufacturer
nu|ga|tory
nug|get
nug|get|ty var. of
  nuggety
nug|gety
nuis|ance
nuit blanche
  nuits blanches

Nuits St George
nuke
  nuk¦ing
Nu¦ku'alofa
nulla var. of nulla-
  nulla
nul¦lah dry river
  bed
nulla-nulla Austra-
  lian Aboriginal club
Null¦ar¦bor Plain
nul¦li¦fi¦ca¦tion
nul¦li¦fier
nul¦lify
  nul¦li¦fies
  nul¦li¦fied
  nul¦li¦fy¦ing
nul¦lipara
nul¦lipar¦ous
null¦ity
  null¦ities
Numa Pom¦pil¦ius
  legendary Roman
  king
numb
num¦bat
num¦ber
num¦ber¦less
numb¦fish
num¦bles
numb¦ly
numb¦ness
numb¦skull
num¦dah
numen
  nu¦mina
nu¦mer¦able
nu¦mer¦ably
nu¦mer¦acy
nu¦mer¦aire
nu¦meral
nu¦mer¦ate
  nu¦mer¦at¦ing
nu¦mer¦ation
nu¦mer¦ator
nu¦mer¦ic
nu¦mer¦ic¦al
nu¦mer¦ic¦al¦ly
nu¦mero¦logic¦al
nu¦mero¦logic¦al¦ly
nu¦mer¦olo¦gist
nu¦mer¦ology
nu¦mero uno +s

nu¦mer¦ous
nu¦mer¦ous¦ly
nu¦mer¦ous¦ness
nu¦merus clau¦sus
Nu¦midia
Nu¦mid¦ian
nu¦mina
nu¦min¦ous
nu¦min¦ous¦ly
nu¦mis¦mat¦ic
nu¦mis¦mat¦ic¦al¦ly
nu¦mis¦ma¦tist
nu¦mis¦mat¦ology
num¦mu¦lar
num¦mu¦lite
nummy
  num¦mier
  num¦mi¦est
num¦nah
num-num shrub
numpty
  nump¦ties
num¦skull var. of
  numbskull
nun member of reli-
  gious community;
  cf. none
nun¦atak
Nuna¦vik
Nuna¦vum¦miut
Nuna¦vut
nun¦bird
Nunc Di¦mit¦tis
nun¦chaku
nun¦ci¦ature
nun¦cio +s
nun¦cle
nun¦cu¦pate
  nun¦cu¦pat¦ing
nun¦cu¦pa¦tion
nun¦cu¦pa¦tive
Nun¦eaton
nun¦hood
nun¦like
nun¦nery
  nun¦ner¦ies
nun¦nish
nunu
nuoc mam
Nupe
  pl. Nupe or Nupes
nup¦tial
nup¦tial¦ity

nur¦agh
nur¦aghi
nur¦aghe var. of
  nuragh
nur¦agh¦ic
nurd var. of nerd
nurd¦ish var. of
  nerdish
nurd¦ish¦ness var.
  of nerdishness
nurdy var. of nerdy
Nur¦em¦berg
Nur¦eyev, Ru¦dolf
  dancer
Nuri¦stan
Nuro¦fen trademark
nurse
  nurs¦ing
nurse¦maid
nur¦sery
  nur¦ser¦ies
nur¦sery¦man
  nur¦sery¦men
nursey
nursie var. of
  nursey
nurs¦ling
nur¦tur¦ance
nur¦tur¦ant
nur¦ture
  nurt¦ur¦ing
nur¦turer
Nus¦selt
Nut Egyptian
  Mythology
nut
  nut¦ted
  nut¦ting
nu¦ta¦tion
nut¦case
nut¦crack¦er
Nut¦crack¦er man
nut¦gall
nut¦hatch
nut¦house
nut¦let
nut-like
nut¦meg
  nut¦megged
  nut¦meg¦ging
nutra¦ceut¦ic¦al
nu¦tria
nu¦tri¦ent
nu¦tri¦ment

nu¦tri¦men¦tal
nu¦tri¦tion
nu¦tri¦tion¦al
nu¦tri¦tion¦al¦ist
nu¦tri¦tion¦al¦ly
nu¦tri¦tion¦ist
nu¦tri¦tious
nu¦tri¦tious¦ly
nu¦tri¦tious¦ness
nu¦tri¦tive
nut¦shell
nutso +s
nutsy
  nuts¦ier
  nutsi¦est
nut¦ter
nut¦ti¦ness
nutty
  nut¦tier
  nut¦ti¦est
Nuu-chah-nulth
  pl. Nuu-chah-nulth
Nuuk
nux vom¦ica
nuz¦zle
  nuz¦zling
nyaff
nyala
  pl. nyala
Nya¦mwezi
  pl. Nya¦mwezi or
  Nya¦mwe¦zis
Nyanja
  pl. Nyanja or
  Nyan¦jas
Nyasa
Nyasa¦land
nyc¦tal¦opia
nyc¦tin¦as¦tic
nyc¦tin¦asty
  nyc¦tin¦as¦ties
nycto¦pho¦bia
Nye¦rere, Ju¦lius
  president of
  Tanzania
nyl¦ghau var. of
  nilgai
nylon
Nyman, Mi¦chael
  composer
nymph
nym¦phaeum
  nym¦phaea
nymph¦al

nym|phalid
nymph|ean
nymph|et
nymph|ette var. of
  nymphet
nymph-like
nym|pho +s
nym|pho|lepsy
nym|pho|lept
nym|pho|lep|tic
nym|pho|mania
nym|pho|maniac
nym|pho|maniac|al
Ny|norsk
Ny|quist, Harry
  engineer
nys|tag|mic
nys|tag|mus
ny|sta|tin
Nyun|gar
Nyx *Greek*
  Mythology; cf. **nix**

O

O *archaic* var. of **oh**
  before name of
  person being
  addressed
oaf|ish
oaf|ish|ly
oaf|ish|ness
Oahu
oak tree; cf. **oke**
oaken
Oak|land
oak leaf let|tuce
Oak|ley, Annie
  markswoman
oakum
oaky
  oak|ier
  oaki|est
oar for rowing; cf.
  or, **ore**
oared
oar|fish
oar|less
oar|lock

oars|man
  oars|men
oars|man|ship
oars|woman
  oars|women
oar|weed
oasis
  oases
oast
oat|cake
oaten
oater
Oates, Titus *clergy-*
  man
oath +s
oat|meal
oaty
  oatier
  oatiest
Oax|aca
oba
Oba|diah *Bible*
Ohan
ob|bli|gato
  ob|bli|gatos or
  ob|bli|gati
ob|con|ic|al
ob|cor|date
ob|duct
ob|duc|tion
ob|dur|acy
ob|dur|ate
ob|dur|ate|ly
ob|dur|ate|ness
obeah
ob|eche
obedi|ence
obedi|ent
obedi|en|tiary
  obedi|en|tiar|ies
obedi|ent|ly
obei|sance
obei|sant
obeli pl. of **obelus**
obe|lia
ob|el|ise *Br.* var. of
  obelize
ob|el|isk
ob|el|ize
  ob|el|iz|ing
ob|elus
  obeli
Ober|am|mer|gau

Ober|hau|sen
Ob|eron character
  in Shakespeare;
  moon of Uranus
obese
obese|ness
obes|ity
obey
obey|er
ob|fus|cate
  ob|fus|cat|ing
ob|fus|ca|tion
ob|fus|ca|tory
obi kimono sash; cf.
  obeah
obit
ob|iter
ob|iter dic|tum
  ob|iter dicta
ob|itu|ar|ial
ob|itu|ar|ist
ob|itu|ary
  ob|itu|ar|ies
ob|ject
ob|ject|ifi|ca|tion
ob|ject|ify
  ob|jecti|fies
  ob|jecti|fied
  ob|jecti|fy|ing
ob|jec|tion
ob|jec|tion|able
ob|jec|tion|able|
           ness
ob|jec|tion|ably
ob|ject|ival
ob|ject|ive
ob|ject|ive|ly
ob|ject|ive|ness
ob|ject|iv|isa|tion
  Br. var. of
  objectivization
ob|ject|iv|ise *Br.*
  var. of **objectivize**
ob|ject|iv|ism
ob|ject|iv|ist
ob|ject|iv|is|tic
ob|ject|iv|ity
ob|ject|iv|iza|tion
ob|ject|iv|ize
  ob|ject|iv|iz|ing
ob|ject|less
ob|ject|or
objet

objet d'art
  ob|jets d'art
objet trouvé
  ob|jets trou|vés
ob|lan|ceo|late
ob|last
ob|late
ob|la|tion
ob|la|tion|al
ob|la|tory
ob|li|gate
  ob|li|gat|ing
ob|li|ga|tion
ob|li|ga|tion|al
ob|li|gato *US*
  var. of **obbligato**
ob|li|ga|tor
ob|liga|tor|ily
ob|liga|tory
ob|lige
  ob|li|ging
ob|li|gee
ob|lige|ment
ob|li|ger generally
ob|li|ging|ly
ob|li|ging|ness
ob|li|gor *Law*
ob|lique
  ob|li|quing
ob|lique|ly
ob|lique|ness
ob|li|quity
ob|lit|er|ate
  ob|lit|er|at|ing
ob|lit|er|ation
ob|lit|era|tive
ob|lit|er|ator
ob|liv|ion
ob|livi|ous
ob|livi|ous|ly
ob|livi|ous|ness
ob|long
ob|lo|quy
ob|nox|ious
ob|nox|ious|ly
ob|nox|ious|ness
ob|nubil|ate
ob|nubil|at|ing
ob|nubil|ation
oboe
oboe d'amore
  oboes d'amore
obo|ist

obol
Obote, Mil'ton
president of
Uganda
ob|ov|ate
O'Brien, Edna
writer
O'Brien, Flann
writer
ob|scene
ob|scene|ly
ob|scene|ness
ob|scen|ity
  ob|scen|ities
ob|scur|ant
ob|scur|ant|ism
ob|scur|ant|ist
ob|scur|ation
ob|scure
  ob|scur|ing
  ob|scurer
  ob|scur|est
ob|scure|ly
ob|scur|ity
  ob|scur|ities
ob|se|quial
ob|se|quies
ob|se|qui|ous
ob|se|qui|ous|ly
ob|se|qui|ous|ness
ob|serv|able
ob|serv|ably
ob|ser|vance
Ob|ser|vant member of Franciscan order
ob|ser|vant
ob|ser|vant|ly
ob|ser|va|tion
ob|ser|va|tion|al
ob|ser|va|tion|al|ly
ob|ser|va|tory
  ob|ser|va|tor|ies
ob|serve
  ob|serv|ing
ob|ser|ver
ob|sess
ob|ses|sion
ob|ses|sion|al
ob|ses|sion|al|ism
ob|ses|sion|al|ly
ob|ses|sive
ob|ses|sive|ly

ob|ses|sive|ness
ob|sid|ian
ob|so|lesce
  ob|so|les|cing
ob|so|les|cence
ob|so|les|cent
ob|so|lete
  ob|so|let|ing
ob|so|lete|ly
ob|so|lete|ness
ob|so|let|ism
obs|tacle
ob|stet|ric
ob|stet|ric|al
ob|stet|ric|al|ly
ob|stet|ri|cian
ob|stin|acy
ob|stin|ate
ob|stin|ate|ly
ob|sti|pa|tion
ob|strep|er|ous
ob|strep|er|ous|ly
ob|strep|er|ous|ness
ob|struct
ob|struc|tion
ob|struc|tion|ism
ob|struc|tion|ist
ob|struct|ive
ob|struct|ive|ly
ob|struct|ive|ness
ob|struct|or
ob|stru|ent
ob|tain
ob|tain|abil|ity
ob|tain|able
ob|tain|er
ob|tain|ment
ob|tect
ob|tect|ed
ob|ten|tion
ob|trude
  ob|trud|ing
ob|truder
ob|tru|sion
ob|tru|sive
ob|tru|sive|ly
ob|tru|sive|ness
ob|tund
ob|tur|ator
ob|tuse
ob|tuse|ly

ob|tuse|ness
ob|tus|ity
ob|verse
ob|verse|ly
ob|ver|sion
ob|vert
ob|vi|ate
  ob|vi|at|ing
ob|vi|ation
ob|vi|ous
ob|vi|ous|ly
ob|vi|ous|ness
oca
oca|rina
O'Casey, Sean playwright
Occam, Wil|liam of
philosopher
oc|ca|sion
oc|ca|sion|al
oc|ca|sion|al|ism
oc|ca|sion|al|ity
oc|ca|sion|al|ly
Oc|ci|dent
Oc|ci|den|tal person
oc|ci|den|tal adj.
oc|ci|den|tal|ise Br. var. of occidentalize
oc|ci|den|tal|ism
oc|ci|den|tal|ist
oc|ci|den|tal|ize
  oc|ci|den|tal|iz|ing
oc|ci|den|tal|ly
oc|cipi|tal
oc|cipito|
      tem|por|al
oc|ci|put
Oc|ci|tan
Oc|ci|tan|ian
oc|clude
  oc|clud|ing
oc|clu|sal
oc|clu|sion
oc|clu|sive
oc|cult
oc|cult|ation
oc|cult|ism
oc|cult|ist
oc|cult|ly
oc|cult|ness
oc|cu|pance

oc|cu|pancy
  oc|cu|pan|cies
oc|cu|pant
oc|cu|pa|tion
oc|cu|pa|tion|al
oc|cu|pa|tion|al|ly
oc|cu|pier
oc|cupy
  oc|cu|pies
  oc|cu|pied
  oc|cu|py|ing
occur
oc|curred
oc|cur|ring
oc|cur|rence
oc|cur|rent
ocean
ocean|ar|ium
  ocean|ar|iums or
  ocean|aria
Ocea|nia
Ocean|ian
Ocean|ic of Oceania
ocean|ic of the ocean
Ocean|id
  Ocea|nids or
  Ocea|ni|des
ocean|og|raph|er
oceano|graph|ic
ocean|og|raphy
oceano|logic|al
ocean|olo|gist
ocean|ology
Ocea|nus Greek Mythology
ocean|ward
ocean|wards
ocel|lar
ocel|late
ocel|lated
ocel|lus
  ocelli
oce|lot
och exclam.
oche line for darts
ocher US
  Br. ochre
ocher|ish US
  Br. ochreish
ocher|oid US
  Br. ochroid
ocher|ous US
  Br. ochreous

ochery *US*
 Br. ochry

och|loc|racy

och|lo|crat

och|lo|crat|ic

och|one

ochre *Br.*
 US ocher

och|rea
 och|reas or
 och|reae

ochre|ish *Br.*
 US ocherish

ochre|ous *Br.*
 US ocherous

och|roid *Br.*
 US ocheroid

och|rous var. of
 ochreous

ochry *Br.*
 US ochery

ocker

Ock|ham var. of
 Occam

o'clock

ocno|phil

O'Con|nell, Dan|iel
 Irish nationalist

O'Con|nor,
 Flan|nery writer

oco|tillo +s

octad

octa|gon

oc|tag|on|al

oc|tag|on|al|ly

octa|he|dral

octa|he|dron
 octa|he|dra or
 octa|he|drons

octal

oc|tam|er|ous

oc|tam|eter

oc|tane

oct|angu|lar

Oc|tans

oc|tant

octa|roon var. of
 octoroon

octa|style

Octa|teuch

octa|va|lent

oct|ave

Oc|ta|via

Oc|ta|vian Roman
 emperor

oc|tavo +s

oc|ten|nial

octet

Oc|to|ber

Oc|to|brist

octo|cen|ten|ary
 octo|cen|ten|ar|ies

octo|cen|ten|nial

octo|decimo +s

octo|foil

octo|gen|ar|ian

oc|topa|mine

octo|pod

Octo|poda

octo|poid

octo|pus
 octo|puses

octo|roon

octo|syl|lab|ic

octo|syl|lable

octo|thorp

octo|thorpe var. of
 octothorp

oc|troi

oc|tu|ple
 oc|tu|pling

octu|plet

octyl

ocu|lar

ocu|lar|ist

ocu|lar|ly

ocu|late

oculi pl. of oculus

ocu|list

ocu|lis|tic

oculo|motor

ocu|lus
 oculi

OD
 OD's
 OD'd
 OD'ing
 = overdose

od hypothetical
 force; also short for
 'God'; cf. odd

odal|isque

odd cf. od

odd|ball

Odd|fel|low

odd|ish

odd|ity
 odd|ities

odd-jobber

odd-jobbing

oddly

odd|ment

odd|ness

odds|maker

odds-on

ode poem

Odense

Odeon cinema

odeon var. of
 odeum

Oder

Odessa

Odets, Clif|ford
 dramatist

odeum
 odeums or odea
 theatre for music;
 cf. odium

Odin Norse god

odi|ous

odi|ous|ly

odi|ous|ness

odium hatred; cf.
 odeum

odom|eter

Odon|ata

odon|ate

odon|tal|gia

odon|tal|gic

odonto|blast

odonto|blast|ic

odon|to|cete

Odon|to|ceti

odon|to|glos|sum

odont|oid

odon|to|logic|al

odon|tolo|gist

odon|tol|ogy

odon|toph|or|al

odon|to|phore

odont|oph|or|ous

odor *US*
 Br. odour

odor|ant

odor|ifer|ous

odor|ifer|ous|ly

odor|ise *Br.* var. of
 odorize

odor|iser *Br.* var. of
 odorizer

odor|ize

odor|iz|ing

odor|izer

odor|less *US*
 Br. odourless

odor|ous

odor|ous|ly

odour *Br.*
 US odor

odour|less *Br.*
 US odorless

Odys|sean of
 Odysseus

odys|sean of an
 odyssey

Odys|seus Greek
 hero

Odys|sey epic poem

odys|sey journey

Oea

oe|dema *Br.*
 US edema

oe|dema|tous *Br.*
 US edematous

Oedi|pal

Oedi|pal|ly

Oedi|pus *Greek
 Mythology*

oeil-de-boeuf
 oeils-de-boeuf

oeno|logic|al *Br.*
 US enological

oen|olo|gist *Br.*
 US enologist

oen|ology *Br.*
 US enology

Oe|none nymph;
 name

oeno|phile

oen|oph|il|ist

o'er = over

Oer|sted, Hans
 Chris|tian physicist

oer|sted unit

oe|sopha|geal *Br.*
 US esophageal

oe|sopha|gitis *Br.*
 US esophagitis

oe|sopha|go|scope
 Br.
 US esophagoscope

oe|sopha|gus *Br.*
 oe|soph|agi or

oe¦sopha¦guses
US esophagus

oes¦tra¦diol Br.
US estradiol

oes¦triol Br.
US estriol

oes¦tro¦gen Br.
US estrogen

oes¦tro¦gen¦ic Br.
US estrogenic

oes¦trone Br.
US estrone

oes¦trous Br. adj.
US estrous

oes¦trum Br.
US estrum

oes¦trus Br. n.
US estrus

oeuvre

ofay offensive white
person; cf. au fait

Ofcom = Office of
Communications

Offa king of Mercia

offal

Of¦faly

off¦beat adj. & n.

off-board

off-brand

off-center US

off-centre Br.

off¦comer

off¦cut piece of
waste

off-cutter cricket
delivery

off-dry

Of¦fen¦bach,
Jacques composer

of¦fence Br.
US offense

of¦fend

of¦fend¦ed¦ly

of¦fend¦er

of¦fense US
Br. offence

of¦fen¦sive

of¦fen¦sive¦ly

of¦fen¦sive¦ness

OFFER = Office of
Electricity
Regulation

offer

of¦fer¦er generally

of¦fer¦or Law and
Finance

of¦fer¦tory
of¦fer¦tor¦ies

off-gas n. & v.
off-gases
off-gassed
off-gassing

off-glide n.

off¦hand adj. &
adv.

off¦hand¦ed

off¦hand¦ed¦ly

off¦hand¦ed¦ness

off-hours n.

of¦fice

of¦fi¦cer

of¦fi¦cial

of¦fi¦cial¦dom

of¦fi¦cial¦ese

of¦fi¦cial¦ise Br. var.
of officialize

of¦fi¦cial¦ism

of¦fi¦cial¦ize

of¦fi¦cial¦iz¦ing

of¦fi¦cial¦ly

of¦fi¦ci¦ant

of¦fi¦ci¦ate

of¦fi¦ci¦at¦ing

of¦fi¦ci¦ation

of¦fi¦ci¦ator

of¦fi¦cin¦al

of¦fi¦cin¦al¦ly

of¦fi¦cious

of¦fi¦cious¦ly

of¦fi¦cious¦ness

offie

off¦ing

off¦ish

off¦ish¦ly

off¦ish¦ness

off-island¦er

off-key

off-kilter

off-licence n.

off-limits

off¦line

off¦load

off-message

off-patent

off-peak

off-piste

off-pitch

off-plan

off-price

off¦print

off-putting

off-putting¦ly

off-ramp

off-roader

off-roading

off-sale

off¦scour¦ings

off-screen

off¦set

off¦set¦ting

off-shears

off¦shoot

off¦shore

off¦shor¦ing

off¦side Football etc.

off side half of
cricket pitch; side
of vehicle

off¦sider

off-spinner

off¦spring

off¦stage

off-tackle

off¦take

off time slack
period; cf. oft-
times

off-track

off-trade

off-white

off-width

offy var. of offie

Ofgem = Office of
Gas and Electricity
Markets

Oflag prison camp

OFSTED = Office
for Standards in
Education

Oftel = Office of
Telecommunica-
tions

often

often¦times

oft-times often; cf.
off times

Ofwat = Office of
Water Services

Oga¦den

ogam var. of ogham

Og¦bo¦mo¦sho

ogee

ogeed

Ogen

ogham

ogival

ogive

ogle

og¦ling

ogler

OGPU Soviet
organization

ogre

ogre¦ish

ogress

ogrish var. of
ogreish

Ogy¦gian

oh exclam.; cf. O,
owe

O'Hig¦gins,
Ber¦nardo Chilean
head of state

Ohio

Ohio¦an

Ohm, Georg
physicist

ohm unit; cf. om

ohmic

ohm¦ic¦al¦ly

ohm¦meter

ohno¦second

ohone var. of
ochone

Ohrid

ohu
pl. ohu or ohus

oi exclam.

oick

oi¦dium
oidia

oik

oil¦bird

oil¦cake

oil¦can

oil¦cloth

oiler

oil¦field

oil¦fish

oil-gilding

oil¦ily

oili¦ness

oil|man
  oil|men
oil|seed
oil|skin
oil|stone
oily
  oili|er
  oili|est
oint|ment
Oire|ach|tas
Oisin
Ojibwa
  pl. Ojibwa or
  Ojib|was
OK
  pl. OKs
  v. OK's
  OK'd
  OKing
Oka cheese
oka unit
okapi
Okara
Oka|vango
okay var. of OK
Oka|yama
oke man; var. of
  oka; cf. oak
Okee|cho|bee
O'Keeffe, Geor|gia
  painter
Oke|fe|no|kee
  Swamp
okey-doke
okey-dokey
Ok|hotsk, Sea of
Okie person from
  Oklahoma
okie man
Oki|nawa
Okla|homa
Okla|homan
okra
okrug
okta
  pl. okta or oktas
Olaf kings of
  Norway
Öland
Ol|bers' Para|dox
old boy net|work
olde *pseudo-archaic*
  old
olden

olde worlde old
  and quaint; cf. old-
  world
Old|ham
oldie
old|ish
old-liner
old-maidish
old|ness
Oldo|wan
old|speak
old|squaw
old|ster
old-timer
Ol|du|vai Gorge
old-womanish
Old World *n. &*
  mod. Europe, Asia,
  and Africa
old-world of former
  times; cf. olde
  worlde
olé *Spanish exclam.*
ole = old
ole|aceous
ole|agin|ous
ole|an|der
ole|as|ter
ole|ate
olec|ra|non
ole|fin *US*
ole|fine *Br.*
ole|fin|ic
ole|if|er|ous
oleo|chem|ical
oleo|graph
oleo|graph|ic
ole|og|raphy
oleo|mar|gar|ine
oleo|resin
oleo|resin|ous
Oles|tra *trademark*
oleum
ol|fac|tion
ol|fac|tive
ol|fact|om|eter
ol|fact|om|etry
ol|fac|tory
oli|ba|num
oli|gaemia *Br.*
  US oligemia
oli|gaem|ic *Br.*
  US oligemic

oli|garch +s
oli|garch|ic
oli|garch|ic|al
oli|garch|ic|al|ly
oli|garchy
  oli|garch|ies
oli|gemia *US*
  Br. oligaemia
oli|gem|ic *US*
  Br. oligaemic
oligo +s
Oligo|cene
Oligo|chaeta
oligo|chaete
oligo|clase
oligo|dendro|cyte
oligo|dendro|glia
oligo|dendro|glial
oligo|dendro|
  gli|oma
oligo|dendro|
  gli|omas
or oligo|dendro|
  gli|omata
oligo|mer
oligo|mer|isa|tion
  Br. var. of
  oligomerization
oligo|mer|ise *Br.*
  var. of oligomerize
oligo|mer|iza|tion
oligo|mer|ize
  oligo|mer|iz|ing
oli|gom|er|ous
oligo|nucleo|tide
oligo|pep|tide
oli|gop|ol|ist
oli|gop|ol|is|tic
oli|gop|oly
oli|gop|olies
oli|gop|son|is|tic
oli|gop|sony
oli|gop|son|ies
oligo|sac|char|ide
oligo|sper|mia
oligo|troph|ic
oli|got|rophy
oli|guria
oli|gur|ic
olingo +s
olio +s
oliv|aceous
oliv|ary
olive

Oli|ver name
oliv|ette
Olivia name
Oliv|ier, Laur|ence
  actor
oliv|ine
olla pod|rida
Ollie name
ollie skate- and
  snowboarding jump
olly|crock
Olmec
  pl. Olmec or
  Olmecs
Olmos
olo|gist
ology
  olo|gies
Olo|mouc
ol|or|oso +s
Ol|sztyn
Olym|pia plain in
  Greece; city, US
Olym|piad
Olym|pian
Olym|pic
Olym|pus mythical
  place; Mount
om mantra; cf. ohm
oma|dhaun
Omagh
Omaha
  pl. Omaha or
  Oma|has
  American Indian
Omaha city, US;
  D-Day beach
Oman
Omani
Omar Muslim
  caliph
Omar Khay|yám
  poet
oma|sum
  omasa
Omay|yad var. of
  Umayyad
ombre card game;
  cf. ombré, hombre
ombré with
  graduated colour;
  cf. ombre, hombre
om|brogen|ous
ombro|troph|ic

om¦buds¦man
  om¦buds¦men
om¦buds¦person
Om¦dur¦man
omega
om¦elet var. of
  omelette
om¦elette
omen
omen¦tal
omen¦tum
omenta
omer
om¦ertà
omi¦cron
om¦in¦ous
om¦in¦ous¦ly
om¦in¦ous¦ness
omis¦sible
omis¦sion
omis¦sive
omit
  omit¦ted
  omit¦ting
om¦ma¦tid¦ium
  om¦ma¦tidia
om¦mato¦phore
omni¦bus
omni¦com¦pe¦tence
omni¦com¦pe¦tent
omni¦dir¦ec¦tion¦al
omni¦far¦ious
Omni¦max
  trademark
om¦nipo¦tence
om¦nipo¦tent
om¦nipo¦tent¦ly
omni¦pres¦ence
omni¦pres¦ent
omni¦range
om¦nis¦ci¦ence
om¦nis¦ci¦ent
om¦nis¦ci¦ent¦ly
omni¦sex¦ual
omni¦sexu¦al¦ity
om¦nium
  gath¦erum
omni¦vore
om¦niv¦or¦ous
om¦niv¦or¦ous¦ly
om¦niv¦or¦ous¦ness
omo¦pha¦gia
omo¦pha¦gic

omopha¦gous
omoph¦agy
Omot¦ic
om¦phalo¦cele
om¦pha¦los
  om¦pha¦loi
Omsk
on¦ager
onan¦ism
onan¦ist
onan¦is¦tic
Onas¦sis, Aris¦totle
  shipping magnate
Onas¦sis, Jackie
  former US First
  Lady
once-over n.
oncer
on¦cho¦cer¦cia¦sis
onco¦gene
onco¦gen¦esis
onco¦gen¦ic
onco¦gen¦icity
onco¦logic¦al
on¦colo¦gist
on¦col¦ogy
on¦com¦ing
on¦cost
On¦daatje, Mi¦chael
  writer
ondes mar¦tenot
  pl. ondes
  mar¦tenot
on dit
one number; single;
  a person; cf. won
one-acter
one-design n.
one-
  dimension¦al¦ity
one-down adj.
one¦fold
Onega
On¦eida
  pl. On¦eida or
  On¦eidas
O'Neill, Eu¦gene
  playwright
oneir¦ic
oneiro¦mancy
one-iron
one-liner
one-lunger

one¦ness
one-nighter
one-off n.
one-on-one
one-piece adj. & n.
oner single act; £1;
  remarkable person
  or thing
oner¦ous
oner¦ous¦ly
oner¦ous¦ness
one¦self
one-step n.
one-to-one
one-two +s n.
one-upmanship
one-worlder
one-worldism
on¦flow
on¦glaze
on-glide
on¦going
on¦going¦ness
onion
on¦iony
onkus
onli¦est
on¦line
on¦look¦er
on¦look¦ing
only
only-begotten
Ono, Yoko artist
ono¦masio¦logic¦al
ono¦masi¦ology
ono¦mast
ono¦mas¦tic
ono¦mato¦poeia
ono¦mato¦poe¦ic
ono¦mato¦poeic¦
  al¦ly
On¦on¦daga
  pl. On¦on¦daga or
  On¦on¦da¦gas
on¦rush
on¦rush¦ing
onset n. beginning
on-set adj. on a film
  set
on¦shore
on¦side Football etc.

on side half of
  cricket pitch; side
  of vehicle
on¦slaught
on¦stage
On¦tar¦ian
On¦tario
ontic
onto = on to, only
  when sense is 'to a
  location on' and is
  otherwise unclear
onto¦gen¦esis
onto¦gen¦et¦ic
onto¦gen¦et¦ic¦al¦ly
onto¦gen¦ic
onto¦gen¦ic¦al¦ly
onto¦logic¦al
onto¦logic¦al¦ly
on¦tolo¦gist
ontol¦ogy
onus
on¦ward
on¦wards
Ony¦choph¦ora
ony¦choph¦oran
onyx
o-o +s bird
oo var. of o-o; cf.
  ooh
oo¦cyst
oo¦cyte
oo¦dles
oofi¦ness
oofy
oof¦ier
oofi¦est
oog¦am¦ous
oog¦am¦ous¦ly
oog¦amy
oo¦gen¦esis
oo¦go¦nium
  oo¦go¦nia
ooh exclam.; cf. oo
oojah
oo¦jama¦flip
ooky
ook¦ier
ooki¦est
oo¦lite
oo¦lith
oo¦lit¦ic

oo|logic|al
oolo|gist
ool'ogy
oo|long
oo|miak var. of
  umiak
oom|pah
Oona
Oo|nagh
oo|phor|ec|tomy
  oo|phor|ec|to|mies
oo|phor|itis
oops-a-daisy
Oort, Jan astron-
  omer
oo|sphere
oo|spore
oo|theca
  oo|the|cae
ootid
ooze
oon|ing
oozi|ness
oozy
ooz|ier
oozi|est
cf. Uzi
opa|ci|fier
opa|cify
  opaci|fies
  opaci|fied
  opaci|fy|ing
opa|city
opah
opal
opal|esce
  opal|es|cing
opal|es|cence
opal|es|cent
opal|ine
opanka
  opan|kas or opanci
opaque
  opaquer
  opaquest
  opaque|ly
  opaque|ness
op|code
ope
  oping
OPEC = Organiza-
  tion of the Petrol-
  eum Exporting
  Countries

op-ed
open
open|able
open|cast
open|er
open|ly
open|ness
open|work
opepe
opera dramatic
  musical work;
  pl. of opus
op|er|abil|ity
op|er|able
opéra bouffe
  opéras bouffes
opera buffa
  opera buffas or
  opere buffe
opéra com|ique
  op|éras com|iques
op|er|and
oper|ant
opera seria
  opera serias or
  opere serie
op|er|ate
op|er|at|ing
op|er|at|ic
op|er|at|ic|al|ly
op|er|ation
op|er|ation|al
op|er|ation|al|ise
  Br. var. of
  operationalize
op|er|ation|al|ism
op|er|ation|al|ist
op|er|ation|al|ize
  op|er|ation|al|iz|ing
op|er|ation|al|ly
op|era|tive
op|era|tive|ly
op|era|tive|ness
op|er|ator
oper|cu|lar
oper|cu|late
oper|cu|lum
  oper|cula
op|er|etta
op|eron
Ophe|lia
ophi|cleide
Oph|idia

oph|id|ian
ophio|lite
ophio|lit|ic
Ophir
oph|it|ic
Ophiu|chus
ophiur|oid
Ophiur|oi|dea
oph|thal|mia
oph|thal|mic
oph|thal|mitis
oph|thal|mo|
    logic|al
oph|thal|molo|gist
oph|thal|mol|ogy
oph|thal|mo|
      ple|gia
oph|thal|mo|
      ple|gic
oph|thal|mo|scope
oph|thal|mo|
    scop|ic
oph|thal|mos|copy
opi|ate
  opi|at|ing
Opie, John painter
opine
  opin|ing
opin|ion
opin|ion|ated
opi|oid
opistho|branch +s
Opistho|bran|chia
opistho|soma
opis|thot|onos
opis|thot|onus var.
  of opisthotonos
opium
opop|anax
opop|onax var. of
  opopanax
Oporto
opos|sum
Op|pen|heimer,
  Rob|ert physicist
op|pi|dum
  op|pida
oppo +s
op|pon|ens
  op|pon|en|tes
  muscle
op|pon|ent
op|por|tune

op|por|tune|ly
op|por|tune|ness
op|por|tun|ism
op|por|tun|ist
op|por|tun|is|tic
op|por|tun|is|tic|
      al|ly
op|por|tun|ity
  op|por|tun|ities
op|pos|able
op|pose
  op|pos|ing
op|poser
op|pos|ite
  op|pos|ite|ly
  op|pos|ite|ness
op|pos|ition
op|pos|ition|al
op|press
op|pres|sion
op|pres|sive
  op|pres|sive|ly
  op|pres|sive|ness
op|press|or
op|pro|bri|ous
  op|pro|bri|ous|ly
op|pro|brium
opp shop var. of op
  shop
op|pugn
op|pug|nance
op|pug|nancy
op|pug|nant
op|pug|na|tion
op|pugn|er
op shop
opsin
op|son|ic
op|so|nin
op|son|isa|tion Br.
  var. of
  opsonization
op|son|ise Br. var.
  of opsonize
op|son|iza|tion
op|son|ize
  op|son|iz|ing
opt|ant
opta|tive
opta|tive|ly
optic of the eye
optic measure for
  spirits trademark

op|tic|al
op|tic|al|ly
op|ti|cian
op|tima pl. of
  optimum
op|ti|mal
op|ti|mal|ity
op|ti|mal|ly
op|ti|mif|ic
op|ti|misa|tion Br.
  var. of
  optimization
op|ti|mise Br. var. of
  optimize
opti|miser Br. var.
  of optimizer
op|ti|mism
op|ti|mist
op|ti|mis|tic
op|ti|mis|tic|al|ly
op|ti|miza|tion
op|ti|mize
  op|ti|miz|ing
opti|mizer
op|ti|mum
  op|tima or
  op|ti|mums
op|tion
op|tion|al
op|tion|al|ity
op|tion|al|ly
opto|coup|ler
opto|elec|tron|ics
op|tom|eter
opto|met|ric
op|tom|etrist
op|tom|etry
opt-out n. & mod.
op|tron|ics
opu|lence
opu|lent
opu|lent|ly
opun|tia
opus
  opuses or opera
Opus Dei
  trademark
  organization
opus Dei worship
or conj.; Heraldry
  gold or yellow; cf.
  oar, ore

orach
  or|aches var. of
  orache
or|ache
or|acle
or|acu|lar
or|acu|lar|ity
or|acu|lar|ly
oracy
Ora|dea
oral verbal; of the
  mouth; exam; cf.
  aural
oral|ism
oral|ist
oral|ity
or|al|ly
Oran
orang
Orang Asli
Or|ange town,
  France; Dutch royal
  house; Order
or|ange fruit; colour
or|ange|ade
Or|ange|ism
Or|ange|man
  Or|ange|men
or|ange|quit
oran|gery
  oran|ger|ies
or|ange|wood
oran|gey
oran|gish
orang-outang var.
  of orang-utan
orang-utan
orang-utang var. of
  orang-utan
orangy var. of
  orangey
Or|anje|stad
orate
  orat|ing
ora|tion
ora|tor
ora|tor|ial of an
  orator
Ora|tor|ian (mem-
  ber) of an Oratory
ora|tor|ic|al of an
  oratory
ora|tor|ic|al|ly
ora|torio +s

Ora|tory
  Ora|tor|ies
  Roman Catholic
  society
ora|tory
  ora|tor|ies
  public speaking;
  chapel
orbat
or|bicu|lar
or|bicu|lar|ity
or|bicu|lar|ly
Or|bi|son, Roy
  singer
orbit
or|bit|al
or|bit|al|ly
or|bit|er
or|bito|sphen|oid
orc fantasy monster;
  cf. auk
orca whale
Or|ca|dian
Or|cagna painter
or|cein
or|chard
or|chard|ist
or|ches|tra
or|ches|tral
or|ches|tral|ly
or|ches|trate
  or|ches|trat|ing
or|ches|tra|tion
or|ches|tra|tor
or|ches|trina
or|ches|trion
or|chid
or|chid|aceous
or|chid|ec|tomy
  or|chid|ec|to|mies
or|chid|ist
or|chid|ology
or|chil
or|chis
or|chi|tis
orcin
or|cinol
Orczy, Baron|ess
  writer
or|dain
or|dain|er
or|dain|ment
or|deal

order
or|der|li|ness
or|der|ly
  or|der|lies
or|din|aire in 'vin
  ordinaire'
or|din|al
or|din|ance decree;
  rite; by-law; cf.
  ordnance,
  ordonnance
or|din|and
or|din|ar|ily
or|din|ari|ness
or|din|ary
  or|din|ar|ies
or|din|ate
or|din|ation
ord|nance guns; cf.
  ordinance,
  ordonnance
Ord|nance Sur|vey
or|don|nance sys-
  tematic arrange-
  ment of parts; cf.
  ordinance,
  ordnance
Or|do|vi|cian
ord|ure
Ore Mountains
ore mineral; cf. oar,
  or
øre
  pl. øre
  Danish or Nor-
  wegian currency
öre
  pl. öre
  Swedish currency
oread
ore|body
  ore|bodies
Öre|bro
orec|chi|ette
orec|tic
ore|gano
Ore|gon
Ore|gon|ian
Orel
Oren|burg
orenda
Oreo +s trademark
Ores|tes Greek
  Mythology

Øre|sund

orf disease of sheep and goats

orfe fish

Orff, Carl composer

organ

or|gan|die Br.

or|gandy
  or|gan|dies US

or|gan|elle

or|gan|ic

or|gan|ic|al|ly

or|gani|cism

or|gani|cist

or|gani|cis|tic

or|gani|gram

or|gan|is|able Br. var. of organizable

or|gan|isa|tion Br. var. of organization

or|gan|isa|tion|al Br. var. of organizational

or|gan|isa|tion|al|ly Br. var. of organizationally

or|gan|ise Br. var. of organize

or|gan|iser Br. var. of organizer

or|gan|ism

or|gan|is|mal

or|gan|is|mic

or|gan|ist

or|gan|iz|able

or|gan|iza|tion

or|gan|iza|tion|al

or|gan|iza|tion|al|ly

or|gan|ize
  or|gan|iz|ing

or|gan|izer

or|gano|chlor|ine

or|gano|gen|esis

or|gano|gram var. of organigram

or|gano|lep|tic

or|gano|met|al|lic

or|ga|non

or|gano|
        phos|phate

or|gano|
        phos|phorus

or|gano|
        thera|peut|ic

or|gano|ther|apy

or|ganum

or|gana

or|ganza

or|gan|zine

or|gasm

or|gas|mic

or|gas|mic|al|ly

or|gas|tic

or|gas|tic|al|ly

or|geat

or|gi|as|tic

or|gi|as|tic|al|ly

or|gone

or|gu|lous

orgy
  or|gies

oribi
  pl. oribi or ori|bis

ori|chalc

ori|chal|cum

oricl

Ori|ent East

ori|ent align; lustrous

orien|tal

orien|talia

orien|tal|ise Br. var. of orientalize

orien|tal|ism

orien|tal|ist

orien|tal|ize
  orien|tal|iz|ing

orien|tal|ly

orien|tate
  orien|tat|ing

orien|ta|tion

orien|ta|tion|al

orien|teer

ori|fice

ori|flamme

ori|gami

ori|ganum

Ori|gen Christian scholar

ori|gin

ori|gin|al

ori|gin|al|ity

ori|gin|al|ly

ori|gin|ate

ori|gin|at|ing

ori|gin|ation

ori|gina|tive

ori|gin|ator

Ori|mul|sion
  trademark

O-ring

Ori|noco

ori|ole

Orion mythical hunter; constellation

Orisha
  pl. Orisha or Orishas
  Nigerian god

ori|son

Orissa state, India

Oriya
  pl. Oriya or Ori|yas

Ork|ney

Or|lando

orle *Heraldry* border; cf. awl

Or|lean|ist

Or|leans
  French Orléans

Orlon *trademark*

orlop

Or|mazd alternative name for **Ahura Mazda**

ormer

or|molu

Ormuz var. of Hormuz

or|na|ment

or|na|men|tal

or|na|men|tal|ism

or|na|men|tal|ist

or|na|men|tal|ly

or|na|men|ta|tion

or|nate

or|nate|ly

or|nate|ness

or|neri|ness

or|nery

or|ni|thine

or|ni|this|chian

or|ni|tho|logic|al

or|ni|tho|logic|al|ly

or|ni|tholo|gist

or|ni|thol|ogy

or|ni|tho|
        mimo|saur

or|ni|tho|pod

or|nith|opter

or|nith|osis

oro|gen

oro|gen|esis

oro|gen|et|ic

oro|gen|ic

or|ogeny

oro|graph|ic

oro|graph|ic|al

or|og|raphy

Oromo
  pl. Oromo or Oromos

Oron|tes

oro|pen|dola

oro|pha|ryn|geal

oro|phar|ynx
  oro|pha|ryn|ges or
  oro|phar|ynxes

oro|tund

oro|tund|ity

or|phan

or|phan|age

or|phan|hood

or|phan|ise Br. var. of orphanize

or|phan|ize

or|phan|iz|ing

or|phar|ion

Orph|ean

Orph|eus mythical poet

Orph|ic

Orph|ism

or|phrey

or|pi|ment

orpin var. of orpine

or|pine

Or|ping|ton

or|rery
  or|rer|ies

orris

Orsk

or|tan|ique

Or|tega, Dan|iel president of Nicaragua

O|rtega y Gas|set, José philosopher

ortho|chro|mat|ic

ortho|clase
ortho|cone
ortho|con|ic
ortho|don|tia
ortho|don|tic
ortho|don|tic|al|ly
ortho|don|tist
Ortho|dox of Judaism or the Eastern Church
ortho|dox generally
ortho|dox|ly
ortho|doxy
  ortho|dox|ies
ortho|drom|ic
ortho|ep|ic
ortho|ep|ist
ortho|epy
ortho|gen|esis
ortho|gen|esist
ortho|gen|et|ic
ortho|gen|et|ic|al|ly
or|thog|nath|ous
or|thog|on|al
or|thog|on|al|ity
or|thog|on|al|ly
or|thog|raph|er
ortho|graph|ic
ortho|graph|ic|al
ortho|graph|ic|al|ly
or|thog|raphy
  or|thog|raph|ies
ortho|morph|ic
ortho|nec|tid
Ortho|nec|tida
ortho|nor|mal
ortho|nor|mal|ity
ortho|nor|mal|iza|tion
ortho|paed|ic Br.
ortho|paed|ic|al|ly Br.
ortho|paed|ist Br.
ortho|ped|ic US
ortho|ped|ic|al|ly US
ortho|ped|ist US
ortho|phos|phate
ortho|phos|phor|ic
ortho|psy|chi|atric
ortho|psych|iatrist
ortho|psych|iatry

orth|opter =
  ornithopter
Orth|op|tera
orth|op|ter|an
orth|op|ter|oid
orth|op|ter|ous
orth|op|tics
orth|op|tist
ortho|pyr|ox|ene
ortho|rexia
  ner|vosa
ortho|rex|ic
ortho|rhom|bic
orth|osis
  orth|oses
ortho|stat
ortho|stat|ic
or|thos|tichy
  or|thos|tich|ies
orth|ot|ic
ortho|tist
ortho|trop|ic
or|to|lan
Orton, Joe playwright
Orton|esque
Oruro
Or|vi|eto town, Italy; wine; cf.
Oviedo
Or|well, George writer
Or|well|ian
oryx
orzo
os
  ossa
  bone
os
  ora
  bodily opening
Osage
  pl. Osage or Osages
Osaka
Os|bert
Os|borne, John dramatist
Oscan
Oscar name; trademark film award
oscar fish
os|cil|late
  os|cil|lat|ing

os|cil|la|tion
os|cil|la|tor
os|cil|la|tory
os|cil|lo|gram
os|cil|lo|graph
os|cil|lo|graph|ic
os|cil|log|raphy
os|cil|lo|scope
os|cil|lo|scop|ic
os|cine
Osco-Umbrian
os|cula pl. of osculum
os|cu|lant
os|cu|lar adj.
os|cu|late
  os|cu|lat|ing
os|cu|la|tion
os|cu|la|tory
os|cu|lum
  os|cula
Osh|awa
oshi
  pl. oshi
osier
Osi|jek
Os|ir|ian
Os|iris Egyptian god
Oslo
Osman founder of Ottoman dynasty
Os|manli
osmic
os|mic|al|ly
os|mium
osmo|lal|ity concentration per kilogram
osmo|lar|ity concentration per litre
os|mom|eter
osmo|met|ric
osmo|met|ric|al|ly
os|mom|etry
osmo|regu|la|tion
osmo|regu|la|tory
os|mose
  os|mos|ing
os|mo|sis
os|mot|ic
os|mot|ic|al|ly
os|mund
os|munda

Os|na|brück
osna|burg
os|prey
Ossa, Mt
os|sein
os|se|ous
Os|sete
Os|se|tia
Os|se|tian
Os|set|ic
Ossi
  Ossis or Os|sies
  offensive East German; cf. Aussie
Os|sian legendary Irish warrior
Os|si|an|ic
os|sicle
Ossie name; cf. Ossi
Ossie var. of Aussie; cf. Ossi
os|sif|ic
os|si|fi|ca|tion
os|sify
  os|si|fies
  os|si|fied
  os|si|fy|ing
Os|sin|ing
osso bucco var. of osso buco
osso buco
os|su|ary
  os|su|ar|ies
Ost|ade, Adri|aen van painter
Oste|ich|thyes
os|te|itis
Ost|end
os|ten|si|bil|ity
os|ten|sible
os|ten|sibly
os|ten|sive
os|ten|sive|ly
os|ten|sive|ness
os|ten|sory
  os|ten|sor|ies
os|ten|ta|tion
os|ten|ta|tious
os|ten|ta|tious|ly
os|ten|ta|tious|ness
osteo|arth|rit|ic
osteo|arth|ritis

osteo|blast
osteo|blast|ic
osteo|clast
osteo|clast|ic
osteo|cyte
osteo|cyt|ic
osteo|gen|esis
osteo|gen|esis
im|per|fecta
osteo|gen|et|ic
osteo|gen|ic
oste|oid
osteo|logic|al
osteo|logic|al|ly
oste|olo|gist
oste|ology
oste|oly|sis
osteo|lyt|ic
osteo|mal|acia
osteo|mal|acic
osteo|mye|litis
osteo|necro|sis
osteo|necrot|ic
osteo|path
osteo|path|ic
osteo|path|ic|al|ly
oste|op|athy
osteo|phyte
osteo|phyt|ic
osteo|por|osis
osteo|por|ot|ic
osteo|sar|coma
osteo|sar|comas or
osteo|sar|co|mata
osteo|sper|mum
osteo|tome
oste|ot|omy
oste|oto|mies
Ostia
os|tin|ato
os|tin|atos or
os|tin|ati
osti|ole
ost|ium
ostia
ost|ler
Ost|mark
Ost|poli|tik
os|tra|cise Br. var.
of ostracize
os|tra|cism
os|tra|cize
os|tra|ciz|ing

ostra|cod
Ostra|coda
os|traco|derm
os|tra|con
os|traca
os|tra|kon var. of
ostracon
Os|trava
os|trich
Os|tro|goth
Os|tro|goth|ic
Ost|wald,
Fried|rich
Wil|helm chemist
Os|wald, St
Os|wald, Lee
Har|vey alleged
assassin
Otago
otaku
otal|gia
other
other|ness
other|where
other|wise
other-worldli|ness
other-worldly
Oth|man var. of
Osman
Otho, Mar|cus
Sal|vius Roman
emperor
otic
oti|ose
oti|ose|ly
oti|os|ity
Otis name
Otis, Eli|sha
inventor
ot|itis ex|terna
ot|itis in|terna
ot|itis media
oto|cyst
oto|laryn|go|
logic|al
oto|laryn|golo|gist
oto|laryn|gol|ogy
oto|lith
oto|lith|ic
oto|logic|al
ot|olo|gist
otol|ogy
Oto|man|guean

Otomi
pl. Otomi
O'Toole, Peter
actor
oto|plasty
oto|plas|ties
oto|rhino|laryn|
golo|gist
oto|rhino|laryn|
gol|ogy
oto|scler|osis
oto|scler|ot|ic
oto|scope
oto|scop|ic
oto|scop|ic|al|ly
oto|toxic
oto|tox|icity
Ot|ranto, Strait of
ot|tava rima
Ot|tawa
otter
Otto king of the
Germans
Otto, Niko|laus
Au|gust engineer
otto attar
otto|cento
Otto|line
Ot|to|man +s dyn-
asty of Osman;
Turk
ot|to|man +s seat
Otway, Thomas
playwright
ou man
ouens or ous
ou bird
oua|bain
Ouaga|dou|gou
ouana|niche
ou|baas
ou|bli|ette
ou|boet
oud Arab lute
Ouden|arde
Oudh region, India
ought as in 'ought
to do something';
archaic nought; cf.
aught
oughtn't
ou|giya var. of
ouguiya
ou|guiya

Ouida novelist
Ouija board
trademark
ou|klip
Oulu
ounce
our belonging to us;
cf. hour
ouro|bor|ic var. of
uroboric
ouro|boros var. of
uroboros
ours the one(s)
belonging to us; cf.
hours
our|self non-
standard
our|selves
Ouse
ousel var. of ouzel
oust|er
out not in etc.; cf.
owt
out|act
out|age
out-and-outer
out|back
out|back|er
out|bal|ance
out|bal|an|cing
out|bid
out|bid|ding
out|board
out|bound
out|box
out|brave
out|brav|ing
out|break
out|breed
out|bred
out|build|ing
out|burst
out|call
out|cast person cast
out
out|caste
out|cast|ing
(cause to be)
Indian without
caste
out|class
out|come
out|com|pete
out|com|pet|ing

out|crop
  out|cropped
  out|crop|ping
out|cross
out|cry
  out|cries
out|curve
out|dance
  out|dan|cing
out|date
  out|dat|ing
out|dated|ness
out|dis|tance
  out|dis|tan|cing
out|do
  out|does
  out|did
  out|do|ing
  out|done
out|door
out|doors|man
  out|doors|men
out|doorsy
out|draw
  out|drew
  out|drawn
out|drink
  out|drank
  out|drunk
out|drive
  out|drove
  out|driving
  out|driven
outer
outer|most
outer|wear
out|face
  out|facing
out|fall
out|field
out|field|er
out|fight
  out|fought
out|fit
  out|fit|ted
  out|fit|ting
out|fit|ter
out|flank
out|flow
out|flung
out|fly
  out|flies
  out|flew
  out|fly|ing
  out|flown

out|fox
out|gas
  out|gases
  out|gassed
  out|gas|sing
out|gen|eral
  out|gen|er|alled Br.
  out|gen|er|aled US
  out|gen|er|al|ling Br.
  out|gen|er|al|ing US
out|go
  out|goes
  out|went
  out|going
  out|gone
out|gross
out-group
out|grow
  out|grew
  out|grown
out|growth
out|guess
out|gun
  out|gunned
  out|gun|ning
out-half +s
out|haul
out|hit
  out|hit|ting
out|house
  out|hous|ing
outie
out|ing
out|jie
out|jockey
out|jump
out|jut|ting
out|land|er
out|land|ish
out|land|ish|ly
out|land|ish|ness
out|last
out|law
out|law|ry
out|lay
out|let
out|lier
out|line
  out|lin|ing
out|liner
out|live
  out|liv|ing

out|look
out|ly|ing
out|man
  out|manned
  out|man|ning
out|man|euver US
out|man|oeuvre
  out|man|oeuv|ring Br.
out|match
out|meas|ure
  out|meas|ur|ing
out|migrant
out|migra|tion
out|moded
out|moded|ly
out|moded|ness
out|most
out|muscle
  out|muscl|ing
out|num|ber
out|pace
  out|pacing
out|patient
out|per|form
out|per|form|ance
out|place|ment
out|play
out|point
out|poll
out|port
out|post
out|pour|ing
out|punch
out|put
  out|put or
  out|put|ted
  out|put|ting
out|put|ter
out|race
  out|racing
out|rage
  out|raging
out|ra|geous
out|ra|geous|ly
out|ra|geous|ness
out|ran
out|range
  out|ran|ging
out|rank
outré
out|reach
Outre|mer

out|ride
  out|rode
  out|rid|ing
  out|rid|den
out|rider
out|rigged
out|rig|ger
out|right
out|rival
  out|rivalled Br.
  out|rivaled US
  out|rival|ling Br.
  out|rival|ing US
outro +s
out|rode
out|run
  out|ran
  out|run|ning
out|rush
out|sail
out|sat
out|score
  out|scor|ing
out|sell
  out|sold
out|sert
out|set
out|shine
  out|shone
  out|shin|ing
out|shoot
  out|shot
out|shop
  out|shopped
  out|shop|ping
out|side
out|sider
out|sing
  out|sang
  out|sung
out|sit
  out|sat
  out|sit|ting
out|size
out|sized
out|skirts
out|smart
out|sold
out|sole
out|source
  out|sour|cing
out|span
  out|spanned
  out|span|ning

out|spend
  out|spent
out|spoken
out|spoken¦ly
out|spoken|ness
out|spread
out|sprint
out|stand|ing
out|stand|ing¦ly
out|stare
  out|star|ing
out|sta¦tion
out|stay
out|stretch
out|strip
  out|stripped
  out|strip|ping
out|swing
  out|swing¦er
out|swing|ing
out-take
out-talk
out-think
  out-thought
out-thrust
out-turn
out|value
  out|valu¦ing
out|vote
  out|vot¦ing
out|wait
out|walk
out|ward
outward-bound
  going away
Out|ward Bound
  organization
  trademark
out|ward¦ly
out|ward|ness
out|wards
out|wash
out|watch
out|wear
  out|wore
  out|worn
out|weigh
out|went
out|wit
  out|wit|ted
  out|wit|ting
out|with
out|wore
out|work

out|work¦er
out|work¦ing
out|world
out|world¦er
out|worn
ouzel
ouzo +s
ova pl. of ovum
oval
ov|albu¦min
oval|ity
oval¦ly
oval|ness
Ov¦ambo
  pl. Ov¦ambo or
  Ov¦am|bos
Ov¦ambo|land
ovar¦ian
ovari|ec¦tomy
  ovari|ec¦to¦mies
ovari|ot¦omy
  ovari|oto¦mies
ovar|itis
ovary
  ovar|ies
ovate
ova|tion
oven
oven|bird
oven|proof
oven|ware
over cf. ova
over-abundance
over-abundant
over-abundant¦ly
over|achieve
  over|achiev¦ing
over|achieve|ment
over|achiever
over|act
over|active
over|activ|ity
over|age surplus;
  over age limit
over|all
over|alled
over|am¦bi¦tion
over|am¦bi¦tious
over|am¦bi¦tious¦ly
over|anx¦iety
over|anx¦ious
over|anx¦ious¦ly
over|arch

over|arm
over|ate past tense
  of overeat; cf.
  overrate
over|awe
  over|aw¦ing
over|bal¦ance
  over|bal|an¦cing
over|bear
  over|bore
  over|borne
over|bear|ing¦ly
over|bear|ing|ness
over|bid
  over|bid|ding
over|bid|der
over|bite
over|blouse
over|blow
  over|blew
  over|blown
over|board
over|bold
over|bold¦ly
over|bold|ness
over|book
over|boot
over|bore
over|borne
over|bought
over|breathe
  over|breath¦ing
over|breed
  over|bred
over|bridge
over|brim
  over|brimmed
  over|brim|ming
over|build
  over|built
over|bur¦den
over|bur¦den|some
over|busy
over|buy
  over|bought
over|call
  over|came
over|cap¦acity
over|cap¦it¦al¦
    isa¦tion
  Br. var. of
  over|capitalization
over|cap¦it¦al¦ise
  Br. var. of

overcapitalize
over|cap¦it¦al¦
    iza¦tion
over|cap¦it¦al¦ize
over|cap¦it¦al¦iz¦ing
over|care|ful
over|care|ful¦ly
over|cast
over|cau¦tion
over|cau¦tious
over|cau¦tious¦ly
over|cau¦tious|ness
over|charge
over|char¦ging
over|check
over|class
over|clock
over|cloud
over|coat
over|come
  over|came
over|com¦ing
over|com¦mit
over|com¦mit¦ted
over|com¦mit|ting
over|com¦mit|ment
over|com¦pen|sate
over|com¦pen|
    sat¦ing
over|com¦pen|
    sat¦ing¦ly
over|com¦pen|
    sa¦tion
over|com¦pen|
    sa¦tory
over|con|fi¦dence
over|con|fi¦dent
over|con|fi¦dent¦ly
over|cook
over|crit¦ic¦al
over|crop
  over|cropped
  over|crop|ping
over|crowd
over|curi¦os|ity
over|curi¦ous
over|damp
over|date
over|dat¦ing
over|deli¦cacy
over|deli¦cate
over|de¦ter¦min|
    ation

over|de|ter|mine
over|de|ter|min|ing
over|de|velop
over|devel|op|ment
over|do
  over|does
  over|did
  over|do|ing
  over|done
over|dog
over|dos|age
over|dose
  over|dos|ing
over|draft
over|dra|mat|ic
over|drama|tise *Br.*
  var. of
  overdramatize
over|drama|tize
  over|drama|tiz|ing
over|draw
  over|drew
  over|drawn
over|dress
over|drink
  over|drank
  over|drunk
over|drive
  over|drove
  over|driv|ing
  over|driven
over|dry
  over|dries
  over|dried
  over|dry|ing
over|dub
  over|dubbed
  over|dub|bing
over|due
over|dye
  over|dye|ing
over|eager
over|eager|ly
over|eager|ness
over|eat
  over|ate
  over|eaten
over|eat|er
over-egg
over-elabor|ate
  over-elaborating
over-elabor|ate|ly
over-elabor|ate|
            ness
over-elabor|ation

over|emo|tion|al
over|emo|tion|al|ly
over|empha|sis
over|empha|sise *Br.*
  var. of
  overemphasize
over|empha|size
  over|empha|siz|ing
over|enthu|si|asm
over|enthu|si|as|tic
over|enthu|si|
          as|tic|al|ly
over|esti|mate
  over|esti|mat|ing
over|esti|mation
over|ex|cit|able
over|ex|cite
  over|ex|cit|ing
over|ex|cite|ment
over-exercise
  over-exercis|ing
over|ex|ert
over|ex|er|tion
over|ex|pose
  over|ex|pos|ing
over|ex|pos|ure
over|ex|tend
over|ex|ten|sion
over|fall
over|fa|mil|iar
over|fa|mil|iar|ity
over|fa|tigue
over|feed
  over|fed
over|fill
over|fine
over|fish
over|flight
over|flow
over|fly
  over|flies
  over|flew
  over|fly|ing
  over|flown
over|fold
over|fond
over|fond|ly
over|fond|ness
over|ful|fil *Br.*
  over|ful|filled
  over|ful|fil|ling
over|ful|fill *US*
over|full
over|fund

over|gar|ment
over|gen|er|al|
          isa|tion
  Br. var. of
  overgeneralization
over|gen|er|al|ise
  Br. var. of
  overgeneralize
over|gen|er|al|
          iza|tion
over|gen|er|al|ize
over|gen|er|al|
          iz|ing
over|gen|er|os|ity
over|gen|er|ous
over|gen|er|ous|ly
over|glaze
over|grain|er
over|graze
  over|graz|ing
over|ground
over|grow
  over|grew
  over|grown
over|growth
over|hand
over|hang
  over|hung
over|hasti|ly
over|hasty
over|haul
over|head
over|hear
  over|heard
over|heat
over|hit
  over|hit|ting
over|hung
over|hype
  over|hyp|ing
Over|ijs|sel
over|in|dulge
  over|in|dul|ging
over|in|dul|gence
over|in|dul|gent
over|in|flated
over|in|fla|tion
over|in|sur|ance
over|issue
  over|issu|ing
over|joyed
over|keen
over|kill
over|laden

over|laid
over|lain
over|land
over|land|er
over|lap
  over|lapped
  over|lap|ping
over|large
over|lay
  over|laid
over|layer
over|leaf
over|leap
  over|leaped
  Br. also over|leapt
over|lie
  over|lay
  over|ly|ing
  over|lain
over|load
over|lock
over|lock|er
over|long
over|look
over|look|er
over|lord
over|lord|ship
over|loud
over|ly
  over|ly|ing
over|man
  pl. over|men
  v. over|mans
  over|manned
  over|man|ning
over|man|tel
over|master
over|mastery
over|match
over|mighty
over|much
over|nice
over|nice|ness
over|night
over|night|er
over-optimism
over-optimis|tic
over-optimis|tic|
            al|ly
over|pack
over|paid
over|paint
over|part|ed

over-particu|lar
over|pass
over|pay
  over|paid
over|pay|ment
over|pitch
over|play
over|plus
over|popu|late
  over|popu|lat|ing
over|popu|la|tion
over|power
over|power|ing|ly
over|pre|scribe
  over|pre|scrib|ing
  over|pre|scrip|tion
over|price
  over|pricing
over|print
over|pro|duce
  over|pro|du|cing
over|pro|duc|tion
over|proof
over|pro|tect
over|pro|tec|tion
over|pro|tect|ive
over|pro|tect|ive|
                ness
over|quali|fied
over|ran
over|rate
  over|rat|ing
  rate too highly; cf.
  overate
over|reach
over|reach|er
over|react
over|reac|tion
over-refine
  over-refining
over-refine|ment
over-report
over-represent
over-
  represen|ta|tion
over|ride
  over|rode
  over|rid|ing
  over|rid|den
over|rider
over|ripe
over|ruff
over|rule
  over|rul|ing

over|run
  over|ran
  over|run|ning
over|sail
over|sam|pling
over|saw
over|scan
over|scru|pu|lous
over|scru|pu|lous|
                ness
over|sea *Br.* var. of
  overseas
over|seas abroad
over|see
  over|sees
  over|saw
  over|see|ing
  over|seen
  supervise
over|seer
over|sell
  over|sold
over|sen|si|tive
over|sen|si|tive|
                ness
over|sen|si|tiv|ity
over|set
  over|set|ting
over|sew
  past participle
  over|sewn or
  over|sewed
over|sexed
over|shadow
over|shirt
over|shoe
over|shoot
  over|shot
over|side
over|sight failure;
  supervision
over|sim|pli|fi|
                ca|tion
over|sim|plify
  over|sim|pli|fies
  over|sim|pli|fied
  over|sim|pli|fy|ing
over|site concrete
  layer
over|size
over|sized
over|skirt
over|slaugh
over|sleep
  over|slept

over|sleeve
over|sold
over|so|lici|tous
over|so|lici|tude
over|soul
over|spe|cial|
                isa|tion
  Br. var. of
  overspecialization
over|spe|cial|ise *Br.*
  var. of
  overspecialize
over|spe|cial|
                iza|tion
over|spe|cial|ize
  over|spe|cial|iz|ing
over|spend
  over|spent
over|spill
over|spin
over|spray
over|spread
over|staff
over|state
  over|stat|ing
over|state|ment
over|stay
  over|stay|er
over|steer
over|step
  over|stepped
  over|step|ping
over|stimu|late
  over|stimu|lat|ing
over|stimu|la|tion
over|stitch
over|stock
over|storey
over|strain
over|stress
over|stretch
over|strike
  over|strik|ing
over|strung
over|study
  over|studies
  over|studied
  over|study|ing
over|stuff
over|sub|scribe
  over|sub|scrib|ing
over|subtle
over|sup|ply
  over|sup|plies

over|sup|plied
over|sup|ply|ing
over|sus|cep|tible
over|sweet
overt
over|take
  over|took
  over|tak|ing
  over|taken
over|task
over|tax
over|tax|ation
over|throw
  over|thrown
over|thrust
over|time
over|tip
  over|tipped
  over|tip|ping
over|tire
  over|tir|ing
overt|ly
overt|ness
over|tone
over|took
over|top
  over|topped
  over|top|ping
over|trade
  over|trad|ing
over|train
over|trick
over|trou|sers
over|trump
over|ture
over|turn
over|type
  over|typ|ing
over|use
  over|us|ing
over|valu|ation
over|value
  over|valu|ing
over|view
over|water
over|wear
over|ween|ing
over|ween|ing|ly
over|ween|ing|ness
over|weight
over|whelm
over|whelm|ing|ly
over|whelm|ing|
                ness

over|wind
  over|wound
over|win|ter
over|work
over|wrap
  over|wrapped
  over|wrap|ping
over|write
  over|wrote
  over|writ|ing
  over|writ|ten
over|wrought
over|zeal|ous
Ovid poet
ovi|ducal
ovi|duct
ovi|duct|al
Ovi|edo city, Spain;
  cf. Orvieto
ovi|form
ovine
ovi|par|ity
ovip|ar|ous
ovi|posit
ovi|pos|ition
ovi|posi|tor
ovoid
ovolo
  ovoli
ovo|tes|tis
  ovo|tes|tes
ovo|vivi|par|ity
ovo|vi|vip|ar|ous
ovu|lar
ovu|late
  ovu|lat|ing
ovu|la|tion
ovu|la|tory
ovule
ovum
  ova
ow exclam.
owe
  owing
  be indebted to
  return; cf. O, oh
Owen, Rich|ard
  anatomist
Owen, Rob|ert phil-
  anthropist
Owen, Wil|fred
  poet
Owens, Jesse ath-
  lete

owl|ery
  owl|er|ies
owlet
owlet-nightjar
owl|ish
  owl|ish|ly
  owl|ish|ness
owl-like
owner
own|er|less
own|er|ship
owt anything; cf.
  out
ox
  oxen
oxa|cil|lin
ox|al|late
ox|alis
oxa|zole
oxbow
Ox|bridge
oxen
oxer
ox-eye daisy
Oxfam
Ox|ford city,
  England
ox|ford shoe; cloth
Ox|ford bags
Ox|ford|ian
Ox|ford|shire
ox|herd
ox|hide
oxic
oxi|dant
oxi|dase
oxi|da|tion
oxi|da|tion|al
oxi|da|tive
oxide
oxi|dis|able Br. var.
  of oxidizable
oxi|disa|tion Br.
  var. of oxidization
oxi|dise Br. var. of
  oxidize
oxi|diser Br. var. of
  oxidizer
oxi|diz|able
oxi|diza|tion
oxi|dize
  oxi|diz|ing
oxi|dizer

ox|im|eter
ox|im|etry
oxi|sol
oxlip
Oxon = Oxfordshire;
  of Oxford
  University
Ox|on|ian
ox|peck|er
ox|tail
oxter
Oxus
oxy|acet|yl|ene
oxy|acid
oxy|an|ion
oxy|codone
Oxy|Con|tin
  trademark
oxy|gen
oxy|gen|ate
oxy|gen|at|ing
oxy|gen|ation
oxy|gen|ator
oxy|gen|ic
oxy|gen|ise Br. var.
  of oxygenize
oxy|gen|ize
oxy|gen|iz|ing
oxy|gen|ous
oxy|haemo|glo|bin
  Br.
oxy|hemo|glo|bin
  US
oxy|moron
oxy|mor|on|ic
ox|yn|tic
oxy|tetra|cyc|line
oxy|to|cic
oxy|to|cin
oxy|tone
oy var. of oi
oyer and
  ter|miner
oyes var. of oyez
oyez
oys|ter
oys|ter|catch|er
oy veh var. of oy
  vey
oy vey
Oz = Australia;
  Australia
Oza|lid trademark

Ozark
ozo|cer|ite var. of
  ozokerite
ozo|ker|ite
ozone
ozon|ic
ozon|ide
ozon|isa|tion Br.
  var. of ozonization
ozon|ise Br. var. of
  ozonize
ozon|iser Br. var. of
  ozonizer
ozon|iza|tion
ozon|ize
  ozon|iz|ing
ozon|izer
ozono|sphere
Ozzie var. of Aussie;
  cf. Ossi

pa father; cf. pah,
  par, parr
paan
pa'anga
  pl. pa'anga
Paarl
pab|lum var. of
  pabulum
pabu|lum
paca rodent; cf.
  packer
paca|mac var. of
  pakamac
paca|rana
PACE = Police and
  Criminal Evidence
  Act
pace
  pacing
pace with due
  respect to
pace|maker
pace|man
  pace|men
pacer
pace|set|ter
pacey var. of pacy

pacha Turkish
officer; var. of
pasha

Pach|el|bel,
Jo|hann composer

pa|chinko

pa|chisi US
trademark

Pa|chuca de Soto

pa|chuco +s

pachy|cephalo|
saur

pachy|derm

pachy|der|mal

pachy|der|ma|tous

pachy|der|mic

pachy|san|dra

pachy|tene

Pa|cif|ic Ocean

pa|cif|ic peaceful

pacif|ic|al|ly

paci|fi|ca|tion

paci|fi|ca|tory

paci|fier

paci|fism

paci|fist

pacify
  paci|fies
  paci|fied
  paci|fy|ing

Pa|cin|ian

Pa|cino, Al actor

pack|able

pack|age
  pack|aging

pack|ager

pack|cloth

pack|er person who
packs; cf. paca

packet

packet|ise Br. var.
of packetize

packet|ize
  packet|iz|ing

pack|frame

pack|horse

pack|man
  pack|men
pedlar; cf. Pac-Man

pack|sack

pack|sad|dle

pack|thread

Pac-Man trademark
fictional character;

cf. packman

pact agreement; cf.
packed

pacu
  pl. pacu

pacy
  paci|er
  paci|est

pad
  pad|ded
  pad|ding

Pa|dang

pa|dauk

Pad|ding|ton

pad|dle

pad|dling

paddle|ball

paddle|fish

pad|dler

pad|dock

Paddy
  Pad|dies
name: offensive
Irishman

paddy
  pad|dies
rage; rice field

paddy|melon gourd
plant

pade|melon wallaby

Pade|rew|ski,
Ig|nacy Jan pianist

pad|kos

pad|lock

pad|loper

Padma

pa|douk var. of
padauk

padre

padri Ind. var. of
padre

pa|drino +s

pa|drona

pa|drone

pad|saw

pad thai

Padua

Pad|uan

padua|soy

paean song of
praise; cf. paeon,
peon

paed|er|ast Br. var.
of pederast

paed|er|as|tic Br.
var. of pederastic

paed|er|asty Br. var.
of pederasty

paedi|at|ric Br.
US pediatric

paedia|tri|cian Br.
US pediatrician

paedi|at|rics Br.
US pediatrics

paedo|don|tics Br.
US pedodontics

paedo|don|tist Br.
US pedodontist

paedo|gen|esis

paedo|gen|etic

paedo|morph|ic

paedo|morph|osis

paedo|phile Br.
US pedophile

paedo|philia Br.
US pedophilia

paedo|phil|iac Br.
US pedophiliac

pa|ella

paeon metrical foot;
cf. paean, pean,
peon

pae|on|ic

pae|ony var. of
peony

Pa|galu

Pagan town, Burma

pagan

Paga|nini, Nic|colò
violinist

pa|gan|ise Br. var.
of paganize

pa|gan|ish

pa|gan|ism

pa|gan|ize
pa|gan|iz|ing

Page, Fred|erick
Hand|ley aircraft
designer

page
  pa|ging

pa|geant

pa|geant|ry

page|boy

pager

Paget's dis|ease

pa|ginal

pa|gin|ate
pa|gin|at|ing

pa|gin|ation

Pa|gnol, Mar|cel
dramatist

pa|goda

pagri

pah exclam.; cf. pa,
par, parr

Pa|hang

Pah|lavi writing
system; Iranian
dynasty

pa|hoe|hoe

paid

pai|deia

Paign|ton

pail bucket; cf. pale

pail|ful

Pai|lin

pail|lasse var. of
palliasse

pail|lette

pain hurt; cf. pane

Paine, Thomas
political writer

Paine Towers

pain|ful

pain|ful|ly

pain|ful|ness

pain|kill|er

pain|kill|ing

pain|less

pain|less|ly

pain|less|ness

pains|tak|ing

pains|tak|ing|ly

pains|tak|ing|ness

paint|able

paint|ball

paint|ball|er

paint|ball|ing

paint|box

paint|brush

paint|er

paint|er|li|ness

paint|er|ly

paint|ing

paint|stick

paint|work

painty
  paint|ier
  painti|est

pair two; cf. pare, pear, *père*

pair|ing forming pair; cf. paring

pair royal
  pairs royal

pair|wise

paisa
  paise
  present-day Indian, Pakistani, and Nepali currency; cf. **pice**

pai|san

pai|sano +s

Pais|ley town, Scotland

pais|ley pattern

Pais|ley|ite

Pai|ute
  pl. **Pai|ute** or **Pai|utes**

pa|jama *US mod. Br.* pyjama

pa|ja|mas *US Br.* pyjamas

paka|mac

Paka|mak *trademark*

paka|poo

pakapu var. of **pakapoo**

pak choi

pa|keha

Pakh|tun var. of **Pashtun**

Paki *offensive*

Paki|stan

Paki|stani

pa|kora

pal
  palled
  pal|ling

pal|ace

pala|din

Palae|arc|tic *Br.*
  US **Palearctic**

palaeo|an|thro|po|logic|al *Br.*
  US **paleoanthropo-logical**

palaeo|an|thro|polo|gist *Br.*

US **paleoanthro-pologist**

palaeo|an|thro|pol|ogy *Br.*
  US **paleoanthropology**

palaeo|bio|logic|al *Br.*
  US **paleobiological**

palaeo|biolo|gist *Br.*
  US **paleobiologist**

palaeo|biol|ogy *Br.*
  US **paleobiology**

palaeo|botan|ic|al *Br.*
  US **paleobotanical**

palaeo|botan|ist *Br.*
  US **paleobotanist**

palaeo|bot|any *Br.*
  US **paleobotany**

Palaeo|cene *Br.*
  US **Paleocene**

palaeo|climate *Br.*
  US **paleoclimate**

palaeo|climat|ic *Br.*
  US **paleoclimatic**

palaeo|climat|olo|gist *Br.*
  US **paleoclimatologist**

palaeo|climat|ology *Br.*
  US **paleoclimatology**

palaeo-conser|va|tive *Br.*
  US **paleo-conservative**

palaeo|current *Br.*
  US **paleocurrent**

palaeo|demog|raphy *Br.*
  US **paleodemography**

palaeo|eco|logic|al *Br.*
  US **paleoecological**

palaeo|ecolo|gist *Br.*
  US **paleoecologist**

palaeo|ecol|ogy *Br.*
  US **paleoecology**

palaeo|envir|on|ment *Br.*

US **paleoenvironment**

palaeo|envir|on|men|tal *Br.*
  US **paleoenviron-mental**

Palaeo-Eskimo +s *Br.*
  US **Paleo-Eskimo**

palaeo|ethno|botan|ic|al *Br.*
  US **paleoethno-botanical**

palaeo|ethno|botan|ist *Br.*
  US **paleoethno-botanist**

palaeo|ethno|bot|any *Br.*
  US **paleoethnobotany**

Palaeo|gene *Br.*
  US **Paleogene**

palaeo|geog|raph|er *Br.*
  US **paleogeographer**

palaeo|geo|graph|ic|al *Br.*
  US **paleogeographical**

palaeo|geog|raphy *Br.*
  US **paleogeography**

palae|og|raph|er *Br.*
  US **paleographer**

palaeo|graph|ic *Br.*
  US **paleographic**

palaeo|graph|ic|al *Br.*
  US **paleographical**

palae|og|raphy *Br.*
  US **paleography**

Palaeo-Indian *Br.*
  US **Paleo-Indian**

palaeo|lati|tude *Br.*
  US **paleolatitude**

Palaeo|lith|ic *Br.*
  US **Paleolithic**

palaeo|mag|net|ic *Br.*
  US **paleomagnetic**

palaeo|mag|net|ism *Br.*
  US

paleomagnetism

palae|onto|logic|al *Br.*
  US **paleontological**

palae|on|tolo|gist *Br.*
  US **paleontologist**

palae|on|tology *Br.*
  US **paleontology**

palaeo|pal|lial *Br.*
  US **paleopallial**

palaeo|pal|lium *Br.*
  palaeo|pal|lia
  US **paleopallium**

palaeo|patho|logic|al *Br.*
  US

paleopathological

palaeo|path|olo|gist *Br.*
  US

paleopathologist

palaeo|path|ology *Br.*
  US **paleopathology**

palaeo|pole *Br.*
  US **paleopole**

Palaeo-Siberian *Br.*
  US **Paleo-Siberian**

palaeo|sol *Br.*
  US **paleosol**

palaeo|temp|era|ture *Br.*
  US

paleotemperature

Palaeo|tropic|al *Br.*
  US **Paleotropical**

Palaeo|zo|ic *Br.*
  US **Paleozoic**

pal|aes|tra

pa|lagi
  pl. **pa|lagi**

pal|ais
  pl. **pal|ais**

pal|ais de danse
  pl. **pal|ais de danse**

palak

pal|am|pore

pal|an|keen var. of **palanquin**

pal|an|quin

pa|lapa

Pa|lare var. of **Polari**

Pa¦lari var. of Polari

pal¦at¦abil¦ity

pal¦at¦able

pal¦at¦able¦ness

pal¦at¦ably

pal¦atal

pal¦at¦al¦isa¦tion *Br.* var. of palatalization

pal¦at¦al¦ise *Br.* var. of palatalize

pal¦at¦al¦iza¦tion

pal¦at¦al¦ize

pal¦at¦al¦iz¦ing

pal¦at¦al¦ly

pal¦ate roof of mouth; cf. palette, pallet

pa¦la¦tial

pa¦la¦tial¦ly

pa¦lat¦in¦ate

pal¦at¦ine

Palau Pacific islands; cf. pelau

Pa¦laung *pl.* Pa¦laung or Pa¦laungs

pa¦la¦ver

Pa¦la¦wan

pa¦lazzo pa¦lazzi or pa¦laz¦zos

pale pal¦ing paler pal¦est lacking colour; become pale; cf. pail

palea

pa¦leae

Pale¦arc¦tic *US Br.* Palaearctic

pale¦face

pale-faced

Pa¦lekh

pale¦ly in a pale way; cf. paly

Pal¦em¦bang

pale¦ness

Pa¦len¦que

paleo¦an¦thro¦po¦logic¦al *US Br.* palaeoanthropological

paleo¦an¦thro¦polo¦gist *US Br.* palaeoanthropologist

paleo¦an¦thro¦pol¦ogy *US Br.* palaeoanthropology

paleo¦bio¦logic¦al *US Br.* palaeobiological

paleo¦biolo¦gist *US Br.* palaeobiologist

paleo¦biol¦ogy *US Br.* palaeobiology

paleo¦botan¦ic¦al *US Br.* palaeobotanical

paleo¦botan¦ist *US Br.* palaeobotanist

paleo¦bot¦any *US Br.* palaeobotany

Paleo¦cene *US Br.* Palaeocene

paleo¦climate *US Br.* palaeoclimate

paleo¦climat¦ic *US Br.* palaeoclimatic

paleo¦climat¦olo¦gist *US Br.* palaeoclimatologist

paleo¦climat¦ology *US Br.* palaeoclimatology

paleo-conser¦va¦tive *US Br.* palaeo-conservative

paleo¦current *US Br.* palaeocurrent

paleo¦demog¦raphy *US Br.* palaeodemography

paleo¦eco¦logic¦al *US Br.* palaeoecological

paleo¦ecolo¦gist *US Br.* palaeoecologist

paleo¦ecol¦ogy *US Br.* palaeoecology

paleo¦envir¦on¦ment *US Br.* palaeoenvironment

paleo¦envir¦on¦ment¦al *US Br.* palaeoenvironmental

Paleo-Eskimo +s *US Br.* Palaeo-Eskimo

paleo¦ethno¦botan¦ic¦al *US Br.* palaeoethnobotanical

paleo¦ethno¦botan¦ist *US Br.* palaeoethnobotanist

paleo¦ethno¦bot¦any *US Br.* palaeoethnobotany

Paleo¦gene *US Br.* Palaeogene

paleo¦geog¦raph¦er *US Br.* palaeogeographer

paleo¦geo¦graph¦ic¦al *US Br.* palaeogeographical

paleo¦geog¦raphy *US Br.* palaeogeography

pale¦og¦raph¦er *US Br.* palaeographer

paleo¦graph¦ic *US Br.* palaeographic

paleo¦graph¦ic¦al *US Br.* palaeographical

pale¦og¦raphy *US Br.* palaeography

Paleo-Indian *US Br.* Palaeo-Indian

paleo¦lati¦tude *US Br.* palaeolatitude

Paleo¦lith¦ic *US Br.* Palaeolithic

paleo¦mag¦net¦ic *US Br.* palaeomagnetic

paleo¦mag¦net¦ism *US Br.* palaeomagnetism

pale¦onto¦logic¦al *US Br.* palaeontological

pale¦on¦tolo¦gist *US Br.* palaeontologist

pale¦on¦tology *US Br.* palaeontology

paleo¦pal¦lial *US Br.* palaeopallial

paleo¦pal¦lium *US* paleo¦pal¦lia *Br.* palaeopallium

paleo¦patho¦logic¦al *US Br.* palaeopathological

paleo¦path¦olo¦gist *US Br.* palaeopathologist

paleo¦path¦ology *US Br.* palaeopathology

paleo¦pole *US Br.* palaeopole

Paleo-Siberian *US Br.* Palaeo-Siberian

paleo¦sol *US Br.* palaeosol

paleo¦tem¦pera¦ture *US Br.* palaeotemperature

Paleo¦trop¦ic¦al *US Br.* Palaeotropical

Paleo¦zo¦ic *US Br.* Palaeozoic

Pa¦lermo

Pal¦es¦tine

Pal¦es¦tin¦ian

pa¦les¦tra var. of palaestra

Pal¦es¦trina, Gio¦vanni Pier¦luigi da composer

pal¦ette in painting; cf. palate, pallet

pal|frey
Pal|grave, Fran|cis
  anthologist
Pali language
pali cliff
  pali or palis
pali|lalia
pali|mony
pal|imp|sest
pal|imp|sest|ic
pal|in|drome
pal|in|drom|ic
pal|in|drom|ist
pal|ing
pal|in|gen|esis
pal|in|gen|et|ic
pal|in|ode
Palio
pal|is|ade
  pal|is|ad|ing
pal|ish
Pa|lissy, Ber|nard
  potter
Palk Strait
pall covering;
  become
  uninteresting; cf.
  pawl
Pal|la|dian
Pal|la|dian|ism
Pal|ladio, An|drea
  architect
pal|la|dium
  pal|la|dia
Pal|las Greek Myth-
  ology; asteroid
pal|las|ite
Pal|las's cat
pal|let mattress;
  platform; cf.
  palate, palette
pal|let|ise Br. var. of
  palletize
pal|let|ize
  pal|let|iz|ing
pal|lia pl. of
  pallium
pal|lial
pal|li|asse
pal|li|ate
  pal|li|at|ing
pal|li|ation
pal|lia|tive
pal|lia|tive|ly

pal|li|ator
pal|lid
pal|lid|ity
pal|lid|ly
pal|lid|ness
pal|lium
  pal|liums or pal|lia
Pall Mall street,
  London
pall-mall game
pal|lor
pally
  pal|lier
  pal|li|est
palm
Palma city, Majorca;
  cf. La Palma,
  Parma
pal|ma|ceous
pal|mar
pal|ma|rosa
Pal|mas town,
  Brazil; cf. Las
  Palmas
pal|mate
pal|mated
palm|cord|er
Palme, Olof prime
  minister of Sweden
Pal|mer, Ar|nold
  golfer
Pal|mer, Sam|uel
  artist
palm|er
Pal|mer|ston,
  Henry, Lord prime
  minister of Britain
pal|mette
pal|metto +s
palm|ful
pal|mier
palm|ist
palm|is|try
palmi|tate
pal|mit|ic
palm|top
palmy
  palm|ier
  palmi|est
Pal|myra ancient
  city, Syria
pal|myra tree
Palo Alto
Palo|mar, Mt

palo|mino +s
pa|looka
Pa|looka|ville
Pal|louse
  pl. Pa|louse or
  Pa|louses
palo|verde
palp|abil|ity
palp|able
palp|ably
palp|al
pal|pate
  pal|pat|ing
pal|pa|tion
pal|pe|bral
pal|pi|tant
pal|pi|tate
  pal|pi|tat|ing
pal|pi|ta|tion
pal|pus
  palpi
pals|grave
pal|stave
palsy
  pal|sies
  pal|sied
  palsy|ing
palsy-walsy
pal|ter
pal|ter|er
pal|tri|ness
pal|try
  pal|trier
  pal|tri|est
pal|udal
Palu|drine
  trademark
paly striped; cf.
  palely
palyno|logic|al
paly|nolo|gist
paly|nol|ogy
Pama-Nyungan
Pam|ela
Pamir Moun|tains
pam|pas
  pl. pam|pas
pam|per
pam|pero +s
pamph|let
pamph|let|eer
Pam|phylia
Pam|phyl|ian

Pam|plona
Pan Greek
  Mythology
pan
panned
pan|ning
  vessel; leaf; swing
  camera; cf. panne
pan var. of paan
pana|cea
pana|cean
pa|nache
pan|ada
Pana|dol trademark
pan-African
pan-African|ism
pan-African|ist
Pa|naji
Pan|ama in Central
  America
pan|ama hat
Pana|ma|nian
Pana|max
pan-American
pan-American|ism
pan-Arab
pan-Arabism
pana|tella
Panay
pan|cake
  pan|cak|ing
pan|cetta
pan|cha|karma
pan|chayat
Pan|chen Lama
pan|chro|mat|ic
pan|creas
pan|crea|tec|tomy
  pan|crea|
    tec|to|mies
pan|cre|at|ic
pan|crea|tin
pan|crea|titis
pan|creo|zymin
pan|cyto|penia
panda animal; cf.
  pander
pan|dal
pan|dan var. of
  pandanus
pan|da|nus
Pan|darus Greek
  Mythology

pan|dect
pan|dect|ist
pan|dem|ic
pan|de|mon|ium
pan|der indulge;
 go-between; cf.
 panda
Pan|dit, Vi|jaya
 Indian politician
pan|dit Hindu
 scholar; cf. **pundit**
Pan|dora *Greek
 Mythology*
pan|dora mollusc
Pan|dora's box
pan|dowdy
 pan|dow|dies
pane in window
 etc.; cf. **pain**
pa|neer
pan|egyr|ic
panel|egyr|ic|al
pan|egyr|ise *Br.* var.
 of panegyrize
pan|egyr|ist
pan|egyr|ize
 pan|egyr|iz|ing
panel
 pan|elled *Br.*
 pan|eled *US*
 pan|el|ling *Br.*
 pan|el|ing *US*
pan|el|list *US*
pan|el|list *Br.*
pan|enthe|ism
pan|enthe|ist|ic
pan|et|tone
 pan|et|toni
pan-European
pan|fish
pan|forte
pan|ful
panga
Pan|gaea
pan-German
pan-German|ic
pan-German|ism
Pan|gloss
Pan|gloss|ian
pan|go|lin
pan|han|dle
 pan|hand|ling
pan|hand|ler
Pan|hel|len|ic

panic
 pan|icked
 pan|ick|ing
pan|icky
pan|icle
pan|icled
pan-Indian
Pa|nini grammarian
pa|nino
 pa|nini
 sandwich
pani puri
panir var. of **paneer**
Pan|jabi var. of
 Punjabi
pan|jan|drum
Pan|jim
Panj|shir
Pank|hurst,
 Em|me|line,
 Chris|ta|bel, and
 Syl|via suffragettes
pan like
pan|mic|tic
pan|mixia
pan|nage
panne velvet; cf.
 pan
pan|nier
pan|ni|kin
pan|nist
Pan|no|nia
Pan|no|nian
pan|nus
pan|op|lied
pan|oply
 pan|op|lies
pan|op|tic
pan|op|ticon
pano|rama
pano|ram|ic
pano|ram|ic|al|ly
pan-pan
pan pipes
pan|psych|ism
pan|psych|ist
pan|sex|ual
pan|sex|ual|ity
pan|si|fied
pan|slav|ism
pan|slav|ist
pan|sper|mia
pan|stick

pansy
 pan|sies
pan|ta|lets *US*
pan|ta|lettes *Br.*
Pan|ta|loon *com-
 media dell'arte*
 character
pan|ta|loons trou-
 sers
Pan|ta|nal
pan|tec
pan|tech var. of
 pantec
pan|tech|ni|con
Pan|tel|le|ria
Pan|tha|lassa
pan|the|ism
pan|the|ist
pan|the|is|tic
pan|theon
pan|ther
pan|tie gir|dle var.
 of **panty girdle**
pan|ties
panti|hose var. of
 pantyhose
pan|tile
pan|tiled
pant|ing|ly
Pant|isoc|racy
Pant|iso|crat|ic
panto +s
Pan|toc|rator
panto|graph
panto|graph|ic
panto|mime
 panto|mim|ing
panto|mim|ic
Pan|tone *trademark*
panto|then|ate
pan|toum
pan|try
 pan|tries
pan|try|man
 pan|try|men
pant|suit
pant|sula
 pant|sulas or
 ma|pant|sula
pan|tun var. of
 pantoum
panty gir|dle
panty|hose

panty|waist
pan|zan|ella
pan|zer
Pao|lozzi, Ed|uardo
 artist
papa
papa|bile
pap|acy
 pap|acies
papad
Pap|ago
 pl. Pap|ago or
 Pap|agos
pa|pain
papal
pa|pa|lagi
 pl. pa|pa|lagi
pap|al|ist
pap|al|ly
Pap|an|dreou,
 An|dreas prime
 minister of Greece
pap|ar|azzo
 pap|ar|azzi
pa|pa|ver|aceous
pa|pa|ver|ine
pa|pa|ver|ous
papaw var. of
 pawpaw
pa|paya
Pa|pe|ete
paper
paper|back
paper|bark
paper|board
paper|chase
pa|per|er
paper|hanger
paper|knife
 pa|per|knives
paper|less
paper|maker
paper|mak|ing
paper|weight
paper|work
pa|pery
Paph|la|gonia
Paph|la|gon|ian
Papie|mento var. of
 Papiementu
Papie|mentu
pa|pier collé
 pa|piers collés

pa¦pier mâché
pa¦pil¦ion¦aceous
pa¦pili¦onid
pa¦pilla
  pa¦pil¦lae
pap¦il¦lary
pap¦il¦late
pap¦il¦loma
  pap¦il¦lo¦mas or
  pap¦il¦lo¦mata
pap¦il¦lon
pap¦il¦lose
pap¦ism
pap¦ist
pap¦is¦tic¦al
pap¦is¦try
pa¦poose child
pa¦pova¦virus
pap¦par¦delle
pap¦pose of a
  pappus
Pap¦pus
  mathematician
pap¦pus
  pappi
  hairs on thistle etc.
pappy
  pap¦pies
  pap¦pier
  pap¦pi¦est
pappy¦show
pap¦rika
Pap test
Pap¦uan
Papua New
  Guinea
Papua New
  Guin¦ean
pap¦ula
  pap¦ulae or
  pap¦ulas
  var. of papule
papu¦lar adj.
pap¦ule
papu¦lose
papu¦lous
papyro¦logic¦al
papyr¦olo¦gist
papyr¦ology
pa¦pyrus
  pa¦pyri or
  pa¦pyr¦uses
par
  parred

par¦ring
  average; equality;
  etc.; cf. pa, pah,
  parr
Pará state, Brazil
para paratrooper;
  paragraph
para-
  aminoben¦zoic
para¦basis
  para¦bases
para¦bi¦osis
para¦bi¦ot¦ic
par¦able
par¦ab¦ola
  par¦ab¦olas or
  par¦ab¦olae
para¦bol¦ic
para¦bol¦ic¦al
para¦bol¦ic¦al¦ly
par¦ab¦ol¦oid
para¦bol¦oid¦al
Para¦cel Is¦lands
para¦cellu¦lar
Para¦cel¦sus physician
para¦cen¦tesis
  para¦cen¦teses
para¦cen¦tric
para¦ceta¦mol
  pl. para¦ceta¦mol
  or para¦ceta¦mols
para¦chron¦ism
para¦chute
  para¦chut¦ing
  para¦chut¦ist
Para¦clete
para¦clin¦ic¦al
para¦crine
para¦crys¦tal
para¦crys¦tal¦line
par¦ade
par¦ad¦ing
par¦ader
para¦did¦dle
para¦digm
para¦dig¦mat¦ic
para¦dig¦mat¦ic¦al¦ly
para¦disa¦ical var.
  of paradisiacal
para¦disal
para¦dise
para¦dis¦iacal

para¦dis¦ical var. of
  paradisiacal
para¦dor
para¦dors or
  para¦dores
para¦dos
para¦dox
para¦dox¦ical
para¦dox¦ic¦al¦ly
para¦drop
  para¦dropped
  para¦drop¦ping
par¦aes¦the¦sia Br.
  par¦aes¦the¦siae or
  par¦aes¦the¦sias
  US paresthesia
par¦af¦fin
para¦gen¦esis
  para¦gen¦eses
para¦gen¦etic
para¦glide
  para¦gliding
para¦glider
para¦goge
para¦gogic
para¦gon model of
  excellence; cf.
  parergon
para¦
  gram¦mat¦ic¦al
para¦gram¦ma¦tism
para¦graph
para¦graph¦ic
Para¦guay
Para¦guay¦an
Para¦íba
para¦influ¦enza
para¦keet
para¦lan¦guage
par¦al¦de¦hyde
para¦legal
para¦leip¦om¦ena
  var. of
  paralipomena
para¦lin¦guis¦tic
para¦lip¦om¦ena
  sing.
para¦lip¦om¦enon
Para¦lip¦om¦enon
  book of Bible
para¦lip¦sis
par¦al¦lac¦tic
par¦al¦lax
par¦al¦lel

par¦al¦lel¦epi¦ped
par¦al¦lel¦isa¦tion
  Br. var. of
  parallelization
par¦al¦lel¦ise Br. var.
  of parallelize
par¦al¦lel¦ism
par¦al¦lel¦is¦tic
par¦al¦lel¦iza¦tion
par¦al¦lel¦ize
  par¦al¦lel¦iz¦ing
par¦al¦lelo¦gram
para¦logic¦al
para¦logic¦al¦ly
par¦alo¦gism
par¦alo¦gist
par¦alo¦gous
par¦alo¦gous¦ly
par¦al¦ogy
Para¦lym¦pics
para¦lyse Br.
  para¦lys¦ing
  US paralyze
para¦lys¦ing¦ly Br.
  US paralyzingly
par¦aly¦sis
  par¦aly¦ses
par¦aly¦sis agi¦tans
para¦lyt¦ic
para¦lyt¦ic¦al¦ly
para¦lyze US
  para¦lyz¦ing
  Br. paralyse
para¦lyz¦ing¦ly US
  Br. paralysingly
para¦mag¦net¦ic
para¦mag¦net¦ism
Para¦ma¦ribo
para¦matta var. of
  parramatta
para¦me¦cium
  para¦me¦cia or
  para¦me¦ciums
para¦med¦ic
para¦med¦ic¦al
par¦am¦eter
par¦am¦eter¦
  isa¦tion
  Br. var. of
  parameterization
par¦am¦eter¦ise Br.
  var. of
  parameterize

par¦am¦eter¦
   iza¦tion
par¦am¦eter¦ize
  par¦am¦eter¦iz¦ing
para¦met¦ric
para¦met¦ric¦al¦ly
par¦am¦et¦risa¦tion
  Br. var. of
  parameterization
par¦am¦et¦rise *Br.*
  var. of
  parameterize
par¦am¦et¦rization
  var. of
  parameterization
par¦am¦et¦rize var.
  of **parameterize**
para¦mili¦tary
  para¦mili¦tar¦ies
par¦am¦nesia
par¦amo +s
para¦motor
  trademark
para¦mount
para¦mount¦cy
para¦mount¦ly
par¦amour
para¦myxo¦virus
Par¦aná
par¦ang
para¦noia
para¦noiac
para¦nol¦ac¦al¦ly
para¦no¦ic
para¦no¦ic¦al¦ly
para¦noid
para¦nor¦mal
para¦nor¦mal¦ly
Par¦an¦thro¦pus
para¦
  numis¦mat¦ica
para¦par¦esis
para¦par¦et¦ic
para¦pente
  para¦pent¦ing
para¦pent¦er
para¦pet
para¦pet¦ed
par¦aph
para¦pha¦sia
para¦pha¦sic
para¦pher¦na¦lia
para¦philia

para¦phil¦iac
para¦phras¦able
para¦phrase
  para¦phras¦ing
para¦phras¦tic
para¦phy¦let¦ic
par¦aphy¦sis
  par¦aphy¦ses
para¦ple¦gia
para¦ple¦gic
para¦po¦dial
para¦po¦dium
  para¦po¦dia
para¦
  pro¦fes¦sion¦al
para¦pro¦tein
para¦psychic
para¦psycho¦
    logic¦al
para¦psycho¦
    logic¦al¦ly
para¦psych¦olo¦gist
para¦psych¦ology
para¦quat
para¦rhyme
para¦sag¦it¦tal
para¦sagittally
para¦sail
par¦as¦cend
par¦as¦cend¦er
para¦se¦lene
  para¦se¦le¦nae
para¦sit¦aemia *Br.*
para¦site
para¦sit¦emia *US*
para¦sit¦ic
para¦sit¦ic¦al
para¦sit¦ic¦al¦ly
para¦siti¦cide
para¦sit¦isa¦tion *Br.*
  var. of
  parasitization
para¦sit¦ise *Br.* var.
  of **parasitize**
para¦sit¦ism
para¦sit¦iza¦tion
para¦sit¦ize
  para¦sit¦iz¦ing
para¦sit¦oid
para¦sito¦logic¦al
para¦sito¦logic¦al¦ly
para¦sit¦olo¦gist
para¦sit¦ology

para¦sol
para¦statal
para¦ster¦nal
par¦as¦tichy
  par¦as¦tich¦ies
para¦sui¦cide
para¦sym¦pa¦thet¦ic
para¦syn¦thesis
  para¦syn¦theses
para¦syn¦thet¦ic
para¦syn¦thet¦ic¦
    al¦ly
para¦tac¦tic
para¦tac¦tic¦al¦ly
para¦taxis
par¦atha
para¦thion
para¦thor¦mone
para¦thy¦roid
para¦troop *mod.*
para¦troop¦er
para¦troops
para¦typhoid
para¦vane
para¦ven¦tricu¦lar
par avion
para¦wing
par¦axial
par¦boil
par¦buckle
  par¦buck¦ling
Par¦cae *Roman*
  Mythology
par¦cel
  par¦celled *Br.*
  par¦celed *US*
  par¦cel¦ling *Br.*
  par¦cel¦ing *US*
parcel-gilt
par¦cheesi
  trademark in the
  US for **pachisi**
parch¦ment
par¦close
par¦da¦lote
pard¦ner
par¦don
par¦don¦able
par¦don¦ably
par¦don¦er
pare
  par¦ing
  trim; peel; cf. **pair**,
  pear, *père*

par¦egor¦ic
par¦eira
paren = parenthesis
par¦en¦chyma
par¦en¦chy¦mal
par¦en¦chy¦mat¦ous
par¦ens pat¦riae
par¦ent
par¦ent¦age
par¦en¦tal
par¦en¦tal¦ly
par¦ent¦craft
par¦en¦teral
par¦en¦teral¦ly
par¦en¦thesis
  par¦en¦theses
par¦en¦the¦sise *Br.*
  var. of
  parenthesize
par¦en¦the¦size
par¦en¦the¦siz¦ing
par¦en¦thet¦ic
par¦en¦thet¦ic¦al
par¦en¦thet¦ic¦al¦ly
par¦ent¦hood
pareo +s var. of
  pareu
pareu
parer
par¦er¦gon
  par¦erga
  supplementary
  work; cf. **paragon**
par¦esis
  par¦eses
par¦es¦the¦sia *US*
  par¦es¦the¦siae *or*
  par¦es¦the¦sias
  Br. paraesthesia
par¦et¦ic
Pa¦reto, Vil¦fredo
  economist
pareu
parev var. of pareve
par¦eve
par ex¦cel¦lence
par¦fait
par¦fleche
par¦fum¦erie
par¦gana
parge
  par¦ging
par¦get
par¦he¦li¦acal
par¦he¦lic

par|he|lion
par|he|lia
pa|riah
Par|ian
par|ietal
pari-mutuel
par|ing piece cut
off; cf. **pairing**
pari passu
Paris capital of
France; Trojan
prince
Paris, Mat|thew
chronicler
par|ish
pari|shad
pa|rish|ion|er
Pa|ris|ian
Pa|risi|enne
pari|son
par|ity
par|ities
parka jacket; cf.
parker
parker
park|ade
park-and-ride *n.*
Park Chung Hee
president of South
Korea
Par|ker, Char|lie
'Bird' saxophonist
Par|ker, Doro|thy
humorist
park|er person who
parks; in 'nosy
parker'; cf. **parka**
par|ker|ised *Br.* var.
of **parkerized**
par|ker|is|ing *Br.*
var. of **parkerizing**
par|ker|ized
par|ker|iz|ing
parkie park-keeper;
cf. **parky**
par|kin
Par|kin|son|ian
Par|kin|son|ism
Par|kin|son's
dis|ease
park|land
park|way
parky
park|ier
parki|est

chilly; cf. **parkie**
par|lance
parl|ando
par|lay bet
par|ley conference;
cf. **pali**
par|lia|ment
par|lia|men|tar|ian
par|lia|men|tarian|
ism
par|lia|men|tary
par|lor *US*
parlor|maid *US*
par|lour *Br.*
par|lour|maid *Br.*
par|lous
par|lous|ly
par|lous|ness
Parma in Italy; P.
ham; P. violet; cf.
La Palma, Palma
parma wal|laby
Par|meni|des
philosopher
Par|men|tier
Par|me|san
Par|mi|giana
Par|mi|gian|ino
painter
Par|mi|giano var. of
Parmigianino
Par|nas|sian
Par|nas|sus
Par|nell, Charles
politician
Par|nell|ite
pa|ro|chial
pa|ro|chial|ism
pa|ro|chi|al|ity
pa|ro|chi|al|ly
par|od|ic
par|od|ic|al|ly
par|od|ist
par|ody
par|odies
par|odied
par|ody|ing
parol oral;
declaration
par|ole
par|ol|ing
release
pa|role *Linguistics*
par|olee

par|ono|masia
paro|nym
paro|nym|ic
par|onym|ous
par|on|ymy
par|on|ym|ies
Paros
par|otid
paro|titis
Par|ou|sia *Theology*
par|ox|ysm
par|ox|ys|mal
par|oxy|tone
par|pen
par|quet
par|queted
par|quet|ry
Parr, Kath|er|ine
wife of Henry VIII
parr salmon; cf. **pa,
pah, par**
parra|keet var. of
parakeet
parra|matta
parri|cidal
parri|cide
par|rot
parrot|bill
parrot|fish
parrot|let
Parry, Hu|bert
composer
parry
par|ries
par|ried
parry|ing
parse
pars|ing
par|sec
Par|see
Par|see|ism
parser
Par|si|fal
par|si|mo|ni|ous
par|si|mo|ni|ous|ly
par|si|mo|ni|ous|
ness
par|si|mony
pars|ley
pars|nip
par|son
par|son|age
parson-bird

par|son|ic
par|son|ic|al
par|son's nose +s
pars pro toto
part portion; com-
ponent; role; to
divide; etc.; cf. **pâte**
par|take
par|took
par|tak|ing
par|taken
par|taker
par|tan
part|er
par|terre
par|theno|carp|ic
par|theno|carpy
par|theno|gen|esis
par|theno|gen|et|ic
par|theno|
gen|et|ic|al|ly
Par|the|non
Par|thia
Par|thian
par|tial
par|ti|al|ity
par|ti|al|ities
par|tial|ly
par|tial|ness
part|ibil|ity
part|ible
par|tici|pant
par|tici|pate
par|tici|pat|ing
par|tici|pa|tion
par|tici|pa|tive
par|tici|pa|tor
par|tici|pa|tory
par|ti|ci|pial
par|ti|ci|pi|al|ly
par|ti|ciple
par|ticle
parti|col|ored *US*
parti|col|oured *Br.*
par|ticu|lar
par|ticu|lar|
isa|tion
Br. var. of
particularization
par|ticu|lar|ise *Br.*
var. of
particularize
par|ticu|lar|ism

par¦ticu¦lar¦ist
par¦ticu¦lar¦is¦tic
par¦ticu¦lar¦ity
  par¦ticu¦lar¦ities
par¦ticu¦lar¦
    iza¦tion
par¦ticu¦lar¦ize
  par¦ticu¦lar¦iz¦ing
par¦ticu¦lar¦ly
par¦ticu¦late
parti pris
  partis pris
par¦ti¦san
par¦ti¦san¦ship
par¦tita
  par¦titas or par¦tite
par¦tite divided
par¦ti¦tion
par¦ti¦tion¦er
par¦ti¦tion¦ist
par¦ti¦tive
par¦ti¦tive¦ly
part¦ly
part¦ner
part¦ner¦less
part¦ners' desk
part¦ner¦ship
Par¦ton, Dolly
  singer
par¦took
par¦tridge
part¦ridge¦berry
  part¦ridge¦berries
part-time
part-timer
par¦turi¦ent
par¦tur¦ition
part¦way
part-work
party
  par¦ties
  par¦tied
  party¦ing
party¦goer
party pol¦it¦ical
  adj.
par¦ure
Par¦vati *Hinduism*
par¦venu
par¦vis
par¦vise var. of
  parvis
parvo¦virus

pas ballet step
  pl. pas
Pasa¦dena
Pas¦cal computer
  language
Pas¦cal, Blaise
  mathematician
pas¦cal unit
pas¦chal of Easter
Paschen ser¦ies
pas de basque
  pl. pas de basque
pas de bour¦rée
  pl. pas de bour¦rée
pas de chat
  pl. pas de chat
pas de deux
  pl. pas de deux
pas de quatre
  pl. pas de quarte
pas de trois
  pl. pas de trois
pas¦eo +s
pas glissé
pasha Turkish offi-
  cer; butterfly
pashka
pashm
pash¦mina
Pashto language
Pash¦tun people
Pašić, Ni¦kola prime
  minister of Serbia
Pas¦ion¦aria, La
  Communist
  politician
Pa¦siphaë *Greek*
  Mythology
pas¦kha var. of
  pashka
paso doble
Paso¦lini, Pier
  Paolo film director
pas¦pa¦lum
pasque flower
pas¦quin¦ade
pass move; go past;
  be accepted; etc.;
  passage between
  mountains; cf. **past**
pass¦able adequate;
  unobstructed; cf.
  passible
pass¦ably

pas¦sa¦caglia
pas¦sade
pas¦sage
  pas¦sa¦ging
pas¦sage¦way
pas¦sage¦work
Passa¦ma¦quoddy
  pl.
  Passa¦ma¦quoddy
  or Passa¦
    ma¦quod¦dies
pas¦sant
pas¦sata
pass¦band
pass¦book
Pas¦schen¦daele
passé
pas¦seg¦giata
  pas¦seg¦giate
pas¦sel
passe¦ment¦erie
Pas¦sen¦dale var. of
  Passchendaele
pas¦sen¦ger
passe¦par¦tout
passe¦pied
pass¦er
passer-by
  passers-by
pas¦ser¦ine
pas seul
pass¦ibil¦ity
pass¦ible capable of
  suffering; cf.
  passable
Pas¦si¦formes
pas¦sim
pass¦ing¦ly
pas¦sion
pas¦sion¦al
pas¦sion¦ate
pas¦sion¦ate¦ly
pas¦sion¦ate¦ness
Pas¦sion¦ist
pas¦sion¦less
Pas¦sion¦tide
pas¦siv¦ate
  pas¦siv¦at¦ing
pas¦siv¦ation
pas¦sive
pas¦sive¦ly
pas¦sive¦ness

pas¦siv¦is¦able *Br.*
  var. of passivizable
pas¦siv¦isa¦tion *Br.*
  var. of
  passivization
pas¦siv¦ise *Br.* var.
  of passivize
pas¦siv¦ity
pas¦siv¦iz¦able
pas¦siv¦iza¦tion
pas¦siv¦ize
  pas¦siv¦iz¦ing
Pass¦over
pass¦port
pas¦sus
  pl. pas¦sus
pass¦word
past gone by in
  time; former time;
  beyond; so as to
  pass; cf. **passed**
pasta
paste
  past¦ing
paste¦board
paste-down *n.*
paste¦l colour; cf.
  pastille
pas¦tel¦ist *US*
pas¦tel¦list *Br.*
pas¦tern
Pas¦ter¦nak, Boris
  writer
paste-up *n.*
Pas¦teur, Louis
  chemist
pas¦teur¦el¦losis
pas¦teur¦isa¦tion
  Br. var. of
  pasteurization
pas¦teur¦ise *Br.* var.
  of pasteurize
pas¦teur¦iser *Br.*
  var. of pasteurizer
pas¦teur¦iza¦tion
pas¦teur¦ize
  pas¦teur¦iz¦ing
pas¦teur¦izer
pas¦tic¦cio +s
pas¦tiche
  pas¦tich¦ing
pas¦ti¦cheur
pas¦tie nipple
  covering; cf. **pasty**

pas|tille lozenge; cf.
  pastel
past|ily
pas|time
pasti|ness
pas|tis
  pl. pas|tis
past mas|ter
past|ness
pas|tor
pas|tor|al of
country life; poem
etc.; letter from
bishop
pas|tor|ale
  pas|tor|ales or
  pas|tor|ali
music; musical play
pas|tor|al|ism
pas|tor|al|ist
pas|tor|al|ity
pas|tor|al|ly
pas|tor|ate
pas|tor|ela var. of
  pastourelle
pas|tor|ship
pas|tour|elle
pas|trami
pas|try
  pas|tries
pas|tur|age
pas|ture
  pas|tur|ing
pas|ture|land
pasty
  pas|ties
  pasti|er
  pasti|est
food; like paste; cf.
  pastie
pat
  pat|ted
  pat|ting
pa|taca
pat-a-cake
pata|gium
pata|gia
Pata|go|nia
Pata|go|nian
Pa|tali|putra
pata-pata
pata|phys|ics
patas mon|key
Patau's syn|drome

Pata|vin|ity
pat|ball
patch|board
patch|er
patch|ily
patchi|ness
patch|ouli
patch|work
patchy
  patch|ier
  patchi|est
pate head
pâte paste for
  porcelain
pâté meat etc. paste;
  cf. pattée
pâté de cam|pagne
pâté de foie gras
patée var. of pattée
pa|tella *n.*
  pa|tel|lae
  pa|tel|lar *adj.*
pa|tel|late
paten shallow dish;
  cf. patten, pattern
pa|tency
pa|tent
pa|tent|able
pa|tent|ee
pa|tent|ly
pa|tent|or
Pater, Wal|ter
  essayist
pater father
pat|era
  pat|erae
  bowl
pater|famil|ias
patres|famil|ias
pa|ter|nal
pa|ter|nal|ism
pa|ter|nal|ist
pa|ter|nal|is|tic
pa|ter|nal|is|tic|
  al|ly
pa|ter|nal|ly
pa|ter|nity
pater|nos|ter
Pa|than
Pathé, Charles film
  pioneer
path|et|ic
path|et|ic|al|ly

path|find|er
path|less
path|name
patho|gen
patho|gen|esis
patho|gen|et|ic
patho|gen|ic
patho|gen|icity
path|ogen|ous
path|og|no|mon|ic
path|og|raphy
  path|og|raph|ies
patho|logic
patho|logic|al
patho|logic|al|ly
path|olo|gist
path|ology
  path|olo|gies
patho|physio|
        logic|al
patho|physio|logic|
        al|ly
patho|physi|
        olo|gist
patho|physi|ology
pathos
path|way
Pa|tience name
pa|tience calm
  endurance
pa|tient
pa|tient Lucy
  pa|tient Lucies
pa|tient|ly
pat|ina
pat|in|ated
pat|in|ation
patio +s
pa|tis|serie
  French pâtisserie
patly
Pat Ma|lone in 'on
  one's Pat Malone'
Pat|more,
  Cov|en|try poet
Pat|mos
Patna
pat|ness
pat|ois
  pl. pat|ois
Paton, Alan writer
pa|tonce
pa|too|tie

Pa|tras
pat|ria
pat|rial
pat|ri|al|ity
patri|arch +s
patri|arch|al
pat|ri|arch|al|ly
patri|arch|ate
patri|archy
  patri|arch|ies
patri|ate
patri|at|ing
Pa|tri|cia
pa|tri|cian
pa|trici|ate
patri|cidal
patri|cide
Pat|rick
patri|lin|eal
patri|local
patri|local|ity
patri|mo|nial
patri|mony
  patri|monies
pat|riot
pat|ri|ot|ic
pat|ri|ot|ic|al|ly
pat|ri|ot|ism
pa|tris|tic
Pa|troc|lus *Greek*
  Mythology
pa|trol
  pa|trolled
  pa|trol|ling
pa|trol|ler
pa|trol|man
  pa|trol|men
pa|trol|ogy
pa|tron
pa|tron|age
pa|tron|al
pat|ron|ess
pat|ron|isa|tion *Br.*
  var. of
  patronization
pat|ron|ise *Br.* var.
  of patronize
pat|ron|iser *Br.* var.
  of patronizer
pat|ron|is|ing|ly *Br.*
  var. of
  patronizingly
pat|ron|iza|tion

pat¦ron|ize
 pat¦ron|iz¦ing
pat¦ron|izer
pat¦ron|iz¦ing¦ly
pa|tronne
patro|nym¦ic
pa¦troon
Patsy name
patsy
 pat|sies
 person easily
 cheated
patta
Pat¦taya
pat¦tée type of
 cross; cf. **pâté**
pat¦ten shoe; cf.
 paten, pattern
pat¦ter
pat¦tern design;
 model; cf. **paten,**
 pattern
pat¦tern|less
pat|tress
Patty name
patty
 pat|ties
 pie; cake
patty|pan
patu|lous
pat|wari
pat¦zer
paua shellfish; cf.
 power
pau|city
 pau|ci¦ties
Paul, St
Paul|ette
Pauli, Wolf|gang
 physicist
Paul|ician
Paul|ician|ism
Paul|ine of St Paul;
 name
Paul|ing, Linus
 chemist
paul|ow¦nia
paunchi|ness
paunchy
 paunch|ier
 paunchi|est
pau|per
pau|per|dom

pau¦per|isa¦tion *Br.*
 var. of
 pauperization
pau¦per|ise *Br.* var.
 of **pauperize**
pau¦per|ism
pau¦per|iza¦tion
pau¦per|ize
 pau¦per|iz¦ing
pau|piette
pau|ra¦que
pauro|pod
Pauro|poda
pauro|pod¦an
Pau|san¦ias geog-
 rapher
pause
 paus¦ing
pav¦age
pavan var. of
 pavane
pav¦ane
Pava|rotti, Lu|ciano
 singer
pave
 pav¦ing
 cover with stones
 etc.
pavé stone setting;
 paved road
pave|ment
paver
Pa¦vese, Ce¦sare
 writer
pa¦vil|ion
pa¦vior *US*
pa¦viour *Br.*
Pav¦lov, Ivan
 physiologist
Pav|lova, Anna
 dancer
pav|lova dessert
Pav¦lov|ian
Pavo
paw animal's foot;
 scrape with foot; cf.
 poor, pore, pour
pawk|ily
pawki|ness
pawky
 pawk|ier
 pawki|est
 drily humorous; cf.
 porky

pawl lever; bar; cf.
 pall
pawn chess piece;
 deposit as security
 for loan; cf. **porn**
pawn|broker
pawn|brok¦ing
Paw¦nee
 pl. **Paw¦nee** or
 Paw|nees
pawn|shop
paw¦paw
Pax goddess of
 peace
pax peace; call for
 truce
Pax Ro¦mana
Pax¦ton, Jo¦seph
 gardener
pay
 paid
pay|able
pay|back
pay|oback US
 Br. pay cheque
pay¦day
payee
payer
pay¦ess sideburns
 on Orthodox Jews
pay|load
pay|master
pay|ment
Payne's grey
pay¦nim
pay-off *n.*
pay¦ola
pay|out *n.*
pay-per-view *n.*
pay|phone
pay|roll
pays|age
pays|agist
pay¦san
pay|slip
Paz, Octa|vio poet
pea vegetable; plant;
 cf. **pee**
pea|berry
 pea|berries
pea-brain
peace quiet; free-
 dom from war; cf.
 piece

peace|able
peace|able|ness
peace|ably
peace|ful
peace|ful¦ly
peace|ful|ness
peace|keep¦er
peace|keep¦ing
peace|maker
peace|mak¦ing
peace|nik
peace|time
peach
peach-bloom
peach-blow
pea|chick
peachi|ness
peach Melba
peachy
 peach|ier
 peachi|est
Pea|cock, Thomas
 Love writer
pea|cock
pea|fowl
pea¦hen
peak summit; reach
 highest value; cf.
 peek, peke, pique
Peake, Mer¦vyn
 writer
peak|ish
peaky
 peak|ier
 peaki|est
peal ring; cf. **peel**
pea-like
pean *US*
 song of praise.
 Br. **paean**; cf.
 paeon, peon
pean fur; cf. **peen**
Peano ax¦ioms
pea¦nut
pear fruit; cf. **pair,**
 pare, *père*
Pearl name
pearl gem; picot; cf.
 Perl, purl
pearl¦er pearl-
 fisher; cf. **purler**
pearl|es¦cent
pearl|eye
pearl|fish

Pearl Har¦bor
pearli|ness
pearl|ised Br. var. of
pearlized
pearl|ite constituent
of steel; cf. **perlite**
pearl|ized
pearl|ware
pearl|wort
pearly
  pearl|ies
  pearl|ier
  pearli|est
Pear|main
Pears, Peter singer
Pear|son, Karl
mathematician
Pear|son, Les¦ter
prime minister of
Canada
peart cheerful; cf.
pert
Peary, Rob¦ert
explorer
peas|ant
peas|ant¦ry
  peas|ant¦ries
peas|anty
pease pud|ding
peat
peat|land
peaty
  peat|ier
  peati|est
peau-de-soie
peau d'orange
pea¦vey
pea|vine
peavy
  pea|vies
var. of **peavey**
peb|ble
peb¦bled
pebble-dash
pebbly
  peb|blier
  peb|bli|est
pec muscle; cf. **pech**,
peck
pecan nut; cf.
pekan
pecca|bil¦ity
pec|cable

pecca|dillo
  pecca|dil¦loes or
  pecca|dil¦los
pec|cancy
pec|cant
pec|cary
  pec|car¦ies
pec|cavi
pech breathe hard;
cf. **pec**, **peck**
Pech|enga
Pe|chora
Peck, Greg|ory
actor
peck strike with
beak; kiss; unit; cf.
pec, **pech**
peck¦er
pecker|head
pecker|wood
peck|ish
Peck|sniff¦ian
pec|or¦ino +s
Pécs
pec|ten
  pec|tens or
  pec|tines
comb-like structure
pec¦tic
pec¦tin polysacchar-
ide
pec¦tin|ate
pec¦tin|ated
pec¦tin|ation
pec|toral
pec|tose
pecu|late
  pecu|lat¦ing
pecu|la¦tion
pecu|la¦tor
pe|cu|liar
pe¦cu|li¦ar|ity
  pe¦cu|li¦ar|ities
pe¦cu|li¦ar¦ly
pe¦cu|ni¦ar¦ily
pe¦cu|ni¦ary
peda|gogic
peda|gogic¦al
peda|gogic¦al¦ly
peda|gogics
peda|gogue
peda|gogy
  peda|gogies

pedal
  ped|alled Br.
  ped|aled US
  ped¦al|ling Br.
  ped|al|ing US
foot lever; rotate a
pedal; cf. **peddle**
pedal|board
ped|al¦er US
person who pedals;
cf. **peddler**
ped¦al|ler Br.
person who pedals;
cf. **pedlar**
ped¦alo
  ped|alos or
  ped|aloes
ped¦ant
pe¦dan|tic
pe¦dan|tic|al¦ly
pe¦dant|ise Br. var.
of **pedantize**
ped¦ant|ize
  ped¦ant|iz¦ing
ped¦ant¦ry
  ped¦ant|ries
ped¦dle
  ped|dling
sell; promote; cf.
pedal
ped|dler US
hawker; drug
pusher;
Br. **pedlar**;
cf. **pedaler**
ped|er¦ast
ped|er¦as¦tic
ped|er¦asty
ped|es¦tal
  ped|es¦talled Br.
  ped|es¦taled US
  ped|es¦tal|ling Br.
  ped|es¦tal|ing US
ped|es¦trian
ped|es¦tri|an|
      isa¦tion
Br. var. of
pedestrianization
ped|es¦tri|an|ise Br.
var. of
pedestrianize
ped|es¦tri|an|
      iza¦tion
ped|es¦tri|an|ize
ped|es¦tri|an|iz¦ing
ped|es¦trian¦ly

Pedi
  pl. Pedi or Pedis
pedi|at¦ric US
Br. paediatric
pedi|at¦ri¦cian US
Br. paediatrician
pedi|at¦rics US
Br. paediatrics
pedi|cab
pedi|cel stalk with
one flower; cf.
pedicle, peduncle
pedi|cel|laria
  pedi|cel|lar|iae
pedi|cel|late
pedi|cle stalk-like
structure; cf.
pedicel, peduncle
pedi|culi|cide
pe|dicu|losis
pedi|cure
  pedi|cur¦ing
pedi|cur¦ist
pedi|gree
pedi|greed
pedi|ment
pedi|men¦tal
pedi|ment¦ed
pedi|palp
pedi|plain
pedi|plan|ation
ped|lar Br.
hawker; drug
pusher;
US peddler;
cf. **pedaller**
ped|lary
pedo|don|tics
Br. paedodontics
pedo|don¦tist
Br. paedodontist
pedo|genic
pedo|logic¦al
ped|olo¦gist
ped|ology
ped|om¦eter
pedo|phile US
Br. paedophile
pedo|philia US
Br. paedophilia
pedo|phil¦iac US
Br. paedophiliac
Pedro Xi|menes
var. of **Pedro**

Ximenez
Pedro Xi|menez
ped|uncle stalk with flowers or fruit; stalk-like attachment; cf. pedicel, pedicle
ped|un|cu|lar
ped|un|cu|late
ped|way
pee
  pees
  peed
  pee|ing
urine; urinate; cf. pea
Peebles|shire
pee|die Scot. small
peek peep; cf. peak, peke, pique
peek|aboo
peek-a-boo var. of peekaboo
Peel, Rob|ert prime minister of Britain
peel skin or rind; shovel; come off; tower; cf. peal
peel|er
Peel|ite
peely-wallie var. of peely-wally
peely-wally
peen part of hammer; cf. pean
Peene|munde
peep-bo
pee-pee
peep|er
peep|hole
peep-toe
pee|pul tree
peer look; noble; equal; cf. pier, pir
peer|age
peer|ess
peerie tiny; cf. peery, peri
peer|less
peer|less|ly
peery
  peer|ies
spinning top; cf. peerie, peri

peeve
peev|ing
pee|ver
peev|ish
peev|ish|ly
peev|ish|ness
pee|wee lapwing; magpie lark; cf. pewee
pee|wit lapwing
peg
  pegged
  peg|ging
Pega|sean
Pega|sus Greek Mythology
Peg-board trademark
peg|board
peg|box
Peggy name
peggy
  peg|gies
ship's steward
peg|mat|ite
pego +s
peg|top
Pegu
Peh|levi writing system; var. of Pahlavi
Pei, I. M. architect
Pei|gan
  pl. Pei|gan or Pei|gans
pei|gnoir
pein var. of peen
peine forte et dure
Peirce, Charles philosopher
Pei|sis|tra|tus var. of Pisistratus
pe|jora|tive
pe|jora|tive|ly
pekan marten; cf. pecan
peke dog; cf. peak, peek, pique
Pe|kin|ese
Pe|king
Pe|king|ese var. of Pekinese
Pekin robin
pekoe

pel|age
Pe|la|gian of Pelagius
Pe|la|gian|ism
pe|la|gic
Pe|la|gius monk adjudged heretical
pel|ar|go|nium
Pe|las|gian member of ancient Mediterranean people
Pe|las|gic
pelau dish; cf. Palau
Pelé footballer
pele tower; var. of peel; cf. peal
pe|lecy|pod
Pelée, Mt
pel|er|ine
Pele's hair
Pel|eus Greek Mythology
pelf
Pel|ham, Henry prime minister of Britain
pel|ham horse's bit
peli|can
pel|ike
peli|kai
Pel|ion
pe|lisse
pel|ite
pel|lagra
pel|lag|rous
pel|let
pel|let|ise Br. var. of pelletize
pel|let|ize
  pel|let|iz|ing
pel|licle
pel|licu|lar
pel|li|tory
  pel|li|tor|ies
pell-mell
pel|lu|cid
pel|lu|cid|ity
pel|lu|cid|ly
Pel|man|ise Br. var. of Pelmanize
Pel|man|ism
Pel|man|ize
  Pel|man|iz|ing

pel|met
Pelo|pon|nese
Pelo|pon|nes|ian
Pe|lops Greek Mythology
pe|lorus
pe|lota game
pelo|ton group of cyclists
pelta
  pel|tae
pel|tate
Pel|tier
pelt|ry
  pel|tries
pel|vic
pelv|im|etry
pel|vis
  pel|vises or pel|ves
pelyco|saur
Pemba
Pem|broke
Pem|broke|shire
pem|mican
pem|phig|oid
pem|phig|ous adj.
pem|phigus n.
PEN = International Association of Poets, Playwrights, Editors, Essayists, and Novelists
pen
  penned
  pen|ning
penal of punishment; cf. penile
pen|al|isa|tion Br. var. of penalization
pen|al|ise Br. var. of penalize
pen|al|iza|tion
pen|al|ize
  pen|al|iz|ing
pen|al|ly
pen|alty
  pen|al|ties
pen|ance
pen|an|cing
Pen|ang
pen|an|nu|lar
pe|na|tes

pence sum of
money
pen|chant
pen|cil
 pen|cilled Br.
 pen|ciled US
 pen|cil|ling Br.
 pen|cil|ing US
pen|cil|er US
pen|cil|ler Br.
pen|dant
pen|dency
pen|dent adj. var. of
 pendant
pen|dente lite
pen|dent|ive
Pen|de|recki,
 Krzysz|tof
 composer
pend|ing
Pen|dragon
pen|du|lar
pen|du|lous
pen|du|lous|ly
pen|du|lum
pene|con|tem|por
 an|eous
pen|ec|tomy
 pen|ec|to|mies
Pe|nel|ope
pe|ne|plain
penes pl. of penis
pene|tra|bil|ity
pene|trable
pene|tra|lia
pene|trance
pene|trant
pene|trate
 pene|trat|ing
 pene|trat|ing|ly
pene|tra|tion
pene|tra|tive
pene|tra|tor
pene|trom|eter
pen|friend
peng|hulu
pengö
 pl. pengö or
 pen|gös
pen|guin
peni|cil|late
peni|cil|lin
peni|cil|lin|ase

peni|cil|lium
 peni|cil|lia
pen|ile of the penis;
 cf. penal
pen|il|lion
pen|in|sula n.
pen|in|su|lar adj.
penis
 pen|ises or penes
peni|stone
peni|tence
peni|tent
peni|ten|tial
peni|ten|tial|ly
peni|ten|tiary
 peni|ten|tiar|ies
peni|tent|ly
pen|knife
 pen|knives
pen|light
pen|man
 pen|men
pen|man|ship
Penn, Wil|liam
 Quaker
pen-name
pen|nant
pen|nate
penne pasta
penni
 pen|niä
 Finnish currency;
 cf. penny
pen|nies
pen|ni|less
pen|ni|less|ly
pen|ni|less|ness
pen|nil|lion var. of
 penillion
Pen|nine Hills
pen|non
pen|noned
penn'orth var. of
 pennyworth
Penn|syl|va|nia
Penn|syl|va|nian
Penny name
penny
 pen|nies or pence
 British currency;
 US cent; cf. penni
penny|cress
penny-farthing
 bicycle

penny|royal
penny|weight
penny wise
penny|wort
penny|worth
Pen|ob|scot
 pl. Pen|ob|scot
peno|logic|al
pen|olo|gist
pen|ology
Pen|rose
pen|sée
pen|sile
pen|sion payment
pen|sion small hotel
 in France
pen|sion|abil|ity
pen|sion|able
pen|sione
 pen|sioni
 small hotel in Italy
pen|sion|er
pen|sion|less
pen|sion|nat
 boarding school in
 France
pen|sive
pen|sive|ly
pen|sive|ness
pen|ste|mon
pen|stock
penta|chloro|
        phe|nol
penta|chord
pent|acle
pen|tad
penta|dac|tyl
penta|dac|tyly
penta|gas|trin
penta|gon
pen|tagon|al
Penta|gon|ese
penta|gram
penta|he|dral
penta|he|dron
 penta|he|dra or
 penta|he|drons
penta|mer
pent|amer|al
pent|amer|al|ly
penta|mer|ic
pen|tam|er|ous
pent|amery

pen|tam|eter
pent|ami|dine
pent|ane
pent|angle
penta|no|ate
penta|ploid
penta|prism
Penta|teuch
Penta|teuchal
pent|ath|lete
pent|ath|lon
penta|tonic
penta|toni|cism
penta|va|lent
pent|azo|cine
Pente|cost
Pente|cos|tal
Pente|costal|ism
Pente|costal|ist
Pen|tel|ic
Pen|the|si|lea Greek
 Mythology
pent|house
penti|mento
 penti|menti
Pent|land Firth
pent|land|ite
pento|bar|bital
pento|bar|bit|one
pen|tode
pen|tose
Pento|thal
 trademark
pent|oxide
pent|ste|mon var.
 of penstemon
pen|tyl
pen|ult
pen|ul|ti|mate
pen|um|bra
 pen|um|brae or
 pen|um|bras
pen|um|bral
pen|uri|ous
pen|uri|ous|ly
pen|uri|ous|ness
pen|ury
Pen|utian
Penza
Pen|zance
peon
 peons or peones
 labourer;

bullfighter;
cf. **paean, paeon,
pean**
peon|age
peony
  peon|ies
people
  peop|ling
  cf. **peepul**
people|hood
Pe|oria
PEP = Personal
  Equity Plan
pep
  pepped
  pep|ping
  vigour; enliven
pep|er|ino volcanic
  rock
pep|er|omia
pep|er|oni var. of
  pepperoni
pe|pino +s
pep|los
  pl. **pep|los** or
  pep|loses
  robe or shawl
pep|lum hanging
  frill; loose tunic
pepo +s fruit
pep|per
pepper|box
pepper|corn
pepper|grass
pep|per|idge
pep|peri|ness
pepper|mint
pepper|minty
pep|per|oni
pepper-shrike
pepper|wort
pep|pery
pep|pily
pep|pi|ness
peppy
  pep|pier
  pep|pi|est
Pepsi-Cola
  trademark
pep|sin
pep|sin|ogen
pep|tic
pep|tid|ase
pep|tide

pep|tido|gly|can
pep|tone
Pepys, Sam|uel
  diarist
Pé|quiste
Pe|quot
  pl. **Pe|quot** or
  Pe|quots
per for each; in 'as
  per'; cf. **purr**
per|acute
per|ad|ven|ture
Perak
per|alka|line
per|alu|min|ous
per|am|bu|late
  per|am|bu|lat|ing
per|am|bu|la|tion
per|am|bu|la|tor
per|am|bu|la|tory
per annum
per|bor|ate
per|cale
per cap|ita
per caput
per|ceiv|able
per|ceive
  per|ceiv|ing
per|ceiver
per|cent US
per cent Br.
per|cent|age
per|cent|ile
per|cept
per|cep|ti|bil|ity
per|cep|tible
per|cep|tibly
per|cep|tion
per|cep|tion|al
per|cep|tive
per|cep|tive|ly
per|cep|tive|ness
per|cep|tiv|ity
per|cep|tron
per|cep|tual
per|cep|tual|ly
Per|ce|val legendary
  hero
Per|ce|val, Spen|cer
  prime minister of
  Britain
per|chance
perch|er

per|cheron
**per|chloro|ethyl|
      ene**
per|cid
perci|form
per|cipi|ence
per|cipi|ent
per|cipi|ent|ly
Per|ci|val
per|coid
per|co|late
  per|co|lat|ing
per|co|la|tion
per|co|la|tor
per cur|iam
per|cuss
per|cus|sion
per|cus|sion|ist
per|cus|sive
per|cus|sive|ly
per|cus|sive|ness
per|cu|tan|eous
per|cu|tan|eous|ly
Percy family name
  of 'Harry Hotspur'
per diem
per|di|tion
per|dur|abil|ity
per|dur|able
per|dur|ably
per|dur|ance
per|dure
  per|dur|ing
père father; cf. **pair,
  pare, pear**
pere|grin|ate
  pere|grin|at|ing
pere|grin|ation
pere|grin|ator
Pere|grine name
pere|grine falcon
pe|reio|pod
Perel|man, S. J.
  humorist
per|emp|tor|ily
per|emp|tori|ness
per|emp|tory
per|en|nate
  per|en|nat|ing
per|en|na|tion
per|en|nial
per|en|ni|al|ity
per|en|ni|al|ly

per|en|tie
per|enty
  per|en|ties
  var. of **perentie**
Peres, Shi|mon
  prime minister of
  Israel
pere|stroika
**Pérez de Cué|llar,
  Ja|vier** UN Secre-
  tary General
per|fect
per|fecta type of
  bet; cf. **perfecter,
  perfector**
per|fect|er person
  or thing that
  perfects; cf.
  perfecta, perfector
per|fect|ibil|ity
per|fect|ible
per|fec|tion
per|fec|tion|ism
per|fec|tion|ist
per|fec|tion|is|tic
per|fect|ive
per|fect|ly
per|fect|ness
per|fecto +s
per|fect|or printing
  press; cf. **perfecta,
  perfecter**
per|fer|vid
per|fer|vid|ly
per|fer|vid|ness
per|fidi|ous
per|fidi|ous|ly
per|fidi|ous|ness
per|fidy
  per|fid|ies
per|fin
per|fo|li|ate
per|for|ate
  per|for|at|ing
per|for|ation
per|fora|tive
per|for|ator
per|force
per|forin
per|form
per|form|abil|ity
per|form|able
per|form|ance
per|forma|tive

per¦forma¦tory
  per¦forma¦tor¦ies
per¦form¦er
per¦fume
  per¦fum¦ing
per¦fumer
per¦fumery
  per¦fumer¦ies
per¦fumy
per¦func¦tor¦ily
per¦func¦tori¦ness
per¦func¦tory
per¦fus¦ate
per¦fuse
  per¦fus¦ing
per¦fu¦sion
per¦fu¦sion¦ist
per¦fu¦sive
Per¦ga¦mene
Per¦ga¦mum
per¦gana var. of
  pargana
per¦gola
per¦gun¦nah var. of
  pargana
per¦haps
peri spirit; cf.
  peerie, peery,
  perry
peri¦anal
peri¦anth
peri¦apsis
  peri¦apses
peri¦apt
peri¦articu¦lar
peri¦astron
peri¦car¦dial
peri¦cardio¦
      cen¦tesis
  peri¦cardio¦
      cen¦teses
peri¦car¦di¦tis
peri¦car¦dium
  peri¦car¦dia
peri¦carp
peri¦cen¦tric
peri¦chon¦drium
  peri¦chon¦dria
peri¦clase
Peri¦clean
Peri¦cles Athenian
  statesman
peri¦clinal
peri¦clin¦ally

peri¦icope
peri¦cra¦nium
peri¦cycle
peri¦cyc¦lic
peri¦derm
peri¦der¦mal
per¦idium
  per¦idia
peri¦dot
peri¦do¦tite
peri¦do¦titic
peri¦gean
peri¦gee
peri¦gla¦cial
Péri¦gord
per¦igyn¦ous
per¦igyny
  per¦igy¦nies
peri¦he¦lion
  peri¦he¦lia
peri¦karyal
peri¦karyon
  peri¦karya
peril
  per¦illed Br.
  per¦iled US
  per¦il¦ling Br.
  per¦il¦ing US
per¦il¦ous
per¦il¦ous¦ly
per¦il¦ous¦ness
peri¦lune
peri¦lymph
peri¦lymph¦at¦ic
peri¦meno¦pausal
peri¦meno¦pause
per¦im¦eter
peri¦met¦ric
per¦im¦etry
peri¦mysial
peri¦mysium
peri¦natal
peri¦natal¦ly
peri¦natolo¦gist
peri¦nat¦ology
per in¦cur¦iam
peri¦neal relating to
  perineum; cf.
  peroneal
peri¦neum
  peri¦nea
peri¦neur¦ial
peri¦neur¦ium

peri¦nuclear
period
peri¦od¦ate
peri¦od¦ic
peri¦od¦ic¦al
peri¦od¦ic¦al¦ly
peri¦od¦icity
peri¦od¦isa¦tion Br.
  var. of
  periodization
peri¦od¦ise Br. var.
  of periodize
peri¦od¦iza¦tion
peri¦od¦ize
  peri¦od¦iz¦ing
peri¦odon¦tal
peri¦odon¦tics
peri¦odon¦tist
peri¦odon¦titis
peri¦odon¦tol¦ogy
peri¦opera¦tive
peri¦os¦teal
peri¦os¦teum
  peri¦os¦tea
peri¦ost¦itis
peri¦pat¦et¦ic
peri¦pat¦et¦ic¦al¦ly
peri¦pat¦eti¦cism
per¦ip¦atus
peri-peri
peri¦pet¦eia
per¦iph¦eral
per¦iph¦er¦al¦
      isa¦tion
  Br. var. of
  peripheralization
per¦iph¦er¦al¦ise Br.
  var. of
  peripheralize
per¦iph¦er¦al¦ity
per¦iph¦er¦al¦
      iza¦tion
per¦iph¦er¦al¦ize
per¦iph¦er¦al¦iz¦ing
per¦iph¦er¦al¦ly
per¦iph¦ery
  per¦iph¦er¦ies
peri¦phrasis
  peri¦phrases
peri¦phras¦tic
peri¦phras¦tic¦al¦ly
peri¦phyt¦ic
per¦iph¦yton
per¦ip¦teral

per¦ique
peri¦scope
peri¦scop¦ic
peri¦scop¦ic¦al¦ly
per¦ish
per¦ish¦abil¦ity
per¦ish¦able
per¦ish¦able¦ness
per¦ish¦er
per¦ish¦ing
per¦ish¦ing¦ly
per¦isperm
per¦isso¦dac¦tyl
Per¦isso¦dac¦tyla
peri¦stal¦sis
peri¦stal¦tic
peri¦stal¦tic¦al¦ly
peri¦stome
peri¦style
peri¦the¦cium
  peri¦the¦cia
peri¦ton¦eal
peri¦ton¦eum
  peri¦ton¦eums or
  peri¦tonea
peri¦ton¦itis
peri-track
per¦itus
  per¦iti
peri¦vas¦cu¦lar
peri¦ven¦tricu¦lar
peri¦wig
peri¦wigged
peri¦win¦kle
per¦jure
per¦jur¦ing
per¦jurer
per¦juri¦ous
per¦jury
  per¦jur¦ies
perk benefit;
  enliven; percolate;
  cf. pirk
perk¦ily
perki¦ness
perky
perk¦ier
perki¦est
Perl computer
  language; cf. pearl,
  purl
perlé

perle|moen
  pl. perle|moen
Per|lis
perl|ite
per|locu|tion
per|locu|tion|ary
Perm city, Russia
perm hair treat-
  ment; permutation
perma|cul|ture
perma|frost
perm|al|loy
per|man|ence
per|man|ency
per|man|ent
per|man|ent|ly
per|man|gan|ate
per|me|abil|
          isa|tion
  Br. var. of
  permeabilization
per|me|abil|ise *Br.*
  var. of
  permeabilize
per|me|abil|ity
  per|me|abil|ities
per|me|abil|ization
per|me|abil|ize
  per|me|abil|iz|ing
per|me|able
per|me|ance
per|me|ate
  per|me|ating
per|me|ation
per|me|ator
per|meth|rin
Per|mian
per|min|er|al|
          isa|tion
  Br. var. of
  permineralization
per|min|er|al|ised
  Br. var. of
  permineralized
per|min|er|al|
          iza|tion
per|min|er|al|ized
per|mis|si|bil|ity
per|mis|sible
per|mis|sibly
per|mis|sion
per|mis|sive
per|mis|sive|ly
per|mis|sive|ness

per|mit
per|mit|ted
per|mit|ting
per|mit|tee
per|mit|ter
per|mit|tiv|ity
Permo–
    Carbon|ifer|ous
Permo–Triassic
per|mu|tate
  per|mu|tat|ing
per|mu|ta|tion
per|mu|ta|tion|al
per|mute
  per|mut|ing
Per|nam|buco
Per|nam|buco
  wood
per|ni|cious
per|ni|cious|ly
per|ni|cious|ness
per|nick|ety
per|noc|tate
  per|noc|tat|ing
per|noc|ta|tion
Per|nod *trademark*
per|oba
per|ogi var. of
  pierogi
Perón, Eva polit-
  ician
Perón, Juan presi-
  dent of Argentina
peru|neal on outer
  side of calf of leg;
  cf. perineal
Peron|ism
Peron|ist
per|or|ate
  per|or|at|ing
per|or|ation
per|ovsk|ite
per|ox|id|ase
per|ox|ide
  per|ox|id|ing
per|oxi|somal
per|oxi|some
per|pend
per|pen|dicu|lar
per|pen|dicu|lar|ity
per|pen|dicu|lar|ly
per|pet|rate
  per|pet|rat|ing
per|pet|ra|tion

per|pet|ra|tor
per|pet|ual
per|petu|al|ism
per|petu|al|ly
per|petu|ance
per|petu|ate
  per|petu|at|ing
per|petu|ation
per|petu|ator
per|petu|ity
  per|petu|ities
*per|pet|uum
  mo|bile*
Per|pi|gnan
per|plex
per|plex|ed|ly
per|plex|ing|ly
per|plex|ity
  per|plex|ities
per pro.
per|quis|ite
Per|rault, Charles
  writer
per|ron
Perry, Fred tennis
  player
perry
  per|ries
  drink; cf. peri
per se
per|se|cute
  per|se|cut|ing
per|se|cu|tion
per|se|cu|tor
per|se|cu|tory
Per|seids
Per|seph|one *Greek
  Mythology*
Per|sep|olis
Per|seus Greek
  hero; constellation
per|se|ver|ance
per|sev|er|ate
  per|sev|er|at|ing
per|sev|er|ation
per|se|vere
  per|se|ver|ing
per|se|ver|ingly
Per|sia
Per|sian
per|si|flage
per|sim|mon
per|sist
per|sist|ence

per|sist|ency
per|sist|ent
per|sist|ent|ly
per|snick|ety
per|son
  per|sons or people
per|sona
  per|so|nas or
  per|so|nae
per|son|able
per|son|able|ness
per|son|ably
per|son|age
per|sona grata
  per|so|nae gra|tae
per|son|al private;
  cf. personnel
per|son|al|isa|tion
  Br. var. of
  personalization
per|son|al|ise *Br.*
  var. of personalize
per|son|al|ism
per|son|al|ist
per|son|al|is|tic
per|son|al|ity
  per|son|al|ities
per|son|al|iza|tion
per|son|al|ize
  per|son|al|iz|ing
per|son|al|ly
per|son|alty
  per|son|al|ties
*per|sona non
  grata*
  *per|so|nae non
  gra|tae*
per|son|ate
  per|son|at|ing
per|son|ation
per|son|ator
per|son|hood
per|soni|fi|ca|tion
per|son|ifier
per|son|ify
  per|soni|fies
  per|soni|fied
  per|soni|fy|ing
per|son|nel
  employees; cf.
  personal
per|spec|tival
per|spec|tive
per|spec|tive|ly

per|spec|tiv|ism
per|spec|tiv|ist
per|spex *trademark*
per|spi|ca|cious
per|spi|ca|cious|ly
per|spi|ca|city
per|spi|cu|ity
per|spicu|ous
per|spicu|ous|ly
per|spir|ation
per|spira|tory
per|spire
　per|spir|ing
per|suad|abil|ity
per|suad|able
per|suade
　per|suad|ing
per|suader
per|sua|sible
per|sua|sion
per|sua|sive
per|sua|sive|ly
per|sua|sive|ness
PERT = programme
　evaluation and
　review technique
pert cheeky; cf.
　peart
per|tain
Per|tex *trademark*
Perth|shire
per|tin|acious
per|tin|acious|ly
per|tin|acious|ness
per|tin|acity
per|tin|ence
per|tin|ency
per|tin|ent
per|tin|ent|ly
pert|ly
pert|ness
per|turb
per|turb|able
per|turb|ation
per|turb|ative
per|turb|ing|ly
per|tus|sis
Peru
Peru|gia
Peru|gian
per|uke
per|usal

per|use
　per|us|ing
per|user
Peru|vian
perv
per|vade
　per|vad|ing
per|vader
per|va|sion
per|va|sive
per|va|sive|ly
per|va|sive|ness
perve
　perv|ing
　var. of perv
per|verse
per|verse|ly
per|verse|ness
per|ver|sion
per|vers|ity
　per|vers|ities
per|ver|sive
per|vert
per|vert|ed|ly
per|vert|er
per|vi|ous
per|vi|ous|ness
pervy
　perv|ier
　pervi|est
pes
　pedes
Pe|sach
pesca|tar|ian
pes cavus
pe|seta
pe|sewa
Pe|sha|war
Pe|shitta
pesh|merga
　pl. pesh|merga or
　pesh|mer|gas
pesk|ily
peski|ness
pesky
　pesk|ier
　peski|est
peso +s
pes pla|nus
pes|sary
　pes|sar|ies
pes|sim|ism
pes|sim|ist

pes|sim|is|tic
pes|sim|is|tic|al|ly
Pesta|lozzi,
　Jo|hann education-
　alist
pes|ter
pes|ter|er
pest-house
pesti|cidal
pesti|cide
pest|ifer|ous
pesti|lence
pesti|lent
pesti|len|tial
pesti|lent|ly
pes|tle
　pest|ling
pesto
pet
　pet|ted
　pet|ting
Peta woman's name;
　cf. Peter
peta|byte
Pé|tain, Phil|ippe
　general
petal
pet|aled *US*
petal|ine
pet|alled *Br.*
petal-like
petal|oid
pé|tanque
pe|tard
peta|sus
pet|cock
pe|techia
　pe|techiae
pe|tech|ial
Peter man's name;
　cf. Peta
peter diminish;
　penis; prison cell
Peter|bor|ough
Peter|loo
peter|man
　peter|men
peter|sham
Peter|son, Oscar
　musician
Peter's pence
Peters pro|jec|tion
peth|id|ine

pé|til|lant
peti|olar
peti|ol|ate
peti|ole
Pe|tipa, Mar|ius
　choreographer
petit *Law* minor
petit batte|ment
　pe|tits batte|ments
petit beurre
　pe|tits beurres
petit bour|geois
　pe|tits bour|geois
petit bour|geoisie
　var. of petite
　bourgeoisie
pe|tite
pe|tite
　bour|geoisie
pe|tite mar|mite
petit four
　pe|tits fours
petit|grain
pe|ti|tion
pe|ti|tion|able
pe|ti|tion|ary
pe|ti|tion|er
pe|ti|tio prin|cipii
petit jeté
　pe|tits jetés
petit-maître
petit mal
　pe|tits mals
petit pain
　pe|tits pains
petit point
　pe|tits pois
Pet|rarch poet
Pet|rarch|an
pet|rel bird; cf.
　petrol
petrol
Petri dish
Pe|trie, Flin|ders
　archaeologist
petri|fac|tion
pet|rify
　petri|fies
　petri|fied
　petri|fy|ing
Pe|trine
pet|ris|sage
petro|chem|ical
petro|chem|is|try
petro|dol|lar

petro|gen|esis
petro|gen|et|ic
petro|glyph
Petro|grad
pet|rog|raph|er
petro|graph|ic
petro|graph|ic|al|ly
pet|rog|raphy
pet|rol fuel; cf.
 petrel
pet|rol|atum
pet|rol|eum
petrol|head
petrol|ifer|ous
petro|logic
petro|logic|al|ly
pet|rolo|gist
pet|rology
Pe|tro|nas Tow|ers
Pe|tro|nius, Gaius
 writer
Petro|pav|lovsk-
 Kamchat|sky
petro|phys|ic|al
petro|physi|cist
petro|phys|ics
pe|tro|sal
petro|tec|ton|ic
petro|tec|ton|ics
pet|rous
Petro|za|vodsk
pe tsai
Pet|samo
pet|ter
petti|coat
petti|coat|ed
petti|fog
 petti|fogged
 petti|fog|ging
petti|fog|ger
petti|fog|gery
pet|tily
petti|ness
pet|tish
pet|tish|ly
pet|tish|ness
petty
 pet|tier
 pet|ti|est
trivial; mean;
minor
petty bour|geois
 var. of petit

bourgeois
petty bour|geoisie
 var. of petite
 bourgeoisie
petu|lance
petu|lant
petu|lant|ly
pe|tu|nia
pe|tun|tse
Pevs|ner, An|toine
 artist
Pevs|ner, Niko|laus
 art historian
pew church seat; cf.
 più
pewee
 tyrant flycatcher;
 cf. peewee
pewit var. of peewit
pew|ter
pew|ter|er
Peyer's patches
pey|ote
Pey|ro|nie's
 dis|ease
pfen|nig
pha|ce|lia
Phae|acian
Phae|dra *Greek
 Mythology*
Phaeo|phy|ceae
Phae|thon *Greek
 Mythology*
phae|ton carriage;
 car
phago|cyte
phago|cyt|ic
phago|cyt|ise *Br.*
 var. of phagocytize
phago|cyt|ize
 phago|cyt|iz|ing
phago|cyt|ose
 phago|cyt|os|ing
phago|cyt|osis
phago|somal
phago|some
Phai|stos
Phal|ange Lebanese
 party; cf. Falange
phal|ange bone
pha|lan|geal
pha|lan|ger

Pha|lan|gist mem-
 ber of Phalange; cf.
 Falangist
phal|an|stery
 phal|an|ster|ies
phal|anx
 phal|anxes troop
 formations
pha|lan|ges bones
phala|rope
phal|era
 phal|erae
phalli pl. of phallus
phal|lic
phal|lic|al|ly
phalli|cism
phal|lism
phallo|cen|tric
phal|lo|cen|tri|city
phal|lo|cen|trism
phall|oc|racy
 phall|oc|ra|cies
phallo|crat|ic
phal|loid|in
phallo|plasty
phal|lus
 phalli or phal|luses
Phan|ariot
phan|ero|gam
phan|ero|gam|ic
phan|er|og|am|ous
Phan|ero|zoic
phan|ta|sise *Br.* var.
 of fantasize
phan|ta|size var. of
 fantasize
phan|tasm
phan|tas|ma|goria
phan|tas|ma|gor|ic
phan|tas|ma|
 gor|ic|al
phan|tas|mal
phan|tas|mic
phan|tast var. of
 fantast
phan|tasy var. of
 fantasy
phan|tom
phar|aoh
phar|aoh ant
Phar|aoh hound
Phar|aoh's
 ser|pent
phar|aon|ic

Phari|sa|ic
Phari|saic|al
Phari|sa|ism
Phari|see
pharma pharma-
 ceutical company or
 sector
pharma|ceut|ical
pharma|ceut|ic|
 al|ly
pharma|ceut|ics
pharma|cist
pharma|co|
 dynam|ics
pharma|co|
 gen|et|ics
pharma|co|
 gen|omi|cist
pharma|co|
 gen|om|ics
pharma|cog|nos|ist
pharma|cog|nosy
pharma|co|
 kin|et|ics
pharma|co|logic
pharma|co|logic|al
pharma|co|logic|
 al|ly
pharma|colo|gist
pharma|col|ogy
pharma|co|peia *US*
 var. of
 pharmacopoeia
pharma|co|peial
 US var. of
 pharmacopoeial
pharma|co|phore
pharma|co|poeia
pharma|co|poeial
pharma|co|
 ther|apy
phar|macy
 phar|ma|cies
pharm|ing
 Biotechnology
Pharos island and
 ancient lighthouse
 off Egypt
pharos any
 lighthouse
pha|ryn|gal var. of
 pharyngeal
pha|ryn|geal

pha|ryn|geal|
 isa|tion
 Br. var. of
 pharyngealization
pha|ryn|geal|ise *Br.*
 var. of
 pharyngealize
pha|ryn|geal|
 iza|tion
pha|ryn|geal|ize
 pha|ryn|geal|iz|ing
pha|ryn|gitis
phar|yn|got|omy
 phar|yn|goto|mies
phar|ynx
 pha|ryn|ges
phas|cog|ale
phase
 phas|ing
 stage; carry out in
 stages; cf. **faze**
phaser device for
 altering sound sig-
 nal; weapon in sci-
 ence fiction; cf.
 phasor
phas|ic
phas|mid
Phas|mida
phasor line
 representing
 complex electrical
 quantity; cf. **phaser**
phat|ic
pheas|ant
pheas|ant|ry
 pheas|ant|ries
Phei|dip|pi|des
 Athenian
 messenger
phen|acetin
phen|an|threne
phen|an|thrid|ine
phen|cyc|lid|ine
phen|el|zine
pheno|bar|bital
pheno|bar|bit|one
pheno|copy
 pheno|copies
pheno|cryst
phe|nol
phen|ol|ic
pheno|logic|al
phen|ology
phe|nol|phthal|ein

phe|nom
phe|nom|ena pl. of
 phenomenon
phe|nom|enal
phe|nom|en|al|ise
 Br. var. of
 phenomenalize
phe|nom|en|al|ism
phe|nom|en|al|ist
phe|nom|en|al|
 is|tic
phe|nom|en|al|ize
 phe|nom|en|al|
 iz|ing
phe|nom|en|al|ly
phe|nom|eno|
 logic|al
phe|nom|eno|logic|
 al|ly
phe|nom|en|
 olo|gist
phe|nom|en|ology
phe|nom|enon
 phe|nom|ena
pheno|thia|zine
pheno|type
pheno|typ|ic
pheno|typ|ic|al
pheno|typ|ic|al|ly
phen|tola|mine
phenyl chemical
 radical; cf. **fennel**
phenyl|alan|ine
phenyl|buta|zone
phenyl|ene|
 di|amine
phenyl|eph|rine
phenyl|ke|ton|uria
phenyl|thio|
 carba|mide
pheny|toin
phero|monal
phero|mone
phew *exclam.*; cf.
 few
phi Greek letter; cf.
 fie
phial small bottle;
 cf. **file**
Phid|ias Athenian
 sculptor
Phila|del|phia
Phila|del|phian
phila|del|phus

phil|an|der
phil|an|der|er
phil|an|thrope
phil|an|throp|ic
phil|an|throp|ic|
 al|ly
phil|an|thro|pise
 Br. var. of
 philanthropize
phil|an|throp|ism
phil|an|throp|ist
phil|an|thro|pize
 phil|an|thro|piz|ing
phil|an|thropy
 phil|an|thro|pies
phila|tel|ic
phila|tel|ic|al|ly
phil|atel|ist
phil|ately
Philby, Kim spy
Phi|le|mon old man
 in Greek myth-
 ology; *Bible*
phil|har|mon|ic
phil|hel|lene
phil|hel|len|ic
phil|hel|len|ism
phil|hel|len|ist
phili|beg var. of
 filibeg
Philip husband of
 Elizabeth II; Mace-
 donian, French,
 and Spanish kings
Philip, St
Phil|ippa
Phil|ippi
Phil|ip|pian
phil|ip|pic
Phil|ip|pine *mod.*
Phil|ip|pines coun-
 try; cf. **Filipina**,
 Filipino
Phil|ip|popo|lis
Phil|is|tine member
 of ancient people
phil|is|tine uncul-
 tured person
phil|is|tin|ism
Phil|lida
Phil|lip name; cf.
 fillip
Phil|lips screw;
 screwdriver

 trademark
Phil|lips curve
phil|lu|men|ist
phil|lu|meny
Philly =
 Philadelphia; cf.
 filly
philo|bat
philo|den|dron
 philo|den|drons or
 philo|den|dra
phil|ogy|nist
phil|ogyny
Philo Ju|daeus
 philosopher
philo|lo|gian
philo|logic|al
philo|logic|al|ly
phil|olo|gise *Br.* var.
 of **philologize**
phil|olo|gist
phil|olo|gize
 phil|olo|giz|ing
phil|ology
Philo|mel *Greek
 Mythology*
Philo|mela var. of
 Philomel
philo|mena
philo|pat|ric
philo|patry
philo|pro|geni|tive
philo|pro|geni|tive|
 ness
phil|oso|pher
*philo|sophia
 per|ennis*
philo|soph|ic
philo|soph|ic|al
philo|soph|ic|al|ly
phil|oso|phise *Br.*
 var. of
 philosophize
phil|oso|phiser *Br.*
 var. of
 philosophizer
philo|soph|ize
phil|oso|phiz|ing
phil|oso|phizer
philo|soph|y
 philo|soph|ies
phil|ter *US*
phil|tre *Br.*
 love potion; cf.

filter
phi|mo|sis
phi|mot|ic
Phin|eas
phish|ing fraudu-
 lent emailing
Phiz illustrator
phiz face; cf. fizz
phizog
phle|bit|ic
phle|bitis
phlebo|graph|ic
phle|bog|raphy
phle|bot|om|ise Br.
 var. of
 phlebotomize
phle|bot|om|ist
phle|bot|om|ize
 phle|bot|om|iz|ing
phle|bot|omy
 phle|boto|mies
phlegm
phleg|mat|ic
phleg|mat|ic|al|ly
phlegmy
phloem
phlo|gis|ton
phlogo|pite
phlox plant; cf.
 flocks
Phnom Penh
pho|bia
pho|bic
Pho|bos son of
 Greek war god;
 moon of Mars
pho|cine
phoco|melia
Phoebe Titaness;
 moon of Saturn
phoebe bird
Phoe|bus Greek sun
 god
Phoe|ni|cia
Phoen|ician
Phoe|nix city, US
phoe|nix
pho|las
Pholi|dota
phon unit of
 loudness
phon|aes|the|sia Br.
 US phonesthesia

phon|aes|thet|ic Br.
 US phonesthetic
phon|aes|thet|ics
 Br.
 US phonesthetics
phon|ate
 phon|at|ing
phon|ation
phon|atory
phone
 phon|ing
phone|card
phone-in n. & mod.
phon|em|atic
phon|eme
phon|em|ic
phon|esthe|sia US
 Br. phonaesthesia
phon|esthet|ic US
 Br. phonaesthetic
phon|esthet|ics US
 Br. phonaesthetics
phon|et|ic
phon|et|ic|al|ly
phon|et|ician
phon|eti|cise Br.
 var. of phoneticize
phon|eti|cism
phon|eti|cist
phon|eti|cize
 phon|eti|ciz|ing
phon|et|ist
pho|ney Br.
 pho|nier
 pho|ni|est
 US phony
phon|ic
phon|ic|al|ly
pho|nily
pho|ni|ness
phono adj.
phono|cardio|
 gram
phono|gram
phono|graph
phono|graph|ic
phono|lite
phono|logic|al
phono|lo|gic|al|ly
phon|olo|gist
phon|ology
pho|non
phono|tac|tic
phono|tac|tics

phony US
pho|nies
pho|nier
pho|ni|est
 Br. phoney
phooey
phor|bol
phor|esy
phor|et|ic
phor|mium
phoro|nid
Phor|on|ida
phos|gene
phos|phat|ase
phos|phate
phos|phat|ic
phos|phat|ide
phos|phat|idyl|
 cho|line
phos|phene sensa-
 tion in eye
phos|phide
phos|phine gas
phos|phite
phospho|crea|tine
phospho|diester
phospho|
 diester|ase
phospho|lip|ase
phospho|lipid
phospho|nate
phos|phon|ic
phos|phon|ium
phospho|pro|tein
phos|phor
phos|phor|esce
 phos|phor|es|cing
phos|phor|es|cence
phos|phor|es|cent
phos|phor|ic
phos|phor|ite
phos|phor|ous adj.
phos|phorus n.
phos|phoryl
phos|phor|yl|ase
phos|phor|yl|ate
 phos|phor|yl|at|ing
phos|phor|yl|ation
phossy jaw
phot unit of
 illumination
phot|ic
pho|tino +s

phot|ism
Pho|tius Byzantine
 scholar
photo
 pl. pho|tos
 v. pho|toes
 pho|toed
 photo|ing
photo|active
photo|biol|ogy
photo|bleach|ing
photo|call
photo|cataly|sis
photo|cata|lyt|ic
photo|cath|ode
photo|cell
photo|chem|ical
photo|chem|ical|ly
photo|chem|is|try
photo|chro|mic
photo|chrom|ism
photo|
 coagu|la|tion
photo|com|
 pos|ition
photo|con|duct|ive
photo|con|duct|
 iv|ity
photo|con|duct|or
photo|copi|able
photo|copier
photo|copy
 photo|cop|ies
 photo|cop|ied
 photo|copy|ing
photo|cur|rent
photo|degrad|able
photo|detect|or
photo|diode
photo|dis|soci|
 ation
photo|dynam|ic
photo|elec|tric
photo|elec|tri|city
photo|elec|tron
photo|elec|tron|ic
photo|emis|sion
photo|emis|sive
photo|emit|ter
photo|essay
photo|fit
photo|gen|ic
photo|gen|ic|al|ly

photo|geo|logic|al
photo|geolo|gist
photo|geol|ogy
photo|gram
photo|
   gram|met|ric
photo|gram|
   met|rist
photo|gram|metry
photo|graph
photo|graph|able
pho|tog|raph|er
photo|graph|ic
photo|graph|ic|
   al|ly
pho|tog|raphy
photo|grav|ure
photo|ion|isa|tion
   Br. var. of
   photoionization
photo|ion|iza|tion
photo|jour|nal|ism
photo|jour|nal|ist
photo|litho
photo|lith|
   og|raph|er
photo|litho|
   graph|ic
photo|litho|
   graph|ic|al|ly
photo|lith|og|raphy
photo|lyse
photo|lys|ing
pho|toly|sis
photo|lyt|ic
photo|map
photo|mask
photo|mech|an|ical
photo|mech|an|ic|
   al|ly
pho|tom|eter
photo|met|ric
pho|tom|et|ric|al|ly
pho|tom|etry
photo|micro|graph
photo|
   microg|raph|er
photo|
   microg|raphy
photo|mon|tage
photo|morpho|
   gen|esis
photo|mosaic

photo|multi|plier
pho|ton
photo|nega|tive
pho|ton|ic
pho|ton|ics
photo-offset
photo-oxidation
photo|period
photo|peri|od|ic
photo|period|ism
photo|pho|bia
photo|pho|bic
photo|phore
pho|top|ic
photo|pig|ment
photo|polar|
   im|eter
photo|poly|mer
photo|posi|tive
photo|prod|uct
photo|pro|tein
photo|real|ism
photo|real|ist
photo|real|is|tic
photo|recep|tive
photo|recep|tor
photo|
   recon|nais|sance
photo|resist
photo|respir|ation
photo|response
photo|sensi|tive
photo|sensi|tiv|ity
photo|set
photo|set|ting
photo|set|ter
photo|sphere
photo|spher|ic
photo|stat
   trademark as n.
   v. photo|stat|ted
photo|stat|ting
photo|stat|ic
photo|story
photo|stories
photo|syn|thate
photo|syn|thesis
photo|syn|the|sise
   Br. var. of
   photosynthesize
photo|syn|the|size
photo|
   syn|the|siz|ing

photo|syn|thet|ic
photo|syn|thet|ic|
   al|ly
photo|system
photo|tac|tic
photo|taxis
photo|taxes
photo|ther|apy
photo|tran|sis|tor
photo|troph
photo|troph|ic
photo|trop|ic
photo|trop|ism
photo|tube
photo|type|set
photo|type|set|ter
photo|type|set|ting
photo|vol|ta|ic
photo|vol|ta|ics
phrag|mites
phrasal
phras|al|ly
phrase
   phras|ing
   cf. fraise
phraseo|logic|al
phrase|ology
   phrase|olo|gies
phratry
   phrat|ries
phreak hacker into
   telecommunica-
   tions; cf. **freak**
phreak|er
phreak|ing hacking
   into telecommuni-
   cations; cf.
   freaking
phre|at|ic
phre|ato|
   mag|mat|ic
phre|ato|phyte
phre|ato|phyt|ic
phren|ic
phreno|logic|al
phren|olo|gist
phren|ology
Phry|gia
Phry|gian
phthal|ate
phthalo|cyan|ine
Phthi|rap|tera
phthi|sic

phthi|sic|al
phthi|sis
Phu|ket
phul|kari
phut
phyco|bilin
phyco|cyan|in
phyco|eryth|rin
phyco|logic|al
phy|colo|gist
phy|cology
phyco|my|cete
phyco|myco|sis
phyla pl. of **phylum**;
   cf. **filer**
phyl|ac|tery
phyl|ac|ter|ies
phy|let|ic
phy|let|ic|al|ly
Phyl|lida
Phyl|lis
phyl|lite
phyllo *US*
   Br. filo
phyllo|clade
phyl|lode
phyl|lo|pod
phyl|lo|quin|one
phyl|lo|tac|tic
phyl|lo|taxis
phyl|lo|taxy
phyl|lox|era
phylo|gen|esis
phylo|gen|et|ic
phylo|gen|et|ic|al|ly
phylo|gen|ic
phylo|gen|ic|al|ly
phyl|ogeny
phy|lum
   phyla
phy|sa|lis
Phy|sep|tone
   trademark
physi|at|rics
physi|at|rist
physic
   phys|icked
   phys|ick|ing
phys|ic|al
phys|ic|al|isa|tion
   Br. var. of
   physicalization
phys|ic|al|ise *Br.*
   var. of **physicalize**

phys|ic|al|ism
phys|ic|al|ist
phys|ic|al|is|tic
phys|ic|al|ity
phys|ic|al|iza|tion
phys|ic|al|ize
 phys|ic|al|iz|ing
phys|ic|al|ly
phys|ic|al|ness
phys|ician
physi|cist
physico-chemical
phys|ics
physio +s
physio|chem|ical
physi|ocracy
 physi|ocra|cies
physio|crat
physio|crat|ic
physio|gnom|ic
physio|gnom|ic|al
physio|gnom|ic|
 al|ly
physio|gnom|ist
physio|gnomy
 physi|ogno|mies
physi|og|raph|er
physio|graph|ic
physio|graph|ic|al
physio|graph|ic|
 al|ly
physi|og|raphy
physio|logic
physio|logic|al
physio|lo|gic|al|ly
physi|olo|gist
physi|ology
physio|ther|ap|ist
physio|ther|apy
phys|ique
physo|stig|mine
phyto|alexin
phyto|chem|ical
phyto|chem|ist
phyto|chem|is|try
phyto|chrome
phyto|estro|gen
phyto|gen|et|ic
phyto|geog|raph|er
phyto|geo|graph|ic
phyto|geo|graph|ic|
 al|ly
phyto|geog|raphy

phyto|haem|agglu|
 tinin *Br.*
phyto|hem|agglu|
 tinin *US*
phyto|lith
phyto|nutri|ent
phyto|patho|
 logic|al
phyto|path|olo|gist
phyto|path|ology
phyt|opha|gous
phyt|oph|agy
phyt|opha|gies
phyto|plank|ton
phyto|sani|tary
phyto|toxic
phyto|tox|icity
phyto|toxin
pi Greek letter;
 pious; cf. pie
pia
Piaf, Edith singer
pi|aff
pi|aff|ing
 dressage movement
pi|aff|er var. of
 piaffe
Pia|get, Jean
 psychologist
pial
pia mater
piani pl. of piano
pi|an|ism
pi|an|is|simo
pi|an|is|simos or
 pi|an|is|simi
pi|an|ist
pi|an|is|tic
pi|an|is|tic|al|ly
piano +s instrument
piano
 pi|anos or piani
 (passage
 performed) softly
pi|ano|forte
pi|an|ola *trademark*
piano no|bile
 piani no|bili
pi|piac
pi|as|sava
pi|aster *US*
pi|astre *Br.*
Piat
Piauí

pi|azza
pi|broch
pic picture; cf. pick
pica printing meas-
 ure; eating of non-
 food substances; cf.
 pika, piker
pica|dor
pi|cante
Pic|ard
Pic|ardy
pic|ar|esque
pic|aro +s
pic|ar|oon
Pi|casso, Pablo
 painter
Pi|casso|esque
pic|ay|une
Pic|ca|dilly
pic|ca|lilli
pic|ca|lil|lies or
 pic|ca|lil|lis
pic|ca|ninny *Br.*
 pic|ca|nin|nies
 offensive;
 US pickaninny
pic|colo +s
piccy
pic|cies
pice
 pl. pice
 former currency in
 Ind. subcontinent;
 cf. paisa
pichi
pick choose; pluck;
 tool; cf. pic
pick|aback var. of
 piggyback
pick|able
pick-and-mix *adj.*
picka|ninny *US*
picka|nin|nies
 offensive;
 Br. piccaninny
pick|ax *US*
pick|axe *Br.*
pick|ax|ing
pick|el|haube
 pick|el|hauben
pick|er
pick|erel
pick|erel|weed
picket person
 supporting strike;

stake; sentry; cf.
 piquet
pick|et|er
Pick|ford, Mary
 actress
picki|ness
pickle
 pick|ling
pick|ler
pick|lock
pick-me-up
pick|ney
pick 'n' mix var. of
 pick-and-mix
pick|off
pick|pocket
pick|pocket|ing
pick|up
Pick|wick|ian
picky
 pick|ier
 picki|est
pic|nic
 pic|nicked
 pic|nick|ling
 meal; cf. pyknic
pic|nick|er
pic|nicky
Pico da Neb|lina
pi|cong
pi|corna|virus
pico|sec|ond
picot
pi|cotee
picquet sentry, var.
 of picket; cf.
 piquet
pic|rate
pic|rite
pi|crit|ic
picro|toxin
Pict|ish
picto|gram
picto|graph
picto|graph|ic
pic|tog|raphy
Pic|tor
pic|tor|ial
pic|tori|al|ly
pic|ture
pic|tur|ing
pic|tur|esque
pic|tur|esque|ly

pic¦tur¦esque¦ness
picture-writing
pic¦tur¦isa¦tion *Br.*
  var. of
  picturization
pic¦tur¦ise *Br.* var.
  of picturize
pic¦tur¦iza¦tion
pic¦tur¦ize
  pic¦tur¦iz¦ing
picu¦let
pid¦dle
  pid¦dling
pid¦dler
pid¦dock
pidgin language; cf.
  pigeon
pi-dog var. of pye-
  dog
pie food; bird;
  former Indian
  currency; cf. pi
pie¦bald
piece
  piecing
  part, coin, etc.;
  assemble; cf. peace
*pièce de
  ré¦sist¦ance
  pièces de
  ré¦sist¦ance*
piece¦meal
piecer
piece¦work
piece¦work¦er
pie¦crust
pied
pied-à-terre
  pieds-à-terre
Pied¦fort
Pied¦mont region,
  Italy
pied¦mont slope
Pied¦mont¦ese
*pied noir
  pieds noirs*
pie-dog var. of pye-
  dog
pie-eyed
Pie¦gan var. of
  Peigan
pie¦man
  pie¦men
pie¦mont¦ite

pier seaside struc-
  ture; pillar; cf.
  peer, pir
Pierce, Frank¦lin
  US president
pierce
  pier¦cing
pier¦cer
pier¦cing¦ly
Pi¦er¦ian
pierid
pieris
Piero della
  Fran¦cesca painter
pier¦ogi dumplings
pier¦ogies var. of
  pierogi
Pierre
Pier¦rette *female*
Pier¦rot *male*
Pies¦porter
pietà work of art
pie¦tas respect for
  an ancestor
Pieter¦maritz¦burg
Pie¦ters¦burg town,
  South Africa
Piet¦ism movement
piet¦ism sentiment
piet¦ist
piet¦is¦tic
piet¦is¦tic¦al¦ly
piet-my-vrou
pi¦etra dura
piety
  piet¦ies
piezo
piezo¦elec¦tric
piezo¦elec¦tric¦al¦ly
piezo¦elec¦tri¦city
pi¦ez¦ometer
pif¦fle
pif¦fling
pig
  pigged
  pig¦ging
pi¦geon bird;
  business; cf. pidgin
pigeon¦hole
  pigeon¦hol¦ing
pigeon¦ite
pi¦geon¦ry
  pi¦geon¦ries
pig¦face

pig¦fish
pig¦gery
  pig¦ger¦ies
pig¦gish
pig¦gish¦ly
pig¦gish¦ness
Pig¦gott, Les¦ter
  jockey
piggy
  pig¦gies
  pig¦gier
  pig¦gi¦est
pig¦gy¦back
pigh¦tle
pig¦let
pig¦like
pig¦ling
pig¦man
  pig¦men
pig¦ment
pig¦men¦tal
pig¦men¦tary
pig¦men¦ta¦tion
pigmy var. of pygmy
pig¦nut
pig¦pen
pig-root
pig¦skin
pig-sticker
pig¦sty
  pig¦sties
pig¦swill
pig¦tail
pig¦tailed
pig¦weed
pi-jaw
pika animal; cf.
  pica, piker
pike
  pik¦ing
pike¦let
pike¦man
  pike¦men
pike¦perch
  pl. pike¦perch
piker person; cf.
  pica, pika
pike¦staff
pikey *offensive*
  Gypsy
piki bread
pik¦kie child
Pik Po¦bedy

pilaf
pi¦laff var. of pilaf
pi¦las¦ter
pi¦las¦tered
Pi¦late, Pon¦tius
Pi¦la¦tes
pilau
pil¦chard
pile
  pil¦ing
pilea
pil¦eate
pil¦eated
pile¦driver
pile¦driv¦ing
piles
pile-up *n.*
pi¦leus
  pilei
pile¦wort
pil¦fer
pil¦fer¦age
pil¦fer¦er
pil¦grim
pil¦grim¦age
  pil¦grim¦aging
pil¦grim¦ise *Br.* var.
  of pilgrimize
pil¦grim¦ize
  pil¦grim¦iz¦ing
Pili¦pino var. of
  Filipino
pil¦lage
  pil¦laging
pil¦la¦ger
pil¦lar
pil¦lared
pil¦laret
pill¦box
pil¦lion
pil¦li¦winks
pill¦lock
pil¦lory
  pil¦lor¦ies
  pil¦lor¦ied
  pil¦lory¦ing
pil¦low
pil¦low¦case
pil¦low¦slip
pil¦lowy
pil¦lule var. of pilule
pill¦wort
pilo¦car¦pine

pil|ose
pill|os|ity
pilot
pi|lot|age
pilot|fish
pi|lot|less
pil|ous
Pils
Pil|sen
Pil|sen|er var. of
  Pilsner
Pils|ner
Pilt|down man
pil|ule
Pima
  pl. Pima or Pimas
pi|mento +s
pi-meson
pi|miento var. of
  pimento
Pimm's trademark
  pl. Pimm's
pim|per|nel
pim|ple
pim|pled
pim|ply
  pim|plier
  pim|pli|est
pimp|mobile
PIN = personal
  identification
  number
pin
  pinned
  pin|ning
pina co|lada
pina|fore
Pin|ang var. of
  Penang
pin|as|ter
Pina|tubo
pin|ball
pin|board
pince-nez
  pl. pince-nez
pin|cer
pin|cette
pinch|beck
pinch-hit
  pinch-hitting
pinch-hitter
pinch|penny
  pinch|pen|nies

pinch-run
  pinch-ran
  pinch-running
pinch-runner
pin|cush|ion
Pin|dar poet
Pin|dar|ic
Pin|dus
pine
  pin|ing
pin|eal
pine|apple
pi|nene
Pin|ero, Ar|thur
  Wing dramatist
pin|ery
  pin|eries
pine|sap
pin|etum
  pin|eta
pine|wood
Pine|wood
  Stu|dios
piney var. of piny
pin|fold
ping|er
pingo +s
ping-pong
pin|guid
pin|guid|ity
pin|guin
ping|wing var. of
  pinguin
pin|head
pin|head|ed
pin|head|ed|ness
pin|hole
pin|ion
Pink|er|ton, Allan
  detective
pink-eye
pinkie little finger;
  white person;
  maggot; cf. pinky
pink|ish
pink|ly
pink|ness
pinko
  pinkos or pink|oes
Pink|ster
pinky
  pink|ier
  pinki|est
  pinkish; cf. pinkie

pinna
pin|nae
pin|nace
pin|na|cle
pin|na|cling
pin|nate
pin|nated
pin|nate|ly
pin|nati|fid
pin|na|tion
pinni|ped
Pinni|pedia
pin|nule
pinny
  pin|nies
Pino|chet, Au|gusto
  president of Chile
pin|ochle
pino|cyt|osis
pin|ole
piñon
pino|tage
Pinot Blanc
Pinot Noir
pin|out
pin|point
pin|prick
Pin|sent, Mat|thew
  rower
pin|spot
pin|stripe
pin|striped
pint
pinta = pint of milk
pin|tail
Pin|ter, Har|old
  dramatist
pin|tle
pinto +s
pin-tuck
pin-up n. & mod.
pin|wheel
pin|worm
piny
Pin|yin
pin|yon var. of
  piñon
pio|let
pion
pi|on|eer
pi|onic
pious
pi|ous|ly

pi|ous|ness
pip
  pipped
  pip|ping
pipa toad; cf. piper
pipal var. of peepul;
  cf. people
pipe
  pip|ing
pipe|clay
pipe|fish
pipe|ful
pipe|less
pipe|line
pipe|lin|ing
Piper, John painter
piper pipe-player;
  cf. pipa
pi|pera|zine
pi|peri|dine
pipe|stone
pip|ette
pip|et|ting
pipe|work
pipe|wort
pipi mollusc
pipi|strelle
pipit
pip|kin
pip|less
pip|pin
pip|sis|sewa
pip|squeak
pipy
pi|quancy
pi|quant
pi|quant|ly
pique
  piquing
  resentment; irri-
  tate; score in card
  games; cf. peak,
  peek, peke
piqué fabric
pi|quet card game;
  cf. picket, picquet
pir Muslim saint; cf.
  peer, pier
pir|acy
  pir|acies
Pi|raeus
pi|ra|gua
Piran|dello, Luigi
  writer

Pira|nesi,
Gio|vanni Bat|tista
engraver
pi|ranha
pir|ate
pir|at|ing
pir|at|ic|al
pir|at|ic|al|ly
piri|form var. of
pyriform
pir|imi|carb
piri|piri plant
piri-piri sauce
pirk fishing hook;
cf. perk
pirog
pi|rogi or pi|rogen
Russian pie
pi|rogi dumplings;
var. of pierogi
pi|rogue canoe
piro|plas|mo|sis
pi|roshki
pirou|ette
pirou|et|ting
pi|rozhki var. of
piroshki
pirri-pirri burr =
piripiri
Pisa
pis aller
pl. *pis aller*
Pisan, Chris|tine de
writer
Pi|sano, An|drea,
Gio|vanni, Ni|cola,
and Nino artists
pisca|tor|ial
pisca|tory
Pi|scean
Pi|sces
pisci|cul|tural
pisci|cul|ture
pisci|cul|tur|ist
pis|cina
pis|ci|nas or
pis|ci|nae
pis|cine
Pi|scis Aus|tra|lis
Pi|scis Aus|tri|nus
pisci|vore
pis|civ|or|ous
pisco
pisé

pish|er
pish|ogue
Pish|pek
pish|rogue var. of
pishogue
Pi|sidia
Pi|sid|ian
pisi|form
Pi|sis|tra|tus tyrant
of Athens
pis|key +s var. of
pisky
pisky
pis|kies
pis|mire
piso|lite
piso|lith
piso|lit|ic
piss|abed
pis|sal|ad|ière
piss|ant
Pis|sarro, Cam|ille
artist
piss|er *vulgar slang*
piss|head *vulgar
slang*
piss-hole *vulgar
slang*
pis|soir
piss|pot *vulgar
slang*
piss-take n. *vulgar
slang*
piss-up n. *vulgar
slang*
pissy *vulgar slang*
pis|ta|chio +s
pis|ta|cite
piste
pis|teur
pis|til of flower; cf.
pistol
pis|til|lary
pis|til|late
pis|til|lif|er|ous
pis|til|line
pis|tol
pis|tolled Br.
pis|toled US
pis|tol|ling Br.
pis|tol|ing US
(shoot with) gun;
cf. pistil
pis|tole coin

pis|tol|eer
pis|tol|ero +s
pis|ton
pis|tou
pit
pit|ted
pit|ting
pita var. of pitta
pita|haya
pit-a-pat
pit|apat var. of
pit-a-pat
Pit|cairn Is|lands
pitch-and-toss
pitch|blende
pitch|er
pitch|er|ful
pitch|fork
pitch|man
pitch|men
pitch|out
pitch-pipe
pitch|pole
pitch|pol|ing
pitch|stone
pitchy
pitch|ier
pitchi|est
pit|eous
pit|eous|ly
pit|eous|ness
pit|fall
pit|head
Pithe|can|thro|pus
pith|ily
pithi|ness
pi|thi|vier
pith|less
pithos
pithoi
pithy
pith|ier
pithi|est
piti|able
piti|able|ness
piti|ably
piti|ful
piti|ful|ly
piti|ful|ness
piti|less
piti|less|ly
piti|less|ness

Pit|man, Isaac
shorthand inventor
pit|man
pit|men
miner
pit|man +s
connecting rod
piton spike
Pi|tons mountains,
St Lucia
pitot
pit|pan
Pitt, Wil|liam two
prime ministers of
Britain
pitta
pit|tance
pitter-patter
Pitti Pal|ace
pitto|sporum
Pitt-Rivers
Mu|seum
Pitts|burgh
pi|tu|it|ary
pi|tu|it|ar|ies
pity
pit|ies
pit|ied
pity|ing
pity|ing|ly
pityr|ia|sis
più *Music* more
Pius popes
pivot
piv|ot|abil|ity
piv|ot|able
piv|otal
pivot|man
pivot|men
pix = pictures; cf.
pyx
pixel
pix|el|ate
pix|el|at|ing
display as or divide
into pixels
pix|el|ation
pix|el|late var. of
pixelate
pix|el|la|tion var. of
pixelation
Pixel|vision
pixie
pixie|ish

pix¦il¦ate var. of
  pixelate
pix¦il¦ated
  bewildered; drunk
pix¦il¦ation film
  technique;
  bewilderment
pix¦il¦lated var. of
  pixilated
pix¦il¦la¦tion var. of
  pixilation
pixy
  pixies
  var. of pixie
pixy¦ish var. of
  pixieish
Pizan, Chris¦tine de
  var. of Pisan
Pi¦zarro, Fran¦cisco
  conquistador
pi¦zazz var. of
  pizzazz
pizza
piz¦zazz
piz¦zeria
pizzi¦cato
  pizzi¦ca¦tos or
  pizzi¦cati
piz¦zle
plac¦abil¦ity
plac¦able
plac¦ably
plac¦ard
pla¦cate
  pla¦cat¦ing
  pla¦cat¦ing¦ly
  pla¦ca¦tion
  pla¦ca¦tory
place
  pla¦cing
  (put in) position;
  cf. plaice
pla¦cebo +s
place¦hold¦er
place-kicker
place¦less
place¦man
  place¦men
place¦ment
pla¦centa
  pla¦cen¦tae or
  pla¦cen¦tas
pla¦cen¦tal
pla¦centa prae¦via
  Br.

pla¦centa pre¦via
  US
pla¦cen¦ta¦tion
pla¦cer
pla¦cet vote
pla¦cid
pla¦cid¦ity
pla¦cid¦ly
pla¦cid¦ness
Placi¦dyl trademark
placket opening in
  garment; cf.
  plaquette
placky bag
placo¦derm
placo¦dont
plac¦oid
Placo¦zoa
pla¦fond
pla¦gal
plage beach; part of
  sun
pla¦giar¦ise Br. var.
  of plagiarize
pla¦giar¦iser Br. var.
  of plagiarizer
pla¦giar¦ism
pla¦giar¦ist
pla¦giar¦is¦tic
pla¦giar¦ize
  pla¦giar¦iz¦ing
pla¦giar¦izer
plagio¦clase
plague
  pla¦guing
  disease; (cause)
  trouble
pla¦guey var. of
  plaguy
pla¦guy
plaice
  pl. plaice
  fish; cf. place
plaid
Plaid Cymru
plaid¦ed
plain flat land; sim-
  ple; not milk (choc-
  olate); not
  self-raising (flour);
  not a court card;
  not trumps;
  complain; cf. plane
plain¦chant

plain sail¦ing
  straightforward
  progress; cf. plane
  sailing
plains¦man
  plains¦men
plains-wander¦er
plain¦tiff
plain¦tive
plain¦tive¦ly
plain¦tive¦ness
plait interlace hair
  etc.; cf. plat
plan
  planned
  plan¦ning
pla¦nar of a plane
  surface; cf. planer
plan¦ar¦ian
plan¦ation
planche
plan¦chet coin
  blank
plan¦chette board
  at seance
Planck, Max physi-
  cist
plane
  plan¦ing
  aircraft; flat (sur-
  face); tool; tree;
  skim; shave; cf.
  plain
planc¦load
plane¦maker
plane¦mak¦ing
planer tool; cf.
  planar
plane sail¦ing form
  of navigation; cf.
  plain sailing
planes¦man
planet
plan¦et¦ar¦ium
  plan¦et¦ar¦iums or
  plan¦et¦aria
planet¦ary
planet¦esi¦mal
planet¦fall
planet¦oid
planet¦olo¦gist
planet¦ology
plan¦form
plan¦gency

plan¦gent
plan¦gent¦ly
plani¦fi¦ca¦tion
plani¦gale
plan¦ig¦raphy
plan¦im¦eter
plani¦met¦ric
plani¦met¦ric¦al¦ly
plan¦im¦etry
plan¦ish
plan¦ish¦er
plani¦sphere
plani¦spher¦ic
plank¦tic
plank¦tiv¦or¦ous
plank¦ton
plank¦ton¦ic
plan¦ner
plano¦con¦cave
plano¦con¦vex
plano¦graph¦ic
plan¦og¦raphy
plan¦om¦eter
plant¦able
Plan¦tagenet
plan¦tain
plan¦tar of the sole
  of the foot
plan¦ta¦tion
plant¦er person;
  container
plant¦er's punch
planti¦grade
Plan¦tin typeface
plant¦let
plant-like
plant¦ocracy
  plant¦oc¦ra¦cies
plants¦man
  plants¦men
plants¦woman
  plants¦women
pla¦nula
  pla¦nu¦lae
plaque
pla¦quette small
  plaque; cf. placket
plashy
plasm var. of
  plasma
plasma
plasma¦lemma
plasma¦lem¦mal

plasma|pause
plasma|pher|esis
plasma|sphere
plas|mat|ic
plas|mic
plas|mid
plas|min
plas|mino|gen
plasmo|desma
  plasmo|des|mata
plas|mo|dial
plas|mo|dium
  plas|modia
plasmo|lyse *Br.*
  plasmo|lys|ing
plas|moly|sis
plasmo|lyze *US*
  plasmo|lyz|ing
plas|mon
Plas|sey
plas|teel
plas|ter
plas|ter|board
plas|ter|er
plas|ter|work
plas|tery
plas|tic
plas|tic|al|ly
plas|ti|cine
  trademark
plas|ti|cisa|tion *Br.*
  var. of
  plasticization
plas|ti|cise *Br.* var.
  of plasticize
plas|ti|ciser *Br.* var.
  of plasticizer
plas|ti|city
plas|ti|ciza|tion
plas|ti|cize
  plas|ti|ciz|ing
plas|ti|cizer
plas|ticky
plas|tid
plas|tique
plas|ti|sol
plas|tral
plas|tron
plat
  plat|ted
  plat|ting
  plot of land; map;
  cf. plait
Pla|taea

platan tree; cf.
  platen
pla|tanna clawed
  toad
plat du jour
  plats du jour
Plate, River
plate
  plat|ing
plat|eau
  pl. plat|eaux or
  plat|eaus
  v. plat|eaus
  plat|eaued
  plat|eau|ing
plate|ful
plate|lay|er
plate|less
plate|let
plate|maker
platen plate in
  printing press;
  roller; cf. platan
plater
plat|er|esque
plat|form
plat|form|er
Plath, Syl|via poet
pla|tin|ic
plat|in|isa|tion *Br.*
  var. of
  platinization
plat|in|ise *Br.* var. of
  platinize
plat|in|iza|tion
plat|in|ize
  plat|in|iz|ing
plat|in|oid
plat|inum
plati|tude
plati|tud|in|ise *Br.*
  var. of
  platitudinize
plati|tud|in|ize
plati|tud|in|iz|ing
plati|tud|in|ous
Plato philosopher
Pla|ton|ic of Plato
pla|ton|ic not sex-
  ual; theoretical
Pla|ton|ic|al|ly in
  the manner of
  Plato
pla|ton|ic|al|ly in a
  platonic way

Pla|ton|ism
Pla|ton|ist
pla|toon
Platt|deutsch
platte|land
platte|land|er
plat|ter
platy
  plat|ies
  fish
platy|hel|minth
Platy|hel|min|thes
platy|pus
platyr|rhine
pla|tysma
  pla|tys|mas or
  pla|tys|mata
plau|dit
plausi|bil|ity
plaus|ible
plaus|ibly
Plau|tus, Titus
  Mac|cius dramatist
playa
play|abil|ity
play|able
play-actor
play|back
play|bill
play|book
play|boy
play-by-play *n.*
play|down
Play|er, Gary golfer
play|er
play|fel|low
play|ful
play|ful|ly
play|ful|ness
play|goer
play|ground
play|group
play|house
play|let
play|list
play|maker
play|mak|ing
play|mate
play-off *n.*
play|pen
play|room
play|scheme

play|school
play|suit
play|thing
play|time
play|wright
play|writ|ing
plaza
plea
pleach
plead
  plead|ed
  US also pled
plead|able
plead|er
plead|ing|ly
pleas|ance
pleas|ant
pleas|ant|ly
pleas|ant|ness
pleas|ant|ry
  pleas|ant|ries
please
  pleas|ing
pleas|ed|ly
pleas|ing|ly
pleas|ur|able
pleas|ur|able|ness
pleas|ur|ably
pleas|ure
  pleas|ur|ing
pleat
plea|ther
pleb ordinary person
plebby
plebe new cadet or
  fresher
ple|beian
ple|bis|cit|ary
pleb|is|cite
Ple|cop|tera
ple|cop|ter|an
plec|trum
  plec|trums or
  plec|tra
pledge
  pledg|ing
pledgee
pledger generally
pledget
pledgor *Law*
pleiad outstanding
  group of seven

Plei|ades seven
  daughters of Atlas;
  star cluster
plein-air adj.
pleio|trop|ic
plei|otrop|ism
plei|otropy
Pleis|to|cene
  trademark
plen|ary
  plen|ar|ies
pleni|po|ten|tiary
  pleni|po|ten|
      tiar|ies
pleni|tude
plent|eous
plent|eous|ly
plent|eous|ness
plen|ti|ful
plen|ti|ful|ly
plen|ti|ful|ness
plen|ti|tude
plenty
ple|num
pleo|chro|ic
ple|och|ro|ism
pleo|cy|to|sis
pleo|morph|ic
pleo|morph|ism
ple|on|asm
ple|on|as|tic
ple|on|as|tic|al|ly
pleo|pod
pler|oma
plero|mat|ic
ple|sio|saur
ples|sor var. of
  plexor
pleth|ora
pleth|or|ic
ple|thysmo|graph
ple|thysmo|
        graph|ic
pleura
  pleurae
  membrane; lateral
  body part
pleura pl. of
  pleuron
pleural
pleur|isy
pleur|it|ic
pleuro|dynia

pleuron
  pleura
pleuro|
        pneu|mo|nia
Ple|ven
plexi|form
plexi|glas
  trademark
plexor
plexus
  pl. plexus or
  plex|uses
pli|abil|ity
pli|able
pli|ably
pli|ancy
pli|ant
pli|ant|ly
plica
  plicae or plicas
pli|cate
pli|cated
pli|ca|tion
plié +s +ed +ing
pli|ers
plight
plim|sole var. of
  plimsoll
plim|soll
Plim|soll line
Plin|ian
plin|ky
Pliny two Roman
  statesmen
Plio|cene
Plio–Pleisto|cene
plio|saur
plissé
plock
plod
  plod|ded
  plod|ding
plod|der
  plod|ding|ly
ploidy
Ploi|eşti
plon|geur
plonk|er
plop
  plopped
  plop|ping
plo|sion
plo|sive

plot
  plot|ted
  plot|ting
  cf. **Plott**, plotz
Plo|tinus
  philosopher
plot|less
Plott hound
plot|ter
plotty
plotz collapse with
  emotion
plough *Br.*
  US plow
plough|able *Br.*
  US plowable
plough|er *Br.*
  US plower
plough|land *Br.*
  US plowland
plough|man *Br.*
  plough|men
  US plowman
plough|share *Br.*
  US plowshare
Plov|div
plover
plow *US*
  Br. plough
plow|able *US*
  Br. ploughable
plow|er *US*
  Br. plougher
plow|land *US*
  Br. ploughland
plow|man *US*
  plow|men
  Br. ploughman
plow|share *US*
  Br. ploughshare
pluck|er
pluck|ily
plucki|ness
pluck|less
plucky
  pluck|ier
  pluck|iest
plug
  plugged
  plug|ging
plug|board
plug|ger
plug|hole
plug-in *adj. & n.*

plug-ugly
  plug-uglies
plum fruit; tree;
  colour; highly
  desirable; cf.
  plumb
plum|age
plum|aged
plumb measure
  depth; vertical;
  exactly; connect to
  pipes; cf. **plum**
plum|bago +s
plum|bate
plum|be|ous
plumb|er
plumb|er's putty
plumb|er's snake
  +s
plum|bic
plum|bism
plumb|less
plum|bous
plume
  plum|ing
plume|less
plume-like
plu|meria
plu|mery
plum|met
plummy
  plum|mier
  plum|mi|est
plum|ose
plump|ish
plump|ly
plump|ness
plumpy
plum|ule
plumy
  plu|mier
  plu|mi|est
plun|der
plun|der|er
plunge
  plun|ging
plun|ger
plu|per|fect
plural
plur|al|isa|tion *Br.*
  var. of
  pluralization
plur|al|ise *Br.* var.
  of pluralize

plur¦al¦ism
plur¦al¦ist
plur¦al¦is¦tic
plur¦al¦is¦tic¦al¦ly
plur¦al¦ity
  plur¦al¦ities
plur¦al¦iza¦tion
plur¦al¦ize
  plur¦al¦iz¦ing
plur¦al¦ly
pluri¦po¦tent
plus
plus ça change
plush¦ly
plush¦ness
plushy
  plush¦ier
  plushi¦est
Plu¦tarch biographer
plu¦teus
  plu¦tei
Plu¦tino
Pluto Greek god of the underworld; planet
plu¦toc¦racy
  plu¦toc¦ra¦cies
plu¦to¦crat
plu¦to¦crat¦ic
plu¦to¦crat¦ic¦al¦ly
plu¦ton
Plu¦to¦nian
Plu¦ton¦ic of the planet Pluto or the underworld
plu¦ton¦ic of type of rock
Plu¦to¦nism theory of rock formation
plu¦to¦nism method of rock formation
Plu¦to¦nist
plu¦to¦nium
plu¦vial
Plu¦vi¦ose
  French Pluviôse
ply
  plies
  plied
  ply¦ing
Ply¦mouth
plyo¦met¦rics
ply¦wood

pneuma
pneu¦mat¦ic of air
pneu¦mat¦ic¦al¦ly
pneuma¦ti¦city
pneu¦ma¦tique Parisian mail system
pneu¦mato¦logic¦al
pneuma¦tol¦ogy
pneuma¦toly¦sis
pneu¦mato¦lyt¦ic
pneu¦mato¦phore
pneumo¦coc¦cal
pneumo¦coc¦cus
  pneumo¦cocci
pneumo¦coni¦osis
pneumo¦cys¦tis
pneumo¦en¦ceph¦alo¦graph¦ic
pneumo¦en¦ceph¦al¦og¦raphy
pneumo¦gas¦tric
pneu¦mon¦ec¦tomy
  pneu¦mon¦ec¦to¦mies
pneu¦mo¦nia
pneu¦mon¦ic
pneu¦mon¦itis
pneu¦mono¦ultra¦micro¦scopic¦silico¦vol¦cano¦coni¦osis
pneumo¦tacho¦graph
pneumo¦thorax
Pnyx assembly place in Athens
Po river, Italy
po +s chamber pot
poach¦er
po¦blano +s
Poca¦hon¦tas princess
po¦chard
po¦chette
pocho +s
pock pockmark; cf. pox
pocked
pocket
pock¦et¦able
pock¦et¦book

pock¦et¦ful
pock¦et¦knife
  pock¦et¦knives
pock¦et¦less
pock¦mark
pocky
poco *Music*
Poco¦mania
pod
  pod¦ded
  pod¦ding
pod¦agra
pod¦ag¦ral
pod¦ag¦ric
pod¦ag¦rous
pod¦cast
pod¦ger
podgi¦ness
Pod¦gor¦ica
podgy
  podgi¦er
  podgi¦est
po¦dia¦trist
po¦dia¦try
po¦dium
  po¦di¦ums or podia
podo¦carp
Pod¦olsk
pod¦sol var. of podzol
pod¦sol¦ic var. of podzolic
pod¦sol¦isa¦tion *Br.* var. of podzolization
pod¦sol¦ise *Br.* var. of **podzolize**
pod¦sol¦iza¦tion var. of **podzolization**
pod¦sol¦ize
  pod¦sol¦iz¦ing var. of podzolize
Pod¦unk
pod¦zol
pod¦zol¦ic
pod¦zol¦isa¦tion *Br.* var. of podzolization
pod¦zol¦ise *Br.* var. of podzolize
pod¦zol¦iza¦tion
pod¦zol¦ize
  pod¦zol¦iz¦ing

Poe, Edgar Allan writer
poem
poens¦kop
poesy
poet
poet¦as¦ter
poète mau¦dit
  poètes mau¦dits
poet¦ess
poet¦ic
poet¦ic¦al
poet¦ic¦al¦ly
poeti¦cise *Br.* var. of poeticize
poeti¦cism
poeti¦cize
  poeti¦ciz¦ing
poet¦ise *Br.* var. of poetize
poet¦ize
  poet¦iz¦ing
poet¦ry
  poet¦ries
po-faced
pogey
pogo
  pl. pogos
  v. po¦goes
  po¦goed
  pogo¦ing
Po¦gon¦oph¦ora
po¦gon¦oph¦or¦an
pog¦rom
Po Hai var. of Bo Hai
po¦hutu¦kawa
poi Hawaiian food
poi
  pl. poi or pois Maori flax ball
poign¦ance
poign¦ancy
poign¦ant
poign¦ant¦ly
poi¦ki¦lit¦ic
poi¦kilo¦blast¦ic
poi¦kilo¦therm
poi¦kilo¦ther¦mal
poi¦kilo¦ther¦mia
poi¦kilo¦ther¦mic
poi¦kilo¦thermy
poilu

Poin|caré, Jules-
  Henri
  mathematician
poin|ci|ana
poind
Poin|de|xter
poin|set|tia
point-blank
point d'appui
  points d'appui
pointe Ballet
Pointe-à-Pitre
point|ed|ly
point|ed|ness
poin|telle
  trademark
Pointe-Noire
point|er
Point|ers two stars
poin|til|lism
poin|til|list
poin|til|lis|tic
point|less
point|less|ly
point|less|ness
points|man
  points|men
point-to-point
point-to-pointer
point-to-pointing
pointy
  point|ier
  point|iest
poise
  pois|ing
Poi|seuille flow
poi|sha
  pl. poi|sha
poi|son
poi|son|er
poi|son|ous
poi|son|ous|ly
poi|son pen let|ter
Pois|son, Siméon-
  Denis mathemat-
  ical physicist
Poi|tier, Sid|ney
  actor
Poi|tiers city, France
Poitou-Charentes
poke
  pok|ing
poker

poker|work
poke|weed
pokey prison; cf.
  pokie, poky
pokey var. of poky
pokie fruit machine;
  cf. pokey, poky
poki|ly
poki|ness
poky
  poki|er
  poki|est
  small; slow; cf.
  pokey, pokie
pol politician; cf.
  poll
Po|lack *offensive*
Pol|and
Pol|an|ski, Roman
  film director
polar
Po|lari theatrical
  slang
po|lar|im|eter
po|lari|met|ric
po|lar|im|etry
Po|laris
po|lar|is|able Br.
  var. of polarizable
po|lari|sa|tion Br.
  var. of polarization
po|lari|scope
po|lari|scop|ic
po|lar|ise Br. var. of
  polarize
po|lar|iser Br. var.
  of polarizer
po|lar|ity
  po|lar|ities
po|lar|iz|able
po|lar|iza|tion
po|lar|ize
po|lar|iz|ing
po|lar|izer
po|laro|graph|ic
po|lar|og|raphy
Po|lar|oid
  trademark
pol|der
Pole Polish person
pole
  pol|ing
  (move with) piece
  of wood; location;

one of two
  opposites; cf. poll
pole|ax US
pole|axe Br.
  pole|ax|ing
pole|cat
polecat-ferret
poleis pl. of *polis*
po|lem|ic
po|lem|ic|al
po|lem|ic|al|ly
po|lemi|cise Br. var.
  of polemicize
po|lemi|cist
po|lemi|cize
  po|lemi|ciz|ing
po|lenta
pole-vaulter
pole|ward
po|lice
  po|licing
po|lice|man
po|lice|men
po|lice|woman
  po|lice|women
poli|cier
pol|icy
  pol|icies
pol|icy|hold|er
pol|icy|maker
pol|icy|making
polio
polio|my|el|itis
polio|virus
polis
  poleis
Poli|sario
Pol|ish of Poland;
  language
pol|ish shine etc.
pol|ish|able
pol|ish|er
pol|it|buro +s
po|lite
  po|liter
  po|litest
po|lite|ly
po|lite|ness
poli|tesse
pol|it|ic
  pol|it|icked
  pol|it|ick|ing
  pol|it|ical

pol|it|ic|al|ly in a
  political way; cf.
  politicly
pol|it|ician
pol|iti|cisa|tion Br.
  var. of
  politicization
pol|iti|cise Br. var.
  of politicize
pol|iti|ciza|tion
pol|iti|cize
  pol|iti|ciz|ing
pol|it|ic|ly judi-
  ciously; cf.
  politically
pol|it|ico +s
pol|it|ics
pol|ity
  pol|ities
polje
Polk, James US
  president
polka
  pol|kas
  pol|kaed or
  polka'd
  pol|ka|ing
polka-dotted
poll vote; head;
  record opinion; cf.
  pol, pole
pol|lack
Pol|lai|uolo,
  An|tonio and Piero
  artists
pol|lan fish; cf.
  pollen
pol|lard
poll|ee person
  questioned in a
  poll; cf. polly, poly
pol|len grains in
  flower; cf. pollan
pol|lex
  pol|li|ces
pol|lie var. of polly
pol|lin|ate
pol|lin|at|ing
pol|lin|ation
pol|lin|ator
pol|lin|ium
pol|lin|ia
polli|wog
pollo +s

Pol|lock, Jack|son
  painter
pol|lock var. of
  pollack
poll|ster
pol|lu|tant
pol|lute
  pol|lut|ing
pol|luter
pol|lu|tion
Pol|lux twin of
  Castor; star
polly
  pol|lies
  politician; cf.
  pollee, poly
Polly|anna
Polly|anna|ish
Polly|anna|ism
polly|wog var. of
  polliwog
Polo, Marco travel-
  ler
polo
pol|oid|al
Polo|kwane
pol|on|aise
po|lo|nium
Po|lon|na|ruwa
po|lony
  po|lo|nies
Pol Pot prime min-
  ister of Cambodia
Pol|tava
pol|ter|geist
Pol|tor|atsk
pol|troon
pol|troon|ery
poly +s polyester;
  polythene;
  polytechnic; cf.
  polly
poly|acet|yl|ene
poly|acryl|amide
poly|adic
poly|amide
poly|amor|ist
poly|amor|ous
poly|amory
poly|an|drous
poly|an|dry
poly|an|thus
  pl. poly|an|thus
poly|atom|ic

poly|bag
Po|lyb|ius historian
poly|car|bon|ate
Poly|carp, St
Poly|chaeta
poly|chaetan
poly|chaete
poly|chaet|ous
poly|chro|mat|ic
poly|chro|ma|tism
poly|chrome
  poly|chrom|ing
poly|chromy
poly|clinic
Poly|cli|tus sculptor
poly|clonal
poly|cot|ton
poly|crys|tal|line
poly|cul|ture
poly|cyc|lic
poly|cys|tic
poly|cy|thae|mia
  Br.
poly|cy|themia *US*
poly|dac|tyl
poly|dac|tyly
Poly|deu|ces *Greek*
  Mythology
poly|dip|sia
poly|drug
poly|elec|tro|lyte
poly|embry|on|ic
poly|embry|ony
poly|ene
poly|es|ter
poly|eth|nic
poly|eth|ni|city
poly|ethyl|ene
Poly|filla *trademark*
poly|gam|ic
pol|yg|am|ist
pol|yg|am|ous
pol|yg|am|ous|ly
pol|yg|amy
poly|gene
poly|gen|esis
poly|gen|et|ic
poly|gen|et|ic|al|ly
poly|gen|ic
poly|gen|ic|al|ly
poly|gen|ism
poly|gen|ist

pol|ygeny
poly|glot
poly|glot|tal
poly|glot|tic
poly|glot|tism
poly|gon
pol|yg|on|al
pol|yg|onum
poly|graph
poly|graph|ic
poly|gyne
pol|ygyn|ous
pol|ygyny
poly|he|dral
poly|he|dric
poly|he|dron
  poly|he|dra or
  poly|he|drons
poly|his|tor
Poly|hym|nia Muse
poly|imide
poly|math
poly|math|ic
pol|ym|athy
poly|mer
poly|mer|ase
poly|mer|ic
poly|mer|is|able *Br.*
  var. of
  polymerizable
poly|mer|isa|tion
  Br. var. of
  polymerization
poly|mer|ise *Br.* var.
  of polymerize
poly|mer|ism
poly|mer|iz|able
poly|mer|iza|tion
poly|mer|ize
poly|mer|iz|ing
poly|mer|ous
poly|met|al|lic
poly|methyl
poly|mict
poly|morph
poly|morph|ic
poly|morph|ism
poly|morpho|
            nuclear
poly|morph|ous
poly|morph|ous|ly
poly|myo|si|tis
poly|myxin

Poly|nesia
Poly|nes|ian
poly|neur|it|ic
poly|neur|itis
poly|ncur|op|athy
poly|no|mial
poly|nuclear
poly|nucleo|tide
po|lynya
poly|oma virus
polyp
polyp|ary
  polyp|ar|ies
poly|pep|tide
pol|ypha|gous
poly|phase
poly|phasic
Poly|phe|mus *Greek*
  Mythology
poly|phe|nol
poly|phenol|ic
poly|phon|ic
poly|phon|ic|al|ly
pol|yph|on|ist
pol|yph|on|ous
pol|yph|ony
  pol|yph|on|ies
poly|phos|phate
poly|phyl|et|ic
polypi pl. of
  polypus
poly|ploid
poly|ploidy
poly|pod
poly|pody
  poly|pod|ies
polyp|oid
poly|pore
polyp|osis
polyp|ous *adj.*
poly|pro|pyl|ene
polyp|tych
poly|pus *n.*
  polypi
poly|rhythm
poly|rhyth|mic
poly|ribo|some
poly|sac|char|ide
poly|sem|ic
poly|sem|ous
poly|semy
poly|some
poly|styr|ene

poly|sul|fide *US*
poly|sul|phide *Br.*
poly|syl|lab|ic
poly|syl|lab|ic|al|ly
poly|syl|lable
poly|symp|tom|
      at|ic
poly|syn|thet|ic
poly|tech|nic
poly|tene
poly|tetra|fluoro|
      ethyl|ene
poly|the|ism
poly|the|ist
poly|the|is|tic
poly|thene
poly|thetic
poly|tonal
poly|ton|al|ity
poly|tunnel
poly|type
poly|typ|ic
poly|typ|ism
poly|un|sat|ur|ate
poly|un|sat|ur|ated
poly|ur|eth|ane
  poly|ur|eth|an|ing
poly|uria
poly|uric
poly|va|lence
poly|va|lent
poly|vi|nyl
poly|vinyl|pyr|roli|
      done
Poly|zoa
poly|zoan
poma *trademark*
pom|ace
po|made
  po|mad|ing
Pomak
po|man|der
poma|rine
po|ma|tum
pombe
pome fruit
pom|egran|ate
pom|elo +s
Pom|er|ania
Pom|er|anian
Pom|erol
pom|fret

pomi|cul|ture
pom|ifer|ous
pom|mel knob; part
  of saddle
pommes frites
Pom|mie var. of
  Pommy
Pommy
  Pom|mies
po-mo =
  postmodern
pomo||logic|al
pom|olo|gist
pom|ology
Pom|pa|dour,
  Ma|dame de mis-
  tress of Louis XV
pom|pa|dour hair-
  style
pom|pano +s
Pom|peii ancient
  city, Italy
Pom|pey Roman
  general; Ports-
  mouth, England
Pom|pi|dou,
  Georges president
  of France
pom|pom woollen
  ball; flower
pom-pom cannon
pom|pon var. of
  pompom
pom|pos|ity
  pom|pos|ities
pom|pous
pom|pous|ly
pom|pous|ness
'pon = upon
ponce
  pon|cing
Ponce de León,
  Juan explorer
poncey
pon|cier
  pon|ci|est
pon|cho +s
poncy var. of
  poncey
pon|der
pon|der|abil|ity
pon|der|able
pon|der|al
pon|der|osa

pon|der|os|ity
pon|der|ous
pon|der|ous|ly
pon|der|ous|ness
Pondi|cherry
pon|dok
pon|dok|kie var. of
  pondok
pond|weed
ponga
pon|gal
pon|gee
pon|gid
pongo +s
pongy
  pong|ier
  pongi|est
pon|iard
pons
  pon|tes
pons as|in|orum
  pon|tes as|in|orum
pons Var|olii
  pon|tes Var|olii
Ponte, Lo|renzo Da
  librettist
Ponte|fract
pon|tes pl. of pons
Pon|tiac
Ponti|anak
Pon|tic
pon|ti|fex
  pon|tifi|ces
Pon|ti|fex
  Max|imus
pon|tiff
pon|tif|ic|al
pon|tif|ic|al|ly
pon|tifi|cate
  pon|tifi|cat|ing
pon|tifi|ces
pon|til
pon|tine
Pont l'Évêque
pon|toon
Pon|tormo, Ja|copo
  da painter
Pon|tus
pony
  po|nies
pony|tail
pony|tailed
pony-trekker

pony-trekking
Ponzi scheme
poo var. of pooh
poo|dle
  pood|ling
poodle|faker
poof *offensive*
  homosexual man;
  exclam.; cf. **pouffe**
poof|ter *offensive*
poofy
  poof|ier
  poofi|est *offensive*
Pooh, Win|nie the
  fictional bear
pooh
pooh-bah
pooh-pooh
Pooh|sticks
pooja var. of **puja**
pooka hobgoblin; cf.
  puka
pool cf. **pul**
Poole town,
  England
pool|room
pool|side
Poona
poon|tang
poop|er scoop|er
poopy
  poop|ier
  poopi|est
poor not rich;
  deserving pity; cf.
  paw, pore, pour
poor|house
poor|ness
poor|will
Poo|ter|ish
poo|tle
  poot|ling
poove var. of **poof**
  offensive
pop
  popped
  pop|ping
popa|dom var. of
  poppadom
pop|corn
Pope, Alex|an|der
  poet
pope
pope|dom

pope|less
Pope|mo|bile
popery
pop|gun
pop-hole
pop|in|jay
pop|ish
pop|ish|ly
pop|lar
pop|lin
pop|lit|eal
Popo|caté|petl
pop-out *n. & adj.*
pop|over
poppa father; cf.
  popper
pop|pa|dom
pop|pa|dum var. of
  poppadom
Pop|per, Karl
  philosopher
pop|per press stud;
  vial; fishing lure; cf.
  poppa
pop|pet
poppet-head
pop|pied
pop|ple
  pop|pling
pop|ply
  pop|plier
  pop|pli|est
poppy
  pop|pies
  pop|pier
  pop|pi|est
poppy|cock
Pop|sicle *trademark*
pop|sie var. of
  popsy
pop|sock
pop|ster
pop|strel
popsy
  pop|sies
pop-top
popu|lace the
  people; cf.
  populous
popu|lar|isa|tion
  Br. var. of
  popularization

popu|lar|ise *Br.* var.
  of popularize
popu|lar|iser *Br.*
  var. of popularizer
popu|lar|ism
popu|lar|ity
popu|lar|iza|tion
popu|lar|ize
  popu|lar|iz|ing
popu|lar|izer
popu|lar|ly
popu|late
  popu|lat|ing
popu|la|tion
popu|lism
popu|list
popu|lis|tic
popu|lous densely
  populated; cf.
  populace
popu|lous|ly
popu|lous|ness
pop-up *adj. & n.*
por|angi
por|bea|gle
por|cel|ain
por|cel|lan|eous
por|cel|lan|ous var.
  of porcellaneous
porched
porch|less
por|cine relating to
  pigs
por|cini mushrooms
por|cu|pine
pore
por|ing
  tiny opening; study
  intently; cf. paw,
  poor, pour
porgy
  por|gies
Pori
Por|if|era
por|if|er|an
porin
pork-barrel|ling
pork|er
pork|ling
porky
  pork|ies
  pork|ier
  pork|iest
  fat; like pork; a lie;

porcupine; cf.
  pawky
porky-pie
porn =
  pornography; cf.
  pawn
porno
porn|og|raph|er
porno|graph|ic
porno|graph|ic|
  al|ly
porn|og|raphy
por|os|ity
por|ous
por|ous|ly
por|ous|ness
por|phy|ria
por|phy|rin
por|phy|rit|ic
por|phyro|blast
por|phyro|blast|ic
Por|phyry
  philosopher
por|phyry
  por|phy|ries
  rock
por|poise
  porpoising
por|ridge
por|ridgy
por|rin|ger
porro prism
Porsche,
  Fer|di|nand car
  designer
Por|senna, Lars
  legendary chieftain
port harbour; wine;
  left side; opening;
  etc.; cf. Porte,
  porte cochère
port|abil|ity
port|able
port|ably
port|age
port|aging
Porta|kabin
  trademark
por|tal
Porta|loo +s
  trademark
por|ta|mento
  por|ta|men|tos or
  por|ta|menti

Porta|studio +s
  trademark
porta|tive
Port-au-Prince
port|cul|lis
port|cul|lised
port de bras
  ports de bras
Porte, the Sub|lime
  or Otto|man Otto-
  man court at
  Constantinople
porte co|chère
  covered entrance
por|tend
por|tent
por|tent|ous
por|tent|ous|ly
por|tent|ous|ness
Por|ter, Cole com-
  poser and lyricist
Por|ter, Kath|er|ine
  Anne writer
Por|ter, Peter poet
por|ter
por|ter|age
por|ter|house
por|ter's knot +s
port|fire
port|folio +s
Port-Gentil
Port Har|court
Port Hed|land
port|hole
Por|tia
por|tico
  por|ti|coes or
  por|ti|cos
por|ti|ère
por|tion
por|tion|less
Port|land port, US;
  peninsula and ship-
  ping area, English
  Channel; cement;
  stone; vase
Port|laoighise var.
  of Portlaoise
Port|laoise
port|let
port|ly
  port|lier
  port|li|est

port|man|teau
  port|man|teaus or
  port|man|teaux
Port Moresby
Pôrto Alegre
porto|bello +s
Port-of-Spain
por|to|lan
por|to|lano +s var.
  of portolan
Porto Novo
Pôrto Velho
Port Pet|rovsk
Port Pirie
por|trait
por|trait|ist
por|trait|ure
por|tray
por|tray|able
por|tray|al
por|tray|er
Port Said
Port Salut
Ports|mouth
Por|tu|gal
Por|tu|guese
Port Vila
port wine stain
po|sada
pose
  pos|ing
Po|sci|don Greek
  god
poser problem
pos|eur person who
  poses
pos|euse female
  poseur
posey
  posier
  posi|est
  pretentious; cf.
  posy
posh|ly
posh|ness
posho +s
posit
posi|tif
pos|ition
pos|ition|al
pos|ition|al|ly
pos|ition|er
posi|tive

posi|tive|ly
posi|tive|ness
posi|tiv|ism
posi|tiv|ist
posi|tiv|is|tic
posi|tiv|is|tic|al|ly
posi|tiv|ity
posi|tron
Posix
posse group of
  people; cf. possie
posse comi|ta|tus
pos|sess
pos|ses|sion
pos|ses|sion|less
pos|ses|sive
pos|ses|sive|ly
pos|ses|sive|ness
pos|ses|sor
pos|ses|sory
pos|set
pos|si|bil|ity
  pos|si|bil|ities
pos|sible
pos|sibly
pos|sie position; cf.
  posse
pos|sum
post cf. poste
  restante
post|age
pos|tal
pos|tal|ly
post|bag
post-bellum
post|box
post|card
post-chaise
post-classic|al
post|code
post|coded
post-coital
post-coital|ly
post-colonial
post-date
  post-dating
post|doc
post|doc|tor|al
pos|ter
poste rest|ante
pos|ter|ior
pos|ter|ior|ity

pos|ter|ior|ly
pos|ter|isa|tion Br.
  var. of
  posterization
pos|ter|ise Br. var.
  of posterize
pos|ter|ity
pos|ter|iza|tion
pos|ter|ize
  pos|ter|iz|ing
pos|tern
post|face
post-feminism
post-feminist
post|fix
post-Fordism
post-Fordist
post-free
post|front|al
post|genom|ic
post|gla|cial
post|grad
post|gradu|ate
post-haste
post hoc
post|hu|mous
post|hu|mous|ly
post-hypnot|ic
pos|tie
pos|til
pos|til|ion
pos|til|lion var. of
  postilion
post-
  Impres|sion|ism
post-
  Impres|sion|ist
post-
  Impres|sion|is|tic
post-industrial
post-industrial|ism
Post-it trademark
post|lap|sar|ian
post|lude
post|man
  post|men
post|mark
post|master
post|master
  gen|eral
  post|masters
  gen|eral
post|mil|len|nial

post|mil|len|nial|
          ism
post|mil|len|nial|
          ist
post|mis|tress
post|mod|ern
post|mod|ern|ism
post|mod|ern|ist
post|mod|ern|ity
post|modi|fi|
      ca|tion
post|modi|fier
post|mod|ify
  post|modi|fies
  post|modi|fied
  post|modi|fy|ing
post-mortem
post|multi|pli|
      ca|tion
post|multi|ply
  post|multi|plies
  post|multi|plied
  post|multi|ply|ing
post-natal
post-natally
post|nup|tial
post-obit
Post Of|fice organ-
  ization
post of|fice individ-
  ual office
post of|fice box
post-op
post-operative
post|orbit|al
post-paid
post-partum
post|pon|able
post|pone
  post|pon|ing
post|pone|ment
post|poner
post|pose
  post|pos|ing
post|pos|ition
post|pos|ition|al
post|posi|tive
post|posi|tive|ly
post|pran|dial
post-produc|tion
post-
  revolu|tion|ary

Post|Script *trademark* computer language
post|script additional remark
post|season
post-structur|al
post-structur|al|ism
post-structur|al|ist
post-synch
post-tax
post-tension
post-traumat|ic
pos|tu|lant
pos|tu|late
  pos|tu|lat|ing
pos|tu|la|tion
pos|tu|la|tor
pos|tural
pos|ture
  pos|tur|ing
pos|turer
post|viral
post|vocal|ic
post-war
post|woman
  post|women
Posy name
posy
  po|sies
  flowers; cf. posey
pot
  pot|ted
  pot|ting
pot|abil|ity
pot|able
pot|age thick soup cf. pottage
pota|ger
pot|am|ology
pot|ash
po|tas|sic
po|tas|sium
po|ta|tion
po|tato
  po|ta|toes
pot-au-feu
  pots-au-feu
Pota|wat|omi
pot|boil|er
po|teen
Po|tem|kin
po|tence

po|tency
  po|ten|cies
po|tent
po|ten|tate
po|ten|tial
po|ten|tial|ise *Br.* var. of potentialize
po|ten|ti|al|ity
  po|ten|ti|al|ities
po|ten|tial|ize
  po|ten|tial|iz|ing
po|ten|tial|ly
po|tenti|ate
  po|tenti|at|ing
po|tenti|ation
po|ten|tilla
po|tenti|om|eter
po|tentio|met|ric
po|tenti|om|etry
po|tent|isa|tion *Br.* var. of potentization
po|tent|ise *Br.* var. of potentize
po|tent|iza|tion
po|tent|ize
  po|tent|iz|ing
po|tent|ly
Po|tenza
pot|ful
pot|head
po|theen var. of poteen
pother
pot-herb
pot|hole
  pot|hol|ing
pot|holer
pot-hook
pot-house
pot|hunt|er
po|tion
Poti|phar *Bible*
pot|jie South African pot or stew
pot|jie|kos South African stew
pot|latch
pot|luck meal or party
pot luck chance
pot|man
  pot|men
Poto|mac

potoo +s
poto|roo +s
Pot|osí
pot|pourri
po|trero +s
Pots|dam
pot|sherd
pot|shot
pot|stick|er
pot|tage *archaic* soup or stew; cf. *potage*
Pot|ter, Bea|trix writer
Pot|ter, Den|nis dramatist
pot|ter *Br.* occupy oneself *US* putter
pot|ter maker of ceramics
pot|ter|er *Br.* *US* putterer
pot|ter's field +s
pot|ter's wheel +s
pot|tery
  pot|ter|ies
pot|ti|ness
pot|tle
potto +s
Pott's frac|ture
potty
  pot|ties
  pot|tier
  pot|ti|est
pot-valour
pou|chong
pouchy
  pouch|ier
  pouchi|est
pouf part of dress; var. of poof, pouffe
pouffe cushion; cf. poof
poufy var. of poofy
poui
  pl. poui or pouis
Pou|lenc, Fran|cis composer
poult-de-soie
poult|er|er
poult|ice
  poult|icing
poult|ry

pou|namu
pounce
  poun|cing
poun|cet box
Pound, Ezra poet
pound|age
pound|al
pound|er
pour flow; rain; cf. paw, poor, pore
pour|able
pour|boire
pour|er
pou|sada
pousse-café
Pous|sin, Nico|las painter
pous|sin chicken
pout|er
pout|ing|ly
pouty
  pout|ier
  pouti|est
pov|erty
povi|done
powan
pow|der
pow|dery
Pow|ell, An|thony novelist
Pow|ell, Colin general and politician
Pow|ell, Enoch politician
Pow|ell, Mi|chael film director
power energy etc.; cf. paua
power|boat
power|ful
power|ful|ly
power|ful|ness
power|head
power|house
power|less
power|less|ly
power|less|ness
power|lift|er
power|lift|ing
power-up *n.*
power-walk
power-walker
Pow|hatan

Powis castle, Wales
pow|wow
Powys county, Wales
pox disease
pox|virus
poxy
  pox|ier
  poxi|est
Pozi|driv *trademark in the UK*
Poz-i-Driv *trademark in the US*
Poz|nań
poz|zo|lana
pozzy var. of possie
praam boat var. of pram
prac|tic|abil|ity
prac|tic|able
prac|tic|able|ness
prac|tic|ably
prac|tical
prac|ti|cal|ity
  prac|ti|cal|ities
prac|tic|al|ly
prac|tice *n.*
prac|tice *US v.*
  prac|ticing
  Br. practise
prac|ticer *US Br.* practiser
prac|ti|cian
prac|ti|cum
prac|tise *Br. v.*
  prac|tis|ing
  US practice
prac|tiser *Br. US* practicer
prac|ti|tion|er
Prader–Willi
Prado
prae|cipe
prae|mu|nire
prae|no|men
prae|pos|tor
Prae|sepe
prae|sid|ium var. of presidium
prae|ter|nat|ural var. of preternatural
prae|ter|nat|ur|al|ism

var. of preternaturalism
prae|ter|nat|ur|al|ly
var. of preternaturally
prae|tor
prae|tor|ial
prae|tor|ian
prae|tor|ship
prag|mat|ic
prag|mat|ic|al|ly
prag|ma|tise *Br.* var. of pragmatize
prag|ma|tism
prag|ma|tist
prag|ma|tis|tic
prag|ma|tize
  prag|ma|tiz|ing
Prague
prahu var. of proa
Praia
Prair|ial month
prairie
praise
  prais|ing
  (give) approval; cf. prase
praise|ful
praiser
praise|wor|thily
praise|worthi|ness
praise|worthy
prajna
Prak|rit
pra|line
prall|tril|ler
pram
prana breath; cf. piranha
pra|nam
prana|yama
prance
  pran|cing
pran|cer
pran|dial
Prandtl, Lud|wig physicist
prank|ish
prank|ish|ness
prank|ster
pra|sad

prase quartz; cf. praise
praseo|dym|ium
prate
  prat|ing
prater
prat|fall
pra|tie
prat|in|cole
prat|ique
Prato
prat|tle
  prat|tling
prat|tler
prau var. of proa
Pravda
prawn
prawn|er
praxis
Prax|it|eles sculptor
pray say prayers; cf. prey
pray|er request etc. to deity; person who prays; cf. preyer
pray|er|ful
pray|er|ful|ly
pray|er|ful|ness
pray|er|less
pray|ing man|tis
prazi|quan|tel
preach|er
preach|ify
  preachi|fies
  preachi|fied
  preachi|fy|ing
preachi|ness
preach|ment
preachy
  preach|ier
  preach|iest
pre|adapt
pre|adap|ta|tion
pre-adoles|cence
pre-adoles|cent
pre-agricul|tur|al
pre-Aids
pre|amble
pre|ambu|lar
pre|amp = preamplifier
pre|amp|li|fied

pre|amp|li|fier
pre|arrange
  pre|arran|ging
pre|arrange|ment
pre|atom|ic
pre|bait|ing
preb|end
preb|endal
preb|end|ary
  preb|end|ar|ies
preb|end|ary|ship
pre|biot|ic
pre-book
pre-bookable
Pre|bor|eal
pre|but|tal
Pre|cam|brian
pre|can|cer|ous
pre|car|ious
pre|car|ious|ly
pre|car|ious|ness
pre|cast
preca|tive
preca|tory
pre|cau|tion
pre|cau|tion|ary
pre|cede
  pre|ced|ing
  go before; cf. proceed
pre|ce|dence
pre|ce|dent
pre|ce|dent|ly
pre|cent lead singing; cf. present
pre|cent|or leader of singing; minor canon; cf. presenter
pre|cen|tor|ship
pre|cept
pre|cep|tive
pre|cept|or
pre|cep|tor|ial
pre|cep|tor|ship
pre|cep|tress
pre|cess move through turning on axis; cf. process
pre|ces|sion movement through turning on axis; cf. procession

pre|ces|sion|al of
precession; cf.
processional
pre-Christian
pre-Christmas
pre|cinct
pre|ci|os|ity
pre|cious
pre|cious|ly
pre|cious|ness
preci|pice
pre|cipit|abil|ity
pre|cipit|able
pre|cipi|tance
pre|cipi|tancy
pre|cipi|tant
pre|cipi|tate
pre|cipi|tat|ing
pre|cipi|tate|ly
pre|cipi|tate|ness
pre|cipi|ta|tion
pre|cipi|ta|tor
pre|cipi|tin
pre|cipi|tous
pre|cipi|tous|ly
pre|cipi|tous|ness
pre|cis
 pl. pre|cis
 v. pre|cises
pre|cised
pre|cis|ing
 (make) a summary;
 French précis
pre|cise exact
pre|cise|ly
pre|cise|ness
pre|ci|sian precise
 person
pre|ci|sian|ism the
 practice of a
 precisian
pre|ci|sion accuracy
pre|ci|sion|ism the
 practice of a
 precisionist
pre|ci|sion|ist
 purist
pre-clas|sic|al
pre|clin|ic|al
pre|clude
 pre|clud|ing
pre|clu|sion
pre|clu|sive
pre|co|cial

pre|co|cious
pre|co|cious|ly
pre|co|cious|ness
pre|co|city
pre|cog|ni|tion
pre|cog|ni|tive
pre|coital
pre|coital|ly
pre-Columbian
pre|con|ceived
pre|con|cep|tion
pre|con|cert
pre|con|di|tion
pre|con|fig|ure
 pre|con|fig|ur|ing
pre-Conquest
pre|con|scious
pre|con|scious|
                ness
pre|cook
pre-cool
pre|cor|dial
pre|cor|dium
pre|cur|sive
pre|cur|sor
pre|cur|sory
pre-cut
 pre-cutting
pre|da|ceous var. of
 predacious
pre|da|cious
pre|da|cious|ness
pre|da|city
pre|date
 pre|dat|ing
 prey on
pre-date
 pre-dating
 be earlier than
pre|da|tion
preda|tor
preda|tor|ily
preda|tori|ness
preda|tory
pre|dawn
pre|de|cease
 pre|de|ceas|ing
pre|de|ces|sor
pre|de|fined
pre|della
pre|des|tin|ar|ian
pre|des|tin|ate
 pre|des|tin|at|ing

pre|des|tin|ation
pre|des|tine
 pre|des|tin|ing
pre|de|ter|min|able
pre|de|ter|min|ate
pre|de|ter|min|
                ation
pre|de|ter|mine
 pre|de|ter|min|ing
pre|de|ter|miner
pre|dial agricul-
 tural; slave
pred|ic|abil|ity
pred|ic|able
pre|dica|ment
predi|cant
 preaching (friar);
 cf. predikant
predi|cate
 predi|cat|ing
predi|ca|tion
pre|dica|tive
pre|dica|tive|ly
predi|ca|tor
pre|dict
pre|dict|abil|ity
pre|dict|able
pre|dict|ably
pre|dic|tion
pre|dict|ive
pre|dict|ive|ly
pre|dict|or
pre|digest
pre|di|ges|tion
predi|kant minister
 of Dutch Reformed
 Church; cf.
 predicant
pre|di|lec|tion
pre|dis|pose
 pre|dis|pos|ing
pre|dis|pos|ition
pred|nis|ol|one
pred|nis|one
pre|dom|in|ance
pre|dom|in|ant
pre|dom|in|ant|ly
pre|dom|in|ate
 pre|dom|in|at|ing
pre|dom|in|ate|ly
pre|doom
pre|dor|sal
pre|dyn|as|tic

pre-echo
pre-echoes
pre-echoed
pre-echoing
pre-eclamp|sia
pre-eclamp|tic
pre-elect
pre-election
pre-elector|al
pre-embryo +s
pre-embryon|ic
pree|mie
pre-eminence
pre-eminent
pre-eminent|ly
pre-empt
pre-emption
pre-emptive
pre-emptor
preen|er
pre-engage|ment
pre-establish
pre-exist
pre-existence
pre-existent
pre-exposure
pre|fab =
 prefabricated
 building
pre|fab|ri|cate
 pre|fab|ri|cat|ing
pre|fab|ri|ca|tion
pref|ace
 pref|acing
prefa|tor|ial
prefa|tory
pre|fect
pre|fect|oral
pre|fect|orial
pre|fec|tural
pre|fec|ture
pre|fer
 pre|ferred
 pre|fer|ring
pref|er|abil|ity
pref|er|able
pref|er|ably
pref|er|ence
pref|er|en|tial
pref|er|en|tial|ly
pre|fer|ment
pre|fetch
pre|fig|ur|ation

pre|fig|ura|tive
pre|fig|ure
  pre|fig|ur|ing
pre|fig|ure|ment
pre|fix
pre|fix|ation
pre|fix|ion
pre|flight
pre|focus
pre|focused
pre|focussed var. of
  prefocused
pre|form
pre|form|ation
pre|form|ation|ist
pre|front|al
pre|geni|tal
preg|gers
pre|gla|cial
preg|nable
preg|nancy
  preg|nan|cies
preg|nant
preg|nant|ly
pre|heat
pre|hen|sile
pre|hen|sil|ity
pre|hen|sion
pre|his|tor|ian
pre|his|toric
pre|his|tor|ic|al|ly
pre|his|tory
pre|human
pre-ignition
pre-industrial
pre-instal Br. var. of
  pre-install
pre-install
pre|judge
  pre|judg|ing
pre|judge|ment
pre|judg|ment var.
  of prejudgement
pre|judi|ca|tion
preju|dice
  preju|dicing
preju|di|cial
preju|di|cial|ly
prel|acy
  prel|acies
pre|lap|sar|ian
prel|ate
prel|at|ic|al

prel|at|ure
pre-launch
pre|lim
pre|lim|in|ar|ily
pre|lim|in|ary
  pre|lim|in|ar|ies
pre|lin|gual|ly
pre|lin|guis|tic
pre|lit|er|ate
pre|load
pre-loved
prel|ude
  prel|ud|ing
prel|ud|ial
pre|mari|tal
pre|mari|tal|ly
pre|master
pre|match
pre|ma|ture
pre|ma|ture|ly
pre|ma|ture|ness
pre|ma|tur|ity
pre|max|il|lary
pre-med
pre|med|ical
pre|medica|tion
pre|medi|tate
  pre|medi|tat|ing
pre|medi|ta|tion
pre|men|strual
pre|men|stru|al|ly
prem|ier first in
  importance etc.;
  head of government
pre|mier cru
pre|miers crus
prem|iere
  prem|ier|ing
  (give) first
  performance
  French première
Prem|ier|ship top
  football division
prem|ier|ship
  headship of
  government
pre|mil|len|nial
pre|mil|len|nial|
        ism
pre|mil|len|nial|ist
Prem|in|ger, Otto
  film director
prem|ise
  prem|is|ing

  base of inference;
  presuppose
prem|ises buildings
  etc.
prem|iss *n. Br.* var.
  of premise
pre|mium
pre|mix
pre|modi|fi|ca|tion
pre|modi|fier
pre|modi|fy
  pre|modi|fies
  pre|modi|fied
  pre|modi|fy|ing
pre|molar
pre|mon|ition
pre|moni|tor
pre|moni|tory
Pre|mon|stra|
      ten|sian
pre|mor|bid
pre|motor
pre|multi|pli|
      ca|tion
pre|multi|ply
  pre|multi|plies
  pre|multi|plied
  pre|multi|ply|ing
pre|natal
pre|natal|ly
pre|nom|inal
pre|nom|in|al|ly
pren|tice
  pren|ticing
pren|tice|ship
pre|nup = prenup-
  tial agreement
pre|nup|tial
pre|occu|pa|tion
pre|occupy
  pre|occu|pies
  pre|occu|pied
  pre|occu|py|ing
pre|ocu|lar
pre-op = preopera-
  tive (treatment)
pre|opera|tive
pre|opera|tive|ly
pre|orbit|al
pre|or|dain
pre-owned
prep
  prepped
  prep|ping

pre-pack
pre-package
  pre-packaging
prep|ar|ation
pre|para|tive
pre|para|tive|ly
pre|para|tory
pre|pare
  pre|par|ing
pre|pared|ness
pre|parer
pre|pay
  pre|paid
pre|pay|able
pre|pay|ment
pre|pense
pre|pense|ly
pre-plan
  pre-planned
  pre-planning
pre|poly|mer
pre|pon|der|ance
pre|pon|der|ant
pre|pon|der|ant|ly
pre|pon|der|ate
  pre|pon|der|at|ing
pre|pone
  pre|pon|ing
pre|pose
  pre|pos|ing
  place in front; cf.
  propose
prep|os|ition word
pre-position put in
  place beforehand
prep|os|ition|al
prep|os|ition|al|ly
pre|posi|tive
pre|pos|sess|ing
pre|pos|ses|sion
pre|pos|ter|ous
pre|pos|ter|ous|ly
pre|pos|ter|ous|
      ness
pre|pos|tor var. of
  praepostor
pre|po|tence
pre|po|tency
pre|po|tent
prep|pie var. of
  preppy
preppy
  prep|pies
  prep|pier

prep¦pi¦est
pre¦pran¦dial
pre-prefer¦en¦tial
pre¦preg
pre-prepare
  pre-prepar¦ing
pre-press
pre¦print
pre¦process
pre¦proces¦sor
pre¦produc¦tion
pre¦program
  pre¦pro¦grammed
  US also
  pre¦pro¦gramed
  pre¦pro¦gram¦ming
  US also
  pre¦pro¦gram¦ing
pre¦puber¦tal
pre¦puberty
pre¦pubes¦cence
pre¦pubes¦cent
pre¦pub¦li¦ca¦tion
pre¦puce
pre¦pu¦tial
pre-qualifier
pre-qualify
  pre-qualifies
  pre-qualified
  pre-qualify¦ing
pre¦quel
Pre-Raphael¦ism
Pre-Raphael¦ite
Pre-Raphael¦it¦ism
pre-record
pre¦regis¦ter
pre¦regis¦tra¦tion
pre-release
pre-requis¦ite
pre-revolu¦tion¦ary
pre¦roga¦tive
pre-Roman
pres¦age
  pres¦aging
pres¦age¦ful
pres¦ager
pres¦by¦opia
pres¦by¦op¦ic
pres¦by¦ter
pres¦by¦ter¦al
pres¦by¦ter¦ate
pres¦by¦ter¦ial
Pres¦by¦ter¦ian

Pres¦by¦ter¦ian¦ism
pres¦by¦ter¦ship
pres¦by¦tery
  pres¦by¦ter¦ies
pre¦school
pre¦school¦er
pres¦ci¦ence
pres¦ci¦ent
pre-scientif¦ic
pres¦ci¦ent¦ly
pre¦scind
pre¦scrib¦able
pre¦scribe
  pre¦scrib¦ing
  advise use of medi-
  cine etc.; impose;
  cf. proscribe
pre¦scriber
pre¦script
pre¦scrip¦tion pre-
  scribing; doctor's
  instruction;
  medicine; cf.
  proscription
pre¦scrip¦tive pre-
  scribing; cf.
  proscriptive
pre¦scrip¦tive¦ly
pre¦scrip¦tive¦ness
pre¦scrip¦tiv¦ism
pre¦scrip¦tiv¦ist
pre¦season
pre¦select
pre¦selec¦tion
pre¦select¦ive
pre¦select¦or
pres¦ence
pre¦senile
pre¦sent give for-
  mally; introduce;
  exhibit; cf. precent
pres¦ent not absent;
  current; time now
  passing; gift
pre¦sent¦abil¦ity
pre¦sent¦able
pre¦sent¦able¦ness
pre¦sent¦ably
pres¦en¦ta¦tion
pres¦en¦ta¦tion¦al
pres¦en¦ta¦tion¦al¦ly
pre¦senta¦tive
pres¦ent¦ee
pres¦ent¦ee¦ism

pre¦sent¦er person
  who presents; cf.
  precentor
pre¦sen¦ti¦ment
  foreboding
pres¦ent¦ism
pres¦ent¦ist
pres¦ent¦ly
pre¦sent¦ment pres-
  entation to court of
  law
pre¦serv¦able
pres¦er¦va¦tion
pres¦er¦va¦tion¦ist
pre¦ser¦va¦tive
pre¦serve
  pre¦serv¦ing
pre¦server
pre-service
pre¦set
  pre¦set¦ting
pre-shrink
  pre-shrank
  pre-shrunk
pre¦side
  pre¦sid¦ing
presi¦dency
  presi¦den¦cies
presi¦dent
president-elect
  presidents-elect
presi¦den¦tial
presi¦den¦tial¦ly
presi¦dent¦ship
pre¦sidio +s
pre¦sid¦ium
Pres¦ley, Elvis
  singer
pre¦soak
Pre¦soc¦rat¦ic
press¦board
pressé
press¦er device that
  presses; cf. pressor
pres¦sie var. of
  prezzie
press¦ing¦ly
press¦man
  press¦men
press¦mark
pres¦sor adj.
  Physiology; cf.
  presser
press-up n.

pres¦sure
pres¦sur¦ing
pres¦sur¦isa¦tion
  Br. var. of
  pressurization
pres¦sur¦ise Br. var.
  of pressurize
pres¦sur¦iza¦tion
pres¦sur¦ize
  pres¦sur¦iz¦ing
press¦work
Pres¦ter John
  legendary king
pres¦ti¦digi¦ta¦tion
pres¦ti¦digi¦ta¦tor
pres¦tige
pres¦tige¦ful
pres¦ti¦gious
pres¦ti¦gious¦ly
pres¦ti¦gious¦ness
pres¦tis¦simo +s
presto +s
Pres¦ton
Pres¦ton¦pans
pre¦stressed
pre¦stress¦ing
Prest¦wick
pre¦sum¦able
pre¦sum¦ably
pre¦sume
  pre¦sum¦ing
pre¦sumed¦ly
pre¦sum¦ing¦ly
pre¦sum¦ing¦ness
pre¦sump¦tion
pre¦sump¦tive
pre¦sump¦tive¦ly
pre¦sump¦tu¦ous
pre¦sump¦tu¦ous¦ly
pre¦sump¦tu¦ous¦
      ness
pre¦sup¦pose
  pre¦sup¦pos¦ing
pre¦sup¦pos¦ition
pre¦synap¦tic
pre¦synap¦tic¦al¦ly
prêt-à-porter
pre-tax
pre-teen
pre¦tence Br.
pre¦tend
pre¦tend¦er
pre¦tense US

pre|ten|sion claim
pre-tension apply
  tension to
  beforehand
pre-tension|er
pre|ten|tious
pre|ten|tious|ly
pre|ten|tious|ness
pret|erit US
pret|er|ite Br.
pret|er|ition
pre|term
pre|ter|mis|sion
pre|ter|mit
  pre|ter|mit|ted
  pre|ter|mit|ting
pre|ter|nat|ural
pre|ter|nat|ur|al|
              ism
pre|ter|nat|ur|al|ly
pre|test
pre|text
pre|tor var. of
  praetor
Pre|toria
pre|tor|ial var. of
  praetorial
pre|tor|ian var. of
  praetorian
pre|tor|ship var. of
  praetorship
pre|treat
pre|treat|ment
pre|trial
pret|ti|fi|ca|tion
pret|ti|fier
pret|tify
  pret|ti|fies
  pret|ti|fied
  pret|ti|fy|ing
pret|tily
pret|ti|ness
pretty
  pret|ties
  pret|tied
  pretty|ing
  pret|tier
  pret|ti|est
pret|ty|ish
pret|ty|ism
pret|zel
  pret|zelled Br.
  pret|zeled US
  pret|zel|ling Br.

pret|zel|ing US
pre|vail
pre|vail|ing|ly
preva|lence
preva|lent
preva|lent|ly
pre|vari|cate
  pre|vari|cat|ing
pre|vari|ca|tion
pre|vari|ca|tor
pre|veni|ent
pre|vent
pre|vent|abil|ity
pre|vent|able
pre|venta|tive
pre|venta|tive|ly
pre|vent|er
pre|ven|tion
pre|vent|ive
pre|vent|ive|ly
pre|ver|bal
pre|view
pre|view|er
Pre|vin, André
  musician
pre|vi|ous
pre|vi|ous|ly
pre|vi|sion fore-
  sight; cf. provision
pre|vi|sion|al of
  foresight; cf.
  provisional
pre|vocal|ic
pre|vocal|ic|al|ly
pre-vocation|al
Pré|vost d'Exiles,
  Antoine-François
  novelist
pre|vue US var. of
  preview
pre-war
pre|wash
pre|wire
  pre|wir|ing
prexy
  prex|ies
prey (kill for) food;
  vulnerable person;
  cf. pray
prey|er animal or
  person that preys;
  cf. prayer
Prez, Jos|quin des
  composer

prez = president
prez|zie = present
prial
Priam Greek
  Mythology
pri|ap|ic
pri|ap|ism
pri|apu|lid
Pri|apu|lida
Pria|pus Greek
  Mythology
Pri|bi|lof Is|lands
Price, Vin|cent
  actor
price
  pri|cing
price|less
price|less|ly
price|less|ness
pricer
pricey
  pricier
  prici|est
pri|ci|ness
prick|er
pricket
prickle
  prick|ling
prickle|back
prick|li|ness
prick|ly
  prick|lier
  prick|li|est
pricy var. of pricey
pride
  prid|ing
pride|ful
pride|ful|ly
pride|less
prie-dieu
  prie-dieux
priest|craft
priest|ess
priest|hood
priest-in-charge
  priests-in-charge
priest|less
Priest|ley, J. B.
  writer
Priest|ley, Jo|seph
  chemist
priest|like
priest|li|ness
priest|ling

priest|ly
priest's hole
prig|gery
prig|gish
prig|gish|ly
prig|gish|ness
prilled
prim
  primmed
  prim|ming
  prim|mer
  prim|mest
prima bal|ler|ina
pri|macy
prima donna
prima donna-ish
pri|maeval var. of
  primeval
pri|maeval|ly var. of
  primevally
prima facie
pri|mal
pri|mal|ly
prima|quine
pri|mar|ily
pri|mary
  pri|mar|ies
pri|mate mammal;
  archbishop
Pri|mates order of
  mammals
pri|ma|tial
pri|mato|logic|al
pri|mato|lo|gist
pri|mat|ology
pri|ma|vera
prime
  prim|ing
prime|ness
pri|mer
pri|meur
pri|meval
pri|mev|al|ly
primi|grav|ida
  primi|grav|idae
prim|ipara
  prim|iparae
prim|ipar|ous
primi|tive
primi|tive|ly
primi|tive|ness
primi|tiv|ism
primi|tiv|ist

prim|ly
prim|ness
primo
 primi or pri|mos
Primo de Ri|vera,
 Mi|guel Spanish
 head of state
primo|geni|tal
primo|geni|tary
primo|geni|tor
primo|geni|ture
prim|or|dial
prim|or|di|al|ity
prim|or|di|al|ly
prim|or|dium
 prim|or|dia
Pri|mor|sky Krai
primo uomo
 primo uomos or
 primi uomini
prim|rose flower
prim|ula
prim|ul|aceous
pri|mum mo|bile
Pri|mus stove
 trademark
pri|mus bishop
*pri|mus inter
 pares*
prince|dom
prince|like
prince|li|ness
prince|ling
prince|ly
 prince|lier
 prince|li|est
prince royal
 princes royal
prince's fea|ther
 plant
prince|ship
prin|cess
*prin|cesse
 loin|taine
 prin|cesses
 loin|taines*
prin|cess royal
 prin|cesses royal
Prince|ton
prin|ci|pal chief; cf.
 principle
prin|ci|pal|ity
 prin|ci|pal|ities
prin|ci|pal|ly

prin|ci|pal|ship
prin|ci|pate
Prín|cipe island
prin|ciple funda-
 mental truth; rule
 of behaviour; etc.;
 cf. principal
prin|cipled
print|abil|ity
print|able
print|er
print|er's devil +s
print|ery
 print|er|ies
print|head
print|ing
print|maker
print|mak|ing
print|out
print-through n.
print|works
prion
prior
pri|or|ate
pri|or|ess
pri|ori|tisa|tion Br.
 var. of
 prioritization
pri|ori|tise Br. var.
 of prioritize
pri|ori|tiza|tion
pri|ori|tize
 pri|ori|tiz|ing
pri|or|ity
 pri|or|ities
prior|ship
pri|ory
 pri|or|ies
Pri|pet var. of
 Pripyat
Pri|pyat
Pris|cian grammar-
 ian
Pris|cilla
Pris|coan
prise Br.
 pris|ing
 force
 US prize
prism
pris|mat|ic
pris|mat|ic|al|ly
pris|moid
pris|moid|al

prison
pris|on|er
pris|sily
pris|si|ness
prissy
 pris|sier
 pris|si|est
Priš|tina
pris|tine
pris|tine|ly
Prit|chett, V. S.
 writer
pri|thee
priv|acy
pri|vate
pri|vat|eer
pri|vat|eer|ing
pri|vat|eers|man
 pri|vat|eers|men
pri|vate|ly
pri|va|tion
pri|vat|isa|tion Br.
 var. of
 privatization
pri|vat|ise Br. var.
 of privatize
pri|vat|iser Br. var.
 of privatizer
pri|vat|ism
priv|ative
pri|vat|iza|tion
pri|vat|ize
 pri|vat|iz|ing
pri|vat|izer
privet
priv|il|ege
 priv|il|eging
priv|ily
priv|ity
 priv|ities
privy
 priv|ies
privy coun|cil|lor
 var. of privy
 counsellor
privy coun|sel|lor
Prix de Rome
 pl. Prix de Rome
prix fixe
 prix fixes
Prix Gon|court
 pl. Prix Gon|court
prize
 priz|ing

 award; cf. prise
prize US
 priz|ing
 force
 Br. prise
prize|fight
prize|fight|er
prize|fight|ing
prize|man
 prize|men
prize-win|ner
prize-win|ning
pro +s
proa
pro|action
pro|active
pro|active|ly
pro|activ|ity
prob|abil|is|tic
prob|abil|is|tic|al|ly
prob|abil|ity
 prob|abil|ities
prob|able
prob|ably
pro|band
pro|bang
pro|bate
 pro|bat|ing
pro|ba|tion
pro|ba|tion|al
pro|ba|tion|ary
pro|ba|tion|er
pro|ba|tive
probe
 prob|ing
probe|able
pro|bene|cid
prober
prob|ing|ly
pro|biot|ic
pro|bit
prob|ity
prob|lem
prob|lem|at|ic
prob|lem|at|ic|al
prob|lem|at|ic|al|ly
prob|lem|atisa|tion
 Br. var. of
 problematization
prob|lem|atise Br.
 var. of
 problematize
prob|lem|atiza|tion

prob¦lem¦atize
  prob¦lem¦atiz¦ing
pro bono pub¦lico
Pro¦bos¦cidea
pro¦bos¦cid¦ean
pro¦bos¦cid¦ian var.
  of proboscidean
pro¦bos¦cis
  pro¦bos¦ces or
  pro¦bos¦cides or
  pro¦bos¦cises
pro¦cain var. of
  procaine
pro¦caine
pro¦cary¦ote var. of
  prokaryote
pro¦ced¦ural
pro¦ced¦ur¦al¦ly
pro¦ced¦ure
pro¦ceed go
  forward; cf.
  precede
pro¦cess go in
  procession; cf.
  precess
pro¦cess¦able
pro¦ces¦sion num-
  ber of moving
  people or vehicles;
  cf. precession
pro¦ces¦sion¦al of
  processions; hymn
  book; cf.
  precessional
pro¦ces¦sion¦ary
  pro¦ces¦sion¦ar¦ies
pro¦ces¦sion¦ist
pro¦ces¦sor
pro¦ces¦sual
procès-verbal
  procès-verbaux
pro¦chlor¦pera¦zine
pro-choice
pro-choicer
pro¦claim
pro¦claim¦er
proc¦lam¦ation
pro¦clama¦tory
pro¦clit¦ic
pro¦clit¦ic¦al¦ly
pro¦cliv¦ity
  pro¦cliv¦ities
Procne *Greek
  Mythology*

pro¦coagu¦lant
Pro¦con¦sul fossil
  primate
pro¦con¦sul gov-
  ernor
pro¦con¦su¦lar
pro¦con¦su¦late
pro¦con¦sul¦ship
Pro¦co¦pius histor-
  ian
pro¦cras¦tin¦ate
  pro¦cras¦tin¦at¦ing
pro¦cras¦tin¦ation
pro¦cras¦tina¦tive
pro¦cras¦tin¦ator
pro¦cras¦tin¦atory
pro¦cre¦ant
pro¦cre¦ate
  pro¦cre¦at¦ing
pro¦cre¦ation
pro¦cre¦ative
pro¦cre¦ator
Pro¦crus¦tean
Pro¦crus¦tes *Greek
  Mythology*
proc¦ti¦tis
procto¦logic¦al
proc¦tolo¦gist
proc¦tol¦ogy
proc¦tor
proc¦tor¦ial
proc¦tor¦ship
procto¦scope
proc¦tos¦copy
  proc¦tos¦co¦pies
pro¦cum¦bent
pro¦cur¦able
pro¦cur¦acy
  pro¦cur¦acies
proc¦ur¦ation
proc¦ur¦ator
proc¦ur¦ator fis¦cal
  proc¦ur¦ators
  fis¦cal
proc¦ura¦tor¦ial
proc¦ur¦ator¦ship
pro¦cure
  pro¦cur¦ing
pro¦cure¦ment
pro¦curer
pro¦cur¦ess
Pro¦cyon
pro¦cyon¦id

prod
  prod¦ded
  prod¦ding
prod¦der
Prod¦die *offensive*
Proddy
Prod¦dies *offensive*
  var. of Proddie
pro Deo
prod¦igal
prod¦ig¦al¦ity
prod¦ig¦al¦ly
pro¦di¦gious
pro¦di¦gious¦ly
pro¦di¦gious¦ness
prod¦igy
  prod¦igies
pro¦dromal
pro¦drome
pro¦drom¦ic
pro¦drug
pro¦duce *n.*
  pro¦du¦cing
prod¦uce *n.*
pro¦du¦cer
pro¦du¦ci¦bil¦ity
pro¦du¦cible
prod¦uct
pro¦duc¦tion
pro¦duc¦tion¦al
pro¦duct¦ive
pro¦duct¦ive¦ly
pro¦duct¦ive¦ness
prod¦uct¦iv¦ity
proem
pro¦em¦ial
pro¦enzyme
pro-European
pro-family
prof¦an¦ation
pro¦fane
  pro¦fan¦ing
pro¦fane¦ly
pro¦fane¦ness
pro¦faner
pro¦fan¦ity
  pro¦fan¦ities
pro¦fer¦ens
  prof¦er¦en¦tes
pro¦fess
pro¦fess¦ed¦ly
pro¦fes¦sion
pro¦fes¦sion¦al

pro¦fes¦sion¦al¦
  isa¦tion
  Br. var. of **profes-
  sionalization**
pro¦fes¦sion¦al¦ise
  Br. var. of
  professionalize
pro¦fes¦sion¦al¦ism
pro¦fes¦sion¦al¦
  iza¦tion
pro¦fes¦sion¦al¦ize
  pro¦fes¦sion¦al¦
  iz¦ing
pro¦fes¦sion¦al¦ly
pro¦fes¦sor
pro¦fes¦sor¦ate
pro¦fes¦sor¦ial
pro¦fes¦sori¦al¦ly
pro¦fes¦sori¦ate
pro¦fes¦sor¦ship
prof¦fer
pro¦fi¦ciency
  pro¦fi¦cien¦cies
pro¦fi¦cient
pro¦fi¦cient¦ly
pro¦file
  pro¦fil¦ing
pro¦filer
pro¦fil¦ist
profit gain; cf.
  prophet
prof¦it¦abil¦ity
prof¦it¦able
prof¦it¦able¦ness
prof¦it¦ably
prof¦it¦eer
pro¦fit¦er¦ole
prof¦it¦less
prof¦li¦gacy
prof¦li¦gate
prof¦li¦gate¦ly
pro-form depend-
  ent word
pro forma (docu-
  ment produced) as
  a matter of form
pro¦found
pro¦found¦ly
pro¦found¦ness
Pro¦fumo, John
  politician
pro¦fund¦ity
  pro¦fund¦ities
pro¦fuse

pro|fuse|ly
pro|fuse|ness
pro|fu|sion
pro|geni|tive
pro|geni|tor
pro|geni|tor|ial
pro|geni|tor|ship
pro|geni|ture
pro|geny
  pro|gen|ies
pro|geria
pro|ges|ter|one
pro|ges|tin
pro|ges|to|gen
pro|glot|tid
pro|glot|tis
  pro|glot|tides
prog|nath|ic
prog|nath|ism
prog|nath|ous
prog|no|sis
  prog|no|ses
prog|nos|tic
prog|nos|tic|able
prog|nos|tic|al|ly
prog|nos|ti|cate
  prog|nos|ti|cat|ing
prog|nos|ti|ca|tion
prog|nos|ti|ca|tive
prog|nos|ti|ca|tor
prog|nos|ti|ca|tory
pro|grad|ation
pro|grade
  pro|grad|ing
pro|gram US
generally; and
Computing in US &
Br.
  pro|grammed
  US also
  pro|gramed
  pro|gram|ming
  US also
  pro|gram|ing
  Br. generally
  programme
pro|gram|a|bil|ity
US var. of
programmability
pro|gram|able US
var. of
programmable
pro|gram|
      ma|bil|ity

pro|gram|mable
pro|gram|mat|ic
pro|gram|mat|ic|
      al|ly
pro|gramme Br.
generally
pro|gram|ming
US & Computing
program
pro|gram|mer
pro|gress
pro|gres|sion
pro|gres|sion|al
pro|gres|sion|ist
pro|gres|sive
pro|gres|sive|ly
pro|gres|sive|ness
pro|gres|siv|ism
pro|gres|siv|ist
pro|gua|nil
pro hac vice
pro|hibit
pro|hib|it|er
Pro|hib|ition US
alcohol ban
pro|hib|ition gener-
ally
pro|hib|ition|ary
Pro|hib|ition|ist
pro|hibi|tive
pro|hibi|tive|ly
pro|hibi|tive|ness
pro|hibi|tor
pro|hibi|tory
pro|insu|lin
pro|ject
pro|ject|ile
pro|jec|tion
pro|jec|tion|ist
pro|ject|ive
pro|ject|ive|ly
pro|ject|or
pro|kary|ote
pro|kary|ot|ic
Pro|kof|iev, Ser|gei
composer
Pro|kop|yevsk
pro|lac|tin
pro|lapse
  pro|laps|ing
pro|lap|sus
pro|late
pro|leg

pro|leg|om|en|ary
pro|leg|om|enon
  pro|leg|om|ena
pro|leg|om|en|ous
pro|lep|sis
  pro|lep|ses
pro|lep|tic
pro|le|tar|ian
pro|le|tar|ian|
          isa|tion
Br. var. of
proletarianization
pro|le|tar|ian|ise
Br. var. of
proletarianize
pro|le|tar|ian|ism
pro|le|tar|ian|
          iza|tion
pro|le|tar|ian|ize
pro|le|tar|ian|iz|ing
pro|le|tar|iat
pro|le|tar|iate var.
of proletariat
pro-life
pro-lifer
pro|lif|er|ate
  pro|lif|er|at|ing
pro|lif|er|ation
pro|lif|era|tive
pro|lif|er|ator
pro|lif|er|ous
pro|lif|ic
pro|lif|ic|acy
pro|lif|ic|al|ly
pro|lif|ic|ness
pro|line
pro|lix
pro|lix|ity
pro|lix|ly
pro|locu|tor
Pro|log computer
language
pro|logue
pro|long
pro|longa|tion
pro|long|ed|ly
pro|long|er
pro|lu|sion
prom|en|ade
  prom|en|ad|ing
prom|en|ader
pro|metha|zine
Pro|me|thean

Pro|me|theus Greek
Mythology
pro|me|thium
prom|in|ence
prom|in|ency
prom|in|ent
prom|in|enti
prom|in|ent|ly
pro|mis|cu|ity
pro|mis|cu|ous
pro|mis|cu|ous|ly
pro|mis|cu|ous|
              ness
prom|ise
prom|is|ing
prom|isee
prom|iser generally
prom|is|ing|ly
prom|isor Law
prom|is|sory
prom|mer
promo +s
prom|on|tory
  prom|on|tor|ies
pro|mot|abil|ity
pro|mot|able
pro|mote
  pro|mot|ing
pro|moter generally
pro|mo|tion
pro|mo|tion|al
pro|mo|tive
pro|mo|tor Scottish
university official
prompt|er
prompti|tude
prompt|ly
prompt|ness
prom|ul|gate
  prom|ul|gat|ing
prom|ul|ga|tion
prom|ul|ga|tor
pro|mulge
  pro|mul|ging
pro|naos
  pro|naoi
pro|nate
  pro|nat|ing
pro|na|tion
pro|na|tor
prone|ness
prong|horn
pro|nom|inal

pro|nom|in|al|
    isa|tion
Br. var. of
  pronominalization
pro|nom|in|al|ise
Br. var. of
  pronominalize
pro|nom|in|al|
    iza|tion
pro|nom|in|al|ize
pro|nom|in|al|
    iz|ing
pro|nom|in|al|ly
pro|noun
pro|nounce
  pro|noun|cing
pro|nounce|abil|ity
pro|nounce|able
pro|noun|ced|ly
pro|nounce|ment
pro|noun|cer
pronto
Pron|to|sil
pro|nuclear
pro|nucleus
  pro|nuclei
pro|nun|cia|mento
  +s
pro|nun|ci|ation
pro-nuncio +s
proof|read
proof|read|er
proof-text Bible
  passage
prop
  propped
  prop|ping
propa|ganda
propa|gand|ise *Br.*
  var. of
  propagandize
propa|gand|ism
propa|gand|ist
propa|gand|is|tic
propa|gand|is|tic|
    al|ly
propa|gand|ize
  propa|gand|iz|ing
propa|gate
  propa|gat|ing
propa|ga|tion
propa|ga|tive
propa|ga|tor
propa|gule

pro|pane
pro|pano|ate
pro|panol
pro|pan|one
pro|pel
  pro|pelled
  pro|pel|ling
pro|pel|lant
pro|pel|ler
propeller-head
  person
pro|pel|lor var. of
  propeller
pro|pene
pro|peno|ate
pro|pen|oic
pro|pen|sity
  pro|pen|sities
proper
pro|per|din
prop|er|ly
prop|er|ness
prop|er|tied
Pro|per|tius,
  Sex|tus poet
prop|erty
  prop|er|ties
pro|phage
pro|phase
proph|ecy *n.*
  proph|ecies
proph|esier
proph|esy *v.*
  proph|es|ies
  proph|es|ied
  proph|esy|ing
prophet inspired
  teacher; visionary;
  cf. **profit**
proph|et|ess
proph|et|hood
pro|phet|ic
pro|phet|ic|al|ly
proph|et|ism
prophy|lac|tic
prophy|lac|tic|al|ly
prophy|laxis
pro|pin|quity
pro|pi|on|ate
pro|pi|oni|
    bac|ter|ium
pro|pi|oni|bac|teria
pro|piti|ate
  pro|piti|at|ing

pro|piti|ation
pro|piti|ator
pro|piti|ator|ily
pro|piti|atory
pro|pi|tious
pro|pi|tious|ly
pro|pi|tious|ness
prop|olis
pro|pon|ent
Pro|pon|tis
pro|por|tion
pro|por|tion|able
pro|por|tion|ably
pro|por|tion|al
pro|por|tion|al|ity
pro|por|tion|al|ly
pro|por|tion|ate
pro|por|tion|ate|ly
pro|posal
pro|pose
  pro|pos|ing
  suggest; cf.
  prepose
pro|poser
prop|os|ition
prop|os|ition|al
pro|pound
pro|pound|er
pro|poxy|phene
pro|pran|olol
pro|pri|etary
pro|pri|etor
pro|pri|etor|ial
pro|pri|etori|al|ly
pro|pri|etor|ship
pro|pri|etress
pro|pri|ety
  pro|pri|eties
pro|prio|cep|tion
pro|prio|cep|tive
pro|prio|cep|tive|ly
pro|prio|cep|tor
prop|shaft
prop|tosis
pro|pul|sion
pro|pul|sive
pro|pul|sive|ly
pro|pul|sor
pro|pyl
propy|laeum
  propy|laea
pro|pyl|ene

pro|pylon
  pro|pylons or
  pro|pyla
pro rata
pro|rate
  pro|rat|ing
pro|ra|tion
pro|roga|tion
pro|rogue
  pro|roguing
pro|sa|ic
pro|saic|al|ly
pro|saic|ness
pro|sa|ism
pro|sa|ist
pro|sauro|pod
pro|scen|ium
  pro|scen|iums or
  pro|scenia
pro|sciutto +s
pro|scribe
  pro|scrib|ing
  forbid; denounce;
  outlaw; cf.
  prescribe
pro|scrip|tion
  action of
  proscribing; cf.
  prescription
pro|scrip|tive that
  proscribes; cf.
  prescriptive
prose
  pros|ing
pro|sec|tor
pros|ecut|able
pros|ecute
  pros|ecut|ing
pros|ecu|tion
pros|ecu|tor
pros|ecu|tor|ial
pros|elyte
pros|elyt|ing
pros|elyt|isa|tion
Br. var. of
  proselytization
pros|elyt|ise *Br.* var.
  of **proselytize**
pros|elyt|iser *Br.*
  var. of **proselytizer**
pros|elyt|ism
pros|elyt|iza|tion
pros|elyt|ize
  pros|elyt|iz|ing
pros|elyt|izer

pros|en|ceph|alon
pros|en|chyma
pros|en|chy|mal
pros|en|chy|ma|
    tous
proser
Pro|ser|pina var. of
  Proserpine
Pro|ser|pine
prosi|ly
pro|sim|ian
pro|si|ness
pro|sit
proso|branch +s
Proso|bran|chia
pro|social
pros|od|ic
pros|od|ist
pros|ody
  pros|od|ies
pro|soma
proso|pag|no|sia
pros|op|og|raph|er
pros|opo|
    graph|ic|al
pros|op|og|raphy
  pros|op|og|raph|ies
pros|opo|poeia
pro|spect
pro|spect|ive
pro|spect|ive|ly
pro|spect|ive|ness
pro|spect|less
pro|spect|or
pro|spec|tus
pros|per
pros|per|ity
pros|per|ous
pros|per|ous|ly
pros|per|ous|ness
Prost, Alain racing
  driver
pros|ta|cyc|lin
pros|ta|glan|din
pros|tate
pros|ta|tec|tomy
  pros|ta|tec|to|mies
pros|tat|ic
pros|ta|titis
pros|thesis
  pros|theses
pros|thet|ic
pros|thet|ic|al|ly

pros|thet|ist
pros|tho|don|tics
pros|tho|don|tist
pros|ti|tute
  pros|ti|tut|ing
pros|ti|tu|tion
pros|ti|tu|tor
pros|trate
  pros|trat|ing
pros|tra|tion
pro|style
pro|sumer
prosy
  prosi|er
  prosi|est
pro|tac|tin|ium
pro|tag|on|ist
pro|tam|ine
pro|tan|drous
pro|tandry
  pro|tandries
pro|tan|ope
pro|tan|opia
pro tanto
prot|asis
  prot|ases
pro|tat|ic
pro|tea
pro|tean
pro|te|ase
pro|te|asome
pro|tect
pro|tect|able
pro|tect|ant
pro|tec|tion
pro|tec|tion|ism
pro|tec|tion|ist
pro|tect|ive
pro|tect|ive|ly
pro|tect|ive|ness
pro|tect|or
pro|tect|or|al
pro|tect|or|ate
pro|tect|or|ship
pro|tec|tress
pro|tégé
pro|té|gée female
  protégé
pro|tein
pro|tein|aceous
pro|tein|ase
pro|tein|ic
pro|tein|ous

pro|tein|uria
pro|teo|gly|can
pro|te|oly|sis
pro|teo|lyt|ic
pro|teo|lytic|al|ly
prote|ome
prote|omic
Pro|tero|zo|ic
pro|test
Prot|est|ant Chris-
  tian
prot|est|ant gener-
  ally
Prot|est|ant|
    isa|tion
  Br. var. of
  Protestantization
Prot|est|ant|ise *Br.*
  var. of
  Protestantize
Prot|est|ant|ism
Prot|est|ant|
    iza|tion
Prot|est|ant|ize
  Prot|est|ant|iz|ing
prot|est|ation
pro|test|er
pro|test|ing|ly
pro|test|or var. of
  protester
Pro|teus minor sea
  god; satellite of
  Neptune
pro|teus bacterium
pro|tha|lam|ion
  var. of
  prothalamium
pro|tha|lam|ium
  pro|tha|lamia
pro|thal|lial
pro|thal|lus
  pro|thalli
pro|thesis
  pro|theses
pro|thet|ic
pro|tho|not|ary var.
  of protonotary
pro|tho|not|ary
  warb|ler
pro|thor|acic
pro|thorax
pro|throm|bin
pro|tist *n.*
Pro|tista

pro|tist|an
pro|tist|ology
pro|tium
proto|cera|tops
proto|col
pro|toc|tist
Pro|toc|tista
proto|gal|ac|tic
proto|gal|axy
  proto|gal|ax|ies
Proto-German|ic
prot|ogyn|ous
prot|ogyny
  prot|ogyn|ies
proto|human
Proto-Indo-
    European
proto|lan|guage
proto|mar|tyr
pro|ton
proton|ate
  proton|at|ing
proton|ation
pro|ton|ic
proto|not|ary
  proto|not|ar|ies
proto|path|ic
proto|plasm
proto|plas|mal
proto|plas|mat|ic
proto|plas|mic
proto|plast
proto|plas|tic
proto|pod
pro|topod|ite
proto|star
proto|stome
Proto|theria
proto|ther|ian
proto|typal
proto|type
  proto|typ|ing
proto|typ|ic
proto|typ|ic|al
proto|typ|ic|al|ly
Proto|zoa
proto|zoa pl. of
  protozoon
proto|zoal
proto|zoan
proto|zo|ic
proto|zoon
  proto|zoa

pro|tract
pro|tract|ed|ly
pro|tract|ed|ness
pro|tract|ile
pro|trac|tion
pro|tract|or
pro|trude
  pro|trud|ing
pro|tru|dent
pro|tru|sible
pro|tru|sile
pro|tru|sion
pro|tru|sive
pro|tu|ber|ance
pro|tu|ber|ant
Pro|tura
pro|tur|an
Proud|hon, Pierre
  Jo|seph social
  philosopher
proud|ly
proud|ness
Proust, Mar|cel
  writer
Proust|ian
prov|abil|ity
prov|able
prov|ably
prove
  past participle
  proved or **proven**
  prov|ing
prov|en|ance
Pro|ven|çal (lan-
  guage or person) of
  Provence
pro|ven|çale cooked
  in Provençal style
Pro|vence
Provence-Alpes-
      Côte d'Azur
prov|en|der
pro|ven|ience
pro|ven|tricu|lus
  pro|ven|triculi
prover
prov|erb
pro|verb|ial
pro|verbi|al|ity
pro|verbi|al|ly
pro-vice-
      chancel|lor
pro|vide
  pro|vid|ing

Provi|dence city,
  US; God
provi|dence care;
  foresight
provi|dent
provi|den|tial
provi|den|tial|ly
provi|dent|ly
pro|vider
Pro|vie
prov|ince
pro|vin|cial
pro|vin|cial|
        isa|tion
  Br. var. of
  provincialization
pro|vin|cial|ise *Br.*
  var. of
  provincialize
pro|vin|cial|ism
pro|vin|cial|ist
pro|vin|ci|al|ity
pro|vin|cial|
        iza|tion
pro|vin|cial|ize
pro|vin|cial|iz|ing
pro|vin|cial|ly
pro|viral
pro|virus
pro|vi|sion provid-
  ing; thing provided;
  food; legal
  requirement; cf.
  prevision
Pro|vi|sion|al of
  IRA
pro|vi|sion|al tem-
  porary; cf.
  previsional
pro|vi|sion|al|ity
pro|vi|sion|al|ly
pro|vi|sion|al|ness
pro|vi|sion|er
pro|vi|sion|less
pro|vi|sion|ment
pro|viso +s
pro|visor
pro|vita|min
Provo +s
provo|ca|tion
pro|voca|tive
pro|voca|tive|ly
pro|voca|tive|ness
pro|vok|able

pro|voke
  pro|vok|ing
pro|voker
pro|vok|ing|ly
pro|vo|lone
prov|ost
prov|ost|ship
prow|ess
prow|fish
prowl|er
prox|em|ics
Prox|ima
  Cen|tauri
prox|imal
prox|im|al|ly
prox|im|ate
prox|im|ate|ly
prox|im|ation
prox|ime ac|ces|sit
prox|im|ity
prox|imo
proxy
prox|ies
Pro|zac *trademark*
pro|zone
prude
pru|dence
pru|dent
pru|den|tial
pru|den|tial|ism
pru|den|tial|ist
pru|den|tial|ly
pru|dent|ly
prud|ery
Prud|hoe Bay
prud|ish
prud|ish|ly
prud|ish|ness
pru|in|ose
prune
  prun|ing
pru|nella
pruner
pru|nus
pruri|ence
pruri|ency
pruri|ent
pruri|ent|ly
pruri|gin|ous
prur|igo
prur|it|ic
prur|itus

prusik climbing
  method; cf. **prussic**
Prus|sia
Prus|sian
prus|si|ate
prus|sic acid cf.
  prusik
pry
  pries
  pried
  pry|ing
pry|ing|ly
pryt|any
pryt|an|ies
Prze|wal|ski's
  horse
psalm
psalm|ic
psalm|ist
psalm|od|ic
psalm|od|ise *Br.*
  var. of psalmodize
psalm|od|ist
psalm|od|ize
  psalm|od|iz|ing
psalm|ody
psal|ter
psal|ter|ium
psal|tery
psal|ter|ies
psepho|logic|al
psepho|logic|al|ly
pseph|olo|gist
pseph|ology
pseud
pseud|epig|rapha
pseud|epig|raph|al
pseud|epi|graph|ic
pseudo +s
pseudo|bulb
pseudo|carp
pseudo|cholin|
        ester|ase
pseudo-classic|al
pseudo-cleft
pseudo|code
pseudo|copu|lation
pseudo|cyesis
  pseudo|cyeses
pseudo|cyst
Pseudo-Dionys|ius
  unidentified
  theologian
pseudo|extinc|tion

pseudo|gene
pseudo|herm¦
  aphro|dit|ism
pseudo|
  mem|brane
pseudo|mem|bran|
  ous
pseudo|monas
pseudo|morph
pseudo|morph|ic
pseudo|morph|ism
pseudo|morph|ous
pseudo|nym
pseudo|nym|ity
pseud|onym|ous
pseud|onym|ous|ly
pseudo|pod
pseudo|po|dium
  pseudo|po|dia
pseudo|preg|nancy
pseudo|
  preg|nan|cies
pseudo|rabies
pseudo|ran|dom
pseudo|ran|dom|ly
pseudo|science
pseudo|scien|tif|ic
pseudo|scien|tist
pseudo|scor|pion
pseudo|urid|ine
psi Greek letter
psilo|cybin
psi|on|ic
psi|on|ic|al|ly
psit¦ta|cine
psit¦ta|cism
psit¦taco|saurus
  psit¦taco|sauri
psit¦ta|cosis
psoas
pso|cid
Pso|cop|tera
pso|cop|ter|an
psor|alen
psor|ia|sis
psori|at|ic
psych +s +ed +ing
  mentally prepare;
  intimidate
Psy¦che *Greek*
  Mythology
psy¦che the soul;
  the mind

psyche var. of psych
psy¦che|delia
psy¦che|del|ic
psy¦che|del|ic|al|ly
psy¦chi|atric
psy¦chi|atric|al|ly
psych|iatrist
psych|iatry
psy¦chic
psych|ic|al
psych|ic|al|ly
psych|ism
psy¦cho +s
psycho|acous|tics
psy¦cho|active
psy¦cho|ana|lyse *Br.*
  psy¦cho|
    ana|lys|ing
  US psychoanalyze
psy¦cho|analy¦sis
psy¦cho|ana|lyst
psy¦cho|ana|lyt|ic
psy¦cho|ana|lyt|
    ic|al
psy¦cho|ana|lyt|ic|
    al|ly
psy¦cho|ana|lyze
    US
  psy¦cho|
    ana|lyz|ing
  Br. psychoanalyse
psy¦cho|bab|ble
psy¦cho|bio|logic|al
psy¦cho|biolo|gist
psy¦cho|biol|ogy
psy¦cho|drama
psy¦cho|dynam|ic
psy¦cho|dynam|ic|
    al|ly
psy¦cho|gen|esis
psy¦cho|gen|ic
psy¦cho|geri|at|ric
psy¦cho|
  geri|atri|cian
psy¦cho|graph|ics
psy¦cho|his|tor|ian
psy¦cho|
  his|tor|ic|al
psy¦cho|his|tory
psy¦cho|his|tor|ies
psy¦cho|kin|esis
psy¦cho|kin|et|ic
psy¦cho|lin|guist

psy¦cho|
  lin|guis|tics
psy¦cho|logic|al
psy¦cho|logic|al|ly
psych|olo|gise *Br.*
  var. of
  psychologize
psych|olo|gism
psych|olo|gist
psych|olo|gize
  psych|olo|giz|ing
psych|ology
psych|olo|gies
psy¦cho|met|ric
psy¦cho|met|ric|
    al|ly
psych|om|etrist
psych|om|etry
psy¦cho|motor
psy¦cho|neuro|
  immun|ology
psy¦cho|neur|osis
  psy¦cho|neur|oses
psy¦cho|path
psy¦cho|path|ic
psy¦cho|path|ic|
    al|ly
psy¦cho|patho|
    logic|al
psy¦cho|path|
    olo|gist
psy¦cho|path|ology
psych|op|athy
psy¦cho|
  phar|maco|
    logic|al
psy¦cho|pharma|
    colo|gist
psy¦cho|pharma|
    cology
psy¦cho|phys|ic|al
psy¦cho|phys|ics
psy¦cho|
  physio|logic|al
psychophysiologist
psy¦cho|
  physi|ology
psy¦cho|pomp
psy¦cho|pom|pos
  var. of psychopomp
psy¦cho|sex|ual
psy¦cho|sexu|al|ly
psych|osis
  psych|oses

  mental disorder; cf.
  sycosis
psy¦cho|social
psy¦cho|social|ly
psy¦cho|somat|ic
psy¦cho|somat|ic|
    al|ly
psy¦cho|sur|gery
psy¦cho|sur|gi|cal
psy¦cho|syn|the|sis
psy¦cho|
  thera|peut|ic
psy¦cho|ther|ap|ist
psy¦cho|ther|apy
psych|ot|ic
psych|otic|al|ly
psych|oto|
    mim|et|ic
psy¦cho|tro|nic
psy¦cho|trop|ic
psy¦chrom|eter
psy¦chro|phile
psyl|lid
psyl|lium
psy-ops psycho-
  logical operations
psy-war psycho-
  logical warfare
Ptah Egyptian god
ptar|migan
pter|ano|don
pter|ido|logic|al
pter|id|olo|gist
pter|id|ology
Pter|ido|phyta
pter|ido|phyte
pter|ido|sperm
ptero|branch +s
ptero|dac|tyl
ptero|pod
ptero|saur
ptero|yl|
    glu|ta|mate
Ptery|gota
ptery|gote
Ptol|em|aic
Ptol|emy
Ptol|emies
  Egyptian kings;
  Greek astronomer
pto|maine
pto|sis
ptot|ic

ptya|lin
pub
  pubbed
  pub|bing
pube +s pubic hair
pu|ber|tal
pu|berty
pubes
  pl. pubes
  part of abdomen
pubes pl. of pubis
pu|bes|cence
pu|bes|cent
pubic
pubis
  pubes
  bone
pub|lic
pub|lican
pub|li|ca|tion
pub|li|cisa|tion *Br.*
  var. of
  publicization
pub|li|cise *Br.* var.
  of publicize
pub|li|cist
pub|li|cis|tic
pub|li|city
pub|li|ciza|tion
pub|li|cize
  pub|li|ciz|ing
pub|lic|ly
pub|lish
pub|lish|able
pub|lish|er
Puc|cini, Gia|como
  composer
puc|coon
puce
pucka var. of pukka
puck|er wrinkle
puck|eroo +s +ed
  +ing
puck|ery
puck|ish
puck|ish|ly
puck|ish|ness
pud|ding
pudding-head
pud|ding|stone
pud|dingy
pud|dle
  pud|dling

pud|dler
pud|dly
pud|dli|er
pud|dli|est
puddy|sticks
pu|dency
pu|den|dal
pu|den|dum
  pu|denda
pu|deur
pudg|ily
pudgi|ness
pudgy
  pudgi|er
  pudgi|est
pudic
pud|sticks
pudu
Pue|bla city and
  state, Mexico
Pue|blo
  pl. Pu|eblo or
  Pu|eblos
  American Indian
pue|blo +s village
puer|ile
puer|ile|ly
puer|il|ity
  puer|il|ities
puer|peral
puer|per|ium
Puerto Cor|tés
Puerto Limón
Puerto Plata
Puerto Rican
Puerto Rico
Puffa *trademark*
puff|back
puff-back shrike
puff|ball
puff|bird
puff|er
puf|fer|fish
puff|ery
puff|ily
puf|fin
puf|fi|ness
puffy
  puff|ier
  puffi|est
pufta|loon
pug
  pugged
  pug|ging

Puget Sound
pug|garee
pug|gish
puggy
  pug|gier
  pug|gi|est
pu|gil|ism
pu|gil|ist
pu|gil|is|tic
Pugin, Au|gus|tus
  architect
Pu|glia
pug|na|cious
pug|na|cious|ly
pug|na|cious|ness
pug|na|city
Pug|wash
puha
puisne *Law*
puis|sance
puis|sant
puis|sant|ly
puja
pu|jari
puka shell
puke
  puk|ing
pu|keko +s
pukey
  pukier
  puki|est
pukka good;
  genuine; cf. pucker
puk|kah var. of
  pukka
puku
puky var. of pukey
pul
  puls or puli
  Afghan currency;
  cf. pool
pula Botswanan
  currency
pulao var. of pilau
pu|laski
pul|chri|tude
pul|chri|tud|in|ous
pule
  pul|ing
  whimper
puli
  pulik
  sheepdog
puli pl. of pul

Pul|it|zer Prize
pull|back *n.*
pull-down *adj.*
pull|er cf. pula
pul|let
pul|ley
pull-in *n.*
Pull|man +s railway
  carriage
Pull|man, Philip
  author
pull-off *adj. & n.*
pull-on *adj. & n.*
pull-out *adj. & n.*
pull|over
pul|lu|lant
pul|lu|late
  pul|lu|lat|ing
pul|lu|la|tion
pull-up *n.*
pul|mon|aria
pul|mon|ary
Pul|mon|ata
pul|mon|ate
pul|mon|ic
pulp|er
pulpi|ness
pul|pit
pulp|wood
pulpy
  pulp|ier
  pulpi|est
pul|que
pul|sar
pul|sate
  pul|sat|ing
pul|sa|tile
pul|satilla
pul|sa|tion
pul|sa|tor
pul|sa|tory
pulse
  puls|ing
pulse|less
pul|trude
  pul|trud|ing
pul|tru|sion
pul|ver|is|able *Br.*
  var. of pulverizable
pul|ver|isa|tion *Br.*
  var. of
  pulverization

pul¦ver¦isa¦tor *Br.*
var. of **pulverizator**

pul¦ver¦ise *Br.* var.
of **pulverize**

pul¦ver¦iser *Br.* var.
of **pulverizer**

pul¦ver¦iz¦able

pul¦ver¦iza¦tion

pul¦ver¦iza¦tor

pul¦ver¦ize
  pul¦ver¦iz¦ing

pul¦ver¦izer

pul¦veru¦lent

pul¦vi¦nus
  pul¦vini

puma

pum¦ice
  pum¦icing

pu¦mi¦ceous

pum¦mel
  pum¦melled *Br.*
  pum¦meled *US*
  pum¦mel¦ling *Br.*
  pum¦mel¦ing *US*
  hit; cf. **pommel**

pum¦melo var. of
pomelo

pump¦er

pum¦per¦nickel

pump¦kin

pump¦kin¦seed

pun
  punned
  pun¦ning

puna

Punan
  pl. **Punan** or
  Punans

punch¦bag

punch¦ball

punch¦board

punch¦bowl

punch¦card

pun¦cheon

punch¦er

punch¦ily

Pun¦chi¦nello +s

punchi¦ness

punch¦line

punch-up *n.*

punchy
  punch¦ier
  punchi¦est

puncta pl. of
punctum

punc¦tae rounded
dots

punc¦tate

punc¦ta¦tion

punc¦tilio +s

punc¦tili¦ous

punc¦tili¦ous¦ly

punc¦tili¦ous¦ness

punc¦tual

punc¦tu¦al¦ity

punc¦tu¦al¦ly

punc¦tu¦ate
  punc¦tu¦at¦ing

punc¦tu¦ation

punc¦tu¦ation¦al

punc¦tu¦ation¦al¦
         ism

punc¦tu¦ation¦al¦ist
adj.

punc¦tu¦ation¦ism

punc¦tu¦ation¦ist *n.*

punc¦tum
  puncta

punc¦ture
  punc¦tur¦ing

pun¦dit expert; cf.
  pandit

pun¦dit¦oc¦racy
  pun¦dit¦oc¦ra¦cies

pun¦dit¦ry

Pune var. of **Poona**

punga var. of **ponga**

pun¦gency

pun¦gent

pun¦gent¦ly

Punic

puni¦ly

pu¦ni¦ness

pun¦ish

pun¦ish¦able

pun¦ish¦er

pun¦ish¦ing¦ly

pun¦ish¦ment

pu¦ni¦tive

pu¦ni¦tive¦ly

pu¦ni¦tive¦ness

pu¦ni¦tory

Pun¦jab

Pun¦jabi

pun¦jabi shirt

punji stick

pun¦kah Indian
cloth fan

punk¦er punk
rocker

punk¦ette

punk¦ish

punky
  punk¦ier
  punki¦est

pun¦ner

pun¦net

pun¦ning¦ly

pun¦ster

Punta Are¦nas

punt¦er

punty
  pun¦ties
  var. of **pontil**

puny
  puni¦er
  puni¦est
  weak; cf. **puisne**

pup
  pupped
  pup¦ping

pupa
  pupae

pupal

pu¦par¦ium
  pu¦paria

pu¦pate
  pu¦pat¦ing

pu¦pa¦tion

pup¦fish

pupil

pu¦pil¦age var. of
  pupillage

pu¦pilar var. of
  pupillar

pu¦pil¦ary var. of
  pupillary

pu¦pil¦lage

pu¦pil¦lar

pu¦pil¦lary

pu¦pip¦ar¦ous

pup¦pet

pup¦pet¦eer

pup¦pet¦eer¦ing

pup¦pet¦ry

Pup¦pis

puppy
  pup¦pies

puppy¦hood

puppy¦ish

Pur¦ana

Pur¦an¦ic

Pur¦beck peninsula,
England; marble

pur¦blind

pur¦blind¦ness

Pur¦cell, Henry
composer

pur¦chas¦able

pur¦chase
  pur¦chas¦ing

pur¦chaser

pur¦dah

pure
  purer
  purest

purée

pur¦ées

pur¦éed

pur¦ée¦ing

pure¦ly

pure¦ness

pur¦fle
  pur¦fling

pur¦ga¦tion

pur¦ga¦tive

pur¦ga¦tor¦ial

pur¦ga¦tory
  pur¦ga¦tor¦ies

purge
  pur¦ging

pur¦ger

puri

puri¦fi¦ca¦tion

puri¦fi¦ca¦tory

puri¦fier

pur¦ify
  puri¦fies
  puri¦fied
  puri¦fy¦ing

Purim

pur¦ine

Pur¦ism artistic
movement

pur¦ism generally

pur¦ist

pur¦is¦tic

Pur¦itan English
Protestant

pur¦itan generally

pur¦it¦an¦ic¦al

pur¦it¦an¦ic¦al¦ly

Pur¦itan¦ism of
Puritans

pur|itan|ism generally

pur|ity

Pur|kinje cell

purl knitting stitch; babble; cf. **pearl**, **Perl**

pur|ler fall; cf. **pearler**

pur|lieu
pur|lieus or
pur|lieux

pur|lin

pur|loin

pur|loin|er

puro +s

puro|mycin

pur|ple
purp|ling

Pur|ple Heart medal

pur|ple heart drug

purple|ness

purp|lish

pur|ply

pur|port

pur|port|ed|ly

pur|pose
pur|pos|ing

pur|pose|ful

pur|pose|ful|ly

pur|pose|ful|ness

pur|pose|less

pur|pose|less|ly

pur|pose|less|ness

pur|pose|ly

pur|pos|ive

pur|pos|ive|ly

pur|pos|ive|ness

pur|pura

pur|pure

pur|pur|ic

pur|purin

purr sound of cat; cf. **per**

purse
purs|ing

pur|ser

purse-seiner

pursi|ness

purs|lane

pur|su|able

pur|su|ance

pur|su|ant

pur|su|ant|ly

pur|sue

pur|su|ing

pur|suer

pur|suit

pur|sui|vant

pursy
purs|ier
pursi|est

puru|lence

puru|lency

puru|lent

puru|lent|ly

pur|vey

pur|vey|ance

pur|vey|or

pur|view

pus matter; cf. **puss**

Pusan

Pusey, Ed|ward theologian

Pusey|ism

Pusey|ite

push|bike

push-button

push|cart

push|chair

push|er

push|ful

push|ful|ly

push|ful|ness

push|ily

pushi|ness

Push|kin, Alek|sandr writer

push|over

push|pin

push|pit

push|rod

push-start

Pushtu var. of **Pashto**

push-up n.

pushy
push|ier
pushi|est

pu|sil|lan|im|ity

pu|sil|lan|im|ous

pu|sil|lan|im|ous|ly

Pus|kas, Fer|enc footballer

puss cat; cf. **pus**

pussy
puss|ies

pussy|cat

pussy|foot

pussy|foot|er

pus|tu|lar

pus|tu|late
pus|tu|lat|ing

pus|tu|la|tion

pus|tule

pus|tu|lous

put
put|ting
place; cf. **putt**

puta

pu|ta|men
pu|ta|mina or
pu|ta|mens

pu|ta|min|al

pu|ta|tive

pu|ta|tive|ly

put-down n.

Putin, Vlad|imir president of Russia

put-in n.

put|lock

put|log

put-off n.

put-on n.

pu|tong|hua

put-put
put putted
put-putting

pu|tre|fac|tion

pu|tre|fac|tive

pu|trefy
pu|tre|fies
pu|tre|fied
pu|tre|fy|ing

pu|tres|cence

pu|tres|cent

pu|tres|cible

pu|trid

pu|trid|ity

pu|trid|ly

pu|trid|ness

putsch

putt **Golf**; cf. **put**

putta|nesca

put|tee

putt|er golf club; golfer; sound of engine

put|ter US occupy oneself
Br. **potter**

put|ter|er US
Br. **potterer**

Putt|nam, David film producer

putto
putti
cherub

putty
put|ties
put|tied
putty|ing
sealant

put-up attrib.

put-upon attrib.

put-you-up n.

putz stupid person; mess about

puy volcanic cone; lentil

puz|zle

puz|zling

puzzle|ment

puz|zler

puz|zling|ly

pya

py|aemia Br.
US **pyemia**

py|aem|ic Br.
US **pyemic**

pyc|nic var. of **pyknic**; cf. **picnic**

pycno|cline

pye-dog

py|el|itis

py|elo|gram

pyel|og|raphy

py|elo|neph|rit|ic

py|elo|neph|ritis

py|emia US
Br. **pyaemia**

py|emic US
Br. **pyaemic**

py|gid|ium
py|gidia

Pyg|ma|lion kings of Tyre and Cyprus

pyg|mean

pygmy
pyg|mies

pygo|style

pyin|kado +s

py|jama *Br. mod.*
  US pajama
py|ja|mas *Br.*
  US pajamas
pyk|nic stocky; cf.
  picnic
pylon
pyl|or|ic
pyl|orus
  pyl|ori
Pyn|chon, Thomas
  novelist
pyo|derma
pyo|gen|ic
Pyong|yang
pyor|rhea *US*
pyor|rhea
  al|veo|laris *US*
pyor|rhoea *Br.*
pyor|rhoea
  al|veo|laris *Br.*
pyra|can|tha
pyra|lid
pyra|mid
pyr|am|idal
pyr|am|id|al|ly
pyra|mid|ic|al
pyra|mid|ic|al|ly
Pyra|mus *Roman*
  Mythology
pyr|ar|gyr|ite
pyre
pyr|ene
Pyr|en|ean
Pyr|en|ees
pyr|eth|rin
pyr|eth|roid
pyr|eth|rum
pyr|et|ic
Pyrex *trademark*
pyr|exia fever
pyr|exial
pyr|exic|al
pyri|dine
pyri|do|stig|mine
pyri|dox|al
pyri|dox|ine
pyri|form
pyri|meth|amine
pyr|imi|dine
pyr|ite
pyr|ites
pyr|it|ic

pyr|it|isa|tion *Br.*
  var. of **pyritization**
pyr|it|ise *Br.* var. of
  pyritize
pyr|it|iza|tion
pyr|it|ize
  pyr|it|iz|ing
pyr|it|ous
pyro +s pyromaniac
pyro|clast
pyro|clas|tic
pyro|elec|tric
pyro|elec|tri|city
pyro|gal|lol
pyro|gen
pyro|gen|ic
pyro|gen|icity
pyr|ogen|ous
pyr|og|raphy
pyro|lus|ite
pyro|lyse *Br.*
  pyro|lys|ing
pyr|oly|sis
pyro|lyt|ic
pyro|lyze *US*
  pyro|lyz|ing
pyro|mania
pyro|maniac
pyro|maniac|al
pyro|man|ic
pyro|metal|
  lur|gic|al
pyro|metal|lurgy
pyr|om|eter
pyro|met|ric
pyro|met|ric|al|ly
pyr|om|etry
pyro|morph|ite
pyr|ope
pyro|phor|ic
pyro|phos|phate
pyro|phos|phor|ic
pyr|osis
pyro|tech|nic
pyro|tech|nic|al
pyro|tech|ni|cian
pyro|tech|nist
pyro|techny
pyr|ox|ene
pyr|ox|en|ite
pyr|oxy|lin
Pyr|rha *Greek*
  Mythology

pyr|rhic
Pyr|rho *Greek*
  philosopher
Pyr|rho|nian
Pyr|rhon|ic
Pyr|rhon|ism
Pyr|rhon|ist
pyr|rho|tite
Pyr|rhus king of
  Epirus
pyr|role
pyr|roli|dine
pyr|roli|done
pyru|vate
Py|thag|oras *Greek*
  philosopher
Py|thag|or|ean
Pythia *Greek*
  priestess
Pyth|ian
Pyth|ias friend of
  Damon
py|thon
Py|thon|esque
py|thon|ess
py|thon|ic
py|uria
pyx box; cf. pix
pyx|id|ium
  pyx|idia
Pyxis constellation
pzazz var. of pizzazz

Qa|ba|lah var. of
  Kabbalah
Qab|al|ism var. of
  Kabbalism
Qab|al|ist var. of
  Kabbalist
Qab|al|is|tic var. of
  Kabbalistic
Qabis var. of Gabès
Qad|dafi var. of
  Gaddafi
qanat
Qara|ghandy
Qatar

Qatari
Qat|tara
  De|pres|sion
qaw|wal
qaw|wali
qi var. of chi (life
  force)
qibla
qi|gong
Qin Chinese dynasty
Qing Manchu
  dynasty
Qing|dao
Qing|hai
qin|tar
  pl. qin|tar or
  qin|tars or
  qin|darka
Qiqi|har
Qom
Q-tip *trademark*
qua in the capacity
  of
Quaa|lude
  trademark
quack|ery
  quack|eries
quack|ish
quad senses relating
  to 'four'; metal
  block used in
  printing; cf. quod
quad|plex
quadra|gen|ar|ian
Quadra|ges|ima
quadra|gesi|mal
quad|ran|gle
quad|ran|gu|lar
quad|rant
quad|ran|tal
Quad|ran|tids
quadra|phon|ic
quadra|phon|ic|
  al|ly
quadra|phon|y
quadra|plex
quad|rat area of
  habitat
quad|rate
  quad|rat|ing
  bone; muscle; rect-
  angular; make
  square
quad|rat|ic

quad¦ra¦ture
quad¦ra¦tus
  quad¦rati
  muscle
quad¦ren¦nial
quad¦ren¦ni¦al¦ly
quad¦ren¦nium
  quad¦ren¦nia or
  quad¦ren¦niums
quad¦ric
quad¦ri¦ceps
  pl. quad¦ri¦ceps
quad¦riga
  quad¦rigae
quad¦ri¦lat¦eral
quad¦rille
quad¦ril¦lion
quad¦ril¦lionth
quadri¦par¦tite
quadri¦ple¦gia
quadri¦ple¦gic
quadri¦plex var. of
  quadraplex
quadri¦va¦lent
quad¦riv¦ium
quad¦roon
quadro¦phon¦ic var.
  of quadraphonic
quadro¦phon¦ic¦
  al¦ly
  var. of
  quadraphonically
quad¦ro¦ph¦ony var.
  of quadraphony
quad¦ru¦man¦ous
quad¦ru¦ped
quad¦ru¦pedal
quad¦ru¦pedal¦ism
quad¦ru¦ple
  quad¦ru¦pling
quad¦ru¦plet
quad¦ru¦pli¦cate
  quad¦ru¦pli¦cat¦ing
quad¦ru¦pli¦ca¦tion
quad¦ru¦pli¦city
quad¦ruply
quad¦ru¦pole
quaes¦tor
quaes¦tor¦ial
quaes¦tor¦ship
quaff¦able
quaff¦er
quag boggy place
quagga zebra

quaggy
  quag¦gier
  quag¦gi¦est
quag¦mire
qua¦haug var. of
  quahog
qua¦hog
quaich +s
Quai d'Orsay
quaigh var. of
  quaich
quail bird; cf. quale
quaint¦ly
quaint¦ness
quake
  quak¦ing
Quaker
Quaker¦ish
Quaker¦ism
Quaker¦ly
quaky
  quaki¦er
  quaki¦est
quale
qualia Philosophy;
  cf. quail
quali¦fi¦able
quali¦fi¦ca¦tion
quali¦fi¦ca¦tory
quali¦fier
qual¦ify
  quali¦fies
  quali¦fied
  quali¦fy¦ing
quali¦ta¦tive
quali¦ta¦tive¦ly
qual¦ity
  qual¦ities
qualm
qualm¦ish
quan¦dary
  quan¦dar¦ies
quan¦dong
quango +s
Quant, Mary fash-
  ion designer
quant pole; quantity
  analyst
quanta pl. of
  quantum
quant¦al
quant¦al¦ly
quant¦ic
quan¦ti¦fi¦abil¦ity

quan¦ti¦fi¦able
quan¦ti¦fi¦ca¦tion
quan¦ti¦fier
quan¦tify
  quan¦ti¦fies
  quan¦ti¦fied
  quan¦ti¦fy¦ing
quan¦tile
quant¦isa¦tion Br.
  var. of
  quantization
quant¦ise Br. var. of
  quantize
quan¦tiser Br. var.
  of quantizer
quan¦ti¦tate
  quan¦ti¦tat¦ing
quan¦ti¦ta¦tion
quan¦ti¦ta¦tive
quan¦ti¦ta¦tive¦ly
quan¦ti¦tive
quanti¦tive¦ly
quan¦tity
  quan¦tities
quant¦iza¦tion
quant¦ize
  quant¦iz¦ing
quant¦izer
quan¦tum
  quanta
quan¦tum mer¦uit
Qua¦paw
quar¦an¦tine
  quar¦an¦tin¦ing
quark
quar¦rel
  quar¦relled Br.
  quar¦reled US
  quar¦rel¦ling Br.
  quar¦rel¦ing US
quar¦rel¦er US
quar¦rel¦ler Br.
quar¦rel¦some
quar¦rel¦some¦ly
quar¦rel¦some¦ness
quar¦rien var. of
  quarrion
quar¦rier
quar¦rion cockatiel
quarry
  quar¦ries
  quar¦ried
  quarry¦ing

quar¦ry¦man
  quar¦ry¦men
quart liquid
  measure
quart fencing
  position; cf. cart,
  kart, khat
quar¦tan
quarte var. of quart
  (Fencing)
quar¦ter
quar¦ter¦age
quar¦ter¦back
quar¦ter¦deck
quarter-final
quarter-finalist
quarter-hour
quarter-light
quar¦ter¦ly
quar¦ter¦lies
quar¦ter¦master
quar¦tern
quarter-pounder
quar¦ter¦staff
quarter-tone
quar¦tet
quar¦tette var. of
  quartet
quar¦tic
quar¦tier
quar¦tile
quarto 19
quartz
quartz¦ite
qua¦sar
quasi-contract
quasi-contrac¦tual
quasi¦crys¦tal
quasi¦crys¦tal¦line
Quasi¦modo fic-
  tional character
Quasi¦modo,
  Sal¦va¦tore Italian
  poet
quasi¦par¦ticle
quas¦sia
quat¦er¦cen¦ten¦ary
  quat¦er¦cen¦ten¦
  ar¦ies
Qua¦ter¦nary
  Geology
qua¦ter¦nary
  fourth; Chemistry

qua¦tern¦ity
  qua¦tern¦ities
quat¦orze
quat¦rain
quatre¦foil
quat¦tro¦cent¦ist
quat¦tro¦cento
qua¦ver
qua¦ver¦ing¦ly
qua¦very
quay place for ships;
  cf. **cay**, **key**
quay¦age
quay¦side
qubit quantum bit;
  cf. **cubit**
quean impudent
  woman; cf. **queen**
queas¦ily
queasi¦ness
queasy
  queas¦ier
  queasi¦est
Que¦bec
  French Québec
Que¦bec¦er var. of
  Quebecker
Que¦beck¦er
que¦bra¦cho +s
Que¦cha var. of
  Quechua
Que¦chan var. of
  Quechuan
Que¦chua
  pl. Que¦chua or
  Que¦chuas
Que¦chuan
Queen, El¦lery
  writer
queen female sover-
  eign etc.; cf. **quean**
queen¦dom
queen¦fish
queen¦hood
Queenie name
queenie male
  homosexual
queen¦less
queen-like
queen¦li¦ness
queen¦ly
  queen¦lier
  queen¦li¦est

Queens¦berry
  Rules
queen¦ship
queen¦side
queen-size
queen-sized
Queens¦land
Queens¦land¦er
queens¦ware
queer¦ish
queer¦ly
queer¦ness
que¦lea
quell¦er
quench¦able
quench¦er
quench¦less
que¦nelle
Quen¦tin
quer¦cetin
Quer¦cia, Ja¦copo
  della sculptor
que¦ren¦cia
Que¦ré¦taro
quer¦ist
quern¦stone
queru¦lous
queru¦lous¦ly
queru¦lous¦ness
query
  quer¦ies
  quer¦ied
  query¦ing
quesa¦dilla
que sera sera
quest¦er
quest¦ing¦ly
ques¦tion
ques¦tion¦abil¦ity
ques¦tion¦able
ques¦tion¦able¦ness
ques¦tion¦ably
ques¦tion¦ary
  ques¦tion¦ar¦ies
ques¦tion¦er
ques¦tion¦ing¦ly
ques¦tion¦less
ques¦tion¦naire
quest¦or var. of
  quester
Quetta
quet¦zal

Quet¦zal¦có¦atl Tol-
  tec and Aztec god
quet¦zal¦co¦atlus
quet¦zal¦co¦atli or
quet¦zal¦co¦atluses
  pterosaur
queue
  queuing or
  queue¦ing
  (get or put in) line;
  cf. **cue**
Que¦vedo y
  Vil¦le¦gas,
  Fran¦cisco Gómez
  de writer
Que¦zon City
Qufu
quib¦ble
quib¦bling
quib¦bler
quib¦bling¦ly
quiche flan
Quiché
  pl. Quiché or
  Quichés
  people; language
Qui¦chua var. of
  Quechua
quick¦beam
quick¦en
quick-fire
quickie
quick¦lime
quick¦ly
quick¦ness
quick¦sand
quick¦set
quick¦sil¦ver
quick¦step
  quick¦stepped
  quick¦step¦ping
  dance
quick step march
quick¦thorn
Qui¦cun¦que vult
quid
  pl. quid or quids
quid¦dity
  quid¦dities
quid¦nunc
quid pro quo +s
qui¦es¦cence
qui¦es¦cency
qui¦es¦cent

qui¦es¦cent¦ly
quiet
quiet¦en
quiet¦ism
quiet¦ist
quiet¦is¦tic
quiet¦ly
quiet¦ness
quiet¦ude
qui¦etus
quila
quill
Quiller-Couch,
  Ar¦thur novelist
quill¦work
quill¦wort
quilt¦er
quin¦acri¦done
quina¦crine
quin¦ary
quin¦ate
quin¦cen¦ten¦ary
  quin¦cen¦ten¦ar¦ies
quin¦cen¦ten¦nial
Quin¦cey, Thomas
  De writer
quin¦cun¦cial
quin¦cun¦cial¦ly
quin¦cunx
Quine, Wil¦lard
  Van Orman
  philosopher
quin¦ella
quini¦dine
quin¦ine
qui¦noa
quinol
quin¦oline
quin¦olone
quin¦one
quin¦qua¦
        gen¦ar¦ian
Quin¦qua¦ges¦ima
quin¦quen¦nial
quin¦quen¦ni¦al¦ly
quin¦quen¦nium
  quin¦quen¦nia or
  quin¦quen¦niums
quin¦que¦reme
quin¦que¦va¦lent
quin¦sied
quinsy

quint five cards;
 quintuplet
quinta large house;
 country estate
quin|tain
quin|tal
Quin|tana Roo
quinte fencing
 position
quint|es|sence
quint|es|sen|tial
quint|es|sen|tial|ly
quin|tet
quin|tette var. of
 quintet
quin|tile
Quin|til|ian Roman
 rhetorician
quin|til|lion
quin|til|lionth
Quin|tin
Quin|ton
quin|tu|ple; cf.
 quad
 quin|tu|pling
quin|tu|plet
quin|tu|pli|cate
 quin|tu|pli|cat|ing
quin|tuply
quip
 quipped
 quip|ping
quip|ster
quipu
quire paper; cf.
 choir
quirk|ily
quirki|ness
quirk|ish
quirky
 quirk|ier
 quirki|est
quis|ling
quis|ling|ite
quit
 quit|ted or quit
 quit|ting
quit|claim
quite completely;
 rather; definitely
Quito
quit-rent
quit|tance
quit|ter
quiver
quiver|ful

quiver|ing|ly
quivery
qui vive in 'on the
 qui vive'
Quix|ote, Don fic-
 tional hero
quix|ot|ic
quix|ot|ic|al|ly
quix|ot|ism
quix|otry
quiz
 quiz|zes
 quizzed
 quiz|zing
quiz|master
quiz|zer
quiz|zical
quiz|zi|cal|ity
quiz|zi|cal|ly
quiz|zi|cal|ness
Qum var. of Qom
Qum|ran
quod prison; cf.
 quad
*quod erat
 dem|on|
        stran|dum*
quod|libet
quod|libet|arian
quoin angle of
 building; corner-
 stone; wedge; cf.
 coin, coign
quokka
quon|dam
Quon|set *trademark*
quor|ate
Quorn *trademark*
quorum
quota
quot|abil|ity
quot|able
quota|tion
quote
 quot|ing
quo|tid|ian
quo|tient
quo war|ranto +s
Quran var. of
 Koran
Qu|ran|ic var. of
 Koranic
qursh
 pl. qursh
Qwa|qwa

qwerty

—————————

R

Ra Egyptian god; cf.
 rah
Rabat
Ra|baul
rab|bet *US*
 (make) groove in
 wood; *Br.* rebate;
 cf. rabbit
rabbi Jewish leader;
 cf. rabi
rab|bin|ate
rab|bin|ic
rab|bin|ic|al
rab|bin|ic|al|ly
rab|bit animal; to
 chatter; cf. rabbet,
 rarebit
rabbit|brush
rabbit|bush
rabbit|fish
rab|bity
rab|ble
Rabe|lais, Fran|çois
 satirist
Rabe|lais|ian
rabi *Ind.* spring
 crop of grain; also
 in 'kohl rabi'; cf.
 rabbi
rabid
ra|bid|ity
ra|bid|ly
ra|bid|ness
ra|bies
Rabin, Yit|zhak
 prime minister of
 Israel
rac|coon
race
 ra|cing
race|card
race|course
race|goer
race|horse
ra|cem|ate
 Chemistry
ra|ceme

ra|cemic
ra|cem|ise *Br.* var.
 of racemize
ra|cem|ize
 ra|cem|iz|ing
ra|cem|ose
racer
race|run|ner lizard
race|track
race|way
Ra|chael
Ra|chel
ra|chid|ial
ra|chis
 ra|chi|des
rach|it|ic
rach|itis
Rach|man|inov,
 Ser|gei composer
Rach|man|ism
ra|cial
ra|cial|ise *Br.* var. of
 racialize
ra|cial|ism
ra|cial|ist
ra|cial|ize
 ra|cial|iz|ing
ra|cial|ly
raci|ly
Ra|cine, Jean
 dramatist
raci|ness
ra|cism
ra|cist
rack framework;
 cogged rail; (instru-
 ment of) torture;
 destruction; joint of
 meat; horse's gait;
 cause anguish to;
 put on rack; draw
 off wine or beer; in
 'rack and ruin' and
 'rack one's brains';
 cf. wrack
racket
rac|ket|ball var. of
 racquetball
rack|et|eer
rack|et|eer|ing
rack|ets game; cf.
 racquetball
racket-tail
 hummingbird
rack|ety

Rack|ham, Ar|thur
   illustrator
rack rent *n.*
rack-rent *v.*
rack-renter
ra|clette
racon
ra|con|teur
ra|con|teuse female
   raconteur
ra|coon var. of
   raccoon
rac|quet bat; var. of
   racket
rac|quet|ball game;
   cf. **rackets**
racquet-tail var. of
   racket-tail
racy
   raci|er
   raci|est
RADA = Royal
   Academy of Dra-
   matic Art
radar
**Rad|cliffe, Mrs
   Ann** novelist
Rad|cliffe, Paula
   runner
rad|dle
   rad|dling
Radha *Hinduism*
**Radha|krish|nan,
   Sar|ve|palli**
   philosopher
ra|dial
ra|di|al|ly
ra|dian
ra|di|ance
ra|di|ancy
ra|di|ant
ra|di|ant|ly
ra|di|ate
   ra|di|at|ing
ra|di|ation
ra|di|ation|al
ra|di|ation|al|ly
ra|dia|tive
ra|di|ator
rad|ical fundamen-
   tal; revolutionary;
   of the root;
   reformer; group of
   atoms; Chinese

character; cf.
   radicle
rad|ic|al|isa|tion
   Br. var. of
   radicalization
rad|ic|al|ise *Br.* var.
   of radicalize
rad|ic|al|ism
rad|ic|al|iza|tion
rad|ic|al|ize
rad|ic|al|iz|ing
rad|ic|al|ly
rad|ic|al|ness
ra|dic|chio +s
rad|ices pl. of radix
rad|icle part of
   plant embryo; sub-
   division of vein; cf.
   radical
ra|dicu|lar
radii pl. of radius
radio
   pl. **ra|dios**
   v. **ra|dioes**
   ra|dioed
   radio|ing
radio|active
radio|active|ly
radio|activ|ity
radio|bio|logic|al
radio|bio|logic|al|ly
radio|biolo|gist
radio|biol|ogy
radio|car|bon
radio|chem|ical
radio|chem|ist
radio|chem|is|try
radio-element
radio|gen|ic
radio|gen|ic|al|ly
radio-goniom|eter
radio|gram
radio|graph
radi|og|raph|er
radio|graph|ic
radio|graph|ic|al|ly
radi|og|raphy
radio|immuno|
                      assay
radio|immuno|
              logic|al
radio|immuno|
          logic|al|ly
radio|immun|ology

radio|iso|tope
radio|iso|top|ic
radio|laria
radio|lar|ian
radio|loca|tion
radio|logic
radio|logic|al
radio|logic|al|ly
radi|olo|gist
radi|ology
radio|lucency
radio|lucent
radi|om|eter
radio|met|ric
radio|metric|al|ly
radi|om|etry
radi|on|ics
radio|nuclide
radio-opacity var.
   of radiopacity
radio-opaque var.
   of radiopaque
radi|opa|city
radi|opaque
radio|phon|ic
radio|scop|ic
radi|os|copy
radio|sonde
radio-telephone
radio-telephon|ic
radio-telepho|ny
radio|telex
radio|thera|peut|ic
radio|thera|pist
radio|ther|apy
rad|ish
ra|dium
ra|dius
   pl. **radii** or
   ra|diuses
   v. **ra|diuses**
   ra|diused
   ra|dius|ing
radix
   ra|di|ces
Rad|nor|shire
Radom city, Poland
ra|dome structure
   for radar
   equipment
radon
rad|ula *n.*
   radu|lae

radu|lar *adj.*
rad|waste
Rae|burn, Henry
   painter
Rael|ian
Raf|fa|ello San|zio
   painter
Raf|fer|ty's rules
raf|fia
raf|fin|ate
raf|fin|ose
raff|ish
raff|ish|ly
raff|ish|ness
raf|fle
   raf|fling
Raf|fles, Stam|ford
   colonial
   administrator
raf|flesia
**Raf|san|jani, Ali
   Akbar Hash|emi**
   president of Iran
raft|er person who
   rafts
raf|ter beam
raf|tered
rafts|man
rafts|men
rag
   ragged
   rag|ging
rag *Ind. Music*; var.
   of raga
raga *Ind. Music*; cf.
   ragga
ragga
raga|muf|fin
rag|bag
rage
   ra|ging
rager
rag|fish
ragga style of popu-
   lar music; cf. **raga**
ragga|muf|fin var.
   of ragamuffin
rag|ged torn, frayed
rag|ged|ly
rag|ged|ness
rag|ged robin
rag|gedy
raggle-taggle
raggy
   rag|gier

rag¦gi¦est
rag|head *offensive*
ragi *cereal*
rag¦ini *melody from raga*
rag¦lan
rag¦man
rag¦men
Rag¦na|rök *Scandinavian Mythology*
ra¦gout +ed +ing *French* ragoût
rag|pick¦er
rag|stone
rag¦tag
rag¦time
rag¦top
rag¦uly *Heraldry*
Ra¦gusa
rag|weed
rag|worm
rag|wort
rah *exclam.*; cf. Ra
Rah¦man, Tunku Abdul *prime minister of Malaysia*
Rah¦man, Mu¦ji|bur *president of Bangladesh*
rah-rah *enthusiastic; enthusiasm; r. skirt*
rai *style of music*; cf. rye, wry
raid¦er
rail *bar; railway; complain; bird*; cf. rale
rail|age
rail-babbler
rail|bus
rail|car
rail|card
rail¦er
rail|head
rail|ing
rail|lery
rail|less
rail|man
rail|men
rail|road
Rail|track *company*
rail|way

rail|way|man
rail¦way|men
rail¦ment
rain *water*; cf. reign, rein
rain|bird
rain|bow
rain|bow|fish
rain|coat
rain|drop
rain|fall
rain|fast
rain|fly
rain|flies
rain|for¦est
Rai¦nier, Mt
rain|ily
raini|ness
rain|less
rain|maker
rain|out
rain|proof
rain|storm
rain|swept
rain|wash
rain|water
rain|wear
rain|worm
rainy
rain¦ier
raini|est
Rai¦pur
rais|able
raise *lift; increase; bring up*; cf. raze
rais|ing
raiser
rai¦sin
rai¦siny
rai¦son d'état
rai|sons d'état
rai¦son d'être
rai|sons d'être
raita *yogurt dish*; cf. rhyta
Raj, the
raja
rajah *var. of* raja
Ra¦jas|than
Ra¦jas|thani
Raj¦kot

Raj|neesh, Bhag|wan Shree *guru*
Raj|poot *var. of* Rajput
Raj¦put
Raj|pu|tana
Raj|shahi
Rajya Sabha
rake
rak¦ing
rake-off *n.*
raker
rakhi *bracelet*
raki *drink*
rak¦ish
rak¦ish|ly
rak¦ish|ness
Rá¦kosi, Mát¦yás *prime minister of Hungary*
Rak¦sha Ban|dhan
raku
rale *sound in lungs*; cf. rail
Ra|leigh *city, US*
Ra|leigh, Wal¦ter *explorer*
ral¦len|tando
ral¦len|tan¦dos *or* ral¦len|tandi
ralli car *horse-drawn vehicle*
ral|lier
rally
ral|lies
ral|lied
rally|ing
rally|cross
rally|ist
RAM = random-access memory
ram
rammed
ram|ming
Rama *Hinduism*
ra¦mada
Ram|adan
Ram|adhan *var. of* Ramadan
Rama|krishna *Hindu mystic*
ramal

Raman, Chan¦dra|sekh¦ara *physicist*
Rama|pith¦ecus
Rama|yana
Ram|bert, Marie *ballet dancer*
ram|ble
ram|bling
ram|bler
ram|bling|ly
Rambo +s *aggressive man*
rambo +s *apple*
Ram|bouil¦let
ram|bunc¦tious
ram|bunc¦tious|ly
ram|bunc¦tious|ness
ram|bu¦tan
Ram|eau, Jean-Philippe *composer*
ram|ekin
ramen *noodles*; cf. ramin
Ram|eses *var. of* Ramses
rami *pl. of* ramus
ramie *fibre; cloth; plant*
ram|ifi|ca¦tion
ram|ify
rami|fies
rami|fied
rami|fy|ing
Ram|il|lies
ramin *tree*; cf. ramen
ram|jet
ram¦kie
ram¦mer
ram|mies *trousers*
rammy
ram|mies *quarrel*
ram¦ose
ram|page
ram|paging
ram|pageous
ram|pager
ram|pancy
ram|pant
ram|pant¦ly
ram|part

ram|pion
Ram|pur
ram|rod
  ram|rod|ded
  ram|rod|ding
Ram|say, Allan
  painter
Ram|say, Wil|liam
  chemist
Ram|ses pharaohs
Ram|sey, Alf
  football manager
ram|shackle
rams|horn snail
ram|sons
ramus
  rami
ranch|er
ranch|era Mexican
  music
ranch|eria settle-
  ment
ranch|ero +s
  rancher
Ran|chi
ran|cid
ran|cid|ity
ran|cid|ly
ran|cid|ness
ran|cor US
ran|cor|ous
ran|cor|ous|ly
ran|cour Br.
  bitterness; cf.
  ranker
Rand, Ayn
  philosopher
Rand Witwaters-
  rand
rand currency; long
  hillock; part of
  shoe
ran|dan
Rand|ers
ran|dily
ran|di|ness
Ran|dolf
Ran|dolph
ran|dom
ran|dom|isa|tion
  Br. var. of
  randomization
ran|dom|ise Br. var.
  of randomize

ran|dom|iza|tion
ran|dom|ize
  ran|dom|iz|ing
ran|dom|ly
ran|dom|ness
Rand|stad
Randy name
randy
  ran|dier
  ran|di|est
ranee archaic var. of
  rani
Raney nickel
  trademark
ran|ga|tira
range
  ran|ging
rangé settled
range|find|er
range|land
ran|ger
Ran|ger Guide
rangi|ness
ran|goli
Ran|goon
rangy
  ran|gier
  ran|gi|est
rani
ra|niti|dine
  trademark
Ran|jit Singh Sikh
  ruler
Ran|jit|sinhji
Vi|bhaji cricketer
rank|er soldier; soil;
  cf. rancour
ran|kle
rank|ling
rank|ly
rank|ness
rank|shift
Rann of Kutch
ran|sack
ran|sack|er
Ran|som, John
  Crowe poet
ran|som
Ran|some, Ar|thur
  writer
Rant|er member of
  Christian sect
rant|er
rant|ing|ly

Ran|ulf
ra|nun|cul|aceous
ra|nun|cu|lus
ra|nun|cu|luses or
ra|nun|culi
Rao, P. V.
  Nara|simha prime
  minister of India
Raoult's law
rap
  rapped
  rap|ping
  knock; criticize;
  (perform) type of
  music; criminal
  charge; smallest
  amount; cf. rapt,
  wrap
ra|pa|cious
ra|pa|cious|ly
ra|pa|cious|ness
rap|acity
rape
  rap|ing
raper
rape|seed
Raph|ael archangel;
  painter
raphe
  raphae
raph|ide
rapid
rap|id|ity
rap|id|ly
rap|id|ness
ra|pier
ra|pine
rap|ist
rap|paree Irish
  bandit
rap|pee snuff
rap|pel
  rap|pelled Br.
  rap|peled US
  rap|pel|ling Br.
  rap|pel|ing US
rap|pen
rap|per
rap|port
rap|por|teur
rap|proche|ment
rap|scal|lion
rapt absorbed; cf.
  rapped, wrapped

rapt|ly
rapt|ness
rap|tor
rap|tor|ial
rap|tor|ial|ly
rap|ture
rap|tur|ing
rap|tur|ous
rap|tur|ous|ly
rap|tur|ous|ness
Ra|quel
rara avis
  rarae aves
rare
  rarer
  rar|est
rare|bit in 'Welsh
  rarebit'
raree-show
rar|efac|tion
rar|efac|tive
rar|efi|ca|tion
rar|efy
  rar|efies
  rar|efied
  rar|efy|ing
rare|ly
rare|ness
rar|ing
rar|ity
  rar|ities
Raro|tonga
Raro|tongan
rasa
Ras al Khai|mah
rasam
ras|cal
ras|cal|ity
  ras|cal|ities
ras|cal|ly
ras|casse
rase var. of raze
ras|gulla
rash
  rash|er
  rash|est
rasher slice of
  bacon
rash|ly
rash|ness
ras malai
rasp|berry
  rasp|berries
rasp|er

rasp|ing|ly
Ras|pu|tin, Gri|gori
　Efimo|vich Russian
　monk
raspy
　rasp|ier
　raspi|est
rass buttocks; cf.
　wrasse
Rasta = Rastafarian;
　cf. raster
Ras|ta|fari
Ras|ta|far|ian
Ras|ta|far|ian|ism
Rasta|man
　Rasta|men
ras|ter Electronics;
　cf. Rasta
ras|ter|isa|tion Br.
　var. of
　rasterization
ras|ter|ise Br. var.
　of rasterize
ras|ter|iser Br. var.
　of rasterizer
ras|ter|iza|tion
ras|ter|ize
　ras|ter|iz|ing
ras|ter|izer
Ras|tya|pino
rat
　rat|ted
　rat|ting
rata tree; in 'pro
　rata'
ratabil|ity var. of
　rateability
rat|able var. of
　rateable
rat|ably var. of
　rateably
rata|fia
rata|ma|cue
Ra|tana,
　Ta|hu|po|tiki
　Wi|remu Maori
　leader
rata|plan
rata|touille
rat|bag
ratchet
rate
　rat|ing
rate|abil|ity
rate|able

rate|ably
ratel
rate|pay|er
rat|fish
rath circular wall;
　chariot for idol; cf.
　wrath
Rat|haus
　Rat|häuser
rathe prompt; early
ra|ther
Rath|lin Is|land
rat|hole
raths|keller
rath yatra
rati|fi|able
rati|fi|ca|tion
rati|fier
rat|ify
　rati|fies
　rati|fied
　rati|fy|ing
ratio +s
rati|ocin|ate
　rati|ocin|at|ing
rati|ocin|ation
rati|ocina|tive
rati|ocin|ator
ratio de|ci|dendi
　ra|tio|nes
　de|ci|dendi
ra|tion
ra|tion|al adj.
ra|tion|ale n.
ra|tion|al|isa|tion
　Br. var. of
　rationalization
ra|tion|al|ise Br.
　var. of rationalize
ra|tion|al|iser Br.
　var. of rationalizer
ra|tion|al|ism
ra|tion|al|ist
ra|tion|al|is|tic
ra|tion|al|is|tic|al|ly
ra|tion|al|ity
ra|tion|al|iza|tion
ra|tion|al|ize
　ra|tion|al|iz|ing
ra|tion|al|izer
ra|tion|al|ly
rat|ite
rat-kangaroo +s

rat|lin var. of
　ratline
rat|line
ra|toon
rats|bane
rat's tails lank hair
rat-tail tail like
　rat's; fish
rat|tan
rat|ter
Ratti|gan, Ter|ence
　dramatist
rat|tily
rat|ti|ness
Rat|tle, Simon con-
　ductor
rat|tle
　rat|tling
rattle|box
rat|tler
rattle|snake
rattle|trap
rat|tly
　rat|tlier
　rat|tli|est
ratty
　rat|tier
　rat|ti|est
rau|cous
rau|cous|ly
rau|cous|ness
rauli
raunch
raunch|ily
raunchi|ness
raunchy
　raunch|ier
　raunchi|est
Rau|schen|berg,
　Rob|ert artist
rau|vol|fia var. of
　rauwolfia
rau|wol|fia
rav rabbi
rav|age
　rav|aging
rav|ager
rave
　rav|ing
Ravel, Maur|ice
　composer
ravel
　rav|elled Br.
　rav|eled US

rav|el|ling Br.
rav|el|ing US
rav|elin
raven
Ra|venna
rav|en|ous
rav|en|ous|ly
rav|en|ous|ness
raver
rave-up n.
Ravi
ravi|gote
ravi|gotte var. of
　ravigote
ravin plunder
ra|vine gorge
ra|vined
ravi|oli
rav|ish
rav|ish|er
rav|ish|ing|ly
rav|ish|ment
raw uncooked;
　unprocessed; etc.;
　cf. roar
Rawal|pindi
raw|hide
raw|ish
Rawl|plug
　trademark
Rawls, John
　philosopher
rawly
raw|ness
Raw|son
Ray, John naturalist
Ray, Man photog-
　rapher
Ray, Sat|ya|jit film
　director
ray
Ray|leigh, John
　physicist
ray|less
ray|let
Ray|mond
Ray|naud's
　dis|ease
rayon
ray|on|nant
raze
　raz|ing
　destroy; cf. raise

razoo +s
razor
razor|back
razor|bill
razor|fish
razz tease; short for
 razzle
raz|za|ma|tazz var.
 of razzmatazz
raz|zia
raz|zle
razzle-dazzle
razz|ma|tazz
Re var. of Ra
re concerning; as
 musical note, var.
 of ray
re|absorb
re|absorp|tion
re|accept
re|accept|ance
re|accus|tom
reach|able
reach|er
reach-me-down
 adj. & n.
re|acquaint
re|acquaint|ance
re|acquire
 re|acquir|ing
re|acqui|si|tion
react
react|ance
react|ant
re|ac|tion
re|ac|tion|ary
 re|ac|tion|ar|ies
re|ac|tion|ist
re|acti|vate
 re|acti|vat|ing
re|acti|va|tion
re|act|ive
re|activ|ity
re|act|or
read
 past tense and
 participle **read**
 interpret writing or
 signs; discern; indi-
 cate measurement;
 study; cf. **reed,**
 rede, red, redd
read|abil|ity
read|able

read|able|ness
read|ably
re|adapt
re|adap|ta|tion
re|address
read|er
read|er|ly
read|er|ship
read|ily
read-in *n.*
readi|ness
Read|ing town,
 England
read|ing
 interpreting writ-
 ing; etc.; cf.
 reeding
re|adjust
re|adjust|ment
re|admis|sion
re|admit
 re|admit|ted
 re|admit|ting
re|admit|tance
re|adopt
re|adop|tion
read|out
read-through *n.*
re-advertise
 re-advertis|ing
re-advertise|ment
ready
 read|ies
 read|ied
 ready|ing
 read|ier
 readi|est
 prepared; available;
 prepare for; cf.
 reddy
ready-mix *n.*
re|affirm
re|affirm|ation
re|affor|est
re|affor|est|ation
Rea|gan, Ron|ald
 US president
Reagan|ism
Reagan|ite
re|agency
re|agent
re|agin
re|agin|ic

real actual; genuine;
 cf. reel, riel
real currency
 reals or **reis** in
 Brazil
 reals or **reales** in
 Spanish-speaking
 countries
re|algar
re|alia
re|align
re|align|ment
real|is|abil|ity *Br.*
 var. of realizability
real|is|able *Br.* var.
 of realizable
real|isa|tion *Br.* var.
 of realization
real|ise *Br.* var. of
 realize
real|iser *Br.* var. of
 realizer
real|ism
real|ist
real|is|tic
real|is|tic|al|ly
real|ity
 real|ities
real|iz|abil|ity
real|iz|able
real|iza|tion
real|ize
 real|iz|ing
real|izer
re|allo|cate
 re|allo|cat|ing
re|allo|ca|tion
re|allot
 re|allot|ted
 re|allot|ting
re|allot|ment
real|ly
realm
real|ness
realo +s
real|poli|tik
real|tor
realty
ream paper; widen
 (hole); cf. **rheme,**
 riem
ream|er
re|ana|lyse *Br.*
 re|ana|lys|ing

re|analy|sis
re|analy|ses
re|ana|lyze *US*
 re|ana|lyz|ing
re|ani|mate
 re|ani|mat|ing
re|ani|ma|tion
reap|er
re|appear
re|appear|ance
re|appli|ca|tion
re|apply
 re|applies
 re|applied
 re|apply|ing
re|appoint
re|appoint|ment
re|appor|tion
re|appor|tion|ment
re|appraisal
re|appraise
 re|apprais|ing
rear back; raise; in
 naval ranks; cf.
 rhea, ria
rear|er
rear|guard
re|arm
re|arma|ment
rear|most
re|arrange
 re|arran|ging
re|arrange|ment
re|arrest
rear|ward
rear|wards
re|ascend
re|ascen|sion
rea|son
rea|son|able
rea|son|able|ness
rea|son|ably
rea|son|er
rea|son|less
re|assem|ble
 re|assem|bling
re|assem|bly
re|assert
re|asser|tion
re|assess
re|assess|ment
re|assign
re|assign|ment

re|assume
re|assum|ing
re|assump|tion
re|assur|ance
re|assure
re|assur|ing
re|assur|ing|ly
re|attach
re|attach|ment
re|attain
re|attain|ment
re|attempt
Ré|aumur
re|au|thor|isa|tion
  Br. var. of
  reauthorization
re|au|thor|ise *Br.*
  var. of **reauthorize**
re|au|thor|iza|tion
re|au|thor|ize
  re|au|thor|iz|ing
reave
reft
  carry out raids;
  rob; cf. **reeve**
reav|er
re|awaken
rebab
re|badge
  re|badg|ing
re|bal|ance
  re|bal|an|cing
re|bar
re|bar|ba|tive
re|base
  re|bas|ing
re|bat|able
re|bate
  re|bat|ing
  partial(ly) refund
re|bate *Br.*
  re|bat|ing
  (make) groove in
  wood;
  US **rabbet**
rebbe
reb|bet|zin
reb|bit|zin var. of
  rebbetzin
rebec
Re|becca biblical
  character; name
re|beck var. of
  rebec

rebel
  pl. reb|els
  v. re|bels
re|belled
re|bel|ling
re|bel|lion
re|bel|li|ous
re|bel|li|ous|ly
re|bel|li|ous|ness
re|bet|ika
re|bid
  re|bid|ding
re|bind
  re|bound
re|birth
re|birth|er
re|birth|ing
reb|lo|chon
re|board
re|book
re|boot
re|bore
  re|bor|ing
re|born
re|bound
re|bound|er
re|bozo +s
re|brand
re|breathe
  re|breath|ing
re|breath|er
rc|broad|cast
re|broad|cast|er
re|buff
re|build
  re|built
re|build|able
re|build|er
re|buke
  re|buk|ing
re|buker
re|burial
re|bury
  re|buries
  re|buried
  re|bury|ing
rebus
rebut
re|but|ted
re|but|ting
re|but|table
re|but|tal
re|but|ter

rec = recreation
  (ground); cf. **reck**,
  wreck
re|cal|ci|trance
re|cal|ci|trant
re|cal|ci|trant|ly
re|cal|cu|late
  re|cal|cu|lat|ing
re|cal|cu|lation
re|cal|es|cence
re|cal|es|cent
re|cali|brate
  re|cali|brat|ing
re|call
re|call|able
re|cant
re|can|ta|tion
re|cant|er
recap
  re|capped
  re|cap|ping
re|cap|it|al|isa|tion
  Br. var. of
  recapitalization
re|cap|it|al|ise *Br.*
  var. of **recapitalize**
re|cap|it|al|iza|tion
re|cap|it|al|ize
  re|cap|it|al|iz|ing
re|cap|itu|late
  re|cap|itu|lat|ing
re|cap|itu|la|tion
re|cap|itu|la|tive
re|cap|itu|la|tory
re|cap|tion
re|cap|ture
  re|cap|tur|ing
re|cast
recce
rec|ces
rec|ced
recce|ing
re|cede
  re|ced|ing
  go back or away
re-cede
  re-ceding
  cede back
re|ceipt
re|ceiv|able
re|ceive
  re|ceiv|ing
re|ceiver
re|ceiv|er|ship

re|cency
re|cen|sion
re|cent
re|cent|ly
re|cent|ness
recep
  pl. recep or receps
  = reception room
re|cep|tacle
re|cep|tion
re|cep|tion|ist
re|cep|tive
re|cep|tive|ly
re|cep|tive|ness
re|cep|tiv|ity
re|cep|tor
re|cess
re|ces|sion
re|ces|sion|al
re|ces|sion|ary
re|ces|sive
re|ces|sive|ly
re|ces|sive|ness
re|ces|siv|ity
Rech|ab|ite
re|charge
re|char|ging
re|charge|able
re|char|ger
ré|chauffé
re|check
re|cher|ché
re|chip|ping
re|chris|ten
re|cid|iv|ism
re|cid|iv|ist
re|cid|iv|is|tic
Re|cife
re|cipe
re|cipi|ency
re|cipi|ent
re|cip|ro|cal
re|cip|ro|cal|ity
re|cip|ro|cal|ly
re|cip|ro|cate
  re|cip|ro|cat|ing
re|cip|ro|ca|tion
re|cip|ro|ca|tor
reci|procity
re|cir|cu|late
  re|cir|cu|lat|ing
re|cir|cu|la|tion

re|cital
re|cital|ist
reci|ta|tion
reci|ta|tive
reci|ta|tivo +s
re|cite
  re|cit|ing
  say aloud; cf. resite
re|citer
reck pay heed; cf.
  rec, wreck
reck|less
reck|less|ly
reck|less|ness
reckon
reck|on|er
re|claim
re|claim|able
re|claim|er
rec|lam|ation
re|clas|si|fi|ca|tion
re|clas|sify
  re|clas|si|fies
  re|clas|si|fied
  re|clas|si|fy|ing
re|clin|able
re|cline
  re|clin|ing
re|cliner
re|clothe
  re|cloth|ing
re|cluse
re|clu|sion
re|clu|sive
re|clu|sive|ness
re|coat
  re|coat|ing
re|code
  re|cod|ing
rec|og|nis|abil|ity
  Br. var. of
  recognizability
rec|og|nis|able Br.
  var. of
  recognizable
rec|og|nis|ably Br.
  var. of
  recognizably
re|cog|ni|sance Br.
  var. of
  recognizance
re|cog|ni|sant Br.
  var. of recognizant

rec|og|nise Br. var.
  of recognize
rec|og|niser Br. var.
  of recognizer
rec|og|ni|tion
rec|og|niz|abil|ity
rec|og|niz|able
rec|og|niz|ably
re|cog|ni|zance
re|cog|ni|zant
rec|og|nize
  rec|og|niz|ing
rec|og|nizer
re|coil
re|coil|less
Rec|ol|lect var. of
  Recollect
rec|ol|lect remem-
  ber
re|col|lect compose
  oneself; collect
  again
rec|ol|lec|tion
rec|ol|lect|ive
Rec|ol|let Francis-
  can
re|col|on|isa|tion
  Br. var. of
  recolonization
re|col|on|ise Br. var.
  of recolonize
re|col|on|iza|tion
re|col|on|ize
  re|col|on|iz|ing
re|color US
re|col|our Br.
re|com|bin|ant
re|com|bin|ase
re|com|bin|ation
re|com|bine
  re|com|bin|ing
re|com|mence
  re|com|men|cing
re|com|mence|
                ment
rec|om|mend
rec|om|mend|able
rec|om|
        men|da|tion
rec|om|
        men|da|tory
rec|om|mend|er
re|com|mis|sion

re|com|mit
  re|com|mit|ted
  re|com|mit|ting
re|com|mit|ment
re|com|mit|tal
rec|om|pense
rec|om|pens|ing
re|com|pil|ation
re|com|pile
  re|com|pil|ing
re|com|pose
  re|com|pos|ing
re|com|pos|ition
recon
  re|conned
  re|con|ning
  = reconnaissance;
  reconnoitre
rec|on|cil|abil|ity
rec|on|cil|able
rec|on|cile
  rec|on|cil|ing
rec|on|cile|ment
rec|on|ciler
rec|on|cili|ation
rec|on|cili|atory
rec|on|dite
re|con|di|tion
re|con|fig|ur|able
re|con|fig|ur|ation
re|con|fig|ure
  re|con|fig|ur|ing
re|con|firm
re|con|firm|ation
re|con|nais|sance
re|con|nect
re|con|nec|tion
rec|on|noiter US
rec|on|noitre
  rec|on|noi|tring Br.
re|con|quer
re|con|quest
re|con|se|crate
  re|con|se|crat|ing
re|con|se|cra|tion
re|con|sider
re|con|sid|er|ation
re|con|sign
re|con|sign|ment
re|con|soli|date
  re|con|soli|dat|ing
re|con|soli|da|tion
re|con|sti|tute
  re|con|sti|tut|ing

re|con|sti|tu|tion
re|con|struct
re|con|struct|able
re|con|struct|ible
  var. of
  reconstructable
re|con|struc|tion
re|con|struct|ive
re|con|struct|or
re|con|vene
  re|con|ven|ing
re|con|ver|sion
re|con|vert
rec|ord n.
re|cord v.
re|cord|able
Re|cord|er barrister
  acting as judge
re|cord|er person or
  thing that records;
  woodwind
  instrument
Re|cord|er|ship
re|cord|ist
re|cork
re|count narrate;
  count again
re|coup
re|coup|able
re|coup|ment
re|course
re|cover return to
  health; regain;
  extract for reuse
re-cover cover again
re|cov|er|abil|ity
re|cov|er|able
re|cov|er|er
re|cov|ery
re|cov|er|ies
rec|re|ancy
rec|re|ant
rec|re|ant|ly
re|cre|ate
  re|cre|at|ing
  create again
rec|re|ate
  rec|re|at|ing
  take recreation
re|cre|ation cre-
  ation again
rec|re|ation
  relaxing activity
rec|re|ation|al

rec¦re¦ation¦al¦ly
rec¦re¦ative
re¦crim¦in¦ate
  re¦crim¦in¦at¦ing
re¦crim¦in¦ation
re¦crim¦ina¦tive
re¦crim¦in¦atory
re¦cross
re¦cru¦desce
  re¦cru¦des¦cing
re¦cru¦des¦cence
re¦cru¦des¦cent
re¦cruit
re¦cruit¦able
re¦cruit¦er
re¦cruit¦ment
re¦crys¦tal¦lisa¦tion
  Br. var. of
  recrystallization
re¦crys¦tal¦lise *Br.*
  var. of recrystallize
re¦crys¦tal¦liza¦tion
re¦crys¦tal¦lize
  re¦crys¦tal¦liz¦ing
recta pl. of rectum;
  cf. **rector**
rec¦tal
rec¦tal¦ly
rect¦angle
rect¦angu¦lar
rect¦angu¦lar¦ity
rect¦angu¦lar¦ly
recti pl. of rectus
rec¦ti¦fi¦able
rec¦ti¦fi¦ca¦tion
rec¦ti¦fier
rect¦ify
  rec¦ti¦fies
  rec¦ti¦fied
  rec¦ti¦fy¦ing
rec¦ti¦lin¦eal
rec¦ti¦lin¦ear
rec¦ti¦lin¦ear¦ity
rec¦ti¦lin¦ear¦ly
rec¦ti¦tude
recto +s
recto¦cele
rec¦tor member of
  clergy; cf. **recta**
rec¦tor¦ate
rec¦tor¦ial
rec¦tor¦ship

rec¦tory
rec¦tor¦ies
rec¦trix
rec¦tri¦ces
rec¦tum
  rec¦tums or recta
  part of intestine
rec¦tus
recti
  muscle
rec¦tus
  ab¦dom¦inis
re¦cum¦bency
re¦cum¦bent
re¦cum¦bent¦ly
re¦cu¦per¦able
re¦cu¦per¦ate
  re¦cu¦per¦at¦ing
re¦cu¦per¦ation
re¦cu¦pera¦tive
re¦cu¦per¦ator
recur
re¦curred
re¦cur¦ring
re¦cur¦rence
re¦cur¦rent
re¦cur¦rent¦ly
re¦cur¦ring¦ly
re¦cur¦sion
re¦cur¦sive
re¦cur¦sive¦ly
re¦cur¦vat¦ure
re¦curve
  re¦curv¦ing
re¦cusal
recu¦sance
recu¦sancy
recu¦sant
re¦cuse
  re¦cus¦ing
re¦cut
  re¦cut¦ting
re¦cyc¦labil¦ity
re¦cyc¦lable
re¦cycle
  re¦cyc¦ling
re¦cyc¦ler
Red Communist
red
  red¦der
  red¦dest
  colour; cf. **redd**,
  read
re¦dac¦tion

re¦dac¦tion¦al
redan
red¦back spider
red-bait *n.*
red¦bone dog
red¦breast robin
red¦bud tree
red¦cap military
  police officer;
  porter
red¦coat soldier;
  entertainer
red¦cur¦rant
redd tidy up; cf.
  red, **read**
red¦den
Red¦ding, Otis
  singer
red¦dish
Red¦ditch
red¦dle
reddy reddish; cf.
  ready
rede
  red¦ing
  advise; advice; cf.
  read, **reed**
re¦dec¦or¦ate
  re¦dec¦or¦at¦ing
re¦dec¦or¦ation
re¦dedi¦cate
  re¦dedi¦cat¦ing
re¦dedi¦ca¦tion
re¦deem
re¦deem¦able
re¦deem¦er
re¦define
  re¦defin¦ing
re¦def¦in¦ition
re¦demp¦tion
re¦demp¦tive
Re¦demp¦tor¦ist
re¦deploy
re¦deploy¦ment
re¦deposit
re¦depos¦ition
re¦design
re¦de¦ter¦min¦ation
re¦de¦ter¦mine
  re¦de¦ter¦min¦ing
re¦develop
re¦devel¦oper
re¦devel¦op¦ment

red-eye effect in
  photograph; fish;
  drink
red¦fish red-
  coloured fish
red fish fish with
  dark flesh
Red¦ford, Rob¦ert
  actor
Red¦grave,
  Mi¦chael, Va¦nessa,
  Corin, and Lynn
  actors
Red¦grave, Steve
  rower
red¦head person;
  duck
re¦dial
  re¦dialled *Br.*
  re¦dialed *US*
  re¦dial¦ling *Br.*
  re¦dial¦ing *US*
re¦did
re¦dif¦fu¦sion
red¦in¦gote
red¦in¦te¦grate
  red¦in¦te¦grat¦ing
red¦in¦te¦gra¦tion
red¦in¦te¦gra¦tive
re¦dir¦ect
re¦dir¦ec¦tion
re¦dis¦count
re¦dis¦cover
re¦dis¦cov¦ery
  re¦dis¦cov¦er¦ies
re¦dis¦play
re¦dis¦solu¦tion
re¦dis¦solve
  re¦dis¦solv¦ing
re¦dis¦trib¦ute
  re¦dis¦trib¦ut¦ing
re¦dis¦tri¦bu¦tion
re¦dis¦tri¦bu¦tion¦
        ism
re¦dis¦tri¦bu¦tion¦
        ist
re¦dis¦tribu¦tive
re¦div¦ide
re¦div¦id¦ing
re¦div¦ision
redi¦vivus
red¦line
  red¦lin¦ing
  (drive at) maximum
  rpm

redly
Red|mond, John
politician
red|neck person
red|necked of
person
red-necked of bird
or other animal
red|ness
redo
re|does
re|did
re|do|ing
re|done
redo|lence
redo|lent
redo|lent|ly
Redon, Odi|lon
painter
re|double
re|doub|ling
re|doubt
re|doubt|able
re|doubt|ably
re|dound
redox *Chemistry*
red|poll finch
red poll cattle
re|draft
re|draw
re|drew
re|drawn
red-raw
re|dress remedy
re-dress dress again
re|dress|able
re|dress|al
re|dress|er
re|dres|sor var. of
redresser
red|shank bird
red|shirt (keep
back) college ath-
lete; supporter of
Garibaldi
red|skin *offensive*
American Indian
red|start
re|duce
re|du|cing
re|ducer
re|du|ci|bil|ity
re|du|cible
re|duc|tant

re|duc|tase
re|*duc*|*tio ad*
ab|*sur*|*dum*
re|duc|tion
re|duc|tion|ism
re|duc|tion|ist
re|duc|tion|is|tic
re|duc|tive
re|duc|tive|ly
re|duc|tive|ness
re|duc|tiv|ism
re|dun|dancy
re|dun|dan|cies
re|dun|dant
re|dun|dant|ly
re|dupli|cate
re|du|pli|cat|ing
re|dupli|ca|tion
re|dupli|ca|tive
redux revived
red|water cattle
disease
red|wing bird
red|wood tree
red|worm specific
worms
ree|bok
re-echo
re-echoes
re-echoed
re-echoing
Reed, Carol film
director
reed grass; part of
musical
instrument; cf.
read, rede
reed|buck
reed|ed
reed|ing architec-
tural moulding; cf.
reading
re-edit
re-edition
reed|ling
re-educate
re-educat|ing
re-education
reedy
reed|ier
reedi|est
reef|er
reef|point

reek smell; cf.
wreak
reeky
reek|ier
reeki|est
reel cylinder for
winding; dance;
wind in, up, etc.;
stagger; cf. real
re-elect
re-election
reel|er
re-eligible
re-embark
re-embark|ation
re-emerge
re-emerging
re-emergence
re-emergent
re-emphasis
re-emphases
re-emphasise *Br.*
var. of
re-emphasize
re-emphasize
re-emphasiz|ing
re-employ
re-employ|ment
re-enact
re-enactment
re-enactor
re-enforce
re-enforcing
enforce again; cf.
reinforce
re-enforce|ment
act of re-enforcing;
cf. reinforcement
re-engineer
re-enlist
re-enlist|er
re-enter
re-entrance
re-entrant
re-entry
re-entries
re-equip
re-equipped
re-equipping
re-equipment
re-erect
re-erection
re-establish
re-establish|ment

re-evaluate
re-evaluat|ing
re-evaluation
reeve
rove or reeved
reev|ing
magistrate; bird; to
thread; cf. reave,
reive
re-examin|ation
re-examine
re-examin|ing
re-export
re-export|ation
re-export|er
re|face
re|fa|cing
re|fash|ion
re|fas|ten
re|fec|tion
re|fec|tory
re|fec|tor|ies
refer
re|ferred
re|fer|ring
re|fer|able
ref|er|ee
ref|er|ees
ref|er|eed
ref|er|ee|ing
ref|er|ence
ref|er|en|cing
ref|er|en|dum
ref|er|en|dums or
ref|er|enda
ref|er|ent
ref|er|en|tial
ref|er|en|ti|al|ity
ref|er|en|tial|ly
re|fer|ral
re|fer|rer
reffo +s
re|fill
re|fill|able
re|fi|nance
re|fi|nan|cing
re|fine
re|fin|ing
re|fine|ment
re|finer
re|finery
re|finer|ies
re|fin|ish

re¦fit
  re¦fit¦ted
  re¦fit¦ting
re¦fix
re¦flag
  re¦flagged
  re¦flag¦ging
re¦flate
  re¦flat¦ing
re¦fla¦tion
re¦fla¦tion¦ary
re¦flect
re¦flect¦ance
re¦flec¦tion
re¦flect¦ive
re¦flect¦ive¦ly
re¦flect¦ive¦ness
re¦flect¦iv¦ity
re¦flect¦om¦eter
re¦flect¦om¦etry
re¦flect¦or
re¦‚flet
re¦flex
re¦flex¦ibil¦ity
re¦flex¦ible
re¦flex¦ion *archaic*
  var. of reflection
re¦flex¦ive
re¦flex¦ive¦ly
re¦flex¦ive¦ness
re¦flex¦iv¦ity
re¦flex¦ly
re¦flex¦olo¦gist
re¦flex¦ology
re¦float
re¦flow
ref¦lu¦ence
ref¦lu¦ent
re¦flux
re¦focus
  re¦focuses or
  re¦focus¦ses
  re¦focused or
  re¦focussed
  re¦focus¦ing or
  re¦focus¦sing
re¦fold
re¦for¦est
re¦for¦est¦ation
re¦forge
  re¦for¦ging
re¦form correct,
  improve
re-form form again

re¦form¦able
re¦format
  re¦format¦ted
  re¦format¦ting
Ref¦or¦ma¦tion in
  Christian Church
ref¦or¦ma¦tion
  reforming
re-formation
  forming again
ref¦or¦ma¦tion¦al
re¦forma¦tive
re¦forma¦tory
  re¦forma¦tor¦ies
re¦form¦er
re¦form¦ism
re¦form¦ist
re¦for¦mu¦late
  re¦for¦mu¦lat¦ing
re¦for¦mu¦la¦tion
re¦found
re¦foun¦da¦tion
re¦fract
re¦frac¦tion
re¦fract¦ive
re¦fract¦ive¦ly
re¦fract¦om¦eter
re¦fracto¦met¦ric
re¦fract¦om¦etry
re¦frac¦tor
re¦frac¦tori¦ness
re¦frac¦tory
  re¦fract¦or¦ies
re¦frain
re¦frain¦ment
re¦frame
  re¦fram¦ing
re¦fran¦gi¦bil¦ity
re¦fran¦gible
re¦freeze
  re¦froze
  re¦freez¦ing
  re¦frozen
re¦fresh
re¦fresh¦er
re¦fresh¦ing¦ly
re¦fresh¦ment
re¦fried
re¦friger¦ant
re¦friger¦ate
  re¦friger¦at¦ing
re¦friger¦ation
re¦frigera¦tive

re¦friger¦ator
re¦frigera¦tory
re¦frin¦gence
re¦frin¦gent
re¦froze
re¦frozen
re¦fuel
  re¦fuelled *Br.*
  re¦fueled *US*
  re¦fuel¦ling *Br.*
  re¦fuel¦ing *US*
ref¦uge
refu¦gee
re¦fu¦gium
  re¦fu¦gia
re¦ful¦gence
re¦ful¦gent
re¦ful¦gent¦ly
re¦fund pay back
re-fund fund again
re¦fund¦able
re¦fur¦bish
re¦fur¦bish¦ment
re¦furn¦ish
re¦fusal
re¦fuse
  re¦fus¦ing
  withhold consent
  etc.
ref¦use rubbish
re-fuse
  re-fusing
  fuse again
re¦fuse¦nik
re¦fuser
re¦fut¦able
refu¦ta¦tion
re¦fute
  re¦fut¦ing
re¦futer
reg = registration
  mark; cf. **regs**
re¦gain
regal of a monarch;
  small organ
re¦gale
  re¦gal¦ing
  entertain; supply
re¦ga¦lia
re¦ga¦lian
re¦gal¦ism
re¦gal¦ist
re¦gal¦ity
  re¦gal¦ities

re¦gal¦ly
re¦gard
re¦gard¦able
re¦gard¦ant
  Heraldry
re¦gard¦ful
re¦gard¦ful¦ly
re¦gard¦less
re¦gard¦less¦ly
re¦gard¦less¦ness
re¦gather
re¦gatta
re¦gel¦ate
  re¦gel¦at¦ing
re¦gel¦ation
Re¦gency of
  19th-century Brit-
  ain or 18th-century
  France
re¦gency
  re¦gen¦cies
  generally
re¦gen¦er¦ate
  re¦gen¦er¦at¦ing
re¦gen¦er¦ation
re¦gen¦era¦tive
re¦gen¦era¦tive¦ly
re¦gen¦er¦ator
re¦gent
re¦ger¦min¦ation
reg¦gae
Reg¦gio di
  Ca¦lab¦ria
reggo var. of rego
regi¦cidal
regi¦cide
re¦gild
re¦gime
regi¦men
regi¦ment
regi¦men¦tal
regi¦men¦tal¦ly
regi¦men¦ta¦tion
Re¦gina
Regi¦nald
Regio¦mon¦ta¦nus,
  Jo¦han¦nes astron-
  omer
re¦gion
re¦gion¦al
re¦gion¦al¦isa¦tion
  Br. var. of
  regionalization

re¦gion¦al¦ise *Br.*
  var. of regionalize
re¦gion¦al¦ism
re¦gion¦al¦ist
re¦gion¦al¦iza¦tion
re¦gion¦al¦ize
  re¦gion¦al¦iz¦ing
re¦gion¦al¦ly
regis¦seur
  French régisseur
regis¦ter
regis¦trable
regis¦trant
regis¦trar
regis¦trar¦ship
regis¦trary
  regis¦trar¦ies
regis¦tra¦tion
regis¦try
  regis¦tries
  place for records
Re¦gius professor
re¦glaze
  re¦glaz¦ing
reg¦let
reg¦nal
reg¦nant
rego +s
rego¦lith
re¦gorge
  re¦gor¦ging
re¦grade
  re¦grad¦ing
re¦gress
re¦gres¦sion
re¦gres¦sive
re¦gres¦sive¦ly
re¦gres¦sive¦ness
re¦gret
  re¦gret¦ted
  re¦gret¦ting
re¦gret¦ful
re¦gret¦ful¦ly
re¦gret¦ful¦ness
re¦gret¦table
re¦gret¦tably
re¦group
re¦group¦ment
re¦grow
  re¦grew
  re¦grown
re¦growth
regs short for
  regulations

regu¦lable
regu¦lar
regu¦lar¦isa¦tion *Br.*
  var. of
  regularization
regu¦lar¦ise *Br.* var.
  of regularize
re¦gu¦lar¦ity
  re¦gu¦lar¦ities
regu¦lar¦iza¦tion
regu¦lar¦ize
  regu¦lar¦iz¦ing
regu¦lar¦ly
regu¦late
  regu¦lat¦ing
regu¦la¦tion
regu¦la¦tive
regu¦la¦tor
regu¦la¦tory
regu¦line
reg¦ulo gas mark
  trademark
Regu¦lus star
regu¦lus
  regu¦luses or
  reg¦uli
  metallic substance
re¦gur¦gi¦tate
  re¦gur¦gi¦tat¦ing
re¦gur¦gi¦ta¦tion
rehab
re¦habbed
re¦habbing
re¦habili¦tate
  re¦habili¦tat¦ing
re¦habili¦ta¦tion
re¦habili¦ta¦tive
re¦han¦dle
  re¦hand¦ling
re¦hang
  re¦hung
re¦hash
re¦hear
  re¦heard
re¦hearsal
re¦hearse
  re¦hears¦ing
re¦hearser
re¦heat
re¦heat¦er
re¦heel
re¦hire
  re¦hir¦ing

Re¦ho¦boam king of
  Israel
re¦ho¦boam wine
  bottle
re¦home
  re¦hom¦ing
re¦house
  re¦hous¦ing
re¦hung
re¦hy¦drat¦able
re¦hy¦drate
  re¦hy¦drat¦ing
re¦hy¦dra¦tion
Reich German state
Reich, Steve
  composer
Reichs¦tag
re¦ifi¦ca¦tion
re¦ifi¦ca¦tory
reify
  re¦ifies
  re¦ified
  re¦ify¦ing
Rei¦gate
reign rule; cf. rain,
  rein
re¦ignite
  re¦ignit¦ing
reiki
Reilly in 'the life of
  Reilly'; var. of Riley
re¦im¦burs¦able
re¦im¦burse
  re¦im¦burs¦ing
re¦im¦burse¦ment
re¦im¦port
re¦im¦port¦ation
re¦im¦pose
  re¦im¦pos¦ing
re¦im¦pos¦ition
Reims
rein strap to control
  horse; restrain; cf.
  rain, reign
re¦incar¦nate
  re¦incar¦nat¦ing
re¦incar¦na¦tion
re¦incor¦por¦ate
  re¦incor¦por¦at¦ing
re¦incor¦por¦ation
rein¦deer
re¦in¦dus¦trial¦
        isa¦tion
  Br. var. of reindus-

trialization
re¦in¦dus¦trial¦ise
  Br. var. of
  reindustrialize
re¦in¦dus¦trial¦
        iza¦tion
re¦in¦dus¦trial¦ize
re¦in¦dus¦trial¦
        iz¦ing
re¦infect
re¦infec¦tion
re¦inflat¦able
re¦inflate
  re¦inflat¦ing
re¦infla¦tion
re¦inforce
  re¦infor¦cing
  strengthen; cf.
  re-enforce
re¦inforce¦ment act
  of reinforcing;
  troops; cf.
  re-enforcement
re¦infor¦cer
re¦inhabit
Rein¦hardt, Django
  guitarist
Rein¦hardt, Max
  theatre director
re¦insert
re¦inser¦tion
re¦inspect
re¦instal *Br.* var. of
  reinstall
re¦install
re¦instal¦la¦tion
re¦install¦ment *US*
re¦instal¦ment *Br.*
re¦instate
  re¦instat¦ing
re¦instate¦ment
re¦insur¦ance
re¦insure
  re¦insur¦ing
re¦insurer
re¦inte¦grate
  re¦inte¦grat¦ing
re¦inte¦gra¦tion
re¦inter
  re¦interred
  re¦inter¦ring
re¦inter¦ment
re¦inter¦pret
re¦inter¦pret¦ation

re|intro|duce
  re|intro|du|cing
re|intro|duc|tion
re|invade
  re|invad|ing
re|inva|sion
re|invent
re|inven|tion
re|invest
re|inves|ti|gate
  re|inves|ti|gat|ing
re|inves|ti|ga|tion
re|invest|ment
re|invig|or|ate
  re|invig|or|at|ing
re|invig|or|ation
reis pl. of real (Brazilian currency)
rei|shi
re|issue
  re|issu|ing
rc|iter|ate
  re|iter|at|ing
re|iter|ation
re|itera|tive
Rei|ter's
  syn|drome
Reith, John director general of the BBC
reive var. of reave; cf. reeve
reiver var. of reaver
rc|ject
re|ject|able
re|jec|ta|menta
re|ject|er person who rejects; var. of rejector
re|jec|tion
re|jec|tion|ist
re|ject|or
re|jig
  re|jigged
  re|jig|ging
re|jig|ger
re|joice
  re|joi|cing
re|joi|cer
re|joi|cing|ly
re|join
re|join|der
re|ju|ven|ate
  re|ju|ven|at|ing
re|ju|ven|ation

re|ju|ven|ator
re|ju|ven|es|cence
re|ju|ven|es|cent
re|key
re|kin|dle
  re|kind|ling
re|label
  re|labelled Br.
  re|labeled US
  re|label|ling Br.
  re|label|ing US
re|laid past tense and participle of relay (lay again); cf. relayed
re|lapse
  re|laps|ing
re|lapser
re|lat|able
re|late
  re|lat|ing
re|lated|ness
re|later person who relates something; cf. relator
re|la|tion
re|la|tion|al
re|la|tion|al|ly
re|la|tion|ship
rela|tival
rela|tive
rela|tive|ly
rela|tiv|isa|tion Br. var. of relativization
rela|tiv|ise Br. var. of relativize
rela|tiv|ism
rela|tiv|ist
rela|tiv|is|tic
rela|tiv|is|tic|al|ly
rela|tiv|ity
rela|tiv|iza|tion
rela|tiv|ize
  rela|tiv|iz|ing
re|la|tor Law; cf. relater
re|launch
relax
re|lax|ant
re|lax|ation
re|lax|ed|ly
re|lax|ed|ness
re|lax|er

re|lax|in
relay +ed
  pass on; race; electrical device
re|lay
  re|laid
  lay again
re|learn
  re|learned
  Br. also re|learnt
re|leas|able
re|lease
  re|leas|ing
re|leasee
re|leaser generally
re|leasor Law
rele|gate
  rele|gat|ing
rele|ga|tion
re|lent
re|lent|less
re|lent|less|ly
re|lent|less|ness
relet
  re|let|ting
rele|vance
rele|vancy
rele|vant
rele|vant|ly
re|levé
re|li|abil|ity
re|li|able
re|li|able|ness
re|li|ably
re|li|ance
re|li|ant
relic
re|li|cence var. of relicense
re|li|cense
  re|licen|sing
rel|ict
re|lief
re|liev|able
re|lieve
  re|liev|ing
re|lieved|ly
re|liever
re|lievo +s
re|light
  re|light|ed or re|lit
re|li|gion
re|li|gion|ism

re|li|gion|ist
re|li|gion|less
re|ligi|ose
re|ligi|os|ity
re|li|gious
re|li|gious|ly
re|li|gious|ness
re|line
  re|lin|ing
re|lin|quish
re|lin|quish|ment
reli|quary
  reli|quar|ies
re|liquiae
rel|ish
rel|ish|able
re|list
re|live
  re|liv|ing
rell|eno +s
rel|lie
rello +s
re|load
re|locate
  re|locat|ing
re|loca|tion
re|lock
re|luc|tance
re|luc|tant
re|luc|tant|ly
rely
  re|lies
  re|lied
  rely|ing
REM = rapid eye movement
rem
  pl. rem
  unit of radiation
re|main
re|main|der
re|make
  re|made
  re|mak|ing
re|man
  re|manned
  re|man|ning
re|mand
rem|an|ence
rem|an|ent
  remaining; cf. remnant
re|map
  re|mapped

re|map|ping
re|mark comment
re-mark mark again
re|mark|able
re|mark|able|ness
re|mark|ably
Re|marque, Erich
  Maria novelist
re|mar|riage
re|marry
  re|mar|ries
  re|mar|ried
  re|marry|ing
re|mas|ter
re|match
rem|bet|ika var. of
  rebetika
Rem|brandt van
  Rijn painter
REME = Royal
  Electrical and
  Mechanical
  Engineers
re|meas|ure
  re|meas|ur|ing
re|meas|ure|ment
re|medi|able
re|med|ial
re|medi|al|ly
re|medi|ate
  re|medi|at|ing
re|medi|ation
rem|edy
  rem|ed|ies
  rem|ed|ied
  rem|edy|ing
re|mem|ber
re|mem|ber|er
re|mem|brance
re|mem|bran|cer
remi|ges
  sing. remex
re|mind
re|mind|er
re|mind|ful
re|min|er|al|
              isa|tion
  Br. var. of
  remineralization
re|min|er|al|ise Br.
  var. of
  remineralize
re|min|er|al|
            iza|tion

re|min|er|al|ize
re|min|er|al|iz|ing
rem|in|isce
rem|in|is|cing
rem|in|is|cence
rem|in|is|cent
rem|in|is|cen|tial
rem|in|is|cent|ly
rem|in|is|cer
re|mise
re|mis|ing
re|miss
re|mis|sible
re|mis|sion
re|miss|ly
re|miss|ness
re|mit
  re|mit|ted
  re|mit|ting
re|mit|table
re|mit|tal
re|mit|tance
re|mit|tee
re|mit|tent
re|mit|ter
remix
re|mix|er
rem|nant small
  remaining quantity;
  cf. remanent
re|model
  re|mod|elled Br.
  re|mod|eled US
  re|mod|el|ling Br.
  re|mod|el|ing US
  re|model|er US
  re|model|ler Br.
re|modi|fi|ca|tion
re|mod|ify
  re|modi|fies
  re|modi|fied
  re|modi|fy|ing
re|mold US
  Br. remould
rem|on|strance
Re|mon|strant
  Arminian in Dutch
  Church
re|mon|strant
  remonstrating
rem|on|strate
  rem|on|strat|ing
  rem|on|stra|tion
  rem|on|stra|tive

rem|on|stra|tor
re|mon|tant
re|mora
re|morse
re|morse|ful
re|morse|ful|ly
re|morse|less
re|morse|less|ly
re|morse|less|ness
re|mort|gage
  re|mort|ga|ging
re|mote
  re|moter
  re|mot|est
re|mote|ly
re|mote|ness
re|mou|lade
re|mould Br.
  US remold
re|mount
re|mov|abil|ity
re|mov|able
re|moval
re|mov|al|ist
re|move
  re|mov|ing
re|move|able var. of
  removable
re|mover
re|mu|age
re|muda
re|mu|ner|ate
  re|mu|ner|at|ing
  re|mu|ner|ation
  re|mu|nera|tive
Remus Roman
  Mythology
REN = ringer
  equivalent number;
  cf. wren, Wren
Re|nais|sance
  European artistic
  revival
re|nais|sance
  revival, renewed
  interest; cf.
  renascence
renal
re|name
  re|nam|ing
Re|namo
Renan, Er|nest
  historian

Re|nas|cence var. of
  Renaissance
re|nas|cence revival
  of something
  dormant; cf.
  renaissance
re|nas|cent
re|nation|al|
              isa|tion
  Br. var. of
  renationalization
re|nation|al|ise Br.
  var. of
  renationalize
re|nation|al|
            iza|tion
re|nation|al|ize
re|nation|al|iz|ing
Ren|ault, Louis car
  manufacturer
Ren|ault, Mary
  novelist
ren|contre n.
  archaic var. of
  rencounter
ren|coun|ter n. &
  v.
Ren|dell, Ruth
  writer
ren|der
ren|der|er
render-set
  render-setting
ren|dez|vous
  pl. ren|dez|vous
  v. ren|dez|vouses
  ren|dez|voused
  ren|dez|vous|ing
ren|di|tion
ren|dzina
rene|gade
  rene|gad|ing
rene|gado
  rene|gadoes
re|nege
  re|neg|ing
  re|neg|er
re|nego|ti|able
re|nego|ti|ate
  re|nego|ti|at|ing
  re|nego|ti|ation
re|negue
  re|neguing
  var. of renege

re|neguer var. of
  reneger
re|new
re|new|abil|ity
re|new|able
re|newal
re|new|er
Ren|frew|shire
renga
  pl. renga or rengas
reni|form
renin enzyme pro-
  ducing angiotensin;
  cf. rennin
ren|minbi
Rennes
ren|net
Ren|nie, John civil
  engineer
ren|nin enzyme
  curdling milk; cf.
  renin
Reno
Ren|oir, Au|guste
  painter
Ren|oir, Jean film
  director
re|nomin|ate
re|nomin|at|ing
re|nomin|ation
re|nor|mal|isa|tion
  Br. var. of
  renormalization
re|nor|mal|ise Br.
  var. of renormalize
re|nor|mal|iza|tion
re|nor|mal|iz|ing
re|nos|ter|bos
re|nos|ter|bosch
  var. of renosterbos
re|nos|ter|veld
re|nounce
  re|noun|cing
re|nounce|able
re|nounce|ment
re|noun|cer
reno|vate
  reno|vat|ing
reno|va|tion
reno|va|tor
re|nown
re|nowned
rent|abil|ity

rent|able
ren|tal
rent|er
ren|tier
re|num|ber
re|nun|ci|ant
re|nun|ci|ation
re|nun|cia|tive
re|nun|ci|atory
ren|vers
ren|verse var. of
  renvers
ren|voi
re|occu|pa|tion
re|occupy
  re|occu|pies
  re|occu|pied
  re|occu|py|ing
re|occur
  re|occurred
  re|occur|ring
re|occur|rence
re|offend
re|offend|er
re|open
re|order
reorg = reorganiza-
  tion; reorganize
re|organ|isa|tion
  Br. var. of
  reorganization
re|organ|ise Br. var.
  of reorganize
re|organ|iser Br.
  var. of reorganizer
re|organ|iza|tion
re|organ|ize
  re|organ|iz|ing
re|organ|izer
re|ori|ent
re|orien|tate
  re|orien|tat|ing
re|orien|ta|tion
reo|virus
rep
  repped
  rep|ping
  (act as) representa-
  tive; repetition,
  repeat; repertory;
  reputation
rep fabric
re|pack

re|pack|age
re|pack|aging
re|pagin|ate
  re|pagin|at|ing
re|pagin|ation
re|paid
re|paint
re|pair
re|pair|able able to
  be repaired; cf.
  reparable
re|pair|er
re|pair|man
  re|pair|men
re|paper
rep|ar|able able to
  be rectified; cf.
  repairable
rep|ar|ation
rep|ara|tive
rep|ar|tee
re|par|ti|tion
re|pass pass again
re|past meal
repat = repatriated
  person
re|pat|ri|ate
  re|pat|ri|at|ing
re|pat|ri|ation
re|pay
  re|paid
re|pay|able
re|pay|ment
re|peal
re|peal|able
re|peat
re|peat|abil|ity
re|peat|able
re|peat|ed|ly
re|peat|er
re|pêch|age
repel
  re|pelled
  re|pel|ling
re|pel|lant var. of
  repellent
re|pel|lence
re|pel|lency
re|pel|lent
re|pel|lent|ly
re|pel|ler
re|pent
re|pent|ance

re|pent|ant
re|pent|er
re|people
  re|peop|ling
re|per|cus|sion
re|per|cus|sive
rep|er|toire
rep|er|tory
  rep|er|tor|ies
rep|et|end
ré|péti|teur
repe|ti|tion
repe|ti|tion|al
repe|ti|tious
repe|ti|tious|ly
repe|ti|tious|ness
re|peti|tive
re|peti|tive|ly
re|peti|tive|ness
re|phrase
  re|phras|ing
re|pine
  re|pin|ing
re|pique
  re|piquing
re|place
  re|placing
re|place|able
re|place|ment
re|placer
re|plan
  re|planned
  re|plan|ning
re|plant
re|plas|ter
re|play
re|plen|ish
re|plen|ish|er
re|plen|ish|ment
re|plete
re|plete|ness
re|ple|tion
re|plevin
re|plevy
  re|plev|ies
  re|plev|ied
  re|plevy|ing
rep|lica
rep|lic|abil|ity
rep|lic|able
rep|lic|ant
rep|lic|ase

rep|li|cate
rep|li|cat|ing
rep|li|ca|tion
rep|li|ca|tive
rep|li|ca|tor
rep|li|con
re|plier
reply
  re|plies
  re|plied
  re|ply|ing
rep|mobile
repo
  pl. repos
  v. repo's
  repo'd
  repo'ing
re|point
re|pol|ish
re|popu|late
  re|popu|lat|ing
  re|popu|la|tion
re|port
re|port|able
rep|or|tage
re|port|ed|ly
re|port|er
rep|or|tor|ial
rep|or|tori|al|ly
re|pos|ado +s
re|pose
  re|pos|ing
re|pose|ful
re|pose|ful|ly
re|pos|ition
re|posi|tory
  re|posi|tor|ies
re|pos|sess
re|pos|ses|sion
re|pos|ses|sor
re|post
re|pot
  re|pot|ted
  re|pot|ting
re|poussé
repp fabric; var. of
  rep
rep|re|hend
rep|re|hen|si|bil|ity
rep|re|hen|sible
rep|re|hen|sibly
rep|re|hen|sion
rep|re|sent act or
  stand for; consti-

tute; depict
re-present present
  again
rep|re|sent|abil|ity
rep|re|sent|able
rep|re|sen|ta|tion
  representing
  something
re-presen|ta|tion
  presenting some-
  thing again
rep|re|sen|
      ta|tion|al
rep|re|sen|
      ta|tion|al|ism
rep|re|sen|
      ta|tion|al|ist
rep|re|sen|ta|tion|
      al|ly
rep|re|sen|ta|tion|
      ism
rep|re|sen|ta|tion|
      ist
rep|re|sen|ta|tive
rep|re|sen|ta|tive|ly
rep|re|sen|ta|tive|
      ness
re|press
re|press|er gener-
  ally
re|press|ible
re|pres|sion
re|pres|sive
re|pres|sive|ly
re|pres|sive|ness
re|pres|sor
  Biochemistry
re|pres|sur|isa|tion
  Br. var. of
  repressurization
re|pres|sur|ise *Br.*
  var. of repressurize
re|pres|sur|iza|tion
re|pres|sur|ize
re|pres|sur|iz|ing
re|price
  re|pricing
re|prieve
  re|priev|ing
rep|ri|mand
re|print
re|print|er
re|prisal

re|prise
  re|pris|ing
repro +s
  reproduction
re|proach
re|proach|able
re|proach|er
re|proach|ful
re|proach|ful|ly
re|proach|ful|ness
re|proach|ing|ly
rep|ro|bate
  rep|ro|bat|ing
rep|ro|ba|tion
re|pro|cess
re|pro|duce
  re|pro|du|cing
re|pro|du|cer
re|pro|du|ci|bil|ity
re|pro|du|cible
re|pro|du|cibly
re|pro|duc|tion
re|pro|duct|ive
re|pro|duc|tive|ly
re|pro|duc|tive|
      ness
re|pro|duct|iv|ity
re|pro|gram
  re|pro|grammed
  US also
  re|pro|gramed
  re|pro|gram|ming
  US also
  re|pro|gram|ing
re|pro|gram|mable
re|pro|gramme var.
  of reprogram
rep|rog|raph|er
repro|graph|ic
repro|graph|ic|al|ly
repro|graph|ics
rep|rog|raphy
re|proof
re|prov|able
re|prove
  re|prov|ing
re|prover
re|prov|ing|ly
rep|tile
Rep|tilia
rep|til|ian
Rep|ton, Hum|phry
  landscape gardener
re|pub|lic

re|pub|lic|an
re|pub|lic|an|ism
re|pub|li|ca|tion
re|pub|lish
re|pudi|ate
  re|pudi|at|ing
re|pudi|ation
re|pudi|ator
re|pudi|atory
re|pug|nance
re|pug|nancy
re|pug|nant
re|pug|nant|ly
re|pulse
  re|puls|ing
re|pul|sion
re|pul|sive
re|pul|sive|ly
re|pul|sive|ness
re|pur|chase
  re|pur|chas|ing
re|puri|fi|ca|tion
re|pur|ify
  re|puri|fies
  re|puri|fied
  re|puri|fy|ing
re|pur|pose
  re|pur|pos|ing
rep|ut|able
rep|ut|ably
repu|ta|tion
re|pute
  re|put|ing
re|puted|ly
re|quali|fi|ca|tion
re|qual|ify
  re|quali|fies
  re|quali|fied
  re|quali|fy|ing
re|quest
re|quest|er
re|quiem
requi|escat
re|quinto +s
re|quire
  re|quir|ing
re|quire|ment
re|quirer
requis|ite
requis|ite|ly
requi|si|tion
requi|si|tion|er
requi|si|tion|ist

re|quital
re|quite
  re|quit|ing
re|ran
re|rate
  re|rat|ing
re|read
re|read|able
re-record
rere|dos
  pl. rere|dos
re-release
  re-releas|ing
re-roof
re-route
  re-routeing or
  re-routing
re|run
  re|ran
  re|run|ning
re|sal|able var. of
  resaleable
re|sale
re|sale|able
re|sat
re|scale
  re|scal|ing
re|sched|ule
  re|sched|ul|ing
re|scind
re|scind|able
re|scis|sion
re|score
  re|scor|ing
re|script
res|cu|able
res|cue
  res|cu|ing
res|cuer
re|seal
re|seal|able
re|search
re|search|able
re|search|er
re|seat
ré|seau
  ré|seaux
re|sect
re|sect|able
re|sec|tion
re|sec|tion|al
re|sec|tion|ist
res|eda
re|seed

re|se|lect
re|se|lec|tion
re|sell
  re|sold
  re|sell|er
re|sem|blance
re|sem|blant
re|sem|ble
  re|sem|bling
re|sent
re|sent|ful
re|sent|ful|ly
re|sent|ful|ness
re|sent|ment
re|ser|pine
re|serv|able
res|er|va|tion
re|serve
  re|serv|ing
  put aside
re-serve
  re-serving
  serve again
re|served|ly
re|serv|ed|ness
re|server
re|serv|ist
res|er|voir
re|set
  re|set|ting
re|set|tabil|ity
re|set|table
re|set|tle
  re|set|tling
re|settle|ment
res ges|tae
re|shape
  re|shap|ing
re|sharp|en
re|shoot
  re|shot
re|shuf|fle
  re|shuf|fling
res|ide
  res|id|ing
resi|dence
resi|dency
  resi|den|cies
resi|dent
resi|den|tial
resi|den|tial|ly
resi|den|tiary
  resi|den|tiar|ies
resi|dent|ship

re|sidua pl. of
  residuum
re|sidual
re|sidu|al|ly
re|sidu|ary
resi|due
re|siduum
  re|sidua
re|sign give up
  employment etc.
re-sign sign again
re|sig|nal
  re|sig|nalled *Br.*
  re|sig|naled *US*
  re|sig|nal|ling *Br.*
  re|sig|nal|ing *US*
res|ig|na|tion
re|signed|ly
re|sign|ed|ness
re|sign|er
re|sile
  re|sil|ing
re|sili|ence
re|sili|ency
re|sili|ent
re|sili|ent|ly
resi|lin
re-silver
resin
res|in|ate
  res|in|at|ing
  treat with resin; cf.
  resonate
res|in|oid
res|in|ous
res ipsa loqui|tur
re|sist
re|sist|ance
re|sist|ant
re|sist|er generally;
  cf. resistor
re|sist|ibil|ity
re|sist|ible
re|sist|ive
re|sist|iv|ity
re|sist|less
re|sist|less|ly
re|sis|tor electrical
  device; cf. resister
re|sit
  re|sat
  re|sit|ting
re|site
  re|sit|ing

reposition; cf.
  recite
re|size
  re|siz|ing
res judi|cata
  res judi|catae
re|skill
re|skin
  re|skinned
  re|skin|ning
Res|nais, Alain film
  director
re|sold
re|sole
  re|sol|ing
re|sol|uble that can
  be resolved
re-soluble that can
  be dissolved again
reso|lute
reso|lute|ly
reso|lute|ness
reso|lution
reso|lu|tive
re|solv|abil|ity
re|solv|able
re|solve
  re|solv|ing
re|solved|ly
re|solv|ent
re|solver
res|on|ance
res|on|ant
res|on|ant|ly
res|on|ate
  res|on|at|ing
  produce or show
  resonance; cf.
  resinate
res|on|ation
res|on|ator
re|sorb
re|sor|cinol
re|sorp|tion
re|sorp|tive
re|sort holiday
  place; recourse;
  turn to
re-sort sort again
re|sort|er
re|sound
re|sound|ing|ly
re|source
  re|sour|cing

re|source|ful
re|source|ful|ly
re|source|ful|ness
re|source|less
re|source|less|ness
re|specify
  re|speci|fies
  re|speci|fied
  re|specify|ing
re|spect
re|spect|abil|ity
re|spect|able
re|spect|ably
re|spect|er
re|spect|ful
re|spect|ful|ly
re|spect|ful|ness
re|spect|ive
re|spect|ive|ly
re|spell
  re|spelled or
  re|spelt
Res|pighi,
  Otto|rino composer
res|pir|able
res|pir|ate
  res|pir|at|ing
res|pir|ation
res|pir|ator
re|spira|tory
re|spire
  re|spir|ing
res|pir|om|eter
res|pite
  res|pit|ing
re|splen|dence
re|splen|dency
re|splen|dent
re|splen|dent|ly
re|spond
re|spond|ence
re|spond|ency
re|spond|ent
re|spond|er
re|sponsa pl. of
  responsum
re|sponse
re|spon|si|bil|ity
  re|spon|si|bil|ities
re|spon|sible
re|spon|sible|ness
re|spon|sibly
re|spon|sive

re|spon|sive|ly
re|spon|sive|ness
re|spon|sor|ial
re|spon|sory
  re|spon|sor|ies
re|spon|sum
  re|sponsa
re|spray
res pub|lica
res|senti|ment
rest repose;
  remainder; cf.
  wrest
re|stage
  re|staging
re|start
re|state
  re|stat|ing
re|state|ment
res|taur|ant
res|taura|teur
re|sten|osis
rest|ful
rest|ful|ly
rest|ful|ness
rest|harrow
res|tio +s
*res|ti|tu|tio in
in|teg|rum*
res|ti|tu|tion
res|titu|tive
rest|ive
rest|ive|ly
rest|ive|ness
rest|less
rest|less|ly
rest|less|ness
re|stock
re|stor|able
Res|tor|ation of
  Charles II
res|tor|ation gener-
  ally
res|tor|ation|ism
res|tor|ation|ist
re|stora|tive
re|stora|tive|ly
re|store
  re|stor|ing
re|storer
re|strain control
re-strain strain
  again

re|strain|able
re|strain|ed|ly
re|strain|er
re|straint
re|strict
re|strict|ed|ly
re|strict|ed|ness
re|stric|tion
re|stric|tion|ism
re|stric|tion|ist
re|strict|ive
re|strict|ive|ly
re|strict|ive|ness
re|string
  re|strung
rest|room
re|struc|ture
  re|struc|tur|ing
re|study
  re|stud|ies
  re|stud|ied
  re|study|ing
re|style
  re|styl|ing
re|sub|mis|sion
re|sub|mit
  re|sub|mit|ted
  re|sub|mit|ting
re|sult
re|sult|ant
re|sulta|tive
re|sum|able
re|sume
  re|sum|ing
  begin or take up
  again
ré|sumé summary;
  curriculum vitae
re|sump|tion
re|sump|tive
re|su|pin|ate
re|su|pin|ation
re|sup|ply
  re|sup|plies
  re|sup|plied
  re|sup|ply|ing
re|sur|face
  re|sur|facing
re|sur|gence
re|sur|gent
res|ur|rect
res|ur|rec|tion
re|sur|vey

re|sus|ci|tate
  re|sus|ci|tat|ing
re|sus|ci|ta|tion
re|sus|ci|ta|tive
re|sus|ci|ta|tor
re|sus|pend
re|sus|pen|sion
ret
  ret|ted
  ret|ting
re|table
re|tablo +s var. of
  retable
re|tail
re|tail|er
re|tain
re|tain|abil|ity
re|tain|able
re|tain|er
re|tain|ment
re|take
  re|took
  re|tak|ing
  re|taken
re|tali|ate
  re|tali|at|ing
re|tali|ation
re|talia|tive
re|tali|ator
re|tali|atory
re|tard
re|tard|ancy
re|tard|ant
re|tar|da|taire
re|tard|ate
re|tard|ation
re|tarda|tive
re|tarda|tory
re|tard|er
retch vomit; cf.
  wretch
rete
  retia
re|teach
  re|taught
re|tell
  re|told
re|ten|tion
re|ten|tive
re|ten|tive|ly
re|ten|tive|ness
re|ten|tiv|ity
  re|ten|tiv|ities

re|test
re|tex|ture
  re|tex|tur|ing
re|thatch
re|think
  re|thought
Reth|ym|non
retia pl. of rete
reti|ar|ius
  reti|arii
  gladiator
reti|cence
reti|cent
reti|cent|ly
ret|icle
re|ticula pl. of
  reticulum
re|ticu|lar of the
  reticulum
re|ticu|late
  re|ticu|lat|ing
re|ticu|la|tion
reti|cule
re|ticu|lin
re|ticu|lo|cyte
re|ticu|lo|endo|
    the|lial
re|ticu|lo|endo|
    theli|osis
re|ticu|lose
Re|ticu|lum con-
  stellation
re|ticu|lum
  re|tic|ula
  network;
  ruminant's stomach
re|tie
  re|tying
re|tight|en
re|tile
  re|til|ing
re-time
  re-timing
ret|ina
  ret|inas or ret|inae
ret|inal
ret|in|itis
ret|in|itis
  pig|ment|osa
ret|ino|blast|oma
ret|in|oic
ret|in|oid
ret|inol
ret|in|op|athy

ret|ino|top|ic
ret|ino|topic|al|ly
ret|inue
re|tiral
re|tire
  re|tir|ing
  end working life;
  withdraw
re|tiré ballet
  movement
re|tired|ness
re|tiree person
  retiring
re|tire|ment
re|tirer
re|tir|ing|ly
re|title
  re|titling
re|told
re|took
re|tool
re|tort
re|tor|tion
re|touch
re|touch|er
re|trace
  re|tracing
re|tract
re|tract|able
re|tract|ile
re|tract|il|ity
re|trac|tion
re|trac|tive
re|tract|or
re|train
re|trans|late
  re|trans|lat|ing
  re|trans|la|tion
re|trans|mis|sion
re|trans|mit
  re|trans|mit|ted
  re|trans|mit|ting
re|tread
  re|trod
  re|trod|den
  tread again
re|tread +ed tyre;
  put fresh tread on
re|treat
re|trench
re|trench|ment
re|trial
ret|ri|bu|tion
re|tribu|tive

re|tribu|tory
re|triev|abil|ity
re|triev|able
re|trieval
re|trieve
  re|triev|ing
re|triever
retro +s
retro|act
retro|action
retro|active
retro|active|ly
retro|activ|ity
retro|bulbar
retro|choir
re|trod
re|trod|den
retro|dic|tion
retro|ele|ment
retro|fit
  retro|fit|ted
  retro|fit|ting
retro|flex
retro|flexed
retro|flex|ion
retro|grad|ation
retro|grade
  retro|grad|ing
retro|grade|ly
retro|gress
retro|gres|sion
retro|gres|sive
retro|lental
retro|perl|ton|cal
retro|reflect|ive
retro|reflect|or
retro|rocket
ret|rorse
ret|rorse|ly
retro|spect
retro|spec|tion
retro|spect|ive
retro|spect|ive|ly
retro|sternal
retro|trans|poson
re|troussé
retro|ver|sion
retro|vert
Retro|vir
  trademark
retro|viral
retro|virus

re|try
  re|tries
  re|tried
  re|try|ing
ret|sina
re|tune
  re|tun|ing
re|turf
re|turn
re|turn|able
re|turn|ee
re|turn|er
re|turn|less
re|tying present
  participle of retie
re|type
  re|typ|ing
Reu|ben
re|uni|fi|ca|tion
re|unify
  re|uni|fies
  re|uni|fied
  re|uni|fy|ing
Ré|union island
re|union
re|unite
  re|unit|ing
re|uphol|ster
re|uphol|stery
re|uptake
re|usable
re|use
  re|us|ing
re|use|able var. of
  reusable
Reu|ters
re|util|isa|tion *Br.*
  var. of reutilization
re|util|ise *Br.* var. of
  reutilize
re|util|iza|tion
re|util|ize
  re|util|iz|ing
rev
  revved
  rev|ving
re|vac|cin|ate
re|vac|cin|at|ing
re|vac|cin|ation
re|val|id|ate
  re|val|id|at|ing
re|val|id|ation
re|valu|ation

re|value
  re|valu|ing
re|vamp
re|vanch|ism
re|vanch|ist
re|var|nish
re|veal
re|veal|able
re|veal|er
re|veal|ing
  re|veal|ing|ly
re|vege|tate
  re|vege|tat|ing
re|vege|ta|tion
re|veille
ré|veil|lon
revel
  rev|elled *Br.*
  rev|eled *US*
  revel|ling *Br.*
  revel|ing *US*
reve|la|tion
reve|la|tion|al
reve|la|tion|ist
rev|ela|tory
rev|el|er *US*
rev|el|ler *Br.*
rev|el|ry
  rev|el|ries
rev|enant
re|venge
  re|ven|ging
re|venge|ful
re|venge|ful|ly
re|venge|ful|ness
re|ven|ger
rev|enue
re|verb =
  reverberation
re|ver|ber|ant
re|ver|ber|ant|ly
re|ver|ber|ate
  re|ver|ber|at|ing
re|ver|ber|ation
re|ver|bera|tive
re|ver|ber|ator
re|ver|ber|atory
Re|vere, Paul
  American patriot
re|vere
  re|ver|ing
  venerate; cf. **revers**
rev|er|ence
  rev|er|en|cing

Rev|er|end title of
  clergy
rev|er|end deserv-
  ing reverence
rev|er|ent feeling or
  showing reverence
rev|er|en|tial
rev|er|en|tial|ly
rev|er|ent|ly
rev|erie
re|vers
  pl. re|vers
  edge of garment
re|ver|sal
re|verse
  re|vers|ing
  back; cf. **revers**
re|verse|ly
re|verser
re|vers|ibil|ity
re|vers|ible
re|vers|ibly
re|ver|sion
re|ver|sion|al
re|ver|sion|er
re|vert
re|vert|ant
re|vert|er
re|vert|ible
revet
  re|vet|ted
  re|vet|ting
  face with masonry
re|vet|ment
re|view assess;
  assessment; cf.
  revue
re|view|able
re|view|al
re|view|er
re|vile
  re|vil|ing
re|vile|ment
re|viler
re|vis|able
re|visal
re|vise
  re|vis|ing
re|viser
re|vi|sion
re|vi|sion|ary
re|vi|sion|ism
re|vi|sion|ist
re|visit

re|vis|ory
re|vi|tal|isa|tion *Br.*
  var. of
  revitalization
re|vi|tal|ise *Br.* var.
  of **revitalize**
re|vi|tal|iza|tion
re|vi|tal|ize
  re|vi|tal|iz|ing
re|viv|able
re|vival
re|vival|ism
re|vival|ist
re|vival|is|tic
re|vive
  re|viv|ing
re|viver
re|vivi|fi|ca|tion
re|viv|ify
  re|vivi|fies
  re|vivi|fied
  re|vivi|fy|ing
rev|oc|abil|ity
rev|oc|able
revo|ca|tion
revo|ca|tory
re|voke
  re|vok|ing
re|voker
re|volt
  re|volt|ing|ly
revo|lute
revo|lu|tion
revo|lu|tion|ary
  revo|lu|tion|ar|ies
revo|lu|tion|ise *Br.*
  var. of
  revolutionize
revo|lu|tion|ism
revo|lu|tion|ist
revo|lu|tion|ize
  revo|lu|tion|iz|ing
re|volve
  re|volv|ing
re|volver
re|vote
revue theatrical
  entertainment; cf.
  review
re|vul|sion
re|vul|sive
re|ward
re|ward|ing|ly
re|ward|less

rewa|rewa
re|wash
re|weigh
re|wind
  re|wound
re|wind|er
re|wir|able
re|wire
  re|wir|ing
re|word
re|work
re|wound
re|wrap
  re|wrapped
  re|wrap|ping
re|writ|able
re|write
  re|wrote
  re|writ|ing
  re|writ|ten
Rex name; cat
  breed; king
rex,
  Tyr|an|no|saurus
Rex|ine *trademark*
Reye's syn|drome
Rey|kja|vik
Rey|nard
Rey|nolds, Al|bert
  prime minister of
  Ireland
Rey|nolds, Joshua
  painter
Reza Shah ruler of
  Iran
rhab|dom
rhab|do|mancy
rhab|dome var. of
  rhabdom
rhabdo|myoly|sis
rhabdo|myo|
        sar|coma
rhabdo|myo|
        sar|co|mas
  or rhabdo|myo|
        sar|co|mata
rha|chis var. of
  rachis
Rhada|man|thine
Rhada|man|thus
  Greek Mythology
Rhae|tian
Rhae|tic
Rhaeto-Romance

Rhaeto-Romanic
Rha|kine
rham|nose
rhap|sode
rhap|sod|ic
rhap|sod|ic|al|ly
rhap|sod|ise Br. var.
of rhapsodize
rhap|sod|ist
rhap|sod|ize
rhap|sod|iz|ing
rhap|sody
rhap|sod|ies
rhat|any
rhat|anies
Rhea Titan; moon
of Saturn
rhea bird; cf. rear,
ria
rhe|bok
rhe|buck var. of
rhebok
Rheims var. of
Reims
rheme Linguistics
part of clause; cf.
ream, riem
Rhem|ish of Reims
Rhen|ish of the
Rhine
rhe|nium
rhe|nos|ter|bos var.
of renosterbos
rheo|logic|al
rhe|olo|gist
rhe|ology
rheo|stat
rheo|stat|ic
rhe|sus
rhe|tor
rhet|oric
rhet|oric|al
rhet|oric|al|ly
rhet|or|ician
rheum watery
discharge
rheum|at|ic
rheum|at|ic|al|ly
rheum|at|icky
rheuma|tism
rheuma|toid
rheum|ato|logic|al
rheuma|tolo|gist

rheuma|tol|ogy
rheumy
rheum|ier
rheumi|est
full of rheum
rhinal
Rhine
Rhine|land
rhine|stone
rhin|itis
rhino +s =
rhinoceros
rhi|noceros
pl. rhi|noceros or
rhi|nocer|oses
rhi|nocer|ot|ic
rhino|plas|tic
rhino|plasty
rhino|plas|ties
rhino|virus
rhi|zo|bium
rhi|zo|bia
rhiz|oc|to|nia
rhi|zoid
rhi|zoid|al
rhi|zome
rhizo|morph
rhizo|pod
Rhizo|poda
rhizo|sphere
rho +s Greek letter
rhoda|mine
Rhode Is|land
state, US
Rhodes Greek
island
Rhodes, Cecil
politician;
R. Scholarship
Rhodes, Wil|fred
cricketer
Rho|desia
Rho|desian
Rho|dian
rho|dium
rhodo|chros|ite
rhodo|den|dron
rhodo|nite
Rho|dope
Moun|tains
Rhodo|phyta
rhodo|phyte
rhod|op|sin
rho|dora

rhomb
rhomb|en|ceph|
alon
rhombi pl. of
rhombus
rhom|bic
rhombo|he|dral
rhombo|he|dron
rhombo|he|dra or
rhombo|he|drons
rhom|boid
rhom|boid|al
rhom|boid|eus
rhom|boidei
Rhombo|zoa
rhombo|zoan
rhom|bus
rhom|buses or
rhombi
Rhon|dda
Rhône
Rhône-Alpes
rhota|cisa|tion Br.
var. of
rhotacization
rhota|cised Br. var.
of rhotacized
rhota|ciza|tion
rhota|cized
rho|tic
rho|ti|city
rhu|barb
Rhum Scottish
island
rhumb imaginary
line; compass point
rhumba var. of
rumba
rhyme
rhym|ing
in poetry; cf. rime
rhyme|less
rhymer
rhyme|ster
rhym|ist
rhyn|cho|saur
rhyn|cho|spor|ium
rhyo|lite
Rhys, Jean writer
rhyta pl. of rhyton;
cf. raita
rhythm
rhyth|mic
rhyth|mic|al

rhyth|mic|al|ly
rhyth|mi|city
rhythm|less
rhy|ton
rhy|tons or rhyta
ria narrow inlet; cf.
rear, rhea
rial Iranian or
Omani currency; cf.
riyal, riel
Ri|alto
rib
ribbed
rib|bing
rib|ald
rib|ald|ry
rib|and
Riba|tejo
Rib|ben|trop,
Joa|chim von Nazi
politician
rib|ber
rib|bie
rib|bon
ribbon|fish
ribbon-grass
ribby
rib|cage
Ri|bera, José de
painter
rib-eye
ribi|tol
rib|less
ribo|fla|vin
ribo|nucle|ase
ribo|nucle|ic
ri|bose
ribo|so|mal
ribo|some
ribo|zyme
ribu|lose
rib|wort
Ri|card trademark
Ric|ard|ian
Ric|ard|ian|ism
Ri|cardo, David
political economist
Ricci ten|sor
Rice, Tim lyricist
rice
ri|cing
rice|paper
ricer

ri¦cer¦car
ri¦cer¦care
ri¦cer¦cari
var. of **ricercar**
Rich¦ard, Cliff pop
singer
Rich¦ards, Gor¦don
jockey
Rich¦ards, I. A.
literary critic
Rich¦ards, Viv
cricketer
Rich¦ard¦son,
Ralph actor
Rich¦ard¦son,
Sam¦uel novelist
Riche¦lieu, duc de
cardinal
rich¦en
riches
Rich¦ler, Mor¦de¦cai
writer
rich¦ly
Rich¦mond
rich¦ness
Rich¦ter scale
Richt¦hofen,
Man¦fred von
fighter pilot
ricin
rick
rick¦eti¦ness
rick¦ets
rick¦ett¦sia
rick¦ett¦siae or
rick¦ett¦sias
rick¦ett¦sial
rick¦ety
rick¦etier
rick¦eti¦est
rickey drink
rickle
rick¦rack
rick¦sha var. of
rickshaw
rick¦shaw
rico¦chet
rico¦cheted or
rico¦chet¦ted
rico¦chet¦ing or
rico¦chet¦ting
ri¦cotta
ric¦rac var. of
rickrack
ric¦tal

ric¦tus
rid
rid¦ding
rid¦able var. of
rideable
rid¦dance
rid¦den
rid¦dle
rid¦dling
rid¦dler
rid¦dling¦ly
ride
rode
rid¦ing
rid¦den
ride¦able
ride-off n.
ride-on adj. & n.
rider
rider¦less
rider¦ship
ridge
ridg¦ing
ridge¦back
ridge¦way
ridgy
ridgi¦er
ridgi¦est
ridgy-didge
ridi¦cule
ridi¦cul¦ing
ri¦dicu¦lous
ri¦dicu¦lous¦ly
ri¦dicu¦lous¦ness
Rid¦ley, Nich¦olas
Protestant martyr
rid¦ley
Rie, Lucie potter
rie¦beck¦ite
Rief¦en¦stahl, Leni
film-maker
Riel, Louis
politician
riel Cambodian
currency; cf. **real,**
rial, riyal
riem
Rie¦mann,
Bern¦hard
mathematician
Rie¦mann¦ian
ri¦empie
Ries¦ling

riet¦bok var. of
reedbuck
Rif Mountains
ri¦fam¦pi¦cin
ri¦fam¦pin
riff
rife¦ness
rif¦fle turn (pages);
search
rif¦fling
rif¦fler
riff-raff
rifle gun
rif¦ling
rifle¦man
rifle¦men
rifle¦scope
rig
rigged
rig¦ging
Riga
riga¦doon
riga¦toni
Rigel
rig¦ger person who
rigs; cf. **rigor,**
rigour
Right Politics
right just; correct;
not left; entitle-
ment; immediately;
completely; restore;
cf. **rite, wright,**
write
right¦able
right¦en
right¦eous
right¦eous¦ly
right¦eous¦ness
right¦er comparative
of **right**; in
'animal-righter'
etc.; cf. **raita, rhyta**
right¦ful
right¦ful¦ly
right¦ful¦ness
right-hander
right¦ish
right¦ism
right¦ist
right¦less
right¦ly
right¦most
right¦ness

righto
right-on adj.
right¦size
right¦siz¦ing
right-to-lifer
right¦ward
right¦wards
right-winger
righty
right¦ies
righty-ho
rigid
ri¦gid¦ify
ri¦gidi¦fies
ri¦gidi¦fied
ri¦gidi¦fy¦ing
ri¦gid¦ity
ri¦gid¦ly
ri¦gid¦ness
Rigil Kent
Rigil Ken¦taurus
rig¦mar¦ole
rigor feeling of cold;
rigor mortis; cf.
rigger, rigour
rigor US
thoroughness;
severity
Br. **rigour**; cf.
rigger
rigor¦ism
rigor¦ist
rigor mor¦tis
rigor¦ous
rigor¦ous¦ly
rigor¦ous¦ness
rig¦our Br.
thoroughness;
severity
US **rigor**; cf.
rigger, rigor
rig-out n.
Rig Veda Hinduism
Rij¦eka
Rijks¦mu¦seum
rijst¦tafel
rik¦ishi
pl. rik¦ishi
Riks¦mål
Rila Moun¦tains
rile
ril¦ing
Riley in 'the life of
Riley'

Riley, Brid|get
 painter
ri|lievo var. of
 relievo
Rilke, Rai|ner
 Maria poet
rill small stream
rille channel on
 moon
ril|lettes
rim
 rimmed
 rim|ming
 edge; cf. riem
Rim|baud, Ar|thur
 poet
rime
 rim|ing
 frost;
 archaic var. of
 rhyme
rim|fire
Rim|ini
rim|land
rim|less
Rim|mon ancient
 deity
rim|ous
rim|rock
rim-shot
Rimsky-Korsakov,
 Niko|lai composer
rimu
rimy
 rimi|er
 rimi|est
rin|der|pest
rind|less
ring +ed circle;
 enclosure; group;
 surround; cf. wring
ring
 rang
 rung
 (make) sound;
 telephone; cf.
 wring
ring-a-ring o'
 roses
ring|bark
ring|bolt
ring|bone
ring|dove
ring|er cf. wringer
Rin|ger's solu|tion

ring|ette
ring|git
 pl. ring|git or
 ring|gits
 Malaysian currency
ring|hals var. of
 rinkhals
ring-in n.
ring|ing|ly
ring|lead|er
ring|less
ring|let
ring|let|ed
ring|let|ted var. of
 ringleted
ring|lety
ring|master
ring|neck
ring-necked
ring|side
ring|sider
ring|ster
ring|tail
ring-tailed
ring|tone
ring|work
ring|worm
rink|hals
rinky-dink
Rin|poche
rinse
 rins|ing
rinser
Rio Branco
Rio de Ja|neiro
Río de la Plata
Río de Oro
Rio Grande river,
 N. America
Rio Grande do
 Norte state, Brazil
Rio Grande do
 Sul state, Brazil
Rioja wine from La
 Rioja, Spain
Rio Muni
Rio Negro
riot disturbance;
 large display; cf.
 ryot
riot|er
riot|ous
riot|ous|ly

riot|ous|ness
rip
 ripped
 rip|ping
ri|par|ian
rip|cord
ripe
 riper
 rip|est
ripe|ly
ripen
ripe|ness
ri|pi|eno
 ri|pi|enos or
 ri|pi|eni
rip-off n.
ri|poste
 ri|post|ing
rip|per
rip|ping|ly
rip|ple
 rip|pling
rip|plet
rip|ply
 rip|plier
 rip|pli|est
rip|rap
 rip|rapped
 rip|rap|ping
rip-roaring
rip-roaringly
rip|saw
rip-snorter
rip-snorting
rip-snorting|ly
rip|stop
Ripu|arian
Rip Van Win|kle
 fictional character
RISC Computing;
 cf. risk
rise
 rose
 ris|ing
 risen
riser
rishi
risi|bil|ity
ris|ible
ris|ibly
risk exposure to
 danger or chance;
 cf. RISC
risk|ily

riski|ness
risky
 risk|ier
 riski|est
Ri|sor|gi|mento
ris|otto +s
ris|qué
ris|sole
Risso's dol|phin
Rit|alin trademark
rit|ar|dando
 rit|ar|dandos or
 rit|ar|dandi
rite solemn act; cf.
 right, wright,
 write
rite de pas|sage
 rites de pas|sage
rite|less
rit|en|uto
 rit|en|utos or
 rit|en|uti
rit|or|nello
 rit|or|nel|los or
 rit|or|nelli
rit|ual
ritu|al|isa|tion Br.
 var. of ritualization
ritu|al|ise Br. var. of
 ritualize
ritu|al|ize
ritu|al|ism
ritu|al|ist
ritu|al|is|tic
ritu|al|is|tic|al|ly
ritu|al|iza|tion
ritu|al|ize
 ritu|al|iz|ing
ritu|al|ly
ritz|ily
ritzi|ness
ritzy
 ritz|ier
 ritzi|est
rival
 ri|valled Br.
 ri|valed US
 ri|val|ling Br.
 ri|val|ing US
rival|rous
ri|val|ry
 rival|ries
rive
 riv|ing
 riven
river

Ri¦vera, Diego
painter

river|bank

river|boat

riv|ered

river|ine

river|less

river|scape

river|side

rivet (fasten with)
pin or bolt; fix; cf.
revet

riv|et¦er

rivet|ing¦ly

rivi|era coast

rivi¦ère necklace

Rivne

rivu|let

rivu|lus

Riy¦adh

riyal Saudi Arabian,
Qatari, or Yemeni
currency; cf. **rial**,
riel

RNase

roach fish
pl. roach

roach cockroach;
marijuana cigarette
butt; curve

road way; part for
vehicles; cf. **rode**,
roed, **rowed**

road|bed

road|block

road|hold¦ing

road|house

roadie
roady|ing

road|kill

road|less

road|man
road|men

road|roll¦er

road|run¦ner

road|show

road|side

road|stead

road|ster

road|way

road|work

road|worthi|ness

road|worthy

roam¦er person who
roams; cf. **Roma**,
romer

roan colour; animal;
cf. **rone**, **rowan**,
rowen

roar animal's deep
cry; prolonged
sound; cf. **raw**

roar¦er

roar|ing¦ly

roast¦er

Rob name

rob
robbed
rob|bing

ro¦bata

Robbe-Grillet,
Alain novelist

Rob¦ben Is¦land

rob¦ber

rob|bery
rob|ber¦ies

Rob¦bia, Luca della
sculptor

Rob¦bie

Rob|bins, Har¦old
novelist

Rob|bins, Je¦rome
choreographer

robe
rob¦ing

Rob¦ert

Rob¦erta

Rob¦erts,
Fred¦erick field
marshal

Robe|son, Paul
singer

Robes|pierre,
Max¦imil¦ian revo-
lutionary

Robey, George
comedian

robin

Ro¦bina

robin-chat

robin-egg var. of
robin's-egg

rob|inia

robin's-egg colour

Rob¦in|son,
Ed¦ward G. actor

Rob¦in|son, Heath
illustrator of absurd
devices

Rob¦in|son, Mary
president of Ireland

Rob¦in|son,
Smokey singer

Rob¦in|son, Sugar
Ray boxer

Rob¦in|son
Cru¦soe fictional
character

robot

ro¦bot¦ic

ro¦bot¦ic|al¦ly

ro¦bot|isa¦tion *Br.*
var. of robotization

ro¦bot|ise *Br.* var. of
robotize

ro¦bot|iza¦tion

ro¦bot|ize
ro¦bot|iz¦ing

Rob|sart, Amy wife
of Robert Dudley

Rob¦son, Flora
actress

ro¦bust +er +est
sturdy; forceful

ro¦busta coffee

ro¦bust¦ly

ro¦bust|ness

roc legendary bird;
cf. **rock**

ro¦caille

roc¦am|bole

Roch|dale

Roche limit

roche mou¦ton|née
roches
mou¦ton|nées

Roch|es¦ter

rochet Christian
vestment

rock cf. roc

rocka|billy

Rock|all

rock and roll

rock and roll¦er

rock|burst

Rocke|fel¦ler, John
industrialist

rock¦er

rock¦ery
rock|er¦ies

rocket

rock¦et|eer

rock¦et¦ry

rock|fall

rock|fish

rock|fowl

Rock|hamp¦ton

rock|hop¦per

rock|hound

rock|hound|ing

Rock|ies

rock¦ily

rocki|ness

rock|less

rock|let

rock-like

rock|ling

rock 'n' roll var. of
rock and roll

rock 'n' roll¦er var.
of rock and roller

rock|slide

rock|steady form of
reggae music

rocku|men¦tary

rocku|men¦tar¦ies

Rock|well,
Nor¦man illustrator

rocky

rock¦ier
rocki¦est

Rocky Moun|tains

ro¦coco

Rod¦den|berry,
Gene television
producer

Rod¦dick, Anita
businesswoman

rode past tense of
ride; cf. **road**,
roed, **rowed**

rode
rod¦ing
fly (of woodcock);
cf. **road**, **roed**,
rowed

ro¦dent

ro¦den¦ti|cide

rodeo +s +ed +ing

Rod|er¦ick

Rodg¦ers, Rich¦ard
composer

ro¦dger|sia

rod¦ham

Rodin, Au|guste
sculptor
rod||less
rod¦let
rod-like
Rod¦ney
rodo|mon|tade
rodo|mon|tad|ing
Ro|drigo, Joa|quin
composer
Ro|dri|guez
soli|taire
Roe, Al||liott
Ver|don aircraft
designer
roe fish eggs or milt;
deer; cf. rho, row
roe|buck
roed having roe; cf.
road, rode, rowed
Roe|dean
Roeg, Nich|olas film
director
roent|gen
roent¦geno|gram
roent¦geno|
            graph|ic
roent¦geno|
            graph|ic|al|ly
roent¦gen|og|raphy
roent¦gen|ology
Roese|lare
rogan josh
ro|ga|tion
ro|ga|tion|al
Ro|ga|tion|tide
Roger name
roger acknowledg-
ing message; also
vulgar slang
Rogers, Gin|ger
actress and dancer
Rogers, Rich|ard
architect
Roget's The|saurus
rogue
roguing
roguery
roguer|ies
roguish
roguish¦ly
roguish|ness
Roh|mer, Eric film-
maker

Ro|hyp|nol
trademark
roily
rois|ter
rois|ter|er
rois|ter|ous
Ro|land paladin of
Charlemagne
role part in play etc.
French rôle
roll turn over; flat-
ten with roller;
reverberate; cylin-
der; movement;
sound; list; bread
roll|able
Rol|land, Ro|main
writer
roll|away n.
roll|back n.
roll-call
roll¦er
roll¦er|ball
Roll¦er|blade n,
trademark
roll¦er|blade v.
roll¦er|blad|ing
roll¦er|blader
roll¦er skate
roller-skate v.
roller-skating
roll¦er skater
roll¦er skat|ing n.
rol|lick behave
exuberantly
rol|lick|ing repri-
mand
roll-in roll-out n.
Computing
roll|mop
roll-neck
rol|lock|ing var. of
rollicking; cf.
rowlock
roll-off n.
roll-on adj. & n.
roll-on roll-off adj.
roll-out n.
roll|over n.
Rolls, Charles
transport pioneer
roll-top
roll-up n. & adj.
Rolo|dex trademark

roly-poly
roly-polies
ROM = read-only
memory
Rom
Roma
(male) Gypsy
Ro|maic
ro|maine lettuce
ro|maji
Roman (citizen) of
Rome; alphabet
roman typeface; fish
roman-à-clef
romans-à-clef
Ro|mance
languages
ro|mance
ro|man|cing
romantic feeling
etc.
ro|man|cer
Ro|manes Romany
language
Ro|man|esque
roman-fleuve
romans-fleuves
Ro|mania
Ro|ma|nian
Ro|man|ic
Ro|man|isa|tion Br.
var. of
Romanization
ro|man|isa|tion Br.
var of
romanization
Ro|man|ise Br. var.
of Romanize
ro|man|ise Br. var.
of romanize
Ro|man|ish
Ro|man|ism
Ro|man|ist
Ro|man|iza|tion
Romanizing
ro|man|iza|tion
romanizing
Ro|man|ize
Ro|man|iz|ing
make Roman or
Roman Catholic
ro|man|ize
ro|man|iz|ing
put into roman

type or the Roman
alphabet
Ro|mano cheese
Romano-British
Rom|anov Russian
dynasty
Ro|mansh dialects
Ro|man|tic of
romanticism
ro|man|tic of
romance
ro|man|tic|al|ly
ro|man|ti|cisa|tion
Br. var. of
romanticization
ro|man|ti|cise Br.
var. of romanticize
ro|man|ti|cism
ro|man|ti|cist
ro|man|ti|ciza|tion
ro|man|ti|cize
ro|man|ti|ciz|ing
Rom|any
Rom|anies
Rom|berg,
Sig|mund
composer
rom|com
Rome
Romeo +s
romer map-reading
device; cf. roamer,
Roma
Rom|ish
Rom|mel, Erwin
field marshal
Rom|ney, George
painter
Rom|ney Marsh
romp|er mod.
romp|ers
Rom|ulus Roman
Mythology
Ron|ald
Ro|naldo footballer
Ronces|valles
ron|da|vel
rond de jambe
ronds de jambes or
ronds de jambe
ronde dance
ron|deau
ron|deaux
poem; cf. rondo

ron|del
rondo +s musical
form; cf. rondeau
Ron|dô|nia
rone gutter; cf. roan
rongo|rongo
ronin
  pl. ronin or ronins
ron|quil
Rönt|gen, Wil|helm
  physicist
rönt|gen var. of
  roentgen
rönt|geno|gram
  var. of
  roentgenogram
rönt|geno|graph|ic
  var. of
  roentgenographic
rönt|geno|graph|ic|
  al|ly
  var. of roentgeno-
  graphically
rönt|gen|og|raphy
  var. of
  roentgenography
rönt|gen|ology var.
  of roentgenology
roo +s = kangaroo;
  cf. roux, rue
rood crucifix; land
  measure; cf. rude
roof
  pl. roofs or rooves
  v. roofs
  roofed
  roof|ing
roof|er
roofie
roof|less
roof|line
roof|scape
roof|top
roof-tree ridge
  piece in roof
rooi|bos
rooi|gras
rooi|kat
rooi|nek *offensive*
rook|ery
  rook|er|ies
rookie
roo|koo +s var. of
  roucou

room space;
  enclosed part of
  building; rent or
  share room; cf.
  rheum
room|er
room|ette
room|ful
roomie room-mate;
  cf. rheumy, roomy
room|ily
roomi|ness
room|mate *US*
room-mate *Br.*
roomy
  room|ier
  roomi|est
  spacious; cf.
  rheumy, roomie
Roo|ney, Mickey
  actor
Roose|velt,
  Elea|nor humani-
  tarian
Roose|velt,
  Frank|lin D. US
  president
Roose|velt,
  Theo|dore
  ('Teddy') US
  president
roost|er
root part of plant;
  source; mathemat-
  ical quantity; take
  root; rummage;
  give support; cf.
  route
root|age
root|ed|ness
root|er supporter;
  cf. router
rootin' tootin'
root-knot disease
roo|tle
  root|ling
root|less
root|less|ness
root|let
root-like
root|stock
rootsy
  root|sier
  root|si|est

rooty
  root|ier
  rooti|est
rooves var. of roofs
rop|able var. of
  ropeable
rope
  rop|ing
rope|able
rope-a-dope boxing
  technique
rope|man|ship
rope-molding *US*
rope-moulding *Br.*
rope|sight
rope-walk
rope-walker
rope-walking
rope|way
ropey var. of ropy
ropi|ly
ropi|ness
ropy
  ropi|er
  ropi|est
roque
Roque|fort
  trademark
ro|quet +s +ed +ing
  strike in croquet
ro|quette the herb
  rocket
Ror|aima
ro-ro = roll-on roll-
  off
ror|qual
Ror|schach test
rort trick; party; cf.
  wrought
rorty
  rort|ier
  rorti|est
Rosa name
Rosa, Sal|va|tor
  painter
ros|ace ornament
ros|acea acne
ros|aceous
Rosa|leen
Rosa|lie
Rosa|lind
rosa|line
Rosa|lyn
Rosa|mond

Rosa|mund
ros|an|il|ine
Ros|anna
Ros|anne
ros|ar|ian
Ros|ario
ros|ar|ium
  ros|ar|iums or
  ros|aria
ros|ary
  ros|ar|ies
  devotion; beads; cf.
  rosery
Ros|cian
Ros|cius Roman
  actor
ros|coe
Ros|com|mon
rose
  ros|ing
  flower; perforated
  spout; make rosy
rose past tense of
  rise
rosé wine
Rose|anne
rose|apple
ros|eate
Ros|eau
rose|bay
Rose|bery, Lord
  prime minister of
  Britain
rose|bud
rose|finch
rose|fish
rose-like
ro|sella
rose|maled
rose|mal|ing
rose|mary
ros|eola
ros|eola in|fan|tum
rose-point
rose|root yellow-
  flowered stonecrop
ros|ery
  ros|er|ies
  rose garden; cf.
  rosary
Ros|etta Stone
ros|ette
ros|et|ted
rose|wood

Rosh Hash|ana
Rosh Hash|anah
var. of Rosh
Hashana
Roshi
Rosi|cru¦cian
Rosi|cru¦cian|ism
Rosie name
Rosie Lee tea
rosi¦ly
rosin
rosi|ness
ros¦iny
Ros|kilde
ro|soglio var. of
rosolio
ro|solio +s
RoSPA = Royal
Society for the Pre-
vention of
Accidents
Ross, Diana singer
Ross, James Clark
explorer
Ross, John explorer
Ros|sel|lini,
Rob|erto film
director
Ros|setti,
Chris|tina poet
Ros|setti, Dante
Gab|riel painter
Ros|sini,
Gioac|chino
composer
Ross|lare
Ross-shire
Ros|tand, Ed¦mond
playwright
ros¦ter
rösti
Ros|tock
Rostov-on-Don
ros¦tra pl. of
rostrum
ros|tral
ros|tral¦ly
ros|trate
ros|trum
ros¦tra or
ros¦trums
Ros|well
rosy
rosi¦er

rosi|est
rot
rot¦ted
rot¦ting
decay; cf. **wrot**
Rota ecclesiastical
court
rota roster; cf. **rotor**
rota|mer
Ro|tar|ian
Ro|tary society
ro|tary
ro¦tar|ies
rotating (machine)
ro|tat¦able
ro|tate
ro|tat¦ing
ro|ta|tion
ro|ta|tion|al
ro|ta|tion|al¦ly
ro|ta|tive
ro|ta|tor
ro|ta|tory
ro|ta|vate
ro|ta|vat¦ing
ro|ta|va|tor
trademark
rota|virus
rote repetition; cf.
wrote
rote|none
rot¦gut
Roth, Philip
novelist
Rother|ham
Rothko, Mark
painter
Roths|child, Meyer
financier
roti bread
ro|ti|fer
Ro|tif¦era
ro|tis|serie
roto|grav¦ure
rotor rotating part;
eddy of air; cf. **rota**
rotor|craft
Ro|to|rua
roto|scope
roto|scop¦ing
roto|till
roto|till¦er
trademark

roto|vate var. of
rotavate
roto|va|tor var. of
rotavator
rot-proof
rot¦ten
rot¦ten|ly
rotten|ness
rotten|stone
rot¦ter
Rot¦ter|dam
Rott|weiler
ro|tund
ro|tunda
ro|tund|ity
ro|tund¦ly
Rou|ault, Georges
painter
rou¦ble
rou¦cou
roué
Rouen
rouge
rou¦ging
rouge et noir
rouget
rough uneven;
coarse; inexact;
rough person; treat
roughly or
imprecisely; cf.
ruff, ruffe
rough|age
rough|cast
rough¦en
rough|house
rough|hous¦ing n.
& v.
roughie hooligan;
outsider in horse
race; unfair act; cf.
roughy
rough|ish
rough¦ly
rough|neck
rough|ness
Rough Rider
volunteer cavalry-
man in Spanish-
American War
rough-rider
frequent rider
rough|shod

roughy
rough|ies
fish; cf. **roughie**
rouille
rou|lade
rou|leau
rou|leaux or
rou|leaus
roule|ment
rou|lette
rou|lett¦ing
Rou|mania archaic
var. of Romania
Rou|ma¦nian
archaic var. of
Romanian
Rou|melia var. of
Rumelia
round
round|about
round|ball
round|ball¦er
roun|del
round|elay
round¦er
round¦ers
Round|head
round|heel
round|heeled
round|house
round|ish
round¦ly
round|ness
rounds|man
rounds|men
Round Tabler
round-up n.
round|wood
round|worm
roup poultry disease
roupy having roup;
cf. **rupee**
rous¦able
rouse
rous|ing
rouse|about
rouser
rous|ette fruit bat
rous|ing¦ly
Rous sar|coma
Rousse var. of Ruse
Rous|seau, Henri
painter

Rous|seau, Jean-
  Jacques
  philosopher
Rous|seau,
  Théo|dore painter
Rous|sil|lon
roust|about
rout defeat; cut a
  groove
route
  route|ing or
  rout|ing
  way taken; direct;
  cf. **root**
rout|er tool; cf.
  rooter
rou|tier mercenary;
  lorry driver
rou|tine
  rou|tin|ing
  rou|tine|ly
rou|tin|isa|tion *Br.*
  var. of
  routinization
rou|tin|ise *Br.* var.
  of **routinize**
rou|tin|ism
rou|tin|ist
rou|tin|iza|tion
rou|tin|ize
  rou|tin|iz|ing
roux
  pl. **roux**
  sauce base;
  cf. **roo, rue**
Ro|van|iemi
rove
  rov|ing
rover
row line; propel
  boat; noise;
  quarrel; cf. **rho,
  roe**
Rowan name
rowan tree; cf.
  rowen
row|boat
row|dily
row|di|ness
rowdy
  row|dies
  row|dier
  row|di|est
rowdy|ism

Rowe, Nich|olas
  dramatist
rowel
  row|elled *Br.*
  row|eled *US*
  row|el|ling *Br.*
  ro|wel|ing *US*
rowen second
  growth of grass; cf.
  rowan
Row|ena
rower
Row|land
Row|land|son,
  Thomas artist
Row|ling, J. K.
  novelist
row|lock
Rown|tree family of
  entrepreneurs
Rox|burgh|shire
royal
roy|al|ism
roy|al|ist
roy|al|ly
roy|alty
  roy|al|ties
Royce, Henry
  engine designer
Roy|ston
roz|zer
rub
  rubbed
  rub|bing
Rub' al Khali
rub-a-dub
  rub-a-dubbed
  rub-a-dubbing
ru|bato
  ru|ba|tos or ru|bati
rub|ber
rub|beri|ness
rub|ber|ise *Br.* var.
  of **rubberize**
rub|ber|ize
  rub|ber|iz|ing
rubber|neck
rubber|neck|er
rubber|oid
rub|bery
rub|bish
rub|bishy
rub|ble
  rub|bled

rub|bly
Rub|bra, Ed|mund
  composer
rubby
  rub|bies
rub-down *n.*
Rube Gold|berg
ru|bella German
  measles; cf.
  rubeola
ru|bel|lite
Ru|bens, Peter
  Paul painter
ru|beola measles;
  cf. **rubella**
ru|bes|cent
Ru|bi|con stream,
  Italy
ru|bi|con in piquet
ru|bi|cund
ru|bi|cund|ity
ru|bid|ium
ru|bigin|ous
Rubik's cube
  trademark
Rub|in|stein,
  Anton composer
Rub|in|stein, Artur
  pianist
ru|bisco
ruble var. of **rouble**
ru|bre|doxin
ru|bric
ru|bric|al
ru|bri|cate
  ru|bri|cat|ing
  ru|bri|ca|tion
  ru|bri|ca|tor
rub-up *n.*
ruby
  ru|bies
Ruby Mur|ray
  curry
ruby-tail wasp
ruby|throat bird
ruche
ruched
ruch|ing
ruckle
  ruck|ling
ruck|sack
ruckus
ruc|tion
ru|da|ceous

rud|beckia
rud|der
rud|der|less
rud|di|ness
rud|dle
  rud|dling
ruddy
  rud|dies
  rud|died
  ruddy|ing
  rud|dier
  rud|di|est
rude
  ruder
  rud|est
  rude|ly
rude|ness
ru|deral
rudery
  ruder|ies
ru|di|ment
ru|di|men|tar|ily
ru|di|men|tari|ness
ru|di|men|tary
rud|ist
ru|dis|tid
Ru|dolf, Lake
Ru|dolph
Rudra Hindu god
Rud|ras sons of
  Rudra
rue
  rue|ing or ruing
  shrub; regret; cf.
  roo, roux
rue|ful
rue|ful|ly
rue|ful|ness
ruf|es|cence
ruf|es|cent
ruff collar; bird;
  Australian fish;
  trump at cards;
  drumming pattern;
  cf. **rough, ruffe**
ruffe European fish;
  cf. **rough, ruff**
ruf|fian
ruf|fian|ism
ruf|fian|ly
ruf|fle
  ruf|fling
ruff-like

rufi|yaa
  pl. **rufi|yaa**
ruf|ous colour
Rufus William II of England
Rug|beian
Rugby town and school, England
rugby football
Rügen
rug|ged
rug|ged|isa|tion *Br.* var. of **ruggedization**
rug|ged|ised *Br.* var. of **ruggedized**
rug|ged|iza|tion
rug|ged|ized
rug|ged|ly
rug|ged|ness
rug|ger
ru|gosa rose
ru|gose wrinkled
ru|gose|ly
ru|gos|ity
Ruhr
ruin
ruin|ation
ruin|ous
ruin|ous|ly
ruin|ous|ness
Ruis|dael, Jacob van painter
Ruiz de Alar|cón y Men|doza, Juan playwright
Rukh Ukrainian movement
rukh var. of **roc**
rule
rul|ing
rule|less
ruler
ruler|ship
Rum var. of **Rhum**
rum
  rum|mer
  rum|mest
  drink; odd; cf. **rhumb**
Ru|mania var. of **Romania**
Ru|ma|nian var. of **Romanian**

Ru|mansh var. of **Romansh**
rumba
  rum|bas
  rum|baed or **rumba'd**
  rumba|ing
rum|ble
  rum|bling
rum|bler
rum|bus|tious
rum|bus|tious|ly
rum|bus|tious|ness
rum|dum
Ru|melia
rumen
  ru|mens or **ru|mina**
ru|min|ant
ru|min|ate
  ru|min|at|ing
ru|min|ation
ru|mina|tive
ru|mina|tive|ly
ru|min|ator
rumly
rum|mage
  rum|ma|ging
rum|ma|ger
rum|mer
rummy
  rum|mier
  rum|mi|est
rum|ness
rumor *US*
ru|mor|mon|ger *US*
ru|mour *Br.*
rumour-monger *Br.*
rum|ple
  rum|pling
rump|less
rum|ply
rum|pot
rump|sprung
rum|pus
rumpy pumpy
run
  ran
  run|ning
run|about *n.*
run-and-gun *adj.*
run|around *n.*

run|away
run|cible spoon
Run|corn
run|down *n.*
run-down *adj.*
rune
run-flat
rung step of ladder; past participle of **ring**; cf. **wrung**
runged
rung|less
runic
run-in *n.*
run|let
run|nable
run|nel
run|ner
runner-up
  runners-up
running-board
runny
  run|nier
  run|ni|est
Runny|mede
run-off *n.*
run-of-the-mill
run-on *adj. & n.*
run-out *n.*
run-through *n.*
run-time
runty
  runt|ier
  runti|est
run-up *n.*
run|way
Run|yon, Damon writer
rupee Indian etc. currency; cf. **roupy**
Ru|pert
ru|pes|trian
ru|piah
rup|tur|able
rup|ture
  rup|tur|ing
rup|ture|wort
rural
rur|al|isa|tion *Br.* var. of **ruralization**
rur|al|ise *Br.* var. of **ruralize**
rur|al|ism

rur|al|ist
rur|al|ity
rur|al|iza|tion
rur|al|ize
  rur|al|iz|ing
rur|al|ly
ruri|decan|al
Rurik Russian dynasty
Ruri|ta|nia
Ruri|ta|nian
rusa
rus|bank
  rus|banks or **rus|banke**
Ruse city, Bulgaria
ruse trick
Rush|die, Sal|man novelist
rush|er
rush|ing|ly
rush|light
rush|like
Rush|more, Mount
rushy
  rush|ier
  rushi|est
rus in urbe
Rus|kin, John critic
Rus|sell, Ber|trand philosopher
Rus|sell, George poet
Rus|sell, John prime minister of Britain
Rus|sell, Ken film director
rus|set
rus|sety
Rus|sia
Rus|sian
Rus|sian|isa|tion *Br.* var. of **Russianization**
Rus|sian|ise *Br.* var. of **Russianize**
Rus|sian|iza|tion
Rus|sian|ize
Rus|sian|iz|ing
Rus|sian|ness
Rus|si|fi|ca|tion
Rus|sify
Rus|si|fies

Rus|si|fied
Rus|si|fy|ing
Russki +s *often
offensive*
Russky
  Russ|kies *often
offensive* var. of
Russki
Russo- Russian
and...
Russo|phile
Russo|philia
Russo|phobe
Russo|pho|bia
rus|sula
rus|tic
rus|tic|al|ly
rus|ti|cate
  rus|ti|cat|ing
rus|ti|ca|tion
rus|ti|city
rust|ily
rusti|ness
rus|tle
  rust|ling
rust|ler
rust|less
rust|proof
rusty
  rust|ier
  rusti|est
rut
  rut|ted
  rut|ting
ru|ta|baga
Ruth, Babe baseball
  player
ruth *archaic* pity
Ru|the|nia
Ru|the|nian
ru|the|nium
**Ruth|er|ford,
  Er|nest** physicist
**Ruth|er|ford,
  Mar|ga|ret** actress
ruth|less
ruth|less|ly
ruth|less|ness
ru|til|ant
ru|tile
rutin
Rut|land
rut|tish

rutty
rut|tier
rut|ti|est
Ru|wen|zori
Ruys|dael var. of
  Ruisdael
Rwanda
Rwan|dan
Rwan|dese
Rya|zan
Ry|binsk
Ryder, Sue philan-
  thropist
Ryder Cup
rye cereal; grain; cf.
  rai, wry
rye|grass
Ryle, Gil|bert
  philosopher
Ryle, Mar|tin
  astronomer
ry|okan
ryot Indian peasant;
  cf. riot
Rysy
ryu
  pl. ryu or ryus
Ryu|kyu Is|lands
Ryurik var. of
  Rurik

———————

S

Saadi var. of **Sadi**
saag
Saale
Saal|ian
Saa|nen
Saar
Saar|brücken
Saar|land
sab
  sabbed
  sab|bing
Saba
Saba|con pharaoh
saba|dilla
Sa|baean of ancient
  Yemen; cf. **Sabian**
Sabah

Saba|ism
Saba|oth
sab|ayon
sab|ba|tar|ian
sab|ba|tar|ian|ism
sab|bath
sab|bat|ic|al
sab|bat|ic|al|ly
Sa|bel|lian
Sa|bel|lian|ism
saber *US*
  Br. sabre
saber|tooth +s *US*
  Br. sabretooth
saber-toothed *US*
  Br. sabre-toothed
Sa|bian of ancient
  religious sect; cf.
  Sabaean
sab|icu
Sab|ina
Sab|ine of ancient
  people of Italy
Sabin vac|cine
sabji var. of sabzi
sab|kha
sable
sabled
sable|fish
sably
sabot
sabo|tage
  sabo|ta|ging
sab|oted
sabo|teur
sabra
Sab|rata var. of
  Sabratha
Sab|ra|tha
sabre *Br.*
  sab|ring
  US saber
sabre|tache
sabre|tooth +s *Br.*
  US sabertooth
sabre-toothed *Br.*
  US saber-toothed
sab|reur
sabre|wing
Sab|rina
sabzi
sac bag-like cavity;
  cf. sack

sac|cade
sac|cad|ic
sac|cate
sac|char|ide
sac|charin n.
sac|char|ine adj.
sac|char|om|eter
sac|char|ose
sac|cu|lar
sac|cu|lated
sac|cu|la|tion
sac|cule
sac|cu|lus
  sac|culi
sacer|dotal
sacer|do|tal|ism
sacer|do|tal|ist
sacer|do|tal|ly
sa|chem
Sach|er|torte
  Sach|er|tor|ten
sa|chet packet; cf.
  sashay
Sa|chev|er|ell
Sachs, Hans poet
sack large bag;
  dress; wine; dis-
  miss; plunder; cf.
  sac
sack|able
sack|but
sack|cloth
sack|ful
sack-like
**Sackville-West,
  Vita** novelist
sac-like
sacra pl. of sacrum
sa|cral
sa|cral|isa|tion *Br.*
  var. of
  sacralization
sa|cral|ise *Br.* var. of
  sacralize
sa|cral|ity
sa|cral|iza|tion
sa|cral|ize
  sa|cral|iz|ing
sac|ra|ment
sac|ra|men|tal
sac|ra|men|tal|ise
  Br. var. of
  sacramentalize

sac¦ra|men¦tal|ism
sac¦ra|men¦tal|ist
sac¦ra|men¦tal|ity
sac¦ra|men¦tal|ize
sac¦ra|men¦tal|
 iz¦ing
sac¦ra|men¦tal¦ly
Sac¦ra|mento
sac¦rar¦ium
 sac¦raria
sacré bleu
sa¦cred
sa¦cred¦ly
sa¦cred|ness
sac¦ri|fice
 sac¦ri¦ficing
sac¦ri|fi¦cial
sac¦ri|fi¦cial¦ly
sac¦ri|lege
sac¦ri|le¦gious
sac¦ri|le¦gious¦ly
sa¦cring
sac¦rist
sac¦ris¦tan
sac¦risty
 sac¦ris¦ties
sacro|iliac
sacro|sanct
sacro|sanct|ity
sa¦crum
 sacra or sa¦crums
sad
 sad¦der
 sad¦dest
Sadat, Anwar al-
 president of Egypt
Sad¦dam Hus¦sein
 president of Iraq
sad¦den
sad¦dish
sad¦dle
 sad¦dling
saddle|back
saddle|backed
saddle|bag
saddle-bow
saddle|bred
saddle|cloth
saddle|less
sad¦dler
sad¦dlery
 sad¦dler¦ies
sad¦dle sore *n.*

saddle-sore *adj.*
saddo +s
Sad¦du|cean
Sad¦du|cee
Sad¦du|cee|ism
Sade, Mar|quis de
 writer
sa|dhana
sadhu
Sadi Persian poet
Sadie name
sad-iron
sad¦ism
sad¦ist
sad¦is¦tic
sad¦is¦tic¦al¦ly
Sad¦ler's Wells
sadly
sad|ness
sado|maso¦chism
sado|maso¦chist
sado|maso¦chis¦tic
sadza
Safa|qis
sa¦fari
Safa|vid
safe
 safer
 saf¦est cf. seif
safe|guard
safe keep|ing
safe|light
safe¦ly
safe|ness
safety
 safe|ties
saf|flower
saf|fron
saf¦ranin var. of
 safranine
saf¦ran¦ine
sag
 sagged
 sag¦ging
 bulge downwards;
 decline
sag *Ind.* vegetable;
 var. of saag
saga
sa|ga¦cious
sa|ga¦cious¦ly
sa|ga¦city
saga|more

Sagan, Carl astron-
 omer
Sagan, Fran|çoise
 writer
saga|naki
sagar
sag|bag
sage|brush
sage¦ly
sage|ness
sag|gar
sag|ger var. of
 saggar
saggy
 sag|gier
 sag|gi|est
Sa|gitta
sa¦git|tal
sa¦git|tal¦ly
Sag¦it|tar¦ian
Sag¦it|tar¦ius
sag¦it|tate
sago +s
sa|guaro +s
Sa|guia el Hamra
sagy
Saha, Megh|nad
 physicist
Sa¦hara
Sa|haran
Sahel
Sa¦hel|ian
sahib
Sahin Line
sa|hi¦tya
Sahi|wal
sa¦huaro var. of
 saguaro
sa¦hu|kar
sai
 pl. sai
 dagger; cf. sigh
Said, Ed|ward W.
 critic
said past tense and
 participle of say
saiga
Sai|gon
sail cf. sale
sail|able
sail|bag
sail|board
sail|board|er

sail|board|ing
sail|boat
sail|cloth
sail¦er ship; cf.
 sailor
sail|fin molly
 sail|fin mol|lies
sail|fish
sail-fluke
sail|less
sail|maker
sail|mak¦ing
sail-off *n.*
sail¦or person; cf.
 sailer
sail|or¦ing
sail|or|less
sail|or¦ly
sail|plane
sain|foin
Sains|bury, John
 grocer
St Al¦bans
St An|drews town,
 Scotland
St An|drew's cross
St Clem|ents
St Croix
Saint-Denis
saint|dom
Sainte-Beuve,
 Charles writer
St Elmo's fire
St Émi|llion
St-Étienne
St Eu|sta¦tius
 Caribbean island
Saint-Exupéry,
 An|toine de
 writer and aviator
St Got|thard Pass
St Helen|ian
St Hel¦ens town,
 England; Mount
St Hel¦ier
saint|hood
St John island, US
 Virgin Islands
Saint John city and
 river, Canada
St John's cities,
 Canada and
 Antigua
St Kilda

St Kitts and Nevis
Saint Lau|rent,
  Yves couturier
St Law|rence River,
  Seaway
St Leger
saint|like
saint|li|ness
saint|ling
St Lucia
St Lu|cian
saint|ly
  saint|lier
  saint|li|est
St Malo
St Mor|itz
St-Nazaire
Saint Nico|las
  town, Belgium
St Pan|cras
saint|paulia
St Peter Port
St Peters|burg
St Pierre and
  Mi|que|lon
St Pöl|ten
Saint-Saëns,
  Ca|mille composer
saint|ship
Saint-Simon,
  Comte de social
  reformer
Saint-Simon, Duc
  de writer
St So|phia
St Ste|phens
St Ste|phen's Day
St Trin|ian's
St-Tropez
Sai|pan
saith *archaic* = says
saithe fish
Saiva
Saiv|ite
saka|bula
Sakai
sake in 'for my sake'
  etc.; Japanese
  drink; cf. **saki**
saker bird
Sakha, Re|pub|lic
  of
Sakh|alin

Sakh|arov, An|drei
  physicist
Saki writer
saki monkey; cf.
  sake
sakkie-sakkie
Sakti var. of **Shakti**
sa|laam
sal|abil|ity *US*
  Br. saleability
sal|able *US*
  Br. saleable
sal|acious
sal|acious|ly
sal|acious|ness
sal|acity
salad
sa|lade ni|çoise
  sa|lades ni|çoises
Sala|din sultan
Sa|lafi
salal
Sala|manca
sala|man|der
sala|man|drian
sala|man|drine
sala|man|droid
sa|lami sausage
Sala|mis island,
  Greece
sal am|mo|niac
Sa|lang Pass
sal|ar|iat
sal|ar|ied
sal|ary
  sal|ar|ies
  sal|ar|ied
  sal|ary|ing
  sal|ary|man
  sal|ary|men
salat Muslim prayer
Sala|zar, An|tonio
  de Oli|veira prime
  minister of Portugal
sal|bu|ta|mol
sal|chow
sale selling; cf. **sail**
sale|abil|ity *Br.*
  US salability
sale|able *Br.*
  US salable
Salem
salep
sal|er|atus

Sal|erno
sale|room
sales|girl
Sal|es|ian
sales|lady
  sales|ladies
sales|man
  sales|men
sales|man|ship
sales|per|son
  sales|per|sons or
  sales|people
sales|room
sales|woman
  sales|women
Sal|ford
Sa|lian
Salic
sali|cin
sal|icion|al
sa|li|cyl|ate
sali|cyl|ic
sa|li|ence
sa|li|ency
sa|li|ent
Sa|li|en|tia
sa|li|en|tian
sa|li|ent|ly
Sali|eri, An|tonio
  composer
sa|lina
sa|line
Sal|in|ger, J. D.
  writer
salin|isa|tion *Br.*
  var. of **salinization**
sal|in|ity
salin|iza|tion
salin|om|eter
Salis|bury
Sa|lish
  pl. **Sa|lish**
Sa|lish|an
sal|iva
sal|iv|ary
sali|vate
  sali|vat|ing
sali|va|tion
Salk, Jonas micro-
  biologist
sal|lee var. of **sally**
  (tree)
sal|len|ders

sal|let helmet
sal|low
sal|low|ish
sal|low|ness
Sal|lust Roman
  historian
Sally name
sally
  sal|lies
  sal|lied
  sally|ing
Sally Lunn
sal|ma|gundi
sal|ma|nazar
salmi
sal|mon
salmon|berry
  salmon|berries
sal|mon|ella
  sal|mon|el|lae
  sal|mon|el|losis
sal|monid
sal|mon|oid
sal|mony
Sal|ome *Bible*
salon
Salon des Re|fusés
Sal|on|ica
sal|oon
Salop
salop|ettes
Sal|op|ian
sa|lotto
  sa|lotti
sal|pi|con
sal|pi|glos|sis
  sal|pi|glos|ses
sal|pin|gec|tomy
  sal|pin|gec|to|mies
sal|pin|gitis
sal|pin|gos|tomy
  sal|pin|gos|to|mies
salsa
salsa verde
sal|sify
  sal|si|fies
SALT = Strategic
  Arms Limitation
  Talks
salt
sal|tar|ello
  sal|tar|el|los or
  sal|tar|elli
sal|ta|tion

sal¦ta¦tor¦ial
sal¦ta¦tory
salt¦box
salt¦bush
salt¦er person
 dealing with salt;
 cf. **psalter**
salt¦ern
Sal¦tillo
salt¦ily
salt¦im¦bocca
salt¦ine
salti¦ness
sal¦tire *Heraldry*
sal¦tire¦wise
salt¦ish
salt¦less
salt¦ness
salt¦peter *US*
salt¦petre *Br.*
sal¦tus
 sal¦tuses
salt water *n.*
salt¦water *adj.*
salt¦wort
salty
 salt¦ier
 salti¦est
sa¦lu¦bri¦ous
sa¦lu¦bri¦ous¦ly
sa¦lu¦bri¦ous¦ness
sa¦lu¦brity
sa¦luki
salut *exclam.*
salu¦tary beneficial
sa¦lu¦ta¦tion
sa¦lu¦ta¦tion¦al
sa¦lu¦ta¦tor¦ian
sa¦lu¦ta¦tory
 sa¦lu¦ta¦tor¦ies
 (address)
 expressing welcome
sa¦lute
 sa¦lut¦ing
sa¦luter
salv¦able
Sal¦va¦dor
Sal¦va¦dor¦ean
sal¦vage
 sal¦va¦ging
sal¦vage¦able
sal¦va¦ger
Sal¦var¦san

sal¦va¦tion
sal¦va¦tion¦ism
Sal¦va¦tion¦ist
 (member) of Salva-
 tion Army
sal¦va¦tion¦ist
salve
 salv¦ing
 ointment; soothe
sal¦ver tray; cf.
 salvor
Salve Re¦gina +s
sal¦via
Salvo +s member of
 Salvation Army
salvo
 salvos or sal¦voes
 discharge of
 weapons; aggressive
 act
salvo +s saving
 clause; excuse
sal vola¦tile
sal¦vor salvager; cf.
 salver
sal¦war
Sal¦ween
Sal¦yut
Salz¦burg
Salz¦git¦ter
Salz¦kam¦mer¦gut
SAM = surface-to-
 air missile
Sam name
sa¦maan var. of
 saman
sam¦adhi
saman
sa¦mango +s
Sam¦an¦tha
Samar island,
 Philippines
Sa¦mara city,
 Russia; cf.
 Samarra
sa¦mara winged
 seed
Sa¦maria
Sam¦ar¦inda
Sa¦mar¦itan
sa¦mar¦ium
Sam¦ar¦kand

Sam¦ar¦qand var. of
 Samarkand
Sam¦arra city, Iraq;
 cf. **Samara**
Sama Veda
 Hinduism
samba
 sam¦baed or
 samba'd
 samba¦ing
 dance
sam¦bal
sam¦bar deer
sam¦bhar spicy dish
Sambo *offensive*
 Sam¦bos or
 Sam¦boes
Sam Browne
sam¦buca
Sam¦buru
 pl. **Sam¦buru**
same¦ness
samey
 samier
 samiest
samey¦ness
samfu
Sam¦hain
Sami
sami¦sen
sam¦ite
sa¦miti
sam¦iz¦dat
sam¦mie sandwich
Sammy name
Sam¦nite
Samoa
Sa¦moan
Samos
sa¦mosa
samo¦var
Sam¦oyed
Sam¦oy¦ed¦ic
sam¦pan
sam¦phire
sam¦pla¦delia
sam¦pla¦delic
sam¦ple
 sam¦pling
sam¦pler
samp¦list
Sam¦pras, Pete
 tennis player

sam¦sara
sam¦sar¦ic
sam¦skara
Sam¦son
Sam¦uel
sam¦urai
 pl. sam¦urai
Sa¦na'a
Sanaa var. of **Sana'a**
San An¦dreas fault
San An¦drés island,
 Caribbean Sea
San An¦tonio
sana¦tive
sana¦tor¦ium
 sana¦tor¦iums or
 sana¦toria
sana¦tory healing;
 cf. **sanitary**
San¦cerre
San¦chi
San¦cho Panza fic-
 tional character
san¦coche
san¦cocho var. of
 sancoche
sanc¦ti¦fi¦ca¦tion
sanc¦ti¦fier
sanc¦tify
 sanc¦ti¦fies
 sanc¦ti¦fied
 sanc¦ti¦fy¦ing
sanc¦ti¦mo¦ni¦ous
sanc¦ti¦mo¦ni¦ous¦ly
sanc¦ti¦mo¦ni¦ous¦
 ness
sanc¦ti¦mony
sanc¦tion
sanc¦tion¦able
sanc¦ti¦tude
sanc¦tity
 sanc¦tities
sanc¦tu¦ary
 sanc¦tu¦ar¦ies
sanc¦tum +s sacred
 or private place
sanc¦tum
 sanc¦torum
 sancta sanc¦torum
 or sanc¦tum
 sanc¦tor¦ums
Sanc¦tus hymn
sanc¦tus bell

Sand, George novelist
sand grains etc.; cf. sans
san|dal
san|daled *US*
san|dalled *Br.*
san|dal|wood
san|darac
san|dar|ach var. of sandarac
San|dawe
  pl. San|dawe or San|dawes
sand|bag
  sand|bagged
  sand|bag|ging
sand|bag|ger
sand|bank
sand|bar
sand|blast
sand|blast|er
sand|board
sand|box
sand|boy
sand|cas|tle
sand|er person or thing that sands
san|der|ling
san|ders timber
san|ders|wood
san|desh
sand|fish
sand|fly
  sand|flies
sand|glass
Sand|groper
sand|grouse
  pl. sand|grouse
san|dhi
sand|hill
sand|hog
sand|hop|per
Sand|hurst
San Diego
sandi|ness
San|di|nista
san|di|ver
sand-like
sand|lot
sand|man
sand|paper
sand|papery

sand|piper
sand|pit
San|dra
San|dring|ham
sand|shoe
sand|stone
sand|storm
sand|veld
Sand|wich town, England
sand|wich food
sand|wich tern
sand|wort
Sandy name
sandy
  sand|ier
  sandi|est
  sandy|ish
sane
  saner
  san|est
  not mad; cf. seine, seiner
sane|ly
sane|ness
San|fi|lippo's syn|drome
San|for|ized *trademark*
San Fran|cisco city, US; cf. **São Francisco**
sang past tense of sing; cf. sangh
sanga var. of sangar
san|gam
san|gar structure for firing from; cf. sangha
san|garee
sang-de-boeuf
Sang|er, Fred|erick biochemist
Sang|er, Mar|ga|ret campaigner
sang|froid
sangh *Ind.* organization
sangha Buddhist monastic order; cf. sangar
Sangho var. of Sango
San|gio|vese

Sango
san|goma
san|grail
san|greal var. of sangrail
san|gria
san|guin|ar|ily
san|guin|ari|ness
san|guin|ary
san|guine
san|guine|ly
san|guine|ness
san|guin|eous
San|hed|rim var. of Sanhedrin
San|hed|rin
san|icle
sani|dine
sani|tar|ian
sani|tar|ily
sani|tari|ness
sani|tar|ium
  sani|tar|iums or sani|taria
sani|tary hygienic; cf. sanatory
sani|tary|ware
sani|tate
sani|tat|ing
sani|ta|tion
sani|ta|tion|ist
sani|tisa|tion *Br.* var. of sanitization
sani|tise *Br.* var. of sanitize
sani|tiser *Br.* var. of sanitizer
sani|tiza|tion
sani|tize
sani|tiz|ing
sani|tizer
san|ity
san|jak
San Joa|quin Val|ley
San Jose city, US
San José capital of Costa Rica
San Juan
San Luis Pot|osí
San Mar|ino
San Mar|tín, José de soldier

san|nyasi
  pl. san|nyasi
san|nya|sin var. of sannyasi
San Pedro Sula
san|pro = sanitary protection
sans without
sansa
San Sal|va|dor
sans-culotte
sans-culott|ism
San Se|bas|tián
san|sei
  pl. san|sei
san|serif var. of sans serif
san|se|veria var. of sansevieria
san|se|vieria
San|skrit
San|skrit|ic
San|skrit|ist
San|so|vino, Ja|copo sculptor
sans serif
Santa = Santa Claus
Santa Ana
Santa Cata|rina
Santa Claus
Santa Cruz
Santa Fe cities, US and Argentina
Santa Fé de Bo|gotá
San|tal
San|tali
San|tan|der
Santa So|phia = St Sophia
San|ta|yana, George philosopher
san|teria
san|tero +s
San|tiago
San|tiago de Com|po|stela
san|tim
santo +s religious symbol
Santo Dom|ingo
san|to|lina
san|ton

san|ton|ica
san|tonin
san|toor
San|to|rini
San|tos
san|yasi var. of
  sannyasi
São Fran|cisco
  river, Brazil; cf. San
  Francisco
saola
São Luís
Saône
São Paulo
São Tomé
sap
  sapped
  sap|ping
sa|pele
sap|ful
sa|phe|nous
sapid
sa|pid|ity
sapi|ence
sapi|ent
sa|pi|en|tial
sa|pi|ent|ly
Sapir, Ed|ward lin-
  guistics scholar
sap|less
sap|ling
sapo|dilla
sap|on|aceous
sa|poni|fi|able
sa|poni|fi|ca|tion
sa|pon|ify
  sa|poni|fies
  sa|poni|fied
  sa|poni|fy|ing
sap|onin
sap|per
Sap|phic of Sappho
sap|phic lesbian
sap|phics verse
sap|phire
sap|phir|ine
sap|phism
Sap|pho Greek poet
sap|pily
sap|pi|ness
Sap|poro
sappy
  sap|pier

sap|pi|est
sapro|gen|ic
sapro|leg|nia
sapro|phage
sap|ropha|gous
sap|roph|agy
sap|roph|il|ous
sapro|phyte
sapro|phyt|ic
sapro|phyt|ic|al|ly
sapro|troph
sapro|troph|ic
sap|suck|er
sap|wood
Saq|qara
sara|band
sara|bande var. of
  saraband
Sara|cen
Sara|cen|ic
Sara|gossa
Sara|jevo
Saran (Wrap)
  trademark
sar|angi
Sar|ansk
sar|ape var. of
  serape
Sara|toga
Sara|tov
Sara|wak
sar|casm
sar|cas|tic
sar|cas|tic|al|ly
sar|cenet var. of
  sarsenet
sarco|cocca
sar|coid
sar|coid|osis
sarco|lemma
sarco|lem|mal
sar|coma
  sar|co|mas or
  sar|co|mata
sar|coma|tosis
sar|coma|tous
sarco|mere
sar|copha|gus
sar|coph|agi
sarco|plasm
sarco|plas|mic
sarc|op|tic mange
sarco|sine

Sard
Sar|da|na|pa|lian
Sar|da|napa|lus
  king of Assyria
sar|dar leader
sar|delle
sar|dine
  sar|din|ing
Sar|dinia
Sar|din|ian
Sar|dis
sar|dius
sar|don|ic
sar|don|ic|al|ly
sar|doni|cism
sard|onyx
saree var. of sari
sar|gasso +s
sar|gas|sum
sarge = sergeant
Sar|gent, John
  Sing|er painter
Sar|gent, Mal|colm
  conductor
Sar|godha
Sar|gon founder of
  Akkad
sari
sarin
Sark Channel Island
sark garment
sar|kar
sark|ily
sarki|ness
sark|ing
sarky
  sark|ier
  sarki|est
Sar|ma|tia
Sar|ma|tian
sar|mie *S. African* =
  sandwich
sar|nie = sandwich
sarod
sar|ong
Sar|on|ic Gulf
saros
sar|panch
sarra|cenia
sar|ruso|phone
sar|sa|par|illa
sar|sen
sar|senet

Sarto, An|drea del
  painter
sar|tor|ial
sar|tori|al|ly
sar|tor|ius
  sar|torii
Sartre, Jean-Paul
  philosopher
Sar|trean
Sarum
sarus crane
sar|vo|daya
Sa|sa|nian var. of
  Sassanian
sa|san|qua
sashay walk osten-
  tatiously; (perform)
  dancing figure; cf.
  sachet
sashed
sash|imi
sash|less
sasin gazelle
sas|ine *Law*
Sas|katch|ewan
Sas|ka|toon
Sas|kia
Sas|quatch
sas|saby
  sas|sa|bies
sassa|fras
Sas|sa|nian
Sas|sanid
Sas|sen|ach +s
sas|si|ly
sas|si|ness
Sas|soon, Sieg|fried
  writer
sassy
  sas|sier
  sas|si|est
sas|tra var. of
  shastra
sas|trugi
SAT = standard
  assessment task;
  trademark Scholas-
  tic Aptitude Test
sat past tense and
  participle of sit
satai var. of satay
Satan
sat|ang
  pl. sat|ang or

sat|angs
sa|tan|ic
sa|tan|ic|al|ly
sa|tan|ism
sa|tan|ist
satay
satchel
sat|com = satellite
    communications
sate
    sat|ing
    gratify; surfeit
saté var. of satay
sat|een
sate|less
sat|el|lite
sat|el|lit|ic
sat|el|lit|ism
sat|el|li|tium
    sat|el|li|tia
Sati wife of Shiva
sati self-immolation
    by widow; commit-
    ter of sati
sa|tiable
sa|ti|ate
    sa|ti|at|ing
sa|ti|ation
Satie, Erik
    composer
sa|ti|ety
satin
sat|inet var. of
    satinette
satin|ette
satin|ise Br. var. of
    satinize
satin|ize
    satin|iz|ing
satin|wood
sat|iny
sat|ire humour
    exposing vice etc.;
    cf. satyr
sa|tir|ic
sa|tir|ic|al
sa|tir|ic|al|ly
sat|ir|isa|tion Br.
    var. of satirization
sat|ir|ise Br. var. of
    satirize
sat|ir|ist
sat|ir|iza|tion

sat|ir|ize
sat|ir|iz|ing
sat|is|fac|tion
sat|is|fac|tor|ily
sat|is|fac|tori|ness
sat|is|fac|tory
sat|is|fi|abil|ity
sat|is|fi|able
satis|fice
    satis|ficing
sat|is|fied|ly
sat|isfy
    sat|is|fies
    sat|is|fied
    sat|is|fy|ing
sat|is|fy|ing|ly
sat|nav = satellite
    navigation
sa|tori
sat|phone
sat|rap
sat|rapy
    sat|rap|ies
sat|sang
Sat|suma former
    province, Japan;
    pottery
sat|suma fruit
sat|ur|able
sat|ur|ant
sat|ur|ate
    sat|ur|at|ing
sat|ur|ation
Sat|ur|day
Sat|urn
Sat|ur|na|lia
    Roman festival
sat|ur|na|lia orgy
Sat|ur|na|lian
sat|ur|na|lian
Sat|urn|ian
sat|urn|ic
sat|urni|id
sat|ur|nine
sat|ur|nine|ly
sat|urn|ism
sat|ya|graha
satyr woodland god;
    lustful man; cf.
    satire
satyr|ia|sis
sa|tyr|ic
sa|tyrid

sauce
    sau|cing
sauce|less
sauce|pan
sauce|pan|ful
sau|cer
sau|cer|ful
sau|cer|less
sau|cier sauce chef
sau|cily
sau|ci|ness
sau|cis|son
saucy
    sau|cier
    sau|ci|est
sau|dade
Saudi
sauer|braten
sauer|kraut
sau|ger
Saul
Sault Sainte Marie
Sau|mur
sauna
saun|ter
saun|ter|er
Sauria
saur|ian
saur|is|chian
sauro|pod
saury
    saur|ies
saus|age
Saus|sure,
    Fer|di|nand de lin-
    guistics scholar
sauté
    sautés
    sautéed or sautéd
    sauté|ing
Sau|ternes
    pl. Sau|ternes
sau|toir
sauve qui peut
Sauve|ter|rian
Sau|vi|gnon
sav|able
Sav|age, Mi|chael
    prime minister of
    New Zealand
sav|age
    sav|aging
sav|age|dom

sav|age|ly
sav|age|ness
sav|agery
    sav|ager|ies
Sa|vai'i
sa|vanna var. of
    savannah
Sa|van|nah port
    and river, US
sa|van|nah grassy
    plain
Sa|van|na|ket var.
    of Savannakhet
Sa|van|na|khet
sav|ant learned per-
    son; in 'idiot savant'
sav|ante female
    savant
sav|arin
sa|vate
save
    sav|ing
save|able var. of
    savable
sav|eloy
saver
Sa|very, Cap|tain
    engineer
savin
sav|ine var. of savin
sa|vior US
sa|viour Br.
sav|oir faire
Sav|ona|rola,
    Gir|ol|amo
    preacher
Sav|on|linna
Sav|on|nerie
savor US
sa|vor|ily US
sa|vori|ness US
sa|vor|less US
sa|vory
    sa|vor|ies
    herb; cf. savoury
sa|vory US
    sa|vor|ies
    not sweet; whole-
    some; snack;
    Br. savoury
sa|vour Br.
sa|vour|ily Br.
sa|vouri|ness Br.

sa|vour|less *Br.*
US savorless

sa|voury

sa|vour|ies *Br.*
not sweet; whole-
some; snack; cf.
savory

Savoy region,
France

savoy cabbage

Sa|voy|ard

Savu Sea

savvy

sav|vies

sav|vied

savvy|ing

sav|vier

sav|vi|est

saw

sawn or sawed
tool; cut; proverb;
cf. soar, sore

saw past tense of
see; cf. soar, sore

saw|bench

saw|bill

saw|bones
pl. saw|bones

saw|buck

saw|cut

saw|dust

sawed-off *US*
adj. & n.
Br. sawn-off

saw|fish

saw|fly

saw|flies

saw|grass

saw|horse

saw|like

saw|log

saw|mill

sawn-off *Br.*
adj. & n.
US sawed-off

saw|tooth

saw|toothed

saw-whet owl

saw-wort

saw|yer

sax saxophone; axe

saxe colour

Saxe-Coburg-
Gotha

sax|horn

saxi|frage

sax|ist

Saxon

Saxon|dom

Saxon|ise *Br. var. of*
Saxonize

Saxon|ism

Saxon|ist

Saxon|ize

Saxon|iz|ing

Sax|ony state,
Germany

sax|ony

sax|on|ies
wool; cloth

Saxony-Anhalt

saxo|phone

saxo|phon|ic

sax|opho|nist

say

said
cf. sei

say|able

sayer

Say|ers, Doro|thy
L. writer

say|on|ara

Say's law *Economics*

say-so *n.*

say|yid

scab

scabbed

scab|bing

scab|bard

scabbard|fish

scab|bi|ness

scabby

scab|bier

scab|bi|est

sca|bies

sca|bi|ous

scab|lands

scab-like

scab|rous

scab|rous|ly

scab|rous|ness

Sca|fell Pike

scaf|fold

scaf|fold|er

scag *var. of* skag

scagli|ola

scal|abil|ity

scal|able

scala media
scalae media

sca|lar *Mathemat-*
ics; cf. scaler

sca|lari|form

scala tym|pani
scalae tym|pani

scala ves|ti|buli
scalae ves|ti|buli

scala|wag *US*
Br. scallywag

scald burn with
liquid or steam;
var. of skald

scald|fish

scal|dic *var. of*
skaldic

scale

scal|ing

scale|abil|ity *var. of*
scalability

scale|able *var. of*
scalable

scale|less

sca|lene

sca|lenus

sca|leni

scaler person or
thing that scales;
cf. scalar

Scali|ger, Jo|seph
Jus|tus scholar of
ancient chronology

Scali|ger, Ju|lius
Cae|sar classical
scholar and
physician

scali|ness

scal|lion

scal|lop

scal|lop|er

scal|lop|ini *var. of*
scaloppine

scally

scal|lies

scally|wag *Br.*
US scalawag

scal|op|pine

scal|pel

scalp|er

scalp|less

scaly

scali|er

scali|est

scaly|foot +s

scam

scammed

scam|ming

scam|mer

scam|mony

sca|morza

scam|per

scampi

scamp|ish

scan

scanned

scan|ning

scan|dal

scan|dal|ise *Br. var.*
of scandalize

scan|dal|ize

scan|dal|iz|ing

scan|dal|mon|ger

scan|dal|ous

scan|dal|ous|ly

scan|dal|ous|ness

scan|dent

Scan|den|tia

Scan|di|navia

Scan|di|navian

scan|dium

scan|nable

scan|ner

scan|sion

scant|ies

scant|ily

scanti|ness

scant|ling

scant|ly

scant|ness

scanty

scant|ier

scanti|est

Scapa Flow

scape|goat

scape|grace

scaph|oid

scapho|pod

Scapho|poda

scap|ula
scapu|lae or
scapu|las
shoulder blade

scapu|lar of the
shoulder; cloak;
bandage; feather

scapu|lary

scapu|lar|ies

scap|uli|mancy

scar
  scarred
  scar¦ring
  (make) mark on
  skin etc.; outcrop;
  cf. **ska**
scarab
scara¦baeid
scara¦bae¦oid
scara¦mouch
Scar¦bor¦ough
scarce
  scar¦cer
  scar¦cest
scarce¦ly
scarce¦ness
scar¦city
  scar¦ci¦ties
scare
  scar¦ing
scare¦crow
scaredy-cat
scare¦mon¦ger
scare¦monger¦ing
scarer
scarf
  scarves or scarfs
  piece of material
  for neck or head
scarf join ends; cut
  whale blubber; con-
  sume greedily
scarfed wearing a
  scarf
scarf-skin
scarf-wise
scari¦fi¦ca¦tion
scari¦fier
scar¦ify
  scari¦fies
  scari¦fied
  scari¦fy¦ing
scari¦ly
scari¦ness
scar¦lat¦ina
Scar¦latti,
  Ales¦san¦dro and
  Do¦men¦ico
  composers
scar¦less
scar¦let colour
scar¦let¦ina var. of
  scarlatina
Scar¦lett name
scar¦per

Scart socket
scarved var. of
  scarfed
scarves pl. of **scarf**
  (for wearing)
scary
  scari¦er
  scari¦est
scat
  scat¦ted
  scat¦ting
  depart; singing;
  droppings; cf. **skat**
Scatch¦ard plot
  Biochemistry
scathe
  scath¦ing
scathe¦less
scath¦ing¦ly
scato¦logic¦al
scat¦ology
scat¦opha¦gous
scat¦ter
scat¦ter¦brain
scat¦ter¦brained
scat¦ter¦er
scat¦ter¦gram
scat¦ter¦graph
scat¦ter¦gun
scat¦ter¦shot
scat¦tily
scat¦ti¦ness
scatty
  scat¦tier
  scat¦ti¦est
scaup duck; cf.
  scorp
scaup¦er var. of
  scorp
scav¦enge
  scav¦en¦ging
  scav¦en¦ger
  scav¦en¦gery
sca¦zon
scena scene in opera
scen¦ario +s
scen¦ar¦ist
scend pitch; surge
scene place; view;
  part of play
scen¦ery
scene¦ster
scenic
scen¦ic¦al¦ly

scen|og¦raph¦er
sceno|graph¦ic
scen|og¦raphy
scent smell;
  perfume; cf. **cent,
  sent**
scent¦less
scep¦ter *US*
  Br. sceptre;
  sovereign's rod; cf.
  septa
scep¦tered *US*
  Br. sceptred
scep¦tic *Br.*
  US skeptic
scep¦tic¦al *Br.*
  US skeptical
scep¦tic¦al¦ly *Br.*
  US skeptically
scep¦ti¦cism *Br.*
  US skepticism
sceptre *Br.*
  US scepter;
  sovereign's rod; cf.
  septa
sceptred *Br.*
  US sceptered
Scha¦den¦freude
Schaff¦hausen
schappe
schedu¦lar *adj.*
sched¦ule
  sched¦ul¦ing
sched¦uler *n.*
Scheele, Carl
  chemist
scheel¦ite
scheff¦lera
Sche¦hera¦zade in
  the *Arabian Nights*
Scheldt
schelly
  schel¦lies
schema
  sche¦mata or
  sche¦mas
  plan;
  cf. **schemer**
sche¦mat¦ic
sche¦mat¦ic¦al¦ly
sche¦ma¦tisa¦tion
  Br. var. of
  schematization
sche¦ma¦tise *Br.* var.
  of schematize

sche¦ma¦tism
sche¦ma¦tiza¦tion
sche¦ma¦tize
  sche¦ma¦tiz¦ing
scheme
  schem¦ing
schemer
schem¦ing¦ly
sche¦moz¦zle var. of
  shemozzle
Schen¦gen
scher¦zando
  scher¦zan¦dos or
  scher¦zandi
scherzo
  scher¦zos or
  scherzi
Schia¦pa¦relli, Elsa
  fashion designer
Schia¦pa¦relli,
  Gio¦vanni
  astronomer
Schick test
Schiele, Egon
  painter
Schiff, Hugo
  chemist
Schil¦ler, Fried¦rich
  von writer
schil¦ling former
  Austrian currency;
  cf. **shilling**
schim¦mel var. of
  skimmel
Schind¦ler, Oskar
  rescuer of Jews
schip¦perke
schism
schis¦mat¦ic
schis¦mat¦ic¦al
schis¦mat¦ic¦al¦ly
schist
schis¦tose
schis¦tos¦ity
schis¦to¦some
schis¦to¦som¦ia¦sis
schiz¦andra
schiz¦an¦thus
schizo +s
schizo-affect¦ive
schizo|carp
schizo|car¦pic
schizo|car¦pous
schizo|gen¦ic
schiz|ogen¦ous

schiz|ogeny forma-
tion of intercellular
space

schiz|ogon|ous

schiz|og|ony asexual
reproduction

schiz|oid

schiz|ont

schizo|phre|nia

schizo|phren|ic

schizo|sty|lis

schizo|typal

schizo|type

schizo|typy

Schle|gel, Au|gust
Wil|helm von poet

Schle|gel,
Fried|rich von
philosopher

schle|mazel var. of
schlimazel

schle|miel

schlen|ter

schlep
schlepped
schlep|ping

schlepp var. of
schlep

schlep|per

Schles|wig

Schlick, Mor|itz
philosopher

Schlie|mann,
Hein|rich
archaeologist

schlier|en

schli|mazel

schlock

schlock|mei|ster

schlocky
schlock|ier
schlocki|est

schloss

schlub

schlump

schmaltz

schmaltzy
schmaltz|ier
schmaltzi|est

schmatte

schmear

schmeer var. of
schmear

Schmidt tele|scope

Schmitt trig|ger

schmo

schmoes

schmooze

schmooz|ing

schmooz|er

schmoozy
schmooz|ier
schmoozi|est

schmuck

schmut|ter

schnapps
pl. schnapps or
schnappses

schnau|zer

Schnei|der,
Jacques flying
enthusiast; S.
Trophy

schnit|zel

schnook

schnor|rer

schnozz

schnoz|zola

Schoen|berg,
Ar|nold composer

scholar

schol|ar|li|ness

schol|ar|ly

schol|ar|ship

scho|las|tic

scho|las|tic|al|ly

scho|las|ti|cism

scho|li|ast

scho|li|as|tic

scho|lium
scho|lia

school|boy

school|child
school|chil|dren

school day, the

school|days

school|er

school|fel|low

school|girl

school|house

schoolie

school|kid

school|man
school|men

school|marm

school|marm|ish

school|master

school|master|ing

school|master|ly

school|mate

school|mis|tress

school|mis|tressy

school|room

school|teach|er

school|teach|ing

school|work

school|yard

schoo|ner

Scho|pen|hauer,
Ar|thur
philosopher

schorl mineral; cf.
shawl

schot|tische

Schottky, Wal|ter
physicist

Schrei|ner, Olive
novelist

Schrö|der,
Ger|hard chancel-
lor of Germany

Schrö|dinger,
Erwin physicist

schtuck var. of
shtook

schtum var. of
shtum

schtup var. of shtup

Schu|bert, Franz
composer

Schu|bert|ian

Schulz, Charles
cartoonist

Schu|macher, E. F.
economist

Schu|macher,
Mi|chael racing
driver

Schu|mann,
Rob|ert composer

schuss

Schütz, Hein|rich
composer

schwa

Schwäb|isch
Gmünd

Schwann, Theo|dor
physiologist

Schwar|zen|egger,
Ar|nold actor

Schwarz|kopf,
Elisa|beth opera
singer

Schwarz|schild,
Karl astronomer

Schwein|furt

Schweit|zer,
Al|bert theologian

Schwe|rin

Schwyz

sci|aen|id

scia|gram

scia|graph

scia|graph|ic

sci|ag|raphy

sci|am|achy

sci|at|ic

sci|at|ica

sci|at|ic|al|ly

sci|ence

sci|en|ter

sci|en|tial

sci|en|tif|ic

sci|en|tif|ic|ally

sci|en|tif|icity

sci|en|tism

sci|en|tist

sci|en|tis|tic

Sci|en|tolo|gist

Sci|en|tol|ogy
trademark

sci-fi = science
fiction

scili|cet

scilla plant; cf.
Scylla

Scil|lies = Scilly
Isles

Scil|lo|nian

Scilly Isles officially
Isles of Scilly

scimi|tar

scimi|tar|bill

scimitar-billed

scin|ti|gram

scinti|graph|ic

scin|tig|raphy

scin|tilla

scin|til|lant

scin|til|late

scin|til|lat|ing

scin|til|lat|ing|ly

scin|til|la|tion

scin¦til¦la¦tor
scin¦ti¦scan
sci¦ol¦ism
sci¦ol¦ist
sci¦ol¦is¦tic
scion
Scipio
  Ae¦mili¦anus
  Roman general
Scipio Af¦ri¦canus
  Roman general
scire fa¦cias
sci¦rocco var. of
  sirocco
scir¦rhoid
scir¦rhos¦ity
scir¦rhous of a
  scirrhus; cf. **cirrous**
scir¦rhus
  scir¦rhi
  carcinoma; cf.
  cirrus
scis¦sel metal
  clippings
scis¦sile able to be
  cut
scis¦sion
scis¦sor
scissor¦bill
scis¦sors
scissors-tail var. of
  scissortail (fish)
scis¦sor¦tail bird;
  fish
scissor-tailed
scis¦sor¦wise
Sci¦uro¦morpha
sclera
  sclerae or scleras
Scler¦ac¦tinia
scler¦ac¦tin¦ian
scler¦al
scler¦en¦chyma
scler¦en¦chy¦ma¦
    tous
scler¦ite
scler¦itis
sclero¦derma
sclero¦phyll
sclero¦phyl¦lous
sclero¦pro¦tein
Sclero¦scope
  trademark in US
scler¦osed

scler¦os¦ing
scler¦osis
  scler¦oses
sclero¦ther¦apy
scler¦otia pl. of
  sclerotium
scler¦ot¦ic
sclero¦tin
scler¦ot¦isa¦tion *Br.*
  var. of
  sclerotization
scler¦ot¦ised *Br.* var.
  of **sclerotized**
sclero¦titis
scler¦otium
scler¦otia
scler¦ot¦iza¦tion
scler¦ot¦ized
sclero¦tome
scler¦otomy
  scler¦oto¦mies
scler¦ous
scoff speak scorn-
  fully; eat greedily;
  cf. **skof**
scoff¦er
scoff¦ing¦ly
scoff¦law
scold¦er
sco¦lex
sco¦li¦ces
scoli¦osis
scoli¦ot¦ic
scol¦lop var. of
  scallop
scom¦broid
sconce
Scone ancient
  settlement, Scot-
  land; stone of S.
scone cake
scoop¦er
scoop¦ful
scoosh
scoot leave quickly;
  cf. **scute**
scoot¦er vehicle; cf.
  scuta
scoot¦er¦ist
scopa
sco¦pae
scope
scop¦ing
sco¦pol¦am¦ine

scopo¦philia
scopo¦pho¦bia
scops owl
scop¦ula
  scopu¦lae
scor¦bu¦tic
scor¦bu¦tic¦al¦ly
scorch¦er
scorch¦ing¦ly
scorda¦tura
score
  scor¦ing
score¦board
score¦book
score¦box
score¦card
score¦less
score¦line
scorer
score¦sheet
scoria
  scor¦iae
scori¦aceous
scorn¦ful
scorn¦ful¦ly
scorn¦ful¦ness
scorp knife; cf.
  scaup
scorp¦er var. of
  scorp
Scor¦pian of Scor-
  pio or Scorpius;
  person
Scor¦pio +s sign of
  zodiac; person
scor¦pi¦oid
scor¦pion arachnid
scor¦pion¦fish
Scor¦pius constella-
  tion
Scor¦sese, Mar¦tin
  film director
scor¦zon¦era
Scot person from
  Scotland; cf. **Scott**
scot tax
Scotch whisky;
  Scottish
scotch put an end
  to; wedge
Scotch¦gard
  trademark
Scotch¦lite
  trademark

Scotch tape
  trademark
sco¦ter
scot-free
Sco¦tia Scotland
sco¦tia architectural
  moulding
Scoti¦cism var. of
  Scotticism
Scot¦ism
Scot¦ist
Scot¦land
scot¦oma
  scot¦omas or
  scot¦omata
sco¦top¦ic
Scots Scottish;
  language
Scots¦man
  Scots¦men
Scots¦woman
  Scots¦women
Scott name; cf. **Scot**
Scott, George
  Gil¦bert and Giles
  Gil¦bert architects
Scott, Peter
  naturalist
Scott, Rid¦ley film
  director
Scott, Rob¦ert
  Fal¦con explorer
Scott, Wal¦ter
  writer
Scot¦ti¦cism
Scot¦tie
Scot¦tish
Scot¦tish¦ness
scoun¦drel
scoun¦drel¦dom
scoun¦drel¦ism
scoun¦drel¦ly
scour¦er
scourge
scour¦ging
scour¦ger
Scouse Liverpudlian
scouse food
Scouser
Scout member of
  Scout Association
scout person sent
  out or ahead;
  search

Scout¦er adult member of Scout Association
scout¦er person who scouts
scout¦master
scowl
scowl¦er
Scrab¦ble game *trademark*
scrab¦ble
  scrab¦bling scratch; grope
scrag
  scragged
  scrag¦ging
scrag-end
scrag¦gily
scrag¦gi¦ness
scrag¦gly
  scrag¦glier
  scrag¦gli¦est
scraggy
  scrag¦gier
  scrag¦gi¦est
scram
  scrammed
  scram¦ming
scrama¦sax
scram¦ble
  scram¦bling
scram¦bler
scram¦jet
Scran¦ton
scrap
  scrapped
  scrap¦ping
scrap¦book
scrape
  scrap¦ing
scraper
scraper¦board
scrap¦heap
scra¦pie
scrap¦per
scrap¦pily
scrap¦pi¦ness
scrap¦ple
scrappy
  scrap¦pier
  scrap¦pi¦est
scrap¦yard
scratch¦board
scratch¦er

scratch¦ily
scratchi¦ness
scratch¦plate
scratchy
  scratch¦ier
  scratchi¦est
scrawly
scrawni¦ness
scrawny
  scraw¦nier
  scraw¦ni¦est
scream¦er
scream¦ing¦ly
scree
screech¦er
screechy
  screech¦ier
  screechi¦est
screed¦ing
screen¦able
screen¦ager
screen¦er
screen¦ful
screen¦play
screen¦shot
screen¦wash
screen¦writer
screen¦writ¦ing
screw¦able
screw¦ball
screw¦ball¦er
screw-down *adj.*
screw¦driver
screw¦driv¦ing
screwed-up *adj.*
screw¦er
screwgate
screw-in *adj.*
screwi¦ness
screw-on *adj.*
screw-up *n.*
screwy
  screw¦ier
  screwi¦est
Scria¦bin, Alek¦sandr composer
scribal
scrib¦ble
  scrib¦bling
scrib¦bler
scrib¦bly
  scrib¦blier

scrib¦bli¦est
scribe
  scrib¦ing
scriber
scrim¦mage
  scrim¦ma¦ging
scrim¦ma¦ger
scrimpy
  scrimp¦ier
  scrimpi¦est
scrim¦shan¦der
scrim¦shank
scrim¦shank¦er
scrim¦shaw
scrip¦ophil¦ist
scrip¦oph¦ily
scrip¦tor¦ium
  scrip¦toria or
  scrip¦tor¦iums
scrip¦tural
scrip¦tur¦al¦ly
scrip¦ture
script¦writer
script¦writ¦ing
scriv¦en¦er
scrof¦ula
scrofu¦lous
scrog¦gin
scroll¦able
scroll¦er
scroll¦work
Scrooge
scro¦tal
scro¦tum
  scrota or
  scro¦tums
scrounge
scroun¦ging
scroun¦ger
scrub
  scrubbed
  scrub¦bing
scrub¦ber
scrub-bird
scrubby
  scrub¦bier
  scrub¦bi¦est
scrub¦fowl
scrub¦land
scrub-turkey
scruff¦ily
scruffi¦ness
scruffy
  scruff¦ier

scruffi¦est
scrum
scrummed
scrum¦ming
scrum¦mage
scrum¦ma¦ging
scrum¦ma¦ger
scrummy
  scrum¦mier
  scrum¦mi¦est
scrum¦ple
  scrump¦ling
scrump¦tious
scrump¦tious¦ly
scrump¦tious¦ness
scrumpy
  scrump¦ies
scrun¦chie *n.* var. of scrunchy
scrun¦chy
  scrun¦chies
scrunch¦ier
scrun¦chi¦est
scru¦ple
  scrup¦ling
scru¦pu¦los¦ity
scru¦pu¦lous
scru¦pu¦lous¦ly
scru¦pu¦lous¦ness
scru¦ta¦tor
scru¦tin¦eer
scru¦tin¦isa¦tion *Br.* var. of scrutinization
scru¦tin¦ise *Br.* var. of scrutinize
scru¦tin¦iser *Br.* var. of scrutinizer
scru¦tin¦iza¦tion
scru¦tin¦ize
  scru¦tin¦iz¦ing
scru¦tin¦izer
scru¦tiny
  scru¦tin¦ies
scry
  scries
  scried
  scry¦ing
scry¦er
SCSI = small computer system interface
scuba
scuba-dive
scuba-diver

scuba-diving
Scud missile
scud
  scud|ded
  scud|ding
  move fast
scuddy
scudo
scudi
scuf|fle
  scuf|fling
scul|dug|gery var.
  of skulduggery
scull oar; row; cf.
  skull
scull|er
scull|ery
  scull|er|ies
scul|lion
sculp var. of sculpt
scul|pin
sculpt
sculp|tor person
  who sculpts; cf.
  sculpture
sculp|tress
sculp|tural
sculp|tur|al|ly
sculp|ture
  sculp|tur|ing
  (make) shaped art;
  cf. sculptor
sculp|tur|esque
scum
  scummed
  scum|ming
scum|bag
scum|ble
  scum|bling
scummy
  scum|mier
  scum|mi|est
scun|cheon
scun|gile var. of
  scungille
scun|gille
  scun|gilli
scungy
  scun|gier
  scun|gi|est
scun|ner
Scun|thorpe
scup|per
scup|per|nong
scurf

scurfy
  scurf|ier
  scurfi|est
scur|ril|ity
  scur|ril|ities
scur|ril|ous
  scur|ri|lous|ly
  scur|ri|lous|ness
scurry
  scur|ries
  scur|ried
  scurry|ing
scur|vied
scur|vily
scurvy
  scur|vier
  scur|vi|est
scuta pl. of scutum;
  cf. scooter
scut|age
scu|tal
Scu|tari
scu|tate
scutch|eon
scutch|er
scute bony plate; cf.
  scoot
scu|tel|lar
scu|tel|late
scu|tel|la|tion
scu|tel|lum
  scutella
scut|ter
scut|tle
  scut|tling
scuttle|butt
scu|tum
  scuta
scut|work
scuzz|bag
scuzz|ball
scuzzy
  scuzz|ier
  scuz|zi|est
Scylla sea monster;
  cf. scilla
scy|phis|toma
  scy|phis|to|mae or
  scyphistomas
Scy|pho|zoa
scy|pho|zoan
scythe
  scyth|ing
Scythia

Scyth|ian
sea ocean; cf. see, si
sea-angel
sea|bag
sea|bed
Sea|bee
sea|bird
sea|board
Sea|borg, Glenn
  nuclear chemist
sea|borg|ium
sea|borne
Sea|Cat trademark
sea|cock
sea|farer
sea|far|ing
sea|food
sea|front
sea|going
sea|grass
sea|gull
sea|kale
sea|keep|ing
SEAL member of
  US Navy force
seal cf. ceiling, seel
seal|able
seal|ant
seal|er cf. selah
sea|lift
seal|point
seal|skin
seal|stone
seal-top
Sealy|ham
seam join; cf. seem
sea|man
  sea|men
  sailor; cf. semen
sea|man|like
sea|man|ly
sea|man|ship
sea|mark
seam|er
seam|free
seami|ness
seam|less
seam|less|ly
sea-moth
sea|mount
seam|stress
Sea|mus

seamy
  seam|ier
  seami|est
Seanad Eir|eann
se|ance
  French séance
sea|plane
sea|port
SEAQ = Stock
  Exchange Auto-
  matic Quotations
sea|quake
sear scorch; fry
  quickly; withered;
  cf. cere, seer, sere
search|able
search|er
search|ing|ly
search|light
sear|ing|ly
Searle, Ron|ald
  artist
Sears Tower
sea|scape
sea|shell
sea|shore
sea|sick
sea|sick|ness
sea|side
sea|son
sea|son|abil|ity
sea|son|able
sea|son|able|ness
sea|son|ably
sea|son|al
sea|son|al|ity
sea|son|al|ly
seat|less
SEATO = South-
  East Asia Treaty
  Organization
Se|attle
sea|ward
sea|wards
sea|water
sea|way
sea|weed
sea|worthi|ness
sea|worthy
se|ba|ceous
Se|bas|tian
Se|bas|to|pol
Sebat

seb|or|rhea *US*
seb|or|rhe|ic *US*
seb|or|rhoea *Br.*
seb|or|rhoe|ic *Br.*
sebum
se|cant
seca|teurs
Sec|chi depth
Sec|chi disc
secco
se|cede
  se|ced|ing
se|ceder
Secer|nen|tea
se|ces|sion with-
  drawal
se|ces|sion|al
se|ces|sion|ism
se|ces|sion|ist
Se|chuana var. of
  Setswana
Seckel
se|clude
  se|clud|ing
se|clu|sion
se|clu|sion|ist
se|clu|sive
Sec|onal *trademark*
sec|ond unit of time
  or angular distance;
  next after first;
  support; cf.
  seconde, secund
se|cond transfer;
  cf. seconde, secund
sec|ond|ar|ily
sec|ond|ari|ness
sec|ond|ary
  sec|ond|ar|ies
se|conde fencing
  position; cf.
  second, secund
se|cond|ee person
  transferred
sec|ond|er person
  seconding a motion
sec|ond hand *n.* on
  clock; in 'at second
  hand'
second-hand *adj.*
  & adv.
sec|ond|ly in the
  second place; cf.
  secundly

se|cond|ment
se|condo
  se|condi or
  se|con|dos
se|crecy
se|cret
se|creta|gogue
sec|re|taire
sec|re|tar|ial
sec|re|tar|iat
sec|re|tary
  sec|re|tar|ies cf.
  secretory
sec|re|tary|ship
se|crete
  se|cret|ing
se|cre|tin
se|cre|tion
se|cret|ive
se|cret|ive|ly
se|cret|ive|ness
se|cret|ly
se|cre|tor
se|cre|tory produ-
  cing by secretion;
  cf. secretary
sect religious group;
  cf. *Sekt*
sect|ar|ian
sect|ar|ian|ise *Br.*
  var. of sectarianize
sect|ar|ian|ism
sect|ar|ian|ize
  sect|ar|ian|iz|ing
sect|ary
  sect|ar|ies
sec|tion
sec|tion|al
sec|tion|al|ise *Br.*
  var. of sectionalize
sec|tion|al|ism
sec|tion|al|ist
sec|tion|al|ize
  sec|tion|al|iz|ing
sec|tion|al|ly
sec|tor
sec|tor|al
sec|tor|ial
secu|lar
secu|lar|isa|tion *Br.*
  var. of
  secularization
secu|lar|ise *Br.* var.
  of secularize

secu|lar|ism
secu|lar|ist
secu|lar|ity
secu|lar|iza|tion
secu|lar|ize
  secu|lar|iz|ing
secu|lar|ly
se|cund of flowers
  on one side only;
  cf. second, seconde
se|cund|ly *Botany*;
  cf. secondly
se|cur|able
se|cure
  se|cur|ing
se|cure|ly
se|cure|ment
se|cure|ness
Se|curi|tate
se|curi|tisa|tion *Br.*
  var. of
  securitization
se|curi|tise *Br.* var.
  of securitize
se|curi|tiza|tion
se|curi|tize
  se|curi|tiz|ing
se|cur|ity
  se|cur|ities
se|curo|crat
Sedan battle site,
  France
sedan car; s. chair
sed|ate
  sed|at|ing
sed|ate|ly
sed|ate|ness
sed|ation
seda|tive
sed|en|tar|ily
sed|en|tari|ness
sed|en|tary
Seder
se|der|unt
Sedge|moor
Sedg|wick, Adam
  geologist
sedgy
se|dilia
  sing. se|dile
sedi|ment
sedi|ment|ary
sedi|men|ta|tion
se|di|tion

se|di|tious
se|di|tious|ly
se|duce
  se|du|cing
se|du|cer
se|du|cible
se|duc|tion
se|duc|tive
se|duc|tive|ly
se|duc|tive|ness
se|duc|tress
se|du|lity
sedu|lous
sedu|lous|ly
sedu|lous|ness
sedum
see
  saw
  seen
  discern with the
  eyes etc.; diocese or
  archdiocese; cf. sea,
  si
see|able
seed part of plant;
  rated competitor;
  cf. cede
seed|bed
seed|corn
seed|eat|er
seed|er cf. cedar
seed|ily
seedi|ness
seed|less
seed|ling
seed-lip
seeds|man
seeds|men
seedy
  seed|ier
  seedi|est
  sordid; cf. cedi
See|ger, Pete musi-
  cian
See|ing Eye dog
seek
  sought
  look for; cf. Sikh
seek|er cf. sika,
  caeca
seel close a person's
  eyes; cf. seal
seem appear to be;
  cf. seam

seem|ing|ly
seem|li|ness
seem|ly
  seem|lier
  seem|li|est
seen past participle
  of see; cf. scene
seep|age
seer prophet; unit of
  weight; cf. cere,
  sear, sere
seer|sucker
see-saw
seethe
  seeth|ing
  seeth|ing|ly
see-through adj.
Sefer
  Sif|rei
seg|ment
seg|men|tal
seg|men|tal|
  isa|tion
  Br. var. of
  segmentalization
seg|men|tal|ise Br.
  var. of
  segmentalize
seg|men|tal|
  iza|tion
seg|men|tal|ize
seg|men|tal|iz|ing
seg|men|tal|ly
seg|men|tary
seg|men|ta|tion
Sego|via city, Spain
Sego|via, An|drés
  guitarist
seg|reg|able
seg|re|gate
  seg|re|gat|ing
seg|re|ga|tion
seg|re|ga|tion|al
seg|re|ga|tion|ist
seg|re|ga|tive
segue
  segue|ing
segui|dilla
Se|guri|dad
Sehn|sucht
sei whale; cf. say
sei|cent|ist
sei|cento
sei|cento|ist

seiche
sei|del
Seid|litz
seif dune
sei|gneur
sei|gneur|ial
sei|gneury var. of
  seigniory
sei|gnior var. of
  seigneur
sei|gnior|age
sei|gnior|ial var. of
  seigneurial
sei|gniory
  sei|gnior|ies
  feudal lordship; cf.
  signory
sei|gnor|age var. of
  seigniorage
Sei|kan Tun|nel
Seine river, France
seine fishing net
seiner fisherman;
  boat
seise in 'be seised
  of'; var. of seize
sei|sin
seis|mal
seis|mic
seis|mic|al
seis|mic|al|ly
seis|mi|city
seis|mo|gram
seis|mo|graph
seis|mo|graph|er
seis|mo|graph|ic
seis|mo|graphy
seis|mo|logic|al
seis|molo|gist
seis|mol|ogy
seis|mom|eter
seis|mo|saurus
sei|tan vegetable
  protein
seiza kneeling
  position
seiz|able
seize
  seiz|ing
seizer
sei|zin var. of seisin
seiz|ure
se|jant Heraldry

Sekh|met Egyptian
  Mythology
Sekt wine; cf. sect
se|lach|ian
se|la|dang
sela|gin|ella
selah exclam. in
  Psalms; cf. sealer
Se|langor
Sel|craig,
  Alex|an|der other
  name of Alexander
  Selkirk
sel|dom
se|lect
se|lect|able
se|lect|ee
se|lec|tion
se|lec|tion|al
se|lec|tion|al|ly
se|lect|ive
se|lect|ive|ly
se|lect|ive|ness
se|lect|iv|ity
se|lect|man
  se|lect|men
se|lect|ness
se|lect|or
Sel|ena name
sel|en|ate
Sel|ene Greek
  goddess
sel|en|ic
sel|en|ide
sel|eni|ous
sel|en|ite
sel|en|it|ic
sel|en|ium
sel|eno|dont
sel|en|og|raph|er
sel|en|og|raphy
sel|en|olo|gist
sel|en|ology
Se|leu|cid
self
  pl. selves
  v. selfs
selfed
self|ing
self-abandon
self-abandoned
self-abandon|ment
self-abasement

self-abnegation
self-absorbed
self-absorp|tion
self-abuse
self-accusa|tion
self-accusa|tory
self-acting
self-activity
self-actual|isa|tion
  Br. var. of self-
  actualization
self-actual|iza|tion
self-addressed
self-adhesive
self-adjust|ing
self-adjust|ment
self-advance|ment
self-
  advertise|ment
self-advertiser
self-advertis|ing
self-advocacy
self-affirm|ation
self-
  aggrand|ise|ment
  Br. var. of self-
  aggrandizement
self-aggrand|is|ing
  Br. var. of self-
  aggrandizing
self-
  aggrand|ize|ment
self-aggrand|iz|ing
self-alienation
self-aligning
self-analys|ing
self-analysis
self-annihil|ation
self-appoint|ed
self-appreci|ation
self-approba|tion
self-approval
self-approv|ing
self-approv|ing|ly
self-assemble
  self-assembling
self-assembly
self-assert|ing
self-assertion
self-assert|ive
self-assert|ive|ness
self-assess|ment
self-assurance

self-assured
self-assured¦ly
self-aware
self-awareness
self-balancing
self-betray¦al
self-build
self-builder
self-cancel¦ling
self-cater
self-catering
self-censor¦ship
self-centered US
self-centered¦ly US
self-centered¦ness US
self-centred Br.
self-centred¦ly Br.
self-centred¦ness Br.
self-certifi¦cate
self-certifi¦ca¦tion
self-certify
  self-certifies
  self-certified
  self-certify¦ing
self-cleaning
self-closing
self-cocking
self-collec¦tion
self-color US
self-colored US
self-colour Br.
self-coloured Br.
self-compat¦ible
self-conceit
self-conceit¦ed
self-concept
self-condem¦na¦tion
self-condemned
self-condemn¦ing
self-confessed
self-confess¦ed¦ly
self-confes¦sion
self-confes¦sion¦al
self-confidence
self-confident
self-confident¦ly
self-congratu¦la¦tion
self-congratu¦la¦tory

self-conscious
self-conscious¦ly
self-conscious¦ness
self-consist¦ency
self-consist¦ent
self-contained
self-contain¦ment
self-contempt
self-contemp¦tu¦ous
self-content¦ed
self-content¦ment
self-contra¦dict¦ing
self-contra¦dic¦tion
self-contra¦dict¦ory
self-control
self-controlled
self-correct
self-correc¦tion
self-created
self-creating
self-creation
self-critical
self-criticism
self-deceit
self-deceiver
self-deceiv¦ing
self-deception
self-deceptive
self-defeat¦ing
self-defence Br.
self-defense US
self-defensive
self-definition
self-delusion
self-denial
self-denying
self-depend¦ence
self-depend¦ent
self-deprecat¦ing
self-deprecat¦ing¦ly
self-depreca¦tion
self-depreca¦tory
self-depreci¦ation
self-deprecia¦tory
self-despair
self-destroy¦ing
self-destruct
self-destruc¦tion
self-destruc¦tive
self-destruc¦tive¦ly

self-determin¦ation
self-develop¦ment
self-devotion
self-diffusion
self-direct¦ed
self-direction
self-discip¦line
self-discip¦lined
self-discov¦ery
self-disgust
self-doubt
self-dramatisa¦tion
  Br. var. of self-dramatization
self-dramatiza¦tion
self-drive
self-educated
self-education
self-efface¦ment
self-effacing
self-effacing¦ly
self-employed
self-employ¦ment
self-enclosed
self-esteem
self-evaluation
self-evidence
self-evident
self-evident¦ly
self-examin¦ation
self-excited
self-existent
self-explana¦tory
self-expres¦sion
self-expres¦sive
self-faced
self-feeder
self-feeding
self-fertile
self-fertil¦isa¦tion
  Br. var. of self-fertilization
self-fertil¦ised Br.
  var. of self-fertilized
self-fertil¦is¦ing Br.
  var. of self-fertilizing
self-fertil¦ity
self-fertil¦iza¦tion
self-fertil¦ized
self-fertil¦iz¦ing

self-financed
self-financing
self-flagel¦la¦tion
self-flatter¦ing
self-flattery
self-forget¦ful
self-forget¦ful¦ness
self-fulfil¦ling
self-fulfill¦ment US
self-fulfil¦ment Br.
self-generat¦ing
self-glorifi¦ca¦tion
self-governed
self-govern¦ing
self-govern¦ment
self-gravita¦tion
self-harm
self-harmer
self-hate
self-hatred
self-heal
self-help
self¦hood
self-identi¦fi¦ca¦tion
self-identity
self-image
self-immola¦tion
self-import¦ance
self-import¦ant
self-import¦ant¦ly
self-imposed
self-improve¦ment
self-incompati¦bil¦ity
self-incompat¦ible
self-induced
self-induct¦ance
self-induction
self-induct¦ive
self-indulgence
self-indulgent
self-indulgent¦ly
self-inflict¦ed
self-insurance
self-interest
self-interest¦ed
self-involved
self-involve¦ment
self¦ish
self¦ish¦ly
self¦ish¦ness

self|ism
self|ist
self-justifi|ca|tion
self-justifi|ca|tory
self-justify|ing
self-knowing
self-knowledge
self|less
self|less|ly
self|less|ness
self-limiting
self-liquidat|ing
self-loader
self-loading
self-loathing
self-locking
self-love
self-made
self-manage|ment
self-managing
self-mastery
self|mate *Chess*
self-medicate
  self-medicat|ing
self-mockery
self-mocking
self-mocking|ly
self-mortifi|ca|tion
self-motivated
self-motivat|ing
self-motiva|tion
self-moving
self-mutila|tion
self-neglect
self|ness
self-obsessed
self-opinion
self-opinion|ated
self-parodic
self-parody
  self-parodies
self-parody|ing
self-perpetu|at|ing
self-perpetu|ation
self-pity
self-pitying
self-pitying|ly
self-policing
self-pollin|ated
self-pollin|at|ing
self-pollin|ation
self-pollin|ator

self-portrait
self-portrait|ure
self-possessed
self-posses|sion
self-preser|va|tion
self-proclaimed
self-propagat|ing
self-propaga|tion
self-propelled
self-propel|ling
self-protec|tion
self-protect|ive
self-raising *Br.*
  US self-rising
self-rating
self-realisa|tion *Br.*
  var. of self-
  realization
self-realiza|tion
self-referen|tial
self-referen|tial|ity
self-referen|tial|ly
self-reflec|tion
self-reflect|ive
self-reflex|ive
self-regard
self-regard|ing
self-regulat|ing
self-regula|tion
self-regula|tory
self-reliance
self-reliant
self-reliant|ly
self-renewal
self-reproach
self-reproach|ful
self-respect
self-respect|ing
self-restrained
self-restraint
self-reveal|ing
self-revela|tion
self-revela|tory
Self|ridge, Harry
  Gor|don business-
  man
self-righteous
self-righteous|ly
self-righteous|ness
self-righting
self-rising *US*
  Br. self-raising
self-rule

self-sacrifice
self-sacrifi|cial
self-sacrifi|cing
self|same
self-satisfac|tion
self-satisfied
self-sealing
self-seed
self-seeder
self-seeker
self-seeking
self-select|ing
self-selection
self-service
self-serving
self-shifter
self-similar
self-similar|ity
self-sow
  past participle self-
  sown or self-sowed
self-starter
self-starting
self-sterile
self-steril|ity
self-stimula|tion
self-styled
self-subsis|tent
self-sufficiency
self-sufficient
self-sufficient|ly
self-sufficing
self-sugges|tion
self-support
self-support|ing
self-surren|der
self-sustained
self-sustain|ing
self-system
self-tailing
self-tanner
self-tanning
self-tapping
self-taught
self-timer
self-
  transcen|dence
self-
  understand|ing
self-will
self-willed
self-winding

self-worth
Sel|ima
Sel|ina
Sel|juk
Sel|juk|ian
sel|kie
Sel|kirk,
  Alex|an|der sailor
Sel|kirk|shire
sell
  sold
  cf. cel, cell
sella
  sel|lae
  depression
  containing gland;
  cf. cellar, seller
sell|able
Sel|la|field
sella tur|cica
  sel|lae tur|cicae
sell|down *n.*
sell|er person who
  sells; cf. cellar,
  sella
Sel|lers, Peter actor
sell-in *n.*
sell-off *n.*
Sel|lo|tape
  Sel|lo|tap|ing
  trademark
sell-out *n. & mod.*
sell-through *n.*
Se|lous, Fred|erick
  explorer
selt|zer
selva
selv|age var. of
  selvedge
selv|edge
selves pl. of self
Sel|wyn
Selz|nick, David O.
  film producer
se|man|teme
se|man|tic
se|man|tic|al|ly
se|man|ti|cian
se|man|ti|cist
se|man|ti|city
sema|phore
  sema|phor|ing
sema|phor|ic
sema|phor|ic|al|ly

Se¦mar¦ang
se¦masio¦logic¦al
se¦masi¦ology
sem¦blable
semb¦lance
seme = semanteme
semé *Heraldry*; cf.
 semi
semée var. of semé
Semei
Sem¦ele mother of
 Dionysus
sem¦eme
semen sperm; cf.
 seaman
se¦mes¦ter
Semey var. of Semei
semi semi-detached
 house; semi-final;
 semi-trailer; cf.
 semé
semi-acoustic
semi-annual
semi-annual¦ly
semi¦aquat¦ic
semi-automat¦ic
semi-autono¦mous
semi-basement
semi¦bold
semi¦breve
semi¦circle
semi¦cir¦cu¦lar
semi-classic¦al
semi¦colon
semi¦con¦duct¦ing
semi¦con¦duct¦or
semi-conscious
semi-conserva¦tive
semi-crystal¦line
semi-cylinder
semi-cylin¦drical
semi-darkness
semi¦demi¦semi¦
 quaver
semi-deponent
semi-detached
semi¦diam¦eter
semi-
 documen¦tary
semi-
 documen¦tar¦ies
semi-dome
semi-double

semi-elliptic¦al
semi-final
semi-finalist
semi-finished
semi-fitted
semi-fluid
semi-independ¦ent
semi-infinite
semi-invalid
semi-lethal
semi-liquid
semi-literacy
semi-literate
Sé¦mil¦lon
semi¦lunar
semi¦major
semi¦metal
semi¦metal¦lic
semi¦minor
semi¦modal
semi-monocoque
semi-monthly
sem¦inal
sem¦in¦al¦ly
sem¦inar
sem¦in¦ar¦ian
sem¦in¦ar¦ist
sem¦in¦ary
 sem¦in¦ar¦ies
sem¦in¦ifer¦ous
Sem¦in¦ole
 pl. Sem¦in¦ole or
 Sem¦in¦oles
semio¦chem¦ical
semi-official
semi-official¦ly
semio¦logic¦al
semi¦olo¦gist
semi¦ology
semi-opaque
semi-opera
semi¦osis
semi¦ot¦ic
semi¦ot¦ic¦al¦ly
semio¦ti¦cian
semi¦ot¦ics
Semi¦pa¦la¦tinsk
semi¦palm¦ated
semi-Pelagian
semi-Pelagian¦ism
semi-perman¦ent

semi-
 perman¦ent¦ly
semi¦per¦me¦able
semi-precious
semi-pro +s
semi-profes¦sion¦al
semi-prone
semi¦quaver
semi¦quin¦one
Se¦mira¦mis *Greek
 Mythology*
semi-retired
semi-retire¦ment
semi-rigid
semi-skilled
semi-skimmed
semi-solid
semi-submers¦ible
semi-sweet
semi-synthet¦ic
Sem¦ite
Sem¦it¦ic
Sem¦it¦isa¦tion *Br.*
 var. of
 Semitization
Sem¦it¦ise *Br.* var. of
 Semitize
Sem¦it¦ism
Sem¦it¦ist
Sem¦it¦iza¦tion
Sem¦it¦ize
 Sem¦it¦iz¦ing
semi¦tone
semi-trailer
semi-transpar¦ent
semi-tropic¦al
semi-tropics
semi¦vowel
Sem¦mel¦weis,
 Ignaz Phil¦ipp
 obstetrician
sem¦mit
semo¦lina
sem¦per fi¦de¦lis
sem¦per¦vivum
sem¦pi¦ter¦nal
sem¦pi¦ter¦nal¦ly
sem¦pi¦ter¦nity
sem¦plice *Music*
sem¦pre *Music*
semp¦stress var. of
 seamstress
Sem¦tex *trademark*

Sena¦nay¦ake, Don
 Ste¦phen prime
 minister of Ceylon
sen¦ar¦ius verse of
 six feet
sen¦arii
sen¦ate legislative
 body; cf. sennet,
 sennit
sen¦ator
sen¦at¦or¦ial
sen¦at¦or¦ship
*sen¦atus
 con¦sul¦tum
 sen¦atus con¦sulta*
send
sent
 cause to go; cf.
 scend
send¦able
Sen¦dai
Sen¦dak, Maur¦ice
 author and
 illustrator
sen¦dal
send¦er
send-off *n.*
send-up *n.*
sene
 pl. sene or senes
Sen¦eca
 pl. Sen¦eca or
 Sen¦ecas
 American Indian
Sen¦eca 'the
 Younger', Roman
 statesman
Sen¦eca 'the Elder',
 Roman rhetorician
se¦necio +s
Sene¦gal
Sene¦gal¦ese
Sene¦gam¦bia
senes pl. of senex
sen¦esce
sen¦es¦cing
sen¦es¦cence
sen¦es¦cent
sene¦schal
senex
 senes
sen¦hor Portuguese-
 speaking man; cf.
 señor

sen|hora
  Portuguese-
  speaking married
  woman; cf. señora
sen|hor|ita
  Portuguese-
  speaking unmarried
  woman; cf.
  señorita
se|nile
sen|il|ity
se|nior
se|ni|or|ity
sen|iti
  pl. sen|iti
Senna, Ayr|ton
  racing driver
senna tree; laxative
Sen|nach|erib king
  of Assyria
sen|net trumpet
  call; cf. senate,
  sennit
sen|night week
sen|nit plaited
  straw; cf. senate,
  sennet
Senoi
  pl. Senoi
señor
  se|ñores
  Spanish-speaking
  man; cf. senhor
se|ñora Spanish-
  speaking married
  woman; cf.
  senhora
se|ñor|ita Spanish-
  speaking unmarried
  woman; cf.
  senhorita
sensa pl. of sensum
sen|sate
sen|sa|tion
sen|sa|tion|al
sen|sa|tion|al|ise
  Br. var. of
  sensationalize
sen|sa|tion|al|ism
sen|sa|tion|al|ist
sen|sa|tion|al|is|tic
sen|sa|tion|al|ize
sen|sa|tion|al|iz|ing
sen|sa|tion|al|ly

sense
sens|ing
sen|sei
  pl. sen|sei
sense|less
sense|less|ly
sense|less|ness
Sensex
sens|ibil|ity
sens|ibil|ities
sens|ible
sens|ible|ness
sens|ibly
sen|sil|lum
sen|silla
sen|si|tisa|tion *Br.*
  var. of
  sensitization
sen|si|tise *Br.* var. of
  sensitize
sen|si|tiser *Br.* var.
  of sensitizer
sen|si|tive
sen|si|tive|ly
sen|si|tive|ness
sen|si|tiv|ity
sen|si|tiv|ities
sen|si|tiza|tion
sen|si|tize
sen|si|tiz|ing
sen|si|tizer
sen|si|tom|eter
sen|sor detecting or
  measuring device;
  cf. censer, censor
sen|sor|ial
sen|sori|al|ly
sen|sori|ly
sen|sori|motor
sen|sori|neural
sen|sor|ium
  sen|soria or
  sen|sor|iums
sen|sory
sen|sual
sen|sual|ise *Br.* var.
  of sensualize
sen|sual|ism
sen|sual|ist
sen|su|al|ity
sen|sual|ize
sen|sual|iz|ing
sen|su|al|ly
sensu lato

sen|sum
  sensa
sen|su|ous
sen|su|ous|ly
sen|su|ous|ness
Sen|sur|round
  trademark
sensu stricto

sent past tense and
  participle of send;
  Estonian currency;
  cf. cent, scent
sente
  li|sente
sen|tence
sen|ten|cing
sen|ten|tial
sen|ten|tious
sen|ten|tious|ly
sen|ten|tious|ness
sen|tience
sen|tiency
sen|tient
sen|tient|ly
sen|ti|ment
sen|ti|men|tal
sen|ti|men|tal|
  isa|tion
  Br. var. of
  sentimentalization
sen|ti|men|tal|ise
  Br. var. of
  sentimentalize
sen|ti|men|tal|ism
sen|ti|men|tal|ist
sen|ti|men|tal|ity
  sentimentalities
sen|ti|men|tal|
  iza|tion
sen|ti|men|tal|ize
sen|ti|men|tal|
  iz|ing
sen|ti|men|tal|ly
sen|ti|nel
sen|ti|nelled *Br.*
sen|ti|neled *US*
sen|ti|nel|ling *Br.*
sen|ti|nel|ing *US*
sen|try
  sen|tries
sentry-go
Se|nufo
  pl. Se|nufo

Se|nussi
  pl. Se|nussi or
  Se|nus|sis
Seoul
sepal
sep|ar|abil|ity
sep|ar|able
sep|ar|able|ness
sep|ar|ably
sep|ar|ate
sep|ar|at|ing
sep|ar|ate|ly
sep|ar|ate|ness
sep|ar|ation
sep|ar|at|ism
sep|ar|at|ist
sep|ara|tive
sep|ar|ator
sep|ar|atory
Se|pedi
Sepha|dex
  trademark
Seph|ardi
Seph|ar|dim
Seph|ar|dic
Seph|ar|ose
  trademark
seph|ira
seph|iroth
sepia
sepoy
sep|puku
sep|sis
septa pl. of septum;
  cf. sceptre
sept|age
sep|tal
sept|ar|ian
sept|ar|ium
  sept|aria
sept|ate
sept|ation
sept|cen|ten|ary
sept|cen|ten|ar|ies
Sep|tem|ber
sep|ten|ar|ius
sep|ten|arii
sep|ten|ary
sep|ten|ar|ies
sep|ten|nial
sep|tet
sept|ette var. of
  septet

sep¦tic
septi¦cae¦mia *Br.*
septi¦caem¦ic *Br.*
sep¦tic¦al¦ly
septi¦cemia *US*
septi¦cem¦ic *US*
sep¦ti¦city
sep¦til¦lion
sep¦timal
sep¦time
septi¦va¦lent
sep¦toria
sep¦tua¦gen¦ar¦ian
Sep¦tua¦ges¦ima
Sep¦tua¦gint
sep¦tum
  septa
sep¦tu¦plet
sep¦ul¦cher *US*
se¦pul¦chral
se¦pul¦chral¦ly
sep¦ul¦chre *Br.*
sep¦ul¦chring
sep¦ul¦ture
se¦qua¦cious
se¦qua¦cious¦ly
se¦qua¦city
se¦quel continuation
  of story; result
se¦quela
se¦que¦lae
  medical condition
se¦quence
se¦quen¦cing
se¦quen¦cer
se¦quent
se¦quen¦tial
se¦quen¦ti¦al¦ity
se¦quen¦tial¦ly
se¦quent¦ly
se¦ques¦ter
se¦ques¦tra pl. of
  sequestrum
se¦ques¦trable
se¦ques¦tral
se¦ques¦trate
se¦ques¦trat¦ing
se¦ques¦tra¦tion
se¦ques¦tra¦tor
se¦ques¦trec¦tomy
se¦ques¦
    trec¦to¦mies

se¦ques¦trum
se¦ques¦tra
se¦quin
se¦quined *US*
se¦quinned *Br.*
se¦quoia
sera pl. of serum
serac
se¦ra¦glio +s
serai
Se¦raing
Seram Sea var. of
  Ceram Sea
se¦rang
se¦rape
ser¦aph
  ser¦aph¦im or
  ser¦aphs
ser¦aph¦ic
ser¦aph¦ic¦al¦ly
Sera¦pis Egyptian
  god
ser¦as¦kier
Serb
Ser¦bia
Ser¦bian
Serbo-Croat
Serbo-Croatian
Ser¦cial
sere sequence of
  animal or plant
  communities; cf.
  cere, sear, seer
Ser¦em¦ban
Ser¦ena
ser¦en¦ade
  ser¦en¦ad¦ing
ser¦en¦ader
ser¦en¦ata
ser¦en¦dip¦it¦ous
ser¦en¦dip¦it¦ous¦ly
ser¦en¦dip¦ity
se¦rene
se¦rener
se¦ren¦est
  calm; cf. serine
se¦rene¦ly
se¦rene¦ness
Ser¦en¦geti
Ser¦en¦is¦sima, La
  Venice
se¦ren¦ity
se¦ren¦ities

serf feudal labourer;
  cf. surf
serf¦age
serf¦dom
serf¦hood
serge cloth; cf.
  sarge, surge
ser¦geancy
ser¦gean¦cies
ser¦geant army, air
  force, or police
  officer; cf. serjeant
sergeant-at-arms
  sergeants-at-arms
  US
  Br. serjeant-
  at-arms
ser¦geant¦ship
ser¦ger
Ser¦gipe
Ser¦gius, St
ser¦ial story in
  episodes; forming a
  series; cf. cereal
seri¦al¦isa¦tion *Br.*
  var. of serialization
seri¦al¦ise *Br.* var. of
  serialize
seri¦al¦ism
seri¦al¦ist
seri¦al¦ity
seri¦al¦iza¦tion
seri¦al¦ize
  seri¦al¦iz¦ing
seri¦al¦ly
seri¦ate
seri¦at¦ing
seri¦atim
seri¦ation
seri¦cite
seri¦cit¦ic
seri¦cul¦tural
seri¦cul¦ture
seri¦cul¦tur¦ist
seri¦ema
ser¦ies
  pl. ser¦ies
serif
ser¦ifed
ser¦iffed var. of
  serifed
seri¦graph
ser¦ig¦raph¦er
ser¦ig¦raphy

serin finch
ser¦ine amino acid;
  cf. serene
serio-comic
serio-comical¦ly
ser¦ious
ser¦ious¦ly
ser¦ious¦ness
ser¦jeant sergeant
  in Foot Guards (in
  official lists); *his-*
  torical barrister; cf.
  sergeant
serjeant-at-arms
  Br.
  serjeants-at-arms
  US sergeant-
  at-arms
serjeant-at-law
  serjeants-at-law
ser¦jeant¦ship
ser¦jeanty
ser¦jeant¦ies
ser¦mon
ser¦mon¦ic
ser¦mon¦ise *Br.* var.
  of sermonize
ser¦mon¦iser *Br.*
  var. of sermonizer
ser¦mon¦ize
ser¦mon¦iz¦ing
ser¦mon¦izer
sero¦con¦ver¦sion
sero¦con¦vert
sero¦diag¦no¦sis
sero¦diag¦nos¦tic
sero¦logic
sero¦logic¦al
sero¦logic¦al¦ly
sero¦olo¦gist
sero¦ology
sero¦nega¦tive
sero¦nega¦tiv¦ity
sero¦posi¦tive
sero¦posi¦tiv¦ity
sero¦preva¦lence
ser¦osa
se¦rosal
sero¦sitis
ser¦os¦ity
sero¦tine
sero¦tonin
sero¦type
  sero¦typ¦ing

sero|typ|ic
ser|ous
serow
Ser|pens constella-
tion
Ser|pens Caput
Ser|pens Cauda
ser|pent
Ser|pen|tes
Ser|pen|tine lake,
London
ser|pen|tine
ser|pen|tin|ing
(move) like a snake
ser|pent|in|isa|tion
Br. var. of
serpentinization
ser|pent|in|ise Br.
var. of serpentinize
ser|pent|in|ite
ser|pent|in|iza|tion
ser|pent|in|ize
ser|pent|in|iz|ing
ser|pigin|ous
SERPS = state
earnings-related
pension scheme
ser|pu|lid
ser|ranid
ser|rano +s
ser|rate
ser|rat|ing
ser|ra|tion
ser|ried
ser|tão +s
Ser|toli cell
serum
sera or ser|ums
ser|val
ser|vant
serve
serv|ing
serve-and-volley|er
ser|ver
serv|ery
serv|er|ies
Ser|vian archaic
var. of Serbian
Ser|vian of Servius
Tullius, king of
Rome
ser|vice
ser|vicing
ser|vice|abil|ity

ser|vice|able
ser|vice|ably
service|berry
service|berries
ser|vice|man
ser|vice|men
ser|vice|woman
ser|vice|women
ser|vi|ette
ser|vile
ser|vile|ly
ser|vil|ity
serv|ing|man
serv|ing|men
serv|ing|woman
serv|ing|women
Ser|vite
ser|vi|tor
ser|vi|tor|ship
ser|vi|tude
serv|let
servo +s
servo|mech|an|ism
servo|motor
ses|ame
ses|am|oid
ses|amum
ses|ama
sesh = session
Se|so|tho
ses|qui|altera
ses|qui|cen|ten|ary
ses|qui|cen|ten|
ar|ies
ses|qui|cen|ten|nial
ses|qui|oxide
ses|qui|ped|alian
ses|qui|ter|pene
sess var. of cess
ses|sile
ses|sion meeting;
bout; cf. cession
ses|sion|al
ses|terce Roman
currency
ses|ter|tius
ses|ter|tii
ses|tina
Set var. of Seth
(Egyptian god)
set
set|ting
put; harden; group;
etc.; cf. sett

set
set|ted
set|ting
group pupils for
teaching; cf. sett
seta
setae
se|ta|ceous
setal
set-aside n.
set|back n.
se-tenant
Seth Egyptian god;
name
Seth, Vik|ram
writer
seth merchant;
banker
SETI = Search for
Extraterrestrial
Intelligence
se|tiger|ous
set-in adj.
set-net
set-netter
set-off n.
seton
se|tose
Set|swana
sett badger's burrow;
paving block; pat-
tern of tartan
set|tee
set|ter
set|tle
set|tling
settle|able
settle|ment
set|tler person who
settles in a place
set|tlor Law
set-to +s n.
Setú|bal
set-up n.
Seu|rat, Georges
French painter
seven
seven|fold
seven-iron
seven|teen
seven|teenth
sev|enth
sev|enth|ly
seven|ti|eth

sev|enty
sev|en|ties
seventy-first,
seventy-second,
etc.
sev|enty|fold
seventy-one,
seventy-two, etc.
Seven Years War
sever
sev|er|able
sev|eral
sev|er|al|ly
sev|er|al|ty
sev|er|ance
se|vere
se|verer
se|ver|est
se|vere|ly
se|ver|ity
se|ver|ities
Sev|ern
Se|ver|naya
Zem|lya
Sev|er|od|vinsk
Se|verus Roman
emperor
sev|ery
sev|er|ies
se|viche
Sev|ille
Sevin trademark
Sèvres
sev|ruga
sew
past participle
sewn or sewed
stitch; cf. so, soh,
sow
sew|age
se|wel|lel
sewen var. of sewin
sewer
sew|er|age
sewin
sewn past participle
of sew; cf. sown
sexa|gen|ar|ian
Sexa|ges|ima
sexa|ges|imal
sexa|ges|im|al|ly
sex|angu|lar
sex|ca|pade

sex|cen|ten|ary
  sex|cen|ten|ar|ies
sex|en|nial
sexer
sex|foil
sex|ily
sexi|ness
sex|ism
sex|ist
sexi|va|lent
sex|less
sex|less|ly
sex|less|ness
sexo|logic|al
sex|olo|gist
sex|ology
sex|par|tite
sex|pert
sex|ploit|ation
sex|pot
Sex|tans
sex|tant
sex|tet
sex|tette var. of
  sextet
sex|tile
sex|til|lion
sex|til|lionth
sexto|decimo +s
sex|ton
sex|tu|ple
  sex|tu|pling
sex|tu|plet
sex|tu|ply
sex|ual
sexu|al|isa|tion Br.
  var. of
  sexualization
sexu|al|ise Br. var.
  of sexualize
sexu|al|ity
  sexu|al|ities
sexu|al|iza|tion
sexu|al|ize
  sexu|al|iz|ing
sexu|al|ly
sexy
  sex|ier
  sexi|est
Sey|chelles
Sey|chel|lois
  pl. Sey|chel|lois

person from the
  Seychelles
Sey|chel|loise
  female Seychellois
Sey|fert gal|axy
Sey|mour, Jane
  wife of Henry VIII
  of England
Sey|mour, Lynn
  ballet dancer
sez non-standard
  spelling of says
Se|zes|sion
Sfax
sforz|ando
  sforz|an|dos or
  sforz|andi
sforz|ato
  sforz|atos or
  sforz|ati
sfu|mato
sgraf|fito
  sgraf|fiti
's-Graven|hage
shaadi
Shaanxi province,
  central China; cf.
  Shanxi
Shaba
Sha|baka pharaoh
sha|bash
Shab|bat
Shab|bes var. of
  Shabbos
shab|bily
shab|bi|ness
Shab|bos
  Shab|bos|im
shabby
  shab|bier
  shab|bi|est
  shab|by|ish
shab|rack
shabti
shabu-shabu
shack|land
shackle
  shack|ling
Shackle|ton,
  Er|nest explorer
shacky
  shack|ier
  shacki|est
shad|bush

shad|chan
shad|chan|im or
  shad|chans
Shad|dai
shad|dock
shade
  shad|ing
shade|less
shader
shadi|ly
shadi|ness
shad|khan var. of
  shadchan
sha|doof
shadow
shadow|er
shadow|graph
shad|owi|ness
shadow|land
shadow|less
shad|owy
  shadow|ier
  shadowi|est
shady
  shadi|er
  shadi|est
Shaftes|bury, Lord
  social reformer
shag
  shagged
  shag|ging
  carpet pile;
  tobacco; bird; also
  vulgar slang
shag|ger *vulgar
  slang*
shag|gily
shag|gi|ness
shaggy
  shag|gier
  shag|gi|est
shag|pile
sha|green
shah
sha|hada
sha|ha|dah var. of
  shahada
Shah Alam
shah|dom
sha|hid
shah|toosh
shaikh var. of
  sheikh

Shai|tan Devil in
  Islam
shai|tan vicious per-
  son or animal
Shaka Zulu chief
shak|able var. of
  shakeable
shake
  shook
  shak|ing
  shaken
  vibrate; jerk about;
  upset; cf. sheikh
shake|able
shake|down
shake-out n.
Shaker religious
  sect member
shaker person or
  thing that shakes
Shaker|ism
Shake|speare,
  Wil|liam dramatist
Shake|spear|ean
Shake|speare|ana
Shake|spear|ian
  var. of
  Shakespearean
Shake|speari|ana
  var. of
  Shakespeareana
shake-up n.
Shakhty city, Russia
shaki|ly
shaki|ness
shako +s
Shakti female prin-
  ciple in Hinduism
sha|kudo
shaku|hachi
shaky
  shaki|er
  shaki|est
shaley var. of shaly
shal|lop
shal|lot plant; cf.
  Shalott
shal|low
shal|low|ly
shal|low|ness
Shal|man|eser
  kings of Assyria
sha|lom

Sha|lott in 'The
Lady of Shalott'; cf.
shallot
shal'war
shaly
  shali'er
  shali'est
sham
  shammed
  sham|ming
shama
sha'mal
sha'man
sha'man'ic
sha'man'ise *Br.* var.
of shamanize
sha'man'ism
sha'man'ist
sha'man'is'tic
sha'man'ize
  sha'man'iz'ing
shama'teur
shama'teur'ism
shamba
sham'ble
  sham'bling
sham'bly
  sham'blier
  sham'bli'est
sham'bol'ic
sham'bol'ic'al'ly
shame
  sham'ing
shame|faced
shame|faced'ly
shame|faced|ness
shame|ful
shame|ful'ly
shame|ful|ness
shame|less
shame|less'ly
shame|less|ness
sha|mi'ana
Sha'mir, Yit'zhak
prime minister of
Israel
shami|sen var. of
samisen
sham|mer
shammy
  sham|mies
sham|poo +s +ed
+ing
sham|rock

sha'mus
Shand|ean
Shan|dong
shandy
  shan|dies
Shan|gaan
  pl. **Shan|gaan** or
  Shan|gaans
Shang|hai city,
China
shang|hai +s +ed
+ing
Shango religious
cult; African god
Shan|gor var. of
Shango (god)
Shangri-La
Shan|kar, Ravi
musician
Shan|kar, Uday
dancer
shanked
Shankly, Bill foot-
ball manager
Shanks's pony
Shan|non
shanny
  shan|nies
Shansi var. of
Shanxi
shan't
shanti peace; cf.
shanty
Shan|tou
Shan|tung var. of
Shandong
shan|tung silk
shanty
  shan|ties
shack; song; cf.
shanti
shanty|man
  shanty|men
Shanxi province,
north central
China; cf. **Shaanxi**
shap'able var. of
shapeable
SHAPE = Supreme
Headquarters
Allied Powers in
Europe
shape
  shap'ing
shape|able

shape|less
shape|less'ly
shape|less|ness
shape|li|ness
shape'ly
  shape|lier
  shape'li|est
shaper
shapka
Shap|ley, Har'low
astronomer
shar'able var. of
shareable
sha|rara
share
  shar'ing
share|able
share|crop
  share|cropped
  share|crop|ping
share|crop|per
share-farmer
share-farming
share|hold'er
share|hold|ing
share-out *n.*
sharer
share|ware
sha'ria
sha'riah var. of
sharia
sha'riat var. of
sharia
Sha'rif, Omar actor
sha'rif descendant
of Muhammad;
Muslim leader
sha'rif|ian
Shar|jah
shark|skin
shark-sucker
**Sharma, Shan|kar
Dayal** president of
India
Sha'ron coastal
plain, Israel; name
Sha'ron, Ariel
prime minister of
Israel
sharon fruit
Shar Pei
sharp'en
sharp|en'er
sharp'er swindler

Sharpe|ville
sharpie
sharp|ish
sharp'ly
sharp|ness
sharp|shoot'er
sharp|shoot'ing
Shar|ron
shash|lik
  pl. **shash|lik** or
  shash|liks
Shasta daisy
shas|tra
Shatt al-Arab
shat|ter
shat|ter|er
shat|ter|ing'ly
shat|ter|proof
shauri
  shauris or
  shaur|ies
shave
  shav'ing
shave|hook
shave|ling
shaven
shaver
shave|tail
Sha|vian
Sha|vuot
Sha|vu|oth var. of
Shavuot
**Shaw, George
Ber|nard** play-
wright
shaw potato stalks
and leaves; thicket;
cf. **shore, sure**
shawl garment; cf.
schorl
shawled
shawlie working-
class woman; cf.
surely
shawm
Shaw|nee
  pl. **Shaw|nee** or
  Shaw|nees
Shay|tan var. of
Shaitan
shay|tan var. of
shaitan
sha|zam
Shcher|ba|kov

shchi soup
she *pron.*
shea tree
shead|ing
sheaf
  pl. sheaves
  v. sheafs
  sheafed
  sheaf|ing
sheal|ing var. of
  shieling
shear
  past tense and
  participle sheared
  or shorn
  cut with shears; cf.
  sheer
Shear|er, Moira
  ballet dancer
shear¦er
shear|ling
shear|water
sheat|fish
sheath *n.*
sheath|bill
sheathe *v.*
  sheath¦ing
sheath|less
sheave
  sheav|ing
Sheba
she|bang
She¦bat var. of
  Sebat
she|been
She|chi|nah var. of
  Shekinah
shed
  past tense and
  participle shed
  shed|ding
  building; throw off,
  spill, etc.
shed
  shed|ded
  shed|ding
  put in shed
she'd = she had; she
  would
shed|der
she-devil
shed|hand
shed|load
Shee|lagh
Sheela-na-gig

sheen
sheeny
  sheen|ies
  sheen|ier
  sheeni|est
sheep|dog
sheep|fold
sheep|ish
sheep|ish¦ly
sheep|ish|ness
sheep|like
sheep's-bit plant
sheep|shank knot
sheeps|head
  pl. sheeps|head
  fish
sheep|skin
sheer unqualified;
  steep; thin; swerve;
  curve of ship; cf.
  shear
sheer legs
  pl. sheer legs
  hoisting apparatus
sheer¦ly
Sheer|ness port,
  England
sheer|ness
sheet|ing
sheet|let
Sheet|rock
  trademark
Shef|field
sheik var. of sheikh
sheik|dom var. of
  sheikhdom
sheikh Arab chief;
  Muslim leader; cf.
  shake
sheikh|dom
Sheila name
sheila young woman
shei|tel
shekel
She|khi¦nah var. of
  Shekinah
She|ki¦nah
She|lagh
shel|drake
shel|duck
shelf
  shelves

  ledge
shelf +s +ed +ing
  inform; informer;
  cf. shelve
shelf-ful
shelf-like
she'll
shel|lac
  pl. shel|lacs
  v. shel|lacks
  shel|lacked
  shel|lack|ing
shell|back
Shel|ley name
Shel|ley, Mary
  writer
Shel|ley, Percy
  Bysshe poet
shell|fire
shell|fish
  pl. shell|fish
shell-less
shell-like
shell|proof
shell shock
shell-shocked
shell|work
shelly
Shelta language
shel|ter
shel|ter|er
shel|ter|less
shel¦ter|wood
shel|tie
shelty
  shel|ties
  var. of sheltie
shelve
  shelv|ing
  put on shelf; set
  aside; fit with
  shelves; cf. shelf
shelver
Shem *Bible*
Shema Hebrew text
she-male
she|moz¦zle
Shen|an|doah
she¦nan|igans
Shensi var. of
  Shaanxi
Shen|yang
Shen|zhen
she-oak

Sheol
shep|herd
shep¦herd|ess
Shep|pey, Isle of
sher¦ard|ise *Br.* var.
  of sherardize
sher¦ard|ize
  sher¦ard|iz¦ing
Shera|ton
sher|bet
she|reef var. of
  sharif
Sheri|dan, Rich|ard
  Brins|ley dramatist
she|rif *Islam*; var. of
  sharif
sher|iff civil or law
  officer
sheriff-depute
  sheriffs-deputes
sher¦iff|dom
sher¦iff|hood
sher|iff prin|ci|pal
  sher|iffs prin|ci|pal
sher¦iff|ship
Sher|lock
Sher|man, Wil|liam
  American general
Sherpa
  pl. Sherpa or
  Sher|pas
Sher|rill man's
  name; cf. Sheryl
Sherry name
sherry
  sher|ries
  drink
's-Hertogenbosch
sher|wani
Sheryl woman's
  name; cf. Sherrill
she's
Shet|land
Shet|land¦er
Shev¦ard|nadze,
  Ed¦uard head of
  state of Georgia
She¦vat var. of
  Sebat
shew *archaic* var. of
  show
shew|bread
Shia
  pl. Shia or Shias

shi|atsu Japanese
therapy; cf. shih-
tzu
shib|bo|leth
shicer
shick|er
shick|ered
shid|duch
  shid|duch|im
shield|less
shiel|ing
shift|able
shift|er
shift|ily
shifti|ness
shift|less
shift|less|ly
shift|less|ness
shifty
  shift|ier
  shifti|est
shi|gella
  pl. shi|gella or
  shi|gellae
shih-tzu dog; cf.
  shiatsu
Shi|ism
shii|take
Shi|ite
Shi|jiaz|huang
shi|kar hunting
shi|kara boat
shi|kari hunter
shik|ker var. of
  shicker
shik|kered var. of
  shickered
Shi|koku
shikra
shiksa often
  offensive
shil|le|lagh
shil|ling African
  and former British
  currency; cf.
  schilling
Shil|long
Shil|luk
  pl. Shil|luk or
  Shil|luks
shilly-shallier var.
  of shilly-shallyer
shilly-shally
  shilly-shallies

shilly-shallied
shilly-shally|ing
shilly-shally|er
shim
shimmed
shim|ming
shimi|yana
shim|mer
shim|mer|ing|ly
shim|mery
shimmy
  shim|mies
  shim|mied
shimmy|ing
shin
shinned
shin|ning
Shin Bet
Shin Beth var. of
  Shin Bet
shin|dig
shindy
  shin|dies
  disturbance
shine
  shone or shined
shin|ing
shiner
shin|gle
shin|gling
shin|gly
shin|glier
shin|gliest
shini|ly
shini|ness
shin|ing|ly
Shin|kan|sen
  pl. Shin|kan|sen
Shin|ner
shinny
  shin|nies
  shin|nied
shinny|ing
  climb; informal ice
  hockey
Shin|ola trademark
shin|plas|ter
Shinto
Shin|to|ism
Shin|to|ist
shinty
  shin|ties
  Scottish game like
  hockey

shiny
shini|er
shini|est
ship
shipped
ship|ping
ship|board
ship-breaker
ship|broker
ship|build|er
ship|build|ing
ship|lap
ship|lapped
ship|lap|ping
ship|less
Ship|ley, Jenny
  prime minister of
  New Zealand
ship|load
ship|master
ship|mate
ship|ment
ship|owner
ship|pable
ship|pen var. of
  shippon
ship|per
ship|pon
ship|shape
ship|way
ship|worm
ship|wreck
ship|wright
ship|yard
shira|lee
Shi|raz city, Iran;
  grape; wine
shire county; cf.
  shyer
shirk|er
Shir|ley
shirr
shirred
shirr|ing
shirt|ed
shirt|ily
shirti|ness
shirt|ing
shirt|less
shirt|lift|er
shirt|sleeve
shirt|sleeved
shirt|waist

shirt|waist|er
shirty
  shirt|ier
  shirti|est
shisham
shish kebab
shiso Japanese herb
shit vulgar slang
  shit|ted or shit or
  shat
  shit|ting
shitake var. of
  shiitake
shit|bag vulgar
  slang
shit|can
  shit|canned
  shit|can|ning
  vulgar slang
shite vulgar slang
shite|poke bird
shit|face vulgar
  slang
shit-faced vulgar
  slang
shit|hole vulgar
  slang
shit|house vulgar
  slang
shit|kick|er vulgar
  slang
shit|less vulgar
  slang
shit|list vulgar
  slang
shit|load vulgar
  slang
shitty
  shit|tier
  shit|ti|est
  vulgar slang
shit|work vulgar
  slang
shiur
shi|ur|im
Shiva var. of Siva
shiva period of
  mourning
shivah var. of shiva
Shi|vaji Indian raja
shiva|ree
shiver
shiv|er|er
shiv|er|ing|ly
shiv|ery

shi|voo +s
Shiv Sena
Shizu|oka
Shko|dër
shlub var. of schlub
shmatte var. of
  schmatte
shmo var. of schmo
Shoah
shoal
shoaly
shoat
shochet
  shoch|et|im
sho|chu
shock|abil|ity
shock|able
shock|er
shock|ing|ly
shock|ing|ness
Shock|ley, Wil|liam
  physicist
shock|proof
shod|ily
shod|di|ness
shoddy
  shod|dies
  shod|dier
  shod|di|est
shoe
  shod
  shoe|ing
  cf. choux, shoo
shoe|bill
shoe-billed
shoe|black
shoe|box
shoe|horn
shoe|lace
shoe|less
shoe|maker
shoe|mak|ing
shoe|pack
shoe|shine
shoe|shiner
shoe|string
sho|far
  sho|fars or
  shof|roth
sho|gun
sho|gun|ate
shoji
Sho|la|pur

Sholo|khov,
  Mikh|ail writer
Shona name
Shona
  pl. Shona or
  Sho|nas
  member of Bantu
  people; language
shone past tense
  and participle of
  shine
shongo|lolo var. of
  songololo
shonky
  shon|kies
  shonk|ier
  shonki|est
shoo +s +ed +ing
shoo|gly
  shoog|lier
  shoog|li|est
shoo-in n.
shoot
  shot
  cf. chute
shoot|able
shoot-'em-up
shoot|er
shoot|ist
shoot-out n.
shop
  shopped
  shop|ping
shop|ahol|ic
shop|fit|ter
shop|fit|ting
shop|front
shop|house
shop|keep|er
shop|keep|ing
shop|less
shop|lift
shop|lift|er
shop|lot
shop|man
  shop|men
shoppe spuriously
  quaint shop
shop|per
shoppy of shops or
  trade
shop-soiled
shop|walk|er
shop|work|er

shop|worn
shore
  shor|ing
  coast; prop; cf.
  shaw, sure
shore|bird
shore|lark
shore|less
shore|line
shore|side
shore|ward
shore|wards
shore|weed
shorn
short|age
short-arse person
short|bread
short|cake
short|com|ing
short|crust
short|en
short|fall
short|hair cat
short|hand
short-handed
short|hold
short|horn
shortie var. of
  shorty
short|ish
short|list
short|ly
short|ness
short|stop
shorty
  short|ies
Sho|shone
  pl. Sho|shone or
  Sho|sho|nes
Sho|shon|ean
Shosta|ko|vich,
  Dmi|tri composer
shot|crete
shote var. of shoat
shot|gun
shot|maker
shot|mak|ing
Sho|to|kan
shot-put
shot-putter
shot-putting
shot|ted weighted
  with shot

shot|tist
should
shoul|der
shoulder-in dress-
  age movement
shouldn't
shout|er
shout-out n.
shouty
  shout|ier
  shouti|est
shove
  shov|ing
shovel
  shov|elled Br.
  shov|eled US
  shov|el|ling Br.
  shov|el|ing US
shovel|board
shov|el|er US
shovel|ful
shovel|head
shov|el|ler Br.
shovel|ware
show
  shown or showed
Showa
show-and-tell
  teaching method
show|band
show|biz
show|biz|zy
show|boat
show|boat|er
show|boaty
show|card
show|case
show|cas|ing
show|down
shower
shower|proof
show|ery
show|girl
show|ground
show|ily
showi|ness
show|jump
show|jump|er
show|man
  show|men
show|man|ship
Show Me State
shown

show-off n.
show|piece
show|place
show|reel
show|room
showy
  show|ier
  show|est
shoyu
shrap|nel
shred
  shred|ded
  shred|ding
  shred|der
Shreve|port
shrewd¦ly
shrewd|ness
shrew|ish
shrew|ish¦ly
shrew|ish|ness
shrew-mole
Shrews|bury
Shri
shriek¦er
shriek|ing¦ly
shrieval
shriev|al¦ty
  shriev|al¦ties
shrill|ness
shrilly
shri|mati
shrimp¦er
shrine
  shrin¦ing
Shriner
shrink
  shrank
  shrunk or
  shrunken
shrink|able
shrink|age
shrink¦er
shrink|ing¦ly
shrive
  shrove
  shriv¦ing
  shriven
shrivel
  shriv|elled Br.
  shriv|eled US
  shriv¦el|ling Br.
  shriv¦el|ing US
shroff

shroom =
  mushroom
Shrop|shire
Shrove|tide
shrub|bery
  shrub|ber¦ies
shrubby
  shrub|bier
  shrub¦bi|est
shrug
  shrugged
  shrug|ging
shrunk¦en
shtetl
  shtet|lach or
  shtetls
shtook
shtum
  shtummed
  shtum|ming
shtup
  shtupped
  shtup|ping
shu|bun¦kin
shuck¦er
shud|der
shud|der|ing¦ly
shud|dery
shuf¦fle
  shuf|fling
shuffle|board
shuf|fler
shufti
shul synagogue
Shu¦men
shun
  shunned
  shun|ning
shunt¦er
shura
shuri|ken
shut
  shut|ting
shut|down
Shute, Nevil
  novelist
shut-in n. & mod.
shut-off n. & mod.
shut|out
shut-out bid
shut¦ter
shut¦ter|bug
shut¦ter|less

shut¦tle
  shut|tling
shuttle|cock
shy
  shies
  shied
  shy¦ing
  shyer
  shy¦est
shyer horse etc. that
  shies; cf. shire
Shy|lock character
  in Shakespeare
shyly
shy|ness
shy|ster
si = te in tonic sol-fa
Sia|chen Gla|cier
sial
siala|gogue
si¦alic
si¦alid|ase
Si¦al|kot
sialo|gogue var. of
  sialagogue
Siam
sia|mang
Siam|ese
Sian var. of Xian
Si¦be|lius, Jean
  composer
Ši|be¦nik
Si|ber¦ia
Si|ber¦ian
sibia
sibi|lance
sibi|lancy
sibi|lant
sibi|lant¦ly
sibi|late
  sibi|lat¦ing
sibi|la¦tion
Sibiu
sib¦li|cide
sib|ling
sib|ship
Sibyl name
sibyl prophetess
sibyl|line of a sibyl;
  prophetic
Sibyl|line books
  Roman oracles
sic correct thus; cf.
  sick

sic bo Chinese game
sic¦ca|tive
sice six on dice; cf.
  syce
Si|chuan
Si¦cil|ian
si¦cili|ana var. of
  siciliano
si¦cili|ano +s
Si¦cily
sick ill etc.; cf. *sic*
sick|bay
sick|bed
sick build|ing
  syn|drome
sick¦en
sick|en¦er
sick|en|ing¦ly
Sick¦ert, Wal¦ter
  painter
sickie
sick|ish
sickle
sickle|bill
sick¦li|ness
sick¦ly
  sick|lier
  sick|li|est
sick|ness
sicko +s
sick-out n.
sick|room
sida
si|dal¦cea
sid¦dha
Sid|dhar¦tha
  Gau|tama founder
  of Buddhism
sid¦dhi
Sid|dons, Sarah
  actress
sid¦dur
side
  sid¦ing
side|arm (throw
  with) sweeping arm
  movement
side arm weapon
side|arm¦er
side|band
side|bar
side|board
side|burn

side|car
side|cut
sided'|ly
sided|ness
side|hill
side|kick
side|lamp
side|less
side|light
side|line
  side|lin|ing
side|long
side|man
  side|men
side|meat
side-on *adv.*
si|der|eal
sid|er|ite
sid|er|it|ic
sid|ero|phore
sid|ero|stat
side-saddle
side|show
side-slip
  side-slipped
  side-slipping
sides|man
  sides|men
side|split house
side-splitting
side|step
  side|stepped
  side|step|ping
  side|step|per
side stream
side|stream smoke
side|stroke
side|swipe
  side|swip|ing
side|track
side|walk
side|wall
side|ward
side|wards
side|ways
side-wheeler
side wind wind
  blowing from one
  side
side|wind move
  sideways
side|wind|er
side|wise

Sidhe
Sidi bel Abbès
sid|ing
sidle
  sid|ling
Sid|ney name
Sid|ney, Philip poet
Sidon
Sidra, Gulf of
Sie|ben|ge|birge
siege
Sieg|fried hero of
  Nibelungenlied
Sieg Heil
Sieg-Heiling
Sie|mens, von;
  Ernst, Karl, and
  Fried|rich
  engineers
sie|mens unit
  pl. sie|mens
Siena city, Italy
Sien|ese
Sien|kie|wicz,
  Hen|ryk novelist
si|enna pigment
Sier|pin|ski
si|erra
Si|erra Leone
Si|erra Leon|ean
Si|erra Madre
Si|erra Ne|vada
si|esta
sieve
  siev|ing
sieve-like
sie|vert
si|faka
Sif|rei
  pl. of Sefer
sift|er
Siga|toka
sigh (emit) long
  audible breath; cf.
  sai
sight vision; see;
  observe; cf. cite,
  site
sight|er
sight|hound
sight|less
sight|less|ly
sight|less|ness

sight|li|ness
sight|ly
sight|see
  sight|sees
  sight|saw
  sight|see|ing
sight|seer
sigil
Sig|int = signals
  intelligence
sig|lum
  sigla
sigma
sig|mate
sig|moid
sig|moid|al
sig|moido|scope
sig|moido|scop|ic
sig|moid|os|copy
sign cf. sine, syne
sign|able
Si|gnac, Paul
  painter
sign|age
sig|nal
  sig|nalled *Br.*
  sig|naled *US*
  sig|nal|ling *Br.*
  sig|nal|ing *US*
sig|nal|er *US*
sig|nal|ise *Br.* var. of
  signalize
sig|nal|ize
  sig|nal|iz|ing
sig|nal|ler *Br.*
sig|nal|ly
sig|nal|man
  sig|nal|men
sig|nary
  sig|nar|ies
  set of signs; cf.
  signory
sig|na|tory
  sig|na|tor|ies
sig|na|ture
sign|board
sign|ee
sign|er
sig|net seal used as
  authentication; cf.
  cygnet
si|gni|fi|ant
sig|nifi|cance
sig|nifi|cant

sig|nifi|cant|ly
sig|ni|fi|ca|tion
sig|nifi|ca|tor
si|gni|fié
sig|ni|fier
sig|nify
  sig|ni|fies
  sig|ni|fied
  sig|ni|fy|ing
sign-off *n.*
si|gnor
  si|gnori
  Italian-speaking
  man
si|gnora Italian-
  speaking married
  woman
si|gnore var. of
  signor
si|gnor|ina Italian-
  speaking unmarried
  woman
si|gnory
  si|gnor|ies
  governing body; cf.
  seigniory, signary
sign|post
sign-up *n.*
sign|writer
sign|writ|ing
sigri
Sig|urd *Norse*
  Legend
Siha|nouk,
  Noro|dom king of
  Cambodia
sika deer; cf. caeca,
  seeker
Sikh adherent of
  Sikhism; cf. seek
Sikh|ism
Si|king
Sik|kim
Sik|kim|ese
Si|kor|sky, Igor air-
  craft designer
Sik|sika
sil|age
  sil|aging
si|lane
si|las|tic *trademark*
Silat
Sil|bury Hill
Sil|ches|ter

si|lence
si|len|cing
si|len|cer
si|lent
si|lent|ly
Si|lenus teacher of
  Dionysus
si|lenus
  si|leni
  woodland spirit
Si|le|sia
Si|le|sian
silex
sil|hou|ette
  sil|hou|et|ting
sil|ica mineral; cf.
  siliqua
sili|cate
si|li|ceous
sil|li|cic
si|lici|clas|tic
sili|cide
si|lici|fi|ca|tion
si|li|cify
  si|lici|fies
  si|lici|fied
  si|lici|fy|ing
si|li|cious var. of
  siliceous
sili|con element
sili|cone
  sili|con|ing
  compound; treat
  with silicone
sili|con|ise Br. var.
  of siliconize
sili|con|ize
  sili|con|iz|ing
sili|cosis
sili|cot|ic
sili|qua
  sili|quae
  seed pod; coin; cf.
  silica
si|lique var. of
  siliqua (seed pod)
sili|quose
sili|quous
silk|en
silkie chicken; var.
  of selkie
silk|ily
silki|ness
silk-like

silk|worm
silky
  silk|ier
  silki|est
sill
sil|la|bub var. of
  syllabub
sil|lily
sil|li|man|ite
sil|li|ness
Sil|li|toe, Alan
  writer
silly
  sil|lies
  sil|lier
  sil|li|est
  foolish; cf. Scilly
silo
  pl. silos
  v. si|loes
  si|loed
  silo|ing
Si|loam *Bible*
si|lox|ane
silt|ation
silt|stone
silty
  silt|ier
  silti|est
Si|lur|ian *Geology*
si|lur|oid fish
sil|van var. of
  sylvan; cf. silvern
Sil|vanus woodland
  god
sil|ver
silver|back
silver|berry
  silver|berries
silver|eye
silver|fish
silveri|ness
silver-line moth
sil|vern of or like
  silver; cf. sylvan
silver|point
sil|ver|side
sil|ver|smith
sil|ver|smith|ing
Sil|ver|stone
silver|sword
sil|ver|ware
sil|ver|weed
sil|very

silvi|cul|tural
silvi|cul|ture
silvi|cul|tur|ist
sima
sima|zine
Sim|birsk
sim|cha
Sime|non, Georges
  novelist
Sim|eon name
Sim|eon Sty|lites,
  St
Sim|fero|pol
sim|ian ape
simi|lar
simi|lar|ity
  simi|lar|ities
simi|lar|ly
sim|ile
si|mili|tude
Simla
Sim|men|tal
sim|mer
Sim|nel, Lam|bert
  pretender to Eng-
  lish throne
sim|nel cake
sim|oleon
Simon, Neil play-
  wright
Simon, Paul singer-
  songwriter
Sim|one
simo|niac
si|mo|ni|ac|al
Si|moni|des Greek
  poet
simon|ise *Br.* var. of
  simonize
simon|ize
simon|iz|ing
simon-pure
si|mony
si|moom
si|moon var. of
  simoom
sim|pat|ico
sim|per
sim|per|ing|ly
sim|ple
  sim|pler
  sim|plest
simple|ness

simple|ton
sim|plex
sim|plici|ter
sim|pli|city
sim|pli|ci|ties
sim|pli|fi|ca|tion
sim|plify
  sim|pli|fies
  sim|pli|fied
  sim|pli|fy|ing
sim|plism
sim|plis|tic
sim|plis|tic|al|ly
Sim|plon
sim|ply
Simp|son, Wal|lis
  Duchess of
  Windsor
simul
simu|lac|rum
  simu|lacra or
  simu|lac|rums
simu|lant
simu|late
  simu|lat|ing
simu|la|tion
simu|la|tive
simu|la|tor
sim|ul|cast
sim|ul|tan|eity
sim|ul|tan|eous
sim|ul|tan|eous|ly
sim|ul|tan|eous|
           ness
sim|urg
sin
  sinned
  sin|ning
sin = sine; cf. sign,
  syne
Sinai
Sina|it|ic
Sina|loa
Sin|an|thro|pus
Sin|atra, Frank
  singer
Sin|bad fictional
  character
sin|cere
  sin|cerer
  sin|cerest
sin|cere|ly
sin|cere|ness
sin|cer|ity

sin|cipi|tal
sin|ci|put
Sin|clair, Clive
  engineer
Sin|clair, Upton
  novelist
Sind
Sind|bad var. of
  Sinbad
Sin|de|bele
Sindhi
sin|door
sin|dur var. of
  sindoor
sine trigonometric
  function; cf. sign,
  syne
Sin|ead
sine anno
sine|cure
sine|cur|ism
sine|cur|ist
sine die
sine qua non
sinew
sin|ew|less
sinewy
sin|fonia
sin|foni|etta
sin|ful
sin|ful|ly
sin|ful|ness
sing
  sang
  sung
sing|able
sing|along
Singa|pore
Singa|por|ean
singe
  singe|ing
Sing|er, Isaac
  Bash|evis novelist
Sing|er, Isaac
  Mer|rit inventor
sing|er
Singh Sikh name
Sing|hal|ese var. of
  Sinhalese
sing|ing|ly
sing-jay
sin|gle
  sin|gling

single-decker
single-hander
single|ness
single seat|er
sing|let
single|ton
single|tree
Sing|lish
sin|gly
Sing Sing
sing-song
sing|song girl
Sing|spiel
  Sing|spiele
sin|gu|lar
sin|gu|lar|ity
  sin|gu|lar|ities
sin|gu|lar|ly
sinh hyperbolic
  tangent
Sin|hala
Sin|hal|ese
Si|ning var. of
  Xining
sin|is|ter
sin|is|ter|ly
sin|is|ter|ness
sin|is|tral
sin|is|tral|ity
sin|is|tral|ly
Sin|it|ic
sink
  sank or sunk
  sink|ing
  sunk
  go below surface or
  down etc.; basin;
  cf. cinque, sync
sink|able
sink|age
sink|er
sink|hole
Sin|kiang var. of
  Xinjiang
sin|less
sin|less|ly
sin|less|ness
sin|ner
sin|net
Sinn Fein
Sinn Fein|er
Sino- Chinese and...
sino|atrial

sin-offering
sino|logic|al
sin|olo|gist
sino|logue
sin|ology
sino|phile
sino|phobe
sino|pho|bia
sin|se|milla
sin|ter
Sint-Niklaas
Sin|tra
Sintu
sinu|ate
Sin|uiju
sinu|os|ity
  sinu|os|ities
sinu|ous
sinu|ous|ly
sinu|ous|ness
sinus
si|nus|itis
si|nus|oid
si|nus|oid|al
si|nus|oid|al|ly
sinus ven|osus
  sinus ven|osi
Sio|bhan
Sion var. of Zion
Siouan
Sioux
  pl. Sioux
sip
  sipped
  sip|ping
sipe
si|phon
si|phon|age
si|phon|al
Si|phon|aptera
si|phon|apter|an
si|phon|ic
Si|phon|ophora
si|phono|phore
siph|uncle
Si|phun|cu|lata
sip|per
sip|pet
sippy cup
Si|pun|cula
si|puncu|lan
si|puncu|lid

sir|dar var. of
  sardar
Sir|daryo
sire
  sir|ing
siree *exclam.*
siren
Si|renia
si|ren|ian
Sir|ius
sir|loin
si|rocco +s
sir|rah
sir|ree var. of siree
sir|taki var. of
  syrtaki
Sirte, Gulf of
sirup *US* var. of
  syrup
sir|upy *US* var. of
  syrupy
sis = sister; *exclam.*;
  cf. cis
sisal
sis|kin
Sis|ley, Al|fred
  painter
sis|si|fied
sis|si|ness
sissy
  sis|sies
  sis|sier
  sis|si|est
sissy|ish
sis|ter
sister-german
  sisters-german
sis|ter|hood
sister-in-law
  sisters-in-law
sis|ter|li|ness
sis|ter|ly
Sis|tine Chapel; of
  popes called Sixtus;
  cf. cysteine, cystine
sis|trum
  sis|tra
Si|swati
Sisy|phean
Sisy|phus *Greek
  Mythology*
sit
  sat
  sit|ting

Sita wife of Rama
sitar
sitar|ist
sita|tunga
sit|com
sit-down *adj. & n.*
site
  sit|ing
  of building etc.;
  locate; cf. **cite**,
  sight
si|tella var. of
  sittella
sit-in *n.*
sit|kamer
sit|rep = situation
  report
Sit|tang
sit|tella
sit|ter
situ in *'in situ'*
situ|ate
  situ|at|ing
situ|ation
situ|ation|al
situ|ation|al|ly
situ|ation|ism
situ|ation|ist
sit-up *n.*
sit-upon *n.*
situs
situs in|ver|sus
Sit|well, Edith,
  Os|bert, and
  Sa|chev|er|ell poets
sitz bath
sitz|fleisch
sitz|krieg
Siva var. of **Shiva**
Siva|ism var. of
  Shivaism
Siva|ite var. of
  Shivaite
Sivaji var. of **Shivaji**
Sivan
Si|walik Hills
Si|wash *derogatory*
  American Indian;
  Chinook Jargon
si|wash camp with-
  out tent
six|ain
sixer
six|fold

six-gun
six-iron
six-pack
six|pence
six|penny
six-pounder
six-shooter
sixte fencing
  position
six|teen
six|teenmo +s
six|teenth
sixth
sixth-former
sixth|ly
six|ti|eth
sixty
  six|ties
sixty-first, sixty-
  second, etc.
six|ty|fold
sixty-fourmo +s
sixty-four
  thou|sand dol|lar
  ques|tion
sixty-one, sixty-
  two, etc.
siz|able var. of
  sizeable
siz|ably var. of
  sizeably
sizar student with
  college grant; cf.
  sizer
siz|ar|ship
size
  siz|ing
size|able
size|ably
size|ism
size|ist
sizer person who
  sizes; cf. **sizar**
Size|well
siz|zle
siz|zling
siz|zler
sjam|bok
sjam|bokked
sjam|bok|king
Sjö|gren's
  syn|drome
ska style of music;
  cf. **scar**

skaap|steker
skag
Skag|er|rak
skald bard; cf. **scald**
skald|ic
Skanda Hindu war
  god
skanky
  skank|ier
  skanki|est
Skara Brae
skarn *Geology*
skat card game; cf.
  scat
skate
  skat|ing
skate|board
skate|board|er
skate|park
skater
skean dagger; cf.
  skein, skene
skean-dhu
ske|benga
sked
  sked|ded
  sked|ding
ske|dad|dle
  ske|dad|dling
ske|donk
skeet|er mosquito;
  var. of **skitter**
skeevy
skeg
skein bundle of
  yarn; flock of geese;
  cf. **skean, skene**
skel|etal
skel|et|al|ly
skel|eton
skel|et|on|ise *Br.*
  var. of **skeletonize**
skel|et|on|ize
  skel|et|on|iz|ing
skelly var. of **schelly**
Skel|ton, John poet
skene structure on
  Greek stage; cf.
  skean, skein
skep beehive
skep|tic *US*
  Br. **sceptic**
skep|tic|al *US*
  Br. **sceptical**

skep|tic|al|ly *US*
  Br. **sceptically**
skep|ti|cism *US*
  Br. **scepticism**
sker|rick
skerry
  sker|ries
sketch|book
sketch|er
sketch|ily
sketchi|ness
sketchy
  sketch|ier
  sketchi|est
skeuo|morph
skeuo|morph|ic
skew|back
skew|bald
skew|er spike; cf.
  skua
skew|ness
skew-whiff
ski +s +ed +ing
ski|able
skia|gram var. of
  sciagram
skia|graph var. of
  sciagraph
skia|graph|ic var. of
  sciagraphic
ski|ag|raphy var. of
  sciagraphy
Ski|athos
ski-bob
ski-bobbed
ski-bobbing
ski-bobber
skid
  skid|ded
  skid|ding
skid|doo var. of
  skidoo
skiddy
  skid|dier
  skid|di|est
Ski|doo +s vehicle
  trademark
ski|doo +s +ed +ing
  ride on Skidoo; go
  away
skid|pad
skid|pan
skid|steer load|er

skier person who
  skis; cf. skyer
skif¦fle
ski-flying
ski¦jorer
ski¦jor¦ing
skil¦fish
skil¦ful Br.
skil¦ful¦ly Br.
skil¦ful¦ness Br.
skil¦let
skill¦ful US
skill¦ful¦ly US
skill¦ful¦ness US
skilly
skim
  skimmed
  skim¦ming
skim¦board
skim¦board¦er
skim¦mel
skim¦mer
skim¦mia
skim¦ming¦ton
ski¦mobile
skimp¦ily
skimpi¦ness
skimpy
  skimp¦ier
  skimpi¦est
skin
  skinned
  skin¦ning
skin¦care
skin¦der
skin-dive
  skin-diving
skin-diver
skin¦flint
skin¦fold
skin¦ful
skin¦head
skin¦less
skin-like
Skin¦ner, B. F.
  psychologist
skin¦ner
skin¦ni¦ness
skinny
  skin¦nier
  skin¦ni¦est
skinny¦ma¦link
skinny¦ma¦links

skinny-rib
skin¦tight
skip
  skipped
  skip¦ping
  bouncing step;
  jump rope; omit;
  var. of skep
skip¦jack
skip¦per
skip¦pet
skirl
skir¦mish
skir¦mish¦er
skirr
skir¦ret
skirt¦ing
skite
  skit¦ing
skit¦ter
skit¦tery
skit¦tish
skit¦tish¦ly
skit¦tish¦ness
skit¦tle
  skit¦tling
skive
  skiv¦ing
skiver
ski¦wear
skoal var. of skol
skof work period;
  stage; cf. scoff
skok¦iaan
skol good health
skolly
  skol¦lies
skoosh var. of
  scoosh
Skopje
skort
Skrae¦ling
Skrya¦bin var. of
  Scriabin
skua bird; cf.
  skewer
skul¦dug¦gery
skulk¦er
skull bone; head; hit
  on head; cf. scull
skull¦cap
skunk¦weed
skunk¦works

skut¦terud¦ite
sky
  skies
  skied
  sky¦ing
sky¦box
sky¦cap
sky¦dive
  sky¦div¦ing
sky¦diver
Skye island; terrier
skyer Cricket high
  hit
skyey
sky¦flower
sky¦glow
sky¦hook
sky¦jack
sky¦jack¦er
Sky¦lab
sky¦lark
sky¦less
sky¦light
sky¦light¦ed
sky¦line
sky¦lit
skyr Icelandic dish
sky¦rocket
sky¦sail
sky¦scape
sky¦scraper
sky¦walk
sky¦ward
sky¦wards
sky¦watch
sky¦watch¦er
sky¦way
sky¦writer
sky¦writing
slab
  slabbed
  slab¦bing
slab¦ber
slabby
  slab¦bier
  slab¦bi¦est
slack¦en
slack¦er
slack¦ly
slack¦ness
slag
  slagged
  slag¦ging

slain past participle
  of slay
slainte
slake
  slak¦ing
sla¦lom
sla¦lom¦er
slam
  slammed
  slam¦ming
slam-bang
slam-dance
  slam-dancing
slam-dancer
slam¦mer
slan¦der
slan¦der¦er
slan¦der¦ous
slan¦der¦ous¦ly
slang¦ily
slangi¦ness
slan¦guage
slangy
  slangi¦er
  slangi¦est
slant¦wise
slap
  slapped
  slap¦ping
slap¦dash
slap¦head
slap¦jack
slap¦per
slap¦stick
slap-up adj.
slash¦er
slasto trademark
slat
  slat¦ted
  slat¦ting
slate
  slat¦ing
slater
slather
slat¦tern
slat¦tern¦li¦ness
slat¦tern¦ly
slaty
  slati¦er
  slati¦est
slaugh¦ter
slaugh¦ter¦er
slaugh¦ter¦house
slaugh¦ter¦ous

Slav
Slava
slave
　slav¦ing
slaver
slav¦ery
Slavey
　pl. **Slavey** or
　Slaveys
　American Indian;
　language
slavey maidservant
Slav¦ic
slav¦ish
slav¦ish¦ly
slav¦ish¦ness
Slav¦ism
Sla¦vo¦nian
Sla¦von¦ic
Slavo¦phile
Slavo¦phobe
slaw
slay
　slew
　slain
　kill; cf. **sleigh, sley**
slay¦er
Slea¦ford
sleaze
　sleaz¦ing
sleaze¦bag
sleaze¦ball
sleaz¦ily
sleazi¦ness
sleazo +s
sleazy
　sleaz¦ier
　sleazi¦est
sled
　sled¦ded
　sled¦ding
sledge
　sledg¦ing
sledge¦ham¦mer
sledger
sleek¦ly
sleek¦ness
sleeky
　sleek¦ier
　sleek¦iest
sleep
　slept
sleep¦er

sleep¦ily
sleep-in *n.*
sleepi¦ness
sleep-learning
sleep¦less
sleep¦less¦ly
sleep¦less¦ness
sleep¦out
sleep¦over
sleep¦suit
sleep¦walk
sleep¦walk¦er
sleepy
　sleep¦ier
　sleepi¦est
sleepy¦head
sleety
　sleet¦ier
　sleeti¦est
sleeved
slee¦veen
sleeve¦less
sleev¦ing
sleigh (travel on)
　sledge; cf. **slay, sley**
sleight dexterity; cf.
　slight
slen¦der
slen¦der¦ise *Br.* var.
　of **slenderize**
slen¦der¦ize
slen¦der¦iz¦ing
slen¦der¦ly
slen¦der¦ness
sleuth
sleuth-hound
slew slide violently;
　past tense of **slay**;
　large number
sley weaving tool; cf.
　slay, sleigh
slice
　sli¦cing
slice¦able
slicer
slicken¦side
slick¦er
slick¦ly
slick¦ness
slid¦able
slid¦ably
slide
　slid
　slid¦ing

slider
slide¦way
slight inconsider-
　able; slender; be
　disrespectful
　towards; instance
　of slighting; cf.
　sleight
slight¦ing¦ly
slight¦ish
slight¦ly
slight¦ness
Sligo
slily var. of **slyly**
slim
　slimmed
　slim¦ming
　slim¦mer
　slim¦mest
slime
　slim¦ing
slime¦ball
slimi¦ly
slimi¦ness
slim jim
slim¦line
slim¦ly
slim¦mer
slim¦ness
slimy
　slimi¦er
　slimi¦est
sling
　slung
sling¦back
sling¦er
sling¦shot
　past tense and
　participle
sling¦shot or
　sling¦shot¦ted
　sling¦shot¦ting
slink¦ily
slinki¦ness
slinky
　slink¦ier
　slinki¦est
slip
　slipped
　slip¦ping
slip-carriage
slip-coach
slip-on *adj. & n.*
slip¦over *n.*
slip-over *adj.*

slip¦page
slip¦per
slip¦per¦ette
　trademark in the
　US
slip¦per¦ily
slip¦peri¦ness
slip¦pery
　slip¦per¦ier
　slip¦peri¦est
slip¦pi¦ness
slippy
　slip¦pier
　slip¦pi¦est
slip¦shod
slip-slop
slip¦stone
slip¦stream
slip-up *n.*
slip¦ware
slip¦way
slit
　slit (generally)
　slit¦ted (of eyes)
　slit¦ting
slither
slith¦ery
slit¦ter
slitty
　slit¦tier
　slit¦ti¦est
Sliven
sliver
slivo¦vitz
Sloane rich young
　person
Sloane, Hans phys-
　ician
Sloaney
　Sloan¦ier
　Sloani¦est
slob
　slobbed
　slob¦bing
slob¦ber
slob¦bery
slob¦bish
slob¦bish¦ness
slobby
　slob¦bier
　slob¦bi¦est
sloe fruit; cf. **slow**
slog
　slogged

slog|ging
slo|gan
slo|gan|eer
slog|ger
sloka
slo-mo = slow motion
sloot gully
slop
slopped
slop|ping
slope
slop|ing
slop|pily
slop|pi|ness
sloppy
slop|pier
slop|pi|est
sloshy
slosh|ier
sloshi|est
slot
slot|ted
slot|ting
slot|back
sloth
sloth|ful
sloth|ful|ly
sloth|ful|ness
slouchy
slouch|ier
slouchi|est
Slough town, England
slough swamp; shed skin
sloughy
slough|ier
sloughi|est
Slo|vak
Slo|vakia
Slo|vak|ian
sloven
Slo|vene
Slo|venia
Slo|ven|ian
slov|en|li|ness
slov|en|ly
slow not fast; reduce speed; cf. **sloe**
slow|coach
slow|down
slow|ish
slow|ly

slow|ness
slow|poke
slow-worm
slub
slubbed
slub|bing
sludgy
sludgi|er
sludgi|est
slue
slu|ing
var. of **slew** (slide)
slug
slugged
slug|ging
slug|abed
slug|fest
slug|gard
slug|gard|li|ness
slug|gard|ly
slug|ger
slug|gish
slug|gish|ly
slug|gish|ness
sluice
slui|cing
sluice|way
sluit var. of **sloot**
slum
slummed
slum|ming
slum|ber
slum|ber|er
slum|ber|land
slum|ber|ous
slum|brous var. of slumberous
slum|gul|lion
slum|lord
slum|mer
slum|mi|ness
slum|mock
slummy
slum|mier
slum|miest
slumpy
slur
slurred
slur|ring
slurpy
slurry
slur|ries
slushi|ness

slushy
slush|ier
slushi|est
slut|tish
slut|tish|ness
sly
slyer
sly|est
sly|boots
slyly
sly|ness
slype covered way
smack bang
smack dab US
smack|er
smack|eroo +s
small|goods delicatessen meats
small|hold|er
small|hold|ing
small|ish
small|mouth fish
small|ness
small|pox
small-reed grass
small-timer unimportant person
smalt
smalt|ite
smarm|ily
smarmi|ness
smarmy
smarm|ier
smarmi|est
smart alec Br.
smart aleck US
smart-alecky
smart-arse Br. n.
smart-ass US n.
smart|en
smart|ing|ly
smart|ish
smart|ly
smart|ness
smart|phone
smart|weed
smarty
smart|ies
smarty-boots
smarty-pants
smash-and-grab adj. & n.
smash|er

smash|ing|ly
smash-up n.
smat|ter
smat|ter|er
smat|ter|ing
smaze smoke and haze
smear|er
smeary
smear|ier
smeari|est
smec|tic
smect|ite
smegma
smeg|mat|ic
smell
smelled or **smelt**
smell|able
smell|er
smelli|ness
smelly
smell|ier
smelli|est
smelt|er
smelt|ery
smelt|er|ies
Smersh
Smet|ana, Bed|řich composer
smet|ana sour cream
smew
smidgen
smidg|eon var. of smidgen
smidgin var. of smidgen
smi|lax
smile
smil|ing
smiler
smiley
smileys
smil|ier
smili|est
smil|ing|ly
smilo|don
smily
smilies
var. of **smiley**
smirk|er
smirk|ily
smirk|ing|ly

smirky
 smirk|ier
 smirki|est
smite
 smote
 smit|ing
 smit|ten
smiter
Smith, Adam
 economist
Smith, Bes|sie
 singer
Smith, David sculp-
 tor
Smith, Ian prime
 minister of
 Rhodesia
Smith, Jo|seph
 founder of Mormon
 Church
Smith, Ste|vie poet
Smith, Syd|ney
 churchman
Smith, Wil|liam
 geologist
smith
smith|er|eens
smith|ers
smith|ery
 smith|er|ies
Smith|field
Smith|son|ian
smith|son|ite
smithy
 smith|ies
smock-frock
smoggy
 smog|gier
 smog|gi|est
smok|able
smoke
 smok|ing
smoke|able var. of
 smokable
smoke|box
smoke-ho var. of
 smoko
smoke|house
smoke|jump|er
smoke|less
smoker
smoker's cough +s
smoke|screen
smoke|stack

smoke|stone
smokie
smoki|ly
smoki|ness
smoko +s
smoky
 smoki|er
 smoki|est
smol|der US
 Br. smoulder
smol|der|ing|ly US
 Br. smoulderingly
Smo|lensk
Smol|lett, To|bias
 novelist
smolt
smooch|er
smoochy
 smooch|ier
 smoochi|est
smoodge
 smoodg|ing
smoodger
smooge var. of
 smoodge
smooger var. of
 smoodger
smooth +s
smooth|able
smooth-bore n. &
 mod.
smoothe v. var. of
 smooth
smooth|er
smoothie
smooth|ish
smooth|ly
smooth|ness
smooth-talker
 charmer; flatterer
smoothy var. of
 smoothie
smor|gas|bord
smorz|ando
smoul|der Br.
 US smolder
smoul|der|ing|ly
 Br.
 US smolderingly
smriti
smudge
 smudg|ing
smudge|less
smudgi|ly

smudgi|ness
smudgy
 smudgi|er
 smudgi|est
smug
 smug|ger
 smug|gest
smug|gle
 smug|gling
smug|gler
smug|ly
smug|ness
smut
 smut|ted
 smut|ting
Smuts, Jan prime
 minister of South
 Africa
smut|tily
smut|ti|ness
smutty
 smut|tier
 smut|ti|est
Smyrna
Smyth, Ethel
 composer
snack|ette
snaf|fle
 snaf|fling
snafu +s +ed +ing
snag
 snagged
 snag|ging
snag|gle
 snag|gling
snaggle-tooth
 snaggle-teeth
 teeth
snaggle-tooths
 fish
snaggy
 snag|gier
 snag|gi|est
snail|fish
snail-like
snake
 snak|ing
snake|bark maple
snake|bird
snake|bite
snake|bitten
snake|board
 trademark
snake|board|er
snake|board|ing

snake|fish
snake|head fish;
 criminal
snake-like
snake|locks
 anem|one
snake|pit
snake|root
snake's head flower
snake|skin
snake|weed
snake|wood
snakey var. of snaky
snaki|ly
snaki|ness
snaky
 snaki|er
 snaki|est
snap
 snapped
 snap|ping
snap|dragon
snap-in adj.
snap-on adj.
snap|pable
snap|per
snap|pily
snap|pi|ness
snap|ping|ly
snap|pish
snap|pish|ly
snap|pish|ness
snappy
 snap|pier
 snap|pi|est
snap|shot
snare
 snar|ing
snarer
snarky
 snark|ier
 snarki|est
snarl|er
snarl|ing|ly
snarl-up n.
snarly
 snarl|ier
 snarli|est
snatch|er
snatchy
snavel
 snav|elled
 snav|el|ling

snavle
  snav|ling
  var. of snavel
snav¦vle
  snav|vling
  var. of snavel
snaz¦zily
snaz¦zi|ness
snazzy
  snaz|zier
  snaz¦zi|est
sneak|box
sneak¦er
sneak|ily
sneaki|ness
sneak|ing¦ly
sneaky
  sneak|ier
  sneaki|est
sneer¦er
sneer|ing¦ly
sneeze
  sneez|ing
sneezer
sneeze|weed
sneeze|wort
sneezy
  sneez|ier
  sneezi|est
Snel|len test
snib
  snibbed
  snib|bing
snicker
snick|er|ing¦ly
snicket
snide
  snider
  snidest
snide¦ly
snide|ness
snidey
sniff¦er
sniff|ily
sniffi|ness
snif¦fle
  snif|fling
snif|fler
snif¦fly
  snif¦flier
  snif¦fli|est
sniffy
  sniff¦ier
  sniffi|est

snif|ter
snift|ing valve
snig
  snigged
  snig|ging
snig|ger
snig|ger¦er
snig¦ger|ing¦ly
snig|gery
snig¦gle
  snig|gling
snip
  snipped
  snip|ping
snipe
  snip|ing
snipe|fish
sniper
snip|pet
snip|pety
snip|pily
snip¦pi|ness
snippy
  snip|pier
  snip¦pi|est
snivel
  sniv|elled Br.
  sniv|eled US
  sniv¦el|ling Br.
  sniv¦el|ing US
sniv¦el¦er US
sniv¦el|ing¦ly US
sniv¦el|ler Br.
sniv¦el|ling¦ly Br.
snob|bery
  snob|ber¦ies
snob|bish
snob|bish¦ly
snob¦bish|ness
snob|bism
snobby
  snob|bier
  snob|bi|est
SNOBOL computer
  language
Sno-cat trademark;
  cf. snowcat
sno-cone var. of
  snow cone
snoek fish; cf.
  snook
snog
  snogged
  snog|ging

snog|ger
snook gesture; cf.
  snoek
snoo|ker
snoop¦er
snoop¦er|scope
snoopy
snoot|ful
snoot|ily
snooti|ness
snooty
  snoot|ier
  snooti|est
snooze
  snooz|ing
snoozer
snoozy
  snooz|ier
  snoozi|est
snore
  snor|ing
snorer
Snor|kel fire-
  fighting platform
  trademark
snor|kel
  snor|kelled Br.
  snor|keled US
  snor¦kel|ling Br.
  snor¦kel|ing US
  (swim under water
  with) breathing
  tube
snor|kel¦er US
snor¦kel|ler Br.
Snorri Stur|lu|son
  Icelandic historian
snort¦er
snot|ter
snot|tily
snot¦ti|ness
snotty
  snot|tier
  snot¦ti|est
snout¦ed
snouty
  snout|ier
  snouti|est
Snow, C. P. novelist
snow
snow|ball
snow|bell
snow|berry
  snow|berries
snow|bird

snow|blade
snow|blader
snow|blad¦ing
snow-blind
snow blind|ness
snow|blink
snow|blow¦er
snow|board
snow|board¦er
snow|bound
snow|cap
snow-capped
snow|cat vehicle
  generally; cf. Sno-
  Cat trademark
snow|cock
Snow|don
Snow|donia
snow|drift
snow|drop
snow|fall
snow|field
snow|flake
snow|ily
snowi|ness
snow-in-summer
  plants
snow|less
snow|like
snow|line
snow|mak¦ing
snow|man
  snow|men
snow|melt
snow|mobile
  snow|mobil¦ing
snow|pack
snow|plough Br.
snow|plow US
snow|scape
snow|shoe
  snow|shoe|ing
snow|shoer
snow|slide
snow|storm
snow|suit
snow|sure
snowy
  snow|ier
  snowi|est
snub
  snubbed
  snub|bing

snub|ber
snuff|box
snuff|er
snuf|fle
  snuf|fling
snuff|ler
snuf|fly
  snuf|flier
  snuf|fli|est
snuffy
  snuff|ier
  snuffi|est
snug
  snugged
  snug|ging
  snug|ger
  snug|gest
snug|gery
  snug|ger|ies
snug|gle
  snug|gling
snug|ly
snug|ness
so *adv. & conj.*; cf.
  sew, soh, sow
soak drench;
  immersion;
  drinker; cf. **soke**
soak|age
soak|away *n.*
soak|er roofing
  metal; liquid for
  soaking; cf. **soca**
so-and-so +s
Soane, John
  architect
soap|berry
  soap|berries
soap|box
soap|fish
soap|ily
soapi|ness
soap|less
soap|stone
soap|suds
soap|wort
soapy
  soap|ier
  soapi|est
soar rise; cf. **saw**,
  sore
soar|away
soar|er cf. **sora**,
  sorer
soar|ing|ly

Soave
Soay sheep
sob
  sobbed
  sob|bing
soba noodles
sob|bing|ly
sober
sober|ing|ly
sober|ly
So|bers, Gary
  cricketer
sober|sided
sober|sides
Sob|ieski, John
  king of Poland
so|bri|ety
so|bri|quet
soc = sociology
soca calypso music;
  cf. **soaker**
soc|age
soc|cage var. of
  socage
soc|cer
Soc|cer|oos
Sochi
so|ci|abil|ity
so|ci|able
so|ci|able|ness
so|ci|ably
so|cial
so|cial|isa|tion *Br.*
  var. of socialization
so|cial|ise *Br.* var. of
  socialize
so|cial|ism
so|cial|ist
so|cial|is|tic
so|cial|is|tic|al|ly
so|cial|ite
so|ci|al|ity
so|cial|iza|tion
so|cial|ize
  so|cial|iz|ing
so|cial|ly
so|ci|etal
so|ci|et|al|ly
so|ci|ety
  so|ci|eties
So|cin|ian
socio|bio|logic|al
socio|bio|logic|al|ly

socio|biolo|gist
socio|biol|ogy
socio|cul|tural
socio|cul|tur|al|ly
socio|eco|logic|al
socio|ecolo|gist
socio|ecol|ogy
socio-econom|ic
socio-
  economic|al|ly
socio|lect
socio-legal
socio|lin|guist
socio|lin|guis|tic
socio|lin|guis|tic|
  al|ly
socio|logic|al
socio|logic|al|ly
soci|olo|gist
soci|ology
socio|met|ric
socio|met|ric|al|ly
soci|om|et|rist
soci|om|etry
socio|path
socio|path|ic
soci|op|athy
socio-politic|al
sock|dol|ager
socket
sock|eye
socko
socle
So|cotra
Soc|ra|tes
  philosopher
So|crat|ic
So|crat|ic|al|ly
So|cred
sod
  sod|ded
  sod|ding
soda
soda|lite
so|dal|ity
  so|dal|ities
sod|bust|er
sod|den
sod|den|ly
sod|den|ness
sodger
sodic
so|dium

Sodom
sod|om|ise *Br.* var.
  of sodomize
sod|om|ite
sod|om|it|ic
sod|om|it|ic|al
sod|om|ize
  sod|om|iz|ing
sod|omy
Sodor
so|ever
sofa
Sofar = sound fixing
  and ranging
sof|fit
Sofia capital of
  Bulgaria; cf.
  Sophia
soft
softa Muslim
  student
soft|back
soft|ball game
soft|cover book
soft|en
soft|en|er
softie
soft|ish
soft|ly
softly-softly
soft|ness
soft|shell
soft-shoe
  soft-shoeing
  (perform) tap
  dance
soft|ware
soft|wood
softy
  soft|ies
  var. of **softie**
SOGAT = Society of
  Graphical and
  Allied Trades
sog|gily
sog|gi|ness
soggy
  sog|gier
  sog|gi|est
Sogne Fjord
sogo shosha
  pl. *sogo shosha*
soh note in tonic
  sol-fa; cf. **sew**, **so**,

sow
Soho
soi-disant
soi¦gné
soi¦gnée female
soi¦gneur
soil-less
soily
soirée
soixante-neuf
so¦journ
so¦journ¦er
Soka Gak¦kai
so¦kaiya
   pl. so¦kaiya
soke district; cf.
   soak
Sokol
Sol sun as Roman
   god
sol var. of soh
sol +s *Chemistry*
sol
   soles
   Peruvian currency
sola plant; in 'sola
   topi'; alone (of
   woman); cf. solar
sol¦ace
   sol¦acing
solan
so¦lan¦aceous
so¦lan¦der
sola¦nin var. of
   solanine
sola¦nine
so¦la¦num plant
solar of the sun; cf.
   sola
so¦lar¦isa¦tion *Br.*
   var. of solarization
so¦lar¦ise *Br.* var. of
   solarize
sol¦ar¦ium
   sol¦ar¦iums or
   sol¦aria
so¦lar¦iza¦tion
so¦lar¦ize
   so¦lar¦iz¦ing
so¦la¦tium
so¦la¦tia
sold past tense and
   participle of sell
sol¦dan¦ella

sol¦der
sol¦der¦able
sol¦der¦er
soldi pl. of soldo
sol¦dier
sol¦dier¦fish
sol¦dier¦ly
sol¦dier¦ship
sol¦diery
sol¦dier¦ies
soldo
soldi
Sole shipping area,
   NE Atlantic
sole
   sol¦ing
   undersurface of
   foot; (fit) underside
   of shoe; fish;
   single; cf. soul
sole¦bar
sol¦ecist
sol¦ecis¦tic
sole¦ly
sol¦emn
sol¦em¦nisa¦tion *Br.*
   var. of
   solemnization
sol¦em¦nise *Br.* var.
   of solemnize
so¦lem¦nity
   so¦lem¦nities
sol¦em¦niza¦tion
sol¦em¦nize
   sol¦em¦niz¦ing
sol¦emn¦ly
solemn¦ness
so¦leno¦don
so¦len¦oid
so¦len¦oid¦al
So¦lent
sole¦plate
so¦lera
so¦leus
sol-fa +s +ed +ing
   Music
sol¦fa¦tara
sol¦fège *US*
sol¦feg¦gio *Br.*
   sol¦feggi
soli pl. of solo
   (*Music; Dancing*)
so¦licit
so¦lici¦ta¦tion

so¦lici¦tor
so¦lici¦tous
so¦lici¦tous¦ly
so¦lici¦tous¦ness
so¦lici¦tude
solid
soli¦dago +s
Soli¦dar¦ity Polish
   movement
soli¦dar¦ity
solid¦ary having
   solidarity
sol¦idi pl. of solidus
so¦lidi¦fi¦ca¦tion
so¦lidi¦fier
so¦lid¦ify
   so¦lidi¦fies
   so¦lidi¦fied
   so¦lidi¦fy¦ing
so¦lid¦ity
sol¦id¦ly
sol¦id¦ness
sol¦idus
sol¦idi
soli¦fluc¦tion
soli¦fuge
soli¦fugid
Soli¦hull
so¦lilo¦quise *Br.* var.
   of soliloquize
so¦lilo¦quist
so¦lilo¦quize
   so¦lilo¦quiz¦ing
so¦lilo¦quy
   so¦lilo¦quies
Soli¦man var. of
   Suleiman
sol¦ip¦sism
sol¦ip¦sist
sol¦ip¦sis¦tic
sol¦ip¦sis¦tic¦al¦ly
soli¦taire
soli¦tar¦ily
soli¦tari¦ness
soli¦tary
   soli¦tar¦ies
soli¦ton
soli¦tude
sol¦mis¦ate *Br.* var.
   of solmizate
sol¦misa¦tion *Br.*
   var. of solmization
sol¦miz¦ate
   sol¦miz¦at¦ing

sol¦miza¦tion
Soln¦hofen
solo
   pl. solos or (*Music;
   Dancing*) soli
   v. soloes
   soloed
   solo¦ing
solo¦ist
Solo¦mon king of
   Israel
Solo¦mon Gundy
Solo¦mon Gun¦dies
Solo¦mon¦ic
Solon Athenian
   statesman
So¦lo¦thurn
sol¦stice
sol¦sti¦tial
Solti, Georg con-
   ductor
solu¦bil¦isa¦tion *Br.*
   var. of
   solubilization
solu¦bil¦ise *Br.* var.
   of solubilize
solu¦bil¦ity
solu¦bil¦iza¦tion
solu¦bil¦ize
   solu¦bil¦iz¦ing
sol¦uble
so¦lunar
solus
sol¦ute
so¦lu¦tion
So¦lu¦trean
solv¦able
solv¦ate
   solv¦at¦ing
solv¦ation
Sol¦vay pro¦cess
solve
   solv¦ing
solv¦ency
solv¦ent
solv¦er
Sol¦way Firth
Soly¦man var. of
   Suleiman
Sol¦zhen¦it¦syn,
   Alek¦sandr
   novelist
som
   pl. som

Kyrgyz or Uzbek
currency
soma
som|aes|thet|ic *Br.*
US **somesthetic**
So|mali
pl. **So|mali** or
So|malis
So|ma|lia
So|ma|lian
So|ma|li|land
soman
som|at|ic
som'at|ic|al|ly
soma|tisa|tion *Br.*
var. of
somatization
soma|tiza|tion
som|ato|medin
som|ato|pleure
som|ato|sen|sory
som|ato|statin
som|ato|troph|in
som|ato|type
som|ato|typ|ing
som|ber *US*
som|ber|ly *US*
som|ber|ness *US*
som|bre *Br.*
sombre|ly *Br.*
sombre|ness *Br.*
som|brero +s
some unspecified
amount or number;
cf. **som, sum**
some|body
some day at some
time in the future
some|day var. of
some day
some|how
some|one
some|place
som|er|sault
Som|er|set
som|es|thet|ic *US*
Br. **somaesthetic**
some|thing
some|time at some
point in time
some time a certain
amount of time
some|times

some|way
some|ways
some|what
some|when
some|where
so|mite
so|mit|ic
Somme
som|mel|ier
som|nam|bu|lant
som|nam|bu|lant|ly
som|nam|bu|lism
som|nam|bu|list
som|nam|bu|lis|tic
som|nam|bu|lis|tic|
al|ly
som|nif|er|ous
som|no|lence
som|no|lency
som|no|lent
som|no|lent|ly
Som|oza,
Ana|sta|sio president of Nicaragua
son male child; cf.
sun
sonar
son|ata
sona|tina
sonde
Sond|heim,
Ste|phen composer
sone unit; cf. **sewn,**
sown
son et lu|mi|ère
Song var. of **Sung**
song
song|bird
song|book
Song|hai
pl. **Song|hai** or
Song|hais
Song|hay var. of
Songhai
songo|lolo +s
song|smith
song|ster
song|stress
song|writer
song|writ|ing
sonic
son|ic|al|ly

son|ic|ate
son|ic|at|ing
son|ic|ation
So|ninke
pl. **So|ninke** or
So|nin|kes
son-in-law
sons-in-law
son|less
son|net
son|net|eer
sonny form of
address; cf. **sunny**
sono|buoy
sono|gram
sono|graph
sono|graph|ic
son|og|raphy
sono|
lumin|es|cence
sono|lumin|es|cent
son|om|eter
Son|ora
Son|oran
son|or|ant
son|or|ity
son|or|ous
son|or|ous|ly
son|or|ous|ness
son|ship
son|sie var. of **sonsy**
sonsy
son|sier
son|si|est
Son|tag, Susan
critic
Soo|chow var. of
Suzhou
sook coward; calf;
cf. **souk**
sool
sool|er
soon|ish
sooth truth
soothe
sooth|ing
calm; ease pain
sooth|er
sooth|ing|ly
sooth|say|er
sooth|say|ing
soot|ily
sooti|ness

sooty
soot|ier
sooti|est
sop
sopped
sop|ping
so|pai|pilla
So|phia name; in 'St
Sophia'; cf. **Sofia**
So|phie name; cf.
Sophy
soph|ism
soph|ist
so|phis|tic
so|phis|tic|al
so|phis|tic|al|ly
so|phis|ti|cate
so|phis|ti|cat|ing
so|phis|ti|cated|ly
so|phis|ti|ca|tion
soph|is|try
soph|is|tries
Sopho|clean
Sopho|cles Greek
dramatist
sopho|more
sopho|mor|ic
Sophy
So|phies
ruler of Persia; cf.
Sophie
sop|or|if|ic
sop|or|if|ic|al|ly
sop|pily
sop|pi|ness
soppy
sop|pier
sop|pi|est
sop|ra|nino +s
sop|rano +s
Sop|with, Thomas
aircraft designer
sora bird; cf. **soarer,**
sorer
Sorb person
sorb fruit
sor|bent
sor|bet
Sorb|ian
sorb|itol
Sorbo *trademark*
Sor|bonne
sor|bus

sor|cer|er
sor|cer|ess
sor|cer|ous
sor|cery
sor|did
sor|did|ly
sor|did|ness
sor|dino
  sor|dini
sor|dor
sore
  sorer
  sor|est
  painful; vexed;
  painful place; cf.
  saw, soar, soarer,
  sora
sore|head
sorel deer; cf. sorrel
sore|ly
sore|ness
sor|ghum
sori pl. of sorus
Sor|op|ti|mist
sor|oral
sor|or|ity
  sor|or|ities
sor|osis
  sor|oses
  multiple fruit; cf.
  cirrhosis
sorp|tion
sor|rel plant; drink;
  horse; cf. sorel
Sor|rento
sor|rily
sor|ri|ness
sor|row
sor|row|er
sor|row|ful
sor|row|ful|ly
sor|row|ful|ness
sorry
  sor|rier
  sor|ri|est
sort category;
  arrangement of
  data; arrange; cf.
  sought
sort|able
sor|tal
sort|er
sor|tes divination
sor|tes Bib|li|cae

sor|tie
  sor|tie|ing
sor|ti|lege
sor|ti|tion
sort-out *n.*
sorus
  sori
so|satie
Sos|no|wiec
so-so neither good
  nor bad
sos|ten|uto +s
sot
  sot|ted
  sot|ting
so|terio|logic|al
so|teri|ology
So|thic
Sotho
  pl. Sotho or
  So|thos
sotol
sot|tish
sotto voce
sou former French
  coin; very small
  sum; cf. sue, xu
sou' = south
sou|bise
sou|bre|saut
sou|brette
sou|bri|quet var. of
  sobriquet
sou|chong
sou|cou|yant
souf|fle murmur
  heard through
  stethoscope
souf|flé food
Sou|frière
sough moan;
  whistle; cf. sow
sought past tense
  and participle of
  seek; cf. sort
souk market; cf.
  sook
sou|kous
soul spirit; music;
  person; cf. sole
souled
soul|ful
soul|ful|ly
soul|ful|ness

soul|less
soul|less|ly
soul|less|ness
soul|mate
soul|ster
Sou|mak
sound|alike
sound|board
sound|box
sound|check
sound|clash
sound|er
sound|hole
sound|ing
sound|less
sound|less|ly
sound|less|ness
sound|ly
sound|ness
sound|proof
sound|scape
sound|track
soup liquid food;
  increase power
soup|çon
souped-up *adj.*
soup|ily
soupi|ness
soupy
  soup|ier
  soupi|est
source
  sour|cing
source|book
sour|dough
sour|ish
sour|ly
sour|ness
sour|puss
sour|sop
sour|veld
sour|wood
Sousa, John Philip
  composer
sousa|phone
sousa|phon|ist
souse
  sous|ing
sous|lik
Sousse
sous vide
sou|tache
sou|tane

sou|tar var. of
  souter
sou|ten|eur
souter shoemaker;
  cf. suiter, suitor
sou|ter|rain
South|amp|ton
south|bound
South|down sheep
South Downs hills,
  England
south-east
south|easter
south-easter|ly
  south-easter|lies
south-eastern
south-eastward
south-eastwards
Southend-on-Sea
south|er|ly
  south|er|lies
south|ern
South|ern blot
south|ern|er
south|ern|most
south|ern|wood
Southey, Rob|ert
  poet
south|ing
south|paw
South|port
south-south-east
south-south-west
south|ward
south|ward|ly
south|wards
south-west
South West
  Af|rica
south|wester wind;
  cf. sou'wester
south-wester|ly
  south-wester|lies
south-western
south-westward
south-westwards
Sou|tine, Chaim
  painter
sou|venir
souv|laki
  souv|la|kia or
  souv|la|kis

sou'|wester hat; cf.
  southwester
sov|er|eign
sov|er|eign|ly
sov|er|eign|ty
  sov|er|eign|ties
So|viet (citizen) of
  Soviet Union
so|viet council
So|viet|isa|tion Br.
  var. of
  Sovietization
So|viet|ise Br. var.
  of Sovietize
So|viet|ism
So|viet|iza|tion
So|viet|ize
  So|viet|iz|ing
So|vieto|logic|al
So|viet|olo|gist
So|viet|ology
sov|khoz
  pl. sov|khoz or
  sov|khozes or
  sov|khozy
sow
  past participle
  sown or sowed
  plant seed etc.; cf.
  sew, so, soh
sow female pig; cf.
  sough
sow|back
sow|bread
sower person who
  sows; cf. sewer
So|wetan
So|weto
sown past participle
  of sow; cf. sewn
sow|this|tle
Sox US = Socks in
  team names
Soxh|let
soya
soy|bean
Soy|inka, Wole
  writer
Soyuz
soz|zled
Spa town, Belgium
spa spring; cf. spar
space
  spa|cing

space|craft
  pl. space|craft
space|farer
space|faring
space-heated
space heat|er
space heat|ing
space|hop|per
  trademark
space|man
  space|men
space|plane
space|port
spa|cer
space|ship
space|suit
space|walk
  space|walk|er
space|woman
  space|women
spacey
  spaci|er
  spaci|est
spa|cial var. of
  spatial
spa|cial|ity var. of
  spatiality
spa|cial|ly var. of
  spatially
spa|cious
spa|cious|ly
spa|cious|ness
spackle trademark
  spack|ling
spacy var. of spacey
spade
  spad|ing
spade|fish
spade|foot +s toad
spade foot
  spade feet
  bottom of chair leg
spade|ful
spade|work
spa|di|ceous
spa|dille
spa|dix
  spa|di|ces
spae
  spae|ing
  foretell; cf. spay
spaetzle
spae|wife
  spae|wives

spa|ghetti
spa|ghetti|fi|cation
spa|ghet|tini
spa|gyr|ic
spahi
Spain
spall
spal|la|tion
spal|peen
spalt|ed
spam
  spammed
  spam|ming
  tinned meat (trade-
  mark); (send)
  unwanted Internet
  messages
spam|mer
span
  spanned
  span|ning
spana|ko|pita
span|dex trademark
span|drel
span|gle
  span|gling
Span|glish
span|gly
  span|glier
  span|gli|est
Span|iard
span|iel
Span|ish
Spanish-American
  n. & adj.
Span|ish|ness
spank|er
spank|ing
span|ner
spans|pek
span|sule
  trademark
span-worm
spar
  sparred
  spar|ring
  fight; dispute; pole;
  mineral; cf. spa
spar|able nail
spa|rag|mos
spa|raxis
spare
  spar|ing
  sparer

spar|est
spare|ly
spare|ness
sparge
  spar|ging
spar|ger
sparid
spar|ing|ly
spar|ing|ness
Spark, Mur|iel
  novelist
spark
spark|ish
spar|kle
  spark|ling
  spark|ler
  spark|less
  spark|ling|ly
  sparkly
  spark|lier
  sparkli|est
sparky
  spark|ies
  spark|ier
  sparki|est
spar|ling
spar|row
spar|row|hawk
sparry
sparse
  sparser
  spars|est
sparse|ly
sparse|ness
spars|ity
Sparta
Spar|ta|cist
Spar|ta|cus gladi-
  ator
Spar|tan (citizen) of
  Sparta; apple
spar|tan austere
spar|tina
spasm
spas|mod|ic
spas|mod|ic|al|ly
spas|mo|lyt|ic
spas|mo|phile
spas|mo|philia
Spassky, Boris
  chess player
spas|tic often
  offensive
spas|tic|al|ly

spas|ti|city
spat
  spat|ted
  spat|ting
spatch|cock
spate
spa|tha|ceous
spathe
spa|tial
spa|tial|isa|tion *Br.*
  var. of
  spatialization
spa|tial|ise *Br.* var.
  of spatialize
spa|ti|al|ity
spa|tial|iza|tion
spa|tial|ize
  spa|tial|iz|ing
spa|tial|ly
spatio-temporal
spatio-tempor|al|ly
Spät|lese
  Spät|leses or
  Spät|lesen
spat|ter
spat|ter|dash
spat|ter|dock
spat|ter|ware
spat|ula
spatu|late
spätzle var. of
  spaetzle
spavin
spav|ined
spawn
spawn|er
spay sterilize; cf.
  spae
spaz *offensive*
  spazes
  spazzed
  spaz|zing
spaza
spazz var. of spaz
  offensive
speak
  spoke
  spoken
speak|able
speak|easy
  speak|easies
Speak|er parlia-
  mentary presiding
  officer

speak|er person
  who speaks;
  loudspeaker
speak|er|phone
Speak|er|ship
spear|fish
spear|grass
spear|gun
spear|head
spear|man
  spear|men
Spear|man's rank
  cor|rel|ation
spear|mint
spear|wort
spec
  specced
  spec|cing
  in 'on spec'; (give)
  specification;
  (*specs*) spectacles;
  cf. speck
speccy var. of
  specky
spe|cial
spe|cial|isa|tion *Br.*
  var. of
  specialization
spe|cial|ise *Br.* var.
  of specialize
spe|cial|ism
spe|cial|ist
spe|cial|is|tic
spe|ci|al|ity
  spe|ci|al|ities
spe|cial|iza|tion
spe|cial|ize
  spe|cial|iz|ing
spe|cial|ly
spe|cial|ness
spe|cial|ty
  spe|cial|ties
spe|ci|ate
  spe|ci|at|ing
spe|ci|ation
spe|cie coins
spe|cies
  pl. spe|cies
  category
spe|cies|ism
spe|cies|ist
spe|ci|fi|able
spe|cif|ic
spe|cif|ic|al|ly

spe|ci|fi|ca|tion
spe|ci|fi|city
spe|cif|ic|ness
spe|ci|fier
spe|cify
  spe|ci|fies
  spe|ci|fied
  spe|ci|fy|ing
spe|ci|men
spe|ci|os|ity
spe|cious
spe|cious|ly
spe|cious|ness
speck spot; smoked
  ham; cf. spec
speckle
  speck|ling
speck|less
specky
specs = spectacles
spec|tacle
spec|tacled
spec|tacu|lar
spec|tacu|lar|ly
spec|tate
  spec|tat|ing
spec|ta|tor
spec|ta|tor|ial
spec|ter *US*
  Br. spectre
spec|tino|mycin
Spec|tor, Phil
  record producer
spec|tra pl. of
  spectrum
spec|tral
spec|tral|ly
spectre *Br.*
  US specter
spec|tro|
    chem|is|try
spec|tro|gram
spec|tro|graph
spec|tro|graph|ic
spec|tro|graph|ic|
    al|ly
spec|trog|raphy
spec|tro|helio|
    graph
spec|tro|helio|
    scope
spec|tro|lite
spec|trom|eter
spec|tro|met|ric

spec|trom|etry
spec|tro|
    pho|tom|eter
spec|tro|photo|
    met|ric
spec|tro|photo|
    met|ric|al|ly
spec|tro|
    pho|tom|etry
spec|tro|scope
spec|tro|scop|ic
spec|tro|scop|ic|
    al|ly
spec|tros|co|pist
spec|tros|copy
spec|trum
  spec|tra
spec|ula pl. of
  speculum
specu|lar of a
  speculum
specu|late
  specu|lat|ing
specu|la|tion
specu|la|tive
specu|la|tive|ly
specu|la|tive|ness
specu|la|tor
specu|lum
  spec|ula
speech|ful
speech|ifi|ca|tion
speechi|fier
speech|ify
  speechi|fies
  speechi|fied
  speechi|fy|ing
speech|less
speech|less|ly
speech|less|ness
speed
  sped
  moved quickly
  speed|ed
  other senses
speed|ball
speed|boat
speed|er
speed|ily
speedi|ness
Speedo +s swim-
  ming costume
  trademark

speedo +s =
  speedometer
speed|om|eter
speed-reader
speed|ster
speed-up n.
speed|way
speed|well
speed|writer
speed|writing
  trademark
speedy
  speed|ier
  speedi|est
Speen|ham|land
Speer, Al¦bert Nazi
  official
speiss metallic
  compound; cf.
  spice
spek|boom
Speke, John
  explorer
speleo|logic|al
spele|olo|gist
spele|ology
spe¦leo|them
spell
  spelled
  Br. also spelt
spell|bind
  spell|bound
spell|bind|er
spell|bind|ing|ly
spell|check
spell|check¦er
spell¦er
spelt *Br.* var. of
  spelled
spel|ter
spe|lunk|er
spe|lunk|ing
Spence, Basil
  architect
Spen|cer, Her¦bert
  philosopher
Spen|cer, Stan|ley
  painter
spen|cer garment;
  sail
Spen|cer|ian
  of style of
  handwriting; cf.
  Spenserian

spend
  spent
spend|able
Spen|der, Ste¦phen
  poet
spend¦er
spend|thrift
spendy
  spend¦ier
  spendi¦est
Spen|gler, Os¦wald
  philosopher
Spen|ser, Ed¦mund
  poet
Spen¦ser|ian of
  Spenser; cf.
  Spencerian
sperm
  pl. sperm or
  sperms
sperma|ceti
sperma|cet¦ic
sperma|theca
  sperma|the¦cae
sperm|at¦ic
sperm¦at|ic|al¦ly
sperm|atid
sperm¦at|id¦al
sperm¦ato|cyte
sperm¦ato|gen¦esis
sperm¦ato|gen|et¦ic
sperm¦ato|gon¦ial
sperm¦ato|gon|ium
  sperm¦ato|gonia
sperm¦ato|phore
sperm¦ato|phor¦ic
sperm¦ato|phyte
sperm¦ato|zoal
sperm¦ato|zoan
  adj.
sperm¦ato|zoid
sperm¦ato|zoon n.
  sperm¦ato|zoa
spermi|cidal
spermi|cidal¦ly
spermi|cide
spermi|dine
sperm|ine
spes¦sart|ine
spew¦er
Spey river, Scotland
sphag|num
sphal¦er|ite
sphene mineral

sphen|oid
sphen|oid¦al
sphen|op¦sid
Sphen|op¦sida
spheral
sphere
  spher¦ing
spher¦ic
spher|ic¦al
spher¦ic|al¦ly
spher¦icity
spher|oid
spher|oid¦al
spher¦oid|icity
sphero|plast
spher|ular
spher|ule
spher¦ul|ite
spher¦ul|it¦ic
sphinc|ter
sphinc|ter¦al
sphinc|ter¦ic
sphin|gid
sphingo|lipid
sphingo|mye¦lin
sphingo|sine
Sphinx monster;
  statue; cf. Sphynx
sphinx enigmatic
  person; hawkmoth;
  cf. Sphynx
sphyg|mo|graph
sphyg|mo|graph¦ic
sphyg|mo|graph¦ic|
      al¦ly
sphyg|mog|raphy
sphyg|mo|logic¦al
sphyg|mol|ogy
sphyg|mo|
  man¦om|eter
sphyg|mo|mano|
     met¦ric
sphyg|mo|
  man¦om|etry
Sphynx cat; cf.
  Sphinx, sphinx
spic *offensive*
  Hispanic; cf. spic
  and span
Spica star
spica bandage
spic and span var.
  of spick and span

spi|cate
spi|cated
spic|cato
spice
  spi¦cing
  flavouring etc.; cf.
  speiss
spice|bush
spicey var. of spicy
spici¦ly
spici|ness
spick and span
spicu|lar
spicu|late
spicu|la¦tion
spic|ule
spicy
  spi¦cier
  spici¦est
spider
spider|ish
spider|man
  spider|men
spider|web
  spider|webbed
  spider|web|bing
spider|wort
spi¦dery
spie¦gel|eisen
spiel
Spiel|berg, Ste¦ven
  film director
spiel¦er
spiff|ily
spif¦fli|cate
spif¦fli|cat|ing
spif¦fli|ca¦tion
spiffy
  spiff|ier
  spiffi|est
spif¦li|cate var. of
  spifflicate
spif¦li|ca¦tion var.
  of spifflication
spig|nel
spigot
spike
  spik¦ing
spike|let
spike|moss
spike|nard
spiki¦ly
spiki|ness

spiky
  spiki|er
  spiki|est
spile
  spil|ing
spi|lite
spi|lit|ic
spill
  spilled
  Br. also spilt
spill|age
Spil|lane, Mickey
  writer
spill|er
spilli|kin
spill|over *n.*
spill|way
spilt *Br.* var. of
  spilled
spin
  past tense spun or
  span
  spin|ning
spina bif|ida
spin|ach
spin|achy
spinal *of the spine;*
  cf. spinel
spinal|ly
spin|dle
spindle-shanks
spindly
  spind|lier
  spind|li|est
spin-down *n.*
spin drier var. of
  spin dryer
spin|drift
spin-dry
  spin-dries
  spin-dried
  spin-drying
spin dryer
spined
spi|nel *mineral; cf.*
  spinal
spine|less
spine|less|ly
spine|less|ness
spi|net
spine|tail
spini|fex
spini|fex|bird
spini|ness

spin|meis|ter
spin|naker
spin|ner
spin|ner|bait
spin|neret
spin|ney
spinny
  spin|nier
  spin|ni|est
spin-off *n. & mod.*
Spi|none
  Spi|noni
spin|ose
spin|ous
spin-out *n. & mod.*
Spin|oza, Bar|uch
  de *philosopher*
Spin|oz|ism
Spin|oz|ist
Spin|oz|is|tic
spin-stabil|isa|tion
  Br. var. of spin-
  stabilization
spin-stabil|iza|tion
spin|ster
spin|ster|hood
spin|ster|ish
spin|ster|ish|ness
spin|thari|scope
spinto +s
spinu|lose
spiny
  spini|er
  spini|est
spir|acle
spir|acu|lar
spir|acu|lum
  spir|acula
spir|aea *Br.*
  US spirea
spiral
  spir|alled *Br.*
  spir|aled *US*
  spiral|ling *Br.*
  spiral|ing *US*
spiral|ity
spir|al|ly
spir|ant
spir|ant|isa|tion *Br.*
  var. of
  spirantization
spir|ant|ise *Br.* var.
  of spirantize
spir|ant|iza|tion

spir|ant|ize
  spir|ant|iz|ing
spire
  spir|ing
spirea *US*
  Br. spiraea
spir|il|lum
  spir|illa
spirit
spir|it|ed|ly
spir|it|ed|ness
spir|it|ism
spir|it|ist
spir|it|ist|ic
spir|it|less
spir|it|less|ly
spir|it|less|ness
spir|it|ous
spir|it|ual *of the*
  spirit or soul; song;
  cf. **spirituel**
spir|itu|al|isa|tion
  Br. var. of
  spiritualization
spir|itu|al|ise *Br.*
  var. of spiritualize
spir|itu|al|ism
spir|itu|al|ist
spir|itu|al|is|tic
spir|itu|al|ity
  spir|itu|al|ities
spir|itu|al|iza|tion
spir|itu|al|ize
  spir|itu|al|iz|ing
spir|itu|al|ly
spir|itu|al|ness
spiri|tuel *witty; cf.*
  spiritual
spiri|tu|elle *witty*
  female
spir|itu|ous
spir|itus
spiro|chaete *Br.*
spiro|chete *US*
Spiro|graph
  trademark toy
spiro|graph
  recording
  instrument
spiro|graph|ic
spiro|graph|ic|al|ly
spiro|gyra
spir|om|eter
spir|om|etry

spir|ono|lac|tone
spiru|lina
spiry
  spir|ier
  spiri|est
spit
  spat or spit
  spit|ting
  eject saliva etc.;
  spatter; rain lightly;
  point of land
spit
  spit|ted
  spit|ting
  (cook on) skewer
spit
  pl. spit or spits
  spade-depth
spit|ball
spit|ball|er
spitch|cock
spite
  spit|ing
spite|ful
spite|ful|ly
spite|ful|ness
spit|fire
Spit|head
Spits|ber|gen
spit|ter
spit|tle
spittle|bug
spit|tly
spit|toon
spitty
spitz *dog*
spiv|vish
spivvy
  spiv|vier
  spiv|vi|est
splanch|nic
splan|chno|pleure
splash|back *n.*
splash|board
splash|down *n.*
splashy
  splash|ier
  splashi|est
splat
  splat|ted
  splat|ting
splat|ter
splat|ter|punk

splay-foot
 splay-feet
spleen|ful
spleen|wort
splen|dent
splen|did
splen|did|ly
splen|did|ness
splen|dif|er|ous
splen|dif|er|ous|ly
splen|dif|er|ous|
 ness
splen|dor US
splen|dour Br.
splen|ec|tomy
 splen|ec|to|mies
splen|et|ic
splen|et|ic|al|ly
sple|nial
splen|ic
splen|itis
sple|nium
 sple|nia
sple|nius
 sple|nii
splen|oid
spleno|meg|aly
splice
 spli|cing
spli|cer
spline
 splin|ing
splin|ter
splin|tery
Split port, Croatia
split
 split|ting
split|ter
split|tism
split|tist
splodge
 splodg|ing
splodgy
 splodgi|er
 splodgi|est
splotchy
 splotch|ier
 splotchi|est
splurge
 splur|ging
splut|ter
splut|ter|er
splut|ter|ing|ly

Spock, Dr
 Ben|ja|min paedia-
 trician
spoddy
 spod|dier
 spod|di|est
spod|ic
spod|osol
spodu|mene
spoil
 spoiled
 Br. also spoilt
spoil|age
spoil|er
spoils|man
 spoils|men
spoil|sport
spoilt Br. var. of
 spoiled
Spo|kane
spoke
 spok|ing
spoken
spoke|shave
 spoke|shav|ing
spokes|man
 spokes|men
spokes|model
spokes|per|son
 spokes|per|sons or
 spokes|people
spokes|woman
 spokes|women
spoke|wise
Spo|leto
spoli|ation
spoli|ator
spoli|atory
spon|da|ic
spon|dee
spon|du|licks
spon|du|lix var. of
 spondulicks
spon|dyl|itis
spon|dyl|osis
sponge
 spon|ging or
 sponge|ing
sponge|able
sponge-like
spon|ger
spongey var. of
 spongy
spongi|form

spon|gily
spon|gin
spon|gi|ness
spongy
 spon|gier
 spon|gi|est
spon|son
spon|sor
spon|sor|ial
spon|sor|ship
spon|tan|eity
spon|tan|eous
spon|tan|eous|ly
spon|tan|eous|ness
spoof|er
spoof|ery
spook|ily
spooki|ness
spooky
 spook|ier
 spooki|est
spool
spoon|bill
spoon|er
spoon|er|ism
spoon|ful
spoon|ily
spooni|ness
spoon|worm
spoony
 spoon|ies
 spoon|ier
 spooni|est
spoor
spoor|er
Spora|des
spor|ad|ic
spor|ad|ic|al|ly
spor|an|gial
spor|angio|phore
spor|an|gium
 spor|an|gia
spore
sporo|cyst
sporo|gen|esis
spor|ogen|ous
spor|ogony
sporo|phore
sporo|phyte
sporo|phyt|ic
sporo|phyt|ic|al|ly
Sporo|zoa
sporo|zoan

sporo|zo|ite
spor|ran
sport|er
spor|tif interested
 in sport; for sports;
 cf. sportive
sport|ily
sporti|ness
sport|ing|ly
sport|ive playful; cf.
 sportif
sport|ive|ly
sport|ive|ness
sports|cast
sports|cast|er
sports|man
 sports|men
sports|man|like
sports|man|ly
sports|man|ship
sports|per|son
 sports|per|sons or
 sports|people
sport|ster
sports|wear
sports|woman
 sports|women
sports|woman|ship
sporty
 sport|ier
 sporti|est
sporu|late
 sporu|lat|ing
sporu|la|tion
spot
 spot|ted
 spot|ting
spot|lamp
spot|less
spot|less|ly
spot|less|ness
spot|light
 spot|light|ed or
 spot|lit
spot on adj. & adv.
spot|ted|ness
spot|ter
spot|tily
spot|ti|ness
spotty
 spot|tier
 spot|ti|est
spot-welder
spou|sal

spouse
spout¦er
spout|less
Sprach\ge¦fühl
sprad¦dle
sprad|dling
sprat
sprat|ted
sprat|ting
Spratly Is¦lands
sprauncy
spraun|cier
spraun|ci|est
sprawl|ing¦ly
spray|able
spray|deck
spray-dryer
spray¦er
sprayey
spray|skirt
spread|able
spread|eagle
spread|eag¦ling
spread eagle *n.*
spread¦er
spread|sheet
Sprech\ge¦sang
Sprech\stimme
spree
  spreed
  spree|ing
spreite
  sprei¦ten or
  spreites
  pattern in burrow
  of fossil; cf. sprite
sprew bird; cf.
  sprue
sprez¦za|tura
sprig
  sprigged
  sprig|ging
spriggy
  sprig|gier
  sprig|gi|est
spright|li|ness
spright¦ly
  spright|lier
  spright|li|est
spring
  sprang
  spring|ing
  sprung
spring|board
spring|bok

spring|buck
  S. African var. of
  springbok
spring¦er
Spring|field
spring|haas
spring|hare
spring|ily
springi|ness
spring|less
spring|let
spring|like
Spring|steen,
  Bruce musician
spring|tail
spring|tide spring-
  time
spring tide tide of
  greatest range
spring|time
springy
  spring|ier
  springi|est
sprin¦kle
  sprink|ling
  sprink|ler
sprint¦er
sprite elf; computer
  graphic; flash in
  atmosphere; cf.
  spreite
sprite¦li|ness var. of
  sprightliness
sprite¦ly var. of
  sprightly
sprit|sail
spritz
spritz¦er
sprocket
sprog
  sprogged
  sprog|ging
spros|ser
spruce
  spru|cing
  spru¦cer
  spru¦cest
spruce¦ly
spruce|ness
spru¦cer
sprue channel in
  mould; disease;
  asparagus; s. grass;
  cf. sprew

spruik
spruik¦er
spruit watercourse
spry +er +est
spry¦ly
spry|ness
spud
  spud|ded
  spud|ding
spu|mante
spume
  spum|ing
spu|mone var. of
  spumoni
spu|moni
spu|mous
spumy
  spumi¦er
  spumi|est
spunk|ily
spunki|ness
spunky
  spunk|ier
  spunki|est
spur
  spurred
  spur|ring
spur-dog fish
spur|fowl
spuri|ous
spuri|ous¦ly
spuri|ous|ness
spur|less
spurn
spurn¦er
spur|rey
spurry
  spur|ries
  var. of spurrey
spurt
sput|nik
sput|ter
sput|ter¦er
spu¦tum
spy
  spies
  spied
  spy¦ing
spy|glass
spy|hole
spy|master
spy|ware
squab

squab¦ble
squab|bling
squab|bler
squad
squad|die
squaddy var. of
  squaddie
squad|ron
squala|mine
squa¦lene
squalid
squal|id|ity
squal|id¦ly
squal¦id|ness
squally
  squall|ier
  squalli|est
squalor
Squa|mata
squa|mate
squamo|
  col¦um|nar
squamo|sal
squa|mous
squa|mule
squa¦mu|lose
squan|der
squan|der¦er
square
  squar¦ing
  squarer
  squar¦est
square dance *n.*
square-dance *v.*
  square-dancing
square dan¦cer
square¦head
  offensive
square-headed
square¦ly
square|ness
squarer
square-rigger
square|tail fish
squar¦ish
squark
squash
  pl. (of vegetable)
  squash or
  squashes
squash|berry
squash|berries
squash|ily
squashi|ness

squashy
squash|ier
squashi|est
squat
squat|ted
squat|ting
cf. squatt
squat|ly
squat|ness
squatt larva used in
angling; cf. squat
squat|ter
squaw
squaw|fish
squawk|er
squaw|root
squeak|er
squeak|ily
squeaki|ness
squeaky
squeak|ier
squeaki|est
squeaky clean
squeal|er
squeam|ish
squeam|ish|ly
squeam|ish|ness
squee|gee
squee|geed
squee|gee|ing
squeez|able
squeeze
squeez|ing
squeezer
squeezy
squelch|er
squelchy
squelch|ier
squelchi|est
squib
squibbed
squib|bing
SQUID =
superconducting
quantum interfer-
ence device
squid sea creature
pl. squid or squids
v. squids
squid|ded
squid|ding
squidge
squidg|ing
squidgy
squidgi|er

squidgi|est
squiffed
squiffy
squif|fier
squif|fi|est
squig|gle
squig|gling
squig|gly
squig|glier
squig|gli|est
squil|lion
squin|ancy|wort
squint|er
squinty
squint|ier
squinti|est
squire
squir|ing
squire|arch +s
squire|arch|ical
squire|archy
squire|arch|ies
squire|dom
squir|een
squire|hood
squire|let
squire|ling
squire|ly
squire|ship
squirm|er
squirmy
squirm|ier
squirmi|est
squir|rel
squir|relled Br.
squir|reled US
squir|rel|ling Br.
squir|rel|ing US
squir|rel|fish
squir|rel|ly
squirt|er
squishy
squish|ier
squishi|est
squit|ters
squiz
squiz|zes
squizzed
squiz|zing
Sra|nan
Sre|bre|nica
Sri var. of Shri
Sri Lanka
Sri Lan|kan

Sri|nagar
stab
stabbed
stab|bing
Sta|bat Mater
stab|ber
sta|bil|ator
sta|bile
sta|bil|isa|tion Br.
var. of stabilization
sta|bil|ise Br. var. of
stabilize
sta|bil|iser Br. var.
of stabilizer
sta|bil|ity
sta|bil|iza|tion
sta|bil|ize
sta|bil|iz|ing
sta|bil|izer
stable
stab|ling
stab|ler
stab|lest
Stable|ford
stable|ful
stable|man
stable|men
stable|mate
stab|lish
sta|bly
stac|cato +s
Sta|cey
stack|able
stack|er
stack|yard
stad|dle
stad|hold|er var. of
stadtholder
stad|hold|er|ship
var. of
stadtholdership
sta|dium
sta|diums or
sta|dia
stadt|hold|er
stadt|hold|er|ship
Staël, Mme de
writer
staff +s personnel;
stick; building
material; provide
with staff; cf. staph
staff
staffs or staves

Music; cf. staph
Staffa
staff|age
staff|er
Staf|ford
Staf|ford|shire
staff|room
stag
stagged
stag|ging
stage
sta|ging
stage|abil|ity
stage|able
stage|coach
stage|craft
stage|hand
stager
stagey var. of stagy
stag|fla|tion
stag|ger
stag|ger|er
stag|ger|ing|ly
stag|horn
stag|hound
stagi|ly
stagi|ness
stag|nancy
stag|nant
stag|nant|ly
stag|nate
stag|nat|ing
stag|na|tion
stagy
stagi|er
stagi|est
staid sedate; cf.
stayed
staid|ly
staid|ness
stain|able
Stain|er, John
composer
stain|er
stain|less
stair set of steps; cf.
stare
stair|case
stair|climb|er
stair|head
stair|lift
stair|way
stair|well

staithe
stake
  stak¦ing
  (support with)
  post; bet; cf. **steak**
stake|build¦ing
stake|hold¦er
stake|hold¦ing
stake-out *n.*
staker
Stakh¦an¦ov|ism
Stakh¦an¦ov|ist
Stakh¦an¦ov|ite
stal¦ac|tic
stal¦ac|ti|form
stal¦ac|tite
stal¦ac|tit¦ic
Stalag
stal¦ag|mite
stal¦ag|mit¦ic
stale
  stal¦ing
  staler
  stal¦est
stale¦ly
stale|mate
  stale|mat¦ing
stale|ness
Sta¦lin, Jo¦seph
  Soviet leader
Sta¦lin|abad
Sta¦lin|grad
Sta¦lin|ism
Sta¦lin|ist
Sta¦lino
stalk stem of plant
  etc.; pursue
  stealthily; cf. **stork**
stalk¦er
stalk|less
stalk-like
stalky
  stalk¦ier
  stalki¦est
stall|age
stall|hold¦er
stal|lion
stal|wart
stal|wart¦ly
stal|wart|ness
Stam|boul
sta¦men
stam|ina

stam¦in|ate
stam¦in|ifer|ous
stam¦in|ode
stam|mer
stam|mer¦er
stam|mer|ing¦ly
stam|pede
  stam|ped¦ing
stam|peder
stamp¦er
stanch var. of
  staunch
stan|chion
stanch¦ly var. of
  staunchly
stanch|ness var. of
  staunchness
stand
  stood
stand|ard
Stand¦ard|bred
stand¦ard|is|able
  Br. var. of
  standardizable
stand¦ard|isa¦tion
  Br. var. of
  standardization
stand¦ard|ise *Br.*
  var. of **standardize**
stand¦ard|iser *Br.*
  var. of
  standardizer
stand¦ard|iz|able
stand¦ard|iza¦tion
stand¦ard|ize
  stand¦ard|iz¦ing
stand¦ard|izer
stand|ard¦ly
stand¦by +s
stand-down *n.*
stand¦ee
stand¦er
stand-in *n. & mod.*
stand|ish
stand-off *n. & mod.*
stand-offish
stand-offish¦ly
stand-offish|ness
stand|out
stand|pipe
stand|point
stand|still
stand-to *n.*

stand-up *adj. & n.*
Stan|ford university,
  US
Stan|ford, Charles
  composer
Stan|hope, Lady
  Hes¦ter traveller
stan|hope carriage
Stan|ier, Will|iam
  railway engineer
Stan¦is|laus patron
  saint of Poland
Stan¦is|lav¦sky,
  Kon¦stan|tin
  theatre director
stank
Stan|ley, Henry
  Mor¦ton explorer
Stan|ley, Mt
Stanley, Port
Stan|ley knife
  trademark
Stan¦ley|ville
stan|nary
  stan|nar¦ies
stan|nate
stan|nic
stan|nous
Stan|sted
stanza
stan|zaed
stan|za¦ic
sta|pe¦dial
sta|pelia
stapes
  pl. stapes
staph
  = staphylococcus;
  cf. **staff**
staph¦yl|in¦id
staphylo|coc¦cal
staphylo|coc¦cus
  staphylo|cocci
staple
  stapl¦ing
stap¦ler
star
  starred
  star|ring
Stara Za¦gora
star|board
star|burst
starch¦er
starch|ily

starchi|ness
starchy
  starch¦ier
  starchi¦est
Starck, Phi¦lippe
  interior designer
star|dom
star|dust
stare
  star¦ing
  gaze fixedly; cf.
  stair
stare de¦ci¦sis
starer
star|fish
star|flower
star|fruit
  pl. star|fruit or
  star|fruits
star|gaze
star|gaz¦ing
star|gazer
star|gazy pie
stark
Stark ef¦fect
stark|ers
stark¦ly
stark|ness
star|less
star|let
star|light
star|like
star|ling
star|lit
Starr, Ringo drum-
  mer
star|rer
star|rily
star|ri|ness
starry
  star|rier
  star¦ri|est
star|ship
START = Strategic
  Arms Reduction
  Talks
start begin;
  beginning
start¦er
star¦tle
  start|ling
start|ler
start|ling¦ly
start-up *n. & mod.*

star|va|tion
starve
  starv|ing
starve|ling
star|wort
Stasi
sta|sis
  sta|ses
stat|able
sta|tant
state
  stat|ing
state|craft
state|hood
state|less
state|less|ness
state|let
state|li|ness
state|ly
  state|lier
  state|li|est
state|ment
Staten Is|land
sta|ter coin; cf.
  stator
state|room
state|side
states|man
  states|men
states|man|like
states|man|ly
states|man|ship
states|woman
  states|women
state|wide
static
stat|ic|al|ly
stat|ice
sta|tin
sta|tion
sta|tion|ari|ness
sta|tion|ary not
  moving; cf.
  stationery
sta|tion|ery paper
  etc.; cf. stationary
sta|tion|master
stat|ism
stat|ist
stat|is|tic
stat|is|tic|al
stat|is|tic|al|ly
stat|is|ti|cian

Sta|tius, Pub|lius
  Pap|in|ius Roman
  poet
sta|tive
stato|blast
stato|cyst
stato|lith
sta|tor part of elec-
  tric motor etc.; cf.
  stater
stato|scope
statu|ary
  statu|ar|ies
statue
stat|ued
statu|esque
statu|esque|ly
statu|esque|ness
statu|ette
stat|ure
stat|ured
sta|tus
sta|tus
  asth|mat|icus
sta|tus
  epi|lep|ticus
sta|tus quo
sta|tus quo ante
stat|ute
statu|tor|ily
statu|tory
staunch
staunch|ly
staunch|ness
stauro|lite
Sta|van|ger
stave
  staved or stove
  stav|ing
staves|acre
Stav|ro|pol
stay remain; cf.
  staid
stay-at-home n.
stay|er
stay|sail
stay-up n.
stead in 'in
  someone's stead', 'in
  good stead'
stead|fast
stead|fast|ly
stead|fast|ness

Steadi|cam
  trademark
stead|ier
stead|ily
steadi|ness
stead|ing
steady
  stead|ies
  stead|ied
  steady|ing
  stead|ier
  steadi|est
steak meat; cf.
  stake
steak au poivre
  steaks au poivre
steak Diane
  steaks Diane or
  steak Dianes
steak|house
steal
  stole
  stolen
  take dishonestly;
  move quietly; cf.
  steel, stele
steal|er thief; cf.
  stela, stelar
stealth|ily
stealthi|ness
stealthy
  stealth|ier
  stealthi|est
steam|boat
steam|er
steamie
steam|ily
steami|ness
steam|roll
steam|roll|er
steam|ship
steamy
  steam|ier
  steami|est
stear|ate
ste|aric
stearin
stea|tite
stea|tit|ic
steato|pygia
stea|topy|gous
stea|tor|rhea US
stea|tor|rhoea Br.
stea|tosis

Sted|man Bell-
  ringing
steed
steel alloy; make
  resolute; cf. steal,
  stele
Steele, Rich|ard
  writer
steel|head fish
steeli|ness
steel|work steel
  articles
steel|work|er
steel|works
  pl. steel|works
  factory
steely
  steel|ier
  steeli|est
  like steel; cf. stelae,
  stele
steel|yard
steen grape; wine
steen|bok antelope
steen|bras
steep|en
steep|ish
steeple
steeple|chase
steeple|chaser
steeple|chas|ing
steepled
steeple|jack
steep|ly
steep|ness
steer guide or dir-
  ect; guidance;
  animal; cf. stere
steer|able
steer|age
steer-by-wire n. &
  mod.
steer|er
steers|man
  steers|men
steeve derrick
Stefan–Boltzmann
  law
stego|saur
stego|saurus
Stein, Ger|trude
  writer
stein beer mug; var.
  of steen

Stein|beck, John
novelist
stein|bock ibex
stein|bok var. of
steenbok
Stei|ner, Ru|dolf
philosopher
Stein|way
stela
ste|lae
pillar; cf. **stealer,
steely, stelar**
ste|lar of a plant's
stele; cf. **stealer,
stela**
Stela|zine
trademark
stele central core of
plant; cf. **steal,
steel, steely**
Stella name
Stella, Frank
painter
Stella Maris
Stel|lae Maris
stel|lar of stars
stel|lar|ator
stel|late
stel|lated
Stel|len|bosch
Stel|ler, Georg nat-
uralist
stelli|form
stel|lium
stel|lia
stem
stemmed
stem|ming
stem|less
stem-like
stemma
stem|mata
stem|mat|ics
stem|ple
stem|ware
stem-winder
sten|cil
sten|cilled *Br.*
sten|ciled *US*
sten|cil|ling *Br.*
sten|cil|ing *US*
Stend|hal novelist
Sten gun
Steno, Nico|laus
geologist

steno +s =
stenographer
sten|og|raph|er
steno|graph|ic
sten|og|raphy
steno|hal|ine
sten|osed
sten|os|ing
sten|osis
sten|oses
steno|ther|mal
sten|ot|ic
steno|top|ic
steno|type
steno|typ|ist
sten|ter framework
for fabric
sten|tor person with
loud voice; single-
celled animal
sten|tor|ian
step
stepped
step|ping
pace; stair; action;
cf. **steppe**
step|brother
step|child
step|chil|dren
step|dad
step|daugh|ter
step|fam|ily
step|fam|ilies
step|father
Step|ford
Steph|anie
steph|an|otis
pl. steph|an|otis or
steph|an|otises
Ste|phen king of
England
Ste|phen, St
**Ste|phen|son,
George** engineer
step-in *adj. & n.*
step|lad|der
step-like
step|mother
step|mum
step-parent
steppe area of
grassland; cf. **step**
step|per
step|sis|ter

step|son
step|wise
ster|adian
ster|ane
ster|cor|aceous
stere unit; cf. **steer**
stereo +s
stereo|bate
stereo|camera
stereo|chem|ical
stereo|chem|ical|ly
stereo|chem|is|try
stereo|gno|sis
stereo|gnos|tic
stereo|gram
stereo|graph
stereo|graph|ic
**stereo|graph|ic|
al|ly**
ster|eog|raphy
stereo|iso|mer
stereo|iso|mer|ic
stereo|isom|er|ism
**stereo|litho|
graph|ic**
**stereo|lith|
og|raphy**
stere|om|etry
stereo|micro|scope
stereo|phon|ic
stereo|phon|ic|al|ly
stere|oph|ony
stere|op|sis
stere|op|tic
stere|op|ticon
stereo|scope
stereo|scop|ic
stereo|scop|ic|al|ly
stere|os|copy
stereo|select|ive
stereo|select|iv|ity
stereo|spe|cif|ic
**stereo|spe|cif|ic|
al|ly**
stereo|speci|fi|city
stereo|spon|dyl
stereo|tac|tic
stereo|tac|tic|al|ly
stereo|taxic
stereo|tax|ic|al|ly
stereo|taxis
stereo|taxy

stereo|type
stereo|typ|ing
stereo|typ|ic
stereo|typ|ical
stereo|typ|ic|al|ly
stereo|typy
steric
ster|ic|al|ly
ster|igma
ster|ig|mata
ster|il|ant
ster|ile
ster|ile|ly
ster|il|is|able *Br.*
var. of **sterilizable**
ster|il|isa|tion *Br.*
var. of **sterilization**
ster|il|ise *Br.* var. of
sterilize
ster|il|iser *Br.* var.
of **sterilizer**
ster|il|ity
ster|il|iz|able
ster|il|iza|tion
ster|il|ize
ster|il|iz|ing
ster|il|izer
ster|let
ster|ling
Ster|lita|mak
stern severe; rear of
ship
ster|nal
**Stern|berg, Jo|seph
von** film director
stern|drive
Sterne, Laur|ence
novelist
sterned
Stern Gang
stern|ite
stern|ly
stern|most
stern|ness
Sterno *trademark*
**sterno|cleido|
mas|toid**
sterno|mas|toid
stern|post
stern|sheets
ster|num
ster|nums or
sterna

ster¦nu¦ta¦tion
ster¦nu¦ta¦tor
ster¦nu¦ta¦tory
  ster¦nu¦ta¦tor¦ies
stern|wards
stern|way
stern|wheel¦er
ster|oid
ster|oid¦al
sterol
ster¦tor|ous
ster¦tor|ous¦ly
stet
  stet|ted
  stet|ting
stetho|scope
stetho|scop¦ic
stetho|scop¦ic¦al¦ly
steth|os¦co|pist
steth|os|copy
Stet|son *trademark*
steve|dore
Ste|ven
Ste¦ven|age
Ste¦ven|graph
Ste¦vens, Wal¦lace
  poet
Ste¦ven|son,
  Rob¦ert Louis
  novelist
ste|via
ste|vio|side
stew|ard
stew|ard|ess
stew|ard¦ry var. of
  stewartry
stew|ard|ship
Stew|art name; var.
  of **Stuart** (royal
  family)
Stew|art, Jackie
  racing driver
Stew|art, James
  actor
Stew|art Is¦land
Stew|art¦ry, The
  district of Galloway
stew¦art¦ry
  stew¦art¦ries
  old territorial
  division
stew|bum
stew|pot
Steyr town, Austria

sthen¦ic
stib|nite
sticho|mythia
stick
  stuck
stick|abil¦ity
stick|ball
stick¦er
Stickie IRA or Sinn
  Fein member
stick¦ily
sticki¦ness
stick-in-the-mud
stickle|back
stick|ler
stick|like
stick|pin
stick|seed
stick-to-it-iveness
stickum
stick-up *n.*
stick|weed
sticky
  stick|ies
  stick¦ier
  sticki¦est cf. **Stickie**
sticky|beak
stic|tion
Stieg|litz, Al¦fred
  photographer
sti|fado +s Greek
  dish
stiff¦en
stiff|en¦er
stif|fie var. of stiffy
stiff|ish
stiff¦ly
stiff|ness
stiff|tail duck
stiff-tailed
stiffy
  stiff|ies
stifle
stif¦ling
stifler
stifl¦ing¦ly
stigma
stig|mas or
  stig|mata
stig|maria
stig|mar¦iae
stig|mar¦ian
stig|mat¦ic

stig¦mat¦ic¦al¦ly
stig¦ma|tisa¦tion
  Br. var. of
  stigmatization
stig¦ma|tise *Br.* var.
  of stigmatize
stig¦ma|tist
stig¦ma|tiza¦tion
stig¦ma|tize
stig¦ma|tiz¦ing
Stijl in 'De Stijl'
stil|bene
stil|bes¦trol *US*
stil|boes¦trol *Br.*
stile steps over
  fence; part of door;
  cf. style
stil|etto +s
still|age
still|birth
still|born
still-hunt *v. & n.*
still life +s *n.*
still|ness
Still|son wrench
stilly
stilt¦ed
stilt¦ed¦ly
stilt¦ed|ness
Stil|ton cheese
  trademark
stimu|lant
stimu|late
stimu|lat¦ing
stimu|lat¦ing¦ly
stimu|la¦tion
stimu|la¦tive
stimu|la¦tor
stimu|la¦tory
stimu|lus
  stim|uli
sting
  stung
sting|aree
sting¦er
stin|gily
stingi|ness
sting|ing¦ly
sting|less
sting|ray
stingy
  stin|gier
  stin|gi¦est

stink
  past tense **stank** or
  stunk
stink|ard
stink¦er
stink|horn
stink|ing¦ly
stinko
stink|pot
stink|weed
stink|wood
stinky
  stink¦ier
  stinki¦est
sti|pend
sti¦pen|diary
  sti¦pen|diar¦ies
sti¦pes
stipi¦tes
stipi|form
stipi|tate
sti¦piti|form
stip|ple
stip|pling
stip|pler
stipu|lar
stipu|late
stipu|lat¦ing
stipu|la¦tion
stipu|la¦tor
stip|ule
stir
  stirred
  stir¦ring
stir|about *n.*
stir-fry
  stir-fries
  stir-fried
  stir-frying
Stir|ling city,
  Scotland
Stir|ling, James
  mathematician
Stir|ling, Rob¦ert
  engineer
stirps
  stir|pes
stir|rer
stir|ring¦ly
stir|rup
stisho|vite
stitch|bird
stitch¦er
stitch|ery

stitch|less
stitch-up *n.*
stitch|wort
sti|ver
Stoa hall in Athens
stoa portico
sto|chas|tic
sto|chas|tic|al|ly
sto|cious
stock|ade
  stock|ad|ing
stock|breed|er
stock|breed|ing
stock|broker
stock|broker|age
stock|brok|ing
stock|er
stock|feed
stock|fish
Stock|hausen,
  Karl|heinz
  composer
stock|hold|er
stock|hold|ing
Stock|holm
stock|horse
stock|ily
stocki|ness
stock|inet
stock|in|ette var. of
  stockinet
stock|ing
stock|inged
stock|ing|less
stock-in-trade
stock|ist
stock|job|ber
stock|job|bing
stock|less
stock|list
stock|man
  stock|men
stock-out *n.*
stock|pile
  stock|pil|ing
stock|piler
Stock|port
stock|pot
stock|room
stock-still
stock|take
stock|taker
stock|tak|ing

Stockton-on-Tees
stocky
  stock|ier
  stocki|est
stock|yard
stodgi|ly
stodgi|ness
stodgy
  stodgi|er
  stodgi|est
stoep veranda; cf.
  stoop, stoup
sto|gie var. of stogy
stogy
  sto|gies
  cigar
Stoic *Philosophy*
stoic stoical person
sto|ic|al
sto|ic|al|ly
stoi|chio|met|ric
stoi|chio|met|ric|
    al|ly
stoi|chi|om|etry
Sto|icism Stoic
  philosophy
sto|icism stoical
  attitude
stoke
  stok|ing
  add fuel to
stoke|hold
stoke|hole
Stoke-on-Trent
Stoker, Bram
  novelist
stoker
stokes unit
  pl. stokes
Stokes' law
Stokes' the|orem
Sto|kow|ski,
  Leo|pold conductor
stok|vel
STOL = short take-
  off and landing
stole long scarf; past
  tense of steal
stolen past
  participle of steal;
  cf. *stollen*
stolid
stol|id|ity
stol|id|ly

stol|id|ness
stol|len cake
sto|lon *Botany*
sto|lon|ate
sto|lon|ifer|ous
stoma
  stomas or sto|mata
stom|ach
stom|ach|er
stom|ach|ful
stom|ach|ic
stom|ach|less
sto|mal
sto|mata pl. of
  stoma
sto|ma|tal
sto|mate
sto|ma|titis
sto|mato|gas|tric
stomp|er
stom|pie
stomp|nose var. of
  stumpnose
stompy
  stomp|ier
  stompi|est
Stone, Oli|ver film
  director
stone
  ston|ing
stone-broke
stone|chat
stone cold *adj.*
stone-cold *adv.* &
  attrib.
stone|crop
stone|cut|ter
stone dead
stone deaf *adj.*
stone-deaf *attrib.*
stone|fish
stone|fly
  stone|flies
stone|ground
stone|hatch
Stone|henge
stone|less
stone|mason
stone|mason|ry
stoner
stone|wall
stone|wall|er
stone|ware

stone|wash
stone|washed
stone|work
stone|work|er
stone|wort
stoni|ly
stoni|ness
stonk|er
stonk|ered
stonk|ing
stony
  stoni|er
  stoni|est
stony broke
stony-iron *adj.* &
  n.
stooge
stoo|ging
stool|ball
stoolie
stoop bend forward;
  stooping posture;
  swoop on prey;
  porch; cf. stoep,
  stoup
stoor var. of stour
stoory var. of stoury
stoosh var. of stush
stoo|shie
stop
  stopped
  stop|ping
stop-and-search *n.*
stop|band
stop|bank
stop|cock
stope
  stop|ing
Stopes, Marie
  birth-control
  campaigner
stop|gap
stop|less
stop-motion *n.* &
  mod.
stop-off *n.*
stop-out *n.*
stop|over
stop|pable
stop|page
Stop|pard, Tom
  playwright
stop|per

stop|ple
　stop|pling
stop|street
stop|watch
stop|word
stor|able
stor|age
storax
store
　stor|ing
store|front
store|house
store|keep|er
store|man
　store|men
storer
store|room
storey *Br.* floor of
　building; cf. story;
　US story
stor|eyed *Br.*
　divided into
　storeys, in 'three-
　storeyed' etc.
stor|ied celebrated
　in stories
stor|ied *US*
　divided into
　storeys, in 'three-
　storied' etc.
stork bird; cf. stalk
storks|bill plant
storm|bound
storm|cock
storm|er
storm|ily
stormi|ness
Stor|mont
storm|proof
stormy
　storm|ier
　stormi|est
Stor|no|way
Stor|ting
story
　stor|ies
　tale; plot; commer-
　cial prospects; cf.
　storey
story *US*
　stor|ies
　floor of building
　Br. storey
story|board

story|book
story|line
story|tell|er
story|tell|ing
stot
　stot|ted
　stot|ting
sto|tin
sto|tinka
　sto|tinki
stot|tie var. of stotty
stotty
　stot|ties
stoup holy-water
　basin; flagon; cf.
　stoep, stoop
Stour rivers,
　England
stour dust
stoury
stout|ish
stout|ly
stout|ness
stove
　stov|ing
stove|pipe
sto|vies
stow
stow|age
stow|away
Stowe, Har|riet
　Bee|cher novelist
Stra|bane
stra|bis|mal
stra|bis|mic
stra|bis|mus
Strabo geographer
strac|cia|tella
Stra|chey, Lyt|ton
　biographer
strad|dle
　strad|dling
strad|dler
Stradi|vari,
　An|tonio violin
　maker
Stradi|var|ius
strafe
　straf|ing
strag|gle
　strag|gling
strag|gler
strag|gly
strag|glier

strag|gli|est
straight not bent
　etc.; straight part;
　heterosexual;
　direct; cf. strait
straight|away mov-
　ing in a straight
　line, straight
　section
straight away
　immediately
straight-eight
　engine; vehicle
straight|en make or
　become straight; cf.
　straiten
straight|en|er
straight|for|ward
straight|
　　　　for|ward|ly
straight|for|ward|
　　　　　　　　ness
straight|ish
straight|jacket var.
　of straitjacket
straight-laced var.
　of strait-laced
straight|ness qual-
　ity of being
　straight; cf.
　straitness
straight-six engine;
　vehicle
straight up *adv.*
straight-up *adj.*
straight|way
strain|able
strain|er
strait water
　connecting seas;
　narrow; trouble; cf.
　straight
strait|en make or
　become narrow; cf.
　straighten
strait|jacket
strait-laced
strait|ly
strait|ness severity;
　hardship; cf.
　straightness
stra|mash
stra|mo|nium

strand|loop|er var.
　of strandloper
strand|loper
strand|wolf
　strand|wolves
strange
　stran|ger
　stran|gest
strange|ly
strange|ness
stran|ger
stran|gle
　stran|gling
strangle|hold
stran|gler
stran|gu|late
　stran|gu|lat|ing
stran|gu|la|tion
stran|guri|ous
stran|gury
Stran|raer
strap
　strapped
　strap|ping
strap-hang
　strap-hung
strap|hang|er
strap|less
strap|line
strap-on *adj. & n.*
strap|pado +s
strap|per
strappy
　strap|pier
　strap|pi|est
strap|work
Stras|berg, Lee
　drama teacher
Stras|bourg city,
　France
strata pl. of
　stratum
strata|gem
stratal
stra|tegic
stra|tegic|al
stra|tegic|al|ly
strat|egise *Br.* var.
　of strategize
strat|egist
strat|egize
　strat|egiz|ing
strat|egy
　strat|egies

Strat|ford|ian
Stratford-upon-
         Avon
Strath|clyde
strath|spey
strati|fi|ca|tion
strati|form
strat|ify
  strati|fies
  strati|fied
  strati|fy|ing
strat|ig|raph|er
strati|graph|ic
strati|graph|ic|al|ly
stra|tig|raphy
strato|cir|rus
strato|cumu|lus
strato|pause
strato|sphere
strato|spher|ic
strato|spher|ic|al|ly
strato|vol|cano
  strato|vol|ca|noes
stra|tum
  strata
stra|tum cor|neum
  strata cor|nea
stra|tus
Strauss, Jo|hann
  father and son,
  composers
Strauss, Rich|ard
  composer
stra|vage
  stra|va|ging
  var. of stravaig
stra|vaig
Stra|vin|sky, Igor
  composer
straw|berry
  straw|berries
straw|board
strawy
stray|er
streak|er
streak|ily
streaki|ness
streaky
  streaki|er
  streaki|est
stream|er
stream|flow
stream|let

stream|line
stream|lin|ing
Streep, Meryl
  actress
street|car
street|ed
street|scape
street|walk|er
street|walk|ing
street|ward
street|wise
Strega *trademark*
Strei|sand, Bar|bra
  singer
stre|litzia
strength|en
strength|en|er
strength|less
strenu|ous
strenu|ous|ly
strenu|ous|ness
Streps|ip|tera
streps|ip|ter|an
strepto|car|pus
  pl. strepto|car|pus
  or
  strepto|car|puses
strepto|coc|cal
strepto|coc|cus
  strepto|cocci
strepto|kin|ase
strepto|my|cete
strepto|mycin
stress|ful
stress|ful|ly
stress|ful|ness
stress|less
stres|sor
stretch|abil|ity
stretch|able
stretch|er
stretchi|ness
stretchy
  stretchi|er
  stretchi|est
stretto
  stretti
streu|sel
strew
  past participle
  strewn or strewed
strew|er
strewth *exclam.*

stria
  striae
stri|at|al
stri|ate
stri|at|ing
stri|ation
stri|atum
  stri|ata
stricken
strickle
strict|ly
strict|ness
stric|ture
stric|tured
stride
  strode
  strid|ing
  strid|den
stri|dency
stri|dent
stri|dent|ly
strider person who
  strides
stri|dor harsh
  sound
stridu|lant
stridu|late
  stridu|lat|ing
stridu|la|tion
stridu|la|tory
stri|gil
stri|gose
strike
  struck
  strik|ing
strike|out
striker
strik|ing|ly
strik|ing|ness
strim|mer
  trademark
Strind|berg,
  Au|gust writer
string
  strung
string|board
stringed
strin|gency
strin|gendo
  strin|gen|dos or
  strin|gendi
strin|gent
strin|gent|ly
string|er

string|halt
string|ily
stringi|ness
string|less
string-like
string|piece
stringy
  string|ier
  stringi|est
stringy|bark
strip
  stripped
  strip|ping
stripe
  strip|ing
striper
stripey var. of stripy
strip|ling
strip|per
strip|per|gram
strip|tease
  strip|teas|ing
strip|teaser
stripy
  stripi|er
  stripi|est
strive
  strove or strived
  striv|ing
  striven or strived
striver
strobe
  strob|ing
stro|bila
  stro|bilae
  segment of tape-
  worm; stack of
  larvae
stro|bil|ation
stro|bilus
  stro|bili
  cone
strobo|scope
strobo|scop|ic
strobo|scop|ic|al|ly
strog|an|off
stroke
  strok|ing
stroke|able
stroker
stroll|er
stroma
  stro|mata
stro|mal

stro|mat¦ic
stro¦mato|lite
stro¦mato|por¦oid
Strom|boli
Strom|boli¦an
strong|box
strong|hold
strong|ish
strong¦ly
strong|man
  strong|men
  forceful leader; cir-
  cus performer
strong|point
strong|room
stron|gyle
stron|gyl|oid|iasis
stron|tia
stron|tian|ite
stron|tium
strop
  stropped
  strop|ping
stro|phan|thin
strophe
stroph¦ic
strop|pily
strop|pi|ness
stroppy
  strop¦pier
  strop¦pi|est
strow
  past participle
  strown or strowed
struc|tural
struc¦tur|al|ism
struc¦tur|al|ist
struc¦tur|al¦ly
struc¦tur|ation
struc|ture
  struc¦tur|ing
struc¦ture|less
stru|del
strug¦gle
  strug¦gling
strug|gler
strum
  strummed
  strum|ming
struma
  stru|mae
strum|mer
stru|mose
stru|mous

strum|pet
strut
  strut|ted
  strut|ting
struth var. of
  strewth
strut|ter
strut|ting¦ly
strych|nic
strych|nine
Stu¦art name; royal
  family
Stu¦art, John
  McDou¦all explorer
stub
  stubbed
  stub|bing
Stub|bies men's
  shorts *trademark*
stub|bily
stub|bi|ness
stub¦ble
stub¦bled
stub¦bly
  stub¦blier
  stub¦bli|est
stub|born
stub|born¦ly
stub|born|ness
Stubbs, George
  painter
Stubbs, Wil|liam
  historian
stubby
  stub|bies
  stub|bier
  stub¦bi|est
stucco
  stuc|coes
  stuc|coed
  stucco|ing
stuck-up *adj.*
stud
  stud|ded
  stud|ding
stud¦ding|sail
stu|dent
student-at-law
  students-at-law
stu¦dent|ship
Stu|dent's t-test
stu|denty
stud|ied¦ly
stud|ied|ness

stu¦dio +s
stu¦di|ous
stu¦di|ous¦ly
stu¦di|ous|ness
stud¦ly
  stud¦lier
  stud¦li|est
stud|muffin
study
  stud|ies
  stud|ied
  study|ing
study-bedroom
stuff|er
stuff|ily
stuffi|ness
stuff|ing
stuffy
  stuff|ier
  stuffi|est
Stuka
stul¦ti|fi|ca¦tion
stul¦ti|fier
stul|tify
  stul¦ti|fies
  stul¦ti|fied
  stul¦ti|fy|ing
stum
  stummed
  stum|ming
stum¦ble
  stum|bling
stumble|bum
stum|bler
stum|bling¦ly
stu|mer
stump¦er
stump|ily
stumpi|ness
stump|nose
  pl. stump|nose
stumpy
  stump¦ier
  stumpi|est
stun
  stunned
  stun|ning
stun|ner
stun|ning¦ly
stun|sail
stuns'l var. of
  stunsail
stunt¦ed|ness
stunt¦er

stunt|man
stunt|men
stunt|woman
stunt|women
stupa shrine; cf.
  stupor
stupe
  stup|ing
stu|pe|fa|cient
stu|pe|fac|tion
stu|pe|fier
stu|pefy
  stu|pe|fies
  stu|pe|fied
  stu|pe|fy|ing
  stu|pe|fy|ing¦ly
stu|pen|dous
stu|pen|dous¦ly
stu|pen|dous|ness
stu|pid
stu|pid|ity
  stu|pid|ities
stu|pid¦ly
stu|pid|ness
stu|por insensible
  state; cf. stupa
stu|por|ous
stur|died
stur|dily
stur¦di|ness
sturdy
  stur|dier
  stur|di|est
stur|geon
Sturm|ab¦teil|ung
Sturm|er
Sturm und Drang
Sturt, Charles
  explorer
stush
stu¦shie var. of
  stooshie
stut|ter
stut|ter¦er
stut|ter|ing¦ly
Stutt|gart
sty
  sties
  stied
  sty|ing
  (keep in) pigsty;
  swelling on eyelid
stye var. of sty (on
  eyelid)

Sty¦gian
sty¦lar
style
  styl¦ing
  fashion; writing
  implement; part of
  flower; design or
  arrange; designate;
  cf. **stile**
style¦less
style¦less¦ness
styler
sty¦let
styli pl. of stylus
styl¦isa¦tion *Br.* var.
  of stylization
styl¦ise *Br.* var. of
  stylize
styl¦ish
styl¦ish¦ly
styl¦ish¦ness
styl¦ist
styl¦is¦tic
styl¦is¦tic¦al¦ly
styl¦ite
styl¦iza¦tion
styl¦ize
  styl¦iz¦ing
stylo +s
stylo¦bate
stylo¦graph
stylo¦graph¦ic
styl¦oid
stylo¦lite
stylo¦met¦ric
styl¦om¦etry
stylo¦phone
  *trademark in the
  US*
styl¦opid
styl¦op¦ised *Br.* var.
  of stylopized
styl¦op¦ized
styl¦ops
  pl. styl¦ops
sty¦lus
  styli or sty¦luses
sty¦mie
  sty¦mies
  sty¦mied
  sty¦mie¦ing
styp¦tic
sty¦rax var. of
  storax

styr¦ene
Styria
Styr¦ian
styro¦foam
  *trademark in the
  US*
Styx river in Hades;
  cf. **sticks**
su¦able
sua¦sion
sua¦sive
suave
  suaver
  suav¦est
suave¦ly
suave¦ness
suav¦ity
  suav¦ities
sub
  subbed
sub¦bing
sub¦acid
sub¦acid¦ity
sub¦acute
sub¦adult
sub¦aerial
sub¦aerial¦ly
sub¦agency
  sub¦agen¦cies
sub¦agent
sub¦alpine
sub¦al¦tern
sub¦ant¦arc¦tic
sub-aqua
sub-aquatic
sub¦aque¦ous
sub¦arach¦noid
sub¦arc¦tic
sub-assembly
  sub-assemblies
Sub-Atlantic
sub¦atom¦ic
sub¦audi¦tion
sub-basement
Sub-Boreal
sub-breed
Sub¦bu¦teo
  trademark
sub¦carrier
sub¦cat¦egor¦isa¦
  tion
  Br. var. of
  subcategorization

sub¦cat¦egor¦ise *Br.*
  var. of
  subcategorize
sub¦cat¦egor¦iza¦
                tion
sub¦cat¦egor¦ize
sub¦cat¦egor¦iz¦ing
sub¦cat¦egory
sub¦cat¦egor¦ies
sub¦class
sub¦clause
sub¦clavian
sub¦clin¦ical
sub¦com¦mit¦tee
sub¦com¦pact
sub¦con¦ic¦al
sub¦con¦scious
sub¦con¦scious¦ly
sub¦con¦scious¦
                ness
sub¦con¦tin¦ent
sub¦con¦tin¦en¦tal
sub¦con¦tract
sub¦con¦tract¦or
sub¦con¦trary
sub¦con¦trar¦ies
sub¦cor¦tical
sub¦cos¦tal
sub¦crit¦ic¦al
sub¦cul¦tural
sub¦cul¦ture
sub¦cuta¦ne¦ous
sub¦cuta¦ne¦ous¦ly
sub¦deacon
sub¦diac¦on¦ate
sub¦dir¦ec¦tory
sub¦dir¦ec¦tor¦ies
sub¦div¦ide
sub¦div¦id¦ing
sub¦div¦ision
sub¦dom¦in¦ant
sub¦du¦able
sub¦duct
sub¦duc¦tion
sub¦due
  sub¦du¦ing
sub¦duer
sub¦dural
sub¦edit
sub¦editor
sub¦editor¦ial
su¦ber¦ic
su¦berin

su¦ber¦isa¦tion *Br.*
  var. of suberization
suber¦ise *Br.* var. of
  suberize
su¦ber¦iza¦tion
su¦ber¦ize
su¦ber¦iz¦ing
sub¦fam¦ily
sub¦fam¦ilies
sub¦floor
sub¦form
sub¦frame
sub¦fusc
sub¦gen¦er¦ic
sub¦genre
sub¦genus
sub¦gen¦era
sub¦gla¦cial
sub¦group
sub¦har¦mon¦ic
sub¦head
sub¦head¦ing
sub¦human
sub¦ja¦cency
sub¦ja¦cen¦cies
sub¦jacent
sub¦ject
sub¦jec¦tion
sub¦ject¦ive
sub¦ject¦ive¦ly
sub¦ject¦ive¦ness
sub¦ject¦iv¦ism
sub¦ject¦iv¦ist
sub¦ject¦iv¦ity
sub¦ject¦less
sub¦join
sub ju¦dice
sub¦jug¦able
sub¦ju¦gate
sub¦jug¦at¦ing
sub¦ju¦ga¦tion
sub¦ju¦ga¦tor
sub¦junct
sub¦junct¦ive
sub¦junct¦ive¦ly
sub¦king¦dom
sub¦lan¦guage
sub¦late
sub¦lat¦ing
sub¦lat¦eral
sub¦la¦tion
sub¦lease
sub¦leas¦ing

sub-lessee
sub-lessor
sub｜let
  sub｜let｜ting
sub｜lethal
sub lieu｜ten｜ant
sub｜lim｜ate
  sub｜lim｜at｜ing
sub｜lim｜ation
sub｜lime
  sub｜lim｜ing
  sub｜limer
  sub｜lim｜est
sub｜lime｜ly
sub｜lim｜inal
sub｜lim｜in｜al｜ly
sub｜lim｜ity
  sub｜lim｜ities
sub｜lin｜gual
sub｜lin｜gual｜ly
sub｜lit｜toral
sub｜lunar
sub｜lun｜ary
sub｜lux｜ation
sub-machine gun
sub｜man
  sub｜men
sub｜man｜dibu｜lar
sub｜mar｜gin｜al
sub｜mar｜ine
sub｜mari｜ner
sub｜medi｜ant
sub｜menu
sub｜merge
  sub｜mer｜ging
sub｜mer｜gence
sub｜mer｜gible
sub｜merse
  sub｜mers｜ing
sub｜mers｜ible
sub｜mer｜sion
sub｜micro｜scop｜ic
sub｜mini｜ature
sub｜mis｜sion
sub｜mis｜sive
sub｜mis｜sive｜ly
sub｜mis｜sive｜ness
sub｜mit
  sub｜mit｜ted
  sub｜mit｜ting
sub｜mit｜ter
sub｜modi｜fi｜ca｜tion
sub｜modi｜fier

sub｜modify
  sub｜modi｜fies
  sub｜modi｜fied
  sub｜modi｜fy｜ing
sub｜mon｜tane
sub｜mucosa
  sub｜muco｜sae
  sub｜muco｜sal
sub｜mul｜tiple
sub｜muni｜tion
sub｜net
sub｜net｜work
sub｜nor｜mal
sub｜nor｜mal｜ity
sub｜nuclear
sub｜opti｜mal
sub｜orbital
sub｜order
sub｜or｜dinal
sub｜or｜din｜ary
  sub｜or｜din｜ar｜ies
sub｜or｜din｜ate
  sub｜or｜din｜at｜ing
  sub｜or｜din｜ate｜ly
sub｜or｜din｜ation
sub｜or｜dina｜tive
sub｜orn
sub｜orn｜ation
sub｜orn｜er
sub｜oscine
sub｜oxide
sub｜par｜al｜lel
sub｜phy｜lum
  sub｜phyla
sub｜plot
sub｜poena
  sub｜poenaed or
  sub｜poena'd
  sub｜poena｜ing
sub｜poena ad
testi｜fi｜can｜dum
sub｜poena duces
tecum
sub-postmaster
sub-postmis｜tress
sub-post of｜fice
sub｜pro｜gram
sub｜region
sub｜region｜al
sub｜ro｜gate
  sub｜ro｜gat｜ing
sub｜ro｜ga｜tion
sub rosa

sub｜rou｜tine
sub-Saharan
sub｜sample
  sub｜samp｜ling
sub｜scribe
  sub｜scrib｜ing
sub｜scriber
sub｜script
sub｜scrip｜tion
sub｜sea
sub｜sec｜tion
sub｜sel｜lium
  sub｜sel｜lia
sub｜sense
sub｜se｜quence
  being subsequent;
  subordinate
  sequence
sub｜se｜quent
sub｜se｜quent｜ly
sub｜serve
  sub｜serv｜ing
sub｜ser｜vi｜ence
sub｜ser｜vi｜ency
sub｜ser｜vi｜ent
sub｜ser｜vi｜ent｜ly
sub｜set
sub｜shrub
sub｜shrubby
sub｜side
  sub｜sid｜ing
sub｜sid｜ence
sub｜sidi｜ar｜ily
sub｜sidi｜ar｜ity
sub｜sidiary
  sub｜sid｜iar｜ies
sub｜sid｜isa｜tion *Br.*
  var. of
  subsidization
sub｜sid｜ise *Br.* var.
  of subsidize
sub｜sid｜iser *Br.* var.
  of subsidizer
sub｜sid｜iza｜tion
sub｜sid｜ize
  sub｜sid｜iz｜ing
sub｜sid｜izer
sub｜sidy
  sub｜sid｜ies
sub｜sist
sub｜sist｜ence
sub｜sist｜ent
sub｜soil
sub｜soil｜er

sub｜song
sub｜son｜ic
sub｜son｜ic｜al｜ly
sub｜space
sub spe｜cie
ae｜terni｜ta｜tis
sub｜spe｜cies
  pl. sub｜spe｜cies
sub｜spe｜cif｜ic
sub｜stage
sub｜stance
sub｜stand｜ard
sub｜stan｜tial
sub｜stan｜tial｜ise *Br.*
  var. of
  substantialize
sub｜stan｜tial｜ism
sub｜stan｜tial｜ist
sub｜stan｜ti｜al｜ity
sub｜stan｜tial｜ize
  sub｜stan｜tial｜iz｜ing
sub｜stan｜tial｜ly
sub｜stan｜ti｜ate
  sub｜stan｜ti｜at｜ing
sub｜stan｜ti｜ation
sub｜stan｜tival
sub｜stan｜tive
sub｜stan｜tive｜ly
sub｜station
sub｜stel｜lar
sub｜stitu｜ent
sub｜sti｜tut｜abil｜ity
sub｜sti｜tut｜able
sub｜sti｜tute
  sub｜sti｜tut｜ing
sub｜sti｜tu｜tion
sub｜sti｜tu｜tion｜al
sub｜sti｜tu｜tion｜ary
sub｜sti｜tu｜tive
sub｜storm
sub｜strate
sub｜stra｜tum
  sub｜strata
sub｜struc｜tural
sub｜struc｜ture
sub｜sum｜able
sub｜sume
  sub｜sum｜ing
sub｜sump｜tion
sub｜sur｜face
sub｜sys｜tem
sub｜ten｜ancy
  sub｜ten｜an｜cies

sub|ten|ant
sub|tend
sub|tense
sub|ter|fuge
sub|ter|minal
sub|ter|ra|nean
sub|ter|ra|ne|ous
sub|ter|ra|ne|ous|ly
sub|text
sub|til|isa|tion *Br.*
  var. of **subtilization**
sub|til|ise *Br.* var. of
  subtilize
sub|til|iza|tion
sub|til|ize
  sub|til|iz|ing
sub|title
  sub|titling
sub|tle
  sub|tler
  sub|tlest
  slight; complex;
  clever; cf. **sutler**
subtle|ness
subtle|ty
  subtle|ties
subtly
sub|tonic *Music*
sub|topia
sub|topian
sub|total
  sub|totalled *Br.*
  sub|totaled *US*
  sub|total|ling *Br.*
  sub|total|ing *US*
sub|tract
sub|tract|er
sub|trac|tion
sub|tract|ive
sub|tract|or var. of
  subtracter
sub|tra|hend
sub|trop|ic|al
sub|trop|ics
sub|type
Subud
subu|late
sub|umbrella *n.*
sub|umbrel|lar *adj.*
sub-underwrite
  sub-underwrote
  sub-underwrit|ing
  sub-underwrit|ten
sub-underwriter

sub|ungu|late
sub|unit
sub|urb
sub|ur|ban
sub|ur|ban|isa|tion
  Br. var. of
  suburbanization
sub|ur|ban|ise *Br.*
  var. of **suburbanize**
sub|ur|ban|ite
sub|ur|ban|iza|tion
sub|ur|ban|ize
  sub|ur|ban|iz|ing
sub|ur|bia
sub|vent
sub|ven|tion
sub|ver|sion
sub|ver|sive
sub|ver|sive|ly
sub|ver|sive|ness
sub|vert
sub|vert|er
sub|vocal
sub|vocal|isa|tion
  Br. var. of
  subvocalization
sub|vocal|ise *Br.*
  var. of **subvocalize**
sub|vocal|iza|tion
sub|vocal|ize
  sub|vocal|iz|ing
sub|vocal|ly
sub|way
sub|woof|er
sub-zero
suc|cah shelter
suc|ced|an|eous
suc|ced|an|eum
suc|ced|anea
suc|ceed
suc|ceed|er
suc|cen|tor
suc|cen|tor|ship
*suc|cès de
  scan|dale*
suc|cès d'es|time
suc|cess
suc|cess|ful
suc|cess|ful|ly
suc|cess|ful|ness
suc|ces|sion
suc|ces|sion|al
suc|ces|sive

suc|ces|sive|ly
suc|ces|sive|ness
suc|ces|sor
suc|cin|ate
suc|cinct
suc|cinct|ly
suc|cinct|ness
suc|cinyl|cho|line
suc|cor; *US*
  Br. **succour**; help;
  cf. **succah, sucker**
suc|cor|less *US*
  Br. **succourless**
suc|cory
suc|cor|ies
  chicory
suc|co|tash
Suc|coth
suc|cour *Br.*
  US **succor**; help;
  cf. **succah, sucker**
suc|cour|less *Br.*
  US **succorless**
suc|cu|bous *adj.*
suc|cu|bus *n.*
suc|cubi
suc|cu|lence
suc|cu|lent
suc|cu|lent|ly
suc|cumb
suc|cur|sal
suc|cuss
suc|cus|sion
such|like
Su|chou var. of
  Suzhou
Su|chow var. of
  Xuzhou
suck|er person or
  thing that sucks;
  gullible person;
  (put out) plant
  shoot; cf. **succah,**
  succour
sucker|fish
sucket spoon
suck|hole
  suck|hol|ing
suck|ing|fish
suckle
  suck|ling
suck|ler
Suck|ling, John
  poet

suck|ling
suck-up *n.*
sucky
  suck|ier
  sucki|est
su|cral|fate
su|cral|ose
su|crase
Sucre city, Bolivia
Sucre, An|tonio de
  president of Bolivia
sucre Ecuadorean
  currency
su|crier
su|crose
suction
suc|tor|ial
suc|tor|ial|ly
suc|tor|ian
Sudan
Su|dan|ese
sudan grass
su|dar|ium
su|daria
suda|tor|ium
suda|toria
Sud|bury
sudd floating vege-
  tation in Nile; cf.
  suds
sud|den
sud|den|ly
sud|den|ness
Su|deten|land
su|dor|ifer|ous
su|dor|if|ic
Sudra Hindu of
  lowest caste
suds lather; cf. **sudd**
sud|ser
sudsy
  suds|ier
  sudsi|est
Sue name
sue
  suing
  take legal
  proceedings
  against; entreat; cf.
  sou, xu
suede
suede|head
suer person who
  sues; cf. **sewer**

suerte
suet
Sueto|nius Roman
  biographer
suety
Suez
suf'fer
suf'fer|able
suf'fer|ance
suf'fer|ation
suf'fer|er
suf|fice
suf|ficing
suf|fi'ciency
  suf|fi'cien|cies
suf|fi'cient
suf|fi'cient|ly
suf'fix
suf'fix|ation
suf'fo|cate
  suf'fo|cat'ing
suf'fo|cat'ing|ly
suf'fo|ca'tion
Suf|folk
suf|fra|gan
suf|fra|gan|ship
suf|frage
suf'fra|gette
suf|fragi waiter
suf|fra|gism
suf|fra|gist
suf|fuse
  suf|fus'ing
suf|fu'sion
Sufi
Sufic
Suf'ism
sug
  sugged
  sug|ging
sugan
sugar
sugar|bird
sugar|craft
sug'ari|ness
sugar|less
sugar|loaf
  sugar|loafs or
  sugar|loaves
Sugar Loaf
  Moun|tain
sugar|plum
sug'ary

sug|gest
sug|gest'er
sug|gest|ibil'ity
sug|gest|ible
sug|ges|tion
sug|gest|ive
sug|gest|ive'ly
sug|gest|ive|ness
Sui Chinese dynasty
sui|cidal
sui|cid|al'ly
sui|cide
  sui|cid'ing
sui gen|eris
sui juris
suint
suit
suit|abil'ity
suit|able
suit|able|ness
suit|ably
suit|case
suit|case|ful
suite set of things;
  cf. sweet
suit'er bag; cf.
  souter, suitor
suitor wooer;
  plaintiff; cf. souter,
  suiter
suk var. of souk; cf.
  sook
Su|karno, Ach'mad
  president of
  Indonesia
sukh var. of souk;
  cf. sook
Sukho|tai
Sukho|thai var. of
  Sukhotai
suki|yaki
suk'kah var. of
  succah
Suk'kur
Su|kuma
Su'lai|man'iya var.
  of Sulaymaniyah
Sula|wesi
Su'lay|man'iyah
sul|cate
sul'cus
sulci
Su|lei|man sultan of
  Ottoman empire

sulfa US
  Br. sulpha; class of
  drugs; cf. sulfur,
  sulphur
sulfa|dia'zine US
  Br. sulphadiazine
sulfa|dimi'dine US
  Br. sulphadimidine
sulfa|mate US
  Br. sulphamate
sulfa|meth|
    oxa'zole US
  Br. sulphameth-
    oxazole
sul|fam'ic US
  Br. sulphamic
sulf|anila'mide US
  Br. sulphanilamide
sulfa|pyri'dine US
  Br. sulphapyridine
sulfa|sala'zine US
  Br. sulphasalazine
sul|fate US
  Br. sulphate
sul|fide US
  Br. sulphide
sul|fite US
  Br. sulphite
sul|fona'mide US
  Br. sulphonamide
sul|fon|ate US
  sul|fon|at'ing US
  Br. sulphonate
sul|fon|ation US
  Br. sulphonation
sul|fone US
  Br. sulphone
sul|fon'ic US
  Br. sulphonic
sul|fonyl US
  Br. sulphonyl
sulf'ox'ide US
  Br. sulphoxide
sul'fur US
  Br. sulphur; chem-
  ical element; cf.
  sulfa, sulpha
sul'fur|ated US
  Br. sulphurated
sul'fur|eous US
  Br. sulphureous
sul'fur'ic US
  Br. sulphuric
sul'fur|iza'tion US
  Br. sulphurization

sul'fur|ized US
  Br. sulphurized
sul'fur|ous US
  Br. sulphurous
sul|fury US
  Br. sulphury
sulk'er
sulk'ily
sulki|ness
sulky
  sulkies
sulk|ier
sulki|est
Sulla Roman
  general
sul|lage
sul'len
sul'len|ly
sul'len|ness
Sulli|van, Ar'thur
  composer
sully
  sul|lies
sul|lied
sully|ing
sulpha Br.
  US sulfa; class of
  drugs; cf. sulfur,
  sulphur
sulpha|dia'zine Br.
  US sulfadiazine
sulpha|dimi'dine
  Br.
  US sulfadimidine
sulpha|mate Br.
  US sulfamate
sulpha|meth|
    oxa'zole Br.
  US
  sulfamethoxazole
sul|pham'ic Br.
  US sulfamic
sulph|anila'mide
  Br.
  US sulfanilamide
sulpha|pyri'dine
  Br.
  US sulfapyridine
sulpha|sala'zine Br.
  US sulfasalazine
sul|phate Br.
  US sulfate
sul|phide Br.
  US sulfide
sul|phite Br.
  US sulfite

sul|phona|mide *Br.*
 US sulfonamide
sul|phon|ate
 sul|phon|at¦ing *Br.*
 US sulfonate
sul|phon|ation *Br.*
 US sulfonation
sul|phone *Br.*
 US sulfone
sul|phon|ic *Br.*
 US sulfonic
sulph|onyl *Br.*
 US sulfonyl
sulph|ox|ide *Br.*
 US sulfoxide
sul|phur *Br.*
 US sulfur; chem-
 ical element; cf.
 sulfa, sulpha
sul|phur|ated *Br.*
 US sulfurated
sul|phur|eous *Br.*
 US sulfureous
sul|phur|ic *Br.*
 US sulfuric
sul|phur|isa|tion
 Br. var. of
 sulphurization
sul|phur|ised *Br.*
 var. of sulphurized
sul|phur|iza|tion
sul|phur|ize
 sul|phur|iz¦ing
sul|phur|ous *Br.*
 US sulfurous
sul|phury *Br.*
 US sulfury
Sul|pi|cian
sul|tan
sul|tana
sul|tan|ate
sul|trily
sul|tri|ness
sul|try
 sul|trier
 sul|tri|est
sulu fabric used as
 sarong
sum
 summed
 sum|ming
 total etc.; cf. some
sumac
su|mach +s var. of
 sumac

Su|ma|tra
Su|ma|tran
Sumba
Sum|bawa
Sum|burgh
Sumer
Su|mer|ian
sumi
sumi-e
summa
 sum|mae
summa cum laude
sum|mand
sum|mar|ily
sum|mari|ness
sum|mar|is|able *Br.*
 var. of
 summarizable
sum|mar|isa|tion
 Br. var. of
 summarization
sum|mar|ise *Br.*
 var. of summarize
sum|mar|iser *Br.*
 var. of summarizer
sum|mar|ist
sum|mar|iz|able
sum|mar|iza|tion
sum|mar|ize
 sum|mar|iz¦ing
sum|mar|izer
sum|mary
 sum|mar|ies
 brief account; with-
 out formalities; cf.
 summery
sum|mery
sum|ma¦tion
sum|ma¦tion|al
sum|ma¦tive
sum|mer
sum|mer|less
sum|mer|ly
sum|mer|sault
 archaic var. of
 somersault
sum|mer|time
 period of summer
sum|mer time time
 advanced during
 summer
sum|mery of or like
 summer; cf.
 summary

summing-up *n.*
 summings-up
sum|mit
sum|mit|eer
sum|mit|less
sum|mon
sum|mon|able
sum|mon|er
sum|mons
sum|mum bonum
sumo +s
sump|ter
sump|tu|ary
sump|tu|os|ity
sump|tu|ous
sump|tu|ous|ly
sump|tu|ous|ness
Sum|qa|yit
Sumy
sun
 sunned
 sun|ning
 star; cf. son
sun|bake
sun|baked
sun|bak¦ing
sunbathe
sun-baked dry and
 hard from the sun
sun|baker
sun|bath
sun|bathe
sun|bath¦ing
sun|bather
sun|beam
sun|bed
sun|belt
sun|bird
sun|bittern
sun|blind
sun|block
sun|bow
sun|burn
 sun|burnt or
 sun|burned
sun|burst
sun|cream
sun|dae ice-cream
 dish; cf. Sunday
Sunda Is|lands
Sun|dan|ese
Sun|dar|bans

Sun|day day of the
 week; cf. sundae
sun|der
Sun|der|land
sun|dew
sun|dial
sun|down
sun|down|er
sun|dress
sun|drops
sun|dry
 sun|dries
 various
sun-dry
 sun-dries
 sun-dried
 sun-drying
 dry in the sun
sun|fast
sun|fish
sun|flower
Sung var. of Song
sung past participle
 of sing; cf. sangh
sun|gazer
sun|glasses
sun|grebe
suni antelope
sunk|en
sun|lamp
sun|less
sun|less|ness
sun|light
sun|like
sun|lit
sun lounge
sun|loun|ger furni-
 ture
Sunna part of Mus-
 lim law
Sunni
 pl. Sunni or
 Sun|nis
 (follower of)
 branch of Islam
sun|nies sunglasses
sun|nily
sun|ni|ness
Sun|nite Sunni
 Muslim
sunny
 sun|nier
 sun|ni|est
 bright with

sunlight; cf. **sonny**
sun|ray
sun|rise
sun|roof
sun|room
sun|screen
sun|set
sun|shade
sun|shine
sun|shiny
sun|space
sun|spot
sun|star
sun|stone
sun|stroke
sun|suit
sun|tan
  sun|tanned
  sun|tan|ning
sun|trap
sunup
sun|ward
sun|wards
sun|yata
Sun Yat-sen
  Chinese leader
Sun Yix|ian var. of
  Sun Yat-sen
sup
  supped
  sup|ping
Supa|driv
  trademark
super
super|able
super|abound
super|abun|dance
super|abun|dant
super|abun|dant|ly
super|acid
super|acid|ity
super|adia|bat|ic
super|alloy
super|altar
super|annu|able
super|annu|ate
  super|annu|at|ing
super|annu|ation
su|perb
super|bike
su|perb|ly
su|perb|ness

Super Bowl
  trademark
super|bug
super|cal|en|der
super|car
super|cargo
  super|cargos or
  super|car|goes
super|charge
  super|char|ging
  super|char|ger
super|cil|iary
super|cili|ous
super|cili|ous|ly
super|cili|ous|ness
super|class
super|clus|ter
super|coil
super|col|lider
super|com|puter
super|com|put|ing
super|con|duct
super|con|duct|ive
super|con|duct|
    iv|ity
super|con|duct|or
super|con|scious
super|con|scious|ly
super|con|scious|
    ness
super|con|tin|ent
super|cool
super|crit|ical
super-duper
super|ego +s
super|eleva|tion
super|emi|nence
super|emi|nent
super|emi|nent|ly
super|eroga|tion
super|eroga|tory
super|ette
super|fam|ily
  super|fam|ilies
super|fat|ted
super|fec|und|
    ation
super|feta|tion
super|fi|cial
super|fici|al|ity
  super|fici|al|ities
super|fi|cial|ly
super|fi|cial|ness

super|fi|cies
  pl. super|fi|cies
super|fine
super|fluid
super|flu|id|ity
super|flu|ity
  super|flu|ities
su|per|flu|ous
su|per|flu|ous|ly
su|per|flu|ous|ness
super|fly
  super|flies
super|fusion
super|gal|axy
  super|gal|ax|ies
super|gene
super|giant
super|glue
  super|glu|ing or
  super|glue|ing
super|grass
super|grav|ity
super|group
super|heat
super|heat|er
super|heavy
super|heavy|
    weight
super|helic|al
super|helix
  super|heli|ces
super|hero
  super|heroes
super|het
super|het|ero|dyne
super|high|way
super|human
super|human|ly
super|im|pos|able
super|im|pose
  super|im|pos|ing
super|im|pos|ition
super|in|cum|bent
super|in|duce
  super|in|du|cing
super|infec|tion
super|in|tend
super|in|tend|ence
super|in|tend|ency
super|in|tend|ent
su|per|ior
su|per|ior|ity
su|per|ior|ly

su|per|ius highest
  voice part
super|jacent
su|per|la|tive
su|per|la|tive|ly
su|per|la|tive|ness
super|lat|tice
super|lumi|nal
super|lun|ary
super|major|ity
  super|major|ities
Super|man cartoon
  character
super|man
  super|men
  exceptional man
super|mar|ket
super|mas|sive
super|mini
super|model
su|per|nal
su|per|nal|ly
super|natant
super|nat|ural
super|nat|ur|al|ise
  Br. var. of
  supernaturalize
super|nat|ur|al|ism
super|nat|ur|al|ist
super|nat|ur|al|ize
  super|nat|ur|al|
    iz|ing
super|nat|ur|al|ly
super|nat|ur|al|
    ness
super|nor|mal
super|nor|mal|ity
super|nova
  super|novae or
  super|novas
super|numer|ary
  super|numer|ar|ies
super|order
super|ordinal
super|ordin|ate
super|oxide
super|phos|phate
super|plas|tic
super|plas|ti|city
super|pose
  super|pos|ing
super|pos|ition
super|power

super|sat|ur|ate
super|sat|ur|at|ing
super|sat|ur|ation
super|scalar
super|scribe
super|scrib|ing
super|script
super|scrip|tion
super|sede
super|sed|ing
super|sed|ence
super|sed|ure
super|ses|sion
super|set
super|size
super|siz|ing
super|sonic
super|son|ic|al|ly
super|space
super|spe|cies
pl. super|spe|cies
super|star
super|star|dom
super|state
super|sta|tion
super|sti|tion
super|sti|tious
super|sti|tious|ly
super|sti|tious|ness
super|store
super|stra|tum
super|strata
super|string
super|struc|tural
super|struc|ture
super|sym|met|ric
super|sym|metry
super|tank|er
super|taster
super|tax
super|title
super|tonic
super|twist
super|unlead|ed
super|user
super|vene
super|ven|ing
super|ven|ient
super|ven|tion
super|vise
super|vis|ing
super|vi|sion
super|visor

super|vis|ory
super|volt|age
super|woman
super|women
su|pin|ate
su|pin|at|ing
su|pin|ation
su|pin|ator
su|pine
su|pine|ly
su|pine|ness
sup|per
sup|per|less
sup|plant
sup|plant|er
sup|ple
sup|pling
sup|pler
sup|plest
supple|jack
sup|ple|ly
sup|ple|ment
sup|ple|men|tal
sup|ple|men|tal|ly
sup|ple|men|tar|ily
sup|ple|men|tary
sup|ple|men|tar|ies
sup|ple|men|ta|tion
supple|ness
sup|ple|tion
sup|ple|tive
Sup|plex *trademark*
sup|pli|ant
sup|pli|ant|ly
sup|pli|cant
sup|pli|cate
sup|pli|cat|ing
sup|pli|ca|tion
sup|pli|ca|tory
sup|plier
sup|ply
sup|plies
sup|plied
sup|ply|ing
provide; provision;
stock; cf. supplely
supply-sider
sup|port
sup|port|abil|ity
sup|port|able
sup|port|ably
sup|port|er

sup|port|ing|ly
sup|port|ive
sup|port|ive|ly
sup|port|ive|ness
sup|port|less
sup|pos|able
sup|pose
sup|pos|ing
sup|posed|ly
sup|pos|ition
sup|pos|ition|al
sup|pos|itious
sup|pos|itious|ly
sup|pos|itious|ness
sup|posi|ti|tious
sup|posi|ti|tious|ly
sup|posi|ti|tious|
ness
sup|posi|tory
sup|posi|tor|ies
sup|press
sup|pres|sant
sup|press|ible
sup|pres|sion
sup|pres|sive
sup|pres|sor
sup|pur|ate
sup|pur|at|ing
sup|pur|ation
sup|pura|tive
supra
supra|chi|as|mat|ic
supra|molecu|lar
supra|mund|ane
supra|nation|al
supra|nation|al|
ism
supra|nation|al|ity
supra|nuclear
supra|optic
supra|orbit|al
supra|renal
supra|seg|men|tal
su|prema|cism
su|prema|cist
su|prem|acy
su|prema|tism
su|prema|tist
su|preme highest;
very great; (dish in)
cream sauce;
French su|prême
(for dish or sauce)

su|preme|ly
su|preme|ness
su|premo +s
su|pre|mum
Mathematics
suq var. of souk; cf.
sook
sura section of
Koran
Sura|baya
surah fabric; var. of
sura
su|rahi
sural
sura|min
Surat
sur|cease
sur|ceas|ing
sur|charge
sur|char|ging
sur|cin|gle
sur|coat
sure
surer
sur|est
certain; cf. shaw,
shore
sure|ly with
certainty; cf.
shawlie
sure|ness
Sû|reté na|tio|nale
surety
sure|ties
surety|ship
surf breaking waves;
go surfing; move
between Internet
sites; cf. serf
sur|face
sur|facing
sur|facer
sur|fac|tant
surf|bird
surf|board
surf|cast|er
surf|cast|ing
surf|feit
surf|er
sur|fi|cial
sur|fi|cial|ly
surfie surfer
surf|perch

surfy
  surf|ier
  surfi|est
  having much surf
surge
  sur|ging
  swell; increase;
  move forward; cf.
  serge
sur|geon
surgeon|fish
sur|geon gen|eral
  sur|geons gen|eral
sur|geon's knot
sur|gery
  sur|ger|ies
sur|gi|cal
sur|gi|cal|ly
suri|cate
su|rimi
Suri|nam var. of
  Suriname
Suri|name
Suri|nam|er
Suri|nam|ese
sur|jec|tion
sur|jec|tive
sur|lily
sur|li|ness
surly
  sur|lier
  sur|li|est
sur|mise
  sur|mis|ing
sur|mount
sur|mount|able
sur|mul|let
sur|name
  sur|nam|ing
sur|pass
sur|pass|able
sur|pass|ing|ly
sur|plice vestment
sur|pliced
sur|plus (amount)
  left over
sur|prise
  sur|pris|ing
sur|prised|ly
sur|pris|ing|ly
sur|pris|ing|ness
surra
sur|real
sur|real|ism

sur|real|ist
sur|real|is|tic
sur|real|is|tic|al|ly
sur|real|ity
sur|real|ly
sur|rebut|tal
sur|rebut|ter
sur|rejoin|der
sur|ren|der
sur|rep|ti|tious
sur|rep|ti|tious|ly
sur|rep|ti|tious|
             ness
Sur|rey county,
  England
sur|rey carriage
sur|ro|gacy
sur|ro|gate
sur|ro|gate|ship
sur|round
sur|tax
Sur|tees, Rob|ert
  writer
sur|title
  sur|titling
sur|tout
Surt|sey
sur|veil|lance
sur|vey
sur|vey|or
sur|vey|or|ship
sur|viv|abil|ity
sur|viv|able
sur|vival
sur|viv|al|ism
sur|viv|al|ist
sur|vive
  sur|viv|ing
sur|vivor
sur|vivor|ship
Surya Hindu sun
  god
sus suspicion; cf.
  suss
Susa ancient city,
  SW Asia; alterna-
  tive name for
  Sousse
Susah var. of Susa
Su|sanna
  Apocrypha
Su|san|nah
Su|sanne

sus|cep|ti|bil|ity
  sus|cep|ti|bil|ities
sus|cep|tible
sus|cep|tibly
sus|cep|tive
sushi
sus|lik var. of
  souslik
sus|pect
sus|pend
sus|pend|er
sus|pense
sus|pense|ful
sus|pen|sible
sus|pen|sion
sus|pen|sive
sus|pen|sive|ly
sus|pen|sive|ness
sus|pen|sory
sus|pi|cion
sus|pi|cious
sus|pi|cious|ly
sus|pi|cious|ness
sus|pir|ation
sus|pire
  sus|pir|ing
Sus|que|hanna
suss figure out;
  knowledge; shrewd;
  cf. sus
Sus|sex
sus|tain
sus|tain|abil|ity
sus|tain|able
sus|tain|ably
sus|tain|ed|ly
sus|tain|er
sus|tain|ment
sus|ten|ance
sus|ten|ta|tion
Susu
  pl. Susu
su|sur|ra|tion
su|sur|rus
Suth|er|land Scot-
  tish region
Suth|er|land,
  Gra|ham painter
Suth|er|land, Joan
  opera singer
Sut|lej

sut|ler army
  provisioner; cf.
  subtler
sutra
sutta var. of sutra
sut|tee var. of sati
Sut|ton Cold|field
Sut|ton Hoo
su|tural
su|ture
  su|tur|ing
Suva
Su|wan|nee
suxa|meth|onium
Su|zanna
Su|zanne
su|zer|ain
su|zer|ainty
Su|zette in 'crêpe
  Suzette'
Su|zhou
Suz|man, Helen
  politician
Su|zuki
Sval|bard
Sved|berg
svelte
Sven Fork|beard
  var. of Sweyn
  Forkbeard
Sven|gali
Sverd|lovsk
Svet|am|bara
Sveti Kon|stan|tin
swab
  swabbed
  swab|bing
swab|bie
Swa|bia
Swa|bian
swacked
swad|dle
  swad|dling
swa|deshi
swag
  swagged
  swag|ging
swage
  swa|ging
swag|ger
  swag|ger|er
  swag|ger|ing|ly
swag|man
  swag|men

Swa|hili
  pl. Swa|hili
swain
swale
Swale|dale
swal|low
swal|low|able
swal|low|er
swal|low|tail
swallow-tailed
swallow-wort
swami
Swam|mer|dam,
  Jan naturalist
swamp|er
swamp|hen
swamp|land
swampy
  swamp|ier
  swampi|est
swan
  swanned
  swan|ning
Swanee var. of
  Suwannee
swank|ily
swanki|ness
swank|pot
swanky
  swank|ier
  swanki|est
swan|like
swan|nery
  swan|ner|ies
swans|down
Swan|sea
Swan|son, Gloria
  actress
swan|song
swan-upping
swap
  swapped
  swap|ping
swap|file
Swapo = South
  West Africa People's
  Organization
swap|pable
swap|per
swap|tion
swa|raj
swa|raj|ist
sward|ed
swarm|er

swar|thily
swar|thi|ness
swar|thy
  swar|thier
  swar|thi|est
swash|buckle
  swash|buck|ling
swash|buck|ler
swas|tika
SWAT team cf.
  SWOT
swat
  swat|ted
  swat|ting
  hit sharply; cf. swot
swath US n.
  swaths or swathes
swathe Br. n.
  swathes or swaths
  v. swath|ing
swather
Swa|tow
sway|back
sway-backed
Swazi
  pl. Swazi or
  Swa|zis
Swazi|land
swear
  swore
  sworn
swear|er
sweat|band
sweat|er
sweat|ily
sweati|ness
sweat|pants
sweat|shirt
sweat|shop
sweat|suit
sweaty
  sweat|ier
  sweati|est
Swede Swedish
  person
swede turnip
Swe|den
Swe|den|borg,
  Eman|uel scientist
Swe|den|borg|ian
swedge
  swedg|ing
Swed|ish
Swee|ney

sweep
  swept
sweep|back
sweep|er
sweep|ing|ly
sweep|ing|ness
sweep|stake
sweet confectionery;
  not bitter; pleasing;
  cf. suite
sweet|bread
sweet|briar Br.
sweet|brier US
sweet|corn
sweet|en
sweet|en|er
sweet|grass
sweet|heart
sweetie
sweetie-pie
sweet|ing
sweet|ish
sweet|lip var. of
  sweetlips
sweet|lips fish
  pl. sweet|lips
sweet|ly
sweet|meal
sweet|meat
sweet|ness
sweet|sop
sweet|veld
sweet wil|liam
swell
  swelled
  swol|len
swel|ter
swel|ter|ing|ly
swept-back adj.
swept-up adj.
swerve
  swerv|ing
swerve|less
swerver
Sweyn Fork|beard
  king of Denmark
swid|den
Swift, Jona|than
  writer
swiftie var. of swifty
swift|let
swift|ly
swift|ness

swifty
  swift|ies
swig
  swigged
  swig|ging
swig|ger
swill|er
swim
  swam
  swim|ming
  swum
swim|feed|er
swim|mable
swim|mer
swim|meret
swim|ming|ly
swim|suit
swim|suit|ed
swim|wear
Swin|burne,
  Al|ger|non Charles
  poet
swin|dle
  swind|ling
swind|ler
Swin|don
swine
  pl. swine animals
  swines or swine
  people
swine|herd
swing
  swung
swing|back
swing|bin
swing|boat
swing|by +s
swinge
  swinge|ing
  swinge|ing|ly
swing|er
swing|ing|ly
swin|gle
  swin|gling
swingle|tree
swing|om|eter
swing-wing
swingy
  swing|ier
  swingi|est
swin|ish
swin|ish|ly
swin|ish|ness

swipe
  swip¦ing
swiper
swip¦ple
swirl
swirly
  swirl¦ier
  swirli¦est
swishy
  swish¦ier
  swishi¦est
Swiss
  pl. Swiss
switch¦able
switch¦back
switch¦blade
switch¦board
switched-on adj.
switch¦er
switch¦eroo +s
switch¦gear
switch¦grass
switch-hitter
switch-hitting
switch-over n.
switch¦yard
swither
Swithin, St
Swithun var. of
  Swithin
Switz¦er¦land
swive
  swiv¦ing
swivel
  swiv¦elled Br.
  swiv¦eled US
  swiv¦el¦ling Br.
  swiv¦el¦ing US
swivet
swiz var. of swizz
swizz
swiz¦zle
  swiz¦zling
swol¦len
swop var. of swap
swop¦pable var. of
  swappable
swop¦per var. of
  swapper
sword
sword¦bill
sword-billed
sword¦fish
sword-like

sword¦play
swords¦man
  swords¦men
swords¦man¦ship
sword¦stick
sword¦tail
SWOT ana¦lysis cf.
  SWAT
swot
  swot¦ted
  swot¦ting
  study hard; cf. swat
swotty
  swot¦tier
  swot¦ti¦est
swy game
syb¦ar¦ite
syb¦ar¦it¦ic
syb¦ar¦it¦ic¦al¦ly
syb¦ar¦it¦ism
Sybil name; cf. sibyl
syca¦mine
syca¦more maple;
  Bible fig
syce groom; cf. sice
syco¦more var. of
  sycamore (fig)
sy¦co¦nium
  sy¦co¦nia
syco¦phancy
syco¦phant
syco¦phan¦tic
syco¦phan¦tic¦al¦ly
sy¦cosis skin
  infection; cf.
  psychosis
Syd¦en¦ham,
  Thomas physician
Syd¦ney city,
  Australia; name
sy¦en¦ite
sy¦en¦it¦ic
Syk¦tyv¦kar
syl¦lab¦ary
  syl¦lab¦ar¦ies
syl¦labi pl. of
  syllabus
syl¦lab¦ic
syl¦lab¦ic¦al¦ly
syl¦labi¦ca¦tion
syl¦lab¦icity
syl¦labi¦fi¦ca¦tion
syl¦labi¦fy

syl¦labi¦fied
syl¦labi¦fy¦ing
syl¦lab¦ise Br. var. of
  syllabize
syl¦lab¦ize
  syl¦lab¦iz¦ing
syl¦lable
  syl¦lab¦ling
syl¦la¦bub
syl¦la¦bus
  syl¦la¦buses or
  syl¦labi
syl¦lep¦sis
  syl¦lep¦ses
syl¦lep¦tic
syl¦lep¦tic¦al¦ly
syl¦lo¦gise Br. var. of
  syllogize
syl¦lo¦gism
syl¦lo¦gis¦tic
syl¦lo¦gis¦tic¦al¦ly
syl¦lo¦gize
  syl¦lo¦giz¦ing
sylph¦like
syl¦van of woods;
  wooded; cf. silvern
Syl¦vaner
syl¦vat¦ic
Syl¦via
Syl¦vian fis¦sure
Syl¦vie
syl¦vine
syl¦vin¦ite
syl¦vite
Syl¦vius
sym¦biont
sym¦bi¦osis
  sym¦bi¦oses
sym¦bi¦ot¦ic
sym¦bi¦ot¦ic¦al¦ly
sym¦bol
  sym¦bolled Br.
  sym¦boled US
  sym¦bol¦ling Br.
  sym¦bol¦ing US
  representation;
  sign; cf. cymbal
sym¦bol¦ic
sym¦bol¦ic¦al
sym¦bol¦ic¦al¦ly
sym¦bol¦isa¦tion Br.
  var. of
  symbolization

sym¦bol¦ise Br. var.
  of symbolize
Sym¦bol¦ism artistic
  movement
sym¦bol¦ism use of
  symbols; symbolic
  meaning
Sym¦bol¦ist adher-
  ent of Symbolism
sym¦bol¦ist user of
  symbols, cf.
  cymbalist
sym¦bol¦is¦tic
sym¦bol¦iza¦tion
sym¦bol¦ize
  sym¦bol¦iz¦ing
sym¦bol¦ogy
sym¦met¦ric
sym¦met¦ric¦al
sym¦met¦ric¦al¦ly
sym¦met¦rise Br.
  var. of symmetrize
sym¦met¦rize
sym¦met¦riz¦ing
sym¦met¦ro¦
  pho¦bia
sym¦metry
  sym¦met¦ries
Sy¦mons, Ju¦lian
  writer
sym¦path¦ec¦tomy
sym¦path¦
  ec¦to¦mies
sym¦pa¦thet¦ic
sym¦pa¦thet¦ic¦al¦ly
sym¦pa¦thique
sym¦pa¦thise Br.
  var. of sympathize
sym¦pa¦thiser Br.
  var. of sympathizer
sym¦pa¦thize
  sym¦pa¦thiz¦ing
sym¦pa¦thizer
sym¦patho¦lyt¦ic
sym¦patho¦
  mimet¦ic
sym¦pathy
  sym¦pa¦thies
sym¦pat¦ric
sym¦patry
  sym¦pat¦ries
sym¦pet¦al¦ous
sym¦pet¦aly
sym¦phon¦ic

sym|phon|ic|al|ly
sym|phon|ist
sym|phony
  sym|phon|ies
Sym|phyla
sym|phyl|an
sym|phys|eal
sym|phys|ial var. of
  symphyseal
sym|phy|sis
  sym|phy|ses
sym|plasm
sym|plas|mic
sym|plast
sym|plas|tic
sym|po|dial
sym|po|dium
  sym|po|dia
sym|po|si|ast
sym|po|sium
  sym|po|sia or
  sym|po|siums
symp|tom
symp|tom|at|ic
symp|tom|at|ic|al|ly
symp|tom|atol|ogy
symp|tom|ise Br.
  var. of symptomize
symp|tom|ize
  symp|tom|iz|ing
symp|tom|less
sympto-thermal
syn|aes|the|sia Br.
  US synesthesia
syn|aes|thete Br.
  US synesthete
syn|aes|thet|ic Br.
  US synesthetic
syna|gogal
syna|gogic|al
syna|gogue
syn|apo|morphy
  syn|apo|morphies
syn|apse
syn|apsid
syn|ap|sis
  synap|ses
syn|ap|tic
syn|ap|tic|al|ly
syn|apto|nemal
syn|arch|ic
syn|arch|ist
syn|archy

syn|arth|rosis
  syn|arth|roses
syn|astry
sync +s +ed +ing =
  synchronization;
  synchronize; cf.
  cinque, sink
syn|carp|ous
syn|chon|drosis
  syn|chon|droses
syn|chro +s
syn|chro|cyclo|tron
syn|chro|mesh
syn|chron|ic
syn|chron|ic|al|ly
syn|chron|icity
syn|chron|isa|tion
  Br. var. of
  synchronization
syn|chron|ise Br.
  var. of synchronize
syn|chron|iser Br.
  var. of
  synchronizer
syn|chron|ism
syn|chron|is|tic
syn|chron|is|tic|
  al|ly
syn|chron|iza|tion
syn|chron|ize
  syn|chron|iz|ing
syn|chron|izer
syn|chron|ous
syn|chron|ous|ly
syn|chrony
syn|chro|tron
syn|clinal
syn|cline
syn|co|pal
syn|co|pate
  syn|co|pat|ing
syn|co|pa|tion
syn|co|pa|tor
syn|cope
syn|cre|tic
syn|cre|tisa|tion Br.
  var. of
  syncretization
syn|cre|tise Br. var.
  of syncretize
syn|cre|tism
syn|cre|tist
syn|cre|tis|tic
syn|cre|tiza|tion

syn|cre|tize
syn|cre|tiz|ing
syn|cyt|ial
syn|cyt|ium
syn|cytia
syn|dac|tyl
syn|dac|tyl|ism
syn|dac|tyl|ous
syn|dac|tyly
syn|des|mosis
  syn|des|moses
syn|det|ic
syn|dic
syn|dic|al|ism
syn|dic|al|ist
syn|di|cate
  syn|di|cat|ing
syn|di|ca|tion
syn|dio|tac|tic
syn|drome
syn|drom|ic
syne since; cf. **sine,
  sign**
syn|ec|doche
syn|ec|doch|ic
syn|ec|doch|ic|al
syn|ec|doch|ic|al|ly
syn|eco|logic|al
syn|ecolo|gist
syn|ecol|ogy
syn|ec|tics
  trademark
syn|ere|sis
  syn|er|eses
syn|er|get|ic
syn|er|gic
syn|er|gism
syn|er|gist
syn|er|gis|tic
syn|er|gis|tic|al|ly
syn|ergy
  syn|er|gies
syn|es|the|sia US
  Br. synaesthesia
syn|es|thete US
  Br. synaesthete
syn|es|thet|ic US
  Br. synaesthetic
syn|fuel
syn|gam|ous
syn|gamy
syn|gas

Synge, J. M. play-
  wright
syn|gen|eic
syn|gen|et|ic
synod
syn|od|al
syn|od|ic
syn|od|ic|al
syno|nym
syno|nym|ic
syno|nym|ity
syn|onym|ous
syn|onym|ous|ly
syn|onym|ous|ness
syn|onymy
  syn|ony|mies
syn|op|sis
  syn|op|ses
syn|op|sise Br. var.
  of synopsize
syn|op|size
  syn|op|siz|ing
Syn|op|tic Gospels
syn|op|tic
syn|op|tic|al|ly
syn|op|tist
syn|os|tosis
  syn|os|toses
syn|ovial
syno|vitis
syn|sacral
syn|sacrum
  syn|sacra or
  syn|sacrums
syn|tac|tic
syn|tac|tic|al
syn|tac|tic|al|ly
syn|tagm
syn|tagma
  syn|tag|mas or
  syn|tag|mata
  var. of syntagm
syn|tag|mat|ic
syn|tag|mat|ic|al|ly
syn|tag|mic
syn|tax
syn|ten|ic
syn|teny
syn|thase
syn|the|sis
  syn|the|ses
syn|the|sise Br. var.
  of synthesize

syn|the|siser *Br.*
　var. of **synthesizer**
syn|the|sist
syn|the|size
　syn|the|siz|ing
syn|the|sizer
syn|thes|pian
　trademark
syn|thet|ic
syn|thet|ic|al
syn|thet|ic|al|ly
syn|the|tise *Br.* var.
　of **synthesize**
syn|the|tize var. of
　synthesize
syn|thon
synth-pop
synthy
syn|tone
syn|ton|ic
syn|type
syph|ilis
syph|il|ise *Br.* var.
　of **syphilize**
syph|il|it|ic
syph|il|ize
　syph|il|iz|ing
syph|il|oid
sy|phon var. of
　siphon
sy|phon|age var. of
　siphonage
sy|phon|al var. of
　siphonal
sy|phon|ic var. of
　siphonic
Syra|cuse
Syrah
syr|ette *trademark*
Syria
Syr|iac language
Syr|ian (citizen) of
　Syria
syr|inga
syr|inge
　syr|in|ging
syr|in|geal
syr|ingo|mye|lia
syr|inx
Syro-Phoeni|cian
syr|phid

syr|taki
syrup
syr|upy
sys|admin = system
　administrator
sysop = system
　operator
sys|tem
sys|tem|at|ic
sys|tem|at|ic|al|ly
sys|tem|atisa|tion
　Br. var. of
　systematization
sys|tem|atise *Br.*
　var. of **systematize**
sys|tem|atiser *Br.*
　var. of **systematizer**
sys|tem|atism
sys|tem|atist
sys|tem|atiza|tion
sys|tem|atize
sys|tem|atiz|ing
sys|tem|atizer
sys|tem|ic
sys|tem|ic|al|ly
sys|tem|isa|tion *Br.*
　var. of
　systemization
sys|tem|ise *Br.* var.
　of **systemize**
sys|tem|iser *Br.* var.
　of **systemizer**
sys|tem|iza|tion
sys|tem|ize
sys|tem|iz|ing
sys|tem|izer
sys|tem|less
sys|tole
sys|tol|ic
syzygy
　syzy|gies
Szcze|cin
Sze|chuan var. of
　Sichuan
Sze|chwan var. of
　Sichuan
Sze|ged
Szent-Györgyi,
　Al|bert biochemist
Szi|lard, Leo physi-
　cist

T

ta = thank you; cf.
　tahr, tar
taal var. of tala
taal Afrikaans
TAB = typhoid-
　paratyphoid A and
　B vaccine
tab
　tabbed
　tab|bing
tabac
ta|banca
tab|ard
tab|aret
Tab|asco
　state, Mexico;
　trademark sauce
tab|bou|leh
tabby
　tab|bies
tab|er|nacle
tab|er|nacled
tabes
tabes dor|salis
tab|et|ic
tabi
　pl. tabi
　Japanese sock;
　cf. **tabby**
Tab|itha
tabla
tab|la|ture
table
　tab|ling
tab|leau
　tab|leaux
tab|leau viv|ant
　tab|leaux viv|ants
table|cloth
table d'hôte
table|ful
table|land
table|spoon
table|spoon|ful
tab|let
table|top
table|ware
tab|lier

tab|loid
tab|loid|isa|tion *Br.*
　var. of
　tabloidization
tab|loid|iza|tion
taboo +s +ed +ing
tabor
tab|oret *US*
tab|ouret *Br.*
Ta|briz
tabu +s +ed +ing
　var. of **taboo**
tabu|lar
tab|ula rasa
　tabu|lae rasae
tabu|lar|ly
tabu|late
　tabu|lat|ing
tabu|la|tion
tabu|la|tor
tabun
taca|ma|hac
tacan
tac-au-tac
tacet *Music* indicat-
　ing silence; cf. **tacit**
tach = tachometer;
　cf. **tack**
tache var. of tash
tachi
Ta|ching var. of
　Daqing
tach|ism
tach|isme var. of
　tachism
tach|is|to|scope
tach|is|to|scop|ic
tach|is|to|scop|ic|
　　　　　　al|ly
tacho +s = tacho-
　graph, tachometer;
　cf. **taco**
tacho|graph
tach|om|eter
tachy|car|dia
tach|yg|raph|er
tachy|graph|ic
tach|yg|raphy
tachy|ki|nin
tach|ym|eter
tachy|met|ric
tach|yon
tachy|phyl|axis

tach|yp|nea *US*
tach|yp|noea *Br.*
tacit understood or
implied; cf. **tacet**
Tacit|ean
tacit|ly
taci|turn
taci|turn|ity
taci|turn|ly
Taci|tus Roman
historian
tack senses except
'tachometer'; cf.
tach
tack|er
tackie
tack|ily
tacki|ness
tackle
tack|ling
tack|ler
tacky
tack|ier
tacki|est
taco +s tortilla; cf.
tacho
tacon|ite
tac|rine
tact
Tac|tel *trademark*
tact|ful
tact|ful|ly
tact|ful|ness
tac|tic
tac|tic|al
tac|tic|al|ly
tac|ti|cian
tac|ti|city
tact|ile
tac|til|ity
tact|less
tact|less|ly
tact|less|ness
tac|tual
tac|tus *Music*
tadger var. of
todger
Ta|djik var. of Tajik
Ta|djiki|stan var. of
Tajikistan
Tad|mor var. of
Tadmur
Tad|mur

tad|pole
Ta|dzhik var. of
Tajik
Ta|dzhiki|stan var.
of Tajikistan
tae-bo *trademark*
tae|dium vitae
Taegu
Tae|jon
tae kwon do
tael weight; cf. **tail**,
tale
tae|nia
tae|niae or tae|nias
Br.
US tenia
tae|niae coli *Br.*
US teniae coli
taenio|dont
taeni|oid *Br.*
US tenioid
Taff *often offensive*
Welsh person
taf|feta
taff|rail
Taffy
Taf|fies
often offensive
Welsh person
taffy
taf|fies
confection; insin-
cere flattery
tafia
Taft, Wil|liam
How|ard US
president
tag
tagged
tag|ging
Taga|log
Taga|met
trademark
Tag|an|rog
ta|gati
pl. ta|gati
v. ta|ga|ties
ta|ga|tied
ta|gati|ing
witch; (practise)
witchcraft
ta|getes plant
ta|gine
taglia|telle

tagma
tag|mata
tag|ma|tise *Br.* var.
of tagmatize
tag|ma|tize
tag|ma|tiz|ing
tag|meme
tag|mem|ic
Ta|gore,
Ra|bin|dra|nath
writer
tagua nut
Tagus
ta|hina var. of
tahini
ta|hini
Ta|hiti
Ta|hi|tian
tahr animal; cf. **ta**,
tar
tah|sil var. of tehsil
Tai language family;
cf. **Thai**
tai fish
pl. tai
Tai'an
t'ai chi (ch'uan)
Tai|chung
Ta'if
Taig *offensive*
taiga forest; cf. **tiger**
taiko +s
taiko|naut
tail part of animal;
end; follow; cf.
tael, **tale**
tail|back
tail|board
tail|coat
tail|drag|ger
tail-ender
tail|gate
tail|gat|ing
tail|gater
taille
Taille|ferre,
Ger|maine
composer
tail|less
tail|leur
tail-off *n.*
tailor
tailor|bird
tailor|fish

tailor-made
tailor's chalk
tailor's twist
tail|piece
tail|pipe
tail|plane
tail|spin
tail|spun
tail|spin|ning
tail|stock
tail|water
tail|wheel
tail|wind
tai|men
pl. tai|men
Tai|myr
Pen|in|sula
Tai|nan
Taino
taint|less
tai|pan
Tai|pei
Tai|ping
Re|bel|lion
Tai|wan
Tai|wan|ese
Tai|yuan
Ta'iz city, Yemen
Taizé
taj
tajes
Tajik person;
language
Ta|jiki Tajik
language
Ta|jiki|stan
ta|jine var. of tagine
Taj Mahal
taka
pl. taka
Bangladeshi
currency; cf. **taker**
tak|able
taka|ful
ta|kahe
take
took
tak|ing
taken
take|able var. of
takable
take|away *n.*
take|down *n.*
take-off *n.*

take|out *n.*
take-out double
take|over *n.*
taker person who
  takes; cf. taka
take-up *n.*
takht
takin
tak|ing|ly
tak|ing|ness
Taki-Taki
tak|kie var. of
  tackie
Takla Makan var.
  of Taklimakan
  Desert
Tak|li|ma|kan
Tako|radi
tala +s *Music;* cf.
  thaler
tala
  pl. tala or talas
  Samoan currency;
  cf. thaler
Ta|laing
  pl. Ta|laing or
  Ta|laings
tala|poin
talaq
tal|aria
Tal|bot, Fox
  photography
  pioneer
tal|bot dog
talc +ed +ing
talc|ose
talc|ous
tal|cum
talcy
tale story; cf. tael,
  tail
Tale|ban var. of
  Taliban
Tale|ban|iza|tion
  var. of
  Talibanization
Tale|ban|ize var. of
  Talibanize
tale|bear|er
tale|bear|ing
ta|leg|gio
tal|ent
tal|ent|ed
tal|ent|less

tales writ
ta|les|man
ta|les|men
  Law; cf. talisman
tale|tell|er
tale-telling
tali *pl.* of talus
Tali|ban
Tali|ban|isa|tion
  Br. var. of
  Talibanization
Tali|ban|ise *Br.* var.
  of Talibanize
Tali|ban|iza|tion
Tali|ban|ize
  Tali|ban|iz|ing
Tali|esin bard
talik
tali|pes
tali|pot
tal|is|man +s lucky
  charm; cf.
  talesman
tal|is|man|ic
talk cf. torc, torque
talka|thon
talk|ative
talk|ative|ly
talk|ative|ness
talk|back *n.*
talk|board
talkee-talkee
talk|er
talk|fest
talkie film; cf.
  torquey
talking-to
talk|time
tall
tall|age
Tal|la|has|see
tall|boy
Tal|ley|rand,
  Charles de French
  statesman
tal|lier
Tal|linn
Tal|lis, Thomas
  composer
tall|ish
tall|lith
tall|ness
tal|low

tallow-wood
tal|lowy
tally
tal|lies
tal|lied
tally|ing
tally-ho
  pl. tally-hos
  v. tally-hoes
tally-hoed
tally-hoing
tally|man
tally|men
Tal|mud
Tal|mud|ic
Tal|mud|ist
talon
tal|oned
taluk
ta|luka var. of taluk
talus
  tali bones
  tal|uses slopes
tal|war
tam|able var. of
  tameable
tama|gotchi
  trademark
tam|ale
tam|an|dua
Ta|mang
  pl. Ta|mang or
  Ta|mangs
Tamar river,
  England
Ta|mara name
tam|ar|ack
tam|arau
ta|mari
tam|ar|illo +s
tam|arin marmoset
tam|ar|ind fruit;
  tree
tam|ar|isk
ta|ma|sha
Tama|shek
Tamau|lipas
tam|bala
  pl. tam|bala or
  tam|ba|las
Tambo, Oli|ver
  politician
tam|botie

tam|bour drum;
  embroidery frame;
  circular structure
tam|boura lute
tam|bourin drum;
  dance
tam|bour|ine jin-
  gling percussion
  instrument
tam|bour|in|ist
Tam|bov
tam|bura var. of
  tamboura
tam|bur|itza
Tam|bur|laine var.
  of Tamerlane
tame
tam|ing
tamer
tam|est
tame|able
tame|ly
tame|ness
tamer
Tam|er|lane
  Mongol ruler
Tamil
Ta|mil|ian
Tamil Nadu
Tamla Mo|town
  trademark
Tam|many
Tam|many|ite
Tam|muz Mesopo-
  tamian god; var. of
  Thammuz
tam-o'-shanter
tam|oxi|fen
Tampa city, US
Tam|pax *trademark*
  pl. Tam|pax
tam|per interfere
Tam|pere city,
  Finland
tam|per|er
Tam|pico
tam|pion
tam|pon
tam|pon|ade
Tam|sin
tam-tam
Tam|worth
tan
  tanned

tan|ning
Tana, Lake
tan|ager
Tan|agra
Tá|naiste
Tanak
Tana|na|rive
tan|bark
tan|dem
tan|door
tan|doori
Tanga port,
 Tanzania
tanga briefs
Tan|gan|yika
Tan|gan|yi|kan
tang|ata whe|nua
Tange, Kenzo
 architect
tan|gelo +s
tan|gency
 tan|gen|cies
tan|gent
tan|gen|tial
tan|gen|tial|ly
tan|ger|ine
tangi
tan|gi|bil|ity
tan|gible
tan|gible|ness
tan|gibly
Tan|gier
tangi|ness
tan|gle
 tan|gling
tangle|foot
tan|gly
 tan|glier
 tan|gli|est
tango
 pl. tan|gos
 v. tan|goes
 tan|goed
 tango|ing
tan|gram
Tang|shan
Tan|gut
 pl. Tan|gut or
 Tan|guts
tangy
 tangi|er
 tangi|est
tanh hyperbolic
 tangent

tania var. of tannia
tan|ist
tan|ist|ry
tani|wha
 pl. tani|wha or
 tani|whas
Tan|jung|ka|rang
tanka Japanese
 poem; cf. tanker
tank|age
tank|ard
tank|er ship; air-
 craft; vehicle; cf.
 tanka
tank-farming
tank|ful
tan|kini
tank|less
tan|nable
tan|nate
tan|ner
tan|nery
 tan|ner|ies
Tann|häu|ser poet
tan|nia
tan|nic
tan|nie
tan|nin
tan|nish
tan|noy trademark
Tannu-Tuva
Ta|noan
tan|pura
Tan|sen musician
tansu
 pl. tansu
tansy
 tan|sies
tan|tal|ic
tan|tal|isa|tion Br.
 var. of
 tantalization
tan|tal|ise Br. var. of
 tantalize
tan|tal|iser Br. var.
 of tantalizer
tan|tal|is|ing|ly Br.
 var. of tantalizingly
tan|tal|ite
tan|tal|iza|tion
tan|tal|ize
 tan|tal|iz|ing
tan|tal|izer
tan|tal|iz|ing|ly

tan|ta|lum
Tan|ta|lus Greek
 Mythology
tan|ta|lus stand for
 decanters
tan|ta|mount
tante
tan|tivy
 tan|tivies
tant mieux
tanto +s
tant pis
tan|tra
tan|tric
tan|trism
tan|trist
tan|trum
Tan|za|nia
Tan|za|nian
tan|zan|ite
Tao
Taoi|seach
Tao|ism
Tao|ist
Tao|is|tic
taonga
 pl. taonga
Taor|mina
Tao-te-Ching
tap
 tapped
 tap|ping
tapa bark; cloth; cf.
 tappa, tapper
tapas Spanish bar
 snacks
tape
 tap|ing
tape-grass
tap|en|ade
 French tapénade
taper thin candle;
 make or become
 thinner; cf. tapir
taper|er
tap|es|tried
tap|es|try
 tap|es|tries
tap|etum
tape|worm
tapho|nom|ic
taph|ono|mist
taph|onomy

tap-in n.
tapi|oca
tapir animal; cf.
 taper
tapis
 pl. tapis
tap|less
tapote|ment
tappa song; cf. tapa,
 tapper
tap|pable
tap|per person or
 thing that taps; cf.
 tapa, tapas, tappa
tap|pet
tap|room
tap|root
tap|ster
tapu
ta|que|ria
tar
 tarred
 tar|ring
 (cover with) dark
 liquid; sailor; cf. ta,
 tahr
Tara hill, Republic
 of Ireland; name
ta-ra goodbye
tara|did|dle
tara|kihi
tar|ama
tara|ma|sa|lata
Tara|naki
tar|an|tass
tar|an|tella
taran|telle var. of
 tarantella
Taran|tino,
 Quen|tin film
 director
tar|ant|ism
Tar|anto
tar|an|tula
ta|rata
Tar|awa
tar|boosh
tar|brush
Tar|den|ois|ian
Tardi|grada
tar|di|grade
tar|dily
tar|di|ness
Tar|dis

tar|dive
dys|kin|esia

tardy
  tar|dier
  tar|di|est

tare weed; unladen
  weight; cf. tear

Targa *trademark*

tar|get

tar|get|able

Tar|gum

Tar|gum|ist

tar|iff

Tarim

ta|riqa

ta|riqat var. of
  tariqa

tarka dhal

Tar|kov|sky,
  An|drei film
  director

tar|la|tan

tar|mac

tar|macked

tar|mack|ing
  trademark

tar|mac|adam +ed

tar|na|tion

tar|nish

tar|nish|able

Tar|nów

taro +s plant

tarot cards

tar|pan horse; cf.
  tarpon

tar|paper

tar|pau|lin

Tar|peia Roman
  Vestal Virgin

Tar|peian Rock

tar|pon fish; cf.
  tarpan

Tar|quin

Tar|quin|ius
  Pris|cus king of
  Rome

Tar|quin|ius
  Su|perbus king of
  Rome

tar|ra|did|dle var.
  of taradiddle

tar|ra|gon

Tar|ra|gona

tar|ras

Tar|rasa

tar|ri|ness

tarry
  tar|rier
  tar|ri|est
  of tar

tarry
  tar|ries
  tar|ried
  tarry|ing
  linger

tar|sal

tarsi pl. of tarsus

tar|sier animal

tarso|meta|tar|sal

tarso|meta|tar|sus

tarso|meta|tarsi

Tar|sus city, Turkey

tar|sus
  tarsi
  group of bones

tar|tan

Tar|tar Asian led by
  Genghis Khan; cf.
  tartar, tartare,
  ta-ta, Tatar

tar|tar deposit on
  teeth etc.; violent-
  tempered person;
  in 'cream of tartar';
  cf. Tartar, tartare,
  ta-ta, Tatar

tar|tare sauce; cf.
  Tartar, tartar,
  ta-ta, Tatar

Tar|tar|ean of
  Tartarus

Tar|tar|ian of
  Tartars

tar|tar|ic

Tar|tarus Greek
  god; part of
  underworld

Tar|tary historical
  region, Asia and E.
  Europe

tarte Tatin
  tartes Tatin

tart|ily

tarti|ness

tart|let

tart|ly

tart|ness

tar|trate

tar|tra|zine

Tar|tuffe hypocrite

Tar|tuf|ferie

Tar|tuf|fery var. of
  Tartufferie

tar|tufo

tar|tufi or
  tar|tu|fos
  truffle

tarty
  tart|ier
  tarti|est

tar|weed

tar|whine

Tar|zan

tasca

taser *trademark*

tash = moustache

Tashi Lama

Tash|kent

task|master

task|mis|tress

Tass Soviet news
  agency

tass cup

tassa drum

tas|sel
  tas|selled *Br.*
  tas|seled *US*
  tas|sel|ling *Br.*
  tas|sel|ing *US*

tas|sie

Tasso, Tor|quato
  writer

taste

tast|ing

taste|ful

taste|ful|ly

taste|ful|ness

taste|less

taste|less|ly

taste|less|ness

taste|maker

taster

tas|te|vin

tasti|ly

tasti|ness

tasty
  tasti|er
  tasti|est

tat

tat|ted

tat|ting

ta-ta goodbye; cf.
  Tartar, tartar,
  tartare, Tatar

tat|ami

Tatar (member of)
  modern Turkic
  people; language;
  cf. Tartar, tartar,
  tartare, ta-ta

Tatar|stan

Tate art collections

Tate, Nahum
  dramatist

tater = potato

Ta|tha|gata

ta|thata

Tati, Jacques film
  director

Tati|ana

tatie = potato

Tatra Moun|tains

tat|ter|de|ma|lion

tat|tered

tat|ters

tat|ter|sall fabric

Tat|ter|salls horse
  auctioneers

tat|tery

tat|tie = potato; cf.
  tatty

tat|tily

tat|ti|ness

tat|ting

tat|tle

tat|tling

tat|tler

tattle|tale

tat|too +s +ed +ing

tat|too|er

tat|too|ist

tatty
  tat|tier
  tat|ti|est
  shabby; of poor
  quality; cf. tattie

Tatum, Art pianist

tau Greek letter; cf.
  taw, tor, tore, torr

taught past tense
  and participle of
  teach; cf. taut,

tort, torte
taunt|er
taunt|ing|ly
Taun|ton
taupe colour; cf.
tope
Taupo town, Lake,
New Zealand
Tau|ranga
Taur|ean person
born under Taurus
taur|ine of bulls
tauro|chol|ate
tauro|chol|ic
Taurus constella-
tion; sign of zodiac;
Mountains; cf.
torus
taut tight; cf.
taught, tort, torte
taut|en
taut|ly
taut|ness
tau|tog
tauto|logic|al
tauto|logic|al|ly
tau|tolo|gise Br.
var. of tautologize
tau|tolo|gist
tau|tolo|gize
tau|tolo|giz|ing
tau|tolo|gous
tau|tol|ogy
tau|tolo|gies
tauto|mer
tauto|mer|ic
tau|to|mer|ism
tau|to|nym
tau|ton|ymy
Tavel
Tav|ener, John
modern composer
tav|ern
tav|erna
Tav|er|ner, John
16th-century
composer
Tav|ern|ers in
'Lord's Taverners'
taw make into lea-
ther; playing
marble; cf. tau, tor,
tore, torr
tawa

taw|drily
taw|dri|ness
taw|dry
taw|drier
taw|dri|est
tawer
taw|ni|ness
tawny
taw|nier
taw|ni|est
taws var. of tawse
tawse
tax
taxa pl. of taxon; cf.
taxer
tax|able
tax|ation
taxer person who
levies a tax; cf. taxa
taxi
pl. taxis
v. tax|ies
tax|ied
taxi|ing or taxy|ing
taxi|cab
taxi|der|mal
taxi|der|mic
taxi|der|mic|al|ly
taxi|der|mist
taxi|dermy
taxi|meter
taxis pl. of taxi
taxis Surgery;
Biology; Linguistics
taxes
taxi|way
tax|man
tax|men
taxol trademark
taxon
taxa
taxo|nom|ic
taxo|nom|ic|al
taxo|nom|ic|al|ly
tax|ono|mist
tax|onomy
tax|on|omies
tax|pay|er
tax-paying
tay|berry
tay|berries
Tay|lor, Eliza|beth
actress

Tay|lor, Jer|emy
churchman
Tay|lor, Zach|ary
US president
Tay|lor|ism
Tay|lor|ist
Tay|myr
Pen|in|sula var. of
Taimyr Peninsula
tayra
Tay|side
tazza
T-back
T-bar
Tbil|isi
T-bill
T-bone
T-boning
T-cell
tchagra
Tchai|kov|sky,
Pyotr Ilich
composer
tchotchke
te Br.
note in tonic sol-fa
US ti; cf. tea, tee
tea
teaed or tea'd
tea|ing
drink; take tea; cf.
te, tee, ti
tea|cake
teach
taught
instruct; cf. taut,
tort, torte
teach|abil|ity
teach|able
teach|able|ness
teach|er
teacher|age
teach|er|ly
teach-in n.
Teachta Dála
Teachti Dála
tea|cup
tea|cup|ful
tea|head
teak
teal
team group; form a
team; cf. teem
team|er

team|mate
team|ster
team-teaching
team|work
tea|pot
tea|poy
tear
tore
torn
rip; pull; move
quickly; cf. tare
tear fluid in eyes; cf.
tier, Tyr
tear|able
tear|away n.
tear|drop
tear|er
tear|ful
tear|ful|ly
tear|ful|ness
tear-jerker
tear-jerking
tear|less
tear|less|ly
tear|less|ness
tear-like
tear-off adj.
teary
tearier
teariest
tease
teas|ing
tea|sel
teaser
teas|ing|ly
Teas|made
trademark
tea|spoon
tea|spoon|ful
teat
tea|time
tea tree Australa-
sian or Mediterra-
nean shrub
tea|zel var. of teasel
tea|zle
teaz|ling
var. of teasel
Tebet
tec = detective
tech = technical col-
lege; technician;
technology

techie technology
  enthusiast
tech|ne|tium
tech|nic
tech|nical
tech|ni|cal|ity
  tech|ni|cal|ities
tech|ni|cal|ly
tech|ni|cian
tech|ni|cist
Tech|ni|color cine-
  matographic
  process *trademark*
tech|ni|color (of)
  vivid colour
tech|ni|colored
tech|ni|col|our *Br.*
  var. of technicolor
tech|ni|col|oured
  Br. var. of
  technicolored
tech|ni|kon
tech|nique
techno
techno|babble
tech|noc|racy
  tech|noc|ra|cies
techno|crat
techno|crat|ic
techno|crat|ic|al|ly
techno|fear
techno|logic|al
techno|logic|al|ly
tech|nolo|gist
tech|nol|ogy
  tech|nolo|gies
techno|phile
techno|philia
techno|philic
techno|phobe
techno|pho|bia
techno|pho|bic
techno|pre|neur
techno|pre|neur|
        ial
techno|pre|neur|
        ship
techno|speak
techno|stress
techno|struc|ture
techy
  tech|ies
  var. of techie
techy var. of tetchy

tecta pl. of tectum
tec|ton|ic
tec|ton|ic|al|ly
tec|tono|phys|ics
tec|tono|strati|
        graph|ic
tec|tor|ial
tec|trix
  tec|tri|ces
tec|tum
  tecta
Ted = Teddy boy;
  name
ted
  ted|ded
  ted|ding
  turn hay etc.
ted|der
Teddy name; in
  'Teddy boy'
teddy
  ted|dies
  toy bear; garment
Te Deum hymn; cf.
  tedium
te|di|ous
te|di|ous|ly
te|di|ous|ness
te|dium boredom;
  cf. Te Deum
tee
  tees
  teed
  tee|ing
  in golf etc.; T-shirt;
  cf. te, tea, ti
tee-hee
  tee-hees
  tee-heed
  tee-heeing
teem be full; cf.
  team
teen|age
teen|aged
teen|ager
teensy
  teen|sier
  teen|si|est
teensy-weensy
  teensy-weensier
  teensy-weensiest
teeny
  teen|ier
  teeni|est
teeny-bop

teeny-bopper
teeny-weeny
  teeny-weenier
  teeny-weeniest
tee|pee var. of tepee
Tees river, England
tee shirt var. of
  T-shirt
Tees|side
Tees|water
tee|ter
teeth pl. of tooth
teethe *v.*
  teeth|ing
tee|total
tee|total|er *US*
tee|total|ism
tee|total|ler *Br.*
tee|totum
te|fil|lin
TEFL = teaching of
  English as a foreign
  language
Tef|lon *trademark*
teg|men
  teg|mina
teg|men|tal
teg|men|tum
  teg|menta
tegu
  pl. tegu or tegus
Tegu|ci|galpa
teg|ula
  tegu|lae
tegu|ment
tegu|men|tal
tegu|men|tary
te-hee var. of tee-
  hee
Teh|eran var. of
  Tehran
Teh|ran
teh|sil
tei|cho|ic
Teil|hard de
  Char|din, Pierre
  philosopher
tein
  pl. tein or teins
  Kazakh currency
tej Ethiopian mead
Te|jano +s
Te Kan|awa, Kiri
  singer

tekke monastery
tek|tite
tela|mon
  tela|mo|nes
tell|angi|ecta|sia
tell|angi|ecta|sis
tell|angi|ectat|ic
Tel Aviv-Jaffa
telco +s
tele-ad
tele|bank|ing
tele|cast
tele|cast|er
tele|cen|ter *US*
tele|centre *Br.*
tele|cine
tele|com
tele|comms var. of
  telecoms
tele|com|mu|ni|
        ca|tion
tele|com|mute
tele|com|mut|ing
tele|com|muter
tele|com|puter
tele|com|put|ing
tele|coms =
  telecommunications
tele|con|fer|ence
tele|con|fer|en|cing
tele|con|nec|tion
tele|con|vert|er
Tele|copier
  trademark
tele|cot|tage
tel|edu
tele-evangel|ic|al
  var. of
  televangelical
tele-evangel|ism
  var. of
  televangelism
tele-evangel|ist var.
  of televangelist
tele|fac|sim|ile
tele|fax *trademark*
tele|feric var. of
  téléphérique
tele|film
tele|gen|ic
tele|gram
tele|graph
tel|eg|raph|er

tele|graph|ese
tele|graph|ic
tele|graph|ic|al|ly
tel|eg|raph|ist
tel|eg|raphy
Tel|egu var. of
    Telugu
tele|kin|esis
tele|kin|et|ic
Tel|ema|chus *Greek*
    Mythology
Tele|mann, Georg
    Phil|ipp composer
tele|mark
tele|mar|ket|er
tele|mar|ket|ing
tele|mat|ics
tele|medi|cine
tele|mes|sage
tel|em|eter
tele|met|ric
tel|em|etry
tel|en|ceph|alon
tele|novela
teleo|logic|al
teleo|logic|al|ly
tele|olo|gism
tele|olo|gist
tele|ology
    tele|olo|gies
tele|oper|ate
    tele|oper|at|ing
tele|oper|ation
tele|oper|ator
tele|ost
tele|path
tele|path|ic
tele|path|ic|al|ly
tel|ep|ath|ise *Br.*
    var. of telepathize
tel|ep|ath|ist
tel|ep|ath|ize
    tel|ep|ath|iz|ing
tel|ep|athy
télé|phé|rique
tele|phone
    tele|phon|ing
tele|phoner
tele|phon|ic
tele|phon|ic|al|ly
tel|eph|on|ist
tel|eph|ony
tele|photo +s

tele|photo|graph|ic
tele|play
tele|port
tele|por|ta|tion
tele|pres|ence
tele|print|er
tele|prompt|er
tele|re|cord
tele|sales
tele|scope
    tele|scop|ing
tele|scop|ic
tele|scop|ic|al|ly
Tele|sco|pium con-
    stellation
tele|shop|ping
tele|soft|ware
tele|tex text
    transmission
    trademark
tele|text text and
    graphics
    transmitted
tele|thon
tele|type *trademark*
    tele|typ|ing
tele|type|writer
tele|van|gel|ical
tele|van|gel|ism
tele|van|gel|ist
tele|view|er
tele|vis|able
tele|vise
    tele|vis|ing
tele|vi|sion
tele|vision|ary
    tele|vision|aries
tele|vis|ual
tele|visu|al|ly
tele|work
tele|work|er
telex
Tel|ford town,
    England
Tel|ford, Thomas
    civil engineer
telic
tel|icity
Tell, Wil|liam
    legendary hero
tell
    told
    tell|able

Tell el-Amarna
tell|er
tel|lin
tell|ing|ly
telling-off
    tellings-off
tell|tale
tel|lur|ate
tel|lur|ian
tel|lur|ic
tel|lur|ide
tel|lur|ite
tel|lur|ium
tel|lur|ous
telly
    tel|lies
tel|net
tel|net|ted
tel|net|ting
tel|net|table
telo|gen
telo|leci|thal
tel|omer|ase
telo|mere
telo|mer|ic
telo|phase
telos
    teloi
tel|pher|age
tel|son
Tel|star
Tel|ugu
    pl. Tel|ugu or
    Tel|ugus
tem|aze|pam
tem|blor
Tembu var. of
    Thembu
tem|enos
    tem|enoi
tem|er|ari|ous
tem|er|ity
Temne
    pl. Temne or
    Tem|nes
temno|spon|dyl
tem|peh
tem|per
tem|pera painting
    medium; cf.
    tempura
tem|pera|ment
tem|pera|men|tal

tem|pera|
        men|tal|ly
tem|per|ance
tem|per|ate
tem|per|ate|ly
tem|per|ate|ness
tem|pera|tive
tem|pera|ture
tem|pcred|ly
tem|per|er
tem|pest
tem|pes|tu|ous
tem|pes|tu|ous|ly
tem|pes|tu|ous|
            ness
tempi pl. of tempo
Tem|plar
tem|plate
Tem|ple, Shir|ley
    actress and
    diplomat
tem|ple
tem|plet
tempo
    tem|pos or tempi
tem|poral
tem|por|alis
tem|por|al|ity
    tem|por|al|ities
tem|por|al|ly
tem|por|ar|ily
tem|por|ari|ness
tem|por|ary
    tem|po|rar|ies
tem|por|isa|tion *Br.*
    var. of
    temporization
tem|por|ise *Br.* var.
    of temporize
tem|por|iser *Br.*
    var. of temporizer
tem|por|iza|tion
tem|por|ize
    tem|por|iz|ing
tem|por|izer
tem|poro|
    man|dibu|lar
Tem|pra|nillo +s
temps levé
    temps levés
tempt|abil|ity
tempt|able
temp|ta|tion
tempt|er

tempt|ing|ly
temp|tress
tem|pura Japanese
dish; cf. **tempera**
ten|abil|ity
ten|able
ten|able|ness
ten|ace
ten|acious
ten|acious|ly
ten|acious|ness
ten|acity
ten|acu|lum
ten|acula
ten|ancy
ten|an|cies
possession as
tenant; cf. **tenency**
ten|ant
ten|ant|able
ten|ant|less
ten|ant|ry
Ten|cel *trademark*
ten|dency
ten|den|cies
ten|den|tious
ten|den|tious|ly
ten|den|tious|ness
ten|der
ten|der|er
ten|der|foot
ten|der|foots or
ten|der|feet
ten|der|ise Br. var.
of tenderize
ten|der|iser Br. var.
of tenderizer
ten|der|ize
ten|der|iz|ing
ten|der|izer
ten|der|loin
ten|der|ly
ten|der|ness
ten|din|itis
ten|din|ous
ten|don
ten|don|itis var. of
tendinitis
tendre
ten|dresse
ten|dril
tendu Ballet
tendu leaf

Tene|brae
tene|bri|onid
tene|brism
tene|brist
tene|brous
tene|ment
tene|men|tal
tene|men|tary
ten|ency in 'locum
tenency'; cf.
tenancy
Ten|er|life
ten|esi
pl. ten|esi
ten|es|mus
tenet
ten|fold
tenge
pl. tenge or tenges
Teng Hsiao-p'ing
var. of **Deng
Xiaoping**
tenia *US*
te|niae or te|nias
Br. taenia
te|niae coli *US*
Br. taeniae coli
Ten|iers, David
painter
teni|oid *US*
Br. taenioid
ten-iron
Ten|nant Creek
ten|nant|ite
tenné *Heraldry*
ten|ner banknote;
cf. **tenor**
Ten|nes|see
Ten|nes|seean
Ten|niel, John illus-
trator
ten|nies tennis
shoes
ten|nis
Tenno +s
Ten|ny|son, Al|fred,
Lord poet
Ten|ny|son|ian
Ten|och|ti|tlán
tenon
ten|on|er
tenor singer; mean-
ing; settled course;
cf. **tenner**

tenor|ino
tenor|ini
tenor|ist
teno|syno|vitis
ten|ot|omy
ten|oto|mies
ten|pin
ten|pound|er
ten|rec
tense
tens|ing
tenser
tens|est
ten|seg|rity
tense|less
tense|ly
tense|ness
ten|sile
ten|sil|ity
ten|sion
ten|sion|al
ten|sion|al|ly
ten|sion|er
ten|sion|less
ten|sive
ten|son
ten|sor
ten|sor|ial
ten|tacle
ten|tac|led
ten|tacu|lar
ten|tacu|late
tent|age
ten|ta|tive
ten|ta|tive|ly
ten|ta|tive|ness
ten|ter
ten|ter|hook
tenth|ly
ten|tor|ium
ten|toria
tenu|ity
tenu|ous
tenu|ous|ly
tenu|ous|ness
ten|ure
ten|ur|ing
ten|ur|ial
ten|uri|al|ly
ten|uto
ten|utos or ten|uti
Ten|zing Nor|gay
mountaineer

ten|zon var. of
tenson
teo|calli
teo|sinte
Teo|ti|hua|cán
te|pache
tepal
te|pary bean
tepee
tephra
tephro|chrono|
logic|al
tephro|
chron|ology
Tepic
tepid
tep|id|ar|ium
tep|id|aria
tep|id|ity
tep|id|ly
tep|id|ness
tep|pan|yaki
te|quila
tera|byte
tera|flop
terai
tera|meter *US*
tera|metre *Br.*
tera|phim
terato|car|cin|oma
terato|
car|cin|omata or
terato|
car|cin|omas
ter|ato|gen
terato|gen|esis
terato|gen|ic
terato|gen|icity
tera|togeny
terato|logic|al
tera|tolo|gist
tera|tol|ogy
tera|toma
tera|to|mas or
tera|to|mata
tera|watt
ter|bium
ter|bu|ta|line
terce religious
service; cf. **terse**
ter|cel
ter|cen|ten|ary
ter|cen|ten|ar|ies
ter|cen|ten|nial

ter|cet
tere|binth
tere|bratu|lid
ter|edo +s
Ter|ence Roman
dramatist; name
Ter|eng|ganu var.
of Trengganu
Te Reo
ter|eph|thal|ate
ter|eph|thal|ic
teres
Ter|esa, Mother
Ter|esa of Ávila, St
Ter|esa of Li|sieux,
St
Ter|esh|kova,
Val|en|tina
cosmonaut
Tere|sina
ter|ete
terga pl. of tergum
ter|gal
ter|gite
ter|gi|ver|sate
ter|gi|ver|sat|ing
ter|gi|ver|sa|tion
ter|gi|ver|sa|tor
ter|gum
terga
teri|yaki
Ter|ma|gant
imaginary deity
ter|ma|gant virago
ter|min|able
ter|min|able|ness
ter|min|al
ter|min|al|ly
ter|min|ate
ter|min|at|ing
ter|min|ation
ter|min|ation|al
ter|min|ator
ter|min|er in 'oyer
and terminer'
ter|mini pl. of
terminus
ter|min|ist
ter|mino|logic|al
ter|mino|logic|al|ly
ter|min|olo|gist
ter|min|ology
ter|min|olo|gies

ter|minus
ter|mini or
ter|min|uses
ter|minus ad
quem
ter|minus ante
quem
ter|minus a quo
ter|minus post
quem
ter|mit|ar|ium
ter|mit|aria
ter|mit|ary
ter|mit|ar|ies
ter|mite
term|ly
tern bird; cf. terne,
turn
tern|ary
tern|ate
tern|ate|ly
terne metal; cf.
tern, turn
tern|let
tero|techno|
logic|al
tero|tech|nolo|gist
tero|tech|nol|ogy
ter|pene
ter|pen|oid
ter|poly|mer
Terp|sich|ore Muse
terp|sich|or|ean
terra alba
ter|race
ter|ra|cing
terra|cotta
terra firma
terra|form
terra|form|er
ter|rain stretch of
land; cf. terrane
terra in|cog|nita
terra|mare
Terra|mycin
trademark
ter|rane fault-
bounded geological
area; cf. terrain
Terra|pin
prefabricated
building trademark
terra|pin turtle
ter|raque|ous

ter|rar|ium
ter|rar|iums or
ter|raria
terra rossa soil
terra sigil|lata
Ter|rassa var. of
Tarrasa
ter|rasse
ter|razzo
Terre Haute
ter|rene of earth;
earthly, worldly; cf.
terrine
terre|plein
ter|res|trial
ter|res|tri|al|ly
ter|ret
terre verte
terri|bil|ità
ter|rible
ter|rible|ness
ter|ribly
ter|rico|lous
Ter|rier member of
Territorial Army
ter|rier dog
ter|rif|ic
ter|rif|ic|al|ly
ter|ri|fier
ter|rify
ter|ri|fies
ter|ri|fied
ter|ri|fy|ing
ter|ri|fy|ing|ly
ter|ri|gen|ous
ter|rine coarse pâté;
earthenware dish;
cf. terrene
ter|ri|tor|ial
ter|ri|tori|al|
isa|tion
Br. var. of
territorialization
ter|ri|tori|al|ise Br.
var. of
territorialize
ter|ri|tori|al|ity
ter|ri|tori|al|
iza|tion
ter|ri|tori|al|ize
ter|ri|tori|al|iz|ing
ter|ri|tori|al|ly
ter|ri|tory
ter|ri|tor|ies

ter|roir environ-
ment for wine
production
ter|ror
ter|ror|isa|tion Br.
var. of
terrorization
ter|ror|ise Br. var.
of terrorize
ter|ror|iser Br. var.
of terrorizer
ter|ror|ism
ter|ror|ist
ter|ror|is|tic
ter|ror|is|tic|al|ly
ter|ror|iza|tion
ter|ror|ize
ter|ror|iz|ing
ter|ror|izer
Terry name
Terry, Ellen actress
terry
ter|ries
fabric
terse
terser
ters|est
brief; curt; cf. terce
terse|ly
terse|ness
ter|tian
Ter|tiary Geology
ter|tiary
ter|tiar|ies
third; monastic
associate
ter|tium quid
Ter|tul|lian
theologian
ter|va|lent
tery|lene trademark
terza rima
ter|zetto
ter|zet|tos or
ter|zetti
TESL = teaching of
English as a second
language
Tesla, Ni|kola
engineer; T. coil
tesla unit
TESOL = teaching
of English to
speakers of other
languages

TESSA = tax-exempt special savings account
tes¦sel¦late
  tes¦sel¦lat¦ing
tes¦sel¦la¦tion
tes¦sera
  tes¦serae
tes¦seral
tes¦si¦tura
Test cricket or rugby match
testa
  tes¦tae
  seed coat; cf. **tester**
test¦abil¦ity
test¦able
test¦aceous
tes¦tacy
  tes¦ta¦cies
tes¦ta¦ment
tes¦ta¦ment¦ary
tes¦tate
tes¦ta¦tion
tes¦ta¦tor
tes¦ta¦trix
  tes¦ta¦tri¦ces
test¦ee
test¦er person or thing that tests; sample; canopy; cf. **testa**
tes¦tes pl. of **testis**
tes¦ticle
tes¦ticu¦lar
tes¦ticu¦late
tes¦ti¦fier
test¦ify
  testi¦fies
  testi¦fied
  testi¦fy¦ing
test¦ily
tes¦ti¦mo¦nial
tes¦ti¦mony
  tes¦ti¦monies
testi¦ness
tes¦tis
  tes¦tes
tes¦tos¦ter¦one
Tes¦tu¦di¦nes order of reptiles
tes¦tudo
  tes¦tu¦dos or
  tes¦tu¦di¦nes

protective screen for troops
testy
test¦ier
testi¦est
tet¦an¦ic
tet¦an¦ic¦al¦ly
tet¦an¦ise Br. var. of **tetanize**
tet¦an¦ize
  tet¦an¦iz¦ing
tet¦an¦oid
tet¦anus
tet¦any
tetch¦ily
tetchi¦ness
tetchy
  tetch¦ier
  tetchi¦est
tête-à-tête
tête-bêche
tête de cuvée
  têtes de cuvées
tether
Te¦thys Greek goddess; moon of Saturn; former ocean
Teton
Té¦touan
tetra
tetra¦chlor¦ide
tetra¦chloro¦ethyl¦ene
tetra¦chord
tetra¦cyc¦lic
tetra¦cyc¦line
tet¦rad
tetra¦dac¦tyl
tetra¦dac¦tyl¦ous
tetra¦dac¦tyly
tetra¦ethyl
tetra¦fluoro¦ethyl¦ene
tet¦rag¦on¦al
tet¦rag¦on¦al¦ly
tetra¦gram
Tetra¦gram¦ma¦ton
tetra¦he¦dral
tetra¦he¦drite
tetra¦he¦dron
  tetra¦he¦dra or
  tetra¦he¦drons
tetra¦hydro¦canna¦binol

tetra¦hydro¦furan
tet¦ral¦ogy
  tet¦ral¦ogies
tetra¦mer
tetra¦mer¦ic
tet¦ram¦er¦ous
tet¦ram¦eter
tetra¦pack var. of **Tetra Pak**
Tetra Pak
  trademark
tetra¦plegia
tetra¦plegic
tetra¦ploid
tetra¦ploidy
tetra¦pod
tet¦rapod¦ous
tet¦rap¦ter¦ous
tet¦rarch +s
tet¦rarch¦ate
tet¦rarch¦ic¦al
tet¦rarchy
  tet¦rarch¦ies
tetra¦spore
tetra¦stich +s
tetra¦style
tetra¦syl¦lab¦ic
tetra¦syl¦lable
tet¦rath¦lon
tetra¦tom¦ic
tetra¦va¦lent
tetra¦zole
tetra¦zo¦lium
tetri
  pl. **tetri** or **tetris**
tet¦rode
tetro¦do¦toxin
tet¦rose
tet¦rox¦ide
tet¦ter
Teuton
Teut¦on¦ic
Teut¦oni¦cism
Tevet var. of **Tebet**
Tewa
  pl. **Tewa** or **Tewas**
Texan
Texas
Texel
text¦book
text¦book¦ish
tex¦tile
text¦less

text¦phone
text¦ual
text¦ual¦ism
text¦ual¦ist
text¦ual¦ity
text¦ual¦ly
tex¦tural
tex¦tur¦al¦ly
tex¦ture
tex¦tur¦ing
tex¦ture¦less
tex¦tur¦ise Br. var. of **texturize**
tex¦tur¦ize
  tex¦tur¦iz¦ing
T-group
Thack¦eray, Wil¦liam Make¦peace novelist
Thad¦daeus Apostle
Thai
  pl. **Thai** or **Thais** (native) of Thailand; a Tai language; cf. **Tai**, **tai**
Thai¦land
Thai¦land¦er
tha¦kur
thal¦am¦ic
thal¦amus
  thal¦ami
thal¦as¦sae¦mia Br.
thal¦as¦semia US
thal¦as¦sic
thal¦as¦so¦ther¦apy
thale cress
thaler German coin; cf. **tala**
Tha¦les Greek philosopher
thali
Tha¦lia Muse; one of the Graces
thal¦ido¦mide
thalli pl. of **thallus**
thal¦lic
thal¦lium
thal¦loid
thal¦lo¦phyte
thal¦lous adj.
thal¦lus n.
  thalli
thal¦weg

Thames
tha|min
Tham|muz Jewish
  month; cf.
  Tammuz
thana
than|age
than|ato|logic|al
thana|tolo|gist
thana|tol|ogy
Thana|tos
thane English or
  Scottish landholder;
  cf. thegn
thane|dom
thank|ful
thank|ful|ly
thank|ful|ness
thank|less
thank|less|ly
thank|less|ness
thank-offering
thanks|giv|ing
thank you +s
thar var. of tahr; cf.
  ta, tar
Thar Des|ert
that|away
Thatch|er,
  Mar|ga|ret prime
  minister of Britain
thatch|er
Thatch|er|ism
Thatch|er|ite
thauma|tin
thauma|trope
thauma|turge
thauma|tur|gic
thauma|tur|gic|al
thauma|tur|gist
thauma|turgy
thaw
thaw|less
the *definite article*;
  cf. thee
the|an|throp|ic
the|archy
  the|arch|ies
the|ater US
theater|goer US
theater-going US
theater-in-the-
      round US

theater|land US
the|atre Br.
theatre|goer Br.
theatre-going Br.
theatre-in-the-
      round Br.
theatre|land Br.
the|at|ric
the|at|ri|cal
the|at|ri|cal|
      isa|tion
  Br. var. of
  theatricalization
the|at|ri|cal|ise Br.
  var. of theatricalize
the|at|ri|cal|ism
the|at|ri|cal|ity
the|at|ri|cal|
      iza|tion
the|at|ri|cal|ize
the|at|ri|cal|iz|ing
the|at|ri|cal|ly
Theban
thebe
  pl. thebe
  Botswanan
  currency
Thebes cities,
  ancient Egypt and
  Greece
theca
the|cae
theca fol|liculi
the|cate
theco|dont
thé dan|sant
  thés dan|sants
thee *archaic* = you;
  cf. the
thegn English
  thane; cf. thane
theine caffeine
their of them; cf.
  there, they're
theirs the one(s)
  belonging to them;
  cf. there's
the|ism
the|ist
the|is|tic
the|ist|ic|al|ly
thek|edar
the|mat|ic
the|mat|ic|al|ly

the|mat|isa|tion Br.
  var. of
  thematization
the|mat|ise Br. var.
  of thematize
the|mat|iza|tion
the|mat|ize
the|mat|iz|ing
Thembu
  pl. Thembu or
  Them|bus
theme
them|ing
The|mis Greek
  goddess
The|mis|to|cles
  Athenian statesman
Themne var. of
  Temne
them|self
them|selves
the|nar
the|nard|ite
thence|forth
thence|for|ward
Theo|bald
theo|bro|mine
theo|cen|tric
The|oc|racy Jewish
  commonwealth
the|oc|racy
  the|oc|ra|cies
  government of or
  by priests
theo|crat
theo|crat|ic
theo|crat|ic|al|ly
The|oc|ri|tus Greek
  poet
theo|di|cean
the|odicy
  the|odi|cies
the|odo|lite
the|odo|lit|ic
Theo|dora Byzan-
  tine empress; name
Theo|dor|akis,
  Mikis composer
Theo|dore
Theo|dor|ic king of
  the Ostrogoths
Theo|dos|ius
  Roman emperor

the|ogony
  the|ogo|nies
theo|lo|gian
theo|logic|al
theo|logic|al|ly
the|olo|gise Br. var.
  of theologize
the|olo|gist
the|olo|gize
the|olo|giz|ing
the|ology
  the|olo|gies
the|om|achy
  the|om|achies
the|ophany
  the|opha|nies
theo|phor|ic
the|oph|or|ous
Theo|phras|tus
  Greek philosopher
theo|phyl|line
the|or|bist
the|orbo +s
the|orem
the|or|em|at|ic
the|or|et|ic
the|or|et|ic|al
the|or|et|ic|al|ly
the|or|et|ician
the|or|isa|tion Br.
  var. of theorization
the|or|ise Br. var. of
  theorize
the|or|iser Br. var.
  of theorizer
the|or|ist
the|or|iza|tion
the|or|ize
the|or|iz|ing
the|or|izer
the|ory
  the|or|ies
theo|so|pher
theo|soph|ic|al
theo|soph|ic|al|ly
theo|so|phist
theo|so|phy
The|oto|kos
Thera
thera|peut|ic
thera|peut|ic|al|ly
thera|peut|ist
ther|ap|ist

ther¦ap¦sid
ther¦apy
  ther¦ap¦ies
Thera¦vada
  Buddhism
there in that place
  etc.; cf. **their,**
  they're
there¦about
there¦abouts
there¦after
there¦anent
there¦at
there¦by
there¦for *archaic*
  for that purpose
there¦fore for that
  reason
there¦from
there¦in
there¦in¦after
there¦in¦before
there¦in¦to
there¦min
there¦of
there¦on
there¦out
there's = there is; cf.
  theirs
Ther¦esa name; cf.
  Teresa
there¦through
there¦to
there¦to¦fore
there¦under
there¦unto
there¦upon
there¦with
there¦with¦al
The¦ria
ther¦iac
ther¦ian
theri¦an¦throp¦ic
therio¦morph¦ic
ther¦mae
ther¦mal
ther¦mal¦isa¦tion
  Br. var. of
  thermalization
ther¦mal¦ise *Br.* var.
  of **thermalize**
ther¦mal¦iza¦tion

ther¦mal¦ize
  ther¦mal¦iz¦ing
ther¦mal¦ly
ther¦mic
Thermi¦dor
Thermi¦dor¦ian
ther¦mion
thermi¦on¦ic
ther¦mis¦tor
ther¦mit var. of
  thermite
ther¦mite
thermo¦bar¦ic
thermo¦chem¦ical
thermo¦chem¦is¦try
thermo¦chro¦mic
thermo¦cline
thermo¦couple
thermo¦dynam¦ic
thermo¦dynam¦ic¦
  al¦ly
thermo¦dynami¦
      cist
thermo-elastic
thermo¦elec¦tric
thermo¦elec¦tric¦
  al¦ly
thermo¦elec¦tri¦city
thermo¦form¦er
thermo¦form¦ing
thermo¦gen¦esis
thermo¦gen¦ic
thermo¦gram
thermo¦graph
thermo¦graph¦ic
therm¦og¦raphy
thermo¦hal¦ine
thermo¦karst
thermo¦labile
thermo¦lumin¦
     es¦cence
thermo¦lumin¦
     es¦cent
therm¦oly¦sis
thermo¦lyt¦ic
therm¦om¦eter
thermo¦met¦ric
thermo¦met¦ric¦
  al¦ly
therm¦om¦etry
thermo¦nuclear
thermo¦phil var. of
  thermophile

thermo¦phile
thermo¦phil¦ic
thermo¦pile
thermo¦plas¦tic
Therm¦opy¦lae
thermo¦regu¦late
thermo¦
     regu¦lat¦ing
thermo¦
     regu¦la¦tion
thermo¦regula¦tory
Ther¦mos
  trademark
thermo¦set
thermo¦set¦ting
thermo¦sphere
thermo¦stable
thermo¦stat
thermo¦stat¦ic
thermo¦stat¦ic¦al¦ly
thermo¦taxis
thermo¦trop¦ic
thermo¦trop¦ism
thero¦pod
the¦saurus
  the¦sauri or
  the¦saur¦uses
these
The¦seus Greek
  hero
Thes¦iger, Wil¦fred
  explorer
the¦sis
  the¦ses
thes¦pian
Thes¦pis Greek poet
Thes¦sal¦ian
Thes¦sa¦lon¦ian
Thes¦sa¦lon¦ica
Thes¦sa¦lon¦íki
Thes¦saly
theta
The¦tis sea nymph
the¦ur¦gic
the¦ur¦gist
the¦urgy
thew
thewed
thewy
  thew¦ier
  thewi¦est
they'd
they'll

they're = they are;
  cf. **their, there**
they've
thia¦ben¦da¦zole
thia¦min var. of
  thiamine
thia¦mine
thia¦zide
thia¦zine
thia¦zole
thick¦en
thick¦en¦er
thicket
thick¦head
thick¦head¦ed
thick¦head¦ed¦ness
thick¦ish
thick-knee bird
thick¦ly
thick¦ness
thick¦ness¦er
thicko +s
thick¦set
thief *n.*
thieves
thieve *v.*
thiev¦ing
thiev¦ery
thiev¦ish
thiev¦ish¦ly
thiev¦ish¦ness
thigh
thighed
thigmo¦tac¦tic
thigmo¦taxis
thigmo¦trop¦ic
thigmo¦trop¦ism
thika¦dar var. of
  thekedar
thill
thill¦er
thim¦ble
thimble¦berry
  thimble¦berries
thimble¦ful
thimble¦rig
thimble¦rig¦ger
Thimbu var. of
  Thimphu
Thim¦phu
thin
  thinned
  thin¦ning

thin|ner
thin|nest
thing|ama|bob
thing|ama|jig
thing|amy var. of
thingummy
thing|uma|bob var.
of thingamabob
thing|uma|jig var.
of thingamajig
thing|ummy
thing|um|mies
thingy
thing|ies
think
thought
think|able
think|er
thinko +s
think-tanker
thin|ly
thin|ner
thin|ness
thin|nish
thio|cyan|ate
thiol
thio|mer|sal
thi|onyl
thio|pen|tal
thio|pen|tone
thi|ori|da|zine
thio|sul|fate US
thio|sul|phate Br.
thio|urea
thiram
third ager
third-hand adj. &
adv.
third|ly
third-rater
thirst|ily
thirsti|er
thirsti|ness
thirst|land
thirsty
thirst|ier
thirsti|est
thir|teen
thir|teenth
thir|ti|eth
thirty
thir|ties
thirty-first, thirty-
second, etc.

thirty|fold
thirty-one, thirty-
two, etc.
thirty-something
thirty-two-mo +s
Thirty Years War
this
these
Thisbe Roman
Mythology
this|tle
thistle|down
this|tly
thither
thixo|trop|ic
thix|otropy
thole
thol|ing
tho|lei|ite
tho|lei|it|ic
tho|los
tho|loi
Thomas, Dylan
poet
Thomas, Ed|ward
poet
Thomas à Kem|pis
theologian
Thomas Aqui|nas,
St
Thom|ism
Thom|ist
Thom|is|tic
Thomp|son, Daley
athlete
Thomp|son, Emma
actress
Thomp|son, Flora
writer
Thomp|son,
Fran|cis poet
Thom|son, James
poet
Thom|son, Roy
newspaper
proprietor
Thom|son's
gaz|elle
thongy
Thor Scandinavian
god
thor|acic
thora|col|um|bar

thora|cot|omy
thora|coto|mies
thorax
thora|ces or
thor|axes
Thora|zine
trademark
Thor|eau, Henry
David writer
thoria
thor|ium
thorn|back
thorn|bill
Thorn|dike, Sibyl
actress
thorn|ily
thorni|ness
thorn|less
thorn|like
thorn|proof
thorn|tail
thorn|veld
thorny
thorn|ier
thorni|est
thor|ough
thor|ough|bred
thor|ough|fare
thor|ough|going
thor|ough|ly
thor|ough|ness
thorough-paced
thor|ough|pin
thorow-wax plant
Thorpe, Ian swim-
mer
Thors|havn var. of
Tórshavn
Thor|vald|sen,
Ber|tel sculptor
those
Thoth Egyptian god
thou archaic = you
thou
pl. thou or thous
thousand; thou-
sandth of an inch
though
thought|crime
thought|ful
thought|ful|ly
thought|ful|ness
thought|less
thought|less|ly

thought|less|ness
thou|sand
thou|sand|fold
thou|sandth
Thrace
Thra|cian
thral|dom Br.
Thrale, Hes|ter
Lynch writer
thrall|dom US
thrash|er
thread|bare
thread|er
thread|fin
thread-like
Thread|nee|dle
Street
thread|worm
thready
thread|ier
threadi|est
threat|en
threat|en|er
threat|en|ing|ly
three|fold
three-iron
three-peat
three|pence
three|penny
three-quarter
three|quel
three|score
three|some
three-wheeler
thren|ode
thren|odial
thren|od|ic
thren|od|ist
thren|ody
thren|odies
threo|nine
thresh|er
thresh|old
threw past tense of
throw; cf. through
thrift|ily
thrifti|ness
thrift|less
thrift|less|ly
thrift|less|ness
thrifty
thrift|ier
thrifti|est

thrill¦er
thrill¦ing¦ly
thrip var. of thrips
thrips
  pl. thrips
thrive
  thrived or throve
  thriv¦ing
  thriven
thro' *literary* or
  informal var. of
  through
throat¦ed
throat¦ily
throati¦ness
throat¦lash var. of
  throatlatch
throat¦latch
throat¦wort
throaty
  throat¦ier
  throati¦est
throb
  throbbed
  throb¦bing
throes pain and
  struggle
thromb¦ec¦tomy
  thromb¦ec¦to¦mies
thrombi pl. of
  thrombus
throm¦bin
thrombo¦cyte
thrombo¦
  cyth¦aemia *Br.*
thrombo¦cyth¦emia
  US
thrombo¦cyto¦
      paenia
  Br. var. of
  thrombocytopenia
thrombo¦cyto¦
      penia
thrombo¦embol¦ic
thrombo¦
    embol¦ism
thrombo¦gen¦ic
thrombo¦gen¦icity
thromb¦oly¦sis
thrombo¦lyt¦ic
thrombo¦phle¦bitis
thrombo¦plas¦tin
throm¦bose
  throm¦bos¦ing

throm¦bosis
  throm¦boses
throm¦bot¦ic
thromb¦oxane
throm¦bus
  thrombi
throne
  thron¦ing
  chair of state; sov-
  ereign power; cf.
  thrown
thros¦tle
throt¦tle
  throt¦tling
throt¦tler
through *prep.*; cf.
  threw
through¦fall
through¦flow
through¦other
through¦out
through¦put
through-ticket¦ing
through¦way var. of
  thruway
throw
  threw
  thrown
  propel etc.; cf.
  throes, through,
  throne
throw¦able
throw¦away
throw¦back
throw¦down
throw¦er
throw-in *n.*
thrown past parti-
  ciple of throw; cf.
  throne
throw-off *n.*
throw-over *adj.*
throw¦ster
thru *US*
  informal var. of
  through
thrum
  thrummed
  thrum¦ming
thrust¦er
thru¦way
Thu¦cydi¦des Greek
  historian
thud
  thud¦ded

thud¦ding
thud¦ding¦ly
Thug Indian robber
  and assassin
thug violent person
thug¦gee
thug¦gery
thug¦gish
thug¦gish¦ly
thug¦gish¦ness
thug¦gism
thuja
Thule
thu¦lium
thumb¦less
thumb¦nail
thumb¦print
thumb¦screw
thumb¦suck¦er
thumb¦tack
thumb¦wheel
Thum¦mim
thump¦er
thumri
thun¦der
thun¦der¦bird
thun¦der¦bolt
thun¦der¦box
thun¦der¦bug
thun¦der¦clap
thun¦der¦cloud
thun¦der¦er
thun¦der¦flash
thun¦der¦fly
thun¦der¦head
thun¦der¦ing¦ly
thun¦der¦less
thun¦der¦ous
thun¦der¦ous¦ly
thun¦der¦ous¦ness
thun¦der¦storm
thun¦der¦struck
thun¦dery
Thur¦ber, James
  humorist
Thur¦gau
thur¦ible
thuri¦fer
Thur¦in¦gia
Thur¦in¦gian
Thurs¦day
Thurso

thus¦ly
thuya var. of thuja
thwaite
thy
Thy¦es¦tean
Thy¦es¦tes *Greek*
  Mythology
thy¦la¦cine
thyla¦koid
thyme herb; cf. time
thym¦ec¦tomy
  thym¦ecto¦mies
thymi pl. of thymus
thym¦ic
thy¦mi¦dine
thy¦mine
thymo¦cyte
thy¦mol
thym¦oma
  thym¦omas or
  thym¦omata
thy¦mus
  thymi
thymy like thyme
thy¦ris¦tor
thyro¦globu¦lin
thy¦roid
thyro¦toxi¦cosis
thyro¦troph¦in var.
  of thyrotropin
thyro¦tropin
thy¦rox¦ine
thyr¦sus
  thyrsi
Thy¦san¦op¦tera
thy¦san¦op¦ter¦an
Thy¦san¦ura
thy¦san¦ur¦an
thy¦self
ti in 'ti tree'
ti *US*
  note in tonic sol-fa
  Br. te
Tia Maria
  trademark
Tia¦mat *Babylonian*
  Mythology
tian
Tian¦an¦men
  Square
Tian¦jin
Tian Shan var. of
  Tien Shan

tiara jewellery
tiare flower
  pl. tiare
tia|rella
Tiber
Ti|ber|ias, Lake
Ti|ber|ius Roman
  emperor
Ti|besti
  Moun|tains
Tibet
Ti|bet|an
Tibeto-Burman
tibia
  tib|iae or tib|ias
tib|ial
tibi|alis
tibio|tar|sus
  tibio|tarsi
Tib|ul|lus Roman
  poet
tic twitch; cf. tick
tic dou|!lour|eux
tich var. of titch
Tich|borne
Ti|cino
tick clock's sound;
  moment; mark;
  parasite; credit; cf.
  tic
tick-bird
tick|er heart; watch;
  text machine; cf.
  tika, tikka
ticket
ticket|less
tickety-boo
tickey coin
tickey-draai dance;
  music
tick|ing
tickle
  tick|ling
tick|ler
tick|lish
tick|lish|ly
tick|lish|ness
tickly
  tick|lier
  tick|li|est
tick|over n.
tick|seed
tick-tack var. of tic-
  tac

tick-tack-toe var. of
  tic-tac-toe
tick-tock
ticky-tacky
tic-tac
tic-tac-toe
tidal
tid|al|!ly
tid|!bit US
  Br. titbit
tiddle|dy|wink US
  var. of tiddlywink
tid|dler
tid|dly
  tid|dlier
  tiddli|est
tiddly|wink
tiddy oggy
  tiddy oggies
tide
  tid|ing
  rise and fall of sea;
  trend; help out; cf.
  tied
tide|land
tide|less
tide|line
tide|mark
tide|wait|er
tide|water
tide|way
tidi|ly
tidi|ness
tid|ings
tidy
  tidies
  tidied
  tidy|ing
  tidi|er
  tidi|est
tie
  ties
  tied
  tying
tie-back n.
tie|break
tie|break|er
tie-down n.
tie-dye
  tie-dyeing
tie-in n. & mod.
tie|less
ti|enda
Tien Shan

ti|ento +s
Tien|tsin var. of
  Tianjin
tie|pin
Tiep|olo, Gio|vanni
  Bat|tista painter
tier level; layer; cf.
  tear, Tyr
tierce organ stop;
  fencing position;
  wine measure; also
  var. of terce
ti|ercé var. of
  tierced
tierced Heraldry
tier|cel var. of tercel
tiered
Tierra del Fuego
tie-up n.
Tif|!fany name
Tif|!fany, Louis
  Com|fort
  glassmaker
tif|fany
tif|fa|nies
  muslin
tif|!fin
Tif|!lis
tig
  tigged
  tig|ging
  (touch in) children's
  game
tiger animal; cf.
  taiga
Tiger balm
  trademark
tiger|ish
tiger|ish|ly
tiger|wood
Tigger|ish
tight-ass n.
tight|en
tight|ly
tight|ness
tight|rope
  tight|rop|ing
tight|wad
Tiglath-pileser
  Assyrian kings
tig|lon
ti|gnon headdress
tigon offspring of
  tiger and lioness

Ti|gray province,
  Ethiopia
Ti|gray|an
Tigre var. of Tigray
Tigre language of
  Eritrea and Sudan
Ti|gre|an var. of
  Tigrayan
tig|ress
Tig|rinya language
  of Tigray
Ti|gris
Tigua var. of Tiwa
Tihwa
Ti|juana
tika Hindu mark on
  forehead; cf. ticker,
  tikka
Tikal
tike var. of tyke
tiki
tikia
tikka food; cf.
  ticker, tika
tilak
til|apia
Til|burg
Til|bury port,
  England
til|bury
  til|bur|ies
  carriage
Tilda name
tilde accent
tile
  til|ing
tile|fish
tiler
till until; drawer for
  money; cultivate
till|able
till|age
till|er
til|leul
til|ley lamp
  trademark
Til|lich, Paul
  theologian
till|ite
Tilly name
tilly lamp var. of
  tilley lamp
Til|!sit
tilt|er

Tim¦aru
tim¦bal *archaic*
  kettledrum
tim¦bale dish;
  paired cylindrical
  drum
tim¦ber
tim¦ber|land
tim¦ber|line
tim¦ber|man
  tim¦ber|men
timbre
tim¦brel
Tim¦buc|too var. of
  Timbuktu
Tim¦buktu
time
  tim¦ing
  progress of events;
  arrange or measure
  time; etc.; cf.
  thyme
time|keep¦er
time|keep¦ing
time|less
time|less¦ly
time|less|ness
time|line
time|li|ness
time¦ly
  time|lier
  time|li|est
tim|eous
tim|eously
time out time off;
  time alone for mis-
  behaving child
time|out break in
  play; computer
  cancellation
time|piece
timer
time|scale
time|share
time-sharing
time|table
  time|tab¦ling
timid
tim¦id|ity
tim|id¦ly
tim|id|ness
Timi¦şoara
tim|oc¦racy
  tim|oc¦ra¦cies

timo|crat¦ic
timo|lol
Timor
Ti¦mor|ese
tim|or|ous
tim|or|ous¦ly
tim|or|ous|ness
Tim|othy name
tim|othy grass
tim|pani
tim|pan|ist
Timur = Tamerlane
tin
  tinned
  tin|ning
tina|mou
Tin|ber¦gen, Jan
  economist
Tin|ber¦gen,
  Niko|laas zoologist
tinc|tor¦ial
tinc|ture
  tinc¦tur|ing
tin¦der
tinder|box
tin|dery
tine prong; cf. Tyne
tinea
tined
tin|foil
ting +ing (make)
  bell-like sound
tinge
  tin|ging or
  tinge|ing
  colour or affect
  slightly; slight trace
tin|gle
  tin|gling
tin|gly
  tin|glier
  tin|gli|est
tin|horn
tini¦ly
tini|ness
tin¦ker
tinker|bird
tin|ker¦er
tin|kle
  tink|ling
tin|kly
  tin|klier
  tin|kli|est
tink|tinkie

tin|ner
tin|nie n. var. of
  tinny
tin|nily
tin|ni|ness
tin|nitus
tinny
  tin|nies
  tin|nier
  tin|ni|est
Tin Pan Alley
tin|plate
  tin|plat¦ing
tin|pot
tin|sel
tin|seled US
tin|selled Br.
tin|sel¦ly
Tin|sel|town
tin|smith
tin|snips
tin|stone
Tin|tagel
tint¦er
tin|tin|nabu|la¦tion
tinto +s
Tin|to|retto painter
tin|type
tin|ware
tiny
  tinies
  tini¦er
  tini|est
tip
  tipped
  tip|ping
tip-and-run n. &
  mod.
tip¦cat
tipi var. of tepee
tip-in n.
tip-off n.
tip|per
Tip¦per|ary
tip|pet
Tip|pett, Mi¦chael
  composer
Tip¦pex
  trademark Tipp-Ex
tip|ple
  tip|pling
tip|pler
tippy
  tip|pier

tip¦pi¦est
tippy-toe
  tippy-toeing
tip|sily
tip|si|ness
tip|staff
tip|ster
tipsy
  tip|sier
  tipsi|est
tip¦toe
  tip¦toe|ing
tip-top
tip-up adj. & n.
tir¦ade
ti¦rail|leur
tira|misu
Ti¦rana
Ti¦ranë var. of
  Tirana
tire
  tir¦ing
  grow weary etc.; cf.
  tyre
tire US
  covering or band
  round wheel;
  Br. tyre
tired¦ly
tired|ness
Tiree
tire|less
tire|less¦ly
tire|less|ness
Tir|esias Greek
  Mythology
tire|some
tire|some¦ly
tire|some|ness
Tîrgu Mureş
Tir¦ich Mir
Tir-na-nog Irish
  Mythology
tiro var. of tyro
tirth var. of tirtha
tir¦tha
Tiru|chi¦ra|palli
'tis archaic = it is;
  cf. tizz
ti¦sane
Tishri
Ti¦siph|one one of
  Furies
Tisri var. of Tishri

tis¦sue

tis¦suey

Tisza

Titan *Greek Mythology*; moon of Saturn

titan person of great strength, intellect, etc.

ti¦tan¦ate salt of titanic acid

ti¦tan¦ess

Ti¦ta¦nia fairy queen; moon of Uranus

Ti¦tan¦ic ship

ti¦tan¦ic of titanium; exceptionally great

ti¦tan¦ic¦al¦ly

titan¦if¦er¦ous

titan¦ite

ti¦tan¦ium

titan¦ous

tit¦bit *Br.* *US* tidbit

titch

titchy
titch¦ier
titchi¦est

titer *US* *Br.* titre

tit¦fer

tith¦able

tithe
tith¦ing

Tith¦onus *Greek Mythology*

titi monkey; tree; cf. titty

Ti¦tian painter

Titi¦caca

titi¦hoya

tit¦il¦late
tit¦il¦lat¦ing
tit¦il¦lat¦ing¦ly
tit¦il¦la¦tion

titi¦vate
titi¦vat¦ing

titi¦va¦tion

tit¦lark

title
tit¦ling

tit¦mouse
tit¦mice

Tito president of Yugoslavia

Tito¦grad

Tito¦ism

Tito¦ist

ti¦trat¦able

ti¦trate
ti¦trat¦ing

ti¦tra¦tion

titre *Br.* *US* titer

ti tree Australasian shrub; var. of tea tree

tit¦ter

tit¦ter¦er

tit¦ter¦ing¦ly

tit¦tie var. of titty

tit¦ti¦vate var. of titivate

tit¦ti¦va¦tion var. of titivation

tit¦tle

tittle-tattle
tittle-tattling

tit¦tup
tit¦tuped or tit¦tupped
tit¦tup¦ing or tit¦tup¦ping

titty
tit¦ties
nipple; breast; cf. titi

titu¦ba¦tion

titu¦lar

titu¦lar¦ly

Titus

Tiv
pl. Tiv or Tivs

Tiv¦oli

Tiwa
pl. Tiwa or Tiwas

tiyin
pl. tiyin or ti¦yins

tizz = tizzy; cf. 'tis

tizzy
tiz¦zies

T-joint

T-junction

Tlax¦cala

Tlem¦cen

Tlin¦git
pl. Tlin¦git or Tlin¦gits

tme¦sis
tme¦ses

to *prep.* in 'to London' etc.; with verb infinitives, e.g. 'to go'; cf. too, tout (= all), two

toad¦fish

toad¦flax

toad-in-the-hole

toad¦ish

toad¦let

toad¦stone

toad¦stool

toady
toad¦ies
toad¦ied
toady¦ing
sycophant; to fawn; cf. tody

toady¦ish

toady¦ism

to and fro

toast

toast¦er

toastie toasted sandwich; cf. toasty

toast¦master

toast¦mis¦tress

toasty
toast¦ier
toasti¦est
like toast; cf. toastie

to¦bacco +s

to¦bac¦con¦ist

To¦bagan

To¦bago

To¦ba¦go¦nian

To¦bias

Tobit *Bible*

to¦bog¦gan

to¦bog¦gan¦er

to¦bog¦gan¦ist

tobra¦mycin

To¦bruk

Toby name

toby
tobies
fishes; jug

Toc¦an¦tins

toc¦cata

Toc H Christian society

Toch¦ar¦ian

to¦chus

toco +s

toc¦oph¦erol

toc¦sin alarm bell; cf. toxin

tod in 'on one's tod'

today

Todd, Swee¦ney fictional character

tod¦dle
tod¦dling

tod¦dler

toddler¦hood

toddy
tod¦dies

todger

to-do +s

tody
to¦dies
bird; cf. toady

toe
toe¦ing
digit on foot; push with toe; cf. tow

toea
pl. toea

toe¦cap

toe¦hold

toe-in *n.*

toe¦less

toe¦nail

toe-out *n.*

toe¦rag

toey

tof¦fee

toffy
tof¦fies
var. of toffee

Tof¦ra¦nil *trademark*

tofu

tog
togged
tog¦ging

toga

toga'd

togaed var. of toga'd

to¦gether

to¦gether¦ness

Tog|gen|burg
tog|gery
tog|gle
  tog|gling
Togli|atti
Togo
Togo|land
Togo|lese
To|hoku
tohu|bohu
toil work
toile cloth
toile de Jouy
toil|er
toi|let WC; washing, dressing, etc.
toi|let|ries
toi|lette *dated* washing, dressing, etc.
toil|some
toil|some|ly
toil|some|ness
toil|worn
toing and fro|ing
to|ings and fro|ings
Tojo, Hi|deki prime minister of Japan
toka|mak
Tokay wine
tokay gecko
toke
  tok|ing
Tok|elau
token
token|ise *Br.* var. of tokenize
token|ism
token|is|tic
token|ize
  token|iz|ing
toker
tok|kin
  pl. tok|kin or tok|kins
toko|loshe
toko|noma
Tok Pisin
tok-tokkie
Toku|gawa
Tokyo
tolar

tol|booth var. of tollbooth
Tol|bu|khin
tol|buta|mide
told past tense and participle of tell; cf. tolled
tole tin plate; *French* tôle; cf. toll
To|le|dan
To|ledo
tol|er|abil|ity
tol|er|able
tol|er|able|ness
tol|er|ably
tol|er|ance
tol|er|ant
tol|er|ant|ly
tol|er|ate
  tol|er|at|ing
tol|er|ation
tol|er|ator
tole|ware
To|lima
Tol|kien, J. R. R. novelist
toll charge; cost; ring; cf. tole, told
toll|booth
toll house
toll|house cookie
Toll|und Man
toll|way
Tol|pud|dle
Tol|stoy, Leo writer
Tol|tec
Tol|tec|an
tolu
To|luca (de Lerdo)
tolu|ene
tol|uic
tolui|dine
tol|uol
Tom name
tom
  tommed
  tomming
  male animal; (work as) prostitute; tomato; cf. tomme
toma|hawk
to|mal|ley
toma|tillo +s

toma|tin var. of tomatine
toma|tine
to|mato
to|ma|toes
to|ma|toey
tomb
Tom|baugh, Clyde astronomer
tom|bola game
tom|bolo +s sandbar
tom|boy
tom|boy|ish
tom|boy|ish|ly
tom|boy|ish|ness
tomb|stone
tom|cat
tom|cod
to|men|tose
to|men|tous var. of tomentose
to|men|tum to|menta
tom|fool
tom|fool|ery
tomme cheese; cf. tom
Tommy
Tom|mies British soldier; name
tommy bar
tommy gun
tommy|rot
tommy ruff
tomo|gram
tomo|graph|ic
tomo|graph|ic|al|ly
tom|og|raphy
Tomor, Mt
to|mor|row
Tom|pion, Thomas clockmaker
tom|pion var. of tampion
tom|pot
Tomsk
tom thumb flower
tom|tit
tom-tom
ton various units of weight; 100; cf. tonne, tun

ton fashionable style
tonal
tonal|ite
tonal|it|ic
ton|al|ity
ton|al|ities
ton|al|ly
Ton|bridge cf. Tunbridge Wells
tondo
tondi
Tone, Wolfe Irish nationalist
tone
  ton|ing
tone|burst
tone-deafness
tone|less
tone|less|ly
ton|eme
ton|em|ic
tone|pad
toner
Tonga country in S. Pacific
Tonga
  pl. Tonga or Ton|gas
  member of three African peoples; languages
tonga horse-drawn vehicle
Ton|gan (native or language) of Tonga
Tonga|riro, Mt
tongs gripping implement
Tong|shan
tongue
  tonguing
  organ in mouth etc.; cf. tung
tongue|fish
tongue-in-cheek
tongue|less
Toni woman's name; cf. Tony
tonic
ton|ic|al|ly
ton|icity
toni|fi|ca|tion
ton|ify
toni|fies

toni|fied
toni|fy|ing
to|night
tonka bean
Ton|kin
Tonlé Sap
ton-mile
ton|nage
tonne 1,000 kg; cf.
  ton, tun
ton|neau
ton|om|eter
tono|plast
ton|sil
ton|sil|lar
ton|sil|lec|tomy
  ton|sil|lec|to|mies
ton|sil|litis
ton|sor|ial
ton|sor|ial|ly
ton|sure
  ton|sur|ing
ton|tine
Ton|ton Ma|coute
  Ton|tons
  Ma|coutes
ton-up
tonus
Tony man's name;
  cf. Toni
Tony +s
  theatre award
tony
  toni|er
  toni|est
  stylish
too adv., in 'too
  much' etc.; cf. to,
  tout (= all), two
toodle-oo
toodle-pip
tool|bar
tool|box
tool|er
tool|kit
tool|maker
tool|mak|ing
tool|set
toot|er
tooth|ache
tooth|brush
tooth|carp
  pl. tooth|carp
tooth|comb

toothed
tooth|fish
tooth|glass
tooth|ily
tooth|ing
tooth|less
tooth|less|ly
tooth|less|ness
tooth-like
tooth|paste
tooth|pick
tooth|some
tooth|some|ly
tooth|some|ness
tooth|wort
toothy
  tooth|ier
  toothi|est
too|tle
  toot|ling
too-too excessively;
  cf. tutu
toot|sie toe; young
  woman; cf. Tutsi
toot sweet
  immediately
tootsy
  toot|sies
  var. of tootsie
Too|woomba
top
  topped
  top|ping
topaz
top|azo|lite
top|coat
top-dress v.
top dress|ing n.
tope
  top|ing
  drink; grove; Bud-
  dhist shrine; shark;
  cf. taupe
topee var. of topi
To|peka
toper
top|gal|lant
To|phet = hell
to|phus
  tophi
topi
topi|ar|ian
topi|ar|ist

topi|ary
  topi|ar|ies
topic
top|ic|al
top|ic|al|isa|tion Br.
  var. of
  topicalization
top|ic|al|ise Br. var.
  of topicalize
top|ic|al|ity
top|ic|al|iza|tion
top|ic|al|ize
  top|ic|al|iz|ing
top|ic|al|ly
Top|kapi
top|knot
top|less
top|less|ness
top|lofty
top|man
  top|men
  sawyer; sailor
top|mast
top|minnow
top|most
top-notcher
topo +s map
top|og|raph|er
topo|graph|ic
topo|graph|ic|al
topo|graph|ic|al|ly
top|og|raphy
  top|og|raph|ies
topoi pl. of topos
topo|iso|mer
topo|isom|er|ase
topo|logic|al
topo|logic|al|ly
top|olo|gist
top|ology
  top|olo|gies
topo|nym
topo|nym|ic
top|onymy
topos
  topoi
  traditional theme
top|per
top|pie
top|ple
  top|pling
top|sail
top-sawyer

top se|cret adj.
top-secret attrib.
top|side
Top|sider
  trademark
top|soil
top|spin
top|spin|ner
top|stitch
topsy-turvily
topsy-turviness
topsy-turvy
topsy-turvydom
top-up n. & mod.
top|water
toque
tor hill; cf. tau, taw,
  tore, torr
Torah
Tor|bay
torc necklace; cf.
  talk, torque
tor|chère
torch-fishing
torch|light
torch|lit
tor|chon
tore past tense of
  tear; cf. tau, taw,
  tor, torr
torea|dor
tor|ero +s
tor|eut|ics
tor|goch
tori pl. of torus; cf.
  Tory
toric
torii
  pl. torii
  Shinto gateway
tor|ment
tor|ment|ed|ly
tor|men|til
tor|ment|ing|ly
tor|ment|or
tor|nad|ic
tor|nado
  tor|na|does or
  tor|na|dos
Tor|nio
toro tuna flesh
tor|oid
tor|oid|al

tor|oid|al|ly
To|ronto
tor|pedo
  tor|pe|does
  tor|pe|doed
  tor|pe|do|ing
torpedo-like
tor|pefy
  tor|pe|fies
  tor|pe|fied
  tor|pe|fy|ing
tor|pid
tor|pid|ity
tor|pid|ly
tor|pid|ness
tor|por
tor|por|if|ic
Tor|quay
torque
  tor|quing
  (apply) turning
  force; var. of torc;
  cf. talk
Tor|que|mada,
  Tomás de Grand
  Inquisitor
tor|quey
  tor|quier
  tor|qui|est
  producing much
  torque; cf. talkie
torr
  pl. torr
  unit of pressure; cf.
  tau, taw, tor, tore
Tor|rens system
tor|rent
tor|ren|tial
tor|ren|tial|ly
Tor|res Strait
tor|reya
Tor|ri|celli,
  Evan|ge|lista
  physicist
Tor|ri|cel|lian
tor|rid
tor|rid|ity
tor|rid|ly
Tor|ri|don|ian
tor|sade twisted
  trimming
tor|sade de pointes
  Medicine
torse *Heraldry*

tor|sel tassel for
  beam or joist
Tórs|havn
tor|sion
tor|sion|al
tor|sion|al|ly
tor|sion|less
torsk fish
torso
  tor|sos
  US also torsi
tort *Law*; cf. taught,
  taut, torte
torte
  tor|ten or tortes
  cake; cf. taught,
  taut, tort
Tor|tel|ier, Paul
  cellist
tor|telli
tor|tel|lini
tort|fea|sor
tor|ti|col|lis
tor|tilla
tor|tious
tor|tious|ly
tor|toise
tortoise-like
tor|toise|shell
Tor|tola
tor|tri|cid
tor|trix
  tor|tri|ces
tor|tu|os|ity
  tor|tu|os|ities
tor|tu|ous
tor|tu|ous|ly
tor|tu|ous|ness
tor|tur|able
tor|ture
  tor|tur|ing
tor|turer
tor|tur|ous
tor|tur|ous|ly
tor|ula
  toru|lae
toru|losis
Toruń
torus
  tori or tor|uses
  ring-shaped object;
  cf. Taurus
Tor|vill, Jayne ice
  skater

Tory
Tor|ies
  Conservative; cf.
  tori
Tory|ism
tosa
Tos|ca|nini, Ar|turo
  conductor
Tosk
  pl. Tosk or Tosks
toss|er *often vulgar*
  slang
toss|pot *vulgar*
  slang
toss-up *n.*
tos|tada
tos|tado +s
  var. of tostada
tos|tone
tosyl
tosyl|ate
tot
  tot|ted
  tot|ting
total
  to|talled *Br.*
  to|taled *US*
  to|tal|ling *Br.*
  to|tal|ing *US*
to|tal|isa|tion *Br.*
  var. of totalization
to|tal|isa|tor *Br.* var.
  of totalizator
to|tal|ise *Br.* var. of
  totalize
to|tal|iser *Br.* var. of
  totalizer
to|tali|tar|ian
to|tali|tar|ian|ism
to|tal|ity
  to|tal|ities
to|tal|iza|tion
to|tal|iza|tor
to|tal|ize
  to|tal|iz|ing
to|tal|izer
to|tal|ly
to|tara
tote
  tot|ing
totem
to|tem|ic
to|tem|ism
to|tem|ist

to|tem|is|tic
toter
tother var. of *t'other*
t'other = the other
toti|potency
toti|potent
tot|ter
tot|ter|er
tot|tery
totting-up
totty
  tot|ties
tou|can
tou|canet
touch|able
touch-and-go
  touch-and-goes
touch|back
touch|down
tou|ché
touch|er
touch|ily
touchi|ness
touch|ing|ly
touch|ing|ness
touch-in-goal
touch|line
touch-me-not plant
touch|paper
touch|stone
touch-tone
  trademark as *n.*
touch-type
  touch-typing
touch-typist
touch-up *n. & mod.*
touch|wood tinder
touchy
  touch|ier
  touchi|est
touchy-feely
tough durable;
  hardy; severe; etc.;
  cf. tuff
tough|en
tough|en|er
toughie
tough|ish
tough|ly
tough|ness
Tou|lon
Tou|louse

Toulouse-Lautrec,
Henri de artist
tou¦pee
tou¦pet var. of
toupee
tour journey; cf. tur
tour¦aco var. of
turaco
Tou¦rane
tour de force
tours de force
tour d'hori¦zon
tours d'hori¦zon
tour en l'air
tours en l'air
tour¦er
Tou¦rette's
syn¦drome
tour¦ism
tour¦ist
tour¦is¦tic
tour¦is¦tic¦al¦ly
tour¦isty
tour¦ma¦line
Tour¦nai
tour¦na¦ment
tour¦ne¦dos
pl. tour¦ne¦dos
tour¦ney
tour¦ni¦quet
tour¦nois
Tours city, France
tour¦tière
tou¦sle
tous¦ling
Tous¦saint
L'Ouver¦ture,
Pierre revolution-
ary
tout attempt to sell;
reseller of tickets
etc.
tout all; cf. to, too,
two
tout court
tout de suite
tout¦er
to¦var¦ich var. of
tovarish
to¦var¦ish
tow pull; fibres; cf.
toe
tow¦able
tow¦age

towai
to¦ward
to¦wards
towel
tow¦elled Br.
tow¦eled US
tow¦el¦ling Br.
tow¦el¦ing US
towel¦ette
towel¦head
tower
tow¦ery
tow-head
tow¦hee
tow¦line
townee var. of
townie
Townes, Charles
physicist
townie
town¦ish
town¦land
town¦less
town¦let
town¦scape
towns¦folk
town¦ship
town¦site
towns¦man
towns¦men
towns¦people
Towns¦ville
towns¦woman
towns¦women
town¦ward
town¦wards
tow¦path
tow¦plane
towy
tow¦ier
towi¦est
tox¦ae¦mia Br.
tox¦aem¦ic Br.
toxa¦phene
tox¦emia US
tox¦em¦ic US
toxic
tox¦ic¦al¦ly
toxi¦cant
tox¦icity
toxi¦co¦logic¦al
toxi¦co¦logic¦al¦ly
toxi¦colo¦gist

toxi¦col¦ogy
toxi¦gen¦ic
toxi¦gen¦icity
toxin poison; cf.
tocsin
toxo¦cara
toxo¦car¦ia¦sis
tox¦oid
tox¦oph¦il¦ite
tox¦oph¦ily
toxo¦plasma
toxo¦plas¦mo¦sis
toyi-toyi
toyi-toyis
toyi-toyied
toyi-toying or
toyi-toyiing
toy¦like
toy¦maker
Toyn¦bee, Ar¦nold
economist;
historian
toyon
toy¦shop
toy¦town
T-piece
tra¦be¦ated
tra¦be¦ation
tra¦bec¦ula n.
tra¦becu¦lae
tra¦becu¦lar adj.
tra¦becu¦late
Trab¦zon
tra¦cas¦serie
trace
tra¦cing
trace¦abil¦ity
trace¦able
trace-horse
trace¦less
tracer
tra¦cer¦ied
tra¦cery
tra¦cer¦ies
Tra¦cey
tra¦chea
tra¦cheae or
tra¦cheas
tra¦cheal
tra¦che¦ate
tra¦cheid
tra¦che¦itis

trache¦os¦tomy
trache¦os¦to¦mies
trache¦ot¦omy
trache¦oto¦mies
trach¦oma
trach¦oma¦tous
trach¦yte
trach¦yt¦ic
track¦age
track¦ball
track¦bed
track¦er
trackie tracksuit
track¦lay¦er
track-laying
trackle¦ment
track¦less
track¦man
track¦men
track¦pants
track¦side
track¦suit
track¦way
track¦work
tract¦abil¦ity
tract¦able
tract¦able¦ness
tract¦ably
Tract¦arian
Tract¦ar¦ian¦ism
trac¦tate
trac¦tion
trac¦tion¦al
trac¦tive
trac¦tor
trac¦tor trail¦er
tract¦otomy
tract¦oto¦mies
trac¦trix
trac¦trices
Tracy, Spen¦cer
actor
trad¦able
trade
trad¦ing
trade¦able var. of
tradable
trade-in n. & mod.
trade-last
trade¦mark
trade-off n.
trader

Trad|es|cant, John
  botanist
trad|es|can|tia
trades|man
  trades|men
trades|people
trades union *Br.*
  var. of trade union
trade union
trade-up *n.*
trad|ition
trad|ition|al
trad|ition|al|ism
trad|ition|al|ist
trad|ition|al|is|tic
trad|ition|al|ly
trad|ition|ary
trad|ition|ist
trad|ition|less
tra|duce
  tra|du|cing
tra|duce|ment
tra|ducer
Tra|fal|gar
traf|fic
  traf|ficked
  traf|fick|ing
traf|fic|ator
traf|fic calm|ing
traf|fick|er
traf|fic|less
traga|canth
tra|ge|dian writer of
  or actor in
  tragedies
tra|gedi|enne
  actress in tragedies
tra|gedy
  tra|ged|ies
Tra|ger *trademark*
tra|ghetto
  tra|ghetti
tragi pl. of tragus
tra|gic
tra|gic|al
tra|gic|al|ly
tragi|com|edy
  tragi|com|ed|ies
tragi|com|ic
tragi|com|ic|al|ly
trago|pan
tra|gus
  tragi

Tra|herne, Thomas
  writer
*trahi|son des
  clercs*
*trahi|sons des
  clercs*
trail|blazer
trail|blaz|ing
trail|er
train|abil|ity
train|able
train|band
train|ee
trainee|ship
train|er
train|load
train|man
  train|men
train|sick
train|spot|ter
train|spot|ting
traipse
  traips|ing
trait characteristic;
  cf. tray, trey
trai|tor
trai|tor|ous
trai|tor|ous|ly
Tra|jan Roman
  emperor
tra|jec|tory
  tra|jec|tor|ies
Tra|kehner
Tra|lee
tram|car
Tra|miner
tram|line
tram|mel
  tram|melled *Br.*
  tram|meled *US*
  tram|mel|ling *Br.*
  tram|mel|ing *US*
tra|mon|tana wind
tra|mon|tane (per-
  son) on the other
  side of the Alps
tramp|er
tramp|ish
tram|ple
  tramp|ling
tramp|ler
tram|po|line
  tram|po|lin|ing
tram|po|lin|ist

trampy
tram|way
trance
  tran|cing
trance-like
tranche
tran|ex|am|ic
tranked
tran|nie var. of
  tranny
tranny
  tran|nies
tran|quil
tran|quil|ity *US*
  Br. tranquillity
tran|quil|ize *US*
  tran|quil|iz|ing
tran|quil|izer *US*
tran|quil|lise *Br.*
  var. of tranquillize
tran|quil|liser *Br.*
  var. of
  tranquillizer
tran|quil|lity *Br.*
  US tranquility
tran|quil|lize *Br.*
  tran|quil|liz|ing
tran|quil|lizer *Br.*
tran|quil|ly
trans|act
trans|ac|tion
trans|ac|tion|al
trans|ac|tion|al|ly
trans|ac|ti|va|tion
trans|act|or
trans|alpine
trans|amin|ase
trans|amin|ate
  trans|amin|at|ing
trans|amin|ation
trans|at|lan|tic
trans|axle
Trans|cau|ca|sia
Trans|cau|ca|sian
trans|ceiver
tran|scend
tran|scend|ence
tran|scend|ency
tran|scend|ent
tran|scen|den|tal
tran|scen|den|tal|
  ise

Br. var. of
  transcendentalize
tran|scen|den|tal|
  ism
tran|scen|den|tal|
  ist
tran|scen|den|tal|
  ize
tran|scen|den|tal|
  iz|ing
tran|scen|den|tal|ly
  in a transcendental
  way
tran|scend|ent|ly in
  a transcendent way
trans|code
  trans|cod|ing
trans|con|duct|
  ance
trans|con|ju|gant
trans|con|tin|en|tal
trans|con|tin|
  en|tal|ly
trans|cor|tical
tran|scribe
  tran|scrib|ing
tran|scriber
tran|script
tran|script|ase
tran|scrip|tion
tran|scrip|tion|al
tran|scrip|tion|al|ly
tran|scrip|tion|ist
tran|scrip|tive
tran|scrip|tome
trans|cu|ta|ne|ous
trans|der|mal
trans|duce
  trans|du|cing
trans|ducer
trans|duc|tion
tran|sect
tran|sec|tion
tran|sept
tran|sep|tal
tran|sex|ual var. of
  transsexual
tran|sexu|al|ism
  var. of
  transsexualism
tran|sexu|al|ity var.
  of transsexuality
trans-fat
trans-fatty acid

trans|fect
trans|fect|ant
trans|fec|tion
trans|fer
  trans|ferred
  trans|fer|ring
trans|fer|abil|ity
trans|fer|able
trans|fer|ase
trans|fer|ee
trans|fer|ence
trans|fer|or *Law*
trans|fer|ral
trans|fer|rer gener-
  ally
trans|fer|rin
trans|fer|ware
trans|fig|ur|ation
trans|fig|ure
  trans|fig|ur|ing
trans|finite
trans|fix
trans|fix|ion
trans|form
trans|form|able
trans|form|ation
trans|form|ation|al
trans|form|ation|
  al|ly
trans|forma|tive
trans|form|er
trans|fuse
  trans|fus|ing
trans|fu|sion
trans|gender
trans|gen|dered
trans|gender|ism
trans|gender|ist
trans|gene
trans|gen|ic
trans|global
trans|gress
trans|gres|sion
trans|gres|sive
trans|gres|sor
tran|ship var. of
  trans-ship
tran|ship|ment var.
  of **trans-shipment**
trans|his|tor|ical
trans|hu|mance
trans|hu|mant
tran|si|ence

tran|si|ency
tran|si|ent
tran|si|ent|ly
trans|illu|min|ate
  trans|illu|min|
        at|ing
trans|illu|min|
        ation
tran|sire
tran|sis|tor
tran|sis|tor|isa|tion
  Br. var. of
  transistorization
tran|sis|tor|ise *Br.*
  var. of
  transistorize
tran|sis|tor|iza|tion
tran|sis|tor|ize
  tran|sis|tor|iz|ing
tran|sit
tran|si|tion
tran|si|tion|al
tran|si|tion|al|ly
tran|si|tion|ary
tran|si|tive
tran|si|tive|ly
tran|si|tive|ness
tran|si|tiv|ity
tran|si|tor|ily
tran|si|tori|ness
tran|si|tory
Trans|jor|dan
Trans|jor|dan|ian
Trans|kei
trans|keto|lase
trans|lata|bil|ity
trans|lat|able
trans|late
  trans|lat|ing
trans|la|tion
trans|la|tion|al
trans|la|tion|al|ly
trans|la|tor
trans|lit|er|ate
  trans|lit|er|at|ing
trans|lit|er|ation
trans|lit|er|ator
trans|lo|cate
  trans|lo|cat|ing
trans|lo|ca|tion
trans|lu|cence
trans|lu|cency
trans|lu|cent

trans|lu|cent|ly
trans|lunar
trans|mar|ine
trans|mem|brane
trans|mi|grant
trans|mi|grate
  trans|mi|grat|ing
trans|mi|gra|tion
trans|mi|gra|tor
trans|mi|gra|tory
trans|mis|si|bil|ity
trans|mis|sible
trans|mis|sion
trans|mis|sive
trans|mis|siv|ity
  trans|mis|siv|ities
trans|mit
  trans|mit|ted
  trans|mit|ting
trans|mit|table
trans|mit|tal
trans|mit|tance
trans|mit|ter
trans|mog|ri|fi|
        ca|tion
trans|mog|ri|fy
  trans|mog|ri|fies
  trans|mog|ri|fied
  trans|mog|ri|fy|ing
trans|mon|tane
trans|mural
trans|mut|abil|ity
trans|mut|able
trans|mu|ta|tion
trans|mu|ta|tion|al
trans|mu|ta|tion|
        ist
trans|mu|ta|tive
trans|mute
  trans|mut|ing
trans|muter
trans|nation|al
trans|nation|al|ism
trans|nation|al|ly
trans|ocean|ic
tran|som
tran|somed
tran|sonic
trans-Pacific
trans|par|ence
trans|par|ency
  trans|par|en|cies
trans|par|ent

trans|par|ent|ly
trans|par|ent|ness
trans-Pennine
trans|per|son|al
trans|pierce
  trans|pier|cing
tran|spir|able
tran|spir|ation
tran|spire
  tran|spir|ing
trans|plant
trans|plant|able
trans|plant|ation
trans|plant|er
trans|pon|der
trans|pon|tine
trans|port
trans|port|abil|ity
trans|port|able
trans|por|ta|tion
trans|port|er
trans|pos|able
trans|posal
trans|pose
  trans|pos|ing
trans|poser
trans|pos|ition
trans|pos|ition|al
trans|posi|tive
trans|poson
trans|puter
trans|racial
trans|sex|ual
trans|sexu|al|ism
trans|sexu|al|ity
trans-ship
  trans-shipped
  trans-shipping
trans-shipment
trans-Siberian
trans-sonic var. of
  transonic
trans-synaptic
tran|sub|stan|ti|ate
  tran|sub|stan|ti|
        at|ing
tran|sub|stan|ti|
        ation
tran|su|date
tran|su|da|tion
tran|sude
  tran|sud|ing
trans|uran|ic

trans|ureth|ral
Trans|vaal
trans|valu|ation
trans|value
   trans|valu|ing
trans|ver|sal
trans|ver|sal|ity
trans|ver|sal|ly
trans|verse
trans|verse|ly
trans|vest|ism
trans|vest|ist
trans|vest|ite
trans|vest|it|ism
Tran|syl|va|nia
Tran|syl|va|nian
trap
   trapped
   trap|ping
trap|ball
trap|door
trapes *archaic* var.
   of traipse
trap|eze
tra|pez|ium
   tra|pezia or
   tra|pez|iums
tra|pez|ius
   tra|pezii
trap|ezo|he|dral
trap|ezo|he|dron
   trap|ezo|he|dra or
   trap|ezo|he|drons
trap|ez|oid
trap|ez|oid|al
trap-like
trap|line
trap|per
trap|pings
Trap|pist
Trap|pist|ine
trap|rock
trash|ily
trashi|ness
trash talk *n.*
trash-talk *v.*
trash talk|er
trashy
   trash|ier
   trashi|est
Trás-os-Montes
trat|toria

trauma
   trau|mas or
   trau|mata
trau|mat|ic
trau|mat|ic|al|ly
trau|ma|tisa|tion
   Br. var. of
   traumatization
trau|ma|tise *Br.* var.
   of traumatize
trau|ma|tism
trau|ma|tiza|tion
trau|ma|tize
   trau|ma|tiz|ing
trav|ail
travel
   trav|elled *Br.*
   trav|eled *US*
   trav|el|ling *Br.*
   trav|el|ing *US*
trav|el|ator
trav|el|er *US*
trav|el|er's check
   US
trav|el|er's joy *US*
trav|el|er's tale *US*
trav|el|ler *Br.*
trav|el|ler's cheque
   Br.
trav|el|ler's joy *Br.*
trav|el|ler's tale *Br.*
trav|el|ogue
travel-sickness
tra|vers dressage
   movement; cf.
   traverse
trav|ers|able
tra|ver|sal
tra|verse
   tra|vers|ing
   move across; rock
   face; structure; sur-
   vey line; cf. travers
tra|ver|ser
trav|er|tine
trav|esty
   trav|es|ties
   trav|es|tied
   trav|esty|ing
tra|vois
   pl. tra|vois
travo|lator var. of
   travelator
trawl|er

trawler|man
   trawler|men
tray container for
   carrying items; cf.
   trait, trey
tray|ful
treach|er|ous
treach|er|ous|ly
treach|er|ous|ness
treach|ery
   treach|er|ies
trea|cle
trea|cly
   trea|clier
   treacli|est
tread
   trod
   trod|den
tread|er
treadle
   tread|ling
tread|mill
tread|wheel
trea|son
trea|son|able
trea|son|ably
trea|son|ous
treas|ure
   treas|ur|ing
treas|urer
treas|urer|ship
treas|ury
   treas|ur|ies
treat|able
treat|er
trea|tise written
   work
treat|ment
treaty
   treat|ies
   agreement
Treb|biano +s
Trebi|zond
treble
   treb|ling
Treb|linka
trebly
   treb|lier
   trebli|est
trebu|chet
tre|cent|ist
tre|cento
tree
   treed

tree|ing
tree|creep|er
tree|hop|per
tree|less
tree|less|ness
tree-like
tree|line
tree|nail
tree|top
tree|ware
trefa
tre|fid var. of trifid
   (spoon)
tref|oil
tref|oiled
tre|hal|ose
trek
   trekked
   trek|king
Trek|ker fan of *Star
   Trek*
trek|ker person who
   treks
Trek|kie
trel|lis
   trel|lises
   trel|lised
   trel|lis|ing
trellis|work
Trema|toda
trema|tode
trem|ble
   trem|bling
trem|bler person
   who trembles
trem|bling|ly
trem|blor earth
   tremor
trem|bly
   trem|blier
   trem|bli|est
tre|men|dous
tre|men|dous|ly
tre|men|dous|ness
tremo|lando
   tremo|landi
tremo|lite
trem|olo +s
tremor
tremu|lous
tremu|lous|ly
tremu|lous|ness
tre|nail var. of
   treenail

tren|chancy
tren|chant
tren|chant|ly
Tren|chard, Hugh
  Marshal of the RAF
trench|er
trench|er|man
  trench|er|men
Tren|de|len|burg
trend|ify
  trendi|fies
  trendi|fied
  trendi|fy|ing
trend|ily
trendi|ness
trend|oid
trend|set|ter
trend|set|ting
trendy
  trend|ies
  trend|ier
  trendi|est
Treng|ganu
trente et qua|rante
Trentino-Alto
  Adige
Trento city, Italy
Tren|ton city, US
tre|pan
  tre|panned
  tre|pan|ning
trep|an|ation
tre|pang
treph|in|ation
tre|phine
  tre|phin|ing
trepi|da|tion
trepi|da|tious
trepi|da|tious|ly
trepo|nema
trepo|nemal
trepo|neme
tres|pass
tres|pass|er
tres|sure
tressy
  tress|ier
  tressi|est
tres|tle
trestle|tree
trestle|work
tre|tin|oin
Tret|ya|kov
  Gal|lery

tre|vally
  tre|val|lies
Tre|vino, Lee golfer
Tre|vira *trademark*
Tre|vith|ick,
  Rich|ard engineer
Trevor name
trews trousers
trey dice or card
  with three spots;
  score of three; cf.
  trait, tray
tri|able
triac
tri|acet|ate
Triad Chinese secret
  society
triad group of three
tri|ad|ic
tri|ad|ic|al|ly
tri|age
triag|ing
trial
  trialled *Br.*
  trialed *US*
  trial|ling *Br.*
  trial|ing *US*
trial|ist
trial|list *Br.* var. of
  trialist
tria|logue
tri|angle
tri|angu|lar
tri|angu|lar|ity
tri|angu|lar|ly
tri|angu|late
  tri|angu|lat|ing
tri|angu|la|tion
Tri|an|gu|lum
Tri|an|gu|lum
  Aus|trale
Tria|non
Trias
Tri|as|sic
tri|ath|lete
tri|ath|lon
tri|atom|ic
tri|axial
tri-axle
tria|zine
tri|azole
trib|ad|ism
tri|bal
tri|bal|ism

tri|bal|ist
tri|bal|is|tic
tri|bal|ly
tri|basic
tribes|man
tribes|men
tribes|people
tribes|woman
  tribes|women
trib|let
tribo|elec|tri|city
tribo|logic|al
trib|olo|gist
trib|ology
tribo|lumin|
      es|cence
tribo|lumin|es|cent
trib|om|eter
tri|brach +s
tri|brach|ic
tribu|la|tion
tri|bu|nal
trib|un|ate
trib|une
trib|une|ship
trib|un|itial
tribu|tar|ily
tribu|tari|ness
tribu|tary
  tribu|tar|ies
trib|ute
tri|car
tri|carb|oxyl|ic
tri|cast
Tri|cel *trademark*
tri|cen|ten|ary
  tri|cen|ten|ar|ies
tri|cen|ten|nial
tri|ceps
  pl. tri|ceps
tri|cera|tops
trich|ia|sis
trich|ina
  trich|inae
Trichi|nop|oly
trich|in|osis
trich|in|ous
tri|chlor|acet|ic var.
  of trichloroacetic
tri|chlor|ide
tri|chloro|acet|ate
tri|chloro|acet|ic
tri|chloro|eth|ane

tri|chloro|ethyl|ene
tri|chloro|phe|nol
tricho|cyst
tricho|logic|al
trich|olo|gist
trich|ology
trich|ome
tricho|monad
tricho|monal
tricho|mon|ia|sis
tricho|path|ic
Trich|op|tera
trich|op|ter|an
tri|chord
tricho|tom|ic
trich|ot|om|ous
trich|ot|omy
  trich|oto|mies
tri|chro|ic
tri|chro|ism
tri|chro|mat|ic
tri|chro|ma|tism
tri|chrome
trick|er
trick|ery
  trick|er|ies
trick|ily
tricki|ness
trick|ish
trickle
  trick|ling
trickle-down *n. &*
  mod.
trick|sily
trick|si|ness
trick|ster
tricksy
  tricks|ier
  trick|si|est
tricky
  trick|ier
  tricki|est
tri|clad
tri|clin|ic
tri|clin|ium
  tri|clinia
tri|color *US*
tri|col|ored *US*
tri|col|our *Br.*
  flag
tri|col|oured *Br.*
tri|corn var. of
  tricorne

tri|corne

tri|cot

tri|co|teuse

tric-trac

tri|cus|pid

tri|cycle

  tri|cyc|ling

tri|cyc|lic

tri|cyc|list

tri|dac|tyl

tri|dac|tyl|ous

tri|dac|tyly

tri|dent

Tri|den|tine

trid|uum

tridy|mite

tried past tense and
  participle of **try**

tri|ene

tri|en|nial

tri|en|ni|al|ly

tri|en|nium

  tri|en|nia or
  tri|en|ni|ums

Trier city, Germany

trier person who
  tries

Tri|este

tri|ethyl

trifa var. of trefa

tri|fecta

trif|fid fictional
  plant

tri|fid in three parts;
  (of spoon) with
  three notches in
  handle

trifle

  trif|ling

trif|ler

trif|ling|ly

tri|fluo|pera|zine

tri|focal

tri|fold

tri|foli|ate

tri|for|ium

  tri|foria

tri|form

tri|formed

tri|fur|cate

  tri|fur|cat|ing

tri|fur|ca|tion

trig

  trigged

  trig|ging

trig|am|ist

trig|am|ous

trig|amy

tri|gem|inus

  tri|gem|ini

trig|ger

trig|ger|fish

Trig|lav

tri|gly|cer|ide

tri|glyph

tri|glyph|ic

tri|glyph|ic|al

tri|gon archaic
  triangle

tri|gon|al

tri|gon|al|ly

tri|gone triangular
  part of body

trig|ono|met|ric

trig|ono|met|ric|al

trig|onom|etry

tri|gram

tri|graph

tri|he|dral

tri|he|dron

  tri|he|dra or
  tri|he|drons

tri|hyd|ric

tri|iodo|methane

tri|iodo|thyr|on|ine

trike

  trik|ing

tri|lat|eral

tril|bied

trilby

  tril|bies

tri|lin|ear

tri|lin|gual

tri|lin|gual|ism

tri|lith

tri|lith|ic

tri|lithon

trill|er

tril|lion

tril|lionth

tril|lium

tri|lo|bite

tril|ogy

trilo|gies

Trim town, Republic
  of Ireland

trim

  trimmed

  trim|ming

  trim|mer

  trim|mest

tri|maran

tri|mer

tri|mer|ic

tri|mer|ous

tri|mes|ter

tri|mes|tral

tri|mes|trial

trim|eter

tri|metho|prim

tri|met|ric|al

tri|mix

trim|ly

trim|mer

trim|ness

Tri|mon|tium

trim|pot

Tri|murti

tri|nal

Trinco|ma|lee

trine

  trin|ing

Trini

Trin|ian in 'St
  Trinian's'

Trini|dad

Trini|dad|ian

Trini|tar|ian

Trini|tar|ian|ism

tri|nitrate

tri|nitro|tolu|ene

trin|ity

  trin|ities

trin|ket

trin|ket|ry

tri|nomial

trio +s

tri|ode

trio|let

tri|ose

tri|ox|ide

trip

  tripped

  trip|ping

tri|par|tite

tri|par|tite|ly

tri|par|ti|tion

tri|pep|tide

tri|phos|phate

triph|thong

triph|thong|al

Tri|pit|aka

tri|plane

triple

  trip|ling
  threefold etc.; cf.
  tripple

trip|let

Trip|lex glass
  trademark

trip|lex with three
  parts; building
  divided into three
  homes; provide in
  triplicate

trip|li|cate

  trip|li|cat|ing

trip|li|ca|tion

triplo|blast|ic

trip|loid

trip|loidy

triply three times;
  cf. tripoli

trip|meter

tri|pod

tri|pod|al

Trip|oli capital of
  Libya; port,
  Lebanon

trip|oli polishing
  powder; cf. triply

Trip|oli|tania

Trip|oli|tan|ian

tri|pos

trip|pant

trip|per

trip|pery

trip|ple

  trip|pling
  horse's gait; move
  with this; cf. triple

trippy

  trip|pier

  trip|pi|est

trip|tych +s art
  work on three
  panels; set of three
  works; cf. tryptic

Trip|ura

trip|wire

tri|quetra

  tri|quet|rae

tri|quet|ral
tri|reme
tris compound
tri|sac|char|ide
Tris|agion
tri|sect
tri|sec|tion
tri|sect|or
tri|shaw
tris|kai|deka|
    pho|bia
tri|skel|ion
tris|mus
tri|somy
Tris|tan
Tris|tan da Cunha
trist|esse
Tris|tram
tri|syl|lab|ic
tri|syl|lable
tri|tag|on|ist
trit|an|ope
trit|an|opia
trite
  triter
  trit|est
trite|ly
trite|ness
tri|ter|pene
tri|ter|pen|oid
tri|the|ism
tri|the|ist
triti|ated
triti|ation
triti|cale
trit|ium
trito|cere|brum
  trito|cere|bra
Tri|ton Greek sea
  god; moon of
  Neptune
tri|ton mollusc;
  nucleus
tri|tone musical
  interval
trit|ur|able
trit|ur|ate
  trit|ur|at|ing
trit|ur|ation
trit|ur|ator
tri|umph
tri|umph|al
tri|umph|al|ism

tri|umph|al|ist
tri|umph|al|ly
tri|umph|ant
tri|umph|ant|ly
tri|um|vir
  tri|um|virs or
  tri|um|viri
tri|um|vir|al
tri|um|vir|ate
tri|une
tri|un|ity
  tri|un|ities
tri|va|lency
  tri|va|len|cies
tri|va|lent
Tri|van|drum
trivet
trivia
triv|ial
trivi|al|isa|tion Br.
  var. of
  trivialization
trivi|al|ise Br. var.
  of trivialize
trivi|al|ity
  trivi|al|ities
trivi|al|iza|tion
trivi|al|ize
  trivi|al|iz|ing
trivi|al|ly
trivi|al|ness
triv|ium
  trivia
Troad
Tro|bri|and
  Is|lands
tro|car
tro|cha|ic
tro|chan|ter
tro|chee metric foot
trochi pl. of trochus
troch|lea n.
  troch|leae
troch|lear adj.
troch|oid
troch|oid|al
trocho|phore
tro|chus
  tro|chi or
  tro|chuses
Trocken|beeren|
    aus|lese
trocto|lite
trod|den

trog
  trogged
  trog|ging
trog|lo|dyte
trog|lo|dyt|ic
trog|lo|dyt|ism
tro|gon
troika
troil|ism
Troi|lus Greek
  Mythology
Tro|jan
troll|er
troll|ey
troll|ey|bus
troll|ius
troll|op woman
Trol|lope, An|thony
  novelist
trom|bone
trom|bon|ist
trom|mel
tromp trudge
trompe l'œil
Tromsø
trona
tronc
Trond|heim
troop armed force;
  group; move in
  large numbers; cf.
  troupe
troop|er soldier;
  police officer;
  troopship; cf.
  trouper
troopie
troop|ship
tro|pae|olum
troph|al|laxis
troph|ecto|derm
troph|ic
tro|phied
tropho|blast
tropho|blast|ic
tropho|zo|ite
tro|phy
  tro|phies
trop|ic
trop|ic|al
trop|ic|al|ly
tropic|bird
trop|ism

tropo|logic|al
trop|ology
tropo|lone
tropo|my|osin
tropo|nin
tropo|pause
tropo|sphere
tropo|spher|ic
troppo
Tros|sachs
Trot = Trotskyist
trot
  trot|ted
  trot|ting
  of horse etc.
tro-tro +s
Trot|sky, Leon
  revolutionary
Trot|sky|ism
Trot|sky|ist
Trot|sky|ite
trot|ter
trou|ba|dour
trouble
  troub|ling
trouble|maker
trouble|making
troub|ler
trouble|shoot
  trouble|shot
trouble|shoot|er
trouble|some
trouble|some|ly
trouble|some|ness
troub|lous
trough
trounce
  troun|cing
troun|cer
troupe company of
  actors etc.; cf.
  troop
trouper member of
  troupe; reliable
  person; cf. trooper
troup|ial
trou|ser mod. & v.
trou|sers
trous|seau
  trous|seaux or
  trous|seaus
trout|ing
trou|vaille

trou|vère

trover

Trow|bridge

trowel

  trow|elled *Br.*

  trow|eled *US*

  trow|el|ling *Br.*

  trow|el|ing *US*

Troy ancient city,
  Turkey

troy weight

Troyes town, France

Troyes, Chré|tien
  de poet

tru|ancy

  tru|an|cies

tru|ant

Tru|cial States

truck cf. Truk
  Islands

truck|age

truck|er

truckie

truckle

  truck|ling

truck|ler

truck|load

trucu|lence

trucu|lency

trucu|lent

trucu|lent|ly

Tru|deau, Pierre
  prime minister of
  Canada

trudge

  trudg|ing

trudgen

trudger

true

  tru|ing or true|ing

  truer

  tru|est

  accurate; genuine;
  faithful; bring into
  exact position; cf.
  trews

true-lover's knot

True|man, Fred
  cricketer

true|ness

Truf|faut, Fran|çois
  film director

truf|fle

  truf|fling

tru|ism

tru|is|tic

Tru|jillo city, Peru

Tru|jillo, Ciu|dad
  former name of
  Santo Domingo

Tru|jillo, Raf|ael
  president of
  Dominica

Truk Is|lands

truly

Tru|man, Harry S.
  US president

tru|meau

  tru|meaux

trump|ery

  trump|er|ies

trum|pet

trum|pet|er

trumpet|fish

trun|cal

trun|cate

  trun|cat|ing

  trun|ca|tion

trun|cheon

trun|dle

  trund|ling

trunk|fish

trunk|ful

trunk|ing

trunk|less

trun|nel

trun|nion

Truro

truss|er

trust|able

Trusta|farian

trust|bust|er

trust|bust|ing

trust|ee administra-
  tor of trust; cf.
  trusty

trustee|ship

trust|er

trust|ful

trust|ful|ly

trust|ful|ness

trust|ily

trusti|ness

trust|ing|ly

trust|ing|ness

trust|wor|thily

trust|worthi|ness

trust|worthy

trusty

  trust|ies

  trust|ier

  trusti|est

  trustworthy;
  prisoner; cf.
  trustee

Truth, So|journ|er
  reformer

truth

truth|ful

truth|ful|ly

truth|ful|ness

try

  tries

  tried

  try|ing

try|ing|ly

try-on *n.*

try-out *n.*

try|pan

tryp|ano|some

tryp|ano|som|ia|sis

tryp|sin

tryp|sino|gen

trypta|mine

tryp|tic of trypsin;
  cf. triptych

tryp|to|phan

try|sail

tryst

tryst|er

tsad|dik

  tsad|dik|im or
  tsad|diks

tsamma

Tsao-chuang var. of
  Zaozhuang

tsar

tsar|dom

tsar|ev|ich

tsar|evna

tsar|ina

tsar|ism

tsar|ist

Tsar|it|syn

tsatske var. of
  tchotchke

Tsavo

Tse|lino|grad

tses|sebe var. of
  tsessebi

tses|sebi

tse|tse

T-shirt

tsim|mes

Tsim|shian
  pl. **Tsim|shian**

Tsi|nan var. of
  Jinan

Tsing|hai var. of
  Qinghai

Tskhin|vali

tsk tsk *exclam.*

Tsonga
  pl. **Tsonga** or
  Tson|gas

tsores var. of tsuris

tsotsi

T-square

tsuba
  pl. **tsuba** or **tsubas**
  Japanese sword
  guard

tsubo
  pl. **tsubo** or **tsubos**
  Japanese unit;
  pressure point

tsuke|mono +s

tsu|nami
  pl. **tsu|nami** or
  tsu|namis

tsuris

Tsu|shima

tsu|tsu|ga|mushi

Tswana
  pl. **Tswana** or
  Tswanas or
  Ba|tswana

T-top

Tua|motu

tuan

Tua|reg
  pl. **Tua|reg** or
  Tua|regs

tua|tara

Tua|tha Dé
  Da|nann

tub

  tubbed

  tub|bing

tuba

tubal

tub|bily

tub|bi|ness

tubby

  tub|bier

  tub|bi|est

tube
  tub¦ing
tub¦ec¦tomy
  tub¦ec¦to¦mies
tube¦less
tube-like
tuber
tuber cin¦er¦eum
tu¦ber¦cle
tu¦ber¦cu¦lar
tu¦ber¦cu¦late
tu¦ber¦cu¦la¦tion
tu¦ber¦cu¦lin
tu¦ber¦cu¦loid
tu¦ber¦cu¦losis
tu¦ber¦cu¦lous
tu¦ber¦ose plant
tu¦ber¦os¦ity
tu¦ber¦ous adj.
tub¦ful
tu¦bico¦lous
tubi¦fex
tubi¦form
tubi¦lin¦gual
tubo¦cur¦ar¦ine
Tu¦buai Is¦lands
tubu¦lar
tu¦bule
Tu¦buli¦den¦tata
tubu¦lin
Tu¦cana
tuck push in;
  stitched fold; food;
  etc.; cf. tux
tucka¦hoe
tucker
tucket
tuck-in n.
tuco-tuco +s
Tuc¦son
tu¦cuxi
  pl. tu¦cuxi
Tudeh
Tudor
Tudor¦bethan
Tudor¦esque
Tues¦day
tufa
tu¦fa¦ceous
tuff rock; cf. tough
tuff¦aceous
tuf¦fet

tufty
tuft¦ier
tufti¦est
Tu Fu Chinese poet
tug
  tugged
  tug¦ging
tug¦boat
tug¦ger
tu¦grik
  pl. tu¦grik or
  tu¦griks
tui
tuile
Tuil¦er¦ies
Tu¦inal trademark
tu¦ition
tu¦ition¦al
tuk-tuk
Tula
tu¦lar¦aemia Br.
tu¦lar¦aem¦ic Br.
tu¦lar¦emia US
tu¦lar¦cm¦ic US
tule plant; cf. tulle
tulip
tulip-root disease of
  oats
tulip¦wood
Tull, Jethro agricul-
  turalist
Tul¦la¦more
tulle fabric; cf. tule
tulli¦bee
  pl. tulli¦bee or
  tulli¦bees
Tulsa
tulsi
Tulsi¦das Indian
  poet
tul¦war var. of
  talwar
tum¦baga
tum¦ble
  tum¦bling
tumble¦bug
tumble¦down
tumble¦home
tum¦bler
tumbler¦ful
tumble¦weed
tum¦brel var. of
  tumbril
tum¦bril

tume¦fa¦cient
tume¦fac¦tion
tu¦mefy
  tu¦me¦fies
  tu¦me¦fied
  tu¦mefy¦ing
tu¦mes¦cence
tu¦mes¦cent
tu¦mes¦cent¦ly
tumid
tu¦mid¦ity
tu¦mid¦ly
tumm¦ler
tummy
  tum¦mies
tumor US
  Br. tumour
tumori¦gen¦esis
tumori¦gen¦ic
tumori¦gen¦icity
tu¦mor¦ous
tu¦mour Br.
  US tumor
tump¦line
tu¦mu¦lar
tu¦muli pl. of
  tumulus
tu¦mult
tu¦mul¦tu¦ous
tu¦mul¦tu¦ous¦ly
tu¦mul¦tu¦ous¦ness
tu¦mu¦lus
  tu¦muli
tun
  tunned
  tun¦ning
  (store in) cask; cf.
  ton, tonne
tuna fish; fruit;
  cactus; cf. tuner
tun¦able
Tun¦bridge Wells
  cf. Tonbridge
tun¦dish
tun¦dra
tune
  tun¦ing
tune¦able var. of
  tunable
tune¦ful
tune¦ful¦ly
tune¦ful¦ness
tune¦less
tune¦less¦ly

tune¦less¦ness
tuner person or
  thing that tunes
  something; cf. tuna
tune¦smith
tune-up n.
tung tree; oil; cf.
  tongue
tung¦state
tung¦sten
tung¦stic
tung¦stite
tung¦stous
Tun¦gus
  pl. Tun¦gus
Tun¦gus¦ian
Tun¦gus¦ic
Tun¦guska
tunic
tu¦nica
  tu¦nicae
tu¦ni¦cate
tu¦nicle
Tunis
Tu¦nisia
Tu¦nis¦ian
tun¦nel
  tun¦nelled Br.
  tun¦neled US
  tun¦nel¦ling Br.
  tun¦nel¦ing US
  tun¦nel¦er US
  tun¦nel¦ler Br.
tunny
  tun¦nies
tup
  tupped
  tup¦ping
Tupa¦maro +s
Tup¦elo city, US
tu¦pelo +s tree
Tupi
  pl. Tupi or Tupis
Tu¦pian
tupik
tuple
tup¦pence
tup¦penny
Tup¦per¦ware
  trademark
tuque
tur wild goat; cf.
  tour
tur¦aco +s

Tur|an|ian
tur|ban
tur|baned
tur|banned var. of
  turbaned
tur|bary
  tur|bar|ies
Tur|bel|laria
tur|bel|lar|ian
tur|bid
tur|bid|im|eter
tur|bidi|met|ric
tur|bid|im|etry
tur|bid|ite
tur|bid|it|ic
tur|bid|ity
tur|bid|ly
tur|bid|ness
tur|bin|al
tur|bin|ate
tur|bin|ation
tur|bine
tur|bit pigeon; cf.
  turbot
turbo +s
turbo|boost
turbo|charge
turbo|char|ging
turbo|char|ger
turbo|fan
turbo|gen|er|ator
turbo|jet
turbo|prop
turbo|shaft
turbo|super|
         char|ger
tur|bot fish; cf.
  turbit
tur|bu|lence
tur|bu|lent
tur|bu|lent|ly
Turco +s
Turco|man var. of
  Turkoman
Turco|phile
Turco|phobe
tur|een
turf
  pl. turfs or turves
  v. turfs
  turfed
  turf|ing

Tur|fan
  De|pres|sion
turf|man
  turf|men
turfy
turf|ier
turfi|est
Tur|ge|nev, Ivan
  writer
tur|ges|cence
tur|ges|cent
tur|gid
tur|gid|ity
tur|gid|ly
tur|gid|ness
tur|gor
Turin city, Italy
Tur|ing, Alan
  mathematician
tur|ion
tur|ista
Tur|kana
  pl. Tur|kana
  person; language;
  Lake
Turk|estan
Tur|key country
tur|key bird; flop;
  stupid person
tur|key|cock
Turk|ic
Turk|ish
Turki|stan var. of
  Turkestan
Turk|men
  pl. Turk|men or
  Turk|mens
Turk|meni|stan
Turko|man +s
Turks and Cai|cos
  Is|lands
Turk's cap plant
Turk's head knot
Turku port, Finland
tur|lough
tur|meric
tur|moil
turn rotate; change;
  etc.; cf. tern, terne
turn|about
turn|around
turn|back
turn|buckle
turn|coat

turn|cock
turn|down
Tur|ner, J. M. W.
  painter
turn|er
turn|ery
tur|nip
tur|nipy
turn|key
turn-off n.
turn-on n.
turn|out
turn|over
turn|pike
turn|round
turn|sole
turn|spit
turn|stile
turn|stone
turn|table
turn|tabl|ism
turn|tabl|ist
turn-up n.
Tur|pan var. of
  Turfan
tur|pen|tine
  tur|pen|tin|ing
Tur|pin, Dick
  highwayman
tur|pi|tude
turps
tur|quoise
tur|ret
tur|ret|ed
tur|ron
tur|tle
turtle-grass
turtle|head
turtle|neck
turtle|shell
Tus|can
Tus|cany
Tus|ca|rora
  pl. Tus|ca|rora or
  Tus|ca|roras
tushy
  tush|ies
tusk|er
tusky
tus|sah var. of
  tussore
Tus|sauds,
  Ma|dame

tussie-mussie
tus|sive
tus|sle
  tus|sling
tus|sock
tus|sock grass
Tus|sock moth
tus|socky
tus|sore
tut
  tut|ted
  tut|ting
Tu|tan|kha|men
  pharaoh
Tu|tan|kha|mun
  var. of
  Tutankhamen
tutee
tu|tel|age
tu|tel|ar
tu|tel|ary
tu|tenag
Tuth|mo|sis
  pharaoh
tutor
tu|tor|age
tu|tor|ial
tu|tori|al|ly
tu|tor|ship
tut|san
Tutsi
  pl. Tutsi or Tut|sis
  person; cf. tootsy
tutti Music
tutti-frutti
Tutu, Des|mond
  archbishop
tutu dancer's skirt;
  plant; cf. too-too
Tuva
Tu|valu
Tu|va|lu|an
tu-whit tu-whoo +s
tux = tuxedo
tux|edo
  tux|edos or
  tux|edoes
tux|edoed
Tux|tla Gu|tiér|rez
tuy|ère
Tuzla
Tver
Twa
  pl. Twa or Twas

twad¦dle
  twad|dling
twad|dler
Twain, Mark writer
twain *archaic* two
twaite shad
twangy
  twang|ier
  twangi|est
'**twas** = it was
twat
  twat|ted
  twat|ting
  vulgar slang as *n.*
tw"ay|blade
tweak
tweak¦er
twee
  tweer
  tweest
Tweed river, Scotland and England
tweed cloth;
  clothing
tweed|ily
tweedi|ness
Tweedle|dum and Tweedle|dee
tweedy
  tweed|ier
  tweedi|est
twee¦ly
Tween *trademark* compound
'**tween** = between
tween|ager
tween¦er
twee|ness
tweeny
  tween|ies
tweet¦er
tweeze
  tweez|ing
twee|zer
twee|zers
twelfth
twelfth¦ly
twelve-bore
twelve|fold
twelve-gauge
twelvemo +s
twelve|month year
twelve-step
  twelve-stepped

twelve-stepping
twelve-stepper
twen|ti|eth
twenty
  twen|ties
twenty-first,
  twenty-second,
  etc.
twenty|fold
twenty-one,
  twenty-two, etc.
'**twere** = it were
twerp
Twi
  pl. **Twi** or **Twis**
twi|bill
Twick¦en|ham
twid¦dle
  twid|dling
twid|dler
twid|dly
  twid|dlier
  twid|dli|est
twig
  twigged
  twig|ging
twiggy
twi|light
  twi|lit or
  twi|light|ed
twill fabric
'**twill** = it will
twin
  twinned
  twin|ning
twine
  twin|ing
twiner
twin|flower
twinge
  twinge|ing or
  twin|ging
twin-jet
twin¦kie
twin¦kle
  twink|ling
twink|ler
twinkle-toed
twinkle|toes
twin¦kly
  twink|lier
  twin¦kli|est
twin|set
twin|spot

twin-tub
twirl¦er
twirly
  twirl|ier
  twirli|est
twirp var. of twerp
twist|able
twisted-stalk plant
twist¦er swindler;
  tornado
twist-grip
twist-lock
twist¦or variable in
  physics
twisty
  twist|ier
  twisti|est
twit
  twit|ted
  twit|ting
twitch¦er
twitchy
  twitch|ier
  twitchi|est
twite
twit|ten
twit|ter
twit|ter|er
twit|tery
twit|tish
'**twixt** = betwixt
twiz¦zle
  twiz|zling
two +s number; cf.
  to, tout (= all), **too**
two-by-four
twoc
  twocced
  twoc|cing
twoc|cer
two¦fer
two|fold
two-hander
two-iron
two|ness
two|pence
two|penn'orth
two|penny
two-piece
two-ply
  two-plies
two-seater
two|some

two-step dance;
  music
two-stroke
two-time
  two-timing
two-timer
two-up gambling
  game
two-up two-down
two-wheeler
twyer
Ty¦burn
tych|ism
Ty¦cho|nian
Tych|on|ic
ty¦coon
tying
tying-up condition
  of horses
tyke
Ty|len|ol *trademark*
Tyler, John US
  president
Tyler, Wat leader of
  Peasants' Revolt
ty¦lo|pod
ty¦lopo|dous
tym¦pan layer in
  printing press;
  architectural
  tympanum
tym|pana pl. of
  tympanum
tym|pani var. of
  timpani
tym|pan¦ic of
  tympanum
tym|pan|ist var. of
  timpanist
tym|pan|ites
  swelling of
  abdomen
tym|pan|it¦ic of
  tympanites
tym|pa¦num
  tym|pa|nums or
  tym|pana
  eardrum; mem-
  brane; *Architecture*
  triangular space
tym|pany var. of
  tympanites
Tyn|dale, Wil|liam
  translator of Bible

Tyn|dall, John
  physicist
Tyne river, England;
  shipping area; cf.
  tine
Tyne|side
Tyne|sider
Tyn|wald
typal
type
  typ|ing
type|cast
type|face
type|script
type|set
  type|set|ting
  type|set|ter
type|writer
type|writ|ing
type|writ|ten
typh|lit|ic
typh|litis
ty|phoid
ty|phoid|al
ty|phon|ic
ty|phoon
typh|ous *adj.*
ty|phus *n.*
typ|ical
typ|ic|al|ity
typ|ic|al|ly
typi|fi|ca|tion
typi|fier
typ|ify
  typi|fies
  typi|fied
  typi|fy|ing
typ|ist
typo +s
typ|og|raph|er
typo|graph|ic
typo|graph|ic|al
typo|graph|ic|al|ly
typ|og|raphy
typo|logic|al
typ|olo|gist
typ|ology
  typ|olo|gies
Tyr Scandinavian
  god
tyr|am|ine
tyr|an|nic|al
tyr|an|nic|al|ly

tyr|an|ni|cidal
tyr|an|ni|cide
tyr|an|nise *Br.* var.
  of tyrannize
tyr|an|nize
tyr|an|niz|ing
tyr|an|no|saur
tyr|an|no|saurus
Tyr|an|no|saurus
  rex
tyr|an|nous
tyr|an|nous|ly
tyr|an|nu|let
tyr|anny
  tyr|an|nies
tyr|ant
Tyre port, Lebanon
tyre *Br.*
  on wheel;
  US tire; cf. tire
Tyr|ian
tyro +s
Tyr|ode's
Tyrol
Tyr|ol|ean
Tyr|ol|ese
Tyr|one
tyro|sin|ase
tyro|sine
Tyr|rhene
Tyr|rhen|ian
Tyson, Mike boxer
tys|tie
Tyu|men
tyuya|mun|ite
tzad|dik var. of
  tsaddik
tzar var. of tsar
Tzara, Tris|tan poet
tzar|dom var. of
  tsardom
tzar|ev|ich var. of
  tsarevich
tzar|evna var. of
  tsarevna
tzar|ina var. of
  tsarina
tzar|ism var. of
  tsarism
tzar|ist var. of
  tsarist
tza|tziki
tze|da|kah

Tzel|tal
  pl. Tzel|tal or
  Tzel|tals
tzi|gane
tzim|mis var. of
  tsimmes
T-zone
Tzo|tzil
  pl. Tzo|tzil or
  Tzo|tzils
Tzu-po var. of Zibo

U

ua|kari
ubac
Ubaid
Uban|ghi Shari
U-bend
uber|babe
über|babe var. of
  uberbabe
Über|mensch
  Über|mensch|en
ubi|ety
ubi|quin|one
ubi|qui|tar|ian
ubi|qui|tar|ian|ism
ubi|qui|tin
ubi|qui|tous
ubi|qui|tous|ly
ubi|qui|tous|ness
ubi|quity
U-boat
UCAS = Universities
  and Colleges
  Admissions Service
Uc|cello, Paolo
  painter
udal
udder
ud|dered
Ud|murt
Ud|mur|tia
udon
udyog
UEFA = Union of
  European Football
  Associations
U-ey

Ufa
Uf|fizi
UFO +s = unidenti-
  fied flying object
ufo|logic|al
ufolo|gist
ufol|ogy
ugali
Uganda
Ugan|dan
Ugarit
Ugar|it|ic
Ugg boot
  trademark var. of
  Ugh boot
ugh expressing
  repulsion
Ugh boot
  trademark
ug|li|fi|ca|tion
Ugli fruit
  trademark
  pl. Ugli fruit
  cf. ugly
uglify
  ugli|fies
  ugli|fied
  ugli|fy|ing
ug|lily
ugli|ness
ugly
  ug|lier
  ugli|est
  repulsive; violent;
  cf. Ugli fruit
Ugrian
Ugric
uh expressing hesita-
  tion; in questions
uh-huh expressing
  assent or
  indifference
uhlan
uh-oh expressing
  alarm or dismay
uh-uh expressing
  negative response
Ui|ghur
Uigur var. of
  Uighur
uil|lean pipes
uinta|there
Uist
uja|maa

Uji¦ya¦mada
Uj¦jain
Ujung Pan¦dang
ukase
uke = ukulele
uke¦lele var. of
  ukulele
ukiyo-e
Ukraine
Ukrain¦ian
uku¦lele
Ulaan¦baatar var.
  of Ulan Bator
Ulala
ulama var. of ulema
Ulan Bator
Ulan¦ova, Gal¦ina
  ballet dancer
Ulan-Ude
ulcer
ul¦cer¦ate
  ul¦cer¦at¦ing
ul¦cer¦ation
ul¦cera¦tive
ul¦cered
ul¦cer¦ous
ulema
ulex¦ite
Ul¦fi¦las bishop and
  translator
Ul¦has¦nagar
ull¦age
Ulm city, Germany
ulmo +s tree
ulna
  ulnae or ulnas *n.*
ulnar *adj.*
U-lock
Ul¦pian Roman
  jurist
Ulsan
Ul¦ster province,
  Ireland
ul¦ster coat
Ul¦ster¦man
  Ul¦ster¦men
Ul¦ster¦woman
  Ul¦ster¦women
ul¦ter¦ior
ul¦ter¦ior¦ly
ul¦tim¦acy
  ul¦tim¦acies
ul¦tim¦ate

ul¦tim¦ate¦ly
ul¦tima Thule
ul¦ti¦ma¦tum
  ul¦ti¦ma¦tums or
  ul¦ti¦mata
ul¦timo
ultimo¦bran¦chial
ulti¦sol
ultra
ultra¦basic
ultra¦cen¦tri¦fu¦
  ga¦tion
ultra¦cen¦tri¦fuge
ultra¦cen¦tri¦
  fu¦ging
ultra¦cold
ul¦tra¦dian
ultra¦fil¦tra¦tion
ultra¦ism
ultra¦ist
ultra¦maf¦ic
ultra¦mar¦ine
ultra¦micro¦scope
ultra¦micro¦scop¦ic
ultra¦mon¦tane
ultra¦mon¦tan¦ism
ultra¦mun¦dane
ultra¦saurus
ultra¦short
ultra¦son¦ic
ultra¦son¦ic¦al¦ly
ultra¦
  son¦og¦raph¦er
ultra¦sono¦graph¦ic
ultra¦son¦og¦raphy
ultra¦sound
ultra¦struc¦ture
ultra¦vio¦let
ultra vires
ulu
ulu¦lant
ulu¦late
  ulu¦lat¦ing
ulu¦la¦tion
Ul¦undi
Uluru
Ul¦ya¦nov original
  surname of Lenin
Ul¦yan¦ovsk
Ulys¦ses Roman
  name for Odysseus
umami
U-matic *trademark*

Umay¦yad
Um¦banda
umbel
um¦bel¦lar
um¦bel¦late
um¦bel¦lif¦er
um¦bel¦lif¦er¦ous
um¦bel¦lule
umber
um¦bil¦ical
um¦bil¦ic¦al¦ly
um¦bil¦icate
um¦bil¦icus
  um¦bil¦ici or
  um¦bil¦ic¦uses
um¦bles
umbo
  umbo¦nes or
  umbos
umbo¦nal
umbo¦nate
umbra
  um¦bras or
  um¦brae
um¦brage
um¦bra¦geous
um¦bral
um¦brella
um¦brella¦bird
um¦brel¦laed
umbrella-like
Um¦bria region,
  Italy
Um¦brian
Um¦briel moon of
  Uranus
um¦brif¦er¦ous
Umeå
um¦faan
um¦fun¦disi
  ba¦fun¦disi
umiak
um¦laut
umma
ummah var. of
  umma
Umm al Qai¦wain
um¦pir¦age
um¦pire
  um¦pir¦ing
um¦pire¦ship
ump¦teen
ump¦teenth

umrah
Um¦tali
umu
Um¦welt
  Um¦welten
'un = one, as in
  'young 'un'
un¦abashed
un¦abashed¦ly
un¦abated
un¦abated¦ly
un¦able
un¦abridged
un¦absorbed
un¦aca¦dem¦ic
un¦accent¦ed
un¦accept¦abil¦ity
un¦accept¦able
un¦accept¦able¦ness
un¦accept¦ably
un¦accept¦ed
un¦accom¦
  mo¦dat¦ing
un¦accom¦pan¦icd
un¦accom¦plished
un¦account¦abil¦ity
un¦account¦able
un¦account¦able¦
  ness
un¦account¦ably
un¦account¦ed
un¦accus¦tomed
un¦accus¦tomed¦ly
un¦achiev¦able
un¦acknow¦ledged
una corda
un¦acquaint¦ed
un¦adapt¦able
un¦adapt¦ed
un¦ad¦dressed
un¦adja¦cent
un¦adjust¦ed
un¦adopt¦ed
un¦adorned
un¦adul¦ter¦ated
un¦ad¦ven¦tur¦ous
un¦ad¦ven¦tur¦
  ous¦ly
un¦ad¦ver¦tised
un¦ad¦vis¦able
un¦ad¦vised¦ly
un¦ad¦vised¦ness

un|aes|thet|ic
un|affect|ed
un|affect|ed|ly
un|affect|ed|ness
un|affec|tion|ate
un|affili|ated
un|afford|able
un|afraid
un|aggres|sive
un|aid|ed
un|aired
un|alien|able
un|aligned
un|alike
un|alive
un|allevi|ated
un|allied
un|allow|able
un|alloyed
un|alter|able
un|alter|able|ness
un|alter|ably
un|altered
un|amazed
un|am|bi|gu|ity
un|am|bigu|ous
un|am|bigu|ous|ly
un|am|bi|tious
un|am|bi|tious|ly
un|am|bi|tious|ness
un|am|biva|lent
un|am|biva|lent|ly
un|amend|ed
un-American
un-American|ism
Unami
un|ami|able
un|amp|li|fied
un|amused
un|ana|lys|able *Br.*
un|ana|lysed *Br.*
un|ana|lyz|able *US*
un|ana|lyzed *US*
un|anchored
un|aneled
  unanointed; cf.
  unannealed
Unani
unan|im|ity
unani|mous
unani|mous|ly

unani|mous|ness
un|annealed not
  heat-treated; cf.
  unaneled
un|announced
un|answer|able
un|answer|able|
       ness
un|answer|ably
un|answered
un|antici|pated
un|apolo|get|ic
un|apolo|get|ic|
      al|ly
un|appar|ent
un|appeal|able
un|appeal|ing
un|appeal|ing|ly
un|appeas|able
un|appeased
un|appe|tis|ing *Br.*
  var. of
  unappetizing
un|appe|tis|ing|ly
  Br. var. of
  unappetizingly
un|appe|tiz|ing
un|appe|tiz|ing|ly
un|applied
un|appre|ci|ated
un|appre|cia|tive
un|appre|hend|ed
un|approach|
     abil|ity
un|approach|able
un|approach|able|
       ness
un|approach|ably
un|appro|pri|ated
un|approved
un|apt
un|apt|ly
un|apt|ness
un|argu|able
un|argu|ably
un|arm
un|arrest|ing|ly
un|articu|lated
un|artis|tic
unary
un|ascer|tain|able
un|ascer|tained
un|ashamed

un|ashamed|ly
un|ashamed|ness
un|asked
un|assail|abil|ity
un|assail|able
un|assail|able|ness
un|assail|ably
un|assert|ive
un|assert|ive|ly
un|assert|ive|ness
un|assign|able
un|assigned
un|assim|il|able
un|assim|il|ated
un|assist|ed
un|associ|ated
un|assuage|able
un|assuaged
un|assum|ing
un|assum|ing|ly
un|assum|ing|ness
un|atoned
un|attached
un|attain|able
un|attain|able|ness
un|attain|ably
un|attempt|ed
un|attend|ed
un|attest|ed
un|attract|ive
un|attract|ive|ly
un|attract|ive|ness
un|attrib|ut|able
un|attrib|ut|ably
un|attrib|uted
un|audit|ed
un|authen|tic
un|authen|tic|al|ly
un|authen|ti|cated
un|author|ised *Br.*
  var. of
  unauthorized
un|author|ized
un|avail|abil|ity
un|avail|able
un|avail|able|ness
un|avail|ing
un|avail|ing|ly
un|avoid|abil|ity
un|avoid|able
un|avoid|able|ness
un|avoid|ably

un|avowed
un|awakened
un|aware
un|aware|ness
un|awares
un|awed
un|backed
un|baked
un|bal|ance
un|bal|an|cing
un|ban
un|banned
un|ban|ning
un|bap|tised *Br.*
  var. of unbaptized
un|bap|tized
un|bar
un|barred
un|bar|ring
un|bear|able
un|bear|able|ness
un|bear|ably
un|beat|able
un|beat|ably
un|beat|en
un|beau|ti|ful
un|beau|ti|ful|ly
un|be|com|ing
un|be|com|ing|ly
un|be|com|ing|ness
un|be|fit|ting
un|be|fit|ting|ly
un|be|fit|ting|ness
un|be|got|ten
un|be|hold|en
un|be|known
un|be|knownst
un|belief
un|believ|abil|ity
un|believ|able
un|believ|able|ness
un|believ|ably
un|believer
un|believ|ing
un|believ|ing|ly
un|be|loved
un|belt
un|bend
un|bent
un|bend|ing|ly
un|bend|ing|ness
un|biased

un|biassed var. of
  unbiased
un|bib|li|cal
un|bid|dable
un|bid|den
un|bind
  un|bound
un|birth|day
un|bleached
un|blem|ished
un|blessed
un|blest var. of
  unblessed
un|blind
un|blink|ing
un|blink|ing|ly
un|block
un|blown
un|blush|ing
un|blush|ing|ly
un|bolt
un|bon|net
un|book|ish
un|born
un|bosom
un|bothered
un|bound
un|bound|ed
un|bound|ed|ly
un|bound|ed|ness
un|bowed
un|brace
  un|bracing
un|braid
un|branched
un|brand|ed
un|breach|able
un|break|able
un|breath|able
un|brib|able
un|bridge|able
un|bridled
un-British
un|broken
un|broken|ly
un|broken|ness
un|bruised
un|buckle
  un|buck|ling
un|build
  un|built

un|bun|dle
un|bund|ling
un|bund|ler
un|bur|den
un|burned
un|burnt *Br.* var. of
  unburned
un|bury
  un|buries
  un|buried
  un|bury|ing
un|busi|ness|like
un|but|ton
un|caged
un|called
un|can|did
un|can|nily
un|can|ni|ness
un|canny
  un|can|nier
  un|canni|est
un|can|on|ic|al
un|can|on|ic|al|ly
un|cap
  un|capped
  un|cap|ping
un|cared
un|car|ing
un|car|ing|ly
un|car|pet|ed
un|case
  un|cas|ing
un|cashed
un|cas|trated
un|catch|able
un|caught
un|ceas|ing
un|ceas|ing|ly
un|cele|brated
un|cen|sored uncut
un|cen|sured
  uncriticized
un|cere|mo|ni|ous
un|cere|mo|ni|
    ous|ly
un|cere|mo|ni|ous|
    ness
un|cer|tain
un|cer|tain|ly
un|cer|tainty
  un|cer|tain|ties
un|cer|tifi|cated
un|cer|ti|fied
un|chain

un|chal|lenge|able
un|chal|lenge|ably
un|chal|lenged
un|chal|len|ging
un|chancy
un|chan|cier
  un|chanci|est
un|change|abil|ity
un|change|able
un|change|able|
    ness
un|change|ably
un|changed
un|chan|ging
un|chan|ging|ly
un|chap|er|oned
un|char|ac|ter|
    is|tic
un|char|ac|ter|
    is|tic|al|ly
un|charged
un|char|is|mat|ic
un|char|it|able
un|char|it|able|
    ness
un|char|it|ably
un|chart|ed
un|char|tered
un|chaste
un|chaste|ly
un|chas|tened
un|chas|tity
un|checked
un|chiv|al|rous
un|chiv|al|rous|ly
un|chosen
un|chris|tian
un|chris|tian|ly
un|church
un|cial
un|ci|form
un|cin|ar|ia|sis
un|cin|ate
un|cir|cu|lated
un|cir|cum|cised
un|cir|cum|ci|sion
un|civil
un|civ|il|ised *Br.*
  var. of uncivilized
un|civ|il|ized
un|civ|il|ly
un|clad
un|claimed

un|clamp
un|clasp
un|clas|si|fi|able
un|clas|si|fied
uncle
un|clean
un|clean|li|ness
un|clean|ly
un|clean|ness
un|clear
un|cleared
un|clear|ly
un|clear|ness
un|clench
un|climb|able
un|climbed
un|clip
  un|clipped
  un|clip|ping
un|cloak
un|clog
  un|clogged
  un|clog|ging
un|clothe
  un|cloth|ing
un|cloud|ed
un|clut|tered
unco +s
un|coat|ed
un|coil
un|col|lect|ed
un|col|ored *US*
un|col|oured *Br.*
un|combed
un|come|ly
un|com|fort|able
un|com|fort|able|
    ness
un|com|fort|ably
un|comfy
  un|comfier
  un|comfi|est
un|com|ment
un|com|mer|cial
un|com|mit|ted
un|com|mon
un|com|mon|ly
un|com|mon|ness
un|com|mu|ni|
    ca|tive
un|com|mu|ni|
    ca|tive|ly

un|com|mu|ni|
    ca|tive|ness
un|com|pan|ion|
    able
un|com|pen|sated
un|com|peti|tive
un|com|peti|tiv|ely
un|com|peti|tive|
    ness
un|com|plain|ing
un|com|plain|
    ing|ly
un|com|pleted
un|com|plexed
un|com|pli|cated
un|com|pli|cated|ly
un|com|pli|cated|
    ness
un|com|pli|
    men|tary
un|com|pound|ed
un|com|pre|hend|
    ing
un|com|pre|hend|
    ing|ly
un|com|pre|hen|
    sion
un|com|prom|
    is|ing
un|com|prom|
    is|ing|ly
un|com|prom|
    is|ing|ness
un|con|cealed
un|con|cern
un|con|cerned
un|con|cern|ed|ly
un|con|cluded
un|con|di|tion|al
un|con|di|tion|
    al|ity
un|con|di|tion|al|ly
un|con|di|tioned
un|con|fessed
un|con|fi|dent
un|con|fi|dent|ly
un|con|fined
un|con|firmed
un|con|form|able
un|con|form|able|
    ness
un|con|form|ably
un|con|form|ity
un|con|gen|ial

un|con|nect|ed
un|con|nect|ed|ly
un|con|nect|ed|
    ness
un|con|quer|able
un|con|quer|able|
    ness
un|con|quer|ably
un|con|quered
un|con|scion|able
un|con|scion|ably
un|con|scious
un|con|scious|ly
un|con|scious|ness
un|con|se|crated
un|con|sent|ing
un|con|sid|ered
un|con|sol|able
un|con|sol|ably
un|con|soli|dated
un|con|sti|
    tu|tion|al
un|con|sti|tu|tion|
    al|ity
un|con|sti|tu|tion|
    al|ly
un|con|strained
un|con|strain|ed|ly
un|con|strict|ed
un|con|struct|ed
un|con|struct|ive
un|con|sult|ed
un|con|sumed
un|con|sum|mated
un|con|tact|able
un|con|tain|able
un|con|tam|in|ated
un|con|ten|tious
un|con|test|ed
un|con|test|ed|ly
un|con|tra|dict|ed
un|con|trived
un|con|trol|lable
un|con|trol|lable|
    ness
un|con|trol|lably
un|con|trolled
un|con|trolled|ly
un|con|tro|ver|sial
un|con|tro|
    ver|sial|ly
un|con|tro|vert|ed

un|con|tro|vert|
    ible
un|con|ven|tion|al
un|con|ven|tion|al|
    ism
un|con|ven|tion|
    al|ity
un|con|ven|tion|
    al|ly
un|con|vert|ed
un|con|vert|ible
un|con|vict|ed
un|con|vinced
un|con|vin|cing
un|con|vin|cing|ly
un|cooked
un|cool
un|co|opera|tive
un|co|opera|tive|ly
un|co|or|din|ated
un|copi|able
un|cord
un|cork
un|cor|rect|ed
un|cor|rob|or|ated
un|cor|rupt|ed
un|count
un|count|abil|ity
un|count|able
un|count|ably
un|count|ed
un|couple
un|coup|ling
un|court|ly
un|couth
un|couth|ly
un|couth|ness
un|cov|en|ant|ed
un|cover
un|crack|able
un|crate
un|crat|ing
un|crease
un|creas|ing
un|cre|ate
un|cre|at|ing
un|crea|tive
un|cred|it|ed
un|crit|ic|al
un|crit|ic|al|ly
un|cropped
un|cross
un|crowd|ed

un|crown
un|crum|ple
un|crump|ling
un|crush|able
un|crushed
UNCTAD = United
    Nations Conference
    on Trade and
    Development
unc|tion
unc|tu|ous
unc|tu|ous|ly
unc|tu|ous|ness
un|culled
un|cul|tiv|able
un|culti|vated
un|cul|tured
un|cured
un|curl
un|cur|tained
un|cut
un|dam|aged
un|damped
un|dated
un|daunt|ed
un|daunt|ed|ly
un|daunt|ed|ness
un|dead
un|dealt
un|deca|gon
un|deceive
un|deceiv|ing
un|decid|abil|ity
un|decid|able
un|decided
un|decided|ly
un|de|cipher|able
un|declared
un|dec|or|ated
un|dee var. of undy
un|defeat|ed
un|defend|ed
un|defiled
un|defin|able
un|defin|ably
un|defined
un|deformed
un|delete
un|delet|ing
un|deliv|ered
un|demand|ing
un|demo|crat|ic

un|demo|crat|ic|
al|ly
un|dem|on|strated
un|demon|stra|tive
un|demon|stra|
tive|ly
un|demon|stra|
tive|ness
un|deni|able
un|deni|able|ness
un|deni|ably
un|denied
un|denom|in|
ation|al
un|dent|ed
un|depend|able
under
under|achieve
under|achiev|ing
under|achieve|
ment
under|achiever
under|act
under|age
under|arm
under|belly
under|bel|lies
under|bid
under|bid|ding
under|bid|der
under|bite
under|blan|ket
under|body
under|bodies
under|boss
under|bred
under|bridge
under|brush
under|cap|acity
under|cap|it|al|
isa|tion
Br. var. of under-
capitalization
under|cap|it|al|ise
Br. var. of
undercapitalize
under|cap|it|al|
iza|tion
under|cap|it|al|ize
under|cap|it|al|
iz|ing
under|card
under|car|riage
under|cart

under|cast
under|charge
under|char|ging
under|class
under|cliff
under|cling
under|clung
under|clothes
under|cloth|ing
under|coat
under|
con|sump|tion
under|cook
under|cool
under|count
under|cover
under|crack|ers
under|croft
under|cur|rent
under|cut
under|cut|ting
under|damp
under|deter|min|
ation
under|deter|mine
under|
deter|min|ing
under|devel|oped
under|devel|op|
ment
under|do
under|does
under|did
under|do|ing
under|done
under|dog
under|draw|ing
under|dress
under|edu|cated
under|empha|sis
under|empha|ses
under|empha|sise
Br. var. of
underemphasize
under|empha|size
under|
empha|siz|ing
under|employed
under|
employ|ment
under|equipped
under|esti|mate
under|esti|mat|ing
under|esti|ma|tion

under|expose
under|expos|ing
under|expos|ure
under|fed
under|felt
under|financed
under|finan|cing
under-fives
under|floor
under|flow
under|foot
under|frame
under|fund
under|fur
under-garden|er
under|gar|ment
under|gird
under|gird|ed or
under|girt
under|glaze
under|go
under|goes
under|went
undcr|go|ing
under|gone
under|grad
under|gradu|ate
under|ground
under|growth
under|hand
under|hand|ed
under|hand|ed|ly
under|heat|ed
under|hung
under|insur|ance
under|insured
under|invest
under|invest|ment
under|lay
under|laid
under|lease
under|leas|ing
under|let
under|let|ting
under|lever
under|lie
under|lay
under|lain
under|lying
under|life
under|lives
under|line
under|lin|ing
under|linen

under|ling
under|lip
under|lit
under|man
under|manned
under|man|ning
under|man|ager
under|men|tioned
under|mine
under|min|ing
under|miner
under|min|ing|ly
under|most
under|neath
under|nour|ished
under|nour|ish|
ment
under|occu|pancy
under|paid
under|paint|ing
under|pants
under|part
under|pass
under|pay
under|paid
under|pay|ment
under|per|form
under|per|form|
ance
under|pin
under|pinned
under|pin|ning
under|plant
under|play
under|plot
under|popu|lated
under|popu|la|tion
under|pow|ered
under|pre|pared
under|price
under|pricing
under|priv|il|eged
under|pro|duce
under|pro|du|cing
under|pro|duc|tion
under|proof
under|prop
under|propped
under|prop|ping
under|quali|fied
under|quote
under|quot|ing
under|rate
under|rat|ing

under-read
under-record
under-rehearsed
under-report
under-represent
under-represen¦ta¦tion
under-resourced
under-resour¦cing
under|ripe
under|satur¦ated
under|satur¦ation
under|score
under|scor|ing
under|sea
under|seal
under|sec¦re¦tary
under|sec¦re¦tar|ies
under|sell
under|sold
under|served
under|sexed
under|sheet
under|sher¦iff
under|shirt
under|shoot
under|shot
under|shorts
under|shrub
under|side
under|signed
under|size
under|sized
under|skirt
under|slung
under|soil
under|sold
under|sow
  past participle
under|sown or
under|sowed
under|spend
under|spent
under|staff
under|stairs
under|stand
under|stood
under|stand|
          abil¦ity
under|stand|able
under|stand|ably
under|stand¦er
under|stand|ing¦ly

under|state
under|stat¦ing
under|stated¦ly
under|state|ment
under|stater
under|steer
under|stocked
under|stood
under|storey *Br.*
under|story
under|stories *US*
under|strap¦per
under|study
under|stud¦ies
under|stud¦ied
under|study|ing
under|sub¦scribed
under|sur¦face
under|swell
under|take
under|took
under|tak¦ing
under|taken
under|taker
under|ten¦ancy
under|ten¦an¦cies
under|ten¦ant
under|things
under|thrust
under|tint
under|tip
under|tipped
under|tip|ping
under|tone
under|took
under|tow
under|trained
under|trial *n.*
under|trick
under|use
under|using
under|util¦isa¦tion
  Br. var. of
  underutilization
under|util¦ise *Br.*
  var. of underutilize
under|util¦iza¦tion
under|util¦ize
under|util¦iz¦ing
under|valu¦ation
under|value
under|valu¦ing
under|vest
under|vote

under|water
under way
under|wear
under weigh
  Nautical var. of
  under way
under|weight
under|went
under|whelm
under|wing
under|wire
under|wood
under|work
under|world
under|write
under|wrote
under|writ¦ing
under|writ¦ten
under|writer
un|des¦cend¦ed
un|deserved
un|deserved¦ly
un|deserv¦ing
un|deserv¦ing¦ly
un|designed
un|design¦ed¦ly
un|desir¦abil¦ity
un|desir¦able
un|desir¦able|ness
un|desir¦ably
un|desired
un|desir¦ous
un|detect|abil¦ity
un|detect|able
un|detect|ably
un|detect¦ed
un|deter¦mined
un|deterred
un|devel¦oped
un|devi¦at¦ing
un|devi¦at¦ing¦ly
un|diag¦nosed
un|did
un|dies
un|dif¦fer¦enced
un|dif¦fer¦en¦
            ti¦ated
un|digest¦ed
un|dig¦ni¦fied
un|diluted
un|dimin¦ished
un|dimmed
un|dine

un|dip¦lo¦mat¦ic
un|dip¦lo¦mat¦ic¦
              al¦ly
un|dir¦ect¦ed
un|dis¦cern¦ing
un|dis¦charged
un|dis¦cip¦lined
un|dis¦closed
un|dis¦cov¦er¦able
un|dis¦cov¦ered
un|dis¦crim¦in¦
              at¦ing
un|dis¦cussed
un|dis¦guised
un|dis¦guised¦ly
un|dis¦mayed
un|dis¦puted
un|dis¦soci¦ated
un|dis¦solved
un|dis¦tin¦guish¦
                able
un|dis¦tin¦guished
un|dis¦tort¦ed
un|dis¦trib¦uted
un|dis¦turbed
un|div¦ided
undo
  pl. un¦dos
  v. un¦does
un¦did
un¦do¦ing
un¦done
un¦dock
un¦docu¦ment¦ed
un¦dog¦mat¦ic
un¦domes¦ti¦cated
un¦done
un¦doubt¦ed
un¦doubt¦ed¦ly
un¦doubt¦ing
un¦drained
un¦dram¦at¦ic
un¦draped
un¦drawn
un¦dreamed
un¦dreamt var. of
  undreamed
un¦dress
un¦drink¦able
un¦driv¦able
un¦drive¦able var.
  of undrivable

UNDRO = United Nations Disaster Relief Office
un¦due
un¦du¦lant
un¦du¦late
  un¦du¦lat¦ing
un¦du¦late¦ly
un¦du¦la¦tion
un¦du¦la¦tory
un¦duly
un¦duti¦ful
un¦duti¦ful¦ly
un¦duti¦ful¦ness
undy *Heraldry*
un¦dyed
un¦dying
un¦dying¦ly
un¦dynam¦ic
un¦earned
un¦earth
un¦earth¦li¦ness
un¦earth¦ly
  un¦earth¦lier
  un¦earth¦li¦est
un¦ease
un¦eas¦ily
un¦easi¦ness
un¦easy
  un¦eas¦ier
  un¦easi¦est
un¦eat¦able
un¦eat¦en
un¦eco¦nom¦ic
un¦eco¦nom¦ic¦al
un¦eco¦nom¦ic¦al¦ly
un¦edify¦ing
un¦edify¦ing¦ly
un¦edit¦ed
un¦educ¦able
un¦edu¦cated
un¦elect¦able
un¦elect¦ed
un¦embar¦rassed
un¦embel¦lished
un¦emo¦tion¦al
un¦emo¦tion¦al¦ly
un¦emphat¦ic
un¦emphat¦ic¦al¦ly
un¦employ¦abil¦ity
un¦employ¦able
un¦employed
un¦employ¦ment

un¦en¦closed
un¦en¦cum¦bered
un¦end¦ing
un¦end¦ing¦ly
un¦end¦ing¦ness
un¦en¦dowed
un¦en¦dur¦able
un¦en¦dur¦ably
un¦en¦force¦able
un¦en¦forced
un¦en¦gaged
un-English
un¦en¦joy¦able
un¦en¦light¦ened
un¦en¦light¦en¦ing
un¦en¦light¦en¦ment
un¦en¦riched
un¦en¦tan¦gle
  un¦en¦tan¦gling
un¦enter¦pris¦ing
un¦en¦thu¦si¦as¦tic
un¦cn¦thu¦si¦as¦tic¦al¦ly
un¦envi¦able
un¦envi¦ably
un¦envied
un¦en¦vir¦on¦men¦tal
UNEP = United Nations Environment Programme
un¦equal
un¦equaled *US*
un¦equal¦ise *Br.* var. of unequalize
un¦equal¦ize
  un¦equal¦iz¦ing
un¦equalled *Br.*
un¦equal¦ly
un¦equipped
un¦equivo¦cal
un¦equivo¦cal¦ly
un¦equivo¦cal¦ness
un¦err¦ing
un¦err¦ing¦ly
un¦err¦ing¦ness
un¦escap¦able
UNESCO = United Nations Educational, Scientific, and Cultural Organization

un¦escort¦ed
un¦essen¦tial
un¦estab¦lished
un¦esthet¦ic *US* var. of unaesthetic
un¦eth¦ic¦al
un¦eth¦ic¦al¦ly
un¦evan¦gel¦ic¦al
un¦even
un¦even¦ly
un¦even¦ness
un¦event¦ful
un¦event¦ful¦ly
un¦event¦ful¦ness
un¦evolved
un¦exam¦ined
un¦exam¦pled
un¦ex¦ca¦vated
un¦ex¦cep¦tion¦able
  acceptable
un¦ex¦cep¦tion¦able¦ness
un¦ex¦cep¦tion¦ably
un¦ex¦cep¦tion¦al
  ordinary
un¦ex¦cep¦tion¦al¦ly
un¦ex¦cit¦abil¦ity
un¦ex¦cit¦able
un¦ex¦cit¦ing
un¦ex¦ecuted
un¦exer¦cised
un¦ex¦haust¦ed
un¦ex¦pect¦ed
un¦ex¦pect¦ed¦ly
un¦ex¦pect¦ed¦ness
un¦ex¦pired
un¦ex¦plain¦able
un¦ex¦plain¦ably
un¦ex¦plained
un¦ex¦ploded
un¦ex¦ploit¦ed
un¦ex¦plored
un¦ex¦posed
un¦ex¦pressed
un¦ex¦pur¦gated
un¦face¦able
un¦fad¦ing
un¦fad¦ing¦ly
un¦fail¦ing
un¦fail¦ing¦ly
un¦fail¦ing¦ness

un¦fair
un¦fair¦er
un¦fair¦est
un¦fair¦ly
un¦fair¦ness
un¦faith¦ful
un¦faith¦ful¦ly
un¦faith¦ful¦ness
un¦fal¦ter¦ing
un¦fal¦ter¦ing¦ly
un¦famil¦iar
un¦famili¦ar¦ity
un¦fan¦cied
un¦fash¦ion¦able
un¦fash¦ion¦able¦ness
un¦fash¦ion¦ably
un¦fash¦ioned
un¦fas¦ten
un¦fathered
un¦father¦li¦ness
un¦father¦ly
un¦fath¦om¦able
un¦fath¦om¦able¦ness
un¦fath¦om¦ably
un¦fath¦omed
un¦favor¦able *US*
un¦favor¦able¦ness *US*
un¦favor¦ably *US*
un¦favor¦ite *US*
un¦favour¦able *Br.*
un¦favour¦able¦ness *Br.*
un¦favour¦ably *Br.*
un¦favour¦ite *Br.*
un¦fazed not disconcerted; cf. unphased
un¦feas¦ibil¦ity
un¦feas¦ible
un¦feas¦ibly
un¦fed
un¦feel¦ing
un¦feel¦ing¦ly
un¦feel¦ing¦ness
un¦feigned
un¦feign¦ed¦ly
un¦felt
un¦fem¦in¦ine
un¦fem¦in¦in¦ity
un¦fenced

un|fer|ment|ed
un|fer|tile
un|fer|til|ised *Br.*
  var. of **unfertilized**
un|fer|til|ized
un|fet|ter
un|fil|ial
un|fili|al|ly
un|filled
un|fil|tered
un|fin|ished
un|fired
un|fit
  un|fit|ted
  un|fit|ting
un|fit|ly
un|fit|ness
un|fit|ting|ly
un|fix
un|flag|ging
un|flag|ging|ly
un|flap|pabil|ity
un|flap|pable
un|flap|pably
un|flat|ter|ing
un|flat|ter|ing|ly
un|fla|vored *US*
un|fla|voured *Br.*
un|fledged
un|fleshed
un|flinch|ing
un|flinch|ing|ly
un|flus|tered
un|focused
un|focussed var. of
  unfocused
un|fold
un|fold|ment
un|forced
un|for|ced|ly
un|ford|able
un|fore|see|able
un|fore|seen
un|forest|ed
un|fore|told
un|for|get|table
un|for|get|tably
un|for|giv|able
un|for|giv|ably
un|for|given
un|for|giv|ing
un|for|giv|ing|ly

un|for|giv|ing|ness
un|for|got|ten
un|formed
un|for|mu|lated
un|forth|com|ing
un|for|ti|fied
un|for|tu|nate
un|for|tu|nate|ly
un|found|ed
un|found|ed|ly
un|found|ed|ness
un|framed
un|free
un|free|dom
un|freeze
  un|froze
  un|freez|ing
  un|frozen
un|fre|quent|ed
un|friend|ed
un|friend|li|ness
un|friend|ly
  un|friend|lier
  un|friendli|est
un|frock
un|froze
un|frozen
un|fruit|ful
un|fruit|ful|ly
un|fruit|ful|ness
un|ful|fil|lable
un|ful|filled
un|ful|fill|ing
un|fund|ed
un|fun|nily
un|fun|ni|ness
un|funny
  un|fun|nier
  un|funni|est
un|furl
un|fur|nished
un|fused
un|fuss|ily
un|fussy
un|gain|li|ness
un|gain|ly
  un|gain|lier
  un|gainli|est
un|gain|say|able
un|gal|lant
un|gal|lant|ly
un|geared
un|gen|er|ous

un|gen|er|ous|ly
un|gen|er|ous|ness
un|gen|ial
un|gen|tle
un|gentle|man|li|
            ness
un|gentle|man|ly
un|gentle|ness
un|gently
unget-at-able
un|gift|ed
un|gird
  un|gird|ed or
  ungirt
un|giv|ing
un|glam|or|ous
un|glazed
un|gloved
un|glued
un|god|li|ness
un|god|ly
  un|god|lier
  un|god|li|est
un|gov|ern|abil|ity
un|gov|ern|able
un|gov|ern|ably
un|grace|ful
un|grace|ful|ly
un|grace|ful|ness
un|gra|cious
un|gra|cious|ly
un|gra|cious|ness
un|graded
un|gram|mat|ical
un|gram|mat|ical|
           ity
un|gram|mat|ical|
          ities
un|gram|
      mat|ical|ly
un|gram|mat|ical|
          ness
un|grasp|able
un|grate|ful
un|grate|ful|ly
un|grate|ful|ness
un|greased
un|green
un|green|ly
un|groomed
un|ground
un|ground|ed
un|group

un|grudg|ing
un|grudg|ing|ly
un|gual
un|guard
un|guard|ed|ly
un|guard|ed|ness
un|guent
un|gues pl. of
  unguis
un|guess|able
un|gulcu|late
un|guided
un|guis
  un|gues
un|gu|late
un|guled
un|hal|lowed
un|ham|pered
un|hand
un|hand|ily
un|handi|ness
un|han|dled
un|hand|some
un|handy
un|hap|pen
un|hap|pily
un|hap|pi|ness
un|happy
  un|hap|pier
  un|happi|est
un|harmed
un|harm|ful
un|har|mon|ious
un|har|ness
un|hasp
un|hatched
un|healed
un|health|ful
un|health|ful|ness
un|health|ily
un|healthi|ness
un|healthy
  un|health|ier
  un|healthi|est
un|heard
un|heat|ed
un|hedged
un|heed|ed
un|heed|ful
un|heed|ing
un|heed|ing|ly
un|heim|lich
un|help|ful

un|help|ful|ly
un|help|ful|ness
un|hemmed
un|her|ald|ed
un|hero|ic
un|hero|ic|al|ly
un|hesi|tat|ing
un|hesi|tat|ing|ly
un|hesi|tat|ing|
         ness
un|hin|dered
un|hinge
  un|hinge|ing or
un|hin|ging
un|hip
  un|hip|per
  un|hip|pest
un|his|tor|ic|al
un|his|tor|ic|al|ly
un|hitch
un|holi|ness
un|hol|ster
un|holy
  un|holi|er
  un|holi|est
un|hood
un|hook
un|hoped
un|horse
  un|hors|ing
un|hous|eled
un|human
un|hung
un|hur|ried
un|hur|ried|ly
un|hurt
un|husk
un|hygien|ic
un|hygien|ic|al|ly
un|hyphen|ated
uni = university
Uniat var. of Uniate
Uni|ate
uni|axial
uni|axial|ly
uni|body
  uni|bodies
uni|cam|eral
UNICEF = United
  Nations Children's
  Fund
uni|cel|lu|lar
uni|color *US*

uni|col|ored *US*
uni|col|our *Br.*
uni|col|oured *Br.*
uni|com
uni|corn
uni|cur|sal
uni|cus|pid
uni|cycle
uni|cyc|list
un|idea'd
un|ideal
un|ideal|ised *Br.*
  var. of unidealized
un|ideal|ized
un|iden|ti|fi|able
un|iden|ti|fied
uni|di|men|sion|al
un|idiom|at|ic
uni|dir|ec|tion|al
uni|dir|ec|tion|
        al|ity
uni|dir|ec|tion|al|ly
UNIDO = United
  Nations Industrial
  Development
  Organization
uni|face
uni|fac|tor|ial
uni|fi|ca|tion
uni|fi|ca|tory
uni|fier
uni|flow
uni|form
uni|formi|tar|ian
uni|formi|tar|ian|
        ism
uni|form|ity
uni|form|ities
uni|form|ly
unify
  uni|fies
  uni|fied
  uni|fy|ing
uni|junc|tion
uni|lat|eral
uni|lat|eral|ism
uni|lat|eral|ist
uni|lat|eral|ly
uni|lin|gual
uni|lin|gual|ism
uni|lin|gual|ly
un|illu|min|ated
un|illu|min|at|ing

un|illus|trated
uni|locu|lar
un|imagin|able
un|imagin|ably
un|imagina|tive
un|imagina|tive|ly
un|imagina|tive|
        ness
un|imagined
uni|modal
uni|modu|lar
uni|mol|ecu|lar
un|im|paired
un|im|pas|sioned
un|im|peach|able
un|im|peach|ably
un|im|peded
un|im|peded|ly
un|im|port|ance
un|im|port|ant
un|im|pos|ing
un|im|pos|ing|ly
un|im|pressed
un|im|pres|sion|
        able
un|im|pres|sive
un|im|pres|sive|ly
un|im|pres|sive|
        ness
un|im|proved
un|in|cor|por|ated
un|indexed
un|in|fect|ed
un|in|flamed
un|inflect|ed
un|influ|enced
un|influ|en|tial
un|in|forma|tive
un|in|formed
un|in|hab|it|able
un|in|hab|it|able|
        ness
un|in|hab|it|ed
un|in|hib|it|ed
un|in|hib|it|ed|ly
un|in|hib|it|ed|ness
un|initi|ated
un|in|jured
un|in|spired
un|in|spir|ing
un|in|spir|ing|ly

un|in|stal
un|in|stalled
un|in|stall|ing
  Br. var. of uninstall
un|in|stall
un|in|stal|ler
un|in|struct|ed
un|insu|lated
un|in|sur|able
un|in|sured
un|inte|grated
un|in|tel|lec|tual
un|in|tel|li|gence
un|in|tel|li|gent
un|in|tel|li|gent|ly
un|in|tel|li|gi|bil|ity
un|in|tel|li|gible|
        ness
un|in|tel|li|gibly
un|in|tend|ed
un|in|ten|tion|al
un|in|ten|tion|al|ly
un|inter|est|ed
un|inter|est|ed|ly
un|inter|est|ed|
        ness
un|inter|est|ing
un|inter|est|ing|ly
un|inter|est|ing|
        ness
un|in|ter|pret|able
un|in|ter|pret|ed
un|inter|rupt|ed
un|inter|rupt|ed|ly
un|inter|rupt|ed|
        ness
un|inter|rupt|ible
un|in|timi|dated
un|inucle|ate
un|in|vent|ive
un|in|vent|ive|ly
un|in|vent|ive|ness
un|in|vest|ed
un|in|ves|ti|gated
un|in|vited
un|in|vited|ly
un|in|vit|ing
un|in|vit|ing|ly
un|in|voked
un|in|volved
union

union|isa|tion *Br.* var. of **unionization**

union|ise *Br.* var. of **unionize**

un-ionised *Br.* var. of **un-ionized**

union|ism

union|ist

union|is|tic

union|iza|tion

union|ize

union|iz|ing bring under trade-union organization

un-ionized not ionized

unip|ar|ous

uni|planar

uni|pod

uni|polar

uni|polar|ity

uni|potent

unique

unique|ly

unique|ness

un|ironed

un|iron|ic

un|iron|ic|al|ly

uni|ser|ial

uni|sex

uni|sex|ual

uni|sexu|al|ity

uni|sexu|al|ly

UNISON trade union

uni|son sound; agreement

unis|on|ant

unis|on|ous

un|issued

unit

UNITA Angolan nationalist movement

UNITAR = United Nations Institute for Training and Research

uni|tard

Uni|tar|ian

Uni|tar|ian|ism

uni|tar|ily

uni|tar|ist

uni|tar|ity

uni|tary

unite

unit|ing

united|ly

unit|hold|er

unit|ise *Br.* var. of **unitize**

uni|tive

uni|tive|ly

unit|ize

unit|iz|ing

Unity name

unity

uni|ties

uni|va|lent

uni|valve

uni|ver|sal

uni|ver|sal|is| abil|ity *Br.* var. of **universalizability**

uni|ver|sal|is|able *Br.* var. of **universalizable**

uni|ver|sal|isa|tion *Br.* var. of **universalization**

uni|ver|sal|ise *Br.* var. of **universalize**

uni|ver|sal|ism

uni|ver|sal|ist

uni|ver|sal|is|tic

uni|ver|sal|ity

uni|ver|sal|iz| abil|ity

uni|ver|sal|iz|able

uni|ver|sal|iza|tion

uni|ver|sal|ize

uni|ver|sal|iz|ing

uni|ver|sal|ly

uni|verse

uni|ver|sity

uni|ver|sities

uni|vocal

uni|vocal|ity

uni|vocal|ly

Unix *Computing, trademark*

un|join

un|just

un|jus|ti|fi|able

un|jus|ti|fi|ably

un|jus|ti|fied

un|just|ly

un|just|ness

un|kempt

un|kempt|ly

un|kempt|ness

un|kept

un|kill|able

un|kind

un|kind|ly

un|kind|ness

un|king

un|kink

un|knit

un|knit|ted

un|knit|ting

un|knot

un|knot|ted

un|knot|ting

un|know|abil|ity

un|know|able

un|know|ing

un|know|ing|ly

un|know|ing|ness

un|known

un|known|ness

un|labeled *US*

un|labelled *Br.*

un|labored *US*

un|laboured *Br.*

un|lace

un|lacing

un|lade

un|laded

un|lad|ing unload; cf. **unlaid**

un|laden

un|lady|like

un|laid past tense and participle of **unlay**; cf. **unlade**

un|lam|ent|ed

un|lash

un|latch

un|law|ful

un|law|ful|ly

un|law|ful|ness

un|lay

un|laid untwist; cf. **unlade**

un|lead|ed

un|learn

un|learned *Br.* also un|learnt

un|learn|ed|ly

un|leash

un|leav|ened

un|less

un|let

un|let|tered

un|lib|er|ated

un|licenced var. of **unlicensed**

un|licensed

un|light|ed

un|lik|able var. of **unlikeable**

un|like

un|like|able

un|like|li|hood

un|like|li|ness

un|like|ly

un|like|lier

un|likeli|est

un|like|ness

un|lim|ber

un|lim|it|ed

un|lim|it|ed|ly

un|lim|it|ed|ness

un|lined

un|link

un|liquid|ated

un|list|ed

un|lis|ten|able

un|lit

un|liv|able *US*

un|live|able *Br.*

un|lived

un|liv|ing

un|load

un|load|er

un|lock

un|looked

un|loose

un|loos|ing

un|loosen

un|lov|abil|ity

un|lov|able

un|love|abil|ity var. of **unlovability**

un|love|able var. of **unlovable**

un|loved

un|love|li|ness

un|lov|ely

un|lov|ing

un|lov|ing|ly

un|lov|ing|ness

un|luck|ily
un|lucki|ness
un|lucky
  un|luck|ier
  un|lucki|est
un|maid|en|li|ness
un|maid|en|ly
un|make
  un|made
  un|mak|ing
un|man
  un|manned
  un|man|ning
un|man|age|able
un|man|age|able|
                ness
un|man|age|ably
un|man|aged
un|man|eu|ver|able
  US
Br. unmanoeuvrable
un|man|li|ness
un|man|ly
un|man|nered
un|man|ner|li|ness
un|man|ner|ly
un|man|oeuv|rable
  Br.
US unmaneuverable
un|mapped
un|marked
un|mar|ket|able
un|marred
un|mar|ried
un|mask
un|mask|er
un|match|able
un|match|ably
un|matched
un|matured
un|mean|ing
un|mean|ing|ly
un|mean|ing|ness
un|meant
un|meas|ur|able
un|meas|ur|ably
un|meas|ured
un|me|di|ated
un|melo|di|ous
un|melo|di|ous|ly
un|melt|ed
un|mem|or|able
un|mem|or|ably

un|men|tion|
            abil|ity
un|men|tion|able
un|men|tion|able|
                ness
un|men|tion|ably
un|men|tioned
un|mer|chant|able
un|mer|ci|ful
un|mer|ci|ful|ly
un|mer|ci|ful|ness
un|mer|it|ed
un|met
un|met|alled
un|metered
un|meth|od|ical
un|meth|od|ic|al|ly
un|met|ric|al
un|mili|tary
un|mind|ful
un|mind|ful|ly
un|mind|ful|ness
un|miss|able
un|mis|tak|abil|ity
un|mis|tak|able
un|mis|tak|ably
un|mis|take|abil|ity
  var. of
  unmistakability
un|mis|take|able
  var. of
  unmistakable
un|mis|take|ably
  var. of
  unmistakably
un|mis|taken
un|miti|gated
un|miti|gated|ly
un|mixed
un|moder|ated
un|mod|ern|ised
  Br. var. of
  unmodernized
un|mod|ern|ized
un|modi|fied
un|modu|lated
un|mol|est|ed
un|moor
un|moral
un|mor|al|ity
un|mothered
un|mother|ly
un|moti|vated

un|mount|ed
un|mourned
un|mov|able
un|move|able var.
  of unmovable
un|moved
un|mov|ing
un|mown
un|muf|fle
  un|muf|fling
un|mur|mur|ing
un|mur|mur|ing|ly
un|music|al
un|music|al|ity
un|music|al|ly
un|music|al|ness
un|mutil|ated
un|muz|zle
  un|muz|zling
un|nail
un|name|able
un|named
un|nat|ural
un|nat|ur|al|ly
un|nat|ur|al|ness
un|nav|ig|abil|ity
un|nav|ig|able
un|neces|sar|ily
un|neces|sari|ness
un|neces|sary
  un|neces|sar|ies
un|need|ed
un|neigh|bor|ly US
un|neigh|bour|ly
  Br.
un|nerve
  un|nerv|ing
un|nerv|ing|ly
un|notice|able
un|notice|ably
un|noticed
un|num|bered
un|oaked
un|ob|jec|tion|able
un|ob|jec|tion|able|
                ness
un|ob|jec|tion|ably
un|ob|li|ging
un|ob|scured
un|ob|serv|able
un|ob|ser|vant
un|ob|ser|vant|ly
un|ob|served

un|ob|served|ly
un|ob|struct|ed
un|ob|tain|able
un|ob|tru|sive
un|ob|tru|sive|ly
un|ob|tru|sive|ness
un|occu|pied
un|offend|ed
un|offend|ing
un|offi|cial
un|offi|cial|ly
un|oiled
un|opened
un|opposed
un|ordained
un|ordered
un|ordin|ary
un|organ|ised Br.
  var. of unorganized
un|organ|ized
un|ori|gin|al
un|ori|gin|al|ity
un|ori|gin|al|ly
un|orna|men|tal
un|orna|ment|ed
un|ortho|dox
un|ortho|dox|ly
un|ortho|doxy
  un|ortho|dox|ies
un|osten|ta|tious
un|osten|ta|tious|ly
un|osten|ta|tious|
                ness
un|owned
un|pack
un|pack|aged
un|pack|er
un|pad|ded
un|paged
un|paid
un|paint|ed
un|paired
un|pal|at|abil|ity
un|pal|at|able
un|pal|at|able|ness
un|pal|at|ably
un|par|al|leled
un|par|don|able
un|par|don|able|
                ness
un|par|don|ably

un|par|lia|
     men|tary
un|pas|teur|ised *Br.*
   var. of
   unpasteurized
un|pas|teur|ized
un|patched
un|pat|ent|ed
un|pat|ri|ot|ic
un|pat|ri|ot|ic|al|ly
un|pat|ron|is|ing
   Br. var. of
   unpatronizing
un|pat|ron|is|ing|ly
   Br. var. of
   unpatronizingly
un|pat|ron|iz|ing
un|pat|ron|iz|ing|ly
un|paved
un|peeled
un|peg
   un|pegged
   un|peg|ging
un|peopled
   un|peop|ling
un|per|ceived
un|per|cep|tive
un|per|cep|tive|ly
un|per|cep|tive|
      ness
un|per|fect|ed
un|per|for|ated
un|per|formed
un|per|fumed
un|per|son
un|per|suad|able
un|per|suad|ed
un|per|sua|sive
un|per|sua|sive|ly
un|per|turbed
un|per|turb|ed|ly
un|phased not
   phased; cf. unfazed
un|philo|soph|ic|al
un|philo|soph|ic|
      al|ly
un|phys|ic|al
un|physio|logic|al
un|physio|logic|
      al|ly
un|pick
un|pic|tur|esque
un|pin
   un|pinned

un|pin|ning
un|pitied
un|pity|ing
un|pity|ing|ly
un|place|able
un|placed
un|planned
un|plant|ed
un|plaus|ible
un|play|able
un|play|ably
un|played
un|pleas|ant
un|pleas|ant|ly
un|pleas|ant|ness
un|pleas|ant|ry
   un|pleas|ant|ries
un|pleas|ing
un|pleas|ing|ly
un|pleas|ure
un|ploughed *Br.*
un|plowed *US*
un|plucked
un|plug
   un|plugged
   un|plug|ging
un|plumb|able
un|plumbed
un|poet|ic
un|poet|ic|al
un|poet|ic|al|ly
un|point|ed
un|polar|ised *Br.*
   var. of unpolarized
un|polar|ized
un|pol|ished
un|pol|it|ic
un|pol|it|ic|al
un|pol|it|ic|al|ly
un|polled
un|pol|luted
un|popu|lar
un|popu|lar|ity
un|popu|lar|ly
un|popu|lated
un|posed
un|pos|sessed
un|pow|ered
un|prac|ti|cal
un|prac|ti|cal|ity
un|prac|ti|cal|ly
un|prac|ticed *US*

un|prac|tised *Br.*
un|pre|ce|dent|ed
un|pre|ce|dent|
      ed|ly
un|pre|dict|abil|ity
un|pre|dict|able
un|pre|dict|ably
un|pre|dict|ed
un|pre|ju|diced
un|pre|medi|tated
un|pre|medi|
      tated|ly
un|pre|pared
un|pre|pared|ly
un|pre|pared|ness
un|pre|pos|sess|ing
un|pre|scribed
un|pre|sent|able
un|pressed
un|pres|sur|ised *Br.*
   var. of
   unpressurized
un|pres|sur|ized
un|pre|tend|ing
un|pre|tend|ing|ly
un|pre|ten|tious
un|pre|ten|tious|ly
un|pre|ten|tious|
      ness
un|priced
un|primed
un|prin|cipled
un|prin|cipled|ness
un|print|able
un|print|ably
un|print|ed
un|priv|il|eged
un|prob|lem|at|ic
un|prob|lem|at|ic|
      al|ly
un|pro|cessed
un|pro|claimed
un|pro|duct|ive
un|pro|duct|ive|ly
un|pro|duct|ive|
      ness
un|pro|fes|sion|al
un|pro|fes|sion|al|
      ism
un|pro|fes|sion|
      al|ly
un|prof|it|abil|ity
un|prof|it|able

un|prof|it|able|
      ness
un|prof|it|ably
un|pro|gres|sive
un|prom|is|ing
un|prom|is|ing|ly
un|prompt|ed
un|pro|nounce|
      able
un|pro|nounce|
      ably
un|prop|er|tied
un|pro|pi|tious
un|pro|pi|tious|ly
un|pros|per|ous
un|pros|per|ous|ly
un|pro|tect|ed
un|pro|test|ing
un|pro|test|ing|ly
un|proud
un|prov|abil|ity
un|prov|able
un|proved
un|proven
un|pro|vided
un|pro|voked
un|pruned
un|pub|li|cised *Br.*
   var. of
   unpublicized
un|pub|li|cized
un|pub|lish|able
un|pub|lished
un|punc|tual
un|punc|tu|al|ity
un|punc|tu|ated
un|pun|ish|able
un|pun|ished
un|puri|fied
un|put|down|able
un|quali|fied
un|quali|fied|ly
un|quan|ti|fi|able
un|quan|ti|fied
un|quench|able
un|quench|ably
un|quenched
un|ques|tion|
      abil|ity
un|ques|tion|able
un|ques|tion|able|
      ness
un|ques|tion|ably

un|ques|tioned
un|ques|tion|ing
un|ques|tion|ing|ly
un|quiet
un|quiet|ly
un|quiet|ness
un|quot|able
un|quote
un|quoted
un|ranked
un|rated
un|ravel
  un|rav|elled *Br.*
  un|rav|eled *US*
  un|rav|el|ling *Br.*
  un|rav|el|ing *US*
un|reach|able
un|reach|able|ness
un|reach|ably
un|reached
un|re|act|ive
un|read
un|read|abil|ity
un|read|able
un|read|ably
un|readi|ness
un|ready
un|real not real; cf.
  unreel
un|real|is|able *Br.*
  var. of unrealizable
un|real|ised *Br.* var.
  of unrealized
un|real|ism
un|real|is|tic
un|real|is|tic|al|ly
un|real|ity
un|real|iz|able
un|real|ized
un|real|ly
un|rea|son
un|rea|son|able
un|rea|son|able|
              ness
un|rea|son|ably
un|rea|soned
un|rea|son|ing
un|rea|son|ing|ly
un|re|cep|tive
un|re|cip|ro|cated
un|reck|oned
un|re|claimed

un|rec|og|nis|able
  Br. var. of
  unrecognizable
un|rec|og|nis|able|
              ness
  Br. var. of unrecog-
  nizableness
un|rec|og|nis|ably
  Br. var. of
  unrecognizably
un|rec|og|nised *Br.*
  var. of
  unrecognized
un|rec|og|niz|able
un|rec|og|niz|able|
              ness
un|rec|og|niz|ably
un|rec|og|nized
un|rec|om|pensed
un|rec|on|cil|able
un|rec|on|ciled
un|re|con|struct|ed
un|re|cord|able
un|re|cord|ed
un|re|cover|able
un|re|cov|ered
un|rec|ti|fied
un|re|deem|able
un|re|deemed
un|re|dressed
un|reel unwind
  from reel; cf.
  unreal
un|reeve
  un|rove
  un|reev|ing
un|re|fined
un|re|flect|ing
un|re|flect|ing|ly
un|re|flect|ive
un|re|formed
un|re|gard|ed
un|re|gen|er|acy
un|re|gen|er|ate
un|re|gen|er|ate|ly
un|regis|tered
un|regu|lated
un|re|hearsed
un|re|inforced
un|re|lated
un|re|lated|ness
un|re|laxed
un|re|leased
un|re|lent|ing

un|re|lent|ing|ly
un|re|lent|ing|ness
un|re|li|abil|ity
un|re|li|able
un|re|li|able|ness
un|re|li|ably
un|re|lieved
un|re|lieved|ly
un|re|li|gious
un|re|mark|able
un|re|mark|ably
un|re|marked
un|re|mem|bered
un|re|mit|ting
un|re|mit|ting|ly
un|re|mit|ting|ness
un|re|morse|ful
un|re|morse|ful|ly
un|re|mov|able
un|re|mu|nera|tive
un|re|mu|nera|
              tive|ly
un|re|mu|nera|tive|
              ness
un|re|new|able
un|re|newed
un|re|pair|able
un|re|pealed
un|re|peat|abil|ity
un|re|peat|able
un|re|peat|ed
un|re|pent|ant
un|re|pent|ant|ly
un|re|port|ed
un|rep|re|sen|
              ta|tive
un|rep|re|sen|
              ta|tive|ness
un|rep|re|sent|ed
un|re|quest|ed
un|re|quit|ed
un|re|quited|ly
un|re|quited|ness
un|re|serve
un|re|served
un|re|served|ly
un|re|serv|ed|ness
un|re|sist|ed
un|re|sist|ed|ly
un|re|sist|ing
un|re|sist|ing|ly
un|re|sist|ing|ness

un|re|solv|able
un|re|solved
un|re|solved|ly
un|re|solved|ness
un|re|spon|sive
un|re|spon|sive|ly
un|re|spon|sive|
              ness
un|rest
un|rest|ed
un|rest|ful
un|rest|ful|ly
un|rest|ing
un|rest|ing|ly
un|re|stored
un|re|strained
un|re|strain|ed|ly
un|re|strain|ed|
              ness
un|re|strict|ed
un|re|strict|ed|ly
un|re|strict|ed|ness
un|re|turned
un|re|vealed
un|re|veal|ing
un|re|versed
un|re|vised
un|re|voked
un|re|ward|ed
un|re|ward|ing
un|rhymed
un|rhyth|mic|al|ly
un|rid|able var. of
  unrideable
un|rid|den
un|ride|able
un|rig
  un|rigged
  un|rig|ging
un|right|eous
un|right|eous|ly
un|right|eous|ness
un|ripe
un|ripe|ness
un|risen
un|rivaled *US*
un|rivalled *Br.*
un|road|worthy
un|robe
  un|rob|ing
un|roll
un|roman|tic
un|roman|tic|al|ly

un|roof
un|root
un|rope
un|rop|ing
un|round|ed
un|rove
un|royal
un|royal|ly
UNRRA = United
Nations Relief and
Rehabilitation
Administration; cf.
UNRWA
un|ruf|fled
un|ruled
un|ru|li|ness
un|ruly
un|ru|lier
un|ruli|est
UNRWA = United
Nations Relief and
Works Agency; cf.
UNRRA
un|sack|able
un|sad|dle
un|sad|dling
un|safe
un|safe|ly
un|safe|ness
un|said
un|sal|abil|ity US
Br. unsaleability
un|sal|able US
Br. unsaleable
un|sal|ar|ied
un|sale|abil|ity
un|sale|able
un|salt|ed
un|salu|bri|ous
un|sanc|ti|fied
un|sanc|tioned
un|sani|tary
un|sat|is|fac|tor|ily
un|sat|is|fac|tori|
ness
un|sat|is|fac|tory
un|sat|is|fied
un|sat|is|fied|ness
un|sat|is|fy|ing
un|sat|is|fy|ing|ly
un|sat|ur|ated
un|sat|ur|ation
un|saved
un|savor|ily US

un|savori|ness US
un|savory US
un|savour|ily Br.
un|savouri|ness Br.
un|savoury Br.
un|say
un|said
un|say|able
un|scal|able
un|scale|able
var. of unscalable
un|scaled
un|scarred
un|scathed
un|scent|ed
un|sched|uled
un|schooled
un|sci|en|tif|ic
un|sci|en|tif|ic|al|ly
un|scram|ble
un|scram|bling
un|scram|bler
un|screened
un|screw
un|script|ed
un|scrip|tural
un|scrip|tur|al|ly
un|scru|pu|lous
un|scru|pu|lous|ly
un|scru|pu|lous|
ness
un|seal
un|search|able
un|search|able|
ness
un|search|ably
un|searched
un|sea|son|able
un|sea|son|able|
ness
un|sea|son|ably
un|sea|son|al
un|sea|soned
un|seat
un|sea|worthy
un|secured
un|see|able
un|seed|ed
un|see|ing
un|see|ing|ly
un|seem|li|ness
un|seem|ly
un|seem|lier

un|seemli|est
un|seen
un|seg|ment|ed
un|seg|re|gated
un|select
un|select|ive
un|self|con|scious
un|self|
con|scious|ly
un|self|con|scious|
ness
un|self|ish
un|self|ish|ly
un|self|ish|ness
un|sen|sa|tion|al
un|sen|sa|tion|al|ly
un|sent
un|sen|ti|men|tal
un|sen|ti|men|tal|ly
un|sep|ar|ated
un|seri|ous
un|served
un|ser|vice|abil|ity
un|ser|vice|able
un|set
un|set|tle
un|set|tling
un|settled|ness
un|settle|ment
un|set|tling|ly
un|sewn not sewn;
cf. unsown
un|sex
un|sexy
un|sex|ier
un|sexi|est
un|shackle
un|shack|ling
un|shaded
un|shad|owed
un|shak|abil|ity var.
of unshakeability
un|shak|able var. of
unshakeable
un|shak|ably var. of
unshakeably
un|shake|abil|ity
un|shake|able
un|shake|ably
un|shaken
un|shaken|ly
un|shaped
un|shape|li|ness

un|shape|ly
un|shared
un|sharp
un|sharp|ened
un|sharp|ness
un|shaved
un|shaven
un|sheathe
un|sheath|ing
un|shed
un|shel|tered
un|shield|ed
un|ship
un|shipped
un|ship|ping
un|shock|abil|ity
un|shock|able
un|shock|ably
un|shod
un|shorn
un|shrink|abil|ity
un|shrink|able
un|shrink|ing
un|shrink|ing|ly
un|shriven
un|shut|tered
un|sight
un|sight|li|ness
un|sight|ly
un|sight|lier
un|sightli|est
un|signed
un|sink|abil|ity
un|sink|able
un|sis|ter|ly
un|sized
un|skil|ful Br.
un|skil|ful|ly Br.
un|skil|ful|ness Br.
un|skilled
un|skill|ful US
un|skill|ful|ly US
un|skill|ful|ness US
un|skimmed
un|slak|able var. of
unslakeable
un|slake|able
un|sleep|ing
un|sleep|ing|ly
un|sliced
un|sling
un|slung
un|smil|ing

un|smil|ing|ly
un|smil|ing|ness
un|smoked
un|snap
  un|snapped
  un|snap|ping
un|snarl
un|soci|abil|ity
un|soci|able
un|soci|able|ness
un|soci|ably
un|social
un|social|ly
un|soiled
un|sold
un|sol|der
un|sol|dier|ly
un|soli|cit|ed
un|soli|cit|ed|ly
un|solv|abil|ity
un|solv|able
un|solv|able|ness
un|solved
un|sophis|ti|cated
un|sophis|ti|
        cated|ly
un|sophis|ti|cated|
        ness
un|sophis|ti|ca|tion
un|sort|ed
un|sought
un|sound
un|sound|ed
un|sound|ly
un|sound|ness
un|soured
un|sown not sown;
  cf. unsewn
un|spar|ing
un|spar|ing|ly
un|spar|ing|ness
un|speak|able
un|speak|able|ness
un|speak|ably
un|speak|ing
un|spe|cial|ised Br.
  var. of
  unspecialized
un|spe|cial|ized
un|spe|cif|ic
un|speci|fied
un|spec|tacu|lar
un|spec|tacu|lar|ly

un|spent
un|spilled
un|spilt Br. var. of
  unspilled
un|spir|it|ual
un|spir|itu|al|ity
un|spir|itu|al|ly
un|spoiled
un|spoilt Br. var. of
  unspoiled
un|spoken
un|spon|sored
un|spool
un|sport|ing
un|sport|ing|ly
un|sports|man|like
un|spot|ted
un|sprayed
un|sprung
un|stable
  un|stab|ler
  un|stab|lest
un|stable|ness
un|stably
un|staffed
un|stage|able
un|stained
un|stamped
un|starched
un|stated
un|stat|ut|ably
un|stayed
un|stead|ily
un|steadi|ness
un|steady
  un|stead|ier
  un|steadi|est
un|step
  un|stepped
  un|step|ping
un|ster|ile
un|ster|il|ised Br.
  var. of unsterilized
un|ster|il|ized
un|stick
  un|stuck
un|stimu|lated
un|stimu|lat|ing
un|stint|ed
un|stint|ed|ly
un|stint|ing
un|stint|ing|ly

un|stirred
un|stitch
un|stop
  un|stopped
  un|stop|ping
un|stop|pabil|ity
un|stop|pable
un|stop|pably
un|stop|per
un|strained
un|strap
  un|strapped
  un|strap|ping
un|streamed
un|stressed
un|string
  un|strung
un|struc|tured
un|stuck
un|stud|ied
un|stud|ied|ly
un|stuffed
un|stuffy
  un|stuff|ier
  un|stuffi|est
un|styl|ish
un|sub|dued
un|sub|ju|gated
un|sub|scribe
  un|sub|scrib|ing
un|sub|sid|ised Br.
  var. of
  unsubsidized
un|sub|sid|ized
un|sub|stan|tial
un|sub|stan|ti|al|ity
un|sub|stan|tial|ly
un|sub|stan|ti|ated
un|subtle
un|subtly
un|suc|cess
un|suc|cess|ful
un|suc|cess|ful|ly
un|suc|cess|ful|
        ness
un|sugared
un|suit|abil|ity
un|suit|able
un|suit|able|ness
un|suit|ably
un|suit|ed
un|sul|lied
un|sum|moned

un|sung
un|super|vised
un|sup|port|able
un|sup|port|ably
un|sup|port|ed
un|sup|port|ive
un|sup|pressed
un|sure
un|sure|ly
un|sure|ness
un|sur|faced
un|sur|mount|able
un|sur|pass|able
un|sur|pass|ably
un|sur|passed
un|sur|prised
un|sur|pris|ing
un|sur|pris|ing|ly
un|sur|viv|able
un|sus|cep|ti|bil|ity
un|sus|cep|tible
un|sus|pect|ed
un|sus|pect|ed|ly
un|sus|pect|ing
un|sus|pect|ing|ly
un|sus|pect|ing|
        ness
un|sus|pi|cious
un|sus|pi|cious|ly
un|sus|pi|cious|
        ness
un|sus|tain|able
un|sus|tain|ably
un|sus|tained
un|swathe
  un|swath|ing
un|swayed
un|sweet|ened
un|swept
un|swerv|ing
un|swerv|ing|ly
un|sworn
un|sym|met|ric|al
un|sym|met|ric|
        al|ly
un|sym|pa|thet|ic
un|sym|pa|thet|ic|
        al|ly
un|sys|tem|at|ic
un|sys|tem|at|ic|
        al|ly
un|tack
un|taint|ed

un|taken
un|tal|ent|ed
un|tam|able var. of
  untameable
un|tame|able
un|tamed
un|tan|gle
  un|tan|gling
un|tanned
un|tapped
un|tar|nished
un|tasted
un|taxed
un|teach
  un|taught
un|teach|able
un|tech|nic|al
un|tem|pered
un|ten|abil|ity
un|ten|able
un|ten|able|ness
un|ten|ably
un|ten|ant|ed
un|tend|ed
un|ten|ured
Un|ter|mensch
  Un|ter|mensch|en
Un|ter|wal|den
un|test|able
un|test|ed
un|tether
un|thanked
un|thank|ful
un|thank|ful|ly
un|thank|ful|ness
un|thatched
un|thaw
un|the|or|ised *Br.*
  var. of untheorized
un|the|or|ized
un|think
  un|thought
un|think|abil|ity
un|think|able
un|think|able|ness
un|think|ably
un|think|ing|ly
un|think|ing|ness
un|thought
un|thread
un|threat|ened
un|threat|en|ing
un|thrift|ily

un|thrifti|ness
un|thrifty
un|throne
un|thron|ing
un|tidi|ly
un|tidi|ness
un|tidy
  un|tidi|er
  un|tidi|est
un|tie
  un|ties
  un|tied
  un|tying
until
un|tilled
un|timed
un|time|li|ness
un|time|ly
  un|time|lier
  un|time|li|est
un|tinged
un|tir|ing
un|tir|ing|ly
un|titled
unto
un|told
un|toned
un|touch|abil|ity
un|touch|able
un|touch|able|ness
un|touched
un|to|ward
un|to|ward|ly
un|to|ward|ness
un|trace|able
un|trace|ably
un|traced
un|tracked
un|trad|ition|al
un|train|able
un|trained
un|tram|meled *US*
un|tram|melled *Br.*
un|trans|fer|able
un|trans|formed
un|trans|lat|abil|ity
un|trans|lat|able
un|trans|lat|ably
un|trans|lated
un|trav|eled *US*
un|trav|elled *Br.*
un|treat|able
un|treat|ed

un|trendy
  un|trend|ier
  un|trendi|est
un|tried
un|trimmed
un|trod|den
un|troubled
un|true
un|truly
un|trust|ing
un|trust|worthi|
                  ness
un|trust|worthy
un|truth
un|truth|ful
un|truth|ful|ly
un|truth|ful|ness
un|tuck
un|tun|able
un|tune|able var. of
  untunable
un|tuned
un|tune|ful
un|tune|ful|ly
un|tune|ful|ness
un|turned
un|tutored
un|twine
  un|twin|ing
un|twist
un|tying
un|typ|ical
un|typ|ic|al|ly
un|usable
un|use|able var. of
  unusable
un|used
un|usual
un|usual|ly
un|usual|ness
un|utter|able
un|utter|ably
un|uttered
un|vac|cin|ated
un|val|id|ated
un|val|ued
un|van|quished
un|var|ied
un|var|nished
un|vary|ing
un|vary|ing|ly
un|vary|ing|ness
un|veil

un|vent|ed
un|ven|til|ated
un|veri|fi|able
un|veri|fied
un|versed
un|viabil|ity
un|viable
un|vio|lated
un|visit|ed
un|viti|ated
un|voiced
un|waged
un|walled
un|want|ed
un|war|ily
un|wari|ness
un|war|like
un|warmed
un|warned
un|war|rant|able
un|war|rant|able|
                  ness
un|war|rant|ably
un|war|rant|ed
un|wary
  un|wari|er
  un|wari|est
un|washed
un|watch|able
un|watched
un|watch|ful
un|watered
un|waver|ing
un|waver|ing|ly
un|waxed
un|weak|ened
un|weaned
un|wear|able
un|wear|ied
un|wear|ied|ly
un|wear|ied|ness
un|weary
un|weary|ing
un|weary|ing|ly
un|wed
un|wed|ded var. of
  unwed
un|wed|ded|ness
un|weed|ed
un|weighed
un|weight
un|wel|come

un|wel|come|ly
un|wel|come|ness
un|wel|com|ing
un|well
un|wept
un|wet|ted
un|whipped
un|whole|some
un|whole|some|ly
un|whole|some|ness
un|wield|ily
un|wieldi|ness
un|wieldy
  un|wield|ier
  un|wieldi|est
un|will|ing
un|will|ing|ly
un|will|ing|ness
un|wind
  un|wound
un|wink|ing
un|wink|ing|ly
un|win|nable
un|wired
un|wis|dom
un|wise
un|wise|ly
un|wished
un|with|ered
un|wit|nessed
un|wit|ting
un|wit|ting|ly
un|wit|ting|ness
un|woman|li|ness
un|woman|ly
un|wont|ed
un|wont|ed|ly
un|wont|ed|ness
un|wood|ed
un|work|abil|ity
un|work|able
un|work|able|ness
un|work|ably
un|worked
un|work|man|like
un|world|li|ness
un|world|ly
un|worn
un|wor|ried
un|worth|ily
un|worthi|ness

un|worthy
un|wor|thier
un|worthi|est
un|wound
un|wound|ed
un|woven
un|wrap
  un|wrapped
  un|wrap|ping
un|wrin|kled
un|writ|able
un|writ|ten
un|wrought
un|yield|ing
un|yield|ing|ly
un|yield|ing|ness
un|yoke
  un|yok|ing
un|zip
  un|zipped
  un|zip|ping
up
  upped
  up|ping
up-anchor *v.*
up-and-comer
up-and-coming
up-and-over *adj.*
up-and-under *n.*
Upani|shad
upas
up|beat
up|braid
up|bring|ing
up|build
  up|built
up|case
  up|cas|ing
up|cast
up|chuck
up|coast
up|com|ing
up|country
up|dat|able
up|date
  up|dat|ing
up|date|able var. of
  updatable
Up|dike, John
  writer
up|dom|ing
up|draft *US*
up|draught *Br.*
up|end

up|field
up|fold
up|front *adj.*
up front *adv.*
up|ful
up|grad|abil|ity var.
  of upgradeability
up|grad|able var. of
  upgradeable
up|grade
  up|grad|ing
up|grade|abil|ity
up|grade|able
up|grader
up|growth
up|haul
up|heav|al
up|heave
  up|heav|ing
Up-Helly-A' var. of
  Up-Helly-Aa
Up-Helly-Aa
up|hill
up|hold
  up|held
up|hold|er
up|hol|ster
up|hol|ster|er
up|hol|stery
up|keep
up|land
up|lift
up|lift|er
up|light
up|light|er
up|light|ing
up|link
up|load
up|mar|ket
up|most
upon
upper
upper|class|man
  upper|class|men
upper|cut
  upper|cut|ting
upper|most
upper|part *mod.* of
  feature of bird etc.
upper part *n.* gen-
  erally
upper|parts *n.* of
  bird etc.

up|pish
up|pish|ly
up|pish|ness
up|pity
Upp|sala
up|raise
  up|rais|ing
up|rate
  up|rat|ing
up|right
up|right|ly
up|right|ness
up|rise
  up|rose
  up|ris|ing
  up|risen
up|river
up|roar
up|roari|ous
up|roari|ous|ly
up|roari|ous|ness
up|root
up|root|er
up|rose
up|rush
ups-a-daisy var. of
  upsy-daisy
up|scale
up|sell
  up|sold
up|set
  up|set|ting
up|set|ter
up|set|ting|ly
up|shift
up|shot
up|side
up|si|lon
up|size
  up|siz|ing
up|slope
up|stage
  up|staging
up|stair
up|stairs
up|stand
up|stand|ing
up|start
up|state
up|stater
up|stream
up|stroke
up|surge

up|swept
up|swing
upsy-daisy
up|take
up|talk
up|tempo
up|throw
    up|threw
    up|thrown
up|thrust
up|tick
up|tight
up|time
up to date *adj.*
up-to-date *attrib.*
up|town
up|town|er
up|trend
up|turn
up|ward
up|ward|ly
up|wards
up|warp
up|well|ing
up|wind
Ur
ura|cil
ur|ae|mia *Br.*
    US uremia
ur|aem|ic *Br.*
    US uremic
ur|aeus
    uraei
Ural
Ural|ic
Ur|ania Muse
Ur|an|ian
ur|an|ic
ur|an|in|ite
ur|an|ium
uran|og|raph|er
urano|graph|ic
uran|og|raphy
uran|om|etry
ur|an|ous *Chemistry*
Ur|anus
ur|anyl
Ur|art|ian
urate
urban of town or
    city
ur|bane courteous
    and refined

ur|bane|ly
ur|ban|isa|tion *Br.*
    var. of
    urbanization
ur|ban|ise *Br.* var.
    of urbanize
ur|ban|ism
ur|ban|ist
ur|ban|ite
ur|ban|ity
ur|ban|iza|tion
ur|ban|ize
    ur|ban|iz|ing
ur|chin
Urdu
urea
ureal
urea|plasma
ure|ide
ur|emia *US*
    Br. uraemia
ur|emic *US*
    Br. uraemic
ur|eter
ur|eter|al
ur|eter|ic
ur|eter|itis
ur|eth|ane
ur|ethra
ur|eth|ral
ur|eth|ritis
Urga
urge
ur|ging
ur|gen|cy
    ur|gen|cies
ur|gent
ur|gent|ly
urger
Uriah
urial
uric
uri|dine
Urim
ur|inal
urin|aly|sis
    urin|aly|ses
urin|ary
urin|ate
    urin|at|ing
urin|ation
urine
urin|if|er|ous

urn vase; vessel for
    tea etc.; cf. earn,
    ern, erne
urn|field
uro|boric
uro|boros
Uro|chord|ata
uro|chord|ate
Uro|dela
uro|dele
uro|dynam|ics
uro|geni|tal
uro|gram
ur|og|raphy
uro|kin|ase
uro|lag|nia
uro|lith|ia|sis
uro|logic
uro|logic|al
ur|olo|gist
ur|ology
ur|onic
uro|philia
uro|pod
uro|pygial
uro|pygium
uros|copy
uro|style bone; cf.
    Eurostyle
Ursa in 'Ursa Major',
    'Ursa Minor'
ur|sine
Ur|sula
Ur|su|line
ur|text
    ur|texte or ur|texts
ur|ti|caria
ur|ti|cate
    ur|ti|cat|ing
ur|ti|ca|tion
Uru|guay
Uru|guay|an
Uruk
Urum|chi var. of
    Urumqi
Urumqi
urus ox
uru|shiol
us|abil|ity
us|able
usage
us|ance

use
    using
    bring into service;
    exploit; cf. youse
use|abil|ity var. of
    usability
use|able var. of
    usable
use|ful
use|ful|ly
use|ful|ness
use|less
use|less|ly
use|less|ness
Use|net
user
user|name
ushabti
U-shaped
usher
ush|er|ette
Ushu|aia
Üskü|dar
usnic
Uso|nian
Us|pa|llata
usque|baugh
Ust-Abakan|skoe
ustad
Usta|shas var. of
    Ustashe
Usta|she
Usta|shi var. of
    Ustashe
Us|ti|nov, Peter
    actor
usual
usu|al|ly
usual|ness
usu|capion var. of
    usucaption
usu|cap|tion
usu|fruct
usu|fruc|tu|ary
    usu|fruc|tu|ar|ies
Usum|bura
us|urer
us|uri|ous
us|uri|ous|ly
usurp
usurp|ation
usurp|er
usury

Utah
Utah|an
utah|rap|tor
Uta|maro,
  Kita|gawa painter
Ute
  pl. Ute or Utes
  American Indian;
  language
ute utility truck
uten|sil
uter|ine
ut|er|itis
uterus
  uteri
Uther Pen|dragon
  Arthurian Legend
util|is|able *Br.* var.
  of utilizable
util|isa|tion *Br.* var.
  of utilization
util|ise *Br.* var. of
  utilize
util|iser *Br.* var. of
  utilizer
utili|tar|ian
utili|tar|ian|ism
util|ity
  util|ities
util|iz|able
util|iza|tion
util|ize
  util|iz|ing
util|izer
ut|most
Uto-Aztecan
Uto|pia
uto|pian
uto|pian|ism
Ut|recht
ut|ricle
ut|ricu|lar
utricu|lus
  utric|uli
Ut|rillo, Maur|ice
  painter
Ut|sire
utta|pam
Ut|tar|an|chal
Uttar Pra|desh
utter
ut|ter|able
ut|ter|ance
ut|ter|er

ut|ter|ly
ut|ter|most
ut|ter|ness
Ut|tley, Ali|son
  writer
U-turn
uvar|ov|ite
uvea
uveal
uve|itis
uvula
  uvu|lae
  part of throat
uvu|lar of the uvula;
  consonant
ux|or|ial
ux|ori|cidal
ux|ori|cide
uxori|local
ux|ori|ous
ux|ori|ous|ly
ux|ori|ous|ness
Uzbek
Uz|beki|stan
Uzi gun

Vaal
Vaasa port, Finland;
  cf. Vasa, *Vasa*
vac = vacation; vac-
  uum cleaner
va|cancy
  va|can|cies
va|cant
va|cant|ly
vac|at|able
vac|ate
  vac|at|ing
vac|ation
vac|ation|er
vac|ation|ist
vac|ation|land
vac|cinal
vac|cin|ate
  vac|cin|at|ing
vac|cin|ation
vac|cin|ator

vac|cine
vac|cinia
Va|che|rin
vacil|late
  vacil|lat|ing
vacil|la|tion
vacil|la|tor
vacua
vacu|ity
vacu|olar
vacu|ol|ation
vacu|ole
vacu|ous
vacu|ous|ly
vacu|ous|ness
vac|uum
  pl. vac|uums or
  vacua
vacuum-clean
vac|uum clean|er
vade mecum
Vado|dara
va|dose
Vaduz
vaga|bond
vaga|bond|age
vagal
va|gary
  va|gar|ies
vagi
va|gina
va|gina den|tata
  va|gi|nae den|tatae
va|gi|nal
va|gi|nal|ly
vagin|ismus
vagin|itis
va|gino|plasty
vagin|osis
va|got|om|ized
va|got|omy
  va|got|omies
va|grancy
  va|gran|cies
va|grant
vague
  vaguer
  vaguest
vague|ly
vague|ness
vaguish
vagus
  vagi

vail doff; yield; cf.
  vale, veil
vain conceited; cf.
  vane, vein
vain|glori|ous
vain|glori|ous|ly
vain|glori|ous|ness
vain|glory
vain|ly
vain|ness
vair
vairy
Vaish|nava
Vai|shya var. of
  Vaisya
Vai|sya
Vaj|payee, Atal
  Bi|hari prime min-
  ister of India
vajra
va|keel var. of vakil
vakil
Val|ais canton,
  Switzerland
val|ance short
  curtain; cf. valence
Val d'Isère
vale valley; cf. vail,
  veil
vale farewell
  pl. val|ete
val|edic|tion
val|edic|tor|ian
val|edic|tory
  val|edic|tor|ies
va|lence *Chemistry*;
  cf. valance
Val|en|cia city and
  region, Spain
Val|en|cian
Val|en|ci|ennes lace
va|lency
  va|len|cies
Val|en|tia weather
  station off Ireland
Val|en|tine, St
val|en|tine
Val|en|tino,
  Ru|dolph actor
Val|era, Eamon de
  president of Repub-
  lic of Ireland
val|er|ate

Val¦er¦ian Roman
emperor
val¦er¦ian plant
Val¦erie
Val¦éry, Paul writer
valet
val¦eta var. of veleta
val¦etu¦din¦ar¦ian
val¦etu¦din¦ar¦ian¦
ism
val¦etu¦din¦ary
val¦etu¦din¦ar¦ies
val¦gus
Val¦halla
vali¦ant
vali¦ant¦ly
valid
val¦id¦ate
val¦id¦at¦ing
val¦id¦ation
val¦id¦ity
val¦id¦ities
val¦id¦ly
val¦ine
val¦ise
Val¦ium trademark
Val¦kyrie
Scandinavian
Mythology
Valla¦do¦lid
val¦lec¦ula
val¦lecu¦lae
val¦lecu¦lar
val¦lecu¦late
Valle d'Aosta
Val¦letta
val¦ley
val¦lum
valli
Val¦ois
Val¦ois, Nin¦ette de
choreographer
val¦onia
valor US
Br. valour
val¦or¦isa¦tion Br.
var. of valorization
val¦or¦ise Br. var. of
valorize
val¦or¦iza¦tion
val¦or¦ize
val¦or¦iz¦ing
val¦or¦ous

val¦our Br.
US valor
Val¦par¦aíso
Val¦poli¦cella
val¦pro¦ate
val¦pro¦ic
Val¦salva
valse
valu¦able
valu¦ably
valu¦ate
valu¦at¦ing
valu¦ation
valu¦ator
value
valu¦ing
value-added mod.
except when used
of tax
value added tax
value¦less
valuer
val¦uta
valv¦ate
valve
valved
valve¦less
valvu¦lar
valv¦ule
valv¦ul¦itis
vam¦brace
vam¦oose
vam¦oos¦ing
vam¦pire
vam¦pir¦ic
vam¦pir¦ism
vamp¦ish
vamp¦ish¦ly
vamp¦ish¦ness
vam¦plate
vampy
vamp¦ier
vampi¦est
Van, Lake
van
van¦ad¦ate
van¦ad¦in¦ite
van¦adium
Van Allen belt/
layer
va¦nas¦pati
Van¦brugh, John
architect

Van Buren,
Mar¦tin US
president
vanco¦mycin
Van¦cou¦ver
Van¦dal member of
Germanic people
van¦dal destructive
person
van¦dal¦ic
van¦dal¦ise Br. var.
of vandalize
van¦dal¦ism
van¦dal¦is¦tic
van¦dal¦ize
van¦dal¦iz¦ing
van de Graaff
Van¦der¦bijl¦park
Van¦der¦bilt,
Cor¦ne¦lius ship-
ping and railway
magnate
Van der Post,
Laur¦ens explorer
van der Waals
forces
van de Velde,
Adri¦aen painter
van de Velde,
Henri architect
van de Velde,
Wil¦lem two Dutch
painters
Van Die¦men's
Land
Van Dyck,
An¦thony painter
Van¦dyke collar;
beard; brown
vane weathervane;
blade; sight on
instrument; part of
feather; cf. vain,
vein
vaned
vane¦less cf.
veinless
Vän¦ern
Va¦nessa
van¦es¦sid
Van Eyck, Jan
painter
vanga
Van Gogh, Vin¦cent
painter

van¦guard
van¦illa
van¦il¦lin
van¦ish
van¦ish¦ing¦ly
vani¦tas
Vani¦tory unit
trademark
van¦ity
van¦ities
van Ley¦den, Lucas
painter
van¦load
van¦quish
van¦quish¦able
van¦quish¦er
Van¦taa
vant¦age
Vanua Levu
Vanu¦atu
Vanu¦atu¦an
vapid
vap¦id¦ity
vap¦id¦ly
vapid¦ness
vapor US
Br. vapour
vapor¦able
va¦por¦er US
Br. vapourer
vap¦or¦etto
vap¦or¦etti or
vap¦or¦ettos
vapori¦form
vapor¦is¦able Br.
var. of vaporizable
vapor¦isa¦tion Br.
var. of vaporization
vapor¦ise Br. var. of
vaporize
vapor¦iser Br. var.
of vaporizer
vapor¦ish US
Br. vapourish
vapor¦iz¦able
vapor¦iza¦tion
vapor¦ize
vapor¦iz¦ing
vapor¦izer
vapor¦ous
vapor¦ous¦ly
vapor¦ous¦ness
vapor¦ware
Br. vapour¦ware

va¦pory *US*
  Br. vapoury
va¦pour *Br.*
  US vapor
va¦pour¦er *Br.*
  US vaporer
vapour¦ish *Br.*
  US vaporish
vapour¦ware
  US vaporware
va¦poury *Br.*
  US vapory
va¦quero +s
var¦actor
Varah, Chad
  founder of the
  Samaritans
Vara¦nasi
Var¦an¦gian
varda var. of vardo
vardo +s
varec
Va¦rese town, Italy
Va¦rèse, Ed¦gard
  composer
Var¦gas, Ge¦tú¦lio
  Dor¦nel¦les presi-
  dent of Brazil
Var¦gas Llosa,
  Mario writer
vari¦abil¦ity
  vari¦abil¦ities
vari¦able
vari¦ably
vari¦ance
vari¦ant
vari¦ate
vari¦ation
vari¦ation¦al
vari¦ation¦ist
vari¦ceal
vari¦cella
vari¦cella zos¦ter
vari¦ces
vari¦co¦cele
vari¦col¦ored *US*
vari¦col¦oured *Br.*
vari¦cose
vari¦cosed
vari¦cos¦ity
var¦ied
varie¦gate
  varie¦gat¦ing
varie¦ga¦tion

var¦ietal
var¦ietal¦ly
var¦iet¦ist
var¦iety
  var¦ieties
vari¦focal
vari¦form
vari¦max
vari¦ola *n.*
vari¦olar *adj.*
vari¦ol¦it¦ic
vari¦ol¦oid
vari¦ol¦ous
vari¦om¦eter
vari¦orum
vari¦ous
vari¦ous¦ly
vari¦ous¦ness
Va¦ris¦can
var¦is¦tor
varix
vari¦ces
var¦let
var¦let¦ry
  var¦let¦ries
var¦mint
Varna port, Bulgaria
varna *Hinduism*
Varne light vessel
var¦nish
var¦nish¦er
Varro, Mar¦cus
  Ter¦en¦tius Roman
  scholar
var¦roa
var¦sity
  var¦sities
Var¦so¦vian
Var¦una Hindu god
varus
varve
varved
vary
  var¦ies
  var¦ied
  vary¦ing
vary¦ing¦ly
vas
  vasa
Vasa Swedish
  dynasty; cf. **Vaasa**
Vasa ship; cf. **Vaasa**
vasal

Vas¦ar¦ely, Vik¦tor
  painter
Va¦sari, Gior¦gio
  painter and
  biographer
Vasco da Gama
  explorer
vas¦cu¦lar
vas¦cu¦lar¦isa¦tion
  Br. var. of
  vascularization
vas¦cu¦lar¦ise *Br.*
  var. of vascularize
vas¦cu¦lar¦ity
vas¦cu¦lar¦iza¦tion
vas¦cu¦lar¦ize
vas¦cu¦lar¦iz¦ing
vas¦cu¦lar¦ly
vas¦cu¦la¦ture
vas¦cu¦lit¦ic
vas¦cu¦litis
vas¦cu¦lit¦ides
vas¦cu¦lum
vas¦cula
vas def¦er¦ens
vasa def¦er¦entia
vase
vas¦ec¦tom¦ise *Br.*
  var. of vasectomize
vas¦ec¦tom¦ize
  vas¦ec¦tom¦iz¦ing
vas¦ec¦tomy
  vas¦ec¦to¦mies
vase¦ful
vas¦el¦ine
  trademark
vas¦el¦in¦ing
vaso¦active
vaso¦con¦stric¦tion
vaso¦con¦strict¦ive
vaso¦con¦strict¦or
vaso¦dila¦ta¦tion
vaso¦dila¦tion
vaso¦dila¦tor
vaso¦dila¦tory
vaso¦motor
vaso¦pres¦sin
vaso¦pres¦sor
vaso¦spasm
vaso¦spas¦tic
vaso¦vagal
vas¦sal
vas¦sal¦age
vas¦ta¦tion

Väs¦ter¦ås
vast¦ly
vast¦ness
VAT = value added
  tax
vat
vat¦ted
vat¦ting
  tank
vat¦ful
vatic
Vati¦can
Vati¦can¦ism
Vati¦can¦ist
VAT¦man
VAT¦men
  tax officer
vat¦man
vat¦men
  paper worker
Vät¦tern
vatu
  pl. vatu
  Vanuatu currency
Vaud canton,
  Switzerland
vaude¦ville
vaude¦vil¦lian
Vaud¦ois
  pl. Vaud¦ois
Vaughan, Henry
  poet
Vaughan, Sarah
  jazz musician
Vaughan
  Wil¦liams, Ralph
  composer
vault arch; under-
  ground chamber;
  jump; cf. **volt, volte**
vault¦er
vaunt
vaunt¦er
vava¦sory
vava¦sor¦ies
vava¦sour
va-va-voom
V-bomber
V-chip
veal
Veb¦len, Thor¦stein
  economist
vec¦tor
vec¦tor¦ial

vec¦tor¦ial¦ly
vec¦tor¦isa¦tion *Br.*
  var. of
  vectorization
vec¦tor¦ise *Br.* var.
  of vectorize
vec¦tor¦iza¦tion
vec¦tor¦ize
  vec¦tor¦iz¦ing
Veda *Hinduism*
ve¦da¦lia beetle
Ve¦danta
Ve¦dan¦tic
Ve¦dant¦ist
Vedda Sri Lankan
  aboriginal
ved¦ette
Vedic
vee
vee¦jay
veena
veep
veer
veery
  veer¦ies
veg
  pl. **veg**
  v. **vegges**
  vegged
  vegging
Vega star
vega grassy region
Vega Car¦pio, Lope
  Felix de dramatist
vegan
Vege¦bur¦ger
  trademark cf.
  veggie burger
Vege¦mite
  trademark
vege¦table
vege¦tal
vege¦tar¦ian
vege¦tar¦ian¦ism
vege¦tate
  vege¦tat¦ing
vege¦ta¦tion
vege¦ta¦tion¦al
vege¦ta¦tive
vege¦ta¦tive¦ly
veg¦gie
veg¦gie bur¦ger cf.
  Vegeburger
vegie var. of **veggie**

vehe¦mence
vehe¦ment
vehe¦ment¦ly
ve¦hicle
ve¦hicu¦lar
veil cover; cf. **vail,**
  vale
veil¦less
vein blood vessel; cf.
  vain, vane
vein¦less cf.
  vaneless
vein¦let
vein-like
vein¦ous
vein¦stone
veiny
  vein¦ier
  veini¦est
veitch¦berry
  veitch¦berries
vela pl. of **velum**; cf.
  velar
ve¦la¦men
  ve¦la¦mina
velar of a veil or
  velum; *Phonetics*;
  cf. **vela**
velar¦isa¦tion *Br.*
  var. of **velarization**
velar¦ise *Br.* var. of
  velarize
ve¦lar¦ium
  ve¦laria
velar¦iza¦tion
velar¦ize
  velar¦iz¦ing
Ve¦láz¦quez, Diego
  Rod¦ríguez de
  Silva y painter
Ve¦láz¦quez de
  Cué¦llar, Diego
  conquistador
Vel¦cro *trademark*
  Vel¦croes
  Vel¦croed
  Vel¦cro¦ing
veld
Velde, van de see
  van de Velde
veld¦skoen
veldt var. of veld
vel¦eta
ve¦li¦ger

vel¦le¦ity
  vel¦le¦ities
Vel¦leius
  Pat¦er¦cu¦lus
  Roman historian
vel¦lum parchment
  etc.; cf. **velum**
Velma
velo¦cim¦eter
velo¦cim¦etry
vel¦oci¦pede
vel¦oci¦ped¦ist
vel¦oci¦rap¦tor
vel¦ocity
  vel¦oci¦ties
velo¦drome
vel¦our
vel¦ours
  pl. and var. of
  velour
vel¦outé
vel¦skoen var. of
  veldskoen
velum
  vela
  membrane; cf.
  vellum
vel¦vet
vel¦vet¦ed
vel¦vet¦een
vel¦vet¦leaf
vel¦vety
vena cava
  venae cavae
venal
ve¦nal¦ity
ve¦nal¦ly
ven¦ation
ven¦ation¦al
Venda person; lan-
  guage; former
  homeland, South
  Africa
ven¦dace
ven¦dange
Ven¦dée depart-
  ment, France
Ven¦demi¦aire
  French
Vendémiaire
vend¦er *US* var. of
  vendor
ven¦detta
vend¦euse

vend¦ible
vend¦or
ven¦due
ven¦eer
vene¦punc¦ture *Br.*
  US venipuncture
ven¦er¦abil¦ity
ven¦er¦able
ven¦er¦able¦ness
ven¦er¦ably
ven¦er¦ate
  ven¦er¦at¦ing
ven¦er¦ation
ven¦er¦ator
ven¦ereal
ven¦er¦eal¦ly
ven¦ereo¦logic¦al
ven¦ere¦olo¦gist
ven¦ere¦ology
ven¦ery
vene¦sec¦tion
Ven¦etia
Ven¦etian
ven¦etian blind
ven¦etianed
Ven¦eto
Vene¦zuela
Vene¦zue¦lan
ven¦geance
venge¦ful
venge¦ful¦ly
venge¦ful¦ness
ve¦nial
veni¦al¦ity
veni¦al¦ly
Ven¦ice
veni¦punc¦ture *US*
  Br. venepuncture
ven¦ison
Ven¦ite
Venn dia¦gram
ven¦nel
veno¦gram
veno¦graph¦ic
veno¦graph¦ic¦al¦ly
ven¦og¦raphy
venom
ven¦omed
ven¦om¦ous
ven¦om¦ous¦ly
ven¦om¦ous¦ness
ven¦os¦ity

ven¦ous
ven|ous¦ly
ven¦ter
vent-hole
venti|duct
venti|fact
ven¦til
ven¦ti|late
  ven¦ti|lat¦ing
ven¦ti|la¦tion
ven¦ti|la¦tor
ven¦ti|la¦tory
vent|less
Ven¦to|lin
  trademark
Ven¦tose
  French Ventôse
ven|touse
ven|tral
ven|tral¦ly
ventre à terre
ven|tricle
ven|tricu¦lar
ven|tri¦cul|
    og¦raphy
ven|tri|lo|quial
ven|trilo|quise *Br.*
  var. of
  ventriloquize
ven|trilo|quism
ven|trilo|quist
ven|trilo|quize
  ven|trilo|quiz¦ing
ven|trilo|quous
ven|trilo|quy
ventro|lat¦eral
ventro|lat¦eral¦ly
ventro|medial
ventro|medial¦ly
ven|ture
  ven¦tur|ing
ven|turer
ven|ture|some
ven|ture|some¦ly
ven|ture|some|ness
Ven|turi, Rob¦ert
  architect
ven|turi
venue
ven¦ule
Venus
Venus|berg
Venus de Milo

Ven¦us|ian
vera causa
  verae cau¦sae
ver|acious truthful;
  cf. voracious
ver|acious¦ly truth-
  fully; cf.
  voraciously
ver|acious|ness
  truthfulness; cf.
  voraciousness
ver|acity truthful-
  ness; cf. voracity
Vera|cruz
ver|anda
ver|an|daed
ver|an|dah var. of
  veranda
ver|ap|amil
vera|trine
ver|atrum
ver|bal
ver|balled
ver¦bal|ling
ver¦bal|is|able *Br.*
  var. of verbalizable
ver¦bal|isa¦tion *Br.*
  var. of
  verbalization
ver¦bal|ise *Br.* var.
  of verbalize
ver¦bal|iser *Br.* var.
  of verbalizer
ver¦bal|ism
ver¦bal|ist
ver¦bal|is¦tic
ver¦bal|iz|able
ver¦bal|iza¦tion
ver¦bal|ize
  ver¦bal|iz¦ing
ver¦bal|izer
ver¦bal¦ly
ver|bas¦cum
ver|ba¦tim
ver|bena
ver¦bi|age
Ver¦bier
verb|less
ver|bose
ver|bose¦ly
ver|bose|ness
ver|bos¦ity
ver|bo¦ten
ver|dancy

ver|dant
verd-antique
ver|dant¦ly
Ver|delho +s
ver|der¦er
Verdi, Giu|seppe
  composer
Verdi¦an
Ver|dic|chio +s
ver|dict
ver|di|gris
ver|din
ver|diter
Ver|dun
ver|dure
ver|dured
ver|dur|ous
Ver|eeni¦ging
Ver|ena
verge
  ver|ging
ver|gence
ver|ger
ver|ger|ship
Ver|gil var. of Virgil
Ver|gil|ian var. of
  Virgilian
ver|glas
ver¦idi|cal
ver¦idi|cal|ity
ver¦idi|cal¦ly
veri|est
veri|fi¦able
veri|fi¦ably
veri|fi|ca¦tion
veri|fier
ver|ify
  veri|fies
  veri|fied
  veri¦fy|ing
ver|ily
Ver|ina
veri|sim|ilar
veri|sim|ili|tude
ver|ism
ver|ismo
ver|ist
ver|is¦tic
ver|it|able
ver|it|ably
vérité
ver|ity
  ver|ities

ver|juice
ver|kramp var. of
  verkrampte
ver|krampte
ver|krampt|heid
Ver|laine, Paul poet
ver|lig var. of
  verligte
ver|ligte
ver|ligt|heid
Ver|meer, Jan
  painter
ver|meil
ver|mian
vermi|celli
vermi|cide
vermi|com|post|
    ing
ver¦micu|lar
ver¦micu|late
ver¦micu|la¦tion
ver¦micu|lite
vermi|cul¦ture
vermi|form
vermi|fuge
ver|mil¦ion
ver|mil¦lion var. of
  vermilion
ver|min
ver|min|ate
  ver|min|at¦ing
ver|min|ation
ver|min|ous
ver|mis
  ver|mes
Ver|mont
Ver|mont|er
ver|mouth
ver|nac¦cia
ver|nacu|lar
ver|nacu|lar|ise *Br.*
  var. of
  vernacularize
ver|nacu|lar|ism
ver|nacu|lar|ity
ver|nacu|lar|ize
  ver|nacu|lar|iz¦ing
ver|nacu|lar¦ly
ver|nal
ver|nal|isa¦tion *Br.*
  var. of
  vernalization

ver|nal|ise *Br.* var.
  of **vernalize**
ver|nal|iza|tion
ver|nal|ize
  ver|nal|iz|ing
ver|nal|ly
ver|na|tion
Verne, Jules
  novelist
Ver|ner's Law cf.
  Werner's
  syndrome
ver|nicle
ver|nier
ver|nis|sage
ver|nix case|osa
Ver|non
Vero board
  trademark
Ver|ona
ver|onal
Vero|nese, Paolo
  painter
Ver|on|ica, St
ver|on|ica plant;
  cloth; matador's
  movement
vero|nique food
Verrazano-
  Narrows Bridge
verre églo|misé
ver|ruca
  ver|ru|cae or
  ver|ru|cas
ver|ru|cose
ver|ru|cous
Ver|sace, Gianni
  fashion designer
Ver|sailles
ver|sal
ver|sant
ver|sa|tile
ver|sa|til|ity
vers de société
verse
  verses
  versed
  vers|ing
  poetry etc.; cf.
  verst
verse|let
ver|set
vers|icle
ver|si|col|ored *US*

ver|si|col|oured *Br.*
ver|sicu|lar
ver|si|fi|ca|tion
ver|si|fier
vers|ify
  ver|si|fies
  ver|si|fied
  ver|si|fy|ing
ver|sin
ver|sine var. of
  versin
ver|sion
ver|sion|al
vers libre
verso +s
verst Russian meas-
  ure of length; cf.
  versed
Ver|stehen
ver|sus
vert
ver|te|bra
  ver|te|brae
ver|te|bral
ver|te|brate
ver|tex
  ver|ti|ces or
  ver|texes
ver|ti|cal
ver|ti|cal|ise *Br.* var.
  of **verticalize**
ver|ti|cal|ity
ver|ti|cal|ize
  ver|ti|cal|iz|ing
ver|ti|cal|ly
ver|ticil|late
verti|cil|lium
  verti|cil|lia
ver|tigin|ous
ver|tigin|ous|ly
ver|tigo
verti|sol
vertu var. of virtu
Veru|la|mium
ver|vain
verve
ver|vet
Ver|viers
Ver|woerd,
  Hen|drik prime
  minister of South
  Africa
Ver|woerd|ian

very
  veri|est
Very light/pis|tol
Vesak
Vesa|lius, An|dreas
  anatomist
ves|ica
vesi|cal of a vesica;
  cf. vesicle
vesi|cant
ves|ica pis|cis
  ves|icae pis|cis
vesi|cate
  vesi|cat|ing
vesi|ca|tion
vesi|ca|tory
  vesi|ca|tor|ies
ves|icle sac; cavity;
  cf. vesical
vesico|ureter|ic
ves|icu|lar
ves|icu|lated
ves|icu|la|tion
Vespa *trademark*
Ves|pa|sian Roman
  emperor
ves|per evening
  (prayer)
ves|pers Christian
  service
ves|per|tili|onid
ves|per|tine
ves|pine
Ves|pucci,
  Amer|igo explorer
ves|sel
Vesta Roman god-
  dess; asteroid
vesta match
Ves|tal of Vesta;
  Vestal Virgin
ves|tal chaste;
  chaste woman
vest|ee
Ves|ter|ålen
ves|ti|ary
  ves|ti|ar|ies
ves|tibu|lar
ves|ti|bule
ves|tibulo|
         coch|lear
vestibulo-ocular
ves|tige
ves|tigial

ves|tigial|ly
ves|ti|men|tary
ves|ti|men|tif|er|an
ves|ti|ture
vest|ment
ves|try
  ves|tries
vestry|man
  vestry|men
ves|ture
  ves|tur|ing
Vesu|vian
vesu|vian|ite
Vesu|vius
vet
  vet|ted
  vet|ting
vetch
vetch|ling
vetchy
vet|eran
Vet|er|ans Day
vet|er|in|ar|ian
vet|er|in|ary
  vet|er|in|ar|ies
veti|ver
veti|vert var. of
  vetiver
veto
  ve|toes
  ve|toed
  veto|ing
veto|er
vex|ation
vex|atious
vex|atious|ly
vex|atious|ness
vex|ed|ly
vexer
vex|il|lo|logic|al
vex|il|lolo|gist
vex|il|lol|ogy
vex|il|lum
vex|illa
vex|ing|ly
via
Via Appia
via|bil|ity
vi|able
vi|ably
Via Cru|cis
Via Dol|or|osa of
  Jesus

via dol¦or¦osa
  via dol¦or¦osas
  generally
via¦duct
Vi¦agra *trademark*
vial glass vessel; cf.
  vile, viol
via media
  via me¦dias
viand
via nega¦tiva
vi¦at¦ic¦al
vi¦at¦icum
  vi¦at¦ica
vibe
vib¦ist
vi¦bracu¦lar *adj.*
vi¦bracu¦lum *n.*
  vi¦brac¦ula
vi¦brancy
  vi¦bran¦cies
vi¦brant
vi¦brant¦ly
vi¦bra¦phone
vi¦bra¦phon¦ist
vi¦brate
  vi¦brat¦ing
vi¦bra¦tile
vi¦bra¦tion
vi¦bra¦tion¦al
vi¦brato +s
vi¦bra¦tor
vi¦bra¦tory
vib¦rio +s
vi¦bris¦sae
vibro¦tac¦tile
vi¦bur¦num
vicar
vic¦ar¦age
vicar apos¦tol¦ic
  vic¦ars apos¦tol¦ic
vicar choral
  vic¦ars choral
vicar gen¦eral
  vic¦ars gen¦eral
vic¦ar¦ial
vic¦ari¦ance
vic¦ari¦ate
vic¦ari¦ous
vic¦ari¦ous¦ly
vic¦ari¦ous¦ness
vic¦ar¦ship

vice immoral behav-
  iour; vice-president
  etc.; cf. **vise**
vice *Br.*
vi¦cing
  clamp;
  US vise
vice- in 'vice-captain'
  etc.
vice ad¦miral
vice chair¦man
vice chan¦cel¦lor
vice con¦sul
vice¦ger¦ency
  vice¦ger¦en¦cies
vice¦ger¦ent
vice¦less
vice-like *Br.*
  US vise-like
vice-marshal in 'air
  vice-marshal'
Vi¦cente, Gil
  dramatist
Vi¦cenza
vice-presidency
  vice-presiden¦cies
vice-president
vice-presiden¦tial
vice¦regal
vice¦regal¦ly
vice¦reine
vice¦roy
vice¦royal
vice¦roy¦alty
  vice¦roy¦al¦ties
vice¦roy¦ship
vice versa
Vichy
vichys¦soise
vicin¦age
vicin¦ity
  vicin¦ities
vi¦cious
vi¦cious¦ly
vi¦cious¦ness
vi¦cis¦si¦tude
vi¦cis¦si¦tu¦din¦ous
Vicks¦burg
Vico, Giam¦bat¦tista
  philosopher
vi¦comte
vi¦com¦tesse
vic¦tim

vic¦tim¦isa¦tion *Br.*
  var. of
  victimization
vic¦tim¦ise *Br.* var.
  of **victimize**
vic¦tim¦iser *Br.* var.
  of **victimizer**
vic¦tim¦iza¦tion
vic¦tim¦ize
  vic¦tim¦iz¦ing
vic¦tim¦izer
vic¦tim¦less
vic¦tim¦ology
  vic¦tim¦olo¦gies
Vic¦tor
vic¦tor
Vic¦tor
  Em¦man¦uel
  kings of Italy
Vic¦toria
Vic¦toria, Tomás
  Luis de composer
Vic¦toria de
  Du¦rango
Vic¦tor¦ian
Vic¦tori¦ana
Vic¦tor¦ian¦ism
vic¦tori¦ous
vic¦tori¦ous¦ly
vic¦tori¦ous¦ness
vic¦tor lu¦dorum
  male
vic¦tory
  vic¦tor¦ies
vic¦trix lu¦dorum
vict¦ual
  vict¦ualled *Br.*
  vict¦ualed *US*
  vict¦ual¦ling *Br.*
  vict¦ual¦ing *US*
vict¦ual¦er *US*
vict¦ual¦ler *Br.*
vi¦cuña
vicus
  vici
Vic-Wells Bal¦let
vid = video
Vidal, Gore writer
vide see
vi¦de¦licet
video
  pl. vid¦eos
  v. vid¦eoes
  vid¦eoed

video¦ing
video¦con¦fer¦ence
video¦con¦fer¦
  en¦cing
video¦disc
video¦fit
video¦gram
vide¦og¦raph¦er
video¦graph¦ics
vide¦og¦raphy
video¦phile
video¦phone
Video¦Plus
  trademark
video¦tape
  video¦tap¦ing
video¦tel¦eph¦ony
video¦tex
video¦text var. of
  videotex
vi¦deshi
vidi¦con
vid¦iot
vie
  vying
vie de Bohème
vi¦elle hurdy-gurdy;
  cf. viol
Vi¦enna capital of
  Austria
Vi¦enne city, France
Vi¦en¦nese of
  Vienna
Vien¦tiane
Viet¦cong
  pl. Viet¦cong
Viet¦minh
  pl. Viet¦minh
Viet¦nam
Viet¦nam¦ese
Viet¦nam¦isa¦tion
  Br. var. of
  Vietnamization
Viet¦nam¦iza¦tion
vieux jeu
view
view¦able
view¦data
  trademark
view¦er
view¦er¦ship
view¦find¦er
view¦graph

view hal|loo
view|less
view|point
view|port
view|screen
viga
Vigée-Lebrun,
  Élisa|beth painter
vigil
vigi|lance
vigi|lant
vigi|lante
vigi|lant|ism
vigi|lant|ly
vi|gneron
vi|gnet|ting
vi|gnet|tist
Vi|gnola, Gia|como
  architect
Vigny, Al|fred,
  Comte de writer
Vigo port, Spain
Vigo, Jean film
  director
vigor US
  Br. vigour
vig|or|ish
vig|oro
vig|or|ous
vig|or|ous|ly
vig|or|ous|ness
vig|our Br.
  US vigor
vi|hara
vi|huela
vi|huela de arco
  vi|hue|las de arco
vi|huela de mano
  vi|hue|las de mano
Vi|jaya|wada
Vi|king
Vila capital of
  Vanuatu
vi|layet
vile
  viler
  vil|est
  loathsome; cf. vial,
  viol
vile|ly
vile|ness
vili|fi|ca|tion
vili|fier

vil|ify
  vili|fies
  vili|fied
  vili|fy|ing
Villa, Pan|cho revo-
  lutionary
villa
Villa|fran|chian
vil|lage
vil|la|ger
vil|la|gey
vil|la|gisa|tion Br.
  var. of villagization
vil|la|giza|tion
Vil|la|her|mosa
vil|lain guilty
  person; cf. villein
vil|lain|ous
vil|lain|ous|ly
vil|lainy
  vil|lain|ies
Villa-Lobos,
  Hei|tor composer
vil|lan|cico +s
vil|lan|ella song
  vil|lan|elle or
  vil|lan|el|las
vil|lan|elle poem
vil|lein feudal
  tenant; cf. villain
vil|lein|age
villi|form
Vil|lon, Fran|çois
  poet
vil|lose
vil|los|ity
vil|lous adj.
vil|lus n.
villi
Vil|nius
Vimy Ridge
vina
vin|aceous
vin|ai|grette
vin|blast|ine
vinca
Vin|cent
Vin|cent de Paul,
  St
Vin|cen|tian
Vinci, Leo|nardo da
  painter
vin|ci|bil|ity
vin|cible

vin|cris|tine
vin|cu|lar adj.
vin|cu|lum n.
vin|cula
vin|da|loo +s
vin de garde
  vins de garde
vin de paille
  vins de paille
vin de pays
  vins de pays
  country wine; cf.
  vin du pays
vin de table
  vins de table
vin d'hon|neur
  vins d'hon|neur
vin|dic|able
vin|di|cate
  vin|di|cat|ing
vin|di|ca|tion
vin|di|ca|tive
vin|di|ca|tor
vin|di|ca|tory
vin|dic|tive
vin|dic|tive|ly
vin|dic|tive|ness
vin du pays
  vins du pays
  local wine; cf. vin
  de pays
Vine, Bar|bara nov-
  elist (pseudonym)
vin|egar
vin|egar|ish
vin|egary
vin|ery
  vin|eries
vine|yard
vingt-et-un
vinho verde
  vin|hos ver|des
vini|cul|tural
vini|cul|ture
vini|cul|tur|ist
vini|fi|ca|tion
vin|ify
  vini|fies
  vini|fied
  vini|fy|ing
vin|ing
vin jaune
  vins jaunes
Vin|land

Vin|ney in 'Blue
  Vinney'
Vin|nyt|sya
vino +s
vino da ta|vola
vin or|din|aire
  vins or|din|aires
vin|os|ity
vin|ous
vin|ous|ly
Vin|son Mas|sif
vin|tage
vin|ta|ger
vint|ner
viny
  vini|er
  vini|est
vin|yasa
vinyl
Vi|ognier
viol stringed musical
  instrument; cf. vial,
  vielle, vile
viola flower; musical
  instrument
viol|able
viol|aceous
viola da brac|cio
  violas da brac|cio
viola da gamba
  violas da gamba
viola d'amore
  violas d'amore
vio|late
vio|lat|ing
vio|la|tion
vio|la|tor
viol da gamba var.
  of viola da gamba
vio|lence
vio|lent
vio|lent|ly
vio|let
violet-ear
vio|lin
vio|lin|ist
viol|ist
vi|olo|gen
vio|lon|cel|list
vio|lon|cello +s
vio|lone
vi|pas|sana
viper

viper|fish ·
vi|per|ine
vi|per|ish
viper|like
vi|per|ous
viper's bu|gloss
viper's grass
vir|aemia *Br.*
  US viremia
vir|aemic *Br.*
  US viremic
vir|ago +s
viral
vir|al|ly
Vir|chow, Ru|dolf
  physician
vir|elay
vire|ment
vir|emia *US*
  Br. viraemia
vir|emic *US*
  Br. viraemic
vireo +s
vir|es|cence
vir|es|cent
virga
  vir|gae
  evaporating rain
vir|gate
Vir|gil Roman poet
Vir|gil|ian
vir|gin
vir|gin|al
vir|gin|al|ist
vir|gin|al|ly
Vir|ginia
Vir|gin|ian
vir|gin|ity
virgin's bower
Virgo
Vir|go|an
virgo in|tacta
  virgo in|tac|tas
vir|gule
viri|des|cence
viri|des|cent
vir|id|ian
vir|ile
vir|il|isa|tion *Br.*
  var. of virilization
vir|il|ism
vir|il|ity
vir|il|iza|tion

viri|local
vir|ino +s
vir|ion
vir|oid
viro|logic|al
viro|logic|al|ly
vir|olo|gist
vir|ology
viro|pexis
virtu knowledge of
  fine arts; in 'article/
  object of virtu'; cf.
  virtue
vir|tual
vir|tual|isa|tion *Br.*
  var. of
  virtualization
vir|tual|ise *Br.* var.
  of virtualize
vir|tual|iser *Br.* var.
  of virtualizer
vir|tu|al|ity
vir|tual|iza|tion
vir|tua|lize
  vir|tual|iz|ing
vir|tual|izer
vir|tu|al|ly
vir|tue moral excel-
  lence etc.; cf. virtu
vir|tue|less
vir|tu|osic
vir|tu|os|ity
vir|tu|oso
  vir|tu|osi or
  vir|tu|osos
vir|tu|oso|ship
vir|tu|ous
vir|tu|ous|ly
vir|tu|ous|ness
viru|lence
viru|lent
viru|lent|ly
virus
visa
  visas
  visaed or visa'd
  visa|ing
  passport
  endorsement; cf.
  visor
vis|age
vis|aged
vis|agiste

Visākha var. of
  Vesak
Visa|kha|pat|nam
vis-à-vis
  pl. vis-à-vis
Visby
vis|cacha
vis|cera
vis|ceral
vis|cer|al|ly
vis|cero|trop|ic
vis|cid
vis|cid|ity
visco|elas|tic
visco|elas|ti|city
visc|om|eter
visco|met|ric
visco|met|ric|al|ly
visc|om|etry
Vis|conti, Lu|chino
  film director
vis|cose
vis|cos|im|eter
vis|cos|ity
vis|cos|ities
vis|count
vis|count|cy
vis|count|cies
vis|count|ess
vis|count|ship
vis|county
vis|count|ies
vis|cous sticky; cf.
  viscus
vis|cous|ly
vis|cous|ness
vis|cus
  vis|cera
  internal organ; cf.
  viscous
vise *US*
vis|ing
  Br. vice
  clamp; cf. vice
vise-like *US*
  Br. vice-like
Vishnu
Vishnu|ism
Vishnu|ite
visi|bil|ity
vis|ible
vis|ibly
Visi|goth
Visi|goth|ic

vi|sion
vi|sion|al
vi|sion|ary
  vi|sion|ar|ies
vi|sion|less
visit
vis|it|able
vis|it|ant
vis|it|ation
vis|it|ator|ial
vis|it|or
vis|it|or|ial
Vis|king *trademark*
vis medi|ca|trix
  na|turae
visna
visor protector for
  eyes; cf. visa
vi|sored
vi|sor|less
Vis|queen
  trademark
vista
vis|taed
Vista|vision *US*
  trademark
Vis|tula
vis|ual
visu|al|is|able *Br.*
  var. of visualizable
visu|al|isa|tion *Br.*
  var. of
  visualization
visu|al|ise *Br.* var. of
  visualize
visu|al|iser *Br.* var.
  of visualizer
visu|al|ity
visu|al|iz|able
visu|al|iza|tion
visu|al|ize
visu|al|iz|ing
visu|al|izer
visu|al|ly
visuo|motor
visuo|spatial
vita curriculum vitae
vital
vi|tal|isa|tion *Br.*
  var. of vitalization
vi|tal|ise *Br.* var. of
  vitalize
vi|tal|ism

vi¦tal¦ist
vi¦tal¦is¦tic
vi¦tal¦ity
vi¦tal¦iza¦tion
vi¦tal¦ize
  vi¦tal¦iz¦ing
vi¦tal¦ly
vita¦min
vita¦min¦ise *Br.* var.
  of **vitaminize**
vita¦min¦ize
  vita¦min¦iz¦ing
vi¦telli
vi¦tel¦lin protein in
  egg yolk
vi¦tel¦line relating to
  egg yolk
Vi¦tel¦lius, Aulus
  Roman emperor
vi¦tello¦genin
vi¦tel¦lus
  vi¦telli
viti¦ate
  viti¦at¦ing
viti¦ation
viti¦ator
viti¦cul¦tural
viti¦cul¦ture
viti¦cul¦tur¦ist
Viti Levu
viti¦ligo
Vi¦toria town, Spain
Vi¦tória port, Brazil
vi¦trec¦tomy
  vi¦trec¦to¦mies
vit¦re¦ous
vit¦ri¦fac¦tion
vit¦ri¦fi¦able
vit¦ri¦fi¦ca¦tion
vit¦ri¦form
vit¦rify
  vit¦ri¦fies
  vit¦ri¦fied
  vit¦ri¦fy¦ing
vi¦trine
vit¦riol
vit¦ri¦ol¦ic
vit¦ri¦ol¦ic¦al¦ly
vitro in *'in vitro'*
Vit¦ru¦vian
Vit¦ru¦vius architect
Vit¦sebsk

vitta
vit¦tae
vit¦tate
vi¦tu¦per¦ate
  vi¦tu¦per¦at¦ing
vi¦tu¦per¦ation
vi¦tu¦pera¦tive
vi¦tu¦per¦ator
Vitus, St in 'St
  Vitus's dance'
viva
  vivas
  viv¦aed or viva'd
  viva¦ing
  oral exam; cf.
  vivers
viva shout; long
  live ...; cf. vivers
viv¦ace
viv¦acious
viv¦acious¦ly
viv¦acious¦ness
viv¦acity
Viv¦aldi, An¦tonio
  composer
viv¦ar¦ium
  viv¦aria
vivat
viva voce *n.*
  viva voces
viva-voce *v.*
  viva-voces
  viva-voced
  viva-voceing
Viveka¦nanda,
  Swami Indian
  spiritual leader
vive la
  dif | fe¦rence
  French *vive la*
  différence
vi¦ver¦rid
vi¦vers food; cf.
  viva, *viva*
Viv¦ian
viv¦ian¦ite
vivid
viv¦id¦ly
viv¦id¦ness
Viv¦ien
Vivi¦enne
vivi¦fi¦ca¦tion
viv¦ify
  vivi¦fies
  vivi¦fied

vivi¦fy¦ing
vivip¦ar¦ity
viv¦ip¦ar¦ous
viv¦ip¦ar¦ous¦ly
viv¦ip¦ar¦ous¦ness
vivi¦sect
vivi¦sec¦tion
vivi¦sec¦tion¦al
vivi¦sec¦tion¦ist
vivi¦sect¦or
vivo in *'in vivo'*
vixen
vix¦en¦ish
vix¦en¦ly
Viy~~ella~~ *trademark*
viz.
viz¦ard
viz¦ier
viz¦ier¦ate
viz¦ier¦ial
viz¦ier¦ship
vizor var. of **visor**
vi¦zored var. of
  visored
vizor¦less var. of
  visorless
vizsla
Vlach +s
Vladi¦kav¦kaz
Vlad¦imir city,
  Russia
Vlad¦imir, St
  Russian prince
Vladi¦vos¦tok
Vla¦minck,
  Maur¦ice de
  painter
vlast
  vlasti
vlei pool
Vlis¦singen
Vlorë
Vltava
V-neck
vobla
voc¦able
vo¦cabu¦lary
  vo¦cabu¦lar¦ies
vocal
vocal cords
vo¦cal¦ese singing to
  instrumental
  music; cf. **vocalise**

vo¦cal¦ic
vo¦cal¦isa¦tion *Br.*
  var. of **vocalization**
vo¦cal¦ise vocal
  music written with
  no words;
  cf. **vocalese**;
  also *Br.* var. of
  vocalize
vo¦cal¦iser *Br.* var.
  of **vocalizer**
vo¦cal¦ism
vo¦cal¦ist
vo¦cal¦ity
vo¦cal¦iza¦tion
vo¦cal¦ize
  vo¦cal¦iz¦ing
vo¦cal¦izer
vo¦cal¦ly
vocal sac
vo¦ca¦tion
vo¦ca¦tion¦al
vo¦ca¦tion¦al¦ise *Br.*
  var. of
  vocationalize
vo¦ca¦tion¦al¦ism
vo¦ca¦tion¦al¦ize
  vo¦ca¦tion¦al¦iz¦ing
vo¦ca¦tion¦al¦ly
voca¦tive
vo¦cif¦er¦ance
vo¦cif¦er¦ant
vo¦cif¦er¦ate
  vo¦cif¦er¦at¦ing
vo¦cif¦er¦ation
vo¦cif¦er¦ator
vo¦cif¦er¦ous
vo¦cif¦er¦ous¦ly
vo¦cif¦er¦ous¦ness
vo¦coder
vodka
vodun
voe
voet¦sak
  voet¦sakked
  voet¦sak¦king
voet¦stoots
vogue
  vogue¦ing or
  vo¦guing
vo¦guish
voice
voi¦cing
voice¦ful
voice¦less

voice|less|ly
voice|less|ness
voice|mail
voice-over
voice|print
voicer
void
void|able
void|ance
void|ness
voila
French *voilà*
voile
voir dire
voire dire var. of
voir dire
voix ce|leste
voix ce|lestes
French **voix céleste**
Voj|vo|dina
Vo|lans constella-
tion
vo|lant
Vola|pük
volar
vola|tile
vola|til|is|able *Br.*
var. of **volatilizable**
vola|til|isa|tion *Br.*
var. of
volatilization
vola|til|ise *Br.* var.
of **volatilize**
vola|til|ity
vola|til|iz|able
vola|til|iza|tion
vola|til|ize
vola|til|iz|ing
vol-au-vent
vol|can|ic
vol|can|ic|al|ly
vol|can|icity
vol|cani|clas|tic
vol|can|ism
vol|cano
vol|ca|noes
vol|cano|logic|al
vol|can|olo|gist
vol|can|ology
vole
volet
Volga
Vol|go|grad

vol|ition
vol|ition|al
vol|ition|al|ly
voli|tive
Volk Germans, in
Nazi ideology
volk Afrikaners
Völker|
wan|der|ung
Völker|
wan|der|ung|en
völk|isch
volk|isch var. of
völkisch
vol|ley
vol|ley|ball
vol|ley|er
Vol|ogda
Volos
vol|plane
vol|plan|ing
Vol|scian
Vol|stead Act
volt *Electricity*; cf.
vault, volte
Volta river, Ghana
Volta, Ales|san|dro
physicist
volt|age
Vol|ta|ic language
vol|ta|ic *Electricity*
Vol|taire writer
volt|ameter
measures electric
charge; cf.
voltmeter
volte *Fencing*;
movement by
horse; cf. vault,
volt
volte-face
volt|meter
measures electric
potential in volts;
cf. voltameter
volu|bil|ity
vol|uble
vol|uble|ness
vol|ubly
vol|ume
vol|umed
volu|met|ric
volu|met|ric|al|ly
vo|lu|min|os|ity

vo|lu|min|ous
vo|lu|min|ous|ly
vo|lu|min|ous|ness
volum|ise *Br.* var. of
volumize
volum|iser *Br.* var.
of volumizer
volum|ize
volum|iz|ing
volum|izer
vol|un|tar|ily
vol|un|tari|ness
vol|un|tar|ism
vol|un|tar|ist
vol|un|tary
vol|un|tar|ies
voluntary-aided
voluntary-
controlled
vol|un|tary|ism
vol|un|tary|ist
vol|un|teer
vol|un|teer|ism
vol|upté
vo|lup|tu|ary
vo|lup|tu|ar|ies
vo|lup|tu|ous
vo|lup|tu|ous|ly
vo|lup|tu|ous|ness
vol|ute
vol|uted
volu|tion
volva
vol|vox
vol|vu|lus
vol|vuli or
vol|vu|luses
Volzh|sky
vomer
vomit
vom|it|er
vom|it|orium
vom|it|oria
vom|it|ous nauseous
vom|itus vomited
matter
von Braun,
Wern|her rocket
designer
V-1 flying bomb
Von|ne|gut, Kurt
novelist

von Neu|mann,
John computer
pioneer
von Reck|ling|
hau|sen's dis|ease
von Stern|berg,
Josef film director
von Wille|brand
factor
von Wille|brand's
dis|ease
voo|doo +s +ed
+ing
voo|doo|ism
voo|doo|ist
Voor|trek|ker
vor|acious greedy;
cf. veracious
vor|acious|ly greed-
ily; cf. veraciously
vor|acious|ness
greed; cf.
veraciousness
vor|acity greed; cf.
veracity
Vor|arl|berg
Vor|on|ezh
Voro|shi|lov|grad
Vor|stel|lung
Vor|stel|lungen
Vor|ster, John
president of South
Africa
vor|tal
vor|tex
vor|texes or
vor|ti|ces
vor|ti|cal
vor|ti|cal|ly
vor|ti|cella
Vor|ti|cism
Vor|ti|cist
vor|ti|city
vor|ti|cose
vor|ticu|lar
Vosges
Vos|tok
vos|tro ac|count
vo|tar|ist
vo|tary
vo|tar|ies
vote
vot|ing
vote|less

voter
vo¦tive
Vot¦yak
vouch
vou|cher
vouch|safe
  vouch|saf¦ing
voulu
vous|soir
Vou|vray
vowel
vow|eled *US*
  Br. vowelled
vow¦el¦ise *Br.* var. of
  vowelize
vow¦el¦ize
  vow¦el¦iz¦ing
vow|elled *Br.*
  US voweled
vow¦el|less
vowel¦ly
vox an|gel|ica
voxel
vox hu¦mana
vox pop
vox pop¦uli
voy¦age
  voy¦aging
voy¦age|able
voy|ager traveller
voy|ageur Canadian
  boatman
voy¦eur
voy¦eur|ism
voy¦eur|is¦tic
voy¦eur|is¦tic|al¦ly
vroom
vrou *S. African*
  woman or wife; cf.
  Frau
vrouw var. of vrou
V-sign
V/STOL = vertical
  and short take-off
  and landing
VTOL = vertical
  take-off and
  landing
V-2 missile
vuggy
vugu¦lar
Vuil|lard, Éd|ouard
  painter
Vul¦can Roman god

Vul¦can|ian
vul¦can|ic var. of
  volcanic
vul¦can|is|able *Br.*
  var. of vulcanizable
vul¦can|isa¦tion *Br.*
  var. of
  vulcanization
vul¦can|ise *Br.* var.
  of vulcanize
vul¦can|iser *Br.* var.
  of vulcanizer
vul¦can|ism
vul¦can|ite
vul¦can|iz|able
vul¦can|iza¦tion
vul¦can|ize
  vul¦can|iz¦ing
vul¦can|izer
Vul¦cano island off
  Italy
vul¦cano|logic¦al
  var. of
  volcanological
vul¦can|olo¦gist var.
  of volcanologist
vul¦can|ology var.
  of volcanology
vul¦gar
vul¦gar|ian
vul¦gar|isa¦tion *Br.*
  var. of
  vulgarization
vul¦gar|ise *Br.* var.
  of vulgarize
vul¦gar|ism
vul¦gar|ity
  vul¦gar|ities
vul¦gar|iza¦tion
vul¦gar|ize
  vul¦gar|iz¦ing
vul¦gar|ly
Vul|gate bible
vul|gate colloquial
  speech
vuln
vul¦ner|abil|ity
  vul¦ner|abil|ities
vul¦ner|able
vul¦ner|ably
vul¦ner|ary
  vul¦ner|ar¦ies
Vul|pec¦ula
vul|pine

vul¦ture
vul¦tur|ine
vul¦tur|ish
vul¦tur|ous
vulva *n.*
vul¦val
vul¦var *adj.*
vulv|itis
Vyatka
vygie
vying
Vyv¦yan

W

Wa people
Waaf *Br.*
  member of
  Women's Auxiliary
  Air Force; cf. WAF
Waal river
wab¦bit
wabi
wa¦boom
WAC = Women's
  Army Corps
wack term of
  address; crazy
  person; cf. wacke,
  whack
wacke rock; cf.
  wack, whack
wacked var. of
  whacked
wack|ily
wacki|ness
wacko
  wackos or
  wack|oes
  crazy (person); cf.
  whacko
wacky
  wack|ier
  wacki|est
wad
  wad|ded
  wad|ding
wad¦able var. of
  wade|able
wad|cut¦ter

wad¦dle
  wad¦dling
wad|dler
waddy
  wad|dies
  war club; cf. wadi
Wade, George
  soldier
Wade, Vir|ginia
  tennis player
wade
  wad¦ing
wade|able
Wade–Giles
wader
wadi watercourse;
  cf. waddy
Wadi Halfa
wady
  wad|ies
  var. of wadi;
  watercourse;
  cf. waddy
WAF *US*
  = Women in the
  Air Force; cf. Waaf
wafer
wafery
Waf¦fen SS
waf¦fle
  waf|fling
waf|fler
waf¦fly
  waf|flier
  waf|fli|est
waft
wag
  wagged
  wag|ging
wage
  wa¦ging
wager
Wagga Wagga
wag|gery
  wag|ger¦ies
wag|gish
wag|gish|ly
wag|gish|ness
wag¦gle
  wag|gling
wag|gler
wag¦gly
  wag|glier
  wag|gli|est

wag¦gon *Br.* var. of
wagon

wag¦gon¦ette *Br.*
var. of wagonette

Wag¦ner, Rich¦ard
composer

Wag¦ner¦ian

wagon

wag¦on¦er

wagon¦ette

wagon-lit
wagons-lits

wagon-roof

wagon-vault

wag¦tail

Wa¦habi var. of
Wahhabi

Wa¦hab¦ism var. of
Wahhabism

Wa¦hab¦ist var. of
Wahhabist

wahey *exclam.*

Wah¦habi

Wah¦hab¦ism

Wah¦hab¦ist

wa¦hine

wahoo +s

wah-wah

waif

waif¦ish

waif¦like

Wai¦kato

Wai¦kiki

wail cry; cf. whale,
wale

wail¦er person who
wails; cf. Waler,
whaler

wail¦ful

wail¦ing¦ly

Wail¦ing Wall

Wain, John writer;
cf. Wayne

Wain constellation

wain wagon; cf.
wane

wains¦cot
wains¦cot¦ed or
wains¦cot¦ted
wains¦cot¦ing or
wains¦cot¦ting

wain¦wright

Waira¦rapa

waist part of body
etc.; cf. waste

waist¦band

waist¦coat

waist¦ed having a
waist; cf. wasted

waist¦less

waist¦line

wait delay action; cf.
weight

wait-a-bit plant

Wai¦tangi

wait¦er

wait¦per¦son +s

wait¦ress

wait¦ron

wait¦staff

waive
waiv¦ing
forgo; cf. wave

wai¦ver act of
waiving; cf. waver

Wajda, An¦drzej
film director

wak¦ame

wake
woke
wak¦ing
woken

wake¦board

wake¦board¦er

Wake¦field

wake¦ful

wake¦ful¦ness

waken

waker

wake-robin

wake-up *n. & mod.*

wakey-wakey

Wa¦khan Sa¦li¦ent

waki¦zashi
pl. waki¦zashi

Waks¦man,
Sel¦man Abra¦ham
microbiologist

Wal¦achia var. of
Wallachia

Wal¦ach¦ian var. of
Wallachian

Wal¦den¦ses

Wal¦den¦sian

Wald¦heim, Kurt
president of Austria

waldo

wal¦does

Wal¦dorf salad

wald¦rapp

wale ridge in fabric;
timber on ship etc.;
w. knot; cf. wail,
whale

Waler horse; person
from New South
Wales; cf. wailer,
whaler

Wales

Wał¦esa, Lech
president of Poland

wali Arab governor

Wal¦ian in 'North
Walian' and 'South
Walian'

walk

walk¦able

walk¦about

walk¦athon

walk¦er

walk¦ies

walkie-talkie

walk-in *adj. & n.*

Walk¦man
trademark
Walk¦mans or
Walk¦men

walk-on *adj. & n.*

walk¦out

walk¦over

walk-through *n. &
adj.*

walk-up *adj. & n.*

walk¦way

wall structure; cf.
waul, whorl

wal¦laby
wal¦la¦bies

Wal¦lace, Al¦fred
Rus¦sel naturalist

Wal¦lace, Edgar
writer

Wal¦lace, Wil¦liam
Scottish national
hero

Wal¦la¦cea

Wal¦la¦cean

Wal¦lachia

Wal¦lach¦ian

wal¦lah

wal¦la¦roo +s

Wal¦la¦sey

wall¦board

wall¦chart

wall¦cover¦ing

wall¦creep¦er

Wal¦len¦berg,
Raoul diplomat

Wal¦ler, Fats jazz
musician

wal¦let

wall eye eye

wall¦eye fish

wall-eyed

wall¦flower

Wal¦lis, Barnes
inventor

Wal¦lis and
Fu¦tuna Is¦lands

wall-less

Wal¦loon

wal¦lop +ed +ing

wal¦lop¦er

wal¦low

wal¦low¦er

wall¦paper

wall¦wash¦er

wally
wal¦lies

wal¦nut

Wal¦pole, Hor¦ace
writer and
politician

Wal¦pole, Hugh
novelist

Wal¦pole, Rob¦ert
prime minister of
Britain

Wal¦pur¦gis night

Wal¦ras' law

wal¦rus

Wal¦sall

Wal¦sing¦ham town

Wal¦sing¦ham,
Fran¦cis politician

Wal¦ter

Wal¦ter Mitty +s

Wal¦ton, Izaak
writer

Wal¦ton, Wil¦liam
composer

waltz

waltz¦er

Wal¦vis Bay
Wam¦pa¦noag
wam¦pum
WAN = wide area
network
wan
  wan¦ner
  wan¦nest
  pale; cf. **won**
wand
Wanda name
wan¦der go
  aimlessly
wan¦der¦er
wan¦der¦lust
wan¦deroo +s
wane
  wan¦ing
  decline; decrease;
  defect in plank; cf.
  wain
waney
Wanga¦nui
wan¦gle
  wan¦gling
wan¦gler
Wan¦kel, Felix
  engineer
Wan¦kel en¦gine
wank¦er *vulgar
slang*
Wan¦kie former
  name for **Hwange**
wanky *vulgar slang*
  worthless
wanly
wanna = want to
wan¦nabe
wan¦ness
want
want¦er
wan¦ton motiveless;
  cf. **wonton**
wan¦ton¦ly
wan¦ton¦ness
wap¦en¦take
wap¦iti
Wap¦ping
war
  warred
  war¦ring
wa¦ragi
wara¦tah

War¦beck, Per¦kin
  pretender to the
  English throne
war¦bird
war¦ble
  warb¦ling
warb¦ler
war¦bonnet
War¦burg, Aby art
  historian
War¦burg, Otto
  biochemist
warby shabby
war¦chalk¦ing
**Ward, Mrs
  Hum¦phry** writer
ward
war¦den
war¦den¦ship
war¦der
Ward¦ian
War¦dour Street
ward¦ress
ward¦robe
ward¦room
ward¦ship
ware articles for
  sale; aware;
  beware; cf. **warez,
  wear, where**
ware¦hou
ware¦house
ware¦hous¦ing
ware¦house¦man
ware¦house¦men
warez pirated
  software
war¦fare
war¦farin
war¦head
War¦hol, Andy
  artist
War¦hol¦ian
war¦horse
wari¦ly
wari¦ness
war¦like
war¦lock
war¦lord
warm¦blood horse
warm-blooded
warm-
    blooded¦ness
warm-down *n.*

warm¦er
warm¦ish
warm¦ly
warm¦ness
war¦mon¦ger
warmth
warm-up *n. & mod.*
warn inform;
  admonish; cf. **worn**
Warne, Shane Aus-
  tralian cricketer
warn¦er
War¦ner Broth¦ers
warn¦ing¦ly
warp bend; pervert;
  haul; rope; threads
  in loom; sediment;
  cf. **whaup**
warp¦age
war¦paint
war¦path
warp¦er
war¦plane
war¦ra¦gal var. of
  warrigal
war¦rant
war¦rant¦able
war¦rant¦ably
war¦rant¦ee person;
  cf. **warranty**
war¦rant¦er person
  giving an
  assurance; cf.
  warrantor
war¦rant¦or *Law*
  person giving a
  warranty
war¦ranty
  war¦ran¦ties
  undertaking; cf.
  warrantee
War¦ren, Earl judge
**War¦ren, Rob¦ert
  Penn** writer
war¦ren
war¦ren¦er
war¦ri¦gal
War¦ring¦ton
war¦rior
War¦saw
war¦ship
wart growth
wart¦hog
war¦time

warty
wart¦ier
wart¦iest
War¦wick
War¦wick¦shire
wary
wari¦er
wari¦est
was
wa¦sabi
wash
wash¦abil¦ity
wash¦able
wash¦bag
wash¦basin
wash¦board
wash¦cloth
wash¦day
wash¦down
wash¦er
washer-drier var.
  of **washer-dryer**
washer-dryer
wash¦er¦man
wash¦er¦men
washer-up
washers-up
wash¦er¦woman
wash¦er¦women
wash¦ery
wash¦er¦ies
wash¦et¦eria
wash-hand basin
wash-hand stand
washi¦ness
Wash¦ing¦ton
**Wash¦ing¦ton,
  Booker T.** educa-
  tionist
**Wash¦ing¦ton,
  George** US
  president
Wash¦ing¦ton¦ian
washing-up *n. &
mod.*
wash¦land
wash¦out
wash¦rag
wash¦room
wash¦stand
wash¦tub
wash-up *n. & mod.*
washy
wash¦ier

washi|est

wasn't

Wasp = White Anglo-Saxon Protestant

wasp insect

waspie corset; cf. Waspy, waspy

Wasp|ish of a Wasp

wasp|ish spiteful

wasp|ish|ly

wasp|ish|ness

wasp-like

Waspy
  Wasp|ier
  Waspi|est
  of a Wasp; cf. waspie

waspy wasp-like; cf. waspie

was|sail

was|sail|er

Was|ser|mann

wast in 'thou wast'

wast|able

wast|age

waste
  wast|ing
  squander; cf. waist

waste|bas|ket

waste|ful

waste|ful|ly

waste|ful|ness

waste|gate

waste|land

waste|less

waster

wast|rel

wat Buddhist temple; cf. watt, what, wot

watch

watch|abil|ity

watch|able

watch|dog
  watch|dogged
  watch|dog|ging

watch|er

watch|fire

watch|ful

watch|ful|ly

watch|ful|ness

watch|keep|er

watch|maker

watch|mak|ing

watch|man
  watch|men

watch|night

watch|tower

watch|word

water

water|bed

water|bird

water|body
  water|bodies

water|borne

water|brash

water|buck

water|cock

water|color *US*

water|col|or|ist *US*

water|col|our *Br.*

water|col|our|ist *Br.*

water|course

water|craft

water|cress

water|dog

water|er

water|fall

Water|ford

water|fowl

water|front

Water|gate US political scandal

water|gate gate to river etc.

water|hen

water|hole

Water|house, Al|fred architect

wateri|ness

water|leaf
  water|leaves

water|less

water|line

water|logged

Water|loo

water|man
  water|men

water|mark

water|melon

water|mill

water|proof

water|proof|er

water|proof|ness

Waters, Muddy blues musician

water|scape

water|shed

water|side

water|ski +s +ed +ing

water|ski|er

water|spout

water|thrush

water|tight

water|way

water|weed

water|wheel

water witch

water-witcher

water-witching

water|works

watery

Wat|ford

Wat|ling Street

Wat|son, James biologist

Wat|son, John psychologist

Watson-Watt, Rob|ert physicist

Watsu *trademark*

Watt, James engineer

watt unit; cf. wat, what, wot

watt|age

Wat|teau, Jean painter

watt-hour

wat|tle
  wat|tling

wattle|bird

wattle-eye

watt|meter

Watts, George Fred|erick painter and sculptor

Watts, Isaac hymn writer

Wa|tusi people

Wa|tusi +s +ed +ing dance

Wa|tutsi var. of Watusi

Waugh, Eve|lyn novelist

Waugh, Steve cricketer

waul cry like cat; cf. wall, whorl

wave
  wav|ing
  gesture; on water; curve; cf. waive

wave|band

wave|form

wave|front

wave|guide

wave|length

wave|less

wave|let

wave-like

waver falter; cf. waiver

waver|er

waver|ing|ly

wav|ery

wave|table

wav|icle

wavi|ly

wavi|ness

wavy
  wavi|er
  wavi|est

wa-wa var. of wah-wah

wax|berry
  wax|berries

wax|bill

wax|cloth

waxen

waxer

wax|head

wax|ily

waxi|ness

wax-like

wax|pod

wax|wing

wax|work

waxy
  wax|ier
  waxi|est

way road etc.; method; cf. **Wei**, weigh, wey, whey

way|bill

way|bread

way|farer

way|far|ing

way in entrance; cf.
　weigh-in
Way|land mythical
　character
way|lay
way|lay|er
way|mark
way|mark|er
Wayne, John actor;
　cf. **Wain**
way out exit
way-out unconven-
　tional
way|point
way|side
way|ward
way|ward|ly
way|ward|ness
wayz|goose
waz var. of wazz
wazir
wazoo +s
wazz
waz|zock
we pl. of **I**; cf. **wee,**
　whee
weak feeble; cf.
　week
weak|en
weak|en|er
weak|fish
weak|ish
weak|ling
weak|ly feebly; cf.
　weekly
weak|ness
weal mark on skin;
　prosperity; in 'the
　common weal'; cf.
　weel, wheel
Weald
Weald|en
wealth
wealth|ily
wealthy
　wealth|ier
　wealthi|est
wean accustom to
　food; cf. ween,
　wheen
wean|er animal; cf.
　wiener
wean|ling
weapon

weapon|isa|tion Br.
　var. of
　weaponization
weapon|ise Br. var.
　of weaponize
weapon|iza|tion
weapon|ize
weapon|iz|ing
weapon|less
weap|on|ry
weap|on|ries
Wear river,
　England; cf. **weir**
wear
　wore
　worn
　have on (clothes
　etc.); cf. ware,
　weir, where
wear|abil|ity
wear|able
wear|er
weari|less
weari|ly
weari|ness
wear|ing|ly
weari|some
weari|some|ly
weari|some|ness
Wear|side
weary
　wear|ies
　wear|ied
　weary|ing
　weari|er
　weari|est
weary|ing|ly
weasel
　weas|elled Br.
　weas|eled US
　weasel|ling Br.
　weasel|ing US
weas|el|ly
wea|sel's snout
　plant
wea|ther atmos-
　pheric conditions;
　cf. wether,
　whether
weather|board
weather|bound
weather|cock
weather|fish
weather|girl
wea|ther|li|ness

wea|ther|ly
weather|man
　weather|men
weather|proof
weather|strip
　weather|stripped
　weather|strip|ping
weather|struck
weather|tight
weather|vane
weave
　wove (fabric)
　woven (fabric)
　weaved moved
　weav|ing
weaver person who
　weaves; bird; ant;
　cf. weever
web
　webbed
　web|bing
Webb, Bea|trice
　socialist
Webb, Mary
　novelist
Webb, Sid|ney
　socialist
webby
　web|bier
　web|bi|est
web|cam trademark
　in the US
web|cast
Weber, Carl Maria
　von composer
Weber, Max
　sociologist
Weber, Wil|helm
　physicist
weber unit
Web|ern, Anton
　composer
web-like
web|log
web|log|ger
web|master
web|site
web-spinner
Web|ster, John
　dramatist
Web|ster, Noah
　lexicographer
web|work
web|worm
web|zine

wed
　wed|ded or wed
　wed|ding
we'd = we had; we
　should; we would
Wed|dell Sea
Wed|dell seal
wed|ding
Wede|kind, Frank
　dramatist
wedge
　wedg|ing
wedge|bill
wedge-like
wedgie
Wedg|wood pottery
　(trademark); colour
wed|lock
Wed|nes|day
wee
　wees
　weed
　wee|ing
　urinate; cf. we,
　whee
wee
　weer
　weest
　tiny; cf. we, whee
wee|bill
weed
weed|er
weed|grown
weedi|cide
weedi|ness
weed|kill|er
weed|less
weedy
　weed|ier
　weedi|est
Wee Free
wee|juns trademark
　in the US
week seven days; cf.
　weak
week|day
week|end
week|end|er
week|ly
week|lies
　once a week; news-
　paper etc.; cf.
　weakly
weel Scot.
　well; cf. weal,

wheel

ween think; cf.
   wean, wheen

weenie sausage; var.
   of wienie

weeny
   ween|ier
   weeni|est
tiny; cf. wienie

weep|er

weepie film etc.;
   var. of weepy

weep|ily

weepi|ness

weep|ing|ly

weepy
   weep|ies
   weep|ier
   weepi|est

wee|ver fish; cf.
   weaver

wee|vil

wee|vily

wee-wee
   wee-wees
   wee-weed
   wee-weeing

We|ge|ner, Al|fred
geologist

Wei Chinese
   dynasties

wei ch'i

Weich|sel

Weich|sel|ian

wei|gela

weigh measure the
   weight of; cf. way,
   wey, whey

weigh|able

weigh|bridge

weigh|er

weigh-in n.
   weighing of boxer;
   cf. way in

weight heaviness
   etc.

weight|ily

weighti|ness

weight|less

weight|less|ly

weight|less|ness

weight|lift|er

weight|lift|ing

weight-watcher

Weight Watch|ers
   trademark

weight-watching

weighty
   weight|ier
   weighti|est

Weil, Sim|one
   philosopher

Weill, Kurt
   composer

Weil's dis|ease

Wei|mar

Wei|mar|aner

Wein|berg, Ste|ven
   theoretical physicist

weir

weird

weirdie

weird|ly

weird|ness

weirdo +s

weirdy var. of
   weirdie

wei|sen|hei|mer
   var. of
   wisenheimer

Weis|mann,
   Au|gust biologist

Weis|mann|ism

Weis|mann|ist

Weiss|mul|ler,
   Johnny swimmer
   and actor

weiss|wurst

Weiz|mann, Chaim
   president of Israel

weka bird

Wel|and var. of
   Wayland

Welch in 'Royal
   Welch Fusiliers'

welch default; var.
   of welsh

welch|er var. of
   welsher

wel|come

wel|com|ing

wel|come|ly

wel|come|ness

wel|com|er

wel|com|ing|ly

weld|abil|ity

weld|able

weld|er

weld|mesh
   trademark

wel|fare

wel|far|ism

wel|far|ist

wel|kin

Wel|kom town,
   South Africa

we'll = we shall; we
   will

Wel|land (Ship)
   Canal

well-being

Welles, Orson actor
   and director

Wel|les|ley, Ar|thur
   Duke of Wellington

well|head

well|ie var. of welly

Wel|ling|ton

wel|ling|ton boot

wel|ling|tonia

well|ness

well-nigh

Wells town,
   England

Wells, H. G.
   novelist

Wells, Fargo, &
   Co.

well|spring

well thought of

well-thought-of
   attrib.

well thought out

well-thought-out
   attrib.

well-to-do

well-wisher

well woman n. &
   mod.

welly
   wel|lies
   wel|lied
   welly|ing

wels fish
   pl. wels

Wels|bach, Carl
   Auer von chemist

Welsh of Wales; cf.
   Welch

welsh default

welsh|er

Welsh|man
   Welsh|men

Welsh|ness

Welsh|pool

Welsh|woman
   Welsh|women

Welt|an|schau|ung
Welt|an|schau|
      ung|en

wel|ter

wel|ter|weight

Welt|schmerz

Welty, Eu|dora
   writer

wel|witschia

Wem|bley

wen boil; runic
   letter; cf. when

Wen|ces|las, St
   'Good King
   Wenceslas'

Wen|ces|laus, St
   var. of Wenceslas

wench

wench|er

Wend people

wend go

wen|digo var. of
   windigo

Wend|ish

Wens|ley|dale

wentle|trap

were in 'we were'
   etc.; cf. weir, whirr

we're

weren't

were|wolf
   were|wolves

Wer|ner, Abra|ham
   Gott|lob geologist

Wer|ner, Al|fred
   chemist

Wer|ner's
   syn|drome
   cf. Verner's Law

Wer|nicke's area
   etc.

wert in 'thou wert';
   cf. wort

Wesak var. of Vesak

Weser

Wes|ker, Ar|nold
   playwright

Wes¦ley, John
 founder of
 Methodism
Wes¦ley¦an
Wes¦ley¦an¦ism
Wes¦sex
West, Ben¦ja¦min
 painter
West, Mae actress
West, Re¦becca
 writer
west¦bound
West Brom¦wich
west¦er¦ing
west¦er¦ly
 west¦er¦lies
west¦ern
West¦ern blot
west¦ern¦er
west¦ern¦isa¦tion
 Br. var. of
 westernization
west¦ern¦ise Br. var.
 of westernize
west¦ern¦iser Br.
 var. of westernizer
west¦ern¦iza¦tion
west¦ern¦ize
west¦ern¦iz¦ing
west¦ern¦izer
west¦ern¦most
Westie
west¦ing
West Irian
West¦mann
 Is¦lands
West¦meath
West¦min¦ster
West¦mor¦land
west-north-west
Weston-super-
      Mare
West¦pha¦lia
West¦pha¦lian
west-south-west
west¦ward
west¦ward¦ly
west¦wards
wet
 wet or wet¦ted
 wet¦ting
 wet¦ter
 wet¦test

moist; moisten; cf.
 whet
weta insect
wet¦back
wether sheep; cf.
 weather, whether
wet¦land
wetly
wet¦ness
wet¦suit
wet¦table
wet¦tish
wet¦ware
we've
Wex¦ford
wey unit; cf. way,
 weigh, whey
Wey¦den, Ro¦gier
 van der painter
Wey¦mouth
whack strike; cf.
 wack, wacke
whack¦er
whack¦ily var. of
 wackily
whacki¦ness var. of
 wackiness
whack¦ing
whacko exclam.; cf.
 wacko
whacky var. of
 wacky
 whack¦ier
 whacki¦est
whale
 whal¦ing
 sea mammal; cf.
 wail, wale
whale¦back
whale¦bird
whale¦boat
whale¦bone
whaler ship; person
 who hunts whales;
 shark; cf. wailer
wham
 whammed
 wham¦ming
wham-bam
whammo
whammy
 wham¦mies
whang
Whan¦ga¦rei

whang¦er
whap var. of whop
whare Maori house
wharf
 wharves or wharfs
wharf¦age
wharfie
wharf¦in¦ger
Whar¦ton, Edith
 writer
wharves
what which thing;
 cf. wat, watt, wot
what¦cha¦ma¦call¦it
what-d'you-call-it
what¦e'er =
 whatever
what¦ever
what¦not
what's-her-name
what's-his-name
whats¦it
what's-its-name
what¦so¦e'er =
 whatsoever
what¦so¦ever
whaup bird; cf.
 warp
wheal var. of weal
wheat
wheat¦ear bird
wheat¦en
wheat¦germ
wheat¦grass
wheat¦meal
wheat¦sheaf
 wheat¦sheaves
Wheat¦stone
 bridge
whee exclam.; cf.
 we, wee
wheech
whee¦dle
 wheed¦ling
wheed¦ler
wheed¦ling¦ly
wheel cf. weal, weel
wheel¦back
wheel¦bar¦row
wheel¦base
wheel¦chair
wheel¦er
wheeler-dealer

wheeler-dealing
wheel¦house
wheelie
wheelie bin
wheel¦less
wheel¦man
 wheel¦men
wheels¦man
 wheels¦men
wheel¦spin
wheel¦wright
wheely bin var. of
 wheelie bin
wheeze
 wheez¦ing
wheez¦er
wheez¦ily
wheezi¦ness
wheez¦ing¦ly
wheezy
 wheez¦ier
 wheezi¦est
whelk
whelm
whelp
when cf. wen
whence
whence¦so¦ever
when¦e'er =
 whenever
when¦ever
when-issued
when¦so¦e'er =
 whensoever
when¦so¦ever
where what place
 etc.; cf. ware, wear,
 weir
where¦abouts
where¦after
where¦as
where¦at
where¦by
wher¦e'er =
 wherever
where¦fore
where¦from
where¦in
where¦of
where¦on

where|so|e'er =
  wheresoever
where|so|ever
where|to
where|upon
wher|ever
where|with
where|withal
wherry
  wher|ries
wherry|man
  wherry|men
whet
  whet|ted
  whet|ting
  sharpen; stimulate;
  cf. wet
whether *conj.*; cf.
  weather, wether
whet|stone
whet|ter
whew
whey part of milk;
  cf. way, weigh, wey
whey-faced
which *pron.*; cf.
  witch, wych
which|away
which|ever
which|so|ever
whicker noise of
  horse; cf. **Wicca**,
  wicker
whiff
whif|fle
  whif|fling
whiffle|tree
whiffy
  whiff|ier
  whiff|fi|est
Whig *Politics*
Whig|gery
Whig|gish
Whig|gism
while
  whil|ing
  period; during;
  pass time; cf. wile
whi|lom
whilst
whim
whim|brel
whim|per
whim|per|er

whim|per|ing|ly
whim|sey var. of
  whimsy
whim|si|cal
whim|si|cal|ity
whim|si|cal|ities
whim|si|cal|ly
whimsy
  whim|sies
whim-wham
whin gorse; rock; cf.
  win, wyn
whin|chat
whine
  whin|ing
  sound; complain;
  cf. wine
whiner
whinge
  whinge|ing or
  whin|ging
whinge|ing|ly
whin|ger
whingy
  whin|gier
  whin|gi|est
whin|ing|ly
whinny
  whin|nies
  whin|nied
  whinny|ing
whin|stone
whiny
  whin|ier
  whini|est
  whining; cf. winey
whip
  whipped
  whip|ping
whip|bird
whip|cord
whip|lash
whip|less
whip-like
whip|per
whipper-in
  whippers-in
whip|per|snap|per
whip|pet
whip|pi|ness
whipple|tree
whip|poor|will
whippy
  whip|pier
  whip|pi|est

whip-round *n.*
whip|saw
  whip|sawn or
  whip|sawed
whip|stitch
whip|stock
whip|tail
whip|worm
whir var. of whirr;
  cf. were
whirl swing round;
  cf. whorl
whirl|er
whirli|gig
whirl|ing|ly
whirl|pool
whirl|wind
whirly|bird
whirr sound; cf.
  were
whisht
whisk
whis|ker
whis|kery
whis|key Irish and
  American
whisky
  whis|kies
  Scotch and
  Canadian
whisky jack bird
whisky mac
whis|per
whis|per|er
whis|pery
whist game; hush;
  cf. wist
whis|tle
  whist|ling
**Whist|ler, James
  Mc|Neill** painter
whist|ler
Whist|ler|ian
whistle-stop
Whit Whitsuntide;
  cf. wit
whit very small
  amount; cf. wit
Whitby
White, Gil|bert
  naturalist
White, Pat|rick
  novelist

white
  whit|ing
  whiter
  whit|est
  cf. wight
white|bait
white|beam
white|board
white|cap bird
white|coat infant
  harp seal
white cur|rant
white-eye bird
white|face make-
  up; cow; bird
white|fish fresh-
  water fish of sal-
  mon family
white fish plaice,
  cod, etc.
white|fly
  white|flies
white|front goose
white-fronted
White|hall
**White|head,
  Al|fred North**
  philosopher and
  mathematician
white|head pimple;
  bird
White|horse city,
  Canada
white|ly
whiten
whit|en|er
white|ness
white-out *n.*
white|smith
white|tail deer
white-tailed
White, T. H.
  novelist
white|thorn
white|throat
white|wall
white|wash
white|wash|er
white|wood pale
  timber
white|work
  embroidery
whitey whitish;
  offensive white

person
whither to where;
  cf. **wither**
whith¦er¦so¦ever
whit¦ing fish
  pl. **whit¦ing**
whit¦ing +s sub-
  stance
whit¦ish
Whit¦lam, Gough
  prime minister of
  Australia
whit¦leather
Whit¦ley Coun¦cil
whit¦low
whitlow-grass
Whit¦man, Walt
  poet
Whit¦ney, Mt
Whit¦sun
Whit Sun¦day *Br.*
Whit¦sun¦day *US*
Whit¦sun¦day
  Is¦lands
Whit¦sun¦tide
Whit¦tier, John
  Green¦leaf poet
Whit¦ting¦ton,
  Dick Lord Mayor
  of London
Whit¦tle, Frank
  aeronautical
  engineer
whit¦tle
  whit¦tling
Whit¦worth
whity
  whit¦ies
  var. of **whitey**
whiz var. of **whizz**
whiz-bang
whiz-kid var. of
  whizz-kid
whizz
whizz-bang var. of
  whiz-bang
whizz-kid
whizzo
whizzy
  whiz¦zier
  whiz¦zi¦est
who
whoa stop; cf. **woe**

who'd = who had;
  who would
who¦dunit *US*
who¦dun¦nit *Br.*
who¦e'er = whoever
who¦ever
whole entire;
  entirety; cf. **hole**
whole¦food
whole¦grain
whole¦heart¦ed
whole¦heart¦ed¦ly
whole¦heart¦ed¦
  ness
whole¦meal
whole¦ness
whole¦sale
  whole¦sal¦ing
whole¦saler
whole¦scale
whole¦some
whole¦some¦ly
whole¦some¦ness
whole¦wheat
whol¦ism var. of
  holism
whol¦is¦tic var. of
  holistic
whol¦ly fully; cf.
  holey, Holi, holy
whom
whom¦ever
whomp
whom¦so
whom¦so¦ever
whoomp
whoomph
whoop shout; cf.
  hoop
whoo¦pee
whoop¦er swan; cf.
  hooper
whoop¦ing cough
whoop¦ing crane
whoops
whoops-a-daisy
whoop¦sie
whoosh
whop
  whopped
  whop¦ping
  hit; cf. **wop**
whop¦per

whore
  whor¦ing
  prostitute; cf.
  haugh, haw, hoar
who're = who are
whore¦dom
whore¦house
whore¦master
whore¦monger
whorer
whore¦son
Whorf, Ben¦ja¦min
  linguist
whor¦ish
whor¦ish¦ly
whor¦ish¦ness
whorl ring; cf. **wall,**
  waul, whirl
whortle¦berry
  whortle¦berries
who's = who is
whose of or
  belonging to whom
  or which
whose¦so
whose¦so¦ever
whoso
who¦so¦ever
who's who +s
who've
wh-question
whump
whup
  whupped
  whup¦ping
wh-word
why +s cf. **wye**
Why¦alla
whyda var. of
  whydah
why¦dah bird; cf.
  wider
Whym¦per,
  Ed¦ward mountain-
  eer
wib¦ble
  wib¦bling
wib¦bly
Wicca cult; cf.
  wicker. whicker
Wic¦can
Wich¦ita
wick
wicked

wick¦ed¦ly
wicked¦ness
wicker basket
  material; cf. **Wicca,**
  whicker
wicker¦work
wicket
wicket¦keep¦er
wicket¦keep¦ing
wicki¦up
Wick¦low
wid¦der¦shins
wid¦dle
  wid¦dling
wide
  wider
  wid¦est
wide¦awake hat
wide awake fully
  awake
wide-bodied
wide¦body
  wide¦bodies
wide¦ly
widen
widen¦er
wide¦ness
wide¦out
wide¦screen
wide¦spread
widg¦eon var. of
  wigeon
widger
widget
wid¦ish
Wid¦nes
widow
widow¦bird
wid¦ow¦er
widow¦hood
widow's weeds
width
width¦ways
width¦wise
wield
wield¦er
wieldy
  wield¦ier
  wieldi¦est
Wie¦ner, Nor¦bert
  mathematician
wie¦ner sausage; cf.
  weaner

Wie|ner schnit|zel
wie|nie sausage; cf.
  weeny
Wies|baden
Wie|sel, Elie
  authority on the
  Holocaust
Wie|sen|thal,
  Simon Nazi war
  crime investigator
wife
  wives
wife|hood
wife|less
wife-like
wife|li|ness
wife|ly
wifey wife
Wif|fle ball
  trademark
wifie Scot. woman
wig
  wigged
  wig|ging cf. Whig
Wigan
wi|geon
wig|ger
wig|gle
  wig|gling
wig|gler
wig|gly
  wig|glier
  wig|gli|est
wiggy
  wig|gier
  wig|gi|est
Wight, Isle of
wight archaic
  person; cf. white
Wight|man Cup
wig|less
Wig|town|shire
wig|wag
  wig|wagged
  wig|wag|ging
wig|wam
Wil|ber|force,
  Wil|liam social
  reformer
Wil|bur
wilco
Wil|cox, Ella
  Whee|ler writer
Wil|coxon test

wild
wild|cat
  wild|cat|ted
  wild|cat|ting
wild|cat|ter
wild|craft
Wilde, Oscar writer
wilde|beest
Wil|der, Billy film
  director
Wil|der, Thorn|ton
  writer
wil|der
wil|der|ness
wild|fire
wild|fowl
wild goose chase
wild|ing
wild|ish
wild|life
wild|ling plant; var.
  of wilding
wild|ly
wild|ness
wild|wood
wile
  wil|ing
  trick; cf. while
Wil|fred
Wil|frid
wil|ful Br.
  US willful
wil|ful|ly Br.
  US willfully
wil|ful|ness Br.
  US willfulness
wilga
Wil|helm emperors
  of Germany
Wil|hel|mina
Wil|helms|haven
wili|ly
wili|ness
Wilkes Land
Wil|kie, David
  painter
Wil|kins, Maur|ice
  biochemist
will wish; impel;
  bequeath; cf. we'll
Willa name
Wil|lard, Emma
  educational
  reformer

willem|ite
Wil|lem|stad
will|er
wil|let
will|ful US
  Br. wilful
will|ful|ly US
  Br. wilfully
will|ful|ness US
  Br. wilfulness
Wil|liam
Wil|liam of Occam
  philosopher
Wil|liam of
  Ockham var. of
  William of Occam
Wil|liam Rufus
  William II of
  England
Wil|liams pear
Wil|liams, Hank
  singer and
  songwriter
Wil|liams, John
  guitarist
Wil|liams, J. P. R.
  rugby union player
Wil|liams, Robin
  actor
Wil|liams, Rowan
  Archbishop of
  Canterbury
Wil|liams, Ser|ena
  tennis player
Wil|liams,
  Ten|nes|see
  dramatist
Wil|liams, Venus
  tennis player
Wil|liams, Wil|liam
  Car|los writer
Wil|liams|burg
Wil|liam|son,
  Henry novelist
wil|lie var. of willy
wil|lies
wil|lie wag|tail
will|ing
will|ing|ly
will|ing|ness
willi|waw
will-o'-the-wisp
wil|low
willow|herb

willow|ware
will|lowy
willow|ier
wil|lowi|est
will|power
Wills, Wil|liam
  explorer
willy
  wil|lies
willy-nilly
willy wag|tail var.
  of willie wagtail
willy-willy
  willy-willies
Wilms' tumor US
Wilms' tu|mour
  Br.
Wil|son, Angus
  writer
Wil|son, Ed|mund
  writer
Wil|son, Har|old
  prime minister of
  Britain
Wil|son, Wood|row
  US president
wilt
Wil|ton
Wilts. = Wiltshire
Wilt|shire
wily
  wili|er
  wili|est
Wim|ble|don
wim|min = women
wimp
wimp|ish
wimp|ish|ly
wimp|ish|ness
wim|ple
  wimp|ling
wimpy
  wimp|ier
  wimpi|est
  feeble
Wims|hurst
win
  won
  win|ning
  cf. whin, wyn
wince
  win|cing
win|cer
win|cey
win|cey|ette

winch
winch¦er
Win¦ches¦ter disk;
  drive; *trademark*
  rifle
win¦ches¦ter bottle
win¦cing¦ly
Winck¦el¦mann,
  Jo¦hann archaeolo-
  gist
wind moving air;
  etc.
  wind¦ed made it
  hard for someone
  to breathe
  wind¦ed or wound
  blew (horn)
wind
  wound coiled;
  cf. wynd
wind¦age
wind¦bag
wind¦bag¦gery
wind¦bound
wind¦break
wind¦break¦er
  trademark in the
  US
wind¦burn
  wind¦burned
  Br. also wind¦burnt
wind¦cheat¦er
wind¦chest
wind-down *n.*
wind¦er
Win¦der¦mere
wind¦fall
wind¦flower
wind¦gall
Wind¦hoek
wind¦hover
Win¦dies West
  Indians
win¦digo
  win¦di¦gos or
  win¦di¦goes
wind¦ily
windi¦ness
wind¦jam¦mer
wind¦lass machine
wind¦less without
  wind
wind¦mill
win¦dow

win¦dow¦less
window¦pane
window-shop
  window-shopped
  window-shopping
window-shopper
window¦sill
wind¦pipe
wind¦proof
wind¦row
wind¦sail
Wind¦scale
wind¦screen
wind¦shield
wind¦slab
wind¦sock
Wind¦sor
wind¦storm
wind¦surf
wind¦surf¦er
  trademark in the
  US for sailboard
wind¦swept
wind-up *adj. & n.*
  clock; conclusion;
  provocation
wind¦ward
windy
  wind¦ier
  windi¦est
wine
  win¦ing
  drink; cf. whine
wine¦berry
  wine¦berries
wine¦bib¦ber
wine¦bib¦bing
wine glass
wine¦glass¦ful
wine¦grow¦er
wine-growing
wine¦maker
wine¦mak¦ing
win¦ery
  win¦eries
Wine¦sap
wine¦skin
winey
  wini¦er
  wini¦est
  like wine; cf. whiny
Win¦frey, Oprah
  chat-show host
wing¦beat

wing chun
Wing¦co +s = Wing
  Commander
wing¦ding
wing¦er
wing¦less
wing¦let
wing¦like
wing¦man
  wing¦men
wing¦over
wing¦span
wing¦spread
wing¦stroke
wing tip tip of wing
wing¦tip shoe
Wini¦fred
wink¦er
win¦kle
  wink¦ling
winkle-picker
wink¦ler
win¦less
win¦nable
Winne¦bago
  pl. Winne¦bago or
  Winne¦bagos
  people; *trademark*
  for camper
win¦ner
Win¦nie
win¦ning¦ly
Win¦ni¦peg
win¦now
win¦now¦er
wino +s
Win¦ona
win¦some
win¦some¦ly
win¦some¦ness
Win¦ston
win¦ter
winter¦berry
  winter¦berries
winter¦bourne
win¦ter¦er
winter¦green plant
  yielding oil; plant
  with spikes of white
  flowers
win¦ter greens
  green vegetables
  available in winter

Win¦ter¦hal¦ter,
  Franz painter
win¦ter¦isa¦tion *Br.*
  var. of
  winterization
win¦ter¦ise *Br.* var.
  of winterize
win¦ter¦iza¦tion
win¦ter¦ize
  win¦ter¦iz¦ing
win¦ter¦less
win¦ter¦ly
winter¦sweet
Win¦ter¦thur
winter¦tide
winter¦time
winter-weight *adj.*
win¦tery var. of
  wintry
win¦trily
win¦tri¦ness
win¦try
  win¦trier
  win¦tri¦est
win-win
winy like wine; var.
  of winey; cf. whiny
wipe
  wip¦ing
wipe¦able
wipe¦out
wiper
wire
  wir¦ing
wire-draw
  wire-drew
  wire-drawing
  wire-drawn
wire-drawer
wire¦frame
wire¦less
wire¦line
wire¦man
  wire¦men
wire¦pull¦er
wire¦pull¦ing
wirer
wire¦tap
  wire¦tapped
  wire¦tap¦ping
wire¦tap¦per
wire-walker
wire¦worm
wir¦ily

wiri|ness

Wir|ral

Wirt|schafts|
    wun|der

Wirts|haus
Wirts|häuser

wiry
  wiri|er
  wiri|est

Wis|con|sin

Wis|con|sin|ite

Wis|den in 'Wisden
  Cricketers'
  Almanack'

wis|dom

wise
  wis|ing
  wiser
  wis|est

wise|acre

wise|crack

wise|crack|er

wise|ly

wisen|hei|mer

wis|ent

wish cf. whisht

wish|bone

wish|er

wish|ful

wish-fulfill|ment
  US

wish-fulfil|ment *Br.*

wish|ful|ly

wish-wash

wishy-washy

wisp|ily

wispi|ness

wispy
  wisp|ier
  wispi|est

wist *archaic* knew;
  cf. whist

wis|taria var. of
  wisteria

Wis|tar rat

wis|teria

wist|ful

wist|ful|ly

wist|ful|ness

wit intelligence;
  humour; person; in
  'to wit'; cf. whit,
  Whit

witan

witch sorceress;
  charm; lure; cf.
  which

witch alder

witch|craft

witch elm var. of
  wych elm

witch|ery

witches' broom

witches' but|ter

witches' sab|bath

witch|etty
  witch|et|ties

witch grass

witch hazel

witch-hunt

witch-hunter

witch|like

witch|weed

witchy
  witch|ier
  witchi|est

wit|ena|gemot

with cf. withe

withal

with|draw
  with|drew
  with|drawn

with|draw|al

withe willow shoot;
  cf. with

wither shrivel; cf.
  whither

wither|ing|ly

wither|ite

with|ers on horse

wither|shins var. of
  widdershins

with|hold
  with|held

with|hold|er

with|in

with it *adj. & adv.*

with-it *attrib.*

with|out

with|stand
  with|stood

with|stand|er

withy
  with|ies

wit|less

wit|less|ly

wit|less|ness

wit|ling *archaic* per-
  son who considers
  themselves witty;
  cf. whittling

wit|loof

wit|ness

wit|ted

Wit|ten|berg

wit|ter

Witt|gen|stein,
  Lud|wig
  philosopher

Witt|gen|stein|ian

witti|cism

wit|tily

witti|ness

wit|ting

wit|ting|ly

wit|tol

witty
  wit|tier
  witti|est

Wit|waters|rand

wives

wiz person
  wizzes
  var. of whizz

wiz|ard

wiz|ard|ly

wiz|ard|ry
  wiz|ard|ries

wiz|ened

wizzo var. of whizzo

wo stop; var. of
  whoa; cf. woe

woad

wobbe|gon var. of
  wobbegong

wobbe|gong

wob|ble
  wob|bling

wobble|board

wob|bler

Wob|blies

wob|bli|ness

wob|bly
  wob|blies
  wob|blier
  wob|bli|est

Wode|house, P. G.
  novelist

Woden
  Scandinavian
  Mythology

wodge

woe grief; cf. whoa

woe|be|gone

woe|ful

woe|ful|ly

woe|ful|ness

wog|gle

wok

woke

woken

Wo|king

wold

Wolf, Hugo
  composer

wolf
  pl. wolves
  v. wolfs
  wolfed
  wolf|ing

Wolfe, James
  general

Wolfe, Thomas
  novelist, d.1938

Wolfe, Tom writer,
  b. 1931

Wolf|en|den
  Re|port

wolf|hound

wolf|ish

wolf|ish|ly

wolf-like

wolf|ram

wolf|ram|ite

wolfs|bane

Wolfs|burg

wolf|skin

Wolf|son, Isaac
  philanthropist

wol|las|ton|ite

Wol|lon|gong

Woll|stone|craft,
  Mary writer

Wolof

Wol|sey, Thomas
  cardinal

Wol|ston|ian

Wol|ver|hamp|ton

wol|ver|ine

wolves

woma

woman
  women

woman|hood

woman|ise *Br.* var.
of **womanize**

woman|iser *Br.* var.
of **womanizer**

woman|ish

woman|ism

woman|ist

woman|ize
   woman|iz|ing

woman|izer

woman|kind

woman|less

woman|like

woman|li|ness

woman|ly

womb

wom|bat

womb-like

women pl. of
   woman

women|folk

women|kind var. of
   womankind

womens|wear

womyn

won
   pl. won
   N. or S. Korean
   currency; cf. **wan**

won past tense and
   past participle of
   win; cf. **one**

Won|der, Ste|vie
   musician

won|der feeling of
   amazement, feel
   curiosity, etc.; cf.
   wander

won|der|er
   cf. **wanderer**

won|der|ful

won|der|ful|ly

won|der|ful|ness

won|der|ing|ly

won|der|land

won|der|ment

wonder-of-the-
         world

wonder-of-the-
         worlds
   plant

wonder|struck

won|drous

won|drous|ly

won|drous|ness

wonga

wonk

wonk|ily

wonki|ness

wonky
   wonk|ier
   wonki|est

wont accustom(ed);
   habit

won't = will not

won|ton dumpling;
   cf. **wanton**

woo +s +ed +ing

woo|able

Wood, Henry con-
   ductor

Wood, Mrs Henry
   novelist

Wood, Nat|alie
   actress

wood timber; forest;
   cf. **would**

wood|bine

wood|block

wood|carv|er

wood|carv|ing

wood|chat

wood|chip

wood|chuck

wood|cock
   pl. wood|cock

wood|craft

wood|cut

wood|cut|ter

wood|cut|ting

wood|ed

wood|en

wooden-head

wooden-headed

wooden-
         headed|ness

wood|en|ly

wood|en|ness

wooden|top

wood|grain

wood-hoopoe

woodi|ness

wood|land

wood|land|er

wood|lark

wood|less

wood|louse

wood|lice

wood|man
   wood|men

wood|note

wood|peck|er

wood|pile

wood|rat American
   rat-like rodent

wood rat S Asian
   forest rat

wood|ruff

Wood|ruff key

wood|rush

Woods, Tiger golfer

wood|screw

wood|shed

wood|shed|ded

wood|shed|ding

woodsia

woods|man
   woods|men

wood|smoke

wood|star

Wood|stock

wood|swal|low

woodsy
   woods|ier
   woodsi|est

wood|turn|er

wood|turn|ing

wood|wasp

wood|wind

wood woolly foot
   +s

wood|work

wood|work|er

wood|work|ing

wood|worm

woody
   wood|ier
   woodi|est

wood|yard

wooer

woof bark; weft

woof|er

woof|ter *offensive*

wool

wool|en *US*
   Br. woollen

Woolf, Vir|ginia
   writer

wool-gather

wool-gather|ing

wool|len *Br.*
   US woolen

Wool|ley, Leon|ard
   archaeologist

wool-like

wool|li|ness

woolly
   wool|lies
   wool|lier
   wool|li|est

woolly-bear
   caterpillar

woolly|butt

woolly foot +s

wool|man
   wool|men

Wool|mark

wool|pack

Wool|sack in House
   of Lords

wool|shed

wool-sorters'
   dis|ease

wool-stapler

Wool|worth, Frank
   Win|field business-
   man

Woo|mera nuclear
   testing site

woo|mera stick

woomph

woo|nerf
   woo|nerven or
   woo|nerfs

woo|pie

Woop Woop
   Austral.
   remote area; cf.
   wop wops

woopy var. of
   woopie

woosh var. of
   whoosh

wooz|ily

woozi|ness

woozy
   wooz|ier
   woozi|est

wop *offensive*
   Italian; cf. **whop**

wop wops *NZ*
   remote area; cf.
   Woop Woop

Wor|ces|ter

Wor|ces|ter|shire

word
word|age
word blind|ness
word|book
word|ily
wordi|ness
word|ing
word|less
word|less|ly
word|less|ness
word-perfect
word|play
word-process v.
word pro|cess|ing
n.
word pro|ces|sor
word|search
word|smith
Words|worth,
Doro|thy diarist
Words|worth,
Wil|liam poet
Words|worth|ian
word wrap
wordy
word|ier
wordi|est
wore past tense of
wear; cf. war
work
wrought archaic
work|abil|ity
work|able
work|ably
work|aday
work|ahol|ic
work|ahol|ism
work|around
work|bench
work|boat
work|book
work|box
work|day
work|er
work|fare
work|flow
work|force
work-harden
work|horse
work|house
work-in n.
Work|ing|ton
work|less
work|load

work|man
work|men
work|man|like
work|man|ship
work|mate
work|out
work|people
work|piece
work|place
work|room
work|sheet
work|shop
work|shopped
work|shop|ping
work-shy
work|site
work|space
work|sta|tion
work|top
work-to-rule
work|up
work|wear
work|week
world
worlde in 'olde
worlde'
world|li|ness
world|ling
world|ly
world|lier
world|li|est
worldly-wise
world-weariness
world-weary
world|wide
World Wide Fund
for Nature
World Wide Web
WORM Computing
= write-once read-
many
worm
worm|er
worm|ery
worm|eries
worm|fish
worm-fishing
worm|hole
wormi|ness
worm-like
Worms town, Ger-
many; Diet of W.
worm|seed
worm's-eye view

worm|wheel
worm|wood
wormy
worm|ier
wormi|est
worn past participle
of wear; cf. warn
wor|ried|ly
wor|rier
worri|ment
wor|ri|some
wor|ri|some|ly
wor|rit
worry
wor|ries
wor|ried
worry|ing
worry|guts
pl. worry|guts
worry|ing|ly
worry|wart
worse
worsen
wor|ship
wor|shipped Br.
wor|shiped US
wor|ship|ping Br.
wor|ship|ing US
wor|ship|er US
Br. worshipper
wor|ship|ful
wor|ship|ful|ly
wor|ship|ful|ness
wor|ship|per Br.
US worshiper
worst most bad; get
the better of; cf.
wurst
worst|ed fabric
wort Brewing;
plant; cf. wart
Worth, Charles
couturier
worth
wor|thily
worthi|ness
Wor|thing
worth|less
worth|less|ly
worth|less|ness
worth|while
worth|while|ness
worthy
wor|thies
wor|thier

wor|thi|est
wot archaic know,
e.g. in 'God wot'; cf.
watt, what
Wotan
Scandinavian
Mythology
wotcha greeting;
also = what are
you; what have
you; what do you
wotch|er greeting;
var. of wotcha
would aux. v.; cf.
wood
would-be +s
wouldn't
wouldst
Woulfe bot|tle
wound
wound|ing|ly
wound|less
wound|wort
wove
woven
wowee
wow|ser
woy|lie
WRAC = Women's
Royal Army Corps
wrack seaweed;
cloud; a wreck; cf.
rack
WRAF = Women's
Royal Air Force
wraith
wraith|like
Wran|gel Is|land
wran|gle
wran|gling
wran|gler
wrap
wrapped
wrap|ping
envelop; cf. rap,
rapt
wrap|around
Computing
wrap-around adj.
& n., generally
wrap-over adj. & n.
wrap|per
wrap-up n. & mod.
wrasse

Wrath, Cape
wrath anger; cf.
  woth
wrath|ful
wrath|ful|ly
wrath|ful|ness
wrathy
wreak inflict; cf.
  reek
wreak|er
wreath +s n.
wreathe v.
  wreathes
  wreathed
  wreath|ing
wreck destroy; ruin
  etc.; cf. rec, reck
wreck|age
wreck|er
wreck|fish
Wren,
  Chris|to|pher
  architect
Wren, P. C. novelist
Wren member of
  Women's Royal
  Naval Service
wren bird
wrench
wren|tit
wrest wrench away;
  cf. rest
wres|tle
  wrest|ling
wrest|ler
wretch wretched
  person; cf. retch
wretch|ed
wretch|ed|ly
wretch|ed|ness
Wrex|ham
wrick v. strain var.
  of rick
wrig|gle
  wrig|gling
wrig|gler
wrig|gly
  wrig|glier
  wrig|gli|est
Wright, Frank
  Lloyd architect
Wright, Or|ville
  and Wil|bur
  aviation pioneers
wright maker or
  builder; cf. right,

rite, write
wring
  wrung
  squeeze tightly
wring|er
wrin|kle
  wrink|ling
wrin|klie n. var. of
  wrinkly
wrin|kli|ness
wrin|kly
  wrink|lies
  wrink|lier
  wrink|li|est
wrist
wrist|band
wrist-drop
wrist|let
wrist|watch
wrist|work
wristy
  wrist|ier
  wristi|est
writ written com-
  mand; archaic past
  participle of write;
  cf. rit.
writ|able
write
  wrote
  writ|ten
  writ|ing
  put words on
  paper; cf. right,
  rite, wright
write|able var. of
  writable
write-back n.
write-down n.
write-in n.
write-off n.
write-once adj.
write-protect v.
writer
writer|ly
writer's block
writer's cramp
write-up n.
writhe
  writh|ing
writhen
writ|ten
WRNS = Women's
  Royal Naval Service
Wroc|ław

wrong
wrong|doer
wrong|doing
wrong|er
wrong-foot v.
wrong|ful
wrong|ful|ly
wrong|ful|ness
wrong|ly
wrong|ness
wrong'un
wrot wrought
  timber; cf. rot
wrote past tense of
  write; cf. rote
wroth angry; cf.
  wrath
wrought worked; cf.
  rort
wrung past tense
  and past participle
  of wring; cf. rung
wry
  wryer or wrier
  wry|est or wri|est
  contorted;
  mocking; cf. rai,
  rye
wry|bill
wryly
wry|mouth fish
wry|neck
wry|ness
wrythen var. of
  writhen
Wu Chinese dialect
wul|fen|ite
Wul|fila var. of
  Ulfilas
wun|der|kind
wun|der|kinds or
  wun|der|kinder
Wundt, Wil|helm
  psychologist
Wup|per|tal
Wur|litz|er
  trademark
Würm Geology
wurst sausage; cf.
  worst
wurtz|ite
Würz|burg
wushu
wuss

wussy
wus|sies
wuz non-standard
  spelling of was
Wy|an|dot person;
  language
Wy|an|dotte
  chicken
Wyatt, James
  architect
Wyatt, Thomas
  poet
wych elm
Wych|er|ley,
  Wil|liam dramatist
wych hazel var. of
  witch hazel
Wyc|lif, John reli-
  gious reformer
Wyc|liffe, John var.
  of Wyclif
Wye river
wye railway track;
  pipe; cf. why
Wyke|ham|ist
wyn runic letter; var.
  of wen; cf. win,
  whin
wynd narrow street;
  cf. wind
Wynd|ham, John
  science fiction
  writer
Wyn|ette, Tammy
  country singer
Wyo|ming
Wyo|ming|ite
WYSIWYG = what
  you see is what you
  get
Wys|tan
wy|vern

X

X-acto knife
  trademark
Xan|adu
Xanax trademark
Xan|kändi
xan|than

xan|thate
Xan|the
xan|thene yellowish compound present in dyes; cf. xanthine
Xan|thian
xan|thic
xan|thin var. of xanthine
xan|thine compound in blood and urine; cf. xanthene
Xan|thippe wife of Socrates
xan|thoma
xan|tho|mas or xan|tho|mata
xan|tho|phyll
Xan|tippe var. of Xanthippe
Xav|ier, St Fran|cis missionary
x-axis
x-axes
xebec
Xen|akis, Ian|nis composer
Xen|ar|thra
xen|ar|thran
Xen|ic|al *trademark*
xeno|biot|ic
xeno|cryst
xeno|crys|tic
xen|og|am|ous
xen|og|amy
xeno|gen|eic
xeno|graft
xeno|lith
xeno|lith|ic
xen|olo|gist
xen|ol|ogy
xenon
Xen|oph|anes philosopher
xeno|phobe
xeno|pho|bia
xeno|pho|bic
Xeno|phon historian
Xen|opus
xeno|time
xeno|trans|plant
xeno|trans|plant|ation

xeric
xeri|scape
xeri|scap|ing
xero|derma
xero|derma pig|ment|osum
xero|graph
xero|graph|ic
xero|graph|ic|al|ly
xer|og|raphy
xero|phile
xer|oph|il|ous
xero|phthal|mia
xero|phyte
xero|phyt|ic
Xerox *n. trademark*
xerox *v.*
Xer|xes king of Persia
x-height
Xhosa
pl. Xhosa or Xho|sas
xi Greek letter
Xia|men
Xian
Xiang
Xi|me|nes de Cis|neros var. of Jiménez de Cisneros
Xing|tai
Xingú
Xi|ning
Xin|jiang
xiphi|ster|num
xiph|oid
X-irradi|ation
Xmas
xoa|non
xoana
X-rated
X-ray
xu
pl. xu Vietnamese currency
Xu|zhou
xylem
xy|lene
xyli|tol
xyl|opha|gous
xylo|phone
xylo|phon|ic

xyl|oph|on|ist
xy|lose
xys|tus
xysti

Y

yab|ber
yab|bie var. of yabby
yabby
yab|bies
yacht
yachtie
yachts|man
yachts|men
yachts|woman
yachts|women
yack chatter; var. of yak
yacker work; var. of yakka
yackety-yak
yackety-yakked
yackety-yakking
yada yada yada
yaf|fle
Ya|gara
yagé
Yagi
yagna var. of yajna
yahoo +s
yahr|zeit
Yah|veh var. of Yahweh
Yah|vist var. of Yahwist
Yah|weh *Bible*
Yah|wist
yajna
Yajur Veda
yak
yakked
yak|king animal; chatter
yaki|tori
yakka
Yakut
pl. Yakut or Ya|kuts
Ya|ku|tia

Ya|kutsk
Ya|kuza
pl. Ya|kuza
Yale lock *trademark*
Yale university, US
Yalie
y'all = you-all; cf. you'll
Yalta
Yalu
Yama *Hindu Mythology*
Yama|moto, Iso|roku admiral
Yama|saki, Min|oru architect
Yamato-e Japanese painting style
yam|mer
yam|mer|er
Yam|ous|sou|kro
Ya|muna
Yan|cheng
yandy
yan|dies
yan|died
yandy|ing
Yang|shao
Yang|tze
Yank American
yank tug
Yan|kee
Yan|kee Doo|dle Dandy
Yano|mami
pl. Yano|mami
Yano|mamö var. of Yanomami
Yan|tai
yan|tra
Yao people
pl. Yao
Ya|oundé
yap
yapped
yap|ping bark; talk noisily
yapok
yapp *Bookbinding*
yap|per
yappy
yap|pier
yap|pi|est
Yaqui
yar|bor|ough

yard|age
yar|dang
yard|arm
yard|bird
Yardie
yard|man
  yard|men
yard|stick
yare
yar|mulka var. of
  yarmulke
yar|mulke
Yaro|slavl
yar|ran
yar|row
yash|mak
Yas|min
yata|ghan
Yates's cor|rec|tion
yatra
yat|ter
yau|pon
yau|tia
yaw deviate; cf.
  yore, your
yawl boat
yawn
yawn|er
yawn|ing|ly
yawp
yawp|er
yaws disease; cf.
  yours
y-axis
  y-axes
yay so; cf. yea
Yayoi
yclept
ye archaic you
yea yes; cf. yay
Yea|ger, Chuck
  pilot
yeah non-standard
  var. of yes
yean
year
year|book
year|ling
year|ly
yearn
yearn|er
yearn|ing|ly
yeast|ily
yeasti|ness

yeast|less
yeast-like
yeasty
  yeast|ier
  yeasti|est
Yeats, W. B. writer
Yeats|ian
yecch var. of yech
yecchy var. of yechy
yech exclam.
  expressing disgust
yechy
yee|haw
  yee|hah
yegg
yeh var. of yeah
Ye|kat|er|in|burg
Ye|kat|er|ino|dar
Ye|kat|er|ino|slav
Ye|liza|vet|pol
yel|low
yellow|back
yellow-belly
  yellow-bellies
yellow|bill
yellow|cake
yellow|fin
yellow|hammer
yellow|head
yellow|ish
Yellow|knife
yellow|legs
  pl. yellow|legs
yel|low|ly
yellow|ness
Yellow|stone
yellow-tail moth
yellow|tail fish
yellow|throat
yellow-wood
yellow-wort
yel|lowy
yelp|er
Yelt|sin, Boris
  president of Rus-
  sian Federation
Yemen
Yem|eni
Yem|en|ite
yen
  pl. yen
  Japanese currency
yen
yenned

yen|ning
  longing
Yen-cheng var. of
  Yancheng
Yeni|sei
yenta
Yen-tai var. of
  Yantai
yeo|man
  yeo|men
yeo|man|ly
yeo|man|ry
  yeo|man|ries
Yeo|vil
yeow
yep non-standard
  var. of yes
yerba
yerba buena
yerba maté
Yere|van
yes
  yeses or yesses
ye|shiva
yes-man
  yes-men
yes|sir
  yes|sirred
  yes|sir|ring
yes|ter|day
yes|ter|year
yeti
Yev|tu|shenko,
  Yev|geni poet
yew tree; cf. ewe,
  you
Y-fronts trademark
Ygg|dra|sil
Yi|chun
Yid|dish
Yid|dish|er
Yid|dish|ism
Yid|dish|ist
Yid|dish|keit
yield
yield|er
yield|ing|ly
yield|ing|ness
yikes
Yin|chuan
Yin|dji|barndi
yip
  yipped
  yip|ping
yip|pee exclam.

yip|pie politically
  active hippy
yips nervousness
Yi|shuv
Yiz|kor
ylang-ylang
ylem
ylid
ylide var. of ylid
Ymir Scandinavian
  Mythology
yob|bery
yob|bish
yob|bish|ly
yob|bish|ness
yobbo
  yob|bos or
  yob|boes
yobby
  yob|bier
  yob|bi|est
yock
yocto|meter US
yocto|metre Br.
yod Hebrew letter
yodel
  yo|delled Br.
  yo|deled US
  yo|del|ling Br.
  yo|del|ing US
yo|del|er US
yo|del|ler Br.
yoga
yogh Middle English
  letter
yog|hurt var. of
  yogurt
yogi
yogic
yo|gini
yo|gism
yog|urt
Yog|ya|karta
yo|himbe
yo|him|bine
yo-ho-ho
yoicks
yok var. of yock
yoke
  yok|ing
  neck-frame; cf.
  yolk
yokel
Yoko|hama

yoko|zuna
  pl. yoko|zuna
Yo|landa
Yo|lande
yolk part of egg; cf.
  yoke
yolked having yolk
yolk|less
yolk sac
yolky
  yolk|ier
  yolki|est
Yom Kip|pur
yon
yon|der
yoni
yonks
yoo-hoo +s +ed
  +ing
yore in 'of yore'; cf.
  yaw, your
York
York, Cape
york *Cricket*
york|er
Yorkie dog
York|ist
York|shire
York|shire|man
  York|shire|men
York|shire|woman
  York|shire|women
York|town
Yor|uba
  pl. Yor|uba or
  Yor|ubas
Yor|vik
Yo|sem|ite
yotta|meter *US*
yotta|metre *Br.*
you *pron.*; cf. ewe,
  yew
you-all
you'd
you-know-what
you-know-who
you'll
Young, Brig|ham
  Mormon leader
Young, Neil singer
young
young|berry
  young|berries
young|ish

young|ling
Young's modu|lus
young|ster
young|stock
young 'un
youn|ker
your belonging to
  you
Your|ce|nar,
  Mar|gue|rite writer
you're = you are
yourn *regional* or
  archaic form of
  yours
yours the one(s)
  belonging to you;
  cf. yaws
your|self
  your|selves
youse you *pl.*
youth
youth|ful
youth|ful|ly
youth|ful|ness
youth hos|tel *n.*
youth-hostel *v.*
  youth-hosteled *US*
  youth-hostelled *Br.*
  youth-hostel|ing
  US
  youth-hostel|ling
  Br.
youth-hostel|er *US*
youth-hosteller
you've
yowl
yo-yo *trademark in
  the UK*
  pl. yo-yos
  v. yo-yoes
  yo-yoed
  yo-yoing
Ypres
yt|ter|bium
yt|trium
Yuan
  Chinese dynasty
yuan
  pl. yuan
  Chinese currency
yuca cassava; cf.
  yucca
Yuca|tán
Yuca|tec
Yuca|tec|an

yucca plant with
  sword-like leaves;
  cf. yuca
yucca moth
yuck *exclam.*; laugh
yucky
  yuck|ier
  yucki|est
Yue
yuga
Yugo|slav
Yugo|slavia
Yugo|slav|ian
Yuit
yuk var. of yuck
yu|kata
  pl. yu|kata or
  yu|ka|tas
yukky var. of yucky
Yukon
yulan
Yule
yule log
Yule|tide
Yuma
Yuman
yummy
  yum|mier
  yum|mi|est
yum-yum
Yun|nan
Yupik
yup|pie
yup|pie|dom
yup|pi|fi|ca|tion
yup|pify
  yup|pi|fies
  yup|pi|fied
  yup|pi|fy|ing
yuppy var. of yuppie
yurt
Yv|ette
Yv|onne

———

Z

zaba|gli|one
Zabrze
Zaca|te|cas
Zac|chaeus

Zach|ary
Zack
zad|dik var. of
  tsaddik
zaf|fer *US*
zaf|fre *Br.*
zaf|tig
zag
  zagged
  zag|ging
Zaga|zig
Zag|reb
Zag|ros
zai|batsu
  pl. zai|batsu
zaide var. of zayde
Zaire
zaire currency
Za|irean
Za|irian var. of
  Zairean
zakat
Za|kin|thos
Zako|pane
za|kouska var. of
  zakuska
za|kuska
za|kuski or
  za|kus|kas
Za|kyn|thos var. of
  Zakinthos
zal|cita|bine
Zam|bezi
Zam|bia
Zam|bian
Zam|bo|anga
zam|bra
zam|buk
zami
zamia
za|min|dar
za|min|dari
za|min|dary
  za|min|daries
  var. of zamindari
Zande
  pl. Zande
zan|der
  pl. zan|der
zani|ly
zani|ness
Zan|skar
Zan|skari
Zan|tac *trademark*

Zante another name for **Zakinthos**

ZANU = Zimbabwe African National Union

Zan¦uck, Dar¦ryl F. film producer

ZANU–PF = Zimbabwe African National Union–Patriotic Front

zany

zanies

zani¦er

zani¦est

Zan¦zi¦bar

Zan¦zi¦bari

Zao¦zhuang

zap

zapped

zap¦ping

Za¦pata, Emili¦ano revolutionary

za¦pa¦te¦ado +s

Zapo¦rizh¦zhya

Zapo¦tec

Zappa, Frank rock musician

zap¦per

zappy

zap¦pier

zap¦pi¦est

ZAPU = Zimbabwe African People's Union

Zaqa¦ziq var. of **Zagazig**

Zara¦goza Spanish name for **Saragossa**

Zara¦thus¦tra Avestan name for **Zoroaster**

Zara¦thus¦trian

zarda chewing tobacco

zar¦dozi

za¦reba var. of **zariba**

zari Indian gold thread

za¦riba

Zarqa

zar¦zuela

Zato¦pek, Emil runner

zax axe; var. of **sax**

zayde grandfather

zazen

Z boson

zeal

Zea¦land island, Denmark; cf. **Zeeland**

Zealot member of ancient Jewish sect

zealot fanatic

zeal¦ot¦ry

zealot¦ries

zeal¦ous

zeal¦ous¦ly

zeal¦ous¦ness

zebec var. of **xebec**

Zebe¦dee

zebra

zebra¦wood

zebu

Zebu¦lon var. of **Zebulun**

Zebu¦lun Bible

Zech¦ar¦iah Bible

Zede¦kiah Bible

zedo¦ary

zedo¦ar¦ies

Zee¦brugge

Zee¦land province, the Netherlands; cf. **Zealand**

Zee¦man ef¦fect

Zef¦fi¦relli, Franco film and theatre director

zein protein

Zeiss, Carl optical-instrument maker

zeit¦geber

zeit¦geist

Zelig

ze¦min¦dar var. of **zamindar**

ze¦min¦dari var. of **zamindari**

ze¦min¦dary

ze¦min¦daries var. of **zamindari**

Zen

ze¦nana

Zend

Zend-Avesta

Zener card; diode

zen¦ith

zen¦ith¦al

Zeno Greek philosopher

Zeno of Cit¦ium Greek philosopher

zeo¦lite

zeo¦lit¦ic

Zepha¦niah Bible

zephyr

Zep¦pe¦lin, Fer¦di¦nand, Count von aviation pioneer

Zep¦pe¦lin airship

zepto¦meter US

zepto¦metre Br.

Zer¦matt

zero

   pl. **zeros**

   v. **zer¦oes**

   zer¦oed

   zero¦ing

zero-graze

zero-grazing

zero-point

zero rate n.

zero-rate v.

zero-rating

zer¦oth before first

zest¦er

zest¦ful

zest¦ful¦ly

zest¦ful¦ness

zesti¦ness

zesty

   zest¦ier

   zesti¦est

zeta Greek letter

zetta¦meter US

zetta¦metre Br.

zeugma

zeug¦mat¦ic

Zeus Greek god

Zeu¦xis Greek painter

Zhang¦jia¦kou

Zhan¦jiang

Zhe¦jiang

Zheng¦zhou

Zhen¦jiang

zho var. of **dzo**

Zhong¦shan city, China

Zhou Chinese dynasty

Zhou Enlai prime minister of China

Zhu¦kov, Ge¦orgi Soviet marshal

Zhyto¦myr

Zia ul-Haq, Mu¦ham¦mad president of Pakistan

Zibo

zi¦dovu¦dine

Zieg¦feld, Flor¦enz theatre manager

ziff beard

ZIF socket

zig

zigged

zig¦ging

zig¦gurat

zig¦zag

zig¦zagged

zig¦zag¦ging

zig¦zag¦ged¦ly

zilch

zilla

zil¦lah var. of **zilla**

zil¦lion

zil¦lion¦aire

zil¦lionth

Zim¦babwe

Zim¦bab¦we¦an

Zim¦mer frame *trademark*

zinc +ed +ing

zinc¦ite

zinco

   pl. **zincos**

   v. **zin¦coes**

zin¦coed

zinco¦ing

zin¦da¦bad

'zine = magazine

zineb

Zin¦fan¦del

zing¦er

zingy

   zing¦ier

   zingi¦est

Zin¦jan¦thro¦pus

Zinne|mann, Fred
film director
zin|nia
Zion
Zion|ism
Zion|ist
zip
zipped
zip|ping
zip code
zip|less
zip|lock
trademark Zip|loc
zip|per
zip|per|head
offensive
zip|pily
zip|pi|ness
Zippo +s *trademark*
cigarette lighter
zippo nothing
zippy
zip|pier
zip|pi|est
zip-up *adj. & n.*
zirc|alloy var. of
zirc|aloy
zir|con
zir|co|nia
zir|co|nium
zither
zither|ist
ziti pasta
zitty
zit|tier
zit|ti|est
spotty
zizz
zloty
pl. **zloty** or **zlotys**
or **zloties**
Zo|an|tharia
zo|an|thar|ian
zo|diac

zo|di|ac|al
zoe|trope
Zof|fany, Jo|hann
painter
zof|tig var. of **zaftig**
Zog king of Albania
Zohar
zois|ite
zokor
Zola, Émile writer
Zollinger–Ellison
Zöllner il|lu|sion
Zoll|ver|ein
zom|bie
zombie|like
zombi|fi|ca|tion
zomb|ify
zombi|fies
zombi|fied
zombi|fy|ing
zonal
zon|al|ly
zona pel|lu|cida
zonae pel|lu|ci|dae
zon|ation
zone
zon|ing
zonk
zon|ule
zo|nure
zoo
zoo|geog|raph|er
zoo|geo|graph|ic
zoo|geo|graph|ic|al
zoo|geo|graph|ic|
   al|ly
zoo|geog|raphy
zooid
zo|oid|al
zoo|keep|er
zoo|logic|al
zoo|logic|al|ly
zo|olo|gist
zo|ology

zoo|morph|ic
zoo|morph|ism
zoo|nosis
zoo|noses
zoo|not|ic
zoo|phile
zoo|philia
zoo|phil|ic
zoo|phyte
zoo|plank|ton
zoo|spore
zoot suit
zoo|xan|thella
zoo|xan|thel|lae
zoo|xan|thel|late
zorb|ing
zori
zor|illa
Zoro|as|ter founder
of Zoroastrianism
Zoro|as|trian
Zoro|as|trian|ism
zorro +s
Zou|ave French
soldier
zou|aves women's
trousers
zouk *Music*
zounds
Zo|virax *trademark*
zowie
Z-plasty
Z-plasties
Zsig|mondy,
Rich|ard chemist
zuc|chetto +s
zuc|chini
pl. **zuc|chini** or
zuc|chi|nis
Zug canton,
Switzerland
zug|zwang
Zui|der Zee
Zulu
Zulu|land

Zuni
pl. **Zuni** or **Zunis**
zuppa in|glese
Zur|ba|rán,
Fran|cisco de
painter
Zur|ich
German **Zü|rich**
Zwickau
zwie|back
Zwingli, Ul|rich
Protestant reformer
Zwing|li|an
zwit|ter|ion
zwit|ter|ion|ic
Zwolle
Zwory|kin,
Vlad|imir Russian-
born American
physicist
Zyban *trademark*
zy|deco
zygo|dac|tyl
zygo|dac|tyl|ous
zygo|dac|tyly
zygo|dac|tyl|ies
zyg|oma
zyg|omas or
zyg|omata
zygo|mat|ic
zygo|morph|ic
zygo|morph|ous
zygo|morphy
Zyg|op|tera
zyg|op|ter|an
zygo|spore
zyg|ote
zyg|ot|ene
zyg|ot|ic
zyg|ot|ic|al|ly
Zy|klon B
zym|ase
zymo|gen
zym|ot|ic
zym|urgy